CHINESE LITERATURE

*

VOLUME II

From 1375

The *Cambridge History of Chinese Literature* gives an account of three thousand years of Chinese literature accessible to non-specialist readers as well as scholars and students of Chinese. From the beginnings of the Chinese written language to the lively world of Internet literature, these two volumes tell the story of Chinese writing, both as an instrument of the state and as a medium for culture outside the state. These volumes treat not only poetry, drama, and fiction, but also early works of history and the informal prose of later eras. Volume II begins with the distinctive Ming culture that emerged around the year 1400, and continues through the Qing (the Manchu dynasty) all the way up to the present day. This period saw an enormuous diversity of writing styles and forms that defied traditional Chinese literary categories. This new and comprehensive treatment covers a wide range of topics, including political censorship and literary creativity, changes in print culture, dynastic transition, courtesans' pleasure quarters, and the rise of women writers. Discussions of lyric poetry, drama, "prosimetric narrative," and the novel are interspersed with in-depth examinations of the complex world of diaspora, the translation of Western literatures, modern "new fiction," and the advent of new media from film adaptations to Web literature.

THE CAMBRIDGE
HISTORY OF
CHINESE LITERATURE

*

Edited by
KANG-I SUN CHANG AND STEPHEN OWEN

*

VOLUME II
From 1375

*

Edited by
KANG-I SUN CHANG

CAMBRIDGE
UNIVERSITY PRESS

CAMBRIDGE UNIVERSITY PRESS

Cambridge, New York, Melbourne, Madrid, Cape Town,
Singapore, São Paulo, Delhi, Dubai, Tokyo

Cambridge University Press
The Edinburgh Building, Cambridge CB2 8RU, UK

Published in the United States of America by Cambridge University Press, New York

www.cambridge.org
Information on this title: www.cambridge.org/9780521855594

First published 2010

Printed in the United Kingdom at the University Press, Cambridge

A catalogue record for this publication is available from the British Library

Library of Congress Cataloguing in Publication data
The Cambridge history of Chinese literature / edited by Kang-i Sun Chang and Stephen Owen.
p.   cm.
Includes bibliographical references and index.
ISBN 978-0-521-85559-4 (v. 2 : hardback)
1. Chinese literature – History and criticism.   I. Chang, Kang-i Sun, 1944–
II. Owen, Stephen, 1946–
PL2265.C36   2010
895.1′09 – dc22   2009024644

ISBN 978-0-521-85559-4 Hardback

only available as a two-volume set:

ISBN 978-0-521-11677-0   2-volume set

Contents

Contents

Contents

Contents

Contents

xi

Contents of Volume I

Illustrations

Contributors

KANG-I SUN CHANG is the inaugural Malcolm G. Chace '56 Professor of East Asian Languages and Literatures at Yale University. Her primary areas of research are classical Chinese literature, lyric poetry, gender studies, and cultural theory/aesthetics. She is the author of *The Evolution of Chinese Tz'u Poetry* (Princeton, 1980), *Six Dynasties Poetry* (Princeton, 1986), and *The Late Ming Poet Ch'en Tzu-lung: Crises of Love and Loyalism* (New Haven, 1991). She is also coeditor (with Ellen Widmer) of *Writing Women in Late Imperial China* (Stanford, 1997), and compiler and coeditor (with Haun Saussy) of *Women Writers of Traditional China* (Stanford, 1999). Her most recent book is *Journey through the White Terror: A Daughter's Memoir* (Taipei, 2006). She has also published several books in Chinese about American culture, feminism, literature, and film.

RONALD EGAN is Professor of Chinese at the University of California, Santa Barbara. His works include book-length studies of Ouyang Xiu and Su Shi, as well as a translation of the selected essays of Qian Zhongshu, *Limited Views: Essays on Ideas and Letters* (Cambridge, MA, 1998). His most recent work is *The Problem of Beauty: Aesthetic Thought and Pursuits in Northern Song Dynasty China* (Cambridge, MA, 2006).

MICHAEL A. FULLER is Associate Professor of Chinese Literature at the University of California, Irvine. He is the author of *An Introduction to Literary Chinese* (Cambridge, MA, 1999), *The Road to Eastslope: The Development of Su Shi's Poetic Voice* (Stanford, 1990), and the chapter "Sung dynasty *Shih* poetry" in *The Columbia History of Chinese Literature* (New York, 2001).

MICHEL HOCKX is Professor of Chinese at SOAS, University of London. His research centers on modern and contemporary Chinese literary media and institutions, as well as modern Chinese poetry and poetics. His major publication is *Questions of Style: Literary Societies and Literary Journals in Modern China, 1911–1937* (Leiden, 2003).

WILT L. IDEMA studied Chinese language and culture at Leiden University. Following study in Japan and Hong Kong, he taught at Leiden University from 1970 to 1999. He has taught Chinese literature at Harvard since 2000. He has published widely in both English and Dutch on Chinese vernacular literature of the last four dynasties. His most recent English-language publications include *The Red Brush, Writing Women of Imperial China* (co-authored with Beata Grant; Cambridge, MA, 2004); *Personal Salvation and Filial Piety:*

Two Precious Scroll Narratives on Guanyin and Her Acolytes (Honolulu, 2008); and *Meng Jiangnü Brings Down the Great Wall: Ten Versions of a Chinese Legend* (Seattle, 2008).

MARTIN KERN is Professor of East Asian Studies at Princeton University. He has published widely on ancient Chinese literature, history, and religion. His current work addresses the intersection of poetic expression, ritual performance, and the formation of Zhou cultural memory and identity. His most recent books are *The Stele Inscriptions of Ch'in Shih-huang: Text and Ritual in Early Chinese Imperial Representation* (New Haven, 2000) and the edited volume *Text and Ritual in Early China* (Seattle, 2005).

DAVID R. KNECHTGES is Professor of Chinese Literature at the University of Washington. His publications include *Two Studies on the Han Fu* (Seattle, 1968), *The Han Rhapsody: A Study of the Fu of Yang Hsiung* (Cambridge, 1976), *The Han shu Biography of Yang Xiong* (Tempe, AZ, 1982), and *Wen xuan: Selections of Refined Literature* (Princeton, 1982, 1987, 1996). He is the editor of Gong Kechang's *Studies on the Han Fu* (New Haven, 1997), and coeditor (with Eugene Vance) of *Rhetoric and the Discourses of Power in Court Culture* (Seattle, 2005).

WAI-YEE LI is Professor of Chinese literature at Harvard University. She is the author of *Enchantment and Disenchantment: Love and Illusion in Chinese Literature* (Princeton, 1993) and *The Readability of the Past in Early Chinese Historiography* (Cambridge, MA, 2007), and coeditor (with Wilt L. Idema and Ellen Widmer) of *Trauma and Transcendence in Early Qing Literature* (Cambridge, MA, 2006). In collaboration with Stephen Durrant and David Schaberg, she also translated *Zuozhuan* (Seattle, forthcoming).

SHUEN-FU LIN is Professor of Chinese Literature at the University of Michigan. Author of *The Transformation of the Chinese Lyrical Tradition: Chiang K'uei and Southern Sung Tz'u Poetry* (Princeton, 1978) and *The Pursuit of Utopias* (in Chinese, 2003), he is also coeditor of *The Vitality of the Lyric Voice: Shih Poetry from the Late Han to the T'ang* (Princeton, 1986), and co-translator (with Larry J. Schulz) of Tung Yueh's *The Tower of Myriad Mirrors: A Supplement to Journey to the West* (Berkeley, 1978; revised edn, Michigan, 2000).

TINA LU is Professor of Chinese Literature at Yale University. She is the author of *Persons, Roles, and Minds: Identity in Peony Pavilion and Peach Blossom Fan* (Stanford, 2001) and *Accidental Incest, Filial Cannibalism, and Other Peculiar Encounters in Late Imperial Chinese Literature* (Cambridge, MA, 2008).

STEPHEN OWEN is James Bryant Conant University Professor at Harvard University, with joint appointments in the Department of Comparative Literature, and in East Asian Languages and Civilizations. His primary areas of research interest are premodern Chinese literature, lyric poetry, and comparative poetics. Much of his previous work has focused on the middle period of Chinese literature (AD 200–1200), and he is currently engaged in a complete translation of the Tang poet Du Fu. His most recent books are: *The Late Tang: Chinese Poetry of the Mid-ninth Century* (Cambridge, MA, 2006), *The Making of Early Chinese Classical Poetry* (Cambridge, MA, 2006), *An Anthology of Chinese Literature: Beginnings to 1911* (New York and London, 1996), *The End of the Chinese "Middle Ages"* (Stanford, 1996),

Readings in Chinese Literary Thought (Cambridge, MA, 1992), *Mi-lou: Poetry and the Labyrinth of Desire* (Cambridge, MA, 1989), *Remembrances: The Experience of the Past in Classical Chinese Literature* (Cambridge, MA, 1986), and *Traditional Chinese Poetry and Poetics* (Madison, WI, 1985).

SHANG WEI is Wm. Theodore and Fanny Brett de Bary and Class of 1941 Collegiate Professor of Asian Humanities and Professor of Chinese Literature at Columbia University. His research interests include print culture, book history, intellectual history, and fiction and drama of the late imperial period. His book *"Rulin waishi" and Cultural Transformation in Late Imperial China* (Cambridge, MA, 2003) addresses the role of ritual and fiction in shaping the intellectual and cultural changes of the eighteenth century. His other publications are mainly concerned with *Jin Ping Mei cihua* (*The Plum in the Golden Vase*), late Ming culture, and fiction commentary in the Ming and Qing periods. He is the coeditor of several books, including (with David Der-wei Wang) *Dynastic Crisis and Cultural Innovation from the Late Ming to the Late Qing and Beyond* (Cambridge, MA, 2005).

XIAOFEI TIAN is Professor of Chinese Literature at Harvard University. Her research interests include Chinese literature and culture, manuscript culture, book history, the history of ideas, and world literature. She is the author of *Tao Yuanming and Manuscript Culture: The Record of a Dusty Table* (Seattle, 2005) and *Beacon Fire and Shooting Star: The Literary Culture of the Liang (502–557)* (Cambridge, MA, 2007). Her Chinese-language publications include a book on the sixteenth-century novel *The Plum in the Golden Vase* (2003; revised ed., 2005); a book on Sappho (2004); a book on the history, culture and literature of Moorish Spain (2006); several works of translations; and a number of collections of poetry and essays. She is currently working on a book about visionary journeys in early medieval and late imperial China.

JING TSU is Assistant Professor of Chinese Literature in the Department of East Asian Languages and Literatures at Yale University. She specializes in modern and contemporary Chinese literature, as well as Chinese intellectual and cultural history. Her research areas include science and popular culture, race, nationalism, dialects, and diaspora from the nineteenth century to the present. She is the author of *Failure, Nationalism, and Literature: The Making of Modern Chinese Identity, 1895–1937* (Stanford, 2005) and *Literary Governance: Sound and Script in Chinese Diaspora* (Cambridge, MA: forthcoming).

DAVID DER-WEI WANG is Edward C. Henderson Professor of Chinese Literature at Harvard University. He specializes in modern and contemporary Chinese literature, late Qing fiction and drama, and comparative literary theory. His works include *Fictional Realism in 20th-Century China: Mao Dun, Lao She, Shen Congwen* (New York, 1992), *Fin-de-siècle Splendor: Repressed Modernities of Late Qing Fiction, 1849–1911* (Stanford, 1997), and *The Monster that Is History: Violence, History, and Fictional Writing in 20th-Century China* (Berkeley, 2004).

STEPHEN H. WEST received his Ph.D. from the University of Michigan in 1972. He began his teaching career at the University of Arizona in 1972 and subsequently taught at the University of California, Berkeley from 1986 to 2004, where he was the Louis Agassiz Professor of Chinese. He currently serves as Director of the Center for Asian Research, and is Foundation Professor of Chinese Language in the School of International Letters and Cultures at Arizona State University. He teaches courses in the prose and poetry of late medieval China (the Song and Yuan dynasties), urban literature of the twelfth and thirteenth centuries, and early Chinese drama. His research specialties are early Chinese theater, and the urban culture and cultural history of the late medieval period.

MICHELLE YEH is Professor of East Asian Languages and Cultures at the University of California, Davis. Her work focuses on modern Chinese poetry, comparative poetics, and translation. She is the author of *Modern Chinese Poetry: Theory and Practice since 1917* (New Haven, 1991), and is the editor and translator of the *Anthology of Modern Chinese Poetry* (New Haven, 1992). She coedited and co-translated *No Trace of the Gardener: Poems of Yang Mu* (New Haven, 1998) and *Frontier Taiwan: An Anthology of Modern Chinese Poetry* (New York, 2001). She has also published several books in Chinese, including *Essays on Modern Chinese Poetry* (1998), *From the Margin: An Alternative Tradition of Modern Chinese Poetry* (2000), and *A Poetics of Aromatics* (2005).

Preface

The two-volume *Cambridge History of Chinese Literature* traces the development of Chinese literary culture over three millennia, from the earliest inscriptions to contemporary works, including the literature of the Chinese diaspora. Our purpose is to provide a coherent narrative that can be read from cover to cover. In order to achieve consistency and readability, our contributors have consulted with one another throughout the writing process, particularly when subject areas and time periods overlap from one chapter to the next. We have carefully considered the structure and goals of each individual chapter, as well as the best point at which to break the history into two volumes so as to add to, rather than detract from, the understanding of the reader.

Literary history as practiced in China has been shaped both by premodern Chinese categories and by nineteenth-century European literary history; historical accounts of Chinese literature in the West have in turn been shaped by Chinese practices, whose categories have become habitual even though the result often seems strange to Western readers. In these volumes, we have the opportunity to question these categories. In particular, we have attempted as much as possible to avoid the division of the field into genres and to move toward a more integrated historical approach, creating a cultural history or a history of literary culture. This is the most natural approach to the earliest time periods, and still relatively easy in the middle period, but becomes increasingly difficult in the Ming, Qing, and modern period. It is possible, however, to achieve our goal by providing a clear framing of the general cultural (and sometimes political) history. For example, the Tang chapter in Volume I has not been divided into the standard categories of "Tang poetry," "Tang prose," "Tang stories," and "Tang *ci*." Rather, we will explore the period in terms of "The age of Empress Wu," "The reign of Emperor Xuanzong and so on," treating poetry, prose, anecdote books, and stories as part of a cohesive historical whole. Similarly, the chapter discussing early and mid-Ming literature in Volume II is divided into "Early Ming to 1450," "The period from 1450 to 1520," and "The period from 1520 to 1572," with each section focusing on topics of literary culture such as "Political persecution and censorship," "New perspectives on place," "Exile literature," and so on. Issues of genre do need to be addressed, but the historical context of a given genre's appearance and its transformations clarifies the role of genre in ways that are made difficult by a genre-based organizational scheme.

A problem one encounters when using this historical approach is that there are a number of works that evolved over a long course of history and as such do not belong to a single historical moment. This primarily involves popular material of the vernacular culture, which appears relatively late in the textual record, but often has older roots. This issue has been handled by Wilt Idema (Chapter 5, Volume II), who has worked to dovetail his treatment with the authors of the historical chapters.

Due to the size and complexity of our undertaking, we have decided not to encourage extended plot summaries, and instead have favored short synopses of novels and longer plays. In addition, much of Chinese literature is in the form of relatively short works. The standard Chinese approach (as well as the approach of other Cambridge histories of literature) has been to focus on individual authors. Inevitably, our approach also involves the discussion of some of the great writers throughout the ages. Apart from those authors whose lives (real or invented) have become part of the reading of their works, however, we have in many cases focused on types of situations or writing rather than on individuals.

Maintaining a coherent narrative becomes more difficult in the Ming, Qing, and modern periods, as literature becomes more diverse and the options for its dissemination increase. In order to restrict this history to a reasonable size and scope, we have chosen not to discuss the literatures of linguistic minorities in the present-day People's Republic of China (PRC). Our historical approach also compels us to exclude literature written in Chinese in Korea, Vietnam, and Japan, although the circulation of literary texts between China and other East Asian countries is touched upon when the exchange is integral to the history of Chinese literary culture itself.

Histories of literature are inevitably shaped by the academic conventions and standard categories of a given national literature, as much as by the material itself. In the case of Chinese literature, the periods, names, generic terms, and conventional translations of Chinese words can occasionally pose a substantial barrier to even the most enthusiastic reader. We have therefore tried as much as possible to find ways to present our material that will not pose unnecessary difficulties to readers familiar only with Anglo-European traditions.

We have tried to be consistent with the translations of terms and titles, although contributors have been urged to use their own best translations for the titles of works confined to their own period. Each initial occurrence of a book title in the text will be given in translation first and then succeeded by a transliteration of the original Chinese title in parentheses. Unless otherwise specified, all translations in these chapters are the work of the contributors. The Chinese characters in book titles, terms, and names are not given in the text; in most cases they can be found in the glossary at the end of book.

Given length and space constraints, sources are not referenced in footnotes but are often mentioned in the text itself. The bibliographies are very selective; in particular, due to the magnitude of publications in Chinese, we have omitted from the bibliographies works of Chinese scholarship to which the editors and authors of these chapters are deeply indebted.

Acknowledgments

After working for several years on the *Cambridge History of Chinese Literature*, I have incurred a great debt of gratitude to many people. First of all, I am grateful to my coeditor Stephen Owen, who was extremely helpful throughout the process of assembling this book, especially in resolving inconsistencies between the two volumes. I am thankful to Linda Bree of Cambridge University Press for inviting us to embark on this project, and also to Edward Kamens of Yale University for his recommendation of us to the Press. The Council on East Asian Studies at Yale University generously supported a workshop in 2004 for the contributors to this book, and subsequently provided grants to help coordinate work on the project. We are all grateful to Mimi Yiengpruksawan, Haun Saussy, and Abbey Newman of the Council for their continuous support.

I also owe special thanks to the editorial consultant, Alice Cheang, who did thoughtful and extensive stylistic editing on the first drafts of these chapters. Although most chapters have since been rewritten, Alice's initial editing remains important. Another individual who deserves special words of gratitude is Eleanor Goodman, whose meticulous copy-editing on these chapters has contributed substantially to the readability of this book. In addition to her copy-editing, I would like to thank her for her work indexing the *History*. Others whose help has been greatly appreciated are Pauline Lin and Matthew Towns, who offered suggestions on early drafts.

Several friends and scholars have also graciously offered aid in various ways and hence my sincere thanks go to them: Lee Chi-hsiang, Chu Hao-i, Wu Chengxue, Liu Zunju, Xue Haiyan, and Wan-wan Huang for providing Chinese reference sources as well as insight into the material; the late historian Frederick W. Mote for offering wise counsel; Yu Ying-shih, Monica Yu, Chinshing Huang, Ayling Wang, Ellen Widmer, Lena Huang, Zhang Hongsheng, Jwo-Farn Chiou, K. C. Sun, and Wang Guojun for their encouragement and practical help during various phases of the project; Guo Yingde, Tian Yuan

Tan, Chen Guoqiu (Leonard Chan), Paize Keulemans, Hung-lam Chu, and Hok-lam Chan for alerting me to some generally ignored facts concerning Ming–Qing literature and culture; Zhang Hui, Zhang Jian, Kang Zhengguo, Sheng Anfeng, and Jeongsoo Shin for assistance in translation; John Treat, Marshall Brown, Wang Ning, Lena Rydholm, Peter Chen-main Wang, Cheng Yu-yu, Olga Lomová, Fan Ming-ju, Choe Yong Chul, and Chen Pingyuan for sharing their views on writing literary history; Ellen Hammond, Sarah Elman, Yang Guanghui, Chi-wah Chan, Tao Yang, David Sensabaugh, Tai-loi Ma, Lie-Chiou Huang, and An Pingqiu for tracking down library and museum research materials; Wang Ao for making referrals and supplying helpful information, often at the last minute; and C. C. Chang for helping with technical problems ranging from computer assistance to bibliographic and glossary compilation, as well as for his constant moral support.

Needless to say, I gratefully acknowledge the sustained efforts of our contributors for devoting considerable time to writing their long chapters, each of which covers an extremely wide range of knowledge. Among our contributors, David Wang and Wilt Idema deserve special thanks for their generosity in offering guidance and advice – in addition to writing their own chapters, they offered invaluable help with the other chapters in the present volume.

Finally, I would like to give thanks to the copy-editor, John Gaunt, and also to the literature editor, Maartje Scheltens, and production manager Jodie Barnes at Cambridge University Press, whose help with this project is very much appreciated.

K. S. C.

Introduction to Volume II

The second volume of the *Cambridge History of Chinese Literature* is comparable in chronological scope to the single-volume Cambridge series in European literatures. Using the year 1375 – rather than the standard date of 1368 (i.e. the first year of the Ming dynasty) – as the temporal division between the first and second volumes brings to light our unique approach to the question of periodization. Thus far, almost all available histories of Chinese literature periodize by dynasty, so we cannot dispense with this habit completely. We have chosen, however, to divide periods differently whenever dynastic periodization becomes problematic. For example, although the Ming dynasty was founded in 1368, in terms of literary history the year 1375 is by far the more important date to remember. By the year 1375, the important surviving intellectuals from the Yuan, such as Yang Weizhen (1296–1370), Ni Can (1301–1374), and Liu Ji (1311–1375), had already died. More importantly, in 1374, Zhu Yuanzhang, the Hongwu Emperor and founding father of the Ming (r. 1368–1398), executed the great poet Gao Qi (1336–1374) and hence inaugurated a reign of terror for intellectuals. To a certain extent, the distinctive early Ming culture began with the advent of Zhu Yuanzhang's brutal political persecution, which would obliterate nearly an entire generation of poets brought up in the last years of Mongol rule.

It was not until around 1400 that literature had the chance to flourish again after a long hiatus, when the Yongle Emperor (r. 1403–1424) began to initiate his many ambitious literary and cultural projects. Given this clear division in the literary history of the period, it seems most useful to commence the second volume of the *Cambridge History of Chinese Literature* with the year 1375, while allowing for some overlap in material. Similarly, we have placed the May Fourth Movement of 1919 not at the beginning of "modernity," as is traditionally done, but rather in the middle of a longer process starting in the latter part of the Qing. (See Chapter 6, "Chinese literature from 1841 to 1937," by David Der-wei Wang.) These examples suggest that literature has its own self-regulating directions that need not be identified with dynastic changes.

This volume also reaffirms the importance of the era that extends from the Ming–Qing period (1368–1912) to the present. In most histories of Chinese literature available today, the period from the Ming–Qing onward has been considered less significant than previous periods, while the modern and contemporary period is largely neglected by Chinese literary historians. In a tradition in which literary works were often judged by how well they emulated the past, individual writers of later times could easily be overlooked. Throughout this volume, however, we will demonstrate that belatedness need not connote derivativeness, providing examples of ways of inheriting and rewriting a tradition that are themselves creative and innovative. In fact, it is during the period from the Ming–Qing to the present that one witnesses the enormous diversity of writing that proved difficult to accommodate within the traditional Chinese categories.

As in the first volume, the emphasis here is not so much on individual writers, but rather on the forms and styles of writing, especially those that characterize increasingly diverse literary directions. Again, the general approach in this volume will be historical. The only exception is Chapter 5, by Wilt L. Idema ("Prosimetric and verse narrative"), which covers a large body of "popular" material, as well as works that evolved over a lengthy course of history and thus cannot be assigned to a single historical moment. In the textual record, these works tend to appear relatively late. Most of these texts have no authors, however; and even in the rare cases in which the author is known, it is often difficult to determine when and where these texts were produced and printed. Wilt L. Idema has done an excellent job in coordinating his chapter with the authors of the historical chapters, judging whether some "popular" works in their various instantiations might have belonged to certain literati culture. All this ensures that our *History* presents a coherent narrative, despite its multi-author approach.

In general, we do not discuss Chinese-language literature that was produced in Korea, Vietnam, and Japan. This is partly due to our unique historical approach, but also because of the fact that readers can find relevant information elsewhere, such as in the *Columbia History of Chinese Literature* (edited by Victor H. Mair). Chapter 1 of this volume ("Literature of the early Ming to mid-Ming, 1375–1572," by Kang-i Sun Chang) is the sole exception. During the early to mid-Ming, the circulation of literary texts between Ming China and other East Asian countries was directly responsive to the important questions of censorship and self-censorship at the time. As such, this is one case where the mutual influences between China and its neighboring countries can be integrated into the history of Chinese literary culture itself. A study of this literary communication also provides insight into the unique power of writers to tell stories across national boundaries. Moreover, it was during the early and mid-Ming, when traffic between China and other East Asian countries became increasingly heavy, that Chinese writers began to produce a large number of literary works about foreign travels. Later, during the mid-Qing, as Shang Wei informs us in his chapter "The literati era and its demise (1723–1840)," China and its neighboring countries continued to maintain close ties in publishing and book marketing.

Although the issue of regionalization is an important topic in this volume, we have decided, aside from the aforementioned examples involving larger regions in East Asia, to keep our regional focus within the boundaries of China. In each chapter, we discuss significant local networks when appropriate – especially when those local networks also serve as a counterbalance to what was recognized as the "national" literary culture. For example, the mid-Ming literary field was at first dominated by a group of writers (the so-called "Early Revivalists") consisting of the "Seven Early Masters" and their associates in the north, but beginning in the early sixteenth century the literary center of China gradually shifted to the Jiangnan region in the south. According to some contemporary reports, this shift was precipitated by the Jiangnan region becoming an important economic and cultural center as early as the late fifteenth century. It is also worth noting that, unlike the Revivalists in the north who all began as high officials in the court, it was the poets and artists in the Jiangnan (especially Suzhou) region who were the first to earn their living by selling paintings and poems. Later Suzhou would also become known for its community of female poets and long-standing tradition of literary men supporting talented women. This feminine side of the Suzhou culture, embodying a quality of delicate romanticism, seems completely opposed to the heroic ideal so characteristic of the "Early Revivalists" in the north.

Print culture is another primary concern of this volume. In each chapter, the author offers commentary on the ways texts were produced and circulated, and, if possible, on the nature of the readership. In particular, the chapter "The literary culture of the late Ming (1573–1644)" by Tina Lu describes how the commercial print industry underwent rapid development during the Wanli reign (1573–1620). This period produced six times more commercial imprints than the preceding fifty years. As a consequence, the readership of literary works became more numerous and dramatically more diverse during the late Ming. As Tina Lu explains, examination aids (with classical commentaries), collections of dramatic songs, and guides to proper female behavior all flourished in an unprecedented way. It was also during this period that the number of courtesans who socialized with male literati and became authors themselves vastly increased. In the meantime, "reconstructed" Yuan dramas were extensively printed – the best example being Zang Maoxun's (1550–1620) *Anthology of Yuan Plays* – although prior to this period the dramatist and lyricist Li Kaixian (1502–1568) had already published many of his "rewritten" texts of the Yuan plays. These examples from the late Ming demonstrate how the literary past was continually re-created and reread in later ages.

Despite our reservations about habitual periodization by dynasty, we believe that the dynastic transition from the Ming to the Qing (the Manchu dynasty) deserves special attention, because early Qing literature was profoundly concerned with the change of dynasty as well as with the meaning of the late Ming legacy. During this transitional period, there was an extraordinary outburst of creative energy in works of historical retrospection. Given this, we have used the year 1644 – despite the various chronological ambiguities about the beginnings of the Qing – as the division between the second and the third chapters in this volume. As Wai-yee Li (in Chapter 3, "Early Qing to 1723") argues, the label "late Ming" was basically a "Qing product," and if early Qing writers "invented" the late Ming, it was only because they were constantly "trying to understand and define their own historical moment." Under great pressure to redefine themselves, writers of the early Qing often faced the difficult decision of whether to align themselves with the Ming loyalists or the Qing conformers – although there were shades of gradation between the two camps. As a result, this period also created an unprecedented number of literary societies and communities centered around the members' political and regional affiliations, which eventually led to new forms of literature. For example, the Jiangnan region, which originally served as the stronghold of a late Ming political party known as the "Revival Society," later became the center of an important theatrical culture (known particularly for political drama) during the Qing.

Biographies of notable late Ming women – in particular, courtesans whose lives paralleled the prosperity and decline of a bygone era – also became popular during the Qing. Works such as Yu Huai's *Miscellaneous Records of the Plank Bridge* and Mao Xiang's *Reminiscences of the Plum Shadows Studio* testify that the romantic ideals of the late Ming continued to survive into the Manchu dynasty. In many ways, their love for the courtesans served to express the early Qing loyalists' need for commemoration. In contrast, writers such as Li Yu (1610–1680) began to invent a new kind of fiction that focused on "compromises, pragmatism, and self-interest."

Political censorship was often a problem for Chinese who lived under Manchu rule, and beginning with the Kangxi reign (1662–1722) the dangers of prosecution posed a constant threat to literary men. It was during this period that loyalist poets developed a special poetics of implicit rhetoric as a style they could use without incurring punishment. As Wai-yee Li explains, however, such literary devices were not reliable safeguards against political persecution. For example, two chief compilers of *Historical Records of the Ming* were put to death for "alleged offenses against the Qing" during the early years of the Kangxi reign. Toward the end of the reign, the prosecution of the famous writer Dai Mingshi (1653–1713) and his eventual execution in response to his *Southern Mountains Collection* stood out among the numerous incidents that foreshadowed the yet more serious "literary inquisition" of the Qianlong reign.

Ironically, Emperor Qianlong (r. 1736–1796), who was responsible for the worst of the literary inquisitions during the Qing, turned out to be the greatest cultural preserver among all the emperors. He led the massive compilation project of *The Complete Library of Four Treasuries*, which comprised an unprecedented number of texts in all branches of Chinese learning. As Shang Wei explains in his chapter on the period from 1723 to 1840, the long and prosperous Qianlong reign was both an age of enormous abundance and one of contradictions. This chapter explores the making of the "literati" novels such as *The Unofficial History of the Scholars* by Wu Jingzi (1701–1754) and *The Story of the Stone* (also known as *The Dream of the Red Chamber*) by Cao Xueqin (1715?–1763). These novels were produced in a unique literary environment in the early years of the Qianlong reign – an environment that was independent of commercial production and consumption – in sharp contrast to the profit-making milieu of the Ming when vernacular novels such as the *Romance of the Three Kingdoms, Water Margin, Journey to the West* (see Chapter 1, by Kang-i Sun Chang), and *The Plum in the Golden Vase* (See Chapter 2, by Tina Lu) were produced and published. This does not mean, however, that commercial publishing was not important during the Qianlong era, for historical and heroic sagas continued to be reprinted and circulated; but it indicates that the "marginalized" literati such as Wu Jingzi and Cao Xueqin were detached from the contemporary market and the popular local theater culture, just as they were disconnected from the official world as well. It is for this reason that their novels were "rediscovered" only decades later. As a result, these authors exercised a much greater influence on readers in the nineteenth and twentieth centuries than on those in their own times, and it was these more modern readers who eventually canonized the "literati" novels produced during the eighteenth century. This interesting case of historic reception has ramifications that go far beyond the aesthetic question of reading and rereading, as it touches on larger issues concerning cultural and sociological changes.

The rise of women writers (often in groups) during the second half of the eighteenth century onward is an important phenomenon in Chinese literature. This period is often considered the "second high tide" in women's literature. Compared with the first high tide of women poets during the seventeenth century, eighteenth-century women writers were more diverse in their literary interests, with an increasing number specializing in the narrative *tanci* (string ballads) and dramatic plays, in addition to traditional poetry – as may be seen in Shang Wei's Chapter 4 and Wilt Idema's Chapter 5 in this volume. Moreover, these women writers were mostly from families among the gentry. Yet, while courtesan poets occupied a prominent position in the literature of the late Ming, courtesans had lost much of their status as respectable writers by the end of the eighteenth century.

This by no means suggests that the courtesan disappeared from Chinese literature after this period. In fact, the courtesan remains one of the archetypal figures in modern Chinese literature. As David Der-wei Wang reminds us in his chapter "Chinese literature from 1841 to 1937," many male writers of the late Qing dedicated full-length novels to courtesans' lives in the pleasure quarters. A case in point is the *Singsong Girls of Shanghai* by Han Bangqing (1856–1894), first translated into English by the novelist Eileen Chang, and recently revised by Eva Hung and published in 2005 by Columbia University Press. David Wang observes that there is a basic difference between the late Qing courtesan narratives and those of earlier times. Whereas the late Ming courtesan quarters often carried a symbolic meaning for the male literati, the late Qing courtesan house was generally represented in terms of its actual social function, and thus represents a new dimension of realism in literature.

Indeed, the practice and discourse of realism, David Wang posits, constitutes "one of the most salient features of the corpus of modern Chinese literature." This is due to a new need to reflect reality, especially at a time when the literati begin to face crises on both the national and the individual levels. According to David Wang, the Late Qing "exposé" (a new fictional genre meant to present eyewitness reports of social realities) strongly anticipated the May Fourth writers' drive to depict the genuine – as Lu Xun,

Lao She, and Zhang Tianyi did in their "new" fiction. In this way, "realism" provided these modern writers with the possibility of looking at life from new perspectives, while at the same time the rise of women writers offered new voices that eventually broadened the scope of this realism. It should be emphasized, however, that in addition to the paradigm of realism, modern Chinese writers have tried their hand at a wide range of genres and styles – from modernism to expressionism, naturalism to lyricism. Even within the canon of realism, there have been various contesting voices and styles. It is this polyphony that makes Chinese literary modernization from the late Qing to the post-May Fourth period such a dynamic phenomenon.

One perennial feature of Chinese literature is that the present is constantly being related to the past. Even in the modern period, writers continued to remind themselves that they could not do away with the literary past. In a sense, China's "modernity" began with the rereading of some major forms of classical literature, such as the poetry written in the Han–Wei and Six Dynasties style, the Late Tang style, and the Song dynasty style, as well as song lyrics (*ci*), and archaic prose (*guwen*). Moreover, as David Wang points out, the idea of "Literary history" (*wenxue shi*) as the Chinese understand it today was actually a modern "invention" of the late Qing. It was not until 1904 that the first history of Chinese literature was finally produced, when studying and writing literary history became a legitimate form of learning. This new discipline of literary history compelled modern writers and readers to view the past as a living part of the future.

Another important aspect of modern Chinese literature is the translation of Western literatures and discourses during the nineteenth and twentieth centuries. (See Jing Tsu, "Translation of Western Literatures and Discourses," in Chapter 6.) Our focus on this is in part intended to fill a gap in modern scholarship, as this fascinating subject has been largely overlooked in literary history. The rediscovery of various kinds of translation (ranging from missionary to literary materials) not only revises our conception of the scope of modern Chinese literature, but also enlarges our knowledge of print culture. As Michel Hockx reminds us in his essay "Print culture and literary societies" (see Chapter 6), the earliest modern printing presses were imported into China by missionaries from the West, and were primarily used for the production of translations, for the most part in the fields of religion and literature. This new Western technology was later adopted by Chinese commercial printing houses. These novel methods of cultural exchange, alongside the growing demand of a new readership in the urban centers, contributed to a richer cultural landscape at the turn of the century.

Finally, we must remind readers again that, unlike the writers of most traditional histories of Chinese literature, we stress a progression toward a more integrated record of literary culture, casting aside the divisions of fixed genres. Genres are important, but they should be viewed in the larger context of literary culture. Thus Michelle Yeh, instead of dividing her chapter into conventional categories of "modern and contemporary fiction," "modern and contemporary poetry," and so on, has decided to organize her sections by topics such as "The Second Sino-Japanese War (1937–1945) and its aftermath," and "The end of the Civil War and the beginning of a new era (1949–1977)," thereby treating various literary phenomena according to major geographical locales. Geography is vital to understanding the literary landscape of the time, since after the repeated division and segregation following the war (e.g. the great retreat of 1937, and the 1949 divide), it was no longer possible for the Chinese to read literature in a monolithic fashion. In particular, the war and its aftermath confronted Chinese writers with an increasingly complex world of diaspora, and consequently led to the creation of new forms of literature. In the process, various political crises caused writers in different regions to make divergent political choices – such as those seen during the Cultural Revolution (1966–1976) in mainland China and the White Terror era (1950–1987) in Taiwan.

The final section of this *History* covers the period from 1978 to the present. This era marks a new direction in the field of modern Chinese studies. (See the third section of Chapter 7.) One of the major concerns during this period is writers' self-redefinition as a response to political and cultural change on the regional and global levels. During this period, Chinese writers' increasing transnational mobility (for example, the emigration of Nobel Prize-winner Gao Xingjian and the renowned novelist Ha Jin) adds to the problem of identifying one's homeland. (See the Epilogue by Jing Tsu.) In the case of Taiwan, the aftermath of the February 28th Incident apparently left many people with shattered identities – as may be seen from the current split among mainlanders, anticolonialists, and nativists in Taiwan. In Hong Kong the question of cultural identity is even more complex, as Hong Kong may seem "Chinese" to foreigners and "foreign" to some Chinese. These problems raise important questions concerning borders and territories in the making of new literature.

The last decade of this period also witnessed the rise of Internet literature. As Michel Hockx describes in his section "Recent changes in print culture and the advent of the new media" (Chapter 7), due to the late arrival of the Internet in mainland China the earliest Chinese-language Web literature was produced outside of China. In particular, Internet literature started in Taiwan at least a decade before its advent in mainland China. During the early and mid-1990s, various Chinese-language literary websites were produced in the United States and other Western countries, which led to the emergence of literary websites in China around 1997. As expected, the Chinese government's effort to control Web literature through policies of censorship has been difficult to carry out, and often backfires, inadvertently promoting the banned work. A case in point is the banning of Hu Fayun's novel *Ruyan@sars.com*. The act of censorship – despite creating problems for the author at first – eventually turned the work into "the hottest novel of 2006." Indeed, as Michel Hockx puts it, "control of Web literature relies heavily on self-censorship and is based on the assumption that those responsible for running the websites want to stay out of trouble."

To date, none of the standard histories of Chinese literature has discussed Web literature, and, given this, our discussion opens up an unprecedented new area of study. Our primary purpose is to provide a widely encompassing narrative history of Chinese literature that addresses the educated general reader in an increasingly global age.

Literature of the early Ming to mid-Ming
(1375–1572)

KANG-I SUN CHANG

Overview

In the available histories of Chinese literature today, early and mid-Ming literature has been largely ignored. This problem is partly due to our obsession with the late Ming (i.e. 1550–1644), which has led us to ignore some equally important, if not more important, literary phenomena occurring before 1550. In fact, many of the important trends that have been associated with the late Ming actually find their origins much earlier. For example, it was during the early Ming – especially the Yongle reign (1403–1424) – that literature began to flourish in the court, when scholar–officials considered themselves to be somewhat like European courtiers.

For the sake of convenience, the literature of the early and middle Ming can be divided roughly into three periods: 1375 to 1450, 1450 to 1520, and 1520 to 1572. The beginning of the first period was far from being a cultural revival. Zhu Yuanzhang, the Hongwu Emperor, was suspicious to the point of paranoia, and was completely unpredictable in his responses to poetry. His persecution of authors whom he believed to have secretly criticized him was often brutal. Once a poor peasant and a local leader during the Red Turban revolt, the emperor assumed that the cultural elite would despise him; thus, reading between the lines for evidence of disloyalty, he brought death or banishment upon countless literary men. Given his persecution of writers and artists, it is ironic that among the past emperors of imperial China, Zhu Yuanzhang is the one whose portraits have been best preserved. At present, twelve portraits of Zhu are kept in the Palace Museum in Taipei, Taiwan, and one is in the Palace Museum in Beijing.

In the following years of his son the Yongle Emperor's reign, scholar officials gradually recovered from decades of terror and finally developed an atmosphere of collegiality in their administrative life as they advised the emperor on matters concerning the Confucian classics and their application in

1. A portrait of the Ming dynasty founder Zhu Yuanzhang (artist unknown). Collection of the National Palace Museum, Taipei, Taiwan.

government policy. Although the Yongle Emperor sometimes liked to punish his officials by putting them in prison – unlike his father Zhu Yuanzhang, who was inclined to kill them – the attitude of intellectuals toward writing literature during the Yongle reign was generally celebratory. At this time, the philosophy of "inherent pattern" (li) as taught by the Song dynasty neo-Confucian scholar Zhu Xi (1130–1200) had already become the basis of the "eight-part" essay (bagu wen) used in the civil service examinations, although it was not until the Chenghua reign (1465–1487) that the eight-part essay finally reached its mature form.

In contrast to the first period, the second period saw a growing weakness in the central government – especially following the battle of Tumu at which the Yingzong Emperor was taken prisoner by the Mongols – but political weakness ironically led to a period of real growth in the field of literature. Freed from the climate of fear and enforced silence that had characterized the previous age, writers now indulged themselves in the uninhibited expression of their thoughts and feelings. As time went by, they began to attack corrupt eunuchs and other high officials, whom they believed had misled the emperors; partly as a result of this focus on criticism and reform, Chinese literary production after 1450 was enormously rich.

The third period of early and middle Ming literature centers on the age of the Jiajing Emperor (r. 1522–1566). The Chinese coast was at this time increasingly troubled by Japanese pirates. In 1550 Mongol forces threatened to break through the wall below Beijing, and the country was saved only by a timely trade settlement with the Mongols. Throughout his long reign, upright officials repeatedly petitioned the Jiajing Emperor, risking their lives to criticize his misrule. In return the emperor enjoyed humiliating his officials in open court; some were even beaten to death. Scenes of beatings in the court were often reproduced in popular fiction. As printing began to thrive, full-length novels and works of various genres enjoyed an ever wider circulation during this period. Certain parallels may be drawn between China of the mid-Ming and Renaissance Europe in terms of their common cultural products.

I. Early Ming to 1450

Political persecution and censorship

This chapter begins in the 1370s with the first few years of the Ming, a transitional time regarded by many as one of the darkest periods for Chinese intellectuals. It should first be mentioned that during the Yuan dynasty (1234–,

1261–, or 1276–1368) Chinese writers enjoyed a certain sense of freedom. (The dates of the Yuan dynasty are still under dispute, depending on whether one calculates the dynastic time span backward from 1368 to the fall of the Jin in 1234, to Khubilai Khan's establishment of the Great Yuan in 1261, or to the fall of the Southern Song in 1276.) As Stephen H. West points out in his chapter (see Volume I of the *Cambridge History of Chinese Literature*), the Yuan is a dynasty in which there appear no literary inquisitions. This is because the Mongol emperors "simply were not interested in the passions of their Chinese officials about writing." In 1368 when Zhu Yuanzhang, the founding emperor of the Ming, expelled the Mongols, he reversed this practice by establishing a government of Confucian ideology based on the new Ming code in order to secure his legitimacy. As mentioned above, during early Ming numerous writers and officials became victims of the "tyrannical despot" Zhu Yuangzhang. Even Liu Ji (1311–1375), the eminent thinker and writer known for his statesmanship – and one of the emperor's faithful longtime senior advisers – eventually evoked the emperor's displeasure and suspicion, and was dismissed from office. Worse yet, Song Lian (1310–1381), another imperial adviser and scholar–official who had won the emperor's respect and had been appointed associate director of the *Yuan History* compilation project, was almost put to death because his grandson was implicated in a plot to overthrow the throne. Empress Ma herself intervened on Song Lian's behalf and reduced his sentence to banishment. Song Lian's grandson was eventually executed along with all his family members, including his parents and one of his uncles. During the initial stages of emperor's purges of his supposed enemies, some reports claim nearly 15,000 people were arrested and executed. Among the intellectuals persecuted by the Hongwu Emperor, the best known was Gao Qi. He was one of the first to be executed, killed by "slashing in half at the waist."

Gao Qi was a close contemporary of Chaucer (ca 1340–1400), but unlike Chaucer, who lived through relatively peaceful times, he had the misfortune of being born in the last few decades of the Yuan, an age of unprecedented disorder, when China was troubled by endless civil wars and natural disasters such as drought and plague. (The disease described in Boccaccio's (1313–1375) *Decameron* was prevalent in China too.) Fortunately, Gao Qi grew up in Suzhou, a city long famous for its great wealth and cultural preeminence, and far more advanced than any other city in either China or Europe. It naturally became a haven to which many writers, artists, and scholars flocked during the tumultuous years of social breakdown in mid-fourteenth-century China. Here the young Gao Qi cultivated his poetic talent and formed associations with a circle of literary colleagues. Though he never sat for the civil service examinations and never took office under the Yuan, by his late teens Gao was already famous as one of the "Four Literary Giants of Suzhou," along with Zhang Yu (1333–1385), Yang Ji (ca 1334–1383), and Xu Ben (1335–1380). These three were also among the greatest painters of the age. Later they were all included in the larger group called "Ten Friends of the North Wall," of which Gao Qi was the unofficial leader. These young poets and artists frequently met in the congenial atmosphere of the city; they gathered to write poems on scenic sights and participated in cultural activities. Their poem series on the Lion Forest Garden is still among the most celebrated works in garden literature. Ironically, it was the troubled times that brought these talented men together within the shelter of Suzhou city.

In 1356, the rebel leader Zhang Shicheng (1321–1367) occupied Suzhou and ruled the city for the next twelve years. Zhang Yu, Yang Ji, and Xu Ben were all forced to take office. Possibly as an escape from political involvement, in 1358 Gao Qi moved his home to the nearby Green Hill and wrote his famous poem "Song of the Man of the Green Hill," in which he describes himself as a recluse "addicted to the search for poetic lines." Later that year, he left Green Hill and spent the next two or three years traveling through the areas of modern Jiangsu and Zhejiang provinces, apparently to avoid further pressure from the rebel regime in Suzhou. His movements are perhaps reflected in his fictional anecdote "The Biography of Master Nangong" (Nangong Sheng zhuan), about a Suzhou knight-errant who manages to escape serving under a certain military governor by traveling around the Jiangnan region. Meanwhile, continuous internecine violence took a heavy toll on Suzhou, although under Zhang Shicheng's government the city seemed to experience a cultural revival of sorts. But when fighting broke out between the future Hongwu Emperor and Zhang Shicheng in 1367, many intellectuals of the area fled Suzhou, leaving the city in desolation. Immediately following the fall of Suzhou, tens of thousands of the local gentry, including the poets Yang Ji and Xu Ben, were banished to faraway regions. The Hongwu Emperor was especially merciless toward Suzhou, no doubt because of his hostility regarding Zhang Shicheng, his fiercest rival. As a member of the Suzhou gentry, Gao Qi suddenly found himself in a politically vulnerable position. He served briefly as one of the editors of the *Yuan History* in the Ming central government in Nanjing, but still could not escape calamity.

Gao Qi was executed mainly because he wrote an essay and a poem to congratulate the new prefect of Suzhou, Wei Guan (1304?–1374), for rebuilding his office on the site of the prefectural offices formerly occupied by Zhang

Shicheng. These congratulatory pieces to Wei Guan, himself an eminent poet, should have been treated for what they were – a routine exchange dictated by convention. Instead, Gao Qi and Wei Guan, along with another local poet, were executed in a public square. Some scholars believe that the real reason for this brutal execution was the emperor's deep-seated hatred of Gao Qi for his refusal to serve in the central government in 1369 after finishing his role in the *Yuan History* project, which was completed that same year. Gao Qi is said to have maintained his composure to the moment of death; he even composed a poem calling for the spirit of the Yangzi river to be his witness. He would, however, have been saddened to know that some years later several of his friends – including Xu Ben – would die as a result of political persecution as well, while Yang Ji and Zhang Yu also came to tragic ends: Yang Ji died in a labor camp, while Zhang Yu drowned himself on his way into exile. Thus, within a few years' time, an entire generation of Suzhou's artistic and literary talent vanished.

The fate of the Suzhou poets lends a terrible poignancy to the early Ming cultural scene. Clearly the tyrant's methods of silencing dissent were effective in frightening the intellectuals of the time. In several poems, Gao Qi expressed deep concern that free poetic expression might one day endanger his life. But bearing witness in poetry was necessary to his art; the deep desire to record the social and political realities of the time was what drove him to write poetry in the first place. What others might have overlooked, or passed over in silence, aroused in Gao Qi a powerful emotional response. Through his poetry we are ineluctably drawn to both a strong sense of the historical significance of the occasion and a deeply personal emotional context. For example, "On Seeing Flowers, I Remember My Departed Daughter, Shu," which refers to the 1367 siege of Suzhou in which Gao Qi's second daughter died, speaks at once of personal tragedy and the cruel reality of war. Eventually, however, Gao Qi found solace through his own writing and his interaction with the classical canon. He displays affinity with the Tang and Song masters, but also understands that inheriting and revising a tradition are in themselves creative and innovative activities. One of the salient characteristics of Gao Qi's poetic art is his mixed style, which conforms to tradition while incorporating elements of "contemporary" vernacular language. The result is an innovative lyrical style. Had Gao Qi lived longer, he might have been able to exercise a greater influence on the development of Ming literature. Instead, his reception in literary history has been marred by the circumstances of his death. After his passing, only his close friends in Suzhou dared to write poems to mourn him, while the local gazetteer referred only discreetly to his poetry. Although

Gao Qi had edited his own poems in a twelve-chapter collection as early as 1370, his nephew did not manage to have them published until thirty years after the poet's death. In the interim, most scholars hesitated to mention Gao Qi for fear of being implicated in his political misadventures, and the lack of obituary notices and detailed biographies led gradually to oblivion for the poet. A century later, the Suzhou painter and poet Shen Zhou (1427–1509) drew belated attention to Gao Qi by honoring his poetic innovations. Other poets, such as Li Dongyang (1447–1516) and Wang Shizhen (1526–1590), also gave high praise to Gao Qi's poetry. But, while critics during the early Qing (i.e. after the Manchu conquest in 1644) recognized Gao as one of the greatest Ming poets, they nonetheless continued to ignore the poetry of the Ming dynasty, and Gao naturally sank once more into obscurity. Only in the eighteenth century did Gao achieve canonical status through the efforts of Zhao Yi (1727–1814). The woman poet Wang Duan (1793–1839) also gave Gao Qi a prominent place in her *Selections of Thirty Poets of the Ming* (*Ming sanshi jia shixuan*). In the twentieth century, however, it was the American historian Frederick W. Mote who brought about a significant "rehabilitation" of Gao Qi as a great poet with the publication of his book on Gao in 1962. As Jonathan Chaves says in his *Columbia Book of Later Chinese Poetry*, Gao became "the best-known Ming poet in the West" mainly because of the work of Mote.

Gao Qi was only one casualty of the Hongwu Emperor's authoritarian approach to rulership, which was to have a profound impact on the subsequent development of Chinese literature. As the emperor gradually built up his new dynasty, he promoted his own legitimacy by establishing a system of education with a general curriculum that centered on the *Four Books* and other Confucian classics. In his puritanical interpretation of these texts, the emperor emphasized the more austere Confucian virtues and strongly prohibited any trifling or self-indulgent extravagances. This was one reason why he often attacked Zhang Shicheng for corrupting the morals of the people of Suzhou and the surrounding cities. The examination system, reestablished in 1370, focused mainly on these texts and was intended to cultivate a moral bond between young scholar–officials and the emperor, who expected absolute obedience from all. Between the stern imposition of Confucian morality and the dangers of serving in his government, literary men were driven into hiding or self-censorship.

One of the writers who adopted self-censorship was Qu You (1347–1433), now best known for his collection of classical fiction, *New Tales Told by Lamplight* (*Jiandeng xinhua*). Qu You began to write these short stories during the last years of the Yuan, finishing the collection ten years after the establishment of the Ming. In his preface he writes that he "secretly stored away the manuscript in a chest" because of its "outlandish," almost "obscene," language. Although the collection was completed by 1378 and circulated in manuscript form among close friends, it was not published until around 1400, perhaps to avoid the danger of persecution. Ironically, despite all his caution, Qu You still could not avoid being persecuted – this time by the Yongle Emperor, the fourth son of the Hongwu Emperor. In the sixth year of Yongle (1408), Qu You was thrown into prison and later spent seventeen years in a labor camp, though for reasons other than the publication of his short stories. It is said that when Qu You was serving as an adviser to Zhu Su, Prince Ding of Zhou – who was the Yongle Emperor's younger brother – Qu You became implicated in his master's missteps. Zhu Su apparently offended his emperor brother (perhaps by plotting a rebellion), and, according to Ming law, his advisers – among them Qu You – were also to be punished. By punishing his brother and the associates, the Yongle Emperor might have been making a political statement by reconfirming his imperial powers at a time when his legitimacy to the throne was still being challenged. When Qu You was finally released from the labor camp in 1425, he was almost eighty years old.

Like Gao Qi, Qu You became known as a literary genius while still a child. At thirteen, he was already writing erudite, elegantly adorned poems, and was hailed by the Yuan poet Yang Weizhen (1296–1370) as a "genius from Heaven." Had he lived in a different era, Qu You would doubtless have enjoyed a brilliant career in office. Instead he and his family, originally based in Hangzhou, were forced to move from one city to another (including Suzhou) as refugees of war. Nevertheless, Qu You's extremely long life allowed him to witness the changes in political climate through the first five reigns of the Ming. One of the most prolific writers of the early Ming, he produced more than twenty books in different genres – including poetry, song lyric (*ci*), prose essay, literary criticism, biography, and fiction. He was a master of the classical language, as is evident in the elegant, mellifluous prose of *New Tales Told by Lamplight*. In this regard, Qu You was a pioneer in reviving the great Tang tradition of the classical tale of the "strange and remarkable" (*chuanqi*). Yet one of the special attractions of *New Tales* is the contemporary setting of the narratives, which are mostly set in the final years of the Yuan and realistically depict a country with a large population decimated by war. We find in these stories a voice raised in passionate outcry against militarization and an overpowering sense of indignation at human suffering, conveyed in a direct, vigorous style. To disguise his criticisms of the Ming government,

Qu You created in his stories the mirror images of the Underworld and the Dragon Kingdom, which are clearly allegorical representations of the governmental bureaucracy with which Qu You was painfully familiar. This allegorical significance becomes clear when wrongdoers are punished in the lowest level of Hell, as in "The record of Scholar Ling Hu's dream of the Underworld" (Linghu Sheng mingmeng lu). In another story entitled "The rural temple of Yongzhou" (Yongzhou yemiao ji), an evil white snake with a red head that had haunted the entire local region for years is eventually captured and punished by the King of the Underworld. It is not too far-fetched to assume that some Ming readers might have secretly compared the snake in the story to the "cruel" founding emperor Zhu Yuanzhang, whose last name, Zhu, literally means "red," and who participated in the Red Turban revolt before overcoming the Yuan. The evident danger of telling this kind of allegory may also account for Qu You's keenness for self-censorship. In any case, stories with such an insistent didactic message might have given pleasure to early Ming readers, aware as they were of the injustice in their own world. Oftentimes these moral lessons are conveyed by evoking a dream world, and Qu You seems to take delight in such vivid and fanciful representation. Most interesting, however, is the author's liberal attitude to love and sex. In this respect, Qu You was certainly influenced by the erotic poems of Yang Weizhen. Qu You's descriptions of love scenes in his *New Tales* are generally characterized by a combination of realism and eroticism, couched in language associated with both classical embellishment and the sensual representation of romantic love. In many cases love arises between a man and a female ghost, yet the sensory experience depicted in the stories is totally convincing. Other stories describe frank sexual encounters between human characters, as in the "Tower of Twofold Fragrance" (Lianfang lou ji), where two sisters make love (and exchange erotic poems) with a young man every night until their father, discovering the affair, agrees to let both of them marry the man. The male protagonist in this story, a young merchant, cares only about his love for these women and gives no thought to the Confucian teachings with which most youths of his family background would be expected to be preoccupied. These stories present a direct challenge to the Confucian values and examination system that the Hongwu Emperor worked so hard to promote.

Qu You's collection of stories became extremely popular during the Yongle reign (1403–1424). One writer, Li Changqi (1376–1452), went so far as to emulate the style of Qu You in his *Sequel to Tales Told by Lamplight* (*Jiandeng yuhua*), which was also an instant success. Indeed, both collections of stories were so widely received by the general public that they were later banned in 1442, when Li Shimian (1374–1450), a high official at theYingzong Emperor's court, expressed grave concern that these works might corrupt the minds of the people. During the more than two decades when the stories were banned in China, Qu You's *New Tales* became popular in Korea, Japan, and Vietnam, and new editions of the book continued to be printed in Korea. (For example, the so-called "Jiajing edition" now preserved in the Naigaku Bunko in Japan – long thought to be a Chinese edition – was recently proven to be a Korean edition first published, with commentaries, by a Korean scholar in 1564.) Writers in Korea, Japan, and Vietnam also competed to create similar stories using Qu You's works as models. This demonstrates how transnational circulation of literary knowledge and texts was enhanced by governmental censorship and the development of print culture. But in fact Chinese readers never stopped taking delight in the story and discourse of the *Jiandeng xinhua*, though many of them read the book as underground literature. After the ban was lifted in China in around 1466, Qu You's *Jiandeng xinhua* was again reprinted and continued to enjoy popularity for at least another century. His stories exercised a great influence on later classical fiction, such as the *Records of the Strange* (*Liaozhai zhiyi*) by Pu Songling (1640–1715), as well as vernacular literature in the late Ming, which often borrowed plots directly from Qu You. However, as Feng Menglong (1574–1646) and Ling Mengchu (1580–1644), the writers of many of these vernacular tales, never acknowledged their sources, Qu You has been unduly neglected ever since.

How did Qu You's contemporaries fare? A number of authors and scholars – especially from remote regional centers – managed to escape political persecution. Of these, the "Ten Talented Men of Min" from Fujian Province were the most prominent, and the list included such leading poets as Lin Hong (ca 1340–ca 1400) and Gao Bing (1350–1423). Lin Hong chose to retire from office before he turned forty and devoted the rest of his life to writing poetry. He became famous for his poetic exchanges with a certain poetess, Zhang Hongqiao, who is said to have died of lovesickness – although this claim has been questioned by recent scholarship. Gao Bing is best remembered for his *Graded Compendium of Tang Poetry* (*Tangshi pinhui*), in which he divides Tang poetry into four periods (early, high, middle, and late), with the poetry of the High Tang (i.e. produced between 713 and 756) considered to be the most superb. The anthology contains 5,769 poems by 620 poets in various subgenres, interspersed with commentary and notes. Gao Bing acknowledges a special debt to Lin Hong, stating that Lin advised him to use High Tang poetry as a model for his own poetic composition. Later Gao Bing gained access to *Canglang's Remarks on Poetry* (*Canglang shihua*), in which the Song Dynasty critic Yan Yu (1191–1241) first canonized High Tang poetry as the definitive standard for all poetry; this, however, did not gain wide currency until after the mid-Ming. Gao Bing's ideas perhaps owed a greater debt to the Yuan critic Yang Shihong (fl. 1340) – Yang's anthology of Tang poetry, *Sounds of the Tang (Tang yin)*, had been popular ever since its first printing in 1344. But, although agreeing with Yang Shihong in the main, Gao nonetheless questioned Yang's criteria of selection – especially his exclusion of Li Bai and Du Fu. Gao believed that his own anthology, being more systematic and complete, would provide a better guide to the new generation of writers. He later selected 1,010 poems out of the original 5,769 to create a shorter version called *The Correct Sounds of Tang Poetry (Tangshi zhengsheng)*, perhaps as a further challenge to Yang Shihong's then "outdated" anthology. Yet Gao's anthologies exercised little influence during the early Ming, whose tastes were still governed by Yang's selections. One reason for this was that although the *Graded Compendium of Tang Poetry* was completed in manuscript form by 1384, the book was not printed until the Chenghua reign (1465–1487), and then only privately by a local official in Fujian. This suggests that the marginal status of one's publisher could do as much harm to an author as political censorship. Gao Bing would have to wait until the sixteenth century to become influential when his shorter anthology, *The Correct Sounds of Tang Poetry*, was printed for the first time. (His *Graded Compendium* was reprinted later.) Compared to his contemporaries, however, Gao Bing was fortunate in that he was never the victim of political persecution or censorship, serving briefly in the Hanlin Academy at the court of Yongle and emerging unscathed. Like Lin Hong, he seems to have enjoyed life in his hometown, associating with the local poets and artists in that remote and comparatively safe region.

Court drama and other forms of literature

If Qu You's classical fiction represents a form of protest against the oppressive political climate of the early Ming, the court drama sanctioned by the central government speaks in a voice that is uncritically laudatory of the new dynasty's glories. Two members of the royal family – Zhu Quan (1378–1448) and Zhu Youdun (1379–1439) – are the best exemplars of this new drama. Zhu Quan, the seventeenth son of the Hongwu Emperor, unabashedly opens his *Record of the Correct Sounds of Great Harmony (Taihe zhengyin pu)* with the following statement: "Ah, great indeed! It has been some time since peace has been brought to this land. The grandeur of ritual and music, the beauty of the musical education . . . have all come as a result of the emperor's benevolent influence." This flattering proclamation, written in a preface dated 1398, the last year of the Hongwu reign, must have fed the old emperor's appetite for praise.

The emperor had always been proud of the accomplishment of establishing the Ming empire by driving away the Mongols. In fact, in 1389, he commissioned an artist to create "The Unified Map of the Great Ming" (Da Ming hunyi tu), which showed Ming territory extending to areas as far as the boundaries of Japan and Western Europe, no doubt as a way to promote his imperial power and influence. Needless to say, other artists found their own means of extolling the new dynasty. Zhu Youdun, Zhu Quan's nephew and Prince Xian of Zhou, staged his dramas in the most elaborate theatrical settings, with complicated arias, all designed to reflect the splendor and magnificence of a new kingdom. Compared with Yuan drama, these works are notable for the confident picture they project of court spectacle and aristocratic extravagance. As one who loved the exuberant play of language itself, Zhu Youdun also created an elaborate descriptive style in his arias so as to convey the proper aura of opulent majesty, and this was further enhanced by an impressive array of dances, presented with fanciful music and flowery costumes, especially in his "Peony" plays.

The author of thirty-two short plays (zaju), Zhu Youdun was regarded as the most distinguished dramatist of the early Ming. He was known especially for his musical talent and lyrical sensibility, which made him one of the best librettists of the dynasty. His invention of a lively vernacular style of dialogue made for a broader realism that delighted audiences. Zhu Youdun's unique achievement in drama was also closely related to his family background, for his father was none other than Zhu Su, Prince Ding of Zhou, the younger (and the only full) brother of the Yongle Emperor. As mentioned above, Zhu Su was the cause of the writer Qu You's imprisonment and exile. A man of exceptional talent, Zhu Su was strongly drawn to literature and learning; he was famous for his song collection, The Palace Lyrics of the Yuan (Yuan gongci). One might assume that Zhu Youdun, who was fascinated by drama and song lyrics throughout life, had been influenced by his father; it may be more correct to say, however, that Zhu Youdun was the one who exerted a powerful influence on the people around him. At his princely court, centered in Kaifeng, even palace ladies were trained in writing poetry and composing music; the woman poet Xia Yunying (1394–1418), who first served as a palace lady but later became Zhu Youdun's consort, is a case in point. Zhu Youdun also lent inspiration to the younger generation of the royal family, including the future Xuanzong Emperor (r. 1426–1435), an unusually skilled painter and poet.

One of the great ironies of life in traditional China is that literary accomplishment was often the outcome of political failure. This applies to both Zhu Youdun and Zhu Quan. Their success in the field of literature was directly linked to the Ming policy of centralization that worked to reduce the powers of the imperial princes. This was especially true after 1402, when Zhu Di usurped the throne from his nephew to become the Yongle Emperor and proceeded systematically to strip the military power of their princedoms as a way of consolidating his own territory. The new emperor's policy was to allow the princes to indulge in luxurious living so long as they did not have political ambitions. Zhu Quan and Zhu Youdun, endowed with rich resources in their respective domains, were particularly vulnerable to suspicion. Zhu Quan, in particular, with more than 80,000 guards and soldiers in his princedom, centered at Daning in what is now Inner Mongolia, was distinguished for his military strength; but after the Yongle Emperor "relieved" him of his military command, Zhu Quan chose to devote himself to the study of dramatic literature. In addition to the critically acclaimed *Record of the Correct Sounds of Great Harmony*, he wrote twelve short plays, of which two are still extant. Zhu Youdun, though politically less prominent than his uncle, was even more distinguished as a dramatist. Succeeding his father in 1425, Zhu Youdun threw himself into the writing and performance of plays for the rest of his life, perhaps also to prove his indifference to politics. Needless to say, his father's political experience may have influenced him.

Viewed in this light, it is easy to understand why Zhu Youdun adopted a celebratory tone in his plays, depicting the shining glories of the Ming. Loyalty to the throne, as Wilt Idema has shown in *The Dramatic Oeuvre of Chu Yu-tun*, is the main theme of Zhu's works. Indeed, both Zhu Youdun and Zhu Quan seem to have faithfully embraced the Confucian moral values promoted by the imperial court. In his play on the romance between the Han poet Sima Xiangru and the young widow Zhuo Wenjun, Zhu Quan goes out of his way to present the young widow as a virtuous woman who helps her future husband drive the carriage during their elopement. Likewise, Zhu Youdun, in several of his plays – "The Very Virtuous Stepmother" (Jimu daxian), the "Dream of Reunion" (Tuanyuan meng), and "Becoming a Singing Girl Again" (Fu luo chang) – honors the "virtuous mother" and the "chaste woman," while duly punishing the "wanton." This moralistic outlook is in keeping with the beliefs of the Hongwu Emperor, who is said to have enjoyed morality plays, especially the Yuan play *The Lute (Pipa ji)*. According to the *Legal Codes of the Great Ming (Da Ming lü)* established by the Hongwu Emperor, "righteous men and chaste women, filial sons and obedient grandsons" were the only acceptable themes in contemporary plays. However, this does not mean that old romantic comedies, such as the famous Yuan play *The Western Wing* (*Xixiang ji*), about the enduring love between a young couple, were prohibited from being performed. Both Zhu Youdun and the playwright Jia Zhongming (1343–after 1422) spoke highly of *The Western Wing*, even though many of their contemporaries denounced the play as "frivolous." Indeed, themes about lovers who were faithful unto death were particularly favored by Zhu Youdun: one typical example is his "Lament upon the Fragrant Sachet" (Xiangnang yuan), in which the heroine commits suicide to express her single-minded devotion to her lover. Zhu Youdun shared some of the moral values of his contemporary Liu Dongsheng. Liu's play, "The Story of Jiao and Hong" (Jiao Hong ji), is a treatment of the devoted love between two cousins, which transforms its source, a work of fiction by the Yuan writer Song Meidong, from a tragedy into a comedy.

Zhu Xi's interpretation of the Confucian classics became orthodoxy in the early years of the dynasty. In particular, the eight-part essay was often used in the civil service examinations to incorporate Zhu Xi's philosophy into expositions of wisdom. Although the structure of the eight-part essay would not be definitively established until after the mid-fifteenth century, even in the early Ming we can already see the influence of this examination system in shaping morals, which became more restrictive and conservative than in any previous period in Chinese history. Most interesting is the high degree of overlap – given the pronounced differences in writing styles – between early instances of eulogies for the emperor in examination essays and contemporary court drama. For example, the essay by Huang Zicheng, the leading candidate in the 1385 examination, applauds the virtues of the "Son of Heaven" and his meritorious officials.

However, it was the cultural projects sponsored by the Yongle Emperor, the third emperor of the Ming, that finally institutionalized these narrower interpretations of Confucian morality. The emperor's passionate support for the publication of Confucian texts was instrumental to the promulgation of moral education. *The Great Compendia of the Principle of Human Nature* (*Xingli daquan*), *The Great Compendia of the Five Classics* (*Wujing daquan*), and *The Great Compendia of Four Books* (*Sishu daquan*), with commentary by Zhu Xi, were all compiled and published by imperial command early in the Yongle reign. Most importantly, the emperor instructed that these texts be used as required reading for scholar–officials and especially for those preparing for the civil service examinations. Moral education, however, was not limited to men. Empress Xu (1362–1407), the Yongle Emperor's chief consort, issued her *Precepts for the Ladies of the Palace* (*Nei xun*) in 1404 to provide instruction with a content similar to the *Four Books*. In a further attempt to bring order and legitimacy to his government, the Yongle Emperor commissioned his grand secretary to compile an encyclopedia of unprecedented dimensions that would include practically every subject as well as all texts that were hard to come by. This monumental work, known as *The Grand Encyclopedia of the Yongle Era* (*Yongle dadian*), involved more than 2,000 scholars and was completed in 1408. Due to its massive size – 50 million characters, 22,938 chapters, and 11,095 volumes, with sources drawn from 7,000 separate works – the encyclopedia was never issued in printed form, although every page of the manuscript is written in beautiful calligraphy. Unfortunately, the original copy was lost before the end of the Ming, and the copy produced in the Jiajing reign (1522–1566) is now incomplete. Today, fifty-one volumes of the original encyclopedia are kept in libraries in the United Kingdom, with numerous others in Japan, Korea, and China. It is the only source for many rare texts, including a number of dramatic works.

In addition to promoting Confusion morals and the recording of cultural history, the Yongle Emperor's ambitions extended to a maritime empire. From 1405 until the end of his reign, an imperial fleet of over three hundred ships made seven expeditions to the countries of the Western Ocean (Southeast Asia, India, and Africa) with the Muslim eunuch Zheng He (1371–1433) as its commander-in-chief. Although the expeditions, which ended with Zheng He's death, did not accomplish much in terms of trade, they sealed the legacy of the Yongle Emperor as a mighty ruler. More than a hundred years later, they became the subject of a play and were also celebrated in the one-hundred-chapter novel *The Journey of Sanbao the Eunuch to the Western Ocean* (*Sanbao taijian Xiyang ji tongsu yanyi*, preface 1597) which remains popular to the present day. Even now, after the six-hundredth anniversary of Zheng He's first voyage, the Chinese are proud of these pioneering expeditions undertaken during the Yongle reign, which pre-dated Columbus's voyages by one hundred years. (For reference, please read "China Has an Ancient Mariner to Tell You About," *New York Times*, July 20, 2005.)

Cabinet-style poetry

Ironically, the cultural projects of the Yongle reign, though intended to enrich the people's scope of learning, failed to usher in a flourishing age of poetry. The spirit of lyricism that once characterized the poetry of Gao Qi's generation had apparently been lost. No longer a vehicle of free lyrical expression and soaring feats of imagination, poetry was now class-determined. By and large, only scholar–officials from the prestigious Hanlin Academy and cabinet members from the posts of grand secretaries were honored as important poets. Moreover, their poetic efforts, known collectively as the "cabinet style" (*taige ti*), were not often noted for linguistic novelty but focused rather on praising the reigning emperor. They expressed the cultural superiority of Confucianism and celebrated the success of a national revival that had been made possible by efficient government. While their major themes echo those of contemporary court dramatists, their writing style is quite different. For the most part, the Yongle cabinet style is plain, monotonous, and often repetitive, with none of the sensory vividness of Zhu Youdun's arias and colloquial songs. It may seem strange that such dull poetry would become the dominant form for so many decades, but the reasons are plain. As a result of the emperor's sponsorship of the civil service, poetry writing gradually came to be centered around the experience of serving in office. At the same time, the uniform development of bureaucratic capacities, the Confucian vision of loyalty and righteousness, and the shared desire for social order all worked to encourage scholar–officials to cultivate a common poetic style that was both politically correct and emotionally satisfying. Like their counterparts at European courts, these scholar–officials considered it one of their main duties to please their ruler. But unlike Castiglione's courtiers, Chinese scholar–officials at the court of Yongle were not required to master the use of weapons or to demonstrate skill in painting and music. Collegiality in office and the desire to serve the emperor were what united them. Thus their poetry dwells mainly on the virtues of the government, and on the whole lacks the lyrical vitality of the poetry of the preceding period. Nevertheless, a few writers managed to create an effective personal style in this new form. The "Three Yangs" – Yang Shiqi (1365–1444), Yang Rong (1371–1440), and Yang Pu (1372–1446) (not related to one another) – are generally considered the great masters of the cabinet style, although they wrote their best poetry at the court of the Renzong (r. 1425) and Xuanzong (r. 1426–1435) emperors, whose benevolent reigns contrasted sharply with the Yongle Emperor's tactics of intimidation. The treatment of Yang Pu under these different reigns provides a telling example. Under Yongle, he was labeled a political criminal and spent ten years in prison, but the Renzong Emperor, upon his accession, rehabilitated Yang Pu along with other officials, promoting them to high positions in the court. Under these conditions, cabinet-style poetry – with its characteristically eulogistic tone – provided an appropriate vehicle of expression for Yang Pu and his colleagues. Though the sickly Renzong died after less than a year on the throne, his son Xuanzong continued to build on his benign policies, and officials at the Ming court experienced a period of genuine peace and harmony for the first time. This explains why the cabinet-style poetry produced during these two short reigns has such emotive power.

Yang Shiqi stands out as the foremost of the cabinet-style poets, and his poetry is said to possess the spirit of "correctness" (*zheng*) essential to this genre. Highly respected in the poetic circles of the day, Yang Shiqi was invited to write the foreword to a newly reprinted edition of Yang Shihong's (fl. 1340) famous anthology of Tang poetry, *The Sounds of the Tang* (*Tang yin*), an anthology that was first published in the Yuan. In his own poetry, Yang Shiqi particularly favored the image of spring, which, as the first season, is a natural symbol for an exemplary government. His overall seriousness and tone of wholehearted praise may sound stilted to modern readers, yet can be seen as a sincere reflection of the gratitude and relief of early Ming scholar–officials, mindful of their country's recent humiliations under the Mongols.

This celebratory attitude also played a role in the revival of another literary form, the *fu* poem, which was used to exalt the virtues of various cities. One fascinating aspect of the revival of this ancient form is that it coincides with the Yongle Emperor's relocation in 1420 of the capital to Beijing, the site of his former princedom and once the capital of the Yuan dynasty. It is possible that in his effort to legitimize his reign, the Yongle Emperor encouraged his courtiers to write compositions in praise of Beijing in the tradition of the "*fu* on metropolises and capitals," which dates back to the Han. Whatever the reason, many high officials at his court – chief among them Li Shimian, Chen Jingzong (1377–1459), and Yang Rong – all composed long, extensive pieces with titles such as "*Fu* on Beijing" (Beijing *fu*) and "*Fu* on the Imperial Capital of the Great Sovereign State" (Huangdu dayitong *fu*). Two themes stand out in these works: the beauty of the city and the grand scale of the Ming court. While they bear some stylistic resemblances to the Han *fu*, the differences are also striking: the *fu* of the early Ming are full of eulogies, with repeated use of ceremonial chants in praise of the moral foundation of the dynasty. Although much longer and more repetitive, these *fu* are thematically reminiscent of cabinet-style poetry. These works may not all have been commissioned by the Yongle Emperor; some scholar–officials may simply have wished to extol the newly reconstructed capital. Other works are possibly exercises in composition, since such writings were occasionally required in the civil service examinations during the Yongle reign. However, the mere fact that both cabinet-style poetry and the *fu* on Beijing were in vogue for such an extended time is enough to suggest that they served a definite political purpose.

II. The period from 1450 to 1520

In the decades following the Yongle reign, the Chinese continued to see Beijing as the symbol of their dynasty's prestige and authority; writings in the *fu* form during this period share their eulogistic tone with those from the beginning of the century. The authors of these *fu* – such as Jin Youzi (1368–1431) and Hu Qixian – claimed that the imperial majesty of Beijing was a living emblem of the heavenly mandate of the Great Ming, an empire that would endure for "tens of thousands of years" and under which China was once again the center of the universe.

In 1449, this newly resurgent sense of confidence was crushed as the twenty-one-year-old Yingzong Emperor was taken prisoner by the Mongols at the Battle of Tumu. The captive emperor was returned to Beijing a year later, only to find that his brother had replaced him. Though eventually restored to the throne in 1457, Yingzong was never fully able to disentangle himself from the growing intricacies of court politics. He died eight years later and was succeeded by his sixteen-year-old son, the Chenghua Emperor. At this time, as the Chinese became ever more concerned about further attacks from the Mongols, the government had begun to spend vast amounts of wealth and manpower to construct defenses in the form of a series of long walls – resulting in today's Great Wall.

But political instability can sometimes lead to cultural prosperity. From 1450 onward, China's growing military debility, far from having a negative impact on its literary productivity, apparently precipitated unprecedented innovations. Following the crisis of Yingzong's captivity by the Mongols, writers and scholar–officials became more courageous in airing their political criticisms – often doing so at the risk of their own lives. In fact, men in public life then were never completely free from political persecution; many suffered from the brutal form of corporal punishment known as *tingzhang* (beating at court) and were often sent into exile, yet unlike their predecessors, they refused to be intimidated. The power center in literature gradually moved from the imperial court to individual writers themselves. The change is owed, in part, to the comparatively enlightened stance of most of the mid-Ming emperors, who, though not particularly competent as rulers, were great supporters of educational and cultural activities. For example, Yingzong, however weak in character, nonetheless made several bold policy changes in the school system, including creating a new rank of provincial teachers, called *tixue guan*, and providing for the expansion of local schools. These reforms led to a significant increase in the number of students at the provincial schools, so that by the early sixteenth century the total number of students enrolled in the schools reached the unprecedented figure of 244,300. This favorable cultural milieu was responsible, to a large extent, for the dramatic rise in literacy during this period. At the same time, many scholar–officials were beginning to develop the ideal of a multidisciplinary literary man who is also well grounded in many fields of knowledge. The Yongle Emperor's policy of promoting an encyclopedic approach to learning may have provided an early stimulus for this new outlook, but it was only in the mid-Ming that this predisposition toward all-inclusiveness began to show itself in the domain of literature and to alter the course of its development.

New perspectives on place

One important form of cultural expression that underwent significant changes after 1450 was the *fu*. We have already seen that many early Ming scholar–officials composed *fu* in praise of Beijing. During the middle years of the Ming, *fu* written about the capital and other cities became far more diverse in both tenor and content. For example, Huang Zuo's (1490–1566) "Fu on Beijing" deploys images of animals such as foxes and rats to represent corrupt officials in the capital, while in his "Fu on Canton" (Yuehui *fu*) he mixes the Han style of visual imagination with his own vision of the local scenery in Canton. Huang's choice of a new and exotic locale in the latter piece distinguishes it from earlier *fu*; although in alternating between lines that use parallelism and lines that do not, he is following a conventional scheme. Another notable example is a *fu* by the famous Confucian scholar and writer Qiu Jun (1420–1495) written about Hainan Island off the coast of south China, entitled "An Extraordinary View Seen from the Outskirts of the South Sea" (Nanming qidian *fu*). In his description, Qiu Jun emphasizes the quality of the "remarkable" (*qi*), as he presents layer upon layer of breathtaking views, and concludes that Hainan Island, though not quite a fairyland, is much more beautiful than any other earthly place. The *fu* also describes the customs and rituals of the local people. Compared to the *fu* of previous decades, the *fu* of the mid-Ming are infinitely more expressive and rich in descriptive imagery. More realistic and convincing, their descriptions are at the same time more sublime in style.

Another area of innovation in writings on place lies in the introduction of descriptions of foreign travels into the genre of *fu*. In general, the *fu* writers of this period exhibit a descriptive prowess that few early Ming writers could equal. Dong Yue's (fl. 1480) "Fu on Korea" (Chaoxian *fu*) is an outstanding example. Upon the accession of the Hongzhi Emperor in 1487, Dong Yue was commanded to visit Korea to renew diplomatic relations, and composed this *fu* soon after his return. It became one of the most interesting pieces of geographical and social discourse. The *fu* describes in great detail Korea's geographical conditions, the location of its cities, and various kinds of agricultural produce; it also narrates the long history of Korean trade with China. In Ming China, trade with neighboring states was never regarded as an exchange of equals, since the Chinese viewed such interactions as a form of tributary relations by which foreign states showed respect to the Chinese empire. However, unlike the Mongols, Korea had long been viewed by the Chinese as a "civilized" state. Thus Dong Yue, in elaborating on the social customs of Korea, attributes the virtues of Korean women to the "sagely influence" of Chinese culture. His view confirms the traditional belief of the Chinese in their own cultural superiority. The same idea appears in Zhan Ruoshui's (1466–1560) "*Fu* on Annam" (*Jiaonan fu*), in which China is credited with cultivating the minds of the "barbarian" people of Annam (today's Vietnam). Zhan composed his rhapsody in 1512, immediately after his official trip to attend the investiture of the new king of Annam. Deeply interested in the history of mysticism in Annam, Zhan explores at great length Chinese cultural influences there, tracing back to such mythological figures as the Red Bird, the Fire God, and Fu Xi (a culture hero who taught the Chinese farming and hunting). In terms of rhetorical style, Zhan's *fu* is not as elegant as Dong Yue's piece on Korea, but even so, it is still a significant literary work, representing the desire of the mid-Ming people to rediscover the larger world. If anything, the mutual influences between China and other East Asian countries as seen in these *fu* deserve special attention.

Stylistically, the *fu* written on the subject of places in the mid-Ming are strongly reminiscent of another emerging genre, the "diary" (*riji*, literally "daily account"), which was intended to record impressions of miscellaneous local topics. In the characteristic mid-Ming manner, men of letters aimed to document everything, and most especially to turn their daily experiences into readable forms of literature. Ye Sheng's (1420–1474) *Diary by the East of the River* (*Shuidong riji*) is a good example, although his diary reads more like a "miscellany" (*biji*). This diary was first published during the Hongzhi reign (1488–1505) in thirty-eight chapters, but the printed edition of 1553 has two additional chapters. The book consists of random sketches of daily experiences and thoughts while traveling. The scope of the diary aims to be "all-encompassing": it ranges from the author's eyewitness account of the momentous Battle of Tumu to comments on the quality of contemporary printed books, and from musings about Tang poetry to his views regarding women. In addition, it includes observations about such varied subjects as the rituals of wine-drinking and the different kinds of tropical fruits in south China. A scholar–official who served three reigns and was constantly on the move from one post to another, Ye Sheng seemed compelled to grasp the outside world in all its multiplicity. He wanted his readers to know what he felt and was concerned about how his views would be judged by posterity. This universalistic approach to diary-writing led later Ming–Qing authors to develop an even more extensive form of miscellany that would encompass contemporary reality in all its detail.

Drama, vernacular lyrics, and popular song culture

One of the most interesting phenomena of this period is imperial sponsorship of dramatic and popular song culture. With the exception of the Hongzhi Emperor, the mid-Ming emperors were on the whole ineffective rulers, many of them coming under the manipulative influence of eunuchs. Their support for song culture, however, provided fertile ground for new developments in literature, until eventually creative endeavors in music would come to share a cultural milieu with oral and written literature. When the late Ming writer Zhuo Renyue (fl. 1606–1636) said that it was popular songs, such as the "Wu Songs" and "Hanging Branch," that "uniquely distinguished" Ming literature – in sharp contrast to other forms of literature produced in the Tang, Song, and Yuan – he was not exaggerating the case.

Anthologies of popular song had begun to be printed as early as the Chenghua reign (1465–1487). For example, four collections of songs (three of which were set to the tune "Staying the Flying Clouds") were published by the Lu Publishing House in Jintai, Beijing. There is no doubt that popular songs – then called "current tunes" (shiqu) – strongly influenced the "colloquial songs" (sanqu) and dramatic arias of elite writers, especially since these different forms all shared the same repertoire. "Colloquial songs" and "current tunes" were sung at private houses or parties at tea houses, while dramatic arias were performed onstage. But audiences learned to enjoy these songs, whatever their context. Some elite writers, such as Kang Hai (1475–1540) and Wang Jiusi (1468–1551), were experts in northern tunes, while others like Chen Duo (1488–ca 1521) and Wang Pan (1470–1530) were skilled in southern tunes. Due to their productivity, the mid-Ming became the most prolific age of the "colloquial song": according to one statistic, some 330 writers specialized in this song form. The form itself goes back to the Yuan, and early Ming drama-tists like Tang Shi (fl. ca 1400) and Zhu Youdun were also known for their "colloquial songs." The publication of an increasingly large number of collo-quial songs during the mid-Ming also indicates a greater audience for reading the song lyrics. The Chenghua Emperor was himself an avid reader of song lyrics: it is said that he was so fond of colloquial songs and dramatic arias that he would try every means to collect all published song lyrics. The notorious Zhengde Emperor, too, loved to listen to all kinds of songs and devoted himself to compiling lyrics. Not surprisingly, during his reign (1506–1521) and the succeeding Jiajing reign (1522–1566), there was a huge increase in the number of collections of colloquial songs published.

Closely related to the popularity of colloquial song was the revival of theater. A new annotated and illustrated edition of the Yuan play *The Western Wing* was published in 1498 (roughly two hundred years after its first appearance). Still extant today, this handsome woodblock edition, produced by a commercial publishing house called the Yue Family in Jintai, Beijing, was meant to be used both as a guide to performance and for reading: throughout the text are distinct black cartouches for song titles and commentator's annotations, along with markers such as small circles for additional notes. According to the publisher's advertisement, the purpose of this special edition was to provide "both song lyrics and visual illustrations so that even those staying at an inn or traveling on a boat could read the book and sing the songs in complete ease and contentment." The publisher's note also indicates that, since contemporary popular songs were often imitations of "the best songs drawn from *The Western Wing*," even those who "lived in small alleys" had all learned the play's arias by heart and knew how to perform them. The advertisement also explains that contemporary songs (of whatever kind) were like the lyrics of ancient times in that their primary purpose was to express human emotions and to purify feelings, and thus always affected "the way of the world" deeply. This shows that people of the mid-Ming not only enjoyed singing (and reading) songs, but tried also to legitimize them as having essential value. The desire to connect contemporary song with the song literature of the past may also explain why the writers of popular songs modeled their works after the arias of *The Western Wing*. One of the earliest Ming anthologies of popular songs, printed in the Chenghua period, was entitled *New Songs on* The Western Wing *and Odes to the Twelve Months: A Compilation to Surpass the Original "Stopping the Flying Clouds" Tunes* (*Xinbian ti Xixiang ji yong shi er yue sai zhuyun fei*). Likewise, extensive excerpts from *The Western Wing* were included in anthologies of colloquial songs and southern plays published later in the sixteenth century, such as *Ballads of an Era of Lasting Peace* (*Yongxi yuefu*, dated 1515) and *The Brocade Sachet of Wind and Moon* (*Fengyue jinnang*, dated 1553). Mid-Ming song culture was indisputably the product of an intermingling of the popular and the elite.

Aside from its vital connection with popular song, the 1498 edition of *The Western Wing* is also significant as evidence of the new reception this Yuan play received roughly two hundred years after its first appearance. As Stephen West and Wilt Idema have noted, controversy had surrounded the play since the beginning of the fifteenth century, mainly because of its notorious status as "a lover's bible." But one of the striking features of the 1498 edition is its open-minded attitude toward the play. First of all, it includes two sets of prefatory materials with general comments on the play. The first is a set of arias praising the author Wang Shifu (ca 1250–1300) for his poetic talent and for creating this great love story. The song-series ends with a word of advice to the reader: "Take full pleasure in this story of *The Western Wing*, / And live as a romantic devil until you die!" The second series of songs, consisting of eight arias set to the tune "Fragrance Filling the Courtyard," elaborates on the various faults of the play. In this section, the "crazy and lascivious" playwright is condemned as being so deficient in the moral qualities of Zhu Xi that he will never make it into the imperial temple. Even the heroine Oriole is judged severely as the "bewitching spirit" who ruins her family's reputation as well as her own. It is precisely these strong words of disapproval, expressed half in jest, that make the play even more appealing to the mid-Ming reader.

We cannot say with certainty that the prefatory materials as outlined above did not pre-date the 1498 edition. Thus far we have only a few small fragments of an unannotated, illustrated edition of *The Western Wing* from around the year 1400. The tradition of annotating *The Western Wing* must have already been established by the beginning of the fifteenth century, as Zhu Youdun comments on this in one of his poems. Be that as it may, the fact that the 1498 edition was published at a time when theatrical performance and popular song culture were becoming increasingly intertwined – and when neo-Confucianism was giving way to other forms of thought – merits our attention.

Not all the plays published during this period drew upon *The Western Wing* (a northern drama) as a model. Southern drama seems to have preferred a different sort of theme. In his play *Record of the Fragrant Sachet* (*Xiangnang ji*), the southern playwright Shao Can (fl. 1465–1505) focuses on the moral relationships enshrined in Confucian teachings, a far cry from the romantic themes of *The Western Wing*. Similar ethical concerns may be found in Qiu Jun's southern play *All Five Moral Relationships Fulfilled* (*Wulun quanbei ji*). (Please note that the authorship of this play is disputed.) In any case, such diversity of theme and treatment reflects the multicultural outlook characteristic of the mid-Ming period.

The examination essay

One genre of mid-Ming literature that especially influenced the lives of scholar–officials was the eight-part essay generally called the "eight-legged essay," the "examination essay," or, because of its relevance to contemporary society, the "current essay" (*shiwen*). According to many modern scholars, it had a crippling effect on the literary imagination, but this judgment is not entirely fair. The eight-part essay was just one of many genres that aspiring scholar–officials were expected to master in order to excel in the civil service examinations and thus advance their careers. The essay developed into its mature form, with firmly established formalistic requirements, during the Chenghua reign. From a modern perspective, the basic form of the essay – with its complicated requirements in the uses of parallel phrases – may seem tedious and restrictive. But anyone familiar with the rhetorical devices of Chinese literature (as in the genres of *fu* and parallel prose) can see that the eight-part essay reflects only a part of the Chinese obsession with parallelism and symmetry. Further, it is not only parallelism that matters in an eight-part essay, since a careful balance between parallel phrases and non-parallel segments is required to create the right configuration. The principle of alternation as embodied in the eight-part essay is in many ways culturally determined: Chinese literary syntax has always shown preference for a judicious interplay between paratactic and hypotactic lines.

Naturally it took rigorous practice for youngsters to master the eight-part essay, involving much repetition and endless drills, as the form became increasingly sophisticated. However, contrary to common assumption, strict requirements of formal style do not always stifle creativity. In fact, new restrictions often stimulated thematic innovation. A good example is the work of the renowned scholar–official Wang Ao (1450–1524), whose eight-part essays were judged to be so excellent that he was the equivalent to a "Du Fu in poetry" or a "Sima Qian in historiography." Wang Ao took first place in both the provincial examination and the metropolitan examination. In one much-quoted essay, "If the People Have Plenty, How Can the Ruler Not Have Enough?" (Baixing zu, jun shu yu buzu), he expounds his views on the problems of heavy taxation using the principle of analogy. The topic for this particular essay comes from the *Analects* (XII, 9); according to Zhu Xi's commentary, the main point of this passage is the ruler's sympathy for his people. But Wang Ao saw in it something new, and focused his argument instead on the importance of conserving the people's wealth. His interpretation reflects the social changes of an age in which China was becoming increasingly commerce-oriented, but what is exciting here is the newness of the subject matter in this eight-part essay, as Wang shifts the focus from the virtue of the ruler to the benefit of the people. Moreover, the author's elegant verbal formulations in both the parallel (amounting to twelve parts rather than the usual eight) and non-parallel segments greatly enhance the logical thrust of his argument. In general, Wang Ao's rhetorical success was closely related to his flawless command of the formal requirements of the genre.

The eight-part essay was not accepted without criticism. In fact, one of its strongest critics was the most distinguished practitioner of the form, namely Wang Ao himself. In 1507, he submitted a petition to the Zhengde Emperor, advising him to recruit a wider range of talent by adding a supplementary examination, such as the "erudite literatus examination" (*boxue hongci ke*) used in previous dynasties, which tested for knowledge of other subjects, including poetry, *fu*, history, philosophy, and Classics. Wang argued that the eight-part essay was simply too limited a form to identify all the qualified men needed to staff the government's higher-level positions. Unfortunately, court politics were then controlled by the eunuch Liu Jin; Wang Ao soon resigned from the Hanlin Academy and his petition to the throne did not receive due attention. Ten years later, after Liu Jin's execution, Wang submitted another petition proposing in even stronger terms the addition of the subjects of poetry and *fu* to the examination. His recommendation was not accepted. However, perhaps in response to these and other criticisms, some later examinations during the Ming – held at both the provincial and the metropolitan levels – began to include a form of expository prose that was not restricted by the same rules as the eight-part essay.

Overall, however, the eight-part essay saw a gradual popularization during this period. The growth of print culture led to the publication of many collections of model examination essays. Rosters of successful candidates from different provinces began to be printed during the Chenghua reign (1465–1487). The examination market of the mid-Ming can in some ways be compared to the boom in scored testing in America today. Over the next few centuries, the form of the eight-part essay continued to undergo changes, although by the eighteenth century it began to be seen as degenerate and problematic. It was finally abolished at the beginning of the twentieth century. Whatever its limitations, we must not forget that the eight-part essay was seen by the Chinese of the Ming and Qing as an important form of cultural expression, from which many gained confidence and power.

Cabinet-style literature after 1450

Apart from mastering the eight-part essay, or "current" prose, the Ming elite also needed to develop a solid background in classical prose and poetry, especially if they wanted to ascend to the top of the social ladder. For the majority of scholar–officials, the most prestigious positions were in the Hanlin Academy, accessible only to the highest-ranking candidates in the civil service examinations. Once admitted to the Hanlin Academy, a successful candidate became one of a body of high officials providing literary services to the imperial court, spending most of his time studying classical texts and writing poems. As the gateway to a life of prestige and leisure, the Hanlin Academy was the highest goal for many young men of ambition, who, if they placed lower in the examinations, might be assigned to provincial offices with much more strenuous administrative duties. As was to be expected, Hanlin academicians were all learned; their reading varied according to their interests, but generally consisted of all the major Classics, including books on poetry and history. Some were also prolific authors, often managing to publish their writings during their tenure. Their published works usually came under the label of "cabinet-style literature," as discussed earlier in this chapter.

However, the definition of "cabinet," as applied to literary style, underwent significant changes during the middle years of the Ming. As the interests of the Hanlin scholar–officials broadened, not all their works could be fitted into the category of "cabinet" literature. From the mid-Ming onward, "cabinet" came to be a stylistic term, referring only to works that are laudatory in tone, especially those written on state and important social occasions. Wang Ao, for example, was known not only for his eight-part essays, but also for the many cabinet-style poems he wrote while at the Hanlin Academy. Upon his resignation at the age of fifty, following the crisis precipitated by the eunuch Liu Jin, his literary style changed radically. His later writings are indeed reminiscent of the works of the late fourth-century recluse-poet Tao Yuanming (also known as Tao Qian, 365?–427). Like Tao Yuanming, who rejoiced in his homecoming after resigning from office, Wang Ao wrote joyfully about his return to Suzhou. His poem series "Coming Home to the East in the Fifth Month of 1509" (Jisi wuyue donggui) is clearly modeled after Tao's seminal work "Returning to My Home in the Country" (Gui yuantian ju). Wang's peculiar gift of descriptive rhetoric is at its best in the nature poetry of his retirement, where his innate love of nature found much fortuitous enhancement in the beauty of the scenery around Suzhou. He began to compose a great number of landscape poems about the nearby mountains and rivers. In the poem on Tiger Hill, Wang elaborates on his impressions of the Thousand-Men Rock on the hilltop: he imagines himself making a toast to heaven as he stands on the gigantic rock on a moonlit night, and then, in a drunken slumber, listening to the sound of the breeze blowing through the bamboo groves. With its lively intermixture of imaginative and descriptive detail, this piece is the very opposite of Wang's earlier "cabinet" poems.

Another important Hanlin official, Wu Kuan (1435–1504), also from Suzhou, took a different approach to widening the scope of his writing. Unlike Wang Ao, who retired early from office, Wu Kuan continued in his powerful position at the Hanlin Academy for thirty years. As a writer, however, he was always conscious of the limitations of the cabinet style, recognizing that in order to become a true poet he first had to attain a genuine freedom of vision. In a manner typical of men from Suzhou, he adopted from the beginning an inclusive approach to literature and art. This wide-ranging perspective is shown in the impressive sweep of his landscape poems, narrative poems, and poems on painting. His poem "Touring the Eastern Park" (You Dongyuan) drew particular praise from his contemporaries for its lively imagery and strongly visualized sensory detail. Wu also produced another type of poetry – including a poem about the flood in south China – that expressed not only his humanitarian concerns but also his interest in mixing colloquial language with classical diction. Wu Kuan's broader approach to literature illustrates the many changes that took place among writers of the "Cabinet" School.

It was Li Dongyang (1447–1516), the highest official in the Hanlin Academy, however, who was the chief arbiter of elite literary taste during this period. As the foremost authority responsible for selecting Hanlin scholars (*shuji shi*) to fill central government positions, Li was the power of literature incarnate. He was also known as a great poet, and produced a significant number of cabinet-style poems, but the mixture of styles in his corpus of literary works is a sign of new directions in the Hanlin Academy. Li preached the importance of an encyclopedic breadth of knowledge. He especially admired the Song poet and scholar Ouyang Xiu (1007–1072), whom he regarded as an ideal example of the scholar–official committed to both public service and literary art. What Li likes most about Ouyang Xiu is the pervasive tranquility and propriety of his writings. Li also expounds extensively on other poets from the Tang, Song, Yuan, and early Ming in his critical commentary, *Poetry Remarks from the Hall of Huailu* (*Huailu tang shihua*), in which he shows rather catholic tastes in poetry, despite his tendency (in letters and prefaces) to favor the Song dynasty writers. Li seems to have played an important role in mentoring the literary development of the younger generation of mid-Ming scholar–officials. He regularly invited junior colleagues to his Eastern Garden for poetry parties, at which all those present engaged in composing and reciting poems, and appreciating paintings. It may have been at one of these gatherings that Wu Kuan wrote his notable "Poem on the Eastern Garden." The two were close friends, and Li composed a long essay on his visit to Wu's beautiful homestead in Suzhou. Full of sensory images and descriptive details, this essay shows how very different the kind of "cabinet" literature practiced by Li Dongyang and his circle was from that of the early Ming.

The Revivalist movement

Although for a long time considered the center of cultural power, Li Dongyang did not go undisputed as an authority. Most notably, the decade between 1496 and 1505 saw a challenge to Li's position in the form of a group of young scholars called the Revivalist (*fugu*) School. Scholars often use the term "Seven Early Masters" (*qian qizi*) to identify the group, which consists of the following seven individuals: Li Mengyang (1475–1530), He Jingming (1483–1521), Kang Hai (1475–1540), Wang Jiusi, Wang Tingxiang (1474–1544), Bian Gong (1476–1532), and Xu Zhenqing (1479–1511). The idea of "seven masters" was adopted only several years after the fact. All "seven masters" were of northern origin, except for Xu Zhenqing, who came from Suzhou. The actual Revivalist School consisted of many more members, and the movement was far more varied and widespread than is commonly assumed. It has been suggested that, since some Revivalists – such as Li Mengyang and He Jingming – had been denied admission to the Hanlin Academy, the establishment of the school might have been triggered by personal grievances. Two of the "seven masters," however – Kang Hai and Wang Jiusi – were from the Hanlin Academy, so the real issues involved may have been much more complicated.

The basic charter of the Revivalist School aimed at creating a new definition of poetry. According to Li Mengyang and his friends, true lyricism had long been lost in poetry. In their view, poetry should be about the expression of emotion (*qing*), but few of their contemporaries were able to write emotionally powerful poems, although they were skillful in inventing diction. Kang Hai and Wang Jiusi were especially critical of cabinet-style poetry for being "flashy" and "weak." It was therefore important to go back to the "roots" of lyricism by learning from great models of the past such as the poets of the High Tang, Du Fu (712–770) in particular. Revivalist notions about High Tang models seem to echo those of the Southern Song critic Yan Yu. They also coincided to a certain extent with those of Gao Bing, although Gao's theories were apparently unknown to the Revivalists, as he goes unmentioned in their writings. The only writer during this period to have made references to Gao seems to be the Fujian poet Sang Yue (1447–1503).

In prose writing, modern scholars have generally understood the Revivalists to have taken their models from the ancient prose style of the Qin (221–207 BC) and Han (206 BC–AD 220), but the Revivalists themselves were not so consistent. For example, while to them the *fu* was a subgenre of prose, most of the *fu* that they composed were in the lyrical style of the Wei–Jin (221–419) and the Southern Dynasties (fourth to sixth centuries), rather than following the epideictic form of the Han *fu*. In experimenting with these shorter and more lyrical models, the Revivalists may have been reacting against the extremely long and monotonous *fu* produced by the cabinet-style writers. Kang Hai's "*Fu* on a Dream Visit to Taibai Mountain" (Mengyou Taibai shan *fu*) is typical of this new style of *fu*, which is both expressive and realistic, as opposed to the often elaborate diction and moral didacticism characteristic of ancient-style *fu*. Kang's piece shares many of the essential features of the *fu* of the Southern Dynasties, particularly in the vital role given to lyricism as an organizational principle. Not all Revivalists approved of the Southern Dynasties style, however. He Jingming, for example, opens his "*Fu* on the Weaving Girl" (Zhinü *fu*) with a criticism of the Southern Dynasties writer Xie Tiao (464–499). Yet on the whole, the Revivalists did not follow the Qin and Han models in writing their *fu* as strictly as other mid-Ming figures like Huang Zuo and Qiu Jun. All this proves that the oft-quoted slogan "in prose one must emulate Qin and Han models, in poetry the High Tang" is far too simplistic and reductive to describe the Revivalist School of the Ming.

For most Revivalists, poetic models included the *Classic of Poetry* (*Shijing*) and the "ancient-style" poetry of the Han and Wei–Jin as well as the much-lauded poets of the High Tang, although it should be emphasized that, again, the Revivalists did not always aim to model their poems after the High Tang as many modern scholars have assumed. Most importantly, they represented a significant departure from writers of the cabinet style, who rarely imitated the *Classic of Poetry*. The Revivalists believed that in composing poetry one should be intimately aware of sound, paying special attention to the art of chanting and singing so as to convey the emotions fully. It was thus important to be able to trace poetry back to its earliest roots in the *Classic of Poetry*, which was compiled in an age when lyric poetry and music were closely intertwined. In this regard, the Revivalist view is similar to the Western concept of lyric poetry, which sees music as an intrinsic element of poetry. Given this perspective, such terms as "rules" (*fa*) and "style and tone" (*gediao*), with which the Revivalists refer to both literary style and sound patterns, become more intelligible. When Li Mengyang (leader of the Revivalist group) claimed that he was learning from Du Fu's "style and tone," he was referring to the self-conscious imitation of the Tang master's use of tonal patterns. Li firmly believed that poetry composition was an art requiring a long process of "practice" (*duanlian*) before one could master its forms. To a certain extent, Li's notion of "practice" seems to echo the European "neoclassical" ideals, especially in regard to the belief in permanent norms, control of the lexicon, attention to flaws, and decorum.

Not all the members of the Revivalist School agreed with Li Mengyang's literal interpretation of the "rules"; many chose to adopt a more liberal approach to the process of learning. For example, He Jingming wrote that learning from the great masters of the past was like taking a raft to the other shore; once the river had been crossed, the raft could be abandoned. Despite divergent approaches, the Revivalist School held certain tenets in common that seem vital to their identity as a group: (1) an attack on the hackneyed and clichéd forms of literature espoused by the Cabinet School; (2) a radical rejection of the neo-Confucian thought of Zhu Xi; (3) an affinity with the new philosophy of Wang Yangming (1472–1529), who advocated the importance of cultivating the intuitive capacity of the mind to awaken itself through introspection; (4) the assumption that poetry should be based on expressing emotion, rather than on manifesting "inherent pattern" (*li*); (5) an emphasis on reviving the spirit of lyricism by acquiring a firm knowledge of the canon and of one's place in it; (6) an ambition to intervene meaningfully in the cultural and political spheres; and (7) a deep appreciation of contemporary popular songs.

The Revivalists' interest in popular songs was rooted in their belief in the ability of these works to express genuine emotion. In the preface to his own *Collected Poems*, printed in 1525, Li Mengyang wrote, "Nowadays true poetry can be found only among the people." On another occasion, Li and He Jingming said of the popular song "Locking the South Branch" (Suo nanzhi) that if all poets learned to sing in this manner, they would "improve the quality of their poems and essays significantly." According to the late Ming writer Xu Wei (1521–1593), Li Mengyang was also the first to give canonical status to *The Western Wing* by putting this comparatively late play alongside the ancient poem "Encountering Sorrow" (Lisao). This interest in drama and popular song encouraged the Revivalists to experiment with new subject matter in their writings. In one of his poems on fishing, He Jingming describes a fisherman's experience of catching and selling fish, along with the quotidian activities of the country folk living in the nearby village, including one woman who is afraid of killing the fish she has purchased from the market. In the same way, Li Mengyang also produced many vivid prose pieces documenting the lives of merchants; several of these are in the form of epitaphs, short biographies, and casual essays. The fact that Li came from a merchant family explains his special interest in the subject. Two other members of the Revivalist School, Kang Hai and Wang Jiusi, were (as previously mentioned) especially distinguished for their colloquial songs.

The Revivalists hoped to nurture through their writings a sense of responsibility for society at large, and this made them critical of government policy. The story of Li Mengyang, who suffered repeated political setbacks and was imprisoned four times, provides a most telling example of the group's dedication to activism. After passing the civil service examination in 1494, Li was appointed to a high post in the central government, where, almost from the beginning, he showed courage under pressure and a special aptitude for leadership. His political troubles began in 1505, when, at the solicitation of the court, he sent a petition to the throne accusing the empress's younger brother of certain wrongdoings. Li was arrested and thrown into jail. In his series of seventeen poems entitled "Expressing My Anger" (Shu fen), Li tells the story of his prison experience – mentioning several kinds of harsh corporal punishment – and expresses unmitigated indignation at his unjust treatment. He was not afraid of exposing corruption in high places, as may be seen in this note to the title of the series: "In the fourth month of 1505, I was put in prison for impeaching the nobleman Shouning." He is no less explicit in his later poems, such as "Encountering Anger" (Li fen) and "Calling to Heaven" (Jiaotian ge), in which he openly airs his outrage at political abuses. Soon afterwards, with the accession of the Zhengde Emperor, the eunuch Liu Jin gained control of the government. In his typically outspoken manner, Li offended Liu Jin and was again put in prison and sentenced to death. Fortunately, Kang Hai interceded in time to save his life. Similar events continued to occur, and eventually Li had to give up his official career altogether, although he refused to remain quiet as a writer.

As mentioned earlier, Wang Yangming's thought greatly influenced the Revivalist movement. Though chiefly remembered as a philosopher, Wang was also a distinguished poet. His family was from Zhejiang but he grew up in Beijing, surrounded by poets, writers, and court officials, thanks to his father's eminent position at the Hanlin Academy. Even in his youth, Wang's poetry attracted considerable attention. Some of his more mature works involve a fusion of philosophical meditation with descriptions of landscape, as in "To

My Students from the Mountains" (Shanzhong shi zhusheng). One of Wang's best friends in Beijing was Li Mengyang; through him, Wang had the chance to exchange poems with members of the Revivalist group and came to share their taste in poetry. More importantly, Wang's emphasis on the intuitive mind inspired the Revivalists' search for lyricism in poetry. Wang also shared Li Mengyang's political affinities. In 1506, he defended two officials who had submitted petitions to the throne condemning the eunuch Liu Jin, and in consequence he was arrested and harshly beaten in prison, and then further punished with banishment to far-flung Guizhou. He was not recalled to the capital until after Liu Jin's downfall in 1510. The years of exile in Guizhou led to Wang's spiritual awakening, out of which grew his radically new philosophy. Li Mengyang, after retiring to his hometown in remote Gansu, began to devote himself to the study of the mind, no doubt under the influence of Wang Yangming.

In addition to Li Mengyang, several other members of the Revivalist School also suffered under the turbulent regime of the eunuch Liu Jin. However, contrary to common assumption, Liu Jin was not an enemy to all members of the Revivalist group. Kang Hai, for example, was successful in interceding on behalf of Li Mengyang because he and Liu Jin were both natives of Shaanxi Province. Later, when Liu Jin fell from power, Kang Hai and his friend Wang Jiusi (also from Shaanxi Province) were both dismissed from the Hanlin Academy for their alleged connection with the eunuch – a great injustice, as their contact had been minimal. Yet, in an age when regional affiliation was regarded as an important personal tie, it is easy to see why both men should have been labeled allies of Liu Jin.

During the long decades of their retirement in Shaanxi, Kang Hai and Wang Jiusi devoted their energies to composing colloquial songs (qu) and plays, gradually becoming distinguished as songwriters and dramatists specializing in northern-style tunes. Bitterly disappointed with their political experience, they found an outlet for their frustration in their writings. Kang Hai published nearly four hundred short vernacular songs and over one hundred longer song-suites. Wang Jiusi, who wrote only a quarter of that number, is considered by later critics to be the better songwriter of the two. Kang, however, is notable for the vivid evocation of landscape in his songs, as in the song "Fragrance Filling the Courtyard" (Manting fang) about viewing the clear sky, or the song "Happiness for All under the Heavens" (Putian le) on the blue sky of autumn. On the whole, the colloquial songs of both men are characterized by powerful rhythms and melodic effect. Couched in a direct and straightforward voice, the songs are often punctuated by lively questions and exclamations, creating an impression of spontaneous speech and heroic abandon.

In their plays, Wang Jiusi and Kang Hai used satire and topical allegory to refer discreetly to political situations. "Du Fu's Spring Outing" (Du Fu youchun), a short play (zaju) by Wang – though based on the historical figure of Du Fu – is actually filled with topical references to contemporary events. The play describes how Du Fu, a disenchanted old retiree who is so poor that he has to pawn his clothes to pay for alcohol, goes out to buy wine on a spring day. Saddened by the desolate atmosphere surrounding the imperial palaces in Chang'an, Du Fu attributes the failures of government policy to the misrule of the chief minister Li Linfu. Meeting the poet Cen Shen and his brother, Du Fu visits the Meipi Pond in their company. Later, when the new prime minister Fang Guan offers him a position at the Hanlin Academy, Du Fu resolutely declines, saying that he would rather spend his days "buying drink, making spring outings, and going to sea on a raft" than put up with "high and mighty" behavior. The main plot of the play is drawn from two of Du Fu's poems, but Wang Jiusi is clearly using the story to describe his own circumstances after his political setback: after his retirement, Wang renamed himself Wang Meipi and went to live near the Meipi Pond, a place once visited by Du Fu around 754. According to some contemporary critics, this play was meant to be a satire about Li Dongyang, who rose to become the head of the Hanlin Academy after Liu Jin's execution. It is difficult to know if such a reading reflects the author's intent, but considering that Wang Jiusi was once a member of the Hanlin Academy (and was among those inclined to find fault with Li's cabinet style of poetry), there may be some truth to this interpretation. In any case, the play was a labor of love that took Wang Jiusi many years to finish. Originally written for his own household troupe, it later became popular in other parts of the country, partly because of its controversial content.

Another theme favored by Wang Jiusi and Kang Hai was a type of satire in fable form, which they learned from their teacher Ma Zhongxi (1446–1512). Ma had also been persecuted by the eunuch Liu Jin, and died in prison. He was famous for his classical tale "The Story of the Wolf of Zhongshan" (Zhongshan lang zhuan), in which a wolf, rescued by a scholar from hunters, wishes to devour his savior. Some Chinese scholars believe the story to be an adaptation from a tale by the Song writer Xie Liang or the Tang poet Yao He (781–846), but it was perhaps Ma Zhongxi's rewriting that made the story popular in the early Ming (although the attribution to

Ma is not without controversy). At a time when public life was complicated by interlocking factional allegiances and shifting political alignments, one can easily understand the appeal of a story about ingratitude. Wang Jiusi and Kang Hai must have felt personal resonance with the tale of the Wolf of Zhongshan, for both men wrote plays based on this story. The authorship of Kang's *Wolf of Zhongshan* has been questioned by some scholars, but several Ming writers, Li Kaixian (1502–1568), Qi Biaojia (1602–1645), and Shen Defu (1578–1642), seemed to be convinced of its authenticity. For the time being we will adopt the term "attributed authorship" – as is used by Tian Yuan Tan in his Harvard dissertation entitled "Qu writing in literati communities" – to refer to such authorship uncertainties.

Wang Jiusi's play about the Zhongshan wolf, in contrast, is a one-act skit (*yuanben*). Here the old man who was one of the judges in Ma Zhongxi's classic tale appears as a local earth god, perhaps to furnish a pretext for more elaborate spectacles for the stage. The play must have come across as intensely funny to the audience, as the figures of Wolf, Buffalo, and Apricot Tree all appear onstage for the first time. At the same time, the comic plot reflects the dark reality of contemporary political life, where the frantic manipulations of factional networks were taking on a more and more animalistic frenzy. Other writers also drew deeply on similar themes. In his classic tale "The Record of the Journey to the East" (Dongyou jiyi), Dong Qi (1483–1546) compares the eunuch Liu Jin to a tiger with a white forehead, and Liu's brother to an old fox. Since the Zhengde Emperor is said to have given himself up day and night to debauchery in his pleasure quarters, which were known as the "Leopard House," these animal fables have a special pertinence to mid-Ming life.

Kang Hai's treatment of the story of the wolf of Zhongshan is much longer – a play in four acts with the addition of extensive dialogue and many more dramatic twists. In his version, the local earth god reverts to the old man of the original story. Although the plot was by this time familiar to the audience, the intensity with which Kang Hai elaborates on the theme of ingratitude is striking. Seizing upon the central moral deficiency of contemporary society, he delivers a searing diatribe through the mouth of the old man: "In this world how many men out there have been ungrateful! Some betrayed their ruler . . . Some let down their parents . . . Some were treacherous to their teachers . . . Some abandoned their dear friends who once assisted them in time of need . . . " These lines provide a glimpse into how Kang Hai may have looked back upon his days in office, when people were constantly betraying each other under political pressure. "You sought after the rich and the powerful, and failed to remember your poor friends," the old man says near the end of the play. These lines are strikingly reminiscent of the elaborate schemes of parallelism and enumeration typical of the *fu*, a genre in which Kang Hai was especially skillful, but the rhetorical devices he uses in his play are different from those found in his *fu*. Here, mixing colloquial language with classical idiom, Kang Hai has created a new elevated style for the northern drama. (The late Ming critic Qi Biaojia judged this play to be "elegant.") Also noteworthy is Kang Hai's reinvention of the stock figure of the old man as a venerable Confucian elder who serves as a ready mouthpiece for the playwright's passionate declarations against the corrupt ways of the world. Kang also adds an element of moral closure at the end of his play, as the wolf is stabbed to death by the same kindly scholar who had saved him. This ending is more in keeping with the classic tale by Ma Zhongxi and quite different from Wang Jiusi's one-act skit, in which the wolf is killed by a ghost.

These dramatic works had ramifications unforeseen by their authors. Once the plays were written, audiences began to speculate on the true identity of the allegorical Zhongshan wolf. Kang's play in particular was suspected to have been directed against Li Mengyang, the head of the Revivalist movement, because, according to hearsay, Li refused to help Kang Hai when the latter was implicated in the Liu Jin incident and consequently banished (along with Wang Jiusi), despite the fact that Kang had once saved Li's life. Many also believed that it was on Li's account that Kang had become involved with Liu Jin in the first place. While it is impossible to prove a direct connection between the play and its historical circumstances, this reading apparently became so popular that it was often uncritically accepted: Shen Defu, for one, commented in an informal piece that Kang Hai intended his *Wolf of Zhongshan* as an "allegory" to "ridicule" Li Mengyang. From the modern point of view, such a literal interpretation would make the play seem less significant as a piece of art. But in the cultural milieu of the mid-Ming, these unfounded allegations served only to enhance the reception of Kang's play, which consequently spawned many imitations; several new plays with the same title appeared in quick succession, and soon the entire literary community was caught up in the rewriting of the wolf story. This was not just an ordinary case of rewriting the past, but rather of making the wolf into an archetypal symbol of vice. The great eighteenth-century novel *The Story of the Stone* (also known as *Honglou meng*, *The Dream of the Red Chamber*), uses the wolf of Zhongshan as an established trope for wicked humanity (see Chapter 5 of the novel).

Although Kang Hai produced many other plays – including the love tragedy of Wang Lanqing, the devoted courtesan who takes her own life after her husband's death – none was so famous as the controversial *Wolf of Zhongshan*.

This demonstrates how literary reception could further complicate a scholar–official's already intricate relationships and factional affiliations. It also shows how much individual members of the Revivalist School differed in both literary theory and practice, and how their views changed at different stages of their lives – especially under the influence of political circumstances. Perhaps the only features they truly shared were a similar educational background and common career goals.

The revival of Suzhou

It took the city of Suzhou more than a century to recover from the devastation caused by the Ming founder. By the beginning of the sixteenth century, however, the cultural and economic center of China had gradually shifted to the Jiangnan region, and Suzhou finally regained its status as the brightest star in the constellation of wealthy cities in the Yangzi delta. The city that had once produced great poets like Gao Qi now gave birth to a new generation of poets. As in the past, most of the poets of mid-Ming Suzhou – such as Shen Zhou (1427–1509), Zhu Yunming (1460–1526), Wen Zhengming (1470–1559), and Tang Yin (1470–1524) – were also famous painters or calligraphers. These men had been taught since early childhood that poetry and painting were two intimately conjoined arts. Tang Yin says in one of his poems, "I spent a lifetime doing painting and poetry." Indeed, to the people of Suzhou, poetry and painting sprang from the same source. Moreover, our modern division between work and leisure simply did not apply to men of letters in Suzhou, for whom writing and painting were two of the greatest enjoyments in life. This explains why the Suzhou poets and artists occupy positions of great significance in both art and literature. The paintings of Shen Zhou, Wen Zhengming, and Tang Yin, along with Zhu Yunming's calligraphy, are well known even in the West, but scholars have largely neglected the importance of these men as poets, an oversight that does little justice to these distinguished writers.

Also essential to our understanding of the culture of Suzhou is its nature as an urban center. From the mid-Ming onward, merchants began to play an increasingly important role in the revival of the city, and their presence greatly enhanced the image of urban life in Suzhou. According to the "*Fu* on Suzhou" (Suzhou *fu*) by Mo Dan (1429–?), the city of Suzhou was full of "rich merchants coming from distant parts of the country," making it into "the center of wealth." In addition to "stores lined up like chessboards and tall bridges all over," Suzhou had "many singing stages, dancing halls, and sundry markets devoted to nighttime business." Similar descriptions can be found in several of Wen Zhengming's and Tang Yin's poems, in which the business district, known as Changmen, is described with particular emphasis on its opulence and luxury. The career of Tang Yin, the son of a merchant, shows how the social destiny of the merchants was gradually coming to merge with that of the elite.

Of all the changes in Suzhou, none is more striking than the introduction of money as an item to be taken account of in cultural life. Unlike the Revivalists in the north, who all started out as high officials at the court, poets and artists in Suzhou often earned their living by selling their paintings and poems. Some were offered positions in government, but in most cases they chose to avoid politics by either turning down the offers or stepping down from office early. But livelihood did not cease to be a concern. In response to the often pressing economic considerations in these poets' lives, we find among their works an unprecedented number of poems on money. For example, in "Speaking My Heart" (Yanhuai), Tang Yin writes, "I am grateful that I've gained celebrity in the realm / Who cares if I have no money to buy wine." In another poem, "Expressing my Intent" (Yanzhi), he justifies his way of making money: "Whenever I had time I would do a painting of blue mountains to sell / I wouldn't allow myself to get money I didn't deserve." Zhu Yunming, on the other hand, considered money harmful because it perverts people's minds: "Mere chance that [silver and gold] became useful to people / But the world has produced no good souls ever since." By far the most interesting statements on money have come from Shen Zhou. In his famous "Odes on Money" (Yong qian *fu*, a series of five poems), Shen writes about the meaning and substance of money. He first elaborates on the power of money, especially the fact that it can purchase everything, including power over ghosts. He then discusses the shape, weight, and uses of coins. Finally, he compares money to a stream of flowing water because of its quality of fluidity and its potential to roll along endlessly. Shen Zhou seems to be one of the few poets and artists in Suzhou who did not sell his paintings and poems "for cash," something he claims to regret in a later song lyric. The honorarium for paintings and literary works was in those days apparently quite high. Wen Zhengming probably earned a good deal of money by writing epitaphs for local families. According to Ye Sheng's *Diary by the East of the River* (*Shuidong riji*), the price for such literary service dramatically increased after the Battle of Tumu in 1449. The mid-Ming period was perhaps the first time in the history of Chinese literature that money was openly discussed in poetry.

It was precisely because of their preoccupation with money that the Suzhou poets and artists managed to free themselves from the burden of officialdom.

In the first place, most of them disliked the form of the examination essay. Shen Zhou never even bothered to take the civil examinations, and when, after achieving fame, he was recommended for a position, he turned it down in good faith. Tang Yin was unjustly implicated in an examination scandal in which his friend Xu Jing was accused of trying to obtain copies of examination questions by bribery, and he decided as a result to abandon an official career altogether. He makes his intentions clear in the following poem: "I wish to grow old and die among flowers and wine / I do not wish to bow down to official carriages." As for Wen Zhengming and Zhu Yunming, neither served in government until after the age of fifty, and both resigned not long after taking office. All this seems to indicate a certain "Suzhou spirit" that valued personal freedom above all else. It would be wrong to conclude, however, that men from Suzhou were completely disinterested in officialdom. During the mid-Ming, Suzhou produced the greatest number of successful examination candidates in the whole country, and more candidates hailed from Suzhou than from any other part of the Jiangnan region. Eminent scholar–officials like Wang Ao and Wu Kuan were from Suzhou. But, though prizing success in the examinations and the pursuit of public office, the men of Suzhou also genuinely respected those who had the courage to give up officialdom. Wang Ao, for example, only gained in prestige when he resigned from the Hanlin Academy and returned to Suzhou. Perhaps it was this dual attitude concerning officialdom that gave the people of Suzhou a special dignity.

This shared attitude also gave men of letters from Suzhou a common regional identity. Like their early Ming predecessor, Gao Qi, Suzhou poets and artists of the mid-Ming preferred to devote their energies to literary and artistic creation. Indeed, in defining the "Suzhou School of Poetry," Shen Zhou (its oldest member) traced the school's origins back to Gao Qi as the first to establish a strong lyrical tradition. Shen also leveled the following criticism: "Since Gao Qi's time, writers of the Suzhou School of Poetry, hindered by their superficial and unrefined style, have been unable to create first-rate poetry. They simply lack the spontaneous expression of feeling [xingqing] characteristic of Gao Qi's poetry . . ." As a remedy, he suggests that his contemporaries should cultivate the "spontaneous expression of feeling." This appeal echoes to some extent the Revivalists' agenda to resurrect the ancient ideal of lyricism. Unlike the Revivalists, who were inclined to single out specific ancient models as their guides, Shen Zhou and his friends in Suzhou did not believe in discriminating certain ancient models from others. There was, to be sure, a degree of overlap between these two groups. Xu Zhenqing, one of the "Four Talented Men of Suzhou" (Wuzhong si caizi), was a Suzhou native but belonged to the Revivalist School. Incidentally, the other members of the "Four Talented Men of Suzhou" were Zhu Yunming, Tang Yin, and Wen Zhengming. The "Four Talented Men of Suzhou" again overlapped with the "Four Masters of Ming" (*Ming sijia*), a term that was used to refer to the four distinguished painters from the Suzhou region – namely Shen Zhou, Wen Zhengming, Tang Yin, and Qiu Ying (ca 1510–1552?).

As a poet, Shen Zhou called for a renewal of lyricism that would make poetry pure and fresh while keeping it down-to-earth. Contrary to the self-image projected in some of his poems (such as, "Alone, I leaned on my cane and gazed into the distance"), he was not a "recluse." The historical Shen Zhou actually enjoyed life in a noisy town, but, as described in the title of one of his poems, he lived in the guise of a "hermit in a city" (*shiyin*). Shen cared deeply about the daily lives of ordinary people, and wrote some of his best poems about the sufferings of the townspeople during the flood season. In "Song of the Filial Woman Zhou" (Zhou xiaofu *ge*), he writes about a poor widow who carried her mother-in-law to safety on her back. His poem series "Eighteen Neighbors" (Shiba lin) tells the story of people who were forced to exchange their children for food and money during the flood. Shen's instinct as a poet is simply to report the facts so as to achieve the effect of spontaneous expression, a quality he felt to be sorely lacking in contemporary poetry. It is in these poems that he shows himself the heir to Gao Qi's poetic acts of bearing witness. This new approach to poetry must have come across as fresh and innovative at a time when the cabinet style was still predominant. When Li Dongyang (1447–1516), leader of the Cabinet School, praised Gao Qi for the "talent and voice" in his poetry, claiming that "for more than a hundred years no one has been able to surpass Gao Qi," he may well have been inspired by Shen Zhou's admiration for the earlier poet. The fact that Shen was a close friend of Wu Kuan, a close associate of Li at the Hanlin Academy, makes this a reasonable assumption. The changes wrought over time in the cabinet-style poetry may also have resulted from the influence of the Suzhou School.

Another great writer famous for his individualistic style in both poetry and calligraphy was Zhu Yunming. In his uninhibited lifestyle, Zhu represented the free-spirited and iconoclastic side of Suzhou culture. Openly critical of Zhu Xi, he admired Wang Yangming's philosophy of mind. His literary style can best be characterized as "wild and eccentric." In the notorious poem series "Slogans" (kouhao), Zhu describes himself as a "wild" (*kuang*) man who "wears no clothes, leaves his shirt unbuttoned, and refuses to comb his hair." "Alone," Zhu continues, "he would walk a hundred times around the winding corridor." Reflected in this description is an emergent sense of self that shows complexity, subtlety, and, above all, subjectivity as Suzhou culture approached maturity during the mid-Ming. Zhu Yunming is also known for a monumental collection of essays in which he criticizes various aspects of traditional Chinese values, a work in some ways comparable to the cultural criticism of today.

In the poet and painter Wen Zhengming we see a more conventional side of Suzhou life that is commonly recognized as its cultural mainstream. With respect to breadth of subject matter and versatility of style, Wen was perhaps the most promising Suzhou poet of his time. His great longevity (Wen lived to the ripe age of eighty-nine) enabled him to produce an unusually large corpus of literary works, among which his poems on painting are especially well known. Not only did he succeed in combining the arts of poetry and painting, but nature and art seem to have become one in his world. This idea appears again and again in Wen's poems, especially those inscribed on his paintings: "All the scenes before my eyes are but new poetry"; "the setting sun is a poem"; "the tip of the tree branch and the hibiscus – both are painted screens"; "unknowingly, I have been taking a walk within the painting." A poem Wen inscribed on his teacher Shen Zhou's painting contains the following couplet: "Gentle breezes on a bright day, such is the emotion of poetry / Thinly scattered trees growing in the marsh, these are paintbrushes." Just as in Wen's imagination nature itself has turned into a series of paintings, so there exists in nature an endless cycle of poems, stringing all the paintings together into a world of harmonious beauty. This pervasive urge to see connections in all aspects of life, art, and nature is characteristic of the Suzhou way of life.

Wen Zhengming was also a contributor to garden literature. Garden poetry was already prominent in Suzhou in Gao Qi's day, as seen in the series of poems exchanged by Gao and his friends on the Lion Forest Garden. But in the mid-Ming, garden literature was to attain an unprecedented importance. We have already shown that Wang Ao, after resigning from the central government, enjoyed touring his private gardens in Suzhou, out of which came a new style of nature poetry that stood in sharp contrast to those of his earlier cabinet style. Wen Zhengming was one of the frequent visitors to the garden at Wang's home, where they often drank wine and composed poems together. One of Wang's poems, "Matching the Rhymes of Zhengming while Drinking at the Happy Old Man's Garden" (Zhengming yin Yilao yuan ciyun), describes the many splendid views at the lake in the garden, while making poignant references to Pei Du (765–839), a prime minister of the Tang who, like Wang himself, retired from office after a political crisis caused by a eunuch. Compared to Wang Ao's poems, Wen's are far more visual and sensory, and the garden usually appears as a self-contained place. Wen's garden pieces are often elaborate affairs including both paintings and poetry. One of these, "Paintings and Odes on the Zhuozheng Garden" (Wen daizhao Zhuozheng yuan tu), consists of a series of thirty-one paintings and poems on different scenes in the garden. The Zhuozheng Garden (literally "Garden of the Inept Official"), the largest garden in Suzhou, was built by Wang Xianchen (dates unknown) after he had been dismissed from the central government. It most likely became famous because of Wen's paintings and poems, and remains a popular tourist site today. One of the poems contains this couplet: "I adore this place where no noise of carriage or horse is heard / Truly one can enjoy hills and woods in the middle of the city." Though clearly inspired by Tao Yuanming's famous series of poems called "Drinking Wine," where the idea of leading a bucolic life "in the midst of people" is celebrated, Wen's poem-series is actually meant to describe the uniqueness of Suzhou, where small-scale "hills and woods" could exist in the heart of a busy city.

Tang Yin lived in just such a garden, called the Peach Blossom Villa (Taohua an), where he spent all day painting, writing poetry, and drinking wine. The villa was also the place where Tang Yin and his literary friends (including Wen Zhengming and Zhu Yunming) gathered for their poetry and drinking parties. Unlike Wen Zhengming, who is often remembered as a high-minded artist, Tang Yin was an idiosyncratic, romantic figure in popular legend. Even in his teen years his paintings and poems had brought him fame as the "number one romantic talent in Jiangnan." Tang Yin also wrote an interesting commentary on *The Western Wing*. Above all, he is best remembered for his "Song of Peach Blossom Villa." The opening lines of the song are filled with audacious repetitions of the words "peach blossom":

> Inside Peach Blossom Villa is my Peach Blossom Studio,
> At the Peach Blossom Studio is the Peach Blossom Immortal,
> The Peach Blossom Immortal planted the peach trees,
> Plucking peach blossoms, I sold them for money to buy wine . . .

Tang Yin sees himself as a flower god who is "half awake and half drunk day after day," while "blossoms bloom, blossoms fall, year after year." The poem reveals the central theme of Tang Yin's poetry: the ephemerality of life captured and embodied in flowers. Falling flowers have always haunted the

Chinese poetic imagination, but in the hands of Tang Yin this image acquires a supreme literary importance. According to numerous biographical accounts, Tang Yin had a special passion for flowers. He worshipped them, and drank to them while working on his paintings, and when the blossoms fell, he would weep for them and bury them in his garden. For this reason, some scholars of *The Story of the Stone* have concluded that Tang Yin was the model for the novel's sentimental heroine, Daiyu, who mourns the faded blossoms and makes a burial mound for them.

Tang Yin's peculiar gifts as a writer and painter broke new ground for the Suzhou tradition. He was especially famous for painting female figures and for the many lyrical poems on women that he inscribed on his own paintings. Before his time, many of the Suzhou poems on women were written by female poets – Meng Shuqing's (fl. 1476) "Viewing the Picture of the Lotus Beauty" (Guan lian meiren tu) is the famous example. But Tang Yin's works came eventually to define the feminine side of Suzhou culture, embodying a surrender to sensual allure that is the very opposite of the ideal proposed by the Revivalists in the north. From this point onward, Suzhou came to represent not only a place in Jiangnan, but a state of mind – most importantly, a dreamland of art and poetry.

III. The period from 1520 to 1572

In 1521, when the Zhengde Emperor died at the age of twenty-nine, the throne was left without an heir. One of his cousins was quickly summoned to the capital to assume the throne. The new Jiajing Emperor, aged fourteen, turned out to be an autocrat who would not easily accept advice from his courtiers. Later he became obsessed with religious Daoism and completely ignored his administrative duties. His administration was progressively crippled as power began to be concentrated in the hands of his eunuchs. Meanwhile, China was increasingly troubled by foreign threats. During his long reign (1522–1566), the Jiajing Emperor received petitions from many scholar–officials. The most famous of these were submitted by Hai Rui (1513–1587), for which he was put in prison and cruelly tortured. Hai Rui later became the hero of several fictional accounts. As late as the 1960s, on the eve of the Cultural Revolution, a popular new play about him was seen as an indirect criticism of Chairman Mao Zedong and was therefore censored. Unlike Mao, however, the teenage Jiajing Emperor was less interested in political censorship than in beatings in open court.

One scholar–official who nearly lost his life to harsh beatings was Yang Shen (1488–1559), son of Chief Grand Secretary Yang Tinghe (1459–1529). Yang Shen topped the lists in the civil service examinations of 1511 and was a distinguished Hanlin academician by the time the Jiajing Emperor ascended the throne. The works of this "number one scholar of the empire" were in great demand. But in 1524 everything changed. The so-called "Great Rites Controversy" was precipitated when the young Jiajing Emperor refused to follow the established Ming ritual of honoring the previous emperor, insisting instead on promoting his own late parents' status. In the flurry of petitions by outraged court officials, more than a hundred officials (including Yang Shen) were arrested and beaten in the court, seventeen dying from injuries sustained during the beatings. Yang Shen survived, but was demoted to the lowly position of soldier and banished for life to Yunnan, the remotest part of the Chinese empire. The other 108 officials were also sent into exile, but Yang Shen, as their leader, received the harshest punishment. According to the *Ming Penal Code*, demotion to the status of soldier was the worst treatment an exile could receive. Yang Shen was then thirty-five, and he would spend the next thirty-five years in exile until his death in 1559. He never received amnesty, though many others did.

Exile literature

It was by virtue of his experience as an exile that Yang Shen became a truly important figure in literature. In Yunnan, he developed expertise in almost every known genre of literature and became a renaissance figure whose works were recited by people "in every corner of the realm," even places where "no well water was available." His exalted place in the popular imagination is no doubt linked to the Chinese respect for talent and, more especially, their sympathy for a gifted man unjustly wronged at the hands of a tyrant. Yang is also a privileged witness of an important age of transition between the mid- and the late Ming. Through Yang's works Ming readers also came to appreciate the diverse cultures of Yunnan, a frontier region that had only become a Chinese province in 1382.

Yang's poetic style was still quite conventional when he first arrived in Yunnan. He wrote several works full of allusions to Qu Yuan, the ancient poet whose "Encountering Sorrow" is still considered the first great masterpiece of Chinese exile literature. Like Qu Yuan, Yang mourned his tragic fate in being banished and estranged from the court (as in "Feelings of Being a Soldier" (Junci shugan), "Poem on Military Exile" (En qian shu Dian jixing)). For Yang, surrounded by "barbaric" non-Chinese, thousands of miles away from his wife and other family members, life in Yunnan must have been extremely difficult. As the hope of amnesty finally died, however, he began to develop a passionate affection for the place. He was in fact able to live in style in Yunnan because his wife Huang E (1498–1569) – who went back to administer his estate in Sichuan – sent him money regularly. The next few decades turned out to be an amazingly productive period for Yang, with numerous works published, frequent travels around the frontier border, and growing celebrity as a writer. At the same time, the unrestrained manner of his life in Yunnan attracted criticism from many. Shen Zizheng, the uncle of the woman poet Ye Xiaoluan (1616–1632), wrote a short play in which the "crazy" Yang Shen dresses up as a woman during an outing with a maid. Not all scholars disapproved of Yang's eccentric behavior, however. Writers like Qi Biaojia were able to see it in a sympathetic light, as a "comical" way of expressing the sorrow and frustration of a political exile. Frederick W. Mote takes the similar view that Yang Shen may have been acting out "a defense against peril" because he was still under the surveillance of the vindictive Jiajing Emperor.

Despite his political problems, Yang Shen was perhaps the most prolific author of the Ming dynasty, publishing in his lifetime more than a hundred titles, including various anthologies that he had compiled and edited. Furthermore, as the governing officials of Yunnan all came to respect him, they allowed him to enjoy the rights of an ordinary citizen, without having to fulfill his assigned military duties. The combined experience of social freedom with the wild scenery of Yunnan awakened a new spirit in him. In his new poetry, we read about such exotic scenes as the "Iron Bridge and Bronze Pillar on the Road to Soul Mountain" near the Tibetan border, or the "clouds of Bo and mists of Cuan" that are home to aboriginal people. In a series of extensive travelogues, he writes about strange mountains and seas that fill readers with great awe. Most importantly, Yang was a great master of the song lyric (ci), a form that had thrived during the Song dynasty but had fallen into obscurity after the Yuan, to which he brought back energy and vigor on a grand scale. As a pioneering champion of this forgotten genre, he produced extensive commentaries on the Song dynasty anthology *The Thatched Cottage Song Lyrics* (*Caotang shiyu*), and compiled two important anthologies drawing upon song lyrics dating back to the Tang. His efforts seem to have stimulated contemporary publications on the same subject, including Zhang Yan's (1487–?) *Graphic Prosodies of Song Lyrics* (*Shiyu tupu*), completed in 1536. Yang Shen's own song lyrics are full of local color, while his sense of an expanded inner world is present everywhere (as in "Fishermen's Pride (Yujia ao): On

Monthly Festivals in South Yunnan"). In his "Ode to the Oriole's Cry" (Ying ti xu), he famously concludes that his beautiful new world in Yunnan is superior to Wang Wei's (699 or 701–761) retreat in Wangchuan. Yang wrote a total of more than three hundred song lyrics during his years in Yunnan. He also produced a book of criticism, *Appreciation of Song Lyrics* (*Ci pin*), discussing the origin and evolution of the genre as well as its relationship with music. Yang became so famous as a song lyricist that in the 1660s, a century after his death, Mao Zonggang (1632–after 1709) used one of his lyrics as the opening passage for his new edition of the *Romance of the Three Kingdoms* (*Sanguo zhi yanyi*). The lyric, set to the tune "Immortal at the River," was taken from Yang's *Songs on Twenty-One Histories* (*Ershi yi shi tanci*). Even to this day, the standard edition of the novel still opens with this song lyric by Yang: "On and on the Great River rolls, racing east / Of proud and gallant heroes its white-tops leave no trace / As right and wrong, glory and decay turn all at once unreal . . ." (translation by Moss Roberts).

Ming readers, however, remembered Yang Shen first and foremost as a romantic lover exchanging poems and songs from exile with his wife in Sichuan. The idea of a long-distance romance based on the exchange of poems was extremely appealing to Ming readers. Huang E, Yang Shen's second wife and the daughter of the respected scholar Huang Ke (1449–1522), was known for her literary gifts. She followed Yang Shen into exile and lived with him in Yunnan for three years, but after his father's death in 1529 she went back to Xindu, Sichuan, to manage the Yang household. The couple had no children, but Huang E educated Yang's sons by concubines as though they were her own. For thirty years, until Yang's death in 1559, the couple's poetic exchanges inspired the adulation of readers throughout all regions of China. Wang Shizhen (1526–1590), in the appendix to his *Remarks on the Arts* (*Yiyuan zhiyan*), cites a poem ("To Send to My Husband") and a song lyric (set to the tune "Yellow Oriole") written by Huang E as testaments to her great talent. He even commented that Huang's song lyrics were superior to her husband's. With praise from an important critic like Wang Shizhen, the leader of the "Seven Late Masters," Huang's reputation as a poet and lyricist was quickly established. However, although her song lyrics (*ci*) were circulated in literary circles, only a very small number of her poems (*shi*) have survived. Like most women of the gentry in her day, Huang probably considered writing poetry to be a private matter and, as far as we know, never published any of her poems during her lifetime. By contrast, her husband had long lived in the spotlight of literary fame, publishing numerous collected works – including a 1540 edition of his song lyrics in seven chapters (followed by a supplement printed in 1543) and a 1551 edition of his collected song lyrics and colloquial songs (*qu*).

In 1570, the year after Huang's death, a small collection of her poems was published as the *Collected Poems of the Wife of Yang Shen* (*Yang Zhuangyuan qi shiji*) by an unknown book dealer. After that the number of poems attributed to her kept growing as more and more came to be discovered by people from different regions. In 1608, a large collection of *Lyrics and Colloquial Songs of Mr. Yang Shen and His Wife* (*Yang Sheng'an xiansheng furen yuefu*) was published; many – including some erotic and burlesque pieces – were attributed to Huang E. This edition had a short preface allegedly written by the famous dramatist Xu Wei (1521–1593). Yang Yusheng, the editor, claimed to have had access to Huang's "handwritten manuscript," which had been "hidden inside a bed-curtain for fifteen years." One of the songs attributed to Huang has continued to appear even in modern Chinese anthologies. Set to the tune "The Fall of a Little Wild Goose," the song expresses the angry thoughts of a jealous wife, who accuses her husband of "making love with someone else" while she remains alone in a "cold room," and contains such provocative lines as "that insufferable little bitch / with her coy tricks" and "this old witch can still / make a furious scene" (translation by Kenneth Rexroth and Ling Chung). Songs of this kind have won Huang E a reputation for being an uninhibited writer who is "not afraid of saying anything." But scholars have long speculated that these songs were false attributions. The 1608 edition may indeed have wrongly (and intentionally?) attributed to Huang E many songs drawn from contemporary songbooks, of which some were by other authors and some perhaps by Yang Shen.

The image of Huang E as a talented woman writer who regularly sent poems and songs to her exiled husband may have been the fabrication of book dealers. The theme of a man and a woman exchanging love poems was a perennial favorite in classical tales (*chuanqi xiaoshuo*) of the time. A case in point is "The Biography of Juanjuan" by the southern writer Yang Yi (1488–1558), a love story consisting entirely of poems exchanged between a man and a woman. Similar romances based on poetic exchanges had already appeared in the classical tales of earlier writers, such as Qu You (1347–1433) and Li Changqi (1376–1451). The appetite of the sixteenth-century reading public for this kind of fiction fueled a boom in the publication of collections of fiction old and new. Both Huang E and Yang Shen later became subjects of romantic fiction, most notably in Feng Menglong's (1574–1646) collection of classical tales, entitled *The Anatomy of Love* (*Qingshi leilue*), where they are models of the passionate individual.

Reconstructing images of women

Around the mid-sixteenth century, scholars began to be actively involved in the reconstruction of women's images in literature. A good illustration can be found in the work of Kang Wanmin (grandson of Kang Hai), who devoted himself to commentary on an elaborate "palindrome of brocade" believed to have been written and embroidered by a fourth-century woman called Su Hui. According to legend, Su Hui was a beautiful and talented woman, who composed a palindrome of 841 characters after being abandoned by her husband, Dou Tao, and then wove it into a brocade of many colors. The palindrome can be read in any order (right to left, left to right, diagonally, and so forth). It is said that her husband, exiled to faraway Dunhuang, was so moved by the palindrome that he left his mistress to be reunited with his gifted wife. Su Hui first became famous during the fifth century as an exemplar of the virtuous woman who was able to combine skill in the feminine arts with literary talent. A few centuries later, a preface attributed to the Tang empress Wu Zetian (624?–705) elevated Su Hui to an "eminent model for all later writers." In all likelihood, the palindrome may not have been the work of Su Hui. Although later readers granted this possibility, efforts were occasionally made in the Song and Yuan dynasties to find new ways of reading the piece. However, it was not until the Jiajing period of the Ming that the palindrome suddenly achieved wide circulation, largely thanks to Kang Wanmin's promotion. In his *Reader's Manual*, Kang claims that Su Hui's palindrome of brocade can yield more than four thousand poems (a Song dynasty monk had counted some three thousand). In an age when the publishing industry was becoming an increasingly prominent influence upon readers, there was pressure on scholars like Kang Wanmin to seek out new topics, such as talented women, especially those who had been marginalized. Even Li Qingzhao (1083–ca 1155), the famous woman poet of the Song, underwent a similar process of "archaeological" reconstruction when Ming scholars found it difficult to determine the authorship of many of the song lyrics attributed to her. Most of the original manuscripts of Li's work had been lost by Ming times and only twenty-three poems were thought to be truly hers. To this day the authenticity of some of her works is still being questioned.

The burgeoning interest of mid-Ming scholars in women's writing did eventually lead to the inclusion of women in the canon of great writers. Perhaps, in their support for the marginalized literary talent of women, some men of letters saw a reminder of their own marginality. Little more is known about the life and work of Kang Wanmin than that he produced a commentary on Su Hui's palindrome in brocade, but one of his reasons for writing the commentary on this almost-forgotten piece may have lain in his sympathy for a talented woman who had been left out of earlier anthologies and literary histories. The realization that female contributions to literature had gone largely unrecognized did in fact prompt many Ming male scholars to compile their own anthologies of women's writings. Some anthologists became obsessed with women writers to the point of idealizing their lives. For example, Tian Yiheng, a mid-sixteenth-century pioneer in this endeavor, declared that he would devote his life to collecting women's works. In his anthology, *Poetic Works of Female Scribes (Shi nüshi)*, Tian argued that since antiquity women had accomplished no less than men in the field of literature, but, due to the negligence of male scholars, their names had remained obscure in literary history. By publishing a reputable anthology of women's works, he hoped to do belated justice to the long and glorious tradition of literary women. Although it would be another century before anthology-making truly began to prosper, Tian Yiheng's anthology, printed sometime during the Jiajing reign, first defined the rationale for separate anthologies dedicated to works by women. In 1618, Qu Juesheng published an even more ambitious anthology in nine chapters entitled *The Feminine Sao (Nü sao)*. Qu emphasized the ideal of literary immortality for women, comparing their works to Confucian classics, in particular the poem "Encountering Sorrow" of Qu Yuan. Women writers of the Ming did indeed often model themselves after Qu Yuan. For example, in the sixteenth century, Madame Wen, a widow from Shaanxi Province, wrote a series of nine poems called "In Imitation of the 'Lisao'," in which she likens her own misfortunes to those of Qu Yuan. In her poem series, Madame Wen demonstrates a thorough familiarity not only with scholarship on the "Lisao," but also with Su Hui's palindromic verses. Madame Wen was honored as "a singular female talent" and her poems were recorded in the gazetteer of her hometown. Here is an example of a woman who acquired literary immortality solely through her writings: nothing else is known about her life, not even her given name.

Inevitably, as scholars assumed the role of editors and anthologists of women's poetry in greater numbers – comparing their own efforts in collecting women's works to Confucius' compilation of the *Classic of Poetry* – more and more women's works came to be discovered. At first, the curatorial function of anthologizing was what drove these men of letters. Later the idea of transmitting women's works became a vital mission to some. These scholars aimed to create a new kind of anthology devoted entirely to women's literature, unlike the traditional anthologies that put women's works at the end alongside those by monks and foreigners – a policy of selection first adopted by the Five Dynasties poet and anthologist Wei Zhuang (836–910). The new strategy of the Ming was meant primarily to reflect pluralism in the arena of women's writings, as well as to develop the techniques necessary to the preservation of women's literature.

One of the problems with women's anthologies of the Ming, however, is the laxity of their criteria for selection. This led Qing scholars to raise doubts about the authenticity of works included in the Ming anthologies. At a time when a tradition of women's anthologies was yet to be established, it is understandable that some book dealers might have felt it necessary to pad the anthologies with additional materials. What is noteworthy is that the entire book publishing industry, starting in the mid-Ming, seemed to be obsessed with this new genre of the "women's anthology." "Authenticity" and "authorship" were no longer issues: all that mattered was for the women included to be appealing to readers. It was perhaps under such conditions that a series of love poems attributed to Zhang Hongqiao, the legendary lover of the fourteenth-century poet Lin Hong, was invented. It could well be that Zhang Hongqiao (whose given name literally means "Red Bridge") never existed, but was fabricated by later readers from the place name "Red Bridge" frequently mentioned in Lin Hong's romantic song lyrics. The *Anatomy of Love* by Feng Menglong, for instance, has a chapter called "Red Bridge" about a woman from the gentry of Fujian Province. As time went by, poems attributed to Red Bridge began to appear and circulate among readers. Eventually these poems came to be included in anthologies like Wang Duanshu's (1621–before 1685) *Classic Poetry by Famous Women* (*Mingyuan shiwei*) and Gu Jingfang's *Orchid Selections of Song Lyrics of the Ming* (*Lan'gao Mingci huixuan*). At the same time, Wang Jiaoluan's "Song of Enduring Sorrow" (Changhen ge) – which first appeared in the *Anatomy of Love* and was perhaps based on a fictional account – ended up in *Poetic Retrospective of Famous Ladies* (*Mingyuan shi gui*), a highly regarded anthology of women's poetry attributed to Zhong Xing (1574–1624). The sensational story associated with Wang Jiaoluan's poem must have been a key reason for its inclusion in Zhong Xing's anthology. According to the editor's note, Wang Jiaoluan wrote her song of resentment immediately after her fiancé married someone else, and then hanged herself after sending her poem to the magistrate in Suzhou. The fiancé was duly punished in accordance with the law. The incident is said to have taken place at the beginning of the Tianshun reign (1457–1464) of the Yongzong Emperor. These anecdotes attest to the presence of a fast-growing publishing industry during the Ming aimed at readers interested in stories about women.

Nevertheless, stories like these were not always untrue. Some "fictional" accounts were based on real events that can be verified from official documents. Such an account, included in one of Feng Menglong's collections of vernacular stories, tells of a young woman named Li Yuying who was put in prison and sentenced to death because her stepmother accused her of writing two poems with improperly erotic content. We read that Li Yuying wrote a petition to the Jiajing Emperor from her prison cell, whereupon the young emperor, usually known for his brutality, played the unaccustomed role of benevolent ruler and pardoned her. The historical Li Yuying did in fact submit a petition to the throne in 1524. The text of the petition as recorded in Feng Menglong's story exactly matches the historical document, which is preserved in a Ming legal casebook, except that only the first half is included in the fictional account. Clearly the story of Li Yuying is based on fact, although, as with anecdotes of all forms, there are layers of ambiguity surrounding the context, which by its nature can never be completely established.

Most Chinese readers, however, have learned to accept the fact that literary and historical writings nearly always contain dimensions that do not conform to reality. What the eighteenth-century novel *The Story of the Stone* says about the ambiguity between truth and untruth captures this fascinating and perplexing attitude of the traditional Chinese reader: "Truth becomes fiction when the fiction's true; Real becomes not-real where the unreal's real" (David Hawkes's translation). Readers of the Ming dynasty seem especially conscious that they lived in an age where the border between fiction and history was often blurred. It was during this period that the genre known as the classical tale gained enormous popularity again. After the reprinting of Qu You's collection of classical tales, *New Tales Told by Lamplight*, many began to write romantic and didactic stories modeled on his example. The title of Shao Jingzhan's (fl. 1560) collection, *Tales of the Searching Lamplight* (*Mideng yinhua*), clearly suggests that it follows the tradition of Qu You. Shao Jingzhan, however, much more than Qu You, was interested in rewriting old stories. For example, "The Tomb of the Chaste and Unyielding Woman" (Zhenliemu ji) is about a brave wife who saves her children's lives and redeems the life of her husband at the cost of her own. The story is based on an old historical account from the Yuan dynasty. Not all the stories in Shao's collection are retellings of real events. His "Story of Prince Yao" (Yao gongzi zhuan) is purely fictional; it was later turned into a vernacular story by the Qing short-story writer Ling Mengchu. Rewriting – that is, creating one's own version of old stories – approached the status of a national obsession among Ming men of letters. Their stories had familiar plots and motifs, and yet the intensity these men invested in casting them into different forms is strikingly original.

Rewriting heroism in fiction

No other project of rewriting can match the scale of the refiguring in the Ming period of three monumental novels: *Romance of the Three Kingdoms* (*Sanguo zhi yanyi*), *Water Margin* (*Shuihu zhuan*), and *Journey to the West* (*Xiyou ji*). All three novels are thought to have evolved from popular oral storytelling followed by a period of maturation in various textual forms. Yet as Andrew H. Plaks has shown, the sixteenth-century texts represent these works in their most fully developed form – essentially the form in which they are known and read today. In other words, it was Ming rewriting that finally shaped the earlier narratives into fully fledged novels.

In contrast to the many love stories that appeared in the form of classical tales (*chuanqi xiaoshuo*) during this period, the novels mentioned above are exceptional for their use of vernacular language. The *Romance of the Three Kingdoms*, the earliest of these novels, mixes vernacular expressions with an otherwise almost purely classical grammar and idiom, but the title, which contains the word "popular" (*su*), calls attention to the vernacular elements of the text. On the whole, we may say that these Ming novels are all written in a language that shows remarkably little difference from modern Chinese usage. Most interestingly, in reworking the earlier narrative sources into polished vernacular fiction, the authors of these novels also invented a new concept of heroism, according to which the distinction between good and evil grew increasingly ambiguous.

The earliest text that we have of the *Romance of the Three Kingdoms* is the 1522 edition. Most sources accept Luo Guanzhong (fl. fourteenth century) as the author of the original work, but the authorship for the 1522 edition remains unknown. During the Wanli period (1573–1620), another edition with commentary by the famous writer and thinker Li Zhi (also known as Li Zhuowu, 1527–1602) became available in print. But it was the Qing edition annotated by Mao Zonggang that eventually became the most popular. The novel in its 1522 edition draws upon materials from both historical texts and earlier popular sources, including books on military tactics. The author breaks new ground in the vivid depiction of battles: altogether it has more than one hundred battle scenes. The basic plot is a retelling of the period between 220 and 265 AD when, after the collapse of the Han dynasty, China was divided into three kingdoms that vied for unified control of the empire. As the leaders of the Three Kingdoms – Liu Bei of the Shu, Cao Cao of the Wei, and Zhou Yu of the Wu – fought for supremacy, they were also concerned with establishing the legitimacy of their claim to power. Thus the concept of heroism evolves through the course of the novel. Perhaps, for Ming readers, the absence of heroes in contemporary life stimulated the need for past heroes worthy of genuine admiration. Even before the Ming, however, the Three Kingdoms period was a favorite subject of dramatic performance, and audiences were said to "burst into tears whenever they heard Liu Bei of the Shu was defeated" and "laugh and sing when Cao Cao of the Wei failed to win victory." This attitude of "exalting Liu Bei and denigrating Cao Cao" reflects the unsophisticated hero worship common among popular audiences. One of the great contributions of the 1522 novel is its attempt to undermine this simplistic understanding of the distinction between hero and villain. (Coincidentally, 1522 was also the year that the teenage Jiajing Emperor ascended the throne.)

In Chinese historiography, the state of Shu has not always been considered the legitimate successor to the Han dynasty. In the *Record of the Three Kingdoms* (*Sanguo zhi*), one of the sources of the novel, the historian Chen Shou (233–297) writes that the state of Wei was the rightful heir to the heavenly mandate after its forfeiture by the Han, and this remained the standard view of historians for centuries. But the neo-Confucian scholar Zhu Xi changed all this by claiming in his *Main Principles of the Comprehensive Mirror to Assist Government* (*Tongjian gangmu*) that the state of Shu was the lawful successor to the Han. Zhu Xi's view was so widely accepted after the Song dynasty that, in the popular imagination, Liu Bei of the Shu became synonymous with the quality of "benevolence" (*ren*), while Cao Cao of the Wei symbolized "despotic cruelty" (*canbao*). The author of the 1522 edition of the *Romance* followed Zhu Xi's interpretation regarding political legitimacy in its general outlines, but he also revised the popular stereotypes so as to make the main characters more realistic and convincing. Nearly every character in the novel is humanized by strengths and weaknesses. Zhuge Liang, the wise minister of Shu and the novel's principal hero, comes the closest to perfection, but even he makes strategic errors and is doomed to die before winning final victory. On his deathbed, he accepts his fate as the will of Heaven.

The author's keen interest in personality is shown in his treatment of the more than 400 characters in this 750,000-word novel. One favored technique is to juxtapose characters representing different types, especially those with deep flaws or personality traits that are mutually contradictory. Indeed, the sense of paradox that haunts the 1522 edition of the novel differentiates it most sharply from its sources. For example, Liu Bei, though a sympathetic character, is portrayed repeatedly as a weak person, who weeps and feels distressed whenever a battle is lost; Cao Cao, by contrast, makes light of defeat. But as the reader soon finds out, it is precisely this overconfidence that leads Cao Cao to lose the decisive Battle of the Red Cliff, while Liu Bei's hypersensitivity enables him to care about the well-being of the common people. Cao Cao, for all his admirable qualities, is at best a "treacherous hero" – one who is capable of great things in an age of peace but who will stoop to treachery in an age of disorder. The characterization of Cao Cao is one of the great achievements of the 1522 rewriting of the *Romance of the Three Kingdoms*. He is a cruel and cold-blooded killer: in one episode he butchers the entire family of a man who has helped him. Calculating and manipulative, he will do anything to get ahead and win popular support. On the other hand, Cao Cao is also capable of acts of great generosity, as when he refrains from killing Chen Lin out of appreciation for his talent, or when he lets Guan Yu – one of Liu Bei's trusted generals – slip away from captivity. (Later, Guan Yu repays him in kind with an "honorable release.") In comparison, Yuan Shao, another "treacherous hero," lacks the strategic brilliance and lionhearted valor of Cao Cao.

The definition of heroism in the *Water Margin* is even more ambivalent and hence more controversial. Growing out of an original story rooted in both historical events and the popular imagination, this novel underwent an even more complicated history of textual formation than the *Romance*. The narrative tells the story of Song Jiang and his band of outlaws who build up a power base in the marshes surrounding Mount Liang during the last years of the Northern Song. They later surrender to the Song court and even help the government to put down a rebellion led by Fang La. Some scholars believe that Shi Nai'an (dates unknown) wrote the original narrative, and his student Luo Guanzhong (fl. 1330–1400) – also credited with the authorship of the *Romance of the Three Kingdoms* – reworked the novel into its definitive version; however, the authorship of the *Water Margin* remains a subject of debate. The main outline of the Mount Liang saga was already well established by the mid-sixteenth century. The earliest extant edition of the novel is a hundred-chapter version, printed around 1550 under the auspices of Guo Xun, marquis of Wuding, and then reprinted in 1589. These were followed by the 1610 edition – whose commentary was attributed to Li Zhuowu, though the authorship of the commentary has become an issue of controversy – and by a seventy-chapter version in 1644 with commentary by Jin Shengtan (1608–1661). Besides these well-known editions, other 100-chapter and 120-chapter editions were also in circulation, as well as an abbreviated version. The novel's reception during the Ming was immensely positive, claiming the Wanli Emperor as one of its most avid readers; it is still popular today.

Unlike the *Romance of the Three Kingdoms,* whose characters are nearly all based on historical figures, the 108 heroes of the *Water Margin* (with the exception of Song Jiang and Yang Zhi) are all fictional creations. The author adopts widely divergent perspectives on heroism, so that contradictory qualities are often found in the same person. Rebels against corrupt government, the outlaws are nevertheless totally committed to brotherhood, believing that "all men are brothers." Nearly all are experts in the martial arts and are dedicated to righting the wrongs of those who are unjustly treated. At the same time, they are merciless killers who will not hesitate to commit acts of extreme violence. Few readers of the novel can forget the gruesome scene in Chapter 31, when Wu Song indiscriminately massacres over a dozen men and women in an act of brutal retaliation at the Mandarin Duck Tower. The recurrent theme of cannibalism, along with the heroes' readiness to kill women, are also puzzling to the modern reader. As C. T. Hsia has put it, "the heroes are at times indistinguishable from the villains." But sixteenth-century commentators like Li Zhuowu (whose authorship is still in doubt) were more interested in the principles of "loyalty" (*zhong*) and "justice" (*yi*) underlying the novel's heroic code. Despite the outlaws' manifest discontent with the government, to late Ming readers they were considered loyal servants of the state so long as the state was willing to use them. In contrast, corrupt court officials such as Gao Qiu and Cai Jing were held to be the real villains, devoid of any redeeming virtues. The fate of the outlaw heroes, killed at the hands of these officials, must have seemed especially tragic to Ming readers. All the sixteenth-century editions of the novel contain the words "loyalty and justice" (*zhong yi*), thereby conferring posthumous honors on the heroes. Only at the end of the Ming, when Jin Shengtan presented a different reading of the novel, were these words taken out of the title. The effect of the *Water Margin* on the Chinese imagination can aptly be described by Oscar Wilde's aphorism, "Life imitates art." Since 1586, it has been fashionable for leaders of rebellions in China to use quotations from the *Water Margin* (e.g. "to implement the Way on behalf of Heaven") as their slogans; some have even adopted the names of individual characters, such as Song Jiang and Li Kui. For this reason the *Water Margin* has been periodically banned by the government.

If the heroes of the *Water Margin* survive on their martial skills while on the road, in the *Journey to the West* we come to see the road itself as an allegorical emblem of the growth of spiritual understanding. This novel, first known in the West as *Monkey* in an abridged translation by Arthur Waley, tells the story of the monk Tripitaka's journey to fetch Buddhist scriptures from India, accompanied by his disciples Monkey, Pigsy, and Sandy. Like the other two novels discussed above, it derives its materials from various earlier sources. As early as the Southern Song, the legend of the pilgrimage already existed in book form. Numerous short versions of the story appeared during the Yuan dynasty in the form of the "kit" (*yuan ben*). Around the mid-fourteenth century, a dramatist named Yang Jingxian produced a series of northern plays (*zaju*) on the subject, but some scholars have argued for an alternative date in the late sixteenth century. In either case, a book version of considerable length written in the colloquial language existed by 1400, as some excerpts were incorporated into the Yongle encyclopedia. A Korean text containing a fragment of the story was printed in 1423. Finally, in the sixteenth century, *Journey to the West* appeared in the form of a novel of one hundred chapters. According to reliable sources, we know that at least two publishers, the Lu and the Dengzhou publishing houses, printed versions of this novel during the Jiajing period (1522–1566). The earliest extant edition, however, was printed in Nanjing in 1592. To this day the authorship of the novel is still in question, although it has been ascribed to Wu Cheng'en (ca 1500–1582), who was also known for his poetry and song lyrics. In any case, the author's skill in transforming the somewhat wooden stock figures of the sources into the unforgettable characters of the novel has won the admiration of readers for centuries. In particular, the reinvention of Monkey added a completely new dimension to the concept of heroism.

With a comic book superhero's magical powers of transformation, Monkey is the only one of the disciples who comes to everyone's rescue in the novel. In his eyes, there are no obstacles that cannot be overcome, nor monsters who cannot be vanquished. To combat the demons that are constantly appearing in their way, Monkey takes on many forms: an insect, a woman, a husband, and so on. The pilgrims must pass through eighty-one ordeals before finally reaching the shores of salvation, and in each calamity it is Monkey's superior energy and wisdom that saves the lives of the whole group. Ironically, Tripitaka – the holy monk of the Tang who in real life single-handedly brought hundreds of sutras from India to China – is portrayed in the novel as an ordinary man, vulnerable and easily intimidated by every obstacle, while it is Monkey who at each encounter helps his master understand that these calamities are only vehicles for spiritual enlightenment. Monkey's superior understanding has not been obtained without a price. He has learned his lesson well because he has already gone through a long process of suffering before becoming one of the pilgrims. Originally a stone monkey who comes to life and acquires magic powers, Monkey wreaks havoc in the Daoist Heavenly Court and has to be subjugated by the Buddha, who imprisons him under the Mountain of Five Phases. It is only after he joins the pilgrims on their journey that he finally learns discipline. First, he removes his six senses so that he may concentrate on the exercise of self-cultivation. In allegorical terms, Monkey represents the mind, and his main responsibility is to remind his master about the importance of cultivating the mind. In Chapter 85, when Tripitaka loses faith once again, Monkey quotes to him from the Heart Sutra: "Seek not afar for Buddha on Spirit Mount / Mount Spirit lives only in your mind" (Anthony C. Yu's translation). The entire novel can therefore be read as an allegory for the progress of the mind, with the eighty-one calamities the means by which one finds enlightenment.

This great emphasis on the mind – with a recurrent underlying theme of combining Buddhist, Daoist, and Confucian thought – has prompted some Chinese scholars to associate *Journey to the West* with Wang Yangming's philosophy of mind. A discussion of a restless "Monkey mind" appears in Wang's own writing. Even though his philosophy was banned by the Jiajing Emperor for almost two decades (from Wang's death in 1529 until 1547), it is possible that the rewriting of the Monkey story was directly related to Wang's idea of "searching within your own mind" for illumination. Government censorship never prevented Wang's thought from being popular throughout the Ming. It is also noteworthy that Li Zhuowu, one of the most enthusiastic promoters of Wang's philosophy of mind in the late Ming, wrote a commentary on the *Journey to the West* (as well as on the *Romance of the Three Kingdoms* and, possibly, the *Water Margin*). In one famous comment, Li states that the demons in the novel are all "illusions" that represent the true "human affairs of this world." His commentary no doubt played a key role in shaping later interpretations of the novel.

Rewriting as a form of creation in drama

In drama, as well as in fiction, the mid-sixteenth-century Chinese ability to absorb elements from a wide range of sources and to transform them into different forms of literature is impressive. Li Kaixian (1502–1568), one of the "Eight Talented Men of the Jiajing Period," was one such writer. (The group also included Tang Shunzhi (1507–1560) and Wang Shenzhong (1509–1559), better known for their prose.) Li was forced out of government service at the comparatively young age of thirty-nine for attacking the eunuch Xia Yan

(1482–1548) in a court petition. He devoted his long years of retirement to the pursuit of literature and the performing arts, specializing in the study of folk songs, dramatic texts, and fiction. His collection of books and sources on these subjects was likely the largest in existence, and he came to be known as the owner of "mountains and seas of lyrics and songs." Li especially admired the "genuine feeling" expressed in contemporary folk songs, saying that they were superb works of literature because "they came directly from the heart." However, his greatest contribution lies in reviving the dramatic traditions of the northern and the southern styles. Li published the definitive texts of the northern drama of earlier periods under the collected title *Revised Plays by Distinguished Yuan Authors* (*Gaiding Yuan xian chuanqi*). The collection contained sixteen Yuan plays, apparently all rewritten by Li Kaixian, of which six are still extant. In fact, several of the Yuan plays known to us, including Bai Pu's (1226–after 1291) "Wutong Rain" (*Wutong yu*) and Ma Zhiyuan's (fl. 1251) "Tears on the Green Shirt" (*Qingshan lei*), are texts reworked by Li, and so, strictly speaking, he should be credited with part of the authorship of these plays. It is, of course, difficult to know how much Li had contributed to the final rewriting of these Yuan plays, but Li's edition of these plays was an important milestone as far as textual transmissions are concerned.

Though a northerner, Li Kaixian was also skillful in composing longer plays in the southern style. In his private troupes at home, most of the singers specialized in performing southern-style arias. His most famous play in the southern style is the *Story of the Sword* (*Baojian ji*), a re-creation of an episode from the *Water Margin*. Finished in 1547, a few years after he resigned from office, the play represents in many ways Li's self-conscious critique of the contemporary political situation. Viewed from the perspective of the cultural and political milieu of the time, it is easy to understand why Li's imagination should have been fired by the *Water Margin*, one of whose main themes explores the process by which law-abiding men are forced to join a band of outlaws. The plot of the *Story of the Sword* is based on chapters 7 through 12 of the *Water Margin*, in which the commoner Lin Chong gets into trouble with the authorities when the son of the evil minister Gao Qiu forcibly takes Lin's beautiful wife. The original story focuses on abuse of power by high officials in the treatment of the common people. In his play, Li Kaixian turns Lin Chong into an upright official who is exiled to a distant region as punishment for his repeated petitions to impeach evil ministers. During Lin's absence, Gao Qiu's son attempts to seduce Lin's wife, Madame Zhang, who resists his advances at the risk of her own life. Meanwhile, the evil ministers make several attempts to murder Lin Chong, so that he is forced to join the rebels on Mount Liang.

Being essentially an upstanding citizen, Lin Chong eventually surrenders to the court and continues to serve in office. At the end of the play, he and his wife are miraculously reunited and the evil minister and his son are put to death. *The Story of the Sword*, written in fluent vernacular prose interspersed with hundreds of elegant arias, is a great artistic achievement. Li Kaixian has made a startling new contribution to the Lin Chong story, encouraging readers to appreciate it in the context of a new genre, while at the same time adding subtle references to contemporary court politics. It should be pointed out that, during the Ming, drama was meant to be read as well as performed. Li's play received great critical acclaim from contemporary readers. In his postscript to the *Story of the Sword*, Wang Jiusi, then eighty-one, recognized Li Kaixian for the supreme craftsmanship of his arias and praised the scale and excellence of his writing as something "never seen before." Only Wang Shizhen (1526–1590), a southerner, felt that Li was somewhat deficient in his knowledge of southern tunes.

The colloquial song (*sanqu*) was even more crucial to the expression of Li Kaixian's creativity. The straightforward style of Li's colloquial songs seems linked to his passion for folk songs, but his unique rhetoric involves a sensual elegance that is lacking in most folk songs. In his day, Li was especially famous for his collection of one hundred "Short Songs of Zhonglu" (*Zhonglu xiaoling*), which are spontaneous and lyrical, even contemplative. Many are intimately personal. He also wrote a special collection of 110 songs during an illness. But the songs in his collection entitled *Mourning My Wife and My Concubine through the Four Seasons* (*Sishi daonei*) are the most moving and hence the best remembered. Li developed strong affinities with older writers like Wang Jiusi and Kang Hai, who apparently influenced his aesthetic thinking. His own exploration in new literary modes was highly influential in shaping new directions in Ming literature, but he was not alone among the writers of his generation in experimenting with new literary forms and styles; the famous songwriter Feng Weimin (1511–1580?) was another such pioneer. Li Kaixian and his friends were the last generation to distinguish themselves in northern songs and drama, before southern drama became dominant in the following decades.

The later Revivalists

Ming poetry, especially poetry after the mid-sixteenth century, has been unjustly neglected by modern scholars. The poets themselves, men like Yang Shen, Wen Zhengming, and Wang Shizhen (1526–1590), were highly regarded in their own time as prolific poets who also worked in many other forms of literature.

The poetic activity of the mid- and late sixteenth century has been called by historians the Late Revival School. This movement was initiated by the efforts of the "Seven Late Masters" (*hou qizi*), headed by Li Panlong (1514–1570), to revive the classical modes of High Tang poetry. Unlike the "Seven Early Masters" (*qian qizi*), who were primarily men of northern origin, the Seven Late Masters – except for Li Panlong himself – all came from the south. They included such famous writers as Wang Shizhen, Xie Zhen (1495–1575), and Zong Chen (1525–1560). Nearly all these men passed the civil service examinations around 1550, and the "neoclassical" revival they espoused dates from the beginning of their official careers in Beijing. We do not know when the name "Seven Late Masters" emerged; at first the group referred to itself as "the Five" or "the Six." Membership, it would appear, was not as fixed as some modern historians think.

The "late" Revivalists eventually came to dominate the literary world in ways that were quite different from the Seven Early Masters. Literary historians have often associated the labels "Seven Early Masters" and "Seven Late Masters" with those who promoted the idea that "poetry must be like that of the High Tang." As has already been discussed, however, while the Seven Early Masters greatly admired the High Tang poets, they also held the *Classic of Poetry* and the poetry of the Han and Wei in high regard. It was the Seven Late Masters who set the seal on the idea that only High Tang poetry was worthy of imitation. Or, to put it more accurately, Li Panlong was the only one among the Seven Late Masters who advocated imitation of the High Tang style to the exclusion of all others.

Li Panlong's poetry was not well received by contemporary readers. His real contribution lies in anthologizing, by means of which he raised High Tang poetry to unparalleled status. Li's compilations were no doubt directly influenced by the reprinting of Gao Bing's (1350–1423) anthologies, the *Graded Compendium of Tang Poetry* and the *Correct Sounds of Tang Poetry*, during this period. Marginalized during his lifetime, Gao Bing's anthologies in reprinted form gained enormous popularity and quickly became the standard texts for Tang poetry, according to contemporary writers such as Huang Zuo (1490–1566). The success of Gao's anthologies naturally inspired new compilations of Tang poetry. Li Panlong published two anthologies of Tang verse, *Correct Edition of Ancient and Modern Poetry* (*Gujin shishan*) and *Selections of Tang Poetry* (*Tangshi xuan*), as companion volumes to Gao Bing. Other anthologists who disagreed with Gao's policy of selection also published rival collections of

Tang poetry. The anthology compiled by Yang Shen under the title *Origins of the Regulated Five-Syllable Line Verse* (*Wuyan lüzu*) is just such an attempt to correct the omissions of Gao Bing. Though essentially agreeing with Gao's division of Tang poetry into four periods, Yang Shen felt that Gao had failed to make appropriate distinctions among important subgenres. Yang also had his own views concerning the origin of the regulated five-syllable line, which he dated back to the Northern and Southern Dynasties period (317–589). Needless to say, the Revivalists disagreed with Yang Shen on these issues.

Regardless of their affiliation, however, most poets of the age cared deeply about the relationship that anthologizing bore to canon formation. It is as though, conscious of their belated arrival upon the literary scene, the Ming poets needed to have a renewed relationship with the canon. To Li Panlong, in particular, Tang verse, as poetry in its purest form, is in a class by itself. For this reason, he wanted to make certain that only those works that are the most typical of the "Tang style" (*Tang ti*), in both spirit and principle, should be included in his anthologies. According to his preface to *Selections of Tang Poetry*, Li's main purpose in making the anthology was "to let gentlemen of posterity exhaust the limits of Tang poetry, for the true essence of the Tang verse is all contained here." By "Tang poetry" Li Panlong meant High Tang poetry. Chen Guoqiu has shown in his study of the Ming Revivalists that more than 60 percent of the selections from the *Correct Edition of Ancient and Modern Poetry* were from the High Tang, with less than 20 percent from the Middle and the Late Tang combined. In Gao Bing's *Graded Compendium of Tang Poetry*, 32 percent is from the High Tang and nearly 35 percent from the Middle Tang. Li Panlong's redefinition of great poetry, which established High Tang poets such as Du Fu and Wang Wei as paragons of the entire tradition, provoked vehement controversy. Li himself imitated the High Tang style to a fault, and the result was poetry that was stale and unoriginal. In fact, it can be said that Li alone of the Seven Late Masters was inflexible in his choice of models for imitation, for his contemporaries adopted a much more multicultural and diverse approach. Years later, Qian Qianyi (1582–1664) lumped together the Early with the Late Revivalists and summarily dismissed the entire Ming Revivalist movement. This sweeping judgment is unfair to the Early Revivalists, who as a group were true innovators, daring to reassert the spirit of classical lyricism against the predominant cabinet style of their day. Unfortunately, Qian's standing as a scholar has led to the wide acceptance of this prejudice.

During the same period, poets in Suzhou – including the famous Huangfu brothers, namely Huangfu Chong (1490–1558), Huangfu Xiao (1497–1546),

Huangfu Pang (1498–1589), and Huangfu Lian (1508–1564) – were creating their own literary traditions outside the sphere of influence of the Late Revivalists. The then ancient Wen Zhengming (1470–1559) continued to be regarded as a major authority in literature and the visual arts, while several of his descendants were distinguishing themselves as writers, artists, and scholars. Gradually, large families such as Wen's came to form an important literary and cultural nexus in the city of Suzhou, a social phenomenon that would become even more pronounced as time went on.

Following the death of Li Panlong in 1570, Wang Shizhen began to be known as the leader of the Seven Late Masters. He eventually became the icon of the Revivalist movement, despite vast differences in his approach from that of Li Panlong. Wang's iconic status did not bring entirely good fortune. When, during the mid- and late sixteenth century, a strong opposing current of anti-Revivalism arose, Wang became the chief target of attack. Warfare among rival literary schools was complicated by the intricate networks of personal, factional, and generational affiliations, as well as intellectual ties, around which members of the elite organized their lives during the Ming. For example, the renowned essayist Gui Youguang (1506–1571) expresses his distaste for the Revivalist School in this belligerent way: "As for today's men of letters, it is really hard to say. These men have hardly acquired classical learning; they have only managed to find one or two self-important mediocre figures to honor as masters. Together they form a gang . . . " The "one or two self-important mediocre figures" clearly referred to younger-generation writers such as Wang Shizhen, and the subsequent battles between Wang and Gui reveal the high degree of animosity that could arise between literary camps. Wang Shizhen did not in fact fit the general description of a Revivalist. Though in his earlier years he had shown affinity for the Revivalists' neoclassical view of literature, Wang was a master of many different poetic styles and forms – ranging from *yuefu* poetry to poetry in the style of the Song dynasty, from palace poetry to poetry on gardens – not to mention that he was also a distinguished composer of song lyrics. As a writer, Wang was an individualist. He wanted to create a poetic style that was unmistakably personal: as he says in his preface to a friend's collected works, "Only when there is a true 'me' can there be true poetry." Thus he disparaged Li Panlong again and again for making lifeless imitations. Wang continued to revise his critical views as he grew older, as may be seen in his many works of literary criticism, including the famous *Remarks on the Arts* (*Yiyuan zhiyan*), which he completed before the age of forty. A man of wide-ranging interests, he accorded high esteem to writers in numerous fields of literature, even those in opposing schools. He befriended Li Kaixian, despite the latter's opposition to the Late Revival School. Like Li, Wang loved to read dramatic texts; his remarks on plays such as *The Pipa Lute* and *The Western Wing* continue to be cited by modern scholars. Wang was also interested in compiling books of fiction, both classical and vernacular. Several classical tales that gained currency at the time came from his *Book of the Beautiful and the Strange (Yanyi pian)*. The most famous of these is the story of the romance between the scholar–official Liu Yaoju and a boat girl, which was later turned into a vernacular story by Ling Mengchu. Clearly Wang Shizhen's literary influence extended far beyond the reach of the Revivalist School, which had much more narrowly defined aims.

Wang Shizhen resembled Yang Shen in many ways: both enjoyed the highest literary influence despite the hardships they suffered in an era of political persecution. Like Yang Shen, who found a new literary life in exile, Wang Shizhen was able to reinvent himself as an author of major importance in the face of great personal suffering, as his father had been put to death through the machinations of enemies at court and he himself was forced to leave office. Both Yang and Wang were witnesses to the unique political culture of the Jiajing reign, in which persecution did not result in silence, but rather stimulated literary expression to attain new heights. These authors served a new class of intelligent and curious readers who were always ready to be informed or even provoked. But this also leads us to reflect on what may be the greatest problem for men of letters at the time: in their attempt to meet the burgeoning demands of the new readership, Ming authors were sometimes tempted to write too much and to dissipate their energies in too many different forms.

2

The literary culture of the late Ming
(1573–1644)

TINA LU

Introduction: the late Ming and the history
of the book

Over the course of these two volumes, the percentage of written material usually called literature steadily decreases in proportion to the body of extant writing as a whole. Earlier chapters deal with virtually all surviving written material from their respective periods. In this chapter, this percentage plummets, as most of what was written, read, and printed in the late Ming dynasty lies outside the purview of literary history.

For generations, scholars have intuited that the way in which commerce and culture mixed in the late Ming was radically different from preceding periods. Recent scholarly work has been able to quantify some of the enormous changes that printing and books – and consequently literature – experienced at this time, when the commercial print industry began to undergo explosive growth. Everywhere we look, we find evidence of an urban reading public, consuming texts at a prodigious rate. Recent studies have shown that only in the beginning of the sixteenth century did printing become the primary mode of textual circulation, so we might even date the beginning of print culture's dominance over manuscripts to this moment. (Nevertheless, manuscript culture remained vital throughout the late Ming, and a number of the important literary texts of this period and later were circulated first in manuscript form.)

Even though commercial printing, which had existed for centuries, did not make any major technological advances in the late Ming, it underwent dramatic and sudden growth during this period. Compare the forty-seven years of the Wanli period (1573–1620) with the fifty-one years of the two preceding reigns, the Jiajing and Longqing periods (1521–1572). Two hundred twenty-five imprints that date from those earlier realms survive from Nanjing and Jianyang, the two primary centers of commercial publishing; from the Wanli reign we have a staggering 1,185 commercial imprints. Year for year, commercial publishing was on average six times more active in the Wanli period than in the fifty years preceding it.

While European book production in the same period was held back by the high cost of paper, in Ming China paper was produced both cheaply and abundantly, out of a variety of different fibers. Local gazetteers record the full panoply of paper products available for purchase: boxes, canopies, blankets, folding fans, window papers, lanterns, even toilet paper. At the same time, woodblock printing itself required a very low initial investment compared to movable type. Throughout the Ming, as the cost of producing books gradually declined and their production became ever more efficient, books themselves became increasingly standardized in terms of size, font, and the relationship between illustration and text. Book prices also declined as workers flooded into professions like woodblock carving and printing.

This proliferation of text transformed life not just for members of the elite, but also for everyone who lived in the cities. Private publishing flourished along with the commercial sphere, so that local officials frequently involved themselves in vanity projects, funding books about their local postings, for example, out of their own pockets. In the space of a few generations, the very appearance of cities had been transformed. Written signs were everywhere in the cities. Not only were books omnipresent, but many other sorts of printed materials were as well: paper currency, religious prints, pictures from plays or novels, government announcements, and ritual paper products for burning.

What precisely were the sorts of books bought by consumers? To readers in premodern China, the blanket term "literature" simply did not exist. Instead, written materials were divided into four categories (the so-called "Four Treasuries" or *siku*): the Classics, histories, philosophy, and belles-lettres (or works by assorted authors). The last of these categories most closely, but still imperfectly, correlates with the texts studied by literary scholars and discussed here.

First, a few comments on the other three categories, which seem to have comprised approximately two-thirds of commercial imprints. Since the state published the Classics and the Four Books in the interests of promoting Confucian values, there was no financial incentive for commercial printers to publish these texts. Instead, commercial printers focused on examination aids, which will be discussed at length later, particularly classical commentaries; essays on the Classics by famous writers; and collected examination essays. Histories occupied only 10 percent or so of all the commercial imprints of the period, with geographical treatises and nonofficial narrative histories taking up the largest share.

What was traditionally classified as philosophy (zi) included some of the most widely distributed reading material in the late imperial period, namely medical texts and encyclopedias (leishu). Encyclopedias often included literary components, whether guides for writing, excerpts from literary works, or handbooks for writing poetry. These materials were organized topically, rather than by author as they might have been in an anthology, and readers who consulted an encyclopedia were hoping for convenient access to information. These two competing forces are visible in many forms in this period: where some genres and texts increasingly foregrounded authors, others turned all written sources into nothing more than fungible bodies of information.

The popularity of other literary genres reveals the dramatic growth in the size and diversity of readership of the period. Printed books were being written for and then marketed to consumers who were not members of the elite and did not associate themselves with the culture of the examinations. In this highly sectarian age, many books were circulated not to make money, or even to entertain, but instead were produced by religious groups or sometimes by individual philanthropists eager to save souls. Perhaps the most widely circulated texts of any sort in this period were "precious scrolls" (baojuan), the principal medium for the spread of certain popular beliefs. Similarly, although morality books (shanshu) had begun to be circulated in the Song dynasty, they flourished in this period in an unprecedented way, written for both the hyperliterate and the semiliterate.

Other didactic writings also reflect the changed readership of the late Ming, specifically the vastly increased numbers of literate women. Guides to proper female behavior and biographies of female exemplars (distinguished by chastity, filial piety, and loyalty) flourished, often in lavish collections filled with illustrations. Some households at this time obviously could afford to spare a significant amount of silver for the edification of their female members.

After excluding these books, less than a third of the surviving imprints remain, and it is these texts and the authors who wrote them that are the subject of this chapter. By far the largest number of texts within this category, outnumbering both fictional narratives and the collected works of individual writers, are dramas and dramatic songs. This category includes complete dramas, volumes of excerpts from different dramas, volumes of arias, and collections of art songs. It was clear even to Ming readers and writers that traditional categories were inadequate to cope with the enormous diversity of writings produced in the Ming. The late Ming was one of the golden ages of genre studies, as various thinkers attempted to work out what was distinctive and important about previously neglected forms of literature. These efforts are particularly visible in writings about drama, but also for other genres. The literary critic and bibliophile Hu Yinglin (1551–1602) wrote at length about fiction as a genre, recognizing how poorly it fit into bibliographies and arguing that within the schema of the four categories, its subject matter most closely approached philosophy, though it also shared characteristics with belles-lettres.

What did the books produced in this period look like? The dominant technology remained, as it had been for centuries and would be until the early twentieth century, that of woodblock printing instead of movable type. Yet it would be wrong to say that the technology of reading remained unchanged. Numerous developments in the material texts seem to indicate the birth of a new kind of reader, who was interested in reading quickly and whose contact with texts began in a marketplace.

With the help of a carver and a printer, the proper tools, and a block of jujube wood, printed pages were fairly easy to produce, but printers were still left with the question of how to assemble the texts. Earlier books tended to be printed in one of two ways, each with its own problems. In the one method, in which pages were printed and then folded so that the text faced inward, the reader would be confronted with two blank pages after every two pages of text. In the other method, a printed sheet was folded in half so that the inside was blank and then the edges were glued to form a spine. The first format did not allow for easy reading, while the second created spines vulnerable to breakage. Of course, neither of these would bother a reader who planned to linger, read aloud, or memorize the contents of a page. Late in the Wanli reign, string-binding (*xianzhuang*) took over and became the format now most commonly associated with traditional books, one that avoided the problems of the previous methods. Robert Hegel points out that it cannot be coincidental that a technology lending itself to fast reading became widespread at precisely the same moment that genres inviting fast reading – namely fiction and drama – gained popularity. Of course, string-binding was just as important to the success of other forms, like encyclopedias, where readers needed to scan contents quickly for information.

Recent scholarship suggests, although some debate remains, that books in this period had become increasingly affordable, even to those from the humbler strata of society; for example, printed materials like calendars or cheap versions of the *Three Character Classic* sold in the 1580s for only a fraction of a manual laborer's daily wages. Rather than claiming that books were available to all, it would be more accurate to say that, by around 1600, publishers were actively engaged in niche marketing. Commercial printers in Fujian

收封事宮女開函近御筵曉漏進趨青瑣闥晴
窻點檢白雲篇楊雄更有河東賦唯待吹噓送
上天

城西陂汎舟

青蛾皓齒在樓船橫笛短簫悲遠天春風自信
牙檣動月徐看錦纜牽魚吹細浪搖歌扇燕
蹴飛花落舞筵不有小舟能盪槳百壺那送酒
如泉

九日藍田崔氏莊

老去悲秋強自寬與來今日盡君歡羞將短髮
還吹帽笑倩旁人為正冠藍水遠從千澗落玉
山高並兩峰寒明年此會知誰健醉把茱萸子
細看

崔氏東山草堂

愛汝玉山草堂靜高秋爽氣相鮮新有時自發
鐘磬響落日更見漁樵人盤剝白鴉谷口栗飯

2. From *Du Fu's Seven-Syllable Regulated Verse* (*Du Zimei qiyanlü*), produced by the famous Ming publisher Min Qiji. Collection of Harvard Yenching Library.

specialized in popular illustrated books, so cheap as to be practically disposable, with cramped printing and inexpensive paper. At the same time, other printers, based primarily in Suzhou, produced whole texts of southern plays generously formatted on the page, complete with woodblock illustrations appended to the beginning and elaborate prefatory materials. Such an edition might sell for a hundred times the price of a thin pamphlet of songs and would have been out of reach to all but the very wealthy.

Other innovations focused on the luxury end of the market as well. While printers in Fujian busily churned out books in large quantities, block cutters elsewhere recorded their names inside books, suggesting that these men were not nameless cogs in a production line, but valued artisans who took pride in their work. Books for the luxury market resisted uniformity in other ways. Even as they became increasingly standardized, extra care and cost were often expended to carve prefatory materials and commentaries so that they appeared to be handwritten. The first Ming example of color printing by woodblock, an art that had died in the last years of the Song dynasty, dates from around the turn of the seventeenth century, and texts involving multiple colors followed soon thereafter. (These two trends often converged, as in the publisher Min Qiji's edition of Du Fu's poetry, where interlinear and marginal comments by Guo Zhengyu appear to be handwritten in red and blue, while the main text appears in standard print font in black.) Other printers specialized in marketing reproductions of earlier books to collectors.

It was in this period that numerous bibliophiles began to refer to their collections as "Libraries of Ten Thousand Chapters." Before the Wanli reign, a collection of even a few dozen volumes was counted a fairly impressive one (at an average of ten chapters a book, that would be a library of a few hundred chapters). By the beginning of the seventeenth century, men of the elite began to record collections that dwarfed these earlier ones. Those who were wealthy and well educated might choose to spend vast amounts of silver on book collecting. The son of an official, the critic Hu Yinglin accumulated a library of 42,384 chapters. One Yangzhou bibliophile owned 10,000 titles, not chapters. The publisher Mao Jin (1599–1659) once paid 200 taels of silver for each page of a prized addition to his collection; his library eventually grew to more than 84,000 chapters. In the space of two generations, a "Library of Ten Thousand Chapters" went from denoting a collection of fabulous size to one of generous, but not fantastic, proportions, in much the same way that the term "millionaire" has become devalued in our own age.

To be sure, more was written in these generations than in those preceding, but the explosion in publishing and book collection may be attributed more directly to repackaging and reorganization. While some publishers specialized and carefully printed a few works, for others, publishing had become big business. Mao Jin began life as one of a new breed of fabulously rich men whose fortunes had been accumulated in the fertile commercial life of urban Jiangnan. In his case, he inherited several pawnshops, as well as an immense rural estate staffed by bondservants. He in turn invested in an enormous publishing business, whose scope would have been unthinkable just a generation earlier. Beginning in 1628 and ultimately publishing more than six hundred titles, his publishing house, named the Jigu ge after one of its buildings, employed and housed more than one hundred workers, including at least forty full-time woodblock carvers. Working alongside them in other buildings in the complex, scholars prepared texts for publication. In the space of twelve years, Mao published all thirteen Classics, all of the dynastic histories, and a compendium (congshu) of 140 works in 746 chapters.

In earlier generations, a writer's work would likely have been published after his death, by his descendants or his students. In a transitional phase, the poet and critic Wang Shizhen (1526–1590) published part of his enormous *oeuvre* himself, while his son published other writings after his death. By the end of the dynasty, however, most important writers published work during their lifetimes, piecemeal and for profit. Writers could hardly avoid considering themselves within the context of the market. This acute awareness of marketability – what would sell, how to package old works to appeal to buyers – colored perceptions of the past as well as the present; the reevaluation of earlier canons characteristic of this period must have been partly a response to the pressure to produce new anthologies for the book market. Other Wanli phenomena are also closely associated with the world of publication. For example, in response to the same market pressures, many thematic collections of classical narrative appeared, arranged around particular topics, such as courtesans, ghosts, or knights-errant, to serve the demands of devotees of these niches.

In the imagination of the Qing, the whole of life in the Ming dynasty took place in Jiangnan, with its urban markets and sophisticated consumers, where beautiful courtesans mingled with artists and writers. For example, Xue Susu (1572–1620), known as one of the Eight Famous Courtesans of the Ming, met and befriended many distinguished men of letters in Jiangnan; in particular, the famous painter Dong Qichang (1555–1636) held her artwork in high esteem. Elegies on the past, like that by the great essayist Zhang Dai (1597–1689) on his lost home in Hangzhou, focused on this area that so uniquely dominated late Ming culture. *Chuanqi*, or southern plays – the theatrical form that most characterizes the period – were performed in a regional style named after the town of Kunshan. But what, after all, was Jiangnan? This ancient name, literally "South of the River" or "the Southland," was redolent of bounty, pleasure, and sensuality. By the last century of the Ming dynasty, however, Jiangnan was widely used in the most prosaic of contexts, as a simple place name. Referring to parts of the two modern provinces of Jiangsu and Zhejiang, it was not an official geographical designation, and its inhabitants did not even share the same topolect (although most spoke the Wu dialect, those in Yangzhou spoke a language much more closely related to Mandarin). Jiangnan referred to a band of wealthy cities and towns in the Yangzi river delta, one of the greatest of which, Yangzhou, was located on the north bank of the river. In the late Ming, its main cities also included Suzhou, Hangzhou, and Nanjing, as well as other flourishing towns and small cities.

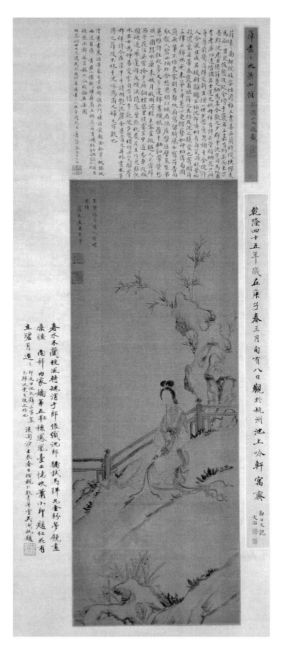

3. Beauty playing a flute by Ming courtesan Xue Susu (perhaps a self-portrait). Collection of the Nanjing Museum (Nanjing bowu yuan), Nanjing, China.

To most modern historians too, Jiangnan stands for what was most distinctive about the late Ming, even as we recognize that many of the changes that transformed Jiangnan were global in scale, propelled partly by the accident of China's poor silver supply. Huge quantities of New World silver flowed into China, in exchange for exports of fine manufactured items, such as textiles and porcelain, sent to Europe. The center of the economic revolution fueled by silver was Jiangnan. Here, luxury items were made, and when they were exchanged for silver, often in Manila, the wealth returned to Jiangnan.

Even the countryside in this region was transformed by money. Jiangnan's legendary fruitfulness made it possible for farmers to grow rice for food and other crops for money. Throughout the countryside of Jiangnan, and to a much lesser extent elsewhere in the empire, farmers entered the cash economy. Their wives and daughters took over the work of textile production, bringing in more money that families increasingly came to rely upon.

It was in the cities that these social changes were most strongly felt. During the late Ming, the city of Suzhou encapsulated many of these trends. In the sixteenth and seventeenth centuries, almost all of the world's great cities, including London, Paris, and Beijing, were also seats of government. Suzhou was the exception; its influence and importance had nothing to do with a centralized government and everything to do with the interaction between culture and commerce. It was both the site where culture was produced and the site of the greatest anxiety about culture. Here, books were produced in the greatest number. Famous for its private gardens, Suzhou was also known for its calligraphers and painters. In Suzhou, an incipient fashion system was at work: new hairstyles, clothing, accessories, and shoes spread from Suzhou across the empire. Even the imperial family assiduously followed Suzhou trends. Contemporaries observed these changes with ambivalence: what to some was luxury and pleasure, to others looked like decadence and decline.

In a typical act of Jiangnan chauvinism, Hu Yinglin claimed that readers from all over the empire read books from Suzhou and Nanjing, but that residents of Suzhou and Nanjing disdained books from elsewhere. The other major area of book production, Beijing, was out of the running, Hu Yinglin explained, because paper there cost three times what it did in Jiangnan. Hu Yinglin's comment has more to do with regional snobbery than with book production.

Publishing centers catering to the wealthy were exactly where one might guess they would be, in Hangzhou, Suzhou, and Nanjing, but others cropped up in all sorts of surprising places, not just Anhui and Fujian, but much further afield in Shanxi, Guangdong, Hunan, and even largely rural Hebei. Recent historical work has shown how complicated the economic ties between different regions in the empire were, and how different areas seemed to have claimed different niches in the production of books. While Suzhou and Nanjing were known for the high quality of their imprints, Fujian was famous for the productivity of its publishers. Anhui was probably where commercial publishing was most profitable and was also the home of some of the most skilled woodblock illustrators. Among printing houses in these regions, there was both competition and collaboration. Moreover, these networks allowed for a surprising degree of geographical mobility, as workers in the publishing industry were highly mobile practitioners of a specialty craft. Whether they were artisans like copyists or cutters, or entrepreneurs who opened up subsidiaries, men employed in publishing often traveled back and forth from Nanjing, where, one guesses, their work was much more lucrative.

Hu Yinglin's comments indicate not the total dominance of one area, but instead an awareness of an empire-wide economy and the creation of a broad readership that covered the most developed parts of the empire. Many historians have observed that over the course of the dynasty the empire had, for all practical purposes, become much smaller: not only did merchants travel for business and rich men travel for pleasure, but the increased use of the mail system and "boat bookshops" (mobile bookshops that sailed the waterways) meant that people had a new awareness of other parts of the empire. The empire, though still unfathomably enormous, was closer knit in the imagination, as readers encountered books printed in distant locations that told of other, even more distant places.

This chapter describes the impact that the growth of publishing and the emergence of a large diverse readership had both on traditional forms like poetry and on the rise of new ones like vernacular short stories and southern plays. Commercialization not only changed the broad outline of the book industry, but also had a profound effect on literary content. Old truisms about the relationship between wealth and cultural status, and about the way in which status itself was defined and achieved, could no longer hold, and even the most recurrent and venerable of literary themes, such as how literature enables a person to articulate his true self, were transformed by this new cultural context. For example, questions of taste and discernment crop up everywhere in the literature of this period, and it is impossible to see this theme outside of its social context: as more and more people mastered the external marks of status – the production (or the simple acquisition) of a tasteful poem, say, or an elegant piece of calligraphy – the guideposts themselves moved.

The chapter is divided into three parts, each one loosely corresponding to a different segment of the late Ming populace. The first section discusses developments in forms of literature traditionally associated with the elite, namely poetry, nonfictional prose, and examination essays. This first section also sketches out a simple political history of the period. The second part covers literature produced by and for a distinctive new group, which the historian Yu Ying-shih calls the *shishang*, or a new elite whose wealth was based on commerce and whose culture was based in the urban centers of Jiangnan. This section treats both long and short fiction, in vernacular and classical Chinese. The final part of this chapter concerns drama, the form that, more than any other, dominated the imagination of the late Ming. Around drama coalesced something approaching an avant-garde, as members of the highest and lowest echelons of society mingled together.

These divisions, meant to correspond with different segments of the population, are heuristic. As Wang Daokun (1525–1593), a writer and high official who was also the scion of a wealthy merchant family, observed, the same people who participated in the traditional elite forms also made their living from mercantile activities. At the same time, one of the most distinctive features of late Ming society was a persistent awareness of class and of the ways that different cultural elements, from the elite to the folk to the urban, could mix together.

In literature, these concerns often manifested themselves as a heightened sensitivity to linguistic and cultural register. Several late Ming collections, the most famous of them the *World-Class Beauty and Heavenly Scents* (*Guose tianxiang*, first edition 1587), arranged texts of different genres all on the same page, sometimes in two rows, sometimes in three. A condensed novel might appear in one row above an excerpted act of a popular drama, both of which were set above a selection of drinking songs. There is in these cheerfully incongruous pastiches a mingling of registers – high and low, elegant and vulgar – that is utterly characteristic of the age, in all of its literary genres. On a broader level, then, this chapter is about the mingling of high and low, the onstage and offstage, the elite and the popular.

I. Elite forms

Literary societies

Premodern China embodied a paradox: by modern standards tiny, rudimentary, and poorly staffed, the central state nonetheless maintained a grasp on the imagination that is impossible to overestimate. This largely had to do with the success of the examination system in defining a whole class of people, the scholar–officials referred to as the *shi*, who defined themselves through participation in the examination system and civil service. The following section concerns the literary genres associated with this elite, and consequently with the state. In general, the more orthodox the form of literature, the more inseparable its concerns and themes were from the state. Compilations of examination essays, among the best-selling and most widely read books of the time, and commentaries on the Four Books and the Classics were obviously imbued with the state ideology. Even traditional lyric poetry – with its aspirations for uniting an individual voice with a cosmic perspective and its history as part of the civil service examinations of an earlier age – reveals how enmeshed the elite, a literary genre, and the state could be.

From the perspective of the Qing dynasty, there were ample signs of dynastic decline in these last decades of the Ming: a government so inefficient in levying taxes that it could neither pay its armies nor adequately defend its borders, and a culture that seemed to have turned licentious and permissive. The period covered by this chapter spans the rule of three different emperors, each hapless in his own way (there was one additional emperor, but he lasted only three weeks before his death, probably of poisoning). None was able to govern effectively. The first, the Wanli Emperor (r. 1573–1620), was almost pathologically apathetic, refusing to meet his ministers even once in thirty years; the second, the semiliterate and perhaps mentally retarded Tianqi Emperor (r. 1620–1627), turned administration over to eunuchs; and the government of the third, the ill-fated Chongzhen Emperor (r. 1627–1644), was so inefficient that he went through almost fifty grand secretaries in the seventeen years of his reign. All three reigns were marked by bitter factional struggles, some self-interested, but many motivated by deeply held ideals.

The impact of this political turmoil on literary culture was tremendous. For one thing, literary themes reflect the turmoil; many of the plays and novels of the period revolve around various political upheavals at court. Not only the content but the very shape of literary culture was determined by the political infighting. By the end of the dynasty, literary culture and political infighting were hardly to be differentiated, and what appeared literary and provincial might have a direct impact on battles at court. Along with other members of his poetry society, the teenaged Chen Zilong (1608–1647), later perhaps the most famous poet of his age, made a straw effigy of the eunuch Wei Zhongxian and shot arrows at it near his home in Songjiang (near present-day

Shanghai). Lucky enough to escape that incident with his life, a few years later a disagreement over proper classical models between the still feisty Chen Zilong and an older scholar led to a violent brawl. In another incident, the grand secretary's brother Wen Yuren viciously satirized an opposition group, the famous Revival Society, in a southern play. A local official retaliated first by banning the play and then ordering local bookstores to destroy their copies of it.

The factionalism that characterized late Ming politics was closely related to one of the most noteworthy features of the contemporary cultural landscape, the prevalence of multiple literary societies (*wenshe*), whose importance continued to grow until the end of the dynasty. Societies for study, schools of poetry, and factional politics were inseparable from each other, all of them central to elite life in the last decades of the Ming dynasty. Membership in a literary society was a potent means of self-identification, composed in equal parts of political affiliation and cultural orientation. Throughout the last reigns of the Ming dynasty, these societies grew larger, more powerful, imbued with an ever stronger sense of group identity. For most of the dynasty, these casual associations, the vast majority of which are now forgotten, had formed and disbanded with equal ease; when members passed the examinations and took up postings far away from home, or when an official assignment sent a member off to a new location, the society would dissolve. By the end of the dynasty, however, the most important of these groups, the Revival Society (Fushe), had members from all over the empire, including more than 15 percent of the successful examination candidates from the wealthiest provinces.

In the 1570s, literary societies customarily had fewer than a dozen members, usually friends or family members who happened to live close by. By the 1590s, groups in Jiangnan had begun to give themselves names, some of them quite grandiose. By the 1620s, especially in Jiangnan, the membership of some of the groups had grown to a hundred men. (Some, however, remained small; in 1628, when the poet Chen Zilong founded the Society for Hope (Jishe), it had only six members, counting himself.) These societies were naturally thickest on the ground in Jiangnan, which had the highest concentration of the elite, but were formed elsewhere as well. Examples include the Society of Rectitude (Duanshe) in Henan and the Society of the District (Yishe) in Shandong.

Late in the Wanli period, in 1604, near the Jiangnan city of Wuxi, Gu Xiancheng (1550–1612), together with his brother and their friend Gao Panlong (1562–1626), restored a long-defunct Song academy called the Eastern Forest (Donglin). The Eastern Forest was a locally based educational institution that sponsored lectures attended by audiences that reached into the thousands, but at the same time the term "Eastern Forest" also referred broadly and almost vaguely to a set of political sympathies. Men with those sympathies established loosely associated groups in other cities. During the Tianqi reign, the powerful eunuch Wei Zhongxian (1568–1627) mercilessly persecuted Eastern Forest supporters, imprisoning, torturing, and executing his political opponents. His attacks make clear that this was a political party. Many of the blacklisted men had never been to the actual academy in Wuxi; the full extent of their connection was through an acquaintance or a friendship with known sympathizers.

Why join a study group if the association was manifestly dangerous? For most of the Ming and the whole of the Qing, passing the civil service examinations was extremely difficult. Although the number of official positions remained relatively constant over the course of the Ming dynasty, the number of examinees greatly increased. At the same time, the quota for candidates from the prosperous Yangzi river delta was kept artificially low, so that candidates from this region must have felt the pressure to join a study group particularly keenly. Apart from providing a venue for socializing with the like-minded, joining a study group improved one's chances at writing a successful essay at a time when any advantage might prove crucial.

Despite their reputation in modern China as aesthetically mannered and intellectually moribund, examination essays were not widely regarded as such in the Ming dynasty. Assigned a quotation from the Four Books, writers crafted in response a highly formalized argument built out of parallelisms. At the beginning of the Wanli period, the eight-part examination essay was only about a century old. Rather than an expression of rote memorization, many writers considered the form a creative challenge, open to stylistic diversity. Among others, the critics Li Zhi (1527–1602) and Yuan Hongdao (1568–1610), both of whom were renowned for championing novelty and innovation in literature, regarded these essays not only as a fair test of literary ability, but also as an important literary form on its own terms. The critic Jin Shengtan (1608–1661), who regarded *Water Margin* as one of the transcendent works of genius in the Chinese tradition, compared the novel to an eight-part essay as a way of praising its ingenious structure.

A successful examination essay depended on certain kinds of privileged knowledge; consequently, the form was almost impossible to master in isolation. This was one reason why so many successful candidates hailed from the same wealthy towns and cities. Candidates from the hinterlands could have no knowledge about what styles examiners might favor or which intellectual trends they followed. In a given year, the use of certain words or phrases might tip off examiners. Such information could best be attained through participation in a literary society whose members had already achieved a toehold in the examination system. In this way, members could help each other pass. These advantages were not considered cheating – which was prevented by such safeguards as the recopying of all completed examinations and submission with the name of the examinee covered.

A close second to the advantages gained by actual participation within a society was the careful perusal of the collected essays that numerous societies began publishing in the 1570s. Before the Wanli period, examination materials were primarily published under the aegis of the state. From the Wanli era to the end of the dynasty, the publication of sample examination essays, along with detailed commentary and criticism, became a central feature of literary societies. Some scholars have argued that these collections were the single greatest mainstay of booksellers. The scholar and writer Fang Yizhi writes in the 1630s about how serious candidates had to commit hundreds of essays to memory and then begin again each year with new essays as new trends emerged. Such a program of study was only possible because of a literary industry that gathered, edited, printed, and distributed these essays. At the same time, the literary industry flourished as the examinations grew ever more competitive.

These anthologies became an increasingly crucial feature of the work of literary societies; the scholar and philosopher Huang Zongxi's (1610–1695) anthology of essays written in the Ming devoted no fewer than eight chapters to the prefaces written for anthologies of examination essays, a small indication of the sheer volume of such materials in the period. There is also evidence that many readers studied examination materials not because they had to, but because they enjoyed them.

The modern historian Kai-wing Chow has made the point that a group like the Revival Society, the most important literary society and political faction of the dynasty, could not have existed before the last years of the Ming. Born at the beginning of the dynasty's last reign, the Revival Society was an independent national organization on a scale that had never before been seen, its operations profoundly shaped not just by printing, but also by improved communications. Similarly, elaborate networks of collaboration and cooperation characterize work in numerous other genres of this period, all of them the beneficiaries of improved mail service and greater ease of travel.

In 1632, a selection of examination essays by Revival Society members, arranged according to province, prefecture, and county, was published. It was, in essence, a literary society brought to its logical conclusion, modeled on the empire, with its own miniature hierarchy. (In reality, almost 90 percent of the members were natives of a fairly narrow swath of the empire: Zhejiang, Jiangxi, Fujian, Huguang, and Nanzhili, which was the district that included Nanjing.) From 1630 to the end of the dynasty, Revival Society members were remarkably successful in the civil service examinations. The examinations had never been so competitive – it is estimated that only one in fifteen recipients of the second degree was able to pass the palace examinations – but Revival Society members took first, second, and third places in the 1637 palace examinations and 18 percent of the total number of degrees.

A cursory glance over their membership rolls reveals that these men represent the intersection between a political and a cultural elite. As successful as they were at the examinations, they even more resoundingly dominated the cultural scene. The Revival Society counted as its members some of the most prominent intellectuals and writers of the period, including Chen Zilong, Huang Zongxi, the poet and playwright Wu Weiye (1609–1672), and the scholar and writer Gu Yanwu (1613–1682). In one measure of the Revival Society's importance, the cultural influence of its members far outlived the dynasty itself. During the first decades of the Qing, virtually all prominent loyalists – those who declared themselves loyal to the old dynasty and refused to serve the new one – were former members of the Revival Society. Many of the same men became pioneers in evidential learning, the new style of philological study that transformed scholarship in the late seventeenth century.

Though often linked to the earlier Eastern Forest, the Revival Society's members were much more ideologically diverse; some shared Eastern Forest conservatism, while others were sympathetic to the ideas of the neo-Confucian reformer Wang Yangming, or even those of radicals like Li Zhi and Wang Gen. Furthermore, the organization of the Revival Society was altogether different. Instead of a vaguely defined network of friends, relatives, and political allies, the Revival Society published lists of its members, making participation a matter of public record. The Revival Society clearly conceived of itself not just as flesh-and-blood associations of acquaintances as the Wuxi-based part of the Eastern Forest Academy or the Seven Late Masters of an even earlier period had, but also as a group formed through the medium of print, as part of a world of printed material. Their group identity was strengthened partly because members needed to pool their resources so as to be able to circulate their writings in print.

By the end of the dynasty, all these circumstances – the strong sense of identity membership in a literary society imparted, the near impossibility of passing the examinations for the vast majority of candidates, and the ever-increasing vigor of the book market – conspired to create some odd effects. Passing had become such a rarity that the actual work of anthologizing the examination essays, not just the selection, but also the editing and commenting, was often done by men who themselves had failed the examinations, usually repeatedly and over the course of decades. Wang Shizhen's son Wang Shisu, who himself never passed, was nonetheless the first to include critical comments in his compilation of essays. Similarly, the critic and anthologist Ai Nanying's (1583–1646) collection of his own heavily annotated essays was widely circulated, praised, and became a model for generations to come, despite his own repeated failure in the examinations.

What gave these men the right to select the best essays and pronounce *ex cathedra* on their virtues and faults? By doing so, they had assumed for themselves the role of the official grader, but they also made clear that these examination essays, like any work of art, could be judged independently as aesthetic objects. The literary world had acquired an independence from the political one, with its own standards and its own officials. Ai Nanying compared the power of the anthologist and commentator to that of the emperor himself. The goal in crafting a beautiful examination essay had become twofold: to pass the examinations and consequently receive a position, and also to be included in an anthology and win the critical acclaim of one's peers.

Li Zhi the professional writer

At first glance, Li Zhi, one of the most influential figures in late Ming literature, was simply an essayist and belletrist like many others; nonetheless, the course of his career reveals some of the new possibilities that had opened up to writers of the mid-sixteenth century. In intellectual histories, he occupies a prominent place as a follower of the Taizhou School, a radical wing of Wang Yangming's teachings. Li Zhi served as an official until he retired from public service in his fifties; later, he shaved his head and became something of a lay Buddhist monk. His notoriety was such that, a year before his death, hoodlums hired by local officials and members of the elite burned his house to the ground. Around the same time, an official in the Ministry of Rites, motivated, it seems, more by sheer annoyance than by political self-interest, had Li Zhi imprisoned for heterodoxy, an unusual charge in that the laws against heterodoxy were almost never enforced in the Ming dynasty. Awaiting trial, Li Zhi slit his own throat.

What made him such a thorn in the side of those officials, but an inspiration to so many writers? Earlier in the sixteenth century, the philosopher Wang Yangming had expanded upon Mencius and argued that all human beings possessed from birth an instinctive moral sense. If everyone was indeed so endowed, it seemed to follow, traditional Confucian education might not provide an exclusive means to self-cultivation. (Not surprisingly, many of Wang Yangming's followers and admirers were also drawn to Buddhist practice and thought.) Along these lines, one might even argue that the uneducated, children, and even women all possessed special claims to knowledge and virtue. Certainly Li Zhi implied that traditional hierarchies should be upended. Perhaps it was not that fathers should teach their sons, men should teach women, and the educated should teach the illiterate, but the other way around. As Li Zhi wrote, "It is fine to say that there are better and worse views – but can it be that men's are always better and women's always worse?"

In some ways, much of what he espoused resembled traditional Daoism, where the primitive had an appeal and a truthfulness that no training and sophistication could approach. To that, he added a strong condemnation of fakery. One of Li Zhi's most famous essays is a paean to the child's mind, by which he means the sincere and unmediated mind:

> The childlike mind is the true mind, the original mind. If it is lost, the true mind is lost and the true person is lost . . . Once people's minds have been given over to received opinions and moral principles, what they have to say is all about these things, and not what would naturally come from their childlike minds. No matter how clever the words, what have they to do with oneself? What else can there be but phony men speaking phony words, doing phony things, writing phony writings? Once the men become phonies, everything becomes phony . . . And the phonies have destroyed so much good literature in the world! . . . The best literature always comes from the childlike mind.

Li Zhi's valorization of the simple and authentic, set in contradistinction to the falsely sophisticated, would prove of enormous cultural influence for the rest of the dynasty.

Within the context of the late Ming, this set of ideas manifested itself in specific but intimately linked ways, first as a frustration with the poverty of elite concerns and forms, and later also as an admiration for folk literature. Even as Li Zhi and others argued that elite culture's traditional forms no longer had the absolute authority that they had once possessed, the strengths and vitality of popular culture were never viewed in isolation from the failures and weakness of elite culture. In other words, popular culture was always the absence of elite culture. By the 1620s, a writer like Feng Menglong (1574–1645) could justify his interest in humble love songs from illiterate peasants precisely on the grounds that these songs were not elite poetry: "Because mountain songs do not vie for social preeminence with poetry, they are not trifling or false." Note that this statement makes no reference to any trait intrinsic to the mountain songs themselves. Instead of simply *being* "authentic" and "sincere," these nonelite genres were *invested* with the qualities of authenticity and sincerity by some of the most sophisticated thinkers of the age.

Later generations of historians and critics, particularly in the politically contentious twentieth century, have imposed anachronistic labels on Li Zhi, as a tragic rebel against traditional society, an advocate for individual rights, or a spokesman for the downtrodden masses. While he did hold some idiosyncratic opinions, Li Zhi at no point set out to mount a critique of the imperial system in general or traditional society as a whole. In fact, his opinions were very much of his age, whether in his call to loyalty to the Wanli Emperor or in his support of widow suicide when the alternative was remarriage. Still, there is no denying that many of his opinions were unusual to the point of being inflammatory. For example, he commended one of the great villainesses in Chinese history, Empress Wu of the Tang, as a wise ruler.

How, then, do we understand Li Zhi's brand of polemic, calculated to raise the hackles of readers with conformist tastes? Did Li Zhi believe everything he wrote? There is no way of knowing. We do know that he was keenly aware of his own status as a polemicist, whose bread and butter was to upset orthodoxies, and that his persona of a man unbridled by convention was highly self-conscious. After all, he called his own collected essays *A Book to Be Burned* (Fenshu).

Li Zhi's career highlights some of the distinctive features of late Ming literary culture. He retired from public service to make a living as a public figure whose fame was established in the sphere of print, and he made a much better living noisily decrying the official establishment than he had ever made while he was part of it. As a student and later as an official, he had lived very humbly; several of his children are said to have died of malnutrition, and his family in Fujian was of extremely modest means. In retirement, however, a number of admirers – some top officials and one as lofty as an imperial prince – sponsored him for years or decades at a time. Even his personality quirks reveal a certain level of material comfort for this quasi-monk: his love of cleanliness was so extreme that several servants were supposedly employed full-time to sweep his quarters.

There was no one earlier in the dynasty whose particular brand of fame could compare to Li Zhi's. He was a literary figure who specialized in no particular genre; instead, at the height of his career, he was famous for being famous or, as became clear at the end of his life, notorious. A man of the marketplace of words, Li Zhi dabbled in more genres than anyone else of his day. Among many other literary endeavors, he published commentaries on the Classics and the Four Books. He authored works both long and short on history and philosophy and collected together his own works in various different combinations, each to be published for profit. He also assembled anthologies of earlier poetry and prose and was involved in numerous influential and highly profitable commentaries of fiction and drama. All of these writings were intended first for the printer and then for the marketplace.

In these works, what was being commodified was partly the opinions and writings themselves, but also a distinctive Li Zhi persona: unconventional, irreverent, polemical. Notably, for one so deeply invested in authenticity, Li Zhi's voice was regularly forged, and there are some writings imputed to him whose real author will probably remain unknown. Perhaps some of these works in numerous genres, including commentary on the Classics and on fiction and drama, are truly his, but almost certainly some were written by people who saw an opportunity for material gain in imitating such a desirable commodity. Li Zhi's concern with authenticity is inseparable from the market forces that shaped the literature of this period. Someone so obsessed with authenticity must recognize his own vulnerability to being forged. Li's self-appointed role as unconventional gadfly was nothing if not replicable and commercially viable.

Poetry and poetics

To the modern reader, one of the most difficult things to understand about late imperial poetry is that the questions one assumes literary history will answer are instead studiously avoided. Who are the best late Ming poets? Which are their best poems? What distinguishes these poetic voices from those of their contemporaries? All of these questions are impossible to answer in a straightforward fashion. Ming critics understood that these questions, easy to answer for an earlier period like the Tang, or even the Song, had become impossible in their own time.

For one thing, there is a great deal more poetry to wade through than in earlier periods. The *Complete Tang Poems* (compiled between 1705 and 1707) comes to 48,000 poems in 12 volumes. For the *Complete Ming Poems*, currently being compiled in Shanghai, more than 400,000 poems have already been collected, and the final work is projected to come to more than 200 volumes. Every educated person in late Ming China could recite hundreds of poems by the score or so most famous Tang poets. There was a consensus about who and which these were. In contrast, not a single Ming poet can be said to have dominated the imagination and entered the canon in the same way.

In the first decades of the Qing dynasty, Huang Zongxi wrote about this overabundance of text:

> Take a look at the collections from the past three centuries that circulate in the world or are kept in libraries. There are no fewer than a thousand writers, each of them having at the very least a few chapters, with the more voluminous running to a hundred chapters. Buried among the works of social exchange and all kinds of phoniness, there must be one or two genuinely moving passages. But they pile up on tables and desks, and no one looks at them. No sooner do you look at them than you find clichés all cut from the same mold, and you toss them aside immediately.

One obvious characteristic of a Tang poem that makes it "better" is the relative scarcity of Tang poems, which makes each individual poem more prized. No ordinary connoisseur will be able to plough through the *Complete Ming Poems* or even to hit all the high points. As much as 90 percent of the great Tang poet Du Fu's *oeuvre* has been lost, while Wang Shizhen singlehandedly left 381 chapters of writings, published in parts, many during his lifetime. In other words, the same features we celebrate when it comes to other parts of late Ming culture – the vitality of the print industry and the radically increased access to writing and publishing – changed the parameters of poetic writing itself.

Late imperial critics recognized that poetry no longer mattered in quite the same way, and they came up with numerous reasons for its decline. Perhaps poetry had been great in the Tang because it had been part of the examination system; it had mattered in a way it did not in a later age. Perhaps the ubiquitous use of poetry in social life had somehow cheapened it. Even as each individual poem and each individual poet became less prized, poetry itself had become an ever more important part of everyday life, written at practically every social gathering and exchanged between people of practically any relation to each other on any occasion, personal or social, that needed commemoration. At the same time, the number of educated people, both men and women, trained to write poetry grew dramatically over the course of the dynasty.

Whatever the reasons, a canon of late Ming poetry has not emerged. Choose any ten anthologies of Ming verse, and you will find remarkably little overlap, even though all of them will contain very good individual poems. In place of canonical poems, we have some canonical poets; but even here, there is significantly less consensus than for an earlier period. What has emerged instead are canonical poetics – all this by way of prefacing a discussion of late Ming poetry that may appear to focus on poets and poetics rather than on poetry itself.

Part of the impact of these generations was to determine a canon of poetry from the Tang and earlier. Anthologies compiled in the middle and late Ming have been largely responsible for creating the sense that the High Tang was the greatest age of Chinese poetry. From the Wanli period onward, the expansion of the print industry made antiquarian interests profitable. The convergence of these two factors made the late Ming the single most important period for canon formation in many genres.

Until the middle of the Ming, there was no clear consensus on either the canon of Tang poems or the pantheon of Tang poets. Midway through the sixteenth century, Li Panlong's (1514–1570) *Correct Edition of Ancient and Modern Poetry (Gujin shishan)* established Li Bai, Du Fu, and Wang Wei as the three greatest poets of the Tang, and hence of all time. This ranking, in which the three stand head and shoulders above all others, was not transmitted as received wisdom from the Tang, but was instead a canon created centuries afterwards for circulation in print. Anthologies like Li Panlong's were followed quickly by Tang Ruxun's fifty-chapter *Explications of Tang Poetry (Tangshi jie)*, published in 1615. Unlike earlier anthologies, these circulated from the beginning in printed commercial editions. Bought and read widely, disseminated to a literate audience many times larger than earlier ones, these anthologies created a canon that by the end of the dynasty had established a consensus about greatness that remains to this day. The canon of Tang poems studied now in schools and universities throughout the Chinese-speaking world dates to the sixteenth century.

Many poets of the late Ming established themselves as either poetic personalities or famous literary figures. When it comes to Tang poets, even an outsized personality like Li Bai's is known almost exclusively though his poetry. In contrast, we know the personality of Yuan Hongdao (1568–1610) through his writings about his poetry, through the writings of contemporaries on him, and only finally through his poetry itself.

To scholars of the early twentieth century, the great conflict of late Ming poetry pitted freethinking heroes who celebrated individualism – most especially the three Yuan brothers, particularly Yuan Hongdao – against hidebound imitators of archaic poets and forms. The actual situation was much more complicated. Instead of debating the importance of literary precedent, debates tended to turn upon such questions as whether Su Shi's poetry was wonderfully spontaneous or prosaic and insipid, or how the Song theorist Yan Yu's philosophy of intuition ought to be understood. In other words, the parties involved agreed far more than they disagreed.

At the beginning of the Wanli period, the dominant voice in poetry was that of Wang Shizhen, the most important of the Seven Late Masters (*hou qizi*). Wang Shizhen foreshadowed some of the innovations of the Yuan brothers, most particularly in his openness to poetic models outside the High Tang and in his increasing emphasis on the expressive potential of poetry. Although he himself was strongly associated with the Revivalists, he urged an expanded canon that included mid-Tang and Song poets like Bai Juyi and Su Shi, who were admired by the Yuan brothers and scorned by most of the Revivalists. Wang Shizhen liked to use the term "native sensibility" (*xingling*), which came to be the hallmark of the Yuan brothers' Gongan School.

Yuan Hongdao was the middle and most famous of the three talented Yuan brothers. Like him, his brothers Zongdao (1560–1600) and Zhongdao (1570–1630) were accomplished poets who passed the examinations and served as officials. Their "school," named after their native place, Gongan in Huguang Province, was not even a loosely organized society. In their youth, the brothers had formed such a society, consisting mainly of themselves and a few other family members, and as adults they established another, called the Grape Society, in Beijing. With its emphasis on spontaneity and individual sensibility, the appeal of the Gongan School resembled a cult of personality more than it did an academy. In these ideas and in their admiration for vernacular forms, the Yuan brothers were heavily indebted to the iconoclastic Li Zhi, whom they admired so much that Yuan Zhongdao even wrote a biography of the older man.

Yuan Hongdao gives his younger brother Zhongdao's poetry an oddly qualified endorsement in this preface:

Among his writings are both excellent spots and faults, but even his faults are full of phrases of his own making and his own original nature. Thus for my part I find the greatest delight in his faults; what are called his excellent spots cannot avoid being in some way repellent by their adornment and imitative qualities – these, I think, have not entirely escaped the manner and practice of literary men of recent times.

At the time that Yuan Hongdao wrote this preface, one of the most popular inclusions in encyclopedias was the poetry manual, which explained rules of meter and parallelism, as well as setting forth aesthetic dos and don'ts. Yuan Hongdao's intent is partly to undermine the homogenizing, dulling effect of such middlebrow, proscriptive poetics; to him, the only good poetry in his brother's poetry is bad poetry. The mistakes are sincere: they emerge from the self and not from imitation and express the self with no artifice. Still, there is something chilling in the elder brother's encomium. Once a culture has reached a point where only bad poetry is good poetry, then poetry itself as a collective pursuit that is also a means of individual expression is clearly at a dead end.

Later in the same preface, Yuan Hongdao writes of what poetry ought to do: "Express only one's native sensibility. Do not be constrained by established patterns. And what does not pour out of one's heart, do not commit it to paper." Yuan Hongdao's poetics have survived and remained profoundly influential, but perhaps they demanded of late Ming poetry what it could no longer do.

Yuan Hongdao's own poetry is quite distinctive, stressing the spontaneous and the quotidian, as did that of his heroes, Bai Juyi and Su Shi. Both Yuan Hongdao's poetry and his highly personal informal prose continue to be read, but his influence has been felt even more strongly in the field of literary criticism, where some of his ideas became widely accepted truisms by the end of the dynasty. Yuan Zongdao and Yuan Hongdao espoused a historicist perspective on literature that without denigrating the past recognized the limitations of modern-day imitations: writers who failed to use the language of their own time could not express themselves with full sincerity. More broadly, even genres themselves could only flourish in their own proper time. (Yuan Zhongdao, the only one of the three to live to old age, was much more moderate in his attitudes.) Though none of the brothers, nor Li Zhi before them, made any huge contribution to the criticism of fiction or drama, all of them laid a groundwork by carving out a space to dignify these vernacular forms.

At the end of the dynasty, no critic defended the dignity of the vernacular more vigorously than Jin Shengtan (1608–1661), for whom it did much more than simply occupy the space left over by poetry. He expressed the sense in which poetry had become obsolete most clearly with his own personal canon, *Six Works of Genius (Liu caizi shu)*. These works of creativity and individuality were, in chronological order: "Encountering Sorrow" (Lisao), the writings of Zhuangzi, Sima Qian's *Records of the Historian (Shiji)*, Du Fu's poetry, the play *The Western Wing*, and the novel *Water Margin*. In his own time, Jin suggested, the spirit of self-expression was to be seen not in poetry, but in vernacular forms like drama and fiction. Poetry of genius and transcendent self-expression was as much a relic of the past as a text like the ancient "Encountering Sorrow," then already more than two thousand years old.

On one level, poetry remained absolutely central to all literary and many social enterprises. The very length of the *Complete Ming Poems* speaks to the ubiquity of poetry in Ming life. The presence of poetry manuals in encyclopedias suggests that the poetic idiom had become important not only for elite men at the highest echelons of society, as in earlier periods, but also increasingly for those in less privileged circumstances too, and even for women. Every figure discussed in the following sections wrote poetry, and poetry appears within the pages of every play and every narrative of the period. In those contexts, both literary and social, poetry will return in this chapter.

Yet poetry had largely become important for secondary reasons, having lost its unique claims to cultural authority. By the late Ming, part of the classical promise of poetry – that it might articulate the poet's intentions in a uniquely privileged and sincere way – had been deferred to other genres. The simple fact that a history of this period can be centered on fiction and drama reflects the displacement of poetry from its central position in the culture. What remained was poetry's place in social interactions and its role in elite lives defined through service to the state. In some important way, poetry's ability to unite the private and public had fractured, never to be restored.

By the end of the sixteenth century, when fame and reputation had become thoroughly commodified, few writers could extricate themselves fully from the network of personal gain surrounding poetry. Elite writers often felt conflicted about writing for commercial purposes. Even as more and more of them came to live off their writing, selling epitaphs, prefaces, and other occasional poetic and prose pieces, many did their best to efface the traces of those commercial transactions by, for example, omitting writings undertaken for profit from their published *oeuvre*. To what extent did a set of courtesies between two men of the elite involve an exchange of money? Figuring out the degree to which a gift exchange was in fact a thinly disguised payment of money demands reconstruction of the social circumstances of each act of writing. At four hundred years' remove, this may be an impossibility.

There were some poets whose writings were untainted by any hint of commerce: for female poets of good family, unlike their male counterparts, poetry and gain were not bound together. Scholars have begun to study the growing interest in the late Ming in the education and writing of women. There is no doubt that female literacy, like literacy in general, became much more widespread; still, in some ways, Ming interest in women's writing had more to do with men's anxieties than with the women themselves. Some men became interested in women's writing out of the same frustration with elite forms that led them to admire vernacular fiction. This was true in other genres as well, most importantly the lyric, as Kang-i Sun Chang has shown. Traditionally written by men in the voice of women, female writers were central to the lyric's revival. The presence of these women writers was practically demanded structurally to unite biological femaleness and stylistic femininity.

The scholar Hu Wenkai's massive bibliography of women's writings lists a wide array of selections from this period, including four major collections of women's poetry. The most important of these, *Poetic Retrospective of Famous Ladies* (*Mingyuan shigui*, published after 1626), deeply influenced the other three, and dedicates twelve chapters to Ming poets. What the preface makes clear is that an appreciation for women's poetry might serve as an oblique way to express frustration with mainstream poetry written by elite men. All the traits attributed to women reflect anxieties about and losses to mainstream poetic culture: women's poetry has privileged access to the natural, the private, and the pure (with which women are especially endowed). Women's poetry also escapes the taint of personal gain (whether of status, capital, or career advancement) and the clichés of tradition. Women – untutored and untainted – have reclaimed some of the self-expressive essence of poetry, since lost by men. The concerns of this preface are those of a belated age.

Poetry and the professional littérateur

Poetic Retrospective of Famous Ladies (*Mingyuan shigui*) is strongly associated with Zhong Xing (1574–1624), one of the two leading lights of the Jingling School. The degree of Zhong Xing's actual involvement with the anthology is impossible to determine; for reasons discussed earlier, false attributions were rife in this period. The Jingling School, named after Zhong Xing and Tan Yuanchun's (1586–1637) native town in Huguang Province, is often associated with the Yuan brothers' Gongan School. The two schools were bound together not just in their theories of poetics, but also through a variety of social ties. Zhong Xing had admired Yuan Hongdao and was a part of the older man's social circle when both were in Beijing, while Tan Yuanchun was a close friend of Yuan Hongdao's eldest son. Typical of relationships between writers at the end of the dynasty, these social ties were also tinged by commerce. Zhong Xing edited the manuscript of Yuan Hongdao's complete works, and Tan Yuanchun was responsible for taking it to a publisher in Hangzhou. Both men made a living by writing, editing, and publishing.

The affiliations and collaborations that tied together so many late Ming intellectuals were far from exclusive. Zhong Xing and Tan Yuanchun are often spoken of in the same breath, but each engaged in numerous literary activities in isolation from the other. Even though the two collaborated on the single most important Ming anthology of Tang poetry, Zhong Xing was involved in other compilations of Tang poetry as a member of the Beautiful City Society (Yecheng she), which focused mostly on study for the examinations.

Almost all the writers in this chapter shared overlapping social circles. Beyond ties of friendship, and often of marriage and family, they were further bound by political alliance and professional interest. Nevertheless, these men, who knew each other either directly or through one or two intermediate connections, were only the tip of the iceberg in relation to the whole of the reading public, and their livelihood depended on a growing, diverse, and anonymous buying public. Scholars estimate that while the population of Ming China probably doubled between the beginning of the dynasty and 1600, the number of recipients of the first (and easiest) examination degree increased twentyfold, from around 30,000 to something around 600,000. These degree recipients, who had dedicated years solely to study, represented only a small percentage of educated readers, and it is reasonable to assume that the reading public, however narrowly or broadly defined, increased by at least that margin, and was therefore to be approximated in the millions, and not in the thousands.

In their critical writings, Tan Yuanchun and Zhong Xing argued that the drive to express native sensibility had to be tempered with a discipline in the ancient forms, lest poetry descend into vulgarity and crudeness. Spontaneity was less important than care. Cultivating a detached air in his own person, Zhong Xing valued the same quality in poems, what came to be called "profundity and aloofness" (shenyou lengqiao).

Ultimately, the poetry of these two men had much less impact than what was said about it. The Jingling School's poetics expressed themselves in practice as a propensity for the difficult and the obscure. Along with sometimes awkward diction and word choice, the poems ended up relying heavily on quirky images a step away from cliché: ancient wisteria, withered pines, faded plum blossoms, shadowed gullies, and lone cranes.

The thrust of these poetics, in valorizing difficulty and obscurity – in short, a quantifiable kind of uniqueness – is hard to separate entirely from a commercial dimension. Much more influential than any poem written by either Zhong or Tan were the two long anthologies, complete with commentaries, on which they collaborated between 1614 and 1617: *A Return to Ancient Poetry* (*Gushi gui*) and *A Return to Tang Poetry* (*Tangshi gui*). These two volumes laid out models for contemporary writing. Explaining the motivations behind this project, Tan Yuanchun focused on the distinctiveness of not only the selections, but the anthologists themselves: "We omit what others have selected and select what others have omitted." Tan goes out of his way to state that in a post-poetic age the work of selection and criticism, far from being passive, is a creative act in itself: "Anthologizing is not merely selecting the writings of the ancients by someone of a later generation but rather the way through which that later person does his own writing."

In the late Ming market, distinctive perspectives with commodity value converged with a print technology through which they could manifest themselves in the form of actual text. If, as some scholars suggest, the Jingling School had a deeper impact than even the Gongan School, the root of that influence was in these two anthologies, since Tan Yuanchun and Zhong Xing lacked the Yuan brothers' ease and ability as poets. The two anthologies had a distinctive appearance in that they were printed in three colors by the publisher Min Qiji, who specialized in producing imprints in many colors. The comments by the two anthologists were printed in two different colors, so that the very form of the books foregrounds the contributions of their editors. That form makes clear that in acquiring *A Return to Tang Poetry*, the late Ming reader purchased not just the writings of the Tang poets, but the two critics' unique take on them.

Following the enormous success of these two anthologies, Zhong Xing's name became attached to at least four editions of the *Classic of Poetry*, all from commercial presses in Nanjing. It is unlikely that he was responsible for all of these; instead, as was the case with famous authors in many genres, his name was attached to these texts as a selling point. His literary reputation had a quantifiable value that booksellers and publishers recognized. Literary historians have observed that individual critical voices appeared in the late Ming in one genre after another, not just in poetry. If market forces go some way towards explaining why so many of the texts from this period are reprints and anthologies, they also show that these critical voices had become a highly prized commodity.

The spread of commercial printing left a mark so deep that it can hardly be overestimated. Examining the lives of poets over the last few decades of the dynasty, we see, to some degree, that what constituted a school of poetry was also changing. The poets of the first half of the dynasty were primarily distinguished officials who received their degrees quite early in life and spent most of their adulthood in the civil service (or, after being cashiered, bemoaning their enforced retirement). Their fame as poets seems to have derived at least in part from their fame as important civil officials. Many of these poets were personal friends. This pattern, true for the Seven Early Masters, remains true for the Seven Late Masters, men like Wang Shizhen and Li Panlong who received their degrees in the same year and came to know each other in Beijing. In contrast, like the Revival Society itself, the friendship between Zhong Xing and Tan Yuanchun seems to have existed chiefly in print.

In an empire in which positions of power were won through written examinations judged partly on the basis of style, the art of writing was a political matter. Until the Wanli reign, arbiters of taste were by and large highly placed officials. In contrast, the famous poets of the last decades of the Ming were famous primarily for their achievements in the world of letters. If they received palace degrees at all, it was generally in middle age or even later, after they had already established some renown as writers. As has been discussed above, before his retirement Li Zhi had served as an official. The three Yuan brothers, though all degree recipients, were chiefly famous as writers, and none served very long in office. Zhong Xing received a degree, but never occupied a very prestigious office; his junior collaborator Tan Yuanchun never even passed the final set of examinations. Men like Tan – who were acclaimed from youth for literary brilliance, but never achieved official success – were a commonplace by the end of the dynasty.

Compared to Qing officials, who often served for decades or else retired for personal reasons, late Ming officials had almost without exception tumultuous careers. Those fortunate enough to pass the examinations at an early age found it nearly impossible to steer clear of political turmoil. Examples span the seventy years covered by this chapter. Some, like Yuan Hongdao, simply retired young. The great playwright Tang Xianzu (1550–1616) had a prestigious post at the Ministry of Rites, and was banished, reinstated, and then fired for good, all in the space of about fifteen years. Only after his retirement did he begin to devote much of his time to playwriting. Qian Qianyi (1582–1664), the poet and critic who later became controversial for serving under the Manchus, was the center of one of the great imbroglios at the Chongzhen court. After returning to court after one factional conflict, he found himself the target of a campaign against Eastern Forest supporters; his candidacy for promotion was blocked and he was accused of corruption. He returned to private life in disgrace.

Poets from the earlier part of the Ming dynasty seem to have expended their literary energies primarily in writing; this pattern does not hold for poets of the Wanli period and later, whose activities were both more commercial and more diffuse. The Yuan brothers' writings about poetry were more influential than their actual poetry. It was Zhong Xing's efforts as an editor and commentator, not as a poet, that attracted the attention of forgers. When Qian Qianyi was not engaged in political infighting, he compiled monumental anthologies of both Tang and Ming verse. These men – broadly learned and engaged simultaneously in multiple literary pursuits, including writing, editing, and commentary – were the precursors to the polymath giants of the eighteenth century, but their efforts were also thoroughly integrated into the world of commercial printing.

Informal writing

Late Ming informal writings, called *xiaopin*, or "lesser works," are often considered a genre, one characteristic of the last few decades of the dynasty. In recent years especially, numerous anthologies of these works have been published by major academic presses in mainland China and Taiwan. Informal writing had been an important part of Chinese literature for centuries; indeed, it was writers of the mid-Ming, Gui Youguang and Tang Shunzhi among them, who created the canon of the eight great Tang and Song writers (*Tang Song badajia*) of ancient prose (*guwen*). This canon still stands largely unquestioned today.

Prose writing had, since the time of the late fourth-century poet Tao Qian, touched on private concerns. What distinguishes the Ming approach to this kind of writing? In the late Ming, the name "lesser works" was used so loosely as to apply to poetry as well; moreover as the name suggests, "lesser works" are defined by what they are not. This definition by exclusion situates these pieces in contradistinction to something else, namely orthodox literature in the service of the state.

There was nothing revolutionary in form about the essays we now call *xiaopin*. The late Ming was a golden age for genre theory as applied to the study of the tradition, with important critical writings on many forms, especially fictional and dramatic, that had hitherto been ignored, and much critical energy was applied to the study of forms that in the late Ming were still quite new. Hu Yinglin and Jin Shengtan essentially invented between them the field of fiction criticism. Southern dramatists invented prosodic rules and created a critical apparatus to talk about this new form. But no such endeavor was undertaken with regard to these "lesser works," so why are they now considered a distinct genre?

Informal writing proves difficult to define by the usual means. Consisting sometimes of only a few lines or pages, at times standing alone and at other times written as the preface to another work or as a letter, these essays vary widely in form. In content, they include rhapsodic descriptions of scenic spots, philosophical queries, epitaphs, inscriptions on paintings, and reminiscences. They are so diverse in both content and form as to seem to have absolutely nothing in common. The genre was established in retrospect, as part of the New Culture movement of the 1920s. Important figures of the May Fourth Movement, like Zhou Zuoren and Lin Yutang, went back to the classical tradition looking for some vindication of certain ideals they thought were otherwise missing. Consequently, unlike late Ming poetry, the canon of *xiaopin* is, because it was formed late by a few highly influential readers, well established and agreed upon.

Throughout the Ming dynasty, much of the debate on prose, as in poetry, centered upon which historical models ought to be imitated, whether the writers of the Tang or those of the Han and even earlier. Prose – specifically, nonparallel "ancient prose" – no less than poetry, carried an enormous theoretical weight. Since neo-Confucianism itself had evolved out of a prose reform movement, prose style was not merely a decorative issue. The question asked of writing was how it could be expressive and still serve as an adequate vessel for the Way.

Consequently, revered prose writers from earlier ages like Han Yu, Liu Zongyuan, and Ouyang Xiu were at once statesmen profoundly engaged with the politics of their own age and important voices in contemporary philosophical disputes. Some of the most formidable intellects of the tradition, they reflected this unity of the personal, the philosophical, and the political in their writings. By the last decades of the late Ming, some of the promise of the classical tradition, both in poetry and in prose, seemed an impossibility. Or rather, poetry's pledged capacity for self-expression had been invested in prose instead, whose own promise of political and philosophical significance had been fractured. Perhaps this is why late Ming prose is so good at expressing a sense of loss.

Part of the difference between prose written in the late Ming and earlier prose was, as in poetry, a matter of sheer quantity. Another difference lay in the changed circumstances of official service. When the giants of the Tang and the Song wrote informal prose, they did so in time taken from an official career, and this writing stood in contrast to the parallel prose in which much of their official work was conducted. Numerous prose masterpieces from the Tang and the Song, for example, concern weighty matters of practical administration. In producing prose, these writers were motivated by career considerations, but probably not by financial ones. The prose writer Chen Jiru (1568–1639), in contrast, never had an official career and made a partial living selling prefaces, epitaphs, and other occasional pieces. The difficulty of achieving officialdom, and the near impossibility of retaining an official career afterwards, combined with the growth in the reading public to allow informal writing to proliferate as it never had before.

Informal writings – which also took place within the parameters of classical genres – present an interesting contrast to poetry, partly because the authors are drawn from precisely the same elite circles of men engaged in multiple literary pursuits even as they remained enmeshed in the examination system and orthodox elite culture. The relationships of these men with the marketplace of words were fraught with complexity. For the most part, however, the informal pieces themselves were not for sale, although in the case of biographies and epitaphs, for example, the line demarcating payment from gifts given in gratitude is a fuzzy one.

Some of the names we find in anthologies of informal writing are already familiar to readers of this chapter as critics and poets: the Yuan brothers, Zhong Xing, and Tan Yuanchun. Other famous writers in this genre include Gui Youguang's grandson Gui Zhuang (1613–1673), and the elegist Zhang Dai, whose greatest writings, circulated in the first decades of the next dynasty, detail his memories of life before the fall of the Ming.

Informal writings do not aim to fulfill the hoary promises of ancient-style prose, in which politics, philosophy, and style were all one. These "lesser works," on the surface a wholly self-deprecatory name, glorify instead the small pleasures of private life and experience. Despite their diversity of form, they share a negative focus, hence their "lesser" status: these are writings by elite men that resolutely avoid focusing on the examinations, or government service, or politics. Even in ancient-style prose, with its long history of political commitment, government service had been displaced from the center.

No writer of informal prose dedicated himself exclusively to the genre; like all men of the elite, these writers also wrote poetry and the eight-part essays they had studied since childhood. Like the poets of the age, the men who achieved renown as prose writers tended to be famous also as literary figures engaged in a wide range of endeavors as editors, anthologists, and collectors. Some dabbled in colloquial song, song lyric, or other genres. Tu Long (1542–1605), for example, wrote southern plays. The three Yuan brothers were famous poets and critics. The troubled but multitalented Xu Wei (1521–1593) was not only a famous essayist, but a painter as well, and was perhaps best known for having written the most famous northern plays of the Ming.

Since they cover nonofficial life, informal writings also provide an excellent window into the amusements of the elite in this sophisticated age. Some are quirky observations about literary texts or historical figures. Many are expressions of connoisseurship. If these writings contrast with their counterparts from an earlier age, such as the ancient-style masterpieces by men like Han Yu and Liu Zongyuan, they were also sometimes written with a contemporary contrast in mind. In the late Ming, manuals and treatises that aimed at guiding the reader in the collection and appreciation of all manner of luxury consumer goods flourished. These texts speak most obviously to the wealth of the age and the growing number of people with disposable income to spend, but they also speak to an increasingly mobile society, whose members needed such books to guide their purchases. This in turn suggests anxieties about status for everyone including those of wealth and privilege. Not coincidentally, although there had been heirlooms and collectibles for centuries, we can trace the use of the word "antique" (*gudong*) to this historical moment, which gave rise not just to collecting, but also to antique dealing and forgery.

The topics of these manuals ranged from the ephemeral and quotidian – food, incense, tea, wine – to costly collector items of the kind preserved in museums to this day, such as high-end housewares, books, and paintings. Some manuals focused on the paraphernalia for a scholar's study, such as inkstones, brushes, and paper, or on the ornaments necessary to beautify his house, like decorative rocks, vases, and flowers. As a whole, these guides deal with general categories, while informal writings concern specific examples and personal history. Manuals tend towards the impersonal, emphasizing what any person with enough money, time, and effort could achieve; informal writings center upon the individual experience, attainable by no one else. The difference between the two is generic; many writers such as Yuan Hongdao, Tu Long, and Chen Jiru, to name a few, dabbled in both forms.

Informal writings frequently mention the dominant literary mode of the age, namely drama. Instead of evaluating libretti, as Lü Tiancheng's (1573–1619) *Classification of Drama (Qupin)* does, their focus is on specific performances savored, of individual performers admired. Some writers describe favorite foods that are distinguished less by rarity, freshness, or special preparation than by something unique to the person, whether a special experience or a memory of the past. Others write of beloved collections or specific *objets* that personal history has made distinctive.

It would have gone against all the unspoken rules to have praised an object on the basis of its monetary worth. This was one way in which these writings helped to define a true aristocracy of taste and discernment against the pretensions of a growing class of men with the money to acquire the same objects. Rather than boast about an object's value, a writer might brag about the opposite, its valuelessness; the object is valuable only because of the excessive love he has lavished on it. The essayist Lu Shusheng (1509–1565) writes, "As for my attachment to my inkstones, it cannot be transferred to other precious, valuable things. The inkstones thus depend on me for being the object of obsession. Who knows whether they may not acquire value that way?" The real subject of the piece is not the inkstones, but the writer's obsession with them. The same unspoken rules hold for even the most expensive objects, like the gardens whose design and maintenance were popular pursuits of the period.

Even in works that do not concern objects, we can still see the mark of the connoisseur. For example, Yuan Hongdao's biography of his four stupid servants hinges on his ability to appreciate something beneath the surface, which is not unlike the beauty a collector finds in stones that appear to others as ugly deformities. The encounter reveals an otherwise hidden affinity between the connoisseur and the object.

With its focus on individuality and quirkiness, informal writing can hardly be detached from ways of thinking about the self. In an age when so many of the old means of self-identification were clearly faltering, many members of the elite cultivated eccentric personae manifested in a variety of ways, some of them literary. The classical short-story writer Song Maocheng (1569–1622), for one, was known as a lover of swords: he carried around a Japanese sword and, according to Chen Zilong, participated in an odd ritual with swordsmen whom he befriended. They would pass around a skull containing wine at an outdoor picnic. After the wine was finished, the friends would then take turns cutting themselves and filling the skull with blood, which was then buried as a sign of their undying loyalty to each other. This sort of behavior would have been considered only slightly less odd in the late Ming than in our own time.

Another popular subject of informal writing was travel for pleasure, a form of entertainment that became increasingly common among the wealthy. Take, for example, the Yangzhou courtesan Wang Wei (1600?–1647), a writer and anthologist of travelogues, who describes herself as "by nature addicted to mountains and waters." Her record of travels describes only secondarily a physical landscape. Primarily it is a landscape of nostalgia that reveals her identity as a travel addict, so that the terrain itself is inseparable from the writer's unique perceptions and experience. Some of the journeys described by Wang Wei and other aficionados of travel covered only a few kilometers and ended in well-known pleasure spots. By the 1620s, some popular destinations, like Mount Huang, had as many as 800,000 visitors a year (accommodated by busy inns and restaurants). Most travels were very far from solitary endeavors, and much of the writing revolves around distinguishing one's own experience from those of myriad others.

Zhang Dai, perhaps the most famous resident of Hangzhou, one of the busiest cities of the time, writes here about an excursion on the city's West Lake, on the night of the full moon. First he details all the other people on the lake: some merrymakers do not even bother to look at the moon; some look at the moon, hoping that others will look at them as they admire it; some come to look at those looking at the moon. Finally all of these lesser sorts clear out, making way for those who truly appreciate the beauty of the full moon on West Lake:

> Only then would people like us move our boats to the shore . . . Those who had been sipping their wine slowly and singing in a low voice came out. Those who had been hiding themselves in the shade of the trees also emerged. We greeted them and pulled them over to sit with us. Poetic friends and famous courtesans arrived on the scene . . . Voices and instruments blended in unison. Only when the moon was fading fast and the east was gradually turning white would our guests take their leave.

The pleasure of the experience is beautifully described. It consists in large part of setting one's own experience apart from those of others and giving a sense of individuality to a generic experience like gazing at the full moon in one of the scenic hotspots of China.

Consider the contrast between such excursions and the famous journeys of Xu Hongzu (better known as Xu Xiake, 1586–1641). At the end of the dynasty, Xu made a series of long journeys, culminating in one that lasted for three years and took him from his home at the mouth of the Yangzi river across the empire to Yunnan Province. Unlike the merchants who were with increasing frequency crisscrossing the empire in search of profit, Xu Xiake undertook his journeys for the sake of disinterested knowledge. Out of these travels, Xu Xiake produced an immense diary more than 600,000 characters in length, which was part geography, part ethnography, and part landscape writing. In the diary, Xu Xiake travels across an unknown landscape, whose interest lies precisely in that it cannot be converted into private space. For each location, he lists notable sites and specific difficulties in traversing the terrain; his journey is to what lies beyond, and not – as was so often the case with late Ming travelers – to some territory located within the self. He makes no mention of childhood memory, of yearnings to merge the self with the landscape, of serendipitous encounters. There is very little here of the main project of informal writings, namely to imbue something fully with an inimitable voice. The very opposite of informal writings, these are writings where the authorial voice has been subsumed by a larger enterprise. Naturally, such a project was not for everyone.

If informal writing was defined in contradistinction to that associated with official business, it was no less often set against writing for profit. The necessity of selling one's writing – to earn money for survival in many cases – sheds additional light on the central drive in informal writing to tie oneself to one's own writing.

After failing the examinations numerous times, Xu Wei took up a job as the secretary, or more accurately the ghostwriter, of a local governor. Later on, Xu gathered together for publication the work of those years, including the celebrated letter to the throne that had won his employer accolades from the emperor himself. To whom did that letter belong – Xu or the man who paid him? Xu Wei was evidently troubled by this question. Compiling the works written in the employ of others, he frets about his relation to them, wondering whether reclaiming those writings has subjected him to mockery.

Inscribing writing with markers of the self could take place by other means as well. Yuan Hongdao wrote a biography of Xu Wei, who seems to have been one of the few contemporaries whom the gregarious Yuan Hongdao did not know either personally or through a friend. Yuan's account of Xu as a man who channels his frustrated official ambitions into art seems at first a clichéd attempt to put Xu Wei into a lineage that begins with Qu Yuan. In an age obsessed with, and thus acutely sensitive to, the possibility of playacting, the private biography (a staple of informal prose) seeks to clear its subject of any possible charge of being a poseur. But how does one imbue the cliché of the unappreciated talent with sincerity? Yuan Hongdao describes how Xu Wei expresses frustration and desperate misery:

> he grabbed an axe and split open his own head. The blood covered his head, and the bones of his skull were fractured. Rubbing them, you could hear the bones move. Another time, he took a sharp awl and poked into his own ears. The wound was more than an inch deep, but he still did not die.

Pathological behavior in any other age, but in this one, such actions take on a different light. Turning the personal into something unquestionably your own could be a painful and serious matter.

II. Fiction and the merchant elite

Introduction to fiction

The last section focused on elite literary forms. This section turns to long and short fiction, in both classical and vernacular, literary forms associated with a new class. According to Yu Ying-shih, the last decades of the Ming dynasty mark a high point in the cultural impact of what he calls the *shishang*, a combination of the old examination-based elite with a new wealthy merchant class. Whatever its complicated status vis-à-vis other genres, fiction was the kind of literature most thoroughly a part of a commercial market at a time when the market itself was viewed with enormous ambivalence. To scholars of the earlier part of the twentieth century, the anonymity of fictional texts spoke to the shame with which late imperial authors would appear to have viewed commercial work and their own low social status. In reality, the relationships between fiction and the market, and between elite writers and folk forms, were much more complicated.

Historians have long noted that, particularly in the Jiangnan area, some families in the late Ming were able to accumulate fortunes of virtually unprecedented magnitude through manufacturing and trade. Whereas the vast majority of wealth in earlier periods had been based on ownership of land, the holders of these new fortunes were based in towns and cities. This wealth was the foundation for many of the cultural pursuits of the late Ming, such as garden design, that would have been virtually unimaginable without it.

Commercial wealth also effected subtler changes, including breaking the exclusive hold of the examination-based elite on both moral and social status. Many members of the new class of *shishang* disdained the idea of a moral hierarchy that elevated scholars above merchants, even though that had been part of traditional thinking for millennia. Wang Daokun wrote about his native Huizhou: "South of the great river, the capital of Xin'an is noted for its rich cultural tradition. It has been the local custom to be either Confucian scholars or merchants, alternating by generations. In short, in what way is a good merchant inferior to a prominent scholar?" Wang Daokun questioned not just the privileged status of the elite, but the very distinction between them and merchants; in an age when the commercial earnings of one brother might support another as he studied for the examinations, the difference was often merely semantic.

In considering the phenomenal growth in fiction writing in the late Ming, we run into the same trends we have seen in other genres. The literary career that merged anthologizing, editing, and creative writing allowed fiction writing to take off. Without those activities in other genres, fiction could not have thrived; in this sense, the rise of fiction was a secondary development. In 1566, in an almost unprecedented feat of antiquarian energy, the retired official and bibliophile Tan Kai edited, assembled, and published the *Extensive Records from the Taiping Reign* (*Taiping guangji*), a massive early Song compendium that included enormous quantities of Tang and pre-Tang materials. The publication of the *Extensive Records*, which provided source material for many of the most famous late Ming stories and tales, reintroduced into wide circulation Tang tales about romance and the arcane, breathing new life into fiction writing in both vernacular and classical forms. The *Extensive Records* also stimulated the growth of numerous secondary collections of classical narratives arranged by theme; this further allowed previously rare texts to be widely read. Several of the men associated with the Gongan School, including Yuan Zhongdao and Jiang Yingke, compiled various collections of jokes and tales, partly culled from the *Extensive Records*. Feng Menglong's collection of jokes draws from more than twenty earlier collections, including the *Extensive Records* and many Ming anthologies.

Another trend that migrated to fiction from other genres was the increasingly "authored" quality of many texts. Earlier, many works of fiction had circulated without mention of an author or an editor; now, they came increasingly to be associated with a single individual. This meant, in some cases, that what had once been either anonymous or the product of group activity was now controlled by a single person and marked with his individual sensibility. This individual could be the author, but was sometimes the editor, or even the publisher. A strong sense of association with an individual had long characterized genres traditionally accorded a high value like poetry, prose, and even the Classics, but now less-esteemed genres also showed this tendency. Paradoxically, the marketing of books seems to have accelerated this process. As we have seen in the case of other genres, books were often given a false attribution so as to attract more buyers. The association of fictional texts with individual authors also had a powerful impact on reading practices; for example, it fed the growth of fiction commentary. Though the trend may have been pushed along by market dynamics, the same trends held for books of fiction that were not written for profit.

This section treats at length the work of two men: the anonymous writer of *The Plum in the Golden Vase (Jin Ping Mei)* and Feng Menglong, the indefatigable collator and editor, who was the seminal figure in the history of the vernacular short story. The contemporary scholar Chen Dakang sees 1590 as the date at which the vernacular novel began to flourish. The preceding seven decades had seen the publication of only eight novels; in the five decades after – from 1590 to the end of the dynasty, that is – we have record of some fifty more. *The Plum in the Golden Vase* was probably written and began circulating around 1590. Feng Menglong's career took off in the 1620s, and he continued to be productive until the end of the dynasty. This section focuses on what these two members of the elite achieved by writing vernacular fiction, and what fiction made possible for them that other forms did not.

Since this approach skips over many texts in favor of texts that have been read widely, I wish to begin with a quick overview of works of fiction not discussed at length here. The vast majority of Ming novels and stories have been either forgotten or lost entirely; some survive in one lone copy in an obscure library. Sometimes whole subgenres faded into obscurity after a few decades of popularity. Court case fiction, to name one, was popular in the last decade of the sixteenth century and the first decade of the seventeenth. After that, nearly two centuries elapsed before more court case fiction was published.

The word "novel" becomes problematic when applied to certain other genres of fiction, showing just how imperfect is the comparison between long vernacular fiction in Chinese and its European counterparts. For example, a number of texts seem to be curiously suspended between cult practice and literature. *Investiture of the Gods (Fengshen yanyi)* was published in 1605 by an unknown scholar who clearly took great pains over its production.

This popular novel, re-created over the centuries in a number of different editions and dramatic adaptations (most recently appearing in video game form), treats the Zhou dynasty's founding from a mythological perspective, integrating human history with the doings of the gods and goddesses. Here myth is transformed into a novel by careful craft.

In other instances, myth works less well as a novel. One publisher collated *Four Journeys* (*Si youji*), a collection of novels named after each of the cardinal directions, including one version of *Journey to the West* (treated in the previous chapter). One of these novels, *Journey to the North* (*Beiyou ji*, first published ca 1602), which tells the story of how one god, the Dark Emperor, came into his position, bears an especially interesting and complicated relationship with religious practice. It is indicative of the looseness of the novel's construction that one modern scholar has argued for its authorship by a spirit medium.

Sometimes even extremely important subgenres have received scant critical attention. Largely unstudied both in China and elsewhere except in evaluations of their accuracy, the historical novel – one rare category to retain its popularity from the late Ming to the present day – was perhaps the single most popular form of reading material in late imperial China. Some of these historical novels are resolutely unrealistic, with elements taken from more fantastical subgenres. For example, *The Journey of Sanbao the Eunuch to the Western Ocean* (*Sanbao taijian Xiyang ji tongsu yanyi*) combines the historical interest of the eunuch Zheng He's fifteenth-century voyages with the excitement of a supernatural quest.

Other historical novels depicted a much more prosaic reality. As the dynasty drew near its close, the period covered by these novels encroached more and more on the present day. By the Chongzhen reign, novels were being written about the very recent past: the corrupt eunuch Wei Zhongxian's rise and fall, for example, was an important topic. In an age that was profoundly politicized, where elite life was in constant turmoil because of factional disputes, these novels may have served to fill in for the lack of newspapers, avoiding fictional convention to present a highly verisimilitudinous version of current events. Of course, a novel could make pointed *sub rosa* commentary about the present in ways that a real history could not: in *The Adventures of Sui Yangdi* (*Sui Yangdi yanshi*), the corrupt seventh-century Emperor Yang is a cipher for the Wanli Emperor. Earlier generations of modern scholars assumed that the anonymous authorship of most novels could only have meant that novels were broadly disdained and that their writers, working solely for profit, wished to be dissociated from their work. In cases like these, however, the novels were closely related to the numerous classical-language unofficial histories that contained potentially seditious content, and through which many readers learned of conflicts at court. There were incentives much stronger than mere embarrassment for such writings to be published anonymously.

Some works of fiction were clearly assembled for financial gain. Jianyang in Fujian Province had, since the Song dynasty, been one of the great centers of commercial publishing, with two families, the Yus and the Lius, particularly prominent. In the Wanli period, the Yus owned more than thirty independent publishing houses; one member of the family, the entrepreneur and publisher Yu Xiangdou (1560–1637), published some twenty titles of fiction, including *The Four Journeys* mentioned above, as well as works of history and philosophy. In addition to employing carvers and printers, Yu Xiangdou also seems to have been involved in the extensive editing and rewriting of materials. Moreover, the books he published were so strongly associated with him that some were sold with a woodblock print of his portrait along with his name. Yu Xiangdou's presence as a publisher was more important to the marketing of a given book than the identity of the book's author.

To early twentieth-century historians of fiction, special value inhered in precisely these rough edges, specifically the loose relationship between authors and texts. For this earlier generation of critics, late Ming vernacular fiction represented the vitality of the folk tradition. Vernacular literature, simple and energetic, was refreshingly free from what they saw as the corrupting influence of elite values. Fiction was written in the vernacular, these critics believed, primarily to appeal to the common people, who were neither educated enough nor wealthy enough to participate in elite culture. Much of the scholarly work of the last few generations has invalidated these assumptions. Or, more accurately, the relationship between folk literature and vernacular forms turns out to be much more complicated than previously imagined.

Some of these assumptions, such as that the common people were the chief audience of vernacular fiction, have easily been debunked by examining surviving copies. For example, a copy of *The Investiture of the Gods*, a novel in one hundred chapters, cost 2 taels in the 1620s, twice the price of a 125-chapter encyclopedia. This case is far from unique, as most extant examples of early printings of fiction are marked by characteristics that indicate an exclusive and privileged audience. Virtually all surviving editions of vernacular fiction from the late Ming are handsomely produced, lavishly illustrated, and printed in clear type with generous margins. In the last decades of the dynasty, interlinear comments were often interspersed in or printed above the text of the novel proper, which must have added to the costs of production. Finally, relatively few copies of any single print run have survived to the present day, suggesting that these novels were never printed in large numbers.

It is virtually impossible to read any fictional text as representing a perspective fully autonomous from elite concerns. Andrew Plaks has noted that all the arts in late imperial China shared an ideological commitment to elite culture. Regardless of who wrote fiction in late Ming China, it is clear that elites were far and away the most active part of the reading audience. From their letters and personal notes, we know that many members of the elite were voracious consumers of all manner of print material, no matter how seemingly humble.

Although wrong in the details, early twentieth-century critics did get one aspect of the big picture right. Vernacular literature, in its long and short forms, as drama and narrative, gained much of its expressive power from not having been traditionally associated with the elites. It was thus able to say things, particularly about the increasingly complicated social world, that poetry and classical prose, no matter how expressive of feeling, simply could not.

The Plum in the Golden Vase

Despite the best efforts of scholars, the exact date of the composition of the Ming dynasty's greatest novel and the identity of its author remain unknown. Even without these specifics, the history of the early transmission and circulation of *The Plum in the Golden Vase* (*Jin Ping Mei*) sheds some light on the complicated relationship between popular forms and the elite around the end of the sixteenth century.

Over the years, more than a score of literary figures from the Wanli period have been proposed as possible authors, most prominent among them Wang Shizhen, Tang Xianzu, Li Kaixian, and Xu Wei. Scholars may never definitively establish the novel's authorship, partly because its anonymity seems to have been the result of deliberate contrivance. Some have posited an early date of composition from the novel's failure to mention southern drama, while others have pointed to possible correspondences between events in the novel and specific political scandals of the Wanli reign. It has even been suggested that the whole novel can be read as a political allegory, but this interpretation has been generally discredited.

Most of the evidence and current scholarly opinion tend to date composition to the middle of the Wanli reign. Though the novel is first mentioned in the 1590s, there are no references to a complete manuscript before 1606. In speaking of the time of composition, therefore, we are referring to a period that probably spans decades, a common pattern in long vernacular fiction.

It is highly unlikely that the novel circulated for long without being mentioned, only then to have been mentioned repeatedly after 1596. In the late fall of that year, Yuan Hongdao wrote to the great painter Dong Qichang (1555–1636) to say what a pleasant diversion the novel had been in his sickness: "Please let me know when I can return it to you, once it has been copied, and exchange it for the other part." The novel was probably passed around before it was complete; readers copied the parts they received and then returned the original. As Dong Qichang was then serving in office in Beijing, it may also be deduced that the manuscripts were being sent by mail, over hundreds of kilometers. The next year, Yuan Zhongdao referred to the partial manuscript in his diary. Later, both brothers made reference to a complete manuscript that they had had copied. Within a decade or so, several famous figures, including the writer Shen Defu (1578–1610) and Feng Menglong, also mentioned the novel, usually in connection with the three Yuan brothers.

Given the tight circles of connection that we observe again and again in this period, and the fact that all early mentions of the novel are made by men connected through Yuan Hongdao and his brothers, current scholarly opinion points to authorship by a single member of the elite, a man who traveled in these circles and began the novel in the years immediately preceding 1596. If this man could be identified, we would almost certainly be able to unearth a fair amount of biographical information about him. One of the paradoxes of research in this period is that even as the forces that powered writing and marked its content became increasingly broad, most of what is covered in this chapter was written by people belonging to overlapping circles of acquaintance.

Famous readers praised this novel at the time, but was it generally esteemed by contemporaries? The text's claim to cultural authority is evident in a number of ways. Some novels, like *Journey to the West*, appear in numerous forms and in different genres, suggesting that publishers and editors felt free to revise and adapt at will. In contrast, *The Plum in the Golden Vase* was treated with a high degree of respect by the publishing world. Redactions of this novel all show a relatively small degree of difference. Rather than haphazard editing or bowdlerization, later efforts to intervene in how a reader might approach the novel came in the form of imitation and sequels instead of direct intervention and rewriting.

While hand-copied manuscripts remained an important way for books to circulate even as printed books became increasingly ubiquitous in the late

Ming, the role of manuscripts had changed as a result of the proliferation of venues for buying books. Robert Hegel has suggested that novels circulating in manuscript – in other words, directly removed from the market economy of the print industry and in such limited numbers as to pique readers' interest – were usually the product of elite pens. Letters exchanged among famous men of arts make clear that books in manuscript wore an intriguingly exclusive air; even the well-connected Yuan Hongdao wanted to know how he could acquire more of this manuscript.

There is no reason, however, to think in terms of a single manuscript being copied and recopied as it was passed from friend to friend before eventually being printed. We cannot tell whether the references mentioned above came from men who were reading the same book or the same parts of the same book. In fact, even though they referred to what they read by the same title, there is evidence to suggest almost the exactly opposite scenario. Furthermore, printed versions did not immediately supplant ones in manuscript; after the novel was printed in 1618, manuscripts continued to circulate.

Transmission by manuscript undermines some easy truisms about texts, unveiling a deceit in which literary histories are often complicit. Scholars often refer to a text as if a single definitive edition exists that perfectly reflects its author's intent. As anyone who has delved into biblical studies, or even Shakespearean studies, knows, often no such version exists; the very notion of the authoritative version is often a product of a whole constellation of contingent factors, including commercial printing and the laws and practices governing the distribution of texts.

Although *The Plum in the Golden Vase* appears to have been conceived by a single mind, none of the multiple extant editions is definitive, and all bear the traces of many editorial hands. While the two major versions both relate the same intricate plot in one hundred chapters, they still differ in significant ways, especially between chapters 53 and 57. The first and longer version is regarded by most modern critics as superior; the other circulated more widely in late imperial China and was the text used by the important early Qing commentator Zhang Zhupo. The modern reader may choose a "better" text or one that was much more influential. Anyway, it is likely that both exist in complicated relationships with other versions that have been lost but may one day resurface.

In elevating the status of the first recension over the second, some scholars have argued that the second recension was cut down from the first to make imprints more commercially viable. One weakness of this theory is that it is not at all clear that any serious money was ever made from this novel. Despite his concern with money and with the lives of merchants, the author of the novel seems not to have expected, and he almost certainly never realized, any financial gain. Paradoxically, genres that were traditionally more respected are much easier to situate within the marketplace. We know from letters and other records how much the elite charged for writing prefaces, epitaphs, and other occasional pieces, but information of that kind for *The Plum in the Golden Vase* will probably elude us forever.

The novel stands as a striking breakthrough on many levels. It was the first novel in the tradition not to be based on a previously existing body of folklore, as were such works as *Water Margin* and *Journey to the West*. Instead, it was based on an earlier text. Like the Yuan brothers and Li Zhi, the novel's author must have admired *Water Margin*, because the first chapters of *The Plum in the Golden Vase* retell a portion of the earlier novel. The licentious Golden Lotus is the sister-in-law of Wu Song, one of the heroes of *Water Margin*; she murders her crippled husband to run off with her lover Ximen Qing. In *Water Margin*, Wu Song avenges his brother's death shortly thereafter; in contrast, most of *The Plum in the Golden Vase* takes place in the years it takes Wu Song to catch up with Golden Lotus. The whole novel is, in other words, a self-aware insertion into an earlier body of work.

This "authored" quality suggests again a rather late date of publication for *The Plum in the Golden Vase*, which, in that sense, has more in common with sequels like Dong Yue's (1620–1686) *Supplement to Journey to the West* (*Xiyou bu*) and commentaries like those of Jin Shengtan than it does with earlier novels. *Supplement to Journey to the West*, completed in 1640, is the first of the sequels that flourished in the early Qing, when all the major novels acquired multiple sequels. Instead of picking up the action where the parent novel ends, the *Supplement* is presented as an insertion between chapters 61 and 62, and takes place in Monkey's mind.

The Plum in the Golden Vase is embedded in a textual world, not just because of its relationship with *Water Margin*, but also in the way the novel makes explicit and highly artificed reference to the enormous diversity of late Ming literary life. No other work in the tradition borrows so heavily from other texts: vernacular stories, works of pornography, histories, dramas, popular songs, jokes, and prosimetric narratives, and even texts far outside of the parameters of the literary, such as official gazettes, contracts, and menus. These quotations are not approximate, as they would be if transmitted orally, but precise, and they are deployed with ironic distance. A novel that initially circulated in manuscript, it is also a profound reflection on the fungibility of all texts in print culture.

The Plum in the Golden Vase is the first – and, together with *The Story of the Stone*, arguably the greatest – novel to focus almost exclusively on the domestic sphere. At the center stands the rich merchant Ximen Qing with his six wives, their children, and their servants. Rich with details about the family's physical surroundings, the novel also describes the interactions of its cast of characters with an unprecedented degree of psychological realism. This image of a family in which the many wives squabble over the unavailable husband, each attempting to gain the upper hand in the household, as the procreative energies of all are squandered on sensuality rather than being engaged in the production of children, became emblematic of late imperial decadence in the eyes of many modern writers. But this impression owes everything to *The Plum in the Golden Vase*.

Within the Chinese tradition, the idea of the family carried an immense political charge: family and state, both hierarchical and headed by a patriarch, mirrored each other. At the same time, the family was also the building block of the polity. A family that engages in incest and adultery cannot simply be a collection of misbehaving individuals; they must also represent something else. Consequently, the dysfunctional family in the novel has been thought to stand in for the Wanli court, and Ximen Qing and his conniving wives to represent the emperor and his bickering ministers. Or, perhaps it is the case that their depravity, and that of other families like theirs all over the empire, causes the dynastic fall depicted at the end of the novel.

Set in the final years of the Northern Song, *The Plum in the Golden Vase* concludes with the collapse of the dynasty and the capture of the emperor by the Jurchens. Since the decline of the family parallels this dynastic history, the historical setting is important; however, the novel makes no effort to describe any reality but its own historical present, the Wanli period. Nearly everything a person could buy in a prosperous late Ming town is described in the novel: clothing, food, all the objects that typically fill a house, and, of course, sex. The novel's whole focus is on urban life. All traces of rural life, which, in traditional Confucian thought, was the moral foundation of society, are thoroughly effaced. By the same token, the world of civil examinations and officialdom is relegated to the margins.

The novel's detailed and highly structured plot is its most significant innovation. The fate not only of Golden Lotus, but of the other characters as well, seems to have been carefully plotted from beginning to end, and there are hints in the last few pages that a sequel might have been planned to cover the adventures of the dead characters after reincarnation. While both *Water*

Margin and *Journey to the West* are easily broken up into episodes for performance, storytelling, or reading for pleasure, *The Plum in the Golden Vase* resolutely resists any such excerpting. This is another indication that *The Plum in the Golden Vase* was conceived from the first as a specifically written text. The novel develops in sets of ten chapters, each covering one major plot, such as the sixth wife Vase's entry into the household, and a number of minor plot elements. Consequently, unlike those earlier texts, it is almost impossible to imagine in a form other than that of the long novel. The very title (as peculiar in Chinese as it is in English translation) can only be understood after reading thirteen chapters: "golden" refers to Golden Lotus, the depraved fifth wife of Ximen Qing; "plum," to Plum Blossom, her maidservant and partner in crime; and "vase," to the name of Ximen Qing's favorite wife.

Either *The Plum in the Golden Vase* perfectly anticipates late Ming critical obsessions, or it was written with these obsessions in mind. One of the earliest printed versions (dating from either the Tianqi reign or the early Chongzhen reign) has a commentary in the style of Li Zhi that is replete with observations about the novel's intricate structure. Narrative structure was the prime concern for late Ming critics, most famously for the great Jin Shengtan, but also for those preceding and following him. Like the pseudonymous commentator of this early edition of the novel, critics looked for repeated patterns, whether in the form of characters who resemble one another or events that foreshadow other events. Critics delighted in finding examples of forward projection of later events (*fubi*, what we might call foreshadowing) and echoes (*zhaoying*, reflections of earlier events). Examples of these are rife in *The Plum in the Golden Vase*. Late imperial and modern critics alike have noticed that the novel is constructed out of carefully constructed patterns of repetition or, to borrow a term used by Plaks, "figural recurrence."

Nonetheless, unsurprisingly for a work of such length and complexity, the novel has some glaring inconsistencies. Moreover, the pacing of the last chapters is strikingly different from that of the middle. These problems stem in part from how the novel was written and then transmitted, but, more importantly, what modern readers may perceive as flaws can also be attributed to reader expectations that were vastly different from our own. As modern readers of masterpieces like *The Plum in the Golden Vase* and *The Story of the Stone* know, some degree of "unfinishedness" was to be expected, and perhaps desired, even in novels of undeniable craft and artistry by tremendously sophisticated authors. Vernacular novels were intentionally circulated not as finished products, but with room for readers, as well as editors and commentators, to contribute their own thoughts. What a literary critic might call open-ended discursive space, a twenty-first-century computer user might compare to an Internet website with space for comments.

Writing a novel like *The Plum in the Golden Vase* required an awesome feat of concentration. Beginning with just a few characters from *Water Margin*, *The Plum in the Golden Vase* draws in their families and then follows those characters to draw in their families and acquaintances, and so on, building up a cast of hundreds to create a simulacrum of a society in its entirety, from the top to the bottom: high officials, wealthy merchants, struggling shopkeepers, manservants, entertainers, doctors, and, of course, women in all stations and stages of life. In tracing the fates of all these characters, interrelated in multiple and intricate ways, any loose threads are for the most part scrupulously tied.

In the Confucian dystopia that is the novel's world, the characters are bound to each other not by filiality, chastity, and loyalty, but through a web of misbehavior and incest. Literature of this period often revolves around exemplars of moral behavior, especially children who sacrifice themselves for their parents and wives who go to all lengths to preserve their chastity. The characters in *The Plum in the Golden Vase* display vices that are the mirror opposite of these virtues: lust, greed, adultery, betrayal, incest, and ultimately murder.

I have left to the end of this section the single feature that most Chinese readers identify with this novel, its explicit descriptions of sexual behavior. Some critics have argued that sexuality is treated no differently in the novel than any other aspect of the household's existence. If the novel describes sex and its social context with an unprecedented degree of detail, it does the same for Ximen Qing's various shady financial dealings. Given the special status of sex in the culture, however, the comparison is necessarily imperfect. Hundreds of years of critical discourse on the novel have focused on how the reader should respond to the sexual content of the novel. Is *The Plum in the Golden Vase* a work of the purest licentiousness, or is its sexual content an angry Confucian's means of railing against the decline in morals? Does the tone of the novel express prurience or contempt for prurience?

Sex is at the core of the novel's treatment of Confucian ethics. Despite his overabundance in wives, Ximen Qing has a dearth of offspring. At the beginning of the novel, he has just one grown daughter, and later, with Vase, a boy who dies in infancy, and, at the novel's end, a single son born posthumously. Issueless sex, conducted with a harem of bickering, adulterous women, is sex divorced from its natural purpose and lies at the heart of the novel's critique of society. Of the novel's hundreds of characters, not a single one is entirely innocent of misdoing, partly because their lives are interwoven. To be related to any of these characters means to be ensnared in a web of iniquity. Take, for example, Lady Lin, a relatively minor character who appears late in the novel after a number of the main characters have died. Though new to the novel, she is immediately connected to a number of other characters. The wealthy widow of a high official, she makes Ximen Qing's acquaintance ostensibly to seek moral guidance for her son. After embarking on an entirely loveless affair with her, Ximen takes her grown son as a godson. This young man himself has sex with the courtesan Cassia, earlier deflowered by Ximen Qing. She in turn is the goddaughter of Ximen Qing's senior wife, Wu Yueniang.

Recall how much weight Confucian moralists invested in family relations: if children treated their parents with respect and wives were true to their husbands, went this mainstream thinking, the human community could hope to arrive at a sort of perfection. *The Plum in the Golden Vase* depicts a world in which those relations, let alone that perfect society, are no longer possible. Looking again at Lady Lin, we see that through her and her son, Ximen Qing has become father, father-in-law, and husband to Cassia. Every relationship among these people turns into a vile act of incest.

On further reflection, the situation only worsens. Many years before, when still a child, Golden Lotus had been a servant in Lady Lin's household; there she grew into a depraved woman who encourages her husband in every sort of vice to prevent him from making any emotional investment in his other wives. In other words, Lady Lin turned Golden Lotus into the emotional monster who then sends her husband out to have sex with women like Lady Lin. Purity is impossible in these circumstances; not a single character in the novel can be extricated from this web.

This corrupt society burns itself out toward the end of the novel. By the time of the Jurchen invasion, all the main characters have died, victims of their own insatiable concupiscence: Golden Lotus is killed by Wu Song for having murdered his brother; Vase is eaten alive by a mysterious female ailment, the result of having sex during her menses; and Ximen Qing is fatally exhausted by what must surely be one of the most grotesque of all sex scenes in world literature.

Fictional commentary

The period covered by this chapter produced one great novel, *The Plum in the Golden Vase*, but also a new field of cultural endeavor, namely fiction commentary, whose rise was encouraged by certain trends in the publishing industry, especially the growing importance of authors and the increasingly complicated position of elites in relation to vernacular literature. How did Ming readers encounter fiction? Typically not in the way modern readers find it, in books where, apart from a few explanatory notes, the novel or the short story is the only text. Instead, virtually all premodern editions of fiction included commentary and numerous illustrations. The illustrations, in particular, seem to have been highly coveted and appreciated.

Punctuated editions with commentary attached (referred to as *pingdian* in Chinese) were a relatively easy way for publishers to make money since separate editions could be produced with little additional work. Editions with this kind of commentary appeared first in the Classics and famous historical works, followed by examination essays, followed then by dramas, and only then moved into fiction. The connections linking commentaries on different genres become clearer when we observe that a number of early editions of novels with commentary were produced by publishers of other types of commentary, and that the pioneers in fiction commentary, in particular Jin Shengtan and Mao Zonggang (ca 1632–after 1709), also wrote important commentaries on drama.

Whatever the genre, the format remained essentially the same. Commentary is a feature of printed texts, almost never appearing in handwritten manuscripts. Like the prefatory material that was sometimes typeset to mimic actual handwriting, commentary might be considered a way of offsetting the anonymity of the printed text by reproducing the reading experience of an expert, who was also an individual full of quirks and eccentricities.

The main text was printed in large characters, with dots and circles added by a commentator to the right to indicate emphasis or approval. One might compare these to the clapping of jazz connoisseurs, which, in addition to denoting approval, also guides how other members of the audience are to appreciate the performance. The commentary was printed in smaller characters, in double rows, immediately under the text to which it referred. Sometimes additional commentary might appear in the top margin, above the main text, or as interlinear interpolations.

The growing importance of commentary reflects how, from the Wanli period to the end of the Chongzhen reign, vernacular novels became more and more deeply integrated into elite culture. David Rolston has traced the origin of these commentaries to the early part of the Wanli reign, when they were rudimentary, often written by the publishers themselves. During the middle and late Wanli reign, commentaries mostly concern the moral rather than the literary qualities of the text. These commentaries often bore Li Zhi's name; scholars are still debating the degree of Li Zhi's involvement and whether the commentaries were in fact mostly the work of Ye Zhou. Li Zhi was a vocal admirer of *Water Margin*, to be sure, but the attribution of other commentaries on the plays *The Western Wing* and *The Lute* rests on much shakier ground. Even his contemporaries thought that these were probably forgeries by an opportunistic publisher wanting to capitalize on Li Zhi's name. Other famous figures, like Zhong Xing and Yuan Hongdao, also had commentaries attributed to them on even more dubious grounds.

Whatever their authorship and the motivation for writing them, these commentaries reveal a shift in opinion on the novel, showing first that novels had risen in general esteem, and then that they had become endowed with authors, whose heartfelt expression (according to the commentators) is represented in them. Li Zhi writes about great artists and the inspiration that moves them to write:

> Had they authored their work without sufferings, hardship, and frustrations at first, they would have behaved as someone who trembled when he was not cold or who groaned when he was not sick. Even if he did author something, what would be the value? *Water Margin* is a work written as a result of great anger.

Over time, vernacular novels literally gained elite authors, in the persons of their editors and commentators. It became increasingly acceptable to work on novels. Wang Daokun was just one well-known figure to involve himself in editing a version of *Water Margin*. For many of the important figures of this period, Feng Menglong the most famous among them, editing and anthologizing were inseparable from activities, like writing, that we generally consider to be more creative. This was also true for Jin Shengtan, for whom being called an editor understates his actual involvement with a text.

Strongly associated with a single, named author and composed in a form inherited from classical commentary, fictional commentary deployed to a large extent the cultural authority of the elite. The novels themselves were, in contrast, often anonymous or pseudonymous, although by the end of the Ming these too came increasingly to be associated with a single author. In accordance with the respective constraints of the two genres, Jin Shengtan put his own name to his commentary, but couched his editorial additions – which are present on almost every page and which reshaped the novel as a whole – as "restorations" of Shi Nai'an's original text.

Published in the last years of the dynasty, Jin Shengtan's commentaries are acts of creative writing in every sense. Jin was the first to assert that there was a single true edition of *Water Margin* and to attribute the authorship of that edition to Shi Nai'an, about whom essentially nothing is known. No longer could the novel be thought of as the product of compilation; it was instead conceived of as a work of painstaking, self-conscious composition by an author who knew exactly what he wanted to do. This is true of Jin's own version of *Water Margin*, but the author of this work was not Shi Nai'an but Jin himself, whose claims of having discovered an older, authoritative edition were manifestly false. Even more transparently untruthful is the preface in Shi's voice that was "discovered" by Jin.

Jin Shengtan's version of *Water Margin*, to this day the most widely read edition of the novel, not only truncates the text, but, in that it concludes with the execution of all the surviving rebels, also invests the novel as a whole with a radically different moral. Jin's changes particularly affect how the reader approaches the novel's unpalatably violent parts. For example, in the hero Song Jiang's murder of the young woman Yan Poxi, Jin's commentary was to date the longest on a novel; at some points there is as much commentary as "original" text.

Why was commentary necessary? For classical texts rife with philological difficulties, the answer was obvious, but commentary served a different function in vernacular fiction. Critics like Jin Shengtan first had to create a need for their work. These texts, they argued, were misunderstood works of genius, full of subtle clues easily missed by ordinary readers. Commentaries would help the reader to distinguish himself from the common run of humanity by being able to plumb the deeper meaning of these texts. This implied that these vernacular texts, on the surface so transparent and pleasurable, possessed hidden depths that could not be illuminated without the help of a commentator who resonated with the author at a profound level.

How should we understand the persistent efforts by commentators to intervene in and shape the way readers encounter the fictional text? According to one scholarly interpretation, these commentaries point to deep-seated anxieties about status that can only be understood in the context of social change in the late Ming. Everyone, elite and merchant, might be able to buy the same book and even to read it, but only some would be able truly to understand it; without commentary, a reader might understand a novel only on the most superficial level. The early Qing critic Liu Tingji neatly encapsulated this perspective when he wrote, "Those who read *The Plum in the Golden Vase* and learned to pity were bodhisattvas; those who read and wanted to imitate were beasts." Commentary had a twofold purpose: to point to the perceived difficulties of the text and to admit some, but not all, into a fellowship of true readers.

There were other means by which elite authors could also take over a text, as in the case of the novel *Quelling the Demons* (*Pingyao zhuan*), whose early history happens to be well documented. Mentioned in an early catalogue, the novel must have been in circulation from the middle of the sixteenth century; a few editions in twenty chapters were published in the middle of the Wanli reign, including one by Shide tang, one of the most active publishing houses in Nanjing. In 1620, a forty-chapter redaction appeared, with a preface claiming that this was the original version. By the 1630s, that claim had been dropped, and the rewritten novel was openly sold as having been edited and revised by Feng Menglong. Feng's interventions point to characteristic elite preferences: he reshaped the narrative to make it generally less folkloric and less repetitive and tied up loose threads and inconsistencies by adding fifteen chapters. Particularly noteworthy is that, until 1620, inconsistencies in the novel were not a matter for concern, but within fifteen years after that, this anonymous novel, containing a mix of folklore and religious practices of possibly folk origin, had acquired one of the most active literary men of the day for its author.

In the early twentieth century, literary historians broadly disdained traditional commentary of late imperial fiction, primarily for its homogeneously orthodox values, but also for its intrusions into the fictional text, and it was at that time that standard editions without commentary began to be issued. Scholarly opinion has now begun to swing the other way, with the increased realization that these editors and commentators were not unwelcome intruders in an autonomous folk discourse. Rather, commentators, editors, and redactors, much vilified in modern times for their conservatism and obvious investment in elite values, turn out not to have been intruders in a folk process, but instead central to the fictional enterprise.

In short, the traditional Chinese novel's openness to rewriting and, in the generations following the Ming dynasty, to sequels, as well as its receptivity to commentary, had less to do with the status of its authors than with the fact that the novel itself was a radically different kind of discursive space from the great classics of Western fiction. In the sixteenth and seventeenth centuries, many of the same issues were being contested both in China and in Europe, perhaps most importantly the relationship between ownership and authorship in an age of widespread commercial imprints. Notwithstanding Jin Shengtan's claims, the experience of reading a novel in the late Ming was like listening not so much to the voice of a single author of genius as to an intimate chamber ensemble of voices – writer, commentator, editor. The sympathetic reader is invited to chime in with his own contribution, whether commentary or sequel. When Jin Shengtan advocated interpretive freedom, this is partly what he had in mind:

> The Western Wing is not a work written by an individual named Wang Shifu alone; if I read it carefully, it will also be a work of my own creation, because all the words in The Western Wing happen to be the words that I want to say and that I want to write down.

Of course, there was something more than a little self-serving in Jin's statement, when he himself was responsible for myriad changes in both Water Margin and The Western Wing. (Moreover, since his editions became standard, his own interpretations necessarily stood in the way of the interpretations of later readers.) Still, for good or ill, this open attitude seems to have characterized the way late Ming readers approached all texts, not just the novel. The supposed disregard of Ming publishers and editors for textual integrity, as they tampered even with the texts of the Classics at will, was frequently bemoaned by Qing scholars, but that condemnation was the attitude of a later age.

The ecology of narrative

To early twentieth-century readers of the vernacular short story, the connection between text and folk tradition seemed perfectly transparent. Even in the vernacular short story, however, the ties between written text and folk form vanish upon closer examination. Instead, it is much easier to reconstruct solid relationships among different genres of written narrative.

Vernacular short stories often situate themselves within the context of professional storytelling, imitating the effect of a transcription of a storyteller's performance. Sometimes the narrator explicitly takes on the voice of the storyteller. For example, the first story of Feng Menglong's first collection of vernacular short stories introduces its subject: "Dear audience, now listen to me tell the story of 'The Pearl Shirt,' which illustrates the never-failing retribution of Heaven as a lesson for all young men." An earlier generation of scholars saw the address to an audience as an incontrovertible marker of authenticity: obviously these stories had been directly transcribed from marketplace performances, or perhaps had been used by professional storytellers as their actual notes, or prompt books. Either way, the stories represented to scholars a direct connection to folk literature, to illiterate storytellers, and to a world untainted by the concerns of the literati.

Despite appearances, the relationship between the professional storyteller and the short story is far from transparent. The same markers taken to be indications of storytelling origin are nowhere to be found in the collection *Sixty Stories* (*Liushi jia xiaoshuo*), published by the scholar Hong Pian around 1560, which suggests that these markers are the doing of Feng Menglong himself, who, with his three major collections of vernacular short stories, practically invented the genre.

How can we be sure that these vernacular short stories were not transcriptions of folk storytellers at work? Such evidence as we have of late Ming storytellers, mentioned in informal writing and the like, seems to indicate that the typical storyteller's stock in trade was not ironic stories that undercut listeners' expectations, but rather set pieces performed with straightforward bravura. The storyteller Liu Jingting, for example, was known for his performance of Wu Song's slaying of the tiger, a famous episode from *Water Margin*.

Even more importantly, Feng Menglong's own prefaces to these collections make it clear from the outset that the stories, far from being naive, were highly self-conscious and mediated by elite concerns. Feng felt it necessary to explain how a short story differed from a novel and to justify it as an independent form: "The kind [of narrative] that concerns itself with a single character in a single action and serves to provide entertainment should not be neglected, any more than the northern plays as compared to the southern." Again, we see a recurrent pattern characteristic of the period, as a new genre defines itself by assuming the status and some of the critical apparatus of older ones.

One might imagine all the different varieties of narrative, both fictional and dramatic, as a kind of ecological system. On a broad level, they share the same pool of source material, a shared stratum of narrative. Many of the same plot elements and character types appear in all kinds of fiction and drama from the period: only daughters, beautiful courtesans, brave and unconventional swordsmen, impoverished young scholars hoping to make their way in the world, to name but a few. Much of the cultural energy of this period was derived from these narratives; cults of both love and heroism seem to have grown out of literature, rather than the other way around. Readers imitated text, and life imitated art.

Long novels were frequently variations on lore cycles, like *Journey to the West* or material from lesser-known myths. Southern plays derived their plots mostly from well-known historical episodes. For example, the very first southern play in the Kun style, *Washing Silk* (*Huansha ji*) by Liang Chenyu (ca 1521–ca 1594), relates an episode from the Warring States period, in which the king of Wu became so entranced by the beauty Xi Shi that his kingdom collapsed. *Crying Phoenix* (*Mingfeng ji*, 1570) tells of political events that took place a mere fifteen years before the time of its writing. Conventionally attributed to Wang Shizhen, the authorship of this politically sensitive play was kept anonymous.

Some plays are derived from classical tales, such as Meng Chengshun's (1600–1682) *Mistress and Maid* (*Jiao Hong ji*), an adaptation of the Yuan dynasty story by the same name. In general, recycling was the norm in drama; some sort of precedent can be found for nearly every play of the period, suggesting that the purpose of dramas was less the denouement of plot than the expression of feeling. A reader immersed in traditional narrative would have been able to guess how a play would end; one read or attended *Mistress and Maid* not to find out that the beautiful and sensitive Jiaoniang was doomed to die and never to marry her cousin Shen Chun, but to be moved again by the songs in which each expressed the emotions of first flirtation and then tragic love.

While vernacular stories and classical tales often relate the same plots, these are almost never taken from canonical narratives found in the Classics, but rather from material that had been recorded because it was unexpected or novel. The more closely associated a classical tale was with the market, the less likely it was to be connected with an author; those least associated with the market were, in contrast, the most closely tied to an author, and even to the circumstances of his life, whether ostensibly overheard in conversation or reported by another member of the elite.

When works in different genres use the same plot, the vernacular story almost always derives from the classical tale or the play and not the other way around. This rule is not inviolate; *Peony Pavilion* (*Mudan ting*), widely regarded as the dynasty's greatest play, probably derives from a vernacular precursor. The conversion from one form to another highlights other differences as well. Vernacular stories tend to draw their characters from the lower orders of society, and are often told in a humorous tone. The action of vernacular stories is more often character-driven than it is in classical tales. Some of the finest vernacular stories, particularly those in the third of Feng Menglong's collections, *Constant Words to Awaken the World* (*Xingshi hengyan*), pay a degree of attention to the actual conditions of urban life and the poor that we find nowhere else in the tradition. Finally, unlike drama (especially southern plays), which often confronts matters of empire-wide significance head-on, vernacular fiction does so only obliquely or ironically.

We might think of vernacular stories not as the lowest in status, but as lying at the end of the food chain of transmission. When earlier scholars assumed that these were the source material for Yuan plays, they mistakenly had the chronology reversed. Even when different genres use the same plots, narratives take on different appearances. Two of the most famous vernacular stories from *Stories Old and New*, "The Pearl Shirt" and "The Courtesan's Jewel Box," were both adapted from classical stories published by the writer of classical tales Song Maocheng in 1612, just a little more than a decade before Feng Menglong published their vernacular versions. Later on, "The Courtesan's Jewel Box" also inspired a southern play.

The two versions of "The Pearl Shirt" tell exactly the same story. In an age when adulteresses were not only the target of vilification but even criminals, Sanqiao is a most unusual character, the sympathetic adulteress. She is a young wife who is seduced while her husband is away on business, and when her husband finds out, he divorces her. She is remorseful but ends up married off as the concubine of a kind official, with whom she later intervenes to save her former husband's life. The two are then reunited and live happily ever after. Song Maocheng's classical version focuses attention on the intricacies of karmic retribution. In contrast, the richness of detail in the vernacular version turns the story into an exploration of the attachment between husband and wife that persists even after their bond has been legally dissolved.

Both versions of "The Courtesan's Jewel Box" tell of the tragic love affair between a beautiful young prostitute and the wealthy scion of an elite family. After the two lovers manage to buy her freedom from her madam, the young man betrays her by promising her to a merchant. In response, she dramatically flings the contents of box after box of priceless jewels (previously hidden from her lover) into the river and then drowns herself. Perhaps there is the kernel of a real-life affair in this story; this sort of complicated relationship between courtesans and elite men was certainly an important part of the culture of the age.

Song Maocheng's classical version concludes with an account of how he got hold of this story. In 1600, hearing what had happened from a friend, Song was determined to write it all down, but that night the girl visited him in a dream and warned him not to make her story public. Years later, Song completed the story after entreating her spirit for forgiveness. Does this mode of transmission seem any more credible than Feng Menglong's implication that the story came from a storyteller? Surely not. As literary historians have noted, classical narrative has always tended to dress itself in apparently factual details even when relating what was fantastic. The differences in alleged provenance between the two narratives, along with most of the other ways in which they diverge, primarily have to do with the two different genres.

Song Maocheng's are among the most carefully crafted and sophisticated of all classical stories, so most likely he made up "The Courtesan's Jewel Box" out of a number of elements that were already in recurrent use in narratives of the period: a courtesan who is a sympathetic heroine, a star-crossed love affair opposed by parents, the casket filled with untold wealth cast aside. Feng Menglong probably came up with his vernacular version after reading Song's tale. The two men came from very much the same small cross-section of Ming society; well-educated members of the elite from neighboring regions, they shared many acquaintances and friends. Feng Menglong was famously well connected, while Song Maocheng was friends with a number of important contemporaries, among them Chen Jiru, Tan Yuanchun, and Chen Zilong. There is no reason to think of the work of one as being of lower or higher social status than that of the other.

It may be more accurate to think of anonymity in vernacular fiction not as a reflection on the author or the genre's social status, but as an intrinsic quality of the genre. Poetry and drama were authored texts whose production was often part of public life. Tang Xianzu openly acknowledged that he spent his retirement from official service writing his four famous plays. Yet while Feng Menglong published many writings under his own name, his vernacular short stories were anonymous.

During the late Wanli period, a number of collections of anecdotes, or, more accurately, short narratives, began to be published. These collections, authored by elite men under their own names, frequently situate themselves in the context of social life by claiming to be the product of casual transmission, as stories told by elite men at parties and then recorded. Some have titles that reflect these claims, as in Wang Tonggui's *Tales Overheard* (*Ertan*, 1597). Other examples of amateur transmission of stories among social equals include Xu Changzuo's *Complete Records of Yanshan* (*Yanshan conglu*, 1602). The new career path of the *littérateur* who was an all-purpose professional man of letters, often distinguished in multiple genres, opened the way to publications of this type.

Sometimes the transmission of these relatively unornamented anecdotes seems to have in fact been casual. Qian Xiyan's *Garden of Cleverness* (*Kuaiyuan*, 1613) is presented as a series of short notes, arranged by topic, that do not resemble stories. While this may be true in some cases, casual transmission is less likely in the case of narratives that are clearly literary. These collections, which are elaborate, longer, and show the earmarks of craft, include Xie Zhaozhe's *Five Assorted Offerings* (*Wuza zu*, 1616), a collection that includes tales written in imitation of the Tang style.

The relationship between Song Maocheng's story and Feng Menglong's version is far from unique. Three of the stories in Ling Mengchu's *Slapping the Table in Amazement (Pai'an jingqi*, 1628) are based on classical tales from *Eternal History (Genshi*, 1626) by Pan Zhiheng, who was also famous as a drama critic. This is an enormous compilation ranging back to the Tang dynasty but consisting mostly of Pan's own work. Pan claims that his stories are based on actual incidents; Ling Mengchu presented his tales as though they were the performance of a storyteller, by this time the standard form for the vernacular story.

Since generic norms were extremely fluid, we may think of these claims of transmission as floating tropes, appropriated in different ways by different genres. Instead of claiming to be simply a collector of folk performances, Ling Mengchu, in a preface signed with his own name, adopts the stance not of the antiquarian or the ethnographer, but of the scholar whose stories are part of his social life, as he makes clear in his explanation of the title, *Slapping the Table in Amazement*: "Whenever my examination classmates visited me, they would ask me for one of my stories to read, and on finishing it, would invariably slap the table and exclaim, 'What an amazing thing!'" By publishing under his own name and placing his stories in the context of elite social life, Ling Mengchu claims for the vernacular story something of the cachet of the classical tale.

Other genres had no part in this ecology. Classical stories modeled on the fourteenth-century collection *New Tales Told by Lamplight (Jiandeng xinhua)* were popular in the late Ming. These stories were romances, closely related to the "scholar-and-beauty" novels that were to become popular in the early decades of the Qing. Writers of other classical tales were eccentric men of the elite like Song Maocheng and Pan Zhiheng, highly respected for their work in other genres. The two most famous writers of vernacular tales, Ling Mengchu and Feng Menglong, were also elite men, involved in but probably not wholly dependent on commercial publishing. In contrast, the writers of these classical romances were largely obscure. They embarked on this work not as an expression of personal idiosyncrasy, but to keep body and soul together. Hu Yinglin, the first critic to direct serious attention to classical fiction, was particularly scornful of them.

Feng Menglong and Ling Mengchu

The amateur ideal, according to which a work of art was a disinterested act of self-expression to be given away as a gift upon completion, was no less vital as a myth in literature than in the visual arts. Increasingly eroded in reality, the ideal retained its pull on the imagination. As we have already seen, how exactly an author ought to be paid for his writing was one of the most heavily fraught concerns of the age, since the taboo against receiving payment continued to exert power even as unprecedented opportunities arose for literate men to make a living with their writing brushes.

Nonetheless, disdain for professionals and admiration for amateurs was not by any means universal. The idea that everyone ought to feel that way is tinged with elite defensiveness and wishful thinking; one could perhaps even say that the late Ming disparagement of professionals should properly be read as anxiety over the increasingly blurred distinctions between professionals and amateurs. Remarkable fluidity in social status was true even for people of traditionally base standing: contemporary accounts by and about professional artists and actors like Liu Jingting the storyteller or Zhu Chusheng the actress make clear that they took their crafts very seriously and regarded themselves in all important respects as the equals of the elites with whom they consorted. New, more flexible ways of thinking about status also applied to men like Feng Menglong, participants in the examination system who made a living from various literary activities. Feng's life history illustrates many of the trends discussed in the first section. Thoroughly imbued with the culture of Suzhou and of the market, he was also what by the late Ming had become a type: a clever, talented man who was a longtime failure in the examination system.

It is easy to confuse the joking tone of vernacular literature with mere frivolity, but whether they were moneymaking enterprises or not, a certain consistency of moral tone does seem to unite all the works of Feng Menglong's *oeuvre*. The titles of all three of the short-story collections associated with him are meant not ironically but seriously, as clarion calls to decent, commonsense behavior in a misbehaving age: *Clear Words to Instruct the World* (*Yushi mingyan*, also known as *Stories Old and New, Gujin xiaoshuo*), *Comprehensive Words to Warn the World* (*Jingshi tongyan*), and *Constant Words to Awaken the World* (*Xingshi hengyan*). Unlike contemporary works of erotica or entertainment, in which the didactic content was secondary (or even ironic), these stories treat the reward of the good and the punishment of the bad as a matter of great seriousness. The protagonists are usually people of humble background, but the moral questions they confront are not in the least trivialized.

The writings of thinkers like Wang Yangming, Li Zhi, and Yuan Hongdao, all cited with some frequency by Feng Menglong, allowed for an ethical earnestness to coexist with a suspicion of traditional elite forms and accepted wisdom. In Feng Menglong's view, the division that makes the most sense lies not between professionals and amateurs, but between ivory-tower pedantry and moral teachings that everyone, no matter how humble, can practice. The stories consistently endorse this morality, the greatest sins in their world being prudishness and hypocritical self-righteousness, while no shame attaches to earning honest money even, for example, as a beggar.

What we know of Feng Menglong's life outside his literary pursuits also shows a certain seriousness of purpose and deep commitment to core Confucian beliefs. He seems to have cultivated close personal friendships, first with Eastern Forest partisans, and later with Revival Society members. At the age of sixty, after decades of failure in the examinations, he happily accepted a courtesy appointment as a lowly official in an impoverished district. There he applied himself in a variety of good works, including distributing medicine to the poor and reducing the rates of female infanticide, all detailed in the gazetteer he compiled in those days. There is no way to be certain, but it seems probable that he and Ling Mengchu, both quite elderly men by this time, died fighting for the lost cause of the Ming dynasty in its last days.

Feng Menglong stands out even in an age when writers worked in multiple genres and involved themselves in every facet of the production of texts. His work, which ranged from classical commentary to ribald folk songs, encompassed great achievements in almost every genre of nonelite literature, including vernacular fiction long and short, jokes, anecdotes, drama, and popular song. These were also all fundamentally commercial endeavors. Feng was sensitive enough to market potential that in 1615 he urged a publisher to offer a high price for the writer Shen Defu's manuscript copy of *The Plum in the Golden Vase*. Three years before the novel's eventual publication, he espied some commercial promise there.

Feng Menglong is now best known for essentially inventing the genre of the vernacular story as we know it. Before Feng, we have only Hong Pian's anthology, *Sixty Stories*, in which it is hard to discern any awareness of the vernacular story as a distinct genre. This collection is strikingly heterogeneous: inconsistently paginated, it includes vernacular narrative, but also some in prosimetric form and a few stories in classical Chinese. It is linked to Feng Menglong's collections, however, by the circumstances of its publication. *Sixty Stories* is very much a part of the world of commercial publishing that was, by the middle of the sixteenth century, becoming so important. A retired official of elite background, Hong Pian nevertheless envisioned his anthology as a moneymaking venture along with his other projects, which included the reprinting of *Yijian zhi*, his ancestor Hong Mai's collection of stories, as well as a collection of anecdotes about Tang poetry.

Feng Menglong's first collection of short stories, *Stories Old and New*, is, even at first glance, quite different from *Sixty Stories*. Most scholars agree that although a number of writers were involved, Feng himself was responsible for the lion's share of the work, whether as author or as editor. The collection as a whole is consistent in tone and in its concerns. For example, its world features many urbanites – traveling merchants, shopkeepers, prostitutes – and few officials. At the same time, according to Feng's preface, his approach is meant to be ostensibly antiquarian: the stories are more frequently set in the Song dynasty than in any other period, and Feng's major formal innovation of a shorter narrative that introduces the main story is ostensibly a return to Song originals now lost.

Feng published three volumes, each with forty stories, known collectively as the *Three Words (Sanyan)*, in the space of seven years in the 1620s. His level of participation in the volumes tapered off with time: he probably wrote nineteen stories for the first volume; in the second, sixteen; in the third, no more than two. Each of the second and third volumes was mostly written by a different collaborator; some of the best-known stories are the work of the collaborator for the third volume.

Our knowledge of Feng's career as a whole comes from twentieth-century reconstructions, mostly because none of the works for which he is best known now was published under his name. In mainstream genres, he achieved only minor distinction. Like all educated men of the period, Feng wrote poetry and prose, now mostly lost. He also wrote two important handbooks on the *Spring and Autumn Annals (Chunqiu)* that were widely circulated and used by students preparing for the examinations.

Certain threads run through much of Feng's work. Even in drama, his concern was always with the pragmatic. He adapted *Peony Pavilion*, among numerous other plays, to make it, in his eyes, more stage-worthy. His collections of poetry and songs implicitly disparaged more mainstream poetry: like others of his time, he felt that the use of poetry in the examinations had tainted it, making creativity and self-expression impossible. In Feng's view, only folk traditions remained vital. He put together collections of lyrics to local tunes, *Hanging Twigs (Guazher)* and *Mountain Songs (Shan'ge)*, the one of northern melodies and the other of local Suzhou melodies, and also compiled an anthology of songs from ancient times to the present called *The Celestial Art Played Anew (Taixia xinzou)*. In terms of longer fiction, he seems to have edited the erotic novel *The Embroidered Couch (Xiuta yeshi)* and worked extensively on two long novels, *Quelling the Demons* and the historical *New Chronicles of the Warring States (Xin lieguozhi*, originally published ca 1570). He reshaped and added sections to both in order to make them more acceptable to elite tastes, making *New Chronicles of the Warring States*, for example, correspond more closely to orthodox historical sources.

The *Three Words* were quickly followed by two collections by Ling Mengchu (1580–1645). Adapted from classical tales, anecdotes, and plays, the stories that constitute *Slapping the Table in Amazement* (*Pai'an jingqi*, 1628) and *Slapping the Table in Amazement, Second Collection* (*Erke pai'an jingqi*, 1632) number seventy-eight in total. The commercial success of *Three Words* no doubt opened the door to men like Ling Mengchu, who was even more open about his participation in the literary marketplace. Ling's father had been a successful official who after retirement took up an active career in publishing in the 1570s and 1580s. Like many men of the elite, he exchanged work as a civil servant for another sort of public work. He collated a number of works on the Classics and wrote commentaries to early histories. When Ling Mengchu was born in 1580, it was into a class that had not existed a generation before: men with impeccable elite credentials who nonetheless openly made their living by writing and publishing.

The Ling family had for generations intermarried with the wealthy Min family, who were invested in publishing concerns, and Ling Mengchu collaborated with his cousin Min Qiji on numerous projects at the high end of the publishing business, putting out deluxe, lavishly illustrated editions of the Classics, drama, and selected works of literature. Other than the vernacular story collections, Ling Mengchu's literary activities were almost as wide-ranging as Feng Menglong's, including plays and dramatic criticism. The list of his connections reads like an all-star cast of the late Ming world of letters: he corresponded or visited with Yuan Zhongdao, Chen Jiru, Tang Xianzu, and other luminaries, while his work was featured in anthologies or commentaries by Feng Menglong, the critic Qi Biaojia, and the playwright Yuan Yuling. The two cosmopolitan cousins wielded their pens for profit, but not to keep starvation at bay.

Other collections of short stories appeared in the years that followed, though none came close to those of Feng and Ling in influence. Some scholars think that Feng Menglong's major collaborator in *Constant Words to Awaken the World* was the sole author of *The Rocks Nod Their Heads* (*Shi diantou*, 1628), which was largely moralistic in tone and focused on either exemplars or miscreants. Some of these later collections experimented with form. *Clap Your Hands and Rid Yourself of Dust* (*Guzhang juechen*, 1630) comprises four long stories, each of ten chapters. Others, following the same pattern seen in classical collections, came to occupy specialized niches, with entire collections centering on narrowly defined themes: to name a few, homosexual love (*Hat and Hairpins Both, Bian er chai*), romance turned ugly (*Antagonists in Love, Huanxi yuanjia*, 1640), and the city of Hangzhou (*Second Collection of West Lake Stories, Xihu Erji*, 1643).

Feng Menglong and Ling Mengchu may have used a folk form as their mouthpiece to criticize orthodoxy (it is no coincidence that Zhu Xi appears as an incompetent magistrate in two of Ling's stories), but their careers as a whole also speak to the culmination of certain broader trends that had begun much earlier in the dynasty. Feng Menglong in particular was an editor of the first importance in an age when such men controlled the tidal movement of texts, where each reorganization and each iteration with new commentary or prefatory materials earned money for its participants. For example, the *Extensive Records of the Taiping Reign* was one of the most important source texts for the *Three Words*. In 1626, between the publication of the second and third of the *Three Words* and sixty years after the initial republication of the *Extensive Records*, Feng Menglong produced a drastically shortened (or, one could argue, necessarily streamlined) version of the *Extensive Records*. He made money at every turn from the *Extensive Records*. He adapted stories he found in it; arranged narratives in it according to late Ming interests, as in *Anatomy of Love* (*Qingshi leilüe*), his anthology of love stories; and finally returned to the original text, cut it apart, and trimmed it down.

Feng Menglong collated other anthologies in the same way. Taking anecdotes from multiple earlier classical sources, he repackaged and sold them as separate collections focusing on a single concept: *Survey of Talk* (*Gujin tan gai*), *Sack of Wisdom* (*Zhinang*), *Treasury of Jokes* (*Xiaolin*), and *Anatomy of Love* all follow essentially the same form. In none of these is the authorship of an individual anecdote important. For example, even though joke books had been assembled by a number of respected authors such as Li Zhi, Xu Wei, and Zhong Xing, the jokes themselves were not associated with an author and so could be copied into other joke collections without a second thought. Indeed, many of the same jokes moved fluidly from collection to collection. The effect shows up even more clearly in *Survey of Talk*, where anecdotes are followed by comments, sometimes Feng's own and sometimes those of others. Not just the anecdotes, but the comments also have been directly copied from earlier texts. Feng was not the first to work along these lines. Even in the sixteenth century, specialized anthologies had begun to appear, and, at the beginning of the seventeenth century, a generation before Feng, the playwright Mei Dingzuo had assembled two thematic anthologies, one on courtesans and the other on ghosts. Other such thematic anthologies on foxes, female divinities, and so on appeared throughout the first half of the seventeenth century.

At any rate, the story of what happened to the vernacular short stories of Feng and Ling ends as it should. In the 1630s, many editions emerged under Feng's name, even though the man himself was too busy serving as a local official to continue his literary work. He was, in other words, the target of much forgery. Until the twentieth century, most readers encountered the work of Feng Menglong and Ling Mengchu not in the anthologies that had earned their authors so much repute and profit, but in *Marvels New and Old* (*Jingu qiguan*), an anthology published in the 1630s that contained stories selected from Feng's *Three Words* and Ling's two *Amazement* collections. This version was apparently not authorized by either man, and the money it earned went into other hands entirely. Live by the sword, die by the sword.

III. Drama

The rise of the southern drama

In speaking of late Ming southern plays, we refer to both a textual and a performance tradition. The literary form of the southern plays was called a *chuanqi*; the most famous of its various musical forms was called *kunqu*, or "song from Kun." The two, *chuanqi* and *kunqu*, found each other just before the period detailed by this chapter. Around 1557, Liang Chenyu wrote *Washing Silk*, the first play to use a style of singing named after Liang's native region in Jiangsu Province, an area near Suzhou called Kunshan. There was nothing new about the theme of *Washing Silk*, but the play's groundbreaking style of performance created an enormous stir. Liang Chenyu had collaborated with a famous musician, Wei Liangfu, who united elements from a number of folk traditions and established rules of rhyme, sets of tunes, and singing styles to create this new kind of opera. Before this time, libretti from the southern plays had been performed in a few other related styles, but Kun style quickly became the favorite of the wealthy and the elite.

A few generations later, Gu Qiyuan (1565–1628) wrote about the impact of this new style and how quickly it displaced older performance styles:

> It is clearer and more mellifluous . . . and yet combines both harmony and sudden changes in melody, extending one word for several breaths. The elite have endowed it with their spirit and greatly enjoy it. As for the other styles,

they seem to make one want to fall asleep in the daytime; and as for northern
plays, it is like blowing on pipes and beating clay pots – people are bored with
it and even scoff at it.

As Gu Qiyuan's comments make clear, this kind of drama continued to
be closely associated with a musical style. Singing a complicated, highly
literary libretto was central in a Kun-style performance, while spectacle and
dance were decidedly secondary, although a number of these plays, including
Washing Silk, did incorporate dancing scenes.

The late Ming was a great age for the theater. The critic Qi Biaojia listed all
of the plays he attended in the space of seven years during the 1630s, totaling an
astonishing eighty-six individual plays, most of which have unfortunately been
lost. It was not only through performance that the public became acquainted
with drama; the modern scholar Zhuang Yifu lists a total of fifty-six publishers
active in the publication of southern plays in this period.

Southern plays had an unparalleled impact on urban culture. At first a
regional form based near Suzhou, they spread through Jiangnan, and by the
beginning of the seventeenth century, the drama critic Wang Jide writes,
they were popular in Beijing and northern China. Some southern plays were
written by famous officials and performed in the homes of the powerful
and highly placed; others, on more popular themes, were performed at local
fairs and temples. One would have been hard pressed to find anyone in the
Jiangnan area – literate or illiterate, male or female – with less than passing
acquaintance with a score of plays and many more famous arias. Older dramas
were adapted to conform to the generic strictures of southern plays, which in
turn were recycled, rewritten, adapted, simplified and transformed into other
regional forms. If we can speak of a single genre as representative of its age,
that form for the late Ming was southern plays.

Nonetheless, as with fiction, the drama covered in this section represents
only a small cross-section of the plays performed in the period. Scholarship on
drama has tended to favor sophisticated, artful works strongly associated with
an elite author. But the vast majority of performances were probably quite
different. The Kun style, adored by the elite, was not for everyone; even in
its heyday, Wang Jide estimated that only two or three out of every ten plays
performed was in the Kun style. Plays written for one style of performance
could be easily adapted to another, and it is often impossible to determine
strictly from the libretto which style of performance the playwright intended.
Some of the related forms were much easier to understand and in consequence

probably more widely performed. There were other performance traditions whose chief focus, like the later Peking opera, was on virtuosic dance or acrobatics. Local folk forms, many of which have not survived in any form, flourished throughout the empire. Feng Menglong's *Mountain Songs* are a rare example of a folk performance tradition that did get recorded, even if in a rudimentary way.

Many plays, such as the famous Mulian plays which dramatize the hero's journey to the underworld to save his sinful mother, were so closely linked to ritual practice and folk religion that it is difficult to characterize them as either literature or liturgy. In 1582, the most influential version of the Mulian drama was written and professionally printed by Zheng Zhizhen, yet another frustrated failed examination candidate. It was performed extensively in many different forms and unquestionably reached a much wider and more diverse audience than any other play discussed in this section, whose audiences were self-selective. Zhang Dai mentions a single performance that lasted three days and three nights and attracted more than ten thousand spectators. At the same time, the drama connoisseur Qi Biaojia loathed the Mulian dramas, complaining of their noisy coarseness.

Sinologists seemingly cannot resist comparing southern plays of the sixteenth and seventeenth centuries to their English contemporaries. This moment was a high-water mark for drama in both cultures. A southern play observes tight structural principles, akin to the five acts of a Shakespearean play. No subplots are left dangling, and all characters are accounted for. No playwright began writing without knowing the ending in advance: the first act summarizes the story; in the second and third, the male and female leads introduce themselves; and the play concludes with a great reunion. The plotting and pacing of the work as a whole carefully alternate the tragic with the comic and solos with choruses.

But southern plays also differ in distinct ways from what those familiar with European traditions might consider normal in drama. Chinese drama connoisseurs were minutely attuned to every detail of singing. Arias alternated with spoken dialogue, and both were performed in a stylized form of Mandarin that bore little resemblance to any language spoken on the streets. (Some acts, intended to speed the narrative along, lack any song at all.) Set to tunes that were part of an established repertory that in part probably long pre-dated southern plays, the arias were written in a poetic language filled with allusions to earlier literature. To connoisseurs and performers, the tune title indicated how an aria was to be sung, including the melody, the number of lines, the number of syllables, and the meter. Playwrights did not write music, only the lyrics.

Other details make it clear that these plays were easily adapted for home performance. Players did not wear elaborate costumes or makeup. Musically, the most important instruments for accompaniment were flute, guitar, and lute, but for home performances, something as simple as a fan for beating time might suffice. In fact, the form of the southern play, in which, for example, each scene is separately titled, suggests that many were from quite early on appreciated at home, in private reading, as what became known as "desktop plays" (*antou ju*). If one can speak of a public sphere associated with the drama at this time, it was not an actual theater, but a virtual one found in the imprints, manuals, and appreciations that circulated plays and discussions about them. Rather than in large theaters charging admission to the public, southern plays tended to be performed in private venues, on a very small scale, either with no stage at all or with a simple rug marking off a space for performance.

Drama was performed by various kinds of troupes, each having its own specialty, with overlapping but distinct repertoires. First, there were the imperial household's private performers, but their audience was limited to the court. Some troupes resided permanently in cities, and their repertoire seems to have consisted of plays with obvious didactic content. An example of such a play would be the sensationalistic *A Handful of Snow* (*Yipeng xue*) by the Suzhou dramatist Li Yu (ca 1591–ca 1671), hereafter referred to as Li Xuanyu to avoid confusion with another Li Yu (1611–1680), in which the decapitated head of a loyal retainer who has sacrificed his life for his master is passed around for much of the play. Other troupes spent part of their time in the city and the rest on tours to country villages. Finally, some troupes were fully itinerant, performing at different local temples and market fairs. Those that focused on performances in temples obviously specialized in plays with strong religious content.

From the late Wanli period to the end of the dynasty, the dramatic troupes with the most cachet were those privately owned by wealthy elite families, performing for their pleasure and that of their guests. Comprising up to thirty actors, actresses, and musicians, these troupes mostly performed the libretti that are still studied as literature today. These private troupes were a trend that took off in the late Wanli period. Owning one of these troupes came to be a status symbol of the highest order, an extravagance for the extremely rich. Recent work has documented how actors were exchanged between elite households, in much the same way as prized antiques, to strengthen friendships or to return favors.

Freed of the obligation to appeal to paying audiences, these private troupes might reflect their owners' rarefied tastes in their repertoire. They typically specialized in dramas by elite playwrights, especially since some troupe owners, like Ruan Dacheng, author of *The Swallow Letter* (*Yanzi jian*), were themselves playwrights. It required erudition to understand many of the scripts and great skill to execute the songs in such a way that they could be understood; in such cases, men of the elite were involved in every step, from the writing of the play, through rehearsals, to the actual performance. Sometimes, troupe owners were able to control virtually every aspect of the production. A wealthy connoisseur might train his performers from the time they were children; he would personally direct the production and sometimes even write the libretto himself. These plays were impossible to write without a solid classical education, and the great playwrights of the age, Tang Xianzu, Shen Jing (1553–1610), Ruan Dacheng, and Li Xuanyu, were often degree holders from elite families. Still, the very highest level of creative control, where impresario and playwright were one, was closed off to all but the very rich.

Like modern-day sinologists, Ming contemporaries also felt compelled to compare southern drama to another form, not, of course, Shakespeare's plays, but northern drama. Many of these comparisons, relying heavily on age-old regional stereotypes of the north and the south, were limited to characterizations of northern plays as lacking in refinement but endowed with energy and vigor, whereas southern plays were regarded as refined, leisurely, soft, and melodious, feminized attributes that had been associated with the Jiangnan region for centuries.

There were indeed obvious differences between northern and southern plays. In terms of performance, they differed in two important respects. First, a southern play was very long, while plays in the northern style were usually limited to four suites of songs, although there were exceptions, like *The Western Wing*. In contrast, southern plays averaged around thirty acts, with a few as long as one hundred acts. Each act might take as long as an hour, although debate continues on precisely how languorous the tempi were in the Ming. So, while most northern plays took up an evening or an afternoon, an entire southern play typically went on for two full days or more. The very length of the form indicates that it was the preserve of leisure and wealth. Consequently, from very early on, southern plays were often performed in excerpts; climactic scenes, or those showcasing the talents of a specific performer, were the ones most often staged.

Second, unlike in northern plays, where only a single role type was allowed to sing in a given act, all the actors in southern plays could have singing parts.

Southern plays included arias sung not just by the leading roles but also by comic players; within acts were interspersed duets, trios, and choruses, much of the pleasure of the play being derived from the shifting focus and point of view. Again, unlike their northern counterparts, southern dramas permitted the use of different rhyme schemes within a single act, which also encouraged increased plot complexity. Early northern plays, those from the Yuan and the early Ming, tended to be formulaic in the way singing was integrated with the rest of the drama and consequently also in the relations among the characters. Northern plays are forced by the constraints of their genre to concentrate on the actions of a single protagonist.

Nevertheless, the two kinds of drama differed more in theory than in practice, and by the late Ming the northern form had changed so much that there is no tidy way to separate the two forms. The best-known northern dramas of the late Ming, *Four Cries of the Gibbon (Sisheng yuan)* by the eccentric, tormented Xu Wei, undermined the old generic constraints to such an extent that Wang Jide, Xu's disciple, considered these plays a premier example of southern plays, to rank alongside Tang Xianzu's work as the greatest of the dynasty. Completed in around 1580, this strikingly creative set of four linked plays is integrated by broad thematic concerns but formally heterogeneous. The first play has one act, the second and third both have two, and the final play has five acts. The first three use northern rhymes and tunes, while the last follows southern conventions. Each of the four dramas toys with a certain preconception about identity. In three of the plays, gender is performed, donned, and divested like a theatrical part. The first two plays take on the question of what identity remains to us after death. All four self-consciously refer to the theater itself, reflecting on the conditions and circumstances of performance. Formal experimentation with the generic rules of drama cannot be separated from the exploration of philosophical questions in these plays.

The Mad Drummer (Kuang gushi yuyang sannong), the first play, presents a showdown in the underworld between two ghosts, with the dead Mi Heng's reenactment of his famous excoriation of the tyrant Cao Cao. The second, *Zen Master Yutong (Yu Chanshi cuixiang yimeng)*, perhaps the oddest of the four, begins with a prostitute whose seduction of a monk leads to his suicide; in the second act, the monk is reincarnated as a female prostitute who watches a performance of that earlier seduction. The third and fourth plays, *A Female Mulan (Ci Mulan tifu congjun)* and *Female Top Candidate (Nü zhuangyuan cihuang defeng)*, both involve girls who cross-dress as young men. Although these two are comparatively straightforward treatments of identity and performance, they have received more critical attention than the others.

The virtuosic experimentation of *Four Cries of the Gibbon* opened the way to even bolder tinkering with the conventions of northern drama. The northern plays that eventually emerged in the late Ming, written in many cases by southerners and often incorporating southern tunes and rhymes, had little to do with the older form. Many playwrights wrote in both forms, or, to put it more accurately, they wrote both short and long plays. In the late Ming, this seems to have been something of the norm. Chen Yujiao (fl. Wanli period, between 1573 and 1620), Ye Xianzu (fl. Tianqi reign, between 1621 and 1627), and Meng Chengshun (fl. Chongzhen reign, between 1628 and 1644) all wrote southern and northern plays, although, as the dynasty wound to an end, the balance tilted more and more heavily towards southern plays. Ling Mengchu wrote both types, but only a few of his northern plays survive. The choice of form seems to have been determined by theme. Chen Yujiao used northern plays to explore border themes. Other playwrights used northern plays for shorter, more tightly structured narratives. The old pattern of four acts gave way to a range from one to ten; the convention of one singer per act was similarly modified. The southern form had in practice become the new norm; in response, as a kind of compensation, the northern play became increasingly playful in its use of formal conventions. For example, Ling Mengchu wrote his dramatic adaptations of the Tang story of Curly Beard in three parts with a different singer in each one: first Li Jing, then Red Whisk, and finally Curly Beard himself.

Drama was a perfect vehicle for many of the concerns of this age to the point that the late Ming sense of reality was profoundly colored by the sensibilities of the theater. While contemporaries complained about the artificiality and emotional disengagement of poetry, no one, not even those critical of drama, would have said such a thing about the theater. Instead, people were too busy recording the intensity of their personal responses to theater. In an age when concerns about status permeated virtually every form of cultural expression, role-playing seemed a particularly apt metaphor for personal identity. The fear that appearance and reality might not correspond, that how one appeared might not correlate with what one was, was a cliché on the stage: boys turned out to be girls, courtesans turned out to be elite daughters and vice versa, servants impersonated their masters, scholars exposed themselves as stupid prigs, and girls knew more about Classics than men. The same cliché also described reality offstage, with parvenus assuming the air of those to the manner born, while many elites were hopeful that their own behavior might manifest a more genuinely refined essence. Onstage and offstage, language – with its age-old promises for self-expression – could also be a means of disguise.

But southern plays touched on other deep concerns as well. Each incorporated action taking place in different locations in the empire (supernatural action, as intervention or a journey to another realm, also contributed to the plot). In this increasingly open society, the southern play was a window onto imaginary travels.

Much more than northern plays, southern plays focused on romance, with which they came to be identified strongly by contemporaries. Typically, the plays feature a young man and a teenaged girl, whose relationship is somehow liminal. They are either engaged or in love. Their feelings are neither wholly sanctioned nor wholly illicit, and the play tells of how the couple pass through various obstacles like travel, family opposition, political turmoil, or rivals in love to come together at the end, their union finally legitimated by society. Both girl and boy demonstrate fidelity, though the young man quite often emerges with another wife as well.

By juxtaposing a domestic plot that involves romance against another plot with geopolitical ramifications, the form of these plays makes an argument about how the domestic and the political are related. Sometimes the domestic plot is of primary importance, and sometimes the political, but they are always interwoven. In traditional China, with its system of arranged marriage, there was always ambivalence about how feeling and passion ought to be integrated into social norms. Southern dramas were able to ask in a way virtually impossible in any other form a question of great importance to late Ming philosophy, namely what the role of personal feeling was in society as a whole.

Many of these plays fetishize a specific object, whether a love token (like the poem written on a maple leaf in Wang Jide's *Written on Red*, *Tihong ji*), an heirloom (like the phoenix hairpin in Shen Jing's *Falling in Love*, *Yizhong qing*), some object of enormous political significance (like the priceless jade cup Li Xuanyu writes about in *Handful of Snow*), or some combination of all three. In every case, the object moves from one person to another, and some of its movements have to be accidental. For example, how does the priceless cup end up in the hands of the penniless maidservant? Through those transfers of objects, the playwright depicts the interconnectedness of society.

Southern plays depict entire societies in cross-section, with the poor, the rich, and the middling classes all in interaction, each commenting on the actions and thoughts of the others. Even when they deal with the gravest subject matter, these plays always involve a blend of comic and tragic, of the low and the high, and quite frequently they meditate on how people of different stations fit together into a single society. This mix was true even on the level of language. Since the development of the lyric in the Song dynasty, the manipulation of registers of language had become one of the main tools of Chinese writers. Shifting register was a way to signify a break in public discourse where intimacy might reside. Nowhere else in Chinese literature was a sensitivity to different kinds and levels of language more important than in southern plays, where scatological humor in the coarsest vernacular imaginable could lie cheek by jowl with quotations from the Classics and allusions to Tang poetry. In one famous act in Tang Xianzu's *Peony Pavilion*, a hermaphrodite gives her X-rated sexual history in a long parody of the *Thousand Word Classic*. The poetry itself constantly shifts: sometimes doggerel, sometimes dreamy lyric, sometimes beautifully constructed parallel couplets. It is as if the lyrics embedded in drama pose an ancient question, central to Chinese poetics, of how poetry as self-expression might function in a new social context.

In drama we also see the culmination of certain trends in the circulation and production of texts that had begun in the middle of the sixteenth century. The volume of publication associated with drama was immense, including not only whole plays, but also anthologies of popular scenes and handbooks of model arias for the multitudes of aficionados who wanted to try their own hand at composition. By the turn of the seventeenth century, a culture of drama appreciation or drama enthusiasm had arisen, generating the production of even more text: guides for drama appreciation, informal writings in which devotion (even obsession) characterized the author, and detailed commentary through which a reader could participate in the textual process as actively as did the playwright.

One pattern we observe repeatedly in this period is how awareness of genre arises out of certain conditions of printing and writing. Not only was the late Ming a golden era for the writing of new plays, it was also a critical period for the rediscovery and reevaluation of earlier drama. As in fiction, some of the most influential writing in drama appeared in the guise of editing, and only in recent generations have scholars come to realize the extent to which editors of this period were also creative writers.

Most notably, the "Yuan drama" was invented in the late Ming, or rather, as with so much of the canon of traditional literature, our modern understanding of Yuan drama is largely a product of the print industry in late Ming China.

Stephen West and Wilt Idema have shown conclusively that Zang Maoxun's (1550–1620) *Anthology of Yuan Plays* (*Yuanqu xuan*) must be understood within its Wanli context. For the last four hundred years, most readers have come into contact with Yuan drama only through the prism of Zang's redactions, and these plays have often mistakenly been understood as a reflection of Yuan concerns. Only now, by examining the few editions that survive from earlier periods, have scholars determined the extent to which Zang freely rewrote and edited, transforming earlier texts both for effect (he liked a big climactic ending) and for ideological reasons (to accord with his sense of Confucian propriety).

Zang Maoxun served as an official in the capital until he was sent home in disgrace for having had a homosexual liaison with a student at the Imperial Academy. From then on, he made a living in the world of letters, specializing in the editing and anthologizing of texts from earlier periods. He was most famous for his *Anthology of Yuan Plays*, but he also compiled anthologies of ancient and Tang poetry. Again, like other figures we have encountered, he was thoroughly involved in the business end of publishing. In his case, he personally hired carvers to produce printing blocks and later sent his own servant to Beijing to sell copies of his books. Published in two batches, one in 1615 and the other in 1616, *Anthology of Yuan Plays* came out in handsome volumes, containing almost four hundred illustrations in all, clearly high-end products for wealthy readers. Although their contents led later readers to mistake these for production or performance copies, the appearance of the volumes confirms what philological research has shown, namely that these one hundred plays, ninety-four ostensibly from the Yuan, were all heavily rewritten by Zang.

Fans of drama also went back in time to create a history for the southern plays. The antecedents to southern plays (*xiwen* or *nanxi*) had been performed to different music, and moreover southern plays only took off in popularity after *Washing Silk*. Nonetheless, in his *Account of Southern Drama* (*Nanci xulu*), Xu Wei catalogues 113 examples from the Song to the mid-Ming, in effect creating a rich history for the genre that was becoming so popular in his day. He even managed to tie southern drama to the glorious (because indigenously Chinese) Song dynasty, contrasting it to the barbaric sounds of northern plays.

Hardly any of the earlier plays mentioned by Xu Wei have survived, and the few that do in their original form, like those in *The Grand Encyclopedia of the Yongle Era*, do not support the idea of a continuous tradition of southern plays. As with northern plays, extant southern plays are not examples of what the genre was in the Song or early Ming, but instead works that have been mediated and thoroughly rewritten by late Ming aficionados. For example, recent tomb finds have enabled scholars to compare late Ming versions of plays like *The White Hare (Baitu ji)* with earlier editions; the late Ming versions, often the only ones that later readers had access to, have clearly been extensively rewritten. These texts were not simply cleaned up, but changed to reflect late Ming aesthetics, concerns, and values.

With some genres, it took centuries for critics to identify a given body of work as a genre and to work out the formal rules governing its composition. In the case of southern plays, born during the printing boom of the late Ming, this critical process was radically accelerated. The genre and its criticism were in fact born together, a highly unusual circumstance in premodern times. Certainly, writers were deeply conscious of the Kun style's novelty. The same Wei Liangfu who invented it also wrote one of its earliest works of criticism, *Rules of Drama (Qulü)*. Within a year or two of *Washing Silk*, Xu Wei had written *An Account of Southern Drama* in lavish praise of the new style, and in the late 1550s he praised the new form's ties to spontaneous folk song. It was, he wrote, derived from "the songs and ballads of the alleys." He argued that to introduce any prosodic regulations would be antithetical to the popular origins of the Kun style. Within a single generation, by the 1580s, Tang Xianzu, Shen Jing, and others were debating the degree to which different arias were singable and how much southern plays needed to be bound by prosodic rules.

To a remarkable extent, there was no line in drama demarcating critics from writers. Virtually all the important playwrights took well-known positions on the important theoretical questions. Perhaps it is more appropriate to think of these men as producers, not just of dramatic texts, but also of all the textual paraphernalia that surrounded drama. Xu Wei was not unusual on this score, and he even integrated playwriting and criticism in his only other major dramatic work, *A Song in Place of Howling (Ge dai xiao)*, which opens with a statement of general principles contrasting this play with Yuan examples of northern plays. Xu Fuzuo (1560–1630), the author of *Discourse on Drama (Qulun)*, wrote four southern plays, including *The Red Pear Blossom (Hongli ji)*, as well as two northern ones. Qi Biaojia, the avid theatergoer who evaluated as many plays as he could get his hands on, also wrote a southern play based on the story of the Han general Su Wu.

More than in other genres of the period, anthologizing, publishing, and writing of drama were profoundly intertwined, bound together by a single culture of connoisseurship. Wang Jide, best known as the author of *Rules of*

Prosody, was also a major anthologist of northern plays (he criticized Zang Maoxun for his editorial liberties), and an author of southern plays. One of his plays, *A Male Queen* (*Nan wanghou*), has received considerable critical scrutiny in recent years. Drama appreciation was closely associated with other sophisticated aesthetic pleasures. *Recompiled Texts on Connoisseurship* (*Chongding xinshang pian*) sets Pan Zhiheng's comments on opera next to those of writers like Yuan Hongdao, Gao Lian (1527–1603), and others on matters like painting, flower arrangement, and food.

Whereas novelists were pseudonymous and associated with a single work, famous playwrights tended to be public literary men, prolific in all forms and especially in their chosen one. They were openly part of the marketplace of words. Li Xuanyu, in addition to thirty-two southern plays, also authored a work on the prosody of northern plays. The growth of dramatic criticism was also related to the rise of manuals in which consumer goods and experiences were evaluated. Though of unparalleled importance in late Ming culture, drama was still only one object for consumption. Lü Tiancheng's *Classification of Drama* (*Qupin*) and Qi Biaojia's *Classification of Drama from Far Mountain Hall* (*Yuanshan tang qupin*) and *Classification of Plays from Far Mountain Hall* (*Yuanshan tang jupin*), in which southern plays were ranked and evaluated, might all be seen to fit into this broader category of manuals.

Drama's self-consciousness had everything to do with the speed at which texts could be disseminated in print. Zang Maoxun's *Selection of Yuan Drama*, published in 1615, covered the Yuan and only the first century of the Ming. In contrast, Shen Tai was able to include contemporary plays in his two anthologies, *Northern Plays of the Great Ming* (*Sheng Ming zaju*, 1629) and the *Second Collection of Northern Plays of the Great Ming* (*Sheng Ming zaju erji*, 1641). Meng Chengshun, author of *Mistress and Maid* (*Jiao Hong ji*) as well as a number of other important southern plays, took this trend to its natural conclusion in his anthology of sixty *Famous Plays Ancient and Modern* (*Gujin mingju*, 1633), which included four by the anthologist himself.

Peony Pavilion *and the cult of love*

At the end of the sixteenth century, the retired official Tang Xianzu (1550–1616) found instant success with *Peony Pavilion* (*Mudan ting*). Within a few years, the play was published in numerous private and commercial editions, read in private, and performed onstage, and had inspired many imitators. The play tells how Du Liniang, a sheltered young girl, takes a walk in her garden and, stirred by the springtime, falls in love with a young man she meets in an erotic dream. Lovesick, she pines away and dies, but not before making a self-portrait of herself. Years later, that portrait is found by Liu Mengmei, the young man in her dream. He in turn falls in love with the girl in the portrait and entreats her to show herself to him. The girl's ghost responds to his summons, and the two begin a passionate love affair. The ghost begs the young man to disinter her body, which turns out to be miraculously preserved. The resurrected girl and the young man marry, and their union is eventually recognized by her initially disbelieving parents.

A plot summary cannot indicate the difficulty of the play's language. The definitive modern edition contains over 1,700 explanatory notes for the play's 55 acts. Numerous passages remain so opaque that scholarly disagreement as to their meaning will never be fully resolved: some are contemporary usages lost in the mists of time, and some allude to obscure texts, but many ambiguities are clearly deliberate on the part of the author. Performed onstage, these passages would be impossible for a live audience to understand, instead contributing to an oneiric, sensuous atmosphere, central to the play's overall effect.

Beloved by some as the literary embodiment of passion itself, *Peony Pavilion*'s distinctive language was the subject of heated contemporary debate. Some contemporaries thought it was virtually unsingable. Shen Jing, an extremely prolific playwright who was almost the exact contemporary of Tang Xianzu, espoused a kind of prosodic fundamentalism, insisting that drama's first duty was to follow strict rules of prosody, which he laid out in *Formulary for the Nine Modes* (*Nan jiugong pu*). He and his followers, the so-called Wujiang School, asserted that the southern play's first priority was the stage; the poetic beauty of a song was a secondary consideration. Tang Xianzu, and his Linchuan School (named after his hometown in Jiangxi), were favorite targets. The two great vernacular short-story writers Feng Menglong and Ling Mengchu were also followers of the Wujiang School, perhaps because of their general predilection for plain diction. Feng Menglong and others, including the drama theorist Lü Tiancheng, rewrote *Peony Pavilion* for stage purposes and to bring it into closer conformity with the rules of prosody.

We know from the comments of hundreds of readers that the play's greatest impact was not on such a theoretical plane; its admirers – men, women, elite, nonelite – were deeply affected on a visceral level. Numerous playwrights rewrote it, not just to correct perceived prosodic transgressions but because they had been deeply inspired by the original. Both male and female readers recopied it by hand and passed it along to friends. In a practice that continued well into the next dynasty, a number of them interspersed their own comments with the text. One actress identified so closely with Du Liniang that she actually died onstage in the middle of a climactic scene. Other sensitive women were said to have been so deeply affected that they fell ill and died after reading it. Two scenes in particular, "Wandering in the Garden" and "Wakened from a Dream," have been an important part of the performance repertoire from the sixteenth century to the present day. The love affair between the young scholar Liu Mengmei and the beauty Du Liniang, equals in both literary talent and looks, left its imprint on nearly every romantic couple in drama and fiction to come.

The play stirred up questions about the proper role of women and the place of feeling in society. One may even consider *Peony Pavilion* as the heart of the cult of romantic love (*qing*) that came to flourish in the period. This fascination with romance was closely related to the interest of Li Zhi and the Yuan brothers in sincerity and authenticity late in the sixteenth century, but it was in the culture that grew up around the southern play, and this play in particular, that passion, love, and sincerity came to be central concerns.

In the play's preface, Tang Xianzu writes a paean to love, according to which the whole play attests to love's power:

> The living may die of love; by its power, the dead live again. Love is not love at its fullest if one who lives is unwilling to die for it, or if it cannot restore to life one who has so died. And must the love that comes in dream necessarily be unreal? For there is no lack of dream lovers in this world.

High praise indeed, but *Peony Pavilion* itself does not take praise of love as far as many later texts would. The play follows Du Liniang in her single-minded pursuit of love only to end with her transformation into a proper Confucian matron who disavows her earlier headstrong behavior. The young lovers do not finish their story with a tragic elopement, but instead with their union legitimated by no less a figure than the emperor himself. The play's conclusion is ultimately conservative, in that it affirms the primacy of the normative bonds between emperor and minister, and between parent and child, which are made vital again by accommodating feeling and passion.

Readers, however, were much more interested in the play's first half. Du Liniang's illicit love and subsequent death so gripped the popular imagination that it was almost as if the second half of the play did not exist. The story of Du Liniang, which ends happily with her marriage and reunion with her parents, was instrumental in sparking a host of imitators who were not so lucky.

These teenaged girls, both fictional and real, were never able to find outward circumstances in which their poetic spirits were recognized and valued. Some of the more extreme elements of the cult of passion were embodied by the young courtesan Xiaoqing, the most famous of these latter-day Du Liniangs, who may or may not have been an actual historical figure.

Published in 1624, the biography of Xiaoqing told the story of a teenager from Yangzhou. Purchased as a concubine by the son of a high official, she invoked the jealousy of the man's wife and was exiled to a villa on West Lake, where she wasted away. Before she died, she commissioned a portrait to be painted and wrote a number of poems in which she compared herself explicitly to Du Liniang.

> Cold rain outside the dark window – such a mournful sound!
> I trim the lamp and leisurely read *Peony Pavilion*.
> In this world there are people even more foolish than I:
> Xiaoqing is clearly not the only one with a broken heart.

By this time, only a few decades after the play was written, *Peony Pavilion* had come to stand for an entire lifestyle. No less a figure than Qian Qianyi doubted Xiaoqing's real existence: one single character, formed by combining the two characters in her name, means "passion," so at the very least this was a pseudonym. Other biographies soon followed, along with more than a dozen dramatic adaptations of her story, all taking a cavalier attitude about specific details and introducing new poems ostensibly by Xiaoqing. These are further indications that, for Ming readers, their subject was not a historical individual but a type, namely the young beauty alluringly ravaged by her own poetic sensitivity. Ye Shaoyuan, a distinguished official and poet, wrote of his daughter, the famous young poetess Ye Xiaoluan, "Whenever she wrote poetry, as soon as she had completed even a single stanza or single line, she would immediately fall ill. This eventually became a debilitating disease, and although she was repeatedly warned by the physician, she never reformed her behavior."

Men and women understood the meaning of Xiaoqing's story differently. To men, she was an emblem of pathos. Numerous women, in contrast, wrote poems in which they compared themselves to Xiaoqing. For them, the very name of Xiaoqing's collection, "Manuscripts Saved from Burning" (*Fenyu cao*), seems to have been an injunction to write poetry and also to preserve it.

All five of Tang Xianzu's plays, of which *Peony Pavilion* was the second to be written, involve pivotal scenes that take place in dreams. Collectively, they are known as *Linchuan's Four Dreams* (*Linchuan simeng*). Later in his career, Tang Xianzu returned to his first play, *The Purple Flute* (*Zixiao ji*), and rewrote it as *The Purple Hairpin* (*Zichai ji*). Both plays dramatized the Tang tale "Huo Xiaoyu." His other two plays, *Handan* (*Handan ji*) and *South Branch* (*Nanke ji*), were also adaptations of two similar Tang tales, in which a whole lifetime takes place within a dream. Running through all his work is a concern with altered states of consciousness, whether that of love or of dream.

Not all late Ming writers were so eager to elevate feeling and other states of consciousness. To Buddhists (and the late Ming was a great age for Buddhist devotion), passion always meant attachment, and consequently illusion, and was thus to be avoided. In *Supplement to Journey to the West*, written at the very end of the dynasty, Dong Yue presents a Buddhist allegory that goes one step beyond *Peony Pavilion* in that it takes place entirely in a dream. The work meditates on the nature of human consciousness, asking the question of whether consciousness is the ultimate ground of reality, or whether something lies beyond it. Passion does not win out. In this novella, Monkey battles with various monstrous instantiations of passion, including the demonic mackerel fish (or *qingyu*, whose name is a homophone for "passion"). The novella's most famous episode places Monkey in a tower with thousands of mirrors in which he sees reflections of other worlds. In *Peony Pavilion*, dreams liberate the consciousness from the limitations of the real world; in *Supplement to Journey to the West*, the mirrors in the tower represent the mind's ability to create infinite illusion. Far from liberating, the mind keeps the self captive.

No text did more than *Peony Pavilion* to make romantic love a matter of profound seriousness, but some of the plays that it influenced most strongly were lighthearted comedies. Two particularly successful examples are Wu Bing's witty comedy of errors, *The Green Peony* (*Lü mudan*), and Ruan Dacheng's romantic comedy *The Swallow Letter*. In this age of heated debate on both prosody and politics, aesthetic allegiance and political allegiance were quite different matters. Tang Xianzu had been a deeply committed (though indifferently successful) official and was throughout life a Revival Society sympathizer. After the Manchu conquest, Wu Bing starved himself out of loyalty to the Ming. The most famous member of the Linchuan School at the end of the dynasty, however, was Ruan Dacheng, protégé of the notorious eunuch Wei Zhongxian and later a Manchu collaborator. *The Swallow Letter*, written in the last year or two of the Ming dynasty and first performed in Nanjing after the Ming court had fled Beijing, tells in sparkling, witty language the story of a young man who is eventually married to two girls who are perfect doubles for each other, one a courtesan and the other the gently reared daughter of a minister of state. Wu Bing and Ruan Dacheng, two famous practitioners of verbal pleasure for its own sake, chose very different paths.

The fake and the cult of the genuine

However much it was intellectualized and rarefied, and though it was often experienced through the medium of print, drama was still very much a performance tradition. The late Ming theater was a place where the very high habitually rubbed shoulders with the very low, not as members of the same audience, but as part of the method by which drama was translated from one person's ideas and words into an onstage experience. In the cult of the theater, the elite playwright and the humble actor were equally valorized. Having begun this chapter on the late Ming with the forms associated with the elite hold on cultural authority, we will conclude with one of the most distinctive features of the period, the mix of high and low.

The playwrights themselves often hailed from the highest echelons of society; many were successful examination candidates and high officials. Professional acting, in contrast, was strongly associated with prostitution, and actors of both sexes were considered to be of the same status as bondservants. Performers were sometimes purchased as small children, to spend the rest of their lives entertaining the wealthy.

More than any other single pursuit, drama invited almost rabid connoisseurship of each of its facets, from singing techniques to performers and even playwrights. The wide range of writing on drama included detailed essays on performance technique, in terms both of the mechanics of singing and of the ways in which feeling might be conveyed. In other words, part of the obsession was with the craft of acting itself.

Elite playwrights not only owned troupes of such actors but also worked side by side with them. The work of staging a performance was regarded as part of the pleasure and status of owning the troupe, and so was usually not outsourced to a professional impresario. Ruan Dacheng was known to have controlled every detail of his troupe's performance: sometimes he wrote the script, he tutored them on every gesture and every trill, he even micromanaged the making of their costumes and the production's staging as well. Many other elite men, and the women of their households as well, were avid amateur performers, devoted to singing the same roles performed by their servants. Elite playwrights wrote openly about donning the costumes of performers to sing in the troupes they owned. Other elite men boasted that they spent all their energies on singing, leaving none for examination study.

Writers of informal prose mention by name numerous late Ming professionals, such as Pan Yingran of Zou Diguang's troupe, Quan of Wu Kun's troupe, and Zhang San of Shen Shixing's troupe, among many others, discussing not just their individual performances, but how they approached playacting in general and the way they tackled specific roles. To describe performers and performances, writers used the refined language of connoisseurship, as opaque now as the words used to describe fine French wine will be four hundred years hence. These actors were themselves *objets d'art*, and also inhabitants of a peculiar social space, at once chattel and admired artist.

One characteristic feature of the age was the combination of two obsessions that seem on the surface mutually exclusive. Late Ming connoisseurs were passionate about genuineness of feeling at the same time that they adored drama – a space dedicated to dissimulation where identities could be assumed and divested with alarming ease. Nowhere was this paradox more apparent than in the status and cultural importance of courtesans. Some courtesans sang arias, but their participation in the culture of theater ran deeper than that. These women, paid to assume a role and to act out fantasy, were central to the romantic ideal of the time and to the culture that grew around the theater.

Xiaoqing's tale was just one of the eight hundred narratives collected in Feng Menglong's *Anatomy of Love*, published only a few years after the appearance of her biography. Some scholars have even attributed the first biography to Feng Menglong as well. In the preface to *Anatomy of Love*, Feng Menglong ranks all other Confucian relations secondary to love:

> I wish to establish a religion of love and teach all living beings: the son faces his father with love; the minister faces the emperor with love; the same holds true for all other relationships. Things in this world are like loose coins; love is the cord.

This grandiose polemic is not meant to be taken literally, but it does suggest something important about how love had come to be regarded. Positing that all relationships ought to be held together by love is one short step away from suggesting that the most noble relationships are held together only by love and not by obligation. In questioning what place there might be for feeling outside of the normative bonds of family and state, women (and courtesans in particular because they were neither wives nor daughters) occupied a central place. A number of plays from this period concern courtesans who sacrifice themselves out of loyalty, whether to their lovers or to the state. That sacrifice, coming from the quintessential outsider, by its very nature speaks to feeling and not to duty.

To people of the Qing, the great flowering of courtesan culture in Jiangnan was one of the late Ming's most distinctive features and a principle object of nostalgic yearning in the puritanical new dynasty. These entertainers were often as well educated as any premodern woman; they were trained, after all, in whatever it took to serve as companions to sophisticated men of the elite. Their appeal and cachet derived precisely from their participation in traditional elite arts: calligraphy, painting, music, and, most importantly, poetry. The culture that grew around them, with its rankings, manuals, and guides to appreciating courtesans, was very much a part of the same culture of connoisseurship so important to the age.

Beginning in the Wanli period, courtesans appear in many literary genres, often as tragic, sympathetic figures, and sometimes as a way for men of the elite to voice their own feeling of helplessness in the face of political turmoil. A number of real-life courtesans who met tragic ends were admired by writers of the period. One such writer, Mei Dingzuo, collected stories about courtesans for an anthology, *Lotuses in the Mud* (*Qingni lianhua ji*, 1602). We might read the different versions of "The Courtesan's Jewel Box" by Feng Menglong and Song Maocheng in just this way. Betrayed by her lover, the young prostitute Du Shiniang dispenses with her wealth in such a way as to overshadow any moral qualms about how exactly that wealth had been accumulated. She represents the essence of the related values of passion and heroism, more so than if she had been a girl of gentle birth. In the late Ming, this tragic single-minded passion has a male counterpart that is equally sympathetic, as in the hero of Feng Menglong's "The Oil Seller and the Courtesan." When his beloved vomits all over him, the humble young man's undimmed ardor is sublime rather than ridiculous.

Courtesans like Bian Sai, Dong Bai, Li Xiang (also known as Li Xiangjun), Chen Yuanyuan, and many others came close to celebrity status in their own time, and, because their presence was recorded in poetry and other writing, they became the object of much nostalgia in later decades. Nonetheless it is important to recall that in a culture where chastity was ranked with loyalty and filiality as a supreme virtue and widows might be vilified for remarrying, a sex worker (which was the essential definition of a courtesan, no matter how glorified, no matter how lofty her clientele and how high her fees) could only achieve a marginal status. The courtesans whose names have been recorded were the most privileged in a hierarchy that also included boys and destitute women forced to sell their bodies for survival.

In general, writing must be seen as a marginal activity in women's lives, and a disproportionate number of women of marginal status seem to have engaged in it. Apart from courtesans and daughters of the elite, the other large category of women writers was Buddhist clergywomen, especially of the Zen school, who have left poems, letters, and sermons. This chapter concludes at the intersection between the elite and the marginal as I explore how the marginal actually inhabited a central cultural space in this period.

In many ways, the cult of love could only find expression in courtesan culture. In an age where arranged marriage, usually between strangers who had never laid eyes on each other, was the norm, passion between two people with complementary tastes, mediated by the exchange of poetry and painting (or, in other words, courtship itself), was generally speaking possible only within the sex trade. Not only were courtesans centrally important in many of the genres so far discussed – poetry, fiction, and drama – they were also absolutely central to the great myth of romantic love.

With a few exceptions like the love affair between the cousins in Meng Chengshun's *Mistress and Maid*, the only affairs between lovers who had chosen each other involved high-end courtesans and their customers. Courtesans often left the profession by marrying, although in a few cases the husbands would allow the courtesan to continue taking lovers, as if recognizing that only a woman allowed to choose other partners could really be in a love match. Such unusual behavior betokened not weakness or stupidity, as it might in a conventional marriage, but a freewheeling heroism (*xia*), a liberation from narrow-minded convention, that was just as much valorized in this period as love.

Some of these courtesans not only inspired some of the best writing of the time, but were also important writers in their own right. The life of Liu Rushi (1618–1664, also known as Liu Shi, among other names), the period's single most famous courtesan, gives some indication of the complicated nature of the courtesan's status. Liu Rushi was successively involved with two of the most talented intellectuals and poets of her time. As a teenager, she was the lover of the poet Chen Zilong, and their relationship became one of the most famous love affairs of the age. The two collaborated in the writing of song lyrics, generating a minor revival of that form. These poems and song lyrics, with their focus on love and yearning, formed the heart of the Yunjian School of poetry. After their relationship was broken up by his family, Chen Zilong helped her to publish a collection of her poetry.

Liu Rushi later married Qian Qianyi, more than three decades her senior, whom she assisted in compiling *Collected Poems of the Successive Reigns (Liechao shiji*), a large anthology that included women's poetry chosen by Liu Rushi herself, which has become the source of much of our knowledge of women's writing from this period. During Qian Qianyi's life, the couple behaved as though she were his senior wife; after his death, however, under pressure from his family, she committed suicide. At the end of the day, she was still nothing but a courtesan in his family's eyes.

Of the constellation of elements that comprised the late-imperial love affair – deeply held emotion, romantic gestures, and the centrality of poetry in the relationship – not a single one could have arisen outside of courtesan culture; at the same time, none remained confined to that culture for long. It is noteworthy that Qian Qianyi's *Collected Poems of the Successive Reigns* itself intersperses poems written by courtesans with those written by elite women (called "wives and daughters"). Some scholars have suggested that the courtesan culture of the late Ming was what made cultural attainments, in particular the ability to write poetry, desirable in women. Certainly, long before men expected to write poetry and talk about literature with their wives, they were doing so with courtesans. Courtesan culture had an enormous and disproportionate impact on mainstream culture, making companionate marriage an ideal, and in many ways coloring female literacy itself. As a poetic theme, courtesans find their way into the writings of girls of impeccable elite origins.

In wealthy families, literacy among girls, who were often taught to read alongside their brothers, had become commonplace, partly because literary pursuits were so much a part of the texture of elite life. When family members exchanged poems or used them to commemorate all manner of occasions, wives and daughters were naturally included as well. By the 1620s, even conservative didactic literature encouraged and assumed female literacy. For example, *Illustrated Biographies of Exemplary Women* (*Huitu lienü zhuan*) is full of pictures of women reading. Elite wives were expected to help teach their children to read and write.

Recent scholarly work has shown the existence of elite women's literary networks, primarily in the Jiangnan region. Just as men joined societies to write poetry, so too did women. In many cases, sisters, cousins, and mothers exchanged writings, and poetry in particular, even after they had married into different families. During the Wanli period, these networks were broader than they ever had been or would be again.

For no one was this more true than for Lu Qingzi (fl. 1590), a daughter of a high official and well respected as a poet during her lifetime, who had a happy companionate marriage with a scholar whose interest in literature mirrored her own. Throughout her life, Lu Qingzi exchanged poems with a miscellany of women writers: numerous courtesans, a prostitute-turned-nun, various Buddhist devotees, and elite women from her own background. The late Ming seems to have been the only period in Chinese history when well-born ladies of the gentry and courtesans socialized with and befriended one another. Poetry was the currency of these relationships.

Lu Qingzi's work suggests some of the distinctive features of personal identity in this period. Did she write about courtesans out of a sense of sympathy, an incipient feminist consciousness? Lu Qingzi wrote as though she herself were their patron, an elite man instead of a woman:

> They begin to sing,
> To move their red lips.
> Hair fixed high, eyebrows just painted,
> Beauties of Handan, worth whole cities,
> Their glamour outshines springtime itself.

The courtesans themselves participated in this shape-shifting. Lu Qingzi projected a persona that was part female and, as a writer, part male. By mingling with elite men almost as equals, but not as gentlewomen, Lu's courtesan correspondents in turn occupied another liminal position.

This was an odd convergence between women belonging to opposite poles of society, with daughters and wives of the elite at one end, and, at the other, women whose identities were so changeable that they often went through name after name. In the hands of many writers – among others, the gently reared Ye Xiaoluan's parents, Xiaoqing's biographers, or Ruan Dacheng, whose *The Swallow Letter* features two physically identical heroines, one a courtesan, the other an official's daughter – the lines between courtesan and young lady were blurred as never before; equally talented and sensitive, these girls might be almost interchangeable. Most real-life women writers of note were also either courtesans or women from elite families, among them Ruan Dacheng's daughter, Ye Xiaowan (younger sister of Xiaoluan), Liang Xiaoyu, and Ma Xianglan.

High-end courtesans of the late Ming owed part of their appeal to the kind of frisson associated in many cultures with cross-dressing and disguise; in some sense they appeared to be well-born young ladies. Sometimes these disguises crossed gender lines as well. Courtesans were the only women who could freely socialize with men in public and who seemed unconfined by restrictive social norms, as women from elite households led much more secluded lives. When traveling in public, courtesans often dressed as elite men. For example, when Liu Rushi first called on her future husband Qian Qianyi, she was dressed as a male scholar, exposing her bound feet on purpose as the one sign of her true gender. Cross-dressing took place more often on a symbolic plane. When Qian Qianyi wrote letters to Liu Rushi, he referred to her as his "younger brother." Writing to others about her work, he sometimes called her "Liuzi" ("Master Liu"), as though she were more than an equal, a literary antecedent. In this way, courtesans were culturally coded as part male, as honorary literati.

An odd world we find ourselves in, at the end of the Ming. These three types – the tragic courtesan, the gentleman loyal to the throne, and the virtuous daughter of the elite – had always been closely related, but their full convergence was revealed in the immediate aftermath of the Ming's fall, when all three, each successively identifying with the others, used poetry to lament their helplessness in the face of political turmoil. After their world collapsed, all three produced their share of martyrs, becoming essentially the same. But the blurring of subjectivities among the three types was already a long-standing trope, dating from the last decades before the dynasty's fall.

Never before and never again in traditional culture would the marginal and the elite so closely abut each other. Courtesan culture acquired its sheen only through its participation in elite forms. Elite culture was equally dependent on courtesan culture, the only place where the cults of love and of sincerity could come into full flower, despite the make-believe and commercial transaction that lay at its heart.

Postscript

In the 1650s, a decade or so after the fall of the dynasty, the writer and entrepreneur Li Yu (1610–1680) wrote *Ideal Marriage Destinies (Yizhong yuan)*, a southern play on four real-life figures from the 1620s. In this farce that is also a fond snapshot, how does Li Yu characterize the bygone dynasty? The play muses on two phenomena discussed above, the obsession with authenticity and the market's impact on art.

The two male leads, writer and calligrapher Chen Jiru (1558–1639) and calligrapher and painter Dong Qichang (1555–1636), find themselves in Hangzhou, in temporary retirement from their official positions. Constantly beleaguered by requests for prefaces, paintings, and inscriptions, the two cannot enjoy their leisure. The play tells how Chen and Dong meet and marry two beautiful young girls also based loosely on historical figures, one a courtesan and the other the daughter of a poor scholar, who specialize in the forgery of Dong's and Chen's highly distinctive styles. This play about different kinds of authenticity begins by posing questions about what it is that ties a style to a particular person.

Dong and Chen happen on a shop selling forged versions of their work. Both men recognize at first glance that these are imitations, but are intrigued by the artists behind the work. Chen Jiru finds and marries his imitator without much trouble, but Dong Qichang is not so fortunate. Knowing of Miss Yang's obsession with Dong Qichang's work, an evil monk deceives her into believing that she will be marrying Dong, when in fact the monk intends to leave orders and marry her himself. The monk then hires a fake Dong Qichang to kidnap Miss Yang. She is too clever to be tricked, however, and the humorous scene that follows foregrounds some of the built-in ironies of the quest for authenticity. The young forger self-righteously grills the fake Dong Qichang to reveal his true identity, even as both parties, accuser and accused, are themselves equally fake: one an impostor of Dong Qichang's style, and the other an impostor of his person.

After she escapes, Miss Yang funds her journey home by selling paintings, not as forgeries, but as the products of that oddest of creatures, a woman painter. Even as she is no longer selling paintings under false auspices, her identity as artist remains central to the marketing of her work, as well as making her vulnerable to challenge. Painting behind a curtain, she is accused of actually being a man, until she invites a few patrons to watch her paint. Like the real-life Liu Rushi, even though as a public person she is part male, her tiny bound feet must be exposed to prove her identity as a female. The fake Dong Qichang turns out to be a real woman.

For his two male protagonists, Li Yu has chosen two of the many late Ming figures who closely approximate brand names. A brilliant writer and official, Chen Jiru engaged in the marketing of his own writing and calligraphy, while his real-life friend Dong Qichang was perhaps the most famous amateur artist of his day, known for his deliberately and distinctively awkward style and also for his sophisticated use of copies of earlier paintings. Both men, in the play as characters and in real life, are producers of styles that are commodities, meant for sale in the open market. Their careers implicitly pose the question of whether they can be said to own their own styles.

Yet the play does not simply abandon art's traditional promises about its expressive powers. Shaped by the market and set onstage, the question of distinguishing the real from the fake has become much more complicated. All four of the main characters, whether elite painter, elite calligrapher, impoverished daughter, or courtesan, make their livings not just with their brushes, but with their ability to convey something distinctively individual, even if fake. Miss Yang's self-portrait, painted in Dong Qichang's style and signed with a forgery of his name, nonetheless manages to capture her essence and communicate it to Dong Qichang. Originating as it does in the market, the connection between each artist and his forger is nonetheless incontrovertibly authentic. A forged painting is no less real in the feelings it communicates.

Early Qing to 1723

WAI-YEE LI

I. Changing contexts

From late Ming to early Qing

There is no easy consensus on what demarcates the beginning of the late Ming period. The conventional date, as followed in this volume, is the year 1573, the beginning of the Wanli reign. Literary historians eager to synchronize changes in literary trends with the "radicalization" of Wang Yangming's (1472–1529) philosophy of introspection and intuitive awakening, however, tend to push the beginning of the late Ming to about the mid-sixteenth century. A certain amount of flexibility is built into any attempt at periodization, but how and where to apply the label of "late Ming" is particularly slippery and problematic. From the 1920s on, efforts have been made to trace the genealogy of the "new literature" or of different versions of modernity back to late Ming oppositional stances and the "romantic" and "individualist" concerns of its literary culture. From that perspective, dynastic decline promised new beginnings. In contrast, in the aftermath of the Manchu conquest, retrospection on the late Ming often yielded negative judgments that tended to conjoin political decline with cultural decadence, and the chief concern lay with pinpointing when that decline became inevitable.

The authors discussed in the previous chapter did not think of themselves as "late Ming writers." There was generally no sense of an ending. Despite forebodings of a deepening crisis, the collapse of the Ming in 1644 caught many by surprise. In any case, dynastic decline did not seem to have undermined the cultural confidence of this period, which was an extraordinarily creative one. The label "late Ming" (*Ming ji, Ming mo*, or *wan Ming*) was a Qing invention that was sometimes accompanied by castigations of heterodoxy, frivolity, and excess. At the same time, early Qing literature was profoundly concerned with the Ming–Qing dynastic transition and the implications of the late Ming legacy. If early Qing writers "invented" the late Ming, they did so under the burden of trying to understand and define their own historical moment.

Compared to the late Ming, the chronological beginnings of the early Qing would seem unproblematic; closer scrutiny, however, reveals ambiguities. According to the official narrative of the Qing, the Ming came to an end when Beijing fell to the rebels and the Chongzhen Emperor (r. 1628–1644) hanged himself on Coal Hill in the suburbs of the capital on the nineteenth of the third month of 1644. Holdovers from the court, such as the Southern Ming in Nanjing, and other attempts at loyalist resistance that lasted until 1662 (or 1683, if we include Zheng Chenggong's (1624–62) force in Taiwan), raised questions on the finality of the official ending. Historians debate when the fall of the Ming was generally accepted as real and irreversible. Likewise, to contemporary observers, the consolidation of Qing rule was a slow and by no means inevitable process. Even as the Kangxi Emperor (r. 1662–1722) came of age and stability had been tentatively restored, the Rebellion of the Three Border Principalities (1673–1681), led by Chinese army leaders who had defected to the Manchus and facilitated the conquest in the 1640s and 1650s, gravely challenged the newly established regime. In 1679, when victory over the rebellion was almost complete, a special examination was held for Eminent Scholars of Vast Learning (*boxue hongru*) nominated by court and local officials. It was designed to mitigate the disaffection of the intellectual elite toward the Qing court; but although many became candidates in the examination, some Ming loyalists staunchly refused to be co-opted. By the end of the Kangxi reign, however, Qing rule was accepted as incontestable.

The Ming–Qing conflict, protracted and tortuous, has almost always been described in apocalyptic terms of unspeakable violence, rupture, and devastation. The Manchu conquest, experienced as a crisis of culture and tradition, forced many to ponder the age-old distinction between "Chinese" and "barbarian." Especially traumatic were the Qing decrees mandating change of costume and hairstyle, as men were forced to shave the fronts of their heads and wear the rest of their hair in a queue; these decrees provoked widespread resistance that was met with ruthless reprisals. There was also a halfhearted ban on foot-binding for women, which lasted only four years (1644–1648). Different regions responded to Qing rule in different ways. As Frederic Wakeman has observed, "the Han members of the early Qing government were likely to be predominantly northerners." Resistance lasted longer in the south, the west, and the southeastern coastal provinces. The major early Qing cases of persecution (spanning the decade from the late 1650s on) all targeted the Jiangnan–Zhejiang literati. Despite all the suffering, or perhaps as a response to it, the early Qing was an extraordinarily creative and vibrant period in Chinese literary history, in part because political disorder and the initial abeyance of centralized control gave writers the freedom to test the boundaries of political, moral, and formal constraints.

On the most basic human level, the Ming–Qing dynastic transition meant that lives were ended, interrupted, redirected, and reassessed, although many also simply continued or eventually resumed their normal lives from before the fall. An unprecedented number among the elite chose to "perish with the country" when the Ming collapsed, amid a chorus of intense debates on the meaning of, and justification for, martyrdom and survival. Those who survived the conquest but "refused to serve two dynasties" are categorized as Ming loyalists (*yimin*). Some were actively involved in anti-Qing resistance, others chose reclusive nonparticipation in the new order. Eremitism in turn encompassed a range of lifestyles, from ascetic withdrawal, even monkhood, to various degrees of social interaction with Qing officials. For Ming officials who also served under the Qing, the Qianlong Emperor (r. 1736–1795) later invented the derogatory biographical category of "officials who served two dynasties" (*erchen*); according to the morality of dynastic order, such "loss of integrity" (*shijie*) was a major blemish. Often, however, more neutral views prevailed, especially in the case of low-level degree holders who had not held office under the Ming. Women, excluded from participation in government, did not face the same stark political choices, but those who chose to ruminate in their writings on dynastic decline and fall sometimes did so with an implied self-definition as loyalist. The designation "female loyalist" placed a woman beyond gender-specific virtues. A woman with loyalist sympathies married to a Qing official might even implicitly criticize his political choice, as in the case of the poetic exchanges between Xu Can (ca 1610s–after 1677) and her husband Chen Zhilin (1605–1668). Loyalism thus seems to have created a sense of common cause and encouraged a measure of independence and self-assertion for a select few female writers.

Obviously, the Qing dynasty was able to consolidate its rule only because enough people accepted this dynastic change as an accomplished fact. Yet the voices of Ming martyrs, loyalists, and their sympathizers hold a special fascination for posterity. The "political integrity" they exemplified has been universalized and made to serve different narratives. Thus the Qianlong Emperor canonized as loyal martyrs those who "died for the Ming dynasty" even as he devised a "literary inquisition" targeting real or imagined subversion. Lynn Struve notes the irony of mid-nineteenth-century scholar–officials "using the anti-Qing resistance saga to reinforce dedication to the Qing state and social order." From the late nineteenth century on, that saga merged with the discourse of nationalism. Stories of loyalist Ming resistance fanned the flames of anti-Manchu sentiment in the last years of the Qing dynasty, inspired the broader quest for national identity in the Republic, and became a rallying cry during the Second Sino-Japanese War (1937–1945). "The loyalist spirit" (yimin jingshen) has also come to represent resistance to oppression and authoritarianism. The romantic idea of creative power embedded within alienation and disempowerment holds unmistakable appeal. Burdened with cultural nostalgia for a lost world destroyed by modernity, war, and revolution, the Chinese of the twentieth century often found metaphors of loss and retrieval in the fall of the Ming – the collapse of the Qing was too recent and messy, and Qing rule was too implicated in the forces of destruction. To a modern Chinese, the consciousness of being "the remnant of a culture" (wenhua yimin, a term used by Yu Ying-shih of the great historian Chen Yinke (1890–1969)) makes for empathy with the Ming loyalists who either died for or outlived a lost world.

The generation that lived through the dynastic transition often felt the need to avow, explain, defend, or lament their political choices. There was intense, self-conscious discussion of the term "loyalist" and of the range of choices it permitted in loyalist communities. The political choices of writers sometimes also determine how literary historians view their period designations. Chen Zilong (1608–1647), who wrote some of his most stirring poems after 1644, is usually classified as a late Ming poet because he died in the anti-Qing resistance. Li Wen (1608–1647), his close friend, exact contemporary, and fellow Yunjian poet, appears in anthologies of Qing literature because he served under the new dynasty, albeit only briefly and after much anguish and soul-searching. By a similar logic, Qian Qianyi (1582–1664) and Wu Weiye (1609–1672), important literary figures during the late Ming, are often classified as Qing poets. In modern histories and anthologies of Qing literature, Ming loyalists are often categorically placed before those who participated in the new order, irrespective of chronology. Thus the Cantonese loyalist poet Qu Dajun (1630–96) comes before Qian Qianyi, almost fifty years his senior.

Political disorder sometimes determined changes in style, sensibility, and subject matter. Gifted with sensuous, ornate diction (yancai) as a young poet, Wu Weiye is said to have developed epic sweep and tragic depth as dynastic upheaval forced him to turn his attention to politics and history. Similar assertions are made about the evolution of the style of Chen Weisong's (1626–1682) lyrics across the dynastic divide. The late Ming play Mistress and Maid (Jiao Hong ji) by Meng Chengshun celebrates romantic passion in the love-suicide and apotheosis of two cousins. During the 1660s, Meng wrote *Chastity and Talent* (*Zhenwen ji*), in which Zhang Yuniang, a historical poet who lived through the Song–Yuan transition, also dies from grief at the death of her betrothed. The two never meet in the play (except in dream and spirit visitation), and Meng turns Zhang's fierce loyalty, divested of romantic–erotic overtones, into an implicit affirmation of Ming loyalism. Li Yu (1611–1680), perceived by many to be largely oblivious to the sufferings of those who lived through that tumultuous era, wrote political poems in 1644 and 1645 to lament the fall of the Ming, and some of his stories and plays turn the traumatic experience of dynastic transition into improbably comic plots of recompense and reconciliation. More to the point, as the postscript to the last chapter has shown, even when Li Yu is not directly addressing political and historical issues, his blend of invention, irreverence, pragmatism, and comedy can be interpreted as responses to the late Ming legacy.

In sum, the literary culture of the early Qing cannot be considered separately from its late Ming counterpart, nor from the history, memory, and representations of the Ming–Qing transition. I will begin with an overview of early Qing perspectives on late Ming thought and culture as a way of juxtaposing cultural self-perceptions and self-definitions before and after the fall of the Ming. I will discuss continuities, transformations, and reversals in ideological terms and then explore their sociological contexts in a brief survey of the conditions facilitating or inhibiting literary production: the shifting functions of literary communities, the developments in printing and publishing, the varying role of censorship, and the changing sociopolitical landscape from the 1640s to the 1720s.

Questions of how and why the Ming dynasty fell dominated the early Qing literary imagination. Literary representations of the Ming–Qing conflict take many forms in different genres: eyewitness accounts, sober reflections, direct engagement, fantastic reenactments, and historical analogies in varying gradations of coded, indirect expression. Closely related to these writings is the literature of remembrance, especially memoirs and poems devoted to retracing the fall of the Ming and recapturing the rich texture of the culture in its last days. I will thus attempt an overview of how late Ming literary and aesthetic sensibility is represented, continued, and transformed. What happened to the late Ming concern with genuineness, self-expression, and imaginative freedom? What is the fate of pleasure and passion in early Qing literature? As noted above, the reversals, resolutions, and compromises in Li Yu's writings can be read as his way of redirecting the energy of the late Ming in playful response to the excesses and contradictions of that earlier period. Li's inventiveness is a heightened form of a more general concern, typical of his era, with reinterpreting tradition. Thus this issue also dominates vernacular fiction, where early Qing reinterpretations take the form of appropriating Ming masterworks through commentaries, sequels, and rewriting.

Needless to say, the aforementioned examples, and early Qing literature in general, also look beyond the late Ming moment to engage with other high points in the literary tradition. For the generation of writers who either came of age or were born after the conquest, late Ming culture was the object of "mediated nostalgia" or "secondhand memory." Often this focus yielded pride of place to other concerns. The early Qing saw an infusion of vibrant new energy in many genres. For song lyrics, classical poetry, parallel prose, classical prose, and classical tales, the revival is especially remarkable. New orthodoxies arose and boundaries were redrawn as evaluation of the late Ming legacy stimulated the quest for new models and inspired self-conscious ruminations on novelty, tradition, and historical purpose. In all genres writers felt impelled to reexamine what is meant by "old" and "new." For example, in his *Records of the Strange* (*Liaozhai zhiyi*) Pu Songling (1640–1715) takes issue with the aesthetics of wonder and the obsession with subjective illumination so characteristic of late Ming culture; at the same time he addresses the entire tradition of imagining other worlds, especially in classical fiction. More generally, historical retrospection on the dynastic transition can also aspire to be meditation on perennial and universal questions. This combination is perhaps best exemplified by the dramatic masterpieces that crown the seventeenth century – Hong Sheng's (1645–1704) *Palace of Eternal Life* (*Changsheng dian*) and Kong Shangren's (1648–1718) *Peach Blossom Fan* (*Taohua shan*).

Early Qing perspectives on late Ming culture

Early Qing intellectual history is dominated by figures identifying themselves as Ming loyalists, most famous among them Huang Zongxi (1610–1695), Gu Yanwu (1613–1682), and Wang Fuzhi (1619–1692). Huang and Gu exerted a powerful influence on their own and succeeding generations; Wang, in some ways more original, did not become widely known until the nineteenth century. Tenacious loyalty to the fallen dynasty coexisted, and may even have prompted, stringent examination of its failures. Aside from specific criticisms of late Ming factionalism, tactical errors, and institutional problems, the proliferation of the literati (*wenren*) was in itself considered a sign of decline. For Gu Yanwu, a person's self-definition as literatus implies political irresponsibility, thus he laments, "From the Tang and Song on, how numerous the literati have become!" He also implicitly compares late Ming speculative philosophical discourses to Wei–Jin "pure conversation" (qingtan), which destroyed not only the state (wangguo) but also all under heaven (wang tianxia).

Keywords in late Ming thought came under scrutiny. Gu Yanwu returns to the memory of words, especially their use in the canonical Confucian classics: against the elevation of subjective consciousness in the teachings of Wang Yangming and his followers, he urges the nonabstract meanings of xin (heart and mind) as understood in the Analects as inclination, application, and mental focus. From the early Qing perspective, doctrines of intuitive awakening threatened socio-ethical norms and opened the way for heterodoxy. Wang Fuzhi accuses Wang Yangming of being "overtly Confucian but secretly Buddhist"; Gu Yanwu describes an elite mired in Chan (Zen) teachings and abstruse speculations. Even Huang Zongxi, whose monumental History of Ming Confucian Thinkers (Mingru xue'an) is largely sympathetic, registers the dangers of radical subjectivity. He describes the later followers of the Taizhou School, who pushed even further Wang Yangming's emphasis on introspection and intuition, as "taking on dragons and snakes with their bare hands" so that their endeavors "could no longer be kept within the bounds of moral teachings."

As an antidote against late Ming excesses, Gu Yanwu proposes simplicity, practical application, broad learning (boxue), and cultivating "a sense of shame in one's conduct" (xingji youchi). That he should present the basic condition of moral self-cultivation in negative terms as the vigilant removal of "causes for shame" is yet another token of his suspicion of high-flown rhetoric and abstraction. Wang Fuzhi, however, instead of eschewing philosophical speculations, envisions transcendence independent of subjective consciousness as he responds to the perceived deleterious concern with mind in late Ming thought. Huang Zongxi, who also affirms the all-encompassing potential of mind, nevertheless reiterates distinctions between "the nature and emotions of the moment" (identified with involuntary affective response) and "the nature and emotions for all ages" (which has an inalienable ethical content). Without "vigilant self-examination in solitude" (shendu), he warns, it is too easy to mistake "private understanding" (sizhi) for "conscience" (liangzhi).

Broad assertions of late Ming moral decline draw upon philological and etymological arguments. Gu Yanwu notes that the word zhen (genuine), so prevalent in late Ming writings, does not appear in the Five Classics, and contrasts its use in Zhuangzi, where it carries implications of Daoist transcendence and immortality, with its meaning of correspondence between name and actuality in early historical writings. He laments, in this context, the frequency with which references to *Zhuangzi* cropped up in late Ming examination essays: "From then on [1569], for the next fifty years, examination essays drew on nothing but Buddhist and Daoist texts. The comet swept aside the Polar and Wenchang constellations [i.e. an evil influence took over the constellations governing official careers and principles of government] and the water in the imperial moat turned to blood." The reasoning and rhetoric here are typical of the period. Using rhetorical elision and by arranging the entries in his *Knowledge Accrued Daily* (*Rizhi lu*), Gu suggests a connection between radical subjectivity and moral license. He accuses Li Zhi (1527–1602) of consorting with female disciples and lecturing to mixed audiences, and criticizes Zhong Xing (1574–1625) for traveling with his concubines while in mourning for his father. In fact, both Li and Zhong seem to have been abstemious characters, and such allegations might have arisen simply because sexual mores represent an easy line of attack.

The grand claims of subjective consciousness are linked in early Qing formulations to sensual indulgence, disequilibrium of the self, and sociopolitical disorder, less in systematic philosophical critiques than by force of association. Thus Gu Yanwu judges apparently disparate developments – such as Li Zhi's flamboyant rebellion against conventional morality or Zhong Xing's alleged immorality and his self-consciously original commentaries on the Classics, histories, and poetry – as omens of the catastrophe to come. Qian Qianyi, in his compendium of Ming poetry, decries Zhong Xing's "poetry of evil omen" (*shiyao*) as "the portent of warfare" (*bingxiang*) and, along with Zhu Yizun (1629–1709), disparages it as "the music of a fallen state" (*wangguo zhi yin*), implying that Zhong's Jingling School of poetry played a role in the collapse of the Ming dynasty. This severe condemnation may have been provoked by the perceived overemphasis on individual expression, dissonance between self and society, and disengagement from history in the work of the Jingling poets. Poets in the Jingling School did, however, write about their time, and some, including the ministers Huang Daozhou (1585–1646) and Ni Yuanlu (1593–1644), became martyrs when the Ming fell. Indeed, the Jingling style of austere obscurity and melancholy reticence was particularly attractive to some early Qing poets who wished to protest their political integrity by underlining alienation from contemporary reality. Perhaps the dark views of the Jingling poets answered the need to seek correspondences between poetic style and national destiny; literary evaluation is thus tied to the quest for historical explanations.

Any easy contrast between late Ming excesses and early Qing restraint and control would be misleading. Anachronistic reconstructions of late Ming "liberation and rebellion" fail to take into account the complexities of that era – its contradictory mixture of hedonism and renunciation, defiance and conformity, iconoclasm and pervasive concern with tradition. For example, Li Zhi, in his famous essay "On the Childlike Mind" (Tongxin shuo), defines *wen* (literature, culture, civilization) as the "spontaneous patterning" (*ziwen*) of those with the pure, free spirit of the childlike mind, but he also valorizes the highly stylized (and later much vilified) eight-part examination essay as one of the forms of recent origin. He dismisses the canonical Confucian classics as "the breeding ground for phony men," but also posits sages untarnished by their learning. His wistful conclusion, "Alas, how can I find a real great sage who has not lost his childlike mind and have a word with him about *wen*!" echoes the line from *Zhuangzi*: "How can I find a man who has forgotten words so that I can have a word with him!" Li Zhi has a similar longing for and skepticism about higher authority, although, unlike in *Zhuangzi*, his philosophical wit is caustic rather than playful and transcendent. Even as he derides reliance on information, moral instruction, and the quest for fame as the enemies of the childlike mind, Li speaks self-consciously as a teacher and a polemicist. In a letter to Jiao Hong (1541–1620), he mocks the officious hypocrisy of "mountain recluses" (*shanren*) and "sages" (*shengren*), but also concludes with this provocative question: "How does one know that I do not have the merchant's actions and mind, that I [might] have donned a Buddhist's robes to deceive the world and steal fame?" In his colophon on a portrait of Confucius, he criticizes the unthinking adherence to ideas about orthodoxy and heterodoxy, but also claims to "follow the multitude" (*cong-zhong*) in avowing devotion to Confucius. Earnestness and self-mockery are here inexorably conjoined; he may yet be immodestly imitating the sage, whose decision to "follow the multitude" on certain rituals (*Analects* 9.3) is premised on judicious deliberation, not blind conformity. A hint of self-doubt seems to motivate this dialectics of heterodoxy and orthodoxy, self-effacement and self-aggrandizement.

To hold genuineness as an ideal has the potential for self-division, since to articulate and seek this ideal is to be already removed from it. Late Ming writers like to unmask the ostentatiously genuine, target the conventionally unconventional, and establish the distinction between themselves and others whom they accuse of bad faith and pretension. Not infrequently, they also turn the irony upon themselves. There are moments of stringent self-criticism. In many of his later writings, Yuan Hongdao (1568–1610) criticizes his own earlier glibness and sensual indulgence from a Buddhist perspective. Yuan Zhongdao (1570–1623) (Hongdao's younger brother) also ruefully upholds self-denial in a letter to Qian Qianyi. One seeks pleasures beyond the world, he writes, because worldly pleasures are unattainable or dangerous: "There are many instances when, being hunchbacked, one assumes the attitude of respect, which then becomes genuine respect." Genuineness is a nexus of correspondences driven by circumstance; it may yet be something imposed from without rather than emanating from within.

In this way, a self-critical edge may have arisen from the late Ming obsession with liminality and encompassing opposites. In the cross-currents of the period, writers constantly evaluate themselves and others. Yuan Zhongdao reveals his ambivalence toward Li Zhi by arguing that Li should not be imitated (by men like himself) even while praising him as inimitable. Many members of the Eastern Forest (Donglin) faction and the Revival Society (Fushe) were critical of the more extreme developments of Wang Yangming's teachings. The Jingling School was targeted in the classical revival of the last two decades of the Ming. Chen Zilong's 1632 poem, in which he deplores the overwhelmingly popular "Chu style" (referring to the Jingling School), already presages early Qing criticism of Zhong Xing (who hailed from Hubei, identified as ancient Chu) and his followers. In other words, critical judgments in the early Qing merely magnify late Ming self-doubt and intimations of negativity.

Even as early Qing writers criticized late Ming intellectual trends and literary styles for their misguided and inflated concern with subjectivity, they continued to ponder the boundaries of selfhood and self-scrutiny. Wang Fuzhi, in *Reflections and Questions* (*Siwen lu*), defines the self (*wo*) as "the condensation of great and just principles" (*da gong li*). By this logic, he goes on to argue in *Reading the Four Books* (*Du sishu daquan*), heavenly principles (*tianli*) can only be realized through human desires (*renyu*). Another philosopher, Chen Que (1604–1677), makes a similar rhetorical move in defending self-interest (*si*) as the fundamental impetus to moral action ("Discourse on self-interest," *Sishuo*). Huang Zongxi, in *Waiting for the Dawn: A Plan for the Prince* (*Mingyi daifang lu*), treats self-interest almost as a nascent consciousness of rights and a bulwark against the claims of absolute political power: in a surprisingly pragmatic twist to this utopian vision, justice (*gong*) becomes a balance of disparate self-interests negotiated through reciprocal recognition of limits. As I will demonstrate below, early Qing writers that purport to bear witness to and recall the trauma of dynastic transition, and to represent how selves and identities are shattered and reconstituted, obsessively stake their truth claim on memory and genuine emotion. In this period, a rich corpus of writings on the discourse of the self – including diaries, memoirs, letters, essays, and biographical and autobiographical accounts, as well as developments in poetry, fiction, and lyrical drama – chart new dimensions in the rhetoric of interiority, genuineness, and role-playing.

Finally, some early Qing literati simply continued late Ming literary trends. The flamboyant wit of Jin Shengtan's (1608–1661) essays, for example, reminds us of the style of Gongan writers. A generation later, the writer and anthologist Zhang Chao (1650–after 1707) still self-consciously emphasizes his empathy with late Ming sensibility in his *Shadows of Secret Dreams* (*Youmeng ying*), which is virtually indistinguishable from late Ming vignettes on the art of living.

The sociological contexts of literature

A comparable picture of continuities, reversals, and transformations emerges in the contexts of literary production and reception. The thriving late Ming publishing industry seems to have survived the turmoil of dynastic transition relatively unscathed. Even though, as Robert Hegel notes, "far fewer illustrated editions of plays were published after 1640," the first decade of Qing rule saw the continued production of many expensive, large-format editions of fiction characteristic of the late Ming. As in the late Ming, prominent men of letters, such as Wang Wan (1624–1691), Zhu Yizun, and Wang Shizhen (1634–1711), printed their own writings. Especially after the establishment of the imperial printer at Wuying Palace in 1673, Hegel observes, government publications became more centralized and more narrowly devoted to canonical and orthodox texts.

There was widespread interest in collectanea (*congshu*) in this period, prompted by nostalgia as well as anxiety about the toll taken by political disorder. Open letters soliciting "rare editions of Tang and Song texts" for republication were not uncommon. New compilations of Ming writings shaped the public memory of the fallen dynasty and defined its legacy. Zhu Yizun published an anthology of Ming poetry (*Ming shi zong*). Huang Zongxi compiled the *Sea of Ming Prose* (*Ming wen hai*) and defended the legacy of Ming thought in his *History of Ming Confucian Thinkers*. The House of Imbibing from the Ancients (Jigu ge) founded by Mao Jin (1599–1659) published Qian Qianyi's *Collective Poems of the Successive Reigns* (*Liechao shiji*) in 1652. In "Song of Jigu ge" (Jigu ge ge), Wu Weiye praises Mao Jin's work in collecting and publishing as the safeguard of cultural continuity and a bulwark against dispersal and destruction. The section devoted to women poets in Qian's anthology was probably edited by his concubine, the courtesan–poet Liu Rushi. Interest in women's writings remained strong; we have more extant anthologies of women's poetry from the early Qing than from any other period of comparable

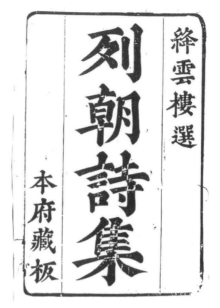

4. From *Collected Poems of the Successive Reigns* (*Liechao shiji*; Changshu: Mao Jin, 1652), compiled by Qian Qianyi and his wife, the famous courtesan Liu Rushi. Collection of Yale University Library.

duration. A notable example is Wang Duanshu's (1621–ca 1701) ambitious *Complementary Canon of Poetry by Notable Women* (*Mingyuan shiwei*, 1667).

Early Qing literary communities show how political and aesthetic concerns intersect in the making of taste, trends, and reputations. Literary schools (*menpai*) continued to be associated with locality. Notable examples include, in poetry, the Yushan School led by Qian Qianyi and the Loudong School led by Wu Weiye, both in Jiangsu; and in song lyric, the Yangxian School in Jiangsu led by Chen Weisong and the Zhexi (western Zhejiang) School led by Zhu Yizun. Women's literary groups were often bound by family and social ties, such as the group that gathered around Shang Jinglan (1604–ca 1680), the widow of the Ming scholar–official and martyr Qi Biaojia (1602–1645), in Kuaiji (Zhejiang). In Hangzhou, the gentry women who formed the Banana Garden Poetry Club (*Jiaoyuan shishe*) were a highly visible part of the cultural landscape and a source of local pride, as Dorothy Ko notes. Canonical aspirations transcended regional ties, and Wang Shizhen's school of "ineffable essence and resonance" (*shenyun*) had a national following. Wang hailed from Shandong, as did Pu Songling, Kong Shangren, Ding Yaokang (1599–1669),

Song Wan (1614–1673), and Zhao Zhixin (1662–1744), among other literary luminaries. The new prominence of writers from the north – as distinct from the late Ming literary scene – is also reflected in the prevalent "south–north" pairing of masters, such as, in poetry, Zhu Yizun and Wang Shizhen (*nan Zhu bei Wang*), and Shi Runzhang (1619–83) and Song Wan (*nan Shi bei Song*); and in drama, Hong Sheng and Kong Shangren (*nan Hong bei Kong*).

Du Dengchun (late seventeenth century) famously remarked in his history of literary societies (*Sheshi shimo*) that the late Ming "brought court politics to literary societies," while the early Qing "brought literary societies to court politics." Written in 1692, Du's obligatory tribute to contemporary literary mores should not be taken as proof that civility replaced factionalism at the Qing court; rather, his need to defend literary societies as having a salutary influence points to real anxiety about threats to their existence. After the fall of the Ming, the Revival Society and its branch organizations supposedly became extinct but enjoyed afterlives under new names, such as the Society of Blue Waves (Canglang hui), the Society of Caution (Shenjiao she), the Society of Common Voice (Tongsheng she), or the Great Society of the Ten Prefectures (Shijun dashe). Members of the Revival Society and their sons and disciples continued to dominate the early Qing cultural landscape, either as loyalists or as officials. The heady blend of politics, scholarship, and literature that had characterized the Revival Society found new life as early Qing literary societies articulated a variety of political directions. Of these the most stirring was loyalism. He Zongmei notes that the regions where anti-Qing resistance was most persistent, namely Jiangsu, Zhejiang, Guangdong, and Fujian, also had the most active literary societies formed by loyalists, such as the Poetry Society of Vigilant Withdrawal (Jingyin shishe) – also called the Covenant of Escape (Tao zhi meng) or the Society of Escape (Taoshe) – of Jiangnan, the West Lake Societies and South Lake Societies of Eastern Zhejiang, and the West Garden Poetry Society (Xiyuan shishe) of Guangdong. Some of these groups, such as the Society of Loyalty and Sincerity (Zhongcheng she) led by former Revival Society members Yang Tinglin (d. 1646) and Liu Tongsheng, were thinly disguised military groups organizing anti-Qing resistance.

Examination essays, which featured prominently in Ming and Qing literary societies, were irrelevant for loyalists, whose very self-definition was based on not taking office under the Qing. Instead, their literary endeavors aimed at preserving memories of the Ming and defining the legacy of loyalism. Members of the Poetry Society of Vigilant Withdrawal, for example, compiled the *Historical Records of the Ming* (*Ming shiji*), *Expanded Records of Song Loyalists* (*Guang Song yimin lu*), and *Anthology of Poems from the Tianqi and Chongzhen*

Eras (*Tianqi Chongzhen liangchao yishi*), in which poems by Ming martyrs have pride of place. Poetry gatherings were sometimes turned into rites of commemoration for the fallen Ming, where political commitment was enshrined in sacrifices to emblems of poetic authority and political integrity, such as Qu Yuan and Tao Yuanming. These networks of literary communities may also have facilitated communication or provided refuge for those involved in resistance. Recognizing their subversive potential, the Qing court issued an edict in 1660 banning "the establishment of covenants and the formation of societies," but literary gatherings continued to have political implications in less tangible ways.

Some loyalist poetry societies, especially those in Eastern Zhejiang, demanded that its members not consort with Qing officials. Their counterparts in Guangdong were less stringent. There Liang Peilan (1629–1705), a Qing official, became involved in the organization of poetry societies whose members were mostly loyalists. In 1653, Wu Weiye presided over a literary gathering, attended by several thousands, at Tiger Mound (near Suzhou). It was convened to reconcile factional struggles between the aforementioned Society of Caution and Society of Common Voice, which apparently included both loyalists and participants in the new order. A leader of the Revival Society during the late Ming, Wu seemed to be harking back to past glories – a famous meeting had been held at Tiger Mound in 1642 – even as he tried to heal present-day divisions. The poems he wrote for the occasion were filled with nostalgia for the fallen dynasty; yet, by coming so much into the public eye, he might have made it more difficult to avoid being pressed to serve the new government, and only a few months later he went north to take office in Beijing. These inconsistencies and ambiguities testify to the unstable, shifting boundaries between "loyalists" and "conformers." The two were not radically separate camps, although political choices sometimes did divide friends and family. Both categories encompassed many different shades of choices and inclinations. Ties of kinship and friendship, literary and social networks, sometimes dating back to the late Ming, often persisted across a spectrum of groups with varying political allegiances, as Xie Zhengguang (Andrew Hsieh) notes.

Although some loyalists, like Wang Fuzhi and the poet Xing Fang (1590–1653), shunned all contact with Qing officials, social interaction between the two groups was common. High-ranking Qing officials, such as Zhou Lianggong (1612–1672), Cao Rong (1613–1685), Gong Dingzi (1616–1673), and Liang Qingbiao (1620–1691), all former Ming officials and important literary figures in their own right, offered help and refuge to loyalists. The latter, for their part, conferred on their protectors the aura of moral authority and cultural capital precisely because of their chosen disempowerment. A Qing official like Zhou Lianggong, suffering the sting of marginalization while negotiating the dangers of political life, would have shared fellow feelings with loyalists. Zhou was especially active in promoting the loyalist poet Wu Jiaji (1618–1684). Wang Shizhen, the most influential Qing poet from the 1670s, actively sought the friendship of poets who refused to participate in the new regime while serving as police magistrate in Yangzhou from 1660 to 1664. In some ways, Wang's place in the canon depended, at least initially, on their support and approval.

Literary gatherings and associations encompassing persons of different political persuasions, such as that of Wu Weiye Tiger Mound or Wang Shizhen in Yangzhou, thus point to the evolution of new literary communities. Collections of writings provide another index. The poems of Liang Peilan, a Qing official, appear alongside the works of his loyalist friends Qu Dajun and Chen Gongyin (1631–1700) in the Kangxi-era anthology compiled by Wang Zhun, *Selections of Poems by Three Masters from Guangdong* (*Lingnan sanjia shixuan*). Mao Xiang (1611–1693), once active in the Revival Society, continued to host literary gatherings on his garden estate after the fall of the dynasty. His anthology of writings by himself, his family members, and his friends, *Collected Writings of Kindred Spirits* (*Tongren ji*), whose compilation spanned the mid-Kangxi period (1673–ca 1692), chronicles similar social interactions between different political groups. Likewise, Deng Hanyi's (1617–1689) *Perspectives on Poetry* (*Shiguan*) anthologizes works by both loyalists and Qing officials as he addresses the memories, hopes, and dilemmas of his era.

Literary communities formed in exile in Manchuria highlight the contradictory nature of the process of political accommodation. These groups included those suspected of involvement in resistance, casualties of factional struggles at court, as well as victims of successive waves of persecution directed especially against the literati of Jiangnan. The common fate of exile may have discouraged political differences, and political caution or the psychology of survival may have tempered loyalist lamentation. Lawrence Yim notes how the loyalist Cantonese monk–poet Hanke (1612–1659) sometimes bravely celebrates new horizons and seeks to domesticate the alien landscape of Manchuria. In the wake of the 1657 examination scandal, Wu Zhaoqian (1631–1684) was exiled to Ningguta (in Manchuria), where, as his mentor Wu Weiye laments, "Mountains are not mountains, waters not waters, / Life is not life, and death not death." Yet the poetic exchanges of the Society of Seven Poets (Qizi zhi hui), of which Wu was a member, often dwell on the familiar contours of literati culture rather than their harsh environment. The Icy Sky Poetry Society (Bingtian shishe) is said to show loyalist sentiments, yet its members, including Hanke, consorted with Gaosai, the Manchu prince presiding over the branch court of Shengjing (Shenyang or Mukden, the pre-conquest capital of the Manchus).

The loyalist poet Yan Ermei (1603–1679) compared Gaosai to Prince Xiao of Liang, patron of belles-lettres in the early Han dynasty. Indeed, as Yan Dichang notes, patronage of literature by the Qing imperial and princely courts reached a level unmatched by any previous dynasty. It was as if the Manchu ruling elite could claim its own distinct heritage only after a confident mastery of the Han Chinese cultural tradition. The Kangxi Emperor has 1,100 extant poems; his grandson, the Qianlong Emperor, left behind more than 40,000. In 1682, the former led a large group of ministers, many of them notable poets, in composing a feast poem in the *boliang* form, whereby each participant contributes one line, following the same rhyme throughout. The emperor's own preface includes copious references to political ideals enunciated in the canonical classics. Imperial literary gatherings thus became occasions to celebrate political harmony and the glory of "government by culture" (*wenzhi*). The literary circles of some Manchu noblemen, most notably Yunduan (1680–1704) and the great lyricist Nara Singde (Nalan Xingde, 1655–1685), included renowned Han Chinese poets and dramatists, although these associations also furnished the pretext for Yunduan's demotion.

The merging of poetic authority and political power embodied in the literary activities of the Manchu elite is also evident in the conferment of high positions at court upon leading Han men of letters, such as Wang Shizhen and Zhu Yizun during the Kangxi reign and Shen Deqian (1673–1769) and Weng Fanggang (1733–1818) during the Qianlong reign. As Yan Dichang points out, however, there was also implied polarity and opposition between scholar–officials at court (*chao*) and those not holding office (*ye*). Many of the most creative and vibrant voices in Qing literature belonged to those caught in failure, alienation, and disempowerment – loyalists and their sympathizers, the exiled, the casualties of factional struggles, literati who hovered at the margins of power.

On one level, the nature and intensity of this opposition can be gauged by the scope of censorship, which seems to have broadened from the 1660s on. Pan Chengzhang (1626–1663) and Wu Yan, the chief compilers of the aforementioned *Historical Records of the Ming*, were put to death in the aftermath of the Ming history case (1661–1663), as alleged defamations of the Qing led to widespread reprisals. The *Anthology of Poems from the Tianqi and Chongzhen*

Eras, referred to above, was proscribed in 1667. As a result of court factional struggles, accusations that Hong Sheng's *Palace of Eternal Life* was performed during national mourning for Empress Dong in 1689 led to Hong's imprisonment and expulsion from the imperial academy. Among those implicated were the poets Zha Silian (1650–1727) and Zhao Zhixin. Zha changed his name to Shenxing ("Cautious Conduct") and henceforth contented himself with insinuating irony and dissatisfaction under a veneer of equanimity. Zhao, barred from office, developed a caustic, discursive bent in his poetry and implicitly attacked the merging of political and poetic authority; hence his dogged criticism of his uncle by marriage, Wang Shizhen. Dai Mingshi (1653–1713) was prosecuted from 1711 to 1713 and eventually executed for sedition in his *Southern Mountain Collection (Nanshan ji)*; possibly linked to the struggle for imperial succession, his case presages the "literary inquisition" of the Qianlong reign. The banning of "immoral" materials (as distinct from the politically subversive) was more sporadic. Successive Qing legal codes categorically banned "licentious fiction and drama." In 1660, the Zhejiang official Zhang Jinyan was demoted for supporting the publication of Li Yu's *Silent Operas (Wusheng xi)*. Significantly, Li Yu himself did not get into trouble. Ding Yaokang was briefly imprisoned in 1665 because his *Sequel to the Plum in the Golden Vase (Xu Jin Ping Mei)* was alleged to have used the Song–Jurchen conflict to criticize the Manchu conquest and not because of its sexual content. Tang Bin (1627–1687), inspector of Jiangsu, made his reputation by assiduously enforcing the banning decrees of the Kangxi reign. Specific titles were usually not listed for proscription until 1778.

II. History and memory in early Qing literature

Historical engagement

To a certain extent censorship determined the survival, direction, and explicitness of historical engagements. Apart from the need to accommodate political constraints, complex and conflicting emotions sometimes seek to be modulated through strategies of indirect expression. The historian Quan Zuwang (1705–1755) enumerates the "inner collections" (*neiji*) of eastern Zhejiang loyalists; either completely hidden or enjoying very limited circulation, these works express the authors' uncensored thoughts and feelings and were hard to find even in Quan's time. Many of our received texts from this period suffered elisions and changes by authors, anthologists, publishers, or the academicians responsible for the compilation of the *Four Treasuries* during the Qianlong reign. Some were rescued from oblivion only during the late Qing and early Republican period. Not surprisingly, references to contemporary or recent history that might have been deemed subversive were likely to be suppressed or else cloaked in obliqueness and ambiguities.

Indirectness and reticence pose special problems for the latter-day reader. When is it legitimate to infer political references? In some cases, biographical context, literary history, and cultural convention provide guidance. Early Qing advocates of the late Tang style championed the affective power and the political-historical significance of an allusive and indirect diction, as evinced by the flourishing of early Qing commentaries on the late Tang poet Li Shangyin (813?–858). The late thirteenth-century anthology *Supplementary Titles for the Music Bureau* (*Yuefu buti*), which contains allusive and mournful song lyrics on objects, was republished to great acclaim in 1679, probably because the late Southern Song style of lamenting the decline and fall of the Song dynasty through indirect expression had contemporary resonance. The philosopher Wang Fuzhi, also an accomplished poet and lyricist, wrote ninety-nine poems on fallen blossoms, grouped in sequences titled "original," "sequels," "extensions," and "supplements." Knowing what we do of his life as a staunch loyalist, and given the established literary precedent of associating the passing of spring with the decline and fall of dynasties, we are justified in reading the poems as laments for the fallen Ming.

Dating is crucial for such context-dependent interpretations. For example, we have two extant song lyrics on willow catkins by Chen Zilong, one dated to the 1630s and the other to 1647. They share a similar diction, drawing on conventional associations of catkins with dispersal, separation, helplessness, and melancholy; both describe the catkins as "floating, drifting" (*piaobo*). In the earlier song lyric, we are prone to read this as referring to the vicissitudes of a courtesan's uncertain fate and the disappointments of love, because between 1632 and 1635 Chen was in the throes of a romantic relationship with the courtesan–poet Liu Rushi. By contrast, the same descriptive compound in the 1647 song lyric summons up associations with Chen Zilong's peregrinations as a resistance fighter and a fugitive after the conquest because, composed shortly before Chen's martyrdom, it is likely to invite a political interpretation.

Modern interpretations are more likely to err on the side of political allegory, especially with reference to Ming loyalism and anti-Qing resistance. Seventeenth-century writers and their audience may have welcomed such indeterminacy as precisely the vehicle allowing the greatest freedom and resonance, both because of the protection it afforded and because of the conflicting emotions it addressed. Perhaps this explains the extraordinary impact of

Wang Shizhen's "Autumn Willows" poems. Composed upon the formation of the Autumn Willows Poetry Society in 1657 at Lake Ming in Lixia (Shandong), they elicited hundreds of poetic responses, including many by women, and immensely enhanced the fame of the twenty-three-year-old poet. The elegiac nature of these poems is confirmed by tantalizing "allegorical indices," such as a lake named "Ming," and ubiquitous references to Jinling, the capital of the Ming under its first two emperors and also of the Southern Ming, as well as by the time-honored tradition of fusing feminized expressions of longing with historical lamentation. Yet there are no specific contemporary references. Critical discussion of these poems has revolved around two overlapping issues: are there any topical allusions, and how deep is the poet's nostalgia and grief for the fallen dynasty? Perhaps what matters is not that there are definitive answers to such questions, but that Wang has renewed a poetic idiom resonant and flexible enough to encompass diverse interpretations. Among the extant response poems, we find gentle melancholy, pointed loyalist lament, universalized regret, and nostalgia for the courtesan world of Qinhuai pleasure quarters near Jinling. Consciously or not, Wang created an elusive, elegiac diction that was capable of negotiating the conflicting demands and expectations of literary communities that made divergent political choices.

That said, the countervailing tendency to strive for historical veracity through direct expression and factual records is also evident. Lynn Struve has extensively documented writings chronicling and remembering the Ming–Qing conflict, in which she notes a great range of rhetorical choices. The eyewitness account best known to modern readers is "An Account of Ten Days in Yangzhou" (Yangzhou shiri ji), which first came to light only in the Daoguang reign (1821–1850). In it, Wang Xiuchu relates the harrowing atrocities visited on Yangzhou in 1645 for resisting the Qing conquest. Nothing is known about Wang, although some clues in "Ten Days" suggest that he was not a Yangzhou native. His account conveys the sense of raw, unmitigated perception and experience, as the narrator suppresses subsequent knowledge, presenting the confusion of each terrifying moment as it unfolds. The late Ming obsession with ways of seeing is given a lurid, traumatic turn as Wang observes from unlikely hiding places the murder of his brothers and the torture of his pregnant wife. Quest for survival seems to override historical reflection or clear-cut ideological concerns. Wang makes few explicit judgments, except to condemn women who shamelessly consorted with the Manchu invaders and their Han collaborators and tried to profit from their looting: "Alas, this is why China is in chaos!" In contrast, many other accounts vindicate Yangzhou women as martyrs who fused chastity with political integrity.

Diaries, letters, and biographical and autobiographical accounts provide a valuable window into the personal experience of the cataclysmic Ming–Qing transition. A notable example is Ye Shaoyuan's (1589–1648) *Daily Records of the Journey Beginning on the Day Jia* (*Jia xing rizhu*). The account begins on the twenty-fifth day of the eighth month of 1645, the *jiachen* day in the sexagenary cycle, when Ye took the tonsure and left his ancestral home. The title also alludes to the line "On the morning of Jia I set forth," from "Elegy for Ying" (*Ai Ying*) in *Verses of Chu* (*Chuci*), where the poet laments the destruction of the ancient Chu capital, Ying, as he goes off into exile. Spanning a little over three years (1645–1648), *Daily Records* continues Ye's annalistic and anecdotal writings about his life (*Autobiographical Annals, Zizhuan nianpu*, 1638; *Sequel to Autobiographical Annals, Nianpu xuzuan*, 1645; *Other Records Related to Tianliao's Autobiographical Annals, Tianliao nianpu bieji*, 1645) in a more fluid, open-ended form. The tone of the diary becomes progressively more gloomy and despairing. Its tragic pathos is forged by the fusion of national calamity with personal loss, as Ye's wife, the poet Shen Yixiu (1590–1635), and four of their children (including the precocious woman poet Ye Xiaoluan discussed in Chapter 2) had died some years before the fall of the Ming. Ye mixes broadly discursive and proclamatory statements on the political situation with private musings on the uncertainties that continued to dog him and his surviving sons as they became fugitive monks in the temples and mountains of Jiangsu. Numerous references to ghosts, spirits, and divination represent attempts to impose provisional order on the experience of chaos and disintegration. In the midst of great suffering and hardship, Ye gives precisely observed and finely delineated vignettes of beauty in nature, expressing keen sensual enjoyment of the modest pleasures that come his way, in a manner reminiscent of late Ming informal writings. Despite Ye's Buddhist vows of renunciation, poetic exchanges and other communications affirm continual ties with his household and literary–social circles. *Daily Records* exemplifies how literati lives and identities were shattered and remade at this juncture.

Contemporary and recent history is also filtered through the so-called novels on current events (*shishi xiaoshuo*) and plays on current events (*shishi ju*), which offer direct representation, uncompromising judgments, and insistent views on moral clarity. Among the twenty or so known novels engaged with contemporary or recent history, about eight were written during the Chongzhen era (1628–1644) and the rest between 1644 and the mid-1660s. These works often choose to personalize evil in the form of iniquitous protagonists, on whom rests the blame for dynastic decline (and, in post-conquest writings, the fall of the Ming). These archvillains include the eunuch Wei Zhongxian (1568–1627), whose abuse of power wrought much havoc in late Ming politics; the rebel Li Zicheng (d. 1645), who precipitated the final collapse of the dynasty; and Ma Shiying (*jinshi* 1619, d. ca 1646) and Ruan Dacheng (1587–1646), self-serving ministers of the short-lived Southern Ming. The accounts of Wei Zhongxian show a lingering fascination with his precipitous rise, as in *Idle Critiques of Monstrous Times* (*Taowu xianping*, ca late 1640s). No such humanizing touches apply to Li, Ma, or Ruan, although in contemporary miscellanies some grudgingly admire Ruan as a playwright and some attempt to defend Ma. One can well imagine the cathartic effect of these novels, in which the downfall of the villains creates a provisional sense of resolution. Among the works in this genre, *History According to the Woodcutter* (*Qiao shi*) by the Woodcutter of the Lower Yangzi (Jiangzuo qiaozi), variously identified as Lu Yingyang (ca 1572–ca 1658) or Li Qing (1602–1683), stands out as a sober yet vivid vernacularization of sources on Ming history from 1620 to 1645. Most of these novels are based on rumors, anecdotes, or official reports in the *Capital Gazette* (*Dibao*). We find the immediacy of eyewitness accounts in a few rare cases presented by Struve, such as *Remnant Accounts from the Yangzi Cape* (*Haijiao yibian*) by the Roaming Unofficial Historian (Manyou yeshi, preface dated 1648) and *Remnant Accounts from the Seven Peaks* (*Qifeng yibian*) by the Woodcutting Daoist of the Seven Peaks (Qifeng qiao daoren, preface dated 1648). Both chronicle Manchu atrocities and anti-Qing resistance in the Changshu area in 1645.

In a parallel development, a spate of plays by a group of dramatists associated with Suzhou address social issues and political developments from late Ming to early Qing. Playwrights from the Suzhou School typically belonged to a lower social echelon and did not hold office; they captured the liveliness of urban culture with a relatively plain diction. Perhaps it was inevitable that Suzhou, as the stronghold of both the Revival Society and theatrical culture, should see the rise of political drama. Wei Zhongxian's struggle with the Eastern Forest faction, the subject of various late Ming and early Qing novels, is also widely enacted on the stage, most notably in Li Xuanyu's *Registers of the Pure and Loyal* (*Qing zhong pu*, preface by Wu Weiye dated 1659). *Registers* glorifies the upright minister Zhou Shunchang (1584–1626), persecuted to death by Wei's faction, and five plebeian heroes martyred for trying to defend Zhou in a popular uprising in 1626. The "view from below" implied in the tribute to the "five righteous men" is also borne out in Li's *Peace for All* (*Wanmin an*, unfortunately no longer extant), which features as heroes the weavers of Suzhou, driven by the oppression of tax collectors to revolt in 1601. As with the novels in which evil is exorcised, plays dealing with contemporary events are eager to distill some version of order from the the reality of chaos, devastation, and dynastic collapse. Thus Li Xuanyu's *Two Manly Heroes* (*Liang xumei*) glorifies the success of a late Ming commander, Huang Yujin, and his wife, Madame Deng, in pacifying and repelling peasant insurgents. They seek refuge in reclusion after the fall of the Ming. In another play, *Union across Ten Thousand Miles* (*Wanli yuan*), Li celebrates Huang Xiangjian as he journeys from Suzhou to Yunnan in search of his parents and returns with them during the chaos of dynastic transition. The historical Huang left a memoir and pictorial record of his filial trek, about which many famous literati wrote eulogistic accounts. Affirmation of familial order, as a kind of recompense for the breakdown of political order, obviously had special resonance during this period. In both fiction and drama, the rapid transition from historical reality to page and stage, so rapid that the person "in the act" could easily become his own audience or reader, created a special sense of urgency, and perhaps also the feeling that aesthetic illusion could augment or influence historical understanding.

Some of the works by the Suzhou dramatists, though not directly tackling contemporary events, offer obvious historical analogies. The violent usurpation of the throne in 1403 by Prince Yan (later the Yongle Emperor, r. 1403–1424) had particular contemporary resonance as a stirring story of "north versus south." The historical Prince Yan came down from the north to Nanjing, ousted and probably killed his nephew, the Jianwen Emperor, and ruthlessly eliminated many officials loyal to Jianwen. Li Xuanyu's *Slaughter of the Ten Thousand Loyal Ones* (*Qianzhong lu*) was but the best known of a number of plays on the martyrs of the Jianwen court. Another favorite "north-versus-south" moment is the Song–Jurchen struggle of the twelfth century. Yue Fei (1103–1141), the national hero who repelled the Jurchen armies, is lionized in plays by Li Xuanyu, Zhang Dafu, and Zhu Zuochao.

Even more than other genres, poetry aspired to bear witness to, keep a true record of, and articulate emotional responses to the Ming–Qing transition. Countless contemporary prefaces to poetry collections laud the very act of writing poetry as a means to defy chaos and destruction. Memory, historical reflection, and poetic self-consciousness converged in new ways in early Qing poetry. Reversing the well-known dictum from *Mengzi*, "after the *Odes* perished, the *Spring and Autumn Annals* was created," Huang Zongxi declares, "How little is it known that, when historical records perished, poetry was created." Poetry rescues from oblivion what is defeated and destroyed, and often what is missing, suppressed, or distorted in the official historiography compiled by the victors. Elsewhere Huang argues that eras of decline and chaos produce great poetry: the absolute disjunction between the poet and his historical reality leads to extreme emotions of anguish and despair, and these in turn make for compelling, involuntary poetic expression.

The epithet of "poet–historian" (shishi) is conferred on or self-consciously embraced by many early Qing poets. First used of Du Fu (712–770) by Meng Qi, the term implies a personal experience of significant (usually traumatic) historical events, the attempt to give a full and accurate account of those events and experiences, the critical acumen to proceed from surface to meaning, and the ability to evoke a world (usually a lost world) with the sweep of totality. Extensive and probing presentation often involved narrative and discursive modes, although some powerful voices also urged the use of subtle and restrained poetic language to convey historical insights and laments. Many early Qing poets modeled their responses to the contemporary crisis on Du Fu's "Autumn Meditations" (Qiuxing), a set of poems famous for their allusive complexity and lyrical involution. This fact alone attests to the importance of indirect expression, metaphorical and allegorical references, and affective intensity in the idea of "poet–historian." Following this logic, Qian Qianyi discourses on how poetry and historical writings are connected by their shared reliance on subtle expression (wei).

In practice, the ideal of the poet–historian encompasses many modes and styles. Wu Jiaji is commended for "using poetry as history" (yi shi wei shi) on account of his stark depictions of human suffering. He chronicles, among other things, the devastation of war, official abuses, and natural disasters. Turning to the ballads of Du Fu and Bai Juyi (772–846) as models, he eschews allusive and elaborate diction. Poets actively involved in anti-Qing resistance, such as Gu Yanwu, Qu Dajun, and Qian Bingdeng (1612–1693), could claim special moral authority as they write about a suppressed history from within, giving their poetic testimony of a doomed cause. More generally, "poetic history" can include elegiac or impassioned commemoration of heroes, martyrs, and victims; modulated perspectives on the historical personages and events of the Ming–Qing transition; and autobiographical journeys of witnessing and remembering. The focus is often contemporary, although genres of "meditations on the past" (huaigu) and "reflections on history" (yongshi) also extend the affective and intellectual space for coping with traumatic historical events. The search for historical authority in poetry often calls for the self-conscious delineation of the processes of memory and historical reflection. To try to tell the truth is to ponder the margins between subjective truth and objective fact, the balance or tension between historical judgment and emotional response. Lyrical engagement with historical crisis thus often presumes the fusion of historical understanding and self-understanding.

One of the best examples of the poetry and poetics of historical engagement is Qian Qianyi. A leader of the Eastern Forest faction, he was deeply involved in the political struggles and cultural debates of the late Ming. When the Southern Ming court in Nanjing fell to Manchu forces in 1645, Qian, then sixty-three and minister of rites, surrendered and served for about five months as a Qing official in 1646 before pleading sickness and resigning. As Kang-i Sun Chang notes, his "loss of integrity" accounts for the unjust dismissal and neglect of his poetry by later generations, although his contemporaries seem to have been more forgiving. The Qianlong Emperor vilified Qian Qianyi and banned his writings, which contain numerous references to the loyalist resistance, either implying or openly avowing anti-Qing sentiments. Compilers of the *Four Treasuries* excluded Qian's works and defamed him through elisions and distortions of other early Qing writings. This vehement denunciation ensured Qian's eclipse for almost two centuries. Ironically, the modern rehabilitation of Qian is built on substantiating Qianlong's suspicion that he was in fact subversive. Reinterpretations of Qian's political choices often lead to more favorable literary evaluations, and he has been readmitted to the canon on the strength of poems that defined him as an "inner" – that is, hidden or misunderstood – Ming loyalist.

It is hard to untangle accusations and self-justifications, intentionality and retrospective construction, in our reading of Qian Qianyi's densely allusive poems. For example, Qian wrote a long and poignant poem mourning the martyrdom in anti-Qing resistance of his disciple and close friend Qu Shisi (1590–1651), the architect of the holdover Ming court of Yongli in the south-west. Responding to the story that Qu had become the city-god of Suzhou, Qian wrote "Twelve Songs Welcoming the Spirit" (Yingshen qu shi'er shou), mixing willful credulity and ironic skepticism with overwhelming grief. These poems commemorating Qu Shisi are complex and moving, yet a suspicious and unsympathetic critic may well regard lamentation as a means of disingenuous self-fashioning, whereby sorrow intimates deep affinity and perhaps even common aspirations and a shared fate. In fact, Qian's covert loyalist activities are attested by Qu's memorial to the Yongli court. The issue, however, is not whether Qian is vindicated by these correct sentiments (explicitly or indirectly expressed); rather, his case demonstrates how compromises and hesitations may produce equally compelling or more complex literary creations, and reminds us not to conflate moral with literary judgment as a matter of course.

During his brief tenure at the Qing court, Qian was assistant overseer in the compilation of the history of the Ming. He continued writing Ming history after he resigned; unfortunately his drafts, along with his vast book collection, were destroyed in a fire. His self-perception as a historian is evident in the *Collective Poems of the Successive Reigns*, which ties the appraisal of Ming poets to the vicissitudes of Ming history. The idea of poet–historian is often linked to longer poetic forms with their abundance of narrative and descriptive detail. Qian favored quatrains and regulated verse, but overcame their brevity to create a mood of sustained meditation by grouping them in poetic sequences. The most impressive example is probably his collection *Throwing down the Brush* (*Toubi ji*, 1659–1663), containing thirteen series of eight poems each, all modeled after Du Fu's series of eight "Autumn Meditations" – hence their alternative title "Later Autumn Meditations" (Hou qiuxing) – plus four poems in which Qian commented on his own act of creation. The series can jointly be read as one long poem chronicling the final throes of Ming resistance from 1659 to 1663, as well as Qian's own hopes, fears, and despair as he reacted to first ephemeral success and then inexorable defeat. In the seventh month of 1659, when Zheng Chenggong's navy was poised to capture Nanjing, Qian was euphoric, as reflected in the first series. Shortly thereafter, Zheng was defeated and retreated to Taiwan. By 1663, Zheng had died and the Yongli court in the southwest had been decisively suppressed. The collection's title, *Toubi*, alludes to the Han dynasty general Ban Chao (32–102), who threw down his brush to undertake military ventures. Qian's self-image in the poetic series is also as one who has embraced heroic endeavor. He seemed to have acted as strategist for Zheng Chenggong. He sounds like a military adviser in the second series when he remonstrates against abandoning the Yangzi area and urges Zheng to bide his time: "The loss of a few chess pieces is no cause for grief" (second series, no. 3, line 2; chess is one of Qian's favorite poetic metaphors for politics and history).

Qian's political aspirations merge with the heroic image of his concubine, the former courtesan Liu Rushi, in the third series, written in the eighth month of 1659, when Qian parted from Liu to join the remnants of Zheng Chenggong's navy near Changshu. The journey was rendered irrelevant by the complete destruction of Zheng's troops. Intended as a tribute to Liu Rushi, these eight poems celebrate her courage and tenacity as a Ming loyalist. In the fourth poem, a chess game by the window, an image of domestic felicity, is charged with political and historical significance:

> She stakes her heart on the chess game of worlds and seas –
> To the squares are tied, unremitting, her joys and sorrows.
> The day news came of troops charging through Southland,
> Was just when, at west window, we faced each other over chess.
> Drops of the water-clock were sparse: we feared the army's waning momentum.
> Blossoms of burnt wicks dropped: we laughed at the slow sound of chess pieces.
> May we together ponder the Jinshan strategy,
> When, beating the war drum in person, you will console my longing.

The "chess game of worlds and seas" and the literal chess game converge as both are caught in a suspended moment: the attention of Qian and Liu is riveted, with great expectation and fear, on the former, so much so that they are drawn into rapt forgetfulness of the latter (lines 5–6). The poet hopes for a reenactment of the Battle of Jinshan, when the Song general Han Shizhong won an important victory over the Jurchens, and he seeks consolation in the image of Liu Rushi beating the war drum to boost morale, just as Han's concubine, the former courtesan Liang Hongyu, has done in stories and plays (lines 7–8). Qian's testimony to Liu's valor and determination is thus also self-redemption, symbolically undoing the shame of his compromise and service under the new regime.

The tone of the poetic sequence grows progressively more anguished, as the sense of displacement and homelessness brought on by the conquest becomes irrevocable: "There is a place, but only for hearing the roaring of waves, / With no sky, how can flying frost be seen?" (twelfth series, no. 3, lines 3–4). Land about to be engulfed by waves recalls the familiar expression of "inundated land," often used to refer to the loss of one's country. Flying frost, visible emblem of heaven's sympathy, cannot be seen in the gathering gloom. Resistance against darkness and disintegration is to be sought in writing. As with Du Fu's "Autumn Meditations," Qian's poems have a self-reflexive dimension. His "lone chants by the marshes," like Qu Yuan's, will turn inward, understood by few: "Like a riddle, like a jest, and perhaps above all like an omen, / From one not mad, not drunk, and also not possessed by demons." Qian is to claim his place in history by following Du Fu's example: "Du Fu, as poet–historian, leaves his name in the annals of history" (first series, no. 8, line 8).

Qian Qianyi, Wu Weiye, and Gong Dingzi are anthologized together in *Poems by the Three Great Masters of the Lower Yangzi* (*Jiangzuo san dajia shichao*,

1667) by Gu Youxiao (1619–1689) and Zhao Yun. All three were former Ming officials who also served under the Qing, Gong's career as a Qing official being the most prolonged and distinguished. Gong has generally been considered a lesser talent, but his greater equanimity and less tormented acceptance of the new order, as compared to Qian and Wu, may have contributed to an impression of glibness.

Wu Weiye held office under the Qing from 1654 to 1656 and later regretted it. He was classified, like Qian Qianyi, under the category of "officials who served two dynasties." Unlike Qian, however, his poetry received the enthusiastic endorsement of the Qianlong Emperor, and he heads the Qing collections in the *Four Treasuries*. Posterity has also been more forgiving towards Wu, and most people have accepted his version of events – that he unwillingly took office under pressure from his family and the Qing authorities. Wu's post-1644 writings are suffused with lamentation for the fall of the Ming dynasty, nostalgia for the world before its collapse, and, after his journey north to take office late in 1653, regret and anguish over his own irresolution and compromises. Wu's sense of guilt turns inward, whereas Qian seems at times to suppress his guilt by passing judgments on the conquest or the early Qing political situation. In neither word nor deed did Wu offend the new dynasty by engaging in or sympathizing with the forces of opposition and resistance, as Qian did. Wu also pruned his early poems of anti-Manchu references before including them in his collection. He thus fit into the Qianlong program of accommodating sorrow at the fall of the Ming with acceptance of the Manchu conquest.

Also honored as a "poet–historian," Wu Weiye often chose to write longer ancient-style poems and ballads, forms that lend themselves to elaboration of descriptive and narrative detail, unfolding arguments, and shifting perspectives. The Meicun (Plum Village) style, named for Wu's abode and cognomen, combines political and historical engagement with romantic myth-making, echoing works such as Bai Juyi's "Song of Enduring Sorrow." Its mournful beauty is characterized by the merging of an ornate, allusive, highly wrought diction (and, by extension, romantic–aesthetic values) with epic sweep and tragic pathos. This style comes out of the poet's need to lament, ponder, or reflect on his tumultuous times. The poems sometimes take on an explorative and investigative dimension, as Wu tries to define how an event or a character is to be remembered.

Whereas modulated perspectives do not actually qualify commemorative intent in his poems on martyrs and heroes, Wu seems reluctant to condemn, even in cases that readily invite negative judgments. An important example is "The Dirge of Mount Song" (Song shan ai, 1655) on the Ming defeat in 1642 at the Battle of Mount Song. After this decisive battle, the Ming commander Hong Chengchou (1593–1665) surrendered and became one of the architects of the new Qing order. Instead of simply condemning Hong, Wu imagines his regrets and marvels at the vicissitudes of his fortunes.

Wu's famous "Song of Yuanyuan" (Yuanyuan qu, ca 1651) shares the same underlying logic of pitting the individual's perspective against historical upheavals found in "The Dirge of Mount Song." The courtesan Chen Yuanyuan is credited with a pivotal role in the conquest. According to various miscellanies and historical sources, Chen was taken captive when Beijing fell to the rebels in 1644. Outraged at this turn of events, her lover Wu Sangui, military commander of the strategic Shanhai guan (the eastern terminus of the Great Wall), joined forces with the Manchus and marched upon Beijing to facilitate the Manchu conquest. In "Song of Yuanyuan," Wu Weiye combines subtle, pointed castigation and deft unmasking of Wu Sangui with measured empathy for Chen Yuanyuan as an unwitting femme fatale:

> At that time when the emperor abandoned the human world,
> Wu crushed the enemy and captured the capital, bearing down from Jade Pass.
> The six armies, wailing and grieving, were uniformly clad in the white of
>   mourning,
> One wave of headgear-lifting anger propelled him, all for the sake of the
>   fair-faced one.
> The fair-faced one, drifting and fallen, was not what I longed for.
> The offending bandits, smote by heaven, wallowed in wanton pleasures.
> Lightning swept the Yellow Turbans, the Black Mountain troops were quelled.
> Having wailed for ruler and kin, I met her again.

To dismantle Wu Sangui's claim of avenging "ruler and kin" is also to expose the hypocrisy of the official Qing version of the dynastic transition, namely that the Manchus avenged the martyred Chongzhen Emperor by fighting the rebels. The focus on Yuanyuan's role goes beyond a specific critique of Wu Sangui; it demonstrates how the concatenation of events leading to the Qing conquest, tied to willful passions and accidental obsessions, was fortuitous and avoidable.

Wu Weiye presents modulated perspectives on Chen Yuanyuan by using temporal shifts and by adopting her voice or point of view in large portions of the poem. Set against a backdrop that accentuates the ephemerality of glory, her precipitous rise is tacitly compared through allusion to that of the ancient beauty Xi Shi, said to have determined the fortunes of two contending states, Wu and Yue (ca fifth century BC). Chen's fate as an object of desire and transaction, being taken across the land against her will, also echoes that of Wang Zhaojun, the Han dynasty palace lady sent to the Xiongnu nomads, ubiquitously invoked in representations of abducted and displaced women in anecdotal, fictional, and historical accounts of the dynastic transition. Wu might have known Chen personally. His own lover, the famous courtesan Bian Sai, certainly did. Wu could have cast "Song of Yuanyuan" as a warning against moral decadence and sensual indulgence, but he chose not to. He remains sympathetic to Chen – in the poem she comes to stand for the helplessness and confusion of the individual caught in cataclysmic turmoil – and focuses instead on Wu Sangui's duplicity and his abuse of the notion of "deep feelings."

The empathic mode of filtering the complexity, confusion, and contradictions of historical events through the perceptions and sufferings of an individual also charges the role of poetic narrator with special significance. "The Old Entertainer of Linhuai" (Linhuai laoji xing), for example, is told in the voice of Dong'er, a former singing girl in the household of Liu Zeqing, a military commander of the Southern Ming. After the fall of Beijing, Dong'er travels there on horseback to learn the fate of the Ming princes, but she witnesses instead the decadent lifestyle of the powerful families there. Returning south, she sees Liu's army in hasty retreat, and again observes and judges the event as one bearing witness to the extent of disorder and suffering in the realm. Her voice merges with the poet's as she exploits her role and transcends it.

Wu Weiye concedes to the narrator the role of poet–historian even more forcefully in "The Song on Listening to the Daoist Bian Yujing [Bian Sai] Playing the Lute" (Ting nü daoshi Bian Yujing tanqin ge, ca 1651). A chance encounter brings him into the presence of a lute-strumming Daoist priestess. Wu makes only passing reference to their former relationship ("Yujing and I met in the southern capital"). His careful distancing of himself as humble listener elevates the authority of Bian's voice as it mediates witnessing and historical reflection, fusing personal suffering with the vicissitudes of history. Bian tells of the plight of the daughter of the lord of Zhongshan, who had been chosen as consort for the Hongguang Emperor of Southern Ming (r. 1644–1645), but was abducted by the Manchus with the fall of Nanjing. When the courtesan quarters are ransacked, Bian herself escapes abduction by becoming a Daoist: "I cut a robe of yellow cloth and embraced the Way, / Carrying a green, patterned lute to tell of the woes of beautiful women." Witnessing and remembering the victimhood of others become the only kind of agency possible for this former courtesan.

Wu Weiye's shame at his own compromises may have deepened his concern with agency and victimhood in history, as he writes during his sickness in a song lyric to the tune "He xinlang":

> And all because in that yesteryear –
> Irresolute, failing to cut ties,
> I have stolen survival among the brambles.

As with Qian Qianyi, poetry represents the final refuge for Wu. Shortly before his death in 1671, Wu asked to be buried in a monk's garb and to have the words "Grave of the poet Wu Meicun" inscribed on his tombstone.

For women writers, historical engagement often means going beyond the boudoir as subject matter and transforming the delicate, romantic diction traditionally characterized as "feminine." Some embraced the compelling model of the poet–historian. Xu Can, for example, wrote "Autumn Thoughts, Eight Poems" and "Ruminations on an Autumn Day, Eight Poems," loosely patterned on Du Fu's "Autumn Meditations." Some poems by Wang Duanshu and Li Yin also chronicle their tumultuous times. Historical judgments by women poets are often tied to reflections on gender roles. In "Song of Grief and Anger" (Beifen xing), after portraying the sufferings and devastation brought on by the conquest, Wang Duanshu depicts herself chanting Han history and asking,

> How did it happen that men, heartless and spineless,
> Set their mind on fame and profit, fishing with the angler's rod?
> With a hammer he tried to strike the First Emperor – he was but frail.
> Though his plot failed, in his heart he had requited the state of Hán.

The would-be assassin here is Zhang Liang (third to second century BC), a noble scion of Hán, one of the states of the Warring States period, which was eliminated by the Qin king (later the First Emperor). Though he fails to avenge the fall of his natal kingdom, he is to topple Qin by becoming Emperor Gaozu's (r. 206–194 BC) chief helper in the founding of the Han dynasty. The Han historian Sima Qian (ca 145–ca 86 BC) describes his surprise on seeing Zhang Liang's portrait. He had expected an image of imposing strength, but Zhang "had the appearance of a gentle lady." In expressing longing for the hero who looks like a woman, Wang Duanshu indicts the collective failure of men. Judging men also means questioning the image of the kingdom-toppling femme fatale. Thus Li Yin absolves Lady Yu of all responsibility for the fall of Xiang Yu. Xu Can, in "Lamenting the Past" (Diaogu, a song lyric to the tune

"Qingyu an"), also exposes the fatuousness of blaming political and historical failures on women:

> Mist and water know not the changes of human affairs.
> Battleships for a thousand miles,
> Banners of defeat in one expanse –
> Blame not the lotus steps.

"Lotus steps" alludes to the story of the Qi ruler (r. 499–500) who had golden lotuses inlaid in the floor to set off the beauty of his consort's delicate steps. Xu Can conjoins this image of effete self-indulgence with one taken from a famous poem by Liu Yuxi (772–842), in which Wu is defeated by Jin forces in 280, only to negate any causal connection between the two: women are not to be blamed for the failures of men.

Political disorder may also have created new possibilities for action or defined an imaginative space for aspirations not admissible in periods when social roles were more stable. Women who were actively involved in loyalist resistance, such as Liu Shu (born ca 1620) or Liu Rushi, transcended traditional gender roles, and some self-consciously developed a martial, heroic self-image as they explored the idea of fluid gender boundaries in their writings. Liu Rushi projects a masculine image in some of her early poems, such as "The Song of Swordsmanship" (Jianshu xing) and "To My Friend" (Zeng youren), where she fuses exhortation of her friends with her own heroic aspirations. According to Chen Yinke, these poems may have been meant for Fang Yizhi (1611–1671) and Sun Lin (1611–1646), who both later died as Ming martyrs. Of her involvement in anti-Qing resistance, we have no textual evidence from Liu's own writings, as few of her poems can be dated to the post-conquest era. Instead, we have Qian Qianyi's moving tribute to her heroic exploits in the third series of his "Later Autumn Meditations" and several poems in his *Youxue ji (To Have Learning)*.

By far the most extensive poetic record on heroic aspirations and the ultimate failure to fulfill heroic ideals made by a woman from this period is the corpus of Liu Shu. She tried to raise an army and offered to join forces with one "commander from Yunnan," but the latter's cowardice (or, according to some sources, unwelcome attentions) forced her to give up. Liu Shu often uses the image of "lone existence" (*gusheng*) to dramatize the disjunction between self and world. "Lone existence" addresses the dilemma of a common humanity; in that sense, it is about carving a space outside gender distinctions. In many of her poems, Liu writes in the voice of a man, or, more precisely, a failed hero, taking on the vocabulary of guilt over survival at this historical moment. The sword (along with a host of other weapons) is often mentioned with words such as *kong*, *man*, and *xu* (in vain); *rao* (superfluous); and *xiu* and *can* (shame). She also uses the gestures and paraphernalia of the male recluse, even while designating her companions as *jiemei* (sisters) and *nongfu* (peasant women).

Martial and military imagery in women's poetry of this period highlights the link between historical engagement and a defiant, unconventional self-image set in an imaginative space that promises escape from the world of the inner chamber. Discontent with gender roles sometimes became the precondition for, as well as the consequence of, political engagement. This was especially true of Zhou Qiong and Gu Zhenli (ca 1620s–1699), great-granddaughter of the Eastern Forest leader Gu Xiancheng mentioned in Chapter 2. Gu Zhenli's song lyric "Hearing the Alarm at the Chuhuang Station" (to the tune "Man jiang hong") begins with a quotation from Jiang Yan's (444–505) "Fu on Sorrow": "I have always been one burdened by sorrow." What is here translated as "I" is literally "servant" (*pu*), a polite self-designation used by men. Gu continues with allusions to the *Nine Disquisitions* attributed to Song Yu (a nebulous figure dated to the third century BC). The opening appropriation of the male poet's lamentation is finally justified by the logic of "universalization" and transmuted into a feminized perspective that makes for heightened awareness of vain endeavors and fruitless aspirations in the throes of national crisis:

> By the river, vain is my pity for the singing girl's oblivious song,
> In the boudoir, for naught the tears I shed for the country.
> Consider: the one in white clothes and grey scarf –
> Why must she be lesser than men?
> It has to be the jealousy of heaven.

In the second half of Du Mu's (803–853) famous quatrain, "Oblivious to the sorrow of losing one's country, the singing girl / Still sings, across the river, 'Flowers in the Rear Courtyard.'" The quoted song title, identified with the court of the last Chen ruler, symbolizes sensual indulgence and political irresponsibility. Whereas Du Mu, as one who consorts with entertainers and courtesans, is himself implicated in the world of heedless pleasures, the poet in her boudoir (*guizhong*) is aloof from all such associations. The contrast between the smallness of her world and the depth of her feelings, highlighted in the juxtaposition of "boudoir" and "country" (literally "divine continent," *shenzhou*), marks her helplessness and implicit protest.

Elsewhere, Gu describes herself as "careless and uncouth" (*cushu*), fit for "hills and streams" rather than female duties and adornment: "Hair combed and coifed, / Tiny bow shoes and narrow sleeves – / Habit has never made these familiar"; "I dread, facing the goddess of needlework, the address of disciple"; "Tumbling chignon, teary style – / What I cannot learn / Are the modes of the boudoir . . . Sickly, I am not equal to the grind of domestic chores. / Lacking talent myself, dare I despise him who exists between Heaven and Earth?" Devotion to household labor, enshrined as an integral part of feminine virtue, is here rejected in the name of sickliness. It irks her, she implies in a parallel construction, as much as her inferior husband. (A talented woman from the fourth century, Xie Daoyun, once referred to her husband as a mediocrity unexpectedly existing "between Heaven and Earth.")

Political engagement and historical understanding changed the rhetoric of friendship, both among women and between men and women. Beyond affinities in sensibility, there was new emphasis on political, intellectual, and spiritual common ground, sometimes tied to an implied sense of "common cause" (or the shared experience of national calamity). The poems addressed by Liu Rushi to Sun Lin and Fang Yizhi, mentioned above, are good examples. For Zhou Qiong, whose social station may have been more dubious, to "masculinize" the rhetoric of friendship or to project the self-image of "female knight-errant" is a way to avoid being taken for "a mere concubine."

This was also a self-reflexive moment. Women writers of the period often dwelt on what it means to write (and to write as a woman) during a moment of national crisis. In some cases the gestures are grandiose, even mythologizing. In "Poem on Losing a Fan" (Shishan shi), Wang Duanshu reverses the conventional association of the autumn fan with an abandoned woman, asserting instead that her fan has disappeared because the poem she wrote on it turned it into a "divine object." Liu Shu conjures a startling vision of writing and reading in a song lyric on the lotus (to the tune "Qing ping le"):

> Blood that has been draining for years
> Still trickles on the tip of the blossoms.
> Shimmering light has now moistened the Heaven-marking brush:
> Just use it to record the unsung heroes of unofficial history.
> On these emerald sheets I read endless drafts of chapters –
> They come unbidden, falling into place line upon line.
> And then dispersal: a pond of mist and clouds,
> Leaving, in vain, scent that rises with the water and the moon.

The red lotus drips with blood from years of war and devastation. The stalk of the lotus is compared to a brush making its marks on Heaven. This brush writes on the lotus leaves, which unfold as chapters, "line upon line" falling into place. Liu thus juxtaposes violence and writing, futility and creation. This is a history dripping with blood, but the lines that fall into place on the lotus leaves give form, order, and meaning to the violence. Their subject is "the unsung heroes of unofficial history," among whom Liu Shu may well count herself. The poet emerges as the person who lives, writes, and reads this history. The sense of power and agency, embodied by the "Heaven-marking brush," is dispersed through the Buddhist images in the last two lines. The poet's vision may be no more than subjective illumination, but it is also no less than that.

The literature of remembrance

"Writing history in poetry" often foregrounds narrative and discursive elements. Other poetic encounters with the past focus on traces, fragments, and the vagaries of memory. Encounters with "objects from the former dynasty" or "the person who remembers" constitute a common theme. Poets might use an object (often one from the Ming palace) as a recurrent poetic topic to demonstrate how webs of social and literary ties had been affected by political change. Recent traumatic events gave new urgency to the established tradition of "meditation on the past." Early Qing poets revisiting political and cultural centers in the lower Yangzi area wrote some of the finest poems in this genre. In 1650, Qian Qianyi wrote twenty poems on West Lake while passing through Hangzhou on his way to try to secure the support of the Jinhua military commander for the loyalist cause. Elegiac longing for the life of pleasure and passion is transmuted into political statement as Qian juxtaposes past glory and present desolation, fusing personal memory with literary memory.

The literature of remembrance often addresses the anguish of forgetting and erasure. Chen Weisong writes of Nanjing (to the tune "Yuchi bei"): "What remains are yellow butterflies shrouded in mist, / Flying with dreams." Yet the past retains a spectral presence:

> After the third watch,
> Under a full, incandescent moon,
> I see countless ghosts speaking as they hold back tears.

Yangzhou, the site of the horrifying massacre of 1645, soon returned to prosperity. In 1653, during Wu Weiye's northward journey to Beijing, he wrote four poems on Yangzhou, pitting memories of bloody destruction against their erasure. The fourth poem juxtaposes two sets of feminine imagery:

one belongs to courtesans and the refinements of the courts of the Southern Dynasties, the other to Wang Zhaojun, an emblem for displaced, abducted, and victimized women in this period. Yangzhou has returned to oblivious good cheer by capitalizing on the first set of images and suppressing the second one. Wu Weiye exposes these elisions: the women of Yangzhou who symbolize its pleasures were once associated with loss, abduction, and the shame of conquest.

In 1664, at one of the literary gatherings at the Vermilion Bridge for which Yangzhou became famous, Wang Shizhen and his friends (including some well-known loyalists) wrote poems on spring, in which they almost uniformly celebrate refined pleasures. Here is Wang Shizhen's own quatrain:

> In yesteryear iron cannons breached the city walls,
> On broken halberds sunk in sand, wild moss grows.
> By Plum Peak, the green, green grass
> Calmly sends off travelers returning on horseback.

The poet dispenses with the carnage of nineteen years earlier in one line – flying cannonballs make the siege of the city swift, faceless, inevitable. The second line echoes Du Mu's meditation on the Battle of Red Cliff, fought in 208: "On the broken halberd sunk in sand, the metal is yet unworn, / Polish and wash it, so as to recognize the former dynasty." If recognition of the "former dynasty" is still possible in Du's poem, in Wang's the memory of war and destruction has been resolutely erased – "wild moss" grows on the broken halberd. Plum Peak, the burial site of the ceremonial gown of Shi Kefa (1601–1645), the commander who died defending Yangzhou, is now the vantage point for pleasure excursions.

Yet the contest for signification is not far beneath the surface. Wu Jiaji, "harmonizing with" Wang Shizhen's poems (that is, writing in the same form and rhyme scheme), gives a stark reminder of how surreal apparent harmony can be:

> North of the mound, south of the mound, a spring day.
> Fallen blossoms, travelers on horseback, all abustle.
> How is it that the clumps of earth beneath the pines
> See no descendants coming to sweep the graves?

Wu's quatrain reverses the logic of Wang's, beginning with images of serenity that are duly dismantled by the repressed violence of unappeased memories. The graves are untended, perhaps because the descendants of the dead had perished during the 1645 massacre.

The desire to combat oblivion, to give voice to the dead, and to relive what is lost provides the impetus behind the memoir literature that thrived in the early Qing. Around 1693, Huang Zongxi, already on the verge of death, wrote *Remembrances of Friends Past* (*Sijiu lu*), a series of vignettes in which he commemorates the courage and integrity of his friends, many of whom died martyrs or loyalists. A gesture, a line, or an anecdote conveys their character; sometimes these are foibles, asides, or witticisms not directly related to larger moral or political purpose. We are told, for example, that the scholar and poet Wu Yingji (1594–1645), a staunch Revival Society member who died in resistance, liked to collect books but was easily deceived by booksellers. Contrary to what one may expect of a moral philosopher, Huang saw no necessary conflict between ethical steadfastness and romantic–aesthetic interests. He recalls how the upright minister Fan Jingwen (1587–1644), who killed himself when Beijing fell, owned a family troupe of musicians who performed for him during meals: "Thus do we know that the path of integrity and righteousness cannot be fully realized by rigid, petty Confucians." Another famous minister, Ni Yuanlu, had even more eccentric obsessions. A great connoisseur of garden design, he took to mixing expensive ink with cinnabar and applying it to walls and window frames. His student, who had been supplying him with specimens of the finest inksticks, wonders, "Although the master soaks his brush often, he should not write as fast as all that." Ni was martyred in 1644 and his garden estate was reduced to rubble. Huang Zongxi's lament stops short of real criticism: "For such was the [unavoidable] blind spot of a man of great understanding." On rare occasions, he made sterner judgments. He criticizes the scholar–literatus Hou Fangyu (1618–1655) (who became the male protagonist of *Peach Blossom Fan*) for drinking with courtesans when his father was in prison. When a mutual friend defends Hou as one who could not bear solitude, Huang replies, "If a person cannot bear solitude, where would he not get to?"

Judgment is also the avowed goal of memoirs of a more autobiographical nature, such as Zhang Dai's (1597–ca 1680) *Dream Memories of Tao'an* (*Tao'an mengyi*). Born into a distinguished and cultivated family in Zhejiang, Zhang was a prolific scholar and writer whose life of leisure and refinement came to an abrupt end in 1644. He proclaims in the confessional preface (1674):

I think over my past life: glory, honor, wealth, all revert to emptiness after passing in the twinkling of an eye. Fifty years amount to one dream . . . From afar I let my thoughts roam over events past, and commit to writing whatever comes to my memory. I bring these recollections in front of the Buddha, repenting of them one by one.

In "An Epitaph for Myself" (Ziwei muzhi ming, 1665), Zhang rationalizes present suffering and deprivation as "just retribution" for past excesses and transgressions. His remembrances and writing could be redemptive, he claims, because of their underlying mood of repentance. His is a paradoxical repentance, however. *Dream Memories* is mostly devoted to summoning and savoring visions of a lost world, with scant regard for critical distance. Many of the entries – on subjects as varied as gardens, theater, fireworks, courtesans, rare and extraordinary objects, artists and artworks, tea and water appreciation – would have fitted effortlessly into the late Ming literature on connoisseurship or the refinements of literati culture.

Zhang Dai's keen sense of irony leads him to expose the sordid reality of transaction behind the pursuit of sensual pleasures. Women raised to be sold as concubines – "the lean mares of Yangzhou" – are treated as mere commodities. Lower-class prostitutes, "numbering as many as five or six hundred, would come out of the alleys every day at dusk. Bathed, adorned, and perfumed, they would linger and mill around tea houses and wine shops, doing so-called 'sentry-duty at the passes.'" Their pathetic ploys to lure customers can barely conceal their despair. Zhang also recognizes the self-indulgent destructiveness of obsessive passions. His cousin, Yanke, is a discerning connoisseur, but shows little remorse when he destroys objects of art in his furious impatience to "improve" them. The huge trees that quickly wither when forcibly transplanted into the cracks of rocks in Yanke's garden become emblems of his wanton wastefulness. Zhang Dai also intermittently considers the theme of retribution. In entries on the incense market of West Lake and the Yue custom of visiting ancestral graves, he observes how past extravagance leads to present devastation. Further, he tries to accept loss with philosophical resignation, as when he sets the destruction of his family book collection against that of the massive Sui–Tang imperial collections.

These ironic, critical, and reflective moments do not, however, give enough of a counterpoint to Zhang Dai's pervasive nostalgia or his implicit invitation to the reader to empathize with his "dream memories." Writing and reading are means to relive a lost world, as Zhang confesses in the preface:

> Picking up a fragment at random is like wandering along old paths and seeing old friends. "The city walls are the same but not the inhabitants" – for all that, I am consoled. Indeed, one should beware of talking to deluded souls about dreams . . . Now I am about to wake up from this great dream called life, but I am still concerned with "the carving of insects" [i.e. trivial literary pursuits], which is just so much somniloquy.

Remembrance and writing allow repossession of what even at the moment of experience seemed evanescent:

> Upon watching a good performance, my only regret was the impossibility of wrapping it in magic brocade and preserving it for eternity. I once compared this to the beautiful moon, or one good cup of properly brewed tea, which can only be savored for a moment even though one treasures it infinitely. When Huan Ziye [d. ca 392] came upon beauty in nature, he would often shout: "What is to be done?" There is indeed nothing to be done – one cannot even speak about it.

Nostalgia can be pervasive; here it is already felt at the moment of experience. Nostalgia also acquires specific political meanings during this period. As Zhang defiantly proclaims in the 1671 preface to another of his books, *The Quest For Dreams of West Lake* (*Xihu mengxun*), the West Lake in his dreams and memory is much more real and compelling than the devastated West Lake of the post-conquest period. To adhere stubbornly to a subjective realm of dreams and memory is also implicitly to reject an oppressive political reality.

In *Dream Memories*, Zhang Dai gives affecting portraits of the actress Zhu Chusheng and the courtesan Wang Yuesheng. Obsessively devoted to the theater, Zhu was worn out by too keen a sensibility and "finally died from [excessive] emotions." Wang was reserved and refined, melancholy and evasive, caught between the burden of deep feeling and the lies of her trade. Vignettes about remarkable women who are also to be pitied, while not the main theme in *Dream Memories*, become the dominant strain in some major examples of the nostalgic literature of remembrance. One of them is Chen Weisong's *Writings on and by Women* (*Furen ji*), which collects anecdotes about the fate of women, many of them poets, during the dynastic transition. In style and spirit it recalls *A New Account of Tales of the World* (*Shishuo xinyu*, ca 430); there are linguistic echoes and a shared sympathy for talented women.

Writings on and by Women contains many anecdotes about chance encounters with women's poetry, its oral transmission and miraculous (albeit sometimes partial) preservation. Wang Shilu (1626–1673), Wang Shizhen's older brother, who contributed a number of entries and provided the source for others, is sometimes said to be quoting from memory. In another entry, when Wang Shizhen fails to recall fully a poem by the woman poet Peng Yan, its curtailed state is justified as an appropriate correlative for intense emotions: "Dark thoughts and feelings of rancor – such things are what precisely makes a person unable to finish a song." Loss, absence, erasure, and ephemerality, made more threatening by political disorder, are thus recurrent themes.

Some anecdotes link women's poetry to the age-old ideal of genuine expression. Kan Yu, trapped in an unhappy marriage and reduced to demeaning labor, "was in deep despair. She raised her head to heaven, wailed, and composed a song." The song is then supposedly overheard and orally circulated. Deliberately archaic, it is reminiscent of well-known Han–Wei ballads about being abused by one's kin and husband. The idea that poetry originates in the elemental, plaintive cry overheard, which lies outside the realm of convention and social function, is one of the abiding myths in Chinese poetics. Kan Yu's sad fate is also tied to the fall of the Ming. Only thirteen when Beijing fell in 1644, she was duped into marrying an uncouth vegetable vendor under the looming threat of being drafted into the harem of the Hongguang Emperor; her plight is thus embroiled in the corruption and decadence of the Southern Ming court. In another example, the artist and poet Zhou Zhao seems at first sight to suffer the familiar fate of the talented, unhappy concubine, but it transpired that she was reduced to concubinage because her father, an official, died a martyr in 1644. Her *fu* mourning his death, with its copious references to Qu Yuan and the *Verses of Chu*, prompts us to compare her to Nüxu, the woman offering advice to the poet in "Encountering Sorrow." Writings on and by women thus become the prism for understanding and remembering this tumultuous era.

The merging of private and public lament is still more evident in other accounts with a more explicit focus on historical judgment, as in this quatrain found "on the walls of the former palace":

> Beyond the Facing Spring Pavilion is limitless distance,
> Beacon fires reaching to the sky shake my heart.
> Ten rounds of long siege are closing in tonight,
> And the emperor is still at Qinhuai.

Chen adds, "The strokes of some characters had been obliterated by moss. Perhaps someone filled in the words as he saw fit. The mournful and restrained tone of the poem suggests that it could have been the words of a palace lady from the Hongguang reign." The quatrain compares the Southern Ming emperor to another pleasure-loving and incompetent last ruler, Chen Houzhu (r. 583–587), and contrasts the palace lady's anguish over the fate of the country with the emperor's oblivious self-indulgence in the Qinhuai pleasure quarters.

Anecdotes about women leaving poems on walls proliferated during the Ming–Qing transition. Several examples are found in *Writings on and by Women*. Some tell of domestic woes and private longings. More typical are poems composed by abducted and victimized women, who, in writing of their personal plight, bear witness to the turmoil of the times as well as to the imperative to remember and to comprehend that historical moment. Many refer repeatedly to the standard topoi of exile, displacement, and victimization embodied in the legends of Wang Zhaojun and Cai Yan.

There are stories of female virtue in *Writings on and by Women*, but chaste women who sometimes find their way into official historiography are included here only if they are also writers. Women's wayward passions, when beautifully crafted and expressed, are also accorded a place and thus implicitly affirmed. The fruits of their artistic and literary talent are all the more treasured for being too easily lost. Words by women and on women have the power to conjure a realm of beauty and pathos; often, as we have seen, these writings also testify to contemporary suffering.

Compared to *Writings on and by Women*, Yu Huai's (1616–1696) *Miscellaneous Records of the Plank Bridge* (*Banqiao zaji*) is more personal and more exclusively focused on courtesans, but the two share a similar dynamic of using women's lives to "sum up the prosperity and decline of an era, the melancholy ruminations of a thousand years." Yu defends the moral purpose of his book: "Although I am compiling these records in order to transmit the fragrant names [of remarkable women], I am also in effect handing down warnings." *Plank Bridge* indeed tells a few stories of famous courtesans coming to ignominious ends, but the supposed "warnings" are elusive. Yu Huai's deep nostalgia for late Ming courtesan culture is compounded of a sense of personal loss and national calamity: mourning lost years and friends who are no more, he also uses the destruction of the Qinhuai pleasure quarters to lament the fall of the Ming.

Perhaps more than any other book, *Plank Bridge* establishes the late Ming courtesan as a cultural ideal. As it chronicles the beauty, wit, and refined taste of the courtesans and their accomplishments as poets, painters, calligraphers, and musicians, the book may seem to resemble the "literature-appraising courtesans" (*pinji*) that flourished from late Ming to late Qing. What sets Yu Huai's work apart is his deep empathy with their plights and dilemmas, successes and failures, unconventionality and free spirit, and above all their role in the political struggles of the period. He shows how, as the Nanjing examination hall and the most select courtesan quarters of Qinhaui faced each other across the Qinhuai river, these pleasure quarters became the site

5. Qinhuai as reconstructed in the 1990s: romantic images of Qinhuai courtesans still appeal deeply to the modern imagination. Photo by Sun Yong.

where the cultural elite articulated their political concerns and aspirations. Consorting with courtesans was "the unofficial chapter on the battles of letters," and examination candidates (often also Revival Society members) gathered in the painted boats of Qinhuai for fervent literary and political discussion.

Plank Bridge offers glimpses into the fascinating ambiguities and permeable boundaries of the Qinhuai world. Though classified as "debased" (*jian*), the courtesan consorted with elite men, sometimes as intellectual equals, and could reclaim respectability through marriage (*congliang*). A courtesan was often born or sold into this class, but Yu Huai reminds us that an elite or even aristocratic woman could also be reduced to that station, as in the case of some family members of ministers opposed to the Yongle Emperor. The world of courtesans represents sensual excess, but Yu notes how some insist on unworldly abstemiousness in the midst of opulence. While their favors can be purchased, they may yet appear unattainable. Yu emphasizes their choice, agency, and loyalty, and also celebrates the passionate, unconventional, and independent spirit that defies prescribed roles and sometimes even gender boundaries. The relationship between patron and courtesan encompasses many gradations of sexual, romantic, and intellectual intimacy. Friendship (with or without nuances of romantic tension) between men and women thrives in the courtesan's world, but *Plank Bridge* also recounts many courtesan–literatus romances. Arranged marriages being the norm in premodern China, the pleasure quarters might well be the only place where agency, tension, yearning, and uncertainty – the ingredients of romance – could come into play. The reality of transaction, however, is never wholly suppressed, and political turmoil rudely shatters the dreams of many courtesans and their literati lovers. The issue is not simply that a glamorous aura masks a sordid and unhappy reality. Rather, the memory of freedom, independence, and splendor is all the more treasured and celebrated precisely because it is recognized as a precariously sustained, carefully wrought, and passionately defended illusion.

Yu Huai asserts the connection between the romantic and the political spheres of experience by comparing himself to Du Mu, the late Tang poet whose romantic dalliances with courtesans did not preclude engagement with political and military issues. One anecdote from *Plank Bridge* tells how Fang Yizhi and Sun Lin pretended to be bandits to frighten Jiang Gai (1611–1653) during his prolonged sojourn with the courtesan Li Shiniang. Fang and Sun reveal their identity only when Jiang piteously begs for mercy. Jiang was known for his integrity and later became a staunch loyalist. The prankster Fang Yizhi was an important thinker, scholar, and poet; he took the tonsure after the fall of the Ming and died a martyr. Yu also records how Sun Lin and his paramour, the courtesan Ge Nen, both died heroic deaths defying their Qing captors. To another courtesan, Li Xiangjun (later made into the heroine of *Peach Blossom Fan*), he pays tribute to the courage of her political convictions. He thus implies that heroism and moral integrity can accommodate romantic liaisons; further, apparently self-indulgent behavior may actually mask or even encourage moral resolve.

Unlike Yu Huai, Mao Xiang does not claim any political significance for his elegiac memoir, *Reminiscences of the Plum Shadows Studio* (*Yingmei'an yiyu*), which chronicles his relationship with the famous courtesan Dong Bai (1624–1651) from their first encounter in 1639 to her early death in 1651. Described as otherwise withdrawn, frail, and long-suffering, though resourceful, Dong actively pursued union with the initially reluctant Mao and, after overcoming many obstacles, finally became his concubine in 1642. Beautiful and talented, she also proved to be a paragon of virtue who, in her devotion to Mao, endured great suffering during the dynastic transition. In the memoir her love becomes conflated with higher moral–political purpose.

Mao's elegiac memoir testifies to how romantic pathos and aestheticized daily life continued to be upheld as ideals in the post-conquest world. Its middle sections on aesthetic and sensual pleasures traverse the traumatic turning points in the dynastic transition. For example, on their 1642 tour of Jinshan, Dong's ethereal beauty, enhanced by a dress made from European gauze, gathers an admiring crowd that follows the couple around, pointing to them as "immortals." Mao continues with two more excursions and concludes the section with their 1645 trip to Lake Yuanyang, whose idyllic scenery betrays no sign of national crisis. Likewise, we are told how Dong compiled a collection of anecdotes and accounts about women, *Beauties by the Boudoir Case* (*Lianyan*), when Mao and his family, having fled the chaos and fighting in Rugao, sought refuge in Yanguan. In 1646, the two "crafted by hand a hundred pellets" of incense, made according to some European prescription and obtained from "the imperial collection." Mao notes how the incense has to be burnt gently, without producing any smoke, and that only a person with Dong's gentle refinement could understand its subtleties. Such a precious commodity presumably became available only with the fall of Beijing and the crumbling of the Southern Ming court, but Mao does not allude to the circumstances of its acquisition. In other words, the narrative of Dong's literary and aesthetic sensibility sometimes seems to defy or ignore calamitous political events, although Mao also chronicles sadly how Dong lost the paintings and calligraphy she loved in the course of their wanderings, in a manner reminiscent of Li Qingzhao's (1083–ca 1155) "Postscript to the Record of Bronzes and Stones" (Jinshi lu houxu). The aesthetic domain, idealized as the locus of marital bliss and domestic order, beckons against all odds as a refuge from the turmoil of history.

Throughout the *Plum Shadows Studio*, Dong Bai is both connoisseur and object of connoisseurship, or, more precisely, her persona as connoisseur turns her into aesthetic spectacle. A great lover of flowers, especially chrysanthemums, Dong takes care to frame herself with chrysanthemum shadows even in her sickness in the autumn of 1650:

> Every night she burned tall bright candles, used six sections of white screens to frame three sides, and set up a small seat among the flowers. The chrysanthemum shadows were positioned in the most expressive and exquisite ways. Only then would she enter. She was among the chrysanthemums, and both the chrysanthemums and she were in the shadows. She returned her gaze to the screen, looked at me, and said, "The spirit of the chrysanthemums is fully expressed. But what is to be done about the person wasting away?" Even now, when I think about it, the scene has the pure grace of a painting.

Here we are still very much in the compass of late Ming sensibility: what is savored is not simply the object, but also the experience and spectacle of aesthetic appreciation; of this logic the connoisseurs themselves are acutely aware.

Dong's artistic pursuits and domestic duties merge in seamless continuity. She masters needlework as perfectly as she does the musical arts of the courtesan; the same zeal sustains her in making copies of famous calligraphic models as in making household lists. Not only does Dong Bai realize traditionally feminine virtues, such as deference, gentleness, and selfless devotion to Mao and his family during the turbulent years of dynastic transition; she is also credited with a broader sense of political morality. She shares Mao's indignation over the plight of Eastern Han scholars opposing corrupt powers, and gives up Zhong Yao (third century) as a calligraphic model when she learns that he denigrated Guan Yu (third century), deified as a paragon of loyalty. In sum, Mao's tribute to Dong emphasizes how romantic–aesthetic values are redeemed by moral exemplarity. Concern with moral justification also colors Mao's self-presentation in the memoir. If he sometimes comes across as a passive and irresolute lover, it may be because he feels the need to affirm the greater claims of filial duty and family honor.

In addition to the *Plum Shadows Studio*, Mao wrote elegies and poems to mourn Dong Bai. His friends contributed at least one portrait, one biography, and innumerable poems and colophons to her memory (some of which are found in Chapter 6 of *Collected Writings of Kindred Spirits*). Mao was able to marry Dong through the intervention of Qian Qianyi and Liu Luding, and both their union and Dong's death became poetic topics among Mao's friends. The courtesan has always defined relationships among men by being the object of their collective desire. In this case, not only passion but nostalgia for late Ming literati–courtesan culture are validated through public display and the reaffirmed bonds among elite men.

The fate of pleasures and passions

As we have seen, nostalgia overrides judgment in the early Qing literature of remembrance. Further, nostalgia for late Ming literati culture or the world of courtesans is presented as a mode of loyalism. Implicit in this is the view that the pleasures and passions of the late Ming are inseparable from political idealism and heroic striving. The long tradition of encoding political meanings in the language of romantic love takes new turns. Hopeless longing and lamentation for lost love fit the allegorical purpose of those mourning the fall of the Ming dynasty. Some choose to express guilt over political compromises as the regret for betraying a lover or the self-castigation of a fallen woman.

As Kang-i Sun Chang points out, love and loyalism are intertwined themes in the writings of Chen Zilong. In "The Song of the Cuckoo" (Dujuan xing), his anguished lament over the crumbling of the Southern Ming court, Chen concludes with an image that gives a romantic tinge to political despair: "I should only hold hands with the goddess of Sunlit Terrace, / And with ink splashed on the walls of Chu, ask questions of Heaven." Traditionally attributed to Qu Yuan, "Questions to Heaven" (Tianwen), in *Verses of Chu*, is thought to convey the poet's despair in the form of questions that test the limits of moral reasoning and historical understanding. In "*Fu* on Gaotang" and "*Fu* on the Goddess," attributed to Song Yu, the goddess of Sunlit Terrace appears in a dream to gratify the Chu king's desires, but remains ultimately elusive and unattainable. In the poetic tradition, this figure comes to embody all the ambiguities and contradictions of desire, but here she holds the poet's hand in empathy. Chen Zilong implies that certainty of higher purpose, as symbolized by the sympathy and recognition of the goddess, can ameliorate his despair over a lost cause.

The political and romantic dimensions of the *Verses of Chu* are also deftly conjoined in You Tong's (1618–1704) short play, *On Reading "Encountering Sorrow"* (Du Lisao). The first three scenes use interlocutors and spectators to dramatize Qu Yuan's composition of "Questions to Heaven," "Nine Songs," and "The Fisherman." Interestingly, although there are many allusions to "Encountering Sorrow," its actual writing is not enacted onstage, as if its stated purpose of self-revelation leaves less room for dramatic invention. In the last scene, Song Yu (here cast as Qu Yuan's disciple), after his empathetic reading of Qu Yuan's "Encountering Sorrow," dreams of the goddess and then composes poems about her. You Tong thus presents romantic–erotic experience and its celebration as the compensatory consequence of pursuing political ideals. Romantic longing also reinstates political goals: the play ends with Song Yu summoning the soul of Qu Yuan (based on allusions to "Great Summons" and "Summoning the Soul" in *Verses of Chu*).

If romantic attachment can be transmuted into political striving, women seen as "objects of desire" are amenable to heroic transformations. Historical and literary sources are full of stories about women who "perished with their country"; many died resisting rape by Manchu soldiers or renegade Ming troops. The female body thus turns into a metaphor for the body politic, even as chastity converges with political integrity. There are also many accounts about courtesans whose moral resolve put men to shame. According to some sources, Liu Rushi, for example, wanted to die as a Ming martyr and urged the same choice upon Qian Qianyi, but Qian demurred.

One remarkable example of how icons of sensual excess can be transformed into heroes is Wu Weiye's short play *Facing Spring Pavilion* (*Linchun ge*). The play's heroines, the consort Zhang Lihua and the commander Lady Xian, leaders respectively of civil and military affairs at the court of Chen Houzhu, manage briefly to stave off ruin for the disintegrating Chen dynasty (557–589). Remembered in official historiography as a devious and pernicious femme fatale, Zhang here gives the court what little legitimacy it can claim. She and Xian, historically unconnected, are brought together as kindred spirits who recognize each other's worth. Combining beauty, poetic talent, administrative ability, military leadership, and strategic genius, they represent, in some ways, the self-redemption of romantic–aesthetic values. Any such grand claim, however, is finally bracketed by irony, for the two cannot turn the tide against inevitable dynastic collapse. In the end, Zhang's ghost can only seek melancholy consolation in karmic cycles and Xian has to take off her martial garb as she "enters the mountains to cultivate the Way."

Other aspects of valorized subjectivity dominate the early Qing imagination. The late Ming was fascinated with the knight-errant (*xia*), an appellation that encompasses independence of spirit and defiant unconventionality, as well as physical courage and martial prowess. Huang Zongxi's spectacular vendetta is a good example. Huang's father had been persecuted and killed during the ascendancy of the eunuch Wei Zhongxian, as had many other Ming officials who tried to adhere to their principles. In 1628, after Wei's downfall, Huang caused a furor at court by attacking members of Wei's clique with a hammer he had hidden in his sleeve. Legal justice would not have sufficed for Huang. The refusal to abide by the constraints of sociopolitical order sometimes appeared as more outrageous eccentricity, as in the case of Fang Yizhi. Even as a fugitive in Guangdong, where he was briefly involved with the Southern Ming Yongli court in 1646, Fang was "given to unrestraint," and once stripped himself naked and let his hair down to reenact the scene of Mi Heng playing the drum to defy Cao Cao (155–220). This famous episode involving Mi Heng was told in the novel *Three Kingdoms* and dramatized in *The Mad Drummer* (*Kuang gushi yuyang sannong*), the first in Xu Wei's (1520–1593) series of four short plays, *Four Cries of the Gibbon* (*Sisheng yuan*). When admonished, Fang Yizhi broke into operatic arias to the accompaniment of his sandalwood clapper. Such apparent self-indulgence may also have masked heroic striving. Quan Zuwang says of a group of Yongshang loyalists who called themselves "the six wild scholars," "To be wild is to disregard the limits of what one can do," while to be mindful of such limits is to let self-interest erode moral courage. Some loyalists thus carried on anti-Qing resistance with the flair and romantic pathos of knights-errant.

Nor did political engagement forestall sensual pleasures. The poet Wei Geng, executed in 1663 for involvement in resistance, insisted on wine and the company of courtesans whenever he discoursed on military strategems. He sought refuge for a time at Yushan, the famous garden estate built by Qi Biaojia. Qi was a Ming scholar–official known for his connoisseurship of the theater and gardens. His exquisite essays, "Notes on Yushan" (Yushan zhu), celebrate shifting perspectives and the interweaving of reality and illusion, dreaming and waking states, in the enjoyment of gardens. When the Nanjing court fell in 1645, Qi drowned himself in a pond at Yushan. Martyrdom marks only the beginning of the politicization of this aesthetic space. Qi's sons, Bansun (b. 1632) and Lisun (1627–ca 1663), used Yushan to foster loyalist activities. Qu Dajun, hiding there in 1660, wrote poems about wandering with immortals and seeking refuge in the world of books, using the vocabulary of late Ming aestheticism and escapism to define an alternative mental space in an alien political reality.

The malleable line between political and romantic–aesthetic spheres was especially noticeable in the lifestyle of those Jiangnan literati who espoused loyalist sentiments without eschewing refinement and sensuality, in contrast to those loyalists who insisted on ascetic withdrawal from society. The former sometimes purported to be making a political statement by continuing or at least remembering the life of refined pleasures before the end of the Ming, because they were remnants not only of the Ming as political entity but also of the late Ming cultural realm. *Plank Bridge* may give the impression that the glories of courtesan culture came to an end with the fall of the Ming, but Yu Huai's *Record of Travels in Wu* (*San Wu youlan zhi*, 1650) shows how gatherings lamenting and commemorating the fallen dynasty were attended by courtesans. He refers repeatedly to one courtesan named Chuyun, with whom he seems to have developed a deep bond.

Yu Huai's friend, Mao Xiang, hosted literary gatherings that harked back to late Ming pleasures and passions. Like Yushan, Mao's famous estate, Painted-in-Water Garden (Shuihui yuan), provided refuge for loyalists wanted by the Qing authorities. In 1654, Mao changed the garden's name to Painted-in-Water Monastery (Shuihui an), and used Buddhist images to convey the sense of inward distance: "The garden is changed into a monastery, / The monastery is returned to its master, the monk. / I come as guest, / Silently listening to the bells and drums." Literary gatherings in the garden reached their height around the late 1650s, as shown in various chapters of *Collected Writings of Kindred Spirits*. The Mao family eventually went into financial difficulties and by the 1670s the garden had fallen into disrepair.

The Mao family kept its own theatrical troupe, and musical and dramatic performances became the topic of many poems and prose accounts in *Kindred Spirits*. In "An Account of the Night Feast in the Hall of Obtaining Perfection" (*Dequan tang yeyan ji*), the Confucian scholar Chen Hu (1613–1675) could not initially be persuaded to sit through a performance of Ruan Dacheng's romantic comedy *The Swallow Letter* (*Yanzi jian*) when he visited Mao in 1660. His host recalls his own denunciation of the play in 1643 (enacted in scene iv of *Peach Blossom Fan*), but defends its present performance as political lament, akin to the dirge of the doomed assassin Jing Ke (third century BC), the flute playing of the Jin general Liu Kun (271–318), and the bamboo scepter of the Song loyalist Xie Ao (1249–1295). Chen Weisong, who "sojourned" for eight years on Mao's estate, wrote many moving poems and song lyrics on how the performances of Mao's singers and actors stirred longings for a lost world. One example is the "Song of the Xu Lad" (Xu lang qu):

> He held the lute aslant his chest, /
> Telling of passes and mountains, layered as sorrows beyond count /
> . . . Mist and flowers of bygone days cannot be embraced, /
> One song of the Xu lad, and the past, like a beautiful body, lays stretched
>   before us.

That the Xu lad (Xu Ziyun) was also Chen's lover underlines how private and public experiences, the romantic and the political spheres, cannot be easily separated. Self-indulgence is also political defiance: "The candles refuse to turn to ashes, / The songs refuse to be brought to an end" (Chen Weisong, "Song of Qinxiao" (Qinxiao qu)).

Encounters with musicians, performers, and artists become a persistent theme in early Qing literature as a whole. Typically, the authors knew these personalities before the fall of the Ming, reencountered them after the fall, sometimes listened to their performances, and either addressed poems to them or wrote about their meeting. Among those most frequently written about were the storyteller Liu Jingting, the musician Su Kunsheng, and the lute player Bai Yuru. Liu and Su, as General Zuo Liangyu's "artists-in-residence" (and, according to some, informal advisers) during the Southern Ming, aroused special pathos as being both inside and outside momentous events, both "in the act" and beyond it as purveyors of memories. As denizens of

Qinhuai, they also summon associations with the romances of the pleasure quarters.

Many of the early Qing works on these subjects bring to mind Du Fu's poems on Li Guinian and Gongsun Daniang's disciple or Bai Juyi's "Song of the Lute." There are also interesting differences. Early Qing literati writing about performers like to emphasize that the latter are their "kindred spirits" (*wobei zhong ren*). Whereas in Bai Juyi's "Song of the Lute," for example, music is still very much the province of the singing girl, in Wu Weiye's eponymous poem scholar–officials like Kang Hai (1475–1540) and Wang Jiusi (1468–1551) also use lute music to lament demotion and exile. By a happy coincidence, the lute players in Wu's poem, Bai Yuru and Bai Zaimei, also share the same surname as Bai Juyi – poet and performer metaphorically merge. In a different poem, Wang Shilu refers to Bai Yuru as "none other than the progeny of old Xiangshan [Bai Juyi]." Chen Weisong says of Su Kunsheng in a song lyric addressed to him: "Consider: if not this one, / Who can be counted as my friend?" Addressing a song lyric to Liu Jingting, Gong Dingzi writes, "You and I, / Have for long tarried together." The affinity of spirit implied here is deepened through the allusion to Yin Hao's (306–356) witticism upon being asked by Huan Wen (312–373) how Huan and Yin compared: "I and myself have for long tarried together, I would rather be myself." The Jiangnan literati's continued immersion in the culture of entertainment and performance accounts in part for this empathic connection. Unstable boundaries between the literatus and the performer may also imply that the trope of performance invades the province of moral certainties. It was probably this disquiet that prompted Huang Zongxi to write a censorious biography of Liu Jingting.

Liu, Su, and other performers are often presented as being capable of heroic action, and when that avenue is closed, their performances make possible historical retrospection and the rites of commemoration. Chen Weisong writes of Su Kunsheng that his song brings forth "the cuckoo's blood / Congealed on the silken sleeve." In Wu Weiye's "Song of the Lute," Bai Yuru's performance reenacts the wars, chaos, and devastation of the dynastic transition. Wu's poem describes a community of mourners listening to the lute player – also a common trope. Many of these poems and song lyrics were written to "harmonize" with each other; often the authors were in the audience together. Irony and self-reflexivity inevitably surface, as these authors compare their own creative endeavors to the performer's reenactment of a lost world. It is in such aesthetic mediation or the promise of aesthetic transcendence that past pleasures and passions find their justification.

III. Continuities, reversals, and new beginnings

Reversals and compromises

The remembrance or continuation of pleasures and passions calls for apology, nostalgia, and, more rarely, self-questioning. The idea that aesthetic mediation fosters historical understanding and self-understanding leaves room for critical reflection but produces no impetus for negating or redefining the past. Yet a powerful current of irreverent revisionism runs through early Qing literature: it combines responses to national trauma, the gathering momentum of renewal and changes in literary genres, social satire, critique of the late Ming legacy, and, in the case of Li Yu, the particular genius of his vibrant wit, inventiveness, and self-invention (to borrow Patrick Hanan's formulation).

The extraordinary outburst of creative energy in historical writings in the early Qing also fueled many literary attempts to retell Chinese history. The fall of the Ming allowed certain taboo subjects, such as the atrocities committed by the Ming founder and the Yongle Emperor or the flaws in the Ming political system, to be tackled openly. Numerous series of ballads on Ming history by You Tong, Pan Chengzhang, and Wan Sitong (1638–1702) direct a sober, critical gaze on the entire course of Ming history. The loyalist poet Gui Zhuang (1613–1673), great-grandson of the prose master Gui Youguang (1506–1571) discussed in Chapter 1 above, sustains an ironic and irreverent tone in his review of all of Chinese history in "Sorrows of Ten Thousand Ages" (Wangu chou) until he gets to the Ming, when the need to lament overrides the urge to debunk exalted narratives. The Shandong literatus and official Jia Fuxi (1590–1674), discussed in Chapter 5 below, takes a similar delight in his prosimetric epitome of Chinese history in unmasking stories of virtue and divine mandate and offers a stringent critique of most Chinese rulers through the ages (including the Ming), but adopts a mournful tone with the Chongzhen Emperor and the remembrance of Jinling (Nanjing) after the fall of the Ming. The last section, added by Jia's friend Kong Shangren, overlaps with Su Kunsheng's song in the last scene of Kong's *Peach Blossom Fan*.

The license to reinterpret history converged with a new satirical edge and formal innovations in vernacular short fiction, which reached a high point in the last decades of the Ming and flourished well into the 1660s before eventually declining. A good example is *Idle Talk under the Bean Arbor* (*Doupeng xianhua*, ca 1660s), by Aina Jushi ("Recluse in a Cassock Woven with Artemisia"), about whom little is known except that he may have hailed from Hangzhou. Twelve meetings under a simple arbor made of bamboo poles constitute the frame story; different narrators and their interactions make for shifting perspectives. Some of the most interesting stories in this collection demystify hallowed historical legends. There had been keen interest in "overturning the case" (*fan'an*) – challenging old interpretations with novel ones – during the late Ming, but resonance with contemporary events gives the *Bean Arbor* stories their special pathos.

The seventh story, "Shuqi Betrayed His Integrity on Mount Shouyang" (Shouyang shan Shuqi bianjie), is a transparent fable on the meanings of service and withdrawal during the Ming–Qing transition. According to *Records of the Historian* (*Shiji*) (in Chapter 61), Boyi and Shuqi were princely brothers who vied to yield rulership to each other and ended up fleeing their kingdom, vaguely understood as being a fief of the Shang. They remonstrated with the Zhou leaders on the evil of "replacing violence with violence" when Zhou marched against Shang. After the Zhou conquest, they "refused to eat the grains of Zhou," gathering wild ferns for food, and finally died of starvation. In *Bean Arbor*, Shuqi's resolve soon weakens, especially after hordes of "fake literati and phony moralists" follow them up Mount Shouyang out of pride, indecision, or opportunism and consume all the available ferns. Shuqi's rhetoric of cynical relativism demonstrates that any position may be justified – the betrayal of integrity (*bianjie*) is whitewashed as a concern with filial piety, and animal bloodlust as a warning for a violent era. Shuqi is obviously to be castigated, but loyalism is also problematic: Boyi seems remote and rigid, and hardly engages our sympathy; the forces that remain loyal to Shang are violent and irrational, nothing more than mutilated ghosts clad in black. The final battle between these ghostly soldiers and Shuqi, defended by animals to which he has given dispensation to eat the fake loyalists of Shouyang, is a confused mess of self-interest, false claims, and misguided judgments. At the end of the story, a god-like Arbiter comes forth to stop the conflict and proclaim the change of dynasties as part of the inevitable flux of things in time. Yet the story is ultimately less about the justifications for rejecting or accepting the new order than about the inevitable compromises, doubts, and confusion that attend all political choices in this period.

The same suspicion of moral absolutes and idealized characters informs two other stories in *Bean Arbor*. In the first, Jie Zhitui – the self-sacrificing minister who, having helped Lord Wen of Jin (seventh century BC) attain hegemony, spurned rewards, refusing to leave his mountain even when it was set on fire – is here shown to be motivated not by lofty purpose but by shame and frustration. Imprisoned by his jealous wife on the mountain, he chooses to perish with her in the flames rather than face his friends. The second story deromanticizes the Xi Shi legend. Xi Shi is said to be a beautiful Yue maiden of humble origins discovered by the Yue minister Fan Li, who offered her to King Fucha of Wu to corrupt him and bring about Wu's downfall. In the romantic apotheosis of the legend, she and Fan Li are lovers and escape together to the Five Lakes after their mission succeeds. In *Bean Arbor*, Xi Shi is merely a fresh-faced, ignorant peasant girl, a passive pawn of Fan Li, and an ingrate who betrays the Wu king. The double-dealing Fan Li (once a Wu subject), fearful that Xi Shi might betray where he has hidden his wealth, drowns her and flees. In the world of *Bean Arbor*, motives are always mixed and questionable, moral clarity is elusive, and disinterestedness and escape are impossible. Sweeping judgments – as when Proctor Chen discourses on Heaven and Earth (with the aid of a crude diagram) in the last chapter, dismissing gods, Daoism, and Buddhism, and offering in their place a pitiless vision of ineluctable purgatorial violence – are bracketed as extreme and untenable even as they promise a glimmer of the author's opinions. The only possible escape may be the fantastic realm that opens up in drunken stupor, as in the eighth story, where two blind men cannot bear the spectacle of violence and destruction once sight is restored to them, and opt to be put in a magical wine jar.

Li Yu is less intent on undermining ideal types from history, but is thoroughly committed to reversing stereotypes and literary conventions. A prolific writer and master of many genres, especially vernacular short stories and plays, Li Yu offers a powerful response to late Ming contradictions and excesses with his comic genius. Sources indicate that Li Yu's father and uncle were in the medicine trade; their once ample family resources were undermined by mid-century political disorder. Li Yu had little success in the civil service examinations before the Ming collapse, and did not take them again under the Qing. In many ways he was the prototypical professional writer of his times. He was actively involved in publishing and publicizing his works, and his literary fame helped him find patronage among his official friends. A best-selling author in his own time, Li Yu was also, despite some detractors, widely admired among the elite, and two well-known women writers, Wang Duanshu and Huang Yuanjie (1618–1685), wrote prefaces and commentaries on his plays. Twentieth-century Chinese critics, however, are often torn between admiration and unease. Li's erotic novella, *The Carnal Prayer Mat (Rou putuan*, written ca 1660s, published 1693), was considered scandalous enough to be excised and preserved only in the form of a summary in the authoritative modern edition of his complete works (1991). His wit borders on levity, his sensuality is unapologetic, and his concern with contemporary turmoil is at best intermittent. In a tradition that prizes lyricism and sincerity, Li mocks the obsession with genuineness and idealized passions, choosing apparently to subsume depth of feeling to the celebration of optimal pleasures and rational self-interest.

Li Yu treats contemporary traumatic events in a comic light. In "The Female Chen Ping Saved Her Life with Seven Ruses" (Nü Chen Ping jisheng qichu, *Silent Operas* (*Wusheng xi*) 5, ca 1654), an illiterate peasant woman, Geng Erniang, outwits the leader of bandit rebels who overrun her village during the Ming–Qing transition. Because of her cleverness, Erniang is said to be as resourceful as the Han strategist Chen Ping, who was famous for his strategems, duplicity, and ruthlessness, hence the term "female Chen Ping." To stave off sexual intercourse with her captor, she devises elaborate schemes that give the author ample opportunities for ribaldry, as he dilates on various bodily functions and Erniang's strategic concessions. Compromised yet intact chastity is an intriguing (and scandalous) proposition holding special significance for this period, in which female chastity was a ubiquitous analogue for male political integrity. The opening premise of the story is the truism that calamity is the test of virtue: the paradox of the test, especially for women, is that it also negates the principle of virtue rewarded, since only false virtue can survive when the truly virtuous usually perish. Li Yu proposes a "live treasure who would not perish in the test" by combining integrity with survival. Here the genuine intention to be virtuous is masked by many ploys of duplicity. Virtue is realized through playacting and public performance: Geng maneuvers her captor into affirming her chastity in front of the assembled villagers. In contrast to the traditional valorization of natural and spontaneous virtue, here virtue is an artifice based on astute calculations of gain and loss. Geng even manages to profit from her ordeal by secretly appropriating her captor's booty. Thus Li Yu in effect calls for a redefinition of virtue to accommodate compromises, pragmatism, and self-interest.

Compromised chastity is also justified in "The Tower for Honoring Ancestors" (Fengxian lou, *Twelve Structures* (*Shi'er lou*) 10). The tower is where the heroine, Madame Shu, calls upon clansmen and ancestors to assist her in the difficult choice between "guarding chastity" and "preserving the orphan" as the Ming collapses and rebels descend on her town. Here again, virtue calls for public display and self-dramatization. Urged to choose to save her son, she endures rape and allows herself to be passed from one man to another until she ends up as the consort of a Manchu general. Reencountering her husband, she restores their son to him and then tries to hang herself. The general recognizes in her "a chaste woman who endured shame to preserve the orphan," and returns her to her husband: "Having died once, you can be said to have kept your promise (of suicide)." He further counsels Shu to claim that his first wife has died, erect an arch to commemorate her chastity, and remarry Madame Shu as his new wife. The finality of death thus becomes reversible, and truth and equivocation are accepted as intertwined. Compromise is again instrumental to survival and reconciliation – indeed, the presumed "first cause" of the story is the good karma engendered by Shu's "half-abstinence" in avoiding beef, which leads to the eventual family reunion.

The comic transformation of traumatic events is even more ingenious in "The House of My Birth" (Shengwo lou, *Twelve Structures* 11). Yin Xiaolou, whose son had been abducted as a child, pretends to be a poor man seeking to be "adopted" as someone's father. The young man who "adopts" him, Yao Ji, turns out to be his lost son. Before this is revealed at the end of the story, Yao Ji also purchases an old woman (his mother) and a girl (his lost fiancée) in the havoc unleashed by the demise of the Song dynasty (a transparent analogue for the Ming collapse). The human market, where women are sold off in sacks, described in contemporary miscellanies as a horrifying symbol of the obliteration of all identity and human dignity during this period, is here facetiously praised as "the fairest of transactions" that facilitates unexpected reunions. Fictional family reunions in the wake of dynastic fall can become the paradigm for imagining how familial, social, and political order is destroyed and reconstituted, as Tina Lu suggests. In this story, economic transactions take the place of natural relationships, but such transactions serve to restore original ties. Again, virtuous actions are good bargains. False appearance, role reversals, mistaken identity, and improbable contrivances all affirm the most basic family bonds. Li Yu is even more insistent in the play based on this story, *Ingenious Finale* (Qiao tuanyuan, preface dated 1668): the idea that everything can be bought and sold marks political collapse yet paradoxically works to reunite the family. The play also features a more determined heroine, who sees the need to take her fate into her own hands in these chaotic times.

In the prologue to "The House of My Birth," Li Yu records a poem by a woman of the elite who laments that she is "fallen" – she seems to have been raped and abducted. Judging people in times of turmoil calls for special discernment, he cautions; one has to "overlook the traces [of their acts] and empathize with their hearts." Contemporary crisis may have added further impetus to what are already dominant concerns in Li Yu's work, namely the precariousness of moral judgments, the delight in paradoxes and unexpected inversions, and the urge to push logical contradictions to their limits. How can a woman be at once chaste and sexually intimate with men other than her husband? How can familial order be rectified through inversions and economic transactions? How can a man be a paragon of female virtue – a chaste "widow" and devoted "mother" ("A Male Mother of Mencius" (Nan Mengmu jiaohe sanqian), *Silent Operas* 6)? What is the ideal domestic arrangement for two women in love with each other (*Women in Love* (*Lianxiang ban*))? Can a maid be loyal to her mistress while usurping her position ("The Cloudscraper" (Fuyun lou), *Twelve Structures* 7)? What happens when gender roles are reversed and a man becomes the object of desire (*Women in Pursuit of a Man* (*Feng qiu huang*))? What should be the karmic consequence of good intentions only half-executed ("The Ingenious Bodhisattva Changes a Girl into a Boy" (Bian nü wei er pusa qiao), *Silent Operas* 9)? Can being incorruptible adversely affect judgments ("A Handsome Lad Raises Doubts by Trying to Avoid Suspicion" (Mei nanzi bihuo fan shengxian), *Silent Operas* 2)?

The paradox dearest to Li Yu's heart may be this: how can the hedonistic pursuit of pleasures and passions be best combined with moral–social order and psychological equilibrium? Of course the problem is hardly new. The late Ming, though it valorized emotions, had felt the need to qualify their excessive claims. Thus the broad comedy in *Peony Pavilion* reconciles grand passion with mundane happiness and social integration. One late Ming parody of *Peony Pavilion* mocks the power of love: in that story a girl who dies from love is resuscitated by a necrophiliac grave robber, only to be killed by her lover when he mistakes her for a ghost ("The Love-lorn Zhou Shengxian Wrought Havoc in Fanlou" (Nao Fanlou duoqing Zhou Shengxian), *Constant Words to Awaken the World* (*Xingshi hengyan*) 14). Accounts of death from excess of feelings usually end on a cautionary note, as in Chen Jiru's (1558–1639) biography of Fan Muzhi. Li Yu does not have the reverence, the scorn, or the anxiety that characterize these late Ming solutions.

Characters rarely die for love in Li Yu's writings. When they do, as in "Tan Chuyu Conveys His Love through the Play, Liu Miaogu Dies to Defend Her Honor as the Song Ends" (Tan Chuyu xili chuanqing Liu Miaogu quzhong sijie, *Priceless Jade* (*Liancheng bi*), 1) and *Sole Mates* (*Bimu yu*), the play based on this story, the focus is less on transcendent passion than on its expression, communication, and vindication through the theater. In both, Li Yu is intent on celebrating the theatricality of life and love. Tan and Liu avow their forbidden love on the quayside stage and then enact a double suicide by jumping into the river. Their magical deliverance returns them to the stage of official success and respectability, from which they finally choose to withdraw.

Li Yu expresses his antiromantic stance as pragmatic calculation that ensures equanimity and sustainable happiness. In "The Hall of the Homing Crane" (Heguilou, *Twelve Structures* 9), a schematic contrast between two friends, Duan (homophonous with "to cut off" and "proper") the prudent stoic and Yu (homophonous with "desire" and "melancholy") the romantic, unfolds as a version of sense versus sensibility. Both are talented scholars married to beautiful women. While Duan in his restraint and detachment is ever mindful of incurring the Creator's (*Zaowu*) jealousy, Yu abandons himself to love. When the two friends are sent on a dangerous mission to the Jurchens and detained for eight years, Yu ages prematurely and his wife dies from pining, while Duan remains unscathed and returns to a wife in blooming health. Prudence turns out to be the obverse of romance, just as Duan's chilly poem of farewell can be read backwards as tender encouragement.

Li Yu continues in the same vein in the play *Be Careful about Love* (*Shen luan jiao*, ca 1666). Its male protagonist, Hua Xiu, holds as ideal the merging of romantic (*fengliu*) and moral (*daoxue*) attributes. Hua is guarded to the point of being unnatural and disingenuous, yet by the logic of the play his repression of emotions – and the comic misunderstandings this produces – deepen the attachment between him and his courtesan lover, the practical and enterprising Wang Youchang. The strategic control of emotions requires low expectations, which Li Yu also lauds as psychological refuge in adverse circumstances, as in "An Ugly Man Fears Beauties but Obtains Them" (Chou langjun pa jiao pian de yan, *Silent Operas* 1), which reverses the "scholar–beauty romance" (*caizi jiaren*) by marrying three beautiful and talented women to an ugly, foul-smelling, and uncouth husband, Que Lihou (the Lord of Flaws, also "Lord of Confucius's Lane (Queli)"; his other name is Que Buquan, homophone for "Flawed and Incomplete"). The third wife devises a scheme for taming Que's demands and sharing the burden of his company, so that even the typical ill-fate of beautiful women can be borne with equanimity. In the play based on this story, *You Can't Do Anything about Fate* (*Naihe tian*), Li Yu breaks all dramatic conventions by casting the male lead in a clown's role. The rule calling for a happy finale still holds enough sway for Li Yu to transform the undeserving Que into a handsome and talented man as transferred karmic recompense for good deeds performed by his loyal servant. More than the story, the play strongly suggests that the first two wives initially find refuge in their love for each other. This is a classic Li Yu twist; in his world, sensual fulfillment and domestic arrangements can take unorthodox turns. Another example is the blissful *ménage à trois* involving three men in a shop selling antiques and art objects ("House of Gathered Refinements" (Cuiya lou), *Twelve Structures 6*).

In Li Yu's world, moral principles are often no more than strategic restraints designed ultimately to legitimize, prolong, and maximize pleasure. Hedonistic pursuits are sometimes guided by calculations that dispense with all moral formulae. For example, in "Tower for Summer Heat" (Xiayi lou, *Twelve Structures 4*), the hero espies through a telescope a beautiful girl admonishing a bevy of pretty maids as they frolic naked in a lotus pond. Through a series of ploys facilitated by telescopic vision, he finally wins the girl and, through the marriage, gains access to all the maids. The celebration of his "technological" coup in creating this de facto harem is unattended by any moral homily.

In the economy of hedonism, there is triumph in numbers. In *The Carnal Prayer Mat*, Li Yu toys with the statistical quantification of pleasure in all forms – the number of lovers, the size of the penis, the types and frequency of movements during sexual intercourse. The male protagonist, Vesperus (literally, "Before Midnight Scholar"), starts by initiating his puritanical wife, Scent, into sexual pleasure. After an operation to enlarge his penis (by implanting a dog's member), he leaves his wife and embarks on a series of increasingly orgiastic sexual adventures. In the end, the statistics of pleasure are overtaken by another mathematical formula, that of karmic retribution. The husbands of all the women with whom Vesperus commits adultery, and many more besides, have slept with Scent, who takes a lover and is then sold by him into prostitution. She kills herself rather than face her erstwhile husband when he unwittingly comes to her as a prospective client. Vesperus becomes an ascetic Buddhist, and when even that does not suffice to quell all desires, resorts to self-castration. While the basic plot of retribution and renunciation is common enough in late imperial erotic fiction, *The Carnal Prayer Mat* is unique in combining humor, self-parody, matter-of-fact excursus on sexual lore, and an intermittently earnest defense of the role of sexual desire in human existence.

The terms of economic transaction inform the karmic scheme in *The Carnal Prayer Mat* and pervade Li Yu's corpus in general. The characters' motives, the narrators' rhetoric, and the author's judgment are formulated through the vocabulary of bargaining, debt, and principal and interest. Mercantile calculations crop up also in Li Yu's treatise on the art of living, *Casual Expressions of Idle Feelings* (Xianqing ouji, 1671), much of which concerns how to make the most of modest resources. Despite some superficial resemblances to late Ming treatises and manuals, *Casual Expressions* is decidedly less rigid and more pragmatic, ironic, and playful. Writing "as a scholar, not a technician," the author rejects normative rigor and humorously presents his own personal preferences as rules of taste. One whole section, "Living Quarters" (Jushi), is devoted to Li Yu's own practical inventions in matters of "home improvement." With the aid of illustrations, he explains his new designs for window frames, furniture, utensils, and calligraphic arrangement. What in late Ming informal writing remains in the realm of suggestion or perceptual organization is concretized as invention in *Casual Expressions*. For instance, the idea of fusing nature and art or artifice, a prevalent late Ming concern, finds its corresponding expression in Li Yu's work in a special window frame design for boats, by which the view looking out from within and the view looking in from without both mimic the effect of a painting. Li Yu calls this "taking the view by borrowing."

Li Yu transforms the late Ming fascination with liminality into a more playfully complacent balance between moral homilies on restraint and half-jesting encouragement of hedonism. In the section on "Nourishment of Life" (Yiyang), he rehearses his philosophy of strategic moderation and psychological distance, but ends with the rather startling suggestion that favorite foods and objects of desire can cure sickness. Most notable of all is the demystification of the object in Li Yu. Even when he writes about his obsessions such as crabs or different flowers in different seasons, the emphasis is on the pleasure he takes in these obsessions, in contradistinction to the late Ming tendency to celebrate the object's aura and the moment of uncontrollable passion for the object.

Casual Expressions abounds with observations on technical means to enhance one's enjoyment of the world of things, thereby divesting it of any intrinsic mystique. An interesting example is Li Yu's treatment of women. In the section "Feminine Charms" (Shengrong), he analyzes the basis of the aesthetic and sensual appeal of women, and offers advice on how women should improve their complexion or choose hairstyles, socks, shoes, and articles of clothing. By showing how women are fashioned into aesthetic objects to enhance male pleasure, he dispels the aura of romantic longing. In writing about drama, Li emphasizes not the lyrical intensity of arias but the importance of structure, staging, and theatrical effect. Effective communication with the audience overrides subtlety. The pragmatic and playful self in *Casual Expressions*, content with optimal pleasures and expedient compromises, is Li Yu's answer to late Ming anxieties about genuineness and excessive emotion.

Reception and appropriation

In the 1670s, the Mustard Seed Garden, Li Yu's bookshop, put out an edition of the *Three Kingdoms* with his commentary. He may also have published and commented on the illustrated Chongzhen-era edition of *The Plum in the Golden Vase*. The most original and compelling expression of Li Yu's literary thought is to be found elsewhere, in the self-referential comments in his own fiction and drama and in his thoughts on the theater in *Casual Expressions*. Ultimately Li is most interested in his own act of creation and in the continuity between commentary and writing. In this he differs from the thriving community of early Qing commentators on fiction and drama, who are focused on the act of reading. For example, Li Yu gives instructions, some of them technical, on how to construct and perform a play in *Casual Expressions*, whereas Jin Shengtan, in his commentary edition of *The Western Wing* (1658), uses the play as the anchor for extensive and often digressive literary and philosophical ruminations.

As Hua Wei observes, commentary on drama by women tends to be more concerned with the credibility and emotional compass of female characters, as in the *Three Wives' Commentary on Peony Pavilion* (*Wu Wushan sanfu heping Mudan ting Huanhun ji*, 1694) by Qian Yi, Tan Ze, and Chen Tong, the prematurely deceased fiancée and wives of Wu Ren. More generally, whereas drama critics touch on issues ranging from stylistics to performance, authors of fiction commentary lay great emphasis on the discerning reader's need to learn the principles of composition (*zuowen zhi fa*) for examination essays and classical essays, especially after Jin Shengtan started the fashion of using the critical vocabulary of those genres to discuss fiction. Early Qing commentators do not as a rule think of themselves, or address their readers, as writers of vernacular fiction. Fiction commentary is instead focused on justifying and elevating itself along with fiction. The heightening prestige of the genre is evident in Lü Xiong's (ca 1640–ca 1722) *Unofficial History of the Female Immortal* (*Nüxian waishi*), which includes comments by such famous literati as the painter Zhu Da (1626–ca 1706), Wang Shizhen, Hong Sheng, and the scholar Liu Tingji (1653–ca 1715). The novel itself gives a mythologized version of the 1403 usurpation mentioned above in connection with the Suzhou dramatists. Here the Jianwen loyalists continue their struggle and flourish in a kind of countergovernment under the leadership of the "woman immortal" Tang

Sai'er, the rebel leader of a messianic cult according to official history and various miscellanies.

Reading is an active, even interventionist, affair in commentarial editions. Although commentators routinely profess to be transmitting long-lost editions that they have discovered, their personal imprint on received works is unmistakable. The commentator appropriates the text and inserts himself as an author. As Zhang Zhupo (1670–1698) says, "I created my book, *The Plum in the Golden Vase*, for myself – why would I have the leisure to write commentary for other people!" Jin Shengtan often gleefully applauds passages he has altered or added in *Water Margin* as strokes of genius.

Throughout the Qing, the masterworks of Ming fiction were known in the form of commentarial editions, mostly produced between the middle and the end of the seventeenth century. These have remained influential, despite the dismissal of May Fourth writers and scholars who sought to free vernacular fiction from the baggage of traditional ideology perceived as all too intrusive in the commentaries. Jin Shengtan's seventy-one-chapter version of *Water Margin* (third preface dated 1641, published 1644?) is still the most widely read, as noted in Chapters 1 and 2 of this volume, and the image of Song Jiang as duplicitous, for which Jin is largely responsible, continues to hold sway. Jin's rhetoric of judging by hidden intention (*zhuxin*) inspired generations of commentators to hunt for subtle clues, as when Zhang Zhupo unmasks the "hidden evil" (*cangjian*) of Wu Yueniang (Ximen Qing's principal wife) in *The Plum in the Golden Vase*.

The commentarial edition of *Three Kingdoms* (preface dated 1679) by Mao Zonggang (ca 1632–after 1709) and his father Mao Lun completes the century-long redaction of the text from 240 to 120 chapters. The Maos excised some passages in the 1522 edition praising Cao Cao's generosity and judiciousness, discoursed extensively on legitimate mandate (*zhengtong*), and polarized the moral dichotomy between Wei and Shu. The song lyric by Yang Shen (1488–1559) that opens *Three Kingdoms*, which most Chinese readers know by heart and accept as a powerful statement of the novel's vision of mutability, was added by the Maos, as noted in Chapter 1 above.

The *Illustrated Ancient Edition of the Way Borne out in Journey to the West* (*Quanxiang guben xiyou zhengdao shu*, dated 1663), with commentary by Wang Xiangxu and possibly Huang Zhouxing (1611–1680), identifies the author as the Daoist patriarch Qiu Chuji (1148–1227) and offers a syncretist vision of the novel with a Daoist slant. Together with the *Illustrated True Explication of Journey to the West* (*Xiuxiang xiyou zhenquan*, preface by You Tong dated 1696), which includes Chen Shibin's avowedly syncretist but essentially Daoist reading, this establishes the trend in allegorical interpretations of *Journey to the West*. Although the May Fourth generation, notably Hu Shi (1891–1962) and Lu Xun (1881–1936), emphasized the novel's comic exuberance and dismissed allegorical readings as overly subtle and ultimately irrelevant, more recent scholarship, such as the studies by Anthony Yu and Andrew Plaks, has renewed the emphasis on the Daoist, Confucian, and Buddhist allegorical meanings. In his commentary on *The Plum in the Golden Vase* (preface dated 1695), Zhang Zhupo effectively refuted accusations of the novel's obscenity. Many later readers share his conviction that the novel has a profound moral vision, although its precise delineation remains open to contention.

Commentators articulated their visions in the name of authors, whom they sometimes consciously invented, as Jin Shengtan did with "Shi Nai'an" and Wang Xiangxu with "Qiu Chuji." The fact that Ming novels are often anonymous works representing long accretions of tradition means that they have built-in inconsistencies, which can yield unity of voice only if opacities or contradictory perspectives are read as conscious irony. Sometimes textual details may not appear to support meanings avowed in the text or imputed by the commentator, and ambiguities and paradoxes have to be reconciled. These are challenges that the commentators gladly take up, for in the problematizing of the text lies their justification. For the modern reader, superior fiction commentaries, such as those by Jin, Mao, or Zhang, afford special pleasure because of their eye for detail ("needle and thread," *zhenxian*) and associations. They also promise an indigenous critical framework for explicating narrative patterns and structures.

At first glance, commentaries may appear to function as "damage control" by assimilating potentially subversive works into the Great Tradition. To counter the accusation of "encouraging banditry" (*huidao*), Li Zhi argues in his preface to *Water Margin* (included in *A Book to Be Burned* (*Fenshu*), 1590) that the novel exemplifies the frustrations of the loyal and just (*zhongyi*) who are relegated to the margins of society. Jin Shengtan, though opposing Li Zhi's view, presents "Shi Nai'an's" censure of the bandit heroes as moral high ground. Zhang Zhupo urges "anguish and rancor" (*beifen*) and "uncompromising filiality" (*kuxiao*) as the main concerns of *The Plum in the Golden Vase* and consistently interprets sexually explicit passages as the author's way of expressing moral outrage.

The apparent "taming" of these novels can also be inconsistent and paradoxical. Thus, in writing his chapter comments, Jin did not follow the directive in his own prefaces. Criticism of Song Jiang functions only to elevate the other bandit heroes, and on a few occasions Jin even expresses admiration for Song

Jiang as a "treacherous hero" (*quanzha zhi xiong*), a formulation that influenced the Maos' fascination with Cao Cao as the "deviant hero" (*jianxiong*) of *Three Kingdoms*. Jin appropriates the orthodox virtues of "integrity and empathy" (*zhongshu*) for "Shi Nai'an," but closer scrutiny reveals that he has redefined those terms to mean natural and spontaneous feeling (third preface, comment in Chapter 42). In both *Water Margin* and *The Western Wing*, Jin's alterations turn dreams into indeterminate closures, so that the boundary between affirmation and negation remains equivocal. It can be argued, for example, that by having the bandit heroes killed in Lu Junyi's dream in Chapter 71, Jin is sparing them the indignity of being betrayed after they accept "pacification." To end *The Western Wing* with the dream encounter of Zhang and Cui is to excise the happy ending that can be viewed as either the vindication of grand passion or its mundane domestication. Equivocation is less evident in the commentaries of the Maos and Zhang Zhupo, but their readings also imply, paradoxically, that "legitimate mandate" is validated through sworn brotherhood and the solidarity of the secret society, and the extensive description of sexual excesses constitutes their negation.

Along with commentaries, sequels define the reception and appropriation of Ming fiction. Commentaries shaped sequels; Jin Shengtan's commentary was especially influential in sequels to *Water Margin*. The built-in commentarial consciousness of sequels becomes metafictional when the parent novels are not only held up as models to be continued or challenged but also enacted as representation, as when Monkey listens to a prosimetric performance of his own exploits in Dong Yue's (1620–1686) *Supplement to Journey to the West* (*Xiyou bu*), or when the surviving heroes of Liangshan watch a play entitled *Water Margin* (*Shuihu ji*) in Chen Chen's (1614–after 1660) *Water Margin: Later Traditions* (*Shuihu houzhuan*, 1664). In this sense, commentaries and sequels mark a new high point in fictional self-consciousness.

Sequels of Ming novels in the form of imitations, continuations, extensions, reworkings, and rebuttals flourished throughout the early Qing. Political disorder in *Water Margin* and *The Plum in the Golden Vase*, both set in the last years of the Northern Song, provides obvious analogies with the fall of the Ming. Li Zhi sees the authors of *Water Margin* as Song loyalists who, "though born during the Yuan, were filled with rancor and frustration over the historical events of Song." It is possible that the novel in its formative stages did carry the memories of the Song–Jin, Song–Yuan, and Yuan–Ming transitions. Dispossessed heroes defying the limits of the law and accomplishing great feats through sheer will and gang solidarity might have held special appeal in such moments of historical crisis, when legitimate political authority was contested and foreign rule justified insurrection. In the 120-chapter *Water Margin*, two Liangshan heroes (Huyan Zhuo and Zhu Tong) and the son of another (Zhang Qing) later go on to fight the Jurchen invaders (Chapters 110 and 120).

The idea that rebellion may embody loyalty and express nationalist strivings is taken up in early Qing sequels to *Water Margin*. One notable example is *Water Margin: Later Traditions*. Adopting the rhetoric of commentary as political camouflage in the preface (deliberately backdated to 1608), Chen Chen, under his usual pen name of Woodcutter of Mount Yandang (Yandang shan qiao), claims to have discovered the book, authored by the anonymous Loyalist of the Ancient Song (Gu Song yimin) during the early Yuan. Chen's formal presence in his own book is therefore as commentator. A staunch loyalist and a member of the Poetry Society of Vigilant Withdrawal mentioned earlier, Chen used the valiant exploits of the surviving bandit heroes in fighting Jurchen invaders, defending the Song dynasty, and escaping to the distant utopia of Siam to express the hopes, fears, and woes of Ming loyalists.

Generally, real or imaginary geographical margins are romanticized because they promise escape from the center, or its corrective revitalization. For early Qing writers, such longings were combined with hopes that the loyalist cause, suppressed and marginalized, might still gather momentum, perhaps through foreign support. Lady Xian, the military commander from the far south in the short play *Facing Spring Pavilion* discussed above, embodies another example of these romances of the margins. Exile is precisely what gives the heroes in Chen Chen's novel the chance to commiserate with Emperor Huizong (r. 1101–1125) in captivity and to rescue Emperor Gaozong (r. 1127–1162), imperiled on the high seas. The bandit heroes' ideal polity in Siam is very different from Liangshan: there is less violence and lawlessness, more appreciation for women and domestic happiness, and greater promotion of civil bureaucracy and literati culture. Ellen Widmer terms this "the irony of civility" – consciousness of being lesser heroes and of having failed to prevail against chaos in their own land dog the rueful fantasy in *Water Margin: Later Traditions*.

In another sequel, *Water Margin Continued (Hou Shuihu zhuan)* by the anonymous Master of the Blue Lotus Chamber (Qinglian shi zhuren), the reincarnated heroes continue their struggle against a corrupt Southern Song government capitulating to the demands of Jurchen invaders. The counter-government ideology is more uncompromising in this novel, with its virulent critique of the emperors and not just of their evil ministers, and of the idea of accepting "pacification." On the other hand, Yang Yao, Song Jiang's reincarnation, protests his loyalty and remonstrates with Emperor Gaozong. In the end, the bandit heroes are defeated by Yue Fei and "turned into black ether." The novel thus embodies the ambivalence toward the bandit heroes evident in both *Water Margin* itself and its interpretive traditions. The line between Yue Fei and the bandit heroes becomes more blurred when the latter are recast as defenders of the realm in Qian Cai's (ca 1662–ca 1721) *The Complete Story of Yue Fei (Shuo Yue quanzhuan)*. In this novel, Yue Fei – who shares a teacher with the Liangshan rebels – encourages the bandits to join the common cause against the Jurchens, and descendants of the bandit heroes become leaders in Yue Fei's army.

Just as sequels to *Water Margin* seek to redirect the errant energy of its bandit heroes by claiming to inherit its true spirit, literary responses to *The Plum in the Golden Vase* also try to contain that novel's fascination with sexuality and other aspects of sensuous existence in the name of buttressing its moral premises. In his *Sequel to the Plum in the Golden Vase*, the Shandong literatus Ding Yaokang meticulously metes out retributions to reincarnations of characters from *The Plum in the Golden Vase*, following the scheme laid out in the imperially sanctioned book of popular morality, *Supreme Retributive Correspondences (Taishang gangying pian)*. Ximen Qing is reincarnated as a rich man's son who squanders his fortune and dies a beggar. He is then reborn into a poor family and made into a eunuch who has to use a small bamboo shaft to urinate because of a botched castration. Golden Lotus, reborn as Golden Cassia, marries an impotent cripple (the reincarnation of Chen Jingji) and, afflicted with the closed vagina of a "stone woman" after a demonic sexual encounter, decides to become a nun. Vase, reborn as Silver Vase, is tricked into prostitution and passed from one man to another until, abandoned and heartbroken, she hangs herself. Plum, reborn as Plum Jade, becomes a Jurchen's concubine; horribly abused by her husband's principal wife (the reincarnated Snow, Ximen Qing's mistreated second wife), she also becomes a nun. In the meantime, Wu Yueniang and Xiaoge (Ximen's principal wife and son) wander through the empire and suffer many tribulations before returning home; they enjoy peace after embracing Buddhist renunciation. The canvas of the narrative is much broader than in *The Plum in the Golden Vase*, as historical figures like Emperor Huizong, the pretender Zhang Bangchang, and the evil minister Qin Kuai (Qin Gui) become part of the story, which also contains extensive descriptions of sociopolitical disorder and its human toll.

Ding claims to explain not only individual fates but dynastic fortune with his retributive scheme. He blames the demise of the Northern Song on factionalism at the Song court and Emperor Huizong's avarice, extravagance, and frivolous obsessions, obvious analogues for the failings of the late Ming and Southern Ming. How then is Yue Fei's unjust death or Qin Kuai's undeserved prosperity to be explained? Ding invokes, rather lamely, their previous lives as winner and loser at the moment of the Song founding. Ultimately, Ding's supposedly precise retributive system is unequal to the burden of historical explanation it is made to bear. Universal suffering, randomly incurred, is observed and delineated too keenly to be reasoned away. Yangzhou may be decadent, but to accept that it deserves the violence the Jurchens inflict on it in the twelfth century (and by analogy the Manchus in 1645) would be callous and offensive, and Ding cannot quite bring himself to draw that "logical" conclusion. The Song (read Ming) may "deserve" to fall, but his description of human suffering in the midst of political turmoil engages our sympathy, which we would withhold if we could accept dynastic collapse as rational historical process.

Ding is highly discursive, especially on the subject of sex. Not only does he comment extensively on the moral and religious purpose of sexual descriptions in *The Plum in the Golden Vase*; he is also eager to control the interpretation of similar passages in his own book. He claims expediency by adopting subdivisions used in Buddhist scriptures and categorizes chapters with sexual content under the "playful division" (*youxi pin*). Sexual encounters in this novel are often painful, unsatisfactory, or delusional, one of the few exceptions being the lesbian relationship between Golden Cassia and Plum Jade (denounced, however, as perverse). Lest his "discourse on emptiness" be misunderstood, Ding emphasizes his method of "seduction and alienation": "A hot bout, a cold bout, making the readers itch [with yearning] and ache [with pain] in turn" (Chapter 31). His pedagogical tone, by turns patient and stern, cannot quite accommodate the aberrant sexuality and sometimes random violence. One may say that such failures of "self-containment" are themselves the legacy of *The Plum in the Golden Vase*, whose moral–religious rhetoric and karmic scheme also fail to dispel our impression of the author's abiding fascination with the meanness, intricacy, and delight of worldly sensuous existence.

The Bonds of Matrimony: A Cautionary Tale (*Xingshi yinyuan zhuan*) by the anonymous Scholar of Western Zhou (Xi Zhou sheng), though not a sequel to *The Plum in the Golden Vase*, inherits its domestic framework and deep concern with the enmities, intrigues, and power struggles in marital and familial relationships. Here all illusions of male power are relentlessly dispelled in the entanglements between the emasculated Di Xichen and his sadistic and domineering wife, Xue Sujie, and only slightly less shrewish concubine, Tong Jijie. As in Ding's novel, karmic retribution drives the plot. Di, Xue, and Tong reenact enmities from former lives described in the first twenty-two chapters: Di was Chao Yuan, an improvident and brutal man who abetted his concubine, Zhen'ge, in hounding his principal wife, Madame Ji, to suicide. Madame Ji, reborn as Tong Jijie, exacts her revenge on Di and the hapless maid Xiao Zhenzhu (Zhen'ge's reincarnation). Di's greatest enemy is Xue, a fox spirit killed and skinned by Chao Yuan in a past life. In the end, order is provisionally restored when Di dispels his evil karma with ten thousand recitations of the Diamond Sutra, Xue dies from illness, and Tong, somewhat tamed, becomes Di's principal wife.

The Bonds of Matrimony carries a preface dated 1661 (or 1721) by one Student of the Way at Eastern Peak (Dongling xuedao ren), but scholars dispute the dating of the text itself, with hypotheses ranging from the 1630s to the 1680s. The turmoil of the Ming–Qing transition may have informed its pervasive sense of societal disintegration and topsy-turviness, of which one clear index is the inversion of marital hierarchy. Compared with this, Sequel to the Plum in the Golden Vase gives a more concrete and forceful portrayal of the sense of traumatic dislocation, in part because the whole plot is built on the continual displacement and wanderings of its characters. Keen observation of manner and mores, however, amply compensates for the more general and theoretical treatment of sociopolitical disorder in The Bonds of Matrimony, whose author seems to have been particularly familiar with Shandong Province and the area around Beijing.

As in Ding's novel, karmic retribution in The Bonds of Matrimony is based on a problematic combination of determinism and human responsibility. The didactic rhetoric likewise fails to contain the waywardness and complexity of the novel, and its moral reasoning is often unconvincing. Supposedly positive characters pale in comparison with the perverse ones, and Di as victim does not really engage the reader's sympathy. The author is deeply interested in female power in all its permutations. Almost all the women are forceful characters. Shrews like Xue and Tong find more positive counterparts in powerful matriarchs, like Chao Yuan's mother, or strong-minded wives, like Di's mother; even victims like Madame Ji are shrewish. Unlike The Plum in the Golden Vase and Ding's sequel, there is no overriding concern with sexual excess. Sexuality is often merely an instrument or a distraction in the power struggle between the sexes. The shrew is sometimes portrayed as lustful in Chinese literature, but Xue Sujie is neither adulterous nor even particularly interested in sex. The narrator hints that she is sexually predatory, but does not press the point. Xue's concern for sex does not seem to go beyond using sexual relations to assert control and augment her power. What makes this long novel of a hundred chapters engrossing is the author's fascination with woman's violence and power (which sometimes results in grotesque sadomasochistic bonds), the densely textured details of daily existence embedded in a panorama of complex family and social relationships, and vivid prose that captures the flow of events and the cadences of individual speech.

Reception and appropriation take other forms in another long novel of a hundred chapters, *Historical Romance of Sui and Tang* (*Sui Tang yanyi*, completed ca 1675, preface dated 1695) by the Suzhou literatus Chu Renhuo (ca 1630–ca 1705), whose publishing house also printed his book. While many major works of Ming fiction are sedimented texts, the accretion of tradition has by this time become more self-conscious and less dependent on oral transmission. Thus Chu in his preface gives details on his friendship with the literatus playwright Yuan Yuling (1592–1674), who wrote one of the source texts and supplied at least one more. While he does not go as far as Ding Yaokang – Ding was among the first writers of vernacular fiction to list an entire bibliography – he readily acknowledges his sources, implying that his own role is to fashion a continuous narrative out of disparate materials. As Robert Hegel observes, *Historical Romance of Sui and Tang*, which owes little to official historiography, is an amalgamation of classical and vernacular fiction and anecdotal literature on court intrigues, love stories, and heroic sagas set roughly between 570 and 770. He suggests that Chu's voice is implied in the ways in which he contrives patterns of balance and contrast in each chapter or cluster of chapters.

Historical Romance of Sui and Tang narrates events from the founding of the Sui dynasty (581–618) to the aftermath of the An Lushan Rebellion (755–763). The rise and fall of dynasties are affirmed as a just and rational historical process, although the saga of Qin Shubao and other warrior heroes of the Sui–Tang transition, largely indebted to Yuan Yuling's *Remnant Writings on Sui History* (*Suishi yiwen*, 1633), introduces a sense of randomness and unpredictability to the portrayal of heroic endeavor. Chu goes further than Yuan, however, in sympathizing with heroes who end up on the wrong side in opposing "the ruler with true mandate," whose ruthless elimination of the rebel heroes is by implication criticized.

The Sui and Tang sections are tied together in a karmic scheme in which Sui Yangdi, last emperor of Sui, is reborn as Prized Consort Yang, the great love of the Tang emperor Xuanzong, himself a reincarnation of Zhu Gui'er, Sui Yangdi's favorite consort, who died a martyr for love and country when the Sui fell. Told in Chapter 100, this is a rather mechanical ploy to unify multifarious strands in the novel. The novel's moral scheme is enforced through stories of exemplarity and warnings against excess. Even so, Sui Yangdi emerges as a sympathetic "romantic emperor" (*fengliu tianzi*) as he presides over the refined pursuits, such as poetry contests, of his harem of talented beauties. In incorporating *The Romance of Emperor Yang of Sui* (*Sui Yangdi yanshi*, 1631) as a source text, Chu Renhuo prunes overt sexual passages that make the emperor more of an exploitative and predatory figure. Yangdi inspires genuine devotion, not only from his consorts but from one Wang Yi, who attempts self-castration in order to serve him as a palace eunuch. His extravagance is described with relish, laced with perfunctory criticism. In general, the love stories between emperors (even "decadent" last rulers) and consorts are told with great sympathy.

Chu takes pains to incorporate many remarkable women into his narrative. In addition to a female ruler, empresses, consorts, and court ladies, he introduces a host of female knights-errant and martial heroines. Romantic elements are woven into heroic sagas – in one memorable scene, the hero and heroine, locked in combat, exchange weapons as love tokens on the battlefield. Martial prowess thus takes the place of matching literary talent as the basis of companionate marriages.

Chu's interest in romance and women may be tied to the contemporary fashion for romances featuring protagonists with literary talent and beauty, which were especially popular from the 1650s to the 1670s. Many are by or associated with the anonymous Master of the Heavenly Flowers Scripture (Tianhua zang zhuren) and Free Man of Mist and Water (Yanshui sanren). Typically short (around twenty chapters) and written in fluent, easy, and elegant vernacular prose, these "scholar–beauty romances" present attractive and gifted young men and women who fall in love, are forced apart by circumstances or assorted villains, and finally achieve union through their literary talent, courage, and resourcefulness. The world of rank and distinction invoked in these novellas, which are almost always set in Jiangnan, is often somewhat abstract, possibly because the authors came from a lower social echelon and could only give categorical descriptions in these exercises in wish fulfillment. Tortuous plot twists, mistaken identity, and cross-dressing are common currency in the genre. Romantic love is fulfilled after many postponements and often crowned with success in the civil service examinations, and young lovers marry with the blessing of family and sometimes the emperor. Perhaps in part to facilitate the integration of love and social order, there are no explicit sexual references, now the province of erotic fiction, which thrived into the early Qing with little interruption. The tone of these romances is alternately playful and moralistic: a good example is *The Fortunate Union* (*Haoqiu zhuan*, ca 1670s) by the Moral Teacher (Mingjiao zhong ren), which calls for an imperially decreed physical examination to vindicate the heroine of all suspicion of premarital relations with the hero. Female protagonists often outshine their mates, as in *Ping Shan Leng Yan* (1658), perhaps part of a broader trend of eulogizing female talent also seen in such works as *Women of Literary Talent* (*Nü caizi shu*, 1659) and *Female Examination Candidates* (*Nü kaike zhuan*, ca 1650s to 1680s). Unproblematic and therefore exportable, scholar–beauty romances were among the first Chinese novels to be translated into European languages in the eighteenth and nineteenth centuries.

New canons and orthodoxies

If early Qing fiction shows consciousness of the burden of containing, redirecting, and responding to Ming masterworks, traditionally elite genres authoritatively proclaim a new revival surpassing Ming precedents. Indeed, the confluence of poetic and political authority discussed earlier made such self-assurance inevitable. Yet this confidence also involves complex negotiations and repressed tensions. Shi Runzhang, like the aforementioned Wu Jiaji, wrote extensively about official corruption and abuses and the suffering of the people. As a distinguished Qing official, however, he tempers his criticism with "gentleness and restraint" (*wenrou dunhou*). One famous poem, "Dodder and Duckweed" (Tusi fuping pian), tells the story of husbands and wives separated and reunited, as in the Li Yu stories discussed earlier. The husband, who sees his former wife riding with a soldier (representative of the Manchu–Han victor) on his horse, is humble and beseeching: "He knelt, straight-backed, and asked the strong man: / Is this not the lowly one's wife?" It turns out that his own new wife is the soldier's former wife, and the encounter ends with amicable "wife-swapping." Given the countless wrenching stories from this period of women "taken away on horseback," this happy exception enacts the fantasy of just recompense, a moment of equal exchange for victor and vanquished, perpetrator and victim, achieved without violence or rancor. The suppression of disquiet, where not offered by the poet, may be supplied by the critic. Thus Song Wan, the Shandong poet–official often paired with Shi Runzhang, wrote many bitter, tragic poems about his own misfortunes (including two stints in prison), but Wang Shizhen commends his "heroic and forceful" (*haojian*) style, comparing him to the expansive Song poet Lu You

(1125–1210), and Wu Weiye opines that extreme suffering has not deflected his course from harmonious equilibrium (*heping*).

The rise of Wang Shizhen to canonical status, signifying a generational shift, illustrates the negotiations underlying the poetic ideal of harmony. Wang was ten years old when the Ming fell. When he was police magistrate in Yangzhou in the early 1660s, Wang befriended older Jiangnan poets, many of them loyalists. In "Fourteen Miscellaneous Poems on Qinhuai" (Qinhuai zashi shisi shou, 1661), he notes how the Qinhuai musician Ding Jizhi introduced him to that lost world. Carefully tracing the process of imagining loss, Wang participates symbolically in the romantic–aesthetic culture of the previous generation. While the loyalist poets facilitated Wang's experience of "mediated nostalgia" and conferred prestige on him through their recognition, he tries to neutralize the political implications of their writings by emphasizing their reclusive disengagement.

Qian Qianyi uses the words "dignity" (*dian*), "distance" (*yuan*), "harmony" (*xie*), and "decorous beauty" (*ze*) to describe Wang Shizhen's poetic style in his 1661 preface to Wang's collection. This early characterization gives a more substantive description of what came to be known as the style of "ineffable essence and resonance" (*shenyun*) associated with Wang's school. In writing of *shenyun*, Wang invokes familiar formulations from Sikong Tu's (837–908) *Twenty-four Categories of Poetry* (Ershisi shipin) and Yan Yu's (fl. thirteenth century) *Canglang's Remarks on Poetry* (Canglang shihua). Here again are intimations of a link between poetry and a Daoist and Buddhist kind of understanding that lies beyond language and conceptual thought. Some of Wang Shizhen's quatrains are reminiscent of the Tang poets Wang Wei (699 or 701–761), Meng Haoran (689–740), and Wei Yingwu (741–830), in which images of light rain, enshrouding mist, faint light, silence, and absence enact the aesthetics of reticence that promises but withholds ineffable meanings. Wang Shizhen compared his poetic ideal to "what painters call the transcendent mode [*yipin*]": "I have contemplated Jing Hao's [fl. 907–923] discourses on landscape painting and found illumination on fundamental principles for poets, so that 'from afar people have no eyes, from afar water has no waves, from afar mountains have no craggy lines.'"

This poetic style of contemplative distance also has political implications. Wang cited Yan Yu, who famously compares poetry's ineffable essence to "antelopes that hang by their horns, leaving no traces that can be sought," and offered his elucidation: "[These are like traces of] dragons hiding in nine abysses, phoenixes soaring above thousands of feet . . . Not only is this a metaphor for poetry, it can also be regarded as the way for a noble man to conduct himself and deal with the world." To "leave no traces" is to avoid danger (like the hidden dragon) and achieve worldly advancement (like the soaring phoenix). By this logic, poetry transcends history and politics, which recede into the distance like mountains and rivers in a painting.

The logic of poetic distance displaces violence, as in Wang Shizhen's poem about Yangzhou cited earlier. It also transforms particulars into universals, as in "Temple of the Lady on Spirit Marshes at Jiao Cliff: Second of Two Poems" (Jiaoji Lingze furen ci ershou qi er, 1685):

> The overlord's spirit, to the river's east, has long since sunk in lonely silence,
> At the Palace of Eternal Peace, desolate brambles sough.
> The endless sorrows of family and country have all been taken
> And entrusted to the rising and ebbing waves of the Xunyang river.

The temple honors Lady Sun, younger sister of Sun Quan (182–252) and consort of Liu Bei (161–223). Legend has it that she drowned herself at Jiao Cliff upon hearing of Liu's death. Another tradition claims that she was so pained by the enmity between her husband's kingdom of Shu and her brother's kingdom of Wu that she killed herself. The conflict of loyalties should speak to the historical sensibilities of an early Qing poet. Wang is, however, more concerned with the melancholy of inevitable loss. Separated from the poet by fourteen centuries, Lady Sun's grief is submerged in the rhythm of inevitable immutability – Sun Quan's hegemonic ambitions are nothing but a vague memory, and brambles choke the Palace of Eternal Peace where Liu Bei died. Such distancing allows the acceptance of loss.

Meditative distance makes possible the qualities of "dignity," "harmony," and "decorous beauty." Apparently artless ineffability is a deliberately self-effacing craft, a kind of aestheticism that distills beautiful images even from suffering and difficulties. On the temple dedicated to a chaste woman who died a gruesome death, Wang writes, "The traveler tied his reins as the moon began to sink. / Outside the gate, in the wind of the wilds, the white lotus opened" ("Again Passing by the Temple of Exposed Sinews" (Zaiguo Lujin Miao), 1660). He sees sympathetic nature in the rugged landscape and difficult roads of Sichuan: "West wind, all of a sudden, sends rustling rain, / Locust flowers fill the road as I leave the old pass" ("Going through the Old Pass in the Rain" (Yuzhong du guguan), 1672).

Wang Shizhen's championship of decorum and orthodoxy (zhengzong) was an integral part of his privileged position in the new order. In 1678, he was promoted from his position as a minor official in Sichuan to the Hanlin Academy for "excellence in both poetry and prose." Imperial recognition was based on the consensus that the Kangxi Emperor gleaned from prior consultation with various officials. His choice seems to have been motivated by deliberate "cultural policy" rather than any specific affinity of poetic sensibilities. The emperor needed to promote a "consensus candidate" who could be the voice of a new cultural confidence. Like the 1679 examination, this was "government by culture." Ironically, though his ability to develop a style that denies or transcends history gained Wang Shizhen canonical status as the voice of a great age, in the end his perceived historical role as one writing "poetry for a great age" led to his being criticized for lack of genuineness. He was seen as too pleasing, decorous, and impersonal.

In terms of literary genealogy, Wang claimed to encompass the Tang without eschewing the Song, and he also tried to mediate the diverse views of Ming poetry espoused by Qian Qianyi, Chen Zilong, and Zhong Xing. He may have regarded the forging of synthesis as requisite for canonicity. In fact, both mid-Ming classicism (as endorsed by Chen) and late Ming interiority (as represented by Zhong) can serve a poetic voice seeking to transcend the trauma of political turmoil. The counterpoint to Wang Shizhen can thus be found not in his Ming predecessors, but among contemporary poets, most of them a generation older, who define their poetic mission in terms of historical engagement.

Wang Shizhen was also at the center of a group of song lyricists in Yangzhou in the early 1660s. Their influential anthologies of late Ming and early Qing song lyrics helped to spark the revival of the form. Wang mastered the art of writing romantic song lyrics that are marked by longing and sensuous appeal, but stopped writing them after he left Yangzhou, possibly because he found it hard to incorporate this "minor art" (*xiaodao*) into his self-defined orthodoxy. It was left to the classical scholar and poet Zhu Yizun to raise the song lyric to new heights of elegance. The rise of Zhu's style and the opposing trends it implicitly addresses paralleled the canonization of "ineffable essence and resonance" in poetry. Chen Weisong was a gifted and prolific lyricist who wrote many lyrics lamenting and reflecting on dynastic transition and sociopolitical disorder, for which he is honored as "lyricist–historian" (*cishi*); but his Yangxian School was ultimately less influential than Zhu Yizun's Zhexi School. The latter, which upheld the Southern Song tradition of Jiang Kui (1155–1235) and Zhang Yan (1248–1320?) in its emphasis on "decorous refinement" (*chunya*) and "reticent resonance" (*qingkong*), had risen to canonical stature by the 1680s.

A decisive year again came in 1679, when *Supplementary Titles for the Music Bureau* was published through the efforts of Zhu Yizun and another lyricist, Jiang Jingqi (1646–1695). *Supplementary Titles* consists of lyrics on objects composed by poets who lived through the Song–Yuan transition. Their elegiac tone is unmistakable, but political meanings are modulated through allusive diction, which presented early Qing lyricists with a potential vehicle for expressing nostalgia and political lament or inferring higher significance through exercises in virtuosity. The divergent uses of *Supplementary Titles* are evident in the prefaces. Whereas Zhu Yizun concisely affirms the collection's "mournful meanings that go beyond words," Chen Weisong, in beautiful and moving parallel prose, pours forth empathetic grief for the "wild words" and "contradictory language" of these "loyalists to the Song." The hundreds of early Qing imitations of *Supplementary Titles*, including Zhu's own, are by and large more allusive than affective. Yet they embody the formal mastery, elegant diction, and feelings intimated rather than expressed that come to characterize the Zhexi School, a designation that became current with the publication of *Song Lyrics by the Six Masters of Zhexi* (*Zhexi liujia ci*), anthologized by the lyricist Gong Xianglin, also in 1679.

Zhu Yizun was involved in anti-Qing resistance, but after becoming the informal adviser (1656–58, 1664–68) of the Qing official and poet Cao Rong, he moved closer to accepting the new order. He was a successful candidate in the 1679 examination, participated in the compilation of Ming history, and became an imperial tutor in 1683. His reputation steadily rose after 1679, after which his chosen mode often became the song lyric on objects, and he also opined that song lyrics should "sing of great peace." His best works, however, were written earlier, when stylistic restraint was a way to deal with more anguished feelings. As he writes in the song lyric about his collection *Taking Wine among Rivers and Lakes* (*Jianghu zaijiu ji*, 1672): "Composing song lyrics in my declining years, / Half of them sorrows transmitted in thin air."

Zhu Yizun's song lyrics on unfulfilled or lost love are among the finest in the tradition. Various sources point to his hopeless passion for his wife's sister, who died young. The tantalizing proximity of what is ultimately unattainable adds complexity to his song lyrics, as in the following one, written to the tune "Guidian xiang":

> Remembrance of events past:
> We passed by riverbanks,
> Her lowered eyebrows a dark light against the blue mountains.
> Sleeping in the same boat, listening to autumn rain –
> Small mat, light coverlet, singly and separately cold.

Some of Zhu's song lyrics juxtapose memories of glances and words furtively exchanged with the irrevocable separation of death, as in the last few lines of a lyric to the tune "Mo yuzi":

> But I do not know:
> The golden casket with locked fragrance – where has it gone?
> Little pond, withered trees.
> I ponder, there is only, from that moment,
> The cold moon's single orb,
> Still shining on the road, deep into the night.

On history and politics, Zhu's tone is typically restrained and melancholy. He writes about the Raining Flowers Terrace in Nanjing, to the tune "Maihua sheng":

> Autumn grass, cold since the Six Dynasties –
> Flowers rain on an empty altar.
> There is not even one person leaning against the balustrade.
> Swallows in the setting sun come and go:
> Rivers and mountains like these.

Verbal echoes of lyrics mourning dynastic collapse by Li Houzhu (a.k.a. Li Yu, 937–978) ("Lean not against the balustrade alone") and Zhang Yan ("Wanderings most bitter: / How much more so, with rivers and mountains like these, / And this moment's feelings") intensify the political lamentation, but the mood remains subdued.

Chen Weisong also passed the 1679 examination and participated in the imperial Ming history project. His death in 1682 meant that his brief official career did not quite counterbalance the awareness of failure and disappointment that pervades his song lyrics. Zhu and Chen once published their song lyrics together (*Zhu Chen cun ci*), but they are usually perceived as leaders of different trends. In his preface to *The Garden of Song Lyrics in Our Time* (*Jin ci yuan*, 1671), Chen articulates the power of song lyrics to convey "finely delineated and profound" (*jingshen*) thoughts comparable in their significance to the canonical classics, history, and poetry. This implied discursiveness is often combined with the flow of powerful diction. Emotions forcefully, sometimes even extravagantly, expressed invite the epithet of "heroic abandon" (*haofang*) most often associated with Su Shi (1036–1101) and Xin Qiji (1140–1207). The sense of alienation, displacement, and despair is, however, more oppressive in Chen's *oeuvre* and in the works of Yangxian lyricists in general. It may be no accident that many of them were minor officials with checkered careers, loyalists and their descendants, men who suffered exile or chose withdrawal from society.

The powerful sweep of Chen Weisong's lyrics can be felt in lines such as: "Unsettled autumn feelings, about to stir, / Have since burst forth, entering the flute's holes on the frosty bridge," "Autumn air, an array of ten thousand horses, / All tethered to the foot of long city walls" ("Autumn Feelings" (Qiuhuai), to the tune "Ye you gong"); "White geese crossed the sky, their cries like arrows, / Crying for all heroes past and present, / Who were yet / By rivers and mountains crushed and erased" ("Autumn Night, Presented to Mr. Gong Zhilu [Dingzi]" (Qiuye cheng Zhilu xiansheng), to the tune "He xinlang").

Sometimes Chen deliberately exploits the tension between conventional romantic imagery and the stark reality of chaos and destruction, as in "Listless" (Wuliao), to the tune "Yu meiren":

> Listless, smiling, toying with a flowering branch, I say:
> Everywhere, blood from the crying cuckoo.
> Lovely flowers should glow against lovely towers and terraces –
> Bloom not by the battlefield, next to distant passes and steep roads!
> Leaning against the tower, gazing afar, my sorrows redouble,
> And yet I address the east wind: A fine wind should not bluster the red
>   banners of war –
> Make haste to send the shad, white as snow, across to the river's east.

In this song lyric, probably written during the Rebellion of the Border Principalities, the ennui and melancholy common in song lyrics quickly give way to political lament, as the cuckoo, transformed from an ancient king who mourns the loss of his kingdom, weeps tears of blood that turn into red flowers. Invocations to flowers and wind, usually playful or suppliant in song lyrics, are here imperative. Rather than heightening the sorrow of wanton destruction, they are to find their proper place and role as the ornaments of the good life.

The young Manchu nobleman Nara Singde stood apart from the traditions represented by Zhu Yizun and Chen Weisong, despite ties of friendship with the latter. Widely hailed as one of the canonical poets in the tradition, he is celebrated for the deep, mournful passion of his song lyrics. Though enjoying imperial favor, he is known for a lyrical voice marked by profound anguish and melancholy, mainly because of the death of his beloved first wife at age twenty-one in 1677. The subgenre of elegy (daowang) receives unprecedentedly intense and extensive attention in his song lyrics:

This grief, when will it end?
Drops on empty steps,
The rain ceasing in the cold night –
Weather fit for burying fallen blossoms.
For three years, endlessly, the spirit in dreams fades.
If dream this is, I should long since have awakened.

. . .

I wish to tie the knot
Of devotion in another life,
Yet fear that, both ill-fated,
We will again be robbed of union,
Left with a remnant of the moon, a fragment of wind.
Pure tears are exhausted,
As the ashes of burnt paper flutter.

Written in 1680 on the anniversary of his wife's death, this song lyric (to
the tune "Jinlüzi") exemplifies how emotional involutions are paradoxically
conveyed through a lucid poetic syntax. Using a similar logic, many of his most
memorable lines follow apparent clichés to their heartbreaking conclusion. He
pleads for the uncertain contours of his wife's dream image to last: "Dreams
too are but hazy – / Why then must / Awakening be hastened?" (to the tune
"Taichang yin"). He dwells on the coldness of the moon and of death: "If
like the moon, it can to the end be clear and bright, / I will brave ice and
snow, and warm you" (to the tune "Die lian hua"). Remembering his wife's
timidity, he writes, "I wish to point the way for her soul, / Leading her in
quest of dreams down winding corridors." Chen Weisong and others compare
Nara Singde to Li Houzhu because both are preoccupied with loss and their
lyrics share an elegiac beauty unencumbered by difficult allusions. Nara's
relatively plain diction also follows complex emotional twists, in a manner
reminiscent of Northern Song masters like Yan Jidao (1030–1106) and He Zhu
(1052–1125).

The romantic aura of Nara Singde, sustained by his obsession with lost
love and his own early death at age thirty, invites suggestions of a "second
innocence." He could be so "genuine and moving" (zhenqie), "using the eye
of nature to observe things, and the tongue of nature to articulate feelings,"
Wang Guowei (1877–1927) claims, because as a Manchu aristocrat "he had
not yet been steeped in Han mores." Li Houzhu, because of the newness
of the song lyric form in his time as well as his own sheltered existence
prior to the fall of his kingdom, could claim innocence of a similar kind,
hence the frequent analogy with Nara Singde. The refreshing vigor of Nara's

work, however, may also derive from his wholehearted embrace of Han literati culture. His exchanges with fellow lyricists Gu Zhenguan (1637–1714, brother of the aforementioned Gu Zhenli), Jiang Chenying (1628–1699), Yan Shengsun (1623–1702), and Chen Weisong yielded some of the most moving song lyrics on friendship in the tradition. He adopted, without irony, the self-image of an "unconventional literatus" (*mingshi*), and empathized with the frustrations and disappointments of his friends, mostly Han poets a generation older: "I am but a scholar unbound who, / Quite by chance, / In the dusty capital, / Belongs to a noble clan" ("To Gu Liangfen [Gu Zhenguan]," to the tune "Jinlü qu"). This "naturalized" melancholy enables him to draw upon the entire tradition of frontier and exile poetry in writing lyrics about attending the emperor on his tour of the frontier. Nara also had enough distance from his estate as a Manchu aristocrat to write with grief and longing about historical vicissitudes, sometimes even with vague references to Ming demise. In the postscript to *Song Lyrics of Our Time: First Collection* (*Jinci chuji*, 1677) compiled by Nara and Gu Zhenguan, Mao Jike (1633–1708) describes their style as "the expression of native sensibility" (*shuxie xingling*). Although the genius of Nara Singde is usually not associated with a school, the consuming sorrow of his song lyrics links him to the major nineteenth-century lyricists Xiang Hongzuo (1798–1835) and Jiang Chunlin (1818–1868).

Compared to other genres, orthodoxy in classical prose was more insistently moral and political. Gu Yanwu declares that only writings elucidating the Classics and dealing with contemporary problems are worthwhile. For early Qing prose masters, such as Wang Youding (1599–ca 1661), Hou Fangyu, or Wei Xi (1624–1680), broad self-identification as Confucians did not preclude interest in characters from the margins of society (such as beggars, servants, knights-errant, actors, entertainers) or wondrous and fantastic realms. Perhaps this was why Wang Wan, also famous for his prose, criticized Hou Fangyu for employing "the techniques of fiction" and decried the fascination with novelty in general. There was also a pervasive concern with commemorating martyrs and moral exemplars from the dynastic transition, not only among loyalists but also among Qing officials like Wang Wan; such topics continued to capture the imagination of members of the next generation, notably Dai Mingshi. The murky case of Dai's alleged literary transgression (1711–13), which resulted in his execution, imposed a much more cautious direction on orthodoxy in prose. Fang Bao (1668–1749), later honored as the first master of the Tongcheng School, was implicated in Dai's case. Both Fang and Dai hailed from Tongcheng in Anhui; Fang wrote the preface for Dai's *Southern Mountain*

Collection, and Dai's "seditious" reference to the Yongli court reiterated an account by his mentor Fang Xiaobiao, Fang Bao's elder clansman. Imprisoned and sentenced to death, Fang Bao was spared and, as a banner slave, started clerical work in the imperial study. He was pardoned in 1724 and subsequently enjoyed a long and distinguished official career.

Chastened by his brush with state power, Fang Bao laid emphasis on "principles and methods" (*yifa*) to affirm his adherence to the orthodox teachings of Zhu Xi (1130–1200) and Cheng Yi (1033–1107) and his goal of "assisting good government by moral precepts." In his preface to an anthology, *Selections of Classical Prose* (*Guwen yuexuan*, 1733), compiled for a Manchu prince, he articulates limpid and austere elegance as a stylistic ideal and points to *The Zuo Tradition* (*Zuozhuan*) and *Records of the Historian*, for which he wrote detailed commentaries, as prime prose models. Elsewhere he uses Han Yu (768–824), Ouyang Xiu (1007–1072), and Gui Youguang to chart the perimeters of an ideal style, but his unease with waywardness and heterodox judgments led him to suppress the more unconventional aspects of these masters; this may also account for his disparagement of Liu Zongyuan (773–819). Even when Fang Bao is writing about contemporary abuses and corruption, as in "Miscellaneous Accounts from Prison" (*Yuzhong zaji*), based on his own imprisonment, his tone is wry, cautious, and deliberately dispassionate. Accounts of martyrs to late Ming political persecution and the Ming–Qing transition such as Zuo Guangdou (1575–1626) and Huang Daozhou, proportionately few in number (compared to, say, Dai Mingshi's corpus), give rare glimpses into his grander passions. All too often, however, he shows feelings only to rein them in under the stylistic imperatives of balance, clarity, and restraint.

IV. Alternative worlds

Fantastic realms

The new orthodoxy in classical prose had little use for the strange, the wondrous, and the fantastic, which flourished throughout the early Qing in poetry, song lyrics, drama, novels, and classical tales. The glorious epitome of this interest is Pu Songling's *Records of the Strange*. We can trace its genealogy to antecedents within the genre ranging from Tang tales to notable Ming examples, discussed in Chapters 1 and 2 of this volume, as well as other early Qing classical tales showing a penchant for the extraordinary and the supernatural. Pu Songling, himself a master of prosimetric narratives (see Chapter 5), was obviously also indebted to vernacular genres.

The late Ming concern with emotions, imagination, and the boundaries between reality and illusion is still evident in *Records of the Strange*. Quite apart from late Ming influence, there were other reasons for the early Qing interest in imaginary realms. Disorder and destruction inspire a longing for escape, sometimes expressed in poems on the quest for immortality (*qiuxian*) or wandering with immortals (*youxian*). Qu Dajun, actively involved in anti-Qing resistance well into the 1670s, wrote many poems and song lyrics in this subgenre. His travels in the Luofu Mountains in Guangdong occasioned many fantasies of escape, but even as a fugitive Qu could transform confined spaces into the realm of immortals. Disquiet, however, is never far beneath the surface. Qu imagines immortals sharing his mourning for a lost world: "All under heaven, just as mountains and rivers are no more, / The immortals, too, must long for the realm of earthly rulers" ("On Mr. Li's Album" (Ti Li sheng hua ce)).

Escape is also tenuous in Ding Yaokang's brilliant fantasy *Wandering with Magicians* (*Huaren you*, 1647). In this play, the protagonist He Gao's quest for enlightenment takes him on a sea journey, whose pleasures and trials have obvious political and religious meanings. Wilt Idema notes that the host of historical beauties and literary geniuses He Gao meets are trivialized to suggest a critique of late Ming self-indulgence. The whale (*jing/qing*) that swallows the boat, opening up phantasmagoric illusions within illusions, is homophonous with "desire" and the Qing dynasty: this invites divergent allegorical interpretations whereby the target can be the conquest or human passions. The final moment of transcendence is defiant but also vaguely melancholy: "As for me, what does it matter if Heaven turns, Earth turns, / Mountains are ruined, waters are ruined" (scene x). The sense of disintegration and uncertainty here is more oppressive than in other early Qing plays, such as You Tong's *Harmony in Heaven* (*Juntian yue*, 1657) and Zha Shenxing's *Judgments in Two Worlds* (*Yinyang pan*, 1701), that delineate immortal realms in order to redress inequities in the human world.

The undead are as prominent as the undying. The poet Jin Bao (Buddhist name Jinshi Dangui, 1614–1680), who took the tonsure in 1650 when the loyalist cause he supported became increasingly hopeless, wrote seven song lyrics on the painting of a skeleton, in which, directly addressing the skeleton, he imagines existence from its perspective. Unlike the encounter with the skeleton in *Zhuangzi* or Zhang Heng's (78–139) "*Fu* on the Skeleton" (*Dulou fu*), philosophical transcendence of mutability offers no consolation. Instead, the skeleton shares the unappeased anguish of the living, whose world is being taken over by the spectacle and the memory of the dead. Cao Zhenji

(1634–1698), who was hailed along with Nara Singde and Gu Zhenguan as one of "the three supreme lyricists of the capital," presents the ghostly realm as a continuation of the devastated human world, as seen in "Speaking on Behalf of Those in the Yellow Springs" (Dai quanxia ren yu, to the tune "Wang Jiangnan"). In 1674, Chen Weisong wrote about "the ghostly wails" he heard in Liangxi: "Just like skeletons, rusty with blood, / A thousand times crying to the moon, / Phantoms choked by moss, / weep in hundreds of ways in the mist" (to the tune "Qinyuan chun"). In the preface, he claims that many had heard these wailing ghosts. Fellow Yangxian lyricists, such as Cao Liangwu and Shi Weiyuan, "harmonized" with him on the same topic, blurring the line between subjective experience and consensual reality in their song lyrics.

Ghostly wails, which seem to represent the voice of past and present traumas unhealed, also appear in a story by Pu Songling, set in the aftermath of the Xie Qian Rebellion of 1646. The ghostly legions only snicker, "laughing through their noses," when an official tries to silence them by proclaiming his official title ("The Ghosts' Wails" (Guiku)). Only a proportionately small number of Pu's stories, however, deal with the chaos and violence of the conquest and early Qing insurrections, encompassing about a dozen out of almost five hundred. Among them are two memorable love stories, "Gongsun Jiuniang" and "Lin Siniang," which exemplify the phantom heroine as inseparable from historical memory, as Judith Zeitlin has noted. Set in 1674, during the bloody aftermath of the Yu Qi Rebellion (1669), "Gongsun Jiuniang" tells of its eponymous heroine's "marriage" with "a scholar from Laiyang" in the realm of ghosts. Upon his return to the human world, the male protagonist tries to fulfill his promise of reburying Jiuniang, but loses his way "among thousands of [unmarked] graves." The silken stocking she gave him "tore into bits in the wind, decaying like ashes." The story ends with the haunting image of a receding, resentful Jiuniang, "shielding herself with her sleeves." The story of Lin Siniang appears in several other early Qing sources, with significant variations. In *Records of the Strange*, she is the ghost of a Ming palace lady who initiates a love affair with the Qing official Chen Baoyao, communicates her lamentation for a lost world through music and stories, and after three years leaves to be reborn. Other early Qing stories of Lin Siniang feature a more martial and initimidating heroine, whereas here she is a figure of intense nostalgia and melancholy. In Pu's story, Lin's death is more specifically associated with the wars of dynastic transition, while at the same time the pathos of loss is romanticized, aestheticized, and thereby divested of dangerous political implications. Chen empathizes with Lin but does not share her lament. The fact that both Pu's stories, unlike most romances in *Records of the Strange*, do not end happily implies that memories of traumatic historical events defy formal or ideological containment.

Pu came of age under the Qing and had no personal memory of the fall of the Ming, although generational difference did not prevent his contemporaries, Zhang Chao and Niu Xiu (1640–1704), from taking a keen interest in the events and personages of the Ming–Qing transition. In Zhang's influential anthology, *New Tales of Yuchu* (*Yuchu xinzhi*, preface dated 1683, postface dated 1700), writers spanning two generations commemorate, sometimes with supernatural twists, the strange fate and extraordinary virtue of many caught in mid-century turmoil. Niu Xiu, though taking pains to affirm the new order, shows similar concerns in his *Leftover Vessel* (*Gusheng*, ca 1700). The Jiangnan roots of Zhang and Niu and their personal ties with loyalists may have accounted for this interest.

Pu was far removed from the Jiangnan literary networks. He lived in rural Shandong almost his entire life. Unable to rise beyond the lowest degree in the civil service examinations, he made a modest living as a tutor for four decades, before being finally granted the degree of senior licentiate at seventy. The autobiographical preface to *Records of the Strange*, dated 1679, marked the first stage in the book's completion, but Pu continued to add stories and make changes for another thirty years. Circulated in manuscript form for decades, the book became known locally, but did not have broad impact until its publication in 1766.

Pu's relative obscurity and marginality gave him insights into the dark side of life in his time. Modern scholarship on *Records of the Strange* often emphasizes its trenchant social criticism. There are indeed many stories that delve into the injustices of the examination system, official incompetence and corruption, the abuses of power by the rich, and intrigues and viciousness in family relations. Indignation stops short of reformist zeal, however, and Pu does not present a coherent vision of a better world based on different principles of social and political organization. "The Kingdom of Rākṣasas [malevolent demons] and the Market in the Sea" (Losha haishi) is a good example of an abrupt shift from public sociopolitical satire to private wish fulfillment. The first half of the story caricatures the reversal of values in contemporary society by imagining a monstrous world that negates beauty. The protagonist Ma Qi, a handsome seafaring youth, is shipwrecked in the Kingdom of Rākṣasas, where advancement hinges on ugliness. Ma's misadventures are told with a biting satirical edge, but midway through the story, he leaves for the Market in the Sea where "immortals played," and finds romantic bliss in a just and beautiful world where he is valued for his literary talent.

Rectification is achieved not by reimagining moral and sociopolitical order, but through the power of individuals, such as the host of sagacious and incorruptible judges in ratiocinative stories, or the god Erlang, who takes on corruption in the underworld in "Xi Fangping." In "Yu Qu'e," Zhang Fei, noted for his uncouth impatience and military prowess in *Three Kingdoms*, becomes the unlikely judge of literary excellence, a deity "who does his round in the underworld once every thirty years and in the human world every thirty-five years" to correct injustices in the examination system. This incongruous choice combines poetic justice with all too real frustration.

The examination system, a Kafkaesque affair that respects neither talent nor industry, provokes deft satire and melancholy reflection. In "Scholar Ye" (Ye sheng), the protagonist, a luckless examination candidate, forgets about his own death in his obsession with gaining just recognition. His soul wanders off to his one-time benefactor and helps his son to succeed, and he himself also passes the examination. It is only when his soul returns home that he realizes he has died, and he sinks to the ground and vanishes. The comments of the "Historian of the Strange" that follow have distinct autobiographical echoes and recall Pu's preface: "I drained my cup and put brush to paper to write the book of lonely anguish and frustration. To use these [fantastic] stories as the vehicle of my thoughts and feelings: is this not lamentable enough!"

The idea of rectifying a flawed existence through writing harks back to Sima Qian, as does Pu's rhetoric of authentication and self-designation as "Historian of the Strange" when he appends comments – by turns earnest, ironic, digressive, and facetious – to the end of his narratives. These comments sometimes assert the analogy, or even identity, between the human world and the fantastic realm, or seek to "naturalize" the latter by establishing its moral, metaphorical, or allegorical connection with the former. Sometimes they make playful twists on what strangeness is: rare virtues and vices, inexplicable motives, or departures from social norms may be singled out as stranger than supernatural occurrences. Pu presents his world of immortals, deities, ghosts, and spirits as being both strange and not strange – strange enough to inspire wonder and interest (but almost never alienation), yet not so strange as to be beyond empathy. In many stories, "the strange" is re-integrated into existent moral and sociopolitical order in conventional happy endings.

Sometimes "the strange" merges with a broader concern with the shifting boundaries between fact and fiction, illusion and reality. Words have magical efficacy. In "Bai Qiulian," lines from famous poems cure sickness and revive the dead. Monkey from *Journey to the West* becomes a deity and overcomes the disbelief of a skeptic, although the "Historian of the Strange" ironically supplies a psychological explanation for apparently divine intervention ("Great Sage Equal to Heaven" (Qitian dasheng)). "Blue Phoenix" (Qingfeng) acquires suprafictional reality when its appreciative reader, Bi Yi'an (Pu's real-life friend), dreams up a fox spirit who regards Blue Phoenix as a model of love and literary fame ("Dream of a Fox" (Humeng), a supposedly real story that Bi related to Pu). In "Flower Goddess" (Jiang fei), Pu is summoned by the Flower Goddess in a dream to write an indictment of the vicious Wind Goddess, in self-parody or rueful compensation for his failures in the real world. In general, however, the status of literary illusion is the subject not of probing questions but of playful celebration.

"Lonely anguish and frustration" suggest intense emotions. Despite Pu's reliance on traditional sources, local lore, and accounts supplied by friends and acquaintances, many of his stories have a lyrical quality. Lyricism here refers not only to elegant, evocative prose or the use of poetry in narrative – although Pu left a sizable corpus of poetry, he did not incorporate many of his poems into his stories, as did his predecessors in the genre – but more importantly refers to emphasis on the transformative powers of feelings and imagination. Tenacious attachment defies obstacles and the boundaries between life and death, the human and the nonhuman realms. Mind triumphs over matter in stories about obsessive devotion. Sun Zichu, hopelessly in love with Abao, thinks that being able to fly will grant him proximity. "Even as his mind was concentrating on this thought, his body had effortlessly turned into a parrot" ("Abao"). Objects respond to obsession by coming to life as lovers and friends, as in several stories about flower spirits. Even a stone, traditionally the symbol of insentience, assumes human form and becomes a martyr to friendship, in requital of its owner's love for its paradoxically ethereal beauty ("Shi Qingxu").

In many cases the object of desire, often a woman from other realms of existence, propels the plot. Successful pursuit typically brings about a happy ending, but there is enough anxiety about the dangers and potential boundlessness of desire to call for built-in mechanisms of control or equivocation. In "Painted Wall" (Huabi), intense contemplation of a wall painting in a Buddhist temple enables the hero to enter the painting and enjoy romantic union with a celestial maiden, "her hair hanging down, holding a flower and smiling"; an icon associated with Buddhist enlightenment here offers sensual gratification. The hero's terrified exit might have made this an allegory on the Buddhist lesson of how desire and its negation are one, but in the end he remains unenlightened, and the only thing that changes is the maiden in the painting – she now displays an elaborate coiffure to mark her passage from innocence to sexual experience. In another story, the spontaneous, irrepressible laughter and unconventional defiance of the fox spirit Yingning turn to sobriety in the interests of reintegrating her into family and society, although her son is said to inherit her laughter ("Yingning"). She also implies that she used her defiant innocence to test the love of her husband and mother-in-law. Pu may have found it just too difficult to imagine a social order that fully accommodates a woman's unconventional spontaneity.

In most of Pu's stories, contradictions are resolved when the fulfillment of desire coincides with the reaffirmation of socio-ethical order. Seductive and assertive female spirits, ghosts, and immortals boldly pursue union with their chosen men, but they become chaste and virtuous wives. Ironic reversal sometimes marks the fulfillment of obsessive passion. A man's passion for chrysanthemums is rewarded by chrysanthemum spirits, who become his wife and best friend, but his wife also forces him to revise his preconception about the flower's inevitable association with unworldliness and lofty disdain for profit ("Yellow Blossoms" (Huangying)). Likewise, a bibliophile is lured away from books by a spirit who embodies the proverbial "beauty inevitably found in books" ("The Bibliophile" (Shuchi)). A common pattern is to reconcile desire and order through triangular relationships with complementary heroines. Passion is paired with restraint, or practicality with ethereal charm, to assure the male protagonist perfect bigamous bliss ("Fragrant Jade" (Xiangyu), and "Chen Yunqi"). A desirable yet unavailable woman can occupy the tantalizing role of intimate friend ("Jiaona") or become the mediating agent for union with a more suitable mate ("Feng Sanniang," "Huanniang," and "Lotus Third Lady" (Hehua san niangzi)). Sometimes one heroine checks the excessive ardor of the other to forestall the destructive consequences of extreme passion, as in "Moon Goddess" (Chang'e) and "Lotus Scent" (Lianxiang). In the latter, the hero lies dying as Lotus Scent, a fox spirit, explains to her ghostly rival, Ms. Li, the different consequences of sexual union with ghosts and fox spirits (the former being invariably deadly, the latter only in cases of excess, a rule that, incidentally, does not apply in other stories) and prescribes an erotic cure. This comic scene demonstrates how desire is both threatening and redemptive. Pu Songling thus pushes the boundaries of desire and imagination but also reaffirms the need for limits.

Dramatic summation

If Pu Songling uses excursions into fantastic realms to explore the claims and limits of emotion and imagination, Hong Sheng and Kong Shangren take up similar issues in the context of historical and political engagement. In some ways, they continue the tradition of early Qing plays, such as Wu Weiye's *Spring in Moling* (*Moling chun*, ca early 1650s), Ding Yaokang's *Fan of West Lake* (*Xihu shan*, 1653), and Li Xuanyu's *Winning the Prize Courtesan* (*Zhan huakui*), that rework the legacy of *Peony Pavilion* by pitting the valorization of romantic love against historical crisis.

Hong Sheng came from an established family in Qiantang (near Hangzhou), but lived for long periods in modest circumstances in Beijing. Of his considerable dramatic corpus, only *Palace of Eternal Life* and four short plays, *Four Beauties* (*Si chanjuan*), are extant. As mentioned above, the ill-fated performance of *Palace of Eternal Life* in 1689 barred many, including Hong Sheng, from office. The play was well received from the first and continues to be one of the most popular works in the *kunqu* opera repertoire.

Hong Sheng quoted in his "Introductory Remarks" Liang Qingbiao's comment that *Palace of Eternal Life* is "*Peony Pavilion* writ large." Indeed, love is mythologized and quotidianized in a conscious effort to "outdo" the earlier play. Romantic passion is tied to artistic (specifically musical) creation and access to the mythic realm. At the same time, rivalries and jealousies in the palace recall a regular polygamous household, performances suggest the world of the pleasure quarters, and maids, acting as voyeurs, give explicit descriptions of sexual passion.

In his preface to the play, Hong describes his earlier plays about Emperor Xuanzong's court and the An Lushan Rebellion: in *The Incense Pavilion* (*Chenxiang ting*), the court recognizes the poet Li Bai's (701–762) defiant genius; *Dance of the Rainbow Skirt* (*Wu Nichang*) describes the restoration of Tang power in the aftermath of the rebellion. Hong's focus thus shifted from personal to political concerns with *Palace of Eternal Life*; there he found his voice in the mythic–romantic affirmation of the love between Emperor Xuanzong and his ill-fated consort Yang Guifei (Yang Yuhuan), the classic example of private passions getting entangled with public collapse. In Bai Juyi's famous poem "Song of Enduring Sorrow" (*Changhen ge*), Xuanzong and Yang swear a secret vow of eternal love in the Palace of Eternal Life. Whereas Bai Juyi's poem and the Yuan play it inspired, namely Bai Pu's (1226–1306) "Rain on the Wutong Trees" (*Wutong yu*), focus on the emperor's passion and longing, Hong balances the perspectives of both Xuanzong and Yang; in some ways he gives more weight to Yang as the agent and victim of passion. She is the artist who creates the "Tune of Rainbow Skirt and Feather Coat," whose different meanings determine various interpretations of the play.

Parallel to the romantic apotheosis of the Xuanzong–Yang love story was a long tradition of moral judgment that castigates Yang as femme fatale and Xuanzong as irresponsible ruler. One early Qing play that exemplifies this view is Sun Yu's *Dramatic History of the Tianbao Era* (*Tianbao qushi*, 1671). Negative portrayals emphasize the impropriety of the union as Yang was married to one of Xuanzong's sons, Prince Shou, invent an adulterous relationship between Yang and the rebel An Lushan, and create a rival and victim of Yang's jealousy, Consort Mei. Hong Sheng rejects these accounts as vulgarization. Consort Mei figures only offstage in his play. Contrary to the usual tendency to denigrate female jealousy in traditional Chinese literature, Yang's jealousy is lauded as evidence of true passion (scene ix). That she suffers abandonment because of her jealousy also invites sympathy (scene viii). Hong Sheng takes pains to dissociate her from her brother, the minister Yang Guozhong guilty of abusing power. In Bai's poem, the emperor, enjoying the pleasures of the night too well, fails to rise for morning audience. Here it is Yang who sleeps late with sensuous languor (scene iv). Her inebriated slumber when news of the rebellion comes to the palace suggests a kind of oblivious innocence (scene xxiv).

When mutinous troops demand Yang's execution at the midpoint of the play (scene xxv), Xuanzong "would rather face ruin of family and country" than abandon Yang, but relents when she insists on giving up her life "to protect the ancestral altar [of the state]." The emperor, praised in other literary works for subordinating private desires to public good, is the irresolute lover here, while Yang becomes the victim embracing martyrdom. In the second half of the play, Yang's ghost is granted the capacity to examine and reflect upon her life. In scene xxx, "Repenting of Passion" (Qinghui), her repentance is redemptive yet ambiguous:

> Tonight I repent of my sins and count my wrongdoings,
> Hoping that high heavens will watch over me and be my witness.
> Yet with that one spark of obsessive attachment,
> I am still submerged in the stream of love, unawakened.
> For this, repentance is of no avail; only heaven can be my witness.

"Sins" and "wrongdoings" may be hard to distinguish from "obsessive attachment," but the local deity declares that "this one act of repentance can erase ten thousand wrongs" and, echoing *Peony Pavilion*, allows Yang's ghost to wander so that she may renew lost love. "Giving up her life for her country," the femme fatale is transformed into a tutelary goddess of a temple (scene xxxii). Reiterating her martyrdom, various deities emphasize that it is the emperor who needs to repent of his cowardice and irresoluteness (scene xxxiii). His regret and mournful remembrance of Yang (scenes xxix, xxxii, xlv), reminiscent of Bai Pu's play, finally earns him reunion with her in Heaven.

Repentance requires self-division and self-questioning, but the second half of the play proceeds on the opposite logic of healing divisions and resolving contradictions. The self is literally reassembled as Yang's undecayed corpse chases her ghost, and body is reunited with spirit:

> Suddenly I wake up from deep sleep,
> Suddenly I wake up from deep sleep.
> My old self long lost –
> Form and spirit are abruptly reunited.
> Looking back in melancholy and confusion,
> Looking back in melancholy and confusion.
> Now unmistakably and irrevocably Zhuang Zhou,
> What more is left of the butterfly?

Her body resurrected, Yang becomes an immortal. Once demoted from her celestial existence because of "earthly desire," she now mysteriously regains her position because of it: "Because of feelings genuine, / she is summoned back to the fairy mountain" (scene xxxvii). The logical inconsistency hardly seems to matter. Hong Sheng is intent on creating a mythic realm that will "make good regrets and sorrows – a love flawed no more in ages to come" (scene xlvii).

The mythic realm facilitates romantic apotheosis through escape from history, but Hong also recognizes the inexorable opposition between passion and duty in historical time. The close juxtaposition of opposites (e.g. inner and outer, private and public, sensual and spiritual), a standard device in *chuanqi* drama, here modulates the alternation of romantic scenes with political scenes that mark the progressive disintegration of empire. Historical and mythic themes intersect. Scenes xi through xvii, for instance, describe the mythic inspiration (as Yang learns the music from a dream visit to the Moon Palace in scene xi), creation (scene xii), transmission (Li Mo, a flute player, overhears and learns the tune outside the palace walls), and performance (scene xvi) of the "Tune of Rainbow Skirt and Feather Coat." This sequence is interwoven with scenes about unrest at the frontier (scenes x, xiii, xvii) and decadence at court (symbolized by the lychee fruit brought posthaste to the capital, Chang'an, from South China in scene xv). Equally striking is the way scene xxxvii, in which Yang's ghost confronts and reunites with her corpse before she is reinstated as an immortal, is framed by two historical scenes. Scene xxxvi dramatizes the fluidity of historical interpretation, as Yang's silk stocking is viewed by a crowd, who debate its diverse meanings as commodity, precious relic, religious offering, and symbol of dynastic decline. In scene xxxviii, Li Guinian, a former court musician, gives a prosimetric performance to tell the story of Xuanzong and Yang in the context of the decline and disintegration of the Tang empire.

The mythic realm increasingly predominates in the last ten scenes, as the play moves toward the grand finale of the lovers' reunion in Heaven. The passion that costs them suffering and separation in the human world earns them their place in the celestial realm, for "immortals are basically souls of deep feelings. / The Fairy Mountain is far, / But with love one can reach it" (scene l). The "Tune of Rainbow Skirt and Feather Coat," traditionally a symbol for sensual indulgence and decadence at Xuanzong's court, becomes a tribute to the sublime passion that facilitates communication between human and divine realms. At the midpoint of the play, Hong Sheng quotes Bai Juyi's lines on how the tune is interrupted by the war drums from Yuyang (scene xxiv). Its transmission is a consequence of political disorder: Li Guinian, in the course of his wanderings, teaches it to the flutist Li Mo in scene xxxviii. By then Li Guinian has to "sell the imperial musical scores, going from door to door, acclaimed by none." Yet at the end of the play, the tune resounds triumphantly to accompany the ascension of Xuanzong and Yang to Heaven – not the original heavenly version, but Yang's interpretation, which the Moon Goddess deems vastly superior (scene l). The triumph of passion in the celestial realm is recompense for its defeat in the human world.

Modern Chinese criticism has tended to emphasize possible references to the Ming–Qing transition in Hong's play. Dynastic decline, a self-indulgent and pleasure-loving court, the foreignness of An Lushan, the eulogy of martyrs (like the musician Lei Haiqing), and Li Guinian's song of remembrance may all have had resonance with recent history. These elements, however, combine to create a nostalgic and mournful mood rather than a political stance. A disciple of Wang Shizhen in poetry, Hong Sheng may be influenced by Wang's aestheticism and techniques of distance in his ambivalent vindication of passion and artistic creation.

If Hong implies analogies between mid-eighth-century Tang dynastic crisis and the fall of the Ming, focus on the latter is direct and unwavering in Kong Shangren's *Peach Blossom Fan*. Kong was a descendant of Confucius. An unexpected opportunity to lecture to the Kangxi Emperor when he was offering sacrifices at the temple of Confucius in Qufu in 1684 launched Kong on a checkered official career, which ended in 1700 with his demotion. His *Little Hulei Lute* (*Xiao hulei*), written in collaboration with the lyricist and dramatist Gu Cai, is generally considered vastly inferior to his masterpiece, *Peach Blossom Fan*, completed around 1699 and first published in 1708.

The central dramatic action of *Peach Blossom Fan* traces Chinese history from the collapse of the Ming to that of the short-lived Southern Ming; that is, from the second month of 1643 to the seventh month of 1645 (scenes ii–xl). The love story of the scholar Hou Fangyu and the famous courtesan Li Xiangjun, set in the world of the Qinhuai pleasure quarters, the political passions of the Revival Society, and intrigues and factional struggles at court, are interwoven with events marking dynastic decline and fall. Hou and Li meet and "marry" – to the extent that the arrangement whereby a client formalizes his union with a virgin courtesan can be called marriage – early in the play (scenes v–vii). Their separation and Hou's peregrinations are linked to the faltering military operations of the collapsing Ming dynasty (scenes xii, xiv, xix–xx). At one point he is put in prison along with other Revival Society members by the evil Southern Ming ministers Ma Shiying and Ruan Dacheng (scene xxxiii). Meanwhile, Li is also victimized by the decadence and self-indulgence of the Southern Ming court. In the central heroic gesture that gives the play its name, Li spatters her fan with blood as she struggles against being forcibly taken to Tian Yang, a Southern Ming minister, as concubine (scene xxii). The bloodstains on the fan, a love token from Hou, are transformed into peach blossoms by the painter Yang Wencong, a morally dubious character who befriends all factions (scene xxiii). (The historical Yang died a martyr to the fallen Ming in 1646.) Li is then recruited against her will into the imperial theatrical troupe in the Southern Ming palace (scenes xxiv–xxv). After enduring many more vicissitudes, Hou and Li unexpectedly meet at a Daoist service commemorating the martyrs of the recently fallen dynasty (scene xl). Just as they are rejoicing over their reunion, Zhang Wei, the Daoist priest conducting the ceremony, tears the peach blossom fan and brutally reminds them of the futility of everything. Hou and Li declare their enlightenment and part for good.

Peach Blossom Fan has an elaborate framing device. In scene i and the additional scene xxi (the beginning and midpoint of the play), both set in 1684, the Master of Ritual, a character in the play, presents himself as a member of the audience and gives monologues on what it means to be both inside and outside the theatrical illusion: "Then reality was like a play, / Now the play seems only too real. / Twice an observer at the side: / Heaven has preserved the one with cold eyes" (additional scene xxi). At the midpoint and the end of the play (extra scene xx, scene xl), which both take place during the Ghost Festival in 1644 and 1645, Zhang Wei proclaims a vision of retributive rewards and punishments for those who died during the dynastic transition. In the very last scene (sequel to scene xl), set in 1648, the Master of Ritual, the storyteller Liu Jingting, and the music teacher Su Kunsheng come on stage to mourn, remember, and commemorate the fallen Ming.

The emphasis on frames and liminal characters, whose passage in and out of the theatrical illusion makes them both actors and interpreters, turns both history and its interpretation into a part of dramatic presentation. The play is premised on two temporal sequences, the order of historical events as lived and experienced, which moves forward in time, and the order in which history is known – the order of memory or historical reconstruction – which moves from the present backward. *Peach Blossom Fan* is thus unique not only because Kong is meticulous about historical references, as evinced by his listing of sources in "Textual Verification of *Peach Blossom Fan*" (*Taohua shan* kaoju), but also because the play treats history as a problem: contradictions to be reconciled, palpable forces shaping the present and the future, something that demands yet resists interpretation.

Why did Kong Shangren choose to problematize history? He was born a Qing subject and wrote about his encounter with the Kangxi Emperor as the most glorious moment in his life, which, incidentally, may explain why scene i and the additional scene xxi are set in 1684. The Master of Ritual, whose namelessness invites identification with Kong, proclaims that the play is performed in the Garden of Peace (additional scene xxi) in an era of prosperity and good government sanctioned by twelve auspicious portents (scene i). Political discretion may have been mixed with the genuine belief that past turmoil is best understood from the perspective of present order. At the same time, the affective power of the play depends on empathy and nostalgia: "The lyricist of Yunting [Kong Shangren], / In his sorrow rests his brush ever so often: / Voice transmitted through gleaming teeth, the song is not yet over; / Wax-tears, dropping on the red plate, are already inch-high." Kong's friendship with well-known Jiangnan Ming loyalists like Mao Xiang, Huang Yun, and Zong Yuanding during the years he was overseeing river management in Yangzhou (1686–1689) may have mediated longing and mourning for the bygone world of late Ming romantic and political passions.

Kong subscribed to the official Qing dynastic narrative that the Ming crumbled for internal reasons. For obvious political reasons, the Manchu conquerors do not appear onstage, and there are only intermittent references to "the great army" or "forces north of the river." Scarcely any mention is made of the bandit rebels. By contrast, mid-Qing plays dealing with the dynastic transition, such as Dong Rong's *Auspicious Shrine* (*Zhikan ji*, 1751) or Huang Xieqing's (1805–1864) *Imperial Daughter* (*Dinü hua*), present the Manchus and the bandits as polarized forces of good and evil. The bandits having destroyed the Ming, the Manchu army marched in to restore order and avenge the fallen dynasty. The comparative reticence of *Peach Blossom Fan* makes for deeper ambiguities.

Despite persistent modern attempts to read nationalist and anti-Manchu sentiments into *Peach Blossom Fan*, there is little convincing evidence of subversive intent. Likewise, the opposite reading – that the play embraces the Ming–Qing transition as a rational, inevitable process by tracing the demise to late Ming excesses and emotionalism – also would not do justice to its complexity and is moreover belied by its elegiac, melancholy mood. To sustain his well-tempered ambivalence toward late Ming cultural attitudes, Kong Shangren turns to metaphors of theater and performance, with their attendant dialectics of self and role, reality and illusion.

The Hongguang Emperor's passion for the theater, abetted by the playwright–minister Ruan Dacheng, becomes the symbol of the frivolity, self-indulgence, and illegitimacy of the Southern Ming court (that is, it has but the simulacrum of mandate). Miscellanies and fictionalized histories from the mid- to the late seventeenth century often refer to rumors about a man claiming to be the son of the late Chongzhen Emperor and Lady Tong, supposedly Hongguang's former consort. Were these "pretenders" or victims of the Southern Ming court? As fitting finale to this matrix of presumed or real lies, the aforementioned *History According to the Woodcutter*, cited in Kong's bibliography, tells how in the chaos following the fall of Nanjing, a crowd took the pretender–crown prince out of prison and made him ascend the throne in theatrical costume found in the Wuying Palace.

Confronted with the bewildering political reverberations of this confusion over reality and illusion, facts and fiction, the well-meaning characters of *Peach Blossom Fan* can only act out their convictions and seek the truth of untrammeled self-expression, as when Revival Society scholars vociferously denounce Ruan Dacheng (scenes iii, iv, viii) or when Li Xiangjun vehemently rejects the trousseau supplied by him (scene vii). Yet these actions are ineffectual and even harmful, insofar as they deepen divisions in the realm. One can also argue that the Qinhuai world of courtesans and entertainers is but a malleable alternate reality, that those who believe in integrity are bedeviled by false appearance and self-deception as they perform roles such as knight-errant, unconventional literatus, loyal official, or romantic heroine. Instead of negative judgments, however, Kong is probably using metaphors of theater and performance to empathize with their dilemmas and confusions when contingency and uncertainty hold sway. If their attempts at meaningful historical action appear theatrical, it is because subjective experience and objective reality are hopelessly disjointed at this historical moment.

This disjunction is especially urgent in light of the Qing dynastic narrative that Ming collapse was inevitable and that Chongzhen was the last legitimate Ming emperor. Political integrity in this context is by definition tragic, private, even delusional. Hou and his fellow Revival Society scholars know that they are against the Southern Ming court but cannot articulate what they do support. The generals Shi Kefa, Zuo Liangyu, and Huang Degong all perceive their actions as expressing loyalty to the Ming, but after the death of the Chongzhen Emperor, the Ming becomes a cipher with different meanings. Liu Jingting uses his storytelling to convince Zuo Liangyu to come to the rescue of imprisoned Revival Society members, but Zuo's eastward march ends up precipitating the fall of the Ming. In the case of Li Xiangjun, her chosen role of the romantic heroine is politicized by historical circumstances. Although her romantic and political passions have to contend with her fate as quasi-commodity, Kong seems to suggest that she closes the perceived gap between role-playing and genuine self-expression. Even if her theatrical gestures are ultimately futile, they are beautiful in the clarity of their conviction. For individuals caught in bewildering historical situations, this may be the only mode of heroic action available.

In the penultimate scene, Hou and Li embrace the Way. One may say that with their exit also go the finality of the religious solution and the use of theater and performance as historical intervention. Instead, theater becomes the venue for memory, nostalgia, and historical retrospection in the last scene as Liu Jingting, Su Kunsheng, and the Master of Ritual, now recluses, gather onstage. Escape from history finally becomes impossible, as the sequence of their three long arias marks the movement from philosophical transcendence to historical engagement and finally to unabashed lamentation, and they are hounded offstage by a petty officer executing the order to ferret out "recluses." In displacing meaningful historical action onto heroic theatrical gestures and dramatized acts of interpretation, Kong pays tribute both to the theater and to historical reflection; hence the convergence of metatheatricality and historical consciousness in *Peach Blossom Fan*.

The literary scene in 1723 and beyond

Dong Rong's *Auspicious Shrine*, the next major dramatic treatment of Ming collapse after *Peach Blossom Fan*, upholds orthodox virtues and unequivocally denounces late Ming culture. By then Xia Lun's (b. 1680) moralistic plays (1740s–1752) had already set the tone of orthodoxy in drama, although plays venting frustrations with autobiographical echoes, following the tradition of Xu Wei's *Four Cries of the Gibbon*, flourished through the Kangxi reign and beyond in the works of Liao Yan (1644–1705), Ji Yongren (d. ca 1682), and Gui Fu (1736–1805), as Wang Ayling notes. Likewise, after 1723, the year in which the Kangxi Emperor died and the Yongzheng Emperor ascended the throne, both triumphant orthodoxy and its discontents continued to flourish in various genres. Fang Bao, though not yet officially pardoned, was promoted to the position of imperial editor in the Wuying Palace in 1722. Liu Dakui (1698–1779), then in his twenties, continued his championship of orthodoxy as the next Tongcheng master, and Liu's contemporary Zheng Xie (1693–1765) voiced in his essays and letters the humor, irony, and intense pathos reined in by Tongcheng orthodoxy. In 1709, Zhao Zhixin attacked Wang Shizhen's impersonal poetic style in *Recorded Conversations about the Dragon* (*Tanlong lu*). The critique signals his own choice to write about disquiet in a supposedly great age: "Even the stars and the moon will be ensnared in the great net!" This path is echoed in more muted tones in the poetry of Zha Shenxing and, in the next generation, that of Li E (1692–1752), although poetic ideals of balance and equanimity will be passed on from Wang Shizhen to Shen Deqian and will continue to hold sway as orthodoxy. In song lyrics, Li E's elegant restraint will find a counterpoint in Zheng Xie's pungent free spirit. In classical fiction, Pu Songling's work will find heirs and detractors, espousing positions from resurgent didacticism to unapologetic fantasy. Probing the many meanings of orthodoxy and the different ways it can be questioned will be the glorious achievement of eighteenth-century fiction, whose masters, Cao Xueqin (1717–1763), Wu Jingzi (1701–1754), and Xia Jingqu (1705–1787), were all born in the final years of the Kangxi reign.

4

The literati era and its demise (1723–1840)

SHANG WEI

Introduction

The years under study in this chapter are often retrospectively called the high Qing or middle Qing era. Following the sixty-one years of the Kangxi reign (1662–1722) was a relatively short rule by the Yongzheng Emperor (1723–1735), which in turn was followed by the Qianlong reign (1736–1796), an era as glorious and almost as long as the Kangxi reign. In 1795, the eighty-four year old Qianlong Emperor decided to abdicate the throne, so as not to surpass the record length of his grandfather's rule. The accession of the Jiaqing Emperor brought a change of reign title but little else; Qianlong continued to rule behind the scenes, though with less vigor and interest, until his death in 1799. His last years, however, proved crucial to the future of the Qing empire. Historians often remind us that the 1790s saw an acceleration of the slide toward chaos, from which the two ensuing reigns – Jiaqing (1796–1820) and Daoguang (1821–1850) – never managed to recover.

The familiar drama of a dynastic cycle coming to an end this time concluded with two cataclysmic events. In 1840, the first Opium War broke out. With modern weaponry, Great Britain blew open the doors of the Qing empire in the name of protecting British citizens and their property. The war brought to the fore problems that can be traced back to the Qianlong years, when the British opium trade began to disturb the balance of currency exchange by creating shortages of silver and produced a large population of opium addicts. Qing's defeat in this war, however, was much more than a military, commercial, and economic event; its profound impact on Chinese political, intellectual, and literary life would become apparent only in the years to come. Even as the British threatened the Qing monarchy from afar, the Taiping Rebellion (1850–1864) came close to bringing the empire to its knees from within. Led by Hong Xiuquan, an aspiring scholar turned cult figure who claimed to be Jesus' brother and God's Chinese son, the Taiping troops swept over nearly two-thirds of the empire, leaving devastation in their wake. This sustained and massive uprising significantly diminished the monarchy's control over the empire and, in Jiangnan, the heart of the rebellion, damaged the infrastructure of local society and the literary community almost beyond repair. Although the Qing dynasty did not officially come to an end until 1911, few of the values and cultural ideals that underpinned its ideology of state emerged unscathed. Thus, in the mid-nineteenth century, Manchu authority faced international and domestic challenges of unprecedented magnitude, with no prospect of easy resolution. The Confucian elite found themselves in a new political and cultural *mise-en-scène*, of which they were only barely beginning to make sense.

The Qianlong era may be characterized as an era in which the literati, by their endeavors and aspirations, and to some extent also their failures and omissions, shaped the trajectory of literary history. The same may be said of preceding eras, beginning with the Tang, if not earlier, but certainly not of the era that followed; in other words, the high Qing was the final phase of traditional literary culture. In the modern era, the literati were super-seded by authors and readers associated with new media and technologies, modern professions and institutions, as well as with the Western calendar, ideas, and way of life. It may be tempting to tell a story about the gradual or even inevitable decline of the cultural traditions held dear by the Confucian elite, but it was precisely in their final stage of cultural hegemony that these literati discovered potential for change from within their own tradition. As shown in some of the novels of the Qianlong era, the best of the literati of the day developed an acute critical consciousness as they came to examine the negative implications of their cherished values and ideals, as well as the limitations of the sources that sustained their own writing and moral imagination. This development is all the more significant because the impetus for it came from within: the challenge from the West was yet to come. When this challenge came in the early and mid-nineteenth century, many thinkers and writers turned once again to indigenous sources, from which they derived a productive framework for negotiating with the West. The future they envisioned, however, was vastly different from what would come to pass in the second decade of the twentieth century, when the moderate views they proposed were eclipsed by the wholesale denunciation of what is called traditional culture. The age of reform gave way to one of revolution.

I. The long Qianlong period: literary and intellectual achievements

The Qianlong era was preceded by the short thirteen-year Yongzheng reign. The Yongzheng Emperor is known for his harsh policies against "seditious books," and his brutal tyranny generated so much terror in the educated literati that the literature and culture of the day were devastated. It would be a mistake, however, to emphasize the imperial court's role in the formation of contemporary literary culture to the exclusion of other contributing factors. For one thing, despite the politically charged environment, "obscene literature" and erotic interpretations of dramatic works seem to emerge without much interruption. The literature and literary discourse of this period were thus more complex and certainly more polarized than generally assumed. Although our knowledge about this period is limited, the changes that took place during the Yongzheng reign do not seem significant enough to characterize it as a distinctive phase in the literary history of the Qing dynasty. Publishing remained as sluggish as before, and aside from poetry and prose, few literary works (such as dramas and novels) can be dated to this period without question. In this chapter, the Yongzheng reign will be considered concurrently with the Qianlong era.

The Qianlong reign has long been seen as both the apex of accumulated prosperity and the beginning of the decline of the Qing dynasty – a superabundant age and one fraught with contradictions. From 1750 onward, literature itself became an endeavor of gigantic proportions that mirrored the empire in all its fertile and fateful complexity. Relentless territorial expansion through conquest, a drastic increase in population, the spread of education and literacy, and a variety of changes experienced by the literati (such as a decrease in opportunities for governmental service, the deflation of their official degrees, and further divisions in professional and intellectual orientation among the educated class) all had a role in shaping the contemporary literary culture.

Modern historians have proposed radically different and even conflicting views of what was happening in the intellectual and cultural circles of the Qianlong era, depending on perspective as well as on which phase and aspect are emphasized. Some see a blossoming of scholarly culture sustained by prolonged peace and opulence: no previous era of comparable length has come close to producing scholarly and literary writings on such a prolific scale across such a broad range of disciplines. Other historians describe the Qianlong reign as a dark age of political repression, with more cases of literary inquisition in its last forty years than in the previous two reigns combined. Not every historian is impressed by the scholarship and poetry of this period, despite or indeed because of its overwhelming abundance; some have found the philological and evidential studies – the prevailing scholarly discourse of the time – trivial, fragmentary, narrow in scope, and lacking interpretive thrust. Simultaneously, too many of the poets of the time sought, with their lackluster imitations of the past, to compensate for quality with quantity. Admirers and followers of Qianjia learning (the learning of the Qianlong and Jiaqing reigns), on the other hand, have gone so far as to laud it as the indigenous precursor of modern science. Even those who discern signs of decline in the literature of this period, however, can hardly deny that the Qianlong years yielded the most sophisticated vernacular novels composed in imperial times.

Each of these views reveals one important aspect of the Qianlong era but glosses over the complex and contradictory nature of the culture. A narrative of continuous decline is as unconvincing as the claim that the Qianlong era is the beginning of the Chinese modern period, not least because similar arguments have already been made about the late Ming and even the Southern Song. Important changes did occur in the Qianlong period whose impact on modern culture is hard to ignore. The question is how to describe them in a way that both does justice to their historical context and illuminates their lingering influences as interpreted and reinterpreted in the modern era.

Intellectual life and literary schools

The Qianlong reign is remarkably long; its main literary figures, including the Qianlong Emperor, enjoyed extraordinary longevity, and there were no major events to mark turning points in the literary history of this period. Changes did occur in a variety of cultural spheres, however. Commercial publishing began to accelerate in the 1750s and reached a new peak in the 1790s, while popular regional theaters flourished across the empire. Simultaneously, the elite culture seemed to experience similar exuberance, as imperial policies, imperial preferences, official and unofficial patronages, literary affiliations, and intellectual and literary discourses interacted with one another in an unfolding process that demands careful consideration.

The state and intellectuals

From the very beginning, the Manchu aristocrats understood that they would never win the support of the Han literary elite without claiming cultural authority for themselves, but it was not until the mid-Qing that they began to make such a claim with confidence. The Qianlong Emperor was well versed in both the Manchu and Chinese cultural traditions, leaving more than 42,640 poems (not counting those composed as a prince and after his abdication), almost as many as all the extant Tang dynasty poems combined. Although he was not solely responsible for all the works that came out under his name, Qianlong rarely missed any opportunity to show off his erudition in front of court officials. He often described himself as a *shusheng* (literally, "book learner"), whose meaning overlaps with a few other terms such as *wenren* and *shi*, all of which may roughly be translated as "literatus."

"Literati" is an elusive category, especially difficult to define during the period in question as it was continuously evolving. As a group, the literati were held together by a collective ethos as well as by cultural prestige and sociopolitical status. Members of or candidates for membership in the ruling class, the literati received the same education, shared certain basic common assumptions and values, and identified themselves with reference to one another. Learning and literary accomplishments were the main components of their shared identity: pedigree and office were, at least in theory, the external manifestations of the internal qualities that defined them as elite. Not many men of culture or learning receive public recognition, and in the Qing, especially the high Qing period, there gradually emerged a glaring gap between the official elite and the cultural elite who had a degree but no official post. Many well-educated men were left without the financial means to claim elite status. To make a living, some took on lesser occupations and became tutors for gentry families, or private advisers and secretaries to local officials, helping keep accounts, enforce tax collection, and handle legal matters and other areas under the jurisdiction of their patrons. Judged by status alone, these men would hardly fit into the category of cultural elite, but they were undeniably literati by dint of their education, and some were even accomplished poets, essayists, and novelists. As self-described – and often so received – bearers of values and culture, the literati fulfilled indispensable social and cultural functions, whatever occupational roles they assumed.

Following his grandfather's example, the Qianlong Emperor announced a special erudite scholar exam in 1736 immediately upon his accession. The regional authorities recommended 270 candidates, of whom 21 declined and the rest were not universally appreciative. Also on his grandfather's model, Qianlong initiated a variety of state-sponsored compilation projects, the largest of which was *The Complete Library of the Four Treasuries* (*Siku quanshu*), formally inaugurated in 1773 and completed in 1782. Unprecedented in scale, this collection comprises 3,450 complete works, and commentaries on 6,750 others, divided into the four categories of Classics, history, philosophy, and miscellaneous literature. More than 360 eminent scholars were summoned to Beijing to work full-time on the project under the supervision of Ji Yun (1724–1805), a leading scholar in evidential studies, but the Manchu authorities and the emperor himself retained ultimate control: as books from all over the empire flowed into the capital for scrutiny and selection, they seized upon the occasion to conduct a literary inquisition. More than 2,400 "seditious" books were destroyed, and their authors, if alive, were put to death along with their family members and relatives. A 1781 report announced that the 52,480 woodblocks used to print these books, weighing 36,530 catties, had been dutifully consumed as firewood in the imperial palace over the previous seven years: "firewood costs two taels seven cash per thousand catties, and thus palace expenses to the tune of 98 taels 6 cash in total have been saved since 1774." What an accomplishment for a *shusheng* – a book learner! Thus the largest imperial project of book preservation commissioned in the Qing was at the same time a project of catastrophic destruction – just one instance of the profound contradictions characteristic of the Qianlong reign.

The Qianlong Emperor ascended the throne determined to amend his father's idiosyncratic approach toward literary inquisition. Headstrong and insecure by turns, the Yongzheng Emperor (1723–1735) had been obsessed with prosecuting what he deemed to be treason by books, not even sparing an apparently innocent or irrelevant poem. In dealing with the case of Zeng Jing, however, he surprised everyone with a sequence of unusual decisions that would turn the literary inquisition into a public drama of furious confrontations and dramatic twists, followed by a cathartic ending of political conversion. In 1728, Zeng Jing, an impoverished licentiate (that is, a holder of the lowest examination degree) from the countryside of Hunan, dispatched a student to Xi'an, trying to persuade General Yue Zhongqi to raise troops against the Yongzheng Emperor. He also wrote two books challenging the legitimacy of the Manchu rulers and charging Yongzheng with the crimes of usurpation and fratricide, as well as accusing him of greed, lust, paranoia, and bloodthirstiness. Outraged, the Yongzheng Emperor wrote a lengthy rebuttal, in which he made an earnest attempt to establish his own righteousness. Instead of executing Zeng Jing, he treated him with deliberate favor, which moved Zeng Jing to make a tearful statement of repentance. As if this were not enough, Yongzheng had his own rebuttal published and distributed along with Zeng Jing's self-criticism and other works; he also sent Zeng Jing on a lecture tour to disseminate this redeeming experience of political conversion. How effective this political melodrama was in changing people's minds is unknown, but Zeng Jing's indictments surely afforded the public a rare glimpse into the darker side of the life of the royal house. Still a young prince at the time, the Qianlong Emperor was repulsed by his father's way of handling the case. As soon as he came to the throne, he put an abrupt end to this seven-year drama by executing Zeng Jing and banning both his accusations and the Yongzheng Emperor's rebuttal. At this, arguably the most ironic, moment in the history of this official literary inquisition, keeping a copy of the previous emperor's writings was a crime.

Compared to his father, the Qianlong Emperor seemed temperate in dealing with seditious books in the early part of his reign. His attitude hardened over time, however, and the most atrocious cases of literary inquisition occurred in the period from 1774 to 1781. Kent Guy has rightly cautioned against seeing the *Four Treasuries* project as linked to a concerted program of literary inquisition, at least not in the way it was carried out. The emperor was obviously agitated by what he considered to be anti-Manchu passages and taboo characters in the books submitted for the compilation. Once he initiated the campaign against "seditious books" in 1774, it soon spiraled beyond his control. Provincial governors were under pressure to turn in as many books as they could, book holders began to indict one another, and some literati took advantage of the situation to pursue personal vendettas. By 1780, an enormous number of cases had been filed, with some provinces sending over five thousand books a year to Beijing for litigation. Driven by almost as many diverse political interests and personal agendas as there were participants, the campaign came so close to the brink of madness that the court eventually had to intervene to reduce the extent of the disruption. A master list of banned books was distributed to provincial officials, and procedural regulations were put in place. The rules of the game had changed, and provincial authorities were reprimanded not for negligence but for overzealousness. The campaign of the 1770s, with all its ironic twists and turns, unveils a much more complex picture of the interaction of literati gentry, bureaucrats, and the imperial court than has been commonly recognized.

The official censorship of obscenity in fiction was related to this literary inquisition, but there are marked differences between the two. Like his predecessors, the Qianlong Emperor issued imperial edicts banning licentious literature, and bawdy songs and dramas, but enforcement of this ban depended mainly on local officials. *Water Margin* and a few earlier novels had already been proscribed in the Ming dynasty for their treatment of rebellions. The Qianlong Emperor promulgated this ruling, but unlike the individual anthologies destroyed by the Qing court, these novels had achieved a much wider circulation through the book market, and their total eradication was impractical. The proliferation of erotic fiction and bawdy songs proved just as difficult to contain. The earliest extant list of banned licentious books was compiled by officials in Jiangsu Province and the district of Suzhou in the 1830s. Although nearly all these titles reappeared on many subsequent lists, the majority of them have survived to the present.

The compilation of the *Four Treasuries* was undertaken at a time when philological and evidential learning was well established as the dominant trend of scholarly discourse, and its execution as an imperial project in turn reinforced the status and influence of this particular mode of scholarship. Evidential scholars traced their philological methodology back to the Han dynasty. Instead of the philosophical discourse that characterized Song neo-Confucianism, they pursued what they saw as empirically verifiable truth through textual studies, producing rich scholarship in such fields as bibliography, collation, epigraphy, phonology, and etymology. So conceived and practiced, this revitalized "Han learning" marked a fundamental shift of scholarly paradigm in the eighteenth century, and many interrelated disciplines – historical geography, astronomy, and historiography – expanded rapidly, reshaping the scope and structure of literary learning as a whole. Although, as Benjamin Elman and Kai-wing Chow have noted, the eight-part essay that required no knowledge of evidential scholarship remained the core of the civil service examination, questions about philological and textual problems appeared with growing frequency in the policy section of examinations at both the provincial and metropolitan levels. Some of the leading scholars in evidential studies served as the examiners or directors of education, and this gave them a legitimate channel for advancing their scholarly agenda.

One should not overemphasize the government's role in facilitating the growth of evidential studies; nor does the argument that literary inquisition drove scholars into the safe haven of politically neutral linguistic and bibliographic scholarship hold up under close scrutiny. Benjamin Elman has shown that evidential studies had already developed a mature form of discourse and a vibrant scholarly community in Jiangnan by 1750. One of the most provocative breakthroughs in evidential scholarship occurred when Yan Ruoqu (1636–1704), in a study completed in the late seventeenth century and published posthumously in 1754, argued that the old text of *Documents (Shangshu)*, one of the Confucian classics, had been forged in the third and fourth centuries. Hui Dong (1697–1758), one of the founders of the Wu School of Han learning, reached a similar conclusion independently. Although evidential scholars did not consciously advocate skepticism, their detailed scholarship often challenged the authenticity of the ancient Classics and undermined the textual foundations of what the neo-Confucians held to be gospel. Cui Shu (1740–1816) and many like-minded contemporaries further applied the methodology of evidential studies to the scrutiny of official historiography, riding roughshod over whatever conventional views stood in their way. So influential were their works that even the practitioners of evidential learning, such as Weng Fanggang (1733–1818), a revered poet and expert in epigraphy, could not help voicing their concerns about the potential of Han learning to disrupt the well-established order of the Confucian world. Other intellectuals of the time like Dai Zhen (1724–1777) went even further in critiquing the issues of neo-Confucian discourse. Zhang Xuecheng (1738–1801) summed up his view on the Confucian classics in his famous epigram "The Six Classics are all histories." In this way he stripped the Confucian classics of their aura of inviolable sanctity by turning them into objects for historical analysis.

Scholarly undertakings of such scale and far-reaching influence as described above require extensive discussion and exchange of opinions within a large scholarly community, as well as access to private libraries and academies, and the support of patrons both within and outside the official arena. Rather than undertaking years of (potentially fruitless) preparations for the civil service examination, many men of learning in Jiangnan opted for a scholarly career under the patronage of merchants – hence the growth of what Elman describes as "the professionalization of academics," a trend that would be suspended by the Taiping Rebellion in the 1850s. Some eminent evidential scholars (including Yan Ruoqu and Dai Zhen) came from merchant families. In Yangzhou and other cities in Jiangnan, wealthy families, especially those of the salt merchants, enjoyed entertaining scholars and literary coteries or hosting sometimes lengthy visits. Semiofficial patronage played a visible role in sustaining a professionalized class of literary scholars. Zhu Yun (1724–1805), Bi Yuan (1730–1797), Ruan Yuan (1764–1849), and other civil officials well versed in evidential scholarship had the custom of hiring private scholars to work on a variety of long-term or short-term compilation projects. When serving in local governmental posts, they were awarded substantial sums as an "allowance for nourishing incorruptibility" (*yanglian jin*) up to ten times the amount of their official salaries, which enabled them to finance book projects as well as to employ the eminent scholars and poets of the day as private advisers or secretaries. Their sponsorship of scholarly pursuits also helped to spread evidential learning beyond Jiangnan.

Scholarly discussions and communications among the literati took place in a variety of mushrooming forms, including large collections, compendia, monographs, treatises, exegeses, and annotations. Letters exchanged between scholars often read like extended scholarly essays. Even those not known for their scholarship were regularly involved in ongoing dialogues on ancient texts, rituals, institutions, geography, astronomy, and antiquarianism. A mere poet seldom got very far within the literary circles of the day. Scholarly learning carried much greater prestige, and it had expanded well beyond the compass of the neo-Confucian curriculum. In the late eighteenth and early nineteenth centuries, notation books (*biji*, literally, "random jottings") reached the apex of their popularity among literary scholars, as no other genre was more congenial to the mode of evidential learning or the contemporary literati's way of life. Inquisitive yet informal, usually lighthearted and with little regard for coherence, a volume of *biji* could include notes on an arbitrary range of topics, along with anecdotes, gossip, hearsay, personal observations, and occasionally fiction. As the chief editor of the *Four Treasuries*, Ji Yun had to find a way to categorize *biji* in this comprehensive imperial project. His solution was to distribute all the *biji* works among six subcategories of "miscellany" (*zajia*) in the philosophy (*zi*) section.

From 1789 to 1798, Ji Yun himself produced five *biji* collections, brought together and published by one of his disciples in 1800 under the general title *Random Notes at the Cottage of Close Scrutiny* (*Yuewei caotang biji*). According to his own account, this enormous book of 1,074 entries was composed during his spare time while writing and revising the entries for the *Annotated Catalogue of the Complete Library of Four Treasuries*. The years Ji Yun spent on his *biji* also coincided, interestingly, with the boom in the creation and publication of *biji* collections, especially the subgenre of *zhiguai*, strange tales or accounts of anomalies concerning foxes, ghosts, and supernatural beings. Reading Ji Yun in the context of the *zhiguai* craze, modern scholars often describe him as conservative, especially in light of his critical appraisal of contemporary trends in *biji* writings, which he traced partly to the influence of Pu Songling's *Records of the Strange*. Ji Yun went so far as to dismiss Pu Songling's stories for mixing together the incompatible modes of the Tang tale (*chuanqi*) and the strange tale of the Six Dynasties (*zhiguai*). He took particular issue with Pu Songling's tendency toward fictionalization (represented by the Tang tale, as Ji Yun understood it); he was also apparently displeased with contemporary *biji* writers who emulated Pu Songling as a means of displaying their own literary brilliance. The latter criticism was most likely aimed at his contemporary and chief competitor, Yuan Mei (1716–1798), who during the same period produced a collection of *zhiguai* tales under the provocative title *Censored by Confucius* (*Zi bu yu*). Whereas, according to *The Analects*, Confucius had refused to talk about prodigies, feats of strength, disorder, and spirits, Yuan Mei took these subjects as the starting point for his extravagant literary adventures. Gratuitous violence and grisly horror are recurring elements in his stories, which are replete with nightmares, mischievous spirits, ghosts, and decapitated heads chasing people around and pounding on closed doors. Playfully unruly and uncanny by turns, Yuan Mei's narratives captivated the imagination of the contemporary literary audience, much to Ji Yun's dismay. Ji Yun's anecdotes, by contrast, were more discursive and didactic, more often than not framed by the concepts of retribution and reincarnation, as well as by other interpretive schemes. Ji Yun also drew on such a broad range of erudite references in his "close scrutiny" of the strange that Leo Chan has described his *zhiguai* collection as taking an "evidential approach to the supernatural."

However, Ji Yun's explanations often sound tentative, and in some cases the frame of reincarnation has become decentralized, if not altogether irrelevant. In one anecdote, a Buddhist monk confides that because he was a butcher in his previous life, he was reincarnated as a pig marked for slaughter. Readers are struck more by the vivid description of the paralyzing terror and pain he experiences in the process of being butchered than by the predictable conceptual frame of the story. In a more discursive piece, a group of anonymous men challenge a self-proclaimed neo-Confucian who aims to discredit the belief in ghosts and spirits. Citing Zhu Xi in an uninterrupted flow, they catalogue a panoply of bizarre incidents about which even the master of neo-Confucianism is hard put to debate. Ji Yun inserts his own voice at the end:

> There are Buddhist ghosts lurking beneath the ground and Confucian ghosts whirling about in midair. The Buddhist ghosts are present every day and the Confucian ghosts gather together spontaneously. How are they to be borne? This is, indeed, not something that an unlearned person like myself is capable of understanding.

Ji Yun claimed that, with pen and notebook ever ready to hand, he heard most of the anecdotes recounted in his collections from his literati friends. He usually opens his tales by dutifully reporting their sources, stating where and when the incident occurred. His raconteurs include the full range of the literary class, from official colleagues on the editorial board of the *Four Treasuries* project to examination candidates, poets, private secretaries, and scholars, as well as the Uygur friends he made in Urumqi during his year of exile in Xinjiang. Permeating his collection is the literati's irrepressible fascination with the supernatural realm, and the stories from Xinjiang add exotic color. Although largely excluded from the sphere of formal discourse, the *biji* of Ji Yun and his contemporaries are indispensable for comprehending the mentality of the literati in the late Qianlong years. Indeed, they disclose an imaginative world that lends itself to no ready explanation, and thus remains both intriguing and unsettling.

Elite decorum and vernacular tendencies

No previous dynasty witnessed the proliferation of more literary schools or groups (*pai*) than the Qing; most of these groups flourished, if not originated, in the long period of stability and prosperity of the Qianlong years. Literary schools usually had regional origins, but their members also defined themselves by their shared views on literature and by an evinced affinity to specific masters, periods, or styles of the past. A few schools achieved prominent national influence, either with or without official endorsement. As leading poets and essayists interacted with one another, a line of demarcation emerged between those who were affiliated with the court and those who, deliberately or otherwise, distanced themselves from the center of officialdom. Their views on literature diverged accordingly.

As shown in Chapter 3 of this volume, Wang Shizhen had been something of a poet laureate under the patronage of the Kangxi Emperor. Although he lost Kangxi's favor six years prior to his death in 1711, his influence lingered on, and his works of "ineffable essence and resonance" or "spiritual resonance" (*shenyun*) set the standard for elite taste. Shen Deqian (1673–1769) occupied a similar position in the early Qianlong years, though he did not obtain the title of provincial graduate until he was sixty-seven, after seventeen attempts. The timing of his success could not have been better: the Qianlong Emperor, still seeking to establish his own poet laureate after a few years upon the throne, immediately introduced Shen Deqian into his inner circle, and composed two prefaces for his works. As a poet, critic, and anthologist, Shen Deqian formulated his poetic theory by stressing the four elements he believed essential: purport (ethical content and concerns), form (style), tone, and spiritual resonance. He enlarged the scope of Wang Shizhen's theory by incorporating the values of the Revivalists. Unlike Wang Shizhen, who wrote mainly in quatrains, Shen traced each subgenre of poetry to its origin and selected several masters in each subgenre as models for emulation. Thanks to his efforts (with the emperor's implicit endorsement), Tang poetry finally gained broader recognition than Song poetry in the early Qianlong era. Shen Deqian lived long enough to enjoy all imaginable imperial favors and privileges, and died before all his honors were stripped in 1778 for his biography of Xu Shukui, whose anthologies were proscribed. In addition to his own poetry, Shen Deqian left an illustrious legacy in the anthologies he compiled and the accomplished disciples he taught. *The Source of Ancient-Style Poetry* (*Gushi yuan*), Shen Deqian's anthology of pre-Tang poetry, is often praised for its extensive scope, while his anthology on Tang poetry (*Tangshi biecai*, literally, "an anthology that removes false forms from Tang poetry" or "a separate anthology of Tang poetry") tries to establish the criteria for orthodoxy (*zhengzong*) in poetry. In 1751, two years after he retired from office, Shen became the principal of the Zhiyang Academy in Shuzhou, where he fostered many outstanding disciples in poetry and evidential learning, such as Wang Mingsheng, Qian Daxin, and Wang Chang, who later became established officials themselves.

Before Shen Deqian's death in 1769, Weng Fanggang (1733–1818) was already regarded as a doyen of classical literature. As the founder and sole representative of the School of Musculature (Jili pai), he proposed to remedy what he saw as the insubstantiality of both Wang Shizhen's and Shen Deqian's poetry by reinstating literary learning and the discursive mode of Song poetry. More specifically, Weng insisted on fleshing out poetic inspiration with scholarly reflection on cosmic patterns and its manifestations in natural and cultural phenomena. He employed the term "musculature" as a broad designation for "patterns" of various kinds, from the proper moral forms and ritual norms to the grain of inscriptions on stones and bronze vessels, thus literally and metaphorically complementing Wang Shizhen's "spirit" and Shen Deqing's "form" (*ge*) and "tone" (*diao*). As was the scholarly fashion of the day, his poems often dwelt in great detail on a specific example of epigraphy, calligraphy, painting, or text, or took as a subject his own scholarly musings and endeavors. Weng Fanggang hoped that these subjects would in turn affect the stylistic profile of his poetry. Understandably, Weng's scholarly poetry thrived in the golden age of evidential learning, when scholarship on epigraphy acquired weighty prestige; it also greatly benefited from crucial institutional changes, as poetry was reinstated as an examination subject in 1757 after an interval of nearly seven centuries. When candidates were required to compose poems on a given topic under strict time constraints, "spiritual resonance" readily gave way to erudition, craftsmanship, and expediency.

Although he was posted to Shandong, Jiangxi, Jiangsu, and other places, Weng Fanggang spent much of his prime in Beijing, where the imperial court, Manchu princes, and Han officials all hosted poetry gatherings. Yao Nai, the founder of the Tongcheng School in Anhui and a colleague of Ji Yun, Shen Deqian, and Weng Fanggang on the editorial board of the *Four Treasuries*, also lived in Beijing for several years, and his exposure to evidential learning left indelible marks on his poetry and prose. Yao Nai's emphasis on rules and norms in literary composition also bore interesting resemblances to Weng Fanggang's conceptualization of "musculature."

Away from the capital, Ruan Yuan and other official elites often assembled their own circles by patronizing private scholars and poets, but such patronage was often short-term, and many poets either chose to detach themselves from politics or had no official connections. During the early years of the Qianlong reign, Li Xian'e (often referred to by his sobriquet, Huaimin) and his brothers formed the Gaomi Group in the region of Qilu (present-day Shandong) and became known for their self-representation as literati outside officialdom. Not everyone, however, appreciated their style, modeled on that of the late Tang poet Jia Dao; Weng Fanggang, not surprisingly, castigated their works for lacking in poise, grace, and decorum. Although the sentiment of the Ming loyalists had been considerably diluted by the first half of the eighteenth century, its influence remained detectable in such regions as Shanxi, where Gu Yanwu, Fu Shan, and other early Qing intellectuals became famous for refusing to cooperate with the Manchu court. Born shortly after the brutal repressions of the Ming–Qing transition, Qu Fu (1668–1744), a native of Shanxi, carried on this legacy. He maintained the status of a commoner throughout his life while traveling extensively. A prolific poet, he also sought comfort in identifying with Qu Yuan and Du Fu through commentary on their works. As in the Kangxi and Yongzheng reigns, Jiangnan remained the main target of the literary inquisition of the Qianlong era, and the Jiangnan literati, who also faced more intense competition in the civil service examinations than candidates from other regions, often ended up following alternative career paths. Li E (1692–1752), a native of Hangzhou, obtained his provincial graduate degree in 1720, but spent much of his life in Yangzhou privately teaching in gentry and merchant households. His main patrons were the Ma brothers, Yueguan (1688–1755) and Yuelu (1695–?), salt merchants who received an elite education and could write poetry and song lyrics. They both declined the opportunity to take the special erudite scholar exam of 1736 and chose to stay in Yangzhou, where they kept an impressive library and gardens, and entertained private scholars and poets.

Li E was the leading poet of the Zhe School (Zhepai) in the Qianlong period, following Huang Zongxi and Zha Shenxing in the preceding generation, and was known for his accomplishments in both poetry and song lyric. Deeply rooted in the Song poetic tradition, the Zhe School, based in Hangzhou, derived its primary creative impetus in the early eighteenth century from connections to the history of the Southern Song: Zhou Jing (1677–1749) organized the Lake Poet Society (Hunan shishe), attracting many like-minded writers to West Lake, while Wu Zhuo (1676–1733), a poet, editor, and book collector, amassed in his private library such rare poetry collections as *The Anthology of Rivers and Lakes (Jianghuji)*, edited by Chen Qi in the Hangzhou of Southern Song days, long thought to be missing or surviving only in fragments. These gatherings, together with the exciting discoveries made under their auspices, fueled a regional consciousness and stimulated the historical memory of the Hangzhou poets, whose poetic musings were epitomized in *Miscellaneous Poems on the Southern Song (Nan Song zashi shi)*, compiled by Wu Zhuo and Shen Jiazhe. Li E, one of the contributors to that volume, also compiled on his own account an impressive collection of source material called *Annals of Song Poetry (Songshi jishi)*. Li's poetry is saturated with the history of the region, which takes the form of wide-ranging textual references and allusions to the Song, by which the landscapes of Hangzhou and Yangzhou are imbued with lingering echoes and traces of the resonant past. Li E is also noted for his autumn scenes replete with images of chilly drizzle, withering lotuses, bamboo leaves shivering in the wind, the glimmering light of a lonely blue lamp, or a transient glimpse of the moon eclipsed by dark clouds. In these works one feels the tension between the mode of presentation and the mood it seeks to evoke, and between pensive melancholy and the fast-paced montage of distinctive snapshots.

Huang Jingren (1749–1783), better known by his sobriquet, Huang Zhongze, represents an anomaly among the poets of the Qianlong era in that he belongs to no particular group. As a descendant of the Song poet Huang Tingjian, he had legitimate grounds for claiming the legacy of the Jiangxi School, but he refused to do so at the expense of artistic freedom and independence. His literary commitments eventually cost him much more. A prodigy from an early age, Huang Jingren nevertheless suffered unusual difficulties in his pursuit of an official career. He served as a private secretary in Zhejiang, Anhui, and Hunan, then as a scribe for the *Four Treasuries* project in Beijing, and died en route to Xi'an where he was going to seek Bi Yuan's patronage. Huang Jingren had rare access to the center of elite culture through his friendship with such eminent figures as Bi Yuan, Wang Chang, and Weng Fanggang, but this did not affect his self-identification as a poor literatus (*hanshi*) with uncompromised personal dignity and cultural ideals. Huang Jingren's poetry is best understood within the context of the time-honored tradition that associated poetry with the expression of righteous anger and outcries against injustice, as seen in this sarcastic observation about the literati's shared misfortune: "Nine out of ten had to endure contemptuous looks, / Cast aside as worthless are none other than the literati." To be a man of letters means to suffer and to be discriminated against: this embittered definition casts an ironic light on the Qianlong Emperor's self-representation as a literatus.

Along with his emotional intensity came a strong sense of devotion to the art of poetry. Whereas the contemporary official elites regarded poetry writing as one among many cultivated pursuits, Huang Jingren saw it as the chief purpose of his life. Poetry was the only enterprise that could engage all his energies, passions, and talents, and at the same time secure him a path to literary immortality. By his death at age thirty-four, Huang had already accumulated nearly 2,000 poems, but no more than 1,300 have survived, in part due to the editorial and anthologizing efforts undertaken by Weng Fanggang and Wang Chang, who were least capable of appreciating his passion and artistic aspirations. Even so, the diversity of Huang Jingren's poetic style remains evident. In his themes of poverty and hardship, he is indebted to the mid-Tang poets Meng Jiao and Jia Dao. Equally impressive are his long lines that move with sweeping, unrestrained momentum reminiscent of Li Bai. Huang Jingren's single-minded devotion to poetry does not seem, however, to detract from his sense of irony. Unlike most of his contemporaries, who wrote with genial ease and a sense of complacency, Huang Jingren saw poetry as the product of estrangement from the mundane world, as shown in his "Offhand Composition: New Year's Eve" (Guisi chuxi oucheng, 1774):

> Laughter and talk in a thousand homes,
>   the water clock drips on,
> yet I feel a misery coming unseen
>   from beyond the world of things.
> Silent, I stand on the market bridge,
>   recognized by none,
> Watching a single star till it grows like the moon
>   such a long, long time.

Detaching himself from the human world, the speaker concentrates on a lonely star in the sky until it looms in his vision as large as the moon, but this imaginative leap verged on hallucination and is thus ridiculed in the following poem: "Year after year I waste the year's end reciting poems, / Beside the lamp my children often secretly laugh at me." Huang Jingren knew how difficult it is to evoke the lyrical from the prosaic without falling into self-absorption, and his poetry conveys such awareness most compellingly through self-mockery. It is not surprising that Huang Jingren became enormously popular in the first half of the twentieth century, especially with Yu Dafu, Zhu Ziqing, and other authors of "new literature" who continued to write classical poetry. Of Huang's contemporary admirers, Yuan Mei, who was thirty-four years his senior and outlived him by forty-eight years, expressed genial appreciation of his poetry, despite their differences in taste and style.

A prominent poet, critic, and essayist, Yuan Mei is perhaps better known in the popular imagination as a man of whimsical humor and wit. Thanks to Arthur Waley's biography, he has also become one of the most accessible Chinese writers for English readers. He is also celebrated for his estate, the Garden of Contentment (Suiyuan), which he designed himself. Located near Little Granary Hill in Nanjing, this site became more than just a residence for Yuan Mei and his family; under Yuan Mei's pen, it grew into a literary myth. Yuan Mei even maintained that his garden provided the model for the utopian garden in Cao Xueqin's novel, *The Story of the Stone*. This claim is not entirely baseless: Cao Xueqin's grandfather, Cao Yin, is alleged to have owned a garden on the same site; however, the garden had already changed hands at least once and was in a state of dilapidation by Yuan Mei's day. Yuan Mei purchased the land in 1749 upon quitting his post as the magistrate of Jiangning district. After a short journey to Shaanxi as a prospective official in 1753, he vowed never to serve in the government again. Not long after this decision to retire permanently to his garden, he announced, "My poetry was no good until after I resigned from office." Associated with Yuan Mei's retirement and renewed literary engagement, the Garden of Contentment became a magnetic center for the literary lights of the second half of the eighteenth century. Its owner's growing reputation attracted visitors from all over the empire. Generous honoraria were offered in exchange for epitaphs for their friends or family members, and envoys from Korea were said to have sought his works at lucrative prices. The garden was fertile ground for an abundant harvest of poetry. In addition to more than 4,400 of his own poems, Yuan Mei gathered nearly 10,000 poems from friends, acquaintances, and visitors over the years. In October 1797, he arranged for all the manuscripts of these poems, the best of which had already appeared in print, to be posted on the wall of a corridor more than a hundred feet long, thus creating a "poetry wall" (*shicheng*) to shield his garden from any intruding forces – a final flare of defiance and wit. Three months later, Yuan Mei passed away.

Yuan Mei's assertion about his well-guarded literary autonomy should not be taken as mere bravado; the claim is substantiated in his discourse on poetry as well as in his disparagement of Shen Deqian and Weng Fanggang. In contrast to their theories on poetry and literature in general, Yuan Mei defined poetry as the spontaneous expression of innate "human nature," as opposed to social and moral constraints, thereby articulating what has been called the School of Natural Wit (Xingling pai). Yuan Mei was not the first to embrace such a perspective on literature, and his concept of "natural wit," a negative construction of that which is bounded by social convention, recalls the ideas of his predecessors in the late Ming, especially Li Zhi's "child mind" and the Yuan brothers' endorsement of spontaneity and immediacy. Yuan Mei's distinctive emphasis is on the importance of natural gifts and inspiration in literary composition. He was not so radical as to denounce the Confucian canon, but certainly went further than his predecessors in proposing a philosophy of pleasure that justifies human desire and the need to enjoy life to the utmost. "Of those who obstruct the fulfillment of human desires," Yuan Mei argued, "few are not crafty and evil people." He chastised the poetry anthologies compiled by Shen Deqian for being rigid in criteria and judgment, and Shen's own poetry for exuding "the air of someone in ritual robes." Weng Fanggang he likened to the owner of an antique store fond of displaying his collections, and expressed detestation for his habit of loading his poetry with so many allusions and references that each line required an erudite note to unravel its sources and implications. Although Yuan Mei did not dismiss book learning and craftsmanship outright, he deplored the consequences of allowing them to dampen one's natural wit, as exemplified by Weng Fanggang's "lifeless" poetry.

Few poets went as far as Yuan Mei to bring classical poetry into intimate contact with everyday experience; indeed, as far as he was concerned, nothing is too trivial or mundane for inclusion in poetry. His poetry was an all-encompassing autobiography, hampered by none of the seriousness and decorum of formal writing. Yuan Mei's scandalous lifestyle, amorous experiences, and exquisite appetite pervaded his writings (he was a gastronome, and his essays on cooking have been translated into several European languages). He was also obsessively concerned with his physical condition and illnesses in ways reminiscent of Bai Juyi and Yang Wanli; even malaria and lost teeth warranted an account in classical poetry. Distinctive hallmarks of his writing include exuberant humor ("The master raises chickens and allows them to indulge in food, / but he has them cooked once they grow fat. The master's plan will work, / unless you leak it to the chickens themselves"), a capacity to discern strangeness or novelty in habitual routines, and the witty inversion of conventional assumptions ("The master painter's fame is so great / that the Central Kingdom appears small by comparison," written in a poem on seeing off the painter Shen Nanpin, who had been invited by the emperor of Japan to assume a post as a teacher). In a sense, Yuan Mei is the Li Yu (1611–1680) of classical poetry, as he did for classical poetry what Li Yu did for vernacular fiction. Aside from wit and humor, Yuan Mei was also noted for incorporating a heavy dose of colloquialisms into his poetry while tampering with its syntax to satisfy the whim of the moment. Canonical poets of the past became handy targets for parodies, and the forms of regulated verse were stretched to their limits. For many of his contemporary followers, Yuan Mei embodied a liberating force that breathed new life into classical poetry, but he also earned a certain amount of ridicule, and his poetry was often criticized for being facile and glib.

In the long Qianlong era, Yuan Mei stands out for his incredible versatility as a writer, with a corpus that includes poetry, prose, remarks on poetry, recipes, and classical tales about ghosts and demons. Yet he left behind few song lyrics, a genre that showed signs of decline in the eighteenth century. He also had little gift for painting, nor is his calligraphy impressive. In this last regard, he was an anomaly, as many of his contemporary poets were also known as painters and calligraphers, such as Zheng Xie (1693–1765), one of the Eight Eccentrics of Yangzhou, whose works move beyond the constraints of the dominant styles and schools. Nevertheless, as a leading poet of the time, Yuan Mei best expressed a shared distaste for the cultural norms of literati. In his *Suiyuan's Poetry Remarks* (*Suiyuan shihua*), Yuan describes how he offended a high-ranking official with the inscription on his seal, "Su Xiaoxiao [a legendary courtesan–poet of the Southern Dynasties] of Qiantang was from my neighborhood," which is a quote from a Tang poet. "He would not stop reprimanding me even after my initial apologies," Yuan Mei writes.

> Fed up with this, I replied with feigned seriousness: "Do you think it is absurd to relate myself to Su Xiaoxiao? Well, seen from today's perspective, you are indeed a top-ranking official, while Su is base. I am afraid, however, that a hundred years from now people will remember Su Xiaoxiao, but not you." Those present all burst into laughter.

This is another instance of Yuan Mei's wit, but underneath the surface play-fulness is a more serious attempt to propose alternative criteria by which to measure an individual.

Although far from being an egalitarian thinker, Yuan Mei went further than most of his contemporaries to reach out to those excluded from the literati. He was proud to have discovered many female talents in poetry, and declared in his later years that Jin Yi, arguably the most gifted of his female disciples, was one of his close friends. Many female family members, including sisters, cousins, daughters-in-law, and granddaughters, were themselves accomplished poets, and brought to bear in their works refreshing perspectives on life experiences that were outside the scope of male poets. Even as Yuan Mei's patronage of women poets won him fame, it also subjected him to condemnation and character assassination, a subject discussed below. Over the fifty years of his retirement in Nanjing, Yuan Mei also made the acquaintance of people from all walks of life. *Shuiyuan's Remarks on Poetry* attests to his genuine interest in their poetry, and, thanks to his anecdotes and comments, their life stories and works have been preserved. For Zhu Hui (1678–1757), a vagrant who spent his last forty years living in Buddhist temples, Yuan Mei wrote the epitaph, "The tomb of Mr. Zhu Caoyi, a late poet of the Qing dynasty." It is noteworthy that Zhu was also the model for a commoner poet in the novel *The Scholars* by Wu Jingzi, who resided in Nanjing in 1733 and 1754. Not unlike Yuan Mei, Wu Jingzi sought to explore the potential for revitalizing literary culture through those outside of the elite. Based on his personal observation of Nanjing commoners, he conjured up four eccentric artists in Chapter 55 of his novel to give a compelling presentation of cultural ideals that he believed had long been lost among the literati.

Yuan Mei's death in 1798 marked the end of a literary era. Although his literary school suffered a setback as many of his disciples abandoned his style, Yuan Mei's influence remained alive through the efforts of a few loyal followers, primarily Zhao Yi and Zhang Wentao. A well-established historian, Zhao Yi (1727–1814) brought a historical perspective to his interpretation of literature, thereby discrediting the concept of the timeless canon. He is especially known for saying that every era brings forth its own talents to establish literary trends, each lasting several hundred years. According to him, even Li Bai and Du Fu could weather changes in time and taste only with difficulty, their works having lost their "freshness" after so many years of transmission. In his own poetry, Zhao Yi further extended the vernacular tendency initiated by Yuan Mei; the outrage it provoked among conservative critics can be gleaned from the following remarks by Zhu Tingzhen (1841–1903):

> Although Zhao Yi uses more allusions in his poetry than Yuan Mei, and the parallel couplets in his regulated verse of the seven-syllable line are more refined, his jocularity and use of burlesque are vulgar to the point of being despicable. His poetry draws its subjects, allusions, and vocabulary from all sorts of street gossip and alley talk, colloquial expressions and local dialects, miscellanies and fiction, plays and dramatic performance, folk songs and common sayings, regional theater and minority songs. Zhao is a harmful enemy of poetry displaying all sorts of vulgarity in ways previously unseen.

Zhang Wentao (1764–1814), also known by his sobriquet, Zhang Chuanshan, was steadfast in following Yuan Mei's theory on natural wit. His poetry often celebrates wine and other hedonistic pleasures, but in his later works the troubled times cast a heavy shadow.

The "Yuan Mei phenomenon" can perhaps be more adequately comprehended if viewed in the larger literary and cultural context. Judged in terms of quantity and social prestige, classical poetry and prose were indeed the dominant literary genres of the Qianlong reign. Though there were some fresh developments in these excessively cultivated and overcrowded fields, the most exciting breakthroughs occurred in the peripheral areas of lesser reputation, primarily that of the vernacular novel.

The making of the literati novel

Particularly in its middle and later phases, the Qianlong era saw a widespread proliferation of vernacular fiction facilitated by commercial publishing. It also witnessed the emergence of what might be called "literati novels" that were largely independent of commercial production and consumption. In the hands of a small number of literati, the vernacular novel acquired a new life as it came to embody literati culture in all its complexity. Although limited in quantity, these works were often enormous in length and scope, incorporating a broad range of literati concerns and sensibilities, as well as individual eccentricities and a variety of intellectual discourses. Some of these works are hopelessly self-indulgent, if not outright self-celebratory; others are fraught with sober and ironic observations. The most outstanding works often register conflicting impulses, as their authors sought to embrace the literati cultural tradition while at the same time questioning its relevance. Thus at their best these novels gave rise to a critical consciousness capable of reflecting upon the limits and dilemmas of their own cultural and intellectual sources. Small wonder that the Chinese intellectuals of the twentieth century often seek in the novels *The Unofficial History of the Scholars* and *The Story of the Stone* the indigenous source of Chinese modernity, however that term is defined. The intellectual history of modern China is reflected to a certain extent in their constant interpretation and reinterpretation of these novels of inexhaustible depth and richness.

Although literati novels were clearly works of enormous cultural importance, the vastness of their authors' ambitions did not translate into immediate success or influence. Occupying the center of these works are, typically, protagonists who are members of the literati making dubious, often doomed, efforts to assert their relevance to worldly affairs, or to search for respite from

society or redemption through religion. Such themes seem to have been recapitulated in the fate of the works themselves: with only limited contemporary
readership, their impact on the cultural scene was as marginal as the status of
their authors.

Vernacular novels and commercial publishing

In the accounts of modern scholars, the mid-Qianlong era produced two
landmark novels, *The Unofficial History of the Scholars* (*Rulin waishi*) and *The
Story of the Stone* (*Shitou ji*, also known as *The Dream of the Red Chamber* or
Honglou meng); their respective authors, Wu Jingzi (1701–1754) and Cao Xueqin
(1715?–1763), have long been hailed as China's most accomplished novelists.
Such illuminating hindsight should not, however, blind us to the reality of the
mid-eighteenth century. Wu Jingzi and Cao Xueqin were authors with at best
local visibility in their own lifetimes. Wu earned a modest reputation mostly
as a poet, and his anthology of poetry and prose was published around 1740. By
contrast, the novel, which took him almost two decades to complete, enjoyed
only limited circulation in hand-copied form and did not appear in print until
1803, nearly half a century after his death. Cao Xueqin did not even finish *The
Story of the Stone*. The hand-copied drafts of early portions were circulated
mainly among his friends and relatives, and their effect on the literary practice
of the time was minimal at best.

A few other literati novels composed between 1750 and 1780 were transmitted in similar ways and thus were barely noticed by contemporary readers.
Discovered or rediscovered years later, they exerted a much more enduring
influence on the intellectual and cultural scene of the nineteenth and twentieth centuries. As such, they belong as much to the modern era as to their
own century. A responsible historical account needs to take into consideration
the complex process whereby these novels came to be considered the highest literary achievements of their day. Such an account should also explore
the significance of their (re)discovery as "events" in the history of modern
China.

Is it appropriate to place at the center of Qianlong-era literary history two
novels largely unknown to contemporary readers? Certain significant changes
did occur during this period, and were recognized even at the time. The fact
that these novels had minimal, if any, exposure among contemporary readers
is itself a sign of historical change, for the vernacular novel had long been
associated with the popular art of storytelling and later with commercial publishing, and thus was noted among literary genres for its greater accessibility
to readers.

Compared with the late Ming period, the Qianlong era seems less innovative in the commercial publication of vernacular fiction. The majority of publications consisted of works from earlier periods, often in editions of low quality, as Robert Hegel's research shows, with crowded texts and crudely rendered illustrations. New novels did occasionally get published, but these were usually popular romances of limited artistic value.

Nor did the vernacular short story fare well in the same period. A narrative genre sharing largely the same origins as the vernacular novel, the vernacular short story had its golden age between 1620 and 1680, with a brief interruption during the Manchu conquest of the 1640s. Even in the early decades of the Qing dynasty, writers of vernacular short stories were still capable of maintaining a small community, especially in Jiangnan. Well connected to publishers, they continued to bring out new works through commercial avenues. This publishing boom barely lasted into the eighteenth century. Writers either died or ceased to produce, and the new generation of writers evinced little interest in this genre. Commercial publishers, for their part, seemed interested only in recycling previously published stories under new titles. More often than not, these texts were put together in haste, and were almost always poorly printed. The vernacular short story languished until the early twentieth century, when a new wave came bearing the compelling influence of modern European literature.

How shall we make sense of this general trend in the commercial publication of vernacular fiction during the Qianlong reign and beyond? Steady growth in population and the unprecedented spread of education and literacy engendered a new demand for printed books. Taking advantage of this socially and geographically expanded market, the commercial publishers of the day tended to target readers and book buyers of modest means. Moreover, as publishing became more localized in terms of scale and the customers it served, or more specialized in the choice of what to print, the extent to which the cultural elite was involved inevitably changed, and in general showed a tendency to decline. Thus, on the one hand, commercial publishers either did not attempt, or failed in the attempt, to engage the most innovative writers of the day in the production of vernacular fiction for a large audience. On the other hand, members of the literati like Wu Jingzi and Cao Xueqin, who remained outside the purview of commercial publishing, continued to indulge in writing novels of unprecedented sophistication and erudition for the appreciation of like-minded friends. These two trends generated an intriguing cultural divide in fiction production over the second half of the eighteenth century.

In the arena of commercial publishing, we may well describe the middle and late Qianlong era as an age of the reproduction and circulation of the vernacular novel. Not only did earlier novels become widespread, but their motifs and values came to inform many other genres. Agglomerations of diverse texts and forms, historical romances (such as *Romance of the Three Kingdoms*) and heroic sagas (as represented by *Water Margin*) often became themselves the source texts for revision and rewriting in a variety of oral and performance literature. For instance, Guan Yu (162–220), a major hero in *Three Kingdoms*, gained remarkable popularity across a wide range of media – oral literature, local operas, official and popular cults, and the lore of secret societies – and served the changing needs of different regions and social groups in the Ming and especially the Qing. Along with the evolution of the Guan Yu myth, there emerged what Prasenjit Duara calls "the arena of superscription," as new interpretations negotiated for dominance without erasing the existing theories on whose symbolic resonances they depended to give them relevance and effectiveness. This common domain of reinterpretation and negotiation was further consolidated from the mid-eighteenth century onward, as the expanded book market and booming regional theater assumed a quintessential role in disseminating the symbols, motifs, and worldviews of the earlier novels.

The transmission of vernacular fiction was not confined to the boundaries of the Qing empire. Chapter 1 of this volume shows that *New Tales Told by Lamplight*, an early Ming collection of classical tales, had already been exported to neighboring countries, such as Japan, Korea, and Vietnam, in the fifteenth century. Facilitated by booming commercial publishing, overseas trade, and long-distance travel, vernacular short stories and novels were introduced to these countries in the latter half of the seventeenth century and in the eighteenth century. A 1762 Korean bibliography, for instance, listed seventy-four works of fiction written in Chinese, including a large number of vernacular novels that had been introduced to Korea from China. This trend in the book trade suffered a setback in 1786, when King Chŏngjo banned the importation of Chinese fiction, but it is unlikely that this official policy was strictly enforced. China and Vietnam, hindered by no significant geographic barriers, developed close ties in publishing and bookselling during the same period. Evidence shows that books were sometimes printed in Guangdong solely for the purpose of export, although the coordination of publishers and book traders across the China–Vietnam border is largely a story yet to be told. The introduction of vernacular fiction into Japan expedited a wide range of changes in reading, writing, and translation practices. Not unlike their counterparts in eighteenth-century Korea and Vietnam, the Japanese elite were trained in reading literary Chinese, especially Confucian texts. As in Korea and Vietnam, the encounter with vernacular Chinese fiction posed a linguistic challenge, which impelled the Japanese to rethink the relationship between the written and the spoken language, and fostered innovations in their use of literary forms. To elucidate what these innovations meant is beyond the scope of this chapter; suffice it to say that the circulation of the vernacular Chinese novel had a profound impact on other East Asian countries, partly because it occurred before the influx of modern French and English novels in the final decades of the nineteenth century. In fact, when Japanese writers and scholars later encountered European novels, they often resorted to vernacular Chinese novels and fiction commentaries (such as Jin Shengtan's commentaries on *Water Margin*) for interpretive models and strategies.

The literati novels of the mid- and late Qianlong era stand out in this age of reproduction and circulation of the vernacular novel fueled by commercial publishing and the book trade. They had so little in common with the earlier novels that their emergence in the mid-eighteenth century could well indicate the rise of a new narrative form. Of course, the term "novel" itself is highly problematic, especially when applied in studies of premodern Chinese literature. During the Ming and Qing eras, various terms (including "unofficial history") were attached to texts that we now cheerfully lump together under the general rubric of "novel." The appellation *zhanghui xiaoshuo*, a catchall phrase for long narrative stories, primarily fictive and in most cases written in the vernacular, which were divided into multiple chapters of varying lengths, was not invented until the first decade of the twentieth century. If these texts can be considered to belong to one common genre or mode of writing, that genre is inevitably a heterogeneous one of different origins and sources, and its history contains more discontinuities than it does continuities.

Early novels, exemplified by *Romance of the Three Kingdoms*, *Water Margin*, and *Journey to the West*, were mainly concerned with historical sagas, dynastic cycles, military affairs, heroic adventures, and religious pilgrimages, with historical or legendary personages occupying the center of the narrative. Derived from written and oral sources, including history and folklore, all of these works underwent extensive revision by multiple hands before they appeared in print form during the mid- or late sixteenth century. Beginning in the final decades of the sixteenth century, individually authored works (such as *The Plum in the Golden Vase*) gradually emerged. Some of these diverged from the common repertory of folklore and historiography. Wu Jingzi, Cao

Xueqin, and other literati novelists of the mid- and late Qianlong period went further by immersing their works deeply in the source of literati culture. In their hands, the vernacular novel is recast in both theme and style. Written by individual literati for a selected and increasingly fragmented literati audience, these works address the literati's wide range of concerns and deal with a variety of literati characters, often with an exquisite display of autobiographical detail. The authors' sophisticated and personal use of narrative and frequent references to literati learning – often the subject of laudatory comments in prefaces written by friends – precluded ordinary readership. Accordingly, they no longer relied on a simulated storyteller who addresses an imagined audience, even though not many literati of the day were ready to espouse the vernacular novel as a respectable literary genre in its own right.

Socially and culturally speaking, these novelists were at the margins of the literati. None had close personal ties with the leading figures in contemporary literature and literary discourse, and few enjoyed success in official careers. With or without the licentiate degree, they often took on jobs such as private tutors in gentry families, or private secretaries in the service of local officials, wandering from one place to another. Wu Jingzi supported his family on a depleted inheritance while Cao Xueqin lived on the verge of poverty after his family's property was confiscated by the Yongzheng Emperor in 1728. Despite their financial difficulties, these writers were rarely motivated by profit. Spending twenty years, as several of them did, on a single work is surely not the way to maximize profits. Unlike most of their predecessors in the late Ming, many of whom were deeply involved in commercial publishing, these mid-Qing novelists were as detached from the book market as they were from the center of officialdom. In a time when the literati as a social group were experiencing deepening crises in self-reproduction and self-representation, they asserted themselves as both the authors and subjects of the vernacular novel, thereby embarking on new avenues of intellectual inquiry.

The early eighteenth century: a flashback

The early decades of the eighteenth century saw a decrease in the creation of the vernacular novel. Shandong-based novelists disappeared from the scene: Ding Yaokang, the author of *The Sequel to the Plum in the Golden Vase*, passed away in 1670; Xizhou Sheng produced no new novels after *Marriage Destinies to Awaken the World* (*Xingsh: yinyuan zhuan*), if in fact he survived into the eighteenth century. These authors' novels of social satire and domestic farce, unfolding against the backdrop of dynastic disintegration or couched as apocalyptic allegories of descent and salvation, seemed to fall out of favor.

Dominating the fiction of the day were popular historical romances of various sorts, erotic novellas, and talent–beauty tales – this last is a highly formulaic subgenre traced to the Ming or earlier, which flourished in the early Qing. These three types of novel created, in part, the immediate preconditions for the writing of *The Story of the Stone*, and, to a certain extent, of *The Unofficial History of the Scholars*.

Cao Xueqin may have begun to write *The Story of the Stone* in 1740. In its opening chapter, he challenges the stone, the alleged author of the novel, to speak in its own defense; the stone responds by distinguishing the novel from all these prevalent types, in which he sees nothing commendable:

> Your so-called "historical romances," consisting, as they do, of scandalous anecdotes about statesmen and emperors of bygone days and scabrous attacks on the reputations of long-dead gentlewomen, contain more wickedness and immorality than I care to mention. Still worse is the "erotic novel," by whose filthy obscenities our young folk are all too easily corrupted. And the talent–beauty romances, those dreary stereotypes with their volume after volume all pitched on the same note and their different characters undistinguishable except by name (all those ideally beautiful young ladies and ideally eligible young bachelors) – even they seem unable to avoid descending sooner or later into indecency.

While the stone's moralistic stance might be strategic, his speech voices Cao Xueqin's discontent with the reigning tendencies of contemporary novels. The stone singles out the talent–beauty romance for further disparagement:

> The trouble with this last kind of romance is that it only gets written in the first place because the author requires a framework in which to show off his love poems. He goes about constructing this framework quite mechanically, beginning with the names of his pair of young lovers and invariably adds a third character, a servant or the like, to make mischief between them, like the clown in a comedy. What makes these romances even more detestable is the stilted, bombastic language – inanities dressed in pompous rhetoric, remote alike from nature and common sense, and teeming with the grossest absurdities.

Cao Xueqin's stone sees no definitive line of demarcation between erotic novels and talent–beauty romances, and he is right to some extent. The romances produced during the Kangxi reign were by and large bowdlerized of sexual connotations, and modern scholars often cite this as evidence of the influence of neo-Confucianism, the orthodox ideology. What was purged from the romances may have found its way into other forms; if anything was lost in the process, it was perhaps a decent guise or pretext for eroticism. In any case, it is surely misleading to characterize the early eighteenth century as an age of neo-Confucian puritanism. Erotic novels and novellas were still circulated through the book market, although it is difficult to determine which ones and how many were written during this period. The recent discovery of *Guwangyan* (*Preposterous Words*) exposed the tip of an iceberg that has yet to be explored. Nearly one million characters in length, *Preposterous Words* is arguably one of the longest novels produced in the Ming and Qing eras. This gigantic work assembles almost all existing motifs and devices of the erotic novel and talent–beauty fiction, with a relentless penchant for parody and hyperbole. Despite its didactic narrative voice and its framework of reincarnation and retribution, the novel invests much of its narrative energy in a seemingly endless parade of sexual sport. The characters show no sign of slowing down until their stories are cut short by sudden death from exhaustion or devastation. Similarly, the author seems to have seen no other option but to end the story when all scenarios had been exhausted and it was no longer possible to prolong the rampage of obscenity and perversion. In the end, the novel reaches its own redemption through exhaustion and death – a fitting farewell to the tradition that fuels its massive narrative.

Despite the frequent collapses of narrative distance throughout *Preposterous Words*, the narrator does not forget to remind us of the fictionality of his stories as well as their travesty of the genre. The title of the novel can be read as an apology – "forgive me for talking recklessly" – but also as a petition for the reader's indulgence – "allow me to mumble on recklessly anyway." The compulsion to garrulity is registered at the novel's beginning in the person of a busybody said to enjoy gossiping more than anything else, one who can memorize lengthy "romances" without missing a single word. This inscribed narrator is fittingly named Daoting ("heard on the roads"), with the alternative name of Tushuo ("street talk"), both of which echo the classical definition of *xiaoshuo* (fiction). The narrator's consciousness of the nature of his speech as fiction-making resonates with his predilection for parody. As we will see, this discourse of the true and the false, and of reality and illusion, recurs in *The Scholars*, *Humble Words*, and especially *The Story of the Stone*, which navigates its young protagonist through a journey of self-discovery that begins with sexual awakening and erotic enchantment but moves well beyond.

The preface to *Preposterous Words* is dated 1730, but the novel left no trace in existing Qing dynasty texts. Nor is there much evidence of its early circulation in manuscript form. An abridged version in three chapters surfaced in 1941 and was published by the Shanghai Eugenics Society in a limited edition. More than twenty years later, the Russian sinologist Boris L'vovich Riftin discovered the complete manuscript in the Lenin Library in Leningrad (now the Russian National Library in St. Petersburg), which had been collected by the astronomer K. I. Skachkov during his sojourn in Beijing from 1848 to 1859. The novel was first published in its entirety in 1997. In a way, this peculiar afterlife is emblematic of the fate of other literati novels of this period. The publication of *Preposterous Words* has evoked much speculation about its possible relationship with *The Story of the Stone*, despite the unmistakable differences between the two works in terms of artistic vision and merit.

Another work worth mentioning here is *Nüxian waishi* (*The Unofficial History of a Female Immortal*). Completed in the early eighteenth century, it is perhaps one of those historical romances castigated by Cao Xueqin's stone, but it almost surely anticipated *The Unofficial History of the Scholars* not least because it is the first full-length vernacular novel to carry the title "Unofficial History." Set in the early Ming period, *The Unofficial History of a Female Immortal* deals with one of the crucial events of that time, the Yongle usurpation, in which the prince of Yan (Zhu Di) overthrew the reigning Jianwen Emperor and took the throne for himself. Rather than following the official narrative in legitimizing the usurpation, the author, Lü Xiong (1640?–1722?), gives a counterfactual account of how this incident might have been put right and the legitimacy of the Jianwen court restored. Interweaving the supernatural into the human realm and combining history with folklore fantasy, Lü Xiong uses the reign title of the Jianwen Emperor throughout the novel, thus erasing the entire Yongle era from Ming chronology. Even as the official *Ming History* was still being composed, this alternative and counterfactual "unofficial history" was already widely circulated among intellectuals, first in hand-copied form and then in print (it was published in 1711, probably with the support of a patron). This printed edition celebrated an imagined community of literary readers by including the commentaries of more than sixty contemporary writers, artists, and scholars, who came from different regions and might not have known one another personally.

Although no literati novels of the Qianlong reign enjoyed similar fame among their contemporary audience, Lü Xiong's adversarial stance toward official histories was by no means an anomaly. Like *The Female Immortal*, *The Unofficial History of the Scholars* is also set in Ming times. Its preface is dated spring 1736, a few months after the completion of the official *Ming History*. According to the preface, "the novel is called an unofficial history because it is not meant to be listed among the official histories."

The Unofficial History of the Scholars

It would be a mistake to characterize *The Unofficial History of the Scholars* (hereafter *The Scholars*) as a historical novel, despite its adoption of the Ming chronology and frequent references to historical personages and incidents. Wu Jingzi offers his own critical comments on the bygone dynasty, as the main part of his novel begins at the end of the Chenghua reign (1465–1488), when major historical changes were already under way, and concludes with the Wanli reign (1573–1620), a time of incipient decline. His implied inquiry into the forces that led to the Ming's demise is suggestive for his own time. As the pattern of the past persisted, the future was only too predictable. Prophetic in vision, *The Scholars* is deeply rooted in its author's personal experiences and his observations on contemporary affairs. In its sweeping display of the deterioration of literati mores, the predicament of official institutions, and the Confucian elite's futile struggle to reassert moral and cultural authority, the novel conveys a sense of crisis. Wu Jingzi uses the term "scholars" in its broadest sense to designate the cultural and sociopolitical elite, as well as those whose promise of joining the elite has yet to be fulfilled. His sarcastic portrayal of the follies and futile aspirations of this motley assortment of characters leaves us wondering what is to become of a society whose leadership is so degenerate or demoralized. Even as most of his contemporaries remained blissfully enchanted with literati culture in its seemingly coherent totality, Wu Jingzi saw a world whose center could no longer hold.

The author of the preface to the 1803 edition of *The Scholars*, the Old Man of the Leisure Studio, was, according to modern scholars, someone who knew Wu Jingzi well, if he was not Wu himself. In either case, the fact that the preface is dated 1736 is of some significance. A few scholars suggest that at that time the novel was in the early stages of composition. The year 1736 marks a watershed in Wu's life: he had finally abandoned the idea of pursuing an official career through the civil service examinations. This personal decision offered him a detached, if not an independent, vantage point from which to represent the literati and officialdom in *The Scholars*. This is echoed in the 1736 preface, which hails the novel for its steadfast denunciation of career, fame, riches, and official rank. In the second month of 1736, more than two hundred literati candidates, including several of Wu Jingzi's personal friends, convened in Beijing for the prestigious erudite scholar examination hosted by the Qianlong Emperor (although the personal audiences that were a part of the examination were eventually postponed to the ninth month of the same year). Wu Jingzi was recommended for the same examination. He sat for a few of its primary sessions, but did not follow through and never made a personal appearance at court.

Wu Jingzi's decision to quit his pursuit of an official career was preceded by another, perhaps equally important, choice: in 1733, Wu left his hometown in Quanjiao, Anhui Province, and settled for the rest of his life in the southeastern metropolis of Nanjing. Separated from his lineage, Wu was free of his obligations as a member of the local gentry. In his novel, no literatus succeeds in living a meaningful and incorrupt life as a member of the gentry, and their putative roles in family, lineage, and local community cease to be fulfilling. Du Shaoqing, Wu Jingzi's fictional alter ego, is weary of his obligations to his lineage and feels only disgust toward his kinsmen; his account likely recapitulates Wu's early trauma of being caught in a vicious dispute over an inheritance. Again echoing Wu's own experiences, Du Shaoqing's departure from his hometown is followed by his refusal of an official recommendation for a special examination. Where Du Shaoqing finds no satisfaction in being a gentleman, other characters experience even greater disillusionment with their pursuit of an official career. In many cases, their lifelong slavery to the civil service examinations drains their vitality and imagination, leaving them in a permanent state of mental impoverishment and moral, if not financial, bankruptcy. Just as Du is estranged from his prescribed roles in both officialdom and the local society, Wu Jingzi had to eke out a place for himself, a search that involved much more than finding a concrete locality. For Wu and his literati characters, the ultimate question is: how should one live one's life in a general climate of disenchantment? His novel shows that the choices are not many, and none is truly satisfactory.

The Scholars is more than an autobiographical novel: the existential anxiety it embodies is collective in nature. Wu Jingzi's fictional alter ego, like many of the other characters in the novel, makes only a fleeting appearance. Here is a novel with neither overarching plot nor one main protagonist to tie the multifarious strands of its narrative together. Anecdotal in design, the book follows its characters in an unfolding series, as one gives way to another, often returning only as a subject of casual conversation. In the early twentieth century, Chinese critics, increasingly exposed to the hegemonic influence of modern European novels and literary concepts, often criticized the novel for lumping together short stories without integrating them into an overarching structure. Even such a negative view overestimates the unity of the novel's constituent parts, for few of its chapters read as self-contained, independent stories. Yet the novel as a whole is not entirely shapeless. Its general design gradually emerges as each episode discloses its meanings through correspondences and contrasts with other episodes. The way the novel is organized is semantically (and thematically) significant. Demoralized and disillusioned, the literati characters are no longer capable of acting out roles consistent with the monolithic narrative characteristic of official histories. Proceeding under the title of an "unofficial history," the novel offers a chronicle of frivolous incidents with no historical significance in the conventional sense of the term; it reduces its subjects to a state of existence that has no possible analogy except with the anecdote.

In exposing the pretensions, hypocrisy, and philistinism of his class, Wu Jingzi makes frequent use of gossip, jokes, and anecdotes, which were circulated orally and in written form among the literati circles of the day. These are insiders' stories that produce the effect of caricature with amusing observations hardly seen in other genres. Largely excluded from official histories and other formal writings, they serve as a major source for Wu Jingzi's novel, which is considered just as marginal. In most cases, jokes are incorporated with a sense of proportion and good judgment; only occasionally do they slip into farcical scenes of burlesque and buffoonery. Moreover, the comic skits are presented, as often in the source material, without the mediation of a narrator or commentator. A sense of irony and humor is generated by the characters' words and deeds, or by the discrepancies between the two, rather than by a narrator's witty remarks. Li Yu and other writers in the comic mode missed no chance to add verbal spin to whatever subjects they laid their hands on, but Wu Jingzi is a minimalist. For him, the art of irony lies in juxtaposition and understatement.

The Scholars is one of the first vernacular novels to minimize reliance on the simulated rhetoric of storytelling typical of novels up until that time. There are no formulaic phrases or verses describing appearance and dress to introduce a character, and no narrator's comments or quoted common sayings to conclude accounts of major incidents. Stripped of the clichés and generic markers of its sources, the prose of *The Scholars* is limpid and straightforward. The differences are not limited to the surface of the text or the narrative style, but also involve the mode of perception and representation itself. No longer presenting stories from the omniscient view of the storyteller–narrator, Wu Jingzi allows readers to experience his narrative world without his guidance. Moments of ambiguity are unavoidable, and readers are often left to form their own judgments. In this sense, *The Scholars* is the first modern Chinese novel that challenges us to see the world anew.

The Scholars comprises three parts, bracketed by a prologue in the first chapter and an epilogue in Chapter 56. The prologue introduces Wang Mian

(?–1357), a self-taught artist who maintains his personal integrity by refusing to serve the government in the tumult of dynastic transition. Wang is not merely an exemplary character, but also a seer; he foresees the calamities that will befall literati culture in the years to follow. As the formulaic eight-part essay becomes the centerpiece of the curriculum for the civil service examinations, literati will altogether neglect the values associated with *wen*, as well as the qualities that would anchor them in an otherwise rootless existence. Wang's prediction becomes reality in Part I (Chapters 2 to 30) of the novel. Literati characters appearing in this part largely fall into two opposing categories: examination candidates and self-proclaimed men of culture who are interested only in such refined affairs as poetry writing. The former regard passing the examinations as the highest reward for their years of struggle. Their repeated failures plunge them into the darkness of pathology and insanity, while success, which often comes as a surprise, generates moments of psychological breakdown, as in the case of Fan Jin in Chapter 3. Overwhelmed by the news of his success in a provincial examination, Fan Jin has trouble maintaining the continuity of his self-identity. His view of himself is entirely subject to the arbitrary rules of the examination system, whose credibility the novel repeatedly challenges. Dismissing the examination candidates as vulgar and without taste, the self-described poets, however, pose no better alternatives, for they are no less obsessed with fame than their counterparts are with the prestige and profit of civil service. These so-called poets, hiding their worldly desires under the guise of culture, surpass the examination essayists only in pretension and hypocrisy. It is noteworthy that poetry was reintroduced as a required subject in the metropolitan examinations in 1757, and in the provincial examinations in 1759, only a few years after Wu Jingzi's death, thus leaving poets like those depicted in his novel with no ground for self-representation as disinterested men of culture. In *The Scholars*, the disparagement of pretense rarely indicates sincerity. Exuding an air of cultivated boredom, Du Shenqing ridicules his fellow poets' earnest claim of cultural distinction for being "so refined as to be vulgar," yet sees no problem at all in embracing the civil service examinations. Kuang Chaoren, a village boy who begins as a diligent student and filial son, comes to embody a dreadful combination of the worst qualities of the two groups – a petty-minded status seeker equipped with the talents of a liar, braggart, and hypocrite. His story ends as he triumphantly sets off on his way to Beijing to assume an official post.

Part II of the novel (Chapters 31 to 37) begins with a journey in the opposite direction. Declining official recommendations to sit for the court examination and other imperial offers to serve in Beijing, several characters converge in

Nanjing, where they construct a temple to make a sacrifice to Wu Taibo, a Confucian sage who was both a culture hero of the Jiangnan region and the legendary founder of the Wu clan (to which Wu Jingzi belonged) so prominent in that region. Nanjing thus emerges in this part of the novel as a ritual and cultural center, in opposition to Beijing, the political center of the empire. It is also set in retrospective contrast to Hangzhou, another southeastern metropolis, portrayed in Part I as the breeding ground for philistines and pretentious poets. No other character is more intimately attached to Nanjing than Du Shaoqing, Wu's fictional alter ego. Detached from his own local lineage yet remaining aloof from official institutions, Du displays an inherent affinity with the natural and cultural landscapes of Nanjing; this affinity is underscored by a change in the narrative voice, which becomes unusually personal, if not self-indulgent. At the most lyrical moments, Du Shaoqing's home is conjured up as a self-contained space for leisure, spontaneity, and genuine feeling, in pointed contrast to the restless, career-oriented life pursued by most literati. More important still is Du Shaoqing's affiliation with his Nanjing friends, especially Yu Yude, through their collective practice of Confucian ritual. The project of constructing a temple to Wu Taibo is announced in Chapter 33, and readers are regularly informed of its progress until Chapter 37, in which an elaborate ceremony is finally carried out. Regarded by Qing dynasty commentators as the climax of the novel, this chapter stands out for its solemn, austere depiction of the ceremony in all its procedural niceties and technical details.

The ceremony is designed to transform society at large, and the full range of its implications slowly unfolds in Part III (Chapters 38 to 55), as several characters embark on individual journeys to extend the moral vision embodied in the Confucian ritual into everyday practice. Their stories, however, are not of moral triumph. The journeys are fraught with ambiguities, and almost always end in frustration. Moreover, the noble vision of Confucian ritual begins to show a darker side in the episodes involving Wang Yuhui in Chapter 48. Wang Yuhui is a belated follower of Yu Yude and Du Shaoqing. Firmly dedicated to the virtues of filial piety and female chastity, he encourages his daughter to follow her husband in death, but is overcome by unexpected sorrow during the memorial ceremony. His trip to Nanjing fails to connect him to the organizers of the Taibo ceremony, and in the empty temple he finds nothing but some locked-away utensils and the ritual program posted on the wall. By having Wang Yuhui read the ritual program, the author casts a retrospective light on Chapter 37, in which the Taibo ceremony took place. Moreover, Wang Yuhui is no ordinary reader, but a dedicated editor of

Confucian ritual texts similar to that he encounters on the wall of the temple. This coincidence does not appear to enlighten him as to what may have gone wrong in his own understanding and practice of ritual. In the aftermath of Wang Yuhui's traumatic experience, this moment places Chapter 37 in a different context and subjects it to unsettling inquiry. Two decades later, in Chapter 55, we see the temple again, this time in ruins.

The Scholars is a work capable of reflecting on the ideas and the ethos that sustain its own narrative through an unfolding process of intellectual inquiry. Its relentless self-reflexivity – a critical impulse that goes against its own grain – helps to define its existence as a new kind of vernacular novel, and indeed a new mode of thinking. Essential to the working out of Wu Jingzi's moral vision is what might be called ritualism. Parts II and III of the novel give an ample account of how the disheartened characters struggle to anchor their lives against the maddening race for status and profit sponsored by official institutions. In the case of the civil service examinations, competition is couched in terms of Confucian moral rhetoric, as each candidate, in composing the eight-legged essay, is required to speak on behalf of Confucius. This allows the candidates to lay claim to moral authority, which, once secured, can easily be converted to political and economic benefit. In response, Wu Jingzi's ritual project consists of two motifs: a withdrawal from the mundane world of politics, and the replacement of discourse with practice. The novel makes clear that Confucian ritual obligations must be fulfilled unconditionally, often at the expense of sociopolitical interest, and that the Confucian life of self-cultivation must be the extension of ritual practice, in which everyone knows his proper position and does what he is supposed to do without conscious effort or verbal negotiation. Wu Jingzi's vision of ritualism is evidently inspired by the rising discourse on Confucian ritual in the Qing dynasty, but his innovative approach to narrative enables him to elucidate the significance of the ritual through the most tangible and in-depth "thick description" (to borrow Clifford Geertz's term). Indeed, Wu Jingzi offers in his novel much more than a narrative illustration of Confucian ritualism. By placing ritual practice in vastly different settings, he ponders its ramifications and exposes it to scrutiny when, as in Wang Yuhui's story, it goes too far and verges on fanaticism.

As ritualism often leads to ethical dilemmas, Wu Jingzi seeks an alternative in lyricism. Here he is concerned primarily with the construction of a poetic subjectivity capable of harmonizing man with nature and transforming life experience, however trivial and fragmentary, into a meaningful totality. It is thus no surprise that the collective effort to strengthen the ethical bonds of Confucian society gives way to individual cultivation of genuineness and artistic sensibility. As Wu Jingzi takes us back to Nanjing in Chapter 55, his cherished city has been diminished to a soulless place. Only four amateur artists, each dedicated to the pursuit of one literary art, continue to uphold the endangered lyrical ideal. Ji Xianian, a self-taught calligrapher, epitomizes what may be called natural spontaneity. Not only does he create a style of his own, he also allows no external forces to dictate his performance, and will write only if he happens to be in the mood. Jing Yuan, a poor tailor, immerses himself in music. He has no friends except an old gardener, who finds in his garden a viable refuge from the outside world of endless commotion and headlong change. At the request of his friend, Jing Yuan brings his zither into the garden and plays a melody that only the two of them can understand and appreciate. Thus conceived, the lyrical vision cannot help but be restricted to the realm of private life, to a sterile kind of solitude. The four artists are eccentric loners, either widowed or unmarried, and remain disengaged from the world at large. They are reminiscent of Wang Mian in the prologue, who retreats into the mountains and perishes in isolation and obscurity.

Wu Jingzi is emotionally invested in his characters' solitary search for home, a place where they belong. His account of Nanjing in Part II registers an intimate personal voice. Whether or not this voice succeeds in absorbing the fragmentary, prosaic world into a cohesive vision, the lyrical subject claims an artistic triumph by infiltrating the mood, rhythm, and tone of Wu Jingzi's narrative, thereby adding a new dimension to a novel noted primarily for its ironic edge. No subsequent imitators have ever managed to achieve the subtle balance between empathy and irony of *The Scholars*. Even as he often turns to lyricism for personal consolation, Wu Jingzi is nevertheless keenly aware of its vulnerability and inadequacy. The account of Du Shaoqing juxtaposes his poetic voice and flamboyant postures against the open derision and unvoiced embarrassment of the onlookers. Evidently, no lyrical subject can come fully into its own when exposed to contextualizing perspectives that constantly erode its autonomy and threaten to engulf its lofty vision. Wu Jingzi's presentation of Du Shenqing, Du Shaoqing's cousin, reveals another, perhaps more troubling aspect of the lyric ideal. Steeping himself in poetry, theater, and the ethos of Nanjing, Du Shenqing personifies literati culture in all its subtleties and refinements, but his lyricism is seriously qualified. Deprived of the vision of the larger organic whole, it operates on the much diminished scale of the individual psyche and deteriorates into narcissism: on a group excursion to Rainflower Mountain, the self-absorbed Du Shenqing seems fascinated more by his own shadow than by the enticing vista.

As a novel of becoming, *The Scholars* sums up the intellectual journey that Wu Jingzi undertook during the last twenty years of his life, and as such inevitably involves a process of growing, repositioning, and self-questioning. In presenting choices to his literati characters, Wu often exposes their least favorable aspects and then juxtaposes these choices with other, equally problematic ones. This habit of always alerting readers to alternative perspectives is the corollary of Wu Jingzi's vocation as an intellectual novelist. Moreover, although he sets his novel within a preconceived historical frame, Wu is often driven by an almost journalistic engagement in the development of the ongoing events. As shown in many studies of the sources of *The Scholars*, Wu's account is remarkably open-ended and to a certain extent contingent on the unfolding drama; that is, the actual lives of his empirical sources. Knowing this helps to explain some of the apparent inconsistencies in the novel's thematic and narrative design and temporal scheme.

Wu Jingzi's authorship of *The Scholars* is confirmed by several unrelated contemporary sources. Although he continued to revise and update his novel until his death, evidence shows that the novel was already in circulation through hand-copied manuscripts no later than 1750. Reception was mixed. One of Wu's friends commended the novel for its artistic achievements, but felt pity for its author, who was now destined to be known as an author of fiction, or rather of "unofficial history." In an epilogue to the 1879 edition, Jin He claimed that the novel was first printed sometime between 1768 and 1779 under the supervision of Jin Zhaoyan, an ancestor closely tied to Wu Jingzi through marriage. This edition has never surfaced, if it ever existed. Little information is available about the circumstances surrounding the 1803 edition and the accompanying commentary. The extant documents show that the novel gained increasing popularity among literati readers from the 1850s on. In Nanhui and Shanghai, several civil officials and men of letters formed a small circle to read, comment on, and circulate the editions they owned. *The Scholars* offered them the vocabulary and reference points with which to make sense of what they observed in officialdom and their everyday surroundings. One commentator claimed that spending time in teahouses helped him to review *The Scholars*. A husband and wife teased each other using allusions to the comic figures of the novel. Still, it was not until the first decade of the twentieth century that novels bearing the marked influence of *The Scholars* began to emerge. The best examples include the four late Qing novels of exposé (*qianze xiaoshuo*), yet their divergences from their putative model are no less marked than their resemblances. The intellectuals of the early twentieth century did more than any of their predecessors to promote

The Scholars. They praised Wu Jingzi for his unmatched command of the vernacular, and recommended his novel as a model for the new literature in opposition to works composed in classical Chinese. They also saw in the novel a ruthless attack on Confucian ritualism and the civil service examination system, which suited the agenda of the May Fourth Movement. It is worth mentioning that the so-called vernacular Chinese was largely genre-specific in pre-twentieth-century literature. No one in Wu Jingzi's time would have charged it with such ideological import, nor have divided all the literary genres into two incompatible modes according to the use of language. Moreover, if *The Scholars* was a milestone in the development of critical consciousness, this consciousness derives from within the tradition of literati culture. In exploring alternatives from all available sources, *The Scholars* indicates how far an insider's critique of Confucianism could go before the Qing empire was exposed to the challenge from the West.

The Story of the Stone

While Wu Jingzi was still working on *The Scholars* in the 1740s, Cao Xueqin had already embarked on his ambitious novel *The Story of the Stone* (also known as *The Dream of the Red Chamber*, hereafter referred to as *The Stone*). Before his death in 1763 or 1764, Cao Xueqin had completed the first eighty chapters and possibly left behind a draft of the remaining chapters. The manuscript of the first eighty chapters was beginning to be circulated among Cao's friends and relatives in 1754, the year Wu Jingzi died. Cao was born in Nanjing into a branch of the clan that had been bondservants to the Manchu emperors and enjoyed imperial favor for generations. Soon after the Yongzheng Emperor dismissed Cao Fu, Cao Xueqin's father (or, according to some scholars, stepfather), from his lucrative post as the textile commissioner of Nanjing and confiscated the family estates in 1728, the Cao family was forced to move to Beijing. No evidence indicates that Wu Jingzi and Cao Xueqin knew about each other, and their novels differ in fundamental ways. *The Stone* is centered around a young man's rite of passage, which is inextricably intertwined with the glory and decline of his privileged family. The hero, Jia Baoyu, a sensitive boy with no worldly ambition, seeks salvation through love and experience, lyrical and theatrical enchantment, and Daoist and Buddhist enlightenment. By tracing different phases of his life's journey and dramatizing various aspects of his experience, the novel epitomizes literati culture in all its charm and intriguing complexity while also registering its weary discontentment. Jia Baoyu's final withdrawal into the emptiness of Buddhism offers no satisfying solutions to the problems that have troubled him all along; it indicates not so much a religious triumph as the stalemate of his obstinate refusal to enter the adult world and embrace the official career expected of a young man with his family background. Having exhausted all the choices available to his protagonist, Cao Xueqin confronts the limitations and inherent dilemmas of the cultural tradition that runs through his narrative. In this sense, *The Stone* is the true intellectual rival of *The Scholars*, despite their differences in theme, sensibility, and narrative style. Together these two novels constitute a critical breakthrough in the literary and intellectual history of early modern China.

The Stone has a complex and involved textual history. Even before Cao Xueqin's death, the eighty-chapter edition was already being circulated in hand-copied form. There are eleven extant versions, which vary greatly in length (one version, for instance, includes only two chapters) and show some textual divergences. What ties them together as a group is the inclusion of comments by Zhiyanzhai ("Red Inkstone Studio"). Scholars have not reached consensus on the identity of Zhiyanzhai. He might have been a member of the Cao family, but comments attributed to him might also encompass those of other commentators, including Jihusou ("Odd Tablet"), whose name is occasionally found in hand-copied manuscripts. In any case, these commentaries often revealed intimate knowledge about Cao Xueqin and identified the empirical sources of his novel. The commentators sometimes claimed to have witnessed the scenes recounted; in several places, they also predict the development of the plot beyond the first eighty chapters.

It is difficult to date the manuscripts with commentary or reconstruct their temporal sequence. Three versions can each be traced to 1754, 1760, and 1761, but the editing and copying process might have stretched well beyond Cao Xueqin's death. Textual variants among these manuscripts shed important light on the process of composition and revision. Pinning down a definitive version that reflects Cao Xueqin's original intent is difficult, however, not least because he continually modified his work, often in response to comments by Zhiyanzhai. Moreover, Cao had little control over the manuscripts already in circulation; his revised versions would immediately be subject to unauthorized changes once in the hands of the copyists and commentators. Even the boundary between narrative discourse and commentary occasionally becomes blurred as parts of the preface or interlineal commentary become integrated into the main body of the novel. What we see in these manuscripts is indeed a novel in progress, and its trajectory, incompletely captured in the extant versions, was influenced by copyists, commentators, and interested readers.

These hand-copied versions of *The Stone* were soon forgotten, and remained unknown until they resurfaced after the 1920s. Throughout the nineteenth century and the early Republican eras, the accepted version was the 120-chapter *The Dream of the Red Chamber*, first published by Cheng Weiyuan and Gao E (1738–1815) in 1791, and revised and reprinted the following year. The Cheng–Gao editions involved significant editing of the first eighty chapters and included another forty chapters, probably developed from existing drafts (a 120-chapter version had already been circulated in hand-copied form prior to the 1791 publication of the Cheng–Gao edition), although it is hard to determine whether they incorporated Cao Xueqin's own drafts of these chapters. The 1792 Cheng–Gao edition has since been the standard text to which readers have responded with commentaries or sequels. The English translation by David Hawkes and John Minford is based primarily on the Cheng–Gao editions, with occasional reference to the early manuscript versions. Since 1982, scholars have produced a number of 120-chapter editions based primarily on the Zhiyanzhai commentary manuscripts, but such editorial practice often results in what might be called an ideal version; that is, an eclectic text based on one version while incorporating certain textual variants from other versions, including the Cheng–Gao editions.

No other literati novels of the eighteenth century were nearly as influential as *The Stone* in nineteenth- and twentieth-century China. It has had a much more colorful afterlife than most contemporary works, as it has been re-incarnated in the form of oral literature, drama, painting, and fiction sequels. It also generated many "paratexts" through the endless proliferation of commentaries, colophons, and anecdotes. Taken together, these derivative discourses on *The Stone* often traversed class and gender boundaries in making their appeal to the public. The result is something much larger and more popular than a specific text called *The Stone*, namely an ever-growing phenomenon that is manifest in a variety of forms and thus undergoing constant transformation.

The Stone is so rich and complex that anyone can find evidence in it to support his own projected interpretation; in this sense, a person's reading of the novel reveals much about himself and his times. As far as intellectual and cultural history is concerned, modern interpretations of *The Stone* are an integral part of the process of constructing and transforming the discourse of Chinese modernity. In other words, the interpretations themselves constitute a legitimate subject for studies of modern intellectual and cultural history. Arguably, modern Chinese literary criticism began with Wang Guowei (1877–1927), who proposed in a 1906 essay a Schopenhauerian reading of *The Stone* as a tragedy of human suffering rooted in the Buddhist view of human desire. Cai Yuanpei, another intellectual leader of the time, adopted a political approach and saw in the novel an anti-Manchu allegory. The unearthing of the Zhiyanzhai versions in the 1920s furnished evidence necessary to interpret *The Stone* as autobiographical. Although the effort to discover historical facts behind the novel are said to be made in a spirit of scientific objectivity, it has so far produced more intriguing hypotheses than convincing arguments. Modern scholarship on *The Stone* is modern in concern, if not always in approach. Essential to Jia Baoyu's love story, according to some critics, is an individual's quest for freedom and liberation from the oppressive system of what these critics call feudalism. Any individual rebellion occurring in the context of traditional society would inevitably start from within the family and lineage. For these critics, Jia Baoyu's passionately professed indifference to patriarchal authority anticipated the youth movement of 1919 that ushered in the modern era for China. Far from seeing the novel as a parable of Buddhist renunciation and enlightenment, these modern scholars read it as the awakening of a modern individual through rebellion and struggle. Accordingly, in the catastrophic fall of the Jia family, they saw the harbinger of the collapse of the traditional social system and the end of dynastic history. We can hardly do justice to the hundred years of modern Chinese scholarship on *The Stone* by summarizing it in one short paragraph, but we must not forget the extent to which the novel became entangled in modern political culture, especially between 1949 and 1976. Mao Zedong was an admirer, instructing his communist cadres to read the novel at least five times, and engineering an ideological campaign against what he saw as bourgeois tendencies in *Stone* scholarship.

How did Cao Xueqin present his own novel? Although he could hardly have foreseen the dramatic afterlife his work was to enjoy, his account of its textual history was sure to frustrate any single and definitive reading. For all his concerns with the intricacies of human sentiments and experiences, Cao traces his work to a divine origin, followed by an ambiguous history of composition and transmission.

Chapter 1 begins with a modified version of the creation myth. When the dome of Heaven was cracked during the war of the titans, the goddess Nüwa, said to have molded human beings from mud, took it upon herself to repair the hole with 36,501 pieces of stone. At the end of her mission one stone was left unused. Refined into sentience in the goddess's fires, the superfluous stone spends much of its time lamenting the oddity of its fortune until one day a Buddhist monk and a Daoist priest decide to take it with them into the human world for experience and knowledge. In one early manuscript, it is the stone who begs them to do so when his mortal desires are stirred by their conversation about worldly glory. What follows is, so to speak, a story of reincarnation as Jia Baoyu makes his journey through mundane experience. Here the stone becomes Jia Baoyu, but it also metamorphoses into a piece of jade, found in Jia Baoyu's (a homophone for "false" or "fake precious jade") mouth at his birth and later worn around his neck as a protective talisman. From the beginning, the jade is intertwined with Jia Baoyu's fate and his sense of self through the use of puns and symbolism. Homophonous with "desire" (yu) in Chinese, the jade is also an emblem of the hero's libido. At one point, the enraged boy violently rejects the jade as the marker of his uniqueness as a male because none of his female cousins was born with a similar thing. As is evident in the later part of the novel, however, the jade's divine origin also suggests the potential for Jia Baoyu's ultimate self-transcendence.

As the narrative moves on to the next paragraph in Chapter 1, eons elapse. Having returned from its trip, the stone is once again found in the same spot where the priest and monk first picked it up, only now bearing a lengthy inscription. Unlike the public documents normally inscribed in this way, the text on the stone's body lacks "the authentication of a dynasty and date." Instead, the inscription "goes into considerable detail about its [the stone's] domestic life, youthful amours, and even the verses, mottoes, and riddles it had written," and concludes with a quatrain begging the reader to copy and transmit it.

To quote Anthony Yu, *The Stone* presents a rare case in traditional Chinese literature by "making its own fictionality a subject of sustained exploration and dramatization." Nowhere is this metafictional consciousness more explicitly manifest than at the beginning of the novel. Cao Xueqin ushers us into a labyrinth of words, texts, metaphors, and symbols, and invites us to ponder the multiplicity of their meanings. In an inquiry of unprecedented complexity into the genesis and history of his own novel, the author highlights several interrelated issues: desire, imagination, memory, the unstable boundaries between the realms of the divine and the human, and the individual's quest for knowledge, experience, redemption, and self-representation. Cao Xueqin presents his novel as the stone's account of its own experience and observations, but only occasionally does the narrator speak in the stone's voice or from a first-person perspective. Moreover, this autobiography of the stone is paradoxically linked to the impulse to make fiction, in turn fueled by human desire, as the stone is emblematically located at the foot of Greensickness Peak (following David Hawkes's rendering of the name, which in Chinese is roughly homophonous with "roots of desire"). The dialectics of true and false, reality and fiction, inform the structure and narrative of *The Stone* at every level. Jia Baoyu, for instance, has a counterpart in the world outside his residential garden named Zhen Baoyu ("real" or "authentic precious jade"). This dichotomy of true and false is not meant to be taken at face value: no one could be less genuine than Zhen Baoyu, whose entire life is oriented toward fame and vanity. In *The Stone*, name rarely corresponds to reality, and the truth can only be approached through paradox.

The divine origin and monumental permanence of the stone do not necessarily guarantee the stability of the text inscribed on its body. Cao Xueqin describes his novel as an unfolding process of constant revisions, involving input from reader–commentators turned editors, under multiple tentative titles. Cao Xueqin's account may well reflect the actual process of composition and transmission, but his inclusion of the convoluted textual history in Chapter 1 serves deeper purposes than acknowledging his friends' work. At least three tentative or alternative titles are deftly woven into the fabric of the narrative, each revealing an aspect or dimension of the novel that is too large and complex to be approached from any one angle. Chapter 5 presents Jia Baoyu's dream visit to the Land of Illusion, where he is introduced to *The Twelve Beauties of Jinling*, picture albums accompanied by riddles predicting the fate of the novel's main female characters. He is also allowed to read part of a manuscript entitled *The Dream of the Red Chamber* (rendered *A Dream of Golden Days* by Hawkes), but the messages coded into the texts elude him. The novel's self-reference yields no epiphany, and prescience cannot substitute for experience. Only toward the end of the novel, after Jia Baoyu has gone through all the events presaged in these texts, does he revisit the Land of Illusion, now the Paradise of Truth, where he realizes that all that has happened was preordained and irreversible. *A Mirror for the Romantic*, yet another title cited in Chapter 1, takes material form in Chapter 12 as a magic bronze mirror capable of evoking illusion while illuminating the truth about death. Jia Rui, the chief protagonist of this chapter, is a slave to his own desires, pathetically addicted to illusion, who dies of exhaustion after repeated sexual encounters with a seductive phantom. Speaking in its own defense, the mirror blames the young man for looking in the wrong side of the mirror and confusing the unreal with the real. Jia Rui dies because he did not read the mirror correctly.

Correlating with its multiple titles, the opening chapters of the novel are composed of discontinuous narratives with several tentative beginnings. With each new approach, Cao Xueqin introduces new characters to fulfill certain narrative and thematic functions. The Buddhist monk and the Daoist priest, who make periodic appearances throughout the work, serve as the agents of an overarching divine scheme by their active intervention in human affairs.

Jia Yucun ("false words preserved") and Leng Zixing ("cool your passion") are the internal narrators whose conversation about the history of the Jia family in Chapter 2 discloses partial or relative truths about what is recounted. Following a tentative examination of the prestige of the Jia family from both within and without, the narrator continues to ponder the issue of "where to begin": "Faced with so exuberant an abundance of material, what principle should your chronicler adopt to guide him in his selection of incidents to record?" The narrator then tells us that the problem has suddenly been solved by the appearance of Grannie Liu, "who turned up at the Rong mansion on the very day of which we are about to write." A distant poor relation of the Jia family, Grannie Liu will visit the family two more times and witness both its glory and its ultimate decline. The sophistication of *The Stone*'s narrative design and structural devices are unprecedented. The closest precedent may be southern plays like *Palace of Eternal Life* and *Peach Blossom Fan*, although there is little evidence of direct influence. As Patrick Hanan and others have shown, *The Stone* became a major source of inspiration for narrative innovations in the nineteenth century, despite the influx of modern European literature in that period.

Cao Xueqin's metafictional manipulation of text and narrative does not prevent him from rendering character and story with unusual psychological depth and convincing realism. Much has been said about Jia Baoyu – the superfluous stone, and by extension "superfluous man" – especially as perceived by those familiar with nineteenth-century Russian novels. Enjoying the blessing of family fortune and prestige, Jia Baoyu shows no interest in fulfilling the duties that come with such privilege; incapable of action with any meaningful consequence, he abandons himself to fancy, idiosyncrasy, and idleness. His life is made up of constant and difficult negotiations between desire and love, experience and knowledge, empathy and detachment, obedience and defiance, and self-indulgence and transcendence. Emphasizing his refusal to grow up, Martin Huang reads the novel as a reluctant *Bildungsroman*. Wai-yee Li, on the other hand, stresses the paradoxical passage of finding enlightenment through love. Either way, Jia Baoyu goes through a life's journey full of distractions and discontinuities, but it is a journey nonetheless.

The Stone's account of Jia Baoyu's life consists of several distinctive stages, each addressing a specific set of issues. The main part of the novel is set in Prospect Garden, which Jia Baoyu shares with his female cousins. Although the garden phase of Jia Baoyu's life seems to be a time of rapt enchantment, with unending poetry parties, banquets, and theater, *The Stone* seems concerned not so much with love as with its elusiveness and the obstructions that stand in its way. The garden is primarily a female domain, in stark contrast to the Jia family mansion, filled with lustful men incapable of empathy and sensitivity. Inside the garden, Jia Baoyu enjoys only the innocent company of his young female cousins, who in his eyes embody ethereal beauty and purity. According to him, girls are made of water, men of mud. Rarely, however, does he extend his admiration and compassion to older women and married women, who have been contaminated by their contact with men. This idealized feminine space gives Jia Baoyu a temporary shelter from approaching adulthood by offering an alternative mode of existence. Though not in love with the girls whom he idolizes, Jia Baoyu is more than willing to repay their kindly presence in his life with friendship and solicitude, knowing that with their inevitable departure his world will become hollow and meaningless. Rejecting the Confucian concept of honor that a scholar–official should die remonstrating the throne and a soldier should die fighting to protect it, Jia Baoyu describes to his maid his idea of a glorious death, mourned by all the girls from the garden: "Then your tears could combine to make a great river that my corpse could float away on, far, far away to some remote place that no bird has ever flown to." Jia Baoyu's narcissistic vision ceases to hold when experience awakens him to the fact that he is not the center of the universe, that everyone has their own destiny in love. After this revelation, Jia Baoyu begins to cherish above all others his relationship with Lin Daiyu, his predestined lover, who shows more understanding than anybody else for his unconventional behavior and contempt for an official career. Even as the two young lovers hardly move beyond the adolescent stage of longing, their relationship, plagued by miscommunications, intolerance, and insecure cravings for assurance, brings them less joy and fulfillment than agony and frustration. Never before in Chinese literature had love been subject to such close scrutiny. The subject was either mythologized, as in *Peony Pavilion*, or more often turned into fantasy in the melodramatic plots of talent–beauty fiction. In either case, obstacles to love invariably came from without and were finally overcome as the young hero conveniently redeemed his imprudent love affairs with success in the civil service examination. Appealing as such denouements may be, they leave little room for pondering the ramifications of love as they play out in individual and social life. Taking love as a subject for open exploration, *The Stone* provides its young lovers with occasion to face not merely each other but ultimately themselves. So conceived, love lies at the core of all the crucial issues of an individual's existence, as well as at that of the mutual understanding of lovers. Ironically, though separated by neither distance nor physical obstacles, Jia Baoyu and Lin Daiyu seldom succeed in expressing themselves or communicating their love. In his agony, Jia Baoyu often resorts to literature, theater, the *Zhuangzi*, and Chan (Zen) Buddhism for comfort, if not solutions. There are moments when he teeters on the brink of revelation, but then falls asleep or, with his usual absentmindedness, simply misses the opportunity.

The garden period of Jia Baoyu's life does not last forever. A scandal breaks out, outsiders intrude, the girls are either married off or forced out, and suffering and deaths ensue. The narrative takes on a eulogistic and nostalgic tone from early on, for Jia Baoyu's attempt to maintain his utopia in defiance of time and human fallibility is doomed from the start. It is noteworthy that Cao Xueqin does not lock his presentation of the garden into the polarity of purity versus pollution. Instead, a dialectical interplay of opposing forces is at work, here as elsewhere in the novel. As Yu Ying-shih has pointed out, the garden is built on the dirt from Jia She's old garden, a site of corruption and sexual transgression. Nor is Jia Baoyu entirely naive and innocent. Before moving into the garden in Chapter 23, he has already experienced both heterosexual and homosexual initiations through his relationships with Qin Keqing and her younger brother Qin Zhong. These episodes are presented in suggestive language through dream and euphemism. In the vagueness of his childish mind, Jia Baoyu has yet to fully comprehend his own experience. Essential to this part of the narrative is his dream visit to the Land of Illusion, the correlate in the mythic realm to the Prospect Garden. At the urgent supplication of Jia Baoyu's deceased ancestors, the goddess Disenchantment (reminiscent of Nüwa, who dismissed the unused stone) comes on a mission to enlighten him. She arranges for her "little sister" Qin Keqing to initiate him in the pleasures of the flesh, hoping that the experience will "shock the silliness out of him" so that he will escape its snares in the future and devote his mind instead to the teachings of Confucianism. Paradoxical as it may seem, this therapy through shock may contain certain wisdom: only by confronting and, if need be, embracing temptation can one master it and leave it behind.

Although modern readers often regard Jia Baoyu's submission to the Confucian order in the last forty chapters of *The Stone* as an outrageous betrayal of Cao Xueqin's intention, this development indicates no more than Jia Baoyu's return to his preordained route. Throughout the novel, Jia Baoyu never manages to put up meaningful resistance. The fall of the garden is followed by numerous tragic incidents, most of which occur during the period when he is reduced to a state of semi-idiocy by the disappearance of his jade talisman. Patriarchal authority is in control, and the Confucian program comes into play. In a melodramatic climax, Jia Baoyu is tricked into marrying Xue Baochai, chosen by his family as the appropriate wife for him, while the devastated Lin Daiyu, his true lover, dies the same night. As it turns out, Jia Baoyu's prolonged idiocy is a necessary precondition for achieving Buddhist enlightenment in that it allows him to endure all these sufferings and coercions with otherworldly indifference. Jia Baoyu disappears on his way home after succeeding in the civil service examinations, leaving his parents, relatives, and pregnant wife in a horror of disbelief. Then, one snowy day, Jia Baoyu makes his final appearance, bowing from afar in a crimson cape to bid farewell to his father before vanishing into the whiteness along with the Buddhist monk and the Daoist priest. In the end, Jia Baoyu's self-salvation is achieved at the expense of human compassion and sensibility, the defining qualities of his consciousness and experience. In reacquiring his spiritual essence, Jia Baoyu, as C. T. Hsia observes, has finally turned into a stone.

It remains a daunting challenge to explain why *The Stone* appeared in the middle of the eighteenth century. Though we are not so naive as to look for a culturally deterministic explanation, there is indeed something special about *The Stone* and its relationship with contemporary culture. As shown above, *The Scholars* also occupied a peripheral position in the cultural scene of the day, but that novel clearly derives from contemporary literati experience and intellectual ethos, and its engagement with Confucian ritualism was an important part of the driving force for its composition. *The Story of the Stone* is as detached as it is marginal; it does not involve much of the philosophical and literary discourse of the time, and its narrative contains few contemporary references. This is not to say that Cao Xueqin did not benefit from contemporary stimuli and the general cultural environment. Yet he evidently cast his eyes far beyond his immediate surroundings, and, perhaps more importantly, he was largely successful in transforming his sources – from the overloaded concepts of passion and genuineness to the form of the novel as he received it – into something new and different. In this sense, Cao Xueqin owes less to his time than his time owes to him. By creating his own cultural and intellectual universe in *The Story of the Stone*, he set the standard by which the accomplishments of the epoch are to be measured.

Other literati novels

The following novels, composed between 1750 and 1780, also merit special attention: Li Baichuan's (ca 1721–1771) *Traces of an Immortal in the Green Wilds* (*Lüye xianzong*), Li Lüyuan's (1707–1790) *Lamp at the Crossroads* (*Qilu deng*), and Xia Jingqu's (1705–1787) *An Old Rustic's Humble Words* (*Yesou puyan*). These authors did not influence one another, nor did their novels subscribe to a common mode of representation, as each in its own way straddles indulgence and irony, fantasy and reality. What holds these works together is their common concern with the fate of literati culture and the possible roles open to literati in family, local society, officialdom, and the empire at large. Sometimes the author's fancy takes us on a cursory flight beyond the empire, into either *Ouluoba* (Europe) or into the land of the supernatural, whether in search of a colonial utopia or an individual escape and salvation. The narrative of these adventures attests to the enormous expansion of the contemporary geopolitical imagination, as well as demonstrating the extension of the novel into an indefinite, all-inclusive form of writing, in direct proportion to the broadened horizons of literati learning as delineated by the evidential scholarship of the time. No other literary genre came close to the vernacular novel in registering the orientation and expansion of literati imagination and aspiration in the Qianlong era.

Li Baichuan, an impoverished man of letters who had little luck in whatever venture he undertook, projected an alternative vision for himself in *Traces of an Immortal in the Green Wilds*. Disillusioned with politics and official institutions, and overwhelmed by the death of his friend and mentor, the protagonist of the novel, Leng Yubing, embarks on his lonely journey in search of Daoist immortality. The author does not dispense with worldly concerns entirely: his hero's command of supernatural forces allows him to intervene in human affairs and court politics in ways otherwise impossible. As the novel unfolds, the author becomes increasingly fascinated by Daoist magic and the art of longevity, dwelling in detail upon the fantasy of the immortal land and citing all manner of esoteric texts. A third of the way into the novel, Leng Yubing ("Colder than Ice") encounters his double, Wen Ruyu ("Warm as Jade"), who is hopelessly caught in the world of red dust (the polarization suggested by the two names recalls Zhang Zhupo's comments on *The Plum in the Golden Vase* as a book about cold and heat). No two characters could be so diametrically opposed in mentality and behavior as these: the higher Leng Yubing ascends in his quest for Daoist purity and transcendence, the deeper his counterpart sinks in the all too human realm of insatiable greed and desire. Yet these characters complement each other in revealing the elusive truth about Daoist transcendence. Wen Ruyu does not succeed in joining Leng Yubing until the end of the novel, and his very existence not only suggests the need for Daoist redemption but also constitutes the necessary precondition for it: who is Wen Ruyu if not the accumulation of all that Leng Yubing cleanses himself of? In a broader sense, these two characters also illustrate the intriguing relationship between two types of novel. The Daoist story aims at doing away with *The Plum in the Golden Vase*'s world of human desire and folly, but it obviously needs the latter to define its vision, to measure its success, and to sustain a narrative in constant danger of being suspended by the eternal bliss of the Daoist utopia.

The experience that Wen Ruyu undergoes is amplified in *Lamp at the Crossroads* (hereafter *Lamp*) with convincing detail, psychological depth, and heavy doses of didacticism. Li Lüyuan began to compose his novel at forty-two, but did not complete it until 1777 when he retired from his official career at the age of seventy. The novel circulated in manuscript form for many years, and was printed in limited quantities in the 1920s and 1930s. A collated and annotated edition became available to general readers only in 1980. Critics embraced this work with enthusiasm, hailing it as one of the most distinguished master-pieces of literary realism produced in Ming–Qing China. Historians have been tempted to use its descriptions to reconstruct the customs and patterns of social lives of the mid-Qianlong period. Few traditional novels are compa-rable to *Lamp* in offering a sweeping array of local society: gentry, officials, clerks, doctors, diviners, private tutors, traveling actors, peddlers, and sundry vagrants. The novel is primarily concerned with the changing fortunes of the local gentry, its characters often showing astonishment when illustrious families decline into obscurity as they fail to produce degree and office holders over a short span of one or two generations. Focusing on the personal jour-ney of Tan Shaowen, a prodigal son reminiscent of Wen Ruyu, the author of *Lamp at the Crossroads* addresses, in his own way, the crisis of the literati's self-reproduction as perceived by many of his contemporaries. Li Lüyuan is at his best in portraying Tan Shaowen's addiction to gambling, his futile resis-tance to temptation, and the overwhelming remorse and guilt he endures as a consequence. To capture the recurring patterns of Tan Shaowen's strug-gles, the narrative develops patterns of repetition and variation: after every near-death experience – an attempted suicide, or a reckless flight to dodge a creditor that reduces him to a homeless beggar – he enjoys a brief period of sanity, only to be lured back again to the gambling table as if bound by an unshakable spell. Although the novel concludes with a happy ending, readers go away impressed by its compelling account of the young man's hopeless descent into the abyss of darkness.

Lamp is a Confucian novel with an unmistakable commitment to narrative specificity and largely uncompromised verisimilitude. Xia Jingqu's *An Old Rus-tic's Humble Words*, a 154-chapter tome completed in 1779, goes much further to glorify Confucianism, projecting the image of a neo-Confucian superman with triumphal and dreary pomposity. Xia's understanding of neo-Confucianism, the state orthodoxy of the Qing, consists of two major elements: belief in self-cultivation, with the objective of achieving the ideal of a sage-king, and belief in the absolute necessity of cleansing the world of Buddhism and other heterodoxies. To animate such a majestic vision through narrative, Xia drastically rewrites earlier romances of heroic adventures and military exploits. Like the itinerant heroes of *Water Margin*, Wen Suchen is a constant traveler on a solitary campaign to correct wrongs and eliminate heresies throughout the empire. Wen is notably different from the typical hero of the literati novel in that he is endowed not merely with intelligence and political ingenuity, but also with physical prowess and an unparalleled command of the martial arts. Equally impressive is his enormous knowledge of military strategy, physiognomy, divination, medicine, astronomy, mathematics, the art of exorcism, and other kinds of magic. The scope of Wen's adventures mirrors the massive expansion of the horizon of literati learning beyond the conventional Confucian curriculum. Despite the government's failure to absorb the literati into public service, Xia Jingqu finds his own way of integrating individual aspiration into the imperial enterprise. Like the author himself, Wen Suchen never manages to acquire a higher degree than that of licentiate and has no formal affiliation with official institutions, but he accomplishes what the government fails in, and his achievements eventually win the recognition of two consecutive rulers and draw him close to the center of power. In the final part of the novel, Wen Suchen's empire-building fantasy reaches an even higher level, when we are told that his followers have reached Europe and converted its population into faithful Confucians. The success of such an undertaking is attributed to the sheer persuasive force of Confucian teaching, since "no blood was shed." In making this enormous leap of the imagination, *Humble Words* may have had an antecedent in *The Sequel to Water Margin* – a Ming loyalist's utopian novel about an overseas Confucian kingdom in what is now Thailand, founded by the survivors of Song Jiang's outlaw band. However, *Humble Words* puts its predecessor to shame by evoking a much grander vision of the Confucian empire on a global scale and also by emphasizing the peaceful nature of this massive conversion. Ironically, the novel was first published in the 1880s, long after the Western powers had brought the Qing empire to its knees with their military muscle.

The irony comes not merely from the contrast between *Humble Words* and the historical circumstances in which it was received; it ultimately arises from within the novel, where fantasy is presented as such, and euphoria often coexists with a troubled sense of foolishness. The final section of Wen

Suchen's utopian pursuits is framed by two intertwined sequences of theatrical performance and dreams that sum up the novel and retrospectively demand to be perceived as doing so. Although Xia Jingqu is clearly aware of the fictionality, even absurdity, of his narrative, he is nevertheless unable to incorporate his occasional forays of wit into a sustained pattern of self-reflection, let alone to question the grounds for his own views and values. This is only one of the areas in which he diverges from Wu Jingzi and Cao Xueqin.

Humble Words is not alone in its concern with the issue of empire. The vast expansion of territory in the Qianlong reign brought about an urgent problem of management. By the end of the eighteenth century, the empire was plagued by internal turmoil: the armed resistance of the Miao people against Qing rule was followed by the uprising of a religious sect called the White Lotus. These events constitute the main subjects of The History of the Bookworm (Yinshi), arguably the longest novel ever written in classical Chinese. Its author, Tu Shen (1744–1801), took part in the crackdown on the Miao rebellion in his capacity as an official in Guangdong and Yunnan, respectively the southern and southwestern frontiers of the empire. Unlike late Ming and early Qing novels dealing with contemporary political and military affairs, The Bookworm is abstruse in style and difficult to read; contemporary references are recast in the guise of shenmo (gods and devils) narrative and further obscured by the author's fascination with magic, supernatural phenomena, and exotic customs. Amid the ongoing crises, Tu Shen could hardly afford to indulge in Xia Jingqu's luxury of taking care of the hearts and minds of "uncivilized" people. Bloody military conquests, aided by magic and mysterious weapons, are recurring events in this novel. As in Humble Words, Europeans make an appearance. Instead of coming from afar to celebrate the hundredth birthday of Wen Suchen's sagely mother, however, the European characters are portrayed as wandering magicians capable of assisting both the rebels and the government. Inevitably, their presence becomes associated with uncertainty and suspicion, if not an immediate threat to the empire. The Bookworm went to print in 1799. One later edition reappeared under the title of New Humble Words (Xin yesou puyan), while Humble Words itself was rewritten in late Qing sequels, fueling political utopianism and science fantasy.

Unlike the literati novelists discussed earlier, Tu Shen seems to have been personally involved in the publication of his novel. Although the 1799 edition of The Bookworm bears only his studio name, it includes his portrait along with those of the printers, publishers, and characters of the novel. Also included are sundry erudite annotations, possibly written by the author himself, under twenty different names. Li Ruzhen (1763–1830), another literati novelist, personally supervised the publication of his own work, *Flowers in the Mirror* (*Jinghua yuan*, hereafter *Flowers*), in 1818. He also had two revised versions published in 1821 and 1828. Evidently, the literati novelists of the time not only cared about authorship but also extended that concern into the realm of book production. Given the nature of the concerns addressed in *The Bookworm* and *Flowers*, as well as their authors' wholehearted immersion in literati learning, getting into print would do little to improve their accessibility beyond the privileged cultural elite. Li Ruzhen did not complete his novel until 1815, but its composition may be traced to the final years of the Qianlong reign. In many ways, *Flowers* can be regarded as the last of the major literati novels written in this period, as well as the most exquisite manifestation in vernacular literature of literati learning and interests.

Set in the Tang dynasty, *Flowers* frames its narrative around the protagonists' peregrinations through the empire. The first half of the novel follows Tang Ao, a disillusioned candidate in the civil service examinations, as he travels overseas to the land of the immortals. The narrative focuses not on this character but on the remote, fantastic kingdoms he passes through. In each place, Tang Ao's acute observation of the folly of human customs and mores as he travels through the Kingdoms of Split-Tongues, Blackened-Teeth, Excellent Wisdom, Women, Dwarves, and Giants serves as derisive commentary on his home country. Even the Kingdom of Gentlemen is not immune from the hypocrisy and vanity that bedevil the literati of the Central Kingdom. This part of the novel teems with caricatures and witty remarks that often prompt comparison with *Gulliver's Travels*, although Li Ruzhen's satire is more lighthearted and much less acerbic.

As the narrative unfolds, Li Ruzhen further complicates the theme of empire as the male protagonists dedicate themselves to overthrowing Empress Wu and restoring the Tang royal house to the throne. This thematic frame becomes ironically misplaced in the remainder of the work, which deals almost exclusively with the concerns of female characters. These are the earthly incarnations of a hundred flower-fairies banished from heaven, who survive countless ordeals to reunite at last in the Central Kingdom to answer a call for a special examination decreed by Empress Wu. Unlike the civil service examinations undertaken in the Tang dynasty or in Li Ruzhen's own time, this fictional examination allows the female candidates to display their skills not only in literature but also in calligraphy, painting, chess, music, medicine, physiognomy, and astrology, among other subjects. Out of the endless games of competition preceding the examination and the extended post-examination revelry emerges an essentially feminine space from which the male characters are conspicuously excluded.

The dominant presence of young female talents in the second half of *Flowers* brings into sharp focus literati concerns with gender, learning, cultivation, and self-representation, the frequent subject matter of contemporary biographies, novels, dramas, poetry, and prose. Along with his fellow literati, Li Ruzhen shows a genuine appreciation for talented women as well as sympathy for their plight; in this way, the design of his novel bears unmistakable traces of *The Stone*'s influence. Li Ruzhen's representation of these female characters fulfills other functions as well. In this novel we encounter what Stephen Roddy has dubbed the feminization of literati knowledge, as philological musings and scholarly discourses are transported into the realm of gentlewomen and become the primary source for their pastimes. The success of these gifted women in examinations leads to no official appointments or public service, nor does their learning serve any other sociopolitical purpose. One recurrent theme in mid-Qing novels is criticism of scholarship insofar as it has been institutionalized into the means for mere personal gain. The four amateur artists who appear at the end of *The Scholars* are far removed from the ladder of social mobility, indicating Wu Jingzi's vision of what it takes to restore genuineness to the ideal of literati culture. Like Wu, Li Ruzhen needs the intervention of others – and in this case, female characters – to rescue literati learning and cultivation from contamination and irony. What his novel presents is not merely political criticism disguised as utopian vision, for its narrative foray into the female domain aptly captures one important aspect of the linguistic scholarship of the time: as the daughters of the gentry families amuse themselves with endless word games and dabble in an immense range of scholarly minutiae, they exhibit both the allure and the self-absorption of literati culture with disarming wit and charm.

Li Ruzhen's self-indulgence was a singular phenomenon in a time of headlong change. New trends in fiction production had already manifested themselves in the final years of the Qianlong reign. Commercial publishing had grown so prolific that its role in shaping the cultural landscape of the day could no longer be ignored. Alongside bookselling and book-lending, the blooming of various forms of urban entertainment also offered additional impetus for the production and consumption of vernacular fiction. Nourished by popular storytelling as practiced in Beijing, Yangzhou, and other cities, martial arts fiction found its way into the print market. The publication of the Cheng–Gao edition of *The Story of the Stone* in 1791 and 1792 sparked another wave of fiction sequels more than a century after the previous one had ebbed. Despite their elitism, many authors showed an unmistakable interest in engaging the expanded and increasingly diversified audience, including female readers from gentry families. Just as striking is the geographical expansion of the literary market, as Guangzhou, a thriving southern port, emerged on the map as a new site for fiction production.

Literati plays and popular regional theaters

The mid-Qing theater scene was shaped by two concurrent and mutually reinforcing changes: the decline of the literati's influence over theater culture and the rise of multiple genres of local opera. These were major events at the time, but they were even more important for their long-term impact on the structural transformation of Chinese culture. The literati dramatists who lived at the end of this period would have seen little to remind them of the world into which their early Qing predecessors had been born: debates among the literati had become much less consequential, and the relations between the center and the periphery had been redefined.

The first two decades of the eighteenth century saw the waning of a glorious age in Chinese theater with the death of Hong Sheng in 1704 and Kong Shangren in 1718. A sluggish period followed, lasting well into the 1740s. The new generation of playwrights emerging in the late 1740s and the 1750s by and large seemed to allow neo-Confucian didacticism to dictate the course of their dramatic imagination. In the years that followed, literati dramatists were forced to negotiate with this dominant moralistic trend on the one hand, and, on the other, to cope with the achievements of dramatic literature in the previous two hundred years, all of which threatened to overshadow them. These concerns were compounded by a perhaps more urgent question: how should one take account of the regional and urban cultures thriving beyond their zone of influence?

This last challenge had serious historical ramifications. Not every literati dramatist of the time responded to it, and those who did often responded poorly, either scorning the bustling regional operas or choosing to ignore them altogether. This response only increased these dramatists' irrelevance to contemporary theater culture. Throughout the mid-Qing period, literati would continue to enjoy the performance of the Kun-style opera while writing and reading dramatic texts – especially southern plays composed primarily in the music mode of the Kun style – but their role in shaping the theater scene was gradually and irreversibly diminishing. The effect of this change is all the more noticeable in light of the indisputable authority the literati once enjoyed in the Kun style. Indeed, due in large part to their championship,

Kun-style opera, which had originated in the Suzhou region in the early sixteenth century, had gradually become a national phenomenon, celebrated by the cultural elite, court officials, merchants, and other urban residents. It was admired for its exquisite lyrics, dramaturgy, music, and dance. Central to the history of the eighteenth-century theater was, however, a steady decline in the popularity of Kun-style opera and the growing appeal of a variety of local operas. In the last decade of the eighteenth century, the rise of Peking opera, a new form that combined elements from several of these regional genres, further marginalized the Kun-style theater. The growth of regional opera was fueled by the boom in commercial theaters and the professional troupes that had come to play a quintessential role in the theater culture of the time. Unlike the troupes kept by elite families, these were often based in a city or a town and toured in the nearby area; their repertoire catered to the needs of the local audience, and could thus reflect a broad range of popular taste.

As Kun-style opera became decentralized, literati playwrights retreated into the sphere of the written text. This development helps to account for the further blurring of the distinction between southern and northern plays during this era, as well as shedding light on the conspicuous lyricism characteristic of both styles. Although the regional operas that mushroomed during this period occasionally made use of scripts, and although Peking opera developed a large print repertoire in later years, none of these produced dramatic texts that came close to the southern and northern plays in sophistication. In this regard, the end of the mid-Qing era marks the end of traditional dramatic literature in imperial times.

We can easily trace the trajectory of literati playwriting up to the 1840s using extant dramatic texts, but a comprehensive history of the regional operas of the same period has yet to be written, in part because they existed primarily in performance and lay outside the sphere of literati culture. Modern scholars have identified over three hundred genres of regional theater, more than half of which can be dated back to the mid-Qing era, if not earlier. The enormous gaps of information about regional theater in the eighteenth century can to a certain extent be filled in by extrapolating from modern Chinese theater. For example, despite the ruptures and changes of the past three centuries, a number of salient characteristics of Qing dynasty regional opera remain deeply embedded in contemporary society. Modern cultural elites have long sought to create new regional and national theaters by drawing on this abundant and extraordinarily diverse Qing legacy. Often politically as well as culturally motivated, they resort to all available institutional means and modern technologies in their ongoing endeavor to contain or rechannel the energy of the different regional theaters.

Southern and northern plays

When a mid-Qing man of letters composed a northern or a southern play, he was working from an established literary form. The northern play has a long history dating back to the Jin and Yuan, but the performance of traditional northern plays had largely come to an end by the early seventeenth century. The majority of southern plays adopted the musical mode of Kun-style opera, which was still alive during the mid-Qing, particularly in Jiangnan, where literati playwrights were sometimes amateur performers as well. Not many playwrights could claim expert command of Kun-style music, however, and even fewer bothered with the technical details necessary to stage their work. In most cases, their texts could not be performed unless they were edited or adapted by musicians – a kind of intervention that the authors themselves often protested.

Chapter 2 of this volume has already introduced the rise of southern plays beginning in the sixteenth century. As far as literary form is concerned, southern and northern plays of course differ in many ways, but it should be pointed out that their distinctions had become less obvious by the second half of the sixteenth century, when Xu Wei (1521–1593) and Liang Chenyu (ca 1521–ca 1594) introduced a new style of northern play. These two southerners were doing what was necessary to keep the northern play alive onstage by adding southern tunes to the repertoire. They also initiated changes that would more directly affect the northern play as a literary genre: instead of the standard four-act format, the plays now varied in length between one and ten acts; the aria lyric also became more important within the play as singing ceased to be limited to only one role type, which was another instance of the southern play's influence. This reformed genre was clearly more flexible in accommodating innovation; in a few extreme cases, it became difficult to distinguish from the southern play proper.

As a literary genre with a long and celebrated tradition, the southern play retained much of its appeal to literati playwrights through most of the mid-Qing era. According to Guo Yingde's statistics, over 187 dramatists produced more than 311 southern plays between 1719 and 1820; to this list must be added fifty-five works by anonymous authors. Fewer than 200 of these, however, have survived to the present day. Impressive in quantity, these mid-Qing southern plays are modest in length and scope as compared with their predecessors in the late Ming and early Qing. The average length of each work ranges from twenty to thirty-nine scenes, while plays of fewer than twenty scenes become much more common. Few mid-Qing playwrights spent their energies composing works of the gigantic proportions of *Peony Pavilion*, *Palace of Eternal Life*, and *Peach Blossom Fan*. Interestingly, reduction in size and scale was accompanied by a decline in productivity: few authors produced more than one play. This suggests that during this period playwriting became a popular casual pursuit of many literati, requiring neither great exertion nor strong commitment.

Nevertheless, the few who did commit themselves to writing plays were often serious, and considered themselves to be on a mission. Indeed, neo-Confucian influence is reflected more pervasively in drama than in any other literary genre of this period. Xia Lun (1680–1752?) best represents this moralistic trend in the southern play. A native of Hangzhou, Xia Lun repeatedly failed the district-level examination and later was given the post of county magistrate, only to resign from public life in 1736 out of frustration from dealing with corrupt local *yamen* (bureaucratic offices). In retirement he concentrated on reading and writing, composing five southern plays from 1744 to 1749. Underlying his work is a coherent design manifesting the primary Confucian virtues of loyalty, filial piety, female chastity, and righteousness. In 1752, he added another play to dramatize the binding power of brotherly love, so that his six works as a whole present a comprehensive illustration of the five basic human relationships (father–son, ruler–subject, husband–wife, elder brother–younger brother, friend–friend) sacred to Confucian social ethics. A strong moralistic thrust was not unprecedented in dramatic literature, as is seen in the famous Ming example of *All Five Moral Relationships Fulfilled*, a southern play attributed to the famous neo-Confucian scholar and statesman Qiu Jun (1421–1495).

Under the dominant influence of the ethical mode of writing, romance gives way to high-minded morality plays, and young male and female lovers yield to hoary Confucian sages. The dramatists of the mid-Qing often drew their protagonists from biographies in the official histories, fleshing out sketchy historical accounts with their own imaginations. Xia Lun's *Flawless Jade* (*Wuxia bi*) takes as its hero Tie Xuan, minister of war to the Jianwen Emperor, whose unflinching loyalty is well documented in the *Ming History*. Xia Lun's account of Tie Xuan holding up the spirit tablet of the Ming founder atop the city wall to demoralize the rebel troops so as to raise the siege, however, is entirely imagined. As is often the case in these morality plays, Tie Xuan's heroic deed is not immune to alternative readings. Here, the rebel turns out to be none other than Prince Yan, who later deposed the ill-fated Jianwen

Emperor and ruled over the empire for twenty-two years as the Yongle Emperor.

Just as the dramatic literature of this period often diverged from romance, it also significantly reduced the comic scenes and language so abundant in southern plays. The clown or fool figures prominently in the earliest extant southern plays preserved in *The Grand Encyclopedia of the Yongle Era*, such as *Top Graduate Zhang Xie (Zhang Xie zhuangyuan)*, a typical comedy about the ungrateful examination candidate. The preponderance of scenes featuring burlesque and buffoonery in these texts is all the more significant given the fact that the printed form of a play tended to underrepresent the number of farcical scenes in actual performance, since these were often improvised or drawn from the existing repertoire. Moreover, the ironic comments and dialogue, and the laughter that comes with them, permeate so deeply a late Ming romance like *Peony Pavilion* that to delete them would dispense with a good part of the irony and ambiguity essential to Tang Xianzu's rendering of the love story. To get a sense of the typical morality play of the mid-Qing era, one must imagine a traditional southern play that has lost its romance and humor – not an appealing prospect.

Not all the southern plays that emerged in this period fall into the above category. Shen Qifeng (1741–1802), for instance, was a playwright whose works have been commended by the modern scholar Wu Mei for their ingenious handling of stage action and dialogue. Shen's talents are perhaps best captured in *The Monkey that Returns Favors (Baoen yuan)*, a comedy of errors with grim, though not irreversible, consequences. The play is based on a story in Hong Pian's *Qingpingshan tang huaben* (1550s) and its revised version in Feng Menglong's collection *Constant Words to Awaken the World*, but by the mid-Qing period numerous variations of the plot had appeared in southern plays, precious scrolls, string ballads, and local operas. To the growing lore surrounding this story, Shen Qifeng added two clowns and wrote scenes including all sorts of jesting. As is often the case in a southern play, dialogue involving clowns or fools (and sometimes other roles as well) is presented in Suzhou dialect – a phenomenon that can be dated back to *Top Graduate Zhang Xie*, if not earlier. In an age of burgeoning regional theaters, Shen Qifeng's southern plays remind us of how Kun-style opera could be rejuvenated by harking back to its local origins.

Over the preceding two centuries, romance had become so entrenched in the southern play style that to do away with romance threatened to suspend the genre altogether. This obviously did not happen in the mid-Qing era, despite the prevailing moral sensibility and intense commitment to didacticism in its dramatic literature. *Peony Pavilion* continued to cast its magic spell by inspiring such romance writers as Zhang Jian (1681–1763), Qian Weiqiao (1739–1806), and Xu Xi (1732–1807). New developments were also under way, the most noticeable being the author's tendency to write himself into the romance as its hero. Xu Xi's *The Destiny of the Mirror Light (Jingguang yuan)*, for instance, is presumably autobiographical, recounting a student's unrequited love for an evasive nun turned courtesan. The hero's name is Yu Xi – Xu Xi with the radical removed from each of the two characters. In his note on the play, Xu Xi made clear that he had written it to vent his personal grief.

This autobiographical mode is not confined to romances and southern plays. As noted earlier, vernacular novels of the same period tend to address the literati's concerns, often with autobiographical touches. Xu Xi went farther in this direction with his northern plays, openly using himself as the protagonist. He produced more than eighteen single-act plays, some dealing with religious issues in the allegorical mode, others addressing everyday concerns. These are works with evident humor, tempering religious revelations with bathos, and in this way glossing over some of the apparent contradictions in theme. Equally impressive is the range of variation in the author–protagonist's tone, as it alternates between cynical and lyrical, and between self-mockery and self-indulgence. In *Dealing with Ghosts (Chougui)*, the character Xu Xi, who practices medicine in his hometown, finds himself haunted by the ghosts of his former patients. A Buddhist monk comes to his rescue; explaining to the ghosts that death is preordained, he shields Xu Xi from any responsibility for their untimely demise. In the end, both the doctor and his dead patients are happily converted to Buddhism, though for different reasons. In *Offering Sacrifices to Fallen Teeth (Jiya)*, Xu Xi dramatizes a sacrifice to his own lost teeth on his sixtieth birthday. Ironically, his servant mistakes a dog's teeth for his. Instead of correcting the mistake, Xu Xi ends up honoring both: after all, dogs and human beings use their teeth in the same way. His other works, such as *Mourning My Younger Brother Xingcan (Ku Xingcan di)* and *Mourning the Fallen Flowers (Daohua)*, read like eulogies because of their poetic rhythm and flamboyant language. This type of drama verges on lyric poetry, so it comes as no surprise that Xu Xi won praises from contemporary poets, including Shen Deqian and Yuan Mei. His collection of playlets, published in the Qianlong years, bears the title *Short Plays to Express My Intent (Xiexin zaju)*, which echoes the classical definition of lyric poetry. The humor Yuan Mei describes as "natural wit" is evident throughout this volume.

Xu Xi's contemporary Yang Chaoguan (1712–1791) produced thirty-two one-act northern plays, anthologized in *Short Plays from the Hall of Singing in the*

Wind (*Yinfengge zaju*). Like Xu Xi, Yang Chaoguan was closely associated with Yuan Mei, despite evident differences of personality and religious orientation, and the latter wrote his biography, celebrating his achievements as a local official as well as their friendship. Yang was a poet at heart: short plays offered him another opportunity to experiment with lyric poetry. His playlets are usually witty, even whimsical, combining verbal spice with humor; some are ornate, filled with prolonged scenic description and poetic musing. Yang often uses poets of the past as the subject of his work, dwelling on their character and eccentricity as they protest in vain against the injustice or absurdity of the world. Yang's anachronistic use of historical and literary references sets these plays apart from what we usually think of as historical drama.

The short play as a literary form goes back to Xu Wei, a late Ming master of poetry, painting, and northern drama, but it was not until the eighteenth century that it joined the mainstream of dramatic literature. Many playwrights of the time thrived on this form, and some of their works featured the poets of the past. The natural affinity between the lyric-like brevity of the form (especially in the case of the one-act play) and the subject (poets) perhaps accounts for the lyrical trend in the mid-Qing dramatic imagination. Gui Fu (1736?–1805?), for instance, composed four playlets in his later years, portraying such poets of the Tang and Song as Bai Juyi, Li He, Su Shi, and Lu You. He gave these works a general title, *The Sequels to Four Cries of the Gibbon*, which built on the work of Xu Wei. Like his contemporary playwrights, Gui Fu was fully aware of the origins and history of this dramatic form. He also showed familiarity with Xu Wei's works by using the poets of the past as the protagonists of his own plays. For most dramatists of the mid-Qing period, however, Xu Wei was perhaps too bold and controversial to be a desirable model. Along with the dramatic form that he initiated, they inherited his eccentricity to a certain extent, but his iconoclasm survived only in vestigial form, as mere gesture.

Reinterpreting Tang Xianzu's legacy

Even as they turned their hand to the ethical mode, the literati authors of the mid-Qing era could hardly ignore the tradition of late Ming dramatic literature. To some extent, the orientation of the southern play in this period can be gauged from the literati attitude toward Tang Xianzu, the most influential of the late Ming dramatists, known for his creation of plays called *Linchuan's Four Dreams*, the most significant of which is *Peony Pavilion*. Over a century after Tang Xianzu's death, playwrights still struggled to emerge from under his shadow. More often than not, their interpretations of Tang's legacy take a conservative tone, most noticeably in their effort to contain the "cult of passion" Tang Xianzu so forcefully articulated in his preface to *Peony Pavilion*. Instead of endorsing the transcendent power of passion or love as the essence of human existence, these playwrights often sought to utilize passion in the service of Confucian ethics, emphasizing its indispensable role in sustaining all human relationships. This tendency can be traced to the strategic justification of passion or love in the statements and literary work of Feng Menglong and other late Ming writers. In the mid-Qing era it found its most potent expression in the dramatic form, where love borders on a kind of moral fanaticism. Whereas *Peony Pavilion* celebrates love as a vital human force capable of transcending death and social distinctions, in these mid-Qing works love manifests itself in a moral heroism characterized by emotional intensity and religious zeal. An act of self-sacrifice requires determination and passion, but passion so represented is no longer a liberating force; instead, it becomes a necessary psychological precondition for an absolute commitment to Confucian moral obligations, and ultimately serves only to perpetuate the hierarchy of social relationships. Carrying this line of thought to its logical extreme, some playwrights abandoned the claim to passion altogether and openly dismissed Tang Xianzu's works for their licentiousness and extravagance. Their dogmatic stance and didactic approach are the most telling evidence of the extent to which neo-Confucian orthodoxy had penetrated the literary discourse.

Not all of the writers and readers of this period shared this view of Tang Xianzu and his *Linchuan's Four Dreams*. Throughout the mid-Qing era, *Peony Pavilion* was often reprinted and staged (though not always in its entirety), despite repeated official prohibition. The emotional response it provoked was often as intense as when the play first appeared in the late sixteenth century. Again, as discussed in Chapter 2 of this volume, the publication and performance of *Peony Pavilion* in the late Ming were sensational events. Many young women were overcome by emotion when they read the text, and an actress even died onstage while performing the role of Du Liniang, the heroine who pines away with unrequited love. In addition, there were a number of accounts of a woman named Xiaoqing, who is said to have replicated in her own life all the major motifs of Du Liniang's story except that of the resurrection, in which Du returns to the human world to reunite with her lover. Thus there emerged around *Peony Pavilion* a wide discourse of anecdotes, comments, colophons, prefaces, poems, and letters, which fed on one another and created a large repository of sources from which new plays and fiction drew material.

The bloody dynastic transition of the mid-seventeenth century seems to have only temporarily subdued the public craze for *Peony Pavilion*. Well into the mid-Qing, literati playwrights like Zhang Jian, Gu Sen, and Qian Weiqiao could not articulate their literary agenda without reference to Tang Xianzu. They either quoted or paraphrased him in the prefaces to their plays, which were also modeled upon his works. As new sequels to or imitations of Tang's plays continued to emerge, so did commentaries and annotated editions of *Peony Pavilion*. In 1694, Wu Wushan published his *Three Wives' Commentary on Peony Pavilion* (*Sanfu heping Mudan ting Huanhun ji*). Another commentary, attributed to Cheng Qiong (d. 1722?) and her husband Wu Zhensheng (1695–1769), was printed in the 1720s or 1730s and reprinted several times. Cheng Qiong had obviously read the *Three Wives' Commentary*, and shared some of its views, but her commentary is different for at least two reasons. First, it is encyclopedic in scope and length (over 300,000 characters), including detailed and often digressive annotations on virtually every subject, however briefly mentioned in the play. According to Cheng Qiong, her commentary was meant to fuel discussions of the play among like-minded female aficionados. Second, it is relentlessly comic, and shows an obsession with an erotic reading of the play. Whereas the three wives are more or less reticent on such subjects, Cheng relentlessly traces the play to its "roots" in sexuality and carnal love. Her annotations of each act always begin with a persistent identification of certain images and metaphors as sexual in nature – "the male and female roots." In her preface, Cheng reveals the origins of her exegeses. Wu Yueshi, a member of her husband's lineage going back to the late Ming, invited renowned literati to expound the deep meanings of *Peony Pavilion* to the actors and actresses of his family troupe. Their interpretations were orally transmitted down through the generations to Wu Zhensheng, who then inspired Cheng Qiong to embark on her gigantic project. Regardless of the reliability of this claim, we cannot miss in Cheng's commentaries the carnivalesque tone and iconoclastic tendency characteristic of late Ming literary culture. Indeed, this commentary shows that, despite the changes in the intellectual and cultural climate in the early and mid-Qing, discursive communities continued to serve as a breeding ground for the (re)production, transmission, and consumption of *Peony Pavilion* lore. That this annotated edition was published and reprinted during the Yongzheng and Qianlong reigns shows the persistent influence of late Ming discourse in an era conventionally known for its cultural conservatism. It is noteworthy that Cheng Qiong's husband, Wu Zhensheng, was himself a playwright. He wrote thirteen southern plays, mostly dealing with historical figures and events, although their concerns often lay elsewhere. In a play entitled *The Traveling Earthly Immortal* (*Dixing xian*), he reintroduces the motif of resurrection and adds idiosyncratic twists, investing much of his interest in the Daoist art of love, portraying it as tantric magic capable of reviving the dead.

Jiang Shiquan and his *Dreams of Linchuan*

The playwrights of the early eighteenth century also lived under the shadow of the formidable legacy left behind by Kong Shangren. What lay at stake, however, went well beyond Kong himself, for, in composing *Peach Blossom Fan*, he had tapped into Tang Xianzu's *Peony Pavilion*. Indeed, essential to Kong's play is a doomed attempt to reenact Du Liniang's role in a time of historical crisis that precluded the possibility of a happy reunion. With this final stroke, Kong undoes the masterpiece he has so admiringly embraced. This is his way of engaging *Peony Pavilion*, and he passes it on as part of his legacy. The question then becomes, how is one to come to terms with the incomparable Tang Xianzu after Kong Shangren's incorporation of his work in the *Peach Blossom Fan*? For Jiang Shiquan (1725–1785), the answer is to put Tang Xianzu himself onstage, which he does in his *Dreams of Linchuan* (*Linchuan meng*). This play pays tribute to the master of the past while registering the author's unsettling awareness of "literary history."

Jiang Shiquan was a man of learning, well respected by his fellow literati, but he was only modestly successful in his official career. In his later years, he participated in compiling the official *Ming History*, as his talents had won the Qianlong Emperor's appreciation, but this led to no further advancement. Within the literary community, he was recognized as one of the three best poets of the time (along with Zhao Yi and Yuan Mei, Jiang's friend). He began to write plays in 1754, and composed eight northern plays and eight southern plays, all of which were published during his lifetime. Like many of his contemporaries, Jiang was fascinated with historical figures and events; he often used them as the subjects of his plays, imputing to the drama the lofty function of Confucian historiography so as to render judgment on the past and set up models for future generations. Though avowedly moralistic, Jiang Shiquan had a lyric streak that proved to be a central part of his dramaturgy.

Dreams of Linchuan stands out among Jiang's plays. By naming the play after Tang Xianzu's *Linchuan's Four Dreams*, he makes an intriguing statement of agenda. Above all, this play creates a world in which the characters from Tang Xianzu's works can interact with Tang and his readers, thereby setting in motion the accumulated discourse surrounding Tang and his plays. Although Tang makes a transitory appearance in a few earlier plays, none can compare with *Dreams of Linchuan* in ingenuity and sophistication. This also raises the question of how Jiang positions himself in relation to Tang and his dramatic works. Finally, the play defines a unique vantage point from which to delve into the intricate relationships between fiction and truth, dream and reality, text and performance, morality and passion, virtue and art, author and audience, as well as between the author and the world of his own creation. These are the same issues at stake in the tradition of dramatic literature going back to Tang Xianzu, if not earlier, and most adeptly presented in the literati novels of the mid-eighteenth century, especially *The Scholars* and *The Story of the Stone*.

Jiang Shiquan felt a deep connection with Tang Xianzu partly because they were both from Linchuan in Jiangxi. A dramatist of tremendous empathic sensibility, Jiang seems to have had more reason than most of his contemporaries to lay claim to Tang's legacy. His claim is not without contention, however. Jiang Shiquan opens his preface to *Dreams of Linchuan* by rebutting the commonly held view that Tang Xianzu was no more than a man of letters, and goes on to state his goal of creating an image of Tang as a Confucian paragon of loyalty and righteousness. To reinforce his point, he presents a biography accentuating Tang's achievements as a local official, Confucian scholar, and upright minister, almost to the exclusion of his artistic creations. Here, as elsewhere, Jiang allows free rein to his instinct as a Confucian historian. When it comes to Tang's dramatic creation, Jiang seems to follow the main trend of his day in moralizing Tang's concept of passion. Moreover, he carefully intertwines Tang's creative acts with the political ordeals he was undergoing in order to illuminate Tang's intentions; he also includes, among the characters of his play, a contemporary reader who claims to have come to know Tang's personality through his *Peony Pavilion*. In this way, Jiang marshals the standard rhetoric of Confucian hermeneutics to support his dramatic agenda.

Despite its apparent moralistic tendency, the play as a whole seems to run in a different, if not the opposite, direction, and the Confucian justification of Tang Xianzu's plays does not go unquestioned in *Dreams of Linchuan*. By having Tang's *dramatis persona* respond to his wife's question about the improbable nature of Du Liniang's resurrection in *Peony Pavilion*, Jiang Shiquan takes the opportunity to introduce the playwright Tang's argument about the opposition between passion and neo-Confucian principle or reason (*li*). This offers Jiang an occasion to reproduce a whole store of criticism on Tang and his plays. Tang is held accountable for the death of a female reader and censured for indulging in the trivial craft of "insect-carving" (literature for its own sake that contributes nothing to the well-being of the state and the people). Elsewhere, he is said to have atoned for his literary offenses by suffering setbacks in his official career, and those who speak in his defense can respond only by saying that his virtues as a man enabled him to escape a more harrowing punishment. Jiang's account of the composition of Tang Xianzu's two other plays in *Linchuan's Four Dreams*, namely *Dreams of Handan* and *Dreams of the Southern Branch*, is no less problematic. In Jiang's account, Tang's frustrations in his official career and the untimely death of his eldest son lead Tang to resign from public life and devote himself to writing the last two *Dreams* to expose the vanity and futility of human aspiration. In the end, Tang, not unlike his own characters, is summoned to the stage to be enlightened by the Heavenly King, who delivers a long lecture in which he dismisses not only literature but also Confucian historiography as an empty and insubstantial dream – criticism that is no less applicable to *Dreams of Linchuan* itself.

Dreams of Linchuan acquires sharp artistic reflexivity through its innovative use of metafictional devices. Jiang conjures up an imaginary space wherein to engage simultaneously with Tang Xianzu, his plays, and the discursive communities of *Peony Pavilion*. Tang's characters are called back to the stage, made to encounter and interact with one another, and comment on their author as well as the unfolding drama itself. Acting on their own volition, they now exist in the same space as Tang, and their conversations with him deprive him of his privilege as an author. Permeating these encounters is an exuberant wit. For example, the characters, trying to identify one another, ask, "Which *Dream* did you come from?" Elsewhere, Tang fails to recognize the characters from his own plays and then has to apologize for having drawn them out of their respective sources to serve his own agenda. Jiang's use of *Peony Pavilion* lore is no less intriguing. According to some widely circulated anecdotes, a young lady named Yu Erniang, having read Tang's *Peony Pavilion*, developed an obsession with the author. In one version of the story, she pines for him until she dies, leaving behind comments on the play that prompt Tang to write a poem lamenting her premature death. In another version, an anonymous young woman insists on visiting Tang Xianzu after reading *Peony Pavilion*, despite his repeated refusals. The encounter, however, wrecks her dream of a romantic union. "I have long admired his talent, and would have been more than willing to entrust my life to him," she says to herself, "but he turns out to be so old and ugly. This is my fate!" Disillusioned and heartbroken, she drowns herself. Jiang Shiquan combines these two versions, revising the scene of their encounter and deleting her suicide from the ending. His Yu Erniang does die from pining, but her restless soul traces her lover from one place to another in a manner not unlike that of Du Liniang.

The most ironical moment occurs at the end of Jiang's *Dreams of Linchuan*, when Tang and the characters of his *Linchuan's Four Dreams* reverse roles. The Spirit of Sleep, en route to call on Tang Xiangzu, delivers this monologue:

> As I think about it, this Old Fellow Tang has been mumbling and playing tricks all his life; how many rumors and lies has he created and how much trouble has he made by producing all this peculiar writing! He once forced me into the role of matchmaker to help Liu and Du achieve their sexual union under the peony pavilion, but I have yet to see the wedding banquet. Little does he know that today he is about to fall into the same trap as I once did. Let me hold him up over there for a while.

In this final scene, Tang turns out to be someone who, like his characters, needs to be awakened from the dream he has created. As the spirit of sleep offers to take him to his deceased son, Tang declines because his own parents are still alive and he is not ready to shake off all his mundane ties, resisting until he is assured that he will be able to return after the meeting, "a small awakening" instead of the ultimate one. The character's hesitation is coded with references, echoing the mental state of Chunyu Fen, the protagonist of *Dreams of the Southern Branch*, as he helplessly clings to the wife he encountered in a dream and refuses enlightenment. It also recalls scene xl of *Peach Blossom Fan*, in which the hero and heroine are subjected to a harangue that shatters their dream of a blissful reunion. Jiang Shiquan tends to conclude his plays with speeches delivered by spirits, gods, and other higher beings. In *Dreams of Linchuan*, he further inscribes his role as an omnipotent author by turning Tang Xianzu and the characters from Tang's plays into the audience of the lecture.

Performance and publishing

Drama is said to live a double life, one onstage and the other in text. In the mid-Qing, these two modes of existence became so separated that the path taken by each rarely intersected with that of the other. To begin with performance, the mid-Qing witnessed a vigorous revival of commercial theaters in urban centers. Commercial theaters had prospered from the eleventh century through the fifteenth century when the northern play dominated the stage, and after more than a century in which the theater had languished in obscurity, large drinking establishments in Beijing and other major cities began once again to offer theatrical performances. Tea houses followed suit with more congenial environments and facilities for staging operas. Thereafter, commercial theaters mushroomed anew. For instance, theater houses (*xiyuan* and *xiguan*) run by merchant organizations or guilds (*huiguan*) burgeoned in Suzhou, becoming a vital part of the urban entertainment scene. Of course, these theaters were only one venue for dramatic performance, and their development was characterized by regional differences; but their revival in the eighteenth century coincided with the rapid growth of professional troupes.

The professional troupe was one of the ways in which actors were organized and managed. There were also troupes owned by elite families and members of the court. Difference in patronage naturally led to divergence in terms of repertoire and audience, but these divergences were by no means absolute and the actors often shifted between groups. Even the professional troupes can be divided into several categories or ranks depending on their relationships with cities, temples, local elites, and officials. As a whole, however, they were more deeply integrated into the fabric of urban culture than the other two groups. Especially noteworthy is that the growth of both professional troupes and commercial theaters was concurrent with the general decline of the troupes kept by the elite families, owing in part to changes in government policy. In comparison to their Ming predecessors, the Manchu emperors adopted stricter taxation policies to contain the wealth of elite families, thereby diminishing the economic foundation of family troupes. Furthermore, the Yongzheng Emperor issued an edict in 1724 prohibiting officials from owning troupes, a rule reissued by the Qianlong Emperor in 1769. In contrast, Yongzheng tended to encourage the development of professional troupes, emphasizing that the theatrical and ritual performances customary at festivals should not be considered illegal activities. Years later, the Jiaqing Emperor specified that local officials should be allowed to hire professional troupes to celebrate these occasions. Not all official families disbanded their troupes immediately. Cao Xueqin's family still kept a large private troupe in Nanjing until their property was confiscated; other gentry and official families put their troupes to use when they entertained the Qianlong Emperor during his journeys through Jiangnan in 1757, 1762, 1765, 1780, and 1784. The emperor himself perhaps set a bad example by keeping in the imperial palace a grand troupe consisting of more than 1,500 actors and musicians. In the long run, however, government restrictions on private troupes had two major effects: the institutional de-linking of theater troupes from the elite, and the reshaping of theater culture on the larger stage of the commercial market and urban entertainment.

The popularity of professional troupes in Nanjing can be seen in *The Scholars*, which was written during the 1730s and 1740s. According to Bao

Tingxi, the head of a professional troupe in the novel, more than 130 such troupes were located in the part of the city near the Qinhuai river alone. Nevertheless, Wu Jingzi still seeks to reassert the literati's prestige and leadership in this changed cultural landscape. In Chapter 30, for instance, Du Shenqing, a man of culture who later passes the palace examination and becomes an official, organizes a Kun-style opera competition. Even in that episode, however, Du is not portrayed as a patron in the conventional sense of the term, and his relationship with the professional troupes is temporary and improvised, dependent to a large extent on his personal connections with Bao Tingxi, the adopted son of his father's steward. Toward the end of the novel, Wu Jingzi cannot help lamenting the degeneration of the theater troupes of Nanjing as they slipped out of literati control. The effort to restore literati leadership of contemporary theater culture came, as he implicitly admits, to naught.

The attenuation of literati influence and the growing professionalization or commercialization of the theater troupes were two interconnected factors that contributed to the rise of multiple new regional operas in the eighteenth century and beyond. These changes had a profound effect on the relationship between literati playwriting and theater performance. In the new age of popular local theaters, it became more difficult to stage southern plays written by literati in the mode of the Kun-style opera. The cultural elite's loss of ownership and control over theater troupes further diminished their chances of performing their own dramatic texts. Evidence suggests that scripts with Kun-style music were occasionally adapted for performance in the new local theaters, but the original texts were altered beyond recognition, a fate their authors deplored.

The dominant trend of the day in the performance of Kun-style opera (and, to varying degrees, other theatrical modes) was to stage the highlights (*zhezixi*) from popular repertoire instead of an entire play. This was due in part to practical concerns, for few literati and officials, not to mention the audiences of the commercial theaters, could spare two whole days to sit through a forty-scene play, even during the holiday season. To present a short program to fit into a single night, a few popular scenes (usually no more than eight) or arias from one play or several unrelated plays were selected. Although this practice was not new to the mid-Qing, it was during this period that it became popular in the commercial theaters, with significant implications for playwriting. As theaters were occupied by the performance of selected scenes from the existing repertoire, literati playwrights tended to compose shorter southern plays. The chance for staging their works remained slim, and most of these were meant to be appreciated through reading.

Thus, for the literati of the mid-Qing, playwriting led more often to the publishing house than to the opera house. It was through publishing, transmitting, reading, and commenting on the dramatic texts that they forged a sense of community. Unlike contemporary literati novelists, whose works either remained unpublished or were published under pseudonyms, dramatists often had their plays published individually or in anthologies, with no effort to hide or disguise their authorship. These dramatic texts, which generally appeared in fine editions and contained prefaces and commentaries by the author's friends, enjoyed the same respect usually accorded poetry and classical prose. Xu Xi, for instance, solicited more than a dozen prefaces for his autobiographical romance *The Destiny of the Mirror Light* from leading poets, including Shen Deqian and Jiang Shiquan. In the author's note, Xu Xi explains that he composed this work as a "desktop play" meant for reading. He also claims to have drafted a stage version in thirty-two scenes and given it to a theater troupe. There is no record of what happened to that version, if it in fact existed.

A different kind of dramatic text was the anthology of highlights or popular scenes. Closely related to the practice of performing selected scenes from the southern plays and a few other genres of regional theater, these anthologies were compiled and published with increasing frequency from the middle of the sixteenth century onward under such titles as *New Pipes from Jade Valley (Yugu xinhuang)*. Some included musical scores and detailed stage directions, which allow us to reconstruct the stage performance. In most cases, the lyrics of the arias are well preserved. *Collected Treasures (Zhui baiqiu)*, compiled and published in the middle of the Qianlong reign, is one of the most comprehensive anthologies of this sort. A more modest version of the work can be dated back to 1688, if not earlier, and the extant texts diverge to varying degrees. The 1774 edition consists of twelve volumes, 429 scenes from Kun-style operas, and fifty-eight scenes from more than thirty regional operas. The inclusion of highlights from regional genres registers their increasing prominence in the theater of the Qianlong period. Regional theaters had by this time developed an impressive repertoire largely independent of the Kun-style opera. Just as important are stage versions of scenes from well-known Kun-style operas that constitute the main body of this anthology. Comparing them with the original texts from other sources shows the changes made to these southern plays as they were adapted for performance. *Collected Treasures* was in high demand by the reading public; it was printed and reprinted numerous times during and after the Qianlong reign.

New directions in playwriting

Though the literati continued to enjoy Kun-style opera and compose their plays in that mode throughout the eighteenth century, they could not entirely ignore the regional operas reverberating in the theaters. To stay on top of the emergent urban culture, they needed engage with it. The didactic, poetic, and autobiographical modes that dominated literati playwriting in the Qianlong reign were of little help in this. Some literati drew on the repertoire of the popular regional theaters, and incorporated local tunes and legends, seeking in this way to push theater culture in the direction they wished it to go. Although contributions of this kind were at best sporadic, taken together they influenced the development of theater culture in fascinating ways.

Tang Ying (1682–1756) was among the earliest literati playwrights to engage systematically with the rising local theaters. Hailing from Fengtian (today's Shenyang), Tang served as a local official in the southeast for many years, where he steeped himself in the local culture. With passion and curiosity, he devoted himself to the study of the regional operas that his fellow literati dubbed "cacophonous strumming" (*luantan*). Tang, however, rarely condescended to local musicians and singers, and he never failed to acknowledge the large segments of local operas that he incorporated into his own plays. He made bold strides in mixing Kun-style melodies with local ones, displaying an eclectic musical sensibility, much to the dismay of his literati contemporaries. Moreover, he almost always offered detailed stage directions in his plays, indicating, for instance, how an actor should be dressed and where a specific musical instrument should be involved, as if he could hear and visualize the performance in his head. He made clear that his works were meant to be performed at banquets and should not be mistaken for "desktop plays."

More than half of his seventeen extant plays derive material from popular local theater. *Crossroad on a Slope* (*Shizi po*), a single-act play that embellishes an episode from *Water Margin*, is a dark physical comedy figuring Sun Erniang as a tigress who brutally dismembers her tenants after seducing them, until she encounters the knight-errant Wu Song and is herself subjected to violent conquest. In contrast, *Predestined Debt* (*Tianyuan zhai*), a twenty-scene play dated to 1754, is a lighthearted comedy full of miscommunications and coincidences. Li Chenglong, an aspiring student and widower, needs money to finance his journey to the capital to take the civil service examination. His parents-in-law refuse Li's access to their dead daughter's dowry unless he marries again. Zhang Gudong ("Antique Zhang"), Li's friend and the hapless son of a bankrupt antique shop owner, volunteers to help. At his urging, his wife agrees to pretend to be Li's new wife so that he may reclaim the dowry. The scheme goes awry as an inconvenient storm keeps Li and Zhang's wife overnight in his parents-in-law's home. Scandal ensues because, regardless of what actually happened between them, the fact that they spent the night together purporting to be husband and wife is itself enough to make a cuckold of poor Zhang. The county magistrate's suggestion that they post an announcement to the contrary would only reinforce the prevailing suspicion. This is a case of perception creating reality: Li Chenglong and Zhang's wife end up becoming involved sexually because they know that they will never be able to claim innocence even if they succeed in overcoming temptation.

Despite the differences in content and tone, these two pieces have at least one thing in common: both derive from the repertoire of the *bangzi* opera (*bangzi xi*), a subgenre of the theater of "cacophonous strumming." *Bangzi* is a block of datewood, which the actors strike with a stick to set the tone and rhythm for the singing and performance. A theatrical form that probably originated in the northwestern provinces of Shaanxi and Shanxi, *bangzi* opera was also known as "songs of Qin." This northwestern style of opera was already popular in Jiangnan by Tang Ying's time, and had even found its way into such anthologies as *Collected Treasures*. Like other physical farces, *Crossroad on a Slope* renders a crude world of moral ambiguities; it concludes in a celebratory tone as Wu Song and Sun Erniang (and her husband Zhang Qing, who returns in time to stop the fight between the two) are reconciled in their common commitment to join the bandits on Mount Liang. Yet violence reigns supreme throughout the play; in most cases, the humor springs from an uneasy mixture of the rhetoric of pleasure and violence. Tang Ying deletes some jokes that are excessively cruel, and reduces violent acts to a minimum. On the whole, however, he is faithful to his source material, and his embellishments further magnify the ambiguous nature of the rhetoric about pleasure. As the seduction scene escalates, the guest, not knowing he is about to die, begs for sex in language that can be read as a petition for death: "This joy is killing me – I am running out of patience with my life!" Then, a moment later: "However you want to treat me, I'll take it. It will be fine even if you kill me. I only beg you to speed up, because I can't wait any longer!"

Predestined Debt works on a more complex plane. Tang significantly rewrites his sources, and makes additions that far exceed the source materials in length and sophistication. In the concluding act, Zhang Gudong encounters a *bangzi* troupe that has been hired to celebrate his wedding with a play called *Lending a Wife*, featuring himself as the chief protagonist. Zhang comments: "I, a decent man Zhang Gudong, have been made fun of by my friends in the *bangzi* troupes, who present *Lending a Wife* everywhere." He ends his protest by pleading with the men of letters to turn the play into a Kun-style opera and represent him in a more positive light, which is precisely what Tang Ying does. This suggests that Tang may have drawn from sources other than the popular anthologies of local operas, for at least one text dated to the early Qianlong period refers to the popularity of *Lending a Wife* in the Yangzhou region. In any event, Tang Ying recasts his sources to create a protagonist who is good-hearted but simple and single-minded; he acts on the strength of his own imagined cleverness, but often ends up getting into trouble.

Tang's most brilliant stroke of revision comes in scene vi of *Predestined Debt*. Here Zhang Gudong, stuck outside the city in the rainy night, speculates about what is going on in the bedroom that his wife is sharing with his friend; meanwhile, those two are struggling to figure out how to handle the awkward situation fraught with temptation and potential for scandal, while anticipating Zhang's possible reaction. All three characters appear onstage simultaneously, with each revealing his or her thoughts in monologues. Outraged and frustrated, Zhang begins by spelling out the worst scenario with a spate of curses, while Li, on the other side of the stage, pledges to maintain his integrity and Zhang's wife roundly condemns her husband for tricking her into a situation from which she can hardly emerge with her reputation intact. Just as Zhang's mood lightens and he shifts to wishful thinking and prayer, the situation in the bedroom takes a drastic turn for the worse: the wife, bereft of options, makes sexual advances and thus seals the marriage with the young student, an assuredly better prospect than her husband. Rarely does a traditional comedy offer such brilliant insight into the fragility of virtue and the unpredictability of human psychology: a fleeting idea can change the course of the action in unforeseeable ways. In *bangzi* theater, this scene is treated in a much cruder fashion: Zhang and his wife dominate the stage, and Li Chenglong barely speaks. When Li finally does speak, his call to heaven to witness his honesty is immediately twisted into a wedding vow by Zhang's wife, who adds her oath to close the deal. Tang Ying rearranges the scene to inject nuance and psychological depth, but his revisions are not always successful. For example, he changes the ending of the play so that Li Chenglong, now a prosperous official, repays Zhang Gudong by arranging a marriage for him, thus meeting the demands of poetic justice. Such an ending is, of course, indicative of the limits Tang Ying encountered as a literati dramatist. As it turns out, the overarching framework of *Predestined Debt* is too conventional and conservative, but this is perhaps the point: equilibrium is precisely what

Tang Ying needs if his mission is to rein in the subversive energy of his sources, and the unruliness of their "cacophonous strumming."

In turning to the repertoire of regional theater for inspiration, Tang Ying may be an anomaly among his contemporaries. He did not, apparently, have any like-minded friends or followers. Elsewhere, a few other playwrights engaged in similar practices, but they encountered unexpected challenges. The adaptation and subsequent rewriting of the widely circulated Hangzhou legend of the White Snake is a case in point.

The femme fatale who seduces an innocent young man and then devours him is a recurring motif in the demon lore of traditional China and other cultures. Exactly when the White Snake from West Lake took on the form of the demon story in anecdotes and oral literature is not known, but by 1550 the White Snake story was already a fully developed "gothic" narrative about obsession, haunting, and nightmare. Based on the existing sources, Feng Menglong produced a vernacular story called "Madame White Eternally Subjugated under the Thunder Peak Pagoda" for his anthology *Common Words to Warn the World* (1624). He faithfully preserves the ending found in the earlier versions of the story, in which the demonic Madame White is imprisoned forever under the Thunder Peak pagoda near West Lake, but the rest of his narrative reads much like an evolving love story until a Daoist priest appears to warn Xu Xuan, the young protagonist, that he has been possessed by a demon. The demonic is palpable even in the early part of the story, but more often than not it is subsumed into the single-mindedness of a woman in love. In a way, it is Madame White's blind and obsessive love that gets Xu Xuan into one predicament after another: she will not hesitate to steal if that is what it takes to dress her man up as a respectable gentleman. The Daoist's revelation of the "truth" about her forces the young man to choose sides and act accordingly, but he resists, vacillates, and is incapable of action. It is not until the final part of the story that terror begins to set in. Where the Daoist fails, the Buddhist monk Fahai successfully intervenes and reveals Madame White in her original snake form with his magic.

The earliest play about the White Snake on record is *Thunder Peak Pagoda* (*Leifeng ji*), presumably written by Chen Liulong of the late Ming, but the text has long been lost. In 1738, Huang Tubi (1700–1771?) produced a play called *Leifeng ta*. It is unclear whether Huang read Chen's work, but he almost certainly drew inspiration from Feng Menglong's story. Huang was active during the same period as Tang Ying, and, like him, served as a local administrator for many years. He too was critical of his source material, which he saw as marred by fallacy and absurdity. The popularity of the White Snake story could hardly be overestimated, however. No sooner did Huang finish his draft than a theater troupe knocked at his door, requesting his permission to perform it. Huang allowed this, but soon regretted the decision. Although the troupes of Suzhou remained faithful to his original text, other groups went out of their way to cater to the tastes of the general audience, and, to his outrage, added a scene in which Madame White gives birth to a son, who later succeeds in the civil service examinations. Similar versions of the story may already have been in circulation, so perhaps these troupes did nothing more than incorporate them into their performance, but Huang found the changes unforgivable. A happy ending is inappropriate to the White Snake story, he argues, because the White Snake is an alien being and thus a source of pollution. In his view, the distinction between human and demon is not negotiable. Huang's protest highlights two larger issues at stake: the conflicting tendencies toward humanizing and demonizing the White Snake on the one hand, and the tensions between literati playwrights and commercial troupes and their audience on the other.

As Huang realized, popularity often comes at a price. Once out of his hands, the play began to evolve according to the whims of the troupes and the audiences to whom they catered. There was little he could do to distance himself from a play attached to his name. Later, when Huang finished another play called *The Cloud-Dwelling Rock* (*Qiyun shi*), he kept it to himself for two years. He did not waver even when troupes begged to be allowed to stage it. In despair, the actors bribed his servants to gain access to the manuscript, and, before Huang knew it, he had another theatrical hit.

Huang Tubi lived long enough to witness an additional twist to this ongoing saga. Despite the success he had enjoyed as a dramatist, *Thunder Peak Pagoda* gradually vanished from theaters in the middle of the Qianlong reign, to be replaced by other versions of the play that deviated significantly from his in further humanizing and redeeming the White Snake. In the final denouement of one version bearing the same title, the Buddha pardons the White Snake and allows her to join her husband, now enlightened, in the Tushita Heaven. According to one source, this manuscript version was hurriedly compiled to entertain the Qianlong Emperor when he visited Jiangnan in 1765. A happy ending is mandatory for such a festive occasion, and the emperor is said to have thoroughly enjoyed the performance. Six years later and possibly coinciding with Huang Tubi's death, another version of the play emerged. The author, Fang Chengpei (1731–?), a student-turned-doctor, was also well versed in music and literature. Despite Huang's earlier warnings against crossing the line between human and demon, Fang did not change the main plot and the ending of the play. As he makes clear in the preface, however, finding that manuscript version vulgar in style and its arias often out of tune, he took the liberty of altering 70 percent of the dialogues and 90 percent of the arias. Fang's *Thunder Peak Pagoda* was printed in 1772, years after Huang Tubi's version had vanished from theaters, but Fang's musical acumen and literary elegance did not necessarily guarantee a success on the stage.

By 1770, the complete set of *Collected Treasures* had been published. It includes highlights taken from the latest popular version of *Thunder Peak Pagoda*, which resembles the manuscript version but is not exactly the same. These textual variations may indicate regional differences as well as differences arising from the choices made by a given troupe, the repertoire it inherited, and its anticipation of and responses to local audiences. The vagaries of editorial practices may also have had a role in shaping these dramatic texts. In an age when theater culture was increasingly dominated by commercial theater and regional operas, dramatic production became inevitably diversified, mediated, and dictated by the market. In this changed and changing theater culture, no one was in a position to have the last word.

The metamorphoses of the White Snake story went well beyond Kun-style opera. The rising regional theaters seized on this theme and subjected it to constant rewritings, as did storytellers working in various forms of performance literature. The proliferation of the story attests to the dynamics of regional culture and urban entertainment. In some regions, the Buddhist elements were downplayed considerably, while Green Fish (Xiaoqing), White Snake's maid, loomed so large in importance as to eclipse nearly all the other characters, as is the case with Yingying's maid in the later reworkings of *The Western Wing*. Interestingly, Green Fish is often portrayed as a vengeful spirit on a mission to assassinate Monk Fahai. At least one nineteenth-century version of string ballads follows a similar story line. Instead of saving the human from the grip of the demon, Fahai is himself turned into a demon and chased by Green Fish, who is just as demonic, at least in her thirst for revenge.

Redrawing the map: local opera in the eighteenth century and beyond

The rise of regional theaters was one of the most significant social and cultural events in the eighteenth and nineteenth centuries, but contemporary literati accounts are sparse and often colored by prejudice. "Cacophonous strumming" is scarcely a reliable guide for understanding these regional operas, a description that captures the literati's contempt as well as their ignorance of what was happening in the local theaters. The literati also used several alternate terms, such as "the miscellaneous" (*hua*), to define regional theater in contrast to "the refined" (*ya*), the Kun-style opera. This dichotomy did not function, as they had hoped, to polarize and segregate the two. Before long, "the miscellaneous" or "the cacophonous" were being performed together with "the refined" on the same stage and often within the same program; actors of the Kun style had to be versed in at least one of the forms of "cacophonous strumming" in order to remain competitive. This state of coexistence did not last long. Xu Xiaochang, in his 1744 preface to Zhang Jian's play *Destiny in Dream* (*Mengzhong yuan*), describes how contemporary audiences in Beijing had grown tired of Kun-style opera. As soon as they heard that the performance would be in the Kun style, everyone would disperse.

The unprecedented blossoming of regional theaters in the Qing dynasty yielded over three hundred local genres, some of which have survived to this day. To this list must be added other forms, such as the puppet theater, which I will not discuss here. Most of these local genres belong to several larger systems or categories, which continued to compete and interact with one another even after Peking opera took center stage in Beijing during the nineteenth century. The oldest of these categories is the Yiyang style, so named because it originated in Yiyang, Jiangxi. This operatic system dates to the Ming dynasty, and its evolving history overlaps with that of Kun-style opera. Yet the literati of mid-Qing, whose tastes had been formed on the slow-paced, soft, and exquisite songs of the Kun style, often dismissed the Yiyang style as high-pitched, noisy, and unpolished. Despite lack of support from the educated elite, the Yiyang style showed remarkable endurance and adaptability through much of the Ming and the early Qing eras, primarily in the lower echelons of society. As this style infiltrated other regions over the years, it gradually gained upward mobility. One of its variants, the capital style, almost outshone the Kun style and other competing regional genres in mid-Qianlong Beijing. Capital style even won official sanction despite the court's repeated prohibition of other regional theaters. Following the boom of the Yiyang style came the *bangzi* opera. Its popularity peaked in the late Qianlong reign, especially from 1779 to the late 1780s, when its leading actor, Wei Changsheng (1744–1802), lived in Beijing. The imperial court banned Wei and his *bangzi* troupe from Beijing stages for their allegedly bawdy performances in 1782 and 1785. Wei eventually retreated to Yangzhou, Suzhou, and Sichuan Province, where *bangzi* opera was as popular as ever. The public celebration of the Qianlong Emperor's eightieth birthday in 1790 opened the capital to many other troupes. The officials of the Salt Administration and the salt merchants of Anhui competed with other regions in dispatching their local troupes to Beijing. The Anhui troupes brought with them the styles called *erhuang* and *xipi* of different regional origins (the *xipi* was, in fact, a variant of the *bangzi* opera), and the two gradually combined to become the *pihuang* style famous in the Qianlong and Jiaqing periods. Out of this long and complex process of hybridization came the Peking opera.

It is not difficult to imagine how much these booming regional theaters shocked the literati, coming as nothing less than an insult, as the literati put it, to their delicate taste and sensibility. After years of tempering, Kun-style theater had become a mature, homogeneous art form in the late Ming, its migration from one area to another leaving few permanent marks on its fully developed forms. The Kun melody embodies what might be called floating Suzhou gracefulness. It is delicately cadenced and extremely rich in nuances, often with a single word melodically prolonged through many subtle variations of tone and enunciation. By contrast, the Yiyang style is less strictly regulated and thus more adaptable to different local dialects and songs. Its regional variants diverged so greatly that people often forgot their common origin. The Yiyang style is noted for vehement, sonorous singing, especially its rapidly paced "rolling" style of singing, chanting, and recitation (*gundiao*), characterized by the irrepressible flow of its "accumulated momentum." It is also known for what is called *bangqiang*, a mounting chorus in which other actors onstage and off join the lead performer in singing or speech by repeating his or her lines, or adding their own in unison. *Gundiao* carried over into other genres of regional theater and had a direct effect on the form of the opera itself: instead of the well-regulated alternation of irregular lines, as seen in the Kun-style arias, the free combination of lines of five and seven syllables, with their many variations, introduced new rhythms that resonated with the popular forms of oral literature. This tendency to break away from the preexisting music suites is also clearly manifest in the *bangzi* and *pihuang* genres. Whereas each scene in Kun-style opera consists of a set of preconceived suites of songs, the *bangzi* and *pihuang* allow much more room for choices and adjustments: scenes can vary greatly in length, and the shifts among them are more frequent and rapid. Such structural flexibility facilitates free borrowing from the repertory of popular regional songs and other forms of performance literature.

This brief account of regional theater in the eighteenth century is not meant to suggest that this genre developed in a linear progression in which one form superseded another. Many of these local operas coexisted and influenced one another. In most cases, each form remained connected to its roots in its own region, large or small, regardless of how it fared in Beijing. For modern anthropologists, literary scholars, and social and cultural historians, a comprehensive study of these regional theaters offers a window into the astonishing regional diversity in eighteenth-century social, cultural, linguistic, and religious practice. Equally impressive is the enormous vitality and creativity displayed in the making and remaking of local operas. Even such peripheral regions as Guizhou and Yunnan in the far southwest were producing their own forms of theater with a robust energy rarely seen before.

Also significant is the cross-regional character of the most influential styles of "local" theater, in that they started out as local phenomena but often migrated far beyond their origins. As a result, each of these major categories spawned numerous variants in other regions. Since some regions were simultaneously exposed to several different styles, there inevitably arose more than one subgenre in each area. For instance, nearly ten different operatic styles were introduced into the Jiangxi region during the Qianlong reign, some of these coming from as far away as Shanxi and Guangdong. A proper account of the development and transformation of the regional theaters of this period would require tracing the restless migrations and reconstructing the complex negotiations with the cultural particularities of each locale that resulted in so much regional variation. Ultimately, such a study would lead to insights into areas long omitted from literary history and help us to redraw the cultural map of the late imperial era.

Needless to say, cities occupy a prominent position on this map. Local operas can be regarded as the products of urban culture, so long as "urban" is understood as not merely standing in contrast to rural. Differences between city and country remained relative during the eighteenth century, with the cities being defined as the core of the social, economic, and cultural activities of the region of which they were an integral part. Commerce was one of the major factors that set cities apart from their rural surroundings, and large commercial troupes were most often based in cities and towns. Sufficient concentrations of population and wealth were necessary preconditions for the growth of regional theaters. Moreover, cities played a key role as hubs in cross-regional transportation networks for the conveyance of food, merchandise, and theater troupes, among other things. Migrating merchants became the inevitable agents facilitating the transmission of regional operas. To some extent, the empire-wide popularity of the *bangzi* and *pihuang* styles can be attributed, respectively, to the long-distance trading activities of Shanxi and Anhui merchants (*Jinshang* and *Huishang*), the two most prominent business communities of the time. The trans-regional cross-fertilization of theater culture would not have been possible had it not been accompanied by the expansion of trade and migration in the Qianlong reign.

The formation of Peking opera demonstrates the results of this constant migration and hybridization of the regional styles. It is not enough to trace the origins of its sources, for these sources were often reshaped as they migrated from one area to another. For instance, while the *xipi* style originated in Shaanxi and Shanxi, it is one of its variant forms developed in Xiangyang of Hubei Province that combined with elements from other styles to create Peking opera. As a latecomer, Peking opera drew its material from many existing sources, including Kun-style opera, and most of these borrowed elements had numerous variations in earlier and contemporary theaters. Most of the recurring stories in Peking opera derive from vernacular novels, including *Romance of the Three Kingdoms* and *Water Margin*, not necessarily in their written or printed forms but by way of derived forms of oral literature and opera. Other popular themes include legends about the generals from the Yang family and the Judge Bao stories, which also had a long history of transmission through sundry genres of fiction and performance literature.

From the second half of the eighteenth century onward, Beijing became the main stage where every major style of opera vied for a place. In 1790, several *xipi* and *erhuang* troupes from Anhui converged on Beijing for the eightieth birthday celebrations of the Qianlong Emperor. The innovations that occurred there resulted in the formation of Peking opera, with the royal house as its most powerful patron. This move from the local to the center conforms to the familiar pattern whereby an artistic or literary form of humble origin is embraced by the imperial court and literati officials, thus becoming part of elite culture. Far from a simple process, as the literati underwent repeated divisions and regroupings, the boundary between the popular and the elite needed to be redrawn again and again.

The imperial court often shifted its position toward different regional theaters. Shortly before Peking opera appeared on the cultural scene of the capital, the *bangzi* opera fell out of favor; Wei Changsheng's troupes were forced to disband, and Wei had to join a Kun-style troupe temporarily before leaving Beijing. Wei was not just another actor lost in the capital city, however, as he is said to have been the homosexual lover of several court officials, including the notorious Heshen. Such liaisons became more common with Peking opera, where young actors play the dominant roles, especially that of the *dan*, in which they serve as female impersonators. Not all the literati were enthusiastic about Peking opera, partly because its reputation had been tarnished by the suspicion of male prostitution. Some complained about the shoddy quality of its arias, some of which made little sense. For others, the golden days of the theater lay in the past, from which Kun-style operas were retrieved from time to time only to show the poverty of recent forms by comparison. Even the imperial patronage of Peking opera made little difference in this regard.

Nearly all the major regional theaters underwent transformations in the modern era. The case of Peking opera represents an extreme that sums up the result of the interaction of political agendas, institutions, ideologies, technologies, and modern media such as the Western-style genres of spoken drama and film (including Broadway shows and Hollywood musicals). The inherited struggles between the elite and the popular are compounded by constant debate between the old and the new, the Chinese and the Western, and preservation and modernization, when each of these terms seems ossified into a rigid dogma. In the current age of globalization, multiculturalism, and the market economy, these controversies are likely to continue, perhaps even intensify. Fundamental structural changes had already occurred in the eighteenth century, however, as the flourishing of regional theater rendered elite participation almost irrelevant. These local styles underwent so many mutations and cross-fertilizations that we cannot generalize about them without taking a historical perspective. Despite all the ruptures of modernization, part of the legacy of regional theater remains and their influence continues to be felt.

II. An age of uncertainty: 1796–1840

The short period that began with the Qianlong Emperor's abdication and concluded with the first Opium War brought changes to the deep structure of the empire that would divert the course of Qing rule. As the European powers imposed a series of treaties leading to the establishment of Western concessions in the major coastal cities such as Shanghai, they fundamentally altered the empire's political and economic life, challenged its elite culture and traditions, and transformed its geopolitical landscape. The effects of the two Opium Wars were compounded by the Taiping Rebellion (1851–1864), which hit Jiangnan especially hard. The rebellion wrought thirteen years of havoc that severely damaged the economy; destroyed private academies, libraries, bookstores, and other parts of the cultural infrastructure in that region; and delivered a fatal blow to the declining Kun-style opera. With wars came refugees and migrations, intellectual centers moved elsewhere, and the devastation of Jiangnan contributed to the rise of Shanghai. Fleeing from Nanjing, Hangzhou, Suzhou, and other nearby cities, many Jiangnan elite struggled to rebuild their homes and reconstitute their culture in a different urban environment shaped in great measure by European colonialism and capitalism.

As much as the empire was weakened by the attack of British warships and undermined by the Taiping Rebellion, many of the problems that would eventually lead to its demise had already begun to take their toll in the 1790s, if not earlier. The British opium trade, which accelerated vastly in the 1790s, generated both fiscal and sociopolitical stresses beyond the remedy of the overtaxed government when opium and foreign currencies infiltrated not merely the coastal cities but also the inland regions. Moreover, uprisings on a national scale were looming on the horizon, while regional turmoil showed no sign of abating. There was a general sense of crisis, but few could pinpoint whence disaster would come or foresee its scope and consequences.

Literati elites were among the first to feel the pressure. For many of them, the first half of the nineteenth century was a period filled with uncertainty and frustration as they were confronted with the general decline of a polity that, in Philip Kuhn's words, seemed increasingly unequal to its tasks. The authority of the state was being fatally eroded by large-scale corruption and factionalism. Heshen, Qianlong's chief grand councilor who was notorious for his abuse of power, was put to death after Qianlong's demise in 1799, but the ingrained patterns of political practice remained unchanged. The Confucian elites were able neither to address the root causes of political corruption and factional conflicts nor to articulate the public interest in ways that would rally the literati, in office and out, to make a collective response to these challenges to their leadership. Official institutions also failed to keep up with the changing circumstances. The mid-Qing era produced unprecedented numbers of educated men, but only a small number could be absorbed into government service, while the bureaucracy, whose size had remained unchanged since the beginning of the dynasty, proved unequal to the tasks of managing a complex society and a population that had more than doubled in fifty years. The court bureaucrats were wretchedly inadequate in coping with predicaments of political participation and administrative management. It would strain credibility to describe the educated literati of the late eighteenth and early nineteenth centuries as belonging to a single community or group, when they were in fact, as some historians have suggested, divided into the official elite and the cultural elite, which could not be easily united by ideas and actions. For concerned literati, the political issues they were facing were inseparable from their reflection on their own roles in state, society, and culture. Schismatized, they were challenged to find common ground and articulate values that would help them to resume leadership. To avert looming domestic and international crises, they had no option but to mobilize all available resources, primarily from their own literary and intellectual traditions.

As the literati elite turned to their traditions in the face of encroaching threats from Western influence, they also needed to come to terms with a robust popular culture. What is called popular literature tends, especially during this period, to develop beyond literati culture, as exemplified by regional theater that fundamentally reshaped the cultural landscape. As in the past, these popular genres were reaching a large illiterate audience through performance, but some of them had also become accessible through commercial print to the growing population of the literate. Literacy was now widespread even among those removed from official institutions and the examination system. Shop assistants, clerks, and women were said to enjoy reading fiction, although their levels of literacy varied. Traditional Confucian education promised official careers and cultural prestige, but for many educated men in this period, this promise remained unfulfilled. Over a million civil licentiates enjoyed far fewer sociopolitical privileges than would merit the name of literati; their cultural status, never high to begin with, would only decline with the growth of their total population. Even larger numbers of educated men took the lowest level of civil service examinations year after year with scant prospect of success. This huge miscellaneous population offered a ready audience for and potential contributors to commercial publishing, and its complex constituency inevitably registered in the broadly expanding cultural scene. It would be premature to describe the developments in the first half of the nineteenth century as a burgeoning mass culture, but commercial publishing was revitalized and the consumption of urban entertainment was on the rise. Later on, this trend was accelerated by the introduction of new media, modern printing technology, and a capitalistic market system, resulting in a booming urban consumer literature that would be denounced by Liang Qichao in his 1905 manifesto of literary reform.

Expanded horizons

Popular entertainment assumed increasingly diverse forms from the mid-Qianlong reign on. Many regions produced not only local operas but also other genres of performance literature, such as *guci* (drum ballads), and *zidishu* in the north and *tanci* (string ballads) in Jiangnan. Moreover, physical farces, comedy shows, bawdy jokes, and love songs of unbridled emotion and erotic connotation became abundant fare along the trade routes and in nearby cities and villages. Only a few anthologies of the short plays and popular songs published in the late Qianlong era have survived, offering a glimpse into a world otherwise inaccessible. Written records about the performance literature of this period are sparse and scattered, but we have enough evidence to sketch in broad outline the activities of storytelling and singing in Yangzhou, Beijing, and other cities. For example, Shi Yukun, a professional *zidishu* performer, made his name in the entertainment quarter of Beijing during the Daoguang reign (1821–1850). His repertoire included stories based on earlier novels and plays, but he was best known for his performance of drum ballads on Judge Bao, which have survived in two hand-copied manuscripts. Differing occasionally in plot and rhetoric, these texts provided the primary sources for a sequence of Judge Bao novels and other criminal court case stories from the late Qing.

The prevalence of various forms of storytelling and singing also contributed to the rise of the martial arts or chivalric novel, another vernacular genre that would reach the peak of its popularity in the second half of the nineteenth century. Two major martial arts novels, *The Green Peony* (*Lü mudan*, 1800) and *A Portrait of Tianbao* (*Tianbao tu*, 1814), were each adapted from a performance-related text of the same title in the *guci* and the *tanci* format respectively. A closer look, however, reveals that these works themselves stemmed from a long-accumulated literary tradition, partially mediated by written or printed texts. The martial arts narrative is a hybrid form of the historical saga, the talent–beauty romance, and the court case story. Each of these subgenres had a long and convoluted history, as will be demonstrated in Chapter 5 of this volume. Court case fiction, which went out of fashion in the early Qing, reemerged nearly a century after its last appearance in print, much changed in structure and content. In *The Court Cases of Judge Shi* (*Shi gongan*, 1798), the episodes are connected in a cohesive narrative sequence, and wandering swordsmen, often known in earlier works for their defiance of the imperial order, now collaborate with judges in a joint effort to crack down on rebellions. The martial arts novels of the same period similarly stressed their protagonists' unflinching loyalty to the throne. These heroes, unlike their counterparts in *The Court Cases of Judge Shi*, are often portrayed as educated men with a superb command of martial arts. Such an image may be partly traced to the talent–beauty romances of the early Qing, so it is not surprising that some elements of the love story also spilled over into the emerging chivalric narrative. Constant interactions and interpenetrations constitute the salient characteristics of these popular texts.

The multiple forms of performance literature, including those of the regional opera, and storytelling and singing, were essential components of the growing urban culture. During the early decades of the nineteenth century, a Beijing resident had easy access to Peking opera; he might also enjoy the performance of other regional operas, as well as *zidishu*, *guci*, and other forms of prosimetric narrative in the entertainment quarter or marketplace. If literate or semiliterate, he could also take advantage of what the bookstores and book rental shops could offer. The improvement in channels for book distribution and circulation provided an additional stimulus to the growth of contemporary urban culture. In Beijing, the book-lending business was booming, and more books (including hand-copied manuscripts) now entered into rapid circulation. A shop owner's note on the title page of a novel, dated 1836, instructed his clients to take care of the book and return it within three days.

The bustling urban culture was not limited to Beijing. It also thrived in Shenyang in the northeast, Guangzhou in the south, and in many Jiangnan cities. From the late eighteenth century on, increasing numbers of new novels were offered through commercial venues; some, composed by authors deeply rooted in local culture, contained identifiable regional references. The burgeoning of the Guangzhou novel in the early nineteenth century is a case in point. Set in the bygone Ming dynasty, as are most novels written in the Qing, *Mirage Tower* (*Shenlou ji*, 1804) offers a panoramic view of contemporary life in this port city, influenced to a large extent by foreign trade. New opportunities that arouse unknown desires and fantasies and lead inevitably to devastation and disillusionment are themes, familiar in earlier novels, that resurface in a changed context with deliberate ambiguity. In *Mirage Tower*, the young protagonist abandons himself to love and sexual adventures. He refuses to follow either the commercial pursuits modeled by his father, a merchant who reaps staggering profits through foreign trade but dies a broken man, or the career of the greedy and malicious customs bureaucrats. The novel paints a lively portrait of this young libertine in a brave new age, describing in meticulous detail life in Guangzhou as it revolves around foreign trade, monetary transactions, and official mismanagement of customs. The unquenchable fascination with cities became more evident in such novels as *Dream of Romance* (*Fengyue meng*, 1848), a Yangzhou novel, and *Singsong Girls of Shanghai* (*Haishanghua liezhuan*, 1894), a more elaborate and innovative work set in Shanghai. Both works acknowledge their origins and sources by representing regional dialect to some extent, and each captures in its own way the larger socioeconomic forces that infiltrate the local community and influence its mores and human relations. In *Dream of Romance*, the brothels of Yangzhou are the site for the exchange of opium and foreign currencies, and Shanghai emerges in the background as the new mecca for pleasure and business.

Along with burgeoning commercial enterprise came a cross-regional community of readers. A few novels became instant best sellers, and contemporary writers wasted no time in responding to and often competing with one another. Coincident with the end of the Qianlong reign, and only five years after the Cheng–Gao edition of *The Story of the Stone* hit the market to enormous popular acclaim, a sequel to *The Stone* appeared in 1796. Several more followed in the next three years. The upsurge of *The Stone* sequels quickly became a national phenomenon, published by different printing houses and often in different cities. Showing keen awareness of their competitors, authors and publishers frequently went out of their way to assert the superiority of their own sequels or to offer a preemptive defense against the attacks of rivals. They were all appealing to the same audience, namely the vast community of readers outside their immediate locale. As shown earlier, *The Stone* was circulated in hand-copied form among limited numbers of contemporary readers. Ironically, once the 120-chapter edition appeared in print, the novel met with commercial success far beyond Cao Xueqin's wildest imagination, giving rise to a whole industry of sequels that would continue, with few interruptions, to the present day. More than a hundred titles have piled up under this general rubric, and the number is still growing.

"Sequel" (*xushu*) is a loose term, embracing a broad range of writing practice from continuations to parodic rewritings. The early sequels to *The Stone* are diverse in both form and agenda. A few authors claimed that their works were based on secret manuscripts of *The Stone*; some set out to ameliorate the unhappiness of its tragic ending, while others seemed more interested in projecting their own fantasies. What is common among these works is their shared desire to take *The Stone* beyond its original ending and present alternative denouements. To sustain the extended narrative, the deceased protagonists are either summoned back to life, return to the human world through reincarnations, or revisit the Jia family mansion as immortals or ghosts. Existing plots were recast, and new episodes were added. The book industry around *The Stone* may be likened to an assembly line that perpetuates itself by churning out a long line of products with the same brand name.

The Stone is not the first novel to be subjected to constant rewriting or to give rise to ensuing narratives. Many novels enjoyed numerous "reincarnations" in the middle of the seventeenth century, and the Ming–Qing transition gave further impetus to the proliferation of *xushu* articulating political antagonism, cultural reflection, and compensatory visions of utopia. The rise of *The Stone* sequels initiated a new wave of fiction sequels that would reach its height in the late Qing. Unlike many earlier fiction *xushu*, these first sequels to *The Stone* showed no overt political concerns and few subversive agendas. Not until the late Qing did the authors of fiction sequels became truly political and even radical as they responded to the deepening crises of the times.

In 1877, *The Six Records of a Floating Life* (*Fusheng liuji*), a personal memoir written some seventy years before, appeared in print for the first time. It has since been commended by generations of Chinese intellectuals and writers for the refreshing sincerity of its portrayal of love, marriage, and private life, as well as what might be called a burgeoning modern subjectivity and sensibility. A closer look, however, reveals something else. Arranged topically instead of chronologically, each of its four extant chapters addresses one aspect of the author's life (love, leisure and arts, misfortunes, and travel) with few areas of overlap or cross-references with other chapters. Disjunctive in representation, the memoir raises more questions than its author answered. This fascinating piece was composed by someone who was hardly a member of the literati, a strong indication in itself of the expanded horizons of literary creation in the early nineteenth century. The author, Shen Fu (1763–?), the scion of a family of declining fortunes, gave up his pursuit of an official career early in life. Alternating between working as a private secretary and running a small business, he struggled constantly to provide for his family. He succeeded, however, in fashioning himself as a man of literati tastes and lifestyle. The memoir, written in classical Chinese of uneven quality, is full of allusions and textual references that assimilate its narrative into the grand tradition of classical poetry and prose. The chapter on travel registers the author's wish to write himself into the landscape defined by and permanently associated with men of letters from the past. Whatever its deficiencies, the memoir is never marred by the lack of sophistication and self-consciousness. Shen Fu often dwells on poetry and the arts of flower arrangement and miniature gardening to discover how they "create illusion out of reality," methods that he himself employed in his memoir. In addition, the memoir is pervaded by lyrical melancholy. Like some of his contemporaries, Shen resigned himself to nostalgic longing for home and pastoral tranquility undisturbed by either family strife or the relentless changes and oppressive barbarity of the outside world. Although not a member of literati, he shared their mentality, if not their aspirations, and his memoir suffered the same fortune as *The Scholars* and *The Stone*, enjoying little, if any, visibility during his lifetime.

Shen Fu's memoir is also noted for its portrayal of his wife as an intelligent woman of refinement and exquisite taste, capable of writing despite her lack of formal education. Here the author was influenced by another contemporary cultural phenomenon, *guixiu* literature or literature composed by gentry women. He even infused into his memoir personal observations of women's culture, as one of his patrons was known, among other things, for his support of gentry women poets.

Gentry women and literature

The scholarship of the last two decades has thrown into relief the contours of women's literature in the Ming and Qing periods. Knowledge of this subject remains constrained by the limited quantity of texts that have survived to the present day, since manuscripts by female authors seemed especially vulnerable to destruction, intentional or otherwise. From the late sixteenth century onward, more and more writings by female authors began to find their way into print, a trend that reached its height during the first half of the seventeenth century before receding in the eighteenth century. In the final decades of the eighteenth century, a second wave of women's literature began to gather momentum, cresting in the first half of the following century. Compared to their predecessors in the late Ming, female writers of the Qing were less diverse in family background, education, and experience. Courtesan poets, who figured conspicuously in the cultural scene of the late Ming, had long since vanished. Few Buddhist nuns stood out for their literary talents. The vast majority of the female authors of the day were *guixiu* or gentlewomen from the Jiangnan region, especially Hangzhou, Suzhou, and Nanjing, although their networks expanded significantly into other regions over time. These women came from elite families and married gentlemen with degrees and often with official titles. As before, lyric poetry remained their favorite genre, but new ground was broken as they directed their attention to such narrative genres as drama and *tanci* – a popular form of prosimetric ballad that became irrevocably associated with women and their literary experience. A few gentlewomen even ventured into commercial publishing, compiling and editing anthologies of poetry and *tanci* by women for a broad audience.

As in the past, the female gentry poets of this period formed a community of ladies of similar background and interests through parties, informal gatherings, and the exchange of poems and letters. They also enjoyed the support of the male members of their families and lineages and benefited from their associations with the eminent literati of the time. Beginning in the final decades of the eighteenth century, prominent literary figures publicly claimed the role of mentors to gentry women poets, embracing them as members of an extended literati community. As Yuan Mei retired to his Garden of Contentment in Nanjing during the final years of his life, he accepted about fifty gentry ladies as disciples, writing prefaces for their anthologies, and publishing in 1796 a collective anthology of their verses entitled *Poems of the Female Disciples of Suiyuan* (*Suiyuan nü dizi shi*). Yuan Mei came to know these female poets through the recommendations of mutual friends or by reputation, as some were already established poets. Yuan's group was loosely knit; not all its members knew one another. Some were also closely associated with Chen Wenshu (1771–1843), who had over thirty female disciples of his own in Hangzhou, including his daughter-in-law, Wang Duan (1793–1839), and the woman playwright Wu Zao (1799–1863). In Suzhou, a group of female poets gathered around Ren Zhaolin (fl. 1776–1823) and his wife, Zhang Zilan, and their collective accomplishments were anthologized as *Recorded Poems of Ten Women of Wu* (*Wuzhong shizi shichao*), published in 1789. Few literary groups operated in isolation or were mutually exclusive; their members moved between groups, or maintained ties with several groups at once. Moreover, the poetry anthologies that emerged out of these interactions included the works of female poets from different circles, regions, and time periods. As such, they played a crucial role in nurturing a sense of community.

Not all the Confucian literati accepted female gentry poets without reservation. Zhang Xuecheng (1738–1801), an important scholar from eastern Zhejiang, where women's literature was not widely appreciated, openly charged Yuan Mei with "poisoning the minds of the young ladies of eminent families" and "showing no respect for the segregation of the sexes and ignoring the fact that they are proper women." In Zhang's mind, these women recalled the courtesan poets of the late Ming in that they formed personal ties to famous literati and were capable of reaching the general reading public through writing and publishing. In doing so, however, they had crossed the line between the private and public world, and their womanly virtue was endangered. Although Zhang put a greater share of the blame on Yuan Mei than on his female disciples, he did not think highly of their poems either. He was afraid that the less talented ladies would end up embarrassing themselves by circulating their works.

While poetry remained the focal point, things were happening on other fronts. The late Ming period had seen a few short plays by female playwrights, and this developed into a visible trend during the mid-Qing, especially from 1736 through 1840. It is no surprise that some gentry ladies would turn their hand to composing plays. Many of these plays read much like extended lyric poems while theatrical devices and the narrative form yielded additional room for negotiating self-representation and expressing the creative imagination. Recurrent in the dramas of female playwrights is the motif of cross-dressing, and female protagonists in male attire are often portrayed as succeeding in the civil service examinations. In Wang Yun's (1749–1819) *Dream of Splendor* (*Fanhua meng*), the female protagonist, Wang Menglin, goes one step further: she dreams of herself as a talented young man who not only achieves success in the examinations but also marries one wife and two concubines. In her one-act play, *The Fake Image* (*Qiaoying*), Wu Zao (1799–1862) depicts her heroine as a frustrated scholar unrecognized in her own time. Sitting in front of a self-portrait that depicts her as a male student, she drinks wine while chanting "Encountering Sorrow" and bemoaning the oddity of her fortune. This play was first transmitted in hand-copied form and then staged in Shanghai in 1825 by a male actor from Suzhou – a rare instance of a female playwright's work being performed in this period.

Although playwriting was an accepted practice among gentry ladies by the mid-Qing, it took them much longer to begin producing vernacular novels. Compared with other genres, vernacular fiction seems to have attracted the least amount of sustained interest from female gentry authors prior to the late eighteenth century. This phenomenon finds ready explanations: the relatively low prestige of vernacular fiction as a literary genre; the predominantly masculine themes of dynastic cycles and military adventures based on historiography and folklore; and the formulaic, impersonal rhetoric of storytelling. Records show that female readers were generally interested in "scholar–beauty romances." Also popular were *The Stone*, which went into widespread circulation in the final decade of the eighteenth century, and *Flowers in the Mirror*, first printed in 1815. These works held irresistible appeal for female audiences with their portrayal of female protagonists in all their subtle complexities. Thus it is no coincidence that the earliest extant novel by a woman writer is *Shadows of Dream of the Red Chamber* (*Honglou meng ying*), a sequel to *The Stone*. The novel was first published under a pseudonym in Beijing in 1877, although composed much earlier. As will be discussed in Chapter 6 of this volume, its author was only recently identified as Gu Chun (or Gu Taiqing, 1799–ca 1877), the daughter of a disgraced Manchu prince, later the concubine of Yihui, a great-grandson of the Qianlong Emperor.

The narrative impulse characteristic of women writers is best captured in the *tanci* or string ballad, as will be elaborated in greater detail in the next chapter (see the section "Female-authored string ballads"). Here it need only be mentioned that although the female gentry authors often refer to string ballad as being "performed" by women, nearly all of their *tanci* works fall into the category of written literature and were read instead of performed. This is one of the ways by which gentry ladies drew a distinction between their *tanci* and those written and performed by professionals. More importantly, they were aware of *tanci* as a territory not yet occupied by male writers, so that their engagement in this genre was subject to fewer traditional constraints. Each major opus of *tanci* would necessitate a whole community, as numerous gentlewomen were involved in its writing, editing, and transmission. In some cases, a woman might spend much of her time hand-copying the work of her mother and then carry the manuscript to her husband's home as if it were part of her dowry. Given their enormous scope, *tanci* were sometimes received as repositories of experience, knowledge, and wisdom, to be passed on from one generation of women to another. Composing a long *tanci* piece is inevitably a complex and time-consuming process, fraught with interruptions and distractions, so some works were left unfinished or were completed by someone other than the original author. While the writing was still under way, a *tanci* would usually be transmitted in hand-copied form among a small coterie of enthusiastic female readers, whose responses and suggestions would help to shape the part yet to be written. To a large extent, each *tanci* may be perceived as the product of an ongoing dialogue. Driven and sustained by this unending discourse, many pieces seem to extend infinitely, with convoluted plots, multiple climaxes, and no prospect of closure, as is seen in the early nineteenth-century *Pomegranate Blossom Dream* (*Liuhua meng*), which runs to nearly five million characters. More often than not, such dialogues were carried on from one work to another, as a large percentage of *tanci* were conceived in response to existing ones, with sequels and rewritings being the dominant modes of composition.

Even a cursory look at a *tanci* piece from the late eighteenth or early nineteenth century ushers us into the larger network of correspondences of which it is an integral part. For instance, Chen Duansheng's (1751–1796) *Karmic Bonds of Reincarnation* (*Zaishengyuan*), arguably the best-known *tanci* by a female author in the Qing dynasty, is itself a sequel to an earlier work. Chen passed away before finishing the book, and it was later completed by Liang Desheng (1771–1857). In fact, even while *Karmic Bonds* was still circulating in manuscript form, it inspired sequels or corrections. The intertextual or transtextual relationships among these works are surely an extension of the relationships among the individual authors or the discursive communities to which they belonged. Even so, *Karmic Bonds* stands out for generating particularly frequent rewritings. One of the most famous rewritings of *Karmic*

Bonds was by Hou Zhi (1764–1829), a gentry woman poet from an eminent scholarly family in Jiangnan.

It might be said that no single writer played a more important role than Hou Zhi in shaping the history of *tanci* literature. In particular, she worked together with publishers to produce definitive versions of several *tanci*, including many that had suffered textual variations from being transmitted in hand-copied form. As an editor, she also influenced the reception of these works through paratextual writings such as prefaces and postscripts. Of course, Hou Zhi was not the first gentlewoman to participate in editing and publishing. Already in the late Ming, female gentry poets were getting involved in compiling, editing, and commenting on women's poetry (and sometimes men's poetry); even greater numbers of anthologies of women's poetry were published during the late eighteenth century and the early nineteenth. In most cases, these publications issued from family presses and were only occasionally circulated through the market. The differences between a commercial press and a family one were less sharply drawn in this period, and some of these anthologies, especially ones that were reprinted, found their way to a general audience.

Hou Zhi, however, did go further than most of her fellow gentlewomen in search of new avenues for participation in the public domain. Unfortunately her forays into commercial publishing had no lasting effect on the production of women's literature. Gentry women were never true participants in, much less beneficiaries of, the gradual professionalization of writing; they remained largely dependent on the infrastructure of the literati community that was to disintegrate in the face of the social and cultural transformations of the years to come. The women writers of the twentieth century emerged amid the convulsions of modernization and commercialization. Writing and publishing in radically altered circumstances, they saw themselves as having little, if anything, in common with the gentry women of the previous century, let alone identifying themselves as their modern descendants. Preoccupied with modern and primarily Western literary genres, they either knew little about *tanci* or else knowingly cast it aside as one of the outmoded forms of a backward legacy that they were eager to disavow.

Consolidating literati culture: outlook and struggle

During the first half of the nineteenth century, the literati were so deeply engaged in intellectual and scholarly discourse that it would be difficult to isolate their literary pursuits. Over the course of the Qianlong reign, several major trends of discourse became reoriented or reinforced; the full range of the implications of these adjustments would become manifest only in the years to come.

Evidential learning, which held sway over Qianlong intellectual discourse, remained a dominant trend until the 1850s, when the Taiping Rebellion severely damaged the infrastructure of the scholarly community in Jiangnan. Representing nothing less than a major shift in scholarly paradigm, evidential learning generated and sustained a great deal of interest in factual knowledge and textual studies, and helped to expand the horizon of literati learning into areas that had received no systematic examination. So pervasive was its influence that even the scholars who opposed its agenda could scarcely undertake a scholarly or intellectual inquiry without engaging textual and linguistic studies in some form. Moreover, as indicated earlier, without the stimulation of evidential learning and the general scholarly climate it engendered, the rise of the erudite, inquisitive literati novel would not have been possible. At their best, evidential scholars facilitated an outlook informed by objectivism and skepticism as their scholarship challenged the textual basis of neo-Confucian orthodoxy. This intellectual orientation was, however, obscured in the practice of many evidential scholars, who seemed engrossed in details and oblivious to the larger issues at stake. Indeed, more than a few intellectuals showed concern about the growing disengagement of evidential inquiry from values and political realities. These critics also questioned its relevance, as scholars of evidential studies seemed incapable of presenting the kind of normative or constructive vision that the Confucian state desperately needed.

Eventually, intellectual and cultural endeavors of lasting importance came from two other sources: the new script school of Confucianism (*jinwen jingxue*), also called the Gongyang School (Gongyang xue), which underwent a revival beginning in the 1770s, and the Tongcheng School (Tongcheng pai), which acquired new appeal for statesmen and men of letters in the early and mid-nineteenth century. The differences between the two schools could not be more marked: the former was based on the exegesis of the Confucian classics, while the latter began as a style of classical prose. Despite their local origins, both grew into schools of national prominence, as each developed a discourse with far-reaching ramifications in contemporary affairs.

Gongyang discourse is so called because it derives from *The Gongyang Tradition (Gongyang zhuan)*, an exegetical text attached to the *Spring and Autumn Annals*, one of the Confucian classics. The Gongyang scholars read the *Spring and Autumn Annals* not as the chronicle that it appeared to be, but as a sacred book containing the codes on which all Confucian institutions, philosophy, and cosmology were founded. Led by Zhuang Cunyu (1719–88), Liu Fenglu (1776–1829), and other scholars of the Changzhou School, Gongyang learning underwent a revival in the Qianlong reign and gradually evolved into a political philosophy, and indeed a comprehensive worldview, that, according to contemporary scholar Wang Hui, addressed urgent contemporary political and cultural issues. Gongyang learning in its rejuvenated form was concerned with the legitimacy of the Qing empire and the historical changes it had to endure. It also offered a theoretical framework for coping with ethnic and regional conflicts within the empire and for negotiating the complex relationships between the empire and the emerging nation states, especially the imperial powers of the West. Sacred to the Gongyang scholars of the time were two assumptions about the *Spring and Autumn Annals*: first, that it provides the ultimate source of legitimacy – the ancient equivalent to a modern constitution – and thus was the foundation for their claim to what might be called Confucian universalism; second, that its partial account of the history of the Eastern Zhou dynasty (771–256 BC) suggests a normative model against which to measure and evaluate the reality, but which was also flexible enough to engage the processes of historical change. After the fall of Jiangnan (in which Changzhou lay) to the Taiping Rebellion in the 1850s, the literati from Guangdong and Hunan began to take the lead in intellectual engagement with current affairs. No one went further than Kang Youwei (1858–1927), a Gongyang scholar from Guangdong, in elaborating the universality of Confucianism. His article "On Confucius's Institutional Reform" (Kongzi gaizhi kao, 1897–1898), described by his disciple Liang Qichao as "a volcanic eruption and an enormous earthquake" that shook up the empire, presents Confucius as a great seer and reformer capable of ingenious ideas comparable to those of modern Western thinkers. *Great Harmony (Datong shu)*, which Kang began writing around 1884 and continued to revise until 1902 (although a complete version was not published until 1935), conjures up an all-inclusive utopian vision of what Kang describes as world governance. Based on core Confucian values, Kang's utopia incorporates a heavy dose of modern European philosophy, science, and institutions, but is ultimately driven by an ideal system of great justice that would transcend both European capitalism and the dynastic history of the Central Kingdom. Fraught with contradictions and internal tensions, this grand vision tested the limits of the Gongyang School's ability to synthesize modern and ancient thoughts of vastly different origins. Surreal and fantastic though it may appear, Kang's theory was nevertheless inseparable from sociopolitical practice; as such, it offered an immediate stimulus for Kang's engagement in the 1898 reform movement.

The tenor of this intellectual trend resonated strongly in literature and literary discourse, which were often noted for their intense political sensibilities and the depth of their historical perspective. Besides Liu Fenglu and his fellow Gongyang scholars, other Changzhou writers, such as Zhang Huiyan (1761–1802) and Hong Liangji (1746–1809), were concerned with contemporary affairs while engaging in poetry, ancient-style prose, and studies of the Confucian classics, including the *Spring and Autumn Annals*. Zhang was especially noted as the founder of what was later called the Changzhou School of song lyrics (Changzhou cipai). His efforts to unravel the deep meaning of song lyrics – a genre mainly associated with the feminine voice and sensibility – by reading them as allegory were taken up by Zhou Ji (1781–1839), who wrote several influential works on the subject. An accomplished poet, Zhou not only expounded Zhang's hermeneutical approach but also emphasized the relevance of "history" in interpreting song lyrics. Along with allegorical interpretation of poetry, his emphasis on history bears the mark of the Gongyang tradition, though mediated, as he explains, by personal experience.

In 1819, Gong Zizhen (1792–1841), a twenty-eight year old poet and scholar who had just failed in his second attempt at the palace examination, encountered Liu Fenglu in Beijing. Gong claimed that he became Liu's follower there and then; his contributions to Gongyang learning in years to come were recognized by Kang Youwei and others. Liu's influence on Gong Zizhen did not end with ideas and learning. Years later, in explaining the recurring themes of his song lyrics, Gong again pointed to Gongyang discourse. It would be misleading and reductive to describe his literary work as lively illustrations of Liu's political philosophy and historical inquiry, yet Gongyang discourse surely furnished Gong Zizhen with a valorized temporal and spatial frame within which to situate the self and the Central Kingdom in his poetry and other writings. His studies of Gongyang scholarship convinced him that he was living in an age of decline. Although fatalistic, this view did not deter him from political engagement and scholarly intervention. Gong spent much time studying geography, and proposed policies regarding the development of the northwest as a way of counterbalancing what he saw as the European threat coming from the ocean. A close associate of Lin Zexu, the governor of Guangdong and Guangxi, and a crucial figure in the coming Opium War, Gong even offered personal advice on the impending clash with the West.

Gong's determination to neutralize the blow from the West was matched by the intensity with which he criticized the political establishment at home and the repressive environment that suffocated individual creativity and imagination. In his more than three hundred quatrains, composed under the collective title *Miscellaneous Cycle of Poems of the Jihai Year* (*Jihai zashi*, referring to the year 1839), Gong ranges effortlessly from the wandering of his free spirit to the turmoil in his private life to the deterioration of state affairs to the doomed fortune of the empire, in ways reminiscent of no less a model than Du Fu in his later years. Rarely has the quatrain as a poetic genre ever been deployed with the scope, energy, and tragic grandeur that characterize Gong's series. Despite the pervasive mood of "decline" in his writings, Gong invested an equal amount of passion in rekindling a "youthful spirit" that, in the context of the nationalistic and revolutionary movements in the years to come, would transform his works into a call for the birth of a new age and a new nation. Gong's literary and intellectual promise was cut short by his accidental death at the age of forty-nine, but he lived long enough to see the first Opium War. He was reluctant to greet the coming era even as he felt estranged from a world that seemed to be eroding under his very feet.

Before Gongyang learning underwent a revival in the Changzhou of the late Qianlong years, the Tongcheng School of ancient-style prose was already well established in Tongcheng, Anhui. Its chief representative was Yao Nai (1731–1815), who created a retrospective genealogy by tracing the movement through Fang Bao (1668–1749) to claim Gui Youguang (1507–1571) of the late Ming as its progenitor. The agenda of the practitioners of the Tongcheng style kept evolving to accommodate changing circumstances and new demands, but its main thrust remained largely the same. In order to appeal to the majority of the literati and consolidate their sense of community, the Tongcheng School developed an all-inclusive discourse by connecting literary culture to the core neo-Confucian values and by negotiating with competing schools. In advocating ancient-style prose as the medium for conveying *yili* (moral reasoning) or the Confucian concept of "principle," the Tongcheng scholars harked back to Han Yu, who was instrumental in the mid-Tang revival of ancient-style prose. They went further than their Tang precursors, however, in their emphasis on the importance of writing to an author's moral self-cultivation, thereby linking the Tongcheng School to Song neo-Confucianism, the state-sanctioned philosophy whose authority had been undercut by the philological and evidential approach of Han learning that had become prevalent in the Qing. Endorsing Song learning did not, however, lead Yao Nai to dismiss Han learning, despite his personal reservations about its growing prominence and the agenda of its practitioners. In addition to *yili*, Yao also emphasized evidential learning (*kaoju*) and literary style (*cizhang*), and developed a comprehensive scheme by which to analyze the tone, texture, and rhetorical devices of ancient-style prose (such as the balanced interaction between "masculine" and "feminine" styles and the appropriate combination of energy, flavor, tone, and other elements). He wished to render these aspects of literary form and style as tangible and accessible as the guiding methods of evidential scholarship.

Insofar as it constituted a response to prevailing styles and modes of discourse, the Tongcheng School also became the focal point against which other schools came to define their positions. Much contemporary literary practice and discourse can be explicated through their negotiations with or opposition to what the Tongcheng writers claimed to represent. For example, to create an alternative to the ancient-style prose of the Tongcheng School, certain writers focused on parallel prose, a semipoetic form that had defined the period style of the Six Dynasties. Dismissing Tongcheng prose as plain and rigid, they produced florid essays that flowed with lyrical cadences and were filled with an enormous range of allusions. Anthologies of parallel prose were published in quick succession. One such work, *Selections of Parallel Prose (Pianti wenchao)*, includes 774 works from the Warring States to the Sui dynasty. The compiler, Li Zhaoluo (1769–1841), was a member of the Yanghu School, which emerged under the influence of the Tongcheng style but reached beyond it by embracing neglected genres. Yanghu is near Changzhou; other members of the Yanghu School included Zhang Huiyan, earlier mentioned as the founder of the Changzhou School of song lyrics.

The prevalence of the Tongcheng School in this period was due in large measure to Yao Nai's multifaceted achievements. A palace graduate, Yao was a member of the national elite as well as the local gentry; he served in Beijing and was involved in the imperial compilation project of the *Four Treasuries*. He also had a huge network of friends, which included Yuan Mei and other luminaries. Perhaps most importantly, he was a prominent editor and teacher, taking full advantage of the institutional framework of both the commercial publishing industry and the private academy to extend the influence of his work. His *Classified Anthology of Ancient-Style Prose (Guwenci leizuan)* was epoch-making in that it redefined the generic categories and the history of ancient-style prose. Yao Nai was equally successful as a scholar and teacher, and spent the last forty years of his life writing and teaching in private academies in Yangzhou, Nanjing, and elsewhere. The Tongcheng style became as widespread as his disciples.

The rise of local elites on the national stage around the 1850s gave the Tongcheng School an additional boost. Zeng Guofan (1811–1872), a prominent statesman and member of the cultural elite from Hunan, reinterpreted the Tongcheng tradition in such a way as to integrate it into his grand project of cultural revival and political salvation. Zeng was the product of neo-Confucian education and a local community regulated by Confucian rituals and customs. After a year of study at Yueyang Academy, one of the four most eminent private academies of the day, he went on to pass examinations at both the provincial and palace levels, and attained the title of Hanlin scholar. In 1852, as the Taiping marched on his hometown, Zeng rose to the occasion by mobilizing the young men from his region and equipping them to block the invasion when the government armies, demoralized and inadequately prepared, failed to stand their ground. No one played a more crucial role in quelling the Taiping Rebellion. Although Zeng disbanded his troops afterwards, his success marked the beginning of the militarization of local communities, which, some historians have claimed, were to destabilize the empire and Republican China in the long run. Nevertheless, the immediate aftermath of this military triumph was an age of reform, as many regional elites moved to the center of national politics and initiated a series of institutional changes. For example, Zeng in 1865 proposed the creation of the Jiangnan Bureau of Manufacture, the national center of military industry, and two years later added the Institute of Translation, the first government organization for the translation of Western works on science and industrial engineering. Thanks to his relentless efforts, the Qing government began in 1872 to send school-age boys to the United States to be educated in modern science and technology. It is thus no surprise that to the tenets of the Tongcheng School Zeng added "statecraft" (*jingji*), which included the management of the emerging modern institutions and organizations. Surrounding himself with such like-minded elites as Li Hongzhang (1823–1901) and Zhang Zhidong (1837–1909), Zeng ensured that his reform project would be carried on after his death.

Like his contemporary Gongyang Confucians, Zeng Guofan saw the Confucian Way as a dynamic force capable of accommodating multifarious changes and reconciling divergent demands. Receptive as he was to modern science, new institutions, and vocational or professional education, Zeng was steadfast in holding on to the core values of neo-Confucianism and classical education. His endorsement of the Tongcheng School is therefore not difficult to understand: the Tongcheng curriculum offered access to the storehouse of literati culture through its syncretic nature and encompassing scope. More importantly, in its adherence to neo-Confucian concepts of moral principle and self-cultivation, it became a vital component of humanistic education, which aimed to build character and conscience on the foundations of Confucian civilization. In this sense, Tongcheng discourse provided Zeng with what he needed to promulgate the qualities essential to the rejuvenation of literati culture as the Confucian gentlemen of the Qing empire were facing daunting challenges from both within and without.

With his prestige and national influence, Zeng brought new life to the Tongcheng School. His legacy was extended by Yan Fu (1854–1921) and Lin Shu (1852–1924), who took inspiration from Zeng in their translations of Western political philosophy and literature. In their hands, ancient-style prose showed remarkable resilience and an unusual adaptability to a wide range of purposes. In the late nineteenth century, Chinese translations of Western science, thought, and fiction invariably appeared in classical Chinese, and their popularity among the general educated audience did not fade until the 1920s. Prolific translators and authors, Yan Fu and Lin Shu were important in mediating and negotiating between traditional literati culture and modern Western culture. They saw values as partly growing out of their own traditions, instead of coming solely from the West, and Lin Shu was especially adept at working with the modern market and through the agency of government and private organizations (including the new national education system). In this way, they combined the high-mindedness of the traditional intellectual with the business acumen of the "organic intellectual" (to borrow Antonio Gramsci's term) who is at home with new technology and modern institutions. Instead of proposing revolution or a wholesale denunciation of the indigenous cultural tradition, this intellectual trend represented a vibrant movement toward modernity that has largely been excluded from the standard account of Chinese literary and intellectual history.

Despite the willingness of the Tongcheng and Gongyang schools to accommodate change in the emerging new world, their contributions to twentieth-century modern Chinese culture have often been cast in a negative light, as they were demonized in the attacks of May Fourth reformers in 1919. As will be discussed in Chapter 6 of this volume, the leaders of the May Fourth Movement, who presented themselves as the only legitimate spokesmen for Chinese modernity, relegated the work of the Tongcheng and Gongyang scholars and writers to an irredeemable past that they associated with the "dead" world of classical Chinese and the hopelessly backward-looking worldview of Confucianism.

5

Prosimetric and verse narrative

WILT L. IDEMA

Introduction

Much of Chinese literature is a historian's delight. Precise dating, an obsession of elite Chinese culture from the beginning, has made the chronological account one of the most popular forms of historical writing. This passion, shared by Confucian literati and Buddhist monks alike, has given us an abundance of historical information in the form of titles, prefaces, and colophons on dates of composition and publication. The voluminous body of historiographical sources also aids in the dating of elite authors and their activities, which allows for a presentation of Chinese literature by period, such as is found in these volumes. This approach, however, runs the danger of failing to do justice to those works that defy attempts at precise dating. As long as such works belong to genres regarded as important, they and their authors (if known) will, with a few ritual caveats, be inserted into the chronological narrative, often at a date somewhat earlier than careful scholarship can justify. Works belonging to genres that fail to achieve canonical status, however, will be allowed to remain in the limbo of timeless oblivion. Such has been the fate of the vast corpus of prosimetric and verse narrative in many genres, including heroic stories, romantic tales, pious legends, and scandalous court cases, works that were written in roughly the last two imperial dynasties, but often were not published in print until the early twentieth century. The overwhelming majority of these texts are not attributed to an author; even in the rare cases where they are, it is often difficult to pinpoint the place and time of composition or first printing. A chapter treating these materials therefore must largely abandon a chronological presentation in favor of a generic and thematic one.

Chinese literary histories often treat this body of texts as one of the many genres of "folk literature" (*minjian wenxue*). "Folk literature" can sometimes be a catchall phrase for all forms of written and oral literature that lie outside of elite literary traditions and also have not been included in the huge depositories of canonical Buddhist and Daoist literature. Used in its widest sense, the term may include all drama and vernacular fiction, although certain forms of drama and vernacular fiction were avidly cultivated by the elite literati from the sixteenth century onward. A more meaningful use of the term "folk literature" would limit it to "oral literature" (*koutou wenxue*). Difficult as it is to define "oral literature" in an extremely literate culture that is at the same time characterized by a high degree of illiteracy in the general citizenry, we can say with some certainty that among the large segment (up to 80 percent) of the Chinese population, especially in the rural areas of the north and west, who were functionally illiterate, there existed a rich body of orally transmitted songs, tales, proverbs, and jokes. By its very nature, orally transmitted literature that pre-dates twentieth-century technology is forever lost. Even with such technology, one still has to distrust the modern scholar who too often feels obliged to "improve" the materials he studies and publishes. This is even more the case in dealing with premodern literature, when attempts to put oral materials into written form involved a scribe who would most likely have been exposed to the basic texts of Confucianism. These scribes may have ranged from barely literate peasants to religious, ritual, medical, and military specialists, and from professional entertainers to literati who had passed the lower-level civil service examinations. To identify this heterogeneous group with "the people," or to assume they all shared the same anti-elite or peasant worldview, would be oversimplifying. Furthermore, there is no reason to believe that these people would have limited themselves to transcribing oral materials. Among them were also creative spirits who, accustomed to composing their own works for performance or reading, would have added something of their own voice into the stories they adapted. Some scholars have called this body of largely anonymous literature in low-status genres *su wenxue*, or "popular literature," to distinguish it from the literature of the literati. I will use this term in preference to "folk literature" and also as distinct from *tongsu wenxue*, which may be rendered as "mass literature," especially when used in a twentieth-century context. While popular literature was written all over China, individual texts often had only local distribution, in contrast to mass literature, which belongs to the age of modern print technology and print capitalism, when a few publishing firms (primarily located in Shanghai) mass-produced titles to be marketed to a national audience.

In the Ming (1368–1644) and Qing (1644–1911) dynasties, works of popular literature were not considered literature at all; at best, such works were tolerated as entertainment. While popular literature was widely read (and in some cases performed before audiences from all walks of life), the texts themselves as physical objects stood only a slim chance of survival. Printed or written on cheap paper, they often would be read and reread until they were reduced to shreds. Scholars would not include these texts in their libraries, and, if they did, would almost certainly not list them in their catalogues. Surprisingly, the largest collections of popular literature of the eighteenth and nineteenth centuries from northern China were held in the Qing imperial palace and the Beijing mansion of the Mongol Princes of Che. Systematic collection of these materials was undertaken only after the May Fourth Movement, when the Academia Sinica brought together a huge collection, largely through the efforts of Liu Fu (Liu Bannong, 1891–1934). Modern scholars subsequently started to study and publish on these materials. These developments came to an end with the political turmoil of the 1930s and the Pacific War. In 1949, the Academia Sinica, with its collection, followed the Guomindang regime to Taiwan, where, for the remainder of the twentieth century, the conservative climate gave little stimulus to research in this field. In the People's Republic of China, a number of volumes collecting different versions of the same tale, such as stories involving the characters of Yue Fei, the White Snake, Liang Shanbo and Zhu Yingtai, and Meng Jiangnü, were published in the 1950s, but distrust in the role of the anonymous but literate authors of these texts turned research toward the oral literature of the countryside as well as the living traditions of "minor arts" (quyi). "Minor arts" refers to any kind of performance involving song, comic dialogue, or prosimetric and verse narrative. At the same time, attempts were made to modernize the repertoire of these genres in the service of Socialist Reconstruction. During the Cultural Revolution (1966–1976), both the performance and the study of "minor arts" were condemned as remnants of feudal ideology and superstition, and came to a halt. Only in recent decades has there been a revival of interest in popular literature in all its variety. Large projects are under way to document and publish all forms of storytelling and song province by province. Beginning with the manuscripts from the mansion of the Princes of Che, major collections are being made available in photographic reprints and/or modern typeset editions, along with up-to-date catalogues. In-depth studies of individual genres, let alone individual works, remain rare. In view of the huge amount of primary materials and the limited and uneven scholarship in this field, any survey at this time must be of a preliminary nature.

I. Early narrative verse, transformation texts, and "all keys and modes"

Genres of written popular literature are more or less closely linked with their counterparts in the tradition of performed narrative. The impulse to tell stories may be an age-old human characteristic, but the formalization of storytelling into literary genres is a more recent phenomenon that varies from culture to culture. In China, the literary tradition began with lyric rather than epic song. While the *Classic of Poetry* does contain a number of narrative songs that, taken together, tell the story of the origin of the Zhou nation and its development into a dynasty, these songs are not presented as a set and, when compared to ancient Greek or Indian epic, their narrative is brief and elliptical. The absence of an epic tradition in early Chinese literature has sometimes been explained as the result of the Chinese ideal of placing *wen* (pattern/order) over *wu* (warfare/violence) and the absence of a class of knights. Given the incessant warfare of the Spring and Autumn period and the Warring States period, when Chinese "gentlemen" (*shi*) were closer to warriors than the scribes into whom they later evolved, such an explanation is unconvincing. One may perhaps infer the existence of an oral epic tradition in these centuries in comparing Sima Qian's (ca 145–ca 86 BC) treatment in his *Records of the Historian* of famous story-cycles, such as the sagas of the travels and tribulations of Prince Chong'er, the flight and revenge of Wu Zixu, or the survival and reinstatement of the Orphan of Zhao, to earlier versions in the *Zuo Tradition* and *Discourses of the States*. Sima Qian does not so much summarize his sources as present accounts that reflect the reorganization of the original materials through generations of oral transmission. He implies this when he says that some of his materials are collected from "local elders" whom he consulted.

The period of the third to fifth centuries AD has left us a number of long narrative songs. Longest and best known of these is "Southeast Fly the Peacocks" (Kongque dongnan fei), which tells the story of a couple who, forced to separate by the husband's mother, eventually both commit suicide. Hans Frankel has shown that this poem had its origins in oral composition, by implication suggesting that many more songs of this kind were current at the time. Indeed, Gan Bao (d. 336), in providing short summaries of popular legends in his *In Search of the Supernatural* (*Soushen ji*), occasionally mentions that "the song" associated with a given legend is still current. "Southeast Fly the Peacocks" is written in five-syllable lines throughout, as are some comparable poems of more modest length, such as "Grief" (Beifen shi), ascribed to Cai

Yan (ca 178–after 206; alternatively ca 170–ca 215). In later centuries, the seven-syllable line would become the prosodic form of choice in prosimetric and verse narrative; it was systematically referred to as *ci*, which in this context might be translated as "ballad verse." *Ci* is more commonly used to designate the genre of allometric song, in which case the term is generally translated "song lyric." The seven-syllable line was used in lyric poetry from the early third century. That it was already in use by professional entertainers for narrative purposes is suggested by a late statement that the poet Cao Zhi (192–232) knew several thousand "entertainer *ci*" by heart. The seven-syllable line would also become the preferred medium for long narrative poems by literati. Bai Juyi's "Song of Enduring Sorrow" and "Ballad of the Lute," and Wei Zhuang's "Ballad of the Wife of Qin," probably the best-known ballads by elite Tang poets, are all written in seven-syllable lines. Compared to the anonymous little epic on Ji Bu found among the Dunhuang manuscripts, these literati compositions tend to be shorter and denser in diction. Verse narrative written completely or primarily in seven-syllable lines continued to be a major component of popular literature from the Ming onward.

The majority of "transformation texts" recovered from Dunhuang, as we have seen in Chapter 4 of the first volume, are written in alternating prose passages and passages in verse. While the more specifically Buddhist genres, such as "sutra-explanation texts" and "tales of causes and conditions," sometimes use rhymeless six-syllable verse, common transformation texts used the seven-syllable line exclusively. The seven-syllable line became the model generally adopted in later prosimetric literature. Victor Mair has argued strongly in favor of an Indian origin for the prosimetric form. Buddhist sutras, circulated and translated in China in increasing numbers from the second century onward, were often written in prosimetric form, but their verse sections were in nonrhyming metrical verse. Chinese translators imitated this by avoiding rhyme and often using a four-syllable or six-syllable line in place of the five-syllable line. From the Chinese perspective, the development of the prosimetric form of transformation texts may have been experienced less as a borrowing than as an improvement upon the original form of the sutras, as the contrast between prose and verse was now accentuated by rhyme. The close link between sutras and transformation texts is further corroborated by the layout of the written texts: unlike Chinese manuscripts of poetry, which do not separate the lines, manuscripts of transformation texts follow the model of the sutras in setting prose and verse apart and clearly separating each line of verse, all to the great practical benefit of anyone reciting or performing these texts.

In the Western traditions, narrative is usually presented exclusively in verse or prose. One of the rare cases of a narrative alternating between prose and verse, for which the Latin term *prosimetrum* is used, is the medieval French *Aucassin et Nicolette*, which calls itself a "chantefable." Some modern sinologists have therefore borrowed "chantefable" to designate prosimetric narrative in the Chinese tradition. The term has the advantage of closely resembling the modern Chinese neologisms *shuochang wenxue* and *jiangchang wenxue*, which both mean "literature for telling and singing," hence focusing on performance rather than textual form. These Chinese terms, however, also include as a rule the various genres of verse narrative.

The Dunhuang transformation texts are examples, fortuitously preserved, of a much wider tradition of prosimetric and verse narrative practiced throughout the Chinese-speaking world, not only in the Tang (618–906) but also throughout the following millennium. Unfortunately, information about professional storytellers in diaries on life in the capital of the Northern Song (960–1126), Kaifeng, and the capital of the Southern Song (1127–1276), Hangzhou, is too scarce to allow us to draw conclusions about the format of their performances. Most of the performers listed in these capital diaries may well have told their stories, irrespective of subject matter, primarily in prose. One late diary mentions the "strumming and singing of tales of causes and conditions," suggesting that this genre, also represented among the Dunhuang narratives, survived at least into the thirteenth century. Another diary contrasts the sophisticated patrons of "cliff ballads" (*yaci*, also "bank ballads") with the more rustic aficionados of "*taozhen* ballads" (a term that has proven difficult to translate), suggesting the existence of different genres of verse narrative, each with its own audience. Further information is, however, lacking.

The only major genre of prosimetric narrative of the twelfth to fourteenth centuries seen in extant texts is the "all keys and modes" (*zhugongdiao*). Reportedly invented in the late eleventh century by Kong Sanzhuan, this genre has verse sections that are written not in isometric seven-syllable lines (most likely set to a simple repetitive melody), but rather to a great variety of often allometric tunes. The genre derives its name from the fact that each verse section is written to a tune or tunes in a different mode from the preceding verse section. In most of these different keys and modes, the verse section is concluded by a coda made up of three seven-syllable lines. In the earliest example, *All Keys and Modes on Liu Zhiyuan* (*Liu Zhiyuan zhugongdiao*), preserved only in fragments and probably dating from the mid-twelfth century, most of the verse sections are limited to two stanzas with a single tune and a coda. This "all keys and modes" tells the story of how Li Sanniang remains faithful to her long-absent husband, Liu Zhiyuan, despite all pressure to remarry. The theme of the wife who remains loyal to her long-absent husband had already been adumbrated in some of the Dunhuang transformation texts; it continues to be a recurrent topic in later prosimetric literature, holding particular appeal for women. The only complete example of the "all keys and modes" is Dong Jieyuan's *The Story of the Western Wing in All Keys and Modes* (*Xixiangji zhugong-diao*). Composed around the year 1200, it has been preserved in a number of fine sixteenth- and seventeenth-century editions. In this work, many verse sections consist of a number of songs followed by a coda. This text not only provided the basis for Wang Shifu's dramatic adaptation, but also became the ancestor of an entire subgenre of tales of romantic love between a dashing student and a beautiful maiden. In the latest known example of the genre, the only partially preserved *Anecdotes of the Tianbao Reign in All Keys and Modes* (*Tianbao yishi zhugongdiao*) by Wang Bocheng of the late thirteenth century, which tells the story of Emperor Xuanzong and Yang Guifei, the song-sets in each verse section closely resemble those in contemporary northern plays (*zaju*). The high demands on the vocal and musical abilities of the performer probably made the "all keys and modes" the elite genre in the world of pro-fessional storytelling. Its texts, especially the works of Dong and Wang, are works of great creative talent, combining a knack for storytelling in verse with a predilection for social satire, as their upper-class heroes are incapacitated by passion and held up to ridicule. Though in later centuries other storytelling genres also employed a variety of melodies, none could approach the musical complexity of the "all keys and modes." For a comparable level of musical complexity, one must turn to drama of the thirteenth century and later. In the early Ming, genres such as "precious scrolls" (*baojuan*) and "ballad narra-tives" (*cihua*) once again use the isometric seven-syllable line in their verse sections.

In addition to the "all keys and modes," we have examples of two minor genres. In "drum lyrics" (*guzici*), the prose narrative is interrupted by songs written to a single allometric melody. Two texts of this type have been preserved. One is an adaptation by Zhao Lingzhi of the late eleventh century of Yuan Zhen's (770–831) famous "Tale of Yingying" (*Yingying zhuan*), partly intended as a corrective to the more popular versions current at the time. The second genre is called "peddler's song" (*huolang'er*). The only example is found in the anonymous northern play *The Peddler: A Female Lead* (*Huolang dan*). Its final act presents the peddler's wife as she tries to make a living by narrating the story of her miserable life in alternating passages of prose and songs set to the tune of "The Peddler" ("Huolang'er"), which varies each time it is repeated. In later centuries, too, shorter genres of ballads will coexist with longer genres of prosimetric and verse narrative.

II. Early precious scrolls and "sentiments of the Way"

Such rare comments on professional storytelling as we have from Ming dynasty authors tend to be limited to general remarks about "ballads by blind women," making it difficult to contextualize the few texts that have been preserved from the fourteenth century onward. The genre about which we have the most information is the "precious scroll." These works, which may be descended directly from Buddhist transformation texts, retained their primarily religious character through the centuries. One example, *The Precious Scroll as Preached by the Buddha about Huaxian'ge and How the Ghost of Madame Yang Embroidered Red Gauze* (*Foshuo Yangshi guixiu hongluo Huaxian'ge baojuan*), preserved in the Shanxi Provincial Museum, claims to be a 1290 reprint of a 1212 edition sponsored by the court of the Jurchen Jin. It tells a complicated story set in the Tang dynasty about a childless couple, Magnate Zhang and Madame Yang, who pray to the Third Lord for a son. When a boy (named Huaxian'ge) is born to them, they forget to repay the god, who then steals the boy's soul at the age of three. As a belated votive offering, Madame Yang over the next three years embroiders a beautiful protective curtain for the god's image. (Elaborate descriptions of women's skill in embroidery and weaving are a favorite feature of later prosimetric literature.) The boy is restored to life, but the four brothers of the Third Lord, who each want a similar curtain, steal Madame Yang's soul. When Magnate Zhang later remarries, the evil stepmother tries to poison Huaxian'ge, killing her own son by mistake. Huaxian'ge eventually marries a princess and rescues his father from prison, and Madame Yang, having finished her embroidery after a lapse of twelve years, comes back to life to be reunited with her husband and son. Scholars have voiced doubts about the date of this text, citing among other reasons the complexity of the story. There can be no doubt, however, about its popularity from an early date; a performance is mentioned in the sixteenth-century novel *The Plum in the Golden Vase*. As late as the second half of the twentieth century, a precious-scroll adaptation of this story was still in circulation in western Gansu. Continued court patronage of the genre of the precious scroll is attested by a partially preserved deluxe manuscript on the legend of Maudgalyayana (Mulian) saving his mother from hell, produced during the early Ming at the court of the Northern Yuan (the Mongol court after its retreat back to the northern grasslands in 1368). The story of Maudgalyayana remained a perennial favorite in the precious-scroll repertoire in later centuries. One such version included the stories of Maudgalyayana's grandfather and father, while another version was expanded to include tales of Mulian's incarnations as the rebel Huang Chao (d. 884) and as a butcher.

From the fifteenth and sixteenth centuries onward, sectarian teachers of new religions used the precious scroll to disseminate their teachings, often printing deluxe editions with the help of subscriptions from palace women and eunuchs. The sectarian precious scrolls are frequently divided into "chapters" (*pin*), each concluded by one or more songs set to a popular tune; ample use is made of ten-syllable verse (*zan*) throughout. Such works hold less interest for the student of literature than for the religious scholar, although some, such as Luo Qing's "five works in six volumes" (*wubu liuce*), contain numerous autobiographical elements. The teachings of these sects often involve the figure of the Eternal Mother (*Wusheng laomu*) who longs for mankind, her errant children, to return. While precious scrolls were regarded by Buddhists as an instrument for popularizing the message of the scriptures, for these sectarian religions the precious scrolls were the scriptures themselves. During the Qing, as sectarian activities came increasingly under suspicion, the authorities actively sought out and destroyed these sectarian works.

One narrative precious scroll, *The Precious Scroll of Incense Mountain* (*Xiangshan baojuan*), which narrates the life of the bodhisattva Guanyin in her human incarnation as the Princess Miaoshan, claims a very early date. The preface states that the text was written in 1103 by the Chan master Puming of the Tianzhu Monastery in Hangzhou. While this attribution is unlikely, we know that the legend of Princess Miaoshan was brought to Hangzhou around this time. Significantly, *The Precious Scroll of Incense Mountain* refers to itself within the text as a "tale of causes and conditions" and not a "precious scroll." As in the Dunhuang tales of causes and conditions, the reciting monk and the listening congregation repeatedly join in invoking the bodhisattva throughout this text. This suggests that the present text of *The Precious Scroll of Incense Mountain* may be derived from one of the "tales of causes and conditions" that were still being performed in the Southern Song. Whatever the actual date of composition, the text was in existence by the late fifteenth century, as it is referred to in an early sixteenth-century source. The earliest extant printing, however, is dated 1773, while the numerous editions in the nineteenth and twentieth centuries are "abbreviated versions."

The story retains the same basic plot in both redactions. Miaozhuang, emperor of the mythical western country of Xinglin, has three daughters but no male heir. When he decides to marry the girls to young men who will move in with the royal family, his youngest daughter Miaoshan stubbornly refuses. Instead she seeks release from the endless cycle of rebirth, with all its attendant suffering, by pursuing a religious life. Unmoved by her parents' pleas, she becomes a novice in the White Sparrow Convent, where the abbess has been instructed to make her life so miserable that she will quickly return to the palace. With divine assistance, the princess accomplishes all the impossible tasks assigned to her. The enraged emperor orders the convent burned to the ground, whereupon the princess douses the fire by spitting out a mouthful of blood that turns into rain. She is brought back to the capital as a criminal, but even the threat of imminent execution cannot change her mind. Following her execution, Miaoshan visits the Underworld but is forced to leave when she disrupts the process of divine justice by saving all sinners. Returned to life, she is taken to Incense Mountain, where she soon achieves enlightenment. In the meantime, her father has been afflicted by a loathsome disease, the description of which must rank as one of the most revolting passages in world literature. A mysterious monk tells him that he can only be cured by the freely donated hands and eyes of one without anger. When the emperor replies that no such person can be found, the monk suggests that he appeal to the hermit of Incense Mountain. Once miraculously healed, the emperor visits the hermit to express his gratitude, and his wife recognizes their daughter in the maimed cripple, who upon the emperor's remorseful prayer is restored to her former beauty. Miaoshan then manifests herself as the Guanyin of a Thousand Hands and Eyes. The long version of 1773, which contains a number of anticlerical passages, is clearly linked to the popularity of the tiny coastal island of Putuoshan as a pilgrimage site; the later, shorter version tries to establish a link between the precious scroll and the Lotus Sutra, the canonical source of the cult of Guanyin, and has been edited to make the text suitable for recitation on the bodhisattva's birthday on the nineteenth day of the Second Month. There also exists a seventeenth-century sectarian rewriting of the Miaoshan legend that is occasionally transmitted under the same title of *The Precious Scroll of Incense Mountain*.

Another early precious scroll that would remain immensely popular in later centuries is the story of Madame Huang, narrated in an abbreviated version in *The Plum in the Golden Vase* by a visiting nun to Ximen Qing's wife Yueniang. Pious from birth, Madame Huang, delights in reciting the Diamond Sutra. She marries a butcher, to whom she bears a boy and a girl. Urged to abandon his sinful profession of killing animals, the butcher refuses for several reasons: he is making good money, he does not believe in Buddhism, and he thinks that women, in that they pollute the gods by the blood they shed in menstruation and childbirth, are far more sinful than men. His wife then refuses to have sexual relations with him, and is soon called to the Underworld by King Yama. Here the narrator takes the opportunity to describe the topography of the Underworld in detail. As Madame Huang passes through the Ten Courts, she is instructed about the cruel punishments meted out to sinners in the hells attached to each of the courts. After she recites the Diamond Sutra for King Yama, he rewards her by allowing her to be reborn as a boy in a rich family (her former identity being conveniently inscribed on her leg). Successful in the examinations, the young man is appointed prefect to his former hometown. In this guise, he persuades the butcher of the truth of Buddhism, and the whole family is enlightened. The above is only one of many hagiographic precious scrolls treating the lives of pious women who are eventually rewarded for their persistent devotion to their faith. The pairing of the devout wife with the insensitive butcher may well have influenced the twentieth-century Taiwanese writer Li Ang's *The Butcher's Wife*.

Just as Buddhist monks and nuns preached their religion using precious scrolls, Daoist priests did so through "sentiments of the Way" (*Daoqing*). Early Daoist traditions had emphasized the secret transmission of scriptures from master to disciple, but the Quanzhen (Perfect Truth) sect, which originated in twelfth-century northern China, had a strong proselytizing element. In its preaching it made ample use of pictures and songs (with a special predilection for the tune "Shuahai'er"). One favorite figure for the unenlightened person – enslaved by greed, lust, riches, and rage – was the skeleton. The most popular narrative in early Quanzhen preaching was the story of Zhuangzi's encounter with a skeleton, elaborated from a famous passage in the *Zhuangzi*. In the earlier text, Master Zhuang laments the fate of a skull he finds by the roadside, only to be chided that night by the skull, who appears to him in a dream to vaunt the incomparable joys of his perfect freedom. In the later tale, Master Zhuang finds a near-complete skeleton, which he brings back to life after filling in its three missing bones with willow branches. The former skeleton turns out to be a traveling merchant, who immediately accuses Master Zhuang of robbing him of all his belongings and drags him to the courthouse. Master Zhuang proves his version of the truth to the judge by turning his accuser into a skeleton once again. This tale is preserved in at least two seventeenth-century adaptations; a third adaptation was included in an abbreviated version by Ding Yaokang (1599–1671) in his *A Sequel to the Plum in the Golden Vase* (*Xu jin ping mei*).

Most representative of the "sentiments of the Way" repertoire from the seventeenth century onwards is the tale of the conversion of the staunch Tang Confucian Han Yu by his nephew Han Xiangzi, one of the Eight Immortals whose legends are recounted in the sixteenth-century novel *Journey to the East* (*Dongyou ji*). A novel on Han Xiangzi's conversion of his uncle appeared in the early seventeenth century, but this never supplanted the prosimetric versions. In the story, Han Xiangzi repeatedly tries to convert his uncle, but even the most spectacular magic cannot dent the latter's Confucian convictions. Only when Han Yu is banished to Chaozhou for protesting against the emperor's veneration of a bone of the Buddha does he awaken to the vanity of all earthly glory and become eager to the pursue the Daoist Way.

The distinctive instrument in the performance of "sentiments of the Way" was the "fish-drum" (*yugu*), a three-foot long bamboo tube covered at one end with a thin membrane. As the main focus of "sentiments of the Way" shifted over time from preaching to entertainment, so its subject matter also broadened in scope. The same holds true of the precious scroll. This development becomes especially noticeable from the nineteenth century on, when "sentiments of the Way" under the names *daoqing*, *yugu*, and *zhuqin* or "bamboo zither" spawned a wide variety of local performative traditions all over China.

III. Ballad-narratives and rustic songs

The term commonly used for non-religious prosimetric narratives between the thirteenth and the sixteenth centuries was "ballad-narratives" (*cihua*). For a long time scholars had little beyond a few lines quoted in plays as a basis for speculation about this genre. In 1967, the dismantling of the grave of a low-ranking official on the outskirts of Shanghai unearthed a set of thirteen ballad-narrative texts, printed in Beijing no later than the late fifteenth century but probably composed in the Suzhou area at some earlier date. (The grave also contained an early printed edition of the southern play *The White Hare* (*Baitu ji*) on the legend of Liu Zhiyuan and Li Sanniang.) With the exception of a single short text composed exclusively in seven-syllable lines, these texts comprise short prose sections alternating with extended sections in seven-syllable verse. A few texts also make sparing use of the ten-syllable line. This ten-syllable line may be an extension of the standard seven-syllable line prefixed with a three-syllable phrase, or, if made up of two sets of three-syllable units followed by one set of four, it may manifest quite a different rhythm. In later centuries the ten-syllable line would become increasingly popular in many genres of prosimetric literature, especially in northern China.

Of the fifteenth-century *cihua* texts discovered in 1967, three deal with episodes from China's military history. The most intensively studied text, possibly dating from the fourteenth century, treats the adventures of Hua Guan Suo. After Zhang Fei and Guan Yu swear brotherhood with Liu Bei, they kill each other's relatives so as to ensure complete dedication to their common cause, but Hua Guan Suo, one of Guan Yu's sons, miraculously survives. The long ballad-narrative gives a full account of the hero's life, from his youth and training, through his wanderings and exploits and his final reunion with his father, to his tragic death in old age. The story, included in some early editions of the *Romance of the Three Kingdoms*, did not make it into Mao Zonggang's edition with commentary in the seventeenth century. Another *cihua* text deals with the adventures of Xue Rengui. Starting out as a common soldier in the Chinese army invading the Korean peninsula in the seventh century, Xue's outstanding feats of arms are claimed by his commanders as their own until he saves the life of Emperor Taizong. The same story, which also was popular on the Yuan stage, is also told in a "plain narrative" (*pinghua*) preserved in *The Grand Encyclopedia of the Yongle Era* and was later developed into the popular military romance *Xue Rengui Chastises the Eastern Regions* (*Xue Rengui zheng dong*). A third tale deals with the founding of the Late Jin dynasty by Shi Jingtang during the tumultuous period of the Five Dynasties (907–960). Shi Jingtang, who has risen from humble beginnings to the rank of governor, is goaded into rebellion by his wife, a sister of the reigning emperor, because she has been slighted by the empress, a former prostitute.

Two other *cihua* texts are moral fables. The most interesting of these tells the story of a filial parrot, whose father has been killed and his mother blinded by hunters. When he leaves the safety of the nest to fetch his mother the cherries she loves, he too is captured, but manages to charm the hunters with his poetic capability. They sell him to the local prefect, who later presents him to the emperor. By refusing to compose any more poems, the little parrot engineers the punishment of the hunters, but on being set free, he returns to the nest only to find that his mother has died. After all the birds have cooperated in providing her with a fine funeral, the little parrot joins the bodhisattva Guanyin as her disciple. This delightful fable was later incorporated into the precious-scroll repertoire and rewritten as a sectarian precious scroll. In contrast, the ballad-narrative version, which stresses humorous elements such as the parrot's doggerel poems, lacks strong religious content.

By far the largest group of ballad-narrative texts features that exemplar of incorruptibility, Judge Bao. The historical Bao Zheng (999–1062) served at the court of the Song emperor Renzong (r. 1023–1063), where he became known for shrewdness and probity. His reputation continued to grow after his death, and soon he was believed to judge criminal cases in this world by day and in the Underworld by night. Over the fourteenth century the Judge Bao character became the main judge portrayed in northern plays, and some of these cases are reencountered in ballad-narratives. One ballad-narrative deals with the judge's miraculous birth and youth. In another he reunites Emperor Renzong with his mother Lady Li, who had been driven from the palace after her baby boy (the future Renzong) was stolen by a concubine, later the empress dowager, who had borne a girl and wanted a son to pass off as her own. In other narratives, the fearless judge confronts imperial relatives who rape and kill innocent women, and monsters who take on the shape of modest maidens to seduce naive young men. The most humorous case involves a talking chamber-pot. In this story, a student on his way to take the examinations in the capital is murdered by two potters. His remains are mixed with clay and made into chamber-pots, one of which the murderers give to an elderly man to whom they owe money. When the old man uses his pot, it protests indignantly and asks him to bring a case before Judge Bao. By the end of the sixteenth century, the cases of Judge Bao were reorganized into a hundred-chapter novel, which was in turn cannibalized to make a collection of short stories. The popularity of Judge Bao helps to explain why many later authors of chantefable literature preferred to set their stories in the reign of Emperor Renzong.

There is no reason to assume that this single set of discovered texts exhausts the themes of fifteenth-century ballad-narratives. The frequent mentioning of Yang Wenguang in the preserved texts suggests that the exploits of the generals of the Yang family in defending the Song dynasty against foreign foes and internal rebels may have been a popular topic in ballad-narratives. Scholars have also suggested that the tales of the heroes of the Liangshan moor may have been treated in ballad-narratives before being reworked into *Water Margin*. The few quotes from ballad-narratives preserved in early works suggest that romantic themes were also treated.

Near the end of the sixteenth century, Zhu Shenglin composed *The Ballad-Narrative of the Prince of Qin of the Great Tang Dynasty* (*Da Tang Qinwang cihua*) in sixty-four chapters, which was printed in an edition of infinitely superior quality to the coarse printings of the fifteenth century. Its subject is the career of Li Shimin, the fourth son of the founder of the Tang dynasty who became the Emperor Taizong. The campaigns and battles leading to the establishment of the dynasty are recounted in great detail, with emphasis given to Li Shimin as the de facto founder of the dynasty. Eventually Li Shimin is compelled by his imperial destiny to accept the murders of his elder brothers by his vassals and his father's subsequent abdication, and the righteousness of these acts is confirmed by a decisive victory over the empire's foreign foes. Prose and verse keep each other roughly in balance in this stirring heroic tale, easily the finest literary adaptation of the story of the young Li Shimin. *The Ballad-Narrative of the Prince of Qin of the Great Tang Dynasty* never enjoyed the same popularity as the novels on the same subject, however, and was generally ignored until its republication in the 1950s.

The composition and printing in a fine edition of the *Da Tang Qinwang cihua* may be seen as part of a general movement from the late sixteenth to the seventeenth century to bring chantefable literature within the ambit of the literati in the wake of drama and vernacular fiction, which, sustained by the publishing boom of this period, had succeeded in becoming minor forms of literati art. Yang Shen (1488–1559), the maverick polymath, is believed to have written, during his banishment to Yunnan, a ballad-narrative summary of Chinese history that, with later additions, has remained in print ever since. The playwright Liang Chenyu (ca 1521–ca 1594) is credited with a comparable work, and the novelist Chen Chen (1614–after 1666) with a sequel, both of which are now lost. In the last century of the Ming, *The Story of the Western Wing in All Keys and Modes* was reprinted a number of times in very fine editions, one with a commentary attributed to the great dramatist Tang Xianzu (1550–1616). Zang Maoxun (d. 1621), better known as the publisher of the *Anthology of Yuan Plays*, also on four occasions published "string ballads" (*tanci*), a term that by this time was common for prosimetric forms in the Jiangnan region. In his prefaces he credited these texts (now lost) to the eccentric poet Yang Weizhen (1296–1370). *The Tale of Cloud-Gate (Yunmen zhuan)*, an anonymous retelling of a Tang dynasty tale, is a chantefable text preserved in a fine edition produced around 1600. Feng Menglong later reworked this text into a vernacular story for his *Three Words (Sanyan)* collection; he also made use of a string ballad on at least one other occasion. Two Cantonese ballad-narratives appeared with extensive commentaries in the style of Jin Shengtan (1610–1661), claiming to be, respectively, the eighth and ninth works in his canon of "books of genius" (*caizi shu*).

In Shandong, the literatus and official Jia Fuxi (Jia Yinchong, 1590–1674) was an enthusiastic amateur performer of chantefable narratives. According to the biography by his fellow provincial Kong Shangren (1648–1718): "He would narrate his tales to students in schools, to the high ministers in their halls, in the offices of the capital officials, and in the marketplace. Carrying his drum, he would perform wherever he found a location." In his play *Peach Blossom Fan*, Kong Shangren has the famous seventeenth-century storyteller Liu Jingting perform a short composition by Jia Fuxi called *The Great Music-Master Zhi Went to Qi* (*Taishi Zhi shi Qi*). Jia Fuxi also composed *A Summary of History: A Drum Ballad* (*Lidai shilüe guci*), in which he lambastes the injustices of this world and ridicules the notion of cosmic justice through posthumous reward and punishment. In a short work entitled "The Chapter 'A Man from Qi'" (Qiren zhang), he satirizes all those who toady to the rich and powerful, using the chapter from *Mencius* about a man who boasts of his high connections to his wife and concubine but in fact makes a living by begging at gravesites. As noted above, both the anonymous author of *The Plum in the Golden Vase* and Jia Fuxi's friend Ding Yaokang, the author of *A Sequel to the Plum in the Golden Vase*, display a remarkable knowledge of prosimetric literature in their novels, even including abbreviated texts as part of their narratives. Ding Yaokang is also credited with the authorship of three short prosimetric compositions of his own. One of these, *Duke Jing of Qi's Treatment of Confucius and Four Other Chapters [from the Analects]* (*Qi Jinggong dai Kongzi wuzhang*), details the failure of Confucius's political program in a corrupt world and his refusal to follow a life of reclusion. The other two short chantefables ascribed to Ding Yaokang are *East of the City Wall* (*Dongguo ji*), a rewriting of "The Chapter 'A Man from Qi'" and *A Dream at the Southern Window* (*Nanchuang meng*). The latter features a fly and a mosquito getting into a fight over a rotten peach; the bookworm who tries to reason with them is berated by a scorpion, and the fly and the mosquito end up in a spider's web.

However, these flirtations between the literati and prosimetric narrative would have no lasting influence. The only famous author with a sizable body of work in this genre is Pu Songling (1640–1715), also from Shandong, who is better known for his collection of classical tales, *Records of the Strange*. Pu Songling, for all his present literary fame, was the private secretary and tutor of a prominent local family and enjoyed only very modest status in his lifetime. Pu's prosimetric narratives, collected as *Rustic Songs of Liaozhai* (*Liaozhai liqu*), were printed only in the twentieth century. Pu seems to have dabbled in this genre both as a young man and towards the end of his life. The youthful compositions, which show his lighter side, include an extended treatment (of disputed authorship) of the joys of newlywed life and a fragment featuring a passionate affair between the beatified Zhu Bajie (Pigsy in *Journey to the West*) and the murdered Pan Jinlian (the nymphomaniac femme fatale in *The Plum in the Golden Vase*). The majority of the rustic songs date from late in Pu's life and reflect the more moralistic tone also observable in the later tales in *Records of the Strange*. This heightened sense of morality may reflect, in addition to a change in the author's outlook, accommodations made to suit his intended audience, as Pu is said to have written some of these texts for the entertainment of his employer's mother. A number of the later works are adaptations of materials earlier treated as classic tales.

In formal terms, Pu's rustic songs differ from contemporary ballad-narratives in that they do not use seven-syllable verse. In many of his rustic songs, the verse sections are written to a single allometric tune that is repeated any number of times; these verses are separated only by short prose passages. This format recalls the drum lyrics of earlier centuries, except that where a drum lyric might repeat the same melody up to twelve times, Pu's melodies may repeat hundreds of times. For instance, in *Expanded Version of the Imperial Progress to Datong (Zengbu Xingyunqu)* in twenty-eight chapters, in which the Zhengde Emperor of the Ming goes incognito to brothels in Datong, Pu exclusively uses "Shuahai'er," the preferred melody in "sentiments of the Way." He does the same in *Underworld Justice (Hansen qu)*. Elsewhere he uses a number of different melodies, but the format remains the same. Several of the rustic songs in one chapter are written in the first person; for example, *The Words of a Poor Man (Qionghan ci)* is the prayer of a poor man addressed to the god of wealth. The two longest texts are, for all intents and purposes, plays.

The rustic songs in three to six chapters tend to focus on family values. *The Song of the Mother-in-law and the Daughter-in-law (Gufu qu)*, adapted from "Shanhu" in *Records of the Strange*, tells the tale of a daughter-in-law who persists in her filial devotion even after her mother-in-law chases her out of the house. *On the Wall (Qiangtou ji)*, actually a short play, recounts how two unfilial sons, having cheated their father out of his property, try to fob him off on each other, until the father ends up on top of the wall between their homes. A clever silversmith eventually tricks them into believing that their father still has money, whereupon the sons vie to take the old man in again. *A Pleasant Song (Kuaiqu)*, in four chapters, is exceptional in taking its characters from the *Romance of the Three Kingdoms*: in Pu Songling's version, after Guan Yu allows Cao Cao to escape once the latter's fleet is wiped out at Red Cliff, Zhang Fei kills Cao Cao, a reversal of historical record. Cao's head is made into a shooting target, and one ear is cooked and eaten by the soldiers.

Pu's longer rustic songs, such as *Underworld Justice*, which is based on "Shang Sanguan" and "Xi Fangping" from *Records of the Strange*, and *Riches and Glory: Divine Immortals* (*Fugui shenxian*), which is an adaptation of "Zhang Hongjian" in *Records of the Strange*, dwell in excruciating detail on the official abuse of power and corruption in the judicial system. *Underworld Justice*, told in eight chapters, combines two stories: a young girl disguises herself as a boy in order to avenge her father after failing to find justice through the courts, and a young man commits suicide and endures horrible tortures in the Underworld in his struggle against a local bully who has managed to buy off the courts both in this world and in the next. The tale is told in a racy vernacular filled with colorful dialect, the characters are presented in simple black-and-white terms, references to sex are bowdlerized while descriptions of violence are expanded, and all the characters get their just deserts in the end. *A Song of Tribulations* (*Monan qu*), a play in thirty-six chapters, focuses on the failure of famine relief, while in another play, *A Mantra to Exorcize Jealousy* (*Rangdu zhou*), Pu Songling returns to his favorite theme of the virago.

Emperors traveling incognito are a popular topic in chantefable literature from the Qing dynasty onward. The widely publicized tours of the Kangxi and Qianlong emperors became the inspiration for an extensive body of narratives in which they are portrayed as roaming about in disguise in order to find out the true condition of the realm, righting miscarriages of justice along the way. These stories evolved into novels, such as *Eternally Flourishing* (*Wannian qing*), also known as *The Qianlong Emperor Roams through Jiangnan* (*Qianlong you Jiangnan*). Whereas these two emperors, like Harun al Raschid in the *Thousand and One Nights* tradition, are depicted as good rulers, the Zhengde Emperor of the Ming is always a wastrel and a fool who has no clue about the life of the common people. In the anonymous novel *The Zhengde Emperor Roams through Jiangnan* (*Zhengde you Jiangnan*, translated in 1843 by Tkin Shen with the assistance of James Legge as *The Rambles of the Emperor Ching Tih in Këang Nan, A Chinese Tale*), a hungry Zhengde Emperor who is enjoying a bowl of rice gruel is easily tricked into believing that the gruel is cooked from pearls. Pu Songling's *Expanded Version of the Imperial Progress to Datong* is evidently an adaptation of an earlier work (now lost), in which the Zhengde Emperor visits Datong disguised as a common soldier after hearing about the charms of the city's three thousand courtesans from the evil minister Jiang Bin. Pu's version emphasizes the emperor's feckless lewdness over his stupidity from the outset:

This Zhengde Emperor was not a ruler of the common sort:
From the moment of his birth he wanted only fun.
The man was a special expert on women and wine.
Too lazy for the work of lord and king on his throne,
But fully conversant with all kinds of sports and games,
He cared nothing for the wide world of rivers and mountains.
But when the Son of Heaven went whoring in Shanxi,
The sufferings of Jiang Bin are hard to tell in full!

The main story, told in a lighthearted vein, features disguises and mistaken identities, feigned foolishness and revelatory hints, and words spoken in jest that become true. "Millionaire" Hu, a dirt-poor student, strikes it rich when he unwittingly befriends the emperor, while the rich bully Wang, who boasts that he can provide the uncouth soldier with a vest made of human skin ("white on the outside, red on the inside") is himself flayed, and the courtesan Fodongxin ("Stirs the Buddha's heart"), who had prayed for the emperor to become her patron but was instead forced to sleep with a mere soldier, finds out that her patron has been the emperor all along.

IV. Performance and text

The previous discussion has dealt with texts. Beginning in the mid-eighteenth century, however, we are able to examine performance traditions in somewhat more detail as well. Early sources for performance usually consist of the lore transmitted by performers of the twentieth century, and are often limited to legends about the high patronage enjoyed by the founder of the lineage, a list of masters and disciples, guidelines for performance, and traditions about the repertoire. The earlier the period in question, the sketchier and more contradictory the sources tend to be. These sources, in combination with current practices of the surviving genres, however, do allow one to reconstruct a world of bewildering variety and constant flux, as genres borrowed themes, techniques, and melodies one from another and readily changed names as they moved from region to region.

In the world of professional storytelling, the basic formal division lies between those performers who told their stories primarily in prose and those who relied on music of some kind to chant or sing all or part of their performance. Storytellers of the first category rarely if ever used scripts. Some of them kept notebooks with outlines of plots, quotable poems, and set descriptions of armor and clothing. While it is highly unlikely that the great novels of the sixteenth century were based on the promptbooks of storytellers, it is entirely possible that storytellers made use of the novels for inspiration, although they certainly did not feel bound by their contents. Nor did storytellers limit themselves to vernacular literature for source material. Pu Songling's *Records of the Strange*, for example, was eagerly mined by storytellers of all kinds once the collection had appeared in print. Prose storytelling flourished throughout China, but the twentieth-century storytellers of Yangzhou became exceptionally famous and have been studied extensively.

Performers in any of the genres of verse or prosimetric narrative likewise did not necessarily rely on scripts. Many were said to be blind and would have had to learn their repertoire by ear; in performing, they must have relied on a combination of memory and improvisational skills, if not on the techniques of oral composition. Significant numbers of performers were either illiterate or barely literate. In some genres, however, texts were frequently used when the music was so complex as to defy improvisation, when there was a constant demand for new titles, or when the performance was entrusted to semiprofessionals, such as monks, nuns, eunuchs, and amateurs. Even so, performers would rarely follow these texts to the letter. Professional performers in particular felt free to develop their sources in their own way. In the case of texts written exclusively in verse, the performer may well have interspersed his performance with improvised sections in prose.

Genres varied greatly in length. Within a given genre, a distinction was usually made between "big books" (extremely long stories, such as the story-cycles *Creation of the Gods*, *Three Kingdoms*, or *Water Margin*) and "small tales" (long tales of romance or of sex and scandal); many genres also featured shorter, often comic, works. Genres that specialized in long tales of war and of romance tended to rely heavily on the seven-syllable line. Tonal contrast was observed within each line, but the rhyme categories were sometimes so broad that one is tempted to speak of assonance rather than rhyme. Most commonly, every other line ends in rhyme, with the same rhyme being maintained for long stretches, although there was a strong tendency to use blocks of four lines. In some genres, the text is composed of four-line stanzas, with all lines sharing the same rhyme, as in the "song booklets" (*gezaice*) of the Minnanese areas, or of two-line stanzas, as in the "pulling songs" (*wan'ge*) of Hunan. The earliest extant verse-narrative on the legend of Liang Shanbo and Zhu Yingtai, printed in around 1660, is written in a rare five-line stanza form. Contemporary genres that still use the five-line stanza, such as the "bamboo-beat song" (*zhuban ge*) from Guangdong, tend to repeat the last line of the preceding stanza as the first line of the following stanza. While some genres adhere strictly to the seven-syllable line, others, such as the "youth books" (*zidishu*), allowed the addition of any number of extra-metrical syllables to the seven-syllable skeleton. Longer forms were judged mainly on the quality of the story, shorter ones in terms of musical performance. Conversely, the more musically demanding genres, involving the use of a number of different allometric melodies, tended to prefer shorter texts.

A degree of fluidity between the genres sometimes results in a baffling complexity of nomenclature. In general, whenever a genre moved to a new region and absorbed the new dialect, it would acquire a new name. The encyclopedic volumes of *China's Minor Arts* (*Zhongguo quyi zhi*) recognize anywhere from twenty to forty different genres in a single province. As performative literature, they tended to be strictly local in nature, each being performed either in the local dialect or in a combination of dialect and the local form of Mandarin. Repertoires, however, show a high degree of overlap. Retellings of the same stories, adapting the contents of the most popular novels and plays, are found all over China. Only a small part of the repertoire of any given genre could be considered unique to that genre.

Traditionally, both men and women could perform as storytellers, with men performing at public venues such as teahouses and theaters, and women performing inside homes at the invitation of the lady of the house. Even Grandmother Jia in *The Story of the Stone*, though at times critical of the silly plots of their stories, indulges herself by inviting female ballad-singers. It is difficult to know how strictly the segregation of male and female performers was observed in early times, but we see it breaking down in the second half of the nineteenth century as female performers of string ballads, in moving from Suzhou to Shanghai, started to perform in public. By the end of the nineteenth century, many performers of "big-drum ballads" (*dagu*) in northern China were young women, inspiring the novelists of their day, from Liu E (1857–1909) to Zhang Henshui (1895–1967), to write long extolments of their musical gifts and physical attractions. Some performers performed alone, others to the accompaniment of one or more musicians.

Performers who did not have to provide their own musical accompaniment while singing were at greater liberty to employ gesture and facial expression; they might also use minimal props, such as a fan. In general, the story would be told by a single performer re-creating the voices of all the characters, but occasionally, as in Suzhou string ballads, two or more performers might be involved, each being responsible for a number of characters. Traditionally, the performers would remain seated, but after 1949 they were encouraged to experiment with standing performances, which allowed for greater movement and more dramatic gestures. Depending on the genre, performers came from a variety of social backgrounds, ranging from professional entertainers, who would transmit their craft through the generations, to amateurs, who included itinerant peasants performing during the slack season and lower literati (or at least people who pretended to that status) telling morality tales in the tradition of the bi-monthly lecture on the *Sacred Edict* (*Shengyu*). Monks, nuns, and priests continued to perform their precious scrolls and "sentiments of the Way," and even when these genres became virtually indistinguishable in content from others, performers would often continue to insist on the ritual settings and on affecting monastic garb.

In the big cities, storytelling was part of the entertainment continuously on offer in the pleasure quarters. Elsewhere, especially in rural areas, performances accompanied seasonal festivals. In a private home, performances would be arranged by the homeowner or his mother or wife. Genres that maintained a religious function might be used to give thanks to the gods, exorcise demons, or subdue an unruly daughter-in-law, as the occasion demanded. Where different genres existed side by side, each would have its own audience. Some held stronger appeal for men, others for women. A given genre might also be linked to a specific ethnic group, as "youth books" were to the Manchus of the capital. As early as the Southern Song, audiences became differentiated by class and educational background. The wealth of chantefable texts in the collections of the imperial palace and the mansion of the Princes of Che are one indication that even if prosimetric literature could not claim literati as its audience, it did charm their womenfolk.

As most performers never made use of texts, for many genres no texts came into circulation until performances were taped and edited for publication in the second half of the twentieth century. In the case of storytelling traditions in prose, these modern editions may indeed be the only texts ever to have existed. The first of these projects to result in major publications were the recording and editing of the saga of Wu Song, as narrated by the Yangzhou storyteller Wang Shaotang (1889–1968), and the recording and editing of stories adapted from the *Records of the Strange* by storytellers from Tianjin and Beijing. Many publications have followed in recent years, including several editions of Suzhou string ballads.

In many genres of verse ballads and prosimetric narrative, texts did exist before modern times, which have less and less of a link to professional performance. Although it is difficult to determine with any certainty, traditional texts for performance might have been derived from an existing item in the repertoire, or they might have been composed as scripts. Some literate performers may have wanted to note down successful items in their repertoire. For instance, many early editions of Suzhou string ballads note on the title page that the text is based on a draft by a famous performer. These performers may have written down the text as an *aide-mémoire*, as study materials for their pupil(s), or at the request of a publisher. In writing out the text, the performer most likely would have relied not only on his memory, but also on his command of the conventional stock phrases and formulae of the genre. Depending on his level of literacy, the final product would have ranged from an incoherent record riddled with misspellings and homophonic substitutions to a fully achieved composition. A text intended for printing would likely first be revised by a (comparatively) literate editor. One can also imagine a scenario in which a performance would be jotted down in shorthand by a clerk. The resulting manuscripts would again have been edited before printing. It is highly unlikely that any extant text from the pre-modern period represents a direct, unedited recording of a performance.

Written texts may also have originated as scripts composed for new performances. The authors would have been either professional and amateur performers or interested non-performers. In both cases they would have been intimately acquainted with the musical and other requirements of the genre, and many of the texts probably reflect changes made following initial performances. These authors often relied on conventional diction, and entire passages are repeated from one work to the next. Limited literacy may have been one reason for this; a more important consideration was how much a listening audience would be able to follow. As twentieth-century experience has amply shown, texts in these genres written by authors who are not intimately acquainted with the needs of performance often have to be intensively edited by the performers.

Some texts were the jealously guarded possessions of performers. Others might circulate outside these closed circles, either in manuscript form or in printed editions. Beijing in the nineteenth century had bookshops specializing in manuscript copies of drum ballads and youth books for rent or purchase. Elsewhere print was the more common mode of distribution. Until the last decades of the nineteenth century, woodblock print was the commonest medium, and texts in local genres were printed locally. In the late nineteenth and early twentieth centuries, woodblock printing was quickly replaced by lithography, which allowed for the production of much cheaper books. Shanghai became the national center for the publication of these materials, including texts in non-local dialects. Later, as lithography became more widespread, regional publishers took over once again. Verse and prosimetric narratives were printed for readers who read the text for their own pleasure or aloud for a group of co-workers or family members. In contrast, there is no record from before the twentieth century that vernacular stories and novels were read aloud. Some publishing firms came to specialize in the printing of verse and prosimetric narratives, and many new works were written for printing without having been part of the repertoire of performers. This applies to the majority of printed southern ballads (*nanci*) and precious scrolls of the nineteenth century, and may also apply to the printed texts of "wooden-fish books" (*muyushu*) and "song booklets" (*gezaice*). Upper-class women who took to the writing of string ballads in the second part of the eighteenth century went one step further in stating explicitly that their works were intended only for reading and, as works of literature, were to be sharply distinguished from the performance-connected song-texts (*changben*). Nevertheless, some of their texts were later adapted for performance.

Most stories, in which vice is punished and virtue rewarded, clearly subscribe to the traditional system of values, although this does not necessarily mean, as is often claimed, that these texts therefore are "didactic." The sheer length of many stories encouraged the detailed development of individual scenes, along with realistic presentation. After all, a virtue that triumphs is a virtue that has been thoroughly tested, allowing ample scope for describing the desperate measures taken by the heroes and heroines to withstand the evil machinations of villains. This emphasis on lurid detail, together with a propensity for sensationalistic plots, full of sudden twists and reversals, exposed these narratives to the charge of immorality. Many authors responded by rewriting well-known stories to remove offensive elements, or else adapted irreproachable subjects, such as *Twenty Four Exemplars of Filial Piety* (*Ershisi xiao*). During the Qing dynasty, the Shandong literatus Cao Hange even wrote a *Drum Ballad on Confucius* (*Kong fuzi gu'erci*), providing a detailed prosimetric account of the life of the Master. At various times throughout history, outsiders to the profession, often with an exaggerated idea of the ability of these genres to influence the public, tried to use verse and prosimetric narrative as an instrument of moral and political education. Lü Kun (1536–1618), while a district magistrate, devised an elaborate scheme to train the blind beggars under his jurisdiction to sing moral ballads specially composed for them, thereby solving at one stroke the problems of vagrancy and loose morals. The reformers and revolutionaries of the final decade of the Qing dynasty, such as the journalist Li Boyuan (Li Baojia, 1867–1906) and the feminist Qiu Jin (1875–1907), on occasion wrote string ballads for a female audience. During the Second Sino-Japanese War (1937–1945), many established writers turned to verse and prosimetric narrative to stir up patriotism. The most successful of these was probably Lao She (1899–1966). Communist leaders both before and after 1949 encouraged the writing of new texts for performance to spread the Party's latest message among the illiterate masses.

The majority of texts dating from premodern times were written in a vernacular of fairly uniform register with dialectal variations smoothed out, thus allowing the texts to circulate far more widely than the performance tradition from which they originated. Editors may indeed have omitted whole sections written in dialect in order to ensure a wider circulation. Where texts were performed wholly or partly in dialect, it is reflected in a performance-connected text. In some performance-connected string ballads, for example, the speeches of lower-class characters, such as servants, are written out in Wu dialect to distinguish them from the upper-class characters, who speak in Mandarin. Wooden-fish book texts, performed and read in Cantonese, include a certain number of common Cantonese words for which special characters had to be created, as no equivalents exist in the northern dialects. While the percentage of these "dialect characters" is relatively low in wooden-fish books, it is much higher in the "song booklets" (*gezaice*) that were performed in various forms of Minnanese, the dialect of southern Fujian and Taiwan. The women of Jiangyong in southernmost Hunan had even developed their own syllabic script of nearly a thousand signs for transcribing both original and borrowed songs and ballads in their own local dialect.

Manuscripts of verse and prosimetric narrative come in many kinds, reflecting the degree of literacy and wealth of the writer or patron. Printed editions of the last few centuries tend to be cheap enough to suit the sub-elite audience at which they were aimed. Sometimes precious scrolls were printed for free distribution as a pious act. Some of the most prestigious editions of wooden-fish books were printed with elaborate literary commentaries of the type popularized by Jin Shengtan.

Texts of verse and prosimetric narrative were also used for purposes other than performing or reading. In Guangdong, wooden-fish books were bought at random at the Mid-Autumn Festival as an augury. In some forms of regional drama, texts of the local form of verse or prosimetric narrative were used as scripts without any editing, simply by dividing up the speeches among the different characters. More developed forms of drama, such as Peking opera, shared so many stories with the local storytelling traditions that is difficult to tell who borrowed what from whom. In the eighteenth and nineteenth centuries, a number of drum ballad and string ballad texts, such as *Green*

Peony (*Lü mudan*), were adapted into vernacular novels, often by the simple expedient of cutting out the verse sections, or, if need be, rewriting them as prose.

V. Drum ballads, youth books, and other northern genres

Drum ballads

The dominant form of long prosimetric narrative, as performed in northern China from the seventeenth century, is known as the drum ballad (*guci*) or drum book (*gushu*). Such works might be performed by a single performer beating out the rhythm of his verse sections on a drum or accompanying himself on the *sanxian* (a three-stringed guitar). In the latter case, the verse sections might, in addition to lines of seven syllables, occasionally include a song to an allometric tune. In the nineteenth century, one also finds performers who drum while being accompanied by a musician on the *sanxian*. Formally speaking, the texts are hardly distinguishable from ballad-narratives, so it is possible to treat drum ballads as a direct continuation of the earlier ballad-narrative tradition, the main difference being that the drum ballad texts tend to be much longer.

The first work to call itself a drum ballad was Jia Fuxi's *A Summary of History: A Drum Ballad* (*Lidai shilüe guci*). Some drum ballads are said to date from the Ming, including *The Glorious Establishment of the Great Ming* (*Da Ming xinglong zhuan*) about the founding of the Ming dynasty by the Hongwu Emperor and the subsequent accession to the throne of his fourth son as the Yongle Emperor, and *Luanchai Ditch* (*Luanchaigou*), celebrating the Yongle Emperor's victorious campaigns against the Mongols. The overwhelming majority of the texts in this genre, however, date from the Qing. The drum ballad's preferred subject matter, described as "bronze lances and iron-clad horses – the affairs of the rise and falls of dynasties," gave rise to a "rough and heroic" style, in contrast to the "tender and delicate" style of the string ballad, the dominant long chantefable genre of the Jiangnan area, with its penchant for love and romance. The best-known of the extant drum ballad texts do indeed deal with the establishment of dynasties or with the wars between imperial China and its northern neighbors. Some texts are relatively faithful adaptations of the vernacular novels' treatment of the same period, while others diverge greatly. The collection from the mansion of the Princes of Che includes a very long prosimetric adaptation of *The Creation of the Gods* as *The List of the Gods* (*Fengshenbang*). The palace collection includes drum ballads on the founding of the Western and Eastern Han; an adaptation of the *Romance of the Three Kingdoms*; and chantefable retellings of the founding of the Tang, the campaigns of Xue Rengui and his descendants, the long and complex wars of the Five Dynasties (907–960), and the exploits of the military families of Hu and Yang as they defended the Song against the Khitan Liao.

A number of drum ballad texts celebrate "pure officials." *The Court Cases of Judge Liu* (*Liu gongan*) recounts the long and illustrious career of Liu Yong (1719–1804). This drum ballad was written in around 1800, while Liu Yong was still alive. Its preface declares: "This book is unlike those tales of ancient times, in which a man can say whatever he wants to say, because there is no one around to bear witness against him. Now that is what I call 'without any foundation!' But this book dares not depart from the truth of which person served in what office, and how His Excellency Liu carried out his arrests and interrogations in every case." Most of the action is set in Nanjing, where Liu served as prefect from 1769 to 1770, periodically donning disguises to investigate cases. When the action returns to Beijing, the narrator takes the opportunity to describe the popular entertainments on offer, including storytellers and their topics. In another drum ballad entitled *The Manchu–Han Struggle* (*Man Han dou*) the hero is Liu Tongxun (1700–1773), Liu Yong's father, who travels incognito to Shandong in order to investigate local conditions. In trying to save the two daughters of a virtuous literatus from a couple of local bullies, he confronts the bullies' patrons, all the way up to the emperor's father-in-law, who is eventually executed by Liu Yong. The material for this tale may derive from Liu Yong's 1782 mission to Shandong province, which resulted in the execution of several high-placed cronies of Heshen (1750–1799), the all-powerful favorite of the aging Qianlong Emperor.

Love and romance were not completely absent from the drum ballad repertoire. One of the most renowned works in this category is the anonymous *The Butterfly Cup* (*Hudie bei*), which still features a fair amount of bloodshed. Lu Shikuan, the son of Lu Lin, governor-general of Huguang (the modern provinces of Hubei and Hunan), goes on an outing outside Wuhan, where he refuses to pay a fisherman for a rare fish and instead has him beaten to death. Tian Yuchuan, the son of the local magistrate, Tian Yunshan, gives Lu Shikuan a beating, from which he dies. When Lu Lin tries to have Tian Yuchuan arrested, the fisherman's daughter Fenglian hides the latter aboard her boat. Sharing many adventures, the couple fall in love, and Tian Yuchuan leaves Fenglian his family heirloom of a butterfly cup as a token of his love. Lu Lin imprisons Tian Yunshan to take revenge, but is then called away on a military campaign. Losing the battle, he is saved by none other than Tian

Yuchuan, who has joined the government troops under an assumed name. A grateful Lu Lin promises Tian Yuchuan his daughter Fengying in marriage. Upon the successful completion of the campaign, Tian Yunshan is freed, and Tian Yuchuan lives happily ever after with his two wives. The same story was popular on the Peking opera stage, and the drum ballad may be an adaptation of the play.

Youth books

In contrast to the drum ballad, the "youth books" (*zidishu*) that flourished in Beijing from the mid-eighteenth to the end of the nineteenth century tended to be short. Typically they consisted of one or more chapters of up to a hundred lines of verse, the same rhyme being maintained within each chapter. The longest work in the genre, the story of Lü Mengzheng's rise from poverty to fame, runs to the modest length of thirty-two chapters. The genre was performed primarily by Manchu amateurs, the "sons and younger brothers of the Eight Banners" (*baqi zidi*), hence its name. Some scholars regard the youth book as an offshoot of the drum ballad, a connection denied by others, who have tried instead to trace the origin of youth book melodies back to Manchu music. Since almost nothing is known about the original music, these attempts remain inconclusive. Sources indicate a division between "eastern tunes," suited to serious subjects, and "western tunes," preferred for romantic themes. In both cases, the music is said to have been very slow, with numerous notes played under each syllable. This may explain why youth books showed greater creativity than drum ballads in manipulating the basic seven-syllable line, as the lines could be expanded freely. Each chapter usually opens with an eight-line poem in seven-syllable lines summarizing the theme and purport of the text. The author may also mention his name or pseudonym. From Beijing, the genre eventually spread to Shenyang and to Tianjin, as amateur performers gave way to professionals.

Some of the earliest youth books are bilingual texts in Manchu and Chinese. The funniest of these is "Eating Crabs" (Pangxie duan'er), in which each line of verse combines words in Manchu (written in Manchu script with Chinese glosses on the side) with words in Chinese. The text tells the story of a Manchu and his Chinese wife, recent arrivals in the city, who buy a crab and then get into a fight about how to go about eating it. The difficulty is resolved only when a more worldly-wise, beautiful female relative arrives to show them how to deal with the uncooperative creature. Some youth books satirize certain Manchu types to be found in Beijing, but the overwhelming majority derive their material from Chinese drama and fiction, including such works as

The Plum in the Golden Vase (a tale avoided by many other genres), *Records of the Strange,* and *The Story of the Stone.* The texts circulated primarily in manuscript form, but from the mid-eighteenth century we also find printed editions. An anonymous five-chapter adaptation of the story of Meng Jiangnü, entitled *Weeping at the Wall (Kucheng),* was printed in around 1750. (A manuscript of the first four chapters containing a full line-by-line Manchu translation has also been preserved.) This adaptation of the legend of Meng Jiangnü, who by her weeping brings down the Great Wall inside which her husband has been buried, focuses on the physical hardships and mental anguish of the heroine as she makes the journey from her hometown through the bleak landscape of northern China to the Great Wall.

Nearly five hundred youth books have been preserved, most of which are available in a number of modern collected editions. This preferential treatment of youth books is due to a large extent to the common conviction among Chinese scholars that youth books are the most literary of all genres of chantefable literature. Indeed, the authors of these texts often stay close to their literary sources in both language and plot. In a literary culture where anonymity is the norm, the authors of approximately 20 percent of the preserved texts are known. Of these, the most productive are Luo Songchuang (active around the mid-eighteenth century), Helü (ca 1770–ca 1850), and Han Xiaochuang (ca 1820–ca 1880).

Luo Songchuang is best known for his rewritings of popular scenes from famous love stories. Three of his works deal with episodes from Tang Xianzu's *Peony Pavilion.* He is also said to have authored *Crossing the Border (Chusai),* which describes the journey of Wang Zhaojun into the barbarian north, and *The Secret Oath under the Magpie Bridge (Queqiao mishi),* based on Hong Sheng's (1645–1704) *Palace of Eternal Life,* on the oath of eternal love taken by Emperor Xuanzong and Yang Guifei on the night of Double Seven. Luo Songchuang's twenty-four-chapter *Green Screen Mountain (Cuipingshan)* is a reworking of the gruesome murder of the adulterous Pan Qiaoyun in Chapters 43 to 45 of *Water Margin.* Helü (Companion of Cranes) was the pseudonym of Yigeng, a member of the high Manchu nobility who served in the 1820s in the Imperial Guard, but later lived in modest circumstances. Most of his works are limited to one chapter, and consist of satirical sketches of members of the Imperial Guard and of quack doctors. In others, he laments his personal misfortune.

Han Xiaochuang traveled between Beijing and Shenyang, doing most of his writing in the latter city. Many of his early works are classified as either "comical" (*xiao*) or "erotic" (*chun*) in an early catalogue. One of his best-known satiric works, *Getting Some Cash and Lording It over Your Wife* (*Dechao aoqi*), is based on Chapter 54 of *The Plum in the Golden Vase*. A poor man, henpecked by his wife, discovers that as soon as he manages to borrow some cash, she is all smiles. Han Xiaochuang later turned to themes listed as "tragic" (*ku*), such as female suicide and other acts of self-sacrifice. His *Long Slope* (*Changbanpo*), based on *Romance of the Three Kingdoms*, tells the story of how Lady Mi, Liu Bei's concubine, risks her life to protect the infant Adou, Liu Bei's son by his wife, and how, after entrusting him to Liu Bei's general Zhao Yun, she finally dies of her wounds. An English translation of this text was provided as early as 1874 by George Carter Stent in his *The Jade Chapelet*. In *Drafting the Summons, Beating out the Teeth* (*Caozhao qiaoya*), Han Xiaochuang celebrates the early Ming official Fang Xiaoru (1357–1402), who, because of his loyalty to the Jianwen Emperor (r. 1399–1402), is brutally killed by Zhu Di, the Yongle Emperor, when the latter takes power in Nanjing. Han Xiaochuang also adapted scenes from *The Story of the Stone*, most famously in *The Karmic Bond of Dew and Tears* (*Lulei yuan*), an adaptation of Chapters 96 to 98, which encompass Jia Baoyu's wedding to Xue Baochai, the death of Lin Daiyu, and Baoyu's subsequent enlightenment. This work is also renowned for the fact that its thirteen chapters make use of all the thirteen rhyme groups ("the thirteen tracks"). Han Xiaochuang, who often chooses a female perspective, has been praised for departing from his sources more readily than other authors in the genre.

Other genres

One of the legendary performers of youth books in the Beijing of the mid-nineteenth century was Shi Yukun, famed for both his performance skills and the erudition he flaunted in his compositions. According to a youth book about his life, his performances attracted a thousand people at a time. He created his own genre of performance, known as the "Shi Yukun style of books" (*Shipai shu*). The texts in this genre are prosimetric, each unit usually consisting of four sections of prose alternating with four sections of seven-syllable verse. Shi also wrote "eulogies" (*zan*) in his own style, short descriptive passages of primarily three-syllable lines, which circulated independently. Shi has left a voluminous *oeuvre* of short and medium-length works, but he is best known for his adaptations of the adventures of Judge Bao and his underlings. It is no longer possible to ascertain which of the Judge Bao chantefables were written by Shi Yukun himself and which by imitators. A prose summary of these stories, *A Record by Ear of Judge Bao Tales* (*Longtu erlu*), was later revised and published as the prose novel *The Three Heroes and Five Gallants* (*Sanxia wuyi*). This was then revised and edited by the famous philological scholar Yu

Yue (1821–1906) as *The Seven Heroes and Five Gallants* (*Qixia wuyi*). The novel enjoyed great popularity and engendered many sequels.

When youth books faded from the scene, their place was taken by "big-drum ballads" (*dagu*). The origin of this genre is a matter of dispute; some scholars see big-drum ballads as originating in the performance of highlights from drum ballads, while others posit an independent origin. Like youth books, big-drum ballads are in verse, but they lack the opening poem and are much less free in their manipulation of the seven-syllable line; also, they were often performed by women. A large part of the repertoire of big-drum ballads was borrowed from youth books. One of the most popular big-drum ballads, *Long Slope* (*Changbanbo*), is based on Han Xiaochuang's youth book of the same title. Many other works by Han were also adopted into the big-drum ballad repertoire. Big-drum ballads were performed in Beijing as well as other parts of northern China, and many localities had their own musical traditions.

The big-drum ballad is said to have given rise to another genre, the "fast book" (*kuaishu*), so called because the tempo accelerated up to the end. Most of the extant "fast books" retell stories from *Romance of the Three Kingdoms* and other well-known traditional novels. This nineteenth-century genre should be distinguished from "fast clapper books" (*kuaibanshu*), which came into maturity in the 1950s and tell stories in lines of unequal length to the rapid beat of bamboo clappers. Representative works include episodes from *Journey to the West*, stories about the Second Sino-Japanese War, and tales of heroic feats of Socialist Reconstruction. Other northern genres that gained visibility in the 1940s and 1950s include "fan-pendant books" (*zhuizi*) from Henan and "fast tales from Shandong" (*Shandong kuaishu*). The latter genre is still performed before enthusiastic crowds.

A much more musically complex verse genre is the *danxian* (named after a kind of one-stringed fiddle) or "songs to different tunes" (*paiziqu*). In Western scholarship, this genre is often called "medley song," as the texts are sung to a sequence of (often allometric) tunes. The invention of this genre is credited to Suiyuanle (Always Happy; real name Si Ruixuan, fl. second half of the nineteenth century), who built on existing traditions of popular song and song-sets. Suiyuanle was the author of a number of texts, but the majority of texts in this genre are anonymous. Many are adaptations of earlier materials (for instance, the story of Du Shiniang, best known in the version found in Feng Menglong's *Three Words*), but the authors of medley songs often show a greater independence from their sources than the authors of youth books. Here too *Records of the Strange* is a popular source, and, as in the youth books, many adaptations greatly simplify the original tale. Ye Shuting, however, writing in the early twentieth century, makes his adaptation of "The Painted Skin" into a clever attack on the modern female student and parodies the newfangled terminology of the day.

VI. String ballads and other genres from the Jiangnan area

From the sixteenth century onward, the term "string ballad" (*tanci*) began to be used as a general designation for verse and prosimetric narratives. Later it came to mean primarily the chantefable literature of Jiangsu and Zhejiang provinces. The earliest recorded use is in Tian Rucheng's (?–ca 1540) *West Lake Excursions* (*Xihu youlan zhi*), which describes the many scenic attractions of Hangzhou and its surroundings. If "drum ballad" suggests a performance accompanied by a drum, a "string ballad" suggests the accompaniment of a plucked stringed instrument such as the *pipa* (lute), as confirmed in the earliest descriptions of string ballad performances in Dong Yue's *Supplement to Journey to the West* (*Xiyou bu*) of 1642 and the southern play *Drunken Moon Bond* (*Zuiyue yuan*) of 1643 by Xue Dan (1620?–1706?). In the following excerpt from *More West Lake Excursions* (*Xihu youlan zhiyu*), Tian Rucheng refers to "string ballads," although he does not use that term:

> Blind men and women in Hangzhou often make a living by learning to play the *pipa* and singing stories and tales of ancient and modern times. This is called *taozhen*. Mostly they tell stories set in the Song dynasty, no doubt a remnant of customs [brought to Hangzhou after the Jin conquest of northern China] from Kaifeng. In his poem "On Passing through Kaifeng," Qu You [1347–1433] writes: "The abandoned parks, all overgrown, serve as pasture for horses, / By the Long Ditch, the willows of old no longer give shelter to the crows. / But the blind woman out in the streets knows no sorrow or sadness, / As she is able to strum the *pipa* and tell of the house of Zhao." The custom in Kaifeng must not have been any different from Hangzhou. Stories such as "Red Lotus," "Liu Cui," "Crazy Ji," "Leifeng Pagoda," and "The Double-Fish Fan-Pendant" all concern strange events that happened in Hangzhou – or that were made up in more recent times.

The term *taozhen* has already been encountered in the discussion of storytelling in Song dynasty Hangzhou. The topics mentioned by Tian Rucheng are all known in the vernacular fiction of the late sixteenth and early seventeenth centuries. The eccentric monk Crazy Ji inspired several novels during this period, then reemerged at the end of the nineteenth century as the central character of *The Adventures of the Reverend Ji (Jigong an)*, a sprawling novel in hundreds of chapters. By far the most popular topic in drama, fiction, and chantefable literature was, however, the legend of the amorous White Snake, buried below Leifeng Pagoda, one of the West Lake's famous landmarks.

The White Snake and Xiaoqing

The earliest developed treatment of the legend of the White Snake appears in an early Ming vernacular story included by Feng Menglong in his *Three Words* collection. It is best read against the background of older classical tales and vernacular stories about monsters that transform themselves into charming girls or beautiful widows in order to seduce gullible young men, robbing their victims of their vital forces and sometimes even devouring them. One of these earlier tales tells of a young man who, charmed by a snake sprite, is reduced to water, leaving only his head. In the White Snake legend, Xu Xian, an apprentice in a relative's apothecary shop in Hangzhou, is caught in a downpour on West Lake, where he meets a captivating widow, dressed in white, attended by her servant who is dressed in blue. She introduces herself as Madame Bai ("Madame White"). He lends her his fine umbrella, and when he visits her some days later to retrieve it, she proposes marriage. She gives him an ingot of silver, which turns out to be stolen from a government treasury. Xu Xian's brother-in-law reports him to the authorities, but as all the silver is recovered, Xu Xian is only banished to Suzhou, where he is allowed to work in a drugstore. Madame White and her servant join him there, and they live as man and wife. A Daoist priest tries to exorcize her, but she only makes fun of him. When some of her gifts to Xu Xian again turn out to be stolen goods, she disappears, and he is banished to Zhenjiang. Here they meet again and she once more convinces him of her innocence. His boss accidentally discovers Madame White's true nature when, spying on her, he sees a monstrous snake. Xu Xian does not believe his boss's story and leaves to start his own business. Later, visiting the famous Jinshan monastery on a little island in the Yangzi river outside Zhenjiang, he is warned by the resident Buddhist monk Fahai that he is in mortal danger because of his attachment to this devilish creature. When Madame White comes to the monastery to claim her husband and Fahai opposes her magic, she disappears into the river. Later, an amnesty allows Xu Xian to return to Hangzhou, where Madame White appears once again. He tries to break off their relationship, but she threatens him, and a snake catcher's attempts to exorcize her again fail. Xu Xian is by now on the point of suicide. At this moment Fahai reappears, and only he is able to subdue the monster. She and her servant (a blue snake) are imprisoned for all eternity below Leifeng Pagoda. Such a fate is not undeserved, given Madame White's demonic nature; yet, though her actions have caused no end of trouble for Xu Xian, she is also described as genuinely devoted to him. Later dramatic versions partly develop this aspect by giving the couple a son, who passes the examinations and achieves high rank.

Zheng Zhenduo (1898–1958), the bibliophile and scholar of popular literature, claimed to possess a late Ming manuscript of A String Ballad of the Legend of the White Snake (Baishe zhuan tanci). In the nineteenth century, a string ballad version circulated as The Legend of the Virtuous Temptress (Yiyao zhuan) or West Lake Bond (Xihu yuan). The earliest extant printing is dated 1869, with a preface dated 1809. This version is allegedly based on an original draft by Chen Yuqian and revised by Chen Shiqi and Yu Xiushan. Chen Yuqian started out as a kunqu actor, but later became a performer of string ballads in Suzhou. He is said to have been a writer, sometimes inviting literati to revise his drafts. Chen Shiqi and Yu Xiushan were famous string ballad performers in the Suzhou tradition as well. In his rewriting of the legend, Chen Yuqian followed the outline of the Three Words version, but amplified the supernatural elements and gave the story a happy ending of sorts. In his version, Madame Bai is a reincarnated white snake sent into the mortal world by the Queen-Mother of the West. Xu Xian reveals her true form when he forces her to drink the traditional realgar wine at the Double Five festival. He collapses in fright, and to save him, she goes to steal the herb of immortality from Mount Kunlun. During her confrontation with Fahai at Jinshan Monastery, her sworn brother the Blackfish sprite submerges Zhenjiang, killing all its inhabitants. The Blackfish sprite is now blamed for all the robberies. Just as Fahai is about to capture Madame Bai under his begging bowl, he discovers that she is pregnant with the Star of Literature and has to let her go. Only after she has given birth to her son Mengjiao is he able to imprison her under Leifeng Pagoda, upon which Xu Xian becomes a monk at Jinshan. Mengjiao later passes the metropolitan examination with the highest honors, and when he announces his success in front of Leifeng Pagoda, his mother's imprisonment comes to an end. This allows for a happy family reunion, after which Madame Bai returns to Heaven and Xu Xian achieves nirvana. The tale would continue to hold a strong fascination for modern and contemporary writers from Lu Xun and Tian Han to Lilian Lee (Li Pik Wah).

By the 1640s, when Xue Dan wrote his Drunken Moon Bond, the repertoire of string ballads had expanded beyond the list of topics mentioned by Tian Rucheng to include such perennial favorites as the tales of Meng Jiangnü, and Zhu Yingtai, who adopted masculine disguise in order to study at an academy. In Xue Dan's play, the female characters, tired of the conventional stories, are treated to a new string ballad on another Hangzhou legend, the tale of Xiaoqing, the young concubine of a Hangzhou magnate. In order to avoid his jealous wife, the magnate installed Xiaoqing in a villa on Orphan Island in the West Lake, where she sought relief from boredom by listening to performances of chantefable narratives. The tale of her patient suffering and early death, and the few poems she was believed to have written, created a considerable stir among educated men and women in the early seventeenth century.

String ballads continued to be performed in Hangzhou throughout the Qing and into the twentieth century. These Hangzhou ballads were later called "southern ballads" (*nanci*), but this term is also used to designate string ballads in general, in contrast to the drum ballads of the north. In the second half of the eighteenth century, Hangzhou would also become a major center for string ballads written by women.

String ballads in performance

Over the centuries, string ballads developed many local performance traditions. By the mid-eighteenth century, Suzhou had established itself as the preeminent center of string ballads, a reputation it has maintained to this day. The most famous performer of the nineteenth century was Ma Rufei. His father was a performer of string ballads and, after working for a time as a clerk, he followed in his father's footsteps. Ma Rufei is best known as a performer of *Pearl Pagoda* (*Zhenzhu ta*), also known as *Nine-Pines Pavilion* (*Jiusong ting*). The plot is relatively simple: when Fang Qing, the grandson of a minister from Kaifeng, falls on hard times, he travels to Xiangyang to borrow money from his aunt, the wife of the high official Chen Lian. She refuses, but her daughter Cui'e secretly gives Fang Qing the family heirloom of a pearl pagoda, hidden in "some pastries for his mother." After Fang Qing has left, Chen Lian, learning what has happened, catches up with Fang at the Nine-Pines Pavilion and promises him his daughter in marriage. On his way home, Fang Qing collapses in a snowstorm, but is found by the governor of Jiangxi, who is on his way to his post. The governor takes him in and also promises him his daughter. In the meantime, Fang Qing's mother has also made her way to Xiangyang and by chance meets with Cui'e while lodging at a local monastery. Fang Qing, having passed the metropolitan exams at the top of the list, is appointed to a high position. He returns to Xiangyang and, dressed as a mendicant Daoist priest, shames his aunt by chanting a "sentiments of the Way" on the venality of worldly sentiment. After Cui'e shows her determination to marry Fang Qing by attempting suicide, the story ends with the wedding of Fang Qing and his two brides.

This string ballad is known in a 1781 printed edition presented as an improvement upon an earlier printed version, which is condemned as "more than enough to make one puke and lacking in any moral message." The 1781 edition continued to be reprinted, but several other printed versions exist, which may be based on the pre-1781 edition. The scene in which the disguised Fang Qing allows his aunt to taunt him before he informs her of his success has been especially popular for its trenchant satire of social snobbery. Another famous scene shows Cui'e descending a staircase, and performers were notorious for extending this simple action to ever greater lengths. We do not have a copy of the text as performed by Ma Rufei, who continued to perfect his performance throughout his lifetime, but an edition based on a taped performance by Wei Hanying, a student of one of Ma's students, was published in 1988. It runs to over one thousand pages of fine print. Ma Rufei published a collection of introductory pieces or *kaipian* in 1886. Such short songs were either narrative or descriptive, and could be performed on their own.

Other perennially popular string ballads in the Suzhou repertoire were *The Jade Dragonfly* (*Yu qingting*), *The Karmic Bond of Three Smiles* (*Sanxiao yinyuan*), and *The Japanese Cloak* (*Wopao ji*). The earliest version of *The Jade Dragonfly*, preserved in *Lingering Echoes of White Snow* (*Baixue yiyin*), a compendium of popular songs dating from the late eighteenth century, is based on the Shaoxing tradition of string ballads. It tells the story of the Suzhou playboy, Shen Guisheng, who, unhappily married to a Madame Zhang, falls in love with the nun Zhishen. The nun hides him in her convent, and soon after he dies. She gives birth to a baby boy, wraps him in a bundle together with the family heirloom of a jade dragonfly fan-pendant left by Shen Guisheng, and orders an elderly nun to take him to the Shen mansion. Running into the cortege of the local prefect, the old woman abandons the infant and flees. The infant is then raised by the prefect, Xu Guozuo. Xu is later accused of embezzlement, and allows Madame Zhang to take the boy, who has been named Yuanzai. Yuanzai grows up and participates in the provincial examinations. His father appears to him in a dream and explains the truth about his origin. Having passed the exams with the highest honors, Yuanzai retrieves the jade dragonfly from his wet nurse and visits Zhishen in her convent. Questioned about the portrait of her lover in her possession, she is forced to confess the truth. Yuanzai is then recognized as the heir of Shen Guisheng, and the nun moves into the Shen mansion. This string ballad was later revised by Chen Yuqian and adopted into the Suzhou repertoire. An edition of the text claiming to be based on his draft was reprinted in 1836. At least two other versions, with many divergent plot elements, have also been preserved. In the Suzhou version, Shen Guisheng is named Jin Guisheng, and the story summarized above is preceded by the tale of Shen Junqing, who is robbed by bandits on the Yangzi before meeting Jin Guisheng at the Lotus Grotto. This addition has given the ballad the alternative title of *The Lotus Grotto (Furong dong)*.

Attempts to identify Shen Yuanzai as the famous Suzhou official Shen Shixing (1535–1614) can easily be dismissed. The real-life Shen Shixing, following the practice of his father and grandfather, used the adopted surname Xu and reverted to the Shen surname as late as 1567. The names of the main characters of *The Karmic Bond of Three Smiles* all belong to well-known historical Suzhou personalities, even if the story itself is entirely fictional. The chief character of this string ballad is the famous painter Tang Yin (1470–1523), whose prospects for a brilliant career in public office were dashed when he became embroiled in a scandal at the metropolitan examinations. Returned to his native Suzhou, he made a living by selling his paintings. Tang's eccentric lifestyle has prompted storytellers to immortalize him as a trickster character in Suzhou folklore. In one of these stories, he falls in love with a slave girl whom he glimpses on the boat of a high official passing through Suzhou and has himself sold as a slave to the official's household so that he may approach her. With the help of his friends, he eventually succeeds in bringing her home. A long vernacular story on this topic had already been included by Feng Menglong in his *Three Words*, and the plot was also popular with playwrights in the first half of the seventeenth century. With its comic exuberance and titillating scenes, *The Karmic Bond of Three Smiles* has long been a favorite. The first artist to cause a sensation with his performance was Wu Yuchang (ca 1800), who is also credited with writing another version of this string ballad, *A New Version of the Three Smiles (Sanxiao xinbian)*. Still another version, edited by Cao Chunjiang, appeared in 1843 as *A Picture of Marital Pleasures (Hehuan tu)*, also known as *A Picture of Nine Beauties (Jiumei tu)* and *A Karmic Bond in a Smile (Xiaozhong yuan)*. There exists yet a third version, simply entitled *The Karmic Bond of Three Smiles*.

The Japanese Cloak made its appearance sometime in the early nineteenth century. Though it has been preserved only in relatively late editions, there can be little doubt about its early popularity. The story, told in one hundred chapters, is set in the reign of the Zhengde Emperor (r. 1506–1521) and interweaves two largely independent plotlines. The Japanese cloak of the title is an heirloom bestowed by the preceding emperor on the Tang family. It invites the jealousy of a competing family, who engineer an accusation of high treason against the Tangs. Many family members lose their lives, but the youngest of the family's seven sons eventually restores the Tang fortune and the Japanese cloak is returned to the family. The other plotline tells the story of an adulterous affair, the husband's murder, and the final punishment of the guilty lovers. The story was immensely popular, and the string ballad was, like the two preceding titles, also reworked into a novel.

The repertoire of Suzhou string ballads was not limited to old favorites, as gifted performers would continuously enrich it with versions of recent scandals or popular bestsellers. *Yang Naiwu and Little Cabbage* (*Yang Naiwu yu Xiaobaicai*) was based on a famous court case of the mid-nineteenth century. The scholar Yang Naiwu confessed under torture to the murder of a bean curd seller, with whose wife Little Cabbage he had had a brief affair, when the murder had in fact been masterminded by Little Cabbage and her long-time lover, the local magistrate's son Zheng Renlai. The case was only cleared up after Yang Naiwu's sister appealed to the higher authorities and numerous officials retried the case. In the twentieth century, the Suzhou author Lu Dan'an (1894–1980) made string ballad adaptations of popular novels, such as *Fate in Tears and Laughter* (*Tixiao yinyuan*) by Zhang Henshui and *Autumn Begonia* (*Qiu haitang*) by Qin Shou'ou (b. 1908).

A glance at a few of these popular string ballads will make it clear why the upper-class women who began to write string ballads in the second part of the eighteenth century were determined to disassociate their works from the texts of performed string ballads. The only string ballad written by a woman specifically for performance, *Linked Rings of Jade* (*Yu lianhuan*) by Zhu Suxian, was printed in 1823 along with a catalogue of conventional plot elements that the reader would *not* encounter in her work: (1) men dressing up as women; (2) secret vows of marriage; (3) premarital sex; (4) elopements of adulterous women; (5) widows losing their chastity; (6) robbery and murder; (7) imprisonments; (8) murder for political motives; (9) secret conspiracies with foreign countries; (10) obsequious flattery of the powerful; (11) instructions in the methods of the immortals; (12) depraved acts by ghosts and monsters; (13) plots hatched by monks and priests; (14) prognostic dreams; (15) burglary and theft; (16) abductions and forced marriages. Most women writers of string ballads simply stated that their compositions were quite different from performed texts and had been written to provide entertaining reading, even though it is clear from their works that some women were eager readers of texts from the performance repertoire too.

The emergence of women writers of string ballads coincided with a revival in the publishing industry in the Jiangnan region, which benefited fiction and other forms of entertainment literature, including string ballads of all kinds. The dates of printed editions previously mentioned tell a clear story: string ballads were printed in increasing numbers from the late eighteenth century onward, often with different versions of the same story appearing in competition. Many of these performance-connected texts are of considerable length and they can often seem bewildering to the uninitiated. The sections in seven-syllable verse are preceded by the instruction "sing" (*chang*); occasional songs to allometric melodies may be introduced as "a song" (*qu*) together with the name of the melody. In the prose sections, a distinction may be made between third-person narrative (*biao*, "to show"), and direct discourse (*bai*, "dialogue"); the style in which each line of direct discourse should be delivered may be indicated by mentioning the appropriate dramatic role type, such as *sheng* (young man) or *dan* (young woman). While parts of the text are written in Mandarin, the dialogue of servants and other lower-class characters is usually given in the Wu dialect, and much of the narrative may be in the Wu dialect as well. Some string ballads dispense with extratextual directions for the performer and are written primarily in Mandarin. Many of these are written entirely in verse, exclusively in seven-syllable lines, or in seven-syllable lines with occasional passages of ten-syllable lines. It has been suggested that the term "southern ballads" (*nanci*), which is occasionally taken as synonymous with string ballads, should be used for this latter category of texts, but other scholars wish to reserve this term to mean the string ballads from Zhejiang (centering on Hangzhou) in contrast to those from Suzhou. Women were perceived to be an important sector of the reading public of string ballads, and publishers not only took the risk of publishing often extremely long string ballads that were written by, for, and about women, but also engaged women to edit them.

Female-authored string ballads

Chinese women seldom ventured into the field of prose fiction, whether classical or vernacular. As has already been mentioned in Chapter 4 of this volume, Gu Chun (Taiqing; 1799–ca 1877) was a rare exception, but even her authorship of *Shadows of Dream of the Red Chamber* (*Honglou meng ying*) was only established more than a century after her death. Among the reasons that may have discouraged women from writing fiction was the fact that most of its subject matter was deemed unsuitable for the proper young lady or matron. Moreover, many Chinese novels feature the figure of a public storyteller, typically male and lower-class, as the narrator. This allowed the literati who indulged in writing vernacular fiction to explore the seamy underside of society using all the registers of the vernacular. When women began to write string ballads in significant numbers, the narratorial persona they usually assumed was that of a young girl writing for the purpose of entertaining her mother and other female relatives. Recently, some scholars have argued that these female-authored string ballads should be studied primarily as women's fiction under the term *tanci xiaoshuo* (fiction in the form of string ballads).

One of the earliest string ballads by a woman is *Rain of Heavenly Flowers* (*Tianyuhua*), with a preface dated 1651 by Tao Zhenhuai, who describes herself as having been raised as a boy by her father. Both the name and the date may be false. The work is first mentioned in 1801 and the earliest known printing dates are a few years later. Given its absolute view of dynastic loyalty and the author's attempt to portray a perfect official whose life is bedeviled by the conflicts inherent in a blind obedience to ethical rules, the work reflects an eighteenth- rather than a seventeenth-century outlook and so is perhaps more safely dated sometime after 1750. The chief male protagonist of *Rain of Heavenly Flowers* is Zuo Weiming ("Support only the Ming"), who stands on the ideologically correct side of every major political struggle of the early seventeenth century. Following the Manchu conquest, he drowns himself and his family in the Yangzi. The most interesting character is, however, his eldest daughter Yizhen, whom he has raised as a boy because he considers her too intelligent to be raised by her mother. Yizhen is shown as eager to get hold of her father's swords, which can expand and contract at will, an obvious symbol of phallic authority. The relationship between father and daughter involves both devotion and rebellion. Yizhen intervenes when her father locks her mother up for a minor impropriety, and again when he tries to drown her younger sister for the gross impropriety of attempting to poison her mother-in-law.

Bold and assertive as she is, Yizhen's range of action is still greatly limited by her gender. This is not true of Meng Lijun, the heroine of Chen Duansheng's (1751–1796) *Karmic Bonds of Reincarnation* (*Zaisheng yuan*). A native of Hangzhou, the author was the granddaughter of the eminent official Chen Zhaolun (1701–1771). Both Duansheng and her younger sister Changsheng were accomplished poets. Changsheng's husband, Ye Shaokui (d. 1821), the son of the well-known woman poet Li Hanzhang, had a long and distinguished official career and rose to be governor of Guangxi. Duansheng's husband, however, got involved in an examination scandal and was banished to Xinjiang, from which he returned only after the death of his wife. Though it has been suggested that *Karmic Bonds of Reincarnation* expresses the author's frustration over her husband's failed career, the often lengthy autobiographical introductions to some of the chapters make it clear that most of the book was written before her marriage.

Karmic Bonds of Reincarnation was written as the sequel to the string ballad *The Jade Bracelet* (*Yuchuanyuan*) by an anonymous mother and daughter. The earlier work is set in the final decades of the Southern Song. Chen Duansheng introduces her characters as reincarnations of the characters in *The Jade Bracelet*, and the action takes place during the Mongol Yuan dynasty. Meng Lijun is the daughter of a minister who has retired to his ancestral estate in Kunming. Huangfu Shaohua, the son of the regional commander-in-chief, and Liu Kuibi, the son of the emperor's father-in-law, both ask for her hand. When Liu Kuibi loses out in the shooting match organized to decide their fate, he appeals to his father in the capital, who levies a charge of treason against the Huangfu family, thus forcing them to flee. Ordered by the emperor to marry Liu Kuibi, Meng Lijun asks her maid to take her place and escapes in male disguise. A rich merchant adopts her as his son and takes her to the capital, where she, now known as Li Mingtang, passes the examinations with flying colors, and, after saving the emperor's life by her superior medical skills, quickly advances to the highest rank. Meanwhile, her former maid attacks Liu Kuibi and tries to drown herself, but is saved and adopted by a passing official, and Huangfu Shaohua, under an assumed name, passes the examinations with Meng Lijun as his chief examiner. Soon Meng Lijun's parents and fiancé come to suspect the true identity of "Li Mingtang", but Meng refuses to give up the pretence. Forced to confess to her parents, she convinces them that she cannot disclose her identity because that would mean admitting to deceiving the emperor, and that the present arrangement is better because it allows her to have her own income and visit her parents freely. She claims it is impossible for her to marry Huangfu Shaohua because she would then be simultaneously his superior as his teacher and his inferior as his wife. Eventually, even the emperor starts to entertain suspicions about his handsome chancellor, and after many further complications, he manages to get her drunk and upon removing her boots discovers her delicately bound feet.

Chen Duansheng's version ends here. Perhaps, though knowing that her readers wanted a happy ending, she was unable to resolve the contradiction between the happy independence of male disguise and the subservient role of wife. It was left to the Hangzhou poet Liang Desheng and her husband Xu Zhongyan (1768–1819) to provide *Karmic Bonds of Reincarnation* with a conventional conclusion. Modern critics have dealt harshly with Liang Desheng for subverting the "feminist" thrust of Chen Duansheng's work by arranging for the marriage of Huangfu Shaohua and Meng Lijun through the intervention of the empress dowager. While it is doubtful that Chen Duansheng was a feminist in the modern sense of the word, she clearly believed that an exceptional woman can outperform any man and deserves the chance to display her talents.

Meng Lijun was clearly perceived as a subversive character by some female readers. One reaction was to create a character embodying all the pitfalls of unbridled ambition in a clever woman, as in Hou Zhi's (1764–1829) *Re-created Heaven* (*Zaizao tian*). Hou Zhi was the daughter of a Nanjing official, and both her husband and son were well-known literati. An established poet in her own right, she turned to the genre of string ballads because it was not dominated by male literati and therefore offered a woman writer a greater chance of making a name for herself. Her motivation may have been in part economic, as she had been engaged to edit *The Jade Bracelet* and *Karmic Bonds of Reincarnation* for commercial publication. The main character in *Re-created Heaven* is Huangfu Feilong, the daughter of Huangfu Shaohua and Meng Lijun. With a name like Feilong (which means "Flying Dragon," commonly associated with a dynastic founder), it comes as no surprise that she is a rambunctious tomboy almost from birth and takes as her role model the empress Wu Zetian, the only woman in Chinese history to have founded a dynasty. After Feilong becomes a consort of the Yuan emperor Yingzong, she immediately sets out to supplant all the other women around the throne, collaborating with eunuchs and traitors. She can only do so, however, because her aunt and mother-in-law, the empress dowager Huangfu Changhua, is temporarily ill. As soon as the empress dowager recovers, she immediately takes action to restore order, though always careful to do so unobtrusively and without claiming credit. If *Re-created Heaven* seems to condemn women who openly pursue power, it also shows, in the words of Ellen Widmer, "a latent respect for the woman who can handle the administration of a household, perhaps even a state, if duty called. This latent respect is Hou's compromise with the far bolder celebration of feminine talent and ambition in *Zaisheng yuan*."

Yet another response to the character of Meng Lijun/Li Mingtang was to create an improved version of the same character who is not subject to the same moral lapses. Qiu Xinru (fl. 1805–1873) attempted this in her *Flowers Made by a Brush* (*Bishenghua*), a massive work that took a lifetime to complete. Here the main character is Jiang Dehua. Like Meng Lijun, she enjoys (in male disguise) a long and distinguished career, which involves marrying a number of wives. Whereas Meng Lijun exposed herself to the charge of unfilial behavior by denying her identity even to her own parents, Jiang Dehua never commits such a heinous sin. She is, however, just as reluctant to give up her position. The figure of the young woman in male disguise who can put any man to shame in the examination hall, on the battlefield, and at the imperial court continued to be a favorite character with women writers of string ballads. As a rule, these characters resume their female identities in the end, but occasionally one carries on as a man also after retiring from court to enjoy the rest of her life with a bride. This is the conclusion of *Goldfish Affinity* (*Jinyu yuan*), written between 1863 and 1868 by Sun Deying, who herself chose to remain unmarried all her life.

Just as Meng Lijun had to fend off an amorous emperor, the issue of unwanted intimacies is explored by Cheng Huiying in much more detail in *Phoenixes Flying in Pairs* (*Feng shuang fei*). Cheng Huiying made her living as a schoolteacher in the late nineteenth century. Her string ballad opens with the story of a handsome young man, who spurns the advances of a male lover and is vindictively accused of homosexuality. This choice of topic is less surprising than it might appear, in view of the treatment of male homosexuality in *The Story of the Stone*, a novel widely read by women, and the enormous popularity in the second part of the nineteenth century of Chen Sen's *Precious Mirror of Graduated Flowers* (*Pinhua baojian*), an extensive catalogue of relations between males. The string ballad, set in the early sixteenth century, develops into a rambling tale of political intrigue, involving the conventional plot elements of treason and adultery, bandits and foreign foes, evil eunuchs and immortal teachers, disguises and adoptions. An act of voluntary castration provides further titillation.

Many of these female-authored string ballads are quite long. *Pacifying the Nation* (*Anbang zhi*), first printed in 1849, runs to 320 chapters. Its sequel *Securing the State* (*Dingguo zhi*) runs to 270 chapters, and the last title in the trilogy, *Phoenix Mountain* (*Fenghuang shan*), first printed in 1874, is of comparable bulk. The action is set in the tumultuous final years of the Tang dynasty, which in these stories become more tumultuous than ever. Many women apparently devoted a lifetime to the writing of a single title, and the plots reach a complexity to put even the longest-running modern soap operas to shame and defy all attempts at summary. The longest female-authored string ballad, written entirely in verse and likely the longest narrative poem in the world, is *Pomegranate Blossom Dream* (*Liuhuameng*), in 360 chapters, by Li Guiyu. Completed in 1841, it was written in Fuzhou, away from the center of ballad-writing in the Jiangnan region, and only circulated in manuscript. The first modern printed edition of *Pomegranate Blossom Dream* consists of ten volumes, each running to six hundred pages, with one hundred lines of verse to a page. The action of the story is set in the second half of the seventh century, but the author hardly makes any attempt at historical veracity. Her exhaustive catalogue of villains and virtuous characters rather reflects contemporary conditions and hopes. One of the central characters is the female hero, Gui Hengkui, who, according to the author's preface,

> possessed the talent to regulate Heaven and Earth and strength enough to manipulate the cosmos, the strategy to set right the times and the tactics to save the world, concentrating all measures and remedies in her single person. She may be called an outstanding hero among women, a uniquely daring champion.

If many female-authored string ballads are works of fantasy, other women tried to provide moral exemplars based on history. Zhou Yingfang's (d. 1891) *Absolute Loyalty* (*Jingzhong zhuan*) is a case in point. The author's mother, Zheng Danruo (d. 1860), like Hou Zhi, was attracted to the genre because it was not dominated by men. She also wrote a string ballad, *Dream Images* (*Mengying yuan*), which clearly shows the influence of the novel *Flowers in the Mirror* (*Jinghua yuan*). It tells the story of how the Immortal Lord of Mount Luofu and twelve flower spirits are born on earth in the early decades of the eleventh century. Some of the flower spirits end up as wives of the reincarnated Immortal Lord of Mount Luofu, while others die spitting blood, or, their honor threatened, commit suicide. Zheng Danruo herself committed suicide when Hangzhou was captured by the Taiping rebels in 1860. Zhou Yingfang's husband, Yan Jin, died in 1865 fighting a local rebellion in Guizhou. Zhou Yingfang devoted her remaining years to the compilation of a string ballad on the life of Yue Fei (1103–1141), a Southern Song general. Legend has it that he was on the verge of recapturing northern China from the Jurchens and bringing back the corpses of the emperors Huizong and Qinzong, when the evil prime minister Qin Kuai (Qin Gui), who was secretly in cahoots with the Jurchens, instigated his recall. Later Qin Kuai, at his wife's suggestion, arranged to have Yue Fei murdered in prison. During the Qing, Yue Fei was widely revered as a symbol of dynastic loyalty; visitors to his temple by Hangzhou's West Lake had the satisfaction of being able to whip the kneeling statues of Qin Kuai and his wife. In the eighteenth century, the greatly embellished feats of Yue Fei and his tragic death were reworked by Qian Cai (ca 1662–ca 1721) into an eighty-chapter novel, *The Complete Story of Yue Fei* (*Shuo Yue quanzhuan*), with an added section in which Yue Fei's sons and former underlings succeed in defeating the barbarians and retrieving the remains of the two emperors. Zhou Yingfang followed the novel closely in her adaptation. For women, the legend of Yue Fei provided the appealing models of his mother and daughter: his mother is said to have tattooed the four characters *jingzhong baoguo* (serve the country with absolute loyalty) on his back on the eve of his departure to join the army, while his daughter is forced to commit suicide following his murder. Zhou Yingfang's string ballad circulated in manuscript until it was printed in 1931, when Yue Fei, transformed by this time from a symbol of dynastic loyalty into the model of a self-sacrificing modern patriot, became useful in counteracting the threat from Japan.

Early twentieth-century reformers and revolutionaries might decry the traditional literary education of elite women as useless, but this did not stop them from using the string ballad to reach a wide female audience. In doing so, they often, like Zhou Yingfang, turned from fantasy to history, sometimes to foreign history. In 1902, the reformist journalist and novelist Li Boyuan (1867–1906) composed *The National Disturbances of the Year Gengzi* (*Gengzi guobian tanci*), a vivid account of the events of 1900 known as the Boxer Rebellion. This work is neglected by modern scholars, largely because it treats the Boxers as frauds and fools, and the officials who supported them as crooks, now a politically incorrect view in China. Other string ballads introduced European female revolutionaries to a Chinese reading public. For instance, Madame Roland (1754–1793), about whom the influential reformist activist Liang Qichao (1873–1929) had written a laudatory biography, is also the subject of *The French Heroine* (*Faguo nüyingxiong tanci*), an anonymous work, presumably by a female author, which was published in 1904 by a bookshop founded by the well-known Francophile novelist Zeng Pu (1872–1935). The aim of the text is to rouse Chinese women out of their pious lethargy and into action through the example of this female revolutionary patriot. Other string ballads feature Jeanne d'Arc and Harriet Beecher Stowe. There are also string ballads on the invention of photography and Fulton's invention of the steamboat, which introduce basic notions of science and encourage perseverance in the pursuit of one's goals. The feminist and revolutionary Qiu Jin (1875–1907) also set out to write a string ballad, *Stones of Jingwei* (*Jingwei shi*), but had finished only five of the planned twenty chapters at the time of her execution. These strongly autobiographical chapters describe how a group of young Chinese women, aware of China's backwardness and its suppression of women, travel to Japan to pursue a modern education. In the first chapter, Qiu Jin includes a long diatribe against the position of Chinese women under Manchu rule as "slaves of slaves."

Following the May Fourth Movement, a few attempts were made to adapt the string ballad as a genre of written literature to suit the new literary environment, but without success. As modern educated women took up the new forms of literature espoused by the May Fourth Movement, such as the short story and the novel, the female-authored string ballad, unable to keep up with the demands for a new realism, quickly came to be seen as a relic of the past.

Pure songs and mountain songs

The Jiangnan region was home to many verse and prosimetric narrative traditions aside from string ballads and southern ballads. In addition to Hangzhou and Suzhou, Yangzhou was also a major center, enjoying its greatest prosperity in the eighteenth century. These days of glory are described in evocative detail by Li Dou (fl. second half of the eighteenth century), who treats the city's entertainment industry in depth in *A Record of the Luxury Barges of Yangzhou* (*Yangzhou huafang lu*). Yangzhou boasted not only a rich tradition of prose storytelling, but also its own local tradition of string ballads, called "stringed ballads" (*xianci*). It was also the home of the "Yangzhou pure song" (*Yangzhou qingqu*), which ranged from simple lyrical and descriptive songs, set to a variety of allometric melodies, to longer narrative songs, written to whole suites of melodies. Most of these songs deal with famous episodes from novels such as *Water Margin* ("Wu Song Kills the Tiger" and "Wu Song Kills his Sister-in-Law"), *Romance of the Three Kingdoms*, and *The Story of the Stone*. There are also a number of fables, such as "The Complaint of the Mouse," about the long-standing animosity between mice and cats. This theme crops up in a number of storytelling genres all over China. Its treatment in Yangzhou pure song is distinctive for its length and humor. The mouse and the rat, boasting to each other about the nobility of their lineage, are surprised by the cat, who kills the mouse. When the soul of the mouse lays plaint before King Yama, the cat is summoned, but he exonerates himself by detailing the destruction wrought by mice and rats. In other genres, the enmity between the mouse and the cat arises because the mouse insists on marrying his daughter to the cat, and the latter swallows the bride as soon as she crosses his threshold. Another pure song text features a dispute between timber and bamboo, and in yet another the phoenix assigns different species of birds to their respective ranks in his army.

If Yangzhou pure song can be seen as the culmination of the professional entertainment culture of a rich and populous city, the "mountain songs" (*shan'ge*) of the rural countryside around Suzhou are our closest approximation to the opposite end of the spectrum. Mountain song here refers to a type of Wu-dialect song, usually made up of four lines of seven syllables, sung to a local tune, each locality having its own distinctive tune. At one time, these songs were also popular in the entertainment quarters of Suzhou. In the early seventeenth century, Feng Menglong published a major collection of such songs, many of them quite bawdy, with love and sex as common themes. In recent decades, scholars have learned that mountain song melodies were used not only for individual songs and sets of songs (e.g. describing the five watches of the night, the twelve months of the year, and the twenty caresses), but also for long narratives of love and romance. Though most of these songs did not circulate in print in modern times until after being collected and published by contemporary scholars, at least one source mentions that such long narrative songs were circulating in print in the 1630s.

VII. Southern traditions

Wooden-fish books

No one can deny that the southern dialects (or southern "Sinitic languages") are very different not only from traditional and modern Mandarin but also from each other. Spoken vernaculars of the south were mutually incomprehensible. One of the largest dialect groups was Cantonese, widely spoken throughout the area of the modern provinces of Guangdong and Guangxi. This was the dialect used in drama, songs, and other forms of performative literature in the region, and these local genres in turn gave rise to a sizable body of writings reflecting the dialect to a greater or lesser degree.

Regional song in Canton went by the name of "wooden-fish songs" (*muyuge*). The term is first found in seventeenth-century sources, which use different characters for their transcription of this term. The Guangdong native Qu Dajun (1630–1696) gives the first detailed description in *New Words from Guangdong* (*Guangdong xinyu*):

> The people of Guangdong love songs . . . The longer of these may reach to a few hundred or even a thousand words, like [Yuan Zhen's] "Song of the Lianchang Palace" and [Bai Juyi's] "Ballad of the Lute" by Tang authors. The songs are accompanied on the three-stringed guitar . . . They are called *moyu* songs. Also, women meeting at annual festivals have blind masters sing for them. These songs are like the string ballads of Yuan dynasty authors, and

are called the "such-and-so story" (*ji*) or the "this-and-that story." These are all tales and legends (*xiaoshuo*), which may or may not have some basis in fact. Mostly they deal with filial sons and loyal servants, chaste wives and virtuous maidens, and it takes a full day to tell one story. Serving as both inspiration and warning, the stories move people so much that they wet their clothes with their tears. The short tunes and stomping songs use no stringed instruments, and often derive a witty metaphor from some object, much like the "Midnight Songs" (*Ziye*) and the "Bamboo Branch" (*Zhuzhi*) songs.

Qu Dajun, who tries to explain Cantonese songs by likening them to song genres of the past, uses "*moyu* songs" ("fish-grabbing songs") here in its broadest possible meaning to embrace all Cantonese songs, including short ditties, longer lyrical and narrative pieces (later referred to as "dragon boats," *longzhou*), and long verse narratives. These long verse narratives are now often referred to as "wooden-fish books" (*muyushu*) or "southern sounds" (*nanyin*). In referring to "the string ballads of the Yuan dynasty," it is conceivable that Qu Dajun had seen the string ballads published by Zang Maoxun and ascribed to Yang Weizhen, but he is more likely making a general reference to ballad-narratives (*cihua*).

The early sources vary in the characters they use to transcribe *muyu*, but the transcription "wooden fish" soon became fixed. As the wooden fish (a hollowed-out block of wood carved in the shape of a fish) is a musical instrument used by Buddhist priests in beating out the rhythm when chanting sutras, some have suggested that wooden-fish books might have derived from precious scrolls. This is unlikely, even though the wooden-fish book repertoire does contain a number of stories on Buddhist themes, such as the legends of Maudgalyayana and of Princess Miaoshan. Other early writers have tried to link the word *muyu* to the Tanka, then a low-caste boat-dwelling ethnic group of the Pearl River delta. Most likely, *muyu* is a general designation for local tunes of popular origin. One local tradition credits the creation of these tunes to the singer Liu Sanjie, herself a creature of myth and the subject of folktales and movies, who can best any challenger in a song competition, even scholars who come armed with boatloads of songbooks.

Whereas "dragon boat" (*longzhou*) songs have texts written in lines of unequal length, with the irregularity of the meter being directly proportional to the amount of Cantonese used in the lyrics, published wooden-fish books are basically written in seven-syllable verse, without any prose. The seven-syllable line allows occasionally for one or more extra-metrical syllables, and the lines are grouped in units of four. The texts tend to be divided into books, which are subdivided in a large number of relatively small chapters. While wooden-fish books are occasionally classified together with string ballads, they tend to be much more modest in length.

Our earliest extant printed editions of wooden-fish books date from the early eighteenth century. Two of these texts, *The Flowered Stationery* (*Huajian ji*) and *The History of the Two Lotus Flowers* (*Er hehua shi*), come with elaborate literary commentaries in the style of Jin Shengtan's commentary on the *Water Margin* and *The Western Wing*, in which frequent reference is made to earlier "vulgar" printings. A third text printed at this time, *Coral Fan and Golden Lock Mandarin Ducks* (*Shanhu shan jinsuo yuanyang ji*), however, lacks such a commentary, and that became the common form of printing. Most of our extant wooden-fish books date from the nineteenth century, when a number of bookshops specialized in their printing. One of these, the Wuguitang bookshop, was still in operation in the early 1970s in Hong Kong. Because of Guangdong's early contacts with the outside world, wooden-fish books may be found in libraries all over the world. Where the date of acquisition is known, it helps to date the text itself.

The Flowered Stationery is, at a casual reading, a somewhat insipid "talented-scholar-and-beautiful-maiden" story, in which Liang Yicang, a dashing Suzhou student, overcomes various plot complications to marry both Yang Yaoxian and Liu Yuqing. Its enduring reputation, as with the other two early titles, is largely due to the literary quality of its verse. The subject matter allows for ample displays of genteel sentiment, and this work has been praised for its delicate fusion of mood and scene. Its local fame, easy availability, and limited length probably go a long way to explain why it was translated in the first half of the nineteenth century into English (by Peter Thoms, as *Chinese Courtship*), as well as into German and Dutch.

The History of the Two Lotus Flowers, at twice the length of *The Flowered Stationery*, is a more ambitious work, although it too is a "talented-scholar-and-beautiful-maiden" romance. As a product of the "Xiaoqing craze" of the seventeenth century, it cannot have been composed much earlier than the final decades of the Ming. In the story, the student Bai Lian reads the biography of Xiaoqing (whose legend later became the subject of a wooden-fish book entitled *The Story of Xiaoqing* (*Xiaoqing ji*)), and writes a text to commemorate her. She appears to him in a dream and gives him two lotus flowers (*he*). He later marries two women with the character *he* in their names, Pei Lihe and He Yinghe, and further expands his family by marrying the courtesan Ziyu and her maid Lingyan. *Coral Fan and Golden Lock Mandarin Ducks* is yet another "talented-scholar-and beautiful-maiden" romance. In its last edition, the plot is summarized as follows:

The student He Qiongrui finds the coral fan and the golden-lock mandarin-ducks fan-pendant which the maiden Zhao Bixian has accidentally dropped, and they thereupon secretly swear eternal love. But later the fan and the pendant are stolen by the villain Chen Qiuke, who also engineers the imprisonment of our student, whereupon Bixian tries to commit suicide but is saved. Eventually the court case is cleared up by the regional censor Wang. He Qiongrui passes the metropolitan examination at the top of the list and marries Bixian.

The majority of the wooden-fish books of the nineteenth century and beyond derive their materials from well-known vernacular novels and plays, especially the military romances of the eighteenth and nineteenth centuries. In some cases, however, the Cantonese version of a well-known tale can diverge greatly from its more common telling. The wooden-fish book version of the legend of Chenxiang furnishes one such instance. This tale is known all over China in many versions. The outline of the story is as follows: Huayue Sanniang (Third Daughter of Mount Hua), the younger sister of the fearsome god Erlang (Second Son), falls in love with the student Liu Xi. When he spurns her, she pursues him, forces him to sleep with her, and has a baby, Chenxiang (Eagle-wood). Erlang, hearing of her gross offence, imprisons her under a mountain, and Chenxiang is raised by his father. Taunted by his schoolfellows for not having a mother, Chenxiang learns the truth from his father, whereupon he sets out to acquire the magical skills needed to free her by studying with the Eight Immortals. Following a fierce battle with his divine uncle, he frees his mother by splitting the mountain with an axe. The legend draws on various elements of early Chinese mythology and can be read as a native Chinese counterpart to the Buddhist legend of Maudgalyayana rescuing his mother from hell.

The Cantonese version of the story of Chenxiang, set in the early Song dynasty, tells a rather different story. A girl named Chen Ruixian is possessed by three heavenly creatures, and all attempts at exorcism fail, even those by Judge Bao. Only Huayue Sanniang, who manifests herself as a young male doctor, is able to offer relief. In return, Ruixian's father undertakes to build a temple with an image of Sanniang made of eagle-wood (*chenxiang*). When the emperor visits the temple, Sanniang appears to him. Smitten with lust, he tries to take her into his harem, but she rejects him violently, leaving him with burned hair and whiskers. Later, Huayue Sanniang has a three-year affair with Liu Xi and bears him a son, Chenxiang. The boy is then raised by Chen Ruixian, who has married Liu Xi. When Chenxiang learns the truth about his origin, he visits his mother, who gives him a divine book of military strategy.

With the help of the book and his friends, he is able to defeat the rebel who has usurped the throne and become emperor himself. Glen Dudbridge has argued that this Cantonese version "takes an intense interest in female kinship, real and assumed," which fits with the primarily female readership of this genre.

The wooden-fish book repertoire also includes a number of texts that are adaptations of local legends. One character who apparently enjoyed considerable popularity in southern China was Zhong Wuyan, the strong and virtuous but extremely ugly wife of King Xuan of Qi in the Warring States period. Her story was expanded in sequel after sequel, each of 150 chapters or more, as the list of her triumphs continued to grow. Some local legends are related to periods when Guangzhou was the capital of an independent state. The story-cycle *Crown Prince Yulong Flees the Capital: The Yin–Yang Precious Fan* (*Yulong taizi zouguo yinyang baoshan*), possibly the longest work in the genre, begins with the marriage of King Ping of the Zhou dynasty with a Jiaozhi princess. This work explores a theme that became prominent in the repertoire of wooden-fish books. His life endangered by powerful politicians, the rightful heir to the throne flees the court and lives in hiding; during his wanderings he is reduced to extreme penury, but eventually he gathers a loyal following and comes back to reclaim his throne from the usurper. In the course of his wanderings, discerning maidens recognize the hero's imperial destiny and marry him even when he appears before them as a beggar or a slave, with the result that the crown prince returns to the capital attended by a bevy of beautiful consorts as well as an army of mighty warriors and wily magicians. An early example of this type of story in the Dunhuang narratives also entered the wooden-fish book repertoire as *Liu Xiu Flees the Capital* (*Liu Xiu zouguo*), but many similar themes can be found in the sagas of Prince Chong'er, Wu Zixu, and the Orphan of Zhao. Most wooden-fish books of this type were probably written and published in quick succession in Foshan during the 1820s and 1830s.

Some wooden-fish books are adaptations of local scandals and court cases. In *The Retribution in This World and the Underworld for Scheming against One's Husband and Killing His Children* (*Moufu sha zi yinyangbao*) we meet the evil stepmother par excellence. Mr. Qu's beautiful wife urges him on her deathbed not to remarry, but he does so anyway with undue haste. His new wife abuses her stepchildren, a boy and a girl, setting them impossible tasks. She then feigns illness, and tells her husband that only the livers of the children will cure her and enable her to give birth to a boy. Her sister bribes a doctor to confirm this claim, and the foolish father agrees. Overhearing this, the girl tells her brother, and he in turn reports it to his teacher, who at first refuses to believe him. Only after the boy has been slaughtered does the teacher come to the house and, after further complications of the plot, the murder is eventually discovered. It becomes clear that the new wife was also responsible for her predecessor's death and further that her husband is an intended victim. Cruel punishments, meticulously described, befall the villain, followed by the tortures of hell. The little girl, the only survivor, later marries the son of the teacher, and her brother is promised a fine career in his next rebirth. Another example is the famous court case of the "seven corpses and eight deaths," about the feuding endemic to the Pearl River delta, which became the wooden-fish book *Liang Tianlai Appeals to the Emperor* (*Liang Tianlai gao yuzhuang*). The same story was also written up as a novel and later reworked by Wu Woyao. A few wooden-fish books also derived their material from Cantonese emigration to the USA.

Bamboo-beat songs and legends

Throughout Guangdong and Guangxi are found large Hakka communities with their own distinctive dialect. There was also a sizable emigration of Hakka-speakers to Taiwan, where their dialect became known as "Cantonese." Hakka communities are renowned for their rich and distinctive oral literature of song and story. In Guangdong, long narrative songs in Hakka are called "bamboo-beat songs" (*zhuban ge*). These are composed in the ubiquitous seven-syllable line, organized into five-line stanzas, with the final line of one stanza being repeated as the first line of the next. One remarkable feature of the repertoire of the bamboo-beat songs is the popularity of material taken from the late Ming anthology of vernacular stories *Marvels New and Old* (*Jingu qiguan*); no fewer than twenty of the forty stories in this collection were adapted as bamboo-beat songs.

On Taiwan, the longer narrative ballads in Hakka are known as "legends" (*zhuanzai*). One of the most popular texts, preserved in a number of printings and manuscripts, is *The Tale of Tang Xian* (*Tang Xian ji*). The newly married Tang Xian leaves his wife to pursue a career at court. He fails to keep his promise of returning at the end of three years, and after nine years his wife dies of longing. Tang Xian, overcome by grief when he eventually returns, is visited by the soul of his wife in a dream. This provides the opportunity for an extensive description of the Underworld and its system of justice, which seems to have been the main point of this text. The legend of Liang Shanbo and Zhu Yingtai was also extremely popular in Hakka communities in both mainland China and Taiwan.

Chaozhou songbooks and Taiwanese song booklets

The region of the old prefecture of Chaozhou in eastern Guangdong does not belong to the Cantonese dialect area, as one part of the population speaks Hakka and another a Minnanese dialect. Chaozhou has produced a large corpus of narrative verse composed in standard written vernacular using the seven-syllable line. Research on Chaozhou songbooks (*Chaozhou gece*) is rare, but has recently been facilitated by the reproduction of a large number of texts. Little is known about authors or publishers; the few known authors appear to have been active in the last years of the nineteenth century and the early years of the twentieth. While it has been suggested that some texts in the repertoire may go back to the Ming dynasty, it is probably safer to assume that the overwhelming majority of extant texts date from the nineteenth century. As with other forms of chantefable literature, Chaozhou songbooks derive most of their content from vernacular novels, plays, precious scrolls, and string ballads. Of material taken from string ballads, both wooden-fish books and Chaozhou songbooks include adaptations of the trilogy *The Jade Bracelet*, *Karmic Bonds in Reincarnation*, and *Re-created Heaven*, testifying to the widespread popularity of these works. The influence of wooden-fish books on the repertoire of Chaozhou songbooks has been considerable.

A perennial favorite among the local Chaozhou stories was the tale of Chen San and Wuniang. The story takes place in Chaozhou, but different versions disagree as to the date, with the Chaozhou songbook version setting the action in the late Southern Song. When Huang Wuniang goes out to watch the illuminations on First Night, she meets Chen Boqing from Quanzhou, who is escorting his sister-in-law to his brother's posting. The two fall in love at first sight. Her father, however, betroths her to a local provincial graduate, Lin Dai, despite her protests, and she falls ill. As Chen passes below her window, she throws him a lychee branch wrapped in a handkerchief. Chen Boqing changes his name to Chen San, and visits her house as a mirror-polisher. He breaks a mirror on purpose so that he can serve in the household as a slave to pay off his debt. Only a year later, when the preparations for the wedding are well under way, does Chen manage with the help of the servant girl Chunyi to arrange a meeting with Wuniang. That very night the couple elopes to Quanzhou. There follows a suit for breach of promise and the judge forces Wuniang's father to reimburse Lin Dai. In the meantime, the lovers reach Quanzhou, where they join Chen's parents and live happily ever after. The story is also known in Minnanese dramatic adaptations from as early as the sixteenth century.

Another favorite tale of star-crossed lovers was the tale of Su Liuniang and Guo Jichun. Su Liuniang is in love with Guo Jichun, to whom she gives a golden hairpin. When Liuniang's parents agree to marry her to someone else, Guo Jichun falls ill, and is only saved from death when Liuniang cuts a piece of flesh from her thigh to make a healing tonic for him. Since one should feed one's flesh only to one's parents in the case of a life-threatening illness, this is an egregious act. As the wedding date approaches, she summons him, but when he shows signs of doubting her love, she promptly commits suicide, whereupon he also hangs himself. The officials in the Underworld, however, taking pity on their love, return them to life. Guo Jichun takes his case to court, and Su Liuniang is awarded to him as bride.

Another local story takes a different view of love and marriage. In *The Complete Song of Prefect Liu of Chaozhou (Chaozhou Liu zhifu quange)*, the childless wife of the prefect of Chaozhou starts an affair with a monk during her husband's temporary absence after visiting the local temple to pray for a son. She conspires with the lover to poison her husband on his return. The prefect manages, however, to drown his wife in a vat of wine and proceeds to arrest the monks. A search of the monastery turns up a number of captive women, who are freed. In *The Case of the Nuns (Nigu an)*, the culprits are not lascivious monks who abuse good women, but nymphomaniac nuns who force unsuspecting young men to become their sex-slaves.

The Minnanese dialect area of southern Fujian and Taiwan has produced its own distinctive body of narrative ballads. These are written in seven-syllable verse, organized in four-line stanzas. In Taiwan, in particular, these songbooks were written more and more exclusively in Minnanese as time went by, so that the later texts are hardly accessible to anyone unacquainted with the dialect or the conventions of its transcription, as many characters are used in a different meaning than they have in Mandarin. In southern Fujian, these Minnanese ballads became known as "brocade songs" (*jin'ge*), while in Taiwan they circulate under the name of "song booklets" (*gezaice*). The earliest extant printed examples were produced in the nineteenth century in Quanzhou and Xiamen. In the late nineteenth and early twentieth centuries, they were also lithographically printed in Shanghai. Beginning in the early twentieth century, song booklets were also produced in Taiwan, and until recently the Zhulin Bookshop in Xinzhu was still printing old and new song booklets in flimsy little editions. In the early days song booklets were also performed; later they were sold primarily to be read. Song booklets also provided the first scripts for the local drama of Taiwan (*gezaixi*) when it made its appearance early in the twentieth century.

Not all song booklets are narrative in nature. A considerable number are moral texts, lamenting the evils of gambling, drinking, and whoring, and extolling diligence, thrift, and filial piety. The "dialogue songs" (*xiangbao ge*) consist mostly of a dialogue, often between a prostitute and a client, in which the prostitute mourns her sad fate. As in other genres, the majority of narrative *gezai* deal with stories popular all over China. By far the longest story in the song booklets repertoire is the legend of Liang Shanbo and Zhu Yingtai, discussed below. Chen San and Wuniang also figure in this repertoire. Distinctive to the song booklets are ballads that deal with the history of emigration from southern Fujian to Taiwan and Southeast Asia, and with the history of Taiwan. Some describe the hardships facing the peasants, others recount successes and failures in setting up a business overseas. We also have song booklet texts about local Taiwanese rebellions during the Qing dynasty.

Of exceptional interest is the ballad entitled *The Song of Taiwanese Democracy* (*Taiwan minzhu ge*), printed in 1897 in Shanghai. It presents an eyewitness account of the events in northern Taiwan following the cession of Taiwan to the Japanese in 1895, including the cowardice of the Qing officials, the arrival of the Japanese troops, and their suppression of local resistance. Song booklets that describe the suffering of the Taiwanese under Japanese occupation all appear to have been written after the departure of the Japanese in 1945. This applies to *The Righteous Robber Liao Tianding* (*Yizei Liao Tianding*), whose career of crime, incidental acts of generosity, and ability to hoodwink the police during the Japanese occupation have made him into a Robin Hood in the eyes of modern admirers in Taiwan. Other song booklets treat more recent crimes of passion and greed, occasionally deriving their material from popular movies.

With the reevaluation of all things Taiwanese in Taiwan in recent years, the fate of song booklets has completely changed: once despised by intellectuals, the entire corpus is now available on the Academia Sinica website.

Women's-script literature

Minnanese songbooks, however difficult to read, are nevertheless written in characters. This is not true of the literature in the "women's script" (*nüshu*) of Jiangyong county in southernmost Hunan province. While claims have been made for an ancient origin of this script, it is probably best understood as a relatively late and highly local phenomenon, the result of an extreme simplification and deformation of traditional Chinese characters, resulting in a system in which one sign was used to transcribe each of the almost one thousand monosyllabic phonemes in the local dialect. As this phonetic writing system was used almost exclusively by women, it was called women's script to distinguish it from "men's script," or regular Chinese characters. The existence of the women's script, first noted by outsiders in the 1930s, began to be studied only in the 1980s, when just a few elderly women were still able to read and write the script.

Women in Jiangyong used their script to record a wide variety of songs and ballads, all composed in the seven-syllable line. Most research has been focused on original compositions by local women in connection with local customs of female friendship and marriage. A significant proportion of these compositions are autobiographical ballads about the authors' sufferings. Some Jiangyong women also had knowledge of regular characters and used the women's script to transcribe popular ballads. With most genres of chantefable literature, the common assumption seems to be that while women formed the primary audience, the authors (except in the case of female-authored string ballads) were men. Here, however, is a case of ballads if not composed by women, then at least selected by women for women, which gives an indication of the kind of story that appealed to women. The first thing one notices is the complete absence of stories in which a male protagonist asserts his manhood, either by defeating a foreign aggressor and safeguarding China's borders with his martial skills, or by impressing large numbers of women with his literary skills or personal charms. This type of story accounts for the overwhelming bulk of Chinese drama, fiction, and chantefable literature. In contrast, nearly all the ballads transcribed into the women's script have a strong female protagonist. In the few stories featuring Judge Bao, the female character whose honor is vindicated or whose murder is avenged tends to be more assertive than in other versions. Readers hoping to find in these texts an alternative system of values governing gender relations will be disappointed, however, as the transcribed ballads include many stories of a wife's continued fidelity despite her husband's protracted absence (up to eighteen years), grinding poverty, and family pressure to remarry. The heroine's unshakable loyalty is, of course, rewarded in the end by the husband's triumphant return. Also, while Jiangyong women show themselves in their writings to be fully aware of the discrimination they suffered, they accept the traditional hierarchical segregation of the sexes. Absent are the tales of maidens in male disguise who outperform any man, which were so popular with the upper-class female authors of string ballads from the Jiangnan region. The story of Madame Huang, locally known as Fifth Daughter Wang, taught the women of Jiangyong that the only hope of escaping the female condition is a pious life, which offers the chance of being reborn as a man and, through this, the possibility of enlightenment and ascension to Heaven.

VIII. Precious scrolls revisited

Following the Cultural Revolution, many parts of China witnessed a spectacular revival of religion and traditional custom. Chinese academics returning to the countryside in the 1980s were surprised to find that, in different regions as far apart as Hebei, Jiangsu, and westernmost Gansu, precious scrolls had been carefully preserved, and their performance, as either ritual or entertainment, was still very much alive. Scholars in Gansu, some of whom have posited an uninterrupted local tradition of chantefable literature from the days before Dunhuang's absorption into China down to the present, were for a time extremely active in the editing and publishing of manuscripts and printed versions of precious scrolls newly encountered in the countryside. More recently, other regions have followed suit.

Precious scrolls were composed in great numbers throughout the nineteenth century; a recent catalogue lists over sixteen hundred titles. Sectarian precious scrolls were also composed, but would gradually be supplanted by records of spirit-writing sessions, which to this day, especially in Taiwan, still account for huge quantities of verse and narrative. Nearly all the precious scrolls of the nineteenth century and later are narratives. Many stories not of an obviously religious nature were included in the genre, along with stories that were of Daoist origin or told the legend of a local deity. Often the only distinctively Buddhist elements would be an opening poem and a closing poem invoking the protection of the Buddha and bodhisattvas on behalf of the audience. Unlike the many genres in which length seems to be a virtue in itself, most of these precious scrolls are of a modest size.

In addition to *The Precious Scroll of Incense Mountain* discussed earlier, one of the most widely circulated precious scrolls of the nineteenth century was *The Precious Scroll of Liu Xiang (Liu Xiang baojuan)*, of which the earliest known edition dates from 1774. When the heroine, Liu Xiang, learns from a nun the horrors of the female condition, she decides to devote herself to a life of religious discipline. Her piety convinces her parents to turn their butcher's shop into a vegetarian restaurant. Married to Ma Yu, the third son of Magnate Ma, she converts him to her way of life, but her refusal to eat meat and wear finery earns her the enmity of her sisters-in-law. They calumniate her before her mother-in-law, who separates the young couple and subjects Liu Xiang to cruel punishments, eventually cutting off her hair and driving her from the house. When Ma Yu returns from the examinations as a top graduate and official, Liu Xiang refuses to come home, and he is forced to go to his post in the company of his second wife. During his absence, all his relatives die from blowfish poisoning. When his soul meets with them in the Underworld in a dream, they implore him to ask Liu Xiang to intercede for them. She does so upon Ma Yu's return, whereupon the couple, the second wife, and a pious servant all become buddhas. The style of this work is considerably simpler than that of *The Precious Scroll of Incense Mountain*, and in many places the text reads like a religious handbook for laywomen.

Another popular *baojuan*, *The Precious Scroll of the Immortal Maiden He* (*He xiangu baojuan*), narrates the deliverance of the Immortal Maiden He, one of the Eight Immortals, by Lü Dongbin. Despite the ostensibly Daoist nature of the text, the narrative features a pious girl who, loathing this world in which "man eats man," refuses to marry and drives her father to such distraction that he eventually beats her to death. Lü Dongbin then takes her to Mount Zhongnan, whence she will later return to deliver her parents. In these later *baojuan*, buddhas and gods, yakshas and Daoist immortals inhabit the same pantheon. In *The Precious Scroll of Xiunü* (*Xiunü baojuan*), the heroine is yet another pious maiden, Tao Xiunü. Kidnapped and sold as a concubine, she refuses to sleep with her owner, for which his wife beats her and eventually scalds her to death. Following her visit to the Underworld, Xiunü comes back to life and, using the magic techniques she has learned from the Immortal Maiden He, she tortures her owners into conversion, after which she is reunited with her parents.

My personal favorite among these later texts is *The Precious Scroll of Shancai and Dragon Daughter* (*Shancai longnü baojuan*) from the mid-nineteenth century. This short text gives an original version of the legend of the young boy Shancai and the granddaughter of the dragon king, the two acolytes who often accompany Guanyin on popular prints. Both figures have their antecedents in Buddhist scripture. The sudden enlightenment of the eight-year-old granddaughter of the dragon king is mentioned in the Lotus Sutra, while the Flower Garland Sutra tells the story of Sudhana (Shancai), who visits fifty-three teachers, including Guanyin, in his quest for wisdom. Shancai's pilgrimage had become the subject of illustrated devotional booklets as early as the Song dynasty. This precious scroll, however, ignores these canonical sources. A childless couple is rewarded for their devotion to Guanyin by the birth of a son, who refuses to study for the examinations and at a tender age leaves the family to study with Master Huang Long (Yellow Dragon, whom Guanyin vanquishes and makes her disciple in *The Precious Scroll of the Immortal Maiden He*). Left alone on the sixtieth birthday of his father, the boy, renamed Shancai, gives in to his lingering attachments and decides to go home. Descending the mountain, he comes upon a little snake trapped inside a bottle. She begs him to set her free, but as soon as he has done so, she turns into a giant serpent who wants to swallow him. As in the sixteenth-century tale of the Wolf of Zhongshan (Zhongshanlang zhuan), they agree to submit their case to three persons to determine whether a favor should be repaid with a favor or with enmity. They consult an old buffalo who complains at length about the ingratitude of men, and then Master Zhuang, who recounts the sorry tale of how he resurrected a skeleton. As the snake prepares to eat Shancai, they consult a young girl who asks the giant monster to show that she can really fit into the small bottle. Once the monster has fallen for this trick, the girl reveals herself as Guanyin. Shancai immediately joins her as her acolyte, and the snake, after a few more years of discipline, is slated to follow. Before the final denouement, the text summarizes a sectarian retelling of the legend of the filial parrot derived from the fifteenth-century ballad-narrative.

The story of the filial parrot is one of the many precious scrolls discovered in western Gansu, also the origin of a precious scroll on the Underworld court case of the mouse versus the cat. Most of the precious scrolls from this region deal with well-known themes: there is even a precious scroll on Wu Song's killing of Pan Jinlian. To the extent that these late texts share a common formal characteristic, it is the frequent use of the ten-syllable line in the verse sections.

IX. The four famous legends

While it is true that many plays and novels were based on chantefable themes or specific texts, chantefable literature from the late Ming onward began to rely heavily on fiction and drama for its material. Some popular stories, however, remained primarily in the domain of chantefable literature and the closely related field of regional drama. Chinese scholars sometimes speak of the "four famous legends" in this context: the myth of Weaver Woman and Oxherd, the legend of Meng Jiangnü, the romance of Liang Shanbo and Zhu Yingtai, and the story of the White Snake. The story of the White Snake has been discussed in connection with the early history and development of the string ballad, but it is important to emphasize that this story spread from Hangzhou and the Jiangnan region all over China and became as popular in Beijing as in Guangdong. The myth of Weaver Woman (Vega) and Oxherd (Altair) began simply as the tale of the two stars falling in love, neglecting their duties, and being placed as a punishment on either side of the Heavenly River (the Milky Way), from which fixed position they are allowed to meet only once a year on the seventh night of the Seventh Month, crossing the Milky Way over a bridge of magpies. Folklorists have recorded more complex versions of this tale, but these were hardly ever retold in chantefable literature. The most popular Weaver Woman story in chantefable literature associates her instead with the paragon of filial piety, Dong Yong.

Dong Yong and the Weaver Woman

One of the works compiled by the imperial librarian Liu Xiang (79–8 BC) was *Biographies of Exemplary Gentlemen* (*Lieshi zhuan*), known in later ages as *Biographies of Filial Sons* (*Xiaozi zhuan*). Unlike the same author's *Biographies of Exemplary Women* (*Lienü zhuan*), this work has not been preserved in its entirety. The tale of Dong Yong is among the extant chapters:

> Dong Yong lost his mother at an early age. He lived with his father. Laboring in the fields, he would take his father along with him in a deer-drawn cart. When his father died, he sold himself to a rich man in order to provide for the funeral. On his way [to his master] he met with a girl, who called out to him: "I want to be your wife." They went on together to the rich man's place. The rich man asked: "Who are you?" She replied: "I am Yong's wife, and I wish to help him repay his debt." The man said: "I will let you go when you have woven three hundred pieces." She finished within ten days. Once they had gone out of the gate, the girl said to Yong: "I am a daughter of Heaven. Heaven ordered me to help you repay your debt." She disappeared as soon as she had said this.

The same story is summarized in a poem by Cao Zhi (192–232), and Dong Yong was also a well-established figure in visual art by the end of the second century AD. From an early date, his divine helpmate has been identified as the Weaver Woman. In later folklore, the Weaver Woman is often said to be the youngest of the seven daughters of the Queen-Mother of the West.

Dong Yong continued to be one of the most popular exemplars of filial piety through the centuries. A verse narrative discovered among the Dunhuang manuscripts tells the tale of Dong Yong and the Weaver Woman, who entrusts him with a baby boy at the moment of her departure. When the boy is taunted by other boys for not having a mother, he hears the truth from his father. A famous soothsayer instructs him on how to meet with his mother: if he goes to a certain pond, he will see three heavenly maidens come down from Heaven, who will disrobe to bathe in the pond. Once he gets hold of her robe, his mother will be forced to speak to him. The Weaver Woman does indeed speak to the boy, but then uses him to take revenge on the soothsayer for betraying her secret. Human knowledge of the affairs of Heaven has been defective ever since.

During the Ming and Qing, the tale of Dong Yong was adapted into every variety of regional drama and rewritten in many genres of chantefable literature. One of these retellings, *Seventh Sister Zhang Descends to the Mortal World: The Tale of the Acacia Shade* (*Zhang Qijie xiafan Huaiyin ji*), from Hunan province, is said to belong to the genre of "pulling songs" (*wan'ge*). In ancient times, pulling songs were meant to be sung while accompanying a hearse as it proceeded from the house of the deceased to the grave; the existing literary examples usually lament the shortness of life and the irrevocability of death. In the Hunan and Hubei of late imperial times, "pulling song" was one of many names for a special style of ritual storytelling in the context of funerary rites, better known as "funeral drumming" (*sanggu*). This genre claims a history of more than two thousand years – tracing its origins back to the *Zhuangzi*, where Master Zhuang is observed to "sing while drumming on a tub" after the death of his wife.

As the story develops over many retellings, Dong Yong, initially devoted to his father, becomes more and more preoccupied with his mother; furthermore, the description of the skills of the Weaver Woman becomes ever more elaborate, and shift from quantity to quality in their focus. The adaptation from Hunan, which remains faithful in its main outline to the older Dunhuang version, is remarkable for being written throughout in seven-syllable lines, with two lines to every stanza. In this retelling, Dong Yong's debtor arranges for his daughter to learn the craft of the Weaver Woman. This daughter marries Dong Yong, raises the baby, and shares in Dong Yong's glory when he is promoted to a high position. The story is further complicated by giving Dong Yong a sworn brother, who later becomes a bandit king and rescues Dong Yong when the debtor's son sends him on a life-threatening mission so that he may have the opportunity to seduce Dong Yong's companion. When the son of Dong Yong and the Weaver Woman is instructed how to locate his mother, he is not told to grab her gown after she has disrobed, but only to grab her gown as she crosses a bridge.

Meng Jiangnü and the Great Wall

If Dong Yong is the perfect example of the filial son, Meng Jiangnü is his female counterpart, the devoted and loyal wife. The legend of Meng Jiangnü goes back over 2,500 years. When Duke Zhuang of Qi in 549 BC tried to take the city of Ju by surprise, his troops were repulsed. One of his men who died in the engagement was Qi Liang, who had earlier refused to take a bribe from the lord of Ju. According to *The Zuo Tradition*, Qi Liang's widow distinguished herself by her strong sense of propriety in refusing the duke's condolences when he offers them on the road and insisting, correctly, that he visit her house. Other Warring States sources mention that she was "good at weeping." In his *Biographies of Exemplary Women*, Liu Xiang adds the detail that her weeping brought down a wall, and extends the story to her suicide after her husband's funeral.

"The Wife of Qi Liang of Qi"

She was the wife of Qi Liang (also known as Zhi) of Qi. Zhi died in battle during the raid of Duke Zhuang on Ju. On his way back, Duke Zhuang encountered his wife, and had a servant offer his condolences to her there on the road. Qi Liang's wife riposted: "Why would our lord take this trouble if Zhi had committed some crime? But if Zhi committed no crime, the humble abode of his father is still standing. It is unacceptable to offer me condolences out in the fields." Thereupon Duke Zhuang had his carriage turn around, and visited her at home, and departed only after all the rites had been completed.

The wife of Qi Liang was without a son, or relatives in any of the five grades of mourning. Resting her head on the corpse of her husband at the foot of the wall, she wept, and her inner sincerity so moved passersby that none failed to shed tears. After ten days the wall collapsed on her account.

After she had completed the burial, she said: "Where can I take refuge? A woman needs a person on whom she can rely. As long as her father is alive, she relies on her father. As long as her husband is alive, she relies on her husband. As long as her son is alive, she relies on her son. Now I have no father, no husband, and no son. Inside the home I have no way to display my sincerity; and outside the home I have no way to display my chastity. And how could I ever marry a second husband? All I can do is die!" She then died by jumping into the river Zi.

A gentleman will call the wife of Qi Liang "chaste and conversant with the rites." The following lines of the *Book of Odes* are apposite: "My heart is wounded by grief, / With you I will seek refuge together."

The encomium reads:

> When Qi Liang died in battle,
> His wife collected his corpse for burial.
> When Zhuang of Qi offered his condolences on the road,
> She refused to accept them there.
> She wept for her husband by the wall,

And the wall tumbled down on her account.
And because she was bereft of relatives,
She committed suicide by jumping into the Zi.

Early authors disagree about which wall fell because of the widow's weeping. The account quoted in the encyclopedic *Imperial Reader of the Taiping Reign* (*Taiping yulan*), compiled in 977, adds that "the people of Ju built a wall of corpses as a victory monument. When his wife went there to bring him back home for burial, she wept before this wall until the earth collapsed on her behalf and she could bury him."

By the Tang dynasty the story had developed into a quite different tale. In this new version, the story is set in the Qin dynasty, and the wall in question is now the Great Wall. Scholars see in this change of scene a reflection of the frantic wall-building of the fifth and sixth centuries. Also, while the Great Wall does not often appear in Han literature, by the third century it had become a common topic in lyric poetry as a site of desolation and misery, depicted with vistas of battlefields strewn with white bones. One popular theme in the lyric poetry of the Tang was the making of winter clothes to send to soldiers serving on the northern borders.

In the Tang version of the legend, the wife of Qi Liang is called Meng Zhongzi or Meng Zi. A relatively complete version is preserved in fragments of a 747 Japanese manuscript of *Carved Jade* (*Diaoyu ji*):

Qi Liang was a man who, in the reign of the First Emperor, [was conscripted to work] on the building of the Great Wall in the north. Fleeing the hardship, he ran away. He entered the garden behind [the house of] Meng Qi [and hid himself] in a tree. [Meng] Qi's daughter, Zhongzi, was bathing in the pond. Looking up, she noticed Qi Liang and called him down. She asked him: "Where are you from? Why are you here?" He answered her: "My name is Qi Liang and I hail from Yan. I was conscripted to work on the building of the Great Wall, but, unable to stand the bitter hardship, I fled to this place." Zhongzi said: "I want to be your wife!" Liang replied: "Young lady, you are the daughter of a rich man and you grew up in the inner apartments. Your beauty is dazzling – how can you be a conscript's wife?" Zhongzi said: "A woman's body cannot be seen by more than one man, so please don't refuse!" She then informed her father of the circumstances, and he assented.

After husband and wife had consummated their marriage, Liang went back to the construction site. His supervisor, furious at his escape, had him beaten to death and buried in the section of the wall that was under construction. [Meng] Qi, who did not know he had died, sent a servant to take his place, and so learned that Liang had died and been buried in the wall. When Zhongzi heard this, she was choked by grief, and went [to the Great Wall]. She wept and wailed before the Great Wall. The wall in front of her suddenly collapsed. The white bones of the deceased were all mixed together, so she could not tell which were the right ones. Zhongzi then pricked her finger in order to drip blood onto the bones. "If these are the bones of Qi Liang, may the blood penetrate them." So saying, she sprinkled the bones with her blood. On meeting Liang's bones, the blood promptly soaked into them. She then brought the bones back with her and buried them. (From *Being with the Wise*)

Yet another Tang source preserved in Japan adds the detail that the girl and the conscript laborer make love before they go to see her parents. Only in the songs from Dunhuang is the wife of Qi Liang named Meng Jiangnü ("the maiden Meng Jiang") and only in the Dunhuang versions does she go to the Great Wall with winter clothes for her husband. A prosimetric version of the legend appears in a badly damaged Dunhuang manuscript that is missing the beginning and ending. All that is left is a fragment in which the husband appears to Meng Jiangnü in a dream to tell her of his death, followed by her discovery of his bones, and a dialogue between Meng Jiangnü and other skeletons. The text can be dated to the ninth or the tenth century.

Of the many adaptations of the legend of Meng Jiangnü from the last few centuries, the one written in the women's script of Jiangyong adheres closely to the outline of the Tang dynasty tale. This version focuses consistently on the inner feelings of the heroine, from her earliest yearnings for love to her grief upon retrieving her husband's bones and taking them back to her home, where "each night she slept alongside her husband's bones, / And never in her life did she marry another man." Many other versions end the tale with a confrontation between the widow and a ruler who behaves inappropriately, in this case not the Duke of Qi, but the First Emperor of Qin, the most redoubtable tyrant in Chinese history, who falls in love with her beauty and is willing to meet any demand she may make in order to make her his own. In some of these versions, this confrontation takes place at Shanhaiguan to the northeast of Beijing, where the Great Wall reaches the Bohai Gulf. Over the years, more and more local features at Shanhaiguan became associated with the legend. Meng Jiangnü and her husband were also venerated as gods in this region. Similar cults in other regions can be traced back as far as the eleventh and twelfth centuries.

Gu Jiegang (1893–1980), a leading scholar of the Folklore Movement of the 1920s, has closely studied the many versions of the legend of Meng Jiangnü. In general, they can be divided into a northern and a southern group. Those in the northern group tend to dispense with the bathing scene. Another element associated with the northern group is the notion that if Meng Jiangnü was such a loyal wife to her husband (renamed Fan Qiliang), she must have been a perfect daughter-in-law as well. One retelling of the story, an "exposition" (*xuanjiang*), gives considerable attention to how Meng Jiangnü cares for her mother-in-law after her husband's departure, waiting until her mother-in-law has died and been properly buried before she sets out to deliver her husband his winter clothes. This attempt to remove any conflict between the heroine's devotion to her husband and her sense of duty as a filial daughter-in-law may be linked to the nature of the exposition genre. Also known as "tales of goodness" (*shanshu*), expositions were a form of prosimetric storytelling that grew out of popular lectures on the *Sacred Edict* as sponsored by the Qing authorities.

In versions from the southern Wu dialect area, the name of Fan Qiliang becomes Wan Xiliang. He is no longer a simple conscript laborer, but a young Suzhou student, who is on the run because the First Emperor, believing that Wan (meaning "ten thousand") can stand for ten thousand men, wishes to bury him in the wall as a sacrificial victim to ensure the stability of the project. These versions retain the bathing scene, but offer elaborate explanations as to why a properly educated upper-class girl like Meng Jiangnü would be bathing naked in the garden pond. As soon as the wedding has taken place, Wan Xiliang is arrested and taken to the north, in some cases even before the wedding has been consummated. As Meng Jiangnü makes her way to the Great Wall, the journey from her hometown of Huating in Songjiang prefecture to Zhenjiang, by way of Suzhou, Wuxi, and Danyang, is developed at length. The versions of the Wu dialect area also retain the servant who travels to the Great Wall and learns of Wan Xiliang's death, but he is increasingly villainous. A crucial episode in Meng Jiangnü's trek is her passage through the Hushu Pass between Suzhou and Wuxi, where she is allowed to go on only after singing "the names of the flowers," that is, singing of her feelings of loneliness in each month of the year. This song also circulated independently. Southern versions from other regions retain the name of Fan Qiliang, and take Meng Jiangnü through a largely mythical landscape filled with giant snakes, ravening tigers, and lascivious bandits.

The precious-scroll versions have their own take on the legend. By far the earliest extant prosimetric adaptation is a long precious scroll from the late Ming. In both form and content, this work belongs in the sectarian tradition – Meng Jiangnü and Fan Qiliang are now avatars of the buddhas Manjusri and Samanthabhadra. Fan Qiliang is not an ordinary conscript laborer in this retelling, but a rising young official in charge of the building of the Great Wall. Fan Qiliang's jealous former supervisor, Meng Tian, suggests that Fan go home to visit his parents. As soon as he sets off, divine intervention takes Fan Qiliang to the garden of Meng Jiangnü. In the meantime, Meng Tian reports Fan's unauthorized absence and the First Emperor orders his arrest. When Fan returns to his post, Meng Tian has him killed and buried in the Great Wall. As Meng Jiangnü comes to claim her husband's remains, she is coveted by Meng Tian. She buys time by giving him an embroidered robe to offer up to the First Emperor. Upon being presented, the robe turns out to be black instead of imperial yellow, and the enraged First Emperor puts Meng Tian to death. Meng Jiangnü then presents the real dragon robe, charming the emperor with her beauty. This plot is maintained in broad outline in a precious scroll from the nineteenth century; a much shorter version, discovered in the 1980s in Gansu, shows evidence of late composition in its inclusion of a long and complicated confrontation between the First Emperor and Meng Jiangnü at Shanhaiguan. Eventually Meng Jiangnü, floating on Fan Qiliang's coffin, drowns herself in the Bohai Gulf. When the First Emperor, robbed of his prize, threatens to dry up the ocean and reduce the dragon king's palace to ashes, a false Meng Jiangnü appears to share his bed. In some versions of the legend, this surrogate is the future mother of Xiang Yu, who grows up to take revenge on Qin by torching its palaces.

In another late precious-scroll adaptation of the legend, the influence of versions of the southern Wu dialect area shows itself. Wan Xiliang and Meng Jiangnü are introduced as minor denizens of Heaven. The god who becomes Wan Xiliang, filled with compassion for the suffering inflicted on the people by the First Emperor, decides on his own authority to descend to Earth to take the place of the ten thousand sacrificial victims needed for the Great Wall. The goddess who becomes Meng Jiangnü decides to follow him, but she is unwilling to be born "in a river of blood," and instead chooses to emerge from a gourd. When, at the end, the emperor gives Wan Xiliang a great state funeral at her request, she jumps into the burning pile of sacrificial offerings and returns to heaven as a puff of smoke.

Liang Shanbo and Zhu Yingtai

Modern interpretations may make Meng Jiangnü into a champion of free love and a rebel against feudal oppression, but in the eyes of tradition she was the embodiment of all feminine virtues. In this respect she is the opposite of Zhu Yingtai, who insists on donning male attire because she wants to pursue an advanced education at an academy for boys. The origin of the tale of Liang Shanbo and Zhu Yingtai can be traced back to the Song dynasty. Zhang Jin (ca 1130–ca 1180) in his *Maps and Facts of Siming in the Qiandao Reign* (*Qiandao Siming tujing*), a description of the Ningbo area, writes,

> The Grave of the Loyal Wife is the place where Liang Shanbo and Zhu Yingtai were buried together. It is found a few miles to the west of the county capital, behind the Court of Reception. There is also a temple there. Old records tell that the two of them studied together in their youth, and that for three years Shanbo did not realize Yingtai was a girl – such was his guileless simplicity!

Zhang Jin proceeds to quote a now lost work of the seventh century as his source. A more detailed account of the couple's love is said to derive from the short-story collection *Records from a Heated Room* (*Xuanshi zhi*) by Zhang Du (fl. second half of the ninth century):

> Yingtai was the daughter of the Zhu family in Shangyu. She disguised herself as a man in order to travel and study, and devoted herself to her studies together with a certain Liang Shanbo from Guiji. Shanbo's style name was Churen. Zhu [Yingtai] returned home first, and only when Shanbo paid her a visit two years later did he realize that she was a girl. He felt greatly disappointed, as if he had lost something. He told his father and mother to ask for her hand, but she had already been promised in marriage to a son of the Ma family.
>
> Later Shanbo served as magistrate of Yin county. After he died of an illness, he was buried on the west side of the city of Yin. Zhu [Yingtai], on her way to marry Ma, passed by his grave in her boat, where wind and waves prevented her from going on. On being told that this was the location of his grave, she left the boat and wept for him. The earth suddenly split open and swallowed her. This was how she was buried together with him.
>
> The chancellor of the Jin, Xie An [320–385], reported this to the throne, which awarded [their grave] the title "Grave of the Loyal Wife."

As this account is first encountered in an eighteenth-century compilation, it is doubtful whether it indeed dates from the ninth century. Be that as it may, the legend was current by Song times and had been enriched by the detail of the transformation of the deceased lovers into butterflies.

One of the first complete extant ballads, *The Song of Liang Shanbo* (*Liang Shanbo ge*), a long narrative ballad written in stanzas of five seven-syllable lines, was printed in around 1660 in Zhejiang province. It survives in a single, slightly damaged copy. The available modern editions of the text do not specify its genre. The main outline of the story up to the moment Zhu Yingtai jumps into Liang Shanbo's grave has acquired the form in which it will be reencountered in countless versions all over China. When Zhu Yingtai has proven to her own father that he cannot recognize her in male dress, she is allowed to leave home to study, having first sworn that she will guard her virginity. On the road she meets Liang Shanbo, also on his way to the academy. They become sworn brothers and share a room. Liang Shanbo suspects her of being a girl, but each time he questions her about a suspicious feature (her breasts, urinating in a squatting position, her refusal to undress at night), she has an explanation that silences him. Eventually he is so thoroughly deceived that, as Zhu Yintai departs, he fails to take any of the none-too-subtle hints she gives to suggest that they should become a couple. Zhu Yingtai tells him to come and ask for the hand of her younger sister in marriage. It is only after Liang Shanbo visits the Zhu mansion that he realizes Yingtai is a girl. By this time, however, her father has already promised her to the Ma family, and Liang Shanbo returns home, where he falls ill with grief. A desperate plea by his mother is of no avail, and Liang Shanbo dies, thus setting the stage for the young couple's union in death.

Only a few traditional versions, such as the one in women's script from Jiangyong, end with the pair being turned into mandarin ducks or butterflies, as is common in modern retellings of the tale. The women's-script version may be read as giving the lesson that however thoroughly a clever girl may be able to deceive a man, in the end her body will reveal the truth (as when Yingtai is expected to bathe with the other students), and that only misery can follow the attempt to join male society. Most traditional versions, however, end with a resurrection or a reincarnation of the couple, in which the star-crossed lovers are finally united in marriage. It is in the resolution that we find the greatest divergence among different versions.

In *The Song of Liang Shanbo*, the disappointed groom Mr. Ma takes his case to court in the Underworld, where we learn that Liang Shanbo and Zhu Yingtai are actually avatars of Oxherd and Weaver Woman. Mr. Ma's suit is duly rejected, and Liang Shanbo and Zhu Yingtai become a happy couple in their next life. In later versions, the lovers are often resurrected from death, sometimes acquiring exceptional military skills and having many adventures before being united. Other versions see them married promptly upon resurrection, only to be separated again when Liang Shanbo passes the examinations and has to fight the barbarians. In Taiwan, the Minnanese version differs drastically from the Hakka version. The Minnanese version adds many episodes in which, following the lovers' resurrection and marriage, Liang Shanbo passes the metropolitan examinations with the highest honors and becomes a commander who defeats China's enemies on all fronts. In the Hakka version, Liang Shanbo spurns the daughter of a high minister and as a punishment is dispatched to buy horses in barbarian lands. Zhu Yingtai dons male disguise again, passes the examinations, and marries the daughter of the prime minister. Upon Liang Shanbo's return, she resumes her female identity and both women bear him sons, who grow up to pass the examinations. With its additions, the Hakka version is closer to the wooden-fish book and Chaozhou songbook versions. While modern readers who read the story as a tragic reflection of the iniquities of the "old society" may find these later developments to be an unnecessary gilding of the lily, premodern readers may have appreciated these adventures, as they allowed Liang Shanbo to reassert his manhood and Zhu Yingtai to display the virtues of a devoted wife, reconfirming the traditional gender values.

In an early string ballad titled *A New Version of the Legend of the Golden Butterflies* (*Xinbian jin hudie zhuan*), which is preserved in a single written copy made by a professional artist in 1769, Liang Shanbo and Zhu Yingtai are said to have studied with Confucius himself in Hangzhou. The omniscient Confucius promptly realizes that Zhu Yingtai is a girl, but takes no action except to honor her request that students should be prohibited from relieving themselves together. This work may have provided the stimulus for an alternative string ballad, titled *A New Version to Eastern Tunes of the Great Paired Butterflies* (*Xinbian dongdiao dashuang hudie*), completed in 1769 but first printed in 1823, in which an attempt is made at a "correct" version of the story. Since the historical Confucius never visited Hangzhou, the couple travels to Qufu, arriving while Confucius is away visiting the other states. Though able to fool the honest disciple left in charge of the school, Zhu Yingtai makes sure to leave as soon as Confucius returns. Both Liang Shanbo and Zhu Yingtai are pictured as perfect embodiments of virtue, impervious to every temptation. As a result, their relationship is a pure friendship, Liang Shanbo never suspecting Zhu Yingtai of being a girl, and Zhu Yingtai never hinting at a future marriage, let alone regretting, as she does in some versions of the story, that she never had sexual relations with Liang Shanbo while she had the opportunity. To make up for the removal of the traditional highlights of the narrative, the plot is enriched with many secondary episodes. Finally, the marriage with Mr. Ma safely averted, the couple end up happily married, and the butterfly transformation is reduced to one line about "the gossip of the villagers." This version of the legend, which is not without merit, appears to have been the one most easily available in print in premodern times. It also seems to have affected the popular mind, as by the 1600s the Confucius Temple at Qufu had acquired a spot "where Liang Shanbo and Zhu Yingtai used to study."

The romance of Liang Shanbo and Zhu Yingtai was extremely popular in all forms of regional opera in the twentieth century. Both Liang and Yingtai would generally be played by actresses. This was also the case when the story was adapted for the screen. The first screen adaptation dates from 1926. Another successful version was produced in China in 1954, while the Shaw Brothers of Hong Kong had a huge hit with their 1963 version. In modern times, the story has often been hailed as an expression of women's desire for equal educational opportunities and as a reflection of the evils of the traditional marriage system. Most recently, the legend has been claimed by the Chinese gay movement.

Conclusion

As a form of popular literature, verse and prosimetric narrative continued to flourish well into the twentieth century. Thanks to the modernization of the Chinese printing industry, many works of popular literature have enjoyed a much wider distribution in print during the first half of the twentieth century than at any earlier period of Chinese history. In the second half of the twentieth century, modern education, mass literature, and the modern media effectively conspired against the continuation of verse and prosimetric narrative as a prominent form of written literature, although some performance traditions, with or without political patronage, managed to survive and, in a few cases, to flourish.

A single-chapter survey can only skim the surface of this voluminous and highly variegated body of literature. While the earliest examples of the different genres have received considerable critical attention, the overwhelming majority of materials remains untouched by scholarship. As access to the major collections has greatly improved in recent years, these texts may finally be given their due in scholarly study and criticism. The results yielded by recent investigations into genres such as youth books and female-authored string ballads show how much may be achieved in the study of other genres as well.

6

Chinese literature from 1841 to 1937

DAVID DER-WEI WANG

This chapter deals with the rise and development of Chinese literature from the end of the First Opium War (1840–1842) to the eve of the Second Sino-Japanese War (1937–1945). During this period, China was in constant turmoil, wracked by military upheaval on the one hand – the Opium Wars, the First and Second Sino-Japanese Wars, the Taiping Rebellion, and the Boxer Rebellion – and on the other hand by cataclysmic social changes running the gamut from technological and commercial advancement to epistemological renovation. Indigenous innovations and foreign stimuli, radical provocations and concilia-tory responses were in drastic contestation. The impact of these multifaceted challenges was such that, by the end of the nineteenth century, officials and intellectuals alike were in agreement that changes were taking place that had been "unthinkable for the past three thousand years."

This was also a period that saw literature conceived, practiced, circulated, and assessed in ways without precedent in Chinese history. Imported printing technology, innovative marketing tactics, increased literacy, widening reader-ship, the boom in diverse forms of media and translation, and the advent of professional writers all created fields of literary production and consumption that in the preceding decades would hardly have been imaginable. Along with these changes, literature – as aesthetic vocation, scholarly discipline, and cultural institution – underwent drastic, often vehemently contested, experimentation to become "literature" as we understand the meaning of the word today. The transformation of literature was indeed one of the most acute symptoms of a burgeoning Chinese modernity.

The conventional view often takes the May Fourth Movement – a nation-wide cultural and political campaign begun on May 4, 1919 that called for self-rejuvenation in response to China's setbacks in post-World War I international politics – as the turning point in China's search for a mod-ern identity. By contrast, the late Qing era, i.e. the last six decades of the Qing dynasty, is seen as a transitional moment between the collapse of the old sociopolitical and literary order and the establishment of a new one.

This approach has been reexamined in recent years. Scholars now suggest that the conception, production, and dissemination of literature during the last decades of the Qing manifested a vigor and variety that can hardly be fitted into the narrow confines prescribed by May Fourth discourse. To be sure, May Fourth writers set in motion a series of paradigm changes that the late Qing literati would not have been able to imagine. But May Fourth claims to modernity may equally have obscured, or even eliminated, much potential that would have thrived in the late Qing; in different circumstances, these possibilities could have given rise to other, richer configurations of literary modernity for China.

We need to ask again: what makes Chinese literature since the mid-nineteenth century "modern"? One way to answer this is to address the historical context in which this inquiry is grounded. Following the story line drawn by political scientists and (literary) historians, one can describe China's literary initiation into the modern as a process of inscribing, and being inscribed by, developments such as the call for constitutional democracy, the discovery of psychologized and gendered subjectivity, the industrialization of military, economic, and cultural production, the rise of an urban landscape, and, above all, the valorization of time as evolutionary sequence. These factors first gained hold in Europe, but, emerging in non-Western civilizations such as China, they took on both global relevance and local urgency.

This imagined scenario, while naming the conditions that gave rise to modern Chinese literature, falls short of addressing the distinctive modernity that characterizes Chinese literature alone. Literary modernity may arise in response to political and technological modernization, but it need not repeat any predetermined order or content in the course of such a response. Hindsight has taught us that the newness of "historical consciousness," as represented in May Fourth literature, may not always seem new, at least not in comparison to the European counterparts it seeks to emulate, and that mere attempts at formalist or formalized rejuvenation do not guarantee a breakthrough onto the global stage where truly new modernities compete for attention.

Instead of highlighting the May Fourth literary revolution and its consequences, this chapter proposes to view Chinese literary modernization as a long and sprawling process traceable to the last decades of the nineteenth century. Literary modernization, at both global and local levels, will not be treated as a monolithic process, each stage leading inevitably toward a higher one in accordance with a certain timetable. Instead, I will argue, one must acknowledge the advent of the modern at any given historical juncture as a fierce competition of new possibilities, where the result does not necessarily reflect the best or even any one of the possibilities. Many innovations, whatever their capacity for generating more positive outcomes, do not withstand the contingency of time. To say this, however, does not mean that literary modernization as a concept is senseless, devoid of any meaningful pattern. Rather, no outcome can be predicted from the outset or seen in retrospect to follow a singular path of evolution; indeed, no actual constituent of the process could ever be replicated, because any pathway to the realization of the modern proceeds through countless mutable and amorphous stages.

I. Towards a new polemics of writing and reading literature: 1841–1894

From Gong Zizhen to Huang Zunxian: a poetics of apocalypse

Unlike orthodox May Fourth literature, which was couched in a discourse that lent itself to transnational circulation, literature in the late Qing represented a yearning for self-renewal at an inchoate stage. Reflecting the capricious circumstances under which China was being pushed into an early phase of modernity, this literature embodied a raw, creative force that was not recapitulated even as Chinese writers achieved mastery of ready-made foreign models. To appreciate the novelty of late Qing literature, therefore, one must truly believe in the capacity of literature to refashion itself, even under adverse conditions, while bearing in mind that manifestations of modernity, in theory as well as in practice, need not be limited to any prefigured formula.

In the midsummer of 1841, the scholar-cum-poet Gong Zizhen died suddenly at an academy in Danyang, Jiangsu. Gong was a controversial figure, thanks to his sharp sociopolitical criticism and his nonconformist views on the literary canon. Though neglected by his contemporaries, Gong's iconoclasm left behind a legacy that would be called on by writers, intellectuals, and politicians in the generations to come.

Gong was born in 1792, the year of Lord George Macartney's (1737–1806) historic voyage to pay tribute to the Qianlong Emperor; he died just as the First Opium War forced China to open her doors to the world. In many ways, Gong's life and works can be seen as a nexus around which early modern Chinese literature developed its most distinctive characteristics. A vociferous critic of contemporary bureaucratic culture, exegetic scholarship, and neo-Confucian dogmatism, Gong promulgated the free expression of *qing*/feeling and "child-heart," thus echoing the tenets of the late Ming "cult of *qing*." His concern about contemporary geopolitics led him to configure history in terms of a spatial redisposition of the individual intellectual and the empire; his study of northwestern China anticipated the revolution in late Qing dynastic cartography. Most importantly, Gong's commitment to the Gongyang School of learning committed him not only to a utopian timetable of progress but to a mytho-poetic vision of change and mutability.

Critics often see Gong Zizhen as the most compelling of the writers observing the first stages of dynastic decline. In inscribing the crisis of early nineteenth-century China, he is said to have brought together two traits of classical Chinese literature: historical engagement, as represented by Sima Qian's (ca 145–ca 86 BC) *Records of the Historian* (*Shiji*), and lyrical pathos, traceable to Qu Yuan's (ca 340–278 BC) "Encountering Sorrow" (Lisao). However, this does not necessarily qualify him as a forerunner of the modern age. What is groundbreaking in Gong's contribution is that he casts his historiographical and lyrical faculties into a form which, deceptively familiar at first glance, projects a radical departure from convention.

Gong Zizhen's poetry is best characterized by an inclination to affective subjectivity, an imaginary historical dynamism, and a political agency underlain by an apocalyptic vision. Liang Qichao (1873–1929), the leading literary reformer at the turn of the twentieth century, has described how he was once captivated by the "electrifying effect" of Gong Zizhen's poetry, although, on a second reading, he found it too "easy and literal." Liang's comment touches on a tension in late Qing literary discourse. The new form of writing is expected to generate a power to move the public, yet it may lack nuance as a result of its popular appeal. In light of Gong's anti-traditionalist posture, one can argue that it was precisely because the poet no longer took the "depth" of the poetic legacy seriously that he could cut through the conventions to lay bare the "nothingness" where meaning was supposed to be at its most profound. Gong Zizhen may have anticipated Liang Qichao's critique when he argued that he meant his poems to be simple and accessible even as the feelings emanating from his brush appeared unfathomable and uncontrollable.

This leads us to the broader question of the evocative power of Gong Zizhen's poetry. In contrast to contemporary evidential scholarship and the discourse of ritualism, Gong Zizhen considered *qing*/feeling the quintessential element of humanity. In this he reveals his indebtedness to late Ming thinkers, such as Li Zhi (1527–1602), as well as to early and mid-Qing literati, such as Wang Shizhen (1634–1711) and Yuan Mei (1716–1797). Gong further believed voice – and its cultural codification, language – to be an immediate manifestation of *qing*; hence his statements, "How can *qing* be channeled? Through voice"; and "Those who are devoid of *qing* cannot express themselves well in language."

But *qing* constitutes only one part of the dialectic of Gong Zizhen's poetics. Whereas it continues, as in the late Ming, to be the innate force modulating human emotional and ethical impulses, for Gong *qing* has to arise in response to ongoing political and cultural dynamics. It is in this context that Gong proposes a re-vision of history. Instead of being a transcendental force prescribing human activities, history appears to Gong as a complex of changes that make sense only when seen in terms of individual engagement and as inscribed in institutional form. For Gong, only someone with chivalric valor can intervene in the set course of history, and only someone with a tender heart can appreciate the melancholy core of history.

Gong Zizhen's juxtaposition of *qing* and history must be understood in light of late Qing historiographical discourse. The first half of the nineteenth century saw Zhang Xuecheng's (1738–1801) view that "the Six Classics are nothing but indices to history" (*liujing jieshi*) gain increasing currency. Even more notable was the emergence of the Gongyang School of learning, which prioritized historical contingency over historical immanence, institutional implementation over moral cultivation, and polity over orthodoxy. A sympathizer with Zhang Xuecheng's iconoclastic historiography, Gong Zizhen found a kindred spirit in the advocates of Gongyang thought. His allegorical reading of the Classics led him to conclude that his was an era of decline (*shuaishi*), while the era of chaos (*luanshi*) was yet to come. Although Gongyang thought foresaw an era of peace and prosperity, Gong Zizhen held that history would first have to take a downward turn, with no hope of reprieve anywhere in sight. Even before the outbreak of the First Opium War, he was already professing an eschatological view: "The heart of autumn ebbs and flows like the sea; the soul of autumn, once gone, can never be summoned back."

Gong Zizhen's poetic endeavor culminated in his *Miscellaneous Cycle of Poems of the Jihai Year* (*Jihai zashi*). This is a collection of 315 poems, all in seven-syllable quatrains, written in the cyclical year *jihai* (1839) when the poet had just quit office for good and was making his homeward journey to Hangzhou. The poems, written on various occasions, touch on a wide spectrum of subjects and moods, ranging from Gong's reflections on his career to his geopolitical proposals, from critiques of social corruption to remembrances of things past, from interactions with family members and friends to romantic encounters with courtesans, and from indulgence in self-abandon to a desire for Buddhist renunciation of the world. As its title suggests, *Miscellaneous*

Cycle of Poems presents not a coherent sequence but a fragmented constellation of timelines, occasions, themes, and sentiments. Though couched in a familiar poetic form that implies closure, its haphazard cross-references and manic-depressive moods threaten to collapse the rhetorical order as well as its contextual grounding at any moment. As a whole, the cycle chronicles a scholar–poet's journey into the darkness of his time – a poignant confession of a wasted life.

Although he inspired certain contemporary literati like Wei Yuan (1794–1857), Gong Zizhen's power would not be recognized until much later. Late Qing poetry after his time can be divided into three schools, all of which in one way or another proposed an antiquarian agenda of emulating the ancients. The Neo-Ancient School, led by poets such as Wang Kaiyun (1833–1916) and Deng Fulun (1828–1893), stressed their affinity to the styles of the Han, Wei, and the Six Dynasties. For Wang Kaiyun, as for his peers, the "return to the ancients" movement championed by such Ming literati as Li Mengyang and He Jingming was a feeble attempt that did not take poetry back far enough. To recapture the essence of Chinese poetry, these poets argued, one had to revisit the models of "truly ancient" periods. Wang Kaiyun's "Song of the Yuanming Garden" (Yuanming yuan ci, 1871), for example, is a seven-syllable ancient-style verse inspired by the poet's visit to the ruins of the Imperial Yuanming Garden demolished by the Anglo-French expeditionary force in 1860. In a pensive, understated tone, Wang describes the weed-covered garden as he contemplates the contingency of history and the ephemerality of civilization.

The second of these schools, the Late Tang School, owes its fame primarily to Fan Zengxiang (1846–1931) and Yi Shunding (1858–1920), both known for their efforts at recapturing the opulent and refined taste of the mid- and late Tang poets from Wen Tingyun (812–870) to Li Shangyin (813–858). Though criticized for indulging in frivolous subjects, the Late Tang School managed to incorporate a historical ethos into their vision of dynastic decadence. Fan Zengxiang's "Song of Colorful Cloud" (Caiyun qu, 1899, 1902), for instance, is a narrative poem about the legendary courtesan Fu Caiyun (better known as Sai Jinhua, 1872–1936), the one-time concubine of the late Qing diplomat Hong Jun (1839–1893) notorious for her alleged affair with Count Waldersee (1832–1904), the German commander-in-chief of the Allied occupation forces in Beijing after the Boxer Rebellion. Fan lavishes sensual images and decadent allusions on his poem, making Fu Caiyun an unlikely witness to the fall of the dynasty. In doing so, he may have been inspired by the early Qing poet Wu Weiye's (1609–1672) "Song of Yuanyuan" (Yuanyuan qu), which describes the late Ming courtesan, Chen Yuanyuan, for whose beauty the general Wu

Sangui was said to have betrayed the Ming. But whereas Chen Yuanyuan is a tragic figure of beauty caught up in dynastic upheaval, Fu Caiyun comes across as a femme fatale, a survivor of her times.

The Song Poetry School was the most accomplished of the three late Qing schools of poetry; its impact continued well into the Republican era, in defiance of the reigning dogmas of the New Literature movement. The poets of this school, also known as the "Tong-Guang Style" (referring to the Tongzhi (1862–1874) and Guangxu (1875–1908) reigns), tried to revive the erudite diction and obscure symbolism characteristic of Song poets like Huang Tingjian (1045–1105), although in practice their interests appear to encompass styles of other periods. Leading names of this school include Chen Sanli (1852–1937), Chen Yan (1856–1937), Zheng Xiaoxu (1860–1938), and Shen Zengzhi (1850–1922).

Chen Sanli came from a scholar's family. His father, Chen Baochen (1831–1900), was a governor-general and a member of the 1898 reform movement headed by Kang Youwei (1858–1927) and Liang Qichao. The failure of the reform brought the family into disgrace, following which Chen Baochen died under mysterious circumstances. Perhaps because of this personal trauma, Chen Sanli's poetry is pervaded by a sense of desolation, making his historical view all the more poignant. Chen Yan was another guiding light of the Song Poetry School. Besides practicing poetry, he was responsible for policing the Song Poetry School with theoretical rigor.

In addition to classical-style poetry, the song lyric (*ci*) enjoyed a brief revival in the late Qing. Wang Pengyun (1849–1904) and Zhu Zumou (1859–1931) are only two of many dedicated to the composition of song lyrics. Once popular in the late Tang, the Song, and the Yuan dynasties, the song lyric has often been regarded as a "feminine" genre despite the fact that most song lyricists are men who often take masculine experience as their subject. This assumption may result from the song lyric's typically elaborate, suggestive style and its strong emphasis on evoking emotional responses.

Song lyric had become popular again in the late eighteenth century, thanks largely to the work of the Changzhou School. Building on the Changzhou School's predilection for allegory and allusion, Wang Pengyun perfected the style and brought it to bear on contemporary realities; for this he is regarded as the key person in reviving the song lyric in the late Qing. Under Wang's influence, Zhu Zumou further cultivated fanciful imagery, topical relevance, and musical subtlety in the song lyric. Equally well-known is Kuang Zhouyi (1859–1926), who was adept not only in metrics and the deployment of imagery but also in song lyric criticism.

For these poets, song lyric provided a crystallized form of language and sensibility that seemed able to withstand the coarsening effect of their era. Yet precisely because of their immersion in this delicate form of poetry, this particular group became more sensitive than others to the threat of cultural vandalism in a time of brutal reforms and spurious modernization. Their works unfailingly convey an elegiac intent, which, together with their exquisite linguistic performance, embodies a tension between self-indulgence and self-denial – a singularly "modern" malaise of exhausted melancholia.

Although all three poetry schools share a common goal of restoring classical-style verse, one should beware of generalizing about them as merely conservative. That each seeks to revive authentic poetry by consulting with different periods and paradigms of antiquity – variously Han, Wei, and the Six Dynasties; Late Tang; Song – already betokens a tradition in meltdown. Instead of one model, these poets find multiple options in the past, each with claims to legitimacy. While they have not invented anything new, by juxtaposing various paradigms of the past in a synchronic constellation, they have "spatialized" distinct temporalities in ways rarely seen before. At the same time, they must cope with increasing pressures from within and without the domain of classical-style poetry, pressures demanding drastic reform or even total denial of the tradition.

The result is a dynamic conflation of voices speaking on behalf of different periods, genres, tastes, subjects, languages, and intended readerships. At their best, the poets of these schools were able to infuse contemporary ethos into the format of classical topics and styles, thus generating a sense of either anachronism or haunting déjà vu. In the case of Chen Sanli and Zhu Zumou, adherence to outdated formalities even serves to dramatize a peculiar existential crisis, as these poets try to come to terms with their modern experience in a negative reflection.

Of the late Qing poets wrestling with the vexed tradition of classical-style poetry, the one who rose to preeminence was Huang Zunxian (1848–1905). In terms of poetic reform, Huang takes up where Gong Zizhen leaves off, while also anticipating Liang Qichao's advocacy of "poetry revolution" in 1899.

Huang's defiant spirit was apparent early in life. In his poem "Mixed Feelings" (Zagan, 1865), he is critical of Confucian antiquarianism, particularly as typified in the eight-part essay. An admirer of Gong Zizhen, Huang argues that the ancients used language that was suitable to their own times; for this reason their poetry need not be treated as something sacrosanct by later generations. He claims in this famous line, "I intend to write in my own language; I cannot be limited by the ancients." On the strength of this conviction, Huang sought to create a new style of verse, which later came to be called "modern-style" poetry.

In 1877, Huang Zunxian made an important career move that had a direct influence on the development of his subsequent poetic vision. Instead of staying in traditional officialdom, he took up a diplomatic appointment. Over the next two decades, he traveled to America, Europe, and other parts of Asia. His overseas experience prompted him to imagine China in a global context, and as a result his poems present a kaleidoscopic vision of divergent cultures, exotic locales, and, most significantly, dynamic temporalities.

In poems like "A Song of Cherry Blossom" (Yinghua ge), "A Song on the Fog of London" (Lundun dawu ge), and "On Climbing the Eiffel Tower" (Deng Bali tieta), Huang excites his readers by the pursuit of new space and sensibilities. His *Assorted Quatrains on Japan* (*Riben zashi shi*) introduces a profusion of foreign items and institutions, from newspapers to electricity, parliamentary institutions to modern schools. Huang tries to incorporate these subjects into the existing repertoire of poetry with as little interpretation as possible. Anomalous in form and exotic in content, his works oblige readers to rethink the aesthetic and cognitive limitations of traditional poetry.

As time went on, Huang became increasingly daring in his experiments with new vocabulary and imagery. Although many poems from this period appear to be obscure, and therefore subject to varied judgments, Huang is determined to yoke together things normally deemed incompatible. In "Parting with My Beloved" (Jin bieli), a set of four poems Huang wrote to his wife from overseas, images such as photographs, telegrams, and even jet lag are invoked to highlight a changed temporal–spatial context of romantic expression, while the longing with which the poems are suffused belongs to the affective world of traditional poetry.

For all his reformist proposals and experiments, Huang believed that "there is really no such thing as ancient and modern in poetry." So long as one is able to take up subjects that are immediate and intimate to one's experience and frame them in a lively form of language, "poetry is already inherent in oneself." With this in view, he is eager to adopt folk songs and colloquial expressions to convey a sense of realism, and persistently registers his personal responses to many topical issues, ranging from the underprivileged position of women to China's recent diplomatic failures. A strong humanist concern permeates Huang's works. "There is a world beyond poetry," he proclaims, "and a human being within the poetry." This explains the title of his major poetic collection, *Poetry from the Human Realm Studio* (*Renjing lu shicao*, 1911).

Huang Zunxian served as Chinese consul-general in Singapore from 1892 to 1894. In the wake of the First Sino-Japanese War of 1894–1895, he became deeply involved in the emerging reform movement. After the failure of the Hundred Days Reform (1898), he lost the conservatives' trust and was forced to retire. Through all these changes, his poetry ever reflected a sense of historical pathos – a motif once compellingly treated by Gong Zizhen.

In 1899, Huang wrote *Miscellaneous Cycle of Poems of the Jihai Year* (*Jihai zashi*) in homage to Gong Zizhen's poetry cycle by the same title of six decades before. Put side by side, the two works constitute a powerful testimony to the changes and continuities of late Qing poetry from the post-Opium War era to the eve of the Boxer Rebellion. Also in 1899, Liang Qichao proposed a "poetry revolution" on his voyage from Japan to Hawaii. The stage was now set for a more radical form of literary rejuvenation.

The revival of wen: the paradox of the Tongcheng School

The revival of the Tongcheng School in the post-Opium War era marks another important moment in late Qing literary modernization. Arguably the most influential literary clique during the Qing dynasty, the Tongcheng School was the brainchild of literati such as Dai Mingshi (1653–1713), Fang Bao (1668–1749), and Liu Dakui (1698–1780), all natives of Tongcheng in Anhui Province, although it did not assume leadership in intellectual trends until after Yao Nai's (1731–1815) systematic promotion in the last decades of his career. Yao Nai's anthology, *Classified Anthology of Ancient-Style Prose* (*Guwenci leizuan*), was aimed at creating a canon. Published posthumously in 1820, it soon became a major source book for literati and scholars. By the eve of the First Opium War, the Tongcheng School was already the most powerful literary force of the time.

The Tongcheng School derived its discursive vigor primarily from its treatise on prose writing. In defiance of contemporary-style writing (*shiwen*), of which the most salient example was the eight-part essay (*baguwen*), Tongcheng scholars upheld archaic prose (*guwen*) as an alternative to the cultural tastes and scholarly attitude of the time. For Fang Bao and his followers, archaic prose conveys the "purport" (*yi*) and "method" (*fa*) crucial to any meaningful form of communication. Fang Bao traced the genealogy of the Tongcheng School to the Tang scholar Han Yu (768–824), an advocate in his own time of an even more archaic form of prose.

The principle issue involved here is the dialogical relationship between *dao* and its formal manifestation in *wen* or letters, something that has occupied Chinese scholars for centuries. For Tongcheng scholars, whereas *dao* stands at the core of intellectual pursuit, *wen* serves as formal evidence to substantiate *dao*. *Wen* is not mere embellishment but an emanation of *dao*. To master archaic prose, accordingly, is a way leading to the truth in all learning.

Though it may sound like trivial hairsplitting within Confucian hermeneutics, this argument points to a significant shift in the late Qing episteme. At the very least, the rise of the Tongcheng School represents a response to three trends of its time: the philological scholarship of Han Learning; the moral reasoning of Song Learning; and the stylistics of the aforementioned eight-part essay as mandated by the imperial examination system. As if seeking a new point of balance in the midst of these trends, Tongcheng scholars promulgated a tripartite methodology of "moral reasoning, evidential learning, and literary style" (*yili, kaozheng, cizhang*); archaic prose was the key to illuminating endeavors in all three directions.

Eclectic as such a tactic might appear to be, this tripartite taxonomy maintains a subtle tilt in favor of *cizhang* or literary style. For it is through the exercise of archaic prose, Tongcheng scholars argue, that one can find a way to remedy the semantic fragmentation inherent in the philological exegesis of Han Learning, provide a formal grounding for the philosophical abstraction of Song Learning, and rectify the pomposity and formularity of the stylistics of the eight-part essay. *Wen* is thus given an unprecedented position in an otherwise familiar Confucian discourse: to elucidate *dao*, one has first to master language and form.

Given its adherence to Confucian tenets, it is small wonder that the Tongcheng School should come under severe attack during the May Fourth era; its emphasis on archaic prose was especially singled out as conservative. The May Fourth modernists, however, overlooked the fact that, in elevating *wen*, the Tongcheng scholars were motivated by their discontent with contemporary discourse, and that the archaic prose they recommended is meant to be less cumbersome than the sanctioned style. The Tongcheng scholars were thus the nonconformists of their own day. Ironically, in order to legitimize their desire for change, the Tongcheng scholars called on the ancients and so placed their undertaking in the long line of "reactionary reforms" in the Chinese literary tradition: reactionary because they valued the past more than the present or future; reform because the antiquity they vowed to restore could not be a revival of the past since it was, at least in part, an imaginary construct.

This kind of reform-cum-antiquarianism was destined to provoke drastic reactions at a time when the temporal paradigms of evolution and revolution were introduced to China. One should not overlook, however, the Tongcheng School's role in the late Qing and early Republican politics of style. In his pioneering study, Theodore Huters points out that the renewed interest in *wen* among Chinese scholars since the late eighteenth century has contributed a great deal to the cognitive grounding and disciplinary rigor of *wenxue* or literature as we understand it today. From this perspective, the Tongcheng School should be viewed as both an impetus and an impediment to Chinese literary modernity. Compared with the calls for total literary reform at the turn of the twentieth century, the Tongcheng School's revisionism may appear feeble, its valorization of classical orthodoxy amounting to little more than anachronism. But, insofar as modern reformers consider literature to be not a mere rhetorical referent but an aesthetic entity embodying moral and intellectual implications, they have not left the Tongcheng teachings too far behind.

Tongcheng stylistics also provides significant clues to the transformation of late Qing cultural practice. It is widely known that the Tongcheng School was established "retroactively" through Yao Nai's efforts. Not only did Yao trace a genealogy of Tongcheng forebears to include such names as Fang Bao and Liu Dakui, he was also responsible for consolidating the school through both pedagogical and conceptual means. Tongcheng had long been a place famous for nurturing scholars and teachers. By dedicating the last four decades of his career to teaching, Yao Nai took up this local tradition and as a result was able to gather a huge number of followers. Four of his disciples, Fang Dongshu (1772–1851), Guan Tong (1780–1831), Yao Ying (1785–1853), and Mei Zengliang (1786–1853), were especially respected at the time. Yao was also at pains to edit the *Classified Anthology of Ancient-Style Prose*, a collection comprising more than seven hundred exemplary prose works from ancient times to the mid-Qing. This became arguably the most popular sourcebook for nineteenth-century Chinese literati.

What Yao Nai and his students undertook was nothing less than the remaking of the canon. From its beginnings on the margins of the mid-Qing scholarly field, the Tongcheng School was, by the start of the next century, headed for the center. By the outbreak of the First Opium War, the Tongcheng tenets of "purport" and "method" had become both intellectual guideline and stylistic manual for contemporary scholars. From the cultivation of a literary "habitus" to the making of a canon, from the formation of a clique to the sanctioning of a style, the rise of the Tongcheng School demonstrates how *wen* means more than mere textual embellishment; it entertains, rather, a whole array of social and cultural implications, referring to both form and content, linguistic trait and cultural mannerism, and, above all, individual choice and institutional establishment.

The Tongcheng School plummeted from its positon of influence after the First Opium War. As China encountered a new system of knowledge and power represented by the West, the Tongcheng School's adherence to *wen* and *dao* came to be seen as impractical. The Taiping Rebellion and other disturbances in the 1850s further shook scholars' confidence in the efficacy of traditional learning and its manifestations in archaic prose.

In the 1860s, however, the school underwent a dramatic reincarnation, thanks to the engagement of Zeng Guofan (1811–1872). A monumental political and historical figure, Zeng is best remembered for his double role as a general quelling the Taiping rebels and a scholar advocating archaic prose. Though not affiliated by direct lineage, Zeng was committed to the Tongcheng School's tripartite guidelines of philosophy, scholarship, and writing. To these he added a fourth element, statecraft (*jingji*), thereby updating the school's agenda in a timely manner. According to Zeng, a good composition should be able to cultivate individual minds as well as remedy dynastic crises, both illuminating one's scholarship and manifesting social commitment.

By highlighting the linkage between writing and statecraft, Zeng Guofan hoped to win for the Tongcheng School a political agency; he did in fact succeed in renewing people's attention to the "usefulness" of Tongcheng prose. As a result, the school enjoyed a revival parallel to the short-lived "restoration" of the Tongzhi reign. But Zeng Guofan's addition of statecraft to the Tongcheng School's already eclectic curriculum may also have eroded its theoretical foundations. In proclaiming that *wen* reflected "the dynamics of the time" and was closely related to "a nation's fate," he had unwittingly called into question the perennial, sacrosanct nature of *dao*, treating it instead as something susceptible to historical change and political judgment.

Nor can one ignore the possible impact of the position Zeng occupied when promoting his version of the Tongcheng style. His close ties to the court, his prestige as a general-cum-scholar, and his capacity to draw into his staff some of the best scholars of his time, all provided the "symbolic capital" needed to make Tongcheng writings into the leading, indeed the canonical, literature in service to the dynasty. Through Zeng Guofan, the Tongcheng School completed its ascent to the apogee of the literary and political field; nevertheless, in its fully established form, the Tongcheng School was a far cry from the school as it was first envisioned in the mid-Qing era.

Of Zeng Guofan's disciples, Zhang Yuzhao (1823–1894), Li Shuchang (1837–1897), Xue Fucheng (1838–1894), and Wu Rulun (1840–1903) were often cited as the most prominent. While they followed their mentor's inculcation of *wen* and *dao*, they were equally wary of the increasing impact of the New Learning. Particularly noteworthy is the fact that Li Shuchang, Xue Fucheng, and Guo Songtao (1818–1891) – another follower of Zeng Guofan's Tongcheng discourse – were among the first group of late Qing diplomats and that they all had extensive overseas careers. Standing on the front line of China's first major encounter with the West, these men sounded the clarion call for reform. At the same time, in writing of their foreign experiences, they uniformly resorted to archaic prose. The novel appeal of their exotic subjects and the antiquarian claim of their native style inevitably brought to Tongcheng discourse a tension absent in the school's earlier writings.

To the extent that language and form constitute the core of Tongcheng stylistic politics, it may not be a coincidence that the last stage of the school's transformation would take place in two translations. In 1898, Yan Fu (1854–1921) published his translation of T. H. Huxley's *Evolution and Ethics* as *Tianyan lun*. The social Darwinism of the book's thesis stunned late Qing intellectual circles. Equally impressive was the fact that Yan Fu rendered Huxley in a prose style reminiscent of the philosophical treatises of the pre-Han period. Yan Fu's translation added a new aspect to the tensions implicit in the Tongcheng School's encounter with the West. Unlike the work of Li Shuchang and Xue Fucheng, Yan Fu's translation represented more an intellectual acquisition than it did an empirical perception of the West. His use of archaic prose, therefore, touched on the epistemological dilemma besetting the Tongcheng School.

When studying in the Royal Naval Academy in Plymouth in 1876, Yan Fu made the acquaintance of Guo Songtao, then ambassador to Britain. Through this connection Yan came to know Guo's friend, Wu Rulun, famed educator and practitioner of Tongcheng prose, whom he later invited to write a preface to his translation of *Evolution and Ethics*. With Wu's endorsement, Yan Fu found his way into the league of Tongcheng writers. For both men, the style of translation meant as much as the matter being translated. Yan argued that he had chosen archaic prose in light of Confucius's dictum, "Language without embellishment will not carry far." "If one uses the vulgar language current today," Yan elaborated, "it is difficult to get the point across. One always suppresses the idea in favor of the expression, and a tiny initial error leads to an infinite error in the end." His motto for a good translation was: faithfulness, precision, elegance.

Wu Rulun believed that only someone as deeply immersed in the practice of *wen* as Yan Fu was qualified to translate because he would be able to give the new learning a discursive form commensurate with that of the ancient

Classics. Compared with the translation of Buddhist texts into Chinese, Yan Fu's undertaking would, in the same way, enrich rather than diminish the eminence of *dao*. At his most polemical, Wu advised Yan to sacrifice semantic fidelity so as to preserve the purity of language. He thus turned the Tongcheng School's antiquarian hermeneutics into a totally formal pursuit. By insisting on an unbreakable linkage between form and content, present and past, Wu paradoxically called attention to the break that had already taken place in those linkages.

Like Wu Rulun, Lin Shu (1852–1924) felt fully justified when he translated Western fiction and drama in an elegant archaic style, without even knowing the languages of the originals. By conventional Tongcheng standards, one cannot emphasize enough the distance between the genres of fiction and prose, and between the indigenous property of *wen* and foreign literary imports. Lin's assimilation of Western literature to the Chinese cultural legacy was an attempt as much to sinicize foreign sources as to exoticize the indigenous tradition. He found in Dickens's fiction a compositional structure reminiscent of *Records of the Historian*, and celebrated Alexandre Dumas's *La Dame aux Camélias* as a supreme model of *qing*/feeling. Through his translation, he brought under one yoke fiction and prose, Chinese thought and Western sensibility, in such a way as to make of them something both new and not new. Perhaps because of their mixture of exoticism and nostalgia, Lin's translations became best sellers in late Qing China. The seemingly obsolete style of Tongcheng prose thus provided Lin as well as his readers with an interface where the cultural and intellectual conflicts embedded in Chinese and non-Chinese literatures are reconciled, something that never could have been foreseen by Lin's Tongcheng predecessors. To this extent, Lin Shu's radical antiquarian exercise constitutes an important part of the late Qing project of literary modernization.

The rise of early modern fiction: the decadent and the chivalric

Compared with poetry and prose, narrative fiction in the late Qing lends itself even more readily to literary modernization. Before translations of Western and Japanese novels and stories were introduced to China, a renovation of fiction was already under way. First came courtesan fiction in the post-Opium War years; examples are *Dream of Yangzhou* (*Yangzhou meng*, 1847) by Ganmeng shangren (dates unknown), and *Precious Mirror for Judging Flowers* (*Pinhua baojian*, 1849) by Chen Sen (1805–1870?). Whereas *Dream of Yangzhou*, couched in a starkly realistic style, features a series of courtesans in pursuit of love and material gain, *Precious Mirror for Judging Flowers* highlights the romance between female impersonators and their patrons in a world illuminated by fantastical theatrics. Other popular titles of this genre include *Traces of Flowers and Moon* (*Huayue hen*, 1859) by Wei Zi'an (1819–1874), *Dream of the Green Chamber* (*Qingloumeng*, 1878) by Yu Da (?–1884), and *Singsong Girls of Shanghai* (*Haishanghua liezhuan*, 1894) by Han Bangqing (1856–1894).

In no other period since the invention of classical fiction – not even the late Ming – did so many literati writers dedicate the full-length novel to life in the pleasure quarters, high and low, or to hetero- and homoerotic daydreams and anxieties. At its best, late Qing courtesan fiction redefines the conventions of romantic and erotic fiction within a social and narrative space, namely the courtesan house. Courtesan narratives of the previous generations, to be sure, made extensive references to the brothel as a symbolic locale, informed by a variety of topoi; but in late Qing fiction the courtesan house calls attention to its own existence and commands a full range of social functions. More than a place capitalizing on the plethora of sexual desire, the courtesan house in late Qing fiction is at once family compound, social hangout, business center, and political arena. In this collapsing of separate moral territories into a single fictive space, it comes as no surprise that revolutionary and reactionary ideologies should be espoused by insouciant singsong girls, or that the supreme virtue of womanhood should be enacted by female impersonators.

Precious Mirror for Judging Flowers (hereafter *Precious Mirror*) chronicles the romances of two Beijing opera singers-cum-courtesans with their patrons. Through their adventures, the true meaning of virtues like love, faithfulness, perseverance, and chastity is made clear. Marred by stale allusion and unimaginative hyperbole, this novel would have been negligible had it set out to recount the romances of ordinary courtesans and scholars. But Chen Sen's teenage courtesans are all opera singers, and in Beijing opera the singers are traditionally male.

The two couples' love affairs demonstrate Chen Sen's indebtedness to three romantic traditions in Chinese literature. In terms of characterization, his novel is nurtured on the tradition of the idealized scholar–courtesan love story, a tradition that can be traced back to such Tang *chuanqi* stories as "The Story of Li Wa" (*Liwa zhuan*). In terms of rhetoric and narration, the love-ridden sentimentality and lyrical extravagance of *Precious Mirror* place it in the grand tradition of the "sentimental-erotic," which includes such poets as Li Shangyin and Du Mu, and such works of drama and fiction as *Peony Pavilion* (*Mudan ting*) and *The Story of the Stone* (*Honglou meng*). Above all, in describing two couples who undergo an array of tests before they can consummate their romance, the novel owes its plot structure to the "talent–beauty" fiction of the late Ming and early Qing eras.

Mediocre as it may be, *Precious Mirror* addresses the transgression and legitimization of sexual norms in a given social context and the ethical pretexts for writing and reading them as such. With its transvestitism and female impersonation, the novel inquires into issues such as masqueraded sexuality versus staged subjectivity, and the theater of power versus the theater of desire. Moreover, as its hidden theme of sexual transvestitism surfaces on the rhetorical level, the novel disturbs the conventional boundaries governing the representation of gender in narrative, and sheds light, however unexpectedly, on woman's position in the formation of romantic conventions.

Traces of Flowers and Moon deals with the contrasting fortunes of two scholar–courtesan pairs against the backdrop of the Taiping Rebellion and other domestic upheavals. One pair rises to prosperity and fame, while the other is hounded to death by ill-health and adversity. As with *Precious Mirror*, the structure and characterization of this novel are also reminiscent of late Ming "talent–beauty" fiction. There is something different, however, in Wei Zi'an's use of convention. *Precious Mirror* subverts the gender and social status of the prototypes of talented young men and beauties; *Traces of Flowers and Moon* rewrites their temperaments and fates. The heroine Liu Qiuhen is a sullen courtesan never popular among brothel-goers, and her patron Wei Chizhu appears to be an abject literatus twice her age. The two meet and find strong mutual attachment, yet, after a series of trials, they are never reunited. Death becomes their doom.

As critics have pointed out, Wei Zi'an wrote *Traces of Flowers and Moon* not so much to narrate a story as to showcase poetry that he had composed over a long span of time before he embarked upon his novel. Some even suspect that he wrote the novel only for the sake of being able to weave the poems into a narrative sequence. In other words, Wei Zi'an "resurrected" his poetry from oblivion by means of a narrative act, his romantic novel becoming a rhetorical reversal of his romantic poetry, creating events for the poems to "trace."

Insofar as the affective and textual "traces" of the flowers and moon take precedence over the "flowers and moon" themselves, one may talk about a derivative aesthetics in Wei Zi'an's novel: derivative in the sense that the original meaning of love cannot be articulated without recourse to its figurative replacement; and aesthetics in the sense that both Wei Zi'an and his characters embrace love in the form not of an act of physical consummation but of a prolonged symbolic substitution of that act.

This derivative aesthetics has a historical dimension. The narrated historical events in the novel, from the Taiping Rebellion to ethnic riots, might signal a national cataclysm of the kind that has traditionally produced both tragic romances and imperial renewals, but the novel's historical narration is no longer able to articulate events in the traditional way, only to recall the "traces" of cataclysm – tributary sensations and trivialized pathos. Compared with the literatus and the courtesan of late Ming and early Qing drama and poetry, Wei Zi'an's protagonists live in a world where grand narratives are in ruin, and they can only experience the traces of bygone sentiments.

Singsong Girls of Shanghai (hereafter *Singsong Girls*) is the greatest of the late Qing courtesan novels and, after *Flowers in the Mirror* (*Jinghua yuan*, 1830), may well be the greatest work of nineteenth-century Chinese fiction. The novel presents a panoramic portrait of life in the Shanghai pleasure quarters in the last decades of the nineteenth century. In the course of its sixty-four chapters, it describes more than two dozen courtesans and their patrons, as seen engaging in the twin sports of desiring and being desired, and inquires into the moral and psychological consequences of their romantic adventures.

Ironically, *Singsong Girls* has never been popular among general readers. This is usually attributed to the fact that it is written in the Wu dialect and is therefore unreadable to readers from other regions. The real reason, however, may lie in the fact that the book does not read like the courtesan novel we generally know. Han Bangqing narrates everything in a matter-of-fact style, to the point where even the most glamorous banquets and the most sensuous rendezvous sound like familiar family routines. In doing so, he pioneers a way of describing desire from a perspective that would later be likened to that of psychological realism.

The courtesans and their customers in *Singsong Girls* appear as a group of amazingly ordinary women and men. They meet, fall in love, quarrel, break up, or are reunited just like ordinary couples; at the same time, they know they are only playing the role of a husband and a wife. Just as they are uninterested in composing love letters and poems to each other, as would have been expected by clichéd formulae, they are equally indifferent to what goes on in bed. The demarcations between love and lust, vanity and disillusionment, so handily drawn in most courtesan novels, can no longer be identified with ease.

Han Bangqing excels in featuring a gallery of courtesans who are not paragons of virtue but first-rate players upon desire in the name of virtue – whether love, fidelity, generosity, or even chastity. Nevertheless, engaging dramas often happen when the girls upset the delicate balance between desire and virtue, fantasy and necessity, by consuming one at the expense of the other. In one case, when the high-minded Li Shufang's plan to become her patron's wife, not concubine, is thwarted by the latter's family, the blow brings out her pride: if she cannot be a wife worthy of a scholar's family, she will be a courtesan proud of her profession. She eventually wastes away and dies a pitiful death. In another case, the country girl Zhao Erbao, lured into the courtesan trade and now a popular success, falls in love with a young man and willingly gives up everything for a marriage proposal. What follows is not difficult to guess. Erbao's sweetheart never comes back, and she finds herself deep in debt for the dowry she has prepared.

In portraying these romantic adventures, Han seems to be saying that the courtesans are only too human when they are deluded by the impossible dreams and virtues that they, of all people, should see through. The sad clichés of fiction do happen and are made to happen repeatedly simply because they are part of the real human condition.

Singsong Girls is a masterpiece that helped to modernize late imperial Chinese fiction in at least three ways, by creating a new typology of desire, an arguable "modern" rhetoric of realism, and a unique instance of the urban novel. As Eileen Chang has observed, in a cultural and ethical environment where the individual pursuit of romantic love can still be overruled in favor of prearranged marriage, Han Bangqing has made the brothel a substitute "Eden," a garden in which the forbidden fruit of "free love" is made available to Chinese intruders. The tragicomedies acted out by the characters of *Singsong Girls* are surprisingly moving: these men and women are shown to be lonely souls, seeking consolation in the most unlikely circumstances and finding bliss, however tentatively, in their fall. Suffice it for critics to conclude that *Singsong Girls* excels most Chinese fiction written since *The Story of the Stone*.

The chivalric and court case novel is another major genre of this period. At a time when China was beset with foreign invasions and domestic rebellions, its reading public (and listening audience) took refuge in the world of chivalric and court case fiction. Here they found a world in which impartial judges and heroic knights join forces to investigate crimes, exorcise demons, oust oppressors, unearth conspiracies, and suppress insurrections. Some of the characters and episodes from late Qing chivalric and court case fiction were so popular that they became a major source of modern Chinese popular culture.

Late Qing chivalric and court case fiction originated as a mixture of two subgenres of the vernacular tradition, chivalric fiction and court case fiction. The chivalric novel portrayed a self-appointed knight transgressing laws in order to right wrongs; the power of this genre lay in its implicit critique of the existing order and its success in projecting the fantasy of overcoming this order. The hero of the court case novel was typically an agent of state power who affirmed the essential rightness of the law by hunting down selfish miscreants; the implicit affirmation of the existing order, and the projected fantasy of purifying it, gave this genre great popularity. The convergence of these two fictional genres in the late Qing points to the uncertainty of the concepts of law and justice at a turbulent historical moment. By flagrantly playing with complicitous relationships between law and violence, justice and terror, late Qing chivalric and court case fiction marks a radical rethinking of legitimacy, whether imperial or ideological.

Three story-cycles demonstrate the popularity of the chivalric and court case novel in the late Qing. *The Court Cases of Judge Shi (Shi gongan)*, often regarded as the progenitor of the new genre, appeared in 1820; by 1903 it had given rise to ten sequels, amounting to a stupendous 528 chapters. The *Sanxia wuyi* cycle, the most popular of all late Qing chivalric and court case fiction, comprises three works – *Three Knights-Errant and Five Sworn Brothers (Sanxia wuyi*, 1879) and its two sequels *The Little Five Sworn Brothers (Xiao wuyi*, 1890) and *Sequel to Little Five Sworn Brothers (Xu xiaowuyi*, 1890) – with a total of 360 chapters. That the renowned philologist Yu Yue (1821–1907) edited the first of these and reissued it under the title *Seven Knights-Errant and Five Sworn Brothers (Qixia wuyi*, 1889) testifies to the novel's abiding popularity. *The Court Cases of Judge Peng (Peng gongan)* was first published in 1892, and has eight sequels, the last one published in the Republican era.

Late Qing chivalric and court case romance originated with Yu Wanchun's (1794–1849) *Quell the Bandits (Dangkouzhi*, 1853). Written as a sequel to Jin Shengtan's (1610–1661) seventy-chapter edition of the *Water Margin*, Yu's *Quell the Bandits* rewrites the story of the reconciliation between the Liangshan band and the Song government. The Liangshan rebels become outright bandits, ever threatening the dynasty's well-being. As the novel's title suggests, the rebels are all eventually put down; their defeat and death represent not tragic downfall, as the conventional reading would have it, but well-earned retribution.

Quell the Bandits is more than a novel about a military crackdown on rebellious uprisings, however. It is also meant to be a literary campaign to "terminate" a novelistic tradition – that of the *Water Margin* – that had allegedly been responsible for propagating or disseminating thoughts of banditry and treason. Although written with the avowed purpose of honoring the institution of imperial power, the novel nevertheless took its inspiration from a narrative cycle known for its subversive themes. Setting out to condemn the recalcitrant acts of chivalric men and women against the law and the state, the author is also tantalized by these nonconformist means for revitalizing a nation's strength. At its most polemical, the novel presents the duplicitous conditions of loyalty and righteousness, two of the most treasured Confucian values, thereby undermining its apparent call for restoring dynastic orthodoxy.

Few novels from mid-nineteenth-century China can match *Quell the Bandits* in the immediate impact it had on current politics. Because of its loyalist agenda, *Quell the Bandits* was widely circulated by the Qing government as propaganda in the period of the Taiping Rebellion; small wonder that it was at the same time banned by the Taiping rebels. Notwithstanding its tendentious conservatism and flagrant anachronism, the novel addresses a range of issues from sovereignty and revolution to the polemics of reading and writing literature, issues that would concern literati in the next century. Thus it effectively gave rise to the polemics of the modern Chinese political novel.

Putting aside the ambiguity of its political vision, *Quell the Bandits* is a striking achievement, as Yu Wanchun mixes elements drawn both from the Chinese fantastic tradition and from his recent encounter with Western technologies. The novel introduces "modern" gadgets and warfare foreign to the traditional military romance; it creates new devices and battle strategies, but puts them in a cosmological (as well as narrative) order that is anything but new. Yu Wanchun appears simultaneously to be promoting new military technology and Daoist mythology. This mixture of the scientific and the fantastic modes may be seen as evidence of the renewed discursive format of Yu's time.

A Tale of Heroes and Lovers is a novel by a poor Manchu aristocrat, Wen Kang (1798?–1872). Wen Kang's family background and his vivid portrait of Manchu lifestyles have led many scholars to liken *A Tale of Heroes and Lovers* to *The Story of the Stone* by Cao Xueqin, though the two writers' assessments of their shared cultural heritage could not be further apart. *The Story of the Stone* may be read as a lyrical remembrance of things past, underlain by a reflective allegory of the impermanence of life, while *A Tale of Heroes and Lovers* celebrates this-worldly glory, orchestrated as a symphony of temporary adversities and eventual fulfillment.

The novel features He Yufeng, a chivalric woman who vows to avenge her father's death at the hands of a villainous general. Through He's adventures, which include accidentally rescuing the young filial scholar An Ji, being frustrated in her plan of revenge by the untimely death of the villain, and finally accepting An Ji's proposal of marriage, the novel explores two ideals of secular life, romantic love (*ernü*) and heroism (*yingxiong*), and the terms under which these two ideals can be harmonized into one. As such, *A Tale of Heroes and Lovers* has long been denigrated by modern critics as spreading feudal Confucian attitudes, although it is valued for Wen Kang's masterful use of Mandarin Chinese.

Even so, one should not underestimate Wen Kang's ambition to authenticate a worldview based on Confucianism. Here love and heroism do not exist as givens, naturally inclusive of each other's terms; rather, they name moral options that should be subsumed in a higher mandate. The novelist extrapolates the meaning of *yingxiong* and *ernü* to the point where the two terms become the source of all virtue and all action. By *yingxiong* and *ernü*, Wen Kang intends not only the philosophical tradition of will and desire, but also the entire fictional tradition of heroes and lovers. His goal is nothing less than to reconcile separate and incommensurate worlds: not theoretical ideals as opposed to real-life practices, but philosophical theories and fictional practices. Thus, given her swordsmanship and her espousal of vendetta, He Yufeng cannot become a complete heroine until she turns to the role prescribed to women by Confucian tradition, namely that of a virtuous wife who can exalt her husband's love to a higher level.

For fans of late Qing chivalric and court case fiction, the *Three Knights-Errant and Five Sworn Brothers* (hereafter *Three Knights-Errant*) is generally regarded as the best. With its impartial Judge Bao, who investigates and solves a series of cases at the risk of his own well-being, and a group of chivalric characters who escort the judge and execute his orders, the novel becomes the model in both theme and characterization for numerous chivalric and court case novels in the following decades.

The "author" (or editor) of *Three Knights-Errant* is usually thought to be Shi Yukun (1810–1871), a popular storyteller who lived in the Xianfeng and Tongzhi reigns. The figure of Judge Bao, undoubtedly the supreme symbol of justice in Chinese popular culture even now, can be traced to Song tales and Yuan drama. Story cycles around famous cases presided over by Judge Bao were already appearing in the Ming dynasty. Shi Yukun is believed to be the key figure who, putting together all the sources about Judge Bao handed down from previous ages, narrated them in an elaborate sequence in his oral performances.

Three Knights-Errant represents the most successful, if not the first, attempt of its time at mixing the chivalric and the court case traditions. In serving the common good, the knights-errant and the judges find that they can collaborate and become the best of partners, agreeing to forget that officials can be corrupted by power and outlaws tainted by disobedience. For this reason, the convergence of the chivalric and the court case traditions betokens for many critics either philistinism or "surrenderism."

But this seeming decadence may equally point to a cynical turn of the public imagination in the post-Taiping Rebellion period. The collaboration between the chivalric heroes and governmental officials in a novel like *Three Knights-Errant* blurs rather than reinforces the concept of justice as spelled out separately in the two fictional traditions. When a chivalric hero trades in his code of honor for an honorable job as law-enforcer, he does so in response to a time in which myths of sovereignty at both personal and national levels are rapidly dissipating. When a judge has to count on ex-outlaws and retired swordsmen to maintain social order, he enacts an overriding cynicism as to how justice is really served.

Though conventional wisdom sees it as a setback in the modernization of Chinese literature, the appearance of late Qing chivalric and court case fiction addresses emphatically a society's urgent need to reconfigure its political and judicial powers. The genre's tongue-in-cheek endorsement of imperial power, while welcomed by conservatives, nevertheless insinuates the impending breakdown of the existing ideology of power. Instead of celebrating the old regime, or a new, purified version of it, to be put in place by some outlaw hero, chivalric and court case fiction envisions a *mise-en-scène* of change by means of various displacements and substitutions of the terms of power. It is amid this reshuffling of terms, in which rebellion and revolution, individualism and loyalism, retribution and justice, moral reciprocity and judicial equality, are reexamined, that a society's yearning for radical change is most clear.

The making of early modern literati

The transformation of late Qing literature would not have been possible without the participation of a group of literati and intellectuals with an early modern outlook. At the same time, changes in the sociopolitical and cultural environment also helped to refashion the image and agency of traditional men of letters. Although the majority of literati still came from a traditional background of Confucian education and many were, like their forebears, members of officialdom, the way in which they carried out their literary and bureaucratic vocations was now pushing them along a rather different path. The desires, experiments, and proposals of this group did not always result in outcomes that fit their expectations, whether favoring tradition or reform, but this in itself may be their contribution to the growth of a modern – and distinctively Chinese – brand of imagination.

Take the case of Gong Zizhen. There might be nothing drastically new in his works upon first reading, but his reenvisioning of history as a cosmic force to be acted out by human agency, his celebration of *qing* as key to unleashing the momentum of change, and his reliance on voice and language to mediate personal sentiment and historical vocation, would occupy reform-minded literati in the subsequent decades. No other writer of his time so movingly pictured China as a land of desolation, where the sun is setting, the winds of sorrow are blowing, and all vegetation has withered under the pall of a fiendish fog, as ferocious beasts and deformed creatures lurk nearby. Roaming this wasteland is a lonely poet who, despite his pessimism and despondence, is driven all the more to express his feelings – anguish, wrath, chivalric desire, and utopian will. In "Ode to Pathos" (Fu youhuan), Gong likens pathos to a romantic passion. He treats his historical melancholy as though it were a mysterious love by which he is possessed and which he will not allow to be exorcised. This is an early symptom of the "obsession with China" that C. T. Hsia believes to underlie the psychic drama of modern Chinese writers.

One of Gong Zizhen's admirers was Kang Youwei, a literatus from Guangdong immersed in both classical and Western learning, and a forceful advocate of reform. Like Gong, Kang was influenced by the Gongyang School of Confucianism in his apocalyptic view of Chinese history. His *Great Harmony* (*Datong shu*) presents a late Qing utopia, an all-inclusive society, prosperous and strong, ineluctably propelled toward the future. Liang Qichao, another admirer, derived from Gong the image of youth (*shaonian*), which he promulgated in his notion of "Youthful China" (*shaonian Zhongguo*), while Lu Xun appears to have recapitulated the poet's predilection for mad genius (*kuangshi*) and crazy words (*kuangyan*) when he made his first fictional character a madman (*kuangren*). Finally, the "sublime figure" of modern Chinese poetics and politics harks back to Gong's iconoclastic poetry. When Mao Zedong set out to promote the People's Commune in 1958, he invoked a poem about cosmic agency by none other than Gong Zizhen.

We have seen how Huang Zunxian rose as a nonconformist poet who confronts the extant paradigm by writing in terms of colloquial expression, personal feeling, and historical urgency, and how he followed the unconventional career of a diplomat. During his consulship in Japan from 1877 to 1882, Huang became acquainted with prominent Japanese *bunjin* (literati), a mixture of reformers and cultural conservatives. These two types of literati did not constitute a simple dichotomy, since both identified with classical learning. Huang's experiences with these literati gave him insight into the intellectual milieu of early Meiji Japan and a model for the Chinese intellectual reformer.

For Huang, the essential question in both cultures was how to accommodate the pressing needs of modernization within the matrix of values and sensibilities associated with classical learning and tradition. Huang's writings at this time bear witness to his own changing attitudes towards modernization as they developed within the context of his continuing commitment to the ideals of tradition.

More intriguing is the Tongcheng School's excursion into the realm of literary modernity. In 1875, Guo Songtao was appointed the first imperial envoy to Britain amid the opposition of the conservatives. Though discharged from the position only two months after his arrival in London, Guo left plenty of writings about his foreign encounters. *An Account of My Mission to the West* (*Shixi jicheng*) features firsthand accounts of British landscapes, civil facilities, and social manners and morals. Li Shuchang was similarly prolific. Assistant to Guo Songtao on the latter's pioneering mission to Britain, he later became a prominent diplomat in his own right, assigned to such places as Japan, Germany, France, Sweden, Belgium, Austria, and Italy. Li may have wished to recapitulate Tongcheng rhetoric in his essays about his foreign experience, but he had a different take on the school's "purport" and "method." In "An Account of Brighton" (Bulaidun ji), for instance, Li seems to be interested not so much in the natural scenery of this British seaside resort as in its vacationing facilities and casual atmosphere. Despite his Confucian outlook, Li found himself no less attracted to cosmopolitanism. However, in ending this essay with an allusion to the *Zuozhuan*, he manages to suggest that Chinese sages long ago realized that only a strong country is capable of properly arranging popular pastimes.

In "An Account of Viewing Oil Paintings in Paris" (Guan Bali youhua ji), Xue Fucheng, Qing court ambassador to Britain between 1890 and 1894, describes how on his visit to a wax museum in Paris he was struck by a simulated scene of the aftermath of the Franco-Prussian War. Although he meant to draw a moral from the French crisis, Xue was obviously more fascinated by the "effect of the real" produced by the museum artifact. His essay takes on an unexpected dimension with regard to the contested claims of mimesis and idealism and the tension between perspective illusionism and empathetic representation. His praise for French craftsmanship sustained the Tongcheng School's preoccupation with form as the vehicle for representing truth.

The late Qing era also witnessed the rise of a new type of literati who did not follow the traditional path in achieving their status. They either found a new source of enlightenment in Western learning or participated in the burgeoning media industry by serving as newspaper editors, columnists, translators, and magazine publishers. The appearance of this type of literati marks a sea-change in Chinese expectations governing men of letters. It also anticipates the advent of the professional writer in the next generation.

Wang Tao (1828–1897) is a prominent example of this new literatus. A native of Suzhou, he first went to Shanghai in 1848 and visited the London Missionary Society Press, where he was offered a job the next year by Walter Henry Medhurst, assisting in Medhurst's translation of the New Testament into Chinese. Wang worked at the Press for the next thirteen years. During the Taiping Rebellion, Wang was a sympathizer with the rebels, and even proposed to a Taiping leader tactics for overcoming the Qing. When the Qing army recaptured Shanghai and ordered his arrest, Wang took refuge in Hong Kong, and remained in exile overseas for the next twenty-two years. In Hong Kong, he began his collaboration with the missionary sinologist James Legge, and eventually assisted Legge in translating eleven Chinese Classics.

In 1867, at Legge's invitation, Wang Tao traveled to Scotland by way of Singapore, Ceylon, Penang, Aden, Messina, Cairo, Marseille, Paris, and London. The trip was an eye-opening experience. He later collected part of his writings on the road into *Jottings from Carefree Travels* (*Manyou suilu*), the first travel book about Europe by a Chinese scholar. In 1872, Wang bought the printing press of the London Mission in Hong Kong and founded the Zhonghua General Printing House. He founded *Circular Daily* (*Xunhuan ribao*), the first Chinese daily newspaper, in 1874. These new forums enabled him to publish hundreds of editorials and treatises calling for political, industrial, and educational reforms. In 1879, Wang made a visit to Japan, where he enjoyed high esteem. His fame as one well versed in foreign learning and reformist thought finally reached such high-ranking officials as Zeng Guofan and Li Hongzhang, paving the way for his pardon by the Qing court in 1884.

The product of a traditional Confucian environment, Wang Tao became a paragon of the first generation of enlightened literati. Instead of joining the bureaucratic system, he forged an unexpected career in Western learning, translation, publication, and journalism – something that would have been unthinkable for Chinese intellectuals and literati only decades before. But this does not mean that he gave up practicing traditional forms of belles-lettres. Wang's seven-syllable regulated verse, classical tales, and prose constitute a sizable portion of his corpus. These may have been outmoded genres, but from time to time Wang Tao was able to infuse them with fresh elements, using foreign settings or innovative themes. His *Random Notes of a Shanghai*

Recluse (*Songyin manlu*, 1884) was a welcome collection because of its mixture of Chinese supernatural narratives with Western motifs and characters.

In this way, Wang Tao presented a double image. Hailed as a champion of the new learning, he was no less renowned for his hobby of frequenting courtesan houses and churning out writings on erotic and fantastic subjects. He was thus as much a pioneer in Chinese journalism and reformist discourse as he was a connoisseur of the fading splendor of traditional literati culture.

Making an interesting pair with Wang Tao is Han Bangqing, the author of *Singsong Girls of Shanghai*. A native of Songjiang Prefecture, Han in his youth lived in Beijing with his father, a low-ranking government official. Despite his reputation as a child prodigy, Han failed repeatedly in the civil service examinations. He eventually gave up hope of an official career and moved to Shanghai, becoming a regular contributor to a column about the demimonde in the newspaper *Shenbao*. Han is said to have been a regular patron of Shanghai brothels and made a study of the boudoirs of select courtesans. *Singsong Girls* is allegedly based on personal experience. Han Bangqing's life may sound much like that led by many other scholars adrift in late Qing Shanghai. Mostly from the lower Yangzi delta, they were either unable or unwilling to advance themselves in officialdom, and, finding their way to Shanghai, they joined the rising media industry. However, two facts merit particular attention in Han's case. In 1892, he founded the magazine *Wonderbook of Shanghai* (*Haishang qishu*), a bi-weekly that featured his collection of short stories, *Sketches of Taixian* (*Taixian man'gao*), and *Singsong Girls* in serial form. The stories in *Sketches of Taixian* are reminiscent of the gothic tradition of *zhiguai* from Six Dynasties tales down to the *Liaozhai*, whereas *Singsong Girls*, as discussed above, represents a breakthrough in depicting Shanghai in realistic terms. Although it lasted only for eight months, *Wonderbook of Shanghai* seems to have been the first literary magazine in Chinese history. For writing fiction and running a literary magazine for commercial purposes, Han Bangqing has also been regarded as the first professional literary writer of modern China.

During the last decades of the nineteenth century, women writers gradually emerged to form a new discourse, though at first it was largely limited to the traditional forms of poetry and long verse narrative. Important names include Wu Zao (1799–1863), a song-lyrics poet, and Qiu Xinru (1811–1860), author of the long verse narrative *Flower Born out of the Pen* (*Bishenghua*). The year 1877 marked the publication of *Shadows of Dream of the Red Chamber* (*Honglou meng ying*), the first extant novel by a Chinese woman. Little is known about the early life of its author, the Manchu lady Gu Taiqing (1799–ca 1877), except that she was the concubine of the Manchu aristocrat Yihui (1799–1838) and that they were both fond of literati activities. Gu was expelled from the family after her husband's death and spent the rest of her life with her children. It is speculated that she may have finished her novel in the 1860s, but set it aside for reasons ranging from family objections to personal reservations.

Scholars have observed Gu's connections to contemporary women writers in Hangzhou and Beijing, such as Liang Desheng, Wang Duan, Wu Zao, and Shen Shanbao (1808–1862). *Shadows of Dream of the Red Chamber* is regarded as a triumph of feminine literary culture in the late Qing. The novel starts where the original 120-chapter edition of *The Story of the Stone* ends, as, following a series of humiliations and tragedies, the Jia family stages a comeback and Baoyu carries on with his marriage to Baochai, all the while making advancements in officialdom. One of the primary goals of Gu Taiqing was to overturn the sad ending of *The Story of the Stone* by depicting subsequent generations of selected major characters as thriving either in worldly achievement or in romantic engagement. But Gu makes a special effort to let us know that Jia Baoyu can never let go his memories of Daiyu, thus underpinning the novel with a note of melancholy. The novel ends with Baoyu's dream encounter with a mirror, in which his women friends wave at him from atop a red chamber and then fade away before he can reach them.

Shadows of Dream of the Red Chamber was not reprinted till 1988, and so far little sign has been found of its influence on other fiction. As one of the many sequels to *The Story of the Stone*, the novel may have come out too late and was perhaps too mild a response to the masterpiece. Nevertheless, though unable to match Cao Xueqin in either lyrical sensibility or romantic imagination, Gu Taiqing's sequel made an important step in joining feminine creativity with the form of the novel. *Shadows of Dream of the Red Chamber* epitomizes a generation of women writers who were ready to embrace the world beyond the fantastic, feminine world of the long verse narrative.

II. Reforming and re-forming literature: 1895–1919

The polemics of literary reform

The last decade of the nineteenth century saw China in the grip of political and social crisis. In the wake of the Chinese defeat in the First Sino-Japanese War (1894–1895), China signed the Treaty of Shimonoseki on April 17, 1895, declaring Korea independent and ceding Taiwan, the Pescadores, and the Liaodong peninsula to Japan. This diplomatic humiliation was only the prelude to a cluster of calamities and perturbations in the next few decades. China was to undergo great challenges as it entered the modern age.

Among the thousands of Chinese intellectuals shocked by the outcome of the First Sino-Japanese War was Liang Qichao, then a young scholar. As he later wrote, "China finally woke up from a four-thousand-year-long dream as a result of her defeat in the Sino-Japanese War and the cession of Taiwan." Liang obtained his *juren* degree in 1889, and in 1890 became a disciple of Kang Youwei. From 1895 to 1898, he worked closely with Kang in promoting reforms, editing important journals and serving as academic director at the reform movement's base, the Academy of Current Events. After the conservative coup that ended the Hundred Days Reform in 1898, Liang started fourteen years of exile in Japan and other countries.

Deeply involved as he was in political activities, Liang Qichao had all along treated literature as a crucial part of reform. During his exile, he came to realize all the more the necessity of refashioning the Chinese soul by means of literature. In 1899, he invented the slogan "poetry revolution" on his voyage from Japan to Hawaii, followed by two others, "prose revolution" (*wenjie geming*) and "fiction revolution" (*xiaoshuo geming*). To be sure, Liang was not the sole advocate of literary reform in a drastic way, but thanks to his rhetorical power and theoretical engagement, his proposals brought forth most emphatically the sentiment of his time.

But the literary reform promoted by Liang Qichao and his followers is only part of the story of the boom in late Qing literature. The emergence of cities and urban culture, the burgeoning of a printing industry, the mushrooming of public media such as newspapers and magazines, and the increasing demand for a literature for public entertainment, all contributed to a new popular reading culture. Without these material factors by which the cultural and social environment had been conditioned, Liang's advocacy of a new form of literature would not have had such an overwhelming effect.

It should be noted that, despite the efforts of Liang and others, old forms of literature – such as Tongcheng School prose and the various genres of classical-style poetry, as well as fictional narrative in parallel discourse – were still practiced and appreciated by a considerable number of writers and readers. They even staged an unlikely comeback around the last years of the Qing and during the early Republican era. The popularity of these forms in the revolutionary years points to a whole range of discontents: from political loyalism to cultural nostalgia, and from *ressentiment* to melancholia to the uncertainties of a new age. These – to the reform-minded "unwelcome" – literary practices have to be included in any configuration of the literary modern. Thus, before the literary revolution was finally launched on May 4, 1919, Chinese literature had already experienced a process of transformation far more dynamic than has been acknowledged by critics still arguing along the lines of May Fourth ideology.

Of the three revolutions proposed by Liang Qichao – poetry revolution, prose revolution, and fiction revolution – fiction revolution was the most enthusiastically received by contemporary literati. By fiction, Liang means vernacular fiction, which may be extended to include popular forms of theater and performing arts. Fiction had traditionally ranked the lowest in the literary canon, but around the turn of the twentieth century it rose to become the most exciting of literary phenomena.

A familiar reconstruction of the rise of late Qing fiction starts with Yan Fu's and Xia Zengyou's (1886–1924) "Announcement of Our Intention to Publish a Supplementary Fiction Section" (Benguan fuyin shuobu yuanqi) in 1897, followed by diatribes against traditional narrative fiction by Liang Qichao and other enlightened elite critics, and their endorsement of the political novel. This wave of literary reform culminated in Liang's founding of the magazine *New Fiction* (Xin xiaoshuo) in Yokohama in 1902. Included in this reconstructed scenario are other factors, such as the phenomenal rise of fiction magazines in the wake of *New Fiction*, the introduction of foreign novels and stories in translation, the radicalization of political thought against the status quo, and the widening of fictional subject matter. Although such critics as Huang Moxi (1866–1913) and Xu Nianci (1875–1908) expressed skepticism at the height of the "new fiction" fever, the conviction that fiction could and should serve as the foremost medium of enlightened discourse has apparently been endorsed by elite and mainstream literary historians ever since.

In their essay, Yan Fu and Xia Zengyou draw upon biological and social Darwinism to account for the intrinsic appeal of fiction. For them, fiction is the genre that most forcefully deals with heroism and romance, the modes with the most universal appeal. Where history falls short in showing what life should be, fiction can rectify history so as to ensure the perpetual valorization of the heroic and romantic ideals of humanity. In response to the view of these two men, Liang's "Foreword to Our Series of Political Novels in Translation" (Yiyin zhengzhi xiaoshuo xu, 1898) introduced the political novel, a genre he believed to be responsible for the success of the Meiji Restoration in Japan, as the type of fiction that would most benefit China. Liang's promotion of the political novel was borne out when he founded *New Fiction* and published the essay "On the Relation between Fiction and Ruling the Public" (Lun xiaoshuo yu qunzhi zhi guanxi) in the inaugural issue of 1902. The essay opens with the famous passage affirming the didactic role of fiction, and its positive political and moral impact: "To renovate the people of a nation, the traditional literature of that nation must first be renovated . . . Why? It is because fiction exercises power of an incalculable magnitude over mankind."

Liang enumerates four ways in which fiction has impact on our emotions – *xun* (diffusing), *qin* (permeating), *ci* (piercing), and *ti* (elevating) – all referring to methods that can disturb one's emotional equilibrium and thus lead one to a changed apprehension of the world. In the wake of the publication of Liang's theory, Dipingzi proclaimed that fiction "dazzles, charms, enchants, intoxicates," Tao Youzeng described fiction as a "monstrous creature" with "a great power beyond imagination and calculation," and Wu Jianren (1866–1910) equated *qing* to all kinds of emotional responses, from patriotism to filial piety.

The discourse spearheaded by Yan Fu, Liang Qichao, and their fellow critics was later recognized as the mainstream of late Qing literature. But did the "new fiction" that Liang and his peers yearned for really become the dominant genre in late Qing society? Were the theories about "new fiction" popular because they brought forth new ideas, or because they rehashed familiar beliefs? Critics have remarked that, despite his employment of Darwinian terms to explain the power of fiction, Yan Fu is very much a traditionalist and was in fact being dishonest with himself in arguing for the greater appeal of fiction over history in strictly Chinese terms. The same criticism may apply to the fiction criticism of Liang Qichao and other contemporaries. For all their affinity for foreign theories and Buddhist concepts, the Confucian idea of "literature as a vehicle for the Way" (*wen yi zai dao*) remains the backbone of their theories about the novel.

One should also keep in mind that, even as the discourse on "new fiction" was on the rise, Liang Qichao's contemporaries were already expressing different views on literature and politics. Wang Guowei (1877–1927), for instance, reinterprets *The Story of the Stone* in the light of theories traceable to Schopenhauer, Nietzsche, and Kant. He sees embodied in Chinese romance a compelling tension between desire and the object of desire, between human suffering and the sublimation of that suffering in art.

Wang Guowei has been accorded a dubious position in modern Chinese literary history on account of his loyalty to the Qing and his taste for classical literature. Only recently have scholars come to assess his works in a different light. As one critic puts it, "Liang Qichao brandishes the banner of 'new fiction,' but the core of his literary concept is old. Wang Guowei recommends classical Chinese fiction, while at the center of his literary thought is something very new." If Liang Qichao is to be praised, it should not be for introducing anything foreign so much as for ingeniously reviving traditional Chinese literary didacticism and utilitarianism by packaging them as Western and Japanese imports. By contrast, Wang Guowei deserves serious attention less because he upholds the traditional Chinese fiction than because he fits Western theories into a radical reading of Chinese Classics, thus adding a new and peculiarly Chinese dimension to what we understand as modern.

Wang Guowei's career reached a turning point in 1907, when, realizing that his strong "emotional powers" could hardly be satisfied by intellectual inquiry, he turned from Western philosophy to Chinese literature and dedicated the following years to the study of literature, particularly the song lyric. Discontented with the didactic Confucian approach, he took inspiration from the intuitive strain of classical poetics found in Yan Yu, Wang Fuzhi, and Wang Shizhen, and formed his own theory of "mental configuration" (*jingjie*), by which he meant a liminal state of reality that is occasioned by but not limited to the lived experience of poetic composition. This "mental configuration" is subjective and aesthetically evocative but also resonates with voices from other moments of epiphanic awakening in history. Above all, Wang tries to modernize the lyrical discourse inherent in traditional poetics.

Wang's search for the lyrical counterpart to "mental configuration" led him to Song and Yuan drama, a field formerly considered unworthy of scholarly attention. Between 1908 and 1912, he wrote several works on the origins and the musical and theatrical elements of Song and Yuan drama, and found in this apparently simple and plebeian genre the source of an aesthetic vision not accessible in the more refined genre of poetry. In this way Wang endeavored to create a paradigm shift in classical Chinese literary studies.

In opposition to Liang Qichao's theory of didacticism and Wang Guowei's theory of mental configuration, Huang Moxi and Xu Nianci approached fiction writing and reading from a formalist perspective. Drawing their inspiration from the aesthetic views of Hegel and Kant and from the Ming–Qing tradition of fiction annotation, they argued that fiction should be above all an aesthetic entity. The effect of beauty, Xu Nianci observes, lies in a rational immersion in nature, a distinctive expression of individuality, an arousal of affective pleasure, a figural form, and a representation of the ideal. Both Huang and Xu were skeptical about the "new fiction" fever; the latter even suggested that the common people constituted no more than 10 percent of its total readership.

As with poetry and fiction, drama underwent a shake-up during the May Fourth era in the areas of performance theory, dramaturgy, generic category, and even theater construction. In promulgating revolution in the genres of poetry, prose, and fiction, Liang Qichao and his followers also had in mind theater reform, holding that, compared with vernacular fiction, traditional popular theatre in various forms reached even wider audiences. As a result, more than 150 new scripts of southern plays and northern plays were produced between 1901 and 1902 with a view to spreading modern ideas. In 1904, *The Great Stage of the Twentieth Century* (*Ershi shiji dawutai*), the first journal for promoting the new theater, was established by Chen Qubing (1874–1933) and the Beijing opera singer Wang Xiaonong (1858–1918). Echoing the agenda of Liang and other reformers, Chen envisions a modern theater that could educate its audience through entertainment, thereby "saving the state and civilizing the land." In 1906, the Enlightenment Dramatic Society was set up, and a historical novel by the renowned fiction writer Wu Jianren was published as a Peking opera libretto. Meanwhile, Wang Xiaonong and Tian Jiyun (1864–1925), another Peking opera singer, strove to rewrite conventional scripts to include new ideas.

At the same time that late Qing reformists were trying to make "use" of fiction for a noble cause, the genre also suffered "misuse." Not only did contemporary writers produce fiction on dubious subjects under the banner of edifying the public, they also wrote, self-reflectively, about the outrageous spectacle of a society that trafficked in the new and the modern. A quick glance at the *oeuvre* of late Qing fiction shows that, for each item of "new fiction," there appear many counterexamples, works that later came to be labeled depravity novels, black-screen novels, chivalric romance, fantasy, and so forth. Although the target audience of "new fiction" imagined by Liang Qichao was the general public, once he became occupied by a political cause he considered more important, his enthusiasm for writing fiction waned.

In the essay "To Fiction Writers" (Gao xiaoshuo jia, 1915), Liang admits that "the past ten years have seen a tremendous degeneration of social morals and manners. What aspect of that degeneration has not been traceable to the influence of the so-called 'new fiction'?" Since the statement was made in 1915, the decline attributed to new fiction could be traced back to 1906, the year Liang's own magazine *New Fiction* folded. In other words, "new fiction" was in decay at the very outset; it was already passé even before its newness had been absorbed by the general public. In picturing the development of late Qing fiction, therefore, one should always be alert to the gap between what writers and critics thought they had achieved and what they in fact achieved, what the elite expected their readers to like and what their readers actually did like.

The production of late Qing literature

We can now take a look at the material circumstances of the production of late Qing fiction. Between the Hundred Days Reform and the fall of the Qing empire, an estimated two thousand or more works of fiction were written and circulated in various forms. Only half this number have been recovered. These works come in a wide range of modes, from detective fiction to science fantasy, from erotic escapades to didactic utopias, and from chivalric cycles to revolutionary romances. But they are most notable for having appropriated these old genres, and mixing, mocking, and collapsing them.

The rush to publish fiction signals a shake-up in cultural production, one more diversified and radical than formerly suspected. The promotion of fiction by the literary elite under the pretext of didacticism was only the most obvious cause of this transformation. Along with the public's insistent demand for new forms of entertainment, setting off a boom in commercial printing, other factors include the capacity of readers to imagine fictional resolutions to historical problems, and willingness on the part of writers to project utopian/dystopian visions onto the future as much as onto the past. The result was an array of imaginary realities that do not square with the newly established orthodoxy for narrating modernity.

By the last decade of the Qing, China boasted more than 170 presses, catering to a potential audience of between two and four million readers. Fiction was published through at least four channels: periodical newspapers, tabloids, fiction magazines, and books. As early as the 1870s, fiction appeared as one of the features of the new publishing medium, the newspaper. The front pages of *Shenbao* (1872–1949), one of the earliest Chinese newspapers, often highlighted reports that combine both journalistic relevance and fictional invention. *Random Sketches of the World* (*Yinghuan suoji*), the monthly literary supplement to *Shenbao*, routinely put narrative fiction side by side with more prestigious genres such as essays and poetry. By 1892, fiction had become such a popular genre that it commanded an exclusive venue of its own in Hang Bangqing's *Wonderbook of Shanghai*.

At the same time, fiction also opened up new territory in tabloids dedicated to *youxi* (recreation) and *xiaoxian* (pastime). Most of the thirty-two tabloids that have been identified, such as *News from the Pleasure Quarters* (*Zhinan bao*) and *News about Recreation* (*Youxi bao*), carried fiction. Wu Jianren and Li Boyuan (1867–1906), two of the most important late Qing writers, started their careers as editors of and regular contributors to these tabloids. In the wake of literati campaigns to promote fiction in the late 1890s, more than thirty presses came to specialize in publishing fiction, and at least twenty-one literary periodicals appeared with *xiaoshuo* or "fiction" in their titles. Four of the most famous are: *New Fiction* (*Xin xiaoshuo*, 1902–1906), *Illustrated Fiction* (*Xiuxiang xiaoshuo*, 1903–1906), *Short Story Magazine* (*Xiaoshuo yuebao*, 1906–1908), and *Fiction Grove* (*Xiaoshuo lin*, 1907–1908).

This was a period in which Western fiction was introduced to China in various forms of translation. Based on the catalogue of late Qing fiction compiled by Ah Ying, one of the pioneers of late Qing fiction studies, mainland Chinese scholars have identified at least 479 original works and 628 translations. Tarumoto Teruo, using a different method of counting, concludes that at least 1,016 kinds of fiction appeared in translation between 1840 and 1911. Charles Dickens, Alexandre Dumas *fils*, Victor Hugo, and Leo Tolstoy, among others, were warmly welcomed by readers, while A. Conan Doyle, H. Rider Haggard, and Jules Verne remained the top three best sellers.

But Chinese fictional renovation was already under way when Western and Japanese texts began to appear in Chinese form. When *Quell the Bandits* became an instrument of propaganda warfare during the Taiping Rebellion, alternately banned by the rebels and promoted by the Qing government, the effect was to reinduct the novel into the service of Chinese political warfare. *Precious Mirror for Judging Flowers*, by bringing the aesthetics of female impersonation to bear on heterosexual romantic conventions, reengendered Chinese sexual subjectivity. Almost all the major classic Chinese novels, from *Water Margin* to *The Story of the Stone*, found second incarnations in parodic doubles at this time.

Two further ways of narrating subjective and social realities appeared with the late Qing publication, in 1877 and 1879 respectively, of two mid-Qing works: Shen Fu's (1762–after 1803) lyrical autobiography *Six Records of a Floating Life* (*Fusheng liuji*), and Zhang Nanzhuang's (dates unknown) ghostly satire *What Sort of Book Is This?* (*Hedian*). In particular, *What Sort of Book Is This?* distinguished itself by using dialect – in this case, the Wu dialect – as part of its realistic effect. It flaunted the colloquial mannerisms of traditional vernacular fiction and anticipated the next generation's experiments with linguistic local color.

By the time Yan Fu and Liang Qichao proposed reforms on the model of Japanese and Western novels, Chinese fictional convention had shown every sign of disintegrating and reinventing itself. The advent of various foreign models did not initiate, but rather compounded, this complex phenomenon, thrusting the whole late Qing practice of fiction into the cross-cultural and interlingual dialogue we know as modernity.

Despite the immense popularity of fiction, however, very few acknowledged masterpieces were produced. Having elevated fiction to the highest place in the literary hierarchy, the enlightened elite could not conceal their disdain for contemporary practitioners of the genre. In spite of all the theories promulgating the didactic functions of fiction, most writers and readers appreciated the genre for a very different reason: fiction was the genre that let them indulge their daydreams, play out their fantasies, and even give in wholeheartedly to "depraved" thoughts.

Nor can one find another period in Chinese literature in which writers invested a discourse with such paradoxical impulses. Many literati made fiction writing their sole profession, but as a group they were most unprofessional: they hurried to get their stories into print but rarely finished them; they pursued one modern topic after another, only to expose their deep-seated parochialism; they fabricated, plagiarized, and sensationalized their materials; they reached out to every social stratum for realistic data, but ended up with an idiosyncratic display of biases and desires; they claimed to expose social abuses and condemn absurdities, but succeeded more in celebrating the pleasures of spectating the one and applauding the other. Despite efforts at the local level to westernize narrative form, rhetorical stance, and subject matter, late Qing fiction remains first and last a corpus of works that attests to the tenacity of a tradition in the face of all attempts to overthrow it. Vacillating between contradictions that range from quantity versus quality, elite ideal versus popular taste, the classical language versus the vernacular language, the central versus the marginal, foreign influence versus indigenous legacy, apocalyptic vision versus decadent desire, exposure versus masquerade, innovation versus convention, enlightenment versus entertainment, and so on, late Qing fiction presents a heterogeneity of voices or noises, making its own cacophony one of the most powerful echoes of a volatile age.

With this understanding, when we revisit the year 1905, the year new fiction was said by Liang Qichao to have suffered its downfall, we see a dynamic fictional world. Whereas *Huang Xiuqiu* introduces a new woman striving to reform the status quo, *A Romance of Hong Xiuquan* (*Hong Xiuquan yanyi*) tells of the arch-rebel of the Taiping Rebellion who almost brought down the Qing empire. In *Voices of Merchants* (*Shisheng*), the popular notion of "business war" is dramatized in the adventures of a group of Shanghai merchants, and education reform becomes the dominant concern of a generation of intellectuals in *A History of Education in the Future* (*Weilai jiaoyushi*). Both *Bitter Society* (*Ku shehui*) and *Bitter Students* (*Ku xuesheng*) describe the hardships of overseas Chinese, while works such as *Splendid Dreams of the Past Twenty*

Years (*Ershizai fanhua meng*) chronicle corruption and abuses in China in the form of exposé. Foreign figures are frequently brought to bear on a social or political issue. In *The Ghost of Rousseau* (*Lusuo hun*), the French thinker teams up with the Ming loyalist Huang Zongxi to overthrow the tyrannical rule of Hell; Madame Roland inspires her Chinese disciple, Huang Xiuqiu, in a dream encounter. In *China's Columbus* (*Zhina gelunbu*), a Chinese explorer sets out to discover the New World and ends up establishing his own republic, and Sherlock Holmes is invoked in *The Travels of Lao Can* (*Lao Can youji*) to highlight his Chinese counterpart's analytical mind and investigative expertise.

The multiple trajectories of fiction

Of the various fictional genres that were popular in the late Qing, the exposé has left the deepest impression on readers. Aimed at revealing social abuses and indicting political corruption, the exposé is characterized by topical urgency, vigorous cynicism, and the compulsive need to laugh at everything high and low. Structurally, it often takes the form of a long string of caricatures, scandals, and comic interludes, mixed in such a way as to convey an effect less of progression than of stagnation.

The traditional approach to late Qing exposé has highlighted the so-called "Four Masterpieces": Wu Jianren's *Eyewitness Reports on Strange Things from the Past Twenty Years* (*Ershinian mudu zhi guaixianzhuang*, hereafter *Eyewitness Reports*), Li Boyuan's *Exposure of Officialdom* (*Guanchang xianxing ji*), Liu E's *The Travels of Lao Can* (*Lao Can youji*), and Zeng Pu's (1872–1935) *Flower in the Sea of Sins* (*Niehai hua*). The trend epitomized in these novels is said to have been inspired by works such as Wu Jingzi's (1750–1754) *The Scholars* (*Rulin waishi*, 1749), but a quick glance at some of the best-known examples indicates otherwise. The self-proclaimed attitude of writers of satirical exposés may have echoed the tenor of "new fiction" and, to that extent, anticipated the moral bearing of the May Fourth writers. However, behind their intent to indict and chastise, ambiguous laughter can be heard, laughter that undermines serious intentions and earnest claims.

Novelist, editor, journalist, political activist, and veteran patron of the demimonde, Wu Jianren was one of the most versatile members of the late Qing literati. His best-known work, *Eyewitness Reports*, was first serialized in Liang Qichao's *New Fiction* in 1903. The novel was an immediate success and, by the time it was finally completed in 1910 to make a total of 108 chapters, it had become one of the most talked-about works of the day. Written in the form of a journal, the novel details how a young man named Jiusi Yisheng is initiated into, and eventually withdraws from, a Chinese society devoid of moral scruples. Jiusi Yisheng has his first bitter lesson at fifteen when his father suddenly dies. He undertakes to settle the family inheritance with his uncle, only to be tricked by the latter out of everything he deserves. He then travels on business, going from Shanghai to Beijing, from Hong Kong to Tianjin. In the course of these travels, he piles up an amazing quantity of "eyewitness reports" on subjects as wide-ranging as political corruption, commercial fraud, intellectual chicanery, and social scandal.

The reader meets government officials who win promotion at the expense of their family members' pain, thieves in the guise of bureaucrats and vice versa, intellectuals who are hypocrites of the most detestable kind, merchants trading not only in goods but in official positions, and deceitful prostitutes who become bureaucrats' wives. These characters, as the narrator describes in his preface, may well be called monsters and goblins, or fox spirits and demons. By the end of the novel, Jiusi Yisheng is forced to escape from society so as to maintain his own sanity; his tale ends up being a bitter parody of a Western *Bildungsroman*.

Doleželová-Velingerová calls attention to two themes that permeate late Qing exposé: "evil always defeats good" and "the greater evil defeats a minor one." In the case of Wu's novel, this gratuitousness stems less from the hero's thwarted integrity as he struggles to cope with reality than from his inertia when faced with the rampant chaos of the world he is thrown into. The hero's "initiation" into knowledge of the world, therefore, serves as a cautionary example to the readers; one learns from his experiences that "social evil" is not something hidden deep behind the scenes, unveiled only at the right moment, but is in fact always with us. If the nineteenth-century European novel typically follows a timeline from the state of ambiguity or innocence to that of truth or knowledge, late Qing exposé tells its audience nothing new but confirms what is all too familiar.

Li Boyuan was a friend of Wu Jianren and another important late Qing satirist. His *Exposure of Officialdom* appeared in serialization in 1903. Unlike *Eyewitness Reports*, which aims at the wholesale ridicule of late Qing society, *Exposure* emphasizes one social stratum – officialdom – treating it as a self-contained miniature world. The novel enumerates the outrageous practices of officials, such as bribery, mismanagement, embezzlement, and, above all, the buying and selling of posts, concluding that these practices have undermined the millennia-old system of civil service examinations and bureaucratic governance.

Liu E's *The Travels of Lao Can* (1906) is one of the most popular novels of the late Qing. Lao Can is a doctor by profession and by avocation a chivalric knight, an enlightened intellectual and a conservative ideologue. Through Lao Can's lonely adventures across natural and human landscapes, as he wanders among different social milieux and engages his friends in debates on political and philosophical issues, the author presents a panorama of late Qing society at the moment before its total disintegration. *The Travels of Lao Can* has been read variously as a great novel of exposé, an intricate allegorical narrative, a unique Chinese picaresque novel, a lyrical novel, and a political novel.

Not unlike his hero, Liu E led a life full of contradictions, being both a self-styled entrepreneur and a conservative scholar, both a connoisseur of ancient curios and a comprador for foreign investors. Fiction writing was never his primary activity, yet *The Travels of Lao Can* places him among the most sensitive literary minds of his time, one who can capture the full spectrum of resentments, frustrations, dreams, and fantasies of a generation of Chinese intellectuals in the face of national crisis.

The Travels of Lao Can has often been cited as a rare example of the late Qing writer's ability to deal with a character's psychology. Lao Can's sorrow at his country's fate, his indignation at innocent suffering, and his lyrical fascination with natural subjects all show a sensitive soul's response to external stimuli. But the novel is at its most powerful when it describes the hero's frustration and amazement as he tries in vain to penetrate beyond the treacherous surface of a given situation. Why are the incorruptible judges more dangerous than the corruptible ones? Why do Chinese people persecute those who can provide the most ready cures for the country's diseases? Such questions function as leitmotifs recurring throughout the novel. They drive the narrator (and the reader) again and again out of Lao Can's inner world to refocus on the outer problems that make Lao Can what he is.

Flower in the Sea of Sins (1907), by Zeng Pu, is based on the legend of Sai Jinhua (Fu Caiyun in fiction). A literatus committed to revolutionary thought, Zeng originally meant *Flower* to be a historical novel presenting a panorama of China's political turmoil from 1870 to the eve of the Republican Revolution. Inspired by the nineteenth-century European historical novel, Zeng Pu intended to relate history, not as the expanded biography of princes, politicians, and generals, but as an account of both important and minor events as experienced by ordinary individuals in a given period. Ironically, in writing his ideal historical novel, Zeng Pu became greatly indebted to the Chinese narrative modes he had hoped to supplant.

The romance between Sai Jinhua and Count Waldersee has been definitively proved by historians to have been unlikely. Taking up the legend in the spirit of suspended disbelief, Zeng Pu creates the courtesan Fu Caiyun as a dynamic character who begins in a house of courtesans and ends up a national heroine. Her protean social roles – including courtesan, concubine and (during their stay abroad) "official" wife of Jin Jun, socialite, and mistress – is deliberately paralleled in her moral resilience. Unscrupulous and promiscuous, she shows herself most adaptable to the rapidly changing world, to the point of saving China with her own body. In the saga of Fu Caiyun's life, Zeng Pu unfolds an unlikely allegory of gender politics and national representation in the late Qing.

The "Four Masterpieces" have obscured other equally notable achievements by writers such as Wu Jianren and Li Boyuan. Unlike Liu E and Zeng Pu, whose reputations were each based on a single work, Wu and Li were versatile and prolific writers. In particular, Li Boyuan's *Modern Times* (*Wenming xiaoshi*, 1906) draws one of the most poignant portraits of China's vexed but hilarious confrontation with modern imports. *Modern Times* was first serialized in 1903, three years after the Boxer Rebellion and five years after the Hundred Days Reform, and recounts bizarre events resulting from the national campaign for reform. Students, native entrepreneurs, nouveaux riches, revolutionaries, technocrats, emancipated women, translators, and others march in legions through this sixty-chapter novel. New-style education, occidentalism, constitutional monarchy, revolution, international trade, women's liberation, military renewal, and technological advancement are some of the topics with which these characters are obsessed.

By highlighting either "strange events" or sordid bureaucratic deals, *Eyewitness Reports* and *Exposure of Officialdom* envision a Chinese society in which anything goes when money or position is at stake. Such motives are also present in *Modern Times*; in order to make money or obtain a position in the modern world, Li Boyuan suggests, even tricksters and imposters have to keep up with the latest trends. The effect is heavily ironic. In satirizing society's pursuit of the latest fashion, which results in nothing new but only the exposure of its inherent greed and opportunism, the novel seems to be expounding a conservative viewpoint, but it also draws our attention to genuine harbingers of the new age – the entrepreneurial spirit and experimental outlook with which people stage their pursuit of the *wenming* or "modern."

In Wu Jianren's sentimental romance, *The Sea of Regret* (*Henhai*, 1906), two pairs of lovers are driven apart during the Boxer Rebellion and brought together later after much suffering, only to find that they no longer suit each other. One of the heroines insists on marrying her fiancé though he is in every sense unworthy of her. She demonstrates a passion less for her fiancé than for her own virtue; this, however, proves to be disastrous for everyone around her. There is nothing to be learned from her experience, only excessive tears to be shed.

Paradoxically, the novel's charm lies precisely in showing the characters of a traditional "talent–beauty romance" in a situation in which all traditional values are dislodged and where they must undergo emotional and conceptual trials as a vain attempt to restore an ideal past. As a mimicry of the "great romance" that can no longer be lived in either the fictional or the historical world, *The Sea of Regret* amounts to a nostalgic gesture – for the characters, the writer, and the audience – in remembrance of a bygone (literary) golden age.

The historical novel was still a popular genre in the late Qing, as illustrated by such novels as *A History of Pain* (*Tongshi*, 1905) and *Romance of the Eastern Jin and the Western Jin* (*Liangjin yanyi*, 1908), both by Wu Jianren. But the "pastness" of narrated events inherent in the historical discourse has lost its power as the "future" emerges to become the new *raison d'être* of narrative and epistemology. This was a natural corollary to the increasingly popular notion that things evolve in a linear fashion, perhaps toward a single natural end.

Science fiction, in particular, provided a setting in which timing and the direction of time could be reconceived. Late Qing fantasists conjured up a world in which previously unimaginable robots, sorcerers, balloons, submarines, airborne vehicles, guided missiles, and spaceships abounded. They were especially eager to write or translate stories about adventures in utopia or dystopia, the flight to the Moon or the Sun, intergalactic space odysseys, and expeditions to the center of the Earth or the bottom of the sea. In these unprecedented spatial–temporal environments, the actions of their characters would either ruin or revive China. By imagining and writing out the incredible and the impractical, late Qing writers laid out the terms of China's modernization project, both as a new political agenda and as a new national myth.

One prominent instance of this is Liang Qichao's *The Future of New China* (*Xin Zhongguo weilai ji*, 1902). The novel opens with an overview of a prosperous China in 1962, sixty years after the novel's publication date. Inspired by the Japanese political novel *Setchubai* (*Plum Blossoms in the Snow*, 1886) and Edward Bellamy's *Looking Backward*, Liang envisions his new China in a "future perfect" mood, imagining things as they will have become with passing time. Ironically, Liang never finished his novel, thus leaving his narrated future in suspension.

More intriguing is Wu Jianren's *The New Story of the Stone* (*Xin Shitouji*, 1908). A rewrite of Cao Xueqin's classic, *The New Story of the Stone* premises the same mythical framework of "mending Heaven," casting Baoyu as a lonely traveler in time. The first part of the novel deals with Baoyu as he travels to the Barbarous World, where he witnesses the atrocities of the Boxer Rebellion and gets arrested for spreading democratic ideas. In the second part, he stumbles upon the Civilized World, a utopia strong in military power, political structure, scientific advancement, and moral cultivation. Baoyu's journey culminates in his visit to the venerable ruler of this world, Dongfang Qiang (literally "Eastern Strength"), who explains his utopia as one based on the Confucian notion of *ren* or benevolence.

Notice how Wu Jianren reinterprets the theme of "mending Heaven" in his work. While Heaven remains the ultimate symbol of the plenitude of Meaning, it is informed not so much by the conventional discourses of compassion or legitimation as by a new telos that justifies China's search for wealth and power. The Heaven that Wu Jianren's Baoyu wishes to mend is at one with the Heaven envisioned in Yan Fu's translation of Huxley's *Evolution and Ethics*. It is a Heaven emblazoned with the new Darwinian slogan of the "survival of the fittest by the grace of Heaven." Situating the Civilized World in a utopia governed by the future perfect mood, Wu Jianren turns his Jia Baoyu into an idealist who has already missed his opportunity by the time he sets out to make amends for his idealism. He can only be a belated spectator of what will already have happened as he sojourns somewhere outside of history. Between the sorrowful past and the fantastic future, a fold in time has occurred, and it is in this parallel moment that the most exhilarating event in China has taken place.

Moon Colony (*Yueqiu zhimindi xiaoshuo*, 1905), by Huangjiang Diaosou, imagines a group of Chinese and Japanese adventurers flying a balloon to the moon when China is no longer suitable for living. Viewing China from a better-than-bird's-eye view, the balloon riders see a land whose scope diminishes in proportion to their widening horizons. The epistemological disorder created by the aerial voyage makes the active reconfiguration of the image of China an urgent priority. Equally daring is Xu Nianci's (Donghai Juewo) "A New Account of Mr. Windbag" (*Xin faluo xiansheng tan*, 1905), a story about a Chinese scientist's one-man expedition to outer space, which culminates in an aborted attempt to fly to the Sun.

Biheguan Zhuren's *New Era* (*Xin jiyuan*, 1908) is set in 1999, when China has become a superpower and is waging a world war against the Western powers. At the center of the narrative is a dispute over who has the right to "time" the world. China wins the war, thanks to superb strategy, fantastic arms, and supernatural intervention, and the Chinese calendar dating back to the Yellow Emperor is adopted globally. A new era is thus established.

Finally, the late Qing saw an upsurge of fiction about women's issues in a variety of genres from exposé to science fiction. Among the most hotly contested issues in late Qing reform, woman's predicament and the emancipation of women were taken not only as a literal goal for gender and social reform but also as a symbol embodying China's struggle for modernity. It is small wonder that once "woman" took on the dimension of national imaginary, male writers should assume a female perspective in addressing their concerns. Granted that the majority of women still had limited opportunities for education and social engagement, fiction about and even written by women pointed to the rise of a feminine/feminist discourse in the next few decades.

Thus, under the male author Luo Pu's (1876–1949) pen, there appeared in *Heroines of Eastern Europe* (*Dong'ou nühaojie*, 1903) a gallery of overseas Chinese and European heroines engaged in nihilist activities. The book particularly highlights the heroic deeds of Sophia Perovskaya (1853–1881), one of the most famous foreign women in late Qing China. An unfinished project, the novel deals only with the early part of Perovskaya's career, but it opens the way for modern Chinese narratives of the Russian heroine by such writers as Qiu Jin, Zeng Pu, Ding Ling, and Ba Jin.

Haitian Duxiaozi's *The Stone of the Goddess Nüwa* (*Nüwashi*, 1904) takes up where *Heroines of Eastern Europe* leaves off. In this novel, a Chinese woman student returns from overseas to assassinate the Empress Dowager and fails. While on the run, she stumbles upon a courtesan house, which turns out to be a scientific utopia, built and ruled by women, as well as the headquarters of an all-female party dedicated to assassinating corrupt politicians and officials.

The year 1904 saw the publication of *A Flower in a Women's Prison* (*Nüyuhua*), by the female author Wang Miaoru, another novel about chivalric women turned revolutionary. We know little about Wang's background except that she lived a short life (roughly from 1878 to 1904). Published posthumously, her novel contains two equally important plots, showing two ways by which women can seek their own rights. Whereas Sha Xuemei, a chivalric woman who accidentally kills her husband, advocates terrorism and immediate action, her friend Xu Pingquan believes that women can achieve independence only through education and continued negotiation with men. That Sha and Xu can talk and disagree with each other in their quest for a new womanhood adds a polemical dimension to late Qing feminist fiction. It shows that, even within the same camp, woman can differ, and that they accept the consequences of such difference. Sha and her comrades burn themselves to death after their resurrection fails. Xu continues to work in Sha's cause, but in her own way, by promoting education. One finds a similar arrangement in Jingguanzi's *Frost in June* (*Liuyue shuang*, 1911), a novel based on the martyrdom of the revolutionary woman Qiu Jin (1875–1907). When Qiu Jin dies a heroic death, her friend Yue Lanshi takes care of Qiu Jin's body and carries on her mission.

Revolution and involution

In the fall of 1911, the revolutionaries succeeded in overthrowing the Qing government, thus bringing the Chinese monarchical tradition to an end. The Republic of China was proclaimed on January 1, 1912, with Sun Yat-sen (1866–1925) as provisional president. Ironically, the "new era" so eagerly anticipated by the reformers came into existence with much less bloodshed and chaos than would have been expected in any grand narrative about revolution. What followed, however, was a series of power struggles, coups, and social disturbances. Lacking substantial military support, Sun Yat-sen was forced to relinquish his post to Yuan Shikai (1859–1916), the Qing military commander responsible for the crackdown on the Hundred Days Reform in 1898. Yuan had become the most powerful strongman in China after the Boxer Rebellion. Taking advantage of the widespread confusion during the founding years of the Republic, he sought to restore the monarchy with himself as emperor in 1915; his attempt was quickly thwarted by the Second Revolution. When Yuan died in 1916, however, no single other political force was strong enough to reconsolidate the fragmented new nation. Over the next ten years, China became embroiled in a succession of civil wars among warlords and political leaders.

Many literati and intellectuals, once the advocates of change, were disillusioned by this incessant turmoil. This begs several questions. How could a revolutionary ideal that had held so much promise have turned rotten so quickly, once exposed to the sunlight of history? In spite of all their efforts at formal renovation, had a drastic reform really been undertaken by the Chinese literati? Should a reformist writer endorse the new regime if it had caused such chaos in China? Meanwhile, a trend of mourning for the bygone period appeared. While this trend may register the longing of a limited number of Qing loyalists, it reflects even more emphatically contemporary misgivings about cultural vandalism, which, bad as it had been in the late Qing, was all the more rampant in the new Republican era.

Prevailing revolutionary discourse was therefore undercut by two rhetorical modes: elegy and cynicism. To that extent, the literature of the early Republican years from 1911 to 1918 may be regarded as either an anticlimax or a mere continuation of late Qing literary reform. The elegiac and cynical modes of early Republican literature, however, should not be read as mere resistance to literary modernity. Rather, they provide a different perspective from which to view the dynamics of the late Qing search for ways of rejuvenating literature. Instead of a Manichean polarity of the old versus the new, one can perhaps talk about revolution in terms of involution, and decadence in terms of de-cadence.

As in politics, the notion of "revolution" or *geming* played a crucial role in mobilizing late Qing literature in a new direction. We have discussed the way in which Liang Qichao and his peers promoted poetry revolution, prose revolution, and fiction revolution as the precondition to other reforms in a society. Nevertheless, instead of saying that revolution informed the current state of Chinese literature, perhaps involution can better describe the circular paths that modern literature had taken. If revolution denotes an overcoming, by means of extreme measures, of that which is established, involution points to a tendency toward introversion, a movement that expands in such a way as to turn inward upon itself.

Though often associated with a regressive action, in contrast to the extroverted direction of revolution, involution cannot be equated with reaction, since it does not seek to return to the point of origin, any more than revolution does; it differs from revolution only in that its trajectory is not perceived as pointing ahead, in an optimistically linear direction. It may indeed be difficult to tell the difference between the two, since the action of both continues indefinitely. In modern Chinese literature, the pattern of involution emerged almost at the same time as revolution became a watchword among the enlightened literati.

By the same token, the modernity of late Qing and early Republican literature manifests itself, not only in the didactic forms conceived by Yan Fu and Liang Qichao, but also in a much more circuitous manner, out of the "decadent" milieu denounced by these men. Decadence, or the decadent, embraces but is not limited to the pejorative connotations of the word – the decay and disintegration of an overripe civilization, together with the artificial and even morbid expressions of this decay and disintegration. Decadence is also de-cadence, a falling away from the established order, a displacement of that which has been taken for granted, and an uncanny "falling together" of conceptual and formal elements that would not have come together in the heyday of the same culture. In this second meaning, decadence is the abnormalization of the normal, and it becomes the hidden presupposition of every discourse touching upon modernity.

The phenomenon of revolution and involution, decadence and de-cadence, can be seen most clearly in the realm of fiction. In view of the fact that fiction before the late Qing had been regarded as a degenerate genre responsible for poisoning Chinese society, it was paradoxical that Yan Fu and Liang Qichao should have embraced it with the hope of transforming this poison into a panacea to cure the ills of Chinese society. It will be remembered that Plato advocated that poets be driven out of the Republic lest their works weaken public morale. In the case of the late Qing critics, the same reasoning led to a rather different conclusion: Yan Fu and Liang Qichao welcomed fiction as something of such incredible potency that it would first purge its own poisonous nature, after which it could then be administered to revive the audience it had earlier poisoned. Theirs is a strange application of the old Chinese medical concept of "using a poison to attack a poison" (*yi du gong du*).

Austere critics who lived in the late Qing and the May Fourth periods could only appreciate the libertinism in late Qing fiction negatively by deploring it. This libertinism is seen not merely in the writers' choice of subjects, but also in their attitude toward the discursive restraints handed down from the past. Some writers are so familiar with the conventions that they can play with them to the point of creating a chiasmatic replica, a hallucinatory mimicry. Thus, in *The Travels of Lao Can*, Liu E turns upside down the formula of the court case novel by declaring that corrupt judges are abominable but incorruptible ones even more so; Li Boyuan's *Exposure of Officialdom* teaches that honest government officials are no more virtuous than prostitutes who call themselves virgins; and Wu Jianren likens the human world to that of goblins, fox spirits, and demons in *Eyewitness Reports*. Decadence does not cease to exist when the campaign for enlightenment begins, nor is it the unfortunate outcome of a modernity project that has gone awry. Decadence happens *within* the campaign for enlightenment, and is a necessary condition of turning the normal into the abnormal.

In contrast to the new political, ethical, economical, and even eugenic boundaries set by the proponents of literary reform, one finds various forms of "excess" in late Qing fiction. Take the most popular genre, exposé, as an example. Late Qing exposé writers universally felt compelled to put social corruption on display, but in many cases they ended up with a paradoxical mode of representation, in which it is recognized that the real can most emphatically be expressed by exaggeration, disfiguration, and metamorphosis. By the early Republican era, this tendency had become spectacular enough to merit a new name, "black-screen" (*heimu*). Writers of "black-screen" narrative ventured to "lay bare" the crisis in the value system, but before all else they exposed the narrative mode of exposé itself as involved in that crisis.

A case in point is Zhang Chunfan's (?–1935) *Nine-Tailed Turtle* (*Jiuwei gui*), a stupendous novel in 192 chapters. Serialized from 1906 to 1910, the novel depicts the merry adventures of a young scholar turned playboy and his heroic subjugation of cunning courtesans. Hu Shi and Lu Xun considered *Nine-Tailed Turtle* an exemplum of the bad taste and frivolity of late Qing literati writers. Ironically, however, they ensured its lasting notoriety by calling it, respectively, a "handbook for brothel-goers" and a "textbook for brothel-goers." These pejorative criticisms touch on an important dimension of *Nine-Tailed Turtle*. Not only does the novel tempt readers with sensual female characters and episodes recounting depraved behavior, it also "teaches" them how to deal with prostitutes high and low, the right way to squander money, and, most importantly, how to become a versatile and responsible libertine.

As Zhang Chunfan painstakingly presents the cases of fraudulent prostitutes and gullible customers, he teases out the "moral" lesson from each case and gives advice on self-improvement. The novel may feature a world preoccupied with erotic impulses, but the way Zhang Chunfan treats them is anything but erotic. In a novel vaunting brothel adventures, the absence of eroticism is something one should not overlook.

In the wake of *Nine-Tailed Turtle* there arose a series of black-screen novels exposing in delicious detail the harsh lessons of politics and the erotic realm. Li Dingyi's *A Dream of New China* (*Xinhua chunmengji*, 1916) chronicles Yuan Shikai's failed attempt to stage a coup to reinstate the imperial system. The same year saw the publication of *A Compendium of Monsters* (*Taowu cuibian*), an episodic novel parading family scandals and political intrigues of the lowest kind. The black-screen trend culminated in 1918 with two cycles of novels, *A Prospectus of the Modern Chinese Black Screen* (*Zhongguo heimu daguan*) and *A Mirror to Expose Monsters in the Human World* (*Renhai zhaoyao jing*). Fragmentary in form and sensational in content, the two cycles sought to cater to the reader's curiosity about contemporary events. Though reveling in the corrupt and absurd, the stories in both sound a didactic note. For early Republican audiences demoralized by unremitting political crises and social turmoil, black-screen fiction purported to be an escape, a palliative to the volatility of the new age. Nevertheless, underneath the nonchalant façade looms an ethos of nihilism and melancholy.

At the opposite extreme to late Qing and early Republican black-screen fiction is fiction that highlights affective extremities. A quick glance at the titles of selected works from the period, such *A New History of Laughter* (*Xin xiaoshi*, 1908), *The World of Folly* (*Hutu shijie*, 1906), *The Sea of Regret*, *The History of Revenge* (*Choushi*, 1905), *The History of Pain*, *Bitter Society*, and *Living Hell* (*Huo diyu*, 1906), shows how late Qing writers could be angry, vengeful, cynical, whimsical, or downright silly.

Above all, tears and melancholia represent a striking sentimental feature of late Qing and early Republican fiction. As mentioned before, weeping is a recurrent motif of *The Travels of Lao Can*; as China is about to collapse, a conscientious literatus like Liu E cannot help shedding tears. He is not alone, however, in infusing personal sentiment into writing. In 1902, Wu Jianren published a series of fifty-seven short observations entitled *Wu Jianren Weeps* (*Wu Jianren ku*), in which he laments a wide range of issues, from national crises, social vulgarities, and romantic stories to his own dissipated past. He also cries in anticipation of his readers' imagined responses, such as "Few people would understand you!" or "Why bother to cry?" Weeping is not always a personal matter. Lin Shu is said to have been so moved when translating *La Dame aux Camélias* that he and his collaborator stopped work from time to time to cry, weeping so profusely that they could be heard even outside their studio.

In the early years of the Republican era, a passion for fiction written in parallel prose suddenly appeared. In 1913, Xu Zhenya (1889–1937) made a tremendous hit with *Jade Pear Spirit* (*Yuli hun*), which tells a tragic tale of love and self-sacrifice involving three principals. Mengxia, a young graduate from a normal college, takes up a teaching job in the Cui family, only to fall in love with his student's mother, the widow Liniang. The tutor and the widow, though rarely seeing each other, express their love by exchanging poems and letters. Their romance is, however, conditioned by Confucian strictures. Upon learning Liniang's determination to remain a widow, Mengxia falls ill and vows perpetual bachelorhood. To ease Mengxia's pain, Liniang arranges to have her sister-in-law Yunqian serve as her substitute. More complications ensue, as a result of which both women die of grief. Heartbroken, Mengxia goes to study in Japan for a few months, then dies a martyr in the October 10, 1911 revolution that topples the Qing.

Though at first glance cliché-ridden, this is a moving work whose power comes not from reinstating but rather from violating the "talent–beauty" tradition. The fate of three characters demonstrates how a society can be paralyzed by self-imposed dogmas, and how, under such circumstances, the young lovers can end up hurting each other with their passion. Artificial as it is, the novel's climax – i.e. Mengxia's martyrdom in the revolution – points to a new twist, representing both a consummation of the death pact of traditional lovers and a vehement negation of feudal restraints, which are sacrificed for the sake of building a new political entity.

The enormous popularity of the novel is not merely the result of the ambiguous tenor of the romance being narrated. Narrated in elegant parallel prose, the romance must have struck audiences as something both familiar and distant. Its ornate symbolism, exquisite rhetoric, and perfectly symmetrical syntactic structure constitute a world in which linguistic and emotional resources appear to resonate with one another as part of a cosmic equilibrium, a universe where prosaic trepidations are redeemable through poetic evocation. But Xu Zhenya's contemporary readers were all too keenly aware of the historical jolt that had brought Chinese civilization to a standstill. Whereas the story being told is one about the sorrowful outcome of a romantic encounter in the talent–beauty genre, the narrative style registers an anachronistic gesture toward a world that was lost even before the Republican Revolution took place. The shared connoisseurship of author and reader in the tradition of parallel prose necessarily becomes an elegiac ritual, one that commemorates, and yet at the same time parodies, the cultural and historical sensibilities of a bygone era.

The prevailing sense of pathos found an individualized manifestation in the case of Su Manshu (1884–1918). Born in Yokohama, Japan, to a Chinese father and a Japanese mother, Su went through many relocations and uncertainties in his childhood and teenage years. He grew up to become a poet, a translator, a revolutionary, and a Buddhist monk. Though much can be said about his idiosyncratic life and literary talent, Su is best remembered for his autobiographical novel, *The Lone Swan* (*Duanhong lingyan ji*, 1912), in which he describes the pathetic experience of growing up, becoming a monk, wandering through exotic lands, and living through two romantic encounters that end in either death or endless regret. Su's alter ego tries to find solace in becoming a monk, only to realize that religious renunciation twice intensifies his attachment to this-worldly passions.

Like *Jade Pear Spirit*, *The Lone Swan* is couched in exuberant classical prose, as if only through an archaic linguistic discourse can this lonely monk convey his unfathomable sadness and authenticate the meaning of his existence. Classical prose, with its apparent compactness and simplicity, seemed for many the appropriate medium for ordering the mixed feelings of a disoriented generation. Other best sellers along these lines include He Zou's *Pavilion of the Broken Zither* (*Suiqin lou*, 1911), Lin Shu's *A Tale of a Bloody Sword* (*Jianxing lu*, 1913), and Wu Shuangre's *A Mirror for a Doomed Romance* (*Nieyuan jing*, 1914). These works anticipated the rise of the Mandarin Ducks and Butterflies fiction (*yuanyang hudie pai*) in the Republican era.

Despite vehement calls for literary reform, schools of classical-style poetry continued to exert their power. After the founding of the Republic, many classical-style poets wrote to commemorate the demise of the Qing; for this they were labeled loyalists. Chen Sanli, for example, once associated with various reforms in the late Qing, wrote to deplore the social and political devastation in the aftermath of the revolution. Wang Guowei composed a series of song lyrics, such as "Yihe Garden" (Yihe yuan ci), to chronicle dynastic change. Jin Zhaofan's narrative poem "A Song of the Imperial Well" (Gongjing pian) laments the forced suicide of the Guangxu Emperor's consort, Zhenfei, at the order of the Empress Dowager on the eve of the court's demarché during the Boxer Rebellion. These poets all bore witness to the finale not only of a dynasty but also of a legacy. Their loyalty should not be understood only in political terms: they were mourning the end of a civilization in the face of nationalist revolution on the one hand and modernist enlightenment on the other.

But the classical style could equally serve as a form for those traditional literati harboring radical thoughts. In 1909, Chen Qubing (1883–?), Gao Xu (1887–1925), and Liu Yazi (1887–1958) founded the Southern Society (Nanshe). Modeled on the late Ming literary society of the same name, this had a clear revolutionary platform; a considerable number of its founding members were related to the League of Unification led by Sun Yat-sen. The Southern Society soon found many followers, eventually developing into a huge organization with more than a thousand members and branches in major cities all over southern China. In many ways, the founding of the Southern Society represented the final culmination of the gathering of classical-style poets in modern times. Apart from their anti-Manchu agenda, members of the Southern Society also proved to be straddling the realms of the traditional and the modern.

The accomplishments of two women poets merit special attention. The poetry of Qiu Jin, the revolutionary martyr and poet executed by the Manchu government in 1907, focuses on swordsmanship and the pathos of the Chinese race, and is based largely on her own experiences. Leaving her husband and children in order to study in Japan, Qiu Jin was a feminist who actively fought for the liberation of women. As a member of the Revolutionary Party and the president of a military academy, she became involved in the attempted assassination of the governor of Anhui. While in prison, she wrote a number of poems about captivity, where she takes full advantage of her surname – Qiu, or "autumn" – to invoke the imagery of desolation and bitterness. She also wrote a series of feminist poems. Perhaps the best of these is "Crimson Flooding into the River" (Manjianghong), championing the liberation of women and the disparagement of men. Qiu Jin is also known for her string ballad *Stones of Jingwei* (*Jingwei shi*, 1905). Inspired by the myth of the Jingwei bird, tirelessly filling the sea with pebbles at the cost of its own life, the ballad calls for women's emancipation in conjunction with racial revolution. Two years later, Qiu Jin sacrificed herself to her cause, and her narrative remained an unfinished project – uncannily reflecting the Sisyphean theme of the Jingwei bird's devotion.

The woman song lyricist Lü Bicheng (1883–1943) broke away from tradition to become a journalist and educator in the last decade of the Qing. Thanks to her business contacts with Westerners in early Republican Shanghai, she amassed a fortune that enabled her to live a luxurious life and travel overseas. Lü showed a talent for composing song lyrics early in life; during the first years of the Republican era she became known for reintroducing feminine consciousness into a genre dominated by male lyricists who, ironically, often assumed female personae, and for expanding the song lyric's traditional repertoire to embrace modern experience.

Classical-style poetry took on a markedly polemical dimension in the cultural politics of Taiwan upon its cession to Japan in 1895. Qiu Fengjia (1864–1912), Hong Qisheng (1867–1929), Lin Chaosong (1875–1915), Xu Nanying (1855–1917), and others wrote profusely about the loss of the island they called home and their fate as "wandering Taiwanese natives" on the Chinese mainland and overseas. Qiu Fengjia, arguably the most talented of the Taiwan poets, was involved in the founding of the short-lived Taiwan Republic (Taiwan minzhuguo) on the eve of the Japanese takeover, only to flee to Guangdong after his attempt failed. In his final years, Qiu wrote hundreds of poems in remembrance of Taiwan, in which he upholds a loyalism that problematizes its own conventions. Instead of asserting Taiwan's ties to the Qing, Qiu's loyalism evokes multiple visions of the island, as both a modern "nation" independent of Qing rule and the last overseas stronghold of Ming orthodoxy, as both a cultural entity thrown outside the track of history and a symbolic landscape encapsulating the nostalgia of a whole generation of Chinese intellectuals.

At the same time, classical-style poetry was vigorously promoted by the Japanese colonial government to facilitate their cooptation of local literati as well as their claim to legitimacy. Between the late 1890s and the mid-1920s, classical-style poetry underwent an unexpected revival on the island. For the loyalists, the genre represented their linkage to cultural China; for the colonizers, the genre functioned as a handy means to demonstrate the shared legacy of Chinese and Japanese civilization and hence served as an emblem of the legitimacy of the Japanese claim to colonial rule over Taiwan.

In 1908, the young Lu Xun observed in "On the Power of Mara Poetry" (Moluo shili shuo), "When a literature shows weakness, the fate of the people has been exhausted; when the voice of the populace ceases, its glory has vanished." Amid the ashes of this civilization, nevertheless, Lu Xun expects to see a devil-like poet – the Mara poet – rise to create a new order. Evoked here is the double image of the poet as both devil and messiah. Lu Xun envisages the predestined downfall of Chinese civilization; at the same time he calls for the resurrection of the dying civilization through the magical incantation of poetry.

Finally, prose also underwent a transformation in the early Republican era. Despite the best efforts of the Tongcheng scholars to adapt to the changing times, vernacular Chinese writing had become the dominant mode of expression by the end of the nineteenth century. In 1902, as Liang Qichao and Yan Fu were debating the feasibility of archaic prose in response to the mounting calls for literary reform, the fiction magazine *New Fiction* was established in Yokohama. Together with dozens of newspapers, propaganda publications, and other literary magazines, this helped to kick off a campaign of literary modernization, at the center of which stood the movement to sanction vernacular Chinese. Liang's own writing was welcomed for its mixture of conventional lexicon and colloquial rhetoric, a style much more accessible to the general reading public. The trend toward vernacular writing was further consolidated in 1905 when the millennia-old civil service examination system was finally abolished.

But the ghost of the Tongcheng School could not so easily be laid to rest. As already noted, the last years of the Qing and the early years of the Republican era actually witnessed a revival of classical-style prose. A Parallel Prose School (Wenxuan pai) emerged, dedicated to the imitation of the style of ancient writers of poetry and prose, as exemplified in *Selections of Refined Literature* (*Wenxuan*) compiled by Xiao Tong (501–531). Central figures of this school are

Huang Kan (1886–1935), Wang Kaiyun (1832–1916), and Zhang Binglin (1868–1936). They saw in this style characterized by dense allusion and ornate parallel prose a way to preserve the essence of Chinese culture. The ultra-conservative agenda of the Parallel Prose School was, however, no less radical than that of the revolutionaries. In their endeavor to preserve the essence of tradition, they introduced to their contemporaries an aesthetic vision of literature that stressed its formal refinement. In so doing, they unwittingly anticipated the rise of the notion of literary autonomy among future generations of writers.

The case of Zhang Binglin amply demonstrates the complex conditions of Chinese intellectual and literary modernization. Besides Confucianism, the system of knowledge he espoused was a hybridization of Kant and Schopenhauer via Japanese translation with Yogacara Buddhism and Daoist thought in the vein of Zhuang Zi. For Zhang, a truly liberated "self" (wo) should be capable of defying not only any intellectual, political, and social establishment but also the assertion of "self" as such. The ultimate "general principle" that he would embrace must end up in its own erasure. Only when everything is reduced to the same level of nothingness does true egalitarianism arise. One could arrive at the state of free will only through the continued practice of self-denial. Paradoxically, this free choice could include such alternatives as nationalism and cultural universalism. Small wonder that Zhang was simultaneously a revolutionary and a conservative, both a strong supporter of anti-Manchu identity politics and an advocate of National Learning and the Parallel Prose School.

Parallel prose was indeed adopted as an official documentary style in the early years of the Republic. When Sun Yat-sen launched the Second Revolution against Yuan Shikai in 1915, his manifesto was written in elegant parallel prose. Meanwhile, the successors to the Tongcheng School, such as Yao Yongpu (1862–1936), Ma Qichang (1855–1930), and Lin Shu were still struggling to carry on the legacy of Tongcheng "purport" and "method." In 1913, Lin Shu published A Tale of the Bloody Sword, which he claimed to be the first full-length novel ever to be written in the Tongcheng style. The novel deals with the romantic tribulations of a young couple against the background of contemporary political events, including the Boxer Rebellion, the Republican Revolution, and Yuan Shikai's attempt to reinstate the monarchical system. Its clichéd plotline notwithstanding, the novel is narrated in a refined style, as though Lin Shu were trying to redeem the chaos of time and give structure to disintegrating human relationships through well-ordered archaic prose. The novel was well received and Lin Shu followed it up by producing several other works of archaic-style prose fiction.

But the resurgence of classical-style prose was soon to be challenged by the champions of the new literature. In 1917, Hu Shi (1891–1962) published "A Proposal for Reforming Literature" (Wenxue gailiang chuyi). Echoing Hu's preamble, Qian Xuantong (1887–1939) set out in 1918 to condemn the Tongcheng School and its confrère, the Parallel Prose School, as "censurable species" and "fiendish monsters" respectively. To further his attack, the next year Qian published a debate in correspondence between one Wang Jing-xuan, the fictitious persona of a Tongcheng pedant played by Qian, and Liu Bannong (1891–1934), Qian's friend and supporter of literary revolution. The debate drew national attention, culminating in Lin Shu's fictional rebuttal in "Monstrous Dream" (Yaomeng) and "Scholar Jing" (Jingsheng), both in archaic prose. But this was already 1919, the year that witnessed the beginning of the May Fourth Movement. When, in 1920, the warlord government in Beijing instituted colloquial Chinese as the language to be taught in primary schools, the pedagogical tradition of classical Chinese came to an end.

Nevertheless, one should not overlook the fact that, as early as the 1920s, certain May Fourth literati already recognized the merits of the Tongcheng School. Hu Shi, for one, contended that, despite its conservative ideology, the Tongcheng School had helped to reorient nineteenth-century prose stylistics in the direction of greater readability. With its claims of clarity, precision, and elegance, the Tongcheng school promoted an "archaic style" that paradoxically served to counteract the convoluted tendency of the "contemporary style," thereby paving the way for the rise of the new writing. Zhou Zuoren (1885–1967) went even further and suggested that the styles of Hu Shi, Chen Duxiu, and Liang Qichao were all derived from the model of Tongcheng prose.

The demise of the Tongcheng School and the relatively minor Parallel Prose School marks the end of the classical language, but not the end of classicism. Looking back, one recognizes that it was the late Tongcheng writers such as Li Shuchang, Xue Fucheng, Yan Fu, and Lin Shu who demonstrated most poignantly the nebulous terms of becoming modern. Alternately labeled conservative and reform-minded, they acted out a negative dialectic that was to propel Chinese literature into the new age. Whereas Tongcheng scholars sanctioned *wen* as that which supported a cultural and social edifice, late Qing and early Republican reformers proposed modern Chinese literature as a distinctive field, one informed as much by the imaginary configuration of the human world as by the moral commitment to it.

III. The age of modern literature: 1919–1937

The May Fourth Movement and the literary revolution

On May 4, 1919, thousands of students in Beijing took to the streets to protest the resolution taken by the Peace Conference in Paris that concluded World War I. Though China had been on the side of the Allies against Germany, the Treaty of Versailles arranged for the German-held concessions in China to be handed over to Japan, another supporter of the Allies, on the basis of a secret agreement between China and Japan dating back to 1915. The Allies' disregard of China's sovereignty and the Chinese government's weak response aroused nationwide indignation. Patriotic protests soon spread to all the major cities, culminating in a national campaign for sociopolitical reform and cultural renovation. Insofar as literature had always been regarded as vital to reforming the mind, literary revolution was held up as one of the movement's major goals, paving the way for the drastic transformation of Chinese literature in the decades to come.

For most of the twentieth century, the May Fourth Movement was celebrated as the harbinger of modern China in almost all domains. More than a historical event or a literary crusade, it took on a mythic dimension, one that signals the magical beginning of Chinese modernity. But, with the further passage of time, we have come to realize that the revolution sparked by the May Fourth Movement did not happen overnight; rather, it resulted from slow and multiple processes of reform in the nineteenth century, as discussed in the preceding sections. Nor did the movement wipe out once and for all the traditional and popular elements deemed reactionary by the May Fourth radicals. On the contrary, traces of tradition continued to haunt the anti-traditional agenda, thus creating some of the most intriguing moments in the forging of modern China.

Still, as compared with the literary reforms of the late Qing era, the May Fourth literary revolution represented a watershed in that it charted a clear, progressive direction for literary discourse and practice. Hu Shi invented "Mr. Science" and "Mr. Democracy," the twin beacons to guide China in her search for wealth and power; "enlightenment" and "revolution" became for many both sociopolitical mandates and pedagogical means. The reformers embraced Western thought – from Marxism to liberalism, from Nietzschean philosophy to Freudian psychology – across the board, and introduced literary concepts, such as romanticism, realism, naturalism, and symbolism, to implement their vision of an irreversible timetable of literary progress.

Although politics and literature had been closely tied since the rise of "new fiction" in the late Qing era, it was in the May Fourth era and subsequent decades that writing was finally transformed into political action, and became a vocation that regularly demanded as much blood as ink. This revolutionary poetics manifests itself in a belief in the immediate link between literary rhetoric and national policy, in a Promethean symbolism of rebellion and sacrifice, in an "obsession with China," and in an apocalyptic vision of national rejuvenation through revolution. Writing could expose social evils, propagate new and progressive thought, illuminate a gendered and politicized subjectivity, and map out a bright future for China.

But, as with late Qing literary reform, one must ask: did the paradigm of revolutionary poetics eclipse other endeavors that could also be called modern? Or, more polemically, did this revolutionary poetics come across as something truly unprecedented and therefore modern, or did it appear to be a renegotiation of something all too familiar, from the point of view of either the Chinese legacy or Western importation?

The conventional narrative of the May Fourth Movement starts with the year 1915, when a group of Chinese students at Cornell University held a series of debates about the viability of language in the context of literary reform. At the climax of their debate, Hu Shi, then majoring in philosophy, came up with the idea of "literary revolution," arguing that, in order to overhaul the outmoded circumstances of Chinese literature, one had to adopt vernacular Chinese as the vehicle of true creativity. This was nothing new. As Hu Shi observes, there had long been a vernacular tradition in premodern literature, and the tendency to merge the spoken and the written languages could be traced as far back as the Yuan dynasty. Had this tendency not been checked by rigid Confucian discourse, most notoriously exemplified in the eight-part essay, Chinese literature might have progressed in a very different direction than the road taken.

Late Qing intellectuals had already promoted the vernacular language to serve the purpose of enlightenment. What distinguishes Hu Shi lies in his vision of the relation of the vernacular to a total literary and cultural renewal. While his Qing predecessors considered vernacular language an efficient tool to enlighten the public, they did not do away with the classical language as a sign system of cultural continuity and intellectual fecundity. The vernacular language reform Hu Shi had in mind involved following Western models, such as Italian literature after Dante, English literature after Chaucer, and German literature after Luther. Little surprise that he should have likened his notion of literary revolution to a Chinese renaissance.

Language reform was the first stage of literary revolution, which in turn was key to a broader project of cultural renovation. In his 1916 letter to Chen Duxiu (1879–1942), Hu Shi spelled out the foundational steps in the creation of a new literature: (1) avoid using classical allusions; (2) discard stale, outworn literary phrases; (3) discard parallel constructions in sentences; (4) do not avoid vernacular words and speech; (5) follow literary grammar; (6) do not write that you are sick or sad when you do not feel sick or sad; (7) do not imitate the writing of the ancients, but make your writing reflect your own personality; (8) what you write should have meaning or real substance.

Although Hu Shi appears to talk only about the linguistic dimension of literary revolution, the notion of vernacular modernity he invoked here had a profound impact on the way later generations of literati envisioned literature. In contrast to the classical language, the vernacular was regarded as innately democratic, transparent, and capable of reflecting the mental activities of the populace. To use the vernacular thus has political, aesthetic, conceptual, and psychological implications. The radical intellectual Chen Duxiu took up where Hu Shi left off when he declared three principles of literary revolution in the February 1919 issue of New Youth (Xin qingnian): (1) overthrow the artificial and self-debasing literature of the artistic few in order to create a plain, simple, and expressive literature of the people; (2) overthrow the stereotyped and heavily ornamented literature of classicism in order to create a fresh and sincere literature of realism; (3) overthrow the pedantic, unintelligible, and obscurantist literature of the hermit and recluse in order to create the plain-speaking and popular literature of society in general.

Meanwhile, Hu Shi had published a treatise of "Constructive Literary Revolution" (Jianshe de wenxue geminglun) promulgating "a literature of national language, a language for national literature." In it he articulated the twin goals of literary revolution, namely vernacularization of language and vernacularization of literature. In 1921, when the Ministry of Education mandated vernacular Mandarin Chinese as the official language for elementary education, the literary revolution had accomplished its first goal.

Other voices had spoken out in favor of literary revolution on the eve of May Fourth. In 1918, Zhou Zuoren published in New Youth an essay on "Human Literature" (Rende wenxue), arguing that, as opposed to premodern literature, which is rife with inhuman elements, modern literature should be devoted to celebrating humanity and committing itself to humanitarian causes. In another essay published in January 1919, he further proposed the notion of a "literature for the people," where he put forward the famous slogan "literature for the sake of life." Li Dazhao (1889–1927), founder of the

Chinese Communist Party (CCP), wrote in 1920 that "the new literature we are asking for is a literature of social realism, not something only in service of individual fame, [a literature grounded in] comprehensive thought and learning, firm ideological commitment, refined artistic skill, compassionate spirit." This laid down the foundations of leftist discourse in modern Chinese literature.

This strident call for a new literature sent resounding echoes through the decade after May Fourth. Literary magazines, journals, and societies mushroomed all over China. By the end of 1919, more than four hundred newspapers had appeared. Between 1921 and 1923, China had about forty literary organizations and fifty magazines; the numbers would double in the next few years. Magazines such as *New Youth*, *Weekly Review* (*Meizhou pinglun*), *New Tide* (*Xinchao*), and *Youthful China* (*Shaonian Zhongguo*) formed a unified front promoting vernacular language, modern forms of writing, and literary revolution. As the most popular magazine, *New Youth*, indicated, nothing was more inspiring than the innovative potential of youth, as national imaginary, political agency, pedagogical momentum, cultural institution, and affective power.

Of the societies founded in the early 1920s, the Society of Literary Studies (Wenxue yanjiu hui) and the Creation Society (Chuangzao she) stood out as the two leading organizations. They embodied the two directions of the May Fourth Movement. Whereas the former highlighted the canon of literature for the sake of life, proposing realism as a way to rectify social injustice, the latter prioritized individual sentiment, favoring the romantic expression of intuition and inspiration. In practice, however, these two societies had overlapping agendas and their differences were matters of degree rather than kind. By the late 1920s, the Creation Society had mutated into a stronghold of revolution with the goal of promoting radical social reform.

The May Fourth Movement also exerted an impact on overseas Chinese communities such as Taiwan. Though a colony of Japan after 1895, Taiwan kept close cultural ties to China, and as late as the 1920s many Taiwanese youth were still traveling to the mainland to acquire an education. Among those studying at the time in Beijing, Zhang Wojun (1902–1955) was particularly inspired by the May Fourth calls for cultural rejuvenation through the reform of language and literature. In 1924, he published an "Open letter to Taiwan Youth" (Zhi Taiwan qingnian de yifeng xin), in which he launched a vehement attack on the "delinquent oldies" of Taiwan's intelligentsia, holding them responsible for the deterioration of Taiwan's society. In a style typical of May Fourth iconoclasm, Zhang couches his attack in terms of the contest between traditional and modern literature, classical and vernacular languages. Zhang and his friends founded the magazine *Youthful Taiwan (Shaonian Taiwan)* in Beijing in 1926, a belated echo of Wang Guangqi's (1892–1936) *Youthful China*, to publicize his reformist platform.

Looking back, one must conclude that the May Fourth Movement represents as much the beginning of a Chinese modernist movement as it does the culmination of the literary reforms that had been developing since the late Qing era. Under the pens of May Fourth writers, traditional norms ranging from the imperial mandate to familial patriarchy are shown as having lost their claims to legitimacy, and, worse, as having revealed themselves to be nothing but rationales for systematic oppression. In Lu Xun's words, for four thousand years the Chinese people had been attending a spectacular banquet that was nothing but "cannibalism." In revulsion against this, modern Chinese literature set about demolishing this obsolete system, even knowing that it might take acts of representational violence to stop the old "cannibalism" and make people see the horrible truth.

But, for all its popularity among youth, the campaign for literary revolution had to deal with the tenacious resistence of the conservatives. Traditionally these conservatives have been seen as mere reactionaries, insensitive to the changing times. A more nuanced view is that, while they followed an agenda in favor of preserving the literary and cultural legacy, these conservatives were equally anxious to find ways to remold China. Some were even thoroughly immersed in Western learning and receptive to things new and innovative. Instead of taking the path of annihilation, however, they turned to safeguard the "national learning" they believed essential to Chinese modernity. Here, too, language and literature became primary concerns.

The battle between the reformists and the conservatives, which had been going on since the late Qing, intensified on the eve of May Fourth. For instance, Lin Shu, the popular translator and self-appointed spokesperson for Tongcheng stylistics, was singled out for public ridicule. But Lin Shu was not fighting alone. As early as 1914, Zhang Shizhao (1881–1973) had already used the magazine *Jiayin* to publicize his antireformist opinions. Zhang and his magazine were eventually to become a major target of people like Lu Xun in the 1920s. In March 1919, just two months before the outbreak of the May Fourth Movement, Liu Shipei and Huang Kan, both professors at Peking University and members of the Parallel Prose School, founded the magazine *National Antiquities (Guogu)* to broadcast the need for restoring classical knowledge and constructing a Chinese nationhood based on an antiquarian idea of cultural essence (*guocui*).

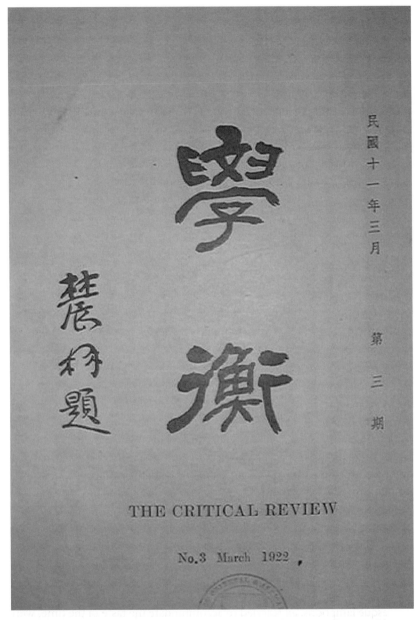

6. Cover from the journal *Xueheng* (*Critical Review*), founded in 1921. Collection of the University of London.

In 1921, a group of scholars based in Nanjing led by Mei Guangdi (1890–1945), Wu Mi (1894–1981), and Hu Xiansu (1894–1968), founded *Critical Review* (*Xueheng*), a magazine dedicated to classical studies. It should be noted that, unlike Lin Shu, Mei Guangdi and Wu Mi had studied in the United States and were familiar with Western intellectual traditions. Inspired by thinkers like Irving Babbitt, they favored a neo-humanist approach to knowledge and culture. Their publications aimed to "promote the national essence so as to integrate new knowledge into the Chinese context" and to "hold a judicious perspective in order to exercise the mission of critique." Their viewpoint is in some ways reminiscent of the motto, popular in the late Qing, "Chinese learning as the basis; Western learning as the application." Not unlike their more radical peers, however, they were enlightened intellectuals, but had chosen a way of implementing their agenda that was more amenable to compromise than wholesale antitraditionalism.

It is noteworthy that Hu Shi, the forerunner of literary revolution, should have come forward to lead a project of "studying national antiquities" in 1923. To many this represented a leap backward, given Hu Shi's radical posture of just a few years before. But, for Hu Shi, a follower of John Dewey, this investigation of the Classics was a pragmatic move to demystify them by tracing the origins and development of classical writings. His study of select Qing vernacular fiction, such as *The Scholars*, *Flowers in the Mirror*, *Singsong Girls of Shanghai*, and *Three Knights-Errant and Five Sworn Brothers*, especially demonstrates his aim of democratizing the subjects and the scope of scholarship.

It must be significant that, of all the issues in the public domain, language and literature figured as the shared concern for both the revolutionaries and the conservatives, and proves that these people were above all engaged in the same episteme, one that hinged on language and literature as indices to other forms of modernity. In this sense, neither side strayed too far from the classical Chinese notion that values literary activities as a manifestation of intellectual cultivation and political engagement.

Even so, popular literature as practiced by the writers of the Mandarin Ducks and Butterflies School commanded an enormous share of the market. At a time when publications such as *New Youth* drew the attention of the "new youth" nationwide, tear-jerkers, chivalric fantasies, detective fiction, and grotesque lampoons, all restyled to accommodate the taste of the time, were equally popular among the general public. The legacy of May Fourth therefore encompasses not merely New Literature but the collective expression of a multitude of voices, styles, locales, and agendas.

*Inchoate modernities: literature and literati
culture in the 1920s*

The May 1918 issue of *New Youth* carried a short story of less than five thousand words entitled "The Diary of a Madman" (Kuangren riji). The story features the diary entries of a Madman who believes that he lives in a society of cannibals. At the climax of his diary, the Madman hopes there may still be children who have not eaten human flesh and cries, "Save the children!" This is framed by a context in which the Madman is said to be cured and to have rejoined the society he formerly condemned.

Lu Xun (1881–1936, real name Zhou Shuren), the author of "The Diary of a Madman," was later hailed as the founding father of modern Chinese literature and the conscience of China. A native of Shaoxing, Zhejiang Province, Lu Xun had an unhappy childhood, owing to his father's untimely death from tuberculosis, and to his grandfather's imprisonment under a charge of taking a bribe at a civil service examination. In 1902, he was awarded an official grant to study medicine in Japan, but changed his career plans in 1906, allegedly as the result of seeing a slide show that contained a famous scene in which a Chinese crowd idly watches as one of their compatriots is beheaded by Japanese soldiers for serving as a spy for the Russian army during the Russo-Japanese war (1904–1905). Dumbfounded, Lu Xun realized that, before saving people's bodies, he had first to save their souls; hence, before practicing ordinary medicine, he must first cure the spirit of China, using the medicine of literature.

Beginning in 1906, Lu Xun wrote a series of essays, including "On the Mara Poet" and "On the Extremity of Culture" (Wenhua pianzhi lun), all reflecting his effort to dissect the malaise of Chinese humanity in symbolic form and his longing for a magical force that would resurrect the Chinese body from the curse of living death. At the same time, he and his brother Zhou Zuoren undertook to translate and publish eastern European stories in the hope of arousing the Chinese public. But Lu Xun's literary career met only with frustrations and setbacks – until the unexpected success of "The Diary of a Madman."

Critics have pointed out that Lu Xun may have drawn inspiration from Gogol's "The Diary of a Madman" and other foreign sources. Equally remarkable, however, is that this Madman may bear a Chinese genealogy traceable to the melancholy poet Qu Yuan of "Encountering Sorrow," the eccentric hermits of the *Zhuangzi*, and the wayward free spirits of the Six Dynasties. But, for May Fourth readers, the Madman embodied a man with forbidden knowledge. Behind the façade of Confucianism lay an orgiastic ritual of barbarism.

After the success of "The Diary of a Madman," Lu Xun went on to write a series of short stories. *The True Story of Ah Q* (*Ah Q zhengzhuan*) depicts in mock-heroic style a small-time hooligan thriving on the "method of spiritual victory": bullying the weak and cowering before the strong. In his "homecoming" stories, such as "My Old Home" (Guxiang), "New Year's Sacrifice" (Zhufu), and "In the Tavern" (Zai jiulou shang), he writes about the painful encounter between the inarticulate peasant and the guilt-ridden intellectual, and the "invisible wall" that makes all attempts at communication futile. "Kong Yiji" (Kong Yiji) and "White Light" (Baiguang) both portray traditional literati trapped in a changing time, while in "Divorce" (Lihun) and "A Small Matter" (Yijian xiaoshi), Lu Xun caricatures human frailties and grotesqueries. These stories were later included in two collections, *Call to Arms* (*Nahan*, 1923) and *Wandering* (*Panghuang*, 1926).

Lu Xun's modernist sensibility can be best appreciated in his ambivalent interaction with tradition. His project to reform the Chinese mind demonstrates a case of what Yü-sheng Lin calls the "cultural, intellectualistic approach" to problems, by which he means the prevalent conviction that China's problems stem solely from the break in cultural and intellectual coherence and can be solved only in immanent, holistic terms. To be sure, Lu Xun sets out to take issue with such an approach; for him, the sanctioned Chinese civilization has long been lost, or, worse, it never existed except as a pretext for a highly developed cannibalism. But, granted his vehement satiric intent, he betrays time and again both a longing to regain a coherent form of meaning and a skepticism about this longing. Out of his desire to "transform the spirit" of the Chinese people and his subsequent disavowal of the possibility of doing this emerges the basic dilemma of his search for modernity.

However eloquent his inquiry into the Chinese national character, there is one dimension Lu Xun remained reticent about, namely the romantic and erotic dynamic in May Fourth subjectivity. He was, of course, not unaware of the consequences of repressed and oppressed sexuality in traditional society. He himself was the victim of an arranged marriage. Although, out of regard for his mother, he never divorced his wife, Lu Xun lived in celibacy for years until his affair with his student Xu Guangping (1898–1968). In his essays and letters, Lu Xun attacked conventional sexual mores violently. Essays like "What Happened after Nora's Departure" (Nala zouhou zenyang, 1923) and "On the Collapse of the Leifeng Tower" (Lun Leifeng ta de daodiao, 1924) stress compellingly the social and ethical need to remold Chinese womanhood. In his fictional writings, however, Lu Xun rarely touches on eroticism and sexuality.

Romantic passion was first fully expressed in the works of Yu Dafu (1896–1945). Like Lu Xun, Yu Dafu studied in Japan and this overseas experience propelled him to write. But whereas Lu Xun was traumatized by China's fate, which he had seen as embodied in the slide showing the decapitation, Yu Dafu occupied himself with romantic longings and sexual frustration. In his first short story, "Sinking" (Chenlun, 1921), a young Chinese student studying in Japan yearns for love, but his romantic longings are continually thwarted by frustrated patriotism, hypochondria, and an inferiority complex. Finally, the protagonist walks into the sea, blaming his impending death on his nation: "O China, my China, you are the cause of my death . . . I wish you could become rich and strong soon! . . . Many, many of your children are still suffering."

"Sinking" scandalized the readers of 1920s China with its unabashed impulse toward confession and its explicit descriptions of erotic fantasy, masturbation, and prostitution. Yu creates a different kind of Madman, one deeply troubled by his libidinous drive, which can become as ferocious as cannibalism. The story presents an almost promiscuous mixture of literary heritages, including the confessional style of the Japanese I-novel, the "superfluous man" of nineteenth-century Russian fiction (such as *Rudin*), and the rebellious posture of Rousseauistic narrative. Yu's predilection for classical Chinese poetry, particularly that which deals with exile and estrangement, lends his narrative a mannerism reminiscent of traditional elite culture.

Even Yu Dafu's personal life enacts the close ties between artifice and life. His unhappy marriages, his extramarital romances, his self-exile to Singapore and Sumatra during the Second Sino-Japanese War, followed by his mysterious death at the hands of the Japanese (allegedly due to his underground patriotic activity) at the end of that war, are all garish elements in the stark portrait of this arch-romantic of modern China.

Despite his narcissistic tendencies, Yu Dafu expresses concern about social and gender problems in such works as "A Night Intoxicated by Spring Breezes" (Chunfeng chenzui de wanshang, 1923) and "Past" (Guoqu, 1927). Consistent throughout these works is a subjective stance, from which Yu projects his own sentiments. Indeed, Yu's melancholia is so pervasive that he seems to have injected into all his characters the same capacity for desolation and sadness. He re-creates historical figures in much the same vein. In "Colored-Rock Cliff" (Caishi ji, 1922), with its profound sense of despair and rootlessness, the character of Huang Zhongze (1749–1783) comes across as Yu's kindred spirit with particular intensity.

Between Lu Xun and Yu Dafu there emerged a wide spectrum of writings about China. Insofar as they set out to expose social injustice and promote humanitarian campaigns, writers like Tai Jingnong (1902–1990), Wang Tongzhao (1897–1957), and others can be read as following Lu Xun's style. They anticipate the rise of critical realism, the mainstream of twentieth-century Chinese literature. Ye Shaojun (1894–1988) stands out for his interest in education and the life of the child as well as his understated style. His "Waterbell Melon" (Maling gua, 1923) is a story about a child's first and last experience attending the civil service examination of 1905, shortly after which the system was abolished. In "Rice" (Fan, 1921), a famine has enshrouded a country school and the students face the impending threat with horror and fascination. For Ye Shaojun, however cruel and hopeless the social reality, there is always a corner where compassion and empathy can redeem the callousness of humanity, and children can be saved, so to speak, from total "cannibalism" because of their innocence. Ye's full-length novel, *Ni Huanzhi* (*Ni Huanzhi*, 1928), is a moving portrait of a young country teacher's aspirations to change the status quo under the banner of May Fourth, and his continued setbacks in career, marriage, revolutionary activity, and health, to the point where death is his only way out. The novel could be read as an anti-*Bildungsroman* about the vagaries in the sentimental education of the May Fourth "new youth."

Xu Dishan (1893–1941), a native of Taiwan, was born into a pious Buddhist family but was drawn to Christianity while studying at Yen-ching University in Beijing. He later traveled to Southeast Asia and taught in Burma. Owing perhaps to his religious background and travel experience, Xu's works express a mixture of exoticism and religious aspiration, a rare combination of themes in post-May Fourth literature. His protagonists are mostly women thrown into adverse circumstances who manage to demonstrate perseverance and forgiveness because they are sustained by their belief, not so much in any religious doctrine as in the magnanimity of human compassion. In "The Bird of Destiny" (Mingming niao, 1921), the heroine is willing to face death in her quest for nirvana; the heroine in "The Merchant's Wife" (Shangren fu, 1921), set in Southeast Asia, undergoes numerous trials as she is deserted by her husband and marries an Indian merchant, though all the while retaining her capacity to endure and love. Most noteworthy is the story "Chuntao" (Chuntao, 1934), in which the title character, a rag picker, is faced with a dilemma when her husband, presumed dead in battle, comes home as an invalid only to find her living with another man. Chuntao, however, believes the three can live under one roof, a powerful testimony to a woman's right to live by her own moral code.

While many of these post-May Fourth writers show the influence of Lu Xun, Yu Dafu's legacy should not be underestimated, even though the current paradigm tends to belittle his decadent manner. As he proclaims, "Feeling is the most important subject of fictional practice." This became the credo of a whole following of writers engaged in romantic writings as well as of romantic posturers. Zhang Ziping (1893–1959) crowds his works with young men and women tempted by illicit passion and carnal adventure, Ni Yide (1901–1970) features artistic characters lost in romantic fantasy, and Tao Jingsun (1897–1952) transmutes into the Chinese context almost all the blatant traits of self-indulgent decadence of the Japanese I-novel. Most notable of all is Ye Lingfeng (1905–1975), who combines gothic motifs with romantic whimsy and perverse sexual psychology with decadent symbolism. Thus a love story is told through a necrophilic conversation with a skull in "Jiulümei" (Jiulümei, 1928), and in "Flu" (Liuxingxing ganmao, 1933) a transient romance is likened to an attack of flu.

After the "Madmen" come the "Madwomen." Women had commanded increasing attention in cultural and social spheres since the late Qing. In addition to Qiu Jin, Wang Miaowu, and Lü Bicheng, already discussed above, Chen Xiefen (1883–1923) was known for her feminist treatise and her editorship of *Women's Studies* (*Nüxuebao*), one of the earliest women's magazines; Xu Zihua (1873–1935) for her poetry and educational career; Shan Shili (1856–1943) for her travelogue from Japan to St. Petersburg in 1903; Xue Shaohui (1868–1911) and Chen Hongbi (1884–1966) for their translation of fiction by diverse European writers ranging from Jules Verne to Emile Gaboriau. These women wrote to articulate their gender consciousness, their desire for education and social engagement, their inquiry into the ties between womanhood and nationhood, and their exploration of fantastic and empirical space beyond traditional closure.

But it was the May Fourth era that saw women actively participating in literary activities. This phenomenon is clearly related to the call made by late Qing and early Republican intellectuals for women's rights in the spheres of education, family, and social position. A survey of women writers at the time shows that they mostly came from families with either cultural heritage or financial advantages and therefore had early access to the new learning. The flourishing modern education system as well as the print industry also helped to disseminate ideas about the "new woman." By the early twenties, a considerable number of women were trying their hand at literary creation.

Take Chen Hengzhe (1890–1976) and Bing Xin (1900–1999), for example. In 1917, Chen Hengzhe published in the *US Student Quarterly* the vernacular short story "One Day" (Yiri), a detailed portrait of the everyday life of young students at a women's college. Published one year before "The Diary of a Madman," "One Day" may well have been regarded as the first example of modern Chinese vernacular literature, as Hu Shi has said, had it been made known to more domestic readers. But, given the prevailing ethos of the May Fourth era, one wonders if "One Day," in which nothing really happens, could have measured up against the shocking effect of "The Diary of a Madman." Chen may, after all, have been limited by her personal experience. Nevertheless, the story points to a different way of depicting reality – a quotidian realism yet to be appreciated by Chinese readers and writers.

Poet, essayist, short-story writer, and author of children's literature, Bing Xin was born in Fujian Province and educated at Yen-ching University and Wellesley College (from 1923 to 1926). She returned to China in 1926 and quickly became involved in the post-May Fourth literary world. Many of Bing Xin's works are utopian in their vision and sentimental in tone. Childlike innocence; motherly love; natural imagery involving stars, flowers, and the sea; and a compassionate embrace of the world are her favorite subjects. Even when depicting the unpleasant aspects of life, she tends to sound idealistic. In "Superman" (Chaoren, 1921), for instance, the hero is a Nietzschean personality who alienates himself from people in the hope of living a self-sufficient life. He eventually learns the importance of love from a poor young boy.

"Notes of a Madman" (Fengren shouji, 1922) is an exception to the general rule. The story, narrated by a mentally deranged person, is full of skeptical observations on society and its values as well as incoherent ramblings about love and hatred, life and death, as if Bing Xin were determined to examine everything that was excluded from her familiar repertoire. Compared to Lu Xun's Madman, Bingxin's Madman cuts a much more amorphous figure and his notes seem to point to no allegorical reading. But in the story's fluid style and disoriented logic, Bing Xin has worked out a counter-discourse to Lu Xun's, available only to a woman who had taken flight from sanctioned feminine conventions into an imaginary space of her own.

Next to Bing Xin is a group of women writers who were all associated with Beijing Women's Normal College: Lu Yin (1898–1934), Su Xuelin (1897–1999), Feng Yuanjun (1900–1974), and Shi Pingmei (1902–1928). Of these,

Lu Yin is the most prominent. She enrolled in the college in 1919, quickly became involved in student politics on campus, and began to publish her writings. She continued writing until her death in childbirth in 1934. If the early works of Bing Xin show a female writer immersed in lyrical imagination and humanitarian concerns, those by Lu Yin point to a woman engaged in the tortured search for the meaning of love and sexuality. Lu Yin is particularly known for her first-person narrators who boldly reveal their emotional agitation in either epistolary or confessional form. The novella *Seaside Friends* (*Haibin guren*, 1923), which follows the adventures of five women college students from graduation to their reunion, presents a melancholy narrative about the liberated woman's encounters with desire and despair. Its convoluted and maudlin style vividly conveys the passions of the writer and her character as they are held at bay. Lu Yin's pessimism is further demonstrated by stories like "After Victory" (Shengli yihou, 1925), in which a young woman seeks the opportunity for love and education against all adversities, only to be thrown into total disillusionment after winning her "victory." Lu Yin's letters to her close friend, the writer Shi Pingmei, who became obsessed by her unfulfilled romance with the revolutionary Gao Junyu (1896–1925), are rendered in such fervent tones as to verge on lesbian passion or even solipsism.

Feng Yuanjun wrote a series of short stories in the early 1920s, including "Separation" (Geli, 1923) and "The Journey" (Lüxing, 1924), in which she depicts romantic liaisons between unmarried men and women and the moral pressures arising therefrom. Though they may hardly raise any eyebrows today, these stories won Feng notoriety in the Beijing of her day. Su Xuelin, Lu Yin's and Feng Yuanjun's classmate at college, studied in France from 1921 to 1925, where she created a semi-autobiographical novel, *Bitter Heart* (*Jixin*, 1929). Not only does the novel present a young woman torn between the romantic attractions of the world and the expectations of her family – stock themes of post-May Fourth writers – it also seeks an alternative solution in the redemptive power of religion, in this case, the heroine's eventual conversion to Catholicism.

Compared with the above, Ling Shuhua (1904–1990) excels in her refined depiction of psychological turbulence and her rhetorical craftsmanship. Ling Shuhua's subjects are mostly drawn from women of the upper class, to which the author herself belonged. In "Embroidered Pillow" (Xiuzhen, 1925), a lovelorn girl is confined to her chamber, her future to be disposed of by her family as if it were real estate. The young married woman in "Intoxicated" (Jiuhou, 1925) develops a sexual attraction for another man when both are slightly drunk after a party. The description of her whimsical desire to kiss the man in the presence of her husband grows into a mini-psychology of love and trust between a woman and her husband. Both stories demonstrate Ling's careful manipulation of irony and symbolism. These and other works won her the nickname "Katherine Mansfield of China."

Modern poetry was born on the eve of the May Fourth Movement. Poetry traditionally occupied the highest position in the literary canon. It deployed a wide spectrum of sensibilities and aesthetic formulations, and associated with a complex repertoire of cultural etiquettes and political agendas. The May Fourth poets' challenge to traditional poetry *in toto* – renouncing its metrical system, rhetorical stance, coded imagery, and conceptual and ideological implications – was a task far more difficult than revolutions in other genres. They had to renegotiate such basic questions as the nature and function of poetry, the convention of language and form, and the relation between the persona of "the poet" and its intended readership, as well as the multiple foreign influences newly introduced to China.

Forerunners of modern poetry include Hu Shi and Shen Yinmo (1883–1971), who both attempted vernacular verse in free style. Guo Moruo (1892–1978) is, however, the most prominent. As early as 1916, while studying in Japan, he wrote numerous passionate poems such as "The Temptation of Death" (Side youhuo) and "The Crescent Moon and White Cloud" (Xinyue yu baiyun). He cofounded the Creation Society, which promoted a romantic style of writing. When the May Fourth Movement took place, Guo was so inspired by the movement that during 1919 and 1920 he published a series of works, including "Phoenix Nirvana" (Fenghuang niepan), "Earth, My Mother" (Diqiu, wode muqin), and "Heavenly Dog" (Tiangou), that would earn him a reputation as an avant-garde poet. By the time he published his poetry collection, *Goddess* (*Nüshen*), in 1921, Guo had become the most provocative voice in modern Chinese literature.

Goddess is the first collection of modern poetry to appear after the beginning of the May Fourth Movement. By all accounts it was representative of the romantic passion and dynamism shared by the new youth of the day. "Phoenix Nirvana" presents a world at a dynamic moment. Earth and sea, our world and the universe are called on to celebrate a new creation energized by the power of destruction and rebirth. The poet borrows the myth of the cyclical death and rebirth of the phoenix to illuminate the ebullience of the era after May Fourth. The evocation of nirvana clearly suggests a religious association. For Guo, May Fourth is not a mere historical event but a religious ritual, one that initiates the new youth into an ecstasy of total self-confidence and self-sacrifice. In "Heavenly Dog," the poet compares himself to the mythological Heavenly Dog who "gallops, shouts, burns" and "swallows the moon; swallows the sun; swallows all the stars; swallows the whole universe." Finally he proclaims: "I worship myself; I am an iconoclast."

Guo Moruo's poetry is crude in form and gushes unabashedly with sentiment. Nevertheless, it exhibits a momentum hitherto unknown among modern poetry practitioners. Critics have discussed his indebtedness to Western Romanticism, in particular the poetry of Walt Whitman, but his imagery also shows the imprint of the apocalyptic poetics of late Qing poets such as Gong Zizhen. Under the pretext of speaking on behalf of the masses, Guo conceives a romantic subjectivity that tends to elevate itself to a cosmic scale; in this way he anticipates the "sublime figure" of Chinese national discourse.

Whereas Guo Moruo overwhelmed post-May Fourth readers with his hyperbolic rhetoric and portentous imagery, it was Xu Zhimo (1897–1931) who truly captured their hearts. A lover of Keats and Shelley, Xu was said to be the first to naturalize Western Romantic poetry in Chinese form successfully. His career spanned only a short period: from 1922 when he returned from study in America and Europe, to his death in a plane crash in 1931. But in those nine years this romantic soul soared high in poetry and in literary and artistic commitment. Deeply immersed in the Anglo-American humanist tradition, Xu Zhimo was the founder of the Crescent Moon Society (Xin yue she, 1928) that oversaw the spread of liberalism in China, a far cry from the increasingly popular leftist discourse.

Xu Zhimo's poetry cannot be separated from his romantic experience. Love played the most important part in his poetry, as in his life. He was intimately connected to three women: his first wife, Zhang Youyi (1900–1988), his first love, Lin Huiyin (1904–1955), and his amorous second wife, Lu Xiaoman (1903–1965). Xu once said that in his first twenty years, he knew nothing about poems. He started to write poems after he met Lin Huiyin while studying in England. Xu abandoned his first wife for Lin, only to suffer a tremendous loss when she decided to marry Liang Sicheng, the son of Liang Qichao. In 1926, Xu fell in love with the socialite Lu Xiaoman, who was at the time married. The two carried on a love affair that was the sensation of the 1920s, and their tempestuous relationship after their eventual marraige may have led indirectly to Xu's untimely death.

Whenever he found himself trapped in feelings of lovesickness, Xu Zhimo wrote poems to express his euphoria and dejection. Works such as "A Night in Venice" (Feilengcui de yiye) and "Goobye again, Cambridge" (Zaibie

Kangqiao) became immediate hits because of their passionate feeling, innovative metrical structure, and subtle imagery:

> But I cannot sing aloud
> Quietness is my farewell music;
> Even summer insects keep silence for me
> Silent is Cambridge tonight!
>
> Very quietly I take my leave
> As quietly as I came here;
> Gently I flick my sleeves
> Not even a wisp of cloud will I bring away.

Xu Zhimo's love poems and romantic stories may appear too sentimental for readers of later generations. But in the turbulent post-May Fourth era, Xu's determination to pursue love and love only, in defiance of all codes of propriety, signified a totally modern posture. To revolutionary critics, Xu might have fallen short for failing to address any progressive agenda, but he easily stood out for the intensity and purity of feeling he chose to express in poetry.

Wen Yiduo (1899–1946) represents yet another type of poet. In 1922, Wen went to America to study fine arts and literature. There he published his first collection of poetry, *Red Candle* (*Hongzhu*). He returned to China in 1925 to take up a university teaching position and to establish a poetry supplement to the *Chenbao* with Xu Zhimo. He also joined the Crescent Moon Society and published essays to promote poetry incorporating images of music, painting, and architecture. These three strands are evident in his second poetry volume, *Dead Water* (*Sishui*, 1928). The poems in this collection have a haunting musicality, while the subject – an exposé of social injustice and corruption – is heartrendingly heavy. The first two stanzas of "Dead Water" read:

> This is a ditch of desperate dead water,
> Where wind can blow but raise no ripples.
> Best just to throw in more scraps of copper and iron,
> Might as well pour in your leftovers of cold porridge.
>
> Perhaps the copper will green into emerald,
> Tin cans rusting out stalks of peach blossoms;
> Then let the grease weave up a sheet of silk,
> While bacteria steam it into the clouds of dawn.
>
> (Translated by Lucas Klein)

For readers well versed in the conventions of classical poetry, Wen's nine-syllable line renders an effect both rhythmically swift and structurally architectonic. Instead of familiar images, one is startled by "earthworms digging in the mud" or the sound of "root hairs of small grasses sucking up water."

In Wen Yiduo, one sees a modern poet's experiments with classical rules and newly possible forms. With Keats, Tennyson, and Browning as his models, he came to recapture the symbolism and ethos of premodern Chinese poetry. Wen Yiduo stopped writing poetry in 1931 and became increasingly engaged in social criticism. With the outbreak of the Second Sino-Japanese War, he moved to Kunming, where he continued to teach and participate in political movements. For his sympathetic stance on the revolutionary cause, he was assassinated in 1946.

The early 1920s also witnessed the rise of a symbolist movement in poetry. Li Jinfa (1901–1974) became attracted to European symbolists while studying sculpture in France at this time. Together with poets like Wang Duqing (1898–1940), Mu Mutian (1900–1971), and Feng Naichao (1901–1983), he helped to forge the first wave of Chinese modernism.

In 1925, Li published *Light Rain* (*Weiyu*), the first volume of Chinese symbolist poetry. Most of his poems deal with subjects typical of his day, such as frustrated romantic longing and gloomy self-indulgence. What makes Li different is his penchant for obscure symbolism, twisted grammar, exotic allusions, and truncated semantic cohesion, all calling forth sensations hitherto unknown in Chinese poetry. Li derived his inspiration from Baudelaire and Verlaine, and was particularly interested in creating a mood of decay and decadence. In his most famous poem, "Deserted Wife" (Qifu, 1925), he re-creates the classical trope of the deserted wife by turning a *fin de siècle* gaze upon a female persona trapped in desolation and unspeakable shame. This and other "bizarre" poems were the target of controversy in the mid-1920s, and by 1927 Li had given up his creative writing.

Modern Chinese drama reform originated in Japan under the influence of the "New Drama" movement there. In 1907, a group of Chinese students in Tokyo formed the Spring Willow Society (Chunliu she) and put on two plays adapted from popular fiction, *La Dame aux Camélias* and *Uncle Tom's Cabin*. The society was an all-male amateur troupe whose performances won favorable responses from the audience, less for stagecraft than for their provocative themes. *Uncle Tom's Cabin*, or, in Chinese, *The Black Slaves' Cry for Heaven* (*Heinu yutianlu*), was especially welcomed for its call to rebellion against (Manchu and foreign) racial oppression, easily read as an allegory of revolutionary sentiment at the time.

A number of dramatic societies and troupes appeared in the aftermath of the 1911 Republican Revolution, dedicated to staging either political topics or newsworthy events. A good example is Ren Tianzhi (dates unknown), a former member of the Spring Willow Society, who organized the Evolution Society (Jinhua tuan) and staged plays such as *Golden Blood* (*Huangjin chixie*, 1911) in support of revolution. These productions were later referred to as "civilized drama" (*wenming xi*). Scripts for civilized drama are mere outlines, and stage performance was largely improvised. But these may not have been perceived as defects for Chinese audiences accustomed to the loose structure of traditional theatre. Instead, they gained an unusual sense of immediacy and excitement when actors staged topical events or even broke with theatrical convention to deliver speeches on political and social issues.

Civilized drama blossomed mainly in cities like Shanghai and Beijing; as it grew in popularity, its subjects expanded to cover a wide range of social and romantic issues, and production came to feature increasingly elaborate mechanical gadgets and special effects. By the eve of May Fourth, it had become a major entertainment attraction for urban audiences, its original pedagogical purpose serving merely as good advertising.

Traditional Peking opera was also undergoing a transformation at this time. The younger generation of actors, such as Mei Lanfang (1894–1961), were engaged not only in revising the extant repertoire by adding modern elements but also in updating stagecraft and dramaturgy. A superb female impersonator, Mei produced his own plays with new scripts, costumes, sets, and theatrical effects, thereby teaching his audience to bring a new attitude to his performances. His *Farewell, My Concubine* (*Bawang biejie*) premiered in 1921 and afterwards became his signature piece. Under the efforts of Mei and his like, Peking opera was elevated from a form of popular entertainment to a genre some said best represented Chinese culture. When Mei was invited to tour America in 1930, he did so in the unofficial guise of China's cultural ambassador.

Meanwhile, debates about the new forms of Chinese drama raged in magazines such as *New Youth*. In a special issue in 1918, Hu Shi and fellow contributors recommended modernizing Chinese drama by closely following such contemporary models as Ibsen, Shaw, Wilde, Chekhov, Maeterlinck, and Galsworthy. For all the divergence in style and subject among these Western masters, their Chinese admirers found in them a consistent strain of social criticism and intellectual enlightenment. Even more, they were fascinated by the mimetic illusionism made possible by the realist stage, which they believed could serve not only as a new literary form but also as a template for new behavioral patterns in life. Ibsen's plays exerted special impact on the

May Fourth intelligentsia. In 1919, Hu Shi put forward *The Greatest Event in One's Life* (*Zhongshen dashi*), depicting a woman, modeled on Ibsen's Nora, who elopes with her Japan-educated fiancé to avoid an arranged marriage. Though primitive in form, Hu Shi's play set the trend for contemporary playwrights to engage social problems in dramatic form, hence the mushrooming of "problem plays."

It was around this time that a new kind of "spoken drama" (*huaju*) came into being. Traditional Chinese drama, its multiple forms notwithstanding, comprises musical, choreographic, and dialogical elements, all orchestrated in a highly stylized presentation. By contrast, spoken drama highlights dialogue-only performance and lifelike action. It aims at a verisimilitude derived from nineteenth-century European realism, though closer reading reveals that playwrights never gave up their interest in melodramatic effect.

Tian Han (1898–1968) was among the most active dramatists of the time. Inspired by modern Western and Japanese as well as traditional Chinese theater, he set out to reform Chinese drama in the early 1920s after studying in Japan. He founded the South China Society (Nanguoshe) in 1925 to experiment with and popularize modern vernacular drama. He also played an active role in the burgeoning movie industry. Among his plays of this period are *Tragedy on the Lakeshore* (*Hushang de beiju*, 1928), *Death of a Famous Actor* (*Mingyou zhi si*, 1929), and *Return to the South* (*Nangui*, 1929).

Hong Shen (1894–1955) was a Harvard-trained dramatist who quickly became involved in drama reform after his return to China in 1922. He directed plays by modern Chinese authors, including his own, and by Western writers he translated, such as Oscar Wilde's *Lady Windermere's Fan* in 1924. Ouyang Yuqian (1889–1961), immersed in Peking opera from his teenage years, was hailed in the 1910s as one of the few female impersonators in the south capable of emulating Mei Lanfang of Beijing. In the wake of the May Fourth Movement, Ouyang stepped into the world of spoken drama, where he wrote, directed, and played in a series of works either by himself or by his colleagues.

Although the general trend was to probe and expose social problems in realist form, we still find select works experimenting with new possibilities from psychological drama to expressionist theater, and from the comedy of manners to the allegorical play. For example, in Tian Han's *The Night the Tiger Was Captured* (*Huohu zhi ye*, 1922), a tragic story of love unrequited is projected onto a mass tiger-hunt in a mountain village. *Yama Zhao* (*Zhao yanwang*, 1923) by Hong Shen shows a runaway soldier as he undergoes a succession of hallucinatory trials in a style inspired by Eugene O'Neill's *Emperor Jones*. In Ouyang Yuqian's *Pan Jinlian* (*Pan Jinlian*, 1928), the murderous adulteress from the Ming novel *The Plum in the Golden Vase* is portrayed as a woman driven to kill her husband as much by patriarchal oppression as by her desire for love. In *Oppression* (*Yapo*, 1923) and *Wasp* (*Yizhi mafeng*, 1923), by Ding Xilin (1893–1974), modern young men and women engage in the sport of love in a playful, Wilde-like manner despite society's moral strictures. Xiong Foxi (1900–1965) uses *The Foreign Graduate* (*Yang Zhuangyuan*, 1927) to depict overseas students as frauds who take advantage of gullible country folk.

Two women playwrights deserve attention for their subversive revision of classical subjects as well as their experimental styles. Yuan Changying's (1894–1973) *Southeast Fly the Peacocks* (*Kongque dongnan fei*, 1929) rewrites the famous narrative poem of the same title about a young couple's suicide pact when the husband's mother compels them to divorce. In her version, Yuan portrays sympathetically not only the couple's love and despair but also the mother's suppressed sexual psychology. In *Linli* (*Linli*, 1926), Bai Wei (1894–1987) depicts the rivalry of two sisters, Linli and Lili, for the love of a young musician, Qinlan. Upon learning that Lili is pregnant with Qinlan's child, Linli commits suicide. Soon after her death Qinlan's body is found, ripped to shreds by a trio of chimpanzees.

Mandarin Ducks and Butterflies

We have discussed the multiple trajectories of modern Chinese literature from the 1910s to the late 1920s. Regardless of differences in popularity, these literary endeavors fall largely within the parameters of May Fourth discourse. Beyond these achievements, however, lies a corpus of literature that has been excluded from the canon despite its popularity in the Republican era. Literary historians have referred to literature of this sort as the Mandarin Ducks and Butterflies School. The term points to the sentimental inclination of the school, which is associated with premodern romantic sensibilities. In practice, however, Mandarin Ducks and Butterflies was never a unified movement. It comprised a huge variety of subjects, such as romance, chivalric fantasy, social exposé, detective novel, and comic writing, as well as genres such as the short story, narrative cycle, essay, anecdotal sketch, translation, and script. In the current paradigm of literary history, the school came into existence primarily to serve as a negative example for the May Fourth writers, so that writers more often than not resented being labeled members of Mandarin Ducks and Butterflies.

There are different stories about the origin of the term "Mandarin Ducks and Butterflies." Although traceable to a poetic couplet in the late Qing novel *Traces of Flowers and Moon*, the term did not become popular until the early

Republican era, along with the appearance of sentimental romances such as *Jade Pear Spirit*. In this type of fiction, the traditional talent–beauty romance was rewritten to fit the ethos of a changing time. Butterfly writers were mostly literati from southern China; though equally immersed in traditional literary training and the new knowledge, their attitude toward the avant-garde was less strict than that of the May Fourth reformers. Instead of belligerent posturing and bombastic rhetoric, their works tend to depict the manners and morals of Chinese society in more minute detail. Observant of the incongruities between present and past, these writers are nevertheless given to a more conciliatory approach to the thorny issues of the modern age. Their discursive style strongly suggests the residual impact of classical literature. Thus, if May Fourth literature represents a distinctive gesture toward modernity, Mandarin Ducks was regularly considered conservative and reactionary, the opposite of modern.

The May Fourth prejudices notwithstanding, the popularity of Butterfly writings prods one to reconsider the multiple conditions of Chinese literary modernity. The popularity of Butterfly writings was the result of at least three factors. First, the growth of a new urban environment, particularly in places like Shanghai and adjacent areas, had given rise to a new reading community often called petty urbanites (*xiao shimin*). These readers constituted the middle or lower-middle strata of urban society, and they wanted a new kind of reading entertainment beyond the routine forms. The spread of vernacular education and the increasing rate of literacy also helped to boost the demand for creative writing that could be consumed on an individual and private basis.

Second, the transformation of mass media and print technology starting in the late Qing had generated a prototype of cultural industry based on mass production and marketing promotion. The emergence of mass publishing houses around 1900 created a modern print culture that incorporated increasingly diverse subject matter. This new media culture indicates both a rising commercial interest on the part of publishers and a growing preference among readers for entertainment over national ideology.

Most importantly, as a form nurtured on both new and not-so-new subjects and styles, Butterfly writings provide a buffer zone for readers in which to negotiate their experience of the modern world. If May Fourth literature aims at defamiliarizing Republican readers from the status quo, Butterfly writing refamiliarizes them with a world that has yet to recede into the past. Thus this literature has been described by Perry Link as a "literature of comfort," in the sense not only of disarming its readers but also of calling on secular images of everyday life.

The assault upon the Mandarin Ducks and Butterflies started as early as the May Fourth era and culminated in the 1930s when "revolutionary literature" was hailed as the progressively modern. Critics like Mao Dun, Zhou Zuoren, and Lu Xun all took issue with the school's noncommittal politics, self-indulgent attitude toward writing, and commercial interest. As a result, Butterfly fiction came to be treated as a reactionary force, a genre that had to be excised from the canon of modern literature.

Looking back, one comes to recognize the uneven quality of Butterfly literature and the circuitous tactics it uses in order to come to terms with modern experience. The formal and thematic ambiguity of these writings may best be said to reflect the psychological ambivalence of the Chinese public as they confronted the inevitable changes of their time. Taking the themes of classical Chinese literature as their precedent, they embody a sentimental yearning for the affirmation of enduring truth and the "moral occult" beneath the spectacle of modern change. At their best, Butterfly fiction writers are observant historians of the quotidian materialism arising from the Chinese encounter with the modern.

Between 1911 and 1949 more than two thousand titles were produced that fall under the rubric of Mandarin Ducks and Butterflies literature. At a conservative estimate, there were at least 113 magazines and more than forty tabloids featuring Butterfly publications in Shanghai. Even major newspapers, such as *Shenbao* and *Shijie ribao*, carried literary supplements featuring Butterfly writings. Writers associated with the school include Bao Tianxiao (1876–1973), a versatile writer, editor, and translator; Wang Dungen (1888–1950), Chen Diexian (1879–1940), and Zhou Shoujuan (1884–1968), editors of the popular magazine *Saturday* (*Libailiu*) and competent romance writers in their own right; Xu Zhuodai (1880–1958), a writer and movie producer known for his slapstick comedy and grotesque caricature; Cheng Xiaoqing (1893–1976), nicknamed "master of detective fiction" for his creation Huo Sang, the Chinese answer to Sherlock Holmes; Sun Liaohong (1897–1958), the creator of Lu Ping, a chivalric bandit modeled after the French gentleman thief Arsène Lupin; and Li Hanqiu (1874–1923) and Zhu Shouju, chroniclers of life in Yangzhou (*Tides of Yangzhou* (*Guangling chao*), 1919) and Shanghai (*Tides of Shanghai* (Xiepuchao), 1921) in the form of exposé and novels of social manners respectively.

One of the pivotal figures of Butterfly fiction is Zhou Shoujuan, best known as the "king of heartbreaking romance." In his drama, *The Flower of Freedom* (*Ziyou hua*, 1911), a young woman betrays her husband and enters into an affair with a military officer; she commits suicide after unwittingly eating her lover's

7. Cover of the journal *Saturday* (*Libailiu*), popular from 1911 to 1949. Collection of the University of London.

heart. "We Shall Meet Again" (Xingzai xiangjian, 1914) tells the story of a girl who falls in love with a British officer, only to realize that he killed her father during the Boxer Rebellion. The girl is persuaded to murder her sweetheart, but she pledges over his body that she will be reunited with him soon. In "A Gramophone Record" (Liushengji pian, 1921), a woman dies heartbroken upon hearing, inscribed on a record, the dying message of her beloved who had been exiled to an island in the Pacific. Romantic passion and filial piety, modern psychology and modern technology tangle together, casting fatal curses on Zhou Shoujuan's lovers. Though they bear the lingering traces of the talents and beauties of premodern fiction, the way the characters cope with their fate reflects the changing mores of a modern age.

In addition to his talent at churning out heartrending stories, Zhou was a competent editor of many popular magazines such as *Saturday*, *Semi-Monthly* (*Banyue*), and *Violet* (*Ziluolan*). Above all, between 1919 and 1932, Zhou served as editor of the literary supplement "Unfettered Talk" (Ziyoutan) in *Shenbao*, one of the largest newspapers in Shanghai, and in this capacity he created the space to accommodate a full spectrum of social critique. The first story by Eileen Chang, the most talented woman writer of twentieth-century China, was published by Zhou Shoujuan in *Violet*.

Zhang Henshui (1895–1967) is the most popular of all the writers of Butterfly fiction. Born in Jiangxi Province to a gentry family from Anhui, Zhang started his career as a journalist, serving as reporter and editor in Anhui, Shanghai, and Beijing from 1917 to 1924. In 1924, Zhang began to serialize *An Unofficial History of the Old Capital* (*Chunming waishi*) in the *Shijie wanbao* in Beijing to immediate popular acclaim. The novel follows a young journalist's sad love affair with two girls through intuitive mutual admiration, exchanges of poems and vows to die together, tuberculosis, and death. The impact of late Qing and early Republican sentimental romance on Zhang's work is conspicuous. What distinguishes Zhang from his predecessors is his seemingly inexhaustible description of the modern and historical sites of Beijing and his meticulous observation of the psychological and behavioral patterns of modern men and women in love. Indeed, Zhang Henshui makes good use of his training in journalism in presenting a *tableau vivant* of Beijing in the early 1920s, and his narratorial stance reflects both an outsider's curiosity about the ancient city and an insider's knowledge of life within the city. In a similar vein, his novel *A Grand Family* (*Jinfen shijia*, 1933) – a family saga modeled on *The Story of the Stone* but with a focus on its female protagonist's search for selfhood – won even greater success.

Zhang Henshui's popularity reached its apex with *Fate in Tears and Laughter* (*Tixiao yinyuan*). First serialized in 1929 in *Xinwen bao*, the daily newspaper with the highest circulation in Shanghai at the time, the novel was most enthusiastically received by readers both there and elsewhere. It tells the story of the romantic adventures of Fan Jiashu, a young southern student in Beijing. Fan falls in love with a street singer, Shen Fengxi, who is nevertheless sold to a warlord and later driven insane by maltreatment. Meanwhile, Fan meets He Lina, a girl from a wealthy family, who is almost Fengxi's twin. A third girl, Guan Xiugu, good at martial arts and endowed with chivalric valor, is also introduced. The plot of *Fate in Tears and Laughter* thus interweaves three basic genres within Butterfly fiction: a sentimental romance with an improbable encounter between lovers from different social backgrounds, a social exposé that foregrounds the brutality of warlord society and the sufferings of people living in the lower depths, and a chivalric narrative that highlights men- and women-at-arms active in the Beijing underworld.

The publication of *Fate of Tears and Laughter* was soon followed by movie and stage adaptations and radio storyteller performances. Zhang Henshui's enormous popularity, the multimedia circulation of his works, and his nationwide appeal all arise from a fortuitous conjunction of developments in technology (newspaper and publishing), popular culture, and capitalism that made *Fate* into a phenomenon never before seen in China.

In chivalric romance, the household name is Xiang Kairan (1890–1957), a native of Hunan who studied in Japan. Xiang first won fame with *An Unofficial History of Studying in Japan* (*Liudong waishi*, 1916), an exposé of the scandalous life of Chinese students in Japan. In 1923, he published *A Tale of Legendary Heroes in the Chivalric World* (*Jianghu qixia zhuan*), which quickly made him the most popular storyteller of chivalric romance in modern China. In this work, Xiang carries on the time-honored tradition of the chivalric novel by presenting a saga full of exciting episodes and distinctive characters. Thanks to his own training in the martial arts, Xiang is able to describe action scenes in a realistic style hitherto unknown in traditional chivalric narratives. Another work, *Chivalric Heroes of Modern Times* (*Jindai xiayi yingxiong zhuan*, 1923), takes the tumultuous late Qing and early Republican eras for its backdrop. The hero, Huo Yuanjia, sets out together with his friend, Wang Wu, to challenge evil forces both within China and overseas. Huo confronts and defeats fighters from Russia and Germany. He dies after a bout with judo experts from Japan as a result of the intentional neglect of a Japanese doctor. The novel successfully injects a modern subject into a narrative tradition often set in the remote past, as such presenting an allegory about nationhood.

The other important chivalric romance writer of this group is Li Shoumin (1902–1961). In 1932, Li began to serialize *Swordsmen in the Shu Mountains* (*Shushan jianxia zhuan*), a cycle of more than 392 chapters in five million characters. Drawing on esoteric notions, outlandish fantasies, and chivalric conventions, Li creates a world in which wizards, immortals, "sword spirits," and magical creatures engage in endless adventures, intrigues, and romances. The saga was still in serialization in 1949 when the Communists took over mainland China, and Li was forced to leave his work unfinished.

Xiang Kairan and Li Shoumin have provoked more criticism from revolutionary-minded critics than other Butterfly fiction writers. Yet, at a time when the Chinese people were struggling to come to grips with modern conditions, the fiction of these two authors enabled them to take flight into a world in which superhuman martial arts rule and sundry *dei ex machina* can always be called on to resolve historical predicaments. Both Xiang and Li exerted a profound impact on chivalric romance writers in Hong Kong and Taiwan after 1949. Jin Yong (1924–), arguably the most popular chivalric romance writer in the second half of the twentieth century, has acknowledged more than once his indebtedness to the two.

From literary revolution to revolutionary literature

Early in April 1927, Chiang Kai-shek and his local allies launched a surprise attack on union workers and leftist activists who had staged a massive strike in the city of Shanghai. The result was a bloody massacre and the collapse of the shaky coalition regime of the Nationalist and Communist Parties based in Wuhan. The incident, later called alternatively the First Chinese Communist Revolution, the Nationalist Party Liquidation, or the 1927 Insurrection, had a profound impact on May Fourth literature. It intensified the political tenor already inherent in the discourse of literary revolution, demanding that writers act out their ideological commitment in both theory and practice. It also compelled other writers to speak out in search of alternatives to such warlike trends. The *discordia concors* created by these voices filled the ensuing decade with sound and fury until the Second Sino-Japanese War broke out in July 1937.

Modern literature showed incipient signs of taking a leftist turn immediately after the May Fourth Movement. Champions of this literary revolution, such as Chen Duxiu, Li Dazhao, and Mao Dun, were all in the vanguard of the Chinese Communist Revolution. In 1923, Deng Zhongxia (1894–1933) and Yun Daiying (1895–1931), members of the newly founded Chinese Communist Party, declared in their journal *Chinese Youth* (*Zhongguo qingnian*) that literature should serve as a weapon to arouse the Chinese people's revolutionary consciousness. Mao Dun (1896–1981), who had joined the Communist Party in 1921, wrote "When Will the Time of Change Come?" (Dazhuanbian shiqi heshi laine, 1925), critiquing the moribund nature of the status quo. The romantic Guo Moruo claimed to have been converted to Marxism in 1924. In 1926, he wrote "Revolution and Literature" (Geming yu wenxue), promoting revolution as the insurrection of the oppressed against their oppressors. The longing for change was best summarized by Cheng Fangwu (1897–1984), who called for a change "from literary revolution to revolutionary literature."

The mounting enthusiasm for revolutionary literature had its external causes. For all the visible reforms and changes in the May Fourth era, China in the early 1920s was trapped in an ongoing crisis. The Nationalist Party was never able fully to control the nation, and colonial powers, warlord forces, and natural disasters continued to shake the foundations of the Republic. A mixed sense of expectation and dejection prevailed in the literary scene. The May Thirtieth Incident of 1925 – a dispute between Shanghai textile workers and their employers that led to a riot, then a bloody crackdown followed by massive protests – provided an occasion for writers to channel their frustration. Meanwhile, the Northern Expedition organized by the Nationalist regime, and the collaboration between the Communists and the Nationalists, further drew young literati into the vortex of revolutionary fervor.

The romantic camp of May Fourth writers were among the first group to promote revolutionary literature. As discussed earlier, the Creation Society, when it was founded in 1921, was a forum in which the romantics could explore intuitive feelings, individualism, and their own nature. But the same group turned out to be more susceptible to ideals representative of the opposite agenda. Though disengaged from immediate political issues, Yu Dafu endorsed terms such as "proletarian spirit" and "class struggle" in 1923. By the late 1920s, the society had transformed into an organization working on behalf of revolutionary literature; its rival, the Sun Society, was even more militant in upholding the revolutionary cause.

Jiang Guangci's (1900–1931) approach to revolution and literature is a typical case. Jiang was among the first batch of recruits of the Chinese Communist Youth League in 1920. In 1921, he was sent to study Marxism and revolutionary tactics at the Oriental University in Moscow. During this period, he made the acquaintance of Qu Qiubai (1899–1935), who later became the Party secretary and the head of the Sun Society in 1928. Life in the Soviet Union, though harsh, kindled Jiang's ideological conviction as well as his literary passion. He published his poems from the Moscow years in *New Dream* (*Xinmeng*, 1925), featuring a persona who yearns fervently for nation, mother, and selfhood, in which he pours out his admiration for such Western romantic models as Byron, Pushkin, and Blok.

In proffering a program to sublimate the desire for revolution into a lofty sacrificial passion for the masses, these romantics were also cultivating solipsism. In Jiang Guangci's words: "Revolution is art . . . The poet – the romantic – is more capable of understanding revolution than anybody else!" Jiang describes an almost erotic delirium at one's embrace of revolution, in which the poet transcends the mundane to rise into a state of supernal ecstasy. "Is there anything," he asks, "that can be more interesting, and more romantic, than revolution?"

Lu Xun had taken a serious interest in the relation between literature and revolution since the mid-1920s, but his skeptical nature kept him from endorsing the burgeoning revolutionary literature movement. On April 8, 1927, he made his first open statement on revolutionary literature at the Whampoa Military Academy, less than a week before Chiang Kai-shek's coup in Shanghai. He acknowledged the importance of literature on the condition that it first serve the purpose of revolution. This is typical of Lu Xun's polemical stance, revealing both his sardonic attitude toward literary formalism and his concern for the dialectical relationship between writing and action. Thus, for him, literature might as well be silenced in the midst of revolution when blood, rather than ink, is spilt. As Lu Xun reiterated in "Revolutionary Literature" (Geming wenxue) later that year, "There is no revolution when revolutionary writers appear in large numbers."

The literary scene of 1928 proved the truth of Lu Xun's words: the revolution was at an ebb so long as revolutionary writers prevailed. These young writers campaigned for the wholesale overhaul of Chinese literature in the name of proletarian liberation. They sneered at Lu Xun and his congeners for their bourgeois taste and political opportunism. Feng Naichao (1901–1983), for instance, caricatured Lu Xun as a senior citizen longing for the past; Li Chuli (1900–1994) likened him to Don Quixote; and Qian Xingcun (1900–1977) ridiculed him as lagging behind the times, proclaiming that "the era of Ah Q has passed." The most devastating charge came from one Du Quan, who labeled Lu Xun a double-counterrevolutionary, a feudal remnant, and a fascist. It was only recently that Du Quan was discovered to be the pseudonym of Guo Moruo.

The charges made by these radicals must have deepened Lu Xun's sense of urgency in regard to the changing times. All along he had been a diligent reader of Soviet literary criticism (via Japanese translation) by such "liberal" Marxists as Leon Trotsky and Aleksandr Voronsky. While engaged in the battle against his critics, he became increasingly convinced of the class nature of art and the imperative for a proletarian literary united front. In other words, despite apparent clashes of opinion, he and his opponents were actually moving closer and closer. One of his sources, the Japanese Marxist Kurahara Korehito, was the proponent of a "new realism," precisely the canonical standard upheld by Qian Xincun and his cohort. By the end of 1928, Lu Xun had turned his attention to such "orthodox" Marxist theoreticians as Plekhanov and Lunacharsky, and he was ready to embark on a pilgrimage to the far left.

The debate among the literati could not have become so volatile had it not been orchestrated, at least to a certain degree, by the Party machine. Critics have called attention to the close ties between the Sun Society and the Communist Party. Qu Qiubai, chief secretary of the Party at the time, was also in charge of the affairs of the Sun Society. With Comintern theoreticians behind him, Qu was able to mobilize a "general intensification of revolutionary policy," as manifested in confrontations on social as well as literary fronts. A more invincible "machine" was set in motion not by the Party but by the revolutionary writers themselves. Hence Guo Moruo's claim in 1928 that revolutionary writers "should do away with their broken bugles – the writers should serve as a megaphone."

The megaphone is invoked as the figure of a loud, persistent noise capable of drowning out the cacophony of individual buglers. Bugles are no match for this mass-produced modern device, which, once awakened to its historical role, blares away relentlessly on a single note. It was perhaps with this under-standing that Lu Xun and others decided to tone down their independent theorizing on revolutionary literature. Under the banner of the united front, they and their opponents joined the Chinese League of Left-Wing Writers, formed on March 2, 1930.

The League was part of the CCP's endeavor to create in urban centers a cul-tural coalition to unify leftist activists and sympathizers like Lu Xun. Several other organizations governing different genres, ranging from drama, film, and art to education, journalism, and Esperanto, were founded at the same time. Though Lu Xun was the League's figurehead, the initiative actually came from the Party machine through its agent Xia Yan (1900–1995), a well-known playwright and moviemaker. Right after its establishment, the League called on its members to commit themselves to solidarity in the "proletariat's struggle for emancipation" as well as the "production of proletarian art." It failed, however, to define either the scope or the meaning of proletarian literature and art, thus giving members no genuine impetus to create a literature of engagement.

Nevertheless, one should not underestimate the League's contribution in the broader arena of literary politics. Under its aegis, numerous publications came out, only to be banned by the Nationalist censors, while these short-lived publications had successfully created a new logic of writing and reading literature: literature was a worthy cause insofar as it could reproduce itself by reiterating the same revolutionary doctrine. More importantly, the League provided a forum by means of which the Party line could be elucidated and Party discipline reinforced. It is in this sense that the League can be said to have provided Mao Zedong and his cohort with the basic guidelines – ideological correctness, organizational discipline, pedagogical means – for using literature for revolutionary purposes in the 1940s.

In its early years, the League's primary enemy was not the censors of the Nationalist Party but rather the humanists and liberals associated with the magazine *Crescent Moon*. As a literary clique, the Crescent Moon Society had been founded by Xu Zhimo and his friends, such as Hu Shi, in 1923. These men, mostly educated in the Anglo-American tradition, celebrated literature as a form of humanism; decorum, taste, and rhetorical rigor were the mottos guiding their literary endeavors. The members of the Creation and Sun Societies followed quite a different charter. Many of them were educated in Japan, and, as romantics-turned-revolutionaries, they saw literature first as uninhibited expression of innermost feelings and individual sentiments, and only later as the uninhibited expression of proletarian solidarity and altruist passion. The animosity between the two camps deepened in 1928 when Xu Zhimo founded the *Crescent Moon* magazine, in which he highlighted the need for a healthy and dignified literary practice, as opposed to one that suffered from thirteen forms of "bacteria," including fanaticism, sentimentalism, and sloganism. Apparently, Xu had in mind the writings of the leftist camp, for which he drew down vitriolic reprisals.

In 1929, Liang Shiqiu (1902–1987) published in *Crescent Moon* "Is Literature Conditioned by Class?" (Wenxue you jiejixing de ma?) and "On Mr. Lu Xun's Hard Translation" (Lun Lu Xun de yingyi). Educated at Harvard under the tutelage of Irving Babbitt, Liang denigrated the excessive claims of Romanticism; instead he favored a literature with decorum and discipline, which he traced back to Matthew Arnold. Underlying Liang's emphasis on the autonomy of literature was a "classical" conviction that literature should rise above contemporary politics to be an arbiter for humanity rather than an instrument of class struggle. Liang further found fault with Lu Xun's translations of Plekhanov and Lunacharsky as examples of "hard" translation and therefore difficult to understand. Above all, he valued creativity over ideology, declaring that "we do not want advertisements, we want goods."

Liang's criticism cut against the grain of leftist revolutionary aesthetics and drew furious responses from Lu Xun and his fellow leftists. Lu Xun pointed out sharply that Liang's promotion of a classless literature reflected nothing but his own bourgeois upbringing. While conceding that the leftists had yet to turn out refined works, Lu Xun reminded Liang that it is not fair to demand that people of illiterate and poor background produce "goods" deemed worthy according to middle-class tastes. As for his "hard" translations, Lu Xun admitted to his own deficiency in language preparation, only to insinuate that his rendition could appear even more faithful to the original in terms not of rhetorical embellishment but of the rough material circumstances that had given birth to the original work.

The fight between Lu Xun and Liang Shiqiu and the *Crescent Moon* group happened right before the formation of the Leftist League. Although neither side could claim a total triumph in the dispute, Lu Xun and his followers did score something of a victory by leaving the public with the impression that the *Crescent Moon* group were gentlemen living in an ivory tower. Later, with the support of the League, they managed to set the tone for revolutionary literature in the 1930s. It is the literature of "tears and blood," they claimed, that engages both readers and writers.

In June 1930, a campaign was mounted against the League, calling for a "nationalist literature" that reflected national spirit and consciousness. This campaign was led by writers such as Wang Pingling (1898–1964) and Huang Zhenxia (1907–1974), who were associated with the Nationalist Party. It exerted almost no impact because its participants were minor figures in literary circles and their slogans sounded both pedantic and vague. But this minor interlude led to a most intriguing episode in the history of modern Chinese literary criticism, namely the dispute over the "free man" (*ziyou ren*) and "the third category of man" (*disanzhong ren*) in literature.

In 1931, Hu Qiuyuan (1910–2004), a young scholar educated in Japan, published an essay attacking "nationalist literature." Central to his argument is that literature should not serve as mere propaganda for political purposes. Instead, it should reflect life by showing its complexities and ambiguities. Hu was immediately attacked by the League. Ironically, Hu was a dedicated

Marxist with a book on Plekhanov's theory of art (1932) to his credit. But, for all his ideological commitment, Hu rejected the "vulgar" version of Marxist reflectionism. He believed that literary creation should not be treated as a "megaphone" in the service of politics. Accordingly, he hoped to see the emergence of a "free man." This free man is not necessarily anti-Marxist or apolitical, as with the *Crescent Moon* members; though politically engaged, he is nevertheless able to exercise his critical powers on the cultural and literary front.

Hu Qiuyuan's idea was echoed by Su Wen (1906–1964), a writer from the modernist camp in Shanghai who was also sympathetic to the leftist cause. In view of the conflict between the two types of Marxist, Hu Qiuyuan's "free man" and the "unfree, Party-dominated" members of the League, as well as between the Communist camp and the Nationalist camp, Su suggests that there should be a "third category of man," referring to those who do not wish to be caught up in these discursive battles. Su believed that the majority of writers of his time, given their concerns about politics, belonged to this third category, one desiring honesty in the depiction of reality as he or she saw it.

Hu Qiuyuan and Su Wen drew waves of attacks from the League, of which Qu Qiubai's was the most cogent if not the most inflammatory. Qu criticized both men for failing to grasp the class basis of Marxist theory and therefore falling prey to the trap of aestheticism. He was at pains to point out that Hu's Soviet model, Plekhanov, was in his own turn criticized for being too idealistic about the aesthetic function of literature, and concluded that Hu's and Su's mistake lay in their fence-sitting attitude where a "true engagement" with the people and with class struggle was in order.

In their subsequent articles on the debate, Qu Qiubai and a fellow League member, the young theoretician Feng Xuefeng (1903–1976), took a much more conciliatory approach. Qu, by invoking Lenin, again stressed the principle of party organization and party literature, but he conceded that, in practice, revolutionary literature should not be coercive but rather "debatable" and "instructional." As for the writers who did not belong to the League, they were asked to recognize the principle. In either case, Qu concludes, creative freedom should be respected as long as the Party mandate remains the general guideline.

By 1932, the League had secured its legitimacy and power in literary circles. The *Crescent Moon* was discontinued in 1931 as a result of Xu Zhimo's death in a plane crash. Following in its footsteps, Lin Yutang (1895–1976) put forward three popular magazines, *Analects* (*Lunyu*), *Human World* (*Renjianshi*), and *Cosmic Wind* (*Yuzhoufeng*), all featuring humor and gentle satire, but they posed no threat to the League. Ironically enough, the League now entered a stage of internecine war that finally ended its ideological unity.

In 1932, Qu Qiubai raised the issue of "mass language," which soon led to heated debate. Qu held that the vernacular language used in May Fourth literature had become a new elite idiom, characterized by new coinages, residual literary Chinese, and imported European and Japanese expressions – a language monopolized by select groups of urban intellectuals. Calling for another "literary revolution" in the name of the proletarian class, he aspired to forge a truly popular language out of a collection of "common idioms" (*putonghua*), something intelligible to all people of the underprivileged classes.

Over the next few years, Qu's proposal, an expression of the utopian desire for a pure language for "the people," ignited a series of debates regarding the viability of the new "common idioms." For people like Mao Dun, the more urgent task in hand was to enrich May Fourth language by incorporating as many dialects and indigenous idioms as possible. For others, such as Lu Xun, however, the debate soon shifted in the direction of latinization. They wanted to promote a new phonetic system, largely based on the Beijing dialect, that did away with tonal indications; even more radically, they wanted to replace the centuries-old written ideographs with an alphabetic script, or latinized Chinese phonetic system, which had purportedly been tried out by the sinologists of the Soviet Union.

But, by 1935, the energy of most League members was being directed into more pressing fights about the Party line. With the departure of Qu Qiubai for the Communist Party base at Ruijin in late 1933, the League's leadership fell into the hands of Zhou Yang (1908–1989) and other ideologues, who simply ignored Lu Xun's authority. In 1936, Zhou Yang announced that the League was to be dissolved in response to the Communist Party's declaration of a national united front against Japanese invasion, and he did so without even consulting Lu Xun, still the League's nominal leader.

What followed was a series of fights later called "the battle of the two slogans." On the Zhou Yang side, the decision to adopt the term "national defense literature" (*guofang wenxue*) as the formal slogan was probably prompted by Mao Zedong's recent call to form a national defense government. Zhou asserted that, in view of the mounting threat of Japanese invasion, national defense should become the central theme in the works of all writers regardless of their political allegiance. This announcement drew immediate opposition from veteran League members, including Guo Moruo and Mao Dun. Both acknowledged the need for a united front in the face of the impending invasion, but they had serious reservations about the dictatorial undertone of Zhou Yang's guideline, however accommodating it appeared to be to the exigencies of the times.

The sudden dissolution of the League struck a fatal blow to Lu Xun, who had already been in frail health. The slogan "national defense literature," with its menacing implication of being both compromising and totalitarian, represented a rebuff to the leftist convictions that Lu Xun had struggled for since the late 1920s. Together with Mao Dun and other friends, he came up with a new slogan, "mass literature of national revolutionary war" (*minzu geming zhanzheng de dazhong wenxue*), as a way to challenge Zhou Yang's line. Lu Xun and his followers insisted that there should be no compromise on the class nature of Marxist revolution, even if the issue of national defense was at stake. Lu Xun was able to launch his retaliation thanks to the assistance of the young Marxist critic Hu Feng (1902–1985), who, returning from Japan a year before, had quickly become Lu Xun's protégé. In 1936, Hu Feng published an essay, "What Do the Masses Demand of Literature?" (Renmin dazhong xiang wenxue yaoqiu shenme?), and thus ignited the battle of the two slogans. In the following months, the camps exchanged fire with increasingly hostile writings full of diatribe, slander, and name-calling.

For readers of today, the "battle of the two slogans" may sound more like a family squabble over something trivial. But close reading reveals that the "battle" came as a result of party sectarianism, jockeying for power, and, most importantly, personality conflicts. For Lu Xun, Zhou Yang and his gang, including men like Xia Yan, Tian Han, and Yang Hansheng (1902–1993), were censurable because, instead of consolidating their fellow League members and sympathizers, they took the slogan and made it into a pretext for sectarian cleansing. As the battle escalated out of control and began to jeopardize the image of leftist writers' solidarity, the Communist Party, now based in Yan'an after the Long March, intervened. As a result, the battle of the two slogans came to an end in early October, shortly before the death of Lu Xun, when twenty writers, including Lu Xun, Mao Dun, and Guo Moruo, signed a joint declaration calling for a united front of all writers.

Nevertheless, the consequences of the battle would continue to influence all the participants of the dispute, first in the Yan'an period of the 1940s, then in the mid-1950s, and finally during the Great Cultural Revolution. It reflects a peculiar feature of the power struggle within the Communist Party: the fastidious dispute over language and slogan proved to be a matter of life and death. In a way, the story of revolutionary literature from the late 1920s to the eve of the Second Sino-Japanese War reflects the haunting effect of language and power that can be traced back to the tradition of politics in literary culture in late Qing China and even earlier eras.

The dialogic of realism

One of the most salient features of the corpus of modern Chinese literature is the practice and imagining of realism, and the endless debate over this. As discussed above, modern Chinese literature arose at a moment when the master narratives vindicating Chinese reality were in a state of disintegration. As intellectuals and literati desperately sought the Way to national strength, the question of how to read and write China ranked high on their agenda. The search for a new narrative paradigm – in the name of realism – was never merely a literary game; it was a crucial part of their campaign to reimagine nationhood, and to reflect and rectify reality.

To be sure, classical Chinese literature had demonstrated a full spectrum of views about and strategies for depicting the real. But realism, as the late Qing and May Fourth literati understood it, derived its canon from such nineteenth-century European models as Balzac, Dickens, Tolstoy, Zola, and eastern European writers, as if only these writers held the secret to the representation of reality. In fact, however, nineteenth-century European realism was never a unified movement, much less one that shared the same aesthetic and ideological origins. That Chinese writers were adhering to realism, at a time when European writers were already experimenting with various forms of modernism, could be regarded either as an anachronism or as the outcome of a peculiar modernist belief of their own.

There was always a gap, however, between what the writers thought they were doing and what they truly did. They set out to break with the old, unrealistic tradition, but ended up reenacting the perennial dialectic: the need to give form to a reality in flux and the commitment to contextualizing that form; the desire to inscribe time and the impulse to transcend time; realism for aesthetic catharsis and realism for normative purposes; realism as historical engagement and realism as myth.

Take Lu Xun as an example. He employs multiple strategies in depicting the real: comic caricature ("Kong Yiji"), mock heroic (*The True Story of Ah Q*), sardonic interlude ("Divorce"), lyrical rendition ("My Old Home"), allegory ("Medicine"), and so on. Underlying all these writings, however, is a theory that emphasizes the representational link between mind and body, language and reality. But Lu Xun's longing for a fully fledged representation of the real ironically nurtures itself on the "break" in this chain of referentiality, as emphatically symbolized by a beheaded body, a split personality ("The Diary of A Madman," "New Year's Sacrifice"), or a living corpse ("In the Tavern"). It is awareness of this break that fuels Lu Xun's nostalgia for the semantic and somatic plenitude of Chinese reality and the polemical power of his writing.

If Lu Xun can be credited as the pioneer of the modern form of the short story, Mao Dun stands out as laying the foundations of the modern Chinese full-length novel. In a way, the rise of the modern Chinese realist novel was more than the advent of a fictional genre; we may see it as representing the zeitgeist of the post-May Fourth sociopolitical dynamic that culminated in the 1927 Communist Revolution. When Mao Dun set out to write his first work, *Eclipse* (*Shi*, 1928) – a trilogy made up of *Disillusionment* (*Huanmie*), *Vacillation* (*Dongyao*), and *Pursuit* (*Zhuiqiu*) – he was in hiding after the failed revolution. Disillusioned by his experience, he meant to use the novel as way to rethink the incongruity between what should have happened and what did happen in the revolution. *Eclipse* describes the vain pursuit by a group of young men and women of love and revolution in the post-May Fourth era. They alternate between romantic and political causes – the May Thirtieth Incident, the Northern Expedition, and the First Chinese Communist Revolution – and end up nowhere. Modeled upon nineteenth-century European novels, *Eclipse* presents a sweeping view of a society in drastic change, showing ordinary men and women encountering the challenge of historical events as they work through moral, emotional, and ideological crises against the linear progression of time. *Eclipse* did not stand alone in dramatizing the sense of the times and idealism in eclipse. Other examples include Ye Shaojun's *Ni Huanzhi* (*Ni Huanzhi*, 1929), Ba Jin's (1904–2005) *Destruction* (*Miewang*, 1928), Jiang Guangci's *Des Sans-Culottes* (*Duanku dang*, 1927), and Bai Wei's *The Bomb and the Expeditionary Bird* (*Zhadan yu zhengniao*, 1928).

While *Eclipse* won instant popularity upon publication, it also received harsh criticism, particularly from radical leftists. This led to a debate about the nature of realism. Mao Dun was faulted for casting a nihilist eye on the revolution, indulging in petit bourgeois sentimentalism, and, most seriously, resorting to the dubious realist aesthetics of distance and noncommitment. Mao Dun argued in "From Guling to Tokyo" (Cong Guling dao Dongjing, 1928) that his characters' romantic exaltation and abjection underscored complex facets of the revolution and that his role as writer was to present reality as it was. He insisted that literature should address issues that most concern its intended readers, the petit bourgeoisie, the goal being to enlighten these readers and convert them to Marxism. In his view, therefore, realist literature plays a self-contradictory role. It chronicles the process through which the revolution has arisen and come to a halt, whereas its existence as such embodies the residual factor that alienates individual talent from collective volition, history from History. It is both a symptom and the cure of a malaise that besets postrevolutionary times.

Chinese realist writings are not limited to these debates over doctrines and slogans, however. By the beginning of the 1930s, at least four directions – social exposé, "revolution-and-romance," nativism, and gender politics – could already be identified. These four directions refer not only to subject matter but also to formal polemics. In practice, they overlap each other and thus result in some of the most powerful works.

To begin with, echoing the May Fourth call for "literature for the sake of life," mainstream realist writers charged their works with a strong humanitarian passion, vowing to expose social evils and deliver poetic justice to the downcast and the wounded. Writers in the leftist camp were particularly keen on the political agency of realism. Rou Shi (1902–1931), Lu Xun's protégé and one of the five leftist writers arrested and executed by the Nationalist regime in 1931, moved his readers with short stories such as "A Slave's Mother" (Wei nuli de muqin, 1930), in which a surrogate mother bears a baby for a rich man at the expense of neglecting her own children. In *February* (*Eryue*, 1929), Rou Shi tells of an idealistic young intellectual's thwarted encounter with feudal practice and provincial customs in a southern Chinese town, a painful testimony to Lu Xun's indictment of "cannibalism."

In Taiwan, Lai He (1894–1943), a doctor turned writer as the result of Lu Xun's inspiration, wrote a series of stories about Taiwanese life under Japanese rule. In "A Steelyard" (Yigan chengzai, 1926), a vegetable vendor is humiliated by Japanese police to the point where he has to take a most violent measure to vent his anger. In "Doctor Snake" (She xiansheng, 1928), the conflict between colonial modernity and Chinese legacy is subtly expressed through the search for a herbal doctor's mysterious prescription. Lai He has been regarded as the founding father of modern Taiwanese literature; for his critical depiction of colonial Taiwan and his engagement in the politics of literature, he is also called the "Lu Xun of Taiwan."

Writings by Rou Shi, Lai He, and others serve to illustrate the "literature of blood and tears" (*xie yu lei de wenxue*), a term coined by Zheng Zhenduo (1898–1958) in the early 1930s. The literature of blood and tears is believed to possess such demonstrative force as both to evoke the blood and tears repressed in the objects of narration, and to induce blood and tears at the site of writing and representing. But tears and blood need not be the only emotional register of the realism of exposé. Able writers can use various narrative modes to accentuate the poignancy of realist effects. Writings of grotesque realism, in the forms of satire, melodrama, and farce, as practiced by writers such as Zhang Tianyi (1906–1985), Wu Zuxiang (1908–1994), and particularly Lao She (1896–1966), readily come to mind.

Zhang Tianyi stands out for his caricatures of the hypocrites, snobs, and quacks who inhabit a society devoid of any integrity; his style clearly reminds us of late Qing exposés. Short stories aside, Zhang's *Ghostland Diary* (*Guitu riji*, 1931), about one Han Shiqian's (homophonous with "Chinese Reality") nightmarish travel to Ghostland, is a rare example of modern dystopia. In *The Unlikely Hero of Shanghai* (*Yangjingbin qixia*, 1933–1934), a young man's wishful adventure to become a knight-errant, played out against the background of anti-Japanese aggression, parodies both the popular genre of chivalric romance and the officially sanctioned genre of patriotic fiction. Zhang proves that excessive laughter can exert more power than excessive tears or excessive enthusiasm.

Although less productive than Zhang Tianyi, Wu Zuxiang shows an even greater talent for modulating narrative device. In "Young Master Gets His Tonic" (Guanguan de bupin, 1932), the weakling son of a landlord literally supports his life on the blood and milk of the peasants. In "Fan Village" (Fanjia pu, 1934), a peasant woman is driven to kill her mother who, having worked too long in the city, has lost any capacity to feel her daughter's despair in a drought. Whereas "Young Master" is narrated like a black comedy, "Fan Village" renders a family catastrophe in a solemn, almost tragic light. In the novella *Eighteen Hundred Bushels* (*Yiqian babai dan*, 1934), poor, hungry peasants are driven to violence by an ever-mounting threat of starvation, thus providing an impetus to the oncoming revolution – all narrated as if in a fiendish theatre of the grotesque.

Lao She (1896–1966) is the most accomplished realist writer of this time. The son of a Manchu soldier who died guarding the Forbidden City in the Boxer Rebellion, Lao She grew up in the slums of Beijing and taught in China and England before becoming a professional writer. In view of his vivid portrayal of Beijing manners and his patriotic fervor and sympathy for lower-class people, one can easily read Lao She as a follower of Lu Xun's kind of critical realism. But Lao She is much less confident in positing a superior, critical position. In a world where the representational order is already broken, any literary practice in the name of realism must call attention to its own formal and conceptual insufficiency. This self-consciousness haunts Lao She, leading him to cross the line that differentiates mimesis from mimicry – the phantasmal displacement and degradation of the mimetic effort. Lao She's realism betrays more nihilist elements than he would admit. Life is at best an absurd comedy of mistaken identities and irrational collisions; "bitter laughter" is the only response.

Vacillating between the excessive lachrymosity of a melodramatic mode and the excessive hilarity of a farcical mode, Lao She's fiction shows an ambiguity rarely emulated by writers in the 1930s. His romantic sentiment finds expression in such works as "Crescent Moon" (Yueyaer, 1935) and "Soul-Shattering Spear" (Duanhun qiang, 1935), with windy, pleading tears or dramatic pronouncements on the mechanism of fate. On the other hand, Lao She's energy of farce drives him to celebrate the victory of clowns and pranksters, as in *The Philosophy of Lao Zhang* (*Lao Zhang de zhexue*, 1929) and *The Biography of Niu Tianci* (*Niu Tianci zhuan*, 1936).

Lao She's laughter often betrays an ontological anxiety as to the closure of the real. In *The Two Mas* (*Erma*, 1931), a novel about the bittersweet relationship between a father and a son stranded in London, and *Divorce* (*Lihun*, 1933), a novel about a group of Beijing bureaucrats in futile pursuit of romantic freedom, Lao She introduces his heroes as victims of their society because of their sobriety and self-esteem. The laughter evoked here has as much to do with a villainous power or a corrupt society as with a basic view of human existence as absurd. This logic of laughter, pushed to an extreme, results in an allegorical novel like *The City of Cats* (*Maocheng ji*, 1933), in which the cartoon-like characters of a Cat Country form a parade of fiendish creatures, reveling on their way to destruction. Thus it would be an oversight to describe Lao She's most celebrated *Camel Xiangzi* (*Luotuo Xiangzi*, 1937) merely as a piece about "tears and blood." In the Sisyphean efforts of the title character, a Beijing rickshaw puller, to obtain and keep a rickshaw, Lao She invests as much bitter tearfulness as horrified laughter. The greater Xiangzi's obsession with his rickshaw grows amid his failures, the larger the element of laughter that creeps into the pathos of the story, and the more the reader begins to suspect the legitimacy of realism as a form of poetic justice.

In drama, *Thunderstorm* (*Leiyu*, 1933) by the young playwright Cao Yu (1910–1996) was staged in Jinan, Shandong in 1934. An immediate hit, the play was staged in cities including Shanghai, Nanjing, and even Tokyo in the next two years. Two film adaptations appeared in 1938. By all accounts, the play's success marked the arrival of the golden era of modern Chinese "spoken drama."

Cao Yu was still a student at Tsinghua University when *Thunderstorm* was published. The play deals with the rise and fall of Zhou Puyuan, a coalmine owner who has built a tyrannical empire both at work and at home. Behind the façade of the Zhou residence there looms a family secret and this triggers a series of explosive subplots involving frustrated passion, incest between stepmother and stepson and half-sister and half-brother, an unwanted orphan, a missing sibling, generational revolt, and class struggle. The play ends in a violent thunderstorm, a moment that unveils all unspeakable taboos and precipitates the destruction of the family.

One can identify traces of Cao Yu's indebtedness to Western models, including Ibsen's *Ghosts*, Racine's *Phèdre*, Ostrovsky's *The Storm*, and O'Neill's *Desire under the Elms*. Still, Cao Yu should be credited for injecting into his play a unique vision of the Chinese affective, ethical, and political systems in shambles. His indictment of stifling Confucian family values, his melancholy contemplation of fate and human frailties, and his insinuation of an apocalyptic force that will bring down the entire establishment, all deeply moved the audiences of the 1930s, themselves trapped in an ongoing historical thunderstorm. Equally noticeable is the literary quality of the script, which, with detailed stage instructions and elaborate rhetoric, brilliantly displays the theatrical as well as literary effect of the spoken drama.

After *Thunderstorm*, Cao Yu produced two scripts, *Sunrise* (*Richu*, 1936) and *Wilderness* (*Yuanye*, 1937), and received more critical acclaim. Whereas *Sunrise* exposes the decadent life of Shanghai through a socialite's degradation and death, *Wilderness* inquires into the human psyche at the primitive level by exploring forbidden love, murder attempts, and an impulse to revolt against reality in the name of justice.

Other playwrights of distinction include Xia Yan and Li Jianwu (1906–1982). Xia Yan's *Sai Jinhua* (*Sai Jinhua*, 1936), inspired by the notorious late Qing courtesan's adventures in the Boxer Rebellion, incited heated debate because of its political satire on "national defense literature." His *Under the Eaves of Shanghai* (*Shanghai wuyan xia*, 1937), however, is a neat play on revolution and love turned into a family melodrama. Li Jianwu was a respected drama critic and playwright. His *It's Only Spring* (*Zhebuguo shi chuntian*, 1933) appears to be a rare comedy of manners about revolutionary zeal and romantic passion betrayed. It brings a fresh, sarcastic take on human fickleness, even on the most serious subjects, to a theatre otherwise immersed in tears and blood.

"Revolution plus romance" (*geming jia lianai*) rose to become a powerful fictional genre in the wake of the succession of events between May Fourth and the 1927 Insurrection. Fiction along these lines deals with the tortuous ways in which young men and women come to terms with their political and romantic commitments. Endeavors of this kind are evidence not only of the writers' use of a narrative ploy to reflect the fragmented post-1927 revolutionary realities, but also of their effort to carry on their engagement with the failed revolution. Between these two narrative poles, one addressing the need for coherence and closure and the other subverting this need, exists a tension; hence more storytelling and the proliferation of plots to fill the expanding space.

Just two weeks after the the 1927 Insurrection in Shanghai ended in fiasco, in May, Jiang Guangci wrote *Des Sans-Culottes*, a *roman-à-clef* about Party members involved in the failed revolution. The novel is replete with dichotomized moral values, high-flown rhetoric, and celebrations of romantic love versus descent into death wish, all in the name of proletarian emancipation. By 1930, Jiang Guangci had become a name synonymous with revolution-and-romance. *The Moon Forces Its Way through the Clouds* (*Chongchu yunwei de yueliang*), his novel about a young girl's passage into womanhood as she turns from student into revolutionary, and her search for political and sexual identity, went through six printings within a year of its publication. Critics were quick to notice the forbidden attractions in Jiang's works. In 1932, Qu Qiubai criticized the novel *Earth Spring* (*Diquan*) by Hua Han (Yang Hansheng, 1902–1990), Jiang Guangci's colleague and follower, as an example of "revolutionary romanticism" (*geming de langman dike*). For Qu, Hua Han had concocted a world of revolution and romance based on self-delusion, allowing his romantic sentiments to obscure the reality.

Mao Dun was among the critics of revolution-and-romance fiction. This did not keep him from taking up the formula. In *Rainbow* (*Hong*, 1931), he tells the story of a woman's pursuit of selfhood through the turbulent years from the May Fourth era to the May Thirtieth Incident. In each of the novel's three parts, the protagonist Mei is seen as undergoing an ideological test parallel to her quest for love. Mei is finally able to sublimate her romantic longing into political action. At the end of the novel, we see her marching in a demonstration to protest the May Thirtieth Incident.

Midnight (*Ziye*, 1933) represents the climax of Mao Dun's novelistic engagement before the Second Sino-Japanese War. A novel of epic scope, its central theme concerns the futile struggle of a group of Chinese capitalists to establish viable industries in competition with foreign economic powers and their involvement in a ferocious native game of stock market speculation. Mao Dun intends to make the world of *Midnight* the dark period before the dawn of revolution. He invests the novel with mythical capital that is the unexpected dividend of the entropic world of speculation and fictitious dealings. The capitalist world of Shanghai will fall, only to beget a new paradise. Speculation, therefore, in its extended sense, is not only a formidable force precipitating the fall of the world, but also part of the grand dialectic of history giving rise to the return of order.

Underlying this plotline is a parodic review of the concept of revolution-and-romance. Not only do men and women in Shanghai's high society gamble on the stock market; they even take romantic love as a kind of currency. They fall in and out of love as if betting on the value of each romance. At Mao Dun's most polemical, he portrays even Communists as speculators in both personal and public spheres. Under the Li Lisan Line, a Party line calling for urban proletariat organization and violent action, these revolutionaries are seen as misinvesting their passion and action at a time least favorable to their agenda, so that their efforts are doomed from the beginning. As the first part of a grand plan that was never carried out, *Midnight* concludes with an open ending, leaving us uncertain as to the outcome of revolution.

Ba Jin (1904–2005) brought the romantic sentiment in revolutionary fiction into full bloom. An anarchist from Sichuan, he wanted to write as a way of professing his conviction of love, equality, and solidarity in humankind, while acknowledging the violent undercurrent of his agenda. In early works such as *Love Trilogy* (*Aiqing sanbuqu*, 1928), revolutionaries martyr themselves as if dying for love unrequited. It is *Family* (*Jia*), Part One of the *Torrent Trilogy* (*Jiliu sanbuqu*), that consummates all the elements of the revolution-and-romance formula. Published in 1933, *Family* is a saga about the Gao family of Sichuan during the May Fourth era, focusing on three Gao brothers in their battle against the feudal family system, their pursuit of love, and their consequent choices of either reconciliation or a total break with the family.

Family was an instant hit among readers, and in the next decades it was to become a celebrated primer for all who were yearning for revolutionary zeal and romantic passion. Compared with his peers, Ba Jin at this stage of his career is not a crafted writer; his narrative is flooded with unbridled passion, melodramatic plotting, and tendentious outcries. His "phenomenon" is not merely a matter of literary taste but a testimony to the shared need of one generation of readers to encode their emotional and ideological outputs. Indeed, Ba Jin embodies in both his works and his own image the symbolism of "youthful China" as envisioned by Liang Qichao and the May Fourth forerunners. A novel like *Family*, therefore, is realistic in the sense that it is not only a reflection of the cannibalistic nature of feudal society but also a timely engagement with the call for articulating the real – justice, love, revolution, and so on – in a strongly dramatic format.

Nativism was one of the most popular themes in realist fiction. When a genealogy of nativist literature is mapped out, Lu Xun again is one of its progenitors. Most of Lu Xun's stories take place in a locale much like his hometown of Shaoxing. "My Old Home," "In the Tavern," and "New Year's Sacrifice" deal directly with his hometown complex: the passage of time, the clash between old and new values, yearning for the lost days of innocence or childhood, (re)encounter with quaint rustic figures, anxiety about impending change, and conflicted feelings of longing for and fear of going home – all part of the bittersweet experience called nostalgia.

Lu Xun is also among the first group of critics looking into the polemics inherent in the realist presentation of the native soil. With Xu Qinwen (1897–1984) and others as his examples, Lu Xun suggests that the concern of native-soil writers for their hometown region can be acutely felt only after the author has been uprooted from the native soil he cherishes so much. Native-soil writers may claim that they derive local color from the objects and moments with which they are or were most familiar, but in rendering these objects and moments they are actually engaged in a task of defamiliarization. By presenting the subject of a vain seeking after lost childhoods or inaccessible homelands, they enact the split in representation and the incongruity between what realist literature proposes to do and what it can do. While the homeland in reality never looks as it does in memory, especially as a native-soil writer would have it remembered, a realist text always takes the risk of betraying the arguable reality it once set out to recover.

But the post-May Fourth nativists were not interested in polemics so much as in the Chinese land as a humanist and ideological symbol. Ever since the 1920s, "native soil" has been associated with peasant hardship and misery. Major writers of this movement included Peng Jiahuang (1898–1933), Tai Jingnong, and Wang Luyan (1901–1944).

For leftist writers, native-soil narratives could even form a typology of the yearning for land and nationhood, as if through calling on the earth they could assert their own ideological roots. Jiang Guangci's *Roaring Earth* (*Paoxiao lede tudi*, 1931) – about a young revolutionary's homecoming trip, not to indulge in nostalgia but to lead revolution against the landlords, including his own father – is a case in point. Another example is Mao Dun's *Village Trilogy* ("Spring Silkworms" (Chuncan), "Autumn Harvest" (Qiushou), and "Winter

Ruins" (Candong), 1932–1934), a moving portrait of traditional rural culture in decline.

The political symbolism of native-soil literature took on a further dimension, thanks to a group of exiled Manchurian writers in the early 1930s. After the seizure of Manchuria by the Japanese and the founding of the puppet Manchukuo regime in 1934, writers such as Xiao Jun (1907–1988) and Xiao Hong (1911–1942) fled their home region and, in Shanghai and elsewhere, produced many writings reminiscing about the Manchurian countryside ravaged by the invaders. Their nostalgia added a nationalist urgency to the native-soil discourse that by then had been assimilated into the leftist theme of class struggle.

Xiao Jun's *Village in August* (*Bayue de xiangcun*) came out in 1934 to immediate popularity. Describing the fall of Manchuria and the heroic resistance of the local people, the novel touched readers with its exuberant descriptions of the immense land beyond the Great Wall and its passionate "call to arms." It was also the first modern Chinese novel to be translated into English. Xiao Jun's wife Xiao Hong was a much more talented writer. Her *Field of Life and Death* (*Shengsichang*, 1934), though less popular at the time of publication, would prove to be a more enduring work in its lyrical rendition of the landscape of Manchuria and the life cycle of its people, their happiness and suffering, their manners and morals, and their determination to regain the lost land. Another writer, Duanmu Hongliang (1912–1996), wrote his first novel, *The Steppe of the Khorchin Banner* (*Keerqinqi de caoyuan*, 1940), at the age of twenty-one, chronicling the rise and fall of a landlord family from the early years of settlement to its patriotic awakening on the eve of the Japanese invasion. Rich symbolism and a panoramic view of the land on which Duanmu grew up make for a novel of epic scope.

Li Jieren (1891–1962) introduces a diffient model of nativist imagination by depicting the changing manners and morals of an urban space, his hometown of Chengdu, Sichuan. Trained in France from 1919 to 1924 and known for his excellent translation of novels such as *Madame Bovary*, Li wrote a trilogy comprising *Ripples in the Dead Water* (*Sishui weilan*), *On the Eve of the Storm* (*Baofengyu qian*), and *Huge Waves* (*Dabo*, Part One) between 1935 and 1937. The trilogy chronicles sociopolitical turmoil during the late Qing and the early Republican era – ranging from bureaucratic corruption to gangster riots, from the Consitutional Reform to the Republican Revolution – but it impresses even more with its detailed, sensuous depictions of everyday life in Chengdu. Mixing sensory data with a distinctive local color, Li manages to make his trilogy a fictional ethnography of the ancient city.

By all accounts, Shen Congwen (1902–1988) must be regarded as the greatest native-soil writer of twentieth-century China. A rebellious son from a western Hunan soldier's family and himself a teenage soldier in service to a warlord, Shen Congwen's early life was full of rustic experiences and rough-and-tumble adventures. This young soldier was as much affected by May Fourth as any urban youth and, in 1922, he made his way to Beijing to pursue a literary career. By the end of the 1920s, he had won fame as an enchanting storyteller.

Before he gave up writing in 1949, Shen produced hundreds of works in the form of short stories, novels, sketches, essays, and travelogues about his homeland, the Miao tribal region of western Hunan. Shen begins his portrait of western Hunan from an ironic perspective, with the thought that although his homeland has been a marginal area on the Chinese map, known for its barbarous ethnic residents and primitive lifestyle, it was also the place that allegedly inspired Qu Yuan's "Encountering Sorrow" and Tao Qian's (365?–427) "Peach Blossom Spring." Western Hunan, accordingly, always appears in a double image in Shen's writing, one that embraces such thematic polarities as geographical locus versus imaginary landscape, reality versus memory, and history versus myth. The author plays with these polarities, showing how they infiltrate each other's domains and thus implement their affinities beneath surface oppositions. At a time when most Chinese writers were committed to a monolithic rendering of reality, Shen Congwen's vision of the native soil was much more avant-garde than it first seemed to be.

Thus Shen Congwen's writing engendered not merely simple nostalgia but an imaginary nostalgia, a self-reflexive display of nostalgia as the fantastic inscription of a hometown and of the memory of a past that is always already mediated. His *Border Town* (*Biancheng*, 1934), perhaps the most popular piece of native-soil of twentieth-century China, is a pastoral about a young girl's involvement with two boatman brothers against the ethereal backdrop of western Hunan scenery; this romance is nevertheless jeopardized by dark family memories, unhappy coincidences, and misunderstandings. The novella projects as much Shen's longing for his hometown at its most romantic as it does his awareness of the contingency and unreality of that longing when thrown into the flux of time and history.

Equally noteworthy is Shen's travelogue *Random Sketches to Hunan* (*Xiangxing sanji*, 1934). A recollection of his homecoming trip in 1934, seventeen years after leaving, *Random Sketches* features a series of vignettes, including a nocturnal stay on the boat, a surprise reunion with a long-lost friend, a sketch of a boatman and a prostitute, and so on. Moving between the past and present, between the utopian legend of "Peach Blossom Spring" and harsh reality, Shen expresses his sensibility in a poetic manner. The best part of his travelogue enacts longing: Shen wants to save a secret place not in the realist reportage of western Hunan, but in the dark realm of imaginary nostalgia for home.

Women writers and the representation of gender politics constitute yet another dimension of realism in the writing of this period. Three writers from Hunan Province serve as examples here. In 1928, Ding Ling (1904–1986) published "The Diary of Miss Sophie" (Shafei nüshi de riji) in Shanghai and created a great sensation in the circle of belles-lettres. The story, a portrait of the young bohemian Sophie's romantic adventures, was regarded as a break-through not only because of its vivid depiction of woman's sexual psychology, but also because of its deft use of the diary as a vehicle to convey a feminine style. Ding Ling may well have derived her heroine's name Sophie from the Russian anarchist heroine Sophia Provoskaya. Confined in a small apartment in Beijing and suffering from tuberculosis, Sophie is nevertheless driven by the desire to find love in her own way, though her pursuit is doomed to failure.

A rebellious woman student from Hunan Province, Ding Ling went to Shanghai with like-minded classmates in 1920. She made it to Beijing in 1924, with the intention of attending Peking University, but ended up befriending two young writers, Shen Congwen and Hu Yepin (1903–1931). She eventually married Hu. "The Diary of Miss Sophie" was Ding Ling's second work. In the wake of its success, she wrote a series of novellas and stories, all in a similar vein of bohemian abandon and romantic melancholy, such as "A Woman and a Man" (Yige nüren he yige nanren, 1928). Tiring quickly of her subjects, she found a new direction in leftist revolution. Her transition can already be seen in the stories "Weihu" (Weihu, 1930) and "Shanghai Spring, 1930" (Yijiu sanling chun de Shanghai), in which her political conversion is brought to bear on the popular theme of revolution and love. Meanwhile, Hu Yepin became increasingly involved in the leftist activities, which led to his arrest and execution in 1931.

The death of Hu Yepin and four other leftist writers in 1931, including Rou Shi, incited the indignation of the international media. For Ding Ling, it marked the watershed of her career between the period of Miss Sophie and that of woman warrior fighting on behalf of the leftist proletarian cause, or between the realism of psychological inquiry and a realism of ideological provocation. For example, "Flood" (Shui, 1931), written after the disastrous flood of 1931, deals with how a natural disaster aroused the political consciousness of Chinese peasants to protest against the status quo. Instead of the diaristic form that highlights Miss Sophie's fluid romantic subjectivity, one finds an apparently genderless and selfless narrative voice that expresses the collective subjectivity of the masses.

In 1933, Ding Ling was put under house arrest by the Nationalists. It coincided with the publication of her novella *Mother* (*Muqin*), a moving biographical account of her mother who rose from widowhood in traditional circumstances to become an independent woman and a resourceful educator. When she miraculously appeared in Yan'an in 1936, Ding Ling became an international icon on behalf of revolutionary women fighting against adversity. This was only the beginning of her saga. The following decades would see her continue to struggle for ideological truth and gendered representation.

Xie Bingying (1907–2000), like Ding Ling, was also a native of Hunan. In 1926, in response to the Nationalist–Communist coalition government's call for youth to join military service, Xie enrolled in the Central Political and Military Academy and was soon selected as one of twenty women to join the revolutionary troops. The diaries and letters Xie wrote as a woman soldier on the Northern Expedition were published under the title *War Diary* (*Congjun riji*) in 1928; it went into nineteen reprints and was translated into numerous languages. In 1936, Xie published her autobiography, which was also a best seller. Although derived from personal experience, Xie's works were generally read as "legends" about a rebellious woman's heroic adventures. In her image of the woman soldier, fiction and reality converge.

Bai Wei (1894–1987) was the eldest daughter of an enlightened scholar who had participated in the 1911 revolution. The father's revolutionary zeal never benefited his daughter, however. She was forced into an arranged marriage; after countless beatings, starvation, and sexual abuse, she ran away and finally ended up studying in Japan, where she met the poet Yang Sao (1900–1957). Their stormy relationship over the next decade would bring Bai Wei endless humiliations and a venereal disease that almost cost her her life.

Bai Wei's ambivalent feelings toward her father and her lover constitute the two strains of her works. It was through her continued struggle against and compromise with these two male figures that she came to terms with the meanings of "woman" and "revolution." Her play, *Breaking out of the Ghost Tower* (*Dachu youlingta*, 1928), is saturated with elements of incest, rape, oppression, and murder, and ends with the father and the daughter shooting and killing each other. In many ways, this anticipates Cao Yu's more famous *Thunderstorm*. As if trying to outbalance the moribund obsession of *The Ghost Tower*, Bai Wei went on to write *Revolutionary God in Danger* (*Geming shen shounan*, 1928), in which a girl sets out to combat a monstrous general who has just crushed a revolution. Bai Wei frames her feminist idealism by dreaming of a revolution carried out by superwomen. Nevertheless, as its title suggests, at the center of the play is the endangered "Revolutionary God," and this God is also our heroine's father.

In 1928, Bai Wei published her first full-length novel, *The Bomb and the Expeditionary Bird*, about two sisters' failed pursuit of revolution and love under the Wuhan coalition regime. While its aesthetic merits remain debatable, the novel teaches us something neither Mao Dun nor Jiang Guangci seems to be concerned with. The two sisters appear to have contradictory personalities and take different paths to revolution, yet they end up with the same recognition that women play no further role in the revolution than that of sexual stimuli for revolutionary men. Then, in 1936, a seriously ill Bai Wei put forward a tell-all autobiographical novel, *My Tragic Life* (*Beiju shengya*), in which she detailed her painful relationship with Yang Sao. The novel stands out as poignant testimony to a woman's trials in literature, love, revolution, and disease.

With Ding Ling, Xie Bingying, and Bai Wei in mind, we now turn to this question: how "realistic" can a realist novel be in regard to the woman writer's search for a truthful representation of revolution and love? The lives and works of these women writers remind us of those of the female characters born under Mao Dun's and Jiang Guangci's pens. Whereas these male writers create an allegory of woman's desire and political commitment, however, their female counterparts substitute an exposé of female suffering and the failure to redeem that suffering through political commitment. The narrative that they present calls into question the realist repertoire concocted by their male colleagues, as it cuts into the nightmarish fears and fantasies shared by women, so haunting as to be denied by many as real. At the same time, their works laid bare subjects so raw as to offend the decorum of verisimilitude. Either way, their writings manifest a wide range of affective responses – from neurosis to catharsis, and from paranoia to euphoria – with regard to a gendered representation of Chinese reality.

Lyricizing China

Alongside all the realist campaigns in modern Chinese literature, there existed a parallel discourse of lyricism in poetry, prose, fiction, and theory. Traditional literary historians have downplayed this lyrical discourse, regarding it as either irrelevant to the "historical consciousness" of the time or secondary to the canon dominated by realism. Nevertheless, lyricism, as a generic attribute, an aesthetic vision, a lifestyle, and even a polemic platform, should be recognized as an important resource for Chinese literati and intellectuals in coping with reality and configuring an alternative modern vision.

Modern Chinese lyrical discourse may have found in Western (and, in select cases, Japanese) romanticism and humanism its models for such traits as evocative sensibility, individualized visions of natural and cultural worlds, and an epiphanic appreciation of the human condition. An equally important source is the classical Chinese dicta "poetry conveys one's intent" and "poetry generates one's feeling." Above all, modern Chinese lyricists are conscientious practitioners of language in re-presenting the world. Whereas realists see language as a transparent tool in reflecting reality, lyrical writers find in refined verbal forms immense possibilities beyond such mimetic endeavors.

In view of the incessant man-made atrocities and natural disasters that beset Republican China, lyricism tends to invite charges of self-indulgence and escapism. In the hands of a competent writer, however, it may entail a polemical dialogue with reality. Through linguistic orchestration, lyricism sanctions human capacity in lending an intelligible form to historical chaos and configuring an aesthetic and ethical order out of human contingencies. Lyricism thus defined, therefore, is as much a medium of cultural engagement as it is an evocative style. Outstanding examples can be found in the poetry of Bian Zhilin (1910–2000), He Qifang (1912–1977), and Feng Zhi (1905–1993); in the prose of Zhou Zuoren, Feng Zikai (1898–1975), and Zhu Ziqing (1898–1948); and in the fiction of Fei Ming (1901–1967), Shen Congwen, and Xiao Hong. On the theoretical front, Zhu Guangqian (1897–1986) and Zong Baihua (1879–1986) provide a framework for modern lyrical aesthetics.

Zhu Guangqian's works, such as *The Psychology of Tragedy* (*Beiju xinlixue*), *On Beauty* (*Tan mei*), *The Psychology of Art* (*Wenyi xinlixue*), and *On Poetry* (*Shilun*), all aim at casting an aestheticized eye upon the Chinese psyche. For Zhu, literature is central to humanity, setting in motion creative activity from which delight and pleasure arise. He rejects the utilitarian purpose of literature in favor of self-expression and imaginative autonomy. Zhu's theory shows the marked influence of Kant, Schopenhauer, and particularly Benedetto Croce. At the same time, he is keen on recapitulating the aesthetic vision conceived by the literati of the Six Dynasties, another tumultuous moment in Chinese history.

Zong Baihua received his advanced education in Germany. In many ways he takes up where Zhu Guangqian leaves off in elaborating on the aesthetic dimension of literary practice. Zong traveled extensively in Europe between 1920 and 1925, an experience that led him to conclude that Western culture is driven by dynamism and intellect. By contrast, he found in Chinese culture an orientation to the "rhythmic force of vitality" or *qiyun*, an aesthetic and behavioral concept traceable to the Six Dynasties. Zong's discovery is admittedly characteristic of the cultural conservatives of the time. He is distinctive, however, in that instead of praising traditional notions as such, he asks how Chinese literati could construct modern sensibilities by renewing the Chinese heritage of music, painting, and literature. Thus he entertains not so much nostalgia for the past as a cosmopolitan search for a "rhythm of life" and a "vision of the future" for the modern Chinese.

Liang Zongdai was a talented poet and translator, known particularly for his rendition of Rilke and Valéry. His most famous treatise is *Poetry and Truth* (*Shi yu zhen*), where he expresses passionately his thoughts on poetry as a "pure form" in light of both Western symbolism and the classical Chinese concept of spontaneous evocation (*xing*).

Modern Chinese lyricism found exuberant expression first in poetry. Among its early practitioners are Xu Zhimo, Wen Yiduo (both discussed above), and Zhu Xiang (1904–1933). Called by Lu Xun the "Keats of China," Zhu Xiang distinguished himself with poems with pristine imagery drawn from nature, concise language, and lingering melancholy. His most important work is *The Stone Gate* (*Shimen ji*, 1934), a volume with subjects ranging from musings on life and nature, and chronicles of the harshness of life and war, to poems dedicated to masters such as Homer, Dante, Rabelais, Auden, and Xu Zhimo. Zhu Xiang drowned himself in 1933.

In 1936, three students of Peking University, Bian Zhilin, He Qifang, and Li Guangtian (1906–1968), published a joint collection, *The Han Garden Collection* (*Hanyuan ji*), featuring some of the most original poems to appear on the eve of the Second Sino-Japanese War. Of the three, the most talented is Bian Zhilin. Inspired as much by Xu Zhimo, Wen Yiduo, and Shen Congwen as by T. S. Eliot and the French symbolists, Bian developed a keen sensibility in observing fleeting human and natural phenomena, which he tries to capture with intricate symbolism. In his early works such as *Scripts of Three Autumns* (*Sanqiucao*, 1933) and *Fish Eyes Collection* (*Yumuji*, 1935), Bian had already shown interest in the musical effect of his poems; through handling prosodic elements, such as the caesura and end-stopped lines, he renewed some of the salient features of classical poetry. Using distinctive imagery drawn from quotidian life, Bian is nevertheless inclined to explore the opaque, multiple layers of human feeling and thought, thereby inviting us to metaphysical contemplation. In "Fragment" (Duanzhang, 1933), for example, Bian writes,

> You are standing on a bridge enjoying the view;
> Someone is watching you from a balcony.
> The moon adorns your window;
> You adorn someone else's dream.

Simple as it is, the poem conveys an intricate shift of visual and interluctionary stances, thus projecting a circulatory relation of love, longing, and illusion. Above all, Bian's poem is tinged with a light melancholy reflection on the imperfection of humanity and its illusory nature.

He Qifang was a diligent student of various Chinese and Western masters, from T. S. Eliot to the late Tang poets Li Shangyin and Li He. His works of the 1930s vividly manifest his effort at bringing together sources of classicism, romanticism, symbolism, modernism, and Russian futurism. As a result, he produced a group of very fine poems using modern meters and subjects while adhering strongly to the sentiments and imagery characteristic of the traditional Chinese poetic repertoire. His fascination with the decadent aesthetics of the late Tang, as shown in select works of *Yuyan* (Prophesy, 1933), enables him to view the desolate existence of a modern Chinese youth in terms of a sensuous yet refined classical context, thus rendering the haunting beauty of the past in the present or vice versa. In 1936, He made his name with *Painted Dreams* (*Huameng lu*), a collection of essays interweaving personal fantasies, classical allusions, and modernist sensibilities into a sequence of subtly articulated essays.

Bian Zhilin, He Qifang, and Li Guangtian all took a leftist turn during the war, when the bitter experience of their exodus from Beijing to southwestern China and their encounters with the atrocities of the war compelled them to adopt a radical strategy. By contrast, Feng Zhi steadily developed his own poetic theory and poetry without regard to political intervention. Also trained at Peking University, Feng grew into a fine poet in the late 1920s, with collections such as *The Northern Journey* (*Beiyou*, 1929), which describes his years of apprenticeship as a poet and his awakening to decayed reality. The title poem, inspired by the Tang poet Du Fu's famous "Northern Journey" (Beizheng), observes a nation ravaged by turmoil. Given its subject, the poem shows incipient signs of Feng's tendency to metaphysical rumination. Feng spent the next five years in Germany. When he returned to China with a doctoral degree from the University of Heidelberg in 1936, he was ready to engage in more ambitious works.

Zang Kejia (1905–2004) and Ai Qing (1910–1996) were poets of the leftist camp, and both took up politics as their favorite subject. Their stress on war, revolution, and the plight of the peasants, however, did not keep them from experimenting with language and form, through which they usher their readers into a poetic beyond the immediate reflection of reality. In works such as "The Brand" (Laoyin, 1934), Zang demands, in raw and unmodulated tones, that his readers look at the predicament of rural China. Ai Qing published only one poetry collection, *Big Dike River* (*Dayan he*, 1936), before the outbreak of the Second Sino-Japanese War. The nine poems in this volume, written in prison between 1932 and 1935, express the poet's longing for his birthplace and intimate figures of bygone years as well as presenting reminiscences about his student days in France (1929–1932). Ai Qing's lifelong penchant for free verse was already strongly evident in these poems.

Shen Congwen is the most important figure to bridge the genres of lyrical poetry and lyrical fiction. Shen's first love was poetry, but the emotional demands of poetic creation were such that he had to take up a less challenging form, namely fiction, as an alternative. Still, he was tireless in experimenting with ways to inject into his narrative practice an element of poetry, which he believed is key to illuminating the "divine nature" of humanity.

Insofar as he invoked a stylized view of life, Shen Congwen is said to have followed in the steps of Fei Ming, a writer known for his idyllic imagination of Chinese rural life and his Daoist musings on the transient human condition. Shen's lyrical narrative is much more than a benign reworking of conventional pastoral themes and rhetoric, however. More often than not, his works deal with subjects that would not ordinarily be classified as lyrical: war, madness, brutal death, political folly, among others. In *Autobiography of Congwen* (*Congwen zizhuan*, 1933), for example, he relates how aboriginal rebels are beheaded by the thousands after the failure of their rebellions. In "Three Men and a Woman" (Sange nanren he yige nüren, 1930), a love triangle ends up in suicide and necrophilia; "Husband" (Zhangfu, 1930) tells how a peasant visits his wife, a prostitute in town, only to be spurned when she is too busy with other appointments on the night she has promised him; in "Sunset" (Huanghun, 1934), a group of innocent peasants are to be executed at supper time, amid the smell of braised pork on the executioner's stove. Even the novella *Border Town* is driven by suicide, accidental death, and inevitable loss, making its idyllic tone equivocal.

Let it not be misunderstood that Shen Congwen lyricizes human misery and injustice at the cost of social conscience. At the surface level, when a lyrical tone is applied to a scene of cannibalism, or when legal injustice and bloody punishment are integrated with casual daily routines like eating and sleeping, Shen's narrative is bound to drive us to question the moral consequences both of a political system that legitimizes brutality and of a literary mode, like lyricism, that is used to delineate brutality. This is where the charm (or horror) of Shen's art lies. In Shen's lyrical agenda, ugly things are neither erased nor reversed as a supplement of the real but only "displaced," as it were, from their roots to enact a dreamlike simulacrum. The most inhuman part of his story may be rendered in the most literal way, whereas the most insensible part may prove the most allegorical.

If one senses a strong irony here, it stems not so much from Shen Congwen's reversal of the cognitive hierarchy of referents in reality as from his exposure of the figurativeness of referentiality itself in presenting the real. In welding together incongruities of rhetorical form and subject matter, Shen merges man's immensely complex emotional capacity to cope with contradiction and in particular the built-in contradictions of any ideal moral/political order. Thus a discourse of lyricism enables him to emphasize the creative force of language and the freedom of human perception, while his sense of irony leads him to bracket, but not to do away with, any lyrical indulgence in life. Only when we recognize how Shen allows both narrative modes to illuminate each other, while putting one another "under erasure," as conventional critics would have it, do we appreciate that, in a most subtle way, his art expresses the humanism of the May Fourth Movement.

Xiao Hong's best works, such as *The Field of Life and Death*, show a similar approach to lyricizing reality. This novel, related in an episodic manner, presents a feminine view of rural life in Manchuria, where a constant round of pregnancy, abuse, backbreaking routines of workaday life, war, and death form woman's cyclical destiny. Xiao Hong weaves sensory images from natural and human phenomena into a narrative fabric, rendering a discordant harmony among them. As a result, however undesirable life is in her homeland, she moves readers by calling forth an imaginary nostalgia.

In deceptively innocent tones, Xiao Hong tells us about the ostracism of an underprivileged student at school ("Hands" (Shou), 1936) and the hasty execution of a deserter in the army ("On the Oxcart" (Niuche shang), 1936). Xiao Hong does not erect a symbolic system around the factual subjects alone; she builds instead associative relations between the subjects and subsidiary empirical and emotional indices, between what exists and what does not. There is an essential simultaneity embedded in her poetic vision of the world, demanding that her reader take multiple perspectives that weave together all sensory impressions.

For Shen Congwen, as for Xiao Hong, an arguable "reality" does not represent itself; it is represented. By describing Chinese reality using the lyrical mode, these two authors call into question the privileged position of realism in representing the world, as well as redrawing the conventional boundaries of lyricism. Emphasis on language and poetic expression is also a confirmation of a writer's choice in "figuring" the world. At its most extreme, their view of text and world dissolves the distinction between realism and lyricism, between prose and poetry, and asserts the fundamentally figurative – that is to say, poetic – nature of all language.

The informal essay represents an attempt to craft a new genre in the post-May Fourth era. In contrast to the tendentious nature of expository prose, writers of the familiar essay adopt a relatively casual style to register everyday life experience, local color and social manners, and the impact of modernity on Chinese reality. The modern Chinese familiar essay is often shown to have evolved under the influence of its British counterpart, but one can discern a linkage between late Ming sketches and casual writings (*xiaopin wen*) and the familiar essay of the modern period.

In contrast to the "miscellaneous essay" (*zawen*), a prose form charged with bombastic rhetoric and the treatment of volatile subjects, the familiar essay has been seen in a disparaging light for its allegedly noncommittal tenor. Not until recent years have we come to understand that rather than manifesting cultural conservatism, the familiar essay may imply a dynamic element in the formation of modern Chinese culture, an element that lies at or beyond the edges of the revolution-centered canon.

The most accomplished familiar essayist at this time is Zhou Zuoren, the brother of Lu Xun. Like Lu Xun, he too spent years studying in Japan (from 1906 to 1911) and showed a wide range of interests in literature, cultural criticism, mythology, and Japanese affairs. Although a strong supporter of the May Fourth campaign, Zhou is at odds with many of his fellow reformists who favor revolution and nationalism. Instead, he seeks to envisage an alternative modernity, one based on individualism, a refined sensibility for local culture, and the connection between Chinese life and a broadly defined Oriental heritage.

Zhou Zuoren puts into practice his cultural and political convictions in the form of the familiar essay. This seemingly effortless, occasional, and personal prose form serves to illuminate his search for a space of one's own. In his early years, Zhou wrote about the need for language reform and the use of the vernacular; he also advocated what he termed a "humane" literature and praised the realism of Western writers. As time went on, Zhou became increasingly engaged in depicting local color, childhood experiences, and leisurely distractions ranging from snacks to casual walks. The titles of his essay collections of the 1920s and 1930s, such as *A Garden of One's Own* (*Ziji de yuandi*), *Mellons and Beans* (*Guadou ji*), *Bitter Tea* (*Kuchaji*), *Looking at Clouds* (*Kanyunji*), *Books for a Rainy Day* (*Yutian deshu*), suggest his philosophy of writing. Through his literary and aesthetic practice as an essayist, Zhou constructs a unique version of Chinese citizenship, affirming the individual's importance in opposition to the normative nationalist project. Perhaps for this reason, he chose to collaborate with the Japanese puppet government when the Second Sino-Japanese War broke out, a treasonous act by patriotic standards. He was sentenced to jail after the war and his works were banned in both mainland China and Taiwan for many years.

Other well-known essayists include Lin Yutang, Feng Zikai, Zhu Ziqing, Shen Congwen, and Lu Xun. Born into a Christian family, Lin Yutang went to mission schools in China and was later educated in America and Europe. A connoisseur with a taste for the leisurely life and consmopolitan worldview, Lin is best known for introducing "humor" to Chinese literature and culture – in fact, the modern Chinese neologism *youmo* was first coined by him. Lin founded three magazines in the mid-1930s, *Analects*, *Human World*, and *Cosmic Wind*, featuring a style strongly suggestive of late Ming leisurely prose. At a time of impending national crisis, the popularity of Lin Yutang and his magazines predictably elicited heated debate about the politics of literature.

Feng Zikai was a gifted artist-cum-essayist who emerged in the 1930s. Much of his writing and painting was rooted in a philosophy of self-expression and compassion. A devout Buddhist, Feng is a close observer of nature and children, yet he is also a romantic often identified with the increasingly politicized intelligentsia. Zhu Ziqing won national acclaim for writings such as "Lotus Pond by Moonlight" (*Hetang yuese*) and "A View of My Father's Back" (*Beiying*). His writings touch on common issues in the ethical and aesthetic domains – familial ties, epiphanies occasioned by natural beauty, and so on – in a meditative and understated style. Both Feng Zikai and Zhu Ziqing are associated with the White Horse Lake Group (*Baimahu pai*), a literary clique brought together by Xia Mianzun (1886–1946) in the 1920s. Their shared goal was to convey through essay writing and reading the need for self-cultivation and education.

Finally, attention is due Lu Xun in this genre. Whereas his miscellaneous essays show biting sarcasm and an aggressive posture, Lu Xun's familiar essays betoken a tenderhearted writer ever fascinated with his own inner darkness, a domain haunted by funeral rites, graves, executions, ghosts, demons, and the death wish. Lu Xun's ghostly obsession finds its starkest manifestation in *Wild Grass* (*Yecao*, 1927), a prose–poetry collection filled with surreal settings, nightmarish encounters, and "lost souls," as well as in *Morning Flowers Plucked at Sunset* (*Zhaohua xishi*, 1927), a collection of essays permeated with his memories of the ghostly ambiance – family deaths, haunted gardens, exorcism rituals, gothic theaters – in which he grew up. Both works render an impression of Lu Xun living life in retrospect, as if only through the perspective of hindsight could he define his existence. Thus, beyond his premonition of ideological and epistemological exclusion for the unreal and the irrational, there always lurks in Lu Xun's work an ambivalent desire to embrace what he denounces and to transgress what he confirms.

The modernists in Shanghai, Beijing, and elsewhere

In 1926, a young Taiwanese named Liu Na'ou (1900–1940) came to Shanghai to study French at Aurora University. There he made the acquaintance of his classmates Shi Zhecun (1905–2003) and Dai Wangshu (1905–1950). These young men shared an interest in avant-garde literature and art, particularly French modernism and Japanese neo-sensationalism. With their support, Liu put out a magazine, *Trackless Train* (*Wugui lieche*, 1928), featuring modernist fiction by such writers as Yokomitsu Rîchi, Kawabata Yasunari, and Paul Morand. *Trackless Train* was soon shut down by the Nationalist censors, and the friends went on to start a second magazine, *La Nouvelle Littérature* (*Xin wenyi*, 1929–30), which included fiction by Liu and Shi, translations of modernist poetry by Dai, and stories by the young writer Mu Shiying (1912–1940). Mu soon joined the circle and became its most prominent member.

These young modernists described their style as neo-sensationalist, a term derived from the Japanese Neo-Sensationalist School (Shinkankakuha). Their aim was to forge a new language so provocative as to arouse the reader's sensibilities as if he had never experienced the words before. Their works, mostly short stories, are characterized by a fragmentary structure, fleeting temporal sequence, vignettes of chance encounters and romantic intrigues, and motifs drawn from the urban material culture of arcades, cafes, and fashion, and the theatre, the racecourse, and the dance hall. The influence of cinema is most salient. Sensations, images, and actions are all incorporated into a fast sequence of cuts and juxtapositions – a textual montage. Underneath their slick style, however, these writers convey a mixture of excitement and melancholy, haunted by the "historical disquiet" of 1930s China.

The appearance of the neo-sensationalist school (Xin ganjue pai) marked the arrival of the first wave of Chinese modernism. Before this, there had already been attempts at a modernist style, as seen in Li Jinfa's poems, Lu Xun's essays in *Wild Grass*, and Tao Jingsun's and Ye Lingfeng's (1905–1975) stories on decadent subjects. But it was the neo-sensationalists who created the signature style and theoretical tenor that define Chinese modernism. Neo-sensationalists depict dangerous liaisons and libertine romances in such a way as to implicate a society deeply devoted to the twin sports of desiring and being desired. Eroticism is an important ingredient in such works, but it is not necessarily generated by sensual episodes or sexually explicit descriptions. For all their apparent interest in nonchalant prurience, these works communicate something else: frenzy in quest of bodily satisfaction; fatigue with quotidian existence, glamorous or not; and an unfathomable thirst for anomaly that transcends ordinary sensuality.

In Liu Na'ou's "Two People Impervious to Time" (Liangge shijian buganzhengzhe, 1929), two dandies encounter a seductive woman at the Shanghai racetrack, and spend the rest of the day falling in and out of love. In Mu Shiying's "Five in a Club" (Yezonghuili de wugeren, 1933), five characters from different walks of life run into each other in a nightclub, where their nocturnal revelry turns into a *danse macabre*, the prelude to a suicidal incident. Shi Zhecun, the most learned of the neo-sensationalists, offers a psychologized view of urban life as a panoply of perversions, hallucinations, and grotesqueries. In "One Evening in the Rainy Season" (Meiyu zhiqi, 1929), a married man meets a mysterious woman on a rainy evening and experiences a sequence of fantasies about an extramarital encounter, a guilty conscience, and fatal threats. In "Magic Track" (Modao, 1933), a man's train ride from Shanghai to Suzhou becomes a journey bewitched by sexual fantasy and horror; "At the Paris Theater" (Zai Bali daxiyuan, 1933) narrates how a young couple's date at the movies deteriorates into a sadomasochistic show full of neurotic quirks.

The city of Shanghai plays a crucial role in sketching out the drama of desire. This is a semicolonial city where hundreds of adventurers and dandies, *flâneurs*, and femme fatales revel in the sport of love. Indeed, with her ever-changing faces, Shanghai can be said to play a ubiquitous character in the neo-sensationalist world, mysterious, seductive, and dangerous. Shanghai becomes the touchstone through which the novel's intelligibility is verified, and this "effect of the real" is nowhere more evident than in the radical circulation of values and desires in the city. In Mu Shiying's famous words, "Shanghai is Heaven built on Hell."

In 1932, Shi Zhezun, Du Heng (1906–1964), and other friends founded the literary magazine *Les Contemporains* (*Xiandai*), which published translations of symbolists, imagists, and modernists from Rémy de Gourmont, Mallarmé, Paul Fort, and Appollinaire to W. B. Yeats, T. S. Eliot, and Ezra Pound. Before it folded in 1935, *Les Contemporains* was the main forum for avant-garde works by a diverse group of poets including Dai Wangshu, Ai Qing, Lin Geng (1910–2006), He Qifang, and Lu Yishi (later known as Ji Xian, 1913–).

Dai Wangshu came to know Liu Na'ou and other neo-sensationalist members while studying at Aurora University. His poetry was influenced by the French symbolists Baudelaire and Verlaine. In 1929, he published his first collection, *My Memories* (*Wode jiyi*), in which "The Rainy Alley" (Yuxiang, 1927) quickly became Dai's signature work. This poem, about the poet's mystical encounter with a girl in a rainy alley, delivers a delicate fusion of hypnotic mood and musical rhythm. Dai continued his experimentation in the 1930s, drawing inspiration from poets like Maeterlinck and François Jammes. In his second collection, *Wangshu's Drafts* (*Wangshu cao*, 1933), Dai creates dreamlike images and fanciful landscapes without losing sight of their realistic associations. The poem "Country Girl" (Cungu), for example, represents for many a fine attempt to bridge the imaginary and real-life worlds. As a whole, the romantic melancholy that marks Dai's early works gives way to an increasingly restless immersion in confusion and delirium. Synesthesia, juxtaposed rhyme schemes, and imagery flaunt the disturbed state of this poetic vision. During the 1940s, Dai's style would undergo a remarkable change as he sought more determinedly for a voice that intervenes with the Chinese reality.

It should be noted that neo-sensationalism thrived at a time when China was beleaguered by mounting crises arising from natural disasters and Japanese aggression. Shanghai was not only a paradise for the modernists but also an incubator for the revolutionaries. Some neo-sensationalists welcomed leftist thought as the newest ideological products, although their indifferent attitude was a far cry from the leftist writers' commitment to a literature of "tears and blood." The interaction between the modernists and the leftists resulted in some of the most dynamic dialogues in modern Chinese literature. The debate over the "Shanghai style" (*haipai*) is one of these moments.

"Shanghai style" had been used since the turn of the century as a pejorative description of the flashy style of theater, painting, and fashion in Shanghai; it became a semiofficial literary term when Shen Congwen adopted it in a polemical essay in *Dagongbao* in 1933. A self-proclaimed "country man" then living in Beijing, Shen was critical of the "city slickers" of Shanghai who did not take literature seriously but rather treated it as a plaything. Shen's attack was rebutted by Su Wen, a regular contributor to *Les Contemporains*. Su Wen sneered at the self-righteous elitism and conservative ideology of Shen and his peers. The quarrel soon developed into one about the geopolitics and geopoetics of Shanghai-based and Beijing-based writers.

His contemptuous critique notwithstanding, Shen Congwen did spell out the distinctive qualities of Shanghai-style writing. The Shanghai School comprises writers who assume postures ranging from the newly imported *flâneur* to the old-style literatus, and features a hybrid of trends as far apart as Mandarin Ducks and Butterflies fiction and neo-impressionist sketches. Genealogically, the Shanghai style can be traced back to the late nineteenth century, when the depravity-fiction writer Han Bangqing composed *Singsong Girls of Shanghai*, to the 1910s, when the Mandarin Ducks and Butterflies writer Zhu Shouju composed *Tides of Shanghai*, and to the 1920s, when Zhang Ziping and Ye Lingfeng composed sentimental romantic fiction. Arising from and nourished by a commercial culture, the Shanghai style is flamboyant and mercurial, with dilettantism and frivolity as its trademark. Yet beneath the flashy surface lies the writers' quivering desire to catch up with time. Tear down the façade of the text, and one finds a desolate city overshadowed by the menacing power of modernization.

The neo-impressionist works of writers like Shi Zhecun, Liu Na'ou, and Mu Shiying have won increasing attention in recent years for their patently modernist sensibility. Eileen Chang (1920–1995), the precocious young writer of wartime Shanghai, was the first to appreciate the modernity of decadent aesthetics in works ranging from *Singsong Girls* to those of the neo-sensationalists and put this aesthetics into practice during the Japanese occupation, while her fondness for Western middle-brow romantic literature further enriched her secular vision of Shanghai. Chang would become the finest interpreter of the *fin de siècle* cult of Shanghai-style fiction in the 1940s, as it blossomed in the shadow of Japanese attack and Communist revolution.

Compared with Shanghai, Beijing seems a less likely site for generating modernist works since, as the capital for more than six dynasties, it had long been associated with traditional legacies. In view of the fact that Beijing was the launching ground of late Qing reforms and the May Fourth Movement, however, modernity and modernism did leave imprints on this ancient city. Unlike Shanghai, which actively embraced colonial and urban elements imported from the West, the prevailing ethos of Beijing was characterized by a tension between acceptance of and resistance to modern lifestyles and thought. Indeed, oscillating between tradition and modernity, China and the West, the country and the city, the old and the new, the zeitgeist of Republican Beijing became an unusual combination of provincialism and cosmopolitanism, traditionalism and modernism. Here was an alternative experience of modernity.

Take the writers of the Beijing School. Like the Shanghai School, the Beijing School was a loosely defined literary group, including writers as different in style as Ba Jin, Bian Zhilin, Lao She, Lin Huiyin, Lin Yutang, Ling Shuhua, Shen Congwen, Zhou Zuoren, Xiao Qian (1910–1999), and Lin Geng. Most of them, however, were not Beijing natives but new residents who had discovered a spiritual affinity with the city. If the Shanghai School was known for its flamboyance and cosmopolitanism, the Beijing School impressed with its adherence to Anglo-American humanism, decorum of literary expression, and urbane sensibility. But for its avant-garde members informed by Western modernists from Baudelaire to Mallarmé, from T. S. Eliot to I. A. Richards (who taught at Peking Univeristy from 1929 to 1930), the ancient city may as well be a Chinese counterpart to the "Waste Land," a locale symbolizing the cultural desolation and historical disorientation of modern China. Beneath the genteel mannerisms of the writers of the Beijing School lurked existential musings on the fate of individual talents vis-à-vis darkening historical forces. Hence Lin Geng's "Night" (Ye, 1933): "Night walks into the land of loneliness / Thus, tears are like wine."

The Beijing School had roots in the Anglo-American humanism that informed post-May Fourth literati culture, but it did not become an institutional force until the early 1930s in media such as the literary supplement of the *Dagongbao* (1933), and the magazines *Literature Quarterly* (*Wenxue jikan*, 1934), *Literature Monthly* (*Wenxue yuekan*, 1936), and *Literature* (*Wenxue*, 1937). At first glance, the writings of the Beijing School come closer to the realism and lyricism discussed above in the sentiments and thematic concerns they express. Yet there existed in select writers a desire not to take either a realist or a lyrical style for granted; instead they focused on striking a note resonant only with the modernist cadence. Lin Huiyin is a case in point. Nicknamed by friends "the most intelligent woman in modern China," Lin Huiyin received solid education both in China and overseas, and became a prominent poet, novelist, essayist, dramatist, and salon hostess, and the founder of architecture as an academic discipline in modern China. To general readers, she is best remembered as the muse of Xu Zhimo, their amorous relationship being one of the most talked-about romances in early modern China.

Perhaps because of her commitment to modern architecture, Lin tends to lend a spatial interpretation to any given subject. In "Spring Scene in the

Ancient City" (Gucheng chunjing, 1937), the poet overlooks Beijing and its environs from the top of the old city wall set off against remote horizons. She juxtaposes colors, images, and even smells from near and far to forge an architectonics of sensations as a way of figuring or embodying a city that is trapped between ancient and modern. In her story "In the Heat of 99 Degrees Fahrenheit" (Jiushijiu du zhong, 1934), she slices the daily life of Beijing into pieces and rearranges them to form a crisscrossing pattern of kaleidoscopic shots. From a rich lady's party to a street vendor's road-side business, and from a rickshaw puller's run through the city to a young woman's romantic dilemma, Lin's story is a dynamic montage of life in Beijing.

The 1930s also saw a small group of literati in Taiwan engaged in modernist experimentation. Japanese influences had penetrated every level of Taiwanese life over thirty years of Japanese occupation; elite youth found it fashionable to emulate the "Tokyo modern" and new European trends coming in via Japanese mediation. Since Taiwan was both a colony and an island, its modernist sensibilities were inevitably determined by a hybrid manifestation of Japanese colonial hegemony, Chinese cultural heritage, and indigenous self-expression.

Yang Chichang (1908–1994) was introduced to surrealism in Japan, where he went to study in 1932. Upon his return to Taiwan, he organized the Windmill Poetry Club (Fengche shishe) and initiated the first wave of modernist poetry on the island. Yang's "Tainan Qui Dort" (Huihuai de chengshi, 1933) is a poem in Japanese about the decaying ancient city of Tainan, wrought with imagery suggestive of a nightmarish experience of death and putrefaction. In a way, surrealism may have lent Yang an obscure but effective channel to express the *ressentiment* and nihilism shared by many Taiwanese youths under colonial rule. Long Yingzong (1910–1999), another Taiwanese writer, was influenced by Japanese neo-sensationalism as well as by Western *fin de siècle* decadent aesthetics. In 1937, he won a literary prize in Japan for his short story in Japanese, "A Town with Papaya Trees" (Zhiyou muguashu de xiaozhen). The story chronicles an idealistic young man's degeneration in a town enshrouded by desolation and boredom. Mixing exoticism and naturalism, Long vividly conveys the spiritual loss and self-alienation of a whole generation of Taiwanese intellectuals living under colonial rule.

In 1936, the Taiwanese musician-cum-poet Jiang Wenye (1910–1983) made his first visit to Beijing and Shanghai. Born in Taiwan and briefly educated in Xiamen, China, Jiang moved to Japan at the age of thirteen; there he found his life's passion in music. By the early 1930s, he had become a promising modernist composer, his models including Ravel, Bartók, and Stravinsky. The 1936 trip, however, changed Jiang's life for good. He was so overwhelmed by the civilization of Beijing that he moved to the ancient city in 1938 and spent the rest of his life there. In addition to music, Jiang composed a number of poetry cycles, such as *Inscriptions of Beijing* (*Bejing ming*, 1942) and *Fu on the Celestial Shrine* (*Fu tiantan*, 1944), in Japanese and Chinese respectively. In these poems, Jiang conveys his immersion in Beijing culture by means of synesthesia and fanciful meditations drawn from French symbolism, while the way in which he modulates between stylistic precision and evasiveness reminds one of Japanese *haiku*. A cosmopolitan, Jiang found in Chinese civilization an awakening to an aestheticized state of nirvana.

IV. Translation, print culture, and literary societies

Translation of Western literatures and discourses
By Jing Tsu

The eclectic nature of fiction and other texts from Western sources that were translated into Chinese in the nineteenth and early twentieth centuries has captured scholarly attention over the past twenty years. This renewed interest is part of an effort to push back the beginnings of modern Chinese literature to a period that has been largely suppressed in its historiography. In the process, however, the array of materials, literary and otherwise, especially from the late Qing period (1880s–1910s), has emerged as a fascinating object of study in its own right. The rediscovery of the different strata of literary production – ranging from popular to elite, missionary to indigenous, and commercial to amateur – prompts one not only to revise the traditional conception of literary formation in the early decades of the twentieth century but also to enlarge the scope of literary studies in order to evaluate the important role of translation in intellectual and cultural history.

Although the process of translation and cultural assimilation has its precedents in the translation of Buddhist scriptures from Sanskrit, the nineteenth and twentieth centuries witnessed something quite different. Most of the materials coming from foreign sources during this period were translated with expediency and involved creative reinterpretations. The influx of Western missionaries and foreigners, later coupled with increasing numbers of commercially motivated writers and a novelty-seeking urban readership, fostered new conditions for experimentation. Scholars have estimated that between 1840 and 1911, 48 percent of all fiction produced was translated from other languages. Though this figure is lower than previously assumed, the majority of these texts were produced after the First Sino-Japanese War of 1894–1895 and before the May Fourth Movement of 1919, particularly between 1902 and 1908.

This periodization, however, gives a limited idea of what was in fact a longer continuum of intercultural transaction at the hands of different agents and representatives. Already in the Ming dynasty, translations by Western missionaries were among the first important exchanges with Europe. Ambitious to spread religious doctrine, the Jesuits quickly learned to use the medium of the science treatise, which was of greater interest to the Chinese. During their two hundred years in China, the Jesuit order introduced 437 works in translation; more than half were religious in nature and 30 percent were related to science. Headed by such figures as Matteo Ricci, Johann Adam Schall von Bell, Nicholas Trigault, and Ferdinand Verbiest, and assisted by native-speaking collaborators, the missionaries targeted the imperial court as their primary audience. They used Western knowledge and some literary texts, such as Trigault's translation of *Aesop's Fables*, as tokens of exchange in establishing initial cultural contact. Yet their reach was limited. For instance, anatomy as a branch of Western science was introduced in the late Ming and early Qing by Johann Terrenz Schreck and Verbiest, but had to wait for the 1851 publication of Benjamin Hobson's *A Treatise on Physiology* (*Quanti xinlun*) in Guangdong to attract wider attention.

The growing urgency of national salvation and the interest of an urban readership made all the difference in the next and most important wave of translation in modern China. The rise to military and colonial dominance by the Western powers in the nineteenth century and China's subsequent turn to Western learning as the necessary means of survival in the modern world brought about a sea of uneven change. Between the Opium Wars and the First Sino-Japanese War, interest in Western science and technological knowledge soared. Considered the secret to power in the modern world, Western learning – referred to as "sound, optics, chemistry, electricity" (*sheng guang hua dian*) – dominated the focus of translation bureaus in Guangzhou, Fuzhou, and Shanghai.

Collaborations, institutions of knowledge, and Western and Chinese translators

One institution of particular significance was the translation bureau, founded in 1867, that was attached to the Jiangnan Arsenal in Shanghai. Under the supervision of the English entrepreneur and educator John Fryer, this bureau produced, in addition to textbooks, a larger body of translations of technical and scientific treatises than any other institution of comparable size. The bureau's publications account for about half of the 660 translations of texts of Western learning from this period, and cover a wide range of subjects, including astronomy, geography, mathematics, medicine, chemistry, electricity, military technology, geology, explosives, medical jurisprudence, metallurgy, and economics. Fryer alone translated more than half of the Arsenal's total output. He was also responsible for the publication of the *Scientific and Industrial Magazine* (*Gezhi huibian*), which, it was hoped, would be to the Chinese what *Scientific American* was to the anglophone world. Reaching a broader readership than previous missionary journals, the *Scientific and Industrial Magazine* introduced and explained subjects like the mechanics of photography, steam engines, and diving-gear science for general and specialized audiences alike. To enhance the magazine's popular appeal, one author tried to explain the halo around the head of Christ as a function of optics. The enthusiasm for the journal can be readily seen in its "Question and Answer" section, which addressed comments from inquisitive Chinese readers who were experimenting with the described techniques at home.

The process of translation cut both ways. The need to adapt the intended message to the conditions of the host language resulted in the transformation of both. Most scholars agree that the process of translation gave rise to new rules of linguistic encounter out of a dialogic necessity. As the brokers of cultural exchange, native informants or collaborators exercised a certain amount of influence as they advised their Western counterparts, sometimes even altering the intended meaning of the text. Protestant missionaries led the way in the mid-nineteenth century with collaborative translations of legal texts, scientific treatises, and novels. Henry Wheaton's *Elements of International Law* (1836), translated by the American missionary W. A. P. Martin in 1864 as *The Public Laws of Myriad Nations* (*Wanguo gongfa*), is one example of the battle not only of words but also of worldviews.

Though the translation process placed greater emphasis on the missionary's initiative, the Chinese informant had the linguistic advantage of being able to exercise discretion in adapting the text into terms more familiar and acceptable to his fellow Chinese. A notable exception to this general practice is the translation of the Bible, which mobilized teams of missionaries, with their Chinese assistants, and resulted in no fewer than five complete translations between the 1820s and 1860s. The tension between the two opposing agendas of translating a text into accessible terms for wider dissemination and preserving the word of God caused severe rifts between the London Missionary

Society and other societies. Henry Medhurst's translation, according to Patrick Hanan, became the object of virulent attacks by fellow missionaries, who saw its use of idiomatic Chinese phraseology as "a profusion of barbarisms" that pandered to the taste of heathens. At the center of the debate was how to translate "God." Whereas Medhurst used *shangdi* (supreme deity), a concept of divinity already familiar to the Chinese, an earlier and less assimilated version preferred the character *shen* (divine spirit) in order to deny that the Chinese had any original access to the knowledge of God prior to the advent of Christianity.

Though the 1870s have been customarily viewed as China's first exposure to foreign fiction on a wide scale, as early as 1819 Western missionaries had recognized the utility of translated fiction in establishing a trusted presence. They translated Western fiction into vernacular Chinese with the assistance of Chinese collaborators. Texts were translated into provincial dialects as well as Mandarin. These early attempts at propagating particular worldviews through translation set a precedent for fiction's ideological use in the later activities carried out by the Chinese themselves. By the time Liang Qichao propagated the importance of fiction and translation in two of his seminal essays, "Preface to the Translation and Publication of Political Novels" (1898) and "On the Relationship between Fiction and Ruling the Public" (1902), the idea was neither wholly novel nor revolutionary. Nationalistic fervor, however, gave it a new impetus.

Even novels that first appeared in Chinese translation in the 1870s, notably in the Shanghai newspaper *Shenbao*, marked a subsequent, rather than the initial, phase in translating foreign fiction. Between May 21 and June 15, 1872, partial Chinese versions of Jonathan Swift's *Gulliver's Travels,* Washington Irving's *The Sketchbook of Geoffrey Crayon, Gent*, and Frederick Marryat's *The Pacha of Many Tales* appeared in literary Chinese. In contrast, the first translated novel of general interest, *Xinxi xiantan* (Edward Bulwer-Lytton's *Night and Morning*), serialized from 1873 to 1875, was rendered in the vernacular.

Using the novel, or fictional narrative, to entertain, educate, and reform the Chinese populace served the purposes of proselytization, as it later did the awakening of national consciousness. Fryer held an essay contest on the advantages and disadvantages of China's intercourse with the West in 1867, when he was editor of a Chinese newspaper founded by the British-owned *North China Herald*. The "new-novel" contest he advertised in 1895, in the well-circulated Chinese-language missionary journal *Review of the Times* (*Wanguo gongbao*), likely inspired subsequent calls for new fiction, including those made by Liang Qichao, who was an avid reader of the newspaper as well as of Fryer's translations of science treatises.

Realizing the broad appeal of fiction, Protestant missionaries like William Milne (1785–1822), Karl Gützlaff (1830–1851), James Legge (1815–1897), and Griffith John (1831–1912) even attempted to write their own original narratives. The most notable missionary-translated novels are William Burns's much truncated version of John Bunyan's *The Pilgrim's Progress* (*Tianlu licheng*), which eventually appeared in complete form over a period of thirteen years, and Edward Bellamy's *Looking Backward, 2000–1887* (*Huitou kan jilue*), rendered into literary Chinese by Timothy Richard and his Chinese assistant in 1888 and then serialized in *Review of the Times*. Republished in 1894 under the title *Asleep for a Hundred Years* (*Bainian yijiao*), the book made an indelible imprint on the leading reformer Kang Youwei, who wrote the utopian social treatise *Great Harmony*, as well as on his student Liang Qichao. Liang's first attempt at fiction writing, *The Future of New China*, his unfinished futuristic novel of 1902, paved the way for the emergence of utopian and science fantasy fiction in the twentieth century.

The works of influential Chinese intellectuals and reformers drew on a wide array of Japanese, Western, and Chinese literary and philosophical sources. Japan was deemed by many to offer a more expedient model for westernization because of its success with rapid modernization. The task of translation was made more efficient, though not necessarily more faithful to the original, if one took advantage of the easily recognized *kanji* – Chinese loanwords – as opposed to having to acquire proficiency in a Western language and an unfamiliar script. However heatedly contested at times, the cultural and racial affinity between Japan and China also meant that their respective encounters with westernization were, in some ways, a shared dilemma. Liang Qichao, in particular, was heavily influenced by Japanese thinkers and writers, such as Inoue Enryō, Yano Ryūkei, Shiba Shirō, and Suehiro Tetchō. Many of their works were translated and published in *New Fiction* (*Xin xiaoshuo*), a seminal journal Liang founded in 1902.

As increasing numbers of Chinese took government-sponsored opportunities to study abroad in Europe, Japan, and America in the late nineteenth century, the study of foreign languages allowed more direct access to the source texts, or at least through a less embellished English or Japanese translation. Prior to the First Sino-Japanese War, interest in Western learning had mainly focused on translations of technical and scientific knowledge; after China's humiliating defeat, intellectuals and political reformers felt an even more profound sense of crisis in which they became concerned with China's spiritual decline in addition to her technical backwardness. This critical period produced a number of new translators, whose works and varied approaches had a huge impact on a new generation of modern writers and intellectuals.

Yan Fu, Lin Shu, and the late Qing literary scene

Often named as the first figure to introduce and systematically translate Western thought into Chinese, Yan Fu, a graduate of the Fuzhou Naval Yard program, went to study in England in 1877 and returned in 1879 with a poignant sense of the urgent need to reverse China's decline. To introduce works that underpinned the contemporary current of change in Western thought, he made critical translations of works such as Thomas Henry Huxley's *Evolution and Ethics*, Adam Smith's *An Inquiry into the Nature and Causes of the Wealth of Nations*, Montesquieu's *The Spirit of Laws*, John Stuart Mill's *A System of Logic* and *On Liberty*, Herbert Spencer's *The Study of Sociology*, and William Stanley Jevons's *Elementary Lessons in Logic*. Though relatively small in volume, Yan Fu's translations were difficult in style. The carefully chosen texts were, as he stated, intended not for the uneducated layman but for men of letters. Of the four dominant styles of prose practiced in the late nineteenth century – parallel prose (*piantiwen*), vernacular, the eight-part style, and the Tongcheng ancient style – he chose the last, insisting on an adherence to classical Chinese thought and writing as a way of assimilating foreign texts. Unlike many others, he did not take from readily available Japanese loanwords or the provisional terms previously used in missionary translations. Instead, he painstakingly revived original terminology from ancient classical texts, some of which were unfamiliar and impenetrable even to his most learned contemporaries. As a testament to his meticulous though arcane approach, he confessed in a letter to Liang Qichao to having spent almost three years brooding over how to translate the Western political concept behind the word "right."

Though scholars have often debated the merits of his difficult style, Yan's translation of social Darwinism offered a compelling theory of a universal scheme of progress and the survival of the fittest. Evolutionism took firm root as the dominant persuasion in the context of China's struggle for national survival.

In terms of having the greatest impact on translation activities in the late Qing, Yan Fu was matched only by Lin Shu. Unlike Yan, Lin never traveled abroad or acquired any foreign-language skills. That, however, did not deter him from collaborating with several Chinese co-translators in producing, astonishingly, more than 180 translations of Western literature over a period of about twenty years. Lin's selection of texts demonstrated an unusual range of interests, reflecting tastes both high and low, historical and romantic. As stated in the prefaces to several of his translations, Lin Shu saw his calling ultimately as "aiding the process of loving the nation and preserving the race," an imperative that had first inspired him to pursue the task of translation. Highlighting and even extending passages that he found relevant to China's predicament, Lin Shu would alter and supplement the original text whenever he thought fit to extrapolate a moral lesson, and especially when he could express indignation at the exploitation of the weaker by the stronger nations.

Like Yan Fu, Lin was committed to the use of terse classical Chinese prose in order to appeal to learned literary sensibilities. He took liberties with the Tongcheng style, however, often mixing in neologisms as well as Western grammar and syntax, and sometimes altering the narrative techniques of the original to suit more traditional Chinese tastes and expectations. In particular, he felt that religious messages or passages that failed to respect the proper Confucian strictures placed on male–female relationships had to be altered. The phrase "Peace on earth, good will to men" in *Uncle Tom's Cabin*, for example, was rendered as "the *qi* of Dao," while "that kingdom which God will set up" became "world union" (*shijie datong*), echoing Kang Youwei's widely influential book the *Great Harmony*.

In general, however, editorial choice in late Qing translations did not always follow a logical process that had the sanctity of the original text in mind. Depending on the input and style of the assistant translators involved, places and characters were usually changed to Chinese settings and surnames in order not to overtax the reader's mind; authors' names and the original titles were often sinicized or transliterated. Often the Chinese rendition bore little resemblance to the original. The lack of standardized guidelines in the general practice of translation in the late Qing also led to a certain amount of confusion, as some texts were translated many times without the translators necessarily being aware of one another's work. For a number of years, for instance, Beecher and Stowe were thought to be two different people, despite Lin Shu's famed 1905 translation of *Uncle Tom's Cabin*.

Advertisements, exotic associations, author brand names, and clever packaging became common practice with the commercialization of fiction. These marketing strategies helped to shape readers' appetites for foreign literature. Literary consumption became much less tied to elite tastes and merged instead with the contemporary urban landscape. That works by Western writers considered second- or third-rate in their own countries were published widely in China during the late Qing craze for translating foreign literature points to a particularity not easily resolved by applying the simple criterion of literary merit. Indeed, the motivation behind translation was not always about endorsing the universal value of great literature, but rather the attempt to establish the very terms by which universalism, and its implied values and distinctions, could be understood and reshaped in the Chinese context. A Victorianist may be surprised that the first translated novel to appear in China should be Edward Bulwer-Lytton's *Night and Morning*, rather than any of the masterpieces of English literature or even Bulwer-Lytton's more famous *The Coming Race*. To the urban audience of Shanghai, however, Bulwer-Lytton was no more or less exotic than a Western scholar named Darwin, whose works were introduced along with Bulwer-Lytton's in the same newspaper, *Shenbao*, in 1873.

The extraordinary translation landscape around the turn of the century, in which classical and vernacular prose, Western syntax, and unknown or even falsified original authorship were mixed together, spread new ideas for popular consumption. Source texts were readily altered during transmission, tolerating a wide range of practices often noted next to the translator's name as "translated and narrated" (*yishu*), "edited and translated" (*bianyi*), or "loosely translated" (*yanyi*). New terminologies were hastily improvised to facilitate new meanings. This widespread openness, not only to the process of transmission but also to the possibilities for creative interpretation in the reception of the transmitted text, gave free rein to a wildly imaginative approach to assimilating Western knowledge. Sometimes, the rate at which people rushed to create neologisms fell behind their perceived novelty. Before an equivalent counterpart in Chinese could be found, new terms appeared as new sounds in the language of intellectuals and fiction writers. Transliterations, such as *demukelaxi* (democracy), *yansipilichun* (inspiration), *laifuqiang* (rifle), and *balimen* (parliament), rolled off the tongues of novelty seekers and political reformers alike, often themselves the objects of parody under the jabbing pens of more conservative writers.

Translated or not, literary genres proliferated along with gender-bending roles. Cross-dressing female assassins, a modern take on the seventeenth-century "string ballads" (*tanci*) that often featured women masquerading as men, formed part of the popular appeal of the political intrigues in nihilist fiction (*xuwudang xiaoshuo*). Rewriting classical novels in the form of modernized sequels provided an effective way to entice a traditional audience with reinvented novelty, as in Wu Jianren's 1905 *The New Story of the Stone*, a science-fantasy rendition of the classical novel *The Story of the Stone*. In Wu's version, Jia Baoyu, the sentimental protagonist turned enlightened intellectual, returns to a futuristic world modernized by technology but where "civilization" (*wenming*) remains a vexing issue. The fiction produced by the writers and translators of this period was as varied in its range as it was outlandish in its subject matter. Well-known genres such as "romance fiction," "depravity fiction," and "fiction of social critique" constituted only one part of a vast spectrum of classifications that included "fishing-industry fiction," "utopian fiction," "navigation fiction," "fiction of the medical world," "racial fiction," "mathematics fiction," "study-of-weaponry fiction," and "advertisement fiction." Few translators and writers were capable of straddling this range. As one of the most prolific writers from this period, Liu Shi'e was an exception, authoring and translating more than a hundred novels, including modern versions of the mid-sixteenth-century novel *Water Margin* as well as science fiction and martial arts fiction.

Apart from the complex landscape of translations and patterns of popular literary consumption of this period, a number of other aspects await further study. Among them is the important role played by women translators. Chen Hongbi, a frequent contributor to the well-known journal *Fiction Grove*, translated mainly detective fiction, such as Emile Gaboriau's *Le Dossier No. 113* (*Di yibai shiyi an*, 1907) and *Electric Crown* (*Dianguan*), both of which appeared in *Fiction Grove*. Another recently excavated figure is Xue Shaohui, who embodied a measured progressivism together with a clear loyalty to traditional learning and values. With no apparent skill in foreign languages, she rendered Jules Verne's *Around the World in Eighty Days* into literary Chinese (*Bashiri huanyou ji*, 1900) on the basis of her husband Chen Shoupeng's oral translation. This was the first translation of Western science fiction in China. The husband–wife team translated other science-related works, such as *A Double Thread* by Ellen Thorneycroft Fowler (translated as *Shuangxian ji*, 1903) and a textbook primer to physics. Concerned with the question of women's rights in the context of the 1898 Reform Movement, Xue also compiled and translated *Biographies of Foreign Women* (*Waiguo lienü zhuan*, 1906). Her brother-in-law, Chen Jitong, was a polyglot particularly well versed in French; a graduate of the Fuzhou Naval Yard, he spent almost twenty years abroad, first as a student and later as an official translator. Chen was responsible for translating tales from *Records of the Strange* (*Liaozhai zhiyi*) into French as *Les Contes Chinois* (1884). Chen's erudite command of Western literature had an influence not only over his brother and his sister-in-law. Zeng Pu, the author of the famous novel *Flower in the Sea of Sins*, praised him for having single-handedly inducted him into the world of reading and translating French literature.

While there existed several different avenues for accessing foreign literature around the turn of the century, it was burgeoning journalism that gave it a unique visibility. A number of literary figures founded journals that provided an important forum for showcasing the latest translated fiction. Liang Qichao's *New Fiction* proclaimed the advent of the "fiction revolution" and led the way by publishing many translations. Wu Jianren, one of the most important writers of the late Qing, edited *Monthly Fiction* (*Yueyue xiaoshuo*), which drew such writers as Zhou Guisheng, a translator of children's fiction and, more famously, the first to introduce detective fiction into Chinese. *A Strange Tale of the Electric Arts* (*Dianshu qitan*), Wu's 1903 vernacular adaptation of a literary Chinese translation of the 1897 Japanese translation of an alleged Victorian detective novel on mesmerism, remains one of the best examples dating from this period of the complex process of translation relayed through multiple linguistic media. That the reference to an English original may have been fabricated highlights all the more the growing allure of translation, whose exoticism was sometimes prized above original composition in Chinese. For example, in order to take advantage of this new market, the real author of the 1903 novel *Freedom of Marriage* (*Ziyou jiehun*) claimed that the novel derived from the work of an American Jewish writer named Vancouver, whom the fictitious Chinese translator, the young daughter of a Chinese watchmaker in Geneva by the name of Liberty Flower, had met by chance.

Recognizing the appeal of translated texts, many editors sought to shape their social vision through them. Zhou Shoujuan, the editor of *Violet* and *Saturday*, translated and published a collection of European and American short stories, praised by Lu Xun as an admirable follow-up to his own pioneering collection, *Fiction from Abroad* (*Yuwai xiaoshuo ji*). Chen Jinghan, a translator who was particularly fascinated by stories dealing with nihilist assassins, founded *Fiction Times* (*Xiaoshuo shibao*) together with the popular writer Bao Tianxiao, who had a strong interest in translating science-related "education fiction." The two editors brought the tales of prolific writers like William le Queux, little remembered in Western literary criticism today, into this lively milieu. The science fiction of Jules Verne and the detective fiction of Conan Doyle were the most popular. Through the fictional worlds of hypnotism, space travel, racial apocalypse, female assassins, and explorations of distant continents, late Qing literary translation sought out new experiences in different corners of the world. The wide array of translators and the diversity of their taste testify to the cultural imagination of this era, marked by unbridled enthusiasm, wonder, sarcasm, and an exceptional zeal to experience their social reality as part of the "modern" rational world.

Ideology, nation-building, and translating the world

Challenging the limitations of traditional and modern cultural sensibilities as they did, the late Qing's experimentations with texts and translation could not long endure. Lin Shu was later criticized for his obstinate adherence to the forms and values of classical prose, increasingly an object of attack in the radicalizing intellectual climate of the early twentieth century. His innovative attempt to open up the classical prose style to accommodate new linguistic forms, concepts, and diction was largely forgotten amidst the antitraditionalist fervor of the May Fourth Movement. As modernization and nation-building got under way in the 1920s and 1930s, the task of translation, like the writing of literature in general, was proclaimed to be the instrument for awakening class consciousness and had to serve other political ideologies.

A serious and doggedly literal approach toward the translation of foreign literature was quietly announced with the publication of two collections of *Fiction from Abroad* by Lu Xun and his brother Zhou Zuoren. Only 1,500 copies of each collection were printed in Tokyo, where the two brothers were studying, in March and July 1909 respectively. No more than twenty-odd copies, however, were sold in Tokyo and Shanghai. Commercial failure aside, the translation was significant for other reasons. It expressed a solemn attitude toward the power of translation as a means of bringing to light the injustices and suffering of the oppressed peoples of other nations. This turn toward global political consciousness demanded a new receptivity on the part of the urban Chinese audience, whose habit of reading translated novels for their sensational value was to the reformist writers a matter for lament. Foreseeing the importance of socially responsible fiction, the Zhou brothers used their anthology as a way of breaking new ground and introducing the works of ten writers of seven nationalities, mainly from eastern, southern, and northern Europe. The collection broke with the focus, dominant since 1897, on translating Anglo-American and western European literature. Bearing the unmistakable imprint of Russia's 1905 White Revolution, which the translators hoped would find resonance in the rebellious sentiments felt by the Chinese against the Manchu government of the Qing dynasty, the collection highlighted tales recounting class oppression and social inequality, especially the works of contemporary Polish and Russian writers, such as Henryk Shienkiewicz (1846–1916), V. Korolenko, Leonid Andrejev (1871–1919),

Mikhail Lermontov (1814–1841), Anton Chekhov (1860–1904), and Vsevolod Michailovitch Garshin (1855–1888).

Readapting the tastes of late Qing readers to a new curriculum of modern literature was not an easy task. The first appearance of *Fiction from Abroad* was greeted with disinterest by the general public, who, among other things, found the length of the short story wanting. Readers complained that "just as things are getting started, it's over." But Lu Xun and Zhou Zuoren, departing from Liang Qichao's narrow vision of translated fiction as political instrument and Lin Shu's preference for style over accuracy, argued for the equal importance of the translator's commitment to social responsibility and fidelity to the original. Whereas Lin Shu often carried out his translations with melodramatic flair and "wept and translated, translated and wept" in the process, the Zhou brothers favored minimal intrusion, opting for a literal, unadorned language. In going against the mainstream, they foreshadowed the ideological direction of what would become the dominant mode of literature in the twentieth century, namely realism. Their concern for the narratives of peoples and races around the world, as they suffered under Western imperialism and economic inequality, set the tone for literary translation and creation alike in the ensuing decades. Realism and its promise of a faithful, reflective narrative held sway over Chinese writers eager for and committed to social change. Though the style of both Lu Xun's earlier translations of Jules Verne and Zhou Zuoren's rendition of Haggard had been heavily influenced by Lin Shu, the two authors proclaimed a new departure for translation in the preface to *Fiction from Abroad*, declaring their collection to be the first transmission of Western literary art into China. It is as if translation finally became, for the first time, a legitimate intellectual, rather than a commercial and sensationalist, pursuit.

From the May Fourth period onward, translation was frequently utilized as a tool for bolstering the ideological claims of writers, intellectuals, and the state. The literary revolution of the 1920s spurred the proliferation of literary journals dedicated to introducing foreign literature as well as literary theories from realism to Russian formalism, imagism, Romanticism, and neo-Romanticism. Pioneering literary journals, such as *New Youth* and *New Tide*, led the way with the translations of Chen Duxiu, Hu Shi, and others, but other publications founded for the exclusive purpose of publishing translations also multiplied. Expanding the spectrum covered by the fiction of oppressed peoples, the Chinese Literary Association focused on works that articulated the theme of "art for life's sake" by writers such as Zola, Maupassant, Dostoevsky, Tagore, and Turgenev, while members of the Creation Society (Guo Moruo,

Yu Dafu, Cheng Fangwu, Tian Han) steered their efforts primarily toward the representative figures of English and German Romanticism. Under Mao Dun's editorship, *Fiction Monthly*, once the forum for late Qing popular fiction of the Mandarin Duck and Butterfly School, now took an ideological turn and began publishing special issues on Russian and French literature and the "literature of the exploited nations."

From the early 1920s through the 1940s, translation activities were focused on Russian literature, followed by English and American, French, German, Japanese, and other languages. While the majority of the texts were still being retranslated from English and Japanese versions, writers and intellectuals began, in recognition of a new literary cosmopolitanism, to place strong emphasis on working with the original languages. At the same time, Ba Jin's translation of his works into Esperanto and continual efforts by language reformers such as Qian Xuantong to romanize the Chinese script remind us that attempts to transform the Chinese language itself through translation were part of a new perception of the modern world that aimed at establishing a relationship with other cultures and literatures rather than merely assimilating them. Lu Xun, whose translation of Gogol's *Dead Souls* remains an important testimonial to foreign influence on modern Chinese literature, remarked that someone with a real background in Russian – like the well-known Marxist critic Qu Qiubai – would have been a more ideal translator. Even as he translated the works of Japanese literary critics Kuragawa Hakuson in the 1920s and 1930s, Lu Xun continued his focus on eastern and northern European literature.

Other translators were more specialized in their choice of authors, often reflecting the influence of earlier experiences of study or residency abroad. Along with Qu Qiubai, Zheng Zhenduo, and Ba Jin, Geng Jizhi was a champion of Russian literature, especially the works of Tolstoy, Turgenev, and Pushkin. His first translation, Tolstoy's *Kreutzer Sonata*, was followed by Dostoevsky's *The Brothers Karamazov* and *Crime and Punishment*, although the galleys for *Crime and Punishment* were destroyed in a fire during the Japanese invasion of the early 1930s. The Du Fu scholar Feng Zhi, a contemporary of Xu Zhimo and Wen Yiduo, introduced the poetry of Rilke, Goethe, Heine, and Novalis after studying in Heidelberg. His 1937 translation of Rilke's *The Sonnets to Orpheus* can be seen as an inspiration for his own collection of sonnets, a new form in Chinese poetry. Fu Lei's more than thirty translations of French literature included Romaine Rolland's *Jean Christophe*; Voltaire's *Candide* and *Zadig*; and Balzac's *Ursule Mirouët*, *Eugénie Grandet*, *César Birotteau*, *La Cousine Bette*, *Le Cousin Pons*, *Le Père Goriot*, and *Les Illusions Perdues*. Yet the credit for introducing the works of Flaubert belongs to Li Jieren, whose 1925 translation of *Madame Bovary* remains one of the most influential works translated into Chinese from European literature.

Despite the view, predominant since the May Fourth Movement, that translation serves ideological purposes, the preceding century puts it in a new light. The importation of foreign literatures and thought was more accurately a reimagination of one's perception of the world through the different eyes of the foreign. The multiple nexuses through which this new "worldliness" unfolded, and the different levels of society in which it found expression, depended not only on the work of intellectuals and reformers but also on the larger cultural topography from which these elite visions were derived. Modern literature is, in this sense, strongly indebted to extraliterary life both inside and outside the national space. Though the cultural history of the nineteenth century is yet to be fully understood, it explored different paths, taken or not, that influenced the ways in which writers and readers perceived themselves in a period of cultural change as China moved toward the modern. In precisely this way, translation offered the whole world, rather than just a nation, in which modern Chinese literature was to find some of its most powerful inspirations.

Print culture and literary societies
By Michel Hockx

As previous chapters in this book have amply demonstrated, print culture existed in China well before the modern period. The importation of Western-style mechanized printing techniques, allowing for large-scale low-cost production, is, however, generally considered a crucial material factor contributing to changes in Chinese literary production from the late nineteenth century onwards. In China, as elsewhere, modern print culture created new markets and new audiences for literature, enabling the emergence of a relatively independent literary community. During the first few decades of the twentieth century, most participants in that community chose to operate in the context of literary societies. These too had had a long prior existence, but their activities now became more public, more independent, and, often, also more professional. The interaction between the media and technologies of print culture and the activities of literary societies are part of the unique context in which the literature of this period, especially the so-called "New Literature," was created. This section details that context to fill in the background against which the authors and works presented in the preceding pages may be read and understood.

Print culture and literary magazines, 1872–1902

The earliest modern printing presses were imported into China by mission-aries in the mid-nineteenth century. They were, of course, used first and foremost for the production of bibles, but the missionaries also published literary works, including the first Chinese translations of modern Western fiction. In the last decades of the nineteenth century, the new technologies were gradually adopted by commercial printing houses. The foreign conces-sions in Shanghai soon became the undisputed center of the printing industry. Throughout the late Qing and Republican periods, the bulk of Chinese print culture was physically produced, or at the very least distributed, by companies in Shanghai. A rich cultural life, including a literary scene (*wentan*), developed as a result, and proved to be a fertile breeding ground for new forms and formats of literary expression.

One particularly influential new format for presenting literary texts was the literary magazine. The first Chinese literary magazine is believed to be *Scattered Notes from around the Universe* (*Yinghuan suoji*), published from 1872 to 1875 by the leading Shanghai newspaper and publishing house, Shenbaoguan, owned by Ernest Major, an Englishman. The literary-journal format was not an immediate success; only five journals came out before the turn of the century, four published by Shenbaoguan, and all short-lived. As far as literature was concerned, early modern print culture focused on publishing books, especially cheap novels. Yet the popularity of such novels and the unprecedented opportunities for widespread low-cost distribution offered by the new printing technologies must have drawn the attention of the late Qing reformist elite. These considerations likely predisposed Liang Qichao to venture the introduction of "new fiction." Given Liang's ambition to turn fiction into a tool of political education, it is not surprising that he chose the magazine format to ensure maximum exposure of his ideas to the largest possible readership. Moreover, Liang's decision to use the journal format may have been influenced by the fact that, at the time he published his first literary journal, he was in Japan, where the magazine was already flourishing as a literary forum.

Fiction journals, 1902–1920

The appearance of Liang Qichao's journal *New Fiction* on the Shanghai market in 1902 not only signaled a key change in the hierarchy of Chinese literary genres, it also heralded the advent of what was to become the standard format for the initial distribution of literary texts. From 1902 onwards, and throughout the Republican period, virtually every work of literature that appeared in book form was first published in a literary magazine. The movement for a new literature spearheaded by Liang Qichao and continued by later generations depended entirely on magazines (as well as newspaper supplements, which will be discussed shortly) for its promotion and vitality. The market for literary journals grew rapidly, as more than twenty new journals – most of them carrying the word *xiaoshuo* ("fiction") in the title and all based in Shanghai – were founded before the end of the decade. These "fiction journals" dominated the market until the early 1920s; after this they met with stiff competition from journals that subscribed to the agenda of the New Culture Movement, many with the word *wenxue* ("literature") in the title. From the 1920s onwards, magazines and works that continued to adhere to the "fiction-journal" format were sometimes disparagingly referred to as part of the "Mandarin Ducks and Butterflies School."

Despite the emphasis on "fiction" as a genre classification, most of these journals offered writings in various genres that reflected the taste of the late imperial and early Republican urban elite. The politically motivated writing advocated by Liang Qichao soon gave way to a range of different styles, including those openly aimed at entertainment or "playfulness" (*youxi*). Moreover, the appeal of these journals was not merely textual. The most popular (and most expensive) magazines were those that also offered visual enjoyment, in the form of cover designs and reproductions of images and photographs on the inside pages. The importance of illustrations is confirmed by the fact that their titles would always be listed in the table of contents. Illustration titles also featured prominently in advertisements for magazines.

A typical issue of a fiction journal of this period had a cover in color featuring a lithographically reproduced painting (often of a young woman) as well as the title of the journal in Chinese calligraphy and in English. Some of the cover paintings were of high artistic and print quality, such as those of the journal *Fiction Times*, which ran from 1909 to 1917. The inside cover and sometimes the first few pages would contain space for advertisements, followed by a series of pages containing images and photographs. Some journals would print photographs of famous Shanghai courtesans, one element that later aroused the disapproval of New Culture advocates. It was also common to carry photographs of some of the contributors to a particular issue in its opening pages.

The images section was typically followed by the table of contents, which in turn was followed by the various sections of the journal. Sections were normally divided by genre: most journals had sections of short fiction, long fiction in serial form, drama (both traditional drama and new-style spoken drama), classical-style poetry, and miscellany (*biji* or *zazu*, or both). The fiction sections were often further divided into subgenres, such as romance fiction, comical fiction, and detective fiction. Much of the fiction included in these journals was translated or adapted from often unacknowledged foreign sources. Most journals published classical and vernacular fiction side by side. "Fiction" was a wide category in this period and could include virtually any type of imaginative prose. The term also encompassed the long verse narrative (*tanci*). It is worth highlighting that new-style spoken drama was developed in this period by contributors to these fiction journals, well before its inclusion into New Culture after 1917.

By the 1910s, the leading commercial publishing houses in Shanghai were all in the hands of Chinese entrepreneurs. Publishing literary journals was only a sideline for these businesses, which derived most of their income either from printing newspapers or from publishing textbooks for the new educational system that had replaced the old system of civil service examinations. Textbook publishing, especially, was the core business underpinning the success of the "big three" Republican-era Chinese publishing houses: the Commercial Press (Shangwu yinshuguan; founded 1904), the Zhonghua Book Company (Zhonghua shuju; founded 1912), and the World Book Company (Shijie shuju; founded 1921). As Christopher Reed describes in detail in *Gutenberg in Shanghai*, these three publishing houses were major commercial operations with distribution networks throughout the country. They were also major employers for writers, editors, proofreaders, and others adept at producing textbooks.

Shanghai had thus become a major source of career opportunities for anyone interested in textual work. Many of the most active contributors to the fiction journals, who also wrote for newspapers and non-literary journals, sustained themselves on fees and royalties. For this reason, this first generation of modern Chinese writers is often referred to as "journalist–*littérateurs*" (a term first proposed by Leo Ou-fan Lee). Their engagement with writing as a profession was one reason why these authors and their journals were denounced by the next generation, who effectively couched their more practical motives for writing in such ideals as "cultural enlightenment" or "art for art's sake."

The Southern Society, 1909–1922

During the heyday of the fiction journal, many of the journalist–*littérateurs* were members of a large professional organization called the Southern Society (Nanshe). Founded in 1909 by three members of the League of Unification

(Tongmenghui), the Southern Society grew in later years to be the largest literary organization of the entire Republican period. Initially, the society appeared to differ little from the traditional literati societies, such as the Revival Society (Fushe) of the late Ming, on which it claimed to be modeled. Like those societies, the Southern Society aimed to bring together men of letters at regularly organized "elegant gatherings" (*yaji*), where they discussed and often wrote classical-style literature, and to bring out a regular publication containing selections of these writings (*shegao*). The difference, however, was that whereas traditional societies had been strongly invested in the civil service examination system and in political patronage, the Southern Society focused its energy on the publication of a professionally edited literary periodical. In order to achieve this, the Society established a number of practices that were to become typical of Republican-era literary societies.

First and foremost, the Southern Society set up ordinances clearly stipu-lating the conditions of membership (including membership fees), rules for the election of officers, and a schedule of meetings and publications. Its most important officers were the editors in charge of putting together the society organ, entitled *The Southern Society Printed Collection* (*Nanshe congke*), each issue of which was divided into sections for prose (*wen*), poetry (*shi*), and song lyric (*ci*). Anyone who was able to contribute to the society's periodical and had the nomination of a quorum of existing members could become a member. Membership was open to everyone in the country, and, since participation in the society's elegant gatherings (which invariably took place in Shanghai) was not a condition of membership, the society soon included members from all over China. New membership lists were published at regular intervals, and elections for the society's officers were held with the aid of announcements in national newspapers. At one point, the society counted more than a thousand members. Even though the number who regularly attended its elegant gath-erings did not exceed two dozen, over three hundred members participated by post in its 1917 vote for a new "manager" (*zhuren*), the results of which were again published in the newspapers. The Southern Society became the proto-type of a nationwide cultural organization with a strong public presence. Its use of national newspapers, especially the Nationalist Party paper, *Republican Daily News* (*Minguo ribao*), to establish its public presence created a precedent that many literary societies were later to follow.

Paradoxically, the Southern Society also created the mold for a very differ-ent type of literary group that was to become a common sight on the literary scene after 1920. Despite its huge membership and formal organization, actual work on the society's publications was done by a small group of associates, most of it by one person, Liu Yazi (1887–1958), a well-connected public figure in Shanghai literary circles.

The *Short Story Magazine* and the Chinese Literary Association

Toward the end of the 1910s, fiction journals were becoming more specialized, with some of the larger journals focusing on one or two particular styles or genres. Most remarkable in this context is the founding, in January 1917, of *Illustrated Novel Magazine* (*Xiaoshuo huabao*) by the well-known journalist–littérateur Bao Tianxiao. This journal contained only writing in the modern vernacular, because, according to its opening manifesto, vernacular literature had been the only true literature throughout Chinese history. Bao Tianxiao's claims pre-dated the much-heralded switch to the vernacular of the Peking University-based journal *New Youth* (*Xin qingnian*, also known as *La Jeunesse*). Nevertheless, it was the latter's programmatic stance that would change the balance of power between classical and modern on the Chinese literary scene from the early 1920s onwards.

In the early 1920s, graduates from Peking University and other new-style higher education institutions started to flock together in Shanghai, forming a new generation of writers and editors for the various newspapers, journals and publishing houses. These "literary intellectuals" (McDougall and Louie's term) brought with them a serious, programmatic, and westernized understanding of literature that was at odds with the more relaxed attitude of many journalist–littérateurs. They also brought with them a knowledge of foreign languages and things foreign that was (or appeared to be) superior to that of the older generation. With these skills, many found their way into the publishing world, where they began to promote New Literature, gradually taking away a share of the market from the fiction journals and their authors.

The first and most famous success for the advocates of New Literature came in 1921, when members of a group calling itself Wenxue yanjiu hui (the Chinese Literary Association) became the editors and key contributors of a well-established fiction journal, the *Short Story Magazine* (*Xiaoshuo yuebao*), which had been in existence for over a decade and was published by the Commercial Press, by this time the largest publishing house in Shanghai. The founding of the Chinese Literary Association in December 1920 had been the result of careful planning and negotiation. This process involved senior literary intellectuals from Beijing (most notably Zhou Zuoren), young literary enthusiasts from various Beijing colleges (most notably Zheng Zhenduo), an equally enthusiastic young editor from Shanghai (Shen Yanbing, who worked for the Commercial Press and would later become famous as the writer and critic Mao Dun), and a few business-minded Commercial Press managers who realized the sales potential of the New Culture movement.

To distinguish its literary program from that of the fiction journals, the Chinese Literary Association asked that the title *Short Story Magazine* be changed to *Literature Journal* (*Wenxue zazhi*), but this was rejected by the publisher for commercial reasons. Though retaining the old title (and presumably at least part of its old subscription base), the journal from 1921 onwards instituted changes in its content and layout that reflected the much more serious and elitist view of literature of its new editorship. Instead of photographs of famous courtesans or of the contributors to the journal, the opening pages featured pictures of famous foreign authors and scenes from foreign cities. Classical poetry, fiction in the classical language or in the old vernacular, long verse narrative, traditional drama, and miscellany all disappeared, to be replaced by sections on modern poetry, literary criticism, literary news, and letters to the editor. Special issues were devoted to the introduction of particular foreign authors. Translated works were now clearly identified as such and their sources acknowledged. Short and long (serialized) fiction continued to make up the bulk of the content. From 1921 until 1932, when it was forced to close down after the Japanese bombing of the Commercial Press, the *Short Story Magazine* was the leading journal for New Literature, especially for fiction. Well-known writers, such as Ding Ling and Lao She, made their debut in its pages. No other New Literature journal of the 1920s came close to being as professionally edited, printed, and distributed as the *Short Story Magazine*.

Like the Southern Society before it, the Chinese Literary Association set up clear rules for membership and for the editing of its publications. It presented itself as a "trade union" for literary workers all over the country, but in reality it was never more than a network of friends and the friends of friends, all devoted to the New Culture program, most of whom ended up working for publishing houses in Shanghai. The association's network was large, though never quite as large as that of the Southern Society. During its heyday in the early 1920s, the association counted 131 members. As was the case with the Southern Society, the actual work of editing publications and maintaining a public presence was undertaken by a very small group of people, especially Zheng Zhenduo and Shen Yanbing.

Apart from periodical publications, the association also published an influential newspaper supplement entitled *Literature Tri-monthly* (*Wenxue xunkan*), in which it unleashed attacks on classical literature and, more particularly, on the kind of literature associated with the fiction journals, which it considered too commercial and lacking in seriousness. The association's most significant and enduring contribution to modern print culture was, however, the editing and production for the Commercial Press of the Chinese Literary Association Series (Wenxue yanjiu hui congshu), which included many well-known works of modern fiction as well as many translations from foreign literature. The association network was especially valued by the Commercial Press because of its members' training in foreign languages. Although it is unclear to what extent the association continued to function as a collective after the mid-1920s, the series continued until 1947.

The bulk of New Literature journals of the 1920s were run on a much smaller scale by groups of friends or associates, often joined in a literary society, working under the auspices of one of the smaller Shanghai publishing houses. These groups brought a number of new practices to the modern Chinese literary scene.

Smaller New Literature collectives and their journals

Shortly after the Chinese Literary Association's attempt to establish itself as the "trade union" for all writers of New Literature, the Chinese literary scene was enlivened by the arrival of the first of a number of small, self-consciously avant-garde groups associated with the Taidong publishing house (Taidong shuju). The Creation Society was founded in Japan by, among others, the well-known poet Guo Moruo and the controversial short-story writer Yu Dafu, both of whom soon left Japan for Shanghai. They announced their intentions in true avant-garde style, with a widely publicized and strongly worded manifesto attacking all established icons of Chinese literature and announcing the society's singular devotion to art. The journals of the Creation Society, including a quarterly, a tri-monthly, and even (briefly) a daily, were soon in competition with those of the Chinese Literary Association. Their first journal, *Creation Quarterly* (*Chuangzao jikan*, 1922–1924), made a conscious attempt at presenting an unconventional format, including the first-ever use of horizontal left-to-right printing in a Chinese literary journal. During the early 1920s, the Creation Society and the Literary Association were engaged in public (and openly antagonistic) discussions about the nature of literature and especially the quality of translations of foreign literature published in their respective organs. The Creation Society's tactics launched its members to fame and aroused the interest of many other Shanghai publishers and newspaper houses in working with small groups of young literary enthusiasts in the production of literary journals and supplements. None of these journals matched the standards of editing and printing quality set by the *Short Story Magazine*, but what they lacked in financial and technological backing they made up for in enthusiasm and romantic (or revolutionary) fervor. That financial backing was not beyond their reach was eventually proved by the Creation Society when, in 1926, with the help of their newfound fame, they established their own publishing operation, partly self-funded and partly supported by the sale of shares. The Creation Society Publishing Department (Chuangzao she chubanbu), which included editorial offices, staff living quarters, and a bookstore, became a landmark on the cultural map of Shanghai until it was closed down by the government in 1930. During this period, it published a number of journals, including *Creation Monthly (Chuangzao yuekan)*, one of the leading journals of its time. Like the Chinese Literary Association, the Creation Society published an influential book series containing both original and translated works for the duration of its existence.

Another influential group that established its own publishing and bookselling operation, though without any avant-garde pretenses, was the Crescent Moon Society (Xin yue she). Founded in 1923 by a group of Beijing intellectuals, including the already famous Hu Shi and the rising poets Xu Zhimo and Wen Yiduo, the society's main activity until 1926 was the organization of social gatherings and literary events on the Beijing scene. After 1926, however, when many of its members had moved to Shanghai, the nature of its activities changed to producing and selling books and journals. Using their own money, they founded the Crescent Moon Bookstore (Xin yue shudian). Their main publication, *Crescent Moon (Xin yue)*, was a professional-looking and expensive journal, catering to the interests of the intellectual elite, especially those interested in Anglo-American literature and culture. The backbone of each issue was its poetry section, especially the famous romantic-formalist works by Xu Zhimo and Wen Yiduo.

Even less avant-garde, but by no means less successful or influential, was the journal *Critical Review (Xueheng)*, a conservative journal for classical-style writing whose lifespan (1922–1933) exceeded that of all the New Literature journals except the *Short Story Magazine*. Edited throughout its existence by Wu Mi, a Harvard graduate and former student of Irving Babbitt who strongly believed in the preservation of China's great literary tradition, the *Critical Review* engaged in a sustained criticism of the New Culture Movement, publishing only works in the classical language and preserving traditional genre divisions in prose and poetry. It also published translations of foreign literature into classical Chinese as well as much literary criticism. Wu Mi and his associates were based in Nanjing and had minimal involvement with the Shanghai scene, although their journal was distributed nationwide by a Shanghai distributor.

The prewar 1930s

Although journals and collectives promulgating programs of westernized literary thought (ranging, as we have seen, from the avant-garde to the conservative) were responsible for an increasing proportion of literary production from the early 1920s onwards, there was no lack of journals to carry on the more relaxed and playful heritage of the 1910s fiction journals. In a striking example of this kind of market segmentation, the Commercial Press ran such a journal, entitled *Story World* (*Xiaoshuo shijie*), alongside the *Short Story Magazine*. The layout of both journals was remarkably similar, and *Story World* enjoyed a more than respectable lifespan (1923 to 1929). The most famous and most successful fiction journal of the entire Republican period, however, is *Saturday* (*Libailiu*), which appeared weekly from 1914 to 1916 and, revived in 1921, appeared again weekly, with short interruptions, until 1937. After the Second Sino-Japanese War, it was revived once more and another 135 issues appeared from 1945 to 1948.

The greatest variety (and the greatest number) of literary journals was produced during the period from 1930 to 1937, when the Nationalist regime was well established (at least in the cities), and the relative political stability and the rising standard of general education enabled businesses like publishing houses to flourish. The mid-1930s, especially, are often seen as the heyday of modern Chinese print culture, in particular of the magazine. Magazine publishing had become a profitable enterprise by this time and publishers were keen to develop it. The prewar 1930s also saw the permeation of the cultural world by political and ideological differences, which have often received exaggerated emphasis in later accounts. The problem with these politicized accounts, which tend to focus on the repressive censorship by the Nationalist government of leftist writing, is that they do little to explain the unprecedented richness of literary production in this period. Below is an attempt to provide a more detached perspective.

Throughout the prewar 1930s, the number of literary journals in circulation was roughly double that of any preceding decade. The diversity of styles was such that it became increasingly difficult to draw clear distinctions between journals for New Literature, pre-1920-style fiction journals, and journals for classical literature. A good example are the journals edited by the famous Lin Yutang, such as *Analects* (*Lunyu*, 1932 to 1937 and 1946 to 1949): their playful style and layout resembled that of the old fiction journals; their preferred genre, the informal essay (*xiaopin*), aligned them with traditional literary sensibilities. In terms of their language and generally pro-Western orientation, however, they must be seen as part of the New Culture. This period also saw a remarkable revival of traditional "tea talk" (*chahua*) gatherings involving painters, poets, and their female companions, but with a distinctly modern twist: the painters were trained in Paris, the poets were writing song lyrics in the modern vernacular, and the female companions were well-educated painters and poets in their own right. Moreover, most of the "tea talks" were held in Shanghai coffeehouses. Some of these activities involved the former Southern Society manager Liu Yazi. The Southern Society itself was briefly resurrected in the context of several large-scale commemorative meetings held in 1935.

A large and influential organization involving members of most groups on the Shanghai scene was the Chinese branch of the International PEN (Guoji bihui Zhongguo fenhui), founded by Xu Zhimo and others in 1930 and chaired by Cai Yuanpei. The Chinese PEN branch hosted regular dinner parties as well as receptions for visiting foreign dignitaries, most famously on the occasion of a visit by George Bernard Shaw in 1933, when even Lu Xun attended. The Chinese PEN itself had no publications, but its events were prestigious and some of its members represented China at International PEN meetings during the 1930s and even during the war, after the Chinese branch itself had already become inactive.

Another large literary organization of the 1930s with a distinctly different style and program was the League of Left-Wing Writers (1930 to 1936). Founded in Shanghai with direct support from the Communist Party, the League was meant to consolidate a stronghold of leftist ideology in urban cultural circles after the Communist Party had lost its political influence there. Lu Xun himself presided over the League, although for most of his presidency he was embroiled in arguments with Communist Party ideologues and their representatives. The League was initially joined by many well-known left-leaning writers, including most of the former members of the Creation Society. The total membership of the League, which included a few branch organizations outside Shanghai, is claimed to have been substantial. Throughout its existence, the League itself was an underground organization and most of its many publications were short-lived and suffered from bad editing, cheap printing, and very limited circulation. Probably its most professionally run journal was the *Big Dipper* (*Beidou*), edited by Ding Ling. Founded in 1931, it was published above ground in Shanghai, but was closed down by government order in 1932. The *Big Dipper* was more literary than most of the League's publications and also contained contributions by non-League members, especially in its first few issues. In its later years, the League was marred by internal problems that hampered the efficiency of its operations and the quality of its output.

Despite its proscribed status, leftist writing was in vogue in the 1930s and commercial publishers were aware of its popularity, especially with younger audiences. Many of the more famous members of the League, such as Lu Xun, Mao Dun, and Ding Ling, never ceased writing for commercially published journals. Some of the best leftist literature was not written for League publications. For instance, Mao Dun's novel *Midnight* (*Ziye*), often hailed as the most successful piece of leftist writing produced by the League, was originally slated for serialization in the *Short Story Magazine*. Although the bombing of the Commercial Press in 1932 and the resultant folding of the *Short Story Magazine* made this impossible, Mao Dun did not offer it to any of the League journals, but published it directly in book form with the Kaiming publishing house (Kaiming shuju) in 1932. It became an instant best seller.

The most influential independent literary journal of the 1930s, not connected to any literary society or organization, was *Xiandai* (*Les Contemporains*, 1932 to 1935). Its format was similar to the *Short Story Magazine*, including extensive opening sections with photographs of things foreign. Enthusiastically edited by Shi Zhecun, *Les Contemporains* published much of the best fiction, poetry, and criticism of its time, including modernist verse by Dai Wangshu, the fiction of the Neo-Sensational School, and critical debates between leftists, conservatives, and independents, Lu Xun among them.

The wartime period and beyond

After the Japanese invasion of 1937, the Chinese literary scene ceased to be concentrated in Shanghai and various new centers arose. Publishing in occupied Shanghai did continue, even after the occupation of the International Settlement (where most publishing houses were located) in 1942. The Shanghai scene included an active group of writers practicing politically innocuous genres, such as the informal *xiaopin* essay and the comedy, published in journals stylistically akin to those published by Lin Yutang in the 1930s. Literary publishing thrived in the wartime capital of Chongqing as well as in Kunming, where many literary intellectuals were teaching at Southwestern Associated University (Xinan lianda). The Communist Party had its own literary base in Yan'an, most famous as the venue of the forum on literature and the arts in 1942 at which Mao Zedong introduced his literary policies. Meanwhile, virtually all authors of all persuasions had joined the All China Federation of

Literature and Arts Circles against the Enemy (Zhonghua quanguo wenyijie kangdi xiehui), a non-partisan patriotic organization chaired by Lao She. The federation promoted the writing of anti-Japanese literature. Its activities included organizing study trips to the front for writers and promoting genres such as reportage literature (*baogao wenxue*). After the Japanese surrender in 1945, when most well-known writers formerly active on the Shanghai scene returned to that city, the federation was renamed the All China Federation for Literature and Arts (Zhonghua quanguo wenyi xiehui) and continued to give representation to all Chinese writers in a non-partisan manner. It ceased to exist when the Communist army took control of Shanghai in 1949.

Newspaper supplements

No description of Republican China's print culture and literary societies would be complete without giving due credit to the crucial role of newspaper supplements in literary debates and literary creation. Varying in length from half a page to eight pages, the newspaper supplement was the ideal medium for bringing the literary thought of particular groups to a nationwide audience. Normally appearing every week (*zhoukan*) or every ten days (*xunkan*), these supplements were by nature suited for the publication of short work and most especially for public debate. In the 1920s, debates between the Chinese Literary Association and the advocates of the older fiction-journal style raged in the pages of *Literature Tri-monthly* (the Association's organ, a supplement of Shanghai's *China Times* (*Shishi xinbao*)) and of the *Shenbao* supplement *Free Talk* (*Ziyou tan*), then under the control of Bao Tianxiao and his associates. By the 1930s, *Ziyou tan* had become the mouthpiece for a group of leftist New Culture advocates, including Lu Xun, who published many of his famous critical essays (*zawen*) in it.

Many newspaper supplements were by nature cliquish. Their regular contributors normally wrote under pseudonyms, their real names known only to insiders, and a considerable amount of space was often dedicated to announcements and/or communications meant only for members of the literary society running the supplement. (Such information is often found printed over the fold between two pages, typically used for advertisements and announcements in Republican-period newspapers and often only partially reproduced in modern reprints, if at all.) Some newspaper supplements were also sold separately from the newspapers that published them and were collected into bound volumes.

Since newspaper printing was to a much lesser degree monopolized by Shanghai publishers, important literary supplements also appeared in other cities, especially Beijing, where the literary supplements to the *Morning News* (*Chenbao*) and *Peking Press* (*Jingbao*) were at the center of the city's literary life. The *Morning News* supplement is most famous for serializing Lu Xun's *The True Story of Ah Q* (*Ah Q zhengzhuan*) in 1922. Shortly afterwards, the editorship of the supplement was taken over by Xu Zhimo, who used it to promote Crescent Moon Society writings.

Apart from these two Beijing-based supplements, two supplements to Shanghai newspapers were considered particularly influential: *Awakening* (*Juewu*), the supplement to the *Republican Daily News*, and *Light of Learning* (*Xuedeng*), the supplement to the *China Times*. Together, these four were known as the "four big supplements" (*si da fukan*), and were widely read by those interested in New Culture and the vernacular movement.

Journal literature: concluding remarks

The vast majority of literary work produced during the late Qing and Republican eras, regardless of style, program, or ideology, was journal literature. This was, by definition, literature that was often written under pressure, its writers mindful of deadlines, and mindful too of the fact that they were being paid by the number of characters. Although, except for the journalist–*littérateurs* of the 1900s and 1910s, few authors in this period were actually able to live off their writing, it was still common for authors to be extremely productive and to write for numerous journals and supplements at the same time. Peer pressure, from fellow members of a literary society, for instance, was part of the reason why authors were so productive. The programmatic character of the New Culture was another reason, as it was considered important to promulgate the New Culture as vigorously as possible. This situation led to certain inevitable consequences: a preponderance of short texts and of serialized texts whose endings were often not yet known even by the authors themselves when they wrote the first installment (Lu Xun's *Ah Q* is again the prime example), a relatively large number of texts that appear either sloppy (due to lack of time for proofreading) or verbose (due to lack of incentives for concision), a tendency for authors to publish everything they wrote almost instantly, and a tendency to stay close to the everyday reality and concerns of the journal's subscription-paying readership. Most journal literature was only cursorily, if at all, revised when republished in book form, so that, even in that much more convenient and durable format, this literature still presents itself to the reader as urgent and passionate, if at times somewhat ill-considered.

V. Coda: modernities and historicities

As a campaign for literary and cultural modernization, the May Fourth Movement derived its polemical momentum and affective power from radical antitraditionalism. By drawing a boundary between the new and the old, advocates of New Literature fostered a discourse involving such thematic axes as decadence versus enlightenment, reaction versus revolution, "cannibalism" versus humanism, and darkness versus brightness. Crossing "the Gate of Darkness," in Lu Xun's terminology, they aspired to a project of modernization that would highlight nationalism, follow a timeline leading to progress, and create a new kind of citizen who could live in complete autonomy.

This agenda, however, could not overlook the fact that modern Chinese literature could not do away with its past. Indeed, the tortuous way in which post-May Fourth literati and intellectuals revoked, invented, and uncannily reinstated Chinese history is the most conspicuous aspect of Chinese literary modernity. If modernity is not to be fetishized into a linear movement unerringly aimed at a prescribed telos, the historicity of the modern had continually to be questioned in response to the outrageous imagination of futures bred in the past, and the unexpected consequences of reducing all imagination to a single task, that of ending history.

This brings us to the paradoxical observation that writing and reading literary history (in the way we understand it) is an "invention" of modern times. In the last decades of the Qing, traditional epistemological and pedagogical systems were shaken up and gradually superseded by a Western-inspired disciplinary matrix. The old model of learning ended when the civil service examination system was abolished and new curricula were institutionalized. In the humanities, this prompted reformers to translate classical Chinese learning into a Europeanized framework.

One of the disciplinary subjects they now addressed was literary history. At a time when national identity was tied to national history, writers and scholars endeavored to forge a discourse reflecting literature as the core of the national heritage. Literary history, in this sense, is a modern project informed by a prescribed timeline and a national imaginary. The earliest Chinese literary history, as newly defined, was *The History of Chinese Literature* (*Zhongguo wenxueshi*) written in 1904 by a young teacher, Lin Chuanjia (1877–1922) of the Great Learning Institute of the Capital (the precursor of Peking University). The writing and publication of the *History of Chinese Literature* had to do with the recent mounting of "literature" as one of the disciplinary subjects of the institute. Lin drafted the history in a rush to meet his teaching needs, and he did so with the institute's curricular policy in mind; that is, studying literature primarily as an aid to prose composition and rhetorical training. Although modeled after the Japanese scholar Sasagawa Rinpū's *History of Chinese Literature* (1898), Lin's version is an eclectic exercise comprising genre classification, philological inquiry, and chronological periodization. This hybrid form reflects Lin's own ambivalent attitude toward literature as an aesthetic construct. He highlights the vicissitudes of intellectual history from Confucius onward and describes the transformations of prose (*wen*) in terms of reaction to historical changes. He pays little attention to poetry and says next to nothing about vernacular fiction and drama. Above all, his vision of literature and literary history is closely related to conventional notions about literature as serving utilitarian and didactic functions.

After Lin Chuanjia's preliminary attempt, the writing of literary history developed in parallel with the New Literature Movement. Reconstructing the past became a way to assert the power of the modern. For instance, in 1922, Hu Shi published *A History of Literature in the Past Fifty Years* (*Wushi nianlai zhi zhongguo wenxue*), in which he pits the new and "living" literature against the old "dead" and "half-dead" literature. Implied in his historical account is a paradigm of evolutionism and organism, while vernacular language is hailed as a springboard for literary rejuvenation. At the same time, Zhou Zuoren proffered a view of literary development based on the perennial dialogue between two classical notions, that "literature is a vehicle of the Dao" and that "literature expresses intent." Zhou also ventures to trace the origin of Chinese literary modernity to the late Ming, when literati sought to express themselves under the inspiration of the Wang Yangming school of Confucianism. Another notable trend appears in *A History of Late Qing Fiction* (*Wanqing xiaoshuo shi*, 1937) by Ah Ying (Qian Xingcun). Classifying late Qing fiction according to political and social topics, the book is the first modern attempt to look back at this period from a leftist, sociological perspective.

Even as literary history was institutionalized as a discipline, a movement arose to try to either discover or disavow the "essence" of Chinese literature and culture. Insofar as they express a heightened anxiety about China's fate as reflected in literature, May Fourth writers show what C. T. Hsia, in his critique of modern Chinese writers, terms an "obsession with China." For Hsia, while Chinese writers share with their Western colleagues a general disgust with the consequences of modern civilization, they are preoccupied by their national crisis and historical malaise to such an extent that they are unable, or unwilling, to expound the moral and political relevance of the fate of the Chinese people to "the state of man in the modern world."

At their best, he argues, Chinese writers feel compelled to display in their works a high moral integrity rarely found among contemporary Western writers, but the price they pay for such an "obsession with China" is "a certain patriotic provinciality and a naiveté of faith with regard to better conditions elsewhere."

Whereas May Fourth reformers try to create a new Chinese identity – be it called national character, national literature, or national culture – by denying the past, the conservatives set out to safeguard the past as the only way of preserving the quintessential legacy of China. One of the earliest and most influential attempts was formulated by Liu Shipei in the context of the "national essence" (*guocui*) movement. Together with his peers, such as Zhang Binglin, Liu forged a grand narrative of ancient Chinese cultural and intellectual history as the foundation of a new national learning. Anachronistic as this radical effort at reviving antiquity may seem, Liu demonstrates an "obsession with China" typical of both the reformers and the conservatives in late Qing and early Republican China.

Another important figure with a revivalist outlook is Liang Shuming (1893–1988), the first prominent scholar of the May Fourth era to defend Confucian tradition in a systematic way. Liang's *Eastern and Western Civilizations and Their Philosophies* (*Dongxi wenhua jiqi zhexue*, 1921) provides an overarching view of the Chinese, Indian, and Western philosophical traditions and their modern ramifications; it would become a harbinger of the neo-Confucian movement.

Meanwhile, there arose a call for classicism by a group of scholars, such as Mei Guangdi and Wu Mi, who also shared a similar educational background and cultural commitment. As mentioned above, they founded the journal *Critical Review* in 1921 to propagate their ideals of humanism, decorum, and cultural rejuvenation based on the classical Chinese heritage. These scholars had mostly been educated overseas and as such were not conservatives in the traditional sense. Their encounter with Western intellectual resources, particularly the new humanism of Irving Babbitt, prodded them to reexamine Chinese culture. They wanted to open a dialogue with the humanist tradition in Western culture, hence their slogan: "Interpret the spirit of Chinese culture and introduce the best elements of Western philosophy and literature."

May Fourth literati also set out to reassess select historical moments so as to find alternative resources for Chinese modernity. For instance, Lu Xun showed a particular interest in the literati culture of the Six Dynasties. In "The Literati Mannerism of the Wei and Jin, and Its Relation to Poetry, Drugs, and

Wine" (Weijin fengdu ji wenzhang yu yao ji jiu de guanxi, 1927), he renders a compelling analysis of the insouciant attitude and apparently decadent lifestyle of the literati of the Six Dynasties, one of the most turbulent periods in premodern Chinese history. The essay implies a critique of contemporary China as well as of behavioral strategies in coping with political perils and cultural crises. Zhu Guangqian, on the other hand, finds in the chaos of the Six Dynasties the unlikely blossoming of an aesthetics of quietude and transcendence, something he believes to be as essential as Kantian aesthetics to remolding modern Chinese subjectivity. And, as discussed earlier, Hu Shi dedicated himself to the rediscovery of vernacular tradition from the Song to the Qing as the origin of the modern Chinese renaissance, while Zhou Zuoren harked back to the late Ming as the incipient moment of Chinese humanist emancipation.

Ironically, mainstream May Fourth writers and critics downgraded late Qing writers while appointing themselves the first-generation promoters of modernity. Yet there were other, subtler reasons for denigrating late Qing literature: more than the remainder of an obsolete literary past, it was also the reminder of the residual tradition always lurking behind the façade of modern discourse. By consigning that which is at present undesirable to a disposable legacy from the past, enlightened Chinese literati hoped to "clean up" their project of modernity. In other words, they explained away the unwelcome aspects of their attempts at modernity by displacing them into a past that was already over. But one might ask these paradoxical questions: is this modern discourse they are protecting from contamination really modern, or does it only seem modern? Is it not possible that the undesirable and unwelcome burdens of modern Chinese literature are derived not from the past but from too radical, or too modern, sources?

In literary practice, what makes writers such as Lu Xun and Shen Congwen outstanding is that their works bear witness to the treacherous terms of articulating modernity under the shadow of tradition. They are aware that, beyond palpable signs of the new and progressive, something else – something that cannot be squared with any ready-made models – has been held back in consensual discourse. Ironically, their constant attempts to come to grips with that underrepresented realm of cultural and political projects of modernity, followed often by their "failures" to do so, brings out some of the most engaging moments of modern Chinese literature.

Though he may play upon the grotesque elements of the late Qing exposé, Lu Xun actually derives his theory of reality and realism from the orthodox treatises of critics such as Yan Fu and Liang Qichao. The Russian scholar

V. I. Semanov calls attention to Lu Xun's creative interpretation of the late Qing literary legacy, particularly the figures and tropes of the exposé. The frame structure of "The Diary of a Madman," for example, reminds one of the opening of Wu Jianren's *Eyewitness Reports*. Nevertheless, Lu Xun's dogged search for a new realm of Chinese reality entails an intense personal drama of moral anxiety and ambiguity. Somewhere behind his Promethean posture, there hovers a prevailing cynicism that successfully combines enlightenment with resignation and apathy. Above all, ghosts and demons from the world of the past find every possible way to haunt this enlightened realist. Exorcism remains the leitmotif of Lu Xun's life and literature.

Lu Xun's creative reinterpretation of antecedents culminates in *Old Stories Retold* (*Gushi xinbian*, 1935), a series of rewrites of classical tales, illuminated by the light of modern political and social circumstances. Here he calls up mythological characters (such as Goddess Nüwa) and historical figures (such as Confucius) and puts them in contemporary circumstances. In so doing, Lu Xun reveals both the contrast between past and present and their paradoxical similitude. Behind the seemingly allegorical intent of these stories is a horrific vacuity filled with resounding laughter. Mixing frivolity and melancholy, *Old Stories Retold* marks Lu Xun's last (anti-)heroic attempt at critiquing Chinese history.

Old Stories Retold created a trend of retelling old stories that went on for decades. Mao Dun, for example, in the early 1930s wrote "Daze County" (Daze xiang, 1931), resurrecting Chen Sheng and Wu Guang of the Qin Dynasty to create a parable about peasant riots of modern times, and "Stone Tablet" (Shijie, 1931), in which the unearthing of a mystical stone tablet in the prelude to *Water Margin* becomes the emblem of the apocalyptic awakening of leftist revolution. By contrast, the neo-sensationalist Shi Zhecun retold classical stories from a decadent, psychological point of view. In "The General's Head" (Jiangjun di tou, 1930), a Tibetan general's hopeless infatuation with a Han Chinese girl ends in his decapitation and symbolic castration. In "Shi Xiu" (Shi Xiu, 1932), drawn from a famous episode of *Water Margin*, the murder of the adulterous Pan Qiaoyun by her husband and his sworn brother Shi Xiu is retold from the perspective of the latter, a misogynist who can consummate his repressed sexual desire only by violence.

Aside from experimenting with new forms, a number of May Fourth writers were able practitioners of various forms of classical-style poetry, the most important genre of premodern literature. This has something to do with the fact that, having grown up in the last decades of the traditional literary canon, they did not lose their deeply ingrained literary sensibilities even after being converted to antitraditionalism. Lu Xun's classical-style poetry, for example, has been well received for its political poignancy, as well as for his ironic use of conventional motifs and metrics. Guo Moruo, the herald of modern poetry, also composed classical-style lines on "youthful pathos" (*shaonian youhuan*) after the model of Gong Zizhen. It was in the hands of a writer like Yu Dafu, however, that classical poetry found a modern resonance in registering the fleeting impressions of the changing times as well as the sense of alienation resulting from the loss of cultural, political, and emotional grounding.

The Czech sinologist Jaroslav Průšek (1906–1980) has described the dynamics of modern Chinese literature as one generated by the pull of two forces: the lyrical and the epic. Whereas the lyrical refers to the discovery of individual subjectivity and a desire for emancipation, the epic refers to the making of social solidarity and a will to revolution. The lyrical and the epic, accordingly, refer not so much to generic traits as to discursive modes, affective capacities, and, most importantly, sociopolitical imaginings. These two modes have fueled the momentum of an entire generation of Chinese writers in their struggle for modernity.

While the "lyrical" may be suggestive of the characteristic traits of Western romanticism and individualism, Průšek is at pains to note that it derives its distinctive orientation no less from premodern Chinese poetic sensibilities. That is to say, granted their antitraditional posture, modern Chinese literati inherited from premodern literature, particularly from poetry and poetic discourse, a style as well as a mannerism in their crafting of a modern subjectivity. In this way, modernity and tradition form a relationship that, though necessarily antagonistic, also puts them in dialogue.

Even for the modernists, the impact of the lyrical is subtly reflected by their creative transformation of the motifs, rhetoric, and imagery of classical poetry. It would be impossible to appreciate Dai Wangshu's "Rainy Alley" without understanding that the lilac, its key image, alludes to a Tang poem; similarly, Li Jinfa's "Deserted Woman" reminds us of the "deserted wife," one of the major tropes in premodern literature. He Qifang and Bian Zhilin, despite their admiration for Western modernists, also resort to the opulent and decadent images of late Tang poetry when conjuring up their own visions of the Chinese wasteland.

Classical-style poets continued to create against the trend of New Literature. Particularly in colonial Taiwan, old-style poetry even underwent a renaissance in the first two decades of the twentieth century. For indigenous literati, classical-style poetry was a vehicle to assert their cultural alliance with China; for Japanese colonials, in that classical-style poetry is also an important part of the Japanese literary tradition, it became a handy means of coopting Taiwanese intellectuals. In China, in addition to names such as Wang Guowei, Chen Sanli, and Liu Yazi, Lü Bicheng merits attention as a major poet of the song lyric. Although Chen had long been hailed the last talented poet in modern China, Liu managed to combine his revolutionary agenda with the posture of the engaged literatus of the classical tradition. Lü was already a well-known woman poet in the late Qing and early Republican era. She reached the peak of her creativity during her travels in Europe in the late 1920s and early 1930s. The spectacle of the Alps and other landscapes enabled Lü not only to expand the thematic repertoire of classical poetry, which had been confined to domestic topoi, but also to generate a modern, feminine vision of the sublime. By focusing on the nexus of space and gender relations, Lü's transgression of geographical and poetical boundaries worked in concert with her feminist consciousness to reshape the whole song lyric genre.

At their most polemical, the practitioners of classical-style literature demonstrated their relevancy to the modern in a negative dialectic. On June 2, 1927, Wang Guowei drowned himself in the Imperial Garden in Beijing. His brief will opens with this ambiguous statement: "After fifty years of living in this world, the only thing that has not yet happened to me is death; having lived through such historical turmoil, nothing further can stain my integrity." Wang's death has been variously attributed to domestic and psychological perturbations, his immersion in Schopenhauer's philosophy, his eschatological visions, and his Qing loyalism. Other factors have also made his suicide compelling to Chinese readers, then and now. As scholars have repeatedly speculated, Wang may have acted out a death wish widely entertained by fellow intellectuals when plunged into despair by historical and cultural crises.

In 1937, Chen Sanli died during a patriotic hunger strike in protest against the Japanese invasion in that year. Chen had been enthusiastic about political reform in his early days, but after seeing the Republican reality he styled himself the "Chinese Onlooker" (Shenzhou Xiushouren). Yet this old "reactionary" poet died for the new China he had chosen to keep at a distance.

One might reprove Chen Sanli and Wang Guowei for lagging behind the spirit of their times, one that was life-affirming and submitted to the discipline of self-renewal. Insofar as their "anachronistic behavior" indicates a (deliberate) blurring of different temporalities as well as paradigms, however, they are arguably more modern than most of the self-proclaimed modern literati of their time. For, even at the beginning of the Chinese modern age, these two had already discerned temporality as something more than the staged realization of enlightenment, revolution, and corporeal transcendence. Faced with radical incompatibilities between the public and private projects of modernity, they asserted their modern freedoms negatively in willful acts of self-annihilation. Thus their suicides paradoxically testified to the emergence of a new, posttraditional Chinese subjectivity.

On July 7, 1937, Japanese troops opened fire on the Chinese army at the Marco Polo Bridge in the suburbs of Beijing. The incident set in motion the Second Sino-Japanese War. The next eight years would see China engulfed in cataclysmic upheavals, including the Nanjing Massacre, the establishment of puppet regimes in Beijing and Nanjing, bloody crackdowns and persecutions, and the exodus of more than twenty million Chinese to southwest China, where the Nationalist regime still held power.

The war brought the development of the various literary movements to a halt. By the mid-1930s, Chinese literature had experienced dynamic growth in multiple directions, in which different streams – literature of engagement and Mandarin Ducks and Butterflies writings, modernism and classicism, the discourse of "humor and laughter" and the discourse of "tears and blood" – crisscrossed and interacted. This vitality was made possible only by the ironic fact of historical uncertainty, and was destined to dissipate once it encountered the brutal force of violence. In view of what modern Chinese writers had already accomplished since the turn of the twentieth century, there is good reason to imagine a more diversified and creative literature had war not broken out. As it was, literature had now to subject itself to a different and, arguably, more tendentious and rigid set of conditions.

Lu Xun died in late 1936 an unhappy man beset by his leftist colleagues as well as by the relentless onrush of sociopolitical circumstances. By then the Chinese Communist Party had completed its Long March into northwest China, which became its wartime base. The Party had drawn aspiring writers such as Ding Ling to join its cause and would continue to build up its political and literary strength in the following decades. Meanwhile, the magazine *Les Contemporains* folded in 1935, marking a tentative coda to Chinese modernism. By the eve of the war, Lin Yutang had embarked on his voyage for the United States. His literature of humor, together with its Anglo-American humanist agenda, would be difficult to carry on in wartime.

Lao She's *Camel Xiangzi*, which ends with the narrator's cynical condemnation of the once hardworking rickshaw puller as a "degenerate, selfish, unfortunate offspring of an ailing society," was completed in 1937, its strident note signaling the changing ethos among even humanitarian writers. Lao She and many other writers, from Shen Congwen to Xiao Hong, Zhang Henshui to Feng Zhi, would soon find themselves on the road with thousands of refugees bound for southwest China and overseas. Zhou Zuoren would choose to stay in Beijing; he ended up collaborating with the puppet regime, for which he had to pay the price after the war. Liu Na'ou and Mu Shiying, the two pillars of Shanghai neo-sensationalism, were assassinated in Shanghai, in 1939 and 1940 respectively, allegedly because of their ties with Japan. Finally, the war itself would bring the career and even the life of many a writer to a premature end, the prominent cases including Xiao Hong and Wang Luyan.

Almost one hundred years earlier, Gong Zizhen, on his road home after quitting office, had written about a China faced with impending change:

> All life in China's nine regions depends on the thundering storm,
> thousands of horses all struck dumb – deplorable indeed.
> I urge the Lord of Heaven to shake us up again
> and grant us human talent not bound to a single kind.

Written on the eve of the First Opium War, the poem imagines the cosmos brought to a standstill, and calls on the natural and supernatural powers to galvanize the current state out of stagnation. Gong's yearning for a new voice anticipates the tenor of modern Chinese literature. For all its radical tonality, however, there lingers in the poem a skepticism about poetry as a viable form of persuasion and agency. As the first half of the poem implies, at a time when the voices of thousands of talents have already been silenced, can a single poet's call for reform really change Heaven's set course?

So, almost a hundred years after Gong Zizhen, Chinese writers were still struggling to respond to the same concerns. In the face of the impending Sino-Japanese war, they were all the more anxious to negotiate issues such as national crisis and cultural renovation, tradition and individual talent, historicity and its modern antithesis. Underlining their search for the meaning of writing is Gong Zizhen's "pathos," Liang Qichao's "new citizenship," Lu Xun's "call to arms" and "wandering," and Shen Congwen's imaginary nostalgia for a lyrical China. Chinese literature was only just entering another stage in redefining its modernity.

7

Chinese literature from 1937 to the present

MICHELLE YEH

I. The Second Sino-Japanese War (1937–1945) and its aftermath

On July 7, 1937, Japanese troops stationed near the Marco Polo Bridge (Lugou Bridge to the Chinese), ten miles southwest of Beijing (Beiping at the time), used the pretext of searching for a soldier who had gone missing during a drill to demand entry into the city. When refused, they fired shots. The Chinese regiment commander Ji Xingwen (1908–1958) ordered his soldiers to return fire, triggering the outbreak of the Second Sino-Japanese War, which was to change China forever.

The military confrontation was not wholly unexpected. Since Japan invaded and occupied Manchuria in September 1931, tension had been mounting. Chiang Kai-shek's (1887–1975) policy of nonresistance had been met with opposition from various quarters, as evidenced in the Xi'an Incident of December 12, 1936, in which Marshal Zhang Xueliang (1901–2001) took Chiang hostage in order to extort a promise from him to form a united front with the Chinese Communist Party (hereafter CCP) against Japanese aggression. Ten days after the Marco Polo Bridge Incident, Chiang issued a statement condemning the violence as "the last straw," and in August declared an all-out war of resistance.

Japan had aimed to take China in three months. Advances in the north went largely unopposed; within a month, Beijing and Tianjin fell. On August 13, Japan attacked Shanghai. Faced with the enemy's superior firepower, Chinese soldiers stood their ground for three months. At Four Banks Storehouse (Sihang cangku) in Shanghai, October 27 to 31, eight hundred soldiers under Commander Xie Jinyuan (1904–1941) held off Japanese offensives, allowing Chinese troops to retreat and Chinese civilians to be evacuated. The campaign ended on November 27. Despite heavy casualties (an estimated 250,000 soldiers died) and eventual defeat, Shanghai's valiant resistance forced Japan to halt military action in Qingdao and, more importantly, shattered all hopes of a "swift conquest" of China.

After Shanghai fell, Japan advanced westward on Nanjing (Nanking), the capital of China. Battle began on December 7; on December 13 Chinese troops retreated, leaving the city open to the enemy. Over the next six weeks, Japanese soldiers, under the command of General Yanagawa Heisuke (1879–1945) and Lieutenant-General Nakajima Kesago (1881–1945), inflicted atrocities on Chinese people indiscriminately; they gang-raped, mutilated, burned, beheaded, and buried civilians alive, often en masse and as a form of sport. According to the Chinese military tribunal held in Nanjing in February 1946, more than 340,000 people were slaughtered during the first six weeks of Japanese occupation. The International Military Tribunal for the Far East set the figure at over 200,000. In addition to the killings, looting was widespread. For example, it is estimated that 880,000 books from Nanjing libraries were shipped to Japan. These war crimes are known to the world as the Nanjing Massacre or the Rape of Nanking.

The Chinese government moved to Wuhan in September 1938, but a month later the city fell, as did Guangzhou (formerly Canton). Moving further west, the government established Chongqing in Sichuan Province as the wartime capital. Japan, in control of most of the north, southeast, and northeast, set up a puppet regime headed by Wang Jingwei (1893–1944), a hero of the 1911 Republican Revolution and at the time vice president of the Nationalist Party (also known as KMT; Guomindang in Chinese, hereafter GMD). On March 30, 1940, a "Republic" under the Wang administration was founded in Nanjing. Japanese invasion spread to British-ruled Hong Kong, which fell in December 1941, and to Guilin, which fell in late 1944.

Literature of resistance

More than any prior act of foreign aggression, the Japanese invasion threatened China's survival. It had a profound impact on the literary scene that was both immediate and long-lasting. Not only were cultural institutions, from universities and museums to publishing houses and newspapers, destroyed or dislocated, many writers were uprooted and forced to live itinerant lives. What was to unfold was a massive diaspora, which would take writers to all corners of the land. Either collectively or individually, they had to come to grips with the irrevocable changes brought about by the war and to chart a new course for their personal and creative lives. While instability and fragmentation describe the geopolitical and psychological conditions in which writers found themselves, literature provided a major source of sanity and hope during the war. Even as prewar activities were disrupted or halted, new networks were formed and new paths ventured upon.

One immediate response to the war was that writers were united by patriotism regardless of their ideological positions. Nationwide, they mobilized to create and promulgate resistance literature. On March 27, 1938, the All-China Resistance Association of Writers and Artists (Zhongguo quanguo wenyijie kangdi xiehui) was formed in Hankou, with Lao She (1899–1966) as its director. In February 1939, the association appointed an International Literary Propaganda Committee (Guoji wenyi xuanchuan weiyuanhui) to garner the support of Western allies. The committee was represented by Lin Yutang (1895–1976) in France, Xiong Shiyi (a.k.a. S. I. Hsiung, 1902–1991) and Jiang Yi (1903–1977) in Britain, Xiao San (1896–1983) in the Soviet Union, and Hu Tianshi in Switzerland.

The association also set up branches in all major cities and launched a national crusade to raise morale and promote patriotism with the slogan "Literature to the countryside! Literature joins the army!" The association's official publication, *Literature of Resistance* (*Kangzhan wenyi*), was to become the longest-running journal in the war period. Young writers were organized into groups of "literary correspondents" (*wenyi tongxun yuan*) to report on cultural activities at the local level. By way of these and other means, literature, along with woodcuts and cartoons, not only bore witness to the war but galvanized the Chinese people in defense of their homeland.

It should come as no surprise that the war led to a golden age of modern theater – "spoken drama" – in light of its accessibility and mass appeal. In August 1937, twelve National Salvation Drama Troupes (Jiu wang yanchu dui) were organized in Shanghai to perform all over China. Two of the most frequently performed plays were *Defend the Marco Polo Bridge* (*Baowei Lugou qiao*, 1937) and *Lay Down Your Whip* (*Fangxia ni de bianzi*, 1936). A team composition, *Defend the Marco Polo Bridge* premiered in Shanghai on August 7, 1937, exactly one month after the incident. *Lay Down Your Whip* gained immense popularity for its simple yet stirring plot. Many of these plays were performed as "street-corner theater" (*jietou ju*), a form popular since 1931.

In the same vein, poetry of resistance employed plain everyday language and singsong rhythm easily learned by heart. Also known as "street-corner poetry" (*jietou shi*), the poetry was literally taken to the street and recited to the public. Other types include "poster poetry" (*chuandan shi*), "slogan poetry" (*kouhao shi*), and "poetry on the wall" (*qiangtou shi*). Tian Jian (1916–1985) and Ke Zhongping (1902–1964) were well known for their work in this genre.

Born in rural Anhui, Tian Jian arrived in Yan'an in summer 1939 and played a major role in promoting a "poetry of national resistance." His poems, typically consisting of very short lines (one to three characters each), were staggered in imitation of Vladimir Mayakovsky's (1893–1930) "ladder poetry." Tian won the accolade "Drummer of Our Time" (Shidai de gushou) from Wen Yiduo (1899–1946) for the "primitive" and "masculine" power of his poetry, as illustrated by "If We Don't Go Fight the War" (Jiashi women bu qu dazhang):

> If we don't go fight the war,
> The enemies, even after killing us
> With their bayonets,
> Will point to our bones and say:
> "Look –
> What slaves!"

Instead of direct exhortation, the poem is a drama of the speaking voice, which taunts the audience by reminding it that the consequence of passivity and cowardice is not just individual deaths but a collective loss of honor and dignity. The last two lines, cast as an apostrophe, capture the enemy's arrogance and contempt. It is not hard to imagine how the poem must have aroused the public when recited out loud in the streets of China.

Aside from populist theater and poetry, reportage literature blossomed. Variously called "report" (baogao), "sketch" (suxie), or "dispatch" (tongxun), reportage was both a necessity – given the ever-changing military situation – and a natural outgrowth of personal experience. Journals devoted significant space to reportage, which was then collected and published in book form. Many produced reportage, but a few stood out: Qiu Dongping (1910–1941, killed by enemy fire), Cao Bai, Luo Binji (b. 1917), and Bi Ye (b. 1916) developed the genre into a gripping mode of writing by incorporating skillfully crafted narrative, dialogue, and characterization.

As different parts of China were affected differently by the war, the following survey focuses on separate regions: the Japanese-occupied area, represented by Beijing and Shanghai; the GMD-ruled interior, including the major cities of Chongqing, Kunming, and Guilin; the CCP bases in the northwest, commonly known as "Three Borders"; Hong Kong before and after Japanese invasion; and colonial Taiwan. The survey will make clear that although war was an inescapable reality, writers did not write about it exclusively. The literature of this period is wide-ranging and extremely diverse in subject matter and style. Moreover, literature of the highest caliber was written. While many established writers reached the peak of their creativity, a new generation of writers emerged on the scene and left indelible marks. This phenomenon is no small miracle when we consider the situation in Europe during World War II.

Chongqing and the United Front

With many playwrights gathering in Chongqing, the wartime capital became a major center for drama. Wu Zuguang (1917–2003) wrote his first play *The City of the Phoenix (Fenghuang cheng)* in 1937, followed by *Song of Righteousness (Zhengqi ge)* based on the life of Wen Tianxiang (1236–1283), the Southern Song dynasty loyalist who died fighting the Mongols. Other long-running plays include *Home on a Snowy Night (Fengxue ye guiren,* 1942) about the tragic love affair between a male Peking Opera singer and a courtesan, *Lin Chong Escapes in the Night (Lin Chong ye ben)* based on the sixteenth-century novel *Water Margin,* and *Weaver Woman and Oxherd* derived from the ancient folktale.

Xia Yan (1900–1995), renowned for his film scripts, wrote *Fascist Germs (Faxisi xijun), Resurrection (Fuhuo,* adapted from Tolstoy's (1828–1910) novel), and *Love at Sky's End (Fangcao tianya). Fascist Germs* explores the clash between idealism and reality, knowledge and patriotism. The protagonist is a Chinese scientist who studies in Japan and marries a Japanese woman. After the war breaks out, he returns to China to devote himself to medical research. Confronted with Japanese fascism, he realizes that he must exterminate "fascist germs" before he can engage in a disinterested pursuit of knowledge.

In 1938, Cao Yu (1910–1996), famous for *Thunderstorm,* moved to Chongqing with the National Drama Academy. In the next few years, he wrote *Metamorphosis (Tuibian), Peking Man (Beijing ren), Family* (based on Ba Jin's (1904–2005) novel), and a Chinese version of Shakespeare's (1564–1616) *Romeo and Juliet. Peking Man* (1941) is considered by many to be his best work. It expresses the May Fourth ideal of enlightenment and modernization, with psychological subtlety and a tone of understatement that suggest the influence of Chekhov (1860–1904).

Peking Man depicts the disintegration of a gentry family in Beijing with a scathing attack on the hypocrisy and inhumanity of traditional society. The coffin that Patriarch Zeng has been preparing for himself for years – having it meticulously lacquered layer by layer – is symbolic of old China. His children suffer in the oppressive family but lack the courage to fight, to change, and to love. The males are either feeble and lethargic, finding temporary escape in genteel hobbies, or cynical and self-loathing, deriving sadistic pleasure from abusing those around them. In contrast, the women are independent and brave. Patriarch Zeng's niece leaves when she realizes that the son whom she loves will never change. The son later commits suicide. The granddaughter-in-law demands release from a loveless arranged marriage and pursues a new life. Only the teenage daughter of an anthropologist who studies Peking Man is uncontaminated by the decaying culture of China. At the end of the play, a robust Peking Man appears on the stage, a poignant reminder of how low his cowardly and selfish descendants have fallen.

After the united front was formed, Guo Moruo was appointed by the GMD to be in charge of propaganda. As relations between the GMD and the CCP deteriorated, however, his power diminished. On January 7, 1941, the GMD's Fortieth Division ambushed the CCP's Fourth New Army in southern Anhui, thus ending the short-lived alliance. In Chongqing, the GMD stepped up censorship to weed out leftist publications.

Chinese literature has a long tradition of evoking the past as a way of alluding to the present. This reflects the Confucian belief in the moral authority invested in historical writing and protects the writer from the wrath of those in power. In Chongqing, many turned to historical drama to critique social and political reality. For example, Guo Moruo wrote three historical plays between December 1941 and February 1942, including *Qu Yuan*, which premiered in April 1942 to critical acclaim. The five-act play dramatizes the conflict between good and evil, personified by a loyal poet–minister and a conniving queen. Yang Hansheng (1902–1993) wrote *Tale of the Heavenly Kingdom* (*Tianguo chunqiu*), about the Taiping Rebellion led by the Christianized Hong Xiuquan (1814–1864), as well as *Hero from the Grassland* (*Caomang yingxiong*), about the peasant leader of an uprising in the Qing dynasty. In both cases, the protagonist meets his downfall because of internecine conflict and his own tragic flaw.

Still others wrote political satires. Song Zhidi's (1914–1956) *Chongqing in Fog* (*Wu Chongqing*, 1940) uses the image of fog, which literally veils the mountain city from October to May, to embody the social climate that corrupts youth. *Portrait of Officialdom* (*Shengguan tu*) by Chen Baichen (1908–1994) pokes fun at the clownish behavior of GMD officials. Similarly, Lao She's *Lingering Fog* (*Can wu*, 1939) satirizes bureaucrats with lively language and memorable characters.

Lao She also wrote novels, such as *Trepidation* (*Huangkong*), *Living Ignominiously* (*Tou sheng*), and *Four Generations under One Roof* (*Sishi tongtang*). Based in part on the suffering that his family witnessed in occupied Beijing, the last story depicts how Patriarch Qi goes to great lengths to maintain the traditional ideal of four generations living under one roof. Tragedy strikes again and again, including the deaths of several of his children and grandchildren.

Re-creating life in the old *hutong* (Beijing backstreets), the novel critiques the traditional, family-based culture. In 1946, along with Cao Yu, Lao She was invited to visit the United States for a year by the State Department. Due to the civil war between the GMD and the CCP, he ended up staying longer and returned to China in late 1949.

Ba Jin tried his hand at drama, but his greatest achievement remains in fiction. *Spring* (1938) and *Autumn* (1940) are sequels to the 1933 *Family*, and complete his magnum opus *Torrent Trilogy* (*Jiliu sanbuqu*). *Autumn* presents the final stage of the disintegration of the Gao family and the coming to maturity of the younger generation. Shorn of sentimentality and didacticism, *Autumn* surpasses the preceding volumes in intensity. Ba Jin also wrote two novellas, *The Fourth Ward* (*Di si bingfang*) and *Leisure Garden* (*Qi yuan*), and what would be his last novel, *Cold Night* (*Han ye*). Written between 1944 and 1946 and published in 1947, *Cold Night* revolves around a middle-class family of four in Chongqing. The triangular relationships between the main characters – husband, wife, and mother-in-law – lead to tragedy; life for each is suffused with an overwhelming sense of powerlessness, especially on the part of the husband, who is too meek and inarticulate to resolve the escalating tension between his wife and his mother. None of the characters is a "bad person," but they are bound ultimately by their personalities, which result in clashing needs and aspirations. In the end, the wife comes back without marrying her boss, but her husband has died of tuberculosis, and her son and her mother-in-law have moved away.

One of the most exciting phenomena on the wartime literary scene is the emergence of young writers. Lu Ling (the pen name of Xu Sixing, 1923–1994) was expelled from middle school for his writing and became a frequent contributor to *July* and *Hope*, both edited by the leftist writer and theorist Hu Feng (the pen name of Zhang Guangren, 1902–1985). *The Hungry Guo Su'e* (*Ji'e de Guo Su'e*) was published in 1942, followed by two collections of short stories and two novels from 1945 to 1948. Lu Ling started writing the novel *Children of the Rich* (*Caizhu de ernü men*) at the age of eighteen. The plot revolves around the three sons of the wealthy Jiang family in Suzhou in decline and disintegration. The eldest son is handsome and smart, but he is too weak to confront his wife's greed and promiscuity. Driven to madness, he burns down the family mansion and drowns himself in a river. The second son loses to his scheming sister-in-law in the fight for the family fortune and turns into a cultural conservative. The youngest son is proud and idealistic; he tries to carve out a new path for himself but experiences nothing but disillusionment and loss of love. He dies alone in a village in Chongqing.

An anti-*Bildungsroman*, *Children of the Rich* paints a bleak picture of lost youth in a time of national crisis. Under the influence of Hu Feng, who opposed shallow romanticism and formulaic writing, Lu Ling developed an unflinching realism in all of his characters. His sympathy lay with the downtrodden in society. *The Hungry Guo Su'e*, written when the author was only nineteen, is about a rural woman martyred by barbaric patriarchy. Su'e is married to a much older man whose opium addiction lands them in poverty. Her need for love cannot be denied, however. She defies the traditional moral code by having an affair with a factory worker and suffers grave consequences. In creating this protagonist, Lu Ling celebrates the irrepressible human lust for life, even though a hypocritical society views her transgression as madness. Fittingly, this is the word with which a passage describing the lovers after making love begins and ends; it evokes both the madness of sexual ecstasy and the madness of despair. Su'e refuses to bow to her community and dies after being brutalized by her husband and neighbors.

Romance continued to be popular and underwent transformation in the hands of a new generation of writers. Interestingly, this occurred when Zhang Henshui (1895–1967), the famous author of Mandarin Ducks and Butterflies fiction, turned away from this style of writing and wrote more than twenty novels on social and political themes. The new romance came into its own with Xu Xu (1908–1980) and Wumingshi ("Mr. No Name," 1917–1986).

Xu Xu received a BA in philosophy from Peking University, where he also did graduate work in psychology. In 1934, he moved to Shanghai and worked as an editor for Lin Yutang's bi-monthly *This Human World* (*Renjian shi*). Xu went to France in 1936 and received a Ph.D. in Philosophy from the the University of Paris. He returned to Shanghai after the war broke out and subsequently moved to Chongqing in 1942 to teach at the National Central Normal College.

In 1943, Xu Xu's *The Soughing Wind* (*Feng xiaoxiao*) came out in Chongqing. The novel takes place in wartime Shanghai and revolves around a male protagonist and three beautiful women with distinctly different attributes: Bai Ping is elegant and sophisticated, Mei Yingzi is sexy and passionate, Helen is innocent and pure. Predictably, the protagonist becomes romantically involved with all three. To further complicate the plot, it turns out that Bai and Mei are undercover agents working for China and the US respectively. They work together to obtain intelligence from Japanese sources. In the process Bai loses her life, and her death is avenged by Mei. The protagonist leaves for Chongqing with Helen so they may dedicate themselves to the resistance movement. Set in glamorous Shanghai, the novel combines the lure of romance with the suspense of spy intrigues. It was so popular that 1943 was named the Year of Xu Xu. In 1944, the author left for the United States to work as a correspondent for the newspaper *News Roundup* (*Saodang bao*) and from there moved to Hong Kong.

Nine years Xu Xu's junior, Wumingshi, the pen name of Bu Naifu, was born in Nanjing in 1917. At age seventeen, he quit middle school and went to Beijing alone. Immersed in May Fourth literature and world literature in translation, he also taught himself English and Russian. Wumingshi acknowledged influences by Romain Roland (1866–1944), Tolstoy, and Nietzsche (1844–1900). His first story, "Collapse" (*Bengkui*, 1937), is based on the mental illness of the German philosopher.

Romance at the North Pole (*Beiji fengqing hua*) was inspired by the love story of Li Fanying, a Korean friend whom Wumingshi met in Chongqing. Serialized in the *North China News* (*Huabei xinwen*) from November 1943 to January 1944 under the title *A Romantic Encounter at the North Pole* (*Beiji yanyu*), the novel features a Korean officer who fights the Japanese in Manchuria alongside Chinese guerrillas. After Manchuria falls, he retreats to Siberia, where on New Year's Eve he meets and falls in love with the daughter of a deceased Polish general. Soon, however, the protagonist is ordered to return to Korea. Passing through Italy, he receives a letter from the mother of the woman he loves. She has committed suicide and left the request that on the tenth anniversary of their first meeting he go to a mountain and look to the North Pole in remembrance of their love.

Romance at the North Pole was an overnight success, as was the sequel *The Woman in the Tower* (*Ta li de nüren*). The same narrator recounts the story of a violinist, Luo Shengti, who gives up true love because he feels morally obligated to his arranged marriage. He not only breaks up with the woman he loves, but pushes her into the arms of a man whom he considers a better choice for her. By the time he realizes that her husband is abusive and base, it is too late. Guilt-ridden, he becomes a Daoist and spends the rest of his life in seclusion on a mountain.

The new romantic genre created by Xu Xu and Wumingshi appealed to readers as much for their fantastic tales of tragic love as for their exotic settings and foreign elements. One character in *The Soughing Wind* is half-Chinese and half-American, and another has an English name. The book also makes many references to Western philosophy. Both protagonists in *Romance at the North Pole* are non-Chinese, and the protagonist in *The Woman in the Tower* plays a Western instrument. Even the image of the "woman in the tower" may have come from medieval European tales of chivalry, with the iconic image of a damsel in distress waiting to be rescued by the knight in shining armor. For Chinese readers, these romances must have been a welcome relief from the dreariness and hardship of wartime life.

After the war, Wumingshi moved to Hangzhou and embarked on the ambitious project of a six-volume work titled *Nameless Book* (*Wuming shu*). He completed the first three volumes between 1946 and 1950 and finished the rest in the 1950s. The work was not published, however, until the early 1980s in Hong Kong. Even during the Cultural Revolution, when Wumingshi was sent to jail, his romances from the war period were circulated in handwritten copies.

Maturing modernism in Kunming and Guilin

The Second Sino-Japanese War led to the displacement of many cultural institutions. The premier universities in North China – Peking, Tsinghua, and Nankai – were relocated first to Changsha in November 1937, and then, in spring 1938, to Kunming in Yunnan Province. Amalgamated as the Southwest Associated University (Xi'nan lianda), they formed a major intellectual center in wartime China. Many prominent thinkers and writers taught there at one time or another. A partial list includes such leading writers as Wen Yiduo, Zhu Ziqing (1898–1948), Shen Congwen (1902–1988), Feng Zhi (1905–1993), Shi Zhecun (1905–2003), Li Guangtian (1906–1960), Bian Zhilin (1910–2000), and Qian Zhongshu (1910–1998), as well as such prominent philosophers and historians as Wu Mi (1894–1981), Jin Yuelin (1895–1984), Feng Youlan (1895–1990), Qian Mu (1895–1990), Zhu Guangqian (1897–1986), and Tang Yongtong (1898–1964). William Empson (Yan Busun, 1906–1984), the eminent British literary critic and poet, also taught there in 1938 and 1939.

During his stint in Kunming, Empson introduced students to modern Anglo-American poets, from Gerard Manley Hopkins (1844–1889) and W. B. Yeats (1865–1939) to T. S. Eliot (1888–1965), W. H. Auden (1907–1973), and Dylan Thomas (1914–1953). Eliot's work had appeared in China as early as 1923; in the 1930s some of his poems and essays were translated by Ye Gongchao (1904–1981), who met Eliot at Cambridge University in 1926, and by Bian Zhilin, Zhao Luorui (b. 1912), and others. A few translations of Yeats and Auden were also available in the prewar period. Auden's wit and satire, as well as his political activism, inspired many students living in the shadow of war. In 1938, Auden and Christopher Isherwood (1906–1986) visited China. Returning to England after a detour in America, they talked about their Chinese experiences on radio and television; these broadcasts formed the core of their book *Journey to a War* (1939). On the cover of the book is a Chinese woodblock portraying a refugee mother carrying a child on her back. As she runs, she looks up fearfully at four Japanese warplanes in the crimson sky.

Before moving to Kunming, Shen Congwen returned to western Hunan for four months in 1937. The experience led to the creation, from 1939 to 1942, of *Long River (Chang he)*. Another "story by the river," *Long River* differs from Shen's earlier work in that instead of presenting rural Hunan as a self-sufficient, idyllic world, the new novel meshes two discourses, or two public spaces, as it ponders the transformation of tradition into modernity. Local culture and oral traditions that bind together a rural community are juxtaposed with the nation state that is both formed and informed by the modern press. Against the backdrop of the New Life Movement launched in 1934 by Chiang Kai-shek, the story reveals ambivalence toward the grand narratives of modernization and nationalism.

The gathering of so many luminaries in Kunming created a stimulating environment. Despite the harsh living conditions and the constant threat of enemy bombs, writers reached the peak of their creativity. One example is Feng Zhi, who wrote *Sonnets (Shisihang ji)* in 1941 and 1942, after a hiatus of twelve years. The sequence of twenty-seven sonnets is a modern landmark not only because it is the first collection of original sonnets in Chinese but also because of its supreme artistry and philosophical depth.

The sonnet had been introduced into China by the early 1920s. Christened *shanglai ti* ("Sonnet-form") by Wen Yiduo, it was also simply known as "fourteen lines." Aside from Wen Yiduo, Zheng Boqi (1895–1979, a noted playwright) and Lu Zhiwei (1894–1970, a pioneer formalist) were among the first to write sonnets. Many associated with the Crescent School in the late 1920s and early 1930s, such as Xu Zhimo (1896–1931), Zhu Xiang (1904–1933), Bian Zhilin, and Liang Zongdai (1903–1983), experimented in the form.

Feng Zhi's sonnets embody the consummate expression of the organic whole of form and content. Written loosely in the Italian form, the sequence of twenty-seven sonnets meditates on life as a process of constant change. Influenced by Goethe (1749–1832) and Rilke (1875–1926), whom Feng had translated as a Ph.D. student in Germany between 1930 and 1935, the poems recognize the frailty and impermanence of humanity in contrast to nature, yet at the same time view life as a paradox. Materiality and spirituality, being and potentiality, form and content are interdependent; the latter in each pair needs the former in order to be concretized. Like a container and a banner, which allow water and wind to be manifested, poetry renders visible that which is hidden in life.

The meaning of life is also the theme of Feng Zhi's *Wu Zixu: From Fatherland to the City of Wu* (*Wu Zixu, cong chengfu dao Wu shi*, 1942–1943). The novel presents Wu's spiritual journey as he escapes from the Kingdom of Chu and seeks to avenge his father's and elder brother's murders by the king. Feng is intent on baring the soul of the avenger, who transforms himself by becoming one with nature and music. The approach is modernist rather than romantic, existentialist rather than naturalist.

While established poets like Feng Zhi were at the the height of their creative powers, a younger generation of poets burst on the scene. Quite a few were students in the Department of Foreign Languages, such as Mu Dan (1918–1977), Yuan Kejia (1921–2008), Du Yunxie (1918–2002), Wang Zuoliang (1916–1995), Zhao Ruihong (b. 1915), Yang Zhouhan (1915–1989), Yu Mingchuan, Lin Pu (1912–1996), Shen Jiping (b. 1927), and Miu Hong (1927–1945). Others came from a background in philosophy (Zheng Min, b. 1920), sociology (He Da, 1915–1994), Chinese literature (Zhou Dingyi, b. 1913), history (Chen Shi, b. 1916), and economics (Luo Jiyi, b. 1920; Ma Fenghua, b. 1922).

Mu Dan, Zheng Min, and Du Yunxie were known as the "Three Stars of the Southwest Associated University." Although Zheng Min did not know the other two personally, it was no accident, given the intellectual climate and literary mentors that they shared, that all three drew on Anglo-American modernism and Western philosophy. The modernist emphases on the interior voice, deep reality, "impersonal" approach, and concrete language set their work apart from both the romantic–idealist poetry before the war and the populist poetry of resistance during the war.

As the war came to an end, journals and literary supplements mushroomed, including *Renaissance* (*Wenyi fuxing*), edited by Zheng Zhenduo (1898–1958) and Li Jianwu (1906–1982); *Poetry Creation* (*Shi chuangzao*) by Zang Kejia (1905–2004) and Cao Xinzhi (1917–1995); and the literary supplement to the *Dagongbao* by Shen Congwen. A group of young poets in Shanghai, including Xin Di (1912–2004, who studied at the University of Edinburgh from 1936 to 1941 and was acquainted with T. S. Eliot, Stephen Spender (1905–1995), and others), Tang Qi (1920–1990), Tang Shi (1920–2005), Chen Jingrong (1917–1989), and Hang Yuehe (the penname of Cao Xinzhi), founded the *Chinese New Poetry Monthly* (*Zhongguo xinshi yuekan*). It attracted former students of the Southwest Associated University, in particular Mu Dan, Du Yunxie, Zheng Min, and Yuan Kejia. They were brought together by a common interest in Anglo-American modernism.

This group of editors and contributors came to be known as the School of Chinese New Poetry, although the monthly folded in five months for financial reasons. After 1949, these poets turned silent and remained unknown until the early 1980s when they were rediscovered. When a collection of their poetry was slated for publication in 1979, Xin Di allegedly dubbed the group the School of Nine Leaves (Jiu ye pai) – since, as he said humorously, they could not call themselves the Nine Flowers. Since the collection appeared in 1981, the Nine Leaves have entered the literary canon and exerted a significant influence on post-Mao generations.

Posthumously recognized as the leading poet of the Nine Leaves, Mu Dan was baptized in the flames of war. In March 1942, when Japanese troops landed in Burma (then a British colony), a Chinese military expedition set out to protect the Burma Road and to aid the British and American allies. The poet, who had graduated from college two years earlier, joined the expedition as a volunteer and served as the interpreter for General Du Yuming (1904–1981). (Du Yunxie also volunteered as an interpreter.) Due to a lack of coordination and support from the Allied forces, the Chinese army suffered a grave defeat and the route of retreat was cut off by the enemy. A small detachment under General Sun Liren (1899–1990) made their way to India to meet up with the British; most went north with General Du across the Wild Man Mountain (*Yeren shan*), through tropical rainforests sprawling more than two hundred miles between Burma and Yunnan Province. Fifty thousand soldiers, half of the expedition army, lost their lives to disease, starvation, torrential rains, poisonous snakes, and wild beasts. Mu Dan survived the "journey of death" to write about it in "Song of the Jungle – In Memory of the Soldiers Who Died on Wild Man Mountain" (Senlin zhi ge – ji Yeren shan sinan de bingshi). The poem is written as a dialogue in which Jungle welcomes Man into his embrace, "to shed all the flesh and blood." All that remains of Man are "aimless eyes," "speechless teeth," and eternal nothingness.

With charged language and paradoxical images, Mu Dan's series "Eight Poems" (Shi ba shou, 1942) contemplates the clash between flesh and spirit, between the quest for love and inevitable disillusionment. Love is but a glimpse of the world lit up by language and surrounded by vast, formless darkness, a world of "sweet words that die before they can be born." Humans can never "own" love because they themselves are, and will always be, incomplete. Insignificant players in the flux of change, human beings will always be transitory as they "grow in the womb of Death." "Eight Poems" cut through all romantic illusions about love, the self, and life.

In addition to the poets, a young fiction writer named Wang Zengqi (1920–1997) also made his debut on the literary scene. Wang Zengqi was a student of Shen Congwen at Southwest Associated from 1939 to 1943. In "Revenge"

(Fuchou), written in Kunming in 1944, a nameless swordsman spends his life looking for his father's killer. He is taken in by an old monk and stays with him at the temple. One day he spots his father's name tattooed on the monk's arm. In the end, he puts his sword back in the scabbard and joins the monk in breaking rocks. The language of "Revenge" is simultaneously colloquial and lyrical, imagistic and terse. The revelation of the monk's identity makes the swordsman realize that they are bound together by their thirst for revenge, which has ostensibly given a purpose to their lives but is meaningless in the final analysis. Daoist–Buddhist overtones underscore this story of resolution and transcendence.

After the war broke out, the renowned physicist and playwright Ding Xilin (1893–1974) moved first to Kunming and later to Guilin. In 1939, he wrote the one-act play *Three Dollars, National Currency (San kuai qian, guobi)*, and the four-act *Wait till the Missus Comes Home (Deng taitai huilai de shihou)*. In 1940, after attending the memorial service of Cai Yuanpei (1868–1940) in Hong Kong, he wrote another four-act play, *Wondrous Peak Mountain (Miaofeng shan)*, in honor of the esteemed educator and scholar. Unlike his prewar comedies, these plays were all based on the grim reality of wartime China, filled with refugees, collaborationists, and militias.

Wen Yiduo had stopped writing modern poetry and devoted himself to the study of Chinese Classics by the end of the 1920s, but he continued to discover and mentor young poets. In 1943 he worked with Robert Payne (Bai En, 1911–1983), a former British diplomat then professor at Southwest Associated, on an English anthology of recent poetry. Wen also compiled the Chinese poets into *Collected Modern Poems (Xiandai shi chao)*, containing 184 poems by sixty-five poets.

Wen Yiduo did not live to see the publication of the English anthology in London in 1947, under the title *Contemporary Chinese Poetry*. After a short spell of jubilation at China's victory in the Second Sino-Japanese War, the country was plunged into turmoil again. Corruption and profiteering were rampant among GMD officials in postwar relocation and restoration efforts. Inflation and devaluation of the currency exacerbated the impoverished living conditions of the masses. Meanwhile, a civil war between the GMD and the CCP seemed imminent. In response to the volatile situation, the GMD adopted draconian measures of repression and assassination. On July 11, 1946, Li Gongpu (1902–1946), leader of the Chinese Democracy League (Zhongguo minzhu tongmeng), was assassinated for his outspoken criticism. Four days later, Wen Yiduo, who had joined the league in 1944, gave two speeches condemning the GMD, even challenging the GMD to take his life too. On his way home afterward, he was gunned down by secret agents.

Guilin was another wartime cultural center in the country's interior. From October 1938 to the first half of 1939, more than a thousand writers, scholars, and artists sojourned here, including Mao Dun (1896–1981), Ouyang Yuqian (1889–1962), Ai Wu (1904–1992), Zhou Libo (1908–1979), Ai Qing (1910–1996), Guo Moruo, Ba Jin, Xia Yan, Tian Han, and Hu Feng. According to the publisher and editor Zhao Jiabi (1908–1997), up to 80 percent of the books and journals published in the interior during the war came from Guilin.

Ai Qing was arguably the most famous wartime poet. Poems such as "Snow Is Falling on the Land of China" (Xue luo zai Zhongguo de tudi shang), "I Love This Land" (Wo ai zhe tudi), and "The North" (Beifang), all written in 1937 and 1938, are moving tributes to the ravaged land and the suffering people. In Guilin, Ai Qing wrote several long narrative poems: "The Bugler" (Chui hao zhe), "He Died the Second Time" (Ta si zai dier ci), and "The Torch" (Huoba). He also published *Discourse on Poetry* (Shi lun, 1939), a collection of remarks on poetry that is often ignored in literary histories perhaps because they seem inconsistent with the image of the patriotic balladeer with which Ai Qing has come to be identified. *Discourse on Poetry* defines poetry as a craft and a distinct art form in a modernist vein. Ai Qing holds that content determines form and that the quality of a poem depends on experience (rather than feeling) and imagination (which reorganizes experience). He compares the poet to Prometheus, who stole language from Zeus. Reflecting this interest in modernism, Ai coedited *Zenith* (*Dingdian*) with the modernist poet Dai Wangshu (1905–1950) in Guilin in 1938. We will never know, however, how Ai Qing would have developed as a modernist. In 1941 he went to Yan'an, where he was to discover the hefty price defiant Prometheus had to pay.

The literary scene in occupied Beijing

Three days after the Marco Polo Bridge Incident, a poem appeared in *New Poetry* (Xin shi):

> As I walk to the street corner
> a car drives by
> so, the loneliness
> of the mailbox
> mailbox PO
> so, I can't remember
> the car's number X
> so, the loneliness

of Arabic numbers
loneliness of the car
loneliness of the street
loneliness of humankind

According to Fei Ming (1901–1967), he composed "Street Corner" (Jie tou) while taking a walk near Huguo Temple in west Beijing. The poet is both amazed and bewildered by the automobile that drives by. The contrast between the speeding car and the immobile mailbox on the street corner – and, by extension, the poet, who cannot remember the car's license plate number – accentuates his feeling of loneliness. Paradoxically, the material advancement in the modern world seems only to lead to greater isolation and estrangement of human beings from their environment.

This sense of alienation also describes the desolation in the ancient capital under occupation, where Japan was to establish a "provisional government of the Republic of China" (Zhonghua minguo linshi zhengfu) headed by Wang Kemin (1879–1945) on December 14, 1937. Renamed the North China Political Affairs Commission (Huabei zhengwu weiyuanhui), it came under the control of the Nanjing puppet government after March 1940.

Fei Ming's poetry was collected in *By the Water* (*Shui bian*). Published in Beijing in April 1944, this slim volume contains sixteen poems by him and seven poems by his friend Kai Yuan (the pen name of Shen Qiwu, 1902–1969, who was an editor of the *Literary Compilation* (*Wenxue jikan*)). The book was published without Fei's knowledge, as he had already left Beijing to return to Hubei Province in December 1937. Fei's critical essays, mostly written when he was teaching at Peking University before the war, were also collected and published as *On New Poetry* (*Tan xin shi*) in Beijing in 1944.

On New Poetry tries to define not only modern poetry but classical poetry as well. Fei Ming goes beyond formal, linguistic, and rhetorical differences between modern and traditional poetry to emphasize the universal essence of poetry, which resides in the quality of the imagination. An expanded edition of the book was published in 1984, and its importance has since been recognized.

Instead of leaving Beijing, Fei Ming's longtime mentor Zhou Zuoren (1885–1967) chose to stay. On January 1, 1939, three young men made an attempt on his life but only wounded him slightly. Shortly thereafter, he took a job as head librarian at the reorganized Peking University (which combined Peking and Beiping Universities), where he was also dean of the College of Letters. In 1941, he was appointed director of the North China Office of Education, a position from which he was dismissed a year later. After the war, Zhou was tried as a collaborationist and sentenced to fourteen years in prison (later reduced to ten). He died after brutal beatings by the Red Guard on May 6, 1967, during the Cultural Revolution.

In occupied Beijing, Zhou Zuoren continued to write "miscellany" or *biji*, a genre that combines the personal essay and textual commentary. In Zhou's hands, it is elevated to a form of belles-lettres showcasing his erudition on a wide variety of topics – classical and modern, Chinese and foreign, scholarly and quotidian. His language is understated, bland, and ingenuous. Friends describe his prose as *ku*, a term which, lacking the negative connotations of its English equivalent ("bitter"), suggests a flavor that may be unpalatable at first but mellows as one gets used to it. Zhou readily agreed with and in fact encouraged this assessment. He used "bitter tea" and "bitter bamboo" to name his books, and his wartime collections bear such titles as *Notes from the Apothecary* (*Yaotang yulu*, 1941), *Collection of Bitter Medicine* (*Yaowei ji*, 1942), and *Miscellaneous Essays from the Apothecary* (*Yaotang zawen*, 1944). Implicit in the essays are Zhou's ideals, in life as well as in writing, of naturalness, moderation, and the absence of affectation.

While Zhou Zuoren stayed in Beijing, Lin Yutang wrote about the ancient capital from France. Spanning more than thirty years from the Boxer Rebellion in 1901 to the Japanese invasion in 1937, *Moment in Peking* weaves a family saga of laughter and tears. Published in the United States in 1939, it sold over fifty thousand copies in six months and was hailed by *Time* as the "classic background novel of modern China." Translated into Chinese as *Fleeting Clouds of the Capital* (*Jinghua yanyun*), the book proved just as popular. *Moment in Peking* was followed by *The Wisdom of China and India* (1942) and *Between Tears and Laughter* (1943), both in English. Lin Yutang made several trips back to China but lived mostly abroad during the war. He never visited his homeland again after 1954.

In Japanese-occupied areas, the publishing industry coined the catchphrase "Ling in the South, Mei in the North" (*Nan Ling bei Mei*). "Ling" refers to Eileen Chang (Zhang Ailing, 1920–2000) in Shanghai, and "Mei" to Mei Niang (b. 1920) in Beijing. The phrase derived from a survey of readers conducted in 1942, in which the two were voted the most popular women writers. Mei Niang was born Sun Jiarui into a wealthy family in Manchuria; her father was the patriotic business tycoon Sun Zhiyuan. When she was two years old, her mother, a concubine, was forced out by Sun's wife and never heard from again. When Mei Niang learned the truth years later, she chose this penname because it was homophonous with "motherless." By the time she graduated from middle school in 1936, Mei Niang had published her first collection of stories, *The Young Miss* (*Xiaojie ji*). After her father passed away, she studied in Japan from 1938 to 1942 before settling in Beijing, where she worked for the *Women's Magazine* (*Funü zazhi*).

Mei Niang's Aquatic Creatures series (*Shuizu xilie*) consists of novellas and short stories titled respectively *Clam* (*Bang*), *Crab* (*Xie*), and *Fish* (*Yu*). The images represent the modern woman: like an aquatic creature, she is "caught in a net" and opens her protective shell only to be eaten. Written in graceful prose, the stories depict how women are still disadvantaged in their relationships with men because of deep-rooted gender inequalities.

Occupied Beijing also witnessed the rise of a young poet named Wu Xinghua (1921–1966). Wu entered the Department of Western Languages at Yen-Ching University in 1937, before he turned sixteen. There he studied English, French, German, Italian, Latin, and Greek, and started to write poetry and translate Western classics. The same year he published his first modern poem, "Silence of the Forest" (Senlin de chenmo), in *New Poetry*. He also published translations, such as a book of Rilke's poems in 1944.

In both content and form, Wu Xinghua combined the classical and modern traditions. He drew subject matter from ancient Chinese history but gave it a distinctly modern, psychological interpretation. Critical of the unbridled freedom exercised by many poets at the time, he advocated formal discipline, creating modern "quatrains" (*jueju*) that are uniform in meter and employ rhymes, such as this poem with the rhyme scheme A-A-B-A:

> Behind the dustless mansion glides the wheel of the full moon
> With each step, the east wind renews peach and plum in bloom
> It looks as if a peacock spreads its tail in the heart of the garden
> Ten thousand eyes, dazzled, are embroidered onto the plume.

Like a colorful tapestry, the images fuse into one another; they evoke rather than define, suggest rather than describe. On a spring night bathed in moonlight, the blossoming peach and plum trees in the courtyard evoke a peacock in all its glory. The image of myriad eyes contains a double entendre: literally, it refers to the "eyes" on peacock feathers, but it also suggests a sense of wonderment experienced by viewers who are transfixed by the splendid sight. Through synesthetic layering, the boundary between the literal and the figurative, the real and the imagined, the visual and the tactile, is blurred.

Understandably, the literary scene in occupied Beijing was rather bleak as a result of the massive exodus of writers. Several Taiwanese writers played a significant role in filling the vacuum, including Zhang Wojun (1902–1955), Hong Yanqiu (1899–1980), Zhang Shenqie (1904–1965), and Zhong Lihe

(1915–1960). Zhang Wojun had studied at the Beijing Normal University, and Hong Yanqiu at Peking University. The playwright Zhang Shenqie escaped to Beijing in 1938 to avoid arrest by the Japanese government in Taiwan. All three had close ties to Zhou Zuoren, who had been their mentor before the war. During the Japanese occupation, Zhang Wojun and Hong Yanqiu were both professors of Japanese at Peking University.

Zhang Wojun, Hong Yanqiu, and Zhang Shenqie were known as the "Three Musketeers of Taiwan" (*Taiwan san jianke*). Their activities revolved around the magazine *Chinese Literature and Art* (*Zhongguo wenyi*) founded by Zhang Shenqie in 1939. The other two were major contributors; Zhang Wojun also acted as editor. They translated a variety of Japanese works into Chinese for both intellectual and financial benefit.

In contrast, Zhong Lihe belonged to a younger generation and came from a working-class background. A native of Pingdong in southern Taiwan, Zhong had only had a primary-school education. In 1940, he eloped with his fiancée Zhong Taimei because they were violating the Hakka ban on marriage between a man and a woman with the same surname. After a brief stay in Shenyang, they settled in Beijing in 1941 and did not return to Taiwan until 1946. In Beijing, Zhong Lihe made a living selling charcoal and translating from Japanese. He published his first and only short-story collection in his lifetime, *Oleander* (*Jiazhutao*), in April 1945.

The title story, written on July 7, 1944, depicts life in a cramped compound shared by sixteen families. It opens with a pot of thriving oleander in contrast to fragile goldfish and a dying pomegranate tree. A common flower in Beijing, oleander not only symbolizes the ordinary citizen but also evokes the cruel reality of "survival of the fittest." Between episodes of exploitation of the weak by the strong are conversations between a young intellectual "from the south" and a student of philosophy. As the story unfolds, the young man's idealism and humanism give way to disillusionment and cynicism.

Zhong Lihe also left a diary from September 9, 1945 to January 16, 1946. Vignettes of life in postwar Beijing are presented with honesty and irony. The author deplores those arrogant Japanese who claimed that they were victorious in China and lost only to other Allied countries. At the same time, he is disheartened by the violence, in the name of patriotism, unleashed by Beijing residents against all Japanese and any Chinese who tried to defend them.

Finally, Zhong Lihe's writing reveals the estrangement of Taiwan from China as a result of Japanese colonization. "The Sorrow of a Sweet Potato" (Baishu de beiai, 1945) laments the fact that mainlanders called the Taiwanese by the derogatory name "sweet potato." (Both Hong Yanqiu and Zhang Shenqie also wrote about the discrimination to which the Taiwanese living in Beijing were subjected.) Lin Haiyin (1918–2001), a Taiwanese who spent the first thirty years of her life in Beijing, recalled in "Sweet Potato People" (Fansu ren),

> At that time, there were forty to fifty Taiwanese in Beijing. They didn't want to live under Japanese rule and came all the way to the mainland, leaving behind their homes. In the household registry, they usually gave their place of origin as Fujian or Guangdong Province. The first reason for doing this was that they hoped to circumvent the attention of the Japanese consulate and other organs; the second was that if they identified themselves as Taiwanese, they would receive discriminatory stares. So when they referred to the Taiwanese among themselves, they would use "sweet potato" because the shape of Taiwan resembles that of a sweet potato. The fact that they used this term to refer to Taiwan revealed the heartache they must have felt away from home.

The heartache that Lin Haiyin described did not go away with the retrocession of Taiwan to China in August 1945. On the contrary, reunification turned into a prelude to historical trauma with profound political, social, and cultural ramifications.

Shanghai the Lone Island

Between November 12, 1937, and the outbreak of the Pacific War on December 8, 1941, when Japan took over the International Settlement following its attack on Pearl Harbor, Shanghai was known as the Lone Island (Gu dao, also translated as Orphan, Solitary, or Isolated Island). During those four years, the foreign concessions – mainly French and British – provided fertile ground for literary activities. Paradoxically, the geopolitical situation gave the city a greater degree of freedom than either the GMD-ruled interior or the CCP-controlled border regions. After an initial period of depression, when many publishing houses folded and bookstores closed, the city witnessed a literary boom. More than a hundred periodicals and newspaper supplements came into circulation. *Magazine* (*Zazhi*, 1938–1945) and *Panorama* (*Wanxiang*, launched in July 1941) enjoyed enormous popularity.

Despite Japanese intervention, Lone Island was a haven for writers from a wide spectrum of political positions and literary persuasions. For example, the first systematic reports on the CCP bases appeared in Shanghai as *Random Notes on the Journey to the West* (*Xi xing man ji*). Traditional poetry, written by such poets as Liu Yazi (1887–1958) of the South Society, also thrived. The leftist writer Ah Ying (pen name of Qian Xingcun, 1900–1977) wrote *The Maritime Hero*

(*Haiguo yingxiong*), a four-act play about the Ming loyalist Zheng Chenggong (1624–1662), later made into a film.

Commercial theater – in particular, modern spoken drama and costume drama – was immensely popular. The four biggest box office successes were *Begonia* (*Qiu Haitang*), *Malice in the Qing Court* (*Qing gong yuan*), *Family* (*Jia*, adapted from Ba Jin's novel), and *Wen Tianxiang*. Three of the four are costume dramas, which, aside from having period settings, incorporate many elements of traditional Chinese theater. Other works of the genre include *The Butterfly Lovers* (*Li hen tian*), *King of Chu* (*Chu bawang*), and *Beauty Trap* (*Meiren ji*, based on an episode from *Romance of the Three Kingdoms*). The predominant themes are loyalty, righteousness, love, and friendship.

Malice in the Qing Court, written in 1941 by Yao Ke (the pen name of Yao Xinnong, 1905–1991), spans the years 1877 to 1900 and focuses on Consort Zhen (1876–1900), who guides the Guangxu Emperor (1871–1908) toward reform and stands up to authority. The story involves the love between Consort Zhen and the emperor and her tragic death by the order of the Empress Dowager (1835–1908). Consort Zhen is portrayed as loyal, courageous, outspoken, and progressive. With lively characterization and meticulous details, the play contributed significantly to the popular imagination about these historical figures for decades to come. Directed by Fei Mu (1906–1951), the play opened in July and ran for four months straight.

Begonia broke all box office records in occupied Shanghai. The script, written by Huang Zuolin, Gu Zhongyi (1903–1965), and Fei Mu, was adapted from the novel by Qin Shouou (1908–1993), first published in *Shenbao* in 1941. Set in Tianjin in the Republican period, the play depicts the tragic love affair between Qiu Haitang ("Begonia"), a Peking Opera singer, and Xiangqi, the third concubine of a ruthless warlord. A melodrama of lovers' trials and tribulations, *Begonia* features Peking Opera prominently. The production is almost four hours long and boasts an impressive cast of fifty-two actors. From December 24, 1942 to May 9, 1943, *Begonia* enjoyed a run of 135 performances at the Carlton Theatre and earned the accolade of "China's First Tragedy." Its popularity continued into the 1950s and beyond, as seen in various adaptations.

In addition to melodrama, comedy of manners was also popular. Yang Jiang (the pen name of Yang Jikang, b. 1911), an important figure in this genre, studied foreign languages at Soochow (Dongwu) and Tsinghua Universities before she went to Oxford University with her husband Qian Zhongshu. Encouraged by friends, she wrote *As You Wish* (*Chen xin ru yi*), *Swindle* (*Nong zhen cheng jia*), and *Wind-Blown Blossoms* (*Feng xu*), which satirize men and women in intellectual circles.

The periodical *July* was an important venue for resistance literature during the war. Founded in Shanghai in September 1937 and later moved to Wuhan, it was edited by Hu Feng and published writers from all over China. The contributing poets were collectively known as the July School, which included Ah Long, Niu Han (b. 1923), Ji Fang (b. 1920), Lu Li (1914–1999), Zeng Zhuo (b. 1922), Lü Yuan (b. 1922), Zou Difan (1915–1995), Sun Dian, Luo Luo, Jia Zhifang (1916–2008), and others. Influenced by Ai Qing and Tian Jian, they wrote free verse in plain speech to address such recurrent themes as homeland, rural life, and patriotism. At its best, the July School appeals to readers with simplicity and directness, as seen in the opening lines from Lü Yuan's "When I Was Young" (Xiao shihou):

> When I was young
> I didn't know how to read
> Mama was my library
> I was reading Mama –
>
> Someday
> When there's peace in the world
> People will fly up . . .
> Wheat will sprout from the snow-covered ground
> Money will be useless . . .

In contrast to the July School are the modernists. Louis (Luyishi), the pen name of Lu Yu (a.k.a. Ji Xian, b. 1913), was trained as a Western-style painter in Suzhou and was drawn to surrealism. He became a frequent contributor to *Les Contemporains* (*Xiandai zazhi*, 1932–1935), edited by Shi Zhecun (1905–2003), Dai Wangshu, and Du Heng. He founded the monthly *Poetry Territory* (*Shi lingtu*) in 1944, and published three collections of poems in two years. The books are no longer in print, but many of the poems were published in Taiwan in the 1950s.

Louis's poetry features a dramatis persona that is explicitly identified with the poet in real life: his tall slim build, signature pipe and walking cane, and pet cat. Neither confessional nor introspective, the poetry is rich in whimsical imagery and self-deprecating humor. What emerges is a fearless individualist who deplores the commercialization of art in modern society and the subordination of literature to politics.

Notwithstanding the considerable achievements in drama and poetry in occupied Shanghai, there is no question that the laurel crown belongs to fiction as represented by two writers of distinct temperament and style: Eileen Chang (Zhang Ailing) and Qian Zhongshu.

Eileen Chang was born into a prominent family; her grandmother was the daughter of Li Hongzhang (1823–1901), an important statesman in the Qing imperial court. According to her autobiographical essay "Dream of Genius" (Tiancai meng, 1939), she could recite Tang poems by the age of three, wrote her first story at seven, and started her first novel at eight. She was admitted to the University of London in 1939, but went instead to the University of Hong Kong when Britain declared war on Germany and her allies. Her study was interrupted when Japan laid siege to the British colony, and she went home in 1942. In Shanghai, Chang published most of her works in popular magazines. Her first collection of stories, Romance (Chuanqi), was published by Magazine Monthly in 1944 and sold out in four days. Her collection of essays titled Written on Water (Liu yan) appeared in 1945 to wide acclaim. By the age of twenty-five, Chang had become a best-selling author and a cultural icon in Shanghai.

Under Eileen Chang's pen, men and women are, above all, social beings caught in a web of family and other complicated relationships. These relationships are primarily economic in that they are based on exchange, "supply and demand," and fluctuating needs and desires. Even in matters of the heart, there are no "pure" motives. It comes as no surprise, then, that Chang's stories have no "heroic" figures. Yet, even as she exposes human foibles and pettiness, she sympathizes with men and women in their earnest but thwarted search for love and happiness. "Life is a splendid gown full of fleas," she writes. Skillfully, Chang captures the paradox of life: splendor and decadence, beauty and desolation.

Women hold a central place in Eileen Chang's oeuvre, portrayed as disadvantaged by their circumstances as well as by their delusions about love. In The Golden Cangue (Jinsuo ji, 1943), Cao Qiqiao, who is from a humble background, is married to the invalid second son of the wealthy Jiang clan. Her sharp tongue and short temper win her nothing but disdain from her in-laws and even the servants. She falls in love with her philandering third brother-in-law, who tries to take advantage of her financially. Embittered by rejection and disappointment, she turns into a monster whose desire to have total control of her two children leads her to ruin their happiness maliciously; they both end up miserable and degenerate like their mother.

In an early scene in which Qiqiao pours her heart out to her third brother-in-law, the narrative zooms in on her gold earrings, which, "like two brass nails, affix her to the door – a butterfly specimen in a glass case, brightly colored, but lonely and desolate." The metaphor echoes the central symbol of the story, the golden cangue (a "cangue" was an instrument of punishment that trapped the hands and head of a criminal in a heavy collar). Qiqiao's ghostly existence does not begin in middle age. The moment she leaves her carefree life in the family-owned sesame oil shop and marries into the Jiang family, she is already dead.

In comparison, Bai Liusu, the heroine of "Love in a Fallen City" (Qing cheng zhi lian, 1943), fares much better. A twenty-eight-year-old divorcee desperately looking for a husband to support her, Bai is introduced to Fan Liuyuan, a notorious playboy who comes from a wealthy overseas Chinese family. Throughout the courtship, which takes place mostly in Hong Kong, neither is willing to commit: she acts reserved because she will not settle for being his mistress; he, unsure if she is just looking for a meal ticket, vacillates between serious and playful. The story ends with Japanese bombings that destroy Hong Kong in December 1941. Bai and Fan find themselves in ruins and decide to get married. As Eileen Chang sees it, love is a delicate balancing act involving insecurity, vanity, and calculation. Ironically, what tips the balance in favor of love in the story is the unforeseeable catastrophe that momentarily renders these factors irrelevant.

Although war plays a key role in the plot, "Love in a Fallen City" does not belong to the literature of resistance extolling patriotism and sacrifice. Chang is interested in the private worlds and personal relationships of ordinary men and women living in an extraordinary time. Her work is filled with keen observations, suggestive details, original metaphors, startling wit, and psychological insights. Aligning herself with popular literature (Zhang Henshui being a favorite author), she readily admits that the meaning, and pleasure, of life is to be found in such trivialities as fashion, food, music, dance, painting, interior design – the sights, sounds, and smells of the city.

In 1943, Chang married Hu Lancheng (1905–1981), writer and chief editor of the *China Daily* (*Zhonghua ribao*) under the Wang Jingwei regime. They divorced three years later. Chang left Shanghai for Hong Kong in 1952, and from there continued on to the United States in 1955. She never returned to the mainland.

There are some striking similarities between Eileen Chang and Qian Zhongshu. Both came from prominent families, both depart from the nationalist discourse in their creative writing, and both deal with love and marriage from a dispassionate, often sardonic, point of view. They differ, however, in focus and tone. A leading scholar, Qian Zhongshu targets intellectuals in his stories – their pretentiousness, vacuity, and blind worship of Western things. Although equally penetrating in his analyses of men and women as social beings, Qian shows less sympathy for his flawed characters than does Chang.

After graduating from Tsinghua University in 1933, Qian Zhongshu studied at Oxford and Paris before returning to China in 1938 to teach at the Southwest Associated University in Kunming. He was visiting Shanghai in 1941 when the Pacific War broke out, making it impossible for him to return. The same year he published a book of essays, *Marginalia of Life* (*Xie zai rensheng bian shang*), displaying remarkable erudition and wit. It was followed in 1946 by *Men, Beasts, Ghosts* (*Ren shou gui*), a collection of short, mostly satirical, stories. *On the Art of Poetry* (*Tan yi lu*, 1948), a book of criticism written in classical Chinese, is highly regarded by scholars.

The title of Qian Zhongshu's novel *Fortress Besieged* (*Wei cheng*) is a metaphor for the predicament of marriage: "People outside the fortress want to get in and people inside want to get out." In matters of the heart, the protagonist Fang Hongjian always lands in an undesirable situation from which he cannot extricate himself. Although he is basically a good person, his relationships with his family, colleagues, and wife deteriorate over time because he is too shy to express his true feelings and too weak to take a stand. Against the backdrop of banal life, he becomes isolated and impotent. Fang's peregrinations from Shanghai to the country's interior and back suggest that another dimension of "fortress besieged" is that of going in circles. At the existential level, this dark picaresque novel is a commentary on the trapped condition of the modern man.

Fortress Besieged is a satire that spares no character, not even the children. The author uses figurative images extensively and turns familiar aphorisms into original analogies. For example, a scantily clad Miss Bao is referred to as "partial truth" since truth is supposed to be "naked." Qian's wit also manifests itself in puns. Courtship is described this way: "If an engagement ring is a lasso that catches him, a button is a pin that nails him." *Fortress Besieged* was first serialized in *Literary Renaissance* from 1944 to 1946 before it was published in book form in 1947; it went through three editions in two years. Unavailable in Maoist China, the novel made a comeback in the 1980s and was made into a television series in 1990.

Su Qing (1917–1982, née Feng Yunzhuang) ranked with Eileen Chang as one of the most popular writers in Shanghai. Su Qing is best known for her autobiographical novel *Ten Years of Marriage* (*Jiehun shi nian*), which was first serialized in the magazine *Words of Wind and Rain* (*Feng yu tan*) in 1943. Published as a book the following year, it went through nine printings in six months; by 1948, it had gone through eighteen printings. The story begins with the wedding announcement of Su Huaiqing and Xu Chongxian, and ends with their divorce. The ten-year marriage takes a heavy toll on Su, who does not get along with her sisters-in-law and discovers that Xu, now a successful lawyer, is having an affair. After the divorce, the protagonist makes a good living by writing fiction. Written in an unaffected style, the story appealed especially to female readers. Eileen Chang, a good friend of the author, praised the work as exhibiting "great simplicity." In 1947 Su Qing produced a sequel, which is, however, overtly didactic. After 1949 she stayed in Shanghai and wrote mainly plays for the Yue Opera.

Hong Kong as sanctuary

During the Second Sino-Japanese War, many writers found shelter in Hong Kong. Some shuttled between the British colony and the mainland. A few, such as the New Sensationist Ye Lingfeng (1905–1975), and the writer and scholar Xu Dishan (1893–1941), became permanent residents of Hong Kong. A diverse group, they ran the gamut of literary styles and political persuasions: left, right, middle-of-the-road. Some were even participants in the Wang Jingwei puppet regime. In addition to the infusion of mainland writers, the local literary scene was enlivened by new or relocated newspapers and journals, such as *Dagongbao*, *Shenbao*, and *Independence* (*Libao*) from the mainland, and locally founded *Hong Kong Daily* (*Xingdao ribao*), *Voice of China* (*Huasheng bao*), *Strong Wind* (*Da feng*), *Pen Talk* (*Bi tan*, edited by Mao Dun), *Literature of the Time* (*Shidai wenxue*, edited by Duanmu Hongliang, 1912–1996), and *Plow* (*Gengyun*, edited by Yu Feng). Between the Marco Polo Bridge Incident and the fall of Hong Kong, literature, especially poetry, thrived.

Hong Kong poets, such as Ou Waiou (1911–1995), Chen Jiangfan (1910–1970), Li Xinruo (1912–1982), Lin Yingqiang (1913–1975), and Hou Ruhua (1910–1938), had published in *Les Contemporains* in Shanghai in the early 1930s. Dai Wangshu, Xu Chi (1914–1996), and Louis also stayed in Hong Kong for varying lengths of time. Others advocated realism from a leftist perspective, such as Huang Yaomian (1903–1987), Chen Canyun (1914–2002), Huang Ningying (1915–1979), Zou Difan, Liu Huozi (1911–1990), Yuan Shuipai (1916–1982), and Lü Jian. Liu Muxia, Peng Yaofen (1923–1942?), Li Yuzhong (b. 1911), and Lü Lun (also a fiction and film scriptwriter, 1911–1988) were also active. Poetry of resistance, urban poetry, pastoral poetry, and romantic lyrics all found expression in Hong Kong.

Ou Waiou (the pen name of Li Zongda) was probably the first Chinese poet to write concrete poetry. The first six lines of "The Second Obituary of the World" (Dierci shijie puwen) consist of the repetition of a single English word:

WAR!
WAR!
WAR!
WAR!
WAR!
WAR! WAR!

Playing with typography, Ou Waiou creates the visual effect of the approaching war as well as an aural simulation of a newspaper boy hawking on the street. Written in early 1937, the poem presages the coming of the Second Sino-Japanese War.

Dai Wangshu edited *Constellations* (*Xingzuo*), the literary supplement to the *Hong Kong Daily*. During the Japanese occcupation, he was imprisoned and tortured. In "With My Maimed Hand" (Wo yong cansun de shouzhang), written in his jail cell on July 3, 1942, the poet touches an imaginary map of China with his injured hand, moving from south to north as he recalls the beauty of his homeland. The large number of tactile images gives the poem a palpable texture. This and other poems written during the war were later collected in *Times of Plight* (*Zainan de suiyue*), published in Shanghai in 1948.

In 1941, Mao Dun came to Hong Kong from Chongqing and served on the editorial board of the weekly *People, Lives* (*Dazhong, shenghuo*), edited by Zou Taobei. At Zou's request, Mao Dun wrote *Corrosion* (*Fushi*), which, unlike his other work, is written in the form of a diary. The first-person narrator is a woman named Zhao Huiming (1895–1944), who is lured into working as a spy for the GMD. Although she lives a life of sin, her spirit has not been "corroded" completely, and she saves a young woman from the GMD. Serialized in Zou Taobei's magazine, the novel was well received in Hong Kong and was made into a film on the mainland in 1950.

One of the most important works published in wartime Hong Kong came from Xiao Hong (1911–1942). In 1938, she had broken up with her first husband Xiao Jun (1907–1988) and married Duanmu Hongliang. The couple arrived in Hong Kong in January 1940 and lived at No. 8 Locke (Ledao) Road in Tsimshasui (Jianshazui), Kowloon. Here she wrote the autobiographical sketches that comprised *Tales of Hulan River* (*Hulan he zhuan*), the satire *Ma Bole*, and other pieces.

Tales of Hulan River, about life in a Manchurian village, is told by a child from a landlord family and portrays the suffering of men and women as a result of superstition and blind conformity to tradition. The bleakness of this world is alleviated only by the joy of the child spending time with her kind and wise grandfather, who teaches her how to read and how to live.

Suffering was a constant in Xiao Hong's own life. In Hong Kong she became frail with tuberculosis and depended on her friends to survive. To make matters worse, she was misdiagnosed with a throat tumor and underwent painful surgery, resulting in the loss of her ability to speak. On January 22, 1942, at the age of thirty-one, she died in a makeshift hospital and was buried in Repulse Bay. Her friend Dai Wangshu wrote this elegy on November 20, 1944:

> Six hours of a lonely journey to lay
> A bouquet of red camellias by your face
> Here I wait, through the endless night
> While you lie listening to the murmuring tide

Like many elegies, there is no mention of death; Xiao Hong is simply described as listening peacefully to the ocean. But her obliviousness to his presence and the contrast, in both color and sound, between the quiet red flowers (evoking a woman's face) and the dark ocean intimates the unbridgeable gap between the living and the dead. After a tumultuous life, Xiao Hong finally finds peace in nature.

Yan'an and the Rectification Campaign

With Yan'an as the center, literature spread to all the communist bases in rural Shanxi, Chakhar, Jehol, Hebei, and Liaoning provinces. Together they form the Three Borders (*San bian*): Jin (northeastern Shanxi), Cha (southwestern Chakhar), and Ji (southern Jehol and most of Hebei). In 1938, the Lu Xun Art Academy (Lu Xun yishu xueyuan) and the Resistance University (Kangzhan daxue) were founded in Yan'an. *Liberation Daily* (*Jiefang ribao*), the Party organ, was launched in 1941. Performance and drama troupes traveled to the countryside to promote resistance and communism; new compositions and old folksongs were published in *Mass Literature and Arts* (*Dazhong wenyi*), *New Poems and Songs* (*Xin shige*), *Poetry Construction* (*Shi jianshe*), and *Poetry Battle Line* (*Shi zhanxian*). Frequent contributors to these journals were collectively known as the Jin-Cha-Ji School of poetry. On July 3, 1941, a poetry society by the same name was formed, with Tian Jian as the chairman; Shao Zinan, Wei Wei, and Chen Hui on the executive committee; and more than thirty members.

One of the most popular poems in the Three Borders was "Wang Gui and Li Xiangxiang" (Wang Gui yu Li Xiangxiang) by Li Ji (1922–1980). First published in the *Liberation Daily* in September 1946, it tells the story of two young peasants in love, who triumph over evil landlords and government officials. If the theme is predictable, the form is noteworthy. Almost a thousand lines long, the narrative poem borrows the staple style of northern Shaanxi folksongs known as sky-roaming (*xin tian you*): a rhymed couplet in which the first line gives a simile or metaphor and the second line explicates it.

Ideological control soon began. In May 1941, Mao Zedong launched the Rectification Campaign in Yan'an (*Yan'an zhengfeng*) to rein in Party members and centralize interpretations of Marxism and the war policy. The campaign went on until April 1945. Its first and most famous victim was Wang Shiwei (1906–1947).

Wang Shiwei, a fiction writer and essayist, was Hu Feng's classmate at Peking University. He went to Yan'an in 1937. In 1942 he published "Wild Lilies" (Ye baihehua) in the *Liberation Daily* and "Politicians and Artists" (Zhengzhijia yishujia) in the *Valley Rain* (*Gu yu*). These essays criticized the preferential treatment (e.g. uniforms and food rations) given to top-ranking cadres. Artists, according to Wang Shiwei, were purer than politicians and it was the artist's right to expose corruption and provide the blueprint for the government.

Zhou Yang led the attack in denouncing Wang Shiwei for thinking that literature served some abstract "human nature," which deviated from CCP policy. In June 1947, Wang Shiwei was convicted as a Trotskyite and secretly executed in July. He was the first writer to be persecuted and murdered by the CCP.

In 1936, Ding Ling was rescued from a GMD prison by the CCP and taken to Yan'an. A collection of her stories, *When I was in Twilight Village* (*Wo zai Xiacun de shihou*), was published in 1944, followed by *A Bullet in the Barrel* (*Yi ke wei chutang de qiangdan*, 1946) and a novel about land reform, *The Sun Shines on the Sanggan River* (*Taiyang zhaozai Sangganhe shang*, 1948). In the title story of the 1944 collection, the narrator is a woman writer who spends two weeks convalescing in a remote mountain village in north China. Zhenzhen, the niece of the narrator's hostess, Mrs. Liu, is raped by the Japanese but voluntarily goes back to live among them in order to gain intelligence. When the story opens, the villagers gather outside Mrs. Liu's home waiting for Zhenzhen to show her face. The villagers feel justified in gawking at, gossiping about, and even openly mocking her because she has been "sullied" by the enemy. Morbid voyeurism and hypocrisy are displayed by men and women alike: "Because of her, [the village women] discover great respect for themselves and recognize their own holy purity; they are proud because they have never been raped." The only exceptions are the narrator and Xia, Zhenzhen's childhood sweetheart. In the end, Zhenzhen declines Xia's marriage proposal and leaves the village to seek medical treatment and education. It is unlikely that she will ever come back.

Ding Ling also critiques the double standard that discriminated against women in an editorial that was published in the *Liberation Daily* on International Women's Day on March 8, 1942. "Thoughts on Women's Day" (Sanbajie you gan) begins with a rhetorical question: "'Woman' – when will the word stop being noticed and needing to be emphasized?" It goes on to lament the difficulty of being a woman in Yan'an and offers four pieces of advice to women: (1) take care of your health and love life; (2) be happy and live a positive, fulfilling life; (3) think for yourself and do not conform to the crowd; (4) persist even in the midst of suffering. Ding Ling was criticized for the editorial. Along with Wang Shiwei and Xiao Jun, they were labeled "exhibitionists" for their outspoken criticisms. But for Mao's help, she might have been subjected to severe persecution.

Concerned about dissent, Mao convened a symposium for writers and artists in May 1942. His opening and concluding remarks are known as "Talks at the Yan'an Forum on Literature and Art" (Zai Yan'an wenyi zuotanhui shang de jianghua, or "Talks"). Mao defines literature and art as, necessarily and without exception, indicative of class origin and ideology. As he puts it, art that transcends class or is independent of politics "does not exist in reality." Quoting Lenin, Mao uses the image of "cogs and screws" to refer to literature and art, explicitly subordinating them to politics. A call for wholesale politicization of artistic creation, the "Talks" were to dictate CCP cultural policy for decades to come.

To counter Mao's "Talks" as they spread to the interior, Zhang Dao-fan (1896–1968), who was in charge of GMD propaganda in Chongqing, penned "The Cultural Policy We Need" (Women suo xuyao de wenyi zhengce) in the inaugural issue of the *Cultural Vanguard* (*Wenhua xianfeng*) on September 1, 1942. He disputes the class nature of literature and emphasizes Confucian virtues and nationalism. Ironically, despite clear differences between GMD and CCP policies, both sides viewed literature as rightly serving political purposes. Zhang's article was followed on October 20 by "About 'Cultural Policy'" (Guanyu 'Wenyi zhengce') by Liang Shiqiu (1903–1987), rejecting the communist doctrine of class struggle. In September 1943, the GMD passed guidelines for cultural activities and, two months later, launched the National Cultural Development Campaign in Chongqing.

Mao's "Talks" led to the composition of many musicals that depicted the triumph of the oppressed. *The White-Haired Girl* (*Baimao nü*) was by far the most successful. A collaborative project drawing on a folktale from Fuping, Hebei Province, the play was penned by He Jingzhi (b. 1924) and Ding Yi (b. 1921), and the music was composed by Ma Ke and Zhang Lu. A peasant girl escapes into the mountains after her father is driven to suicide and she is raped by a landlord. Lacking sunlight and salt, her hair turns white. The locals mistake her for a ghost when she is spotted stealing food from the temple. At last, she is rescued by the People's Liberation Army. The play incorporated different styles of regional folk music and underwent many revisions before it premiered in Yan'an in May 1945.

The most successful fiction writer to come out of Yan'an is Zhao Shuli (1906–1970). A native of Shanxi Province, Zhao established himself with the novella *Xiaoerhei Gets Married* (*Xiaoerhei jiehun*) in 1943. The story depicts two peasants who overcome the opposition of their backward parents in pursuit of love. In this and other works such as "The Tale of Li Youcai's Rhymes" (Li Youcai banhua, 1946), Zhao captures the flavor of language used by Shanxi peasants and avoids the Europeanized Chinese often found in May Fourth literature.

Zhao Shuli won high praise from Mao Dun and Zhou Yang; his work was hailed as ushering in a "people's literature" written in the "national form." "Zhao Shuli direction" – a term coined in 1946 – represented a new paradigm and inspired a large following. Together with Xi Rong (the pen name of Xi Chengzheng, b. 1922), Ma Feng (the pen name of Ma Shuming, b. 1922), Li Shuwei (b. 1918), Hu Zheng (b. 1924), and Sun Qian (the pen name of Sun Huaiqian, b. 1920), all of whom either came from Shanxi or worked there, Zhao formed the Mountain Potato School (Shanyaodan pai) in the late 1950s.

Colonial Taiwan

The year 1937 marked a new page in the history of Taiwan. The colonial government conscripted hundreds of thousands of Taiwanese men as "volunteers" to serve with Japanese troops fighting in Southeast Asia. Taiwanese (as well as Korean and mainland Chinese) women were forced to serve as sex slaves under the euphemistic appellation of "comfort women" (*wei an fu*). Censorship was stepped up, and the use of Chinese was banned. One exception, however, was poetry written in classical Chinese in newspapers, which suggests the long-standing esteem in which Chinese poetry was held in Japanese culture. Although prior to the ban many Taiwanese writers were already writing in Japanese, from 1937 to the end of the Second Sino-Japanese

War all literature was written in the language of the colonial power. The policy was part of the Kōminka (*huangmin hua*, literally "to Japanize") Movement to transform Taiwanese people into "royal subjects."

For Taiwanese writers, it was not always easy to stay clear of politics. Zhang Wenhuan (1909–1978) was one of the most prolific writers during the war. Like many of his generation, he studied in Japan, receiving his secondary and tertiary education there. Back in Taiwan, he was enlisted by the Association of Law-Abiding Royal Subjects (Huangmin fenggong hui) and was a representative at the Conference of Writers of Great East Asia in 1942. For this he was later regarded as a collaborationist. Yet his literary endeavors suggest otherwise. In 1941, Zhang Wenhuan launched *Taiwan Literature* (*Taiwan wenxue*) to counter the *Literary Art of Taiwan* (*Wenyi Taiwan*, renamed from *Beautiful Island* (*Huali dao*)) founded by the Japanese writer Nishikawa Mitsuru (1908–1999). Financed by the restaurateur Wang Jingquan, *Taiwan Literature* published ten issues in two and a half years before it folded under political pressure in 1943. It served as an important venue for Taiwanese writers who refused to cooperate with the colonial government.

Camellia (*Shanchahua*), Zhang Wenhuan's most famous work, was serialized from January 23 to May 14, 1940 in *New Citizens of Taiwan* (*Taiwan xinmin bao*). Beautifully illustrated and well advertised, the novel became a best seller; a teahouse was even named after it. A semi-autobiographical *Bildungsroman*, the story revolves around the journey of a young man from the rural south to the city. He experiences ambivalence as he deals with two languages (Chinese and Japanese) and lifestyles (traditional and modern, pastoral and urban).

Zhang also founded the Housheng Drama Research Society (Housheng yanju yanjiuhui). The most important drama troupe during the war, it produced plays with strong local color and native consciousness, such as *Capon* (*Yan ji*), adapted by Lin Boqiu (1920–1998) from Zhang's novella. For its articulation of a Taiwanese identity, the society was shut down by the authorities.

Lü Heruo (1914–1951), known as "the most talented man of Taiwan" (*Taiwan diyi caizi*), wrote his first story, "Ox Cart" (Niu che), in 1935; the story was published in Japan in 1936. Hu Feng included it in *Collected Short Stories from Korea and Taiwan: Mountain Spirit* (*Chaoxian Taiwan duanpian ji: shanling*), making Lü Heruo, along with Yang Kui (1905–1985), one of the first two Taiwanese writers to be introduced to mainland readers. In 1939, Lü went to Tokyo to study singing at a conservatory and performed on the stage for over a year. During this time he also wrote two novellas, *An Illustrated Guide to the Seasons* (*Jijie tujian*) and *Girl in Blue* (*Lanyi shaonü*), and the novel *Women of Taiwan* (*Taiwan nüxing*), which show great sensitivity to the plight

8. The name of the Taiwanese writer Lü Heruo (1914–1951) is still remembered today; an inscription about him by the scholar Hsu Chun-ya has been engraved on a busy walkway in Taipei, Taiwan. Photo by Wan-wan Huang.

of women in traditional society. Lü returned to Taiwan in 1942 and joined Zhang Wenhuan in editing the *Taiwan Literature* while working as a reporter. His plays and fiction were collected in *Clear Autumn* (*Qingqiu*).

After the war, Lü Heruo worked as a reporter for the *People's Guide* (*Renmin daobao*) and started writing fiction in Chinese. His last work, "Winter Night" (Dong ye, 1947), exposed the problems of corruption and bureaucracy, and presaged the February 28th Incident. Disillusioned by the incident, Lü edited the leftist newspaper *Light* (*Guangming bao*) and opened a print shop to promulgate socialism. In 1949, the GMD retreated to Taiwan and started arresting leftists on the island. Then a music teacher at a high school in Taipei, Lü escaped to the Luku Mountains, where he died from a poisonous snakebite. The name of Lü Heruo is still remembered today; an inscription about him by the scholar Xu Junya (Hsu Chun-ya) is engraved on a busy walkway in Taipei.

The Silver Bell Society (Yinling hui) was formed in 1942 by three classmates at Taizhong First Middle School: Zhang Yanxun (pen name Hong Meng,

1925–2004), Zhu Shi, and Xu Qingshi (pen name Xiaoxing). By 1944, there were more than thirty members. The society launched a mimeograph journal, *Affinity Grass (Yuan cao)*, which published mainly poetry in traditional and modern forms, as well as literary criticism. After the war, Silver Bell closed down temporarily but was revived in January 1948 with new blood – Lin Hengtai (pen name Hengren, b. 1924), Zhan Bing (pen name Lü Yuan, b. 1921), Xiao Xiangwen (pen name Danxing), and Xu Longshen (pen name Ziqian). The revived journal had a new name, *Current (Chaoliu)*, and published works in both Chinese and Japanese. It folded in spring 1949 after five issues; leaders of the Silver Bell Society were arrested and some were imprisoned.

Of Hakka origin, Wu Zhuoliu (1900–1976) was a primary-school teacher in the Japanese education system. In 1940 he resigned in protest against discrimination and went to Nanjing, where he made a living as a reporter. Two years later, he returned to Taiwan and continued to work for newspapers. Wu wrote his first short story at the age of thirty-six. In "The Doctor's Mother" (Xiansheng ma) a stingy doctor tries hard to become Japanese so as to feel superior. Blindly imitating all things Japanese, he loses touch with his roots, which are personified by his mother, who becomes more and more isolated in the family. When she dies, the doctor holds a lavish Japanese-style funeral against her explicit wishes.

Wu Zhuoliu wrote *The Orphan of Asia (Yaxiya de guer)* in Japanese in 1945 and 1946. Like an orphan, Taiwan had been abandoned by China in 1895. By the time the island was returned to China under the Cairo Agreement in 1945, vast linguistic and cultural differences existed between the mainland and Taiwan. In April 1946, the Committee on Popularization of the National Language (Guoyu puji weiyuanhui) was formed and branches were set up in every county in Taiwan. More than two hundred new journals and newspapers appeared, many in both Chinese and Japanese. Bilingual publications did not last long, however. On October 24, 1946, on the eve of the first anniversary of the retrocession of Taiwan, Japanese was banned as part of the GMD policy of "re-Sinicization" and decolonization. The ban deprived many Taiwanese of access to information and deepened their distrust toward the government.

Compounded by inflation, devaluation of the old currency, supply shortages, unemployment, and mismanagement under the administration of the GMD general Chen Yi (1883–1950), discontent exploded in Taiwan in 1947. On February 28, an inspector from the Bureau of Tobacco and Alcohol arrested an old woman peddling contraband cigarettes in Taipei. The inspector fired his gun, accidentally killing a bystander. The angry crowd attacked him, and a riot spread like wildfire. Armies were sent in from the GMD (at that time, its headquarters were still on the mainland) to suppress the riot, in which many innocent Taiwanese and mainlanders were killed. The GMD also used the incident to ferret out dissenting intellectuals who were sympathetic to communism or socialism. Chen Yi was dismissed from office on March 22 and returned to the mainland; at the end of the Civil War he was executed in Taipei for planning to defect to the CCP.

The February 28th Incident created a rift between the native Taiwanese (known as *benshengren*) and the GMD (and, by extension, recent émigrés from the mainland, or *waishengren*). A taboo subject for four decades, the event had a profound impact on the future of Taiwan.

II. The end of the Civil War and the beginning of a new era (1949–1977)

The People's Republic of China

"Time has begun": cultural policy and thought control

In July 1949, three months before the founding of the People's Republic of China (PRC), the CCP held a congress of 824 representatives of literature and the arts to consolidate cultural policy and approve the establishment of the Federation of Writers and Artists, with Guo Moruo as president, Mao Dun and Zhou Yang as vice presidents, and Ding Ling and Ai Qing as editor and associate editor respectively of the Federation's *Literary Gazette* (*Wenyi bao*). In his opening address, Premier Zhou Enlai (1898–1976) urged all cultural workers to follow the guidelines laid down in Mao Zedong's 1942 "Talks at the Yan'an Forum on Literature and the Arts." Literature was to serve the state, and the state would be the sole arbiter of literature.

To eradicate independent thinking, a rectification campaign was launched in 1951 to reorient intellectuals toward Soviet theories and scholarship, and away from the Western ideas in which many of them had been trained. A case in point was the attack, triggered by Mao's letter to the *People's Daily*, on the film *The Life of Wu Xun* (*Wu Xun zhuan*). Scripted and directed by the American-trained Sun Yu (1900–1990), the film was accused of glorifying Wu Xun – a beggar in the late Qing who saved up enough pennies to found schools for poor children – when he was in fact a "reformist" complicit with the feudal order. Other measures of thought reform included the reorganization of universities on the Soviet model, revamping college curricula, and criticisms and self-criticisms of such leading scholars as Liang Shuming (1893–1988), Yu Pingbo (1900–1990), and Zheng Zhenduo.

In July 1954, Hu Feng submitted to Mao Zedong, Zhou Enlai, and Liu Shaoqi (1898–1969) the *Report on the Practice of Literature and Art in Recent Years* (*Guanyu jinnianlai wenyi shijian qingkuang de baogao*), also known as *The Book of 300,000 Words* (*Sanshiwan yan shu*). Hu castigates the dogmatism of the cultural establishment, the incompetence of the cadres in charge, and the formulaic writing produced under their cultural policy. For his outspoken dissent, Hu was labeled a counterrevolutionary voicing views that were anti-Party, anti-Marxist, bourgeois–idealist, and factionalist. A national campaign was launched in January 1955 to ferret out Hu's "accomplices," which, according to one estimate, implicated as many as one hundred thousand people, of whom more than ten thousand went to jail. Ironically, some of them had never even met Hu Feng but had only read his works. Among those persecuted were writers such as Lu Ling, Lü Yuan, Niu Han, and Jia Zhifang. Hu Feng himself was arrested in May 1956 and was not released from prison until 1979.

Historical fiction and critical realism

Land reform and the establishment of cooperatives in the 1940s and 1950s gave rise to "land reform fiction," represented by Zhao Shuli's *Three Mile Bay* (*Sanli wan*), Liu Qing's *History of the Pioneers* (*Chuangye shi*), Ding Ling's award-winning *The Sun Shines on the Sanggan River*, and Zhou Libo's (1908–1979) *Rainstorms* (*Baofeng zouyu*). The last work, featuring vivid characters and a language rich in local color, is based on Zhou Libo's experiences in Manchuria. His *Great Changes in a Mountain Village* (*Shan xiang jubian*) is essentially a sequel with a focus on a village in Hunan.

Revolutionary history was also memorialized in fiction, as seen in *Sea of Forests and Prairies of Snow* (*Lin hai xue yuan*, 1956) by Qu Bo (1923–2002), *Protecting Yan'an* (*Baowei Yan'an*) by Du Pengcheng (1921–1991), *The Red Sun* (*Hong ri*) by Wu Qiang (1910–1990), *Riverside at Dawn* (*Liming de hebian*) by Jun Qing (1922–1991), *Lilies* (*Baihehua*) by Ru Zhijuan (b. 1925), and *Red Boulder* (*Hong yan*, 1961) by Luo Guangbin (1924–1967) and Yang Yiyan (b. 1925). Many of these works depict the Civil War. *Sea of Forests and Prairies of Snow* relates Qu Bo's military expedition in winter 1946, when he led thirty-six men to battle GMD troops around the Peony River. Although vastly outnumbered, his men won. *Red Boulder* is a fictionalized account of CCP underground resistance in postwar Chongqing based on the authors' personal experience.

Luo Guangbin and Yang Yiyan were both imprisoned by the GMD but escaped the 1949 massacre to write about betrayal and valor. The novel was hailed as an epic "history of the Party."

On the literary scene dominated by revolutionary romanticism, Zong Pu's "Red Bean" (Hong dou) stood out for its characters (intellectuals) and subject matter (romantic love). Zong Pu, the pen name of Feng Zhongpu, is the daughter of the philosopher Feng Youlan, and majored in English literature at Nankai University. In "Red Bean," set in 1948, Jiang Mei, a college student, falls in love with Qi Hong, a banker's son. The difference in their class background leads to divergent paths in life. Jiang Mei makes the painful choice of communism over love, but she will always treasure the red beans – known as the "love bean" in Chinese culture – that Qi Hong gave her. Published in *People's Literature* in 1957, the story was a huge success, but it was targeted by the establishment for its sympathetic treatment of politically incorrect love. The work remained banned until 1979, when it was reprinted.

In the repressive environment, only works that conformed strictly to the official Party line were permitted. Many writers who had been active before 1949 stopped writing altogether. Some devoted themselves to classical scholarship, others became translators. In spring 1956, Nikita Khrushchev (1894–1971) denounced Stalin and ushered in a period of "thaw" in the Soviet Union; diverse and critical works appeared. The CCP responded by inviting Chinese intellectuals to speak their minds. In April, Mao announced: "Let a hundred flowers bloom; let a hundred schools [of thought] compete!" The former referred to literature, the latter to scholarship. Intellectuals were reassured by the government that they were free "to think independently, debate, create and critique, publish, uphold and reserve [their] own views." Known as the Hundred Flowers Movement, the campaign marked several new directions in literature.

One was the emergence of "critical realism," advocated by Qin Zhaoyang (1916–1994), the new editor of *People's Literature*. This new mode was exemplified by Liu Binyan (1925–2005) and Wang Meng (b. 1934). Another development was the appearance of new journals, including the *Poetry Journal* (*Shi kan*). Founded on January 28, 1957, it was edited by Zang Kejia; the inaugural issue published eighteen classical-style poems and a letter by Mao, as well as works by such veteran poets as Ai Qing, Feng Zhi, and Chen Mengjia (1911–1966, also a philologist and archaeologist). With an initial press run of fifty thousand, *Shi kan* became the leading poetry journal in China. Suspended in 1964, it was revived in January 1976 and has been in print to this day.

Born and educated in Beijing, Wang Meng joined the CCP in 1948 and in 1949 began working for the Communist Youth League. It took him three years to complete *Long Live Youth* (*Qingchun wansui*) in 1956, but the novel was not published until 1979. Instead, Wang Meng became famous overnight with "A Young Newcomer in the Organization Department" (Zuzhibu lai de nianqing ren). Through a young cadre-member's battle with bureaucracy, the story shows how bureaucrats are more concerned with maintaining their power than with addressing the people's needs. Wang also managed to weave into the story a romantic relationship even though love was considered an undesirable theme by the official policy.

Growing up in Harbin, Liu Binyan joined the CCP in 1944. Living in Manchuria after the Civil War, he taught himself Russian and translated Russian plays into Chinese. Having established his reputation as a translator, Liu began working as an investigative journalist in 1951 for the *Chinese Youth News* (*Zhongguo qingnian bao*). In 1956 he contributed two reportage pieces to *People's Literature*. "At the Bridge Construction Site" (Zai qiaoliang de gongdi shang) and "Internal News at the Newspaper" (Benbao neibu xiaoxi) attracted much attention for their penetrating analyses of problems in the CCP. The first tells the story of a young engineer who makes suggestions to improve efficiency at a construction site. His superior accuses him of being anti-Party and has him transferred. Similarly, the woman reporter in "Internal News at the Newspaper" is frustrated in her quest of truth and justice under a conservative boss.

The Anti-Rightist Campaign and the prelude to the Cultural Revolution

Alarmed by the avalanche of grievances in response to the Hundred Flowers Movement, the CCP reversed its policy in 1957 and launched the Anti-Rightist Campaign to silence the critics. By the end of 1958, over 300,000 intellectuals had been labeled rightists. For example, Wang Meng was sent to the country-side to do manual labor. After returning to Beijing to teach, he was exiled again three years later, this time to Xinjiang. Wang Meng did not return to Beijing until 1979. Liu Binyan was also a target during the Anti-Rightist Campaign; his work was banned until the late 1970s.

The purge of rightists swept the entire country. In order to meet the "quota" set by the central government (or to exceed it to earn extra merit), work units went to absurd lengths to trump up charges. In January 1957, a young Sichuan poet named Liu Shahe (b. 1931) published a sequence of prose poems titled

"On Plants and Trees" (Caomu pian) in the magazine *Stars* (*Xingxing*). The allegorical poems won considerable recognition. When the political climate changed in a few months, however, Liu was accused of satirizing Party cadres and harboring treasonous thoughts, and was severely punished.

Prominent figures did not escape persecution; if anything, they became the obvious targets. Ding Ling, for instance, won the Stalin Prize in 1951 and donated all the prize money (fifty thousand rubles) to benefit children. In 1957, however, she was accused of being the leader of the "Ding Ling–Feng Xuefeng Rightist Anti-Party Group" and exiled to the Great Northern Wilderness (*Beidahuang*) in Heilongjiang Province. Ai Qing was also sent to Heilongjiang, and then to Xinjiang; he was allowed to return to Beijing in 1979.

As the Anti-Rightist Campaign silenced intellectuals, Zhou Yang, the culture tsar of the CCP, promoted "true proletarian literature." His "New Folk Songs Have Blazed a Trail for Poetry," published in *Red Flag* (*Hongqi*) in 1958, launched a mass poetry movement. Millions of peasants, workers, and soldiers were encouraged to compose "new folksongs." An anthology of 305 of these was compiled in *Songs of the Red Flag*.

Guided by Mao's formula of "classical + folksong," poets wrote "political lyrics" to pay homage to the Revolution and to New China. Boasting an oratorical style, these lyrics lent themselves to public recitation and were filled with images of the fatherland, the red flag, the red sun, and the like. Many poets came from the military, such as Li Ying (b. 1926), Gong Liu (the pen name of Liu Renyong, 1927–2003), Lei Shuyan (b. 1942), and Zhou Liangpei (b. 1949). Some of the best-known works were "Song of Lei Feng" (Lei Feng zhi ge) and "A Window of the Westbound Train" (Xiqu lieche de chuangkou) by He Jingzhi; and "A General's Trilogy" (Jiangjun sanbuqu), "A Eulogy of White Snow" (Baixue de zan'ge), and "Deep Valley" (Shenshen de shangu) by Guo Xiaochuan (the pen name of Guo Enda, 1910–1970).

Guo Xiaochuan joined the CCP in 1937. He wrote many patriotic poems during the Second Sino-Japanese War and earned a reputation as a "soldier–poet." "Gazing at the Starry Sky" (Wang xingkong, 1959) celebrates the completion of the Great Hall of the People in Tiananmen Square. With more than 230 lines divided into four sections, the poem expresses, in the first two sections, man's realization of his own insignificance vis-à-vis the grandeur and permanence of the universe. The rest of the poem presents an uplifting outlook on the future under the CCP. Yet there is a subtle, unresolved tension between the individual vision and the collective vision, which is uncommon in political lyrics.

The most popular piece of fiction in New China at this time was *The Song of Youth* (*Qingchun zhi ge*) by Yang Mo (1914–1996). Yang was born into a landlord family in Beijing. In 1928 she had to quit school when her father went bankrupt; to escape an arranged marriage, she ran away from home. In 1936 she became a CCP member and went to the northwest, where she worked with women's associations and CCP newspapers during the Second Sino-Japanese War. *The Song of Youth*, written between 1950 and 1955, was published in 1958 while being simultaneously serialized in the *Beijing Daily* (*Beijing ribao*).

Originally titled *Ever-Burning Wildfire* (*Shao bujin de yehuo*), the autobiographical novel details the turbulent life of a young revolutionary in the 1920s and 1930s. The protagonist, Lin Daojing, falls in love with Yu Yongze, a student at Peking University. She then meets Lu Jiachuan, who is involved in the underground student movement. She is converted to the communist cause and leaves Yu. She is then imprisoned by the GMD for leftist activities but is inspired by her fellow prisoners. The story ends with her joining anti-Japanese demonstrations on December 9, 1935.

The Song of Youth is a revolutionary *Bildungsroman* whose roots may be traced to works like Mao Dun's *Rainbow* in the 1930s. Yang Mo's ability to delve into the emotional world of the heroine as she matures into a communist made the work a great success. Although it dealt with one of the few acceptable themes at the time, namely the CCP underground movement before 1949, it did not escape criticism both before and during the Cultural Revolution for the bourgeois nature of the main characters and the lack of attention to peasants and workers. In response, Yang Mo revised the story by adding elements of class struggle in rural China. The revisions did not appease all the critics, but the popularity of the novel continued to grow, especially after it was made into a film in October 1959.

Drama was comparatively free to incorporate elements that had been removed from other genres; increasingly it became the sole source of criticism of Mao's policies. Formerly a film actress in Shanghai, Jiang Qing (1914–1991), or Madame Mao, took it upon herself to point out hidden criticisms to Mao as a means of expanding her own power. One of her targets was the 1961 opera written by the historian Wu Han (1909–1969), then deputy mayor of Beijing. *Hai Rui's Dismissal from Office* (*Hai Rui ba guan*) tells the story of Hai Rui (1513–1587) of the Ming dynasty, mentioned in the first chapter of this volume. Hai Rui is a man who places principle above personal loyalties, and this quality results in his dismissal from office when justice calls for the execution of the son of his former superior. The work received praise from Mao at first, but Jiang Qing interpreted it as a veiled criticism of Mao's dismissal of General

Peng Dehuai (1898–1974) and orchestrated a purge of Wu Han and two of his co-authors of a widely read newspaper column in 1965. The purge was a prelude to the Cultural Revolution.

Underground literature and the Cultural Revolution

The failed economic reform known as the Great Leap Forward (*Da yuejin*) resulted in "Three Years of Natural Disasters" in from 1959 to 1962. Famine spread all over China and an estimated thirty-eight million people died. At the Lushan meeting of the Party's Central Committee in 1959, Peng Dehuai criticized the Great Leap Forward for its gross mismanagement and "petty-bourgeois fanaticism." Mao made repeated self-criticisms in speeches and called for the dismantling of the communes, but he insisted that his policy was 70 percent correct. Under pressure, Mao resigned as chairman of the PRC but remained chairman of the CCP. The PRC government was now led by the new chairman, Liu Shaoqi, as well as by Premier Zhou Enlai and General Secretary Deng Xiaoping (1919–1997).

To restore his power and eliminate opposition, Mao initiated the Socialist Education Movement in 1963, which prompted grassroots action mainly among schoolchildren. Although it did not have any immediate political impact, it influenced the younger generation, from whom Mao would later draw support. In 1963, Mao began attacking Liu Shaoqi openly for his "revisionist" policy and called for class struggle to be applied on a daily basis. By 1964, the Socialist Education Movement had morphed into the Four Cleanups Movement to eradicate "undesirable elements" in politics, economy, thought, and organization. This was clearly directed at Liu Shaoqi.

On May 16, 1966, Mao issued a "circular," later published in the *People's Daily*, that denounced the "counterrevolutionary revisionists" in the CCP and called for a "thorough critique" of five professions: academia, education, journalism, literature and art, and publishing. On May 25, a young philosophy teacher at Peking University named Nie Yuanzi (b. 1921) wrote a "big-character poster" (*dazibao*), naming the rector and some professors as "black anti-Party gangsters." A few days later, Mao ordered the text of the poster to be broadcast nationwide, prasing it as "the first Marxist big-character poster in China." On May 29, the Red Guard was formed at the Middle School of Tsinghua University. On July 28, representatives of the Red Guard submitted a letter to Mao stating that mass purges were justified; Mao responded by giving them full support in his call to "bombard the headquarters." On August 16, approximately eleven million Red Guards from all over the country gathered in Tiananmen Square to show their loyalty to Chairman Mao, who commended their contributions to the promulgation of socialism and democracy. Thus began the Great Proletarian Cultural Revolution (*wuchan jieji wenhua da geming*), abbreviated as the Great Cultural Revolution (*wenhua da geming*) or simply Cultural Revolution (*wen'ge*).

What began as a power struggle in the highest echelon of the CCP grew into a national campaign involving central government and local party cadres, who seized the opportunity to accuse rivals of counterrevolutionary activities. At the height of the Cultural Revolution, the whole country was caught up in purges, carried out with all forms of abuse and violence. It affected every sector of Chinese society and wrought irreparable destruction. Although Mao officially declared the Cultural Revolution to be over in 1969, havoc continued much longer. The term is used to refer to the period from May 1966 to October 1976, when the Gang of Four – Jiang Qing, Zhang Chunqiao (1917–2005), Yao Wenyuan (1932–2005), and Wang Hongwen (1934–1992) – were arrested.

The impact on the literary scene was both immediate and wide-ranging. Many writers, condemned as "cow-ogres and snake-spirits," were locked up in "cowsheds"; others were sent to May Seventh Cadre Schools. Named after Mao's 1966 directive to Lin Biao, the first cadre school was established in Heilongjiang in October 1968. They soon spread all over China, and intellectuals were sent there to be "reeducated" through hard labor and the study of Marxism and Maoism. To give one example, the cadre school in Xianning in Hubei Province housed six thousand intellectuals from Beijing; among them were such prominent figures as Bing Xin (1900–1999), Shen Congwen, Zang Kejia, Xiao Qian, Li Guangtian, Chen Baichen (1908–1994), Feng Xuefeng (1903–1976), and Guo Xiaochuan. Countless writers and intellectuals endured mental and physical abuse. Some were killed, others driven to insanity or suicide.

Teahouse (*Chaguan*), widely accepted as Lao She's most accomplished play, was written in 1956 and first performed in 1957. The play in three acts tells the story of a teahouse in Beijing at three critical moments in history. The first act takes place in 1898 after the aborted reform led by the Guangxu Emperor; the second in 1916, after the death of Yuan Shikai (1859–1916), when warlords were dividing up China; and the third, in 1946, when Beijing was terrorized by American soldiers and GMD secret police. As time goes on, the teahouse declines and the stage looks barer and barer, while the banners that line the teahouse – "Discussion of State Affairs Is Prohibited" – become more and more prominent.

As early as 1958, the play was criticized for its lack of a positive ending. Much harsher criticism came during the Cultural Revolution, which led to

Lao She's suicide after he was beaten by the Red Guard. Chen Mengjia, Deng Tuo (1912–1966, one of Wu Han's co-authors), Fu Lei (1908–1966), Zhou Shoujuan (1894–1968), and Wen Jie (1923–1971) all chose the same end. Others, such as Wu Xinghua, Zhao Shuli, Luo Guangbin, and Li Guangtian (1906–1968, whose death was declared a suicide at the time) were killed by the Red Guard.

The devastation of cultural institutions was equally profound and widespread. Schools, research institutes, publishing houses, libraries, and museums became paralyzed as teachers, scholars, editors, journalists, and other professionals were persecuted. Most periodicals were suspended. By 1969, only some twenty journals remained in circulation, down from 295 in 1950. This is the lowest number in modern Chinese history.

Jiang Qing had begun opera reform before the Cultural Revolution. In February 1966, with Lin Biao's support, she put forward the idea of Model Plays (*yangban xi*) and the theory of the Three Prominences (*san tuchu*), ordering that literary works should give prominence to positive characters, even greater prominence to heroic characters, and the greatest prominence to the principal hero or heroine. By December 1966, the Eight Model Plays were chosen, consisting of the plays *The Red Lantern (Hong deng ji)*, *Taking Tiger Mountain by Strategy (Zhi qu Weihu shan)*, *Shajiabang*, *On the Docks (Haigang)*, *Raid on White Tiger Regiment (Qixi Baihu tuan)*; two ballets, *The Red Detachment of Women (Hongse niangzijun)* and *The White-Haired Girl*; and one symphonic suite based on *Shajiabang*. These Model Plays incorporated aspects of Peking Opera and Western theater, such as realist backdrop, Western music, and Western singing styles. Characters were based on "tall – great – perfect" (*gao da quan*), leaving no room for "middle characters," to the point where the heroes showed no traces of bourgeois thought, and villains no hint of redeeming qualities. Between 1969 and 1972, these pieces were adapted to other media, such as radio, film, and television, and a few more operas and ballets were added to the repertoire. Throughout the Cultural Revolution, the people were force-fed an exclusive diet of these Model Plays, sarcastically summed up by the catchphrase "eight plays for 800,000,000 people."

Mao Dun described the desolation of the literary scene as "Eight Model Plays and One Writer." The "one writer" refers to Hao Ran (1932–2008). Born a poor peasant in Hebei and orphaned before the age of ten, Hao Ran received only three and a half years of formal schooling. He began to write in 1949 and worked for newspapers and journals throughout the 1950s. Hao Ran has published about eighty books in his career but is best known for two novels: *Bright Sunny Sky (Yan yang tian,* 1962–1965) and *The Golden Highway (Jinguang dadao,* 1972–1977).

Bright Sunny Sky sold three and a half million copies during the Cultural Revolution. The story takes place in summer 1957 at the time of the wheat harvest, as progressive poor peasants struggle against their rich neighbors, who greedily seek profit at the expense of the community. The novel in three volumes offers a broad view of the peasants' lives and succeeds in creating a number of memorable characters. *The Golden Highway* focuses on how peasants overcome poverty with organized collective endeavors. Typical of the literature of the Cultural Revolution, the protagonist Gao Daquan is perfect, and the story highlights the class struggle between idealized peasants and villainous ex-landlords, rich peasants, and their cohort.

Hao Ran's novels were lauded by Jiang Qing, who even gave him instructions on his future writings. After the arrest of the Gang of Four in 1976, Hao Ran was dismissed from his official positions. Although he continues to write, his later work is overshadowed by the past and has received scant attention from readers and critics.

In December 1968, to contain the havoc wrought by the Red Guard, Mao launched the Down to the Countryside Movement (*xiaxiang yundong*). The so-called "educated youth" (*zhi qing*) – primarily students in urban middle schools – were ordered to the countryside far away from home to work alongside peasants. It is estimated that more than fifteen million young men and women were "sent down" to places as remote as the Great Northern Wilderness in the northeast, Yunnan and Guizhou in the south, Inner Mongolia in the north, and Xinjiang and Qinghai in the northwest. Not until the late 1970s were most of them allowed to return to their home cities. The experience would become a major theme in post-Mao literature.

Even extreme repression could not completely stifle young voices of freedom. In February 1963, Guo Shiying (1942–1968), son of Guo Moruo and a philosophy student at Peking University, formed an underground poetry group called X with three high school friends: Zhang Heci (grandson of the philosopher Zhang Dongsun (1886–1973)), Sun Jingwu, and Ye Rongqing. Others, like Jin Die and Mou Dunbai (b. 1947), were also associated with the group. In three months, they published three issues of a hand-copied journal that contained their own writings and were circulated among friends. They were arrested in mid-May for counterrevolutionary activities; their writings were accused of being anti-Party and anti-Marxist. Ye Rongqing was released; Jin Die escaped to Hong Kong; and Guo Shiying, Zhang Heci, Sun Jingwu, and Mou Dunbai were sentenced to labor reform. Five years later, on April 19, 1968, Guo Shiying, then a student at the Beijing Agriculture University, was kidnapped by the Red Guard; after three days of torture and interrogation, he was thrown out of a third-floor window. It was alleged that he committed suicide, another "counterrevolutionary act against the people."

Like the X group, Zhang Langlang (b. 1943), a student at Central Arts Academy (Zhongyang meishu xueyuan) and son of the painter Zhang Ding (b. 1917), gathered with fellow students in private homes. At a poetry recital that they organized at school in 1962, Zhang Langlang read his long poem "The Burning Heart" (Ranshao de xin), which ended with the line "We – the Sun Column!" After the recital, they decided to christen their group the Sun Column (Taiyang zongdui). Along with Zhang, many young writers and artists, such as Mou Dunbai, Dong Shabei, Zhang Wenxing, Zhang Xinhua, Yu Zhixin, Zhou Qiyue, Zhang Liaoliao, Jiang Dingyue, Wu Erlu, Yuan Yunsheng, Ding Shaoguang (b. 1939), Zhang Shiyan, and Wu Hong (b. 1945), participated at one time or another.

Consisting mostly of children of high-ranking Party cadres and prominent cultural figures, the Sun Column enjoyed access to private libraries of literature, art books, philosophy, and music, as well as to the so-called "yellow-covered books" and "gray-covered books" – translations of works from Western Europe, North America, and the Soviet Union that were published for "internal circulation" as objects of critique for their "imperialist" or "revisionist" contents. A yellow cover designated literature, while a gray cover generally referred to books of political science. Among the literary works that the group read were *The Decameron* by Boccaccio (1313–1375), *The Count of Monte Cristo* by Alexandre Dumas père (1802–1870), *The Trial* by Kafka (1883–1924), *The Thaw* and *People, Years, Life* by Ilya Ehrenburg (1891–1967), *Nausea* by Jean-Paul Sartre (1905–1980), *The Chair* by Samuel Beckett (1906–1989), *The Catcher in the Rye* by J. D. Salinger (b. 1919), *On the Road* by Jack Kerouac (1922–1969), and *Look back in Anger* by John Osborne (1929–1994). They also encountered the writings of Baudelaire (1821–1867), Hemingway (1899–1961), and Balzac (1799–1850). According to Zhang Langlang, they even listened to, and were fascinated by, the Beatles. In 1966, the Sun Column was labeled a "reactionary organization." Zhang Langlang fled to the south but was caught; he received a death sentence that was later commuted. He spent ten years in prison. Eventually he left China and has been living in the United States since. Some members of the group committed suicide, while others went on to have successful careers – for example, Wu Hung is currently professor of Chinese Art History at the University of Chicago.

Before Zhang Langlang fled to the south, he wrote down four characters in his friend Wang Dongbai's notebook: "believe in the future." These words so deeply touched another young poet who had attended some of the Sun

Column's meetings that he wrote a poem with this title, expressing an innocent idealism and optimism despite the surrounding desolation:

> When spider webs seal off my stove without mercy,
> When smoke from the cinders sighs in sad poverty,
> Stubbornly I spread out a blanket of dejected ashes
> And write with fair snowflakes: Believe in the future!

The poet is Guo Lusheng (b. 1948), also known by his pen name Shizhi, or "Index Finger." A youngster from a soldier's family, Guo Lusheng had befriended Guo Shiying and Zhang Langlang. On December 20, 1968, he boarded a train that was taking him to the countryside, an experience captured in "This Is Beijing at Eight past Four" (Zhe shi si dian ling ba fen de Beijing). Along with "Believe in the Future" (Xiangxin weilai), this poem captivated urban youths in exile, who hand-copied and circulated, memorized and recited, the poems. In the early 1970s, Guo Lusheng suffered a mental breakdown and was institutionalized briefly. In the 1980s, after a divorce and his mother's death, he was institutionalized again. Since the late 1990s, Guo has been recognized as a leading figure of underground poetry and has achieved cult status.

Underground literary activities were by no means limited to Beijing before or during the Cultural Revolution. For example, Wu Wenxian (b. 1935), Song Zirong, and Zhou Zexian formed the Petöfi Club (Peiduofei julebu) in Guiyang as early as the 1950s. Wu Wenxian came from a wealthy family in Guizhou Province. Well-versed in classical Chinese, he was also an avid reader of Russian and English literature, especially Aleksandr Pushkin (1799–1937) and Walt Whitman (1819–1892). He wrote poetry in both classical and modern styles, and circulated it among friends. Wu was caught trying to cross the southern border and spent years in jail.

Huang Xiang was born in Hunan in 1942. His father was a GMD general secretly executed in Manchuria shortly after 1949. Huang started writing poetry in 1958 and published his first poems in the then-dominant folksong style in 1959. In 1963, while working on a tea farm in Guizhou, he and several friends, including Xiong Qingtang, Zhu Yan, and Su Xiaoyi, formed a literary salon. During the Cultural Revolution, Huang Xiang lived in the attic of an abandoned Catholic church, which became the meeting place for a group of aspiring writers, including Ya Mo (b. 1942, the pen name of Wu Lixian, Wu Wenxian's younger brother), Li Jiahua, and Qu Xiaosong, among others. Later, this group met at Ya Mo's home near Guiyang. Huang named their gathering Wild Duck Salon (*Yeya shalong*) after the primary school where Ya Mo was teaching.

Huang Xiang has been persecuted since childhood, having been denied formal education and incarcerated six times for a total of twelve years between 1959 and 1995. In "Beast" (Yeshou, 1968), he compares himself to a beast being chased and trampled on by the world. Yet the inhumanity he has suffered cannot destroy his indomitable will to speak out against it: "Even if I have only one bone left / I will stick it in the throat of this abominable age."

In 1971, Lin Biao died in an airplane crash after a failed coup. Despite the Anti-Lin Anti-Confucius Campaign that began soon afterward, the underground literary scene thrived. In Beijing, Xu Haoyuan and Lu Yansheng formed groups; two years later, Shi Kangcheng started his own group. They interacted with one another, sharing forbidden books that were hard to come by. The books were passed from one person to another by bicycle in a kind of relay known as "book chasing" (*pao shu*). One participant, Zhao Yifan (1935–1988), had been collecting underground writings and publications since the beginning of the Cultural Revolution.

In Baiyangdian, the lake country in central Hebei, a community formed of more than six hundred "educated youths," many from Beijing and Tianjin. Mang Ke (the pen name of Jiang Shiwei), Duo Duo (the pen name of Li Shizheng), and Genzi (the pen name of Yue Chong), all born in 1951, had gone to high school together and were living in Baiyangdian from 1969 to 1976. They were visited by friends from Beijing, such as Bei Dao (the pen name of Zhao Zhenkai, b. 1949), Jiang He (the pen name of Yu Youze, b. 1949), Chen Kaige (b. 1952), and Yan Li (b. 1954). Along with fellow residents in Baiyangdian, including Lin Mang (the pen name of Zhang Jianzhong, b. 1949), Fang Han, and Song Haiquan, these young men would all begin to write poetry.

The existence of literary salons during the Cultural Revolution is proof of the irrepressible human yearning for freedom of expression. Similarly, readers longed for genuine feeling, not illustrated dogma, in literature. Because of its relative brevity and mnemonic features (such as rhyme), poetry was easily reproduced and circulated underground. A few novels also enjoyed immense popularity in handwritten copies, however. They include *An Embroidered Shoe* (*Yi zhi xiuhua xie*) by Zhang Baorui (b. 1952), *The Second Handshake* (*Dierci woshou*) by Zhang Yang (b. 1944), *When Lotuses Bloom Again* (*Dang furonghua chongxin kaifang de shihou*) by Gan Huili, *Ninth Wave* (*Jiu ji lang*) by Bi Ruxie, and *Escape* (*Taowang*) by an anonymous author.

Both *Ninth Wave* and *Escape* take an unflinching look at the cruel reality of the Cultural Revolution, especially with regard to the "educated youth."

Yet the earliest stories in print about the Cultural Revolution did not come from the mainland. Chen Ruoxi (a.k.a. Lucy Jo-hsi Chen, the pen name of Chen Xiumei) was born in Taiwan in 1939 and, while a student at the National Taiwan University, began publishing fiction. After graduation, she went to Johns Hopkins University to major in creative writing. In 1966, she and her husband (also a student from Taiwan) decided to go to mainland China to raise their family. There, Chen experienced the Cultural Revolution firsthand. In 1973, she and her family managed to get out. *Mayor Yin* (*Yin xianzhang*) was published in Taiwan in 1976.

The collection contains six stories about the Cultural Revolution, with characters ranging from CCP cadres and intellectuals to old people and children. Without directly depicting physical violence, Chen Ruoxi's stories reveal the psychological horror and human tragedies of life in an ironclad dictatorship. Denied love, dignity, and freedom, people are ruled by the instinct for survival, which in extreme circumstances takes sinister forms. In "Jingjing's Birthday" (Jingjing de shengri), people live in paranoia under the cult of Mao. Paranoia is manifest in daily life in many ways: the utter lack of personal privacy, the sense of shame imposed on intellectuals (especially Western-educated intellectuals like Chen) for their "capitalist" ideas, the scared look on children's faces when they hear the word "counterrevolutionary," and parents' precautionary act of tearing out pages that contain Mao's images from new comic books before giving them to children for fear that they might soil those images and incur grave consequences. Understandable as such acts may be, paranoia inevitably leads to distrust, hypocrisy, opportunism, and apathy. The "friendship" between the protagonist and her neighbor is built not on trust or affection but on a shared secret, or, more precisely, their helpless complicity in the "crime" of their children, who innocently call Chairman Mao a "rotten egg" at play.

Taiwan

Anticommunism and homesickness

As the GMD lost ground in the Civil War, its rule in Taiwan became more heavy-handed. In May 1949, martial law was declared and an embargo was imposed on the two major ports of Jilong (Keelung) and Gaoxiong (Kaohsiung). Thus began the era of White Terror (*baise kongbu*). Internationally, Taiwan's strategic importance was brought to the fore by the Korean War, which broke out on June 25, 1950. Two days later, President Truman ordered the Seventh Fleet to patrol the Taiwan Strait to stop the spread of communism. In 1952, the Republic of China on Taiwan signed the Sino-Japanese

Peace Treaty, and on December 2, 1954, it signed the Sino-American Mutual Defense Treaty. Taiwan was to be an important partner to the US in the Cold War.

In the cultural sphere the GMD also turned a new page. The GMD was painfully aware of the CCP's success in mobilizing and controlling writers and artists in the pre-1949 period. Further, the threat of CCP invasion was substantial throughout the 1950s, with frequent aerial bombings across the Taiwan Strait. To prevent communist infiltration of the last GMD stronghold was of critical importance. A dual approach was adopted: suppress undesirable elements on the one hand, and, on the other, offer incentives to cultural workers to cooperate.

As a "hard" measure, censorship not only applied to contemporary publications but also to pre-1949 literature. All works by writers who stayed on the mainland after the Civil War were labeled "leftist" and banned. Thus the bulk of May Fourth literature was out of reach. Only the few writers who had either died before 1949 (such as Xu Zhimo and Zhu Ziqing) or moved to Taiwan with GMD ties (such as Hu Shi and Liang Shiqiu) were considered safe, and their works were readily available. During the White Terror, clandestine possession or reading of "communist literature" was cause for arrest and imprisonment.

Taiwanese literature from the colonial period, the majority of which was written in Japanese, was also censored as part of the GMD's policy of decolonization and re-Sinicization. As a result, the indigenous tradition was suppressed and unavailable to the recent migrants and those born after 1949.

In this artificially created vacuum, the GMD implemented the "soft" measure of rewarding literature consistent with the official ideology. It did this by first identifying and organizing specific groups, namely the military, youth, and women. The prominent role played by the military in cultural policy is understandable in view of both its loyalty to the regime and its importance as a human resource. Among the nearly one million migrants who came with the GMD, military personnel numbered six hundred thousand. In 1951, Chiang Ching-kuo (1910–1988), the eldest son of President Chiang Kai-shek and head of the Political Department of the Ministry of National Defense from 1950 to 1954, issued "A Respectful Address to Writers and Artists" (Jing gao wenyijie renshi shu). Echoing the slogan of taking literature "to the masses" during the Second Sino-Japanese War, he encouraged writers to "take literature to the military." Many journals were published by the military; almost every unit had its own. In addition, literary competitions were held at all levels of the military and literary prizes were awarded. Many servicemen, such as Chu

Ge (the pen name of Yuan Dexing, b. 1931) and Yin Di (b. 1937), went on to become renowned writers and artists.

The Chinese Literature and Art Association (Zhongguo wenyi xiehui) was formed in 1950 under the leadership of Zhang Daofan. This was a national organization of writers with branches throughout the island. For the young, the Corps of Patriotic Chinese Youth against Communism (Zhongguo qing-nian fangong jiuguo tuan) was founded in 1952, and the Chinese Young Writers Association (Zhongguo qingnian xiezuo xiehui) was founded in 1953, with its official journal *Young Lions Literary Art* (*Youshi wenyi*). For women, the Chinese Women Writers Association (Zhongguo funü xiezuo xiehui) was formed in 1955; the monthly *Chinese Women* (*Zhonghua funü*) was launched by the United Anti-Communist Chinese Women's Association in 1960.

The Chinese Literature and Art Prizes Committee (Zhonghua wenyi jiangjin weiyuanhui) was set up in spring 1950 to award literary prizes and offer generous honoraria to writers. The criterion for selection was that a work must "use literary and artistic techniques to raise nationalist consciousness" and convey the goals of "opposing the Communists and countering the Soviets." By the time the committee was dissolved in July 1957, it had rewarded more than a thousand writers.

As early as October 1949, the literary supplement to the *New Life Daily* (*Xin sheng bao*), edited by Feng Fangmin, initiated discussions on "combat literature and art" (*zhandou wenyi*), which favored works that were "combative" (*zhandouxing*) and "entertaining" (*quweixing*). In November 1949, Sun Ling wrote "Song of Protecting Great Taiwan" (Baowei da Taiwan ge) and coined the term "anticommunist literature" (*fangong wenxue*). On December 16, 1949, the inaugural issue of the literary supplement to the *National Daily* (*Minzubao*, the previous incarnation of the *United Daily* (*Lianhebao*)), announced: "It is the responsibility of all who work in literature and art today to engage in combat and fight back the enemies."

In September 1953, Chiang Kai-shek published "Supplement to Two Chapters on Education and Entertainment under the Principle of People's Livelihood" (Mingzhu zhuyi yule liang pian bushu). It upholds nationalism as the guiding principle for literature whereas "yellow" (pornographic), "red" (communist), and "black" (morbid) elements are to be eradicated. In response to the edict, the Chinese Literature and Art Association organized a research group on May 4, 1954, which paved the way for the Cultural Cleansing Movement (*wenhua qingjie yundong*) a few months later.

Collectively, the above organizations and publications supported the official ideology of nationalism, anticommunism, and traditionalism. Most native

Taiwanese writers were linguistically hamstrung: they could not publish in Japanese, which was banned, or write in Chinese, of which they had yet to achieve full command. Some simply gave up while a few would continue to write in Japanese for the drawer or to publish in Japan. These we might call "the silenced generation." Most writers would need a full decade to acquire enough proficiency in Chinese to write and publish. The last group constitutes "the translingual generation" (*kuayue yuyan de yidai*) – an epithet coined by Lin Hengtai in 1967.

There were still others who chose silence because of their old ties with mainland writers. Tai Jingnong (1902–1990), for example, was an accomplished fiction writer who had published two collections of short stories in the 1930s. As a young man, he formed close friendships with Lu Xun (1881–1936) and Chen Duxiu (1879–1942) and was imprisoned three times by the GMD. He went to Taiwan to teach at the National Taiwan University in 1946 and could not return to the mainland when the Civil War broke out. Because of his personal history, he never wrote fiction again. His pre-1949 fiction was not available in Taiwan until the 1990s.

The lacuna in the literary scene in postwar Taiwan was filled mostly by recent émigré writers, with a few exceptions. In fiction, many writers came from the military; the so-called "Three Musketeers" referred to Zhu Xining (1927–1998), Sima Zhongyuan (b. 1933), and Duan Caihua (b. 1933). Zhu's "Molten Iron" (Tie jiang) is a moving elegy for Old China. Set in north China at the turn of the twentieth century, the story centers on the competition between two local clans for a lucrative salt contract with the government. To prove their valor, the heads of the clans engage in an upward spiral of self-immolation until, in the ultimate dare, Patriarch Meng swallows molten iron and wins the contract for his son. Within a few years, with the completion of the railroad, salt is no longer hard to come by and no profit can be made on the contract. Family wealth only corrupts Meng's son and leads to the clan's demise. Irony is conveyed with symbolic images: just as the hot-blooded patriarch is killed by molten iron, so the old way of life is transformed forever by the modern world represented by the monstrous, unstoppable train. Despite Patriarch Meng's honorable but "primitive" valor, his self-sacrifice is rendered meaningless by the onslaught of modernity.

Sima Zhongyuan's stories also take place in the old north China. Filled with outlaws, riffraff, peasants, prostitutes, and ghosts, and rich in local color and folklore, his gripping tales of betrayal, revenge, and retribution evoke traditional notions of justice and heroism. Sima remains one of the most popular writers in Taiwan; some of his stories have been made into films.

In light of GMD cultural policy, it is understandable that works that looked to the lost homeland were lauded. It is important to keep in mind, however, that writing about nostalgia and condemnation of communism should not necessarily be regarded as prompted by slavish conformity to the official ideology, but rather as a natural outgrowth of the writers' personal experiences of wars and diaspora. Their works constitute a kind of "scar literature" that grew out of political turmoil and historical trauma. At their best, these works go beyond political correctness and achieve considerable artistry. Classic examples in poetry are Yu Guangzhong's (Kwang-chung Yu, b. 1928) "Nostalgia" (Xiangchou) and "Four Stanzas of Nostalgia" (Xiangchou si yun), which employ concise metaphors and musical language to express a longing for the motherland. Novels in a similar vein were legion, including *Fool in the Reeds* (*Dicun zhuan*, 1951) by Chen Jiying (1917–1997), later translated into English by Eileen Chang; *Cousin Lianyi* (*Lianyi biaomei*, 1952) by Pan Renmu (1919–2005); *The Roaring Liao River* (*Gungun Liaohe*, 1952) by Ji Gang (b. 1920); *Lingering Tune* (*Yu yin*, 1952) by Xu Zhongpei (1917–2006); *Tale of Tears and Blood* (*Enchou xielei ji*, 1952) by Liao Qingxiu (b. 1927); and *Blue and Black* (*Lan yu hei*, 1958) by Wang Lan (1922–2003).

Pan Renmu (a.k.a. Pan Fobin) graduated from the Central University in Nanjing with a major in English. In 1949 she moved to Taiwan and worked for many years in the Bureau of Education. An award-winning author of fiction, she also edited and wrote children's literature. *Cousin Lianyi*, in two parts, is told by Lianyi's cousin. Proud, idealistic, and hopeful, Lianyi breaks off her engagement and gets expelled from school for taking part in student protests. Finding herself pregnant, she goes to Shaanxi with the CCP, parting ways with her cousin and friends. Part Two shows Lianyi fourteen years later, having suffered greatly in post-1949 China. The novel gives a touching portrayal of individual lives and downplays politics. When the novel was reprinted in 1985, however, Pan not only wrote a new preface condemning the CCP, but also rewrote Part Two to have Lianyi, instead of her cousin, as the first-person narrator. The revision was motivated by the news of her parents' death on the mainland.

Wang Lan's *Blue and Black*, published in 1958, is one of the most popular novels in postwar Taiwan. The story spans the years 1937 to 1950 and revolves around Tang Qi, a woman who grew up as an orphan, is raped by her boss at the hospital where she works as a nurse, and subsequently makes a living by singing. The tearjerker ends happily. Tang Qi is reunited with her disabled soldier lover, whose wife has left him for another man. The novel was made into a popular film in 1966, as well as a play and a television series.

Arguably the most memorable anticommunist fiction came from Jiang Gui, the pen name of Wang Lindu (1908–1980). His signature work *Whirlwind* (*Xuanfeng*) was completed in 1952 and self-published in 1957. Written in the modern vernacular but incorporating elements of traditional fiction, the novel chronicles the decline of the Fang clan in Shandong Province after the rise of communism. Published under the new title *A New Biography of Monster Taowu* (*Jin taowu zhuan*), the story presents a microcosmic China in transition, comparing communism to a whirlwind, which touches everyone in its path but leaves people with nothing. *The Double Ninth Day* (*Chongyang*, 1961) may be seen as a companion piece to *Whirlwind*. With a cast of almost a hundred characters, the story is set primarily in Wuhan in 1927 when the GMD split over whether or not to cooperate with the CCP and the Comintern. In their single-minded effort to stage class struggle, the communists overthrow traditional morality only to create a new dogmatism. Implicitly the novel warns against the destructive utopianism that underlies communism.

Aside from poetry and fiction, many writers turned to lyrical prose or the familiar essay to articulate their identification with traditional Chinese culture in lieu of the physical homeland that had been lost. Women stand out in this genre, such as Zhang Xiuya (1919–2001), Zhong Meiyin (1922–1984), Xu Zhongpei, Ai Wen (b. 1923), and, above all, Qi Jun (1918–2005). The author of more than twenty books, Qi Jun wrote mostly about childhood memories and the life of the old gentry defined by taste and sensitivity. Well-versed in classical literature, she wrote in a lucid, elegant language studded with literary allusions. Qi Jun also wrote fiction, but it is her familiar essays that have made her one of the most popular writers in Taiwan for more than half a century.

Modernist experiments

Other writers were less interested in traditional Chinese literature than in recent trends in Europe and America. Although censorship was rigorously enforced, as long as artistic experimentation did not touch political taboos, it was tolerated, even if not completely accepted. The close alliance with the United States and the economic development of Taiwan also created an environment that was receptive to Western, especially American, cultural influences. The appeal of modernism – including Freudian psychoanalysis and the existentialism of writers from Schopenhauer (1788–1860) and Nietzsche to Sartre and Camus (1913–1960) – cannot be completely explained by political and economic forces, however. In the repressive sociocultural milieu, modernism, with its emphasis on individuality, the unconscious, and alienation, struck a resonant chord in many writers and artists.

Experimentation in the modernist vein found fertile ground in small, privately run journals. *Modern Poetry Quarterly* (*Xiandaishi jikan*) was founded by Ji Xian, previously known as Louis, in 1953. In the thirteenth issue on February 1, 1956, he announced the founding of the Modernist School (Xiandai pai), whose "six creeds" (*liu da xintiao*) appeared on the cover. Describing themselves as "Modernists who selectively promote the spirit of all new poetic schools since Baudelaire" (creed 1), the six creeds define modern poetry as "a horizontal transplant, not a vertical inheritance" (creed 2), "intellectual" (creed 4), and "pure" (creed 5).

The loosely organized Modernist School claimed a large membership, from eighty to over one hundred writers. The driving force behind it was the charismatic and energetic Ji Xian, with Lin Hengtai and Fang Si (b. 1925) as major players. Of the six creeds, the second was the most controversial and would become a target of criticism in decades to come. The sixth creed originally read "anarchy" but was changed to "anticommunism" in print. Ji Xian was an ardent critic of communism because it suppressed creative freedom, but the substitution also suggests a precautionary measure in light of his associations with "leftist" writers in the pre-1949 period.

Modern Poetry Quarterly showed signs of decline by the late 1950s and in February 1964 it folded after forty-five issues. After retiring from Chenggong High School where he was a teacher, Ji Xian moved to the United States in 1972 and has been living in northern California. *Modern Poetry Quarterly* was revived in 1982 under the new leadership of Mei Xin (1935–1997) and remained in print for another decade or so.

In reaction to the "antitraditional" stance of the Modernist School, a group of poets – Qin Zihao (1912–1963), Xia Jing (b. 1925), Yu Guangzhong, and Deng Yuping – founded the Blue Star Poetry Club (Lanxing shishe) in March 1954 and launched several periodicals. Well-versed in Western poetry, they were not opposed to experimentation – for example, Qin promoted French symbolism and Yu translated English poetry into Chinese – but they emphasized lyricism to counter the "intellectual poetry" that the Modernist School advocated. The difference between the two clubs led to a heated debate in 1957 and 1958.

In October 1954, three naval officers stationed at Zuoying near Gaoxiong – Zhang Mo (b. 1931), Luo Fu (a.k.a. Lo Fu, b. 1928), and Ya Xian (b. 1931) – formed the Epoch Poetry Club (Chuangshiji shishe). At the beginning, the club advocated a "new form of national poetry," but in 1958 it began to embrace surrealism. Superficially understood at the time, "surrealism" was more a code word for radical experiments than a well-defined literary concept. The quarterly journal folded in 1969 but was revived in 1972; in its new incarnation led by Luo Fu, it endorsed a return to the Chinese poetic tradition.

Despite their differences, these poetry clubs shared a common disaffection for anticommunist literature, an aversion to traditionalism, and a commitment to creative freedom. They sought to win legitimacy for modern poetry – still marginalized in the cultural arena – as distinct from the privileged classical poetry. This attitude notwithstanding, quite a few poets, including Ji Xian and Ya Xian, participated in the official discourse by competing for, and winning, government-sponsored literary prizes. If the prestige of the prizes gave the poets some symbolic capital in the eyes of the establishment, the substantial prize money no doubt provided them with a coveted resource with which to finance poetry journals of a radically different nature.

In sharp contrast to the mainland, where successive political campaigns choked writers into silence, Taiwan in the 1950s and 1960s witnessed a flourishing modernist movement, in both literature and art, with comparatively few restrictions. Shang Qin (b. 1930) is arguably the greatest Chinese surrealist to date. A serviceman with a basic education and no family, he creates a world in which conventional values are deconstructed with the devices of defamiliarization and allegory. His poetry – mainly prose poetry – is characterized by a straightforward narrative frame, rambling sentences, and a low-key, matter-of-fact tone, as seen in his signature piece "Giraffe" (Changjinglu):

> When the young prison guard notices that at each monthly physical all the height increases for the prisoners take place in the neck, he reports to the warden: "Sir, the windows are too high." The reply he receives is: "No, they look up at Time."
>
> Not knowing the face, origin, or whereabouts of Time, the young, kind-hearted prison guard goes to the zoo night after night, to patrol and wait outside the giraffe pen.

The deadpan way in which the poet fuses the mundane and the fantastic, the commonsensical and the literal, finds a parallel in the structure of the prosaic, rambling sentences. The human condition, the poem suggests, is hopeless and absurd, as suggested by the images of prison and zoo. The pathos of the situation is heightened, rather than diminished, by the figure of the prison guard, whose implausible naïveté, ostensibly due to his youth, makes a poignant comment on reality.

Similarly dark interpretations of life are found in the poetry of Luo Fu. Interest in surrealism and existentialism led his work from melancholy lyricism to agonizing contemplations of death and redemption in *Death in the Stone Chamber* (*Shishi zhi siwang*). A sequence of sixty-four poems, ten lines each, the poem was written between 1959 and 1963, when the poet worked as a military reporter in Quemoy (Jinmen) under frequent CCP bombardment.

Under the influence of He Qifang and Rilke, Ya Xian wrote melodious, wistful lyrics about north China in his early career. His mature work (which ended abruptly in 1964) consists of characters caught in degrading circumstances, such as the retired colonel who lives in wretched poverty and the Peking Opera diva who is objectified by men and cursed by women. With economy of language, suggestive imagery, mesmerizing musicality, and a detached point of view, Ya Xian laments the vacuity and absurdity of modern life. "Cantabile Andante" (Ruge de xingban) juxtaposes thirty-eight lines, all beginning with "The necessity of . . ." The catalogue gives a kaleidoscopic view of urban life that is simultaneously lighthearted and menacing, enjoyable and monotonous, carefree and chaotic. The poem ends with the image of the river and the lines "Guanyin is on the distant mountain / Poppies are in the poppy field." Guanyin, the Buddhist Goddess of Mercy, is also a mountain on the outskirt of Taipei. Against the backdrop of the ever-flowing river – a symbol of life – the juxtaposition of bodhisattva and the beautiful but potentially deadly poppies evokes good versus evil, beauty versus horror. They coexist in life; it is impossible to have the one without the other.

Like the above three poets, Zheng Chouyu (a.k.a. Wen-tao Cheng, b. 1933) also came from a military background. He distinguished himself early on with lyrics that blended, seemingly without effort, classical phrasing and images with a modern sensibility. A skilled mountain-climber, he also wrote about the mountains and indigenous peoples of Taiwan. After obtaining an MA from the University of Iowa, Zheng taught at Yale University as a Chinese-language instructor for many years.

Zhou Mengdie is the pen name of Zhou Qishu (b. 1920). A serviceman from Shandong, he went to Taiwan in 1948, leaving behind his wife and three children. From 1959 to 1980, he ran a bookstall, selling mostly books of poetry on a sidewalk in downtown Taipei, near Star Café, a popular hangout for writers. His poetry blends classical and modern Chinese and is informed by Daoist and Buddhist philosophies. His pen name "Mengdie" literally means "dreaming of butterflies," an allusion to the Daoist text *Zhuangzi*. Notions of karma and impermanence permeate his poetry about love and life, while

Zen-like insights are often expressed through paradoxical images: "All eyes are covered with eyes / Who can fetch fire from snow and meld fire into snow?" Zhou Mengdie lives a stoic life of material scarcity. Even after winning the National Literature and Art Award in 1997, he has not changed his lifestyle.

Also active on the postwar literary scene were young poets who started writing in the 1950s while still in college or high school, such as Lin Ling (b. 1933), Bai Qiu (b. 1937), Xiong Hong (b. 1938), Huang Hesheng (b. 1938), Huang Yong, Fang Qi, Fang Xin (b. 1939), Duo Si (b. 1939), and Ye Shan (b. 1940). They display an impressive range and depth. Some stopped writing after a few years; others went on to become major figures in Taiwanese literature.

Foremost among the younger poets is Ye Shan, the pen name of Wang Jingxian (Ching-hsien Wang). Blending vernacular and classically flavored Chinese, his early work is melancholy yet unsentimental, intense yet restrained. In 1966, after receiving an MFA from the University of Iowa, he went to the University of California at Berkeley to study with Chen Shixiang (Hsi-hsiang Ch'en) and received a Ph.D. in comparative literature. He has been a professor in the United States, Hong Kong, and Taiwan since 1970.

Equally conversant with Chinese and European classics, Ye Shan – renamed Yang Mu in the early 1970s – shows a versatility and maturity that mark him as a major poet not only in Taiwan but in the Chinese-speaking world in general. "Jizi of Yanling Hangs up His Sword" (Yanling Jizi gua jian, 1972) fictionalizes Jizi, a prince and diplomat of the state of Wu in the Eastern Zhou dynasty. In 544 BC, while on a state mission to the state of Lu, Jizi passes through Xu and befriends its ruler. The lord of Xu eyes Jizi's sword admiringly; Jizi makes up his mind to give it to him on his way back. By the time he returns a year later, however, the lord has passed away. Jizi goes to his grave and hangs the sword on a tree. Rather than repeating the standard Confucian interpretation (of faithfulness), the poem creates an ambience of solitude and forlornness as Jizi laments the decline of Chinese culture, symbolized by the decline of swordsmanship in Confucianism.

Written in the same year, Yang Mu's "Etudes: The Twelve Earthly Branches" (Shier xingxiang lianxiqu) is a critical reflection on the Vietnam War. The sequence of twelve poems matches the twelve Chinese double-hours with the twelve signs in the Western zodiac, thus pairing Earth with Heaven. The poems juxtapose the dehumanizing effect of war with the humanizing moments of lovemaking. Composed of intense, surreal images, the sequence ends with the death of the soldier–narrator.

If the poets in the 1950s created the first wave of modernism in Taiwan, fiction soon blossomed in its own right. The phenomenon owed much to the fertile ground offered by journals and literary supplements to newspapers. Foremost among them was the *Literary Magazine* (*Wenxue zazhi*) founded by T. A. Hsia (Xia Ji'an, 1916–1965) in September 1956. The elder brother of the literary critic C. T. Hsia (Xia Zhiqing, b. 1921), T. A. Hsia taught at Southwest Associated University and Peking University in the 1940s; after 1949 he became a professor of English literature at the National Taiwan University. After he returned to Taiwan from a semester at Indiana University in 1955, Hsia founded the *Literary Magazine*, which called for a literature that "does not instigate" but "tells the truth." The journal played a significant role in introducing Western modernism – from Kafka and Dostoevsky to Hemingway and Faulkner – to a Taiwanese readership and exerted a formative influence on young writers, many of whom were Hsia's students in the Department of Foreign Languages and Literatures. The journal folded in August 1960.

March 1960 witnessed the founding of *Modern Literature* (*Xiandai wenxue*) by several of T. A. Hsia's students, with Bai Xianyong (Hsien-yung Pai, a.k.a. Kenneth Pai, b. 1937) as director and Wang Wenxing (Wen-hsing Wang, b. 1939) and Chen Ruoxi as editors. The journal folded in September 1963 (and was revived in August 1977 only to fold again in March 1984), but by then this new generation of fiction writers had transformed Taiwanese literature forever.

Of Muslim background, Bai Xianyong came from a prominent family in Guangxi Province; his father, General Bai Chongxi (1893–1966), was minister of defense in 1946. Bai Xianyong entered the National Taiwan University in 1957 and published his first story in the *Literary Magazine*. In 1963, he went to study in the United States and wrote a series of stories under the title *New Yorkers* (*Niuyue ke*). In 1965 he started writing stories that would be collectively known as *Taipei People* (*Taibei ren*). In the opening story, "The Eternal Snow Beauty" (Yongyuan de Yin Xueyan), Snow Beauty is a scandalous socialite from Shanghai who uncannily never ages. Throwing mahjong parties for recent mainland émigrés, she is the perfect hostess, re-creating the elegance and opulence of Old Shanghai down to the last detail. Her home in Taipei provides a cozy haven for those men and women who have lost everything: wealth and power, youth and beauty. Like a goddess watching mortals play their petty games, Snow Beauty is emotionally detached and subtly condescending to her "guests," whose generous tips support her lifestyle. Her "coldness" is demonstrated by her affair with a middle-aged businessman, who is stabbed to death by a disgruntled employee. The evening after his funeral, at which she puts in a brief appearance, she hosts a mahjong game at her house; all is business as usual.

Whether concerning recent émigrés or overseas Chinese professionals, Bai's stories often deal with the traumatic consequences of uprootedness and the loss of self-identity. They also address the universal theme of enduring the vicissitudes of life. Another signature piece, "Wandering in the Garden, Waking from a Dream" (You yuan jing meng), draws its title from a famous scene in the Kun-style opera *Peony Pavilion* (*Mudan ting*) about the power of love over death. The story takes place at a party in postwar Taipei and centers on General Dou's widow, who used to be a *kunqu* diva in Shanghai renowned for her performance of the leading role in *Peony Pavilion*. She was fortunate enough to marry General Dou, an opera aficionado, as his wife rather than as his concubine, as was the common fate of opera singers. The one thing that she could never have is love. At the party given by her former "sister" in the opera troupe, Madame Dou finds herself distracted by the handsome, attentive attaché, who brings back memories of her fleeting affair with her husband's attaché back in Nanjing. The amateur opera performance at the party thus brings to the fore the unbridgeable gap between fantasy and reality, desire and fate. The use of stream of consciousness, color symbolism, and suggestive details bring to life Madame Dou's poignant "waking."

Wang Wenxing started writing stories in his junior year in college. After receiving an MFA from the University of Iowa in 1965, he returned to Taiwan to teach at his alma mater. Wang began to work on his first novel *Family Catastrophe* (*Jia bian*) in 1966 and published it in 1973. The work sparked controversy for both its form and its content. The "catastrophe" in the title ostensibly refers to the disappearance of the protagonist's aging father, who walks out on his wife and son with nothing but the shirt on his back. The fruitless search for his whereabouts is interspersed with vignettes from the past, which reveal the escalating tension between the man and his son, who has come to see him as a failure and the family system as hypocritical and oppressive. Ironically, in the absence of the father, the family thrives.

Family Catastrophe was criticized for its "heretical" ideas as well as for its experimental language that was sprinkled with neologisms, erratic syntax, and Chinese phonetic symbols. Even bolder linguistic experiments characterize Wang Wenxing's second novel, *Backed against the Sea* (*Bei hai de ren*), which took him over twenty years to complete. The first volume came out in 1981, the second in 1997. The protagonist is a half-blind veteran who is dishonorably discharged for embezzlement. To escape gambling debts, he hides in a fishing village, where he resorts to swindling and theft to survive. In the end, he is hunted down and killed by the villagers. In Joycean language, the novel probes the absurdity of the existential condition.

Other journals that played an important role include *Literary Star* (*Wen xing*, 1957); *Pen Monthly* (*Bi hui*, 1959), founded by Yu Tiancong (b. 1936); *Literature Quarterly* (*Wenxue jikan*, 1966), founded by Yu Suqiu and edited by Yu Tiancong; and *Pure Literature* (*Chun wenxue*, 1967), edited by Lin Haiyin.

Lin Haiyin was born in Japan and was taken to Taiwan shortly after her birth. When she was five years old, her father, refusing to live under Japanese occupation, moved the family to Beijing. After graduating from Beiping Journalism Academy, Lin worked as an editor at the *World Journal* (*Shijie ribao*) and married her colleague Xia Chengying (educator, editor, and columnist under the pen name He Fan, 1910–2002). They moved back to Taiwan with their three children in August 1948. In 1953, Lin Haiyin became the editor of the literary supplement to the *United Daily*, a post she held for ten years. Her short story "The Candlewick" (Zhu xin) presents a psychological drama about women in traditional society. The wife makes herself sick so as to torment the maid, whom her husband favors and eventually marries as a concubine, by making her wait on her day and night. She outlives the maid, but it is a hollow victory, as she lies in bed like a flickering candle, pained by the knowledge of a loveless life.

Lin Haiyin's autobiographical stories, written between 1957 and 1960, were collected in *Old Tales in South City* (*Chengnan jiu shi*). Seen through the eyes of young Yingzi (Lin's own childhood name), the novel re-creates Beijing in the 1920s with memorable characters and touching episodes. It was made into a film in mainland China in 1980 and brought Lin immense popularity there.

Under Lin's watch, the literary supplement to the *United Daily* published veteran native Taiwanese writers who had been neglected in the postwar period. Thanks to her, Zhong Lihe's magnum opus, *Bamboo Hat Mountain Ranch* (*Lishan nongchang*), completed in 1956, was published posthumously in 1961. She also helped build a museum in Zhong's memory in 1979. Equally important was Lin Haiyin's discovery of native talents, including Zheng Qingwen (b. 1932), Huang Chunming (b. 1939), Chen Yingzhen (b. 1937), Wang Zhenhe (1940–1990), and Qidengsheng (b. 1939).

Qidengsheng is the pen name of Liu Wuxiong, who started writing in 1962. The pen name is possibly derived from the Seven Sages of the Bamboo Grove, a group of eccentric neo-Daoists in the third century. In April 1967, he published "I Love Black Eyes" (Wo ai hei yanzhu) in the *Literature Quarterly*, which became controversial. The story could not be simpler. On a rainy afternoon, the protagonist, Li Longdi, goes to the city to meet his wife at the theater. As the city suddenly floods, people trample on one another in a panic to get to safety. Li carries a sick woman (who turns out to be a prostitute) on his back to a rooftop and stays with her all night. The next morning, he spots his wife on another rooftop but ignores her calling and waving. Angry, she tries to swim to him but is carried away by the water. All the while Li denies to the prostitute that the angry woman is his wife. After the flood subsides, he goes home, not knowing if he will ever find his wife.

The title of the story is intentionally ambiguous: both Li's wife and the prostitute have black eyes. Thrown into an unexpected situation, Li is forced to confront the quintessential condition of existence. If he seems apathetic and irresponsible to his wife, the decision to stay with the prostitute originates in his disgust with the selfishness that people display and results from his choice of universal love over personal relations.

Huang Chunming published his first story in 1956, before graduating from Pingdong Normal College. Many of his stories paint a sympathetic picture of the men and women in the lower echelon of society, depicting their dignity and hope as they eke out a living. In "Days by the Sea" (Kan hai de rizi, 1966), White Plum, an aging prostitute, builds a new life by having a baby with an unwitting client and going back to her seaside hometown. The fish-rich ocean evokes the primal life force, cleansing, rebirth, and the community into which she is reintegrated through her baby boy and hard work. "Our Son's Big Doll" (Erzi de da wanou), written in 1969, is less hopeful. A "sandwich man" makes a living by dressing up as a clown and wearing two large boards on the front and back of his body to advertise the movie being shown at the local theater. Exhausted from walking all day, he comes home to his wife and baby son. The baby only recognizes him with his clown face on and cries when he sees his father's real face.

In other stories, Huang Chunming examines, with an ironic and critical eye, Taiwan as it undergoes rapid economic development and social transformation in the 1960s and 1970s. The price of modernization is evident in "Sayonara, Goodbye" (Shayonala zaijian), "The Taste of Apples" (Pingguo de ziwei), and "Little Widow" (Xiao guafu), stories which satirize the blind worship of foreign things and the forfeiture of national pride in the race for economic gain. "The Drowning of an Old Cat" (Nisi yi lao mao) is set in a rural community where a new swimming pool is to be built to take advantage of the local natural springs. Old Uncle Ah Sheng opposes it vehemently because the pool will destroy the *fengshui* and corrupt youth. In the clash between tradition and modernity, age-old beliefs (like *fengshui*) and new concepts (such as tourism), Ah Sheng inevitably loses. He jumps into the newly built pool and drowns. At the end of the story, the splashing sound of kids playing in the pool drowns out the music of the funeral procession. While Uncle Ah Sheng's superstition is laughable, the loss of a culture based on personal loyalty and close-knit community is lamented.

Wang Zhenhe is another master of satire. A native of Hualian, Wang studied in the Department of Foreign Languages and Literatures at the National Taiwan University. He worked at television companies for many years and wrote numerous film reviews. The short story "An Oxcart for a Dowry" (Jiazhuang yi niuche) was first published in the *Literature Quarterly* in 1967. The protagonist, Wanfa (the name means "All Prosperity"), makes a living by delivering goods with a rented oxcart. His poverty is exacerbated by the addictive gambling of his wife, who has no compunction about selling their daughters to pay off her gambling debts. To supplement his meager income, they rent out the shack behind their house to a street clothes vendor. When Wanfa finds out that his wife and the street vendor are having an affair, he kicks him out. But a series of misfortunes lands the family in dire straits; the vendor comes to their rescue, moves back into the shack, and resumes the affair with the wife – this time with Wanfa's tacit approval. On the "designated night" each week, Wanfa stays away from home and drinks alone at a local eatery.

The story captures the pained resignation with which Wanfa accepts the humiliating situation. His impaired hearing takes on symbolic significance as the story progresses, just as the street vendor's "stinking armpits" and Wanfa's wife's unsightly face and figure signal character flaws. With a generous sprinkling of native Taiwanese (or Hoklo) words and phrases, the vivid dialogue in the story enhances the effect of this verisimilitude.

Chen Yingzhen, the pen name of Chen Yongshan, came from a Christian family and graduated from the English Department of Tamkang University. He published his first short story in 1959 and worked as an editor for the *Literature Quarterly* in 1961. In July 1968, just as he was about to leave for Iowa to attend the International Writing Program, he was arrested and sentenced to ten years in prison. A member of the Democratic Taiwan League, Chen was charged with reading "leftist books" and engaging in "communist propaganda." He was released from prison in 1975 under the amnesty in honor of President Chiang Kai-shek's death, but was imprisoned again in 1978.

Chen's stories from the 1960s deal with two types of characters: young intellectuals and the downtrodden of society. We see the first in "My Younger

Brother Kangxiong" (Wo de didi Kangxiong) and "My First Assignment" (Diyijian chaishi), and the second in "The Tribe of Generals" (Jiangjun zu). In the last story, the two protagonists do not even have names: the middle-aged veteran from the mainland is known by his nickname Triangle Face, while the young girl from south Taiwan, with a limp from polio, is simply called "she" and "skinny little girl." They first meet as members of a traveling band. Triangle Face learns that the girl had been sold by her family to a pimp but ran away and became a clown in the band. One morning he leaves her his entire pension to pay off her family debt and disappears. Five years later, they meet again in a marching band; fully grown now, she is a baton twirler. He learns that his pension did not save her as he had intended; instead, she was sold off to another pimp, who blinded her in one eye and forced her to work as a prostitute. Eventually, she saved enough money to redeem herself and went looking for him so that she could pay him back. The next morning, their dead bodies are discovered in the field, lying side by side, dressed in their shining band uniforms.

Death is a choice made by many of Chen Yingzhen's protagonists. If the belief in innocence and sacrifice for love in "The Tribe of Generals" smacks of romantic idealism, Kangxiong's suicide in "My Younger Brother Kangxiong" expresses guilt over moral transgression and despair at life's vacuity and futility. In another story, "My First Assignment," a young policeman's first case is to investigate the suicide of a thirty-four-year-old businessman in a small hotel. Like pieces of a puzzle, his interviews with the hotel owner, the mistress, and the PE teacher with whom the deceased had contact before he died reveal different attitudes toward life.

Like Lin Haiyin, Nie Hualing (b. 1925) also played the dual role of editor and writer. A student refugee from the mainland, Nie published her first novel *The Lost China Tree* (*Shiqu de jinlingzi*) in 1960. For eleven years, Nie edited the literary section of the liberal *Free China* (*Ziyou Zhongguo*), whose nominal founder was Hu Shi, until the journal was shut down in 1960 and its chief editor, Lei Zhen (1897–1979), was arrested. In 1964, Nie Hualing was invited to attend the Iowa Writers' Workshop, then directed by the American poet Paul Engle (1908–1991), whom she later married. In 1967 the couple started the International Writing Program; among the first writers they invited were Ya Xian from Taiwan and Dai Tian (b. 1939) from Hong Kong.

Nie's second novel, *Mulberry and Peach: Two Women of China* (*Sangqing yu taohong*), was serialized in 1970 in the *United Daily* and was censored for touching on taboo political subjects. It was later serialized in the *Mingbao Monthly* (*Mingbao yuekan*) in Hong Kong, where the book was published in

1976. The book is divided into four parts, each containing a letter by Peach and an excerpt from Mulberry's diary. Juxtaposing the letters written in the present and the diary excerpts from 1945 to 1970, the novel reveals the transformation of the young, innocent Mulberry in war-torn China into the promiscuous, disillusioned Peach in exile in the US. Unlike most works written in Taiwan at the time, the book critiques the moral collapse of China, whether under the CCP or the GMD. It also views the diaspora from a feminist point of view, depicting the heroine's sexual escapades with no apology.

Before Nie Hualing, female sexuality had been explored by a seventeen-year-old writer named Li Ang, the pen name of Shi Shuduan (b. 1952). "The Flower Season" (Huaji, 1969) is the first-person narrative of a teenager who skips school one morning to buy a Christmas tree. Not finding what she wants in the shop, she takes a motorcycle ride with the florist to his nursery in the country. As she is taken farther and farther away from the familiar environment, she imagines him attempting to rape her. In the end, nothing happens. Simple in plot, the story captures a teenage girl's simultaneous fascination and trepidation toward sex. The nightmare of rape is no less a product of fantasy than is her dream of love influenced by the fairytales that she enjoys reading.

Popular literature

Although there is no hard-and-fast line between "serious" and "popular" literature, most avant-garde journals mentioned above consciously distinguished themselves from commercially oriented literature for mass consumption. Popular literature thrived in postwar Taiwan and may be divided into two categories: romance (sometimes called the New Mandarin Ducks and Butterflies) and martial arts sagas. The former is best represented by *Crown* (*Huangguan*), a magazine founded in 1954 by Ping Jintao. *Crown* published such popular writers as Feng Feng, Sima Zhongyuan, Hua Yan, and, above all, Qiong Yao (the pen name of Chen Zhe, b. 1933).

Qiong Yao published her first novel, *Outside the Window* (*Chuang wai*), in 1963. The story of a tragic affair between a high school student and her teacher, it was an instant best seller. By the end of the decade, she had written fifteen novels and become the most popular writer in Taiwan. She remained prolific in the ensuing decades: nineteen novels in the 1970s, nine in the 1980s, and nine in the 1990s. Many of her novels were translated into films that enjoyed box office success. In 1976 she formed her own film studio, Superstar, featuring Brigitte Lin (Lin Qingxia, b. 1954) in many of the productions. In the 1980s her popularity spread to mainland China, where many of her novels have been adapted for television series and movies.

Guo Lianghui (b. 1929), another popular writer, graduated from the University of Sichuan in 1948. After moving to Taiwan in 1949, she started publishing stories, some of which were broadcast on the radio. Her 1962 novel *Padlock on the Heart* (*Xinsuo*) was banned after it came out for its depictions of sex and incestuous relationships, and Guo Lianghui was expelled from state-sponsored writers' associations. The ban was lifted in 1988 and the novel was reprinted in 2002. For years Guo continued to write, mostly about modern relationships; she was also among the first to deal with homosexuality in fiction.

Martial arts sagas have a long tradition in China. After 1949, they were dismissed as "feudal" on the mainland but continued to thrive in Hong Kong and Taiwan. In postwar Taiwan, Wolong Sheng, Zhuge Qingyun, and Sima Ling were known as the Three Musketeers. Serialized daily in newspapers, their works employed the formula of "family tragedy – miraculous encounter – revenge" and were immensely popular. In the 1960s, new models began to emerge. Writing since 1960, Liu Canyang, the pen name of Gao Jianji (b. 1941), is known for graphic descriptions of violence; his work focuses on the lives of hired assassins who are stoic loners rather than genteel swordsmen.

Also writing in the 1960s, a young man named Xiong Yaohua (1936–1980) developed a new style by integrating elements of *Miyamoto Musashi* by Eiji Yoshikawa (1892–1962), pre-1949 sagas by the Master of the Returned Pearl (Huanzhu louzhu), contemporary sagas by Jin Yong (the pen name of Zha Liangyong or Louis Chia, b. 1924), and even James Bond stories. In contrast to the conventional mode, Xiong created a fast-paced plot, less detailed but more evocative fighting scenes, and terse and even lyrical language. Under the pen name Gu Long ("Ancient Dragon"), he produced his best works from the mid-1960s through the 1970s; many were made into films and television series.

The most popular prose writer to emerge in the 1970s is San Mao, the pen name of Chen Maoping (1943–1991). She became a phenomenal success with the publication in 1976 of *Tales of the Sahara* (*Sahala de gushi*). This and other autographical accounts touched the hearts of millions with tales of her exotic adventures in North Africa, romance with her Spanish husband José, and the image of a rebellious, romantic heroine. San Mao's popularity spread to mainland China in the 1980s. In 1991 she hanged herself in a hospital ward while waiting for surgery.

In postwar Taiwan, a number of native poets, including Wu Yingtao (1916–1971), Lin Hengtai, Zhan Bing, Jin Lian, and Zhang Yanxun, published in

Chinese. However, the dominance of émigré writers on the literary scene eventually provoked a reaction. In April 1957, Zhong Zhaozheng (b. 1925) launched the *Literary Friends Newsletter* (*Wenyou tongxun*), which provided a venue for native writers. In April 1964, Wu Zhuoliu founded *Taiwan Literary Art* (*Taiwan wenyi*). In June 1964, *Bamboo Hat* (*Li*) was founded by twelve poets: in addition to Wu Yingtao, Lin Hengtai, Zhan Bing, and Jin Lian were Huan Fu (b. 1922), Bai Qiu (1939), Zhao Tianyi (b. 1935), Xue Bogu, Huang Hesheng, Wang Xianyang (b. 1941), Du Guoqing (Kuo-ching Tu, b. 1941), and Gu Bei. Lin Hengtai chose the name for its obvious association with rural Taiwan. Following the modernist vein in its early issues, *Bamboo Hat* embraced a nativist stance from the 1970s onward. The journal, with its emphasis on the local and the vernacular (including the use of Hoklo), was a precursor to the nativist literature that began appearing in the 1970s. Another poetry club was the Vineyard (Putaoyuan), founded in 1962 by Wen Xiaocun (b. 1928), Chen Minhua, and Wang Zaijun. In contrast to the modernists, the Vineyard Poetry Club advocated clarity of language and fidelity to the Chinese tradition.

Identification with traditional Chinese culture had always been at the core of the official nationalist discourse. In November 1966, to counter the Cultural Revolution raging on the mainland, the Chinese Cultural Renaissance Movement (*Zhongguo wenhua fuxing yundong*) was launched by leading intellectuals under state sponsorship. In January 1970, *Renaissance* (*Wenyi fuxing*) was founded by Zhang Qiyun. In March 1971, the *Chinese Literature and Art Monthly* (*Zhonghua wenyi yuekan*) was founded, with Sima Zhongyuan as director and Yin Xueman (b. 1918) as chief editor.

The Cultural Renaissance Movement coincided with an emerging identity crisis in Taiwan. In the early 1970s, the Republic of China suffered a series of setbacks in the international arena, which shook the foundation of its identity. In 1971, the territorial dispute with Japan over Diaoyutai Island in the East China Sea sparked the Protect Diaoyutai Movement (abbreviated to Baodiao) among Taiwanese students studying in the United States. Disappointed at the GMD's failure to take a stronger stand, the students gravitated toward mainland China. A bigger blow to Taiwan occurred on October 25, 1971, when the General Assembly of the United Nations passed Resolution 2758, recognizing the People's Republic as the sole legitimate Chinese nation in place of the Republic of China, a founding member of the UN and a permanent member on its Security Council. The recognition was followed by President Nixon's historic visit to China on February 21–28, 1972 (diplomatic relations were established in 1979), and the establishment of diplomatic relations between Japan and the PRC in September of the same year.

Already in 1971, the Longzu ("Dragon Race") Poetry Society had been formed by a group of young poets: Chen Fangming (b. 1947), Lin Huanzhang (b. 1939), Xiao Xiao (b. 1947), Su Shaolian (b. 1949), and Gao Xinjiang (editor of the literary supplement to the *China Times* from 1973 onward). Named after the ancient symbol of China, the Dragon Race proclaims in its manifesto, "We strike our own gong, beat our own drum, dance with our own dragon." Taiwan's setbacks in international politics stimulated further reflections on national identity and were a significant force behind the Modern Poetry Debate of 1972–1974.

The Modern Poetry Debate and the Native Literature Movement

Throughout the 1950s and 1960s, modern poetry never ceased to be criticized for its difficulty and foreignness. Both the *Bamboo Hat* and the Vineyard Poetry Club positioned themselves as offering an alternative poetics. As the identity and even the legitimacy of Taiwan came into doubt in the early 1970s, poetry became a target. Two essays in the literary supplement to the *China Times* in February and September 1972 triggered the Modern Poetry Debate. In these essays, John Kwan Terry (Guan Jieming), a Chinese-Singaporean professor of English, lamented the wholesale Westernization of modernist poetry and its loss of cultural identity. Echoing such sentiments, Tang Wenbiao (1936–1985), a poet and mathematician, published scathing attacks on such leading poets as Yu Guangzhong, Zhou Mengdie, and Ye Shan (Yang Mu). In the next year or two, numerous articles, both for and against modernist poetry, would follow.

The defenders were clearly outnumbered by the opponents in the debate. Modernism was characterized by its critics as colonial, narcissistic, obscurantist, escapist, and decadent; metaphors of sickness and impotency were used repeatedly to describe it. In its place, the critics called for a poetry that would embrace Chinese roots on the one hand and address the social reality of Taiwan on the other. Instead of "horizontal transplant" – in Ji Xian's words – they advocated a return to the Chinese tradition; instead of modernism, they advocated realism; instead of experimentation, they advocated plain, accessible language.

In the wake of this debate, a host of new poetry societies emerged on the scene, questioning the limitations of modernism and embracing a distinctly Chinese identity. Some of the poetry societies are: Coming Tide (Hou lang, 1972), founded by Su Shaolian, Hong Xingfu (1949–1982), Chen Yizhi (b. 1953), and Xiao Wenhuang; Sirius (Tianlangxing, 1973); Autumn River (Qiu shui, 1974), founded by Gu Ding, Tu Jingyi, and Lü Di; Grassroots (Caogen, 1975), founded by Luo Qing (b. 1948), Zhang Xianghua (b. 1939), and Zhan Che

(b. 1954), among others; Great Ocean (Da haiyang, 1975), founded by Zhu Xueshu and Wang Qijiang (b. 1944); Green Earth (Lü di, 1976), founded by Fu Wenzheng; Poetry Genealogy (Shi mai, 1976), founded by Yan Shang (b. 1938); and Tide of Poetry (Shi chao, 1977), founded by Gao Zhun. Several members of Green Earth, including Xiang Yang (b. 1955), Ku Ling, and Li Changxian, went on to form Bouquet of Sunshine (Yangguang xiao ji, 1979).

These and other poetry societies emphasized either the continuity of Chinese culture or the rural roots and local history of Taiwan. An example of the former is the Sirius Poetry Society led by Wen Ruian (b. 1954) and Fang Ezhen (the pen name of Liao Yan, b. 1954). Wen and Fang had joined the Oasis Poetry Society (Lüzhou shishe) in Malaysia. In 1973, they founded Sirius and in 1974 went to Taiwan to attend college. There they formed the Sacred Land Poetry Society (Shenzhou shishe) in 1976. Like Sirius, Sacred Land was not only a literary organization, but also aimed at "promoting the national spirit and renewing Chinese culture." In addition to studying Chinese literature, its members also trained in martial arts and ran martial arts studios. With branches in Taiwan, Hong Kong, Singapore, and Malaysia, Sacred Land caught the attention of the Taiwan authorities. In 1980, military police arrested Wen Ruian and Fang Ezhen and charged them with treason and "engaging in communist propaganda." Thanks to the intervention of Yu Guangzhong, Jin Yong, and Gao Xinjiang, they were released and deported, eventually settling in Hong Kong. Since the early 1980s, Wen Ruian has been a best-selling author of martial arts sagas.

Tribute to rural Taiwan is represented by Wu Sheng and Zhan Che. The pen name of Wu Shengxiong (b. 1944), Wu Sheng graduated from the Pingdong Agriculture College (now Pingdong University of Science and Technology) and has worked as a middle school teacher most of his life. In the mid-1970s he published "Vignettes of My Hometown" (Wuxiang yinxiang), a poem sequence that presents daily life in rural Taiwan. With realistic images and colloquial language (including Hoklo words and expressions), Wu Sheng's poems are simple yet refreshing. Zhan Che, who graduated from the same college, was inspired by Wu Sheng's early work to write "Earth, Please Stand up and Speak" (Tudi qing zhan qilai shuohua). The poem was based on the poet's real-life encounter with a woman sugarcane farmer. Squatting at the edge of the field, the single mother was worried that the low price of sugarcane would not bring in enough income to feed her children. The poet identifies the farmer with Mother Taiwan, who is weighed down by injustice, and urges her to stand up and speak out. Zhan Che has become an advocate for farmers in recent decades.

Rejection of wholesale Westernization and the espousal of the language of everyday life were also manifest in music, as seen in the Campus Folksong (or New Folksong) Movement of the mid-1970s. The New Folksongs were mostly composed and performed by college students. They often adapted modern poems, such as those by Xu Zhimo, Yu Guangzhong, Zheng Chouyu, and Wu Sheng, to serve as lyrics. The movement in turn inspired poets to integrate poetry into popular culture by using multiple media, such as dance, pantomime, and drama. Since the 1980s, not only have poems been set to music, but quite a few poets have written lyrics for popular songs.

The Modern Poetry Debate of 1972–1974 was a precursor of the Native Literature Movement. In April 1977, fiction writer Wang Tuo (b. 1944) published "It's 'Realist Literature', Not 'Native Literature'" (Shi 'xianshi zhuyi wenxue', bushi 'xiangtu wenxue') in *Cactus* (*Xianrenzhang*). Native literature, according to Wang Tuo, should not limit itself to rural life but should depict urban reality as well. Two rejoinders came in the same issue from Yin Zhengxiong and Zhu Xining. Whereas Yin criticized Wang Tuo's view as based on an "ideology of hate," Zhu expressed concern that an overemphasis on the native land would create regionalism and separatism. In May, Ye Shitao (b. 1925) published the introduction to his *History of Native Taiwan Literature* (*Taiwan xiangtu wenxue shi*) in the *China Tide* (*Xia chao*), pointing out that native literature should be "Taiwan-centered." Shortly thereafter, the journal held a symposium on "Current Taiwanese Literature" and published essays on native literature by Yang Qingchu (b. 1940), Wang Tuo, and Huang Chunming, among others. In August, Peng Ge (the pen name of Yao Peng, b. 1926), a veteran writer, journalist, and columnist for the GMD-run *Central Daily* (*Zhongyang ribao*), published "Where Is Literature without Human Nature?" (Bu tan renxing he you wenxue?). He condemned nativist literature for its exclusive focus on "class," singling out Chen Yingzhen, Wang Tuo, and Yu Tiancong for criticism. The essay was followed by "Cry Wolf" (Lang lai le) by Yu Guangzhong, also published in the *Central Daily*. Yu equated nativist literature with the "literature of workers, peasants, and soldiers." To refute these charges, Yu Tiancong published "Native Literature and Nationalism" (Xiangtu wenxue yu minzu zhuyi), and Chen Yingzhen penned "Literature Comes from Society and Reflects Society" (Wenxue laizi shehui fanying shehui). The debate went on throughout 1977 and had petered out by January 1978.

The political implications of the Native Literature Movement did not escape the GMD. On August 29, 1977, the government held a symposium with more than 270 writers in attendance; none in the nativist camp was invited. President

Yan Jiagan (1905–1993) urged the writers to "stand firm on anticommunist literature." The following January, the military sponsored a conference at which General Wang Sheng (1917–2006), director of political warfare, emphasized the unity of the land and called upon writers to extend their love for the native land to the rest of the nation.

The subtext of the Native Literature Movement was the growing discontent among Taiwanese intellectuals with GMD rule and their increasingly vocal demand for democracy in the 1970s. The 1973 incident in the Philosophy Department at the National Taiwan University, in which eight faculty members were denied reappointment because of their liberal views, was indicative of widespread disenfranchisement. Many had begun to openly challenge the official ideology which for decades had defined Taiwan exclusively in Chinese terms and suppressed native history and culture. To the extent that the repressed history and literature of Taiwan were rediscovered and brought to the attention of the public, the movement was a "roots-searching" enterprise. Insofar as it was critical of Taiwan's economic dependence on, and cultural subordination to, the United States, it was an expression of postcolonial awareness. If native Taiwanese topics and issues appeared earlier in the works of Zhong Lihe, Zhong Zhaozheng, Li Qiao (b. 1934), Yang Qingchu, Huang Chunming, Chen Yingzhen, Wang Zhenhe, and so on, the movement also inspired many younger writers, such as Zeng Xinyi (b. 1948), who satirized women who worshipped foreign cultures and material comfort; Song Zelai (b. 1952), who wrote about economic hardship in his rural hometown; and Wu Jinfa (b. 1954), who depicted the plight of indigenous peoples. The Native Literature Movement changed the course of Taiwan's literature and helped to shape its development in decades to come.

Hong Kong

In-betweenness

On October 10, 1949, Guangzhou witnessed a sudden influx of people coming from Shanghai, Nanjing, Wuhan, Chongqing, Kuming, and other major cities. The influx went on unabated until October 14 when, after the 2:00 p.m. train had left for Hong Kong, the Pearl Sea Bridge (Zhuhai da qiao) was blown up by the GMD to cut off the land passage between Guangzhou and Hong Kong. On the morning of October 15, soldiers of the People's Liberation Army were seen patrolling the main streets of Guangzhou. Over the next six months, refugees continued to take the train from Guangzhou to Shenzhen and then walk across the Lake Luo Bridge to Hong Kong. After April 30, 1950, the PRC forbade its citizens to exit the mainland; the "iron curtain" had fallen and was to stay down until 1979.

Before May 1949, Hong Kong had about 1.6 million people. By April 30, 1950, the population had grown to 2.6 million. In other words, the tiny island at the southeastern edge of the Asian continent had received one million refugees from the mainland, increasing the population by more than half of its original number. Although Hong Kong had been a haven for mainlanders during the Second Sino-Japanese War (1937–1945), the exodus in 1949 and 1950 was far more massive and the impact of this diaspora far more significant.

A British colony since 1843, Hong Kong was a thriving trade port in the early twentieth century, but its position as an entrepôt declined considerably after the United Nations imposed a trade embargo against the PRC during the Korean War. In response, Hong Kong developed a textile industry, taking advantage of the new pool of labor from the mainland. The economy grew rapidly and became more diversified and international in the 1960s. In 1967, labor disputes led to a wave of strikes organized by Hong Kong's leftist union, known as "May Storm." Under Governor Murray MacLehose (Mai Lihao, 1917–2000), new social programs to address problems in housing, medical care, education, and workers' compensation were put in place between 1971 and 1982. These improvements paved the way for Hong Kong's development into an international banking and financial center in the 1980s and beyond.

In the cultural sphere, the British government adopted a policy of noninterference. It did not impose English, nor did it ban Chinese. Efforts to carry on the Chinese cultural tradition led to the founding of New Asia College (Xinya shuyuan) in 1950, and of the New Asia Institute of Advanced Chinese Studies in 1953, by Qian Mu (1895–1990), Tang Junyi (1909–1978), and Zhang Pijie. In 1958, Tang Junyi, along with Xu Fuguan (1903–1982), Mou Zongsan (1909–1995), and Zhang Junmai (1887–1968), jointly authored "Declaration to the World on Behalf of Chinese Culture" (Wei Zhongguo wenhua jinggao shijie renshi xuanyan), which is regarded as the manifesto of New Confucianism. In 1963, New Asia College was merged with Chung Chi (Chongji, founded in 1950) and United (Lianhe, founded in 1956) Colleges to form the Chinese University of Hong Kong.

Beginning in the 1950s, the Hong Kong government encouraged the teaching of English in school as the official language and required English for entrance into the civil service. In response, intellectuals and students organized in 1970 to demand that Chinese be legitimized as an official language.

As a result, Chinese was recognized by the colonial government in 1972 and has since enjoyed equal status with English.

Compared with mainland China and Taiwan, Hong Kong enjoyed a greater degree of civil liberty, including freedom of speech. With no censorship and rare interference from the authorities, a wide spectrum of ideological positions coexisted. More importantly, Hong Kong was situated between the mainland and Taiwan, and had access to both. So long as the mainland remained closed behind the Iron Curtain, Taiwan benefited from extensive exchanges with Hong Kong. Exchanges took one of two forms. First, banned works from pre-1949 China were smuggled from Hong Kong to Taiwan and were privately circulated. This kind of underground transmission played a significant role in the modernist movement in postwar Taiwan.

Second, Hong Kong provided a venue for Taiwan writers to publish their works. For example, Ya Xian's first poetry collection, *One Night in Kulinglin* (*Kulinglin de yi ye*), came out in Hong Kong in 1959, although it was never published in Taiwan. In 1956, when Ji Xian founded the Modernist School in Taipei, Ma Lang (the pen name of Ma Boliang, a.k.a. Ronald Mar, b. 1936) launched the *New Literary Currents* (*Wenyi xin chao*) in Hong Kong. The two journals cooperated extensively in terms of distribution and contributions. Fiction writers, such as Nie Hualing, Guo Lianghui, and Gao Yang (1926–1992), published their works in Hong Kong newspapers and journals. In 1964, the Cape of Good Hope Literary Prizes in Hong Kong all went to Taiwan writers: Ya Xian and Guan Guan (the pen name of Guan Yunlong, b. 1929) in poetry and Chen Yingzhen in fiction. From 1974 to 1985, Yu Guangzhong taught at the Chinese University of Hong Kong, located in Shatin. His friendship with, and influence on, Huang Guobin (b. 1946), Huang Weiliang (b. 1947), and Liang Xihua (b. 1947) earned them the nickname the Shatin Gang of Four.

Conversely, as Free China, Taiwan attracted many young men and women from Hong Kong and Southeast Asia, who attended college and developed a literary career there. "Overseas students" in the 1960s included Ye Weilian (Wai-lim Yip, b. 1937), Dai Tian, Ao Ao (the pen name of Zhang Zhen'ao, a.k.a. Dominic Cheung, b. 1943), Zheng Zhen (the pen name of Zheng Shusen, a.k.a. William Tay, b. 1948), and Wen Jianliu (1944–1976). Ye Weilian was not only a member of the Epoch Poetry Society but also its major theorist in the 1960s and 1970s. Ao Ao formed the Constellations Poetry Society (Xingzuo shishe) in 1964 with fellow overseas students at the National Chengchi (Zhengzhi) University, including Lin Lü, Wang Runhua (Yoon-wah Wong, b. 1941), Dan Ying (b. 1943), and Chen Huihua (b. 1942). Zheng Zhen wrote fiction in college but became best known as a translator and editor of world literature, as well as a literary and film scholar. Wen Jianliu also attended the National Chengchi University. After receiving an MA from the University of Iowa, he returned to Hong Kong in 1974 and taught at Hong Kong University until he died at thirty-two.

Hong Kong also hosted writers from both sides of the Taiwan Strait. For instance, the PRC cultural delegation to India, headed by Zheng Zhenduo, passed through Hong Kong in December 1954. The delegation to the Congress of Asian Nations, led by Guo Moruo and counting among its members Ding Xilin and Ba Jin, stayed briefly in Hong Kong in April 1954. In May 1956, the Peking Opera Delegation to Japan, led by Mei Lanfang (1894–1961) and Ouyang Yuqian, also passed through.

European writers, including Graham Greene (1904–1991) and Somerset Maugham (1874–1965) from Britain, and Pierre Benoît (1886–1962) from France, visited Hong Kong in the early 1950s. In 1955, English writer Richard Mason (1919–1997) spent three months in Hong Kong; after he returned to Britain, he wrote *The World of Suzie Wong*, a love story set in Hong Kong about an American painter and a Chinese bar girl. The novel was made into a film in 1960, featuring the Hollywood heartthrob William Holden (1918–1981) and the Hong Kong beauty Nancy Kwan (Guan Nanqian, b. 1939). In 2005, a ballet based on the novel premiered in Hong Kong.

The unique geopolitical position of Hong Kong enabled leftist (including Trotskyite) and rightist (including US-backed) camps to coexist. Among writers, Ye Lingfeng, Cao Juren (1900–1972, literary historian), and He Da belonged to the former; Xu Xu and Xiong Shiyi (playwright) to the latter. Leftist periodicals include the *Wenhuibao, Dagongbao, New Evening Post (Xin wanbao), Little Friends (Xiao pengyou), Youth Paradise (Qingnian leyuan), Ocean Light Literary Art (Haiguang wenyi), Literary Companion (Wenyi banlü), Ocean Literature (Haiyang wenyi), Pangu, The 1970s (Qishi niandai)*, and *Literature and Art (Wenxue yu meishu)*, among others. Most of the journals were short-lived and had limited distribution. Right-leaning periodicals include the *Hong Kong Times (Xianggang shibao), Literary Scene (Wen tan), Hong Kong Daily (Xingdao ribao), Overseas Chinese Daily (Huaqiao ribao)*, and others. The most influential periodicals came from US-financed publishing houses such as United (Lianhe, founded in 1951), World Today (Jinri shijie, founded in 1952), and Asia (Yazhou, also founded in 1952). Asia Press published several magazines, including *Chinese Students Weekly (Zhongguo xuesheng zhoubao*, founded in 1952). Until it folded in July 1974, it was instrumental in introducing avant-garde literature and art (including film) from around the world and providing fertile ground for young writers.

Literature of the exodus

Much postwar literature in Hong Kong was written by émigré writers, who either looked back on the recent wars, depicting the heroism and suffering of the people, or sang of the homeland in a nostalgic mode. Nostalgia was represented by such poets as Li Kuang (the pen name of Zheng Jianbo, 1927–1991), Xu Su, Xu Xu, and Li Su, all of whom inherited the romantic lyricism of May Fourth poetry. Their work influenced the first poetry society in postwar Hong Kong, New Thunder Poetry Scene (Xinlei shitan), whose members included Lin Renchao, Murong Yujun, and Lu Ganzhi.

Also a fiction writer, Xu Su published *Star, Moon, Sun* (*Xingxing, yueliang, taiyang*) in 1955. Spanning the Second Sino-Japanese War, the novel revolves around the relationships between a young man from a well-to-do, conservative family and three beautiful women with distinctive personalities: one is melancholy like a lone star, one bright like the moon, and one passionate like the sun. The work was so popular that in 1961 it was made into an epic film (running 214 minutes) in color, with a star-studded cast and scenes shot in Taiwan. Such phenomenal success was repeated with the publication of Wang Lan's *Blue and Black* in 1958 and the making of the film in 1966.

Among the recent émigré writers, Eileen Chang made the most profound and enduring impact on Chinese literature. Chang moved to Hong Kong from Shanghai in 1952 and was commissioned by the US Information Service to write anticommunist literature. The result was two novels: *Rice Sprout Song* (*Yang ge*) and *The Naked Earth: A Novel about China* (*Chi di zhi lian*). Set in a village not far from Shanghai, *Rice Sprout Song* exposes the negative impact of land reform in China. Despite good harvests, incessant and unreasonable demands on the peasants to contribute to the Korean War effort leave them with barely enough to eat. Driven by unbearable hunger, the peasants demand more grain from the public granary but are suppressed by soldiers. In the end, the protagonist's entire family is destroyed: his daughter is trampled to death by the crowd, he dies from a gunshot wound, and his wife ends her own life after setting fire to the granary in revenge. Ironically, in the name of "peasant revolution," the CCP created a new dictatorship that forced peasants to the verge of starvation. Originally a communal harvest song, "Rice Sprout Song" turns out to be a dirge for the oppressed. Neither didactic nor melodramatic, the novel unfolds in visceral images and in a low key, laying bare the despair of those caught in a dogmatic and hypocritical system.

Rice Sprout Song was written in both English and Chinese. The Chinese version was serialized in *World Today* in the first half of 1954. The English version was published by Charles Scribner's Sons in New York and was reviewed in the *New York Times Book Review* on April 3, 1955. It did not, however, make a splash. It was not until 1961, when C. T. Hsia published his magisterial *History of Modern Chinese Fiction*, that the novel received the attention it deserved. Hsia called *Rice Sprout Song* a classic and named Chang as the most original writer in modern China.

In the 1950s and 1960s, Chang also translated American literature and wrote film scripts for major studios in Hong Kong. In 1955, she left for the US, paying a visit to Hu Shi in New York. She married the American playwright Ferdinand Reyher (1891–1967) in 1956. Many of her stories were serialized in the *Crown* and published in Taiwan in the 1960s and 1970s. By then a living legend, Chang exerted a formative influence on new generations of writers, especially women writers, in Taiwan and Hong Kong. Many of her works would be made into films from the 1980s on. The most recent film rendition is *Lust, Caution* (*Se jie*), directed by Ang Lee (Li An, b. 1954), based on her short story by the same name. On September 8, 1995, Chang was found dead from heart failure in her Los Angeles apartment.

As émigré writers settled in, they began to write about their new lives in Hong Kong. A prime example is Zhao Zifan's (1924–1986) *Half Down* (*Ban xialiu shehui*). Published by Asia Press in November 1953, the novel depicts recent émigrés, mostly intellectuals and servicemen, who live in slums and do manual work to survive. Although impoverished, they are neither selfish and coldhearted like the rich, nor have they lost their integrity and idealism. The novel enjoyed immense popularity in Hong Kong and Taiwan and was made into a film in Mandarin in 1957. Other works depicting the harsh reality of living in Hong Kong in the 1950s and 1960s include Lü Lun's *Dead-End* (*Qiong xiang*, 1952), Cao Juren's *Tavern* (*Jiudian*, 1954), and Zhang Yifan's *Spring Comes to Diaojing Peak* (*Chun dao Diaojingling*).

The moral struggle for many living in Hong Kong is the theme of *The Drinker* (*Jiutu*) by Liu Yichang. Born Liu Tongyi in Shanghai in 1918, Liu Yichang graduated from St. John's University in 1941 and worked as a journalist and editor in Shanghai and Chongqing during the Second Sino-Japanese War. He returned to Shanghai after the war and founded his own publishing house and the literary supplement to *Peace Daily* (*Heping ribao*). In 1948 he moved to Hong Kong, and in February 1960 took over the editorship of *Repulse Bay* (*Qianshui wan*), the literary supplement to the *Hong Kong Times*. Under his editorship, new Hong Kong literature thrived.

The Drinker was published in 1963. The first-person narrator is a young writer from the mainland who lives in Hong Kong. To make a living, he has to give up his idealism and writes crude martial arts sagas and erotic stories for newspapers. He tries to start a literary journal with friends but in the end is unable to extricate himself from a decadent life. *The Drinker* employs the stream of consciousness extensively. It inspired director Wong Kar-wai (Wang Jiawei, b. 1958) to make the film *2046* in 2004, just as the same author's *Reversed* (*Dui dao*) inspired Wong Kar-wai's *In the Mood for Love* (*Huayang nianhua*) in 2000.

Everyman's Literature (*Renren wenxue*), edited by Huang Sicheng, Qi Huan, Li Kuang, and Xu Su from 1952 to 1954, was one of the first literary journals in postwar Hong Kong. Traditional in its orientation, it defined poetry as the direct expression of personal emotion cast in regular forms and rhymes. A different approach was articulated by Lin Yiliang, the pen name of Song Qi (a.k.a. Stephen C. Soong, 1916–1996). A poet, literary critic, and translator from Shanghai, Lin settled in Hong Kong in 1948. He became a major contributor to *Everyman's Literature*, for which he wrote a column, "Talks on Western Literature." Contrary to the traditionalist bent of the journal, Lin objected to "light lyricism" and "heavy didacticism" and advocated psychological nuance and organic form. Using his friend Wu Xinghua as a model, Lin Yiliang published Wu's poems and critical essays (under the pseudonym Liang Wenxing) in Hong Kong and Taiwan in the 1950s. Ironically, even as Wu was being silenced by the CCP, he found a new audience outside the mainland. Lin's theory of poetry as well as the translations he did for World Today Press – including *Anthology of American Poetry* (*Meiguo shixuan*), which he edited in 1961 – strongly influenced younger poets. He also helped to establish the Research Centre for Translation at the Chinese University of Hong Kong in 1964 and founded the journal *Renditions* in 1974.

Modernism

The coexistence of right- and left-leaning literary traditions, extensive introduction to world literature, and cross-pollination with the literary scene of Taiwan all contributed to the rise of a new generation of Hong Kong writers in the 1960s and 1970s. Again, periodicals provided a major venue. For example, the first poetry journal born in postwar Hong Kong, *Poetry Blossoms* (*Shi duo*), was founded in August 1955 by Kun Nan (under Disiai, the pen name of Cen Kunnan, b. 1935), Ye Weilian, and Wuxie (Wang Wuxie, a.k.a. Wucius Wong, b. 1936). Among its major contributors were Lu Yin (b. 1935), Du Hong (the pen name of Cai Yanpei, b. 1936), and Lanzi (a.k.a. Xi Xi, b. 1938), in addition to the founding editors. *Poetry Blossoms* pioneered modernist literature. Many of the writers associated with the journal went on to found others, such as *New Currents* (*Xin sichao*, 1959–1960), edited by Ma Lang and Kun Nan; *Modern Editions* (*Haowangjiao*, 1963–1964), edited by Kun Nan, Li Yinghao, Ye Weilian, and Wu Xie; *Poetic Style* (*Shi feng*, 1972–1984), edited by Dai Tian, Wen Jianliu, Ji Hun, Huang Guobin, Ma Jue (b. 1943), Li Zongheng, and Cai Yanpei; *Compass* (*Luopan*, 1976–1978), edited by Ye Hui (b. 1952), He Furen (b. 1950), Kang Fu, and Zhou Guowei; *Creator* (*Pangu*, 1967), edited by Dai Tian, Gu Cangwu (b. 1945), and Cen Yifei; *Burning Wind* (*Fen feng*, 1970–1978); *Autumn Glowworm* (*Qiu ying*, 1970–1972, 1978–1988), edited by Li Jiasheng, Guan Mengnan (b. 1946), Lan Liu, Luo Guixiang, and Ye Hui; and *Big Thumb* (*Damuzhi*, 1975–1987), edited by Ye Si (b. 1947) and Fan Junfeng. Some of the journals were explicitly modernist, others more eclectic. Some emphasized experimentation while others favored traditional Chinese lyricism.

In contrast to Taiwan and mainland China, Hong Kong was faced with a different kind of identity issue. In an overtly "apolitical" environment, there was no "official ideology" to conform to or rebel against. The omnipresence of the British colonial government and the English language also meant a stark juxtaposition of Chinese and Western cultures. Not surprisingly, it is in a Hong Kong poem from the 1960s that we find a "postmodern" pastiche, as seen in "Where the Flag Flutters" (Qi xiang) by Kun Nan. Arranged in different typefaces, the poem consists of disparate elements that point to a variety of registers – linguistic (classical Chinese prose, business Chinese, Cantonese, English), sociocultural (business letter, pop music, advertising, stock market, horse race, traditional literary criticism, *Analects of Confucius*), and political (national anthem of the PRC). Similar experiments can also be seen in Kun Nan's novel *Earth Gate* (*Di de men*).

Of course, not all writers who wrote about the reality of Hong Kong life were modernists. Shu Xiangcheng (the pen name of Wang Shenquan, 1923–1999), for example, wrote realist poetry and fiction about urban life. Yet the contributions of modernist writers in the 1960s and 1970s are undeniable. Two in particular stand out. Ye Si, the pen name of Liang Bingjun (Ping-kwan Leung), was born in Guangzhou, grew up in Hong Kong, and graduated from Baptist College. After working as a newspaper editor and schoolteacher, he went to the University of California at San Diego in 1978 and received a Ph.D. in comparative literature in 1984. He has taught at Hong Kong University and Lingnan University since then. A versatile writer, Ye Si has published numerous stories, poems, translations, and scholarly essays on literature and cultural criticism, as well as film, art, and food reviews. Writing in a variety of styles, genres, and media, he has transcended conventional boundaries and often created hybrid forms to articulate his singular artistic vision. In his early fiction, Ye Si was equally adept in realism and magical realism. His poetry is deceptively simple, even prosaic, but derives from seemingly trivial details of quotidian life, moving insights into the relationship between the self and the world.

Xi Xi, the pen name of Zhang Yan, was born into a Cantonese family in Shanghai. In 1950 she moved to Hong Kong with her parents. After graduating from a teachers' college, she taught primary school but has been a full-time writer since the 1980s. Xi Xi has written poetry, fiction, children's stories, essays, film reviews, and film scripts. Her first collection, *Stories of East City* (*Dongcheng gushi*), was published in March 1966; her first book of poetry, *Stone Cymbal* (*Shi qing*), was published in 1982. She was also a cofounder and editor of the *Chinese Student Weekly* in the 1960s, *Big Thumb* in the 1970s, and *Leaf Literary* (*Suye wenxue*) from 1981 to 1984.

"A Woman like Me" (Xiang wo zheyang de yige nüzi, 1982) is a monologue of a young cosmetician at a funeral home. An orphaned child, she learned the craft from her aunt, who has remained single since her boyfriend left her because of her line of work. Now in a relationship of her own, the protagonist prepares herself for the same fate by telling herself repeatedly, "A woman like me should not fall in love." In the last scene of the story, she sits in a coffee shop, ready to take her boyfriend to her workplace. She sees him crossing the street with a big bouquet of flowers and thinks, "He doesn't know that in my profession flowers mean goodbye."

The story takes a detached and ironic look at love – its frailty, transience, and blindness. All the protagonist's friends slowly drift away because she reminds them of death. She is a mirror in which they see their own fear of death, and she expects the same response from her boyfriend. He loves her distinctive scent, not knowing that she wears perfume to cover up the pungent smell of formaldehyde. The ominous ending intimates that the relationship will end, like her aunt's did, when he finds out what she does for a living. The calmness with which she accepts this is reminiscent of Daoist transcendence of mundane values.

A Daoist-like respect for nature finds expression in the work of Wu Xubin (b. 1949). A cofounder of *Big Thumb*, Wu received her MS in ecology from the University of California at San Diego. Her stories from the 1970s, such as "Watch" (Shoubiao), "The Hunter" (Lieren), and "Ox" (Niu), are distinguished by a wholehearted acceptance and appreciation of nature – including the fact that animals kill each other – expressed in a serene and lyrical language. Wu stopped writing in 1986.

Popular literature

Unlike Taiwan or mainland China, Hong Kong has seen few debates or controversies about literature. One reason is perhaps the marginalized position of literature in a society with a predominantly commercial and apolitical ethos. Writers are left alone to engage in experimentation as they please. This is at least one reason why some Hong Kong writers either publish their work or become well-known first in Taiwan. It is popular literature rather than highbrow literature that flourishes in Hong Kong, best represented by the genres of pseudohistorical fiction, romance, detective story, science fiction, and martial arts saga. Nangong Bo's historical fiction, Yao Ke's historical plays, and Tang Ren's (the pen name of Ruan Lang) *Spring Dream of Nanking* (*Jinling chun meng*), a pseudobiographical exposé of Chiang Kai-shek, are all examples of pseudohistorical fiction from the 1950s. In the genre of romance, Yi Da and Zheng Hui were the most popular authors in the 1950s and 1960s. Ni Kuang (the pen name of Ni Yiming, b. 1935) was the best-known writer of detective fiction, although he also wrote romance, supernatural tales, and martial arts sagas. (Ni wrote parts of Jin Yong's *Heavenly Dragon in Eight Parts*, which Jin Yong deleted or rewrote later.) Ni Kuang's younger sister, Yi Shu, with more than 250 novels and books of essays to date, was also immensely popular.

The popularity of martial arts sagas in Taiwan in the 1960s was to a large extent owed to two pioneers. In Hong Kong in the mid-1950s, the so-called new martial arts saga came into being with the publication of works by Liang Yusheng (b. 1924) and Jin Yong. Liang Yusheng, the pen name of Chen Wentong, came from Mengshan, Guangxi Province. During the Second Sino-Japanese War, he studied literature and history with such prominent scholars as Rao Zongyi (b. 1917) and Jian Youwen, who had come to Mengshan as refugees. In 1949, Liang Yusheng moved to Hong Kong, where he worked as a newspaper editor. There, he and two colleagues, Luo Fu (a Hong Kong-based journalist) and Jin Yong, edited the literary supplement to the *New Evening Post* (*Xin wanbao*) and jointly wrote a column called "Notes from the Mansion of Three Swords" (Sanjianlou suibi). It was Luo Fu's idea, in 1952, that they should start writing martial arts sagas. Luo Fu stopped after writing one, but Liang Yusheng and Jin Yong went on to become seminal figures who transformed the genre. From 1952 to 1984, Liang wrote thirty-five sagas, among them *Tale of the White-Haired Demon Girl* (*Baifa monü zhuan*) and *Seven*

Swordsmen from Mount Heaven (Qijian xia Tianshan). Also a writer of essays on poetry, history, and the game of chess, he has been living in Australia in recent years.

Jin Yong came from Haining in Zhejiang Province. A journalist for the *Dagongbao*, he wrote film scripts and essays under several other pen names. It was in 1955 or 1956, when his first martial arts saga, *The Book and the Sword (Shujian enchou lu)*, was serialized, that he adopted the pen name Jin Yong by splitting the second character in his given name into two. Thus began his legendary career as the most widely read writer of the genre and one of the most widely read Chinese authors of all time.

A Jin Yong martial arts saga combines romantic love stories, fantastic adventures, and intrigue in a quasi-historical setting. He draws on traditional Chinese literature for vivid and elegant language, Western literature for character development, and Chinese culture for philosophical and moral values. His heroes embody a code of honor based on righteousness, honesty, and selfless brotherhood, confronting and ultimately triumphing over power. Instead of holding on to power, they walk away from it with nonchalance. Jin Yong's last work, *The Deer and the Cauldron (Lu ding ji)*, is the ultimate expression of such spirit. The protagonist, Wei Xiaobao, is a young boy who never masters martial arts. Unlike the noble and brave protagonists in Jin Yong's other novels, Wei is a punk with no grander ambition than living a good life with plenty of money and beautiful women. He uses his street-smarts to survive the treacherous world of court intrigues and in the end leaves the emperor because he knows well that power corrupts character and destroys friendship.

From 1955 to 1972, already a successful publisher, Jin Yong wrote fourteen martial arts sagas, many of which have been made into films and television series. Raising the genre to a height hitherto unimaginable, Jin Yong transformed the genre from entertainment for the literate to a literary art appealing to the educated and the masses alike. The popularity of his work spread to Taiwan and Southeast Asia and, from the 1980s on, to the mainland as well. His works have also become the subject of scholarly studies and are translated into other languages.

III. Intersections and contestations (1978 to the present)

From 1978 to the present, all three geopolitical regions – mainland China, Taiwan, and Hong Kong – have undergone dramatic transformations in response to, and in interaction with, historic changes. Transformations originated in the political realm, but they impact every aspect of society. In each case, change involves the transfer of power from the old guard as well as shifts in social, economic, and cultural structures.

Mainland China transitioned into the post-Mao era in the late 1970s and into the post-Deng era in the mid-1990s, characterized by liberalizing trends in economic and sociocultural, if not political, arenas. The past three decades have witnessed China transform from a closed society behind the Iron Curtain to the largest market in the world, from a primarily agricultural to a rapidly urbanizing society, from a repressive monolith to a porous, multifaceted society. With impressive economic development and increasing international clout, China is poised to be a superpower in the twenty-first century. Issues such as uneven modernization and the widening gap between the rich and the poor, the 1989 Tiananmen Massacre, and ethnic tensions in Xinjiang and Tibet, however, are more than growing pains and pose a potential threat to stability and progress.

Taiwan marched steadily toward democratization in the 1980s. Martial law was lifted in 1987 and, for the first time since 1949, contact was reopened between Taiwan and mainland China. Ironically, contact took place as nativist consciousness surged to polarize the population as *benshengren* versus *waishengren*. The first truly democratic presidential election took place in 1996. The GMD lost the presidency in 2000 and 2004, but regained it in 2008. A fully fledged democracy since 1987, Taiwan has faced the dual challenge of resolving tensions between, on the one hand, pro-independence and pro-reunification, and, on the other, establishing a peaceful and mutually beneficial relationship with China while maintaining autonomy.

Hong Kong, a British colony since 1842, was returned to Chinese rule on July 1, 1997. Under Deng Xiaoping's formula of "One Country, Two Systems" (*yiguo liangzhi*), Hong Kong was given the status of Special Administrative Region (SAR) and was to maintain its capitalist way of life for fifty years. Since the handover, a number of institutional changes, such as the reformation of the education system, have been put in place. Having survived the Asian Financial Crisis of 1998 and the SARS epidemic of 2003, Hong Kong has bounced back economically. As investors, tourists, and immigrants from the mainland are slowly but surely changing the demographics and sociocultural makeup, tensions with Beijing have surfaced from time to time. What concerns many in Hong Kong is as much prosperity as it is political and intellectual freedom.

Since the early 1980s, the mainland, Taiwan, and Hong Kong have become inextricably connected. As the old barriers are removed, interaction resumes, information and goods flow, people move across regional boundaries, and mutual influences grow through trade, tourism, intermarriage, immigration, cultural and intellectual exchanges, and political negotiations. Significant differences notwithstanding, the three regions have more in common, and their fates are more intertwined, than ever before.

More than a direct reflection of external reality, literature takes the pulse of the changing Chinese-speaking world and captures the spirit of the time. Through their works writers ask, what does it mean to be Chinese, Taiwanese, or Hongkongnese? How did they get to where they are and where are they going? Although these questions are not new, the new historical context in which they are raised gives them unique significance and a sense of urgency.

The rapidly urbanizing and globalizing environment and the widespread use of computer and information technology in the three regions also generate new experiences and inspire new experimentation. Such issues as urban life, gender, sexuality, ethnicity, aboriginal cultures, and minorities' rights have come to the fore. A wide range of styles and approaches, under the rubrics of modernism, nativism, neorealism, new historicism, and postmodernism, have also found their way into literature. If the rise of visual culture has been correlated with a decline in readership, the alleged "death of literature" cannot be farther from the truth. The Internet has democratized the cyberspace in which literature thrives. Fiction continues to inspire film and television series, while poetry enjoys a loyal, albeit smaller, following.

Finally, since the early 1980s, Chinese literature has attracted much international attention as more translations become available and more interaction with the international literary scene is made possible by immigration, scholarly exchanges, and literary festivals. As Sinophone literature around the world grows, the boundary between the local and the global seems blurred. In the year 2000, Gao Xingjian (b. 1940), the novelist and playwright who left China in 1987 and has since been living in Paris, became the first Chinese writer to win the Nobel Prize in Literature.

Mainland China

The thaw in the New Era

The engine of transformation was started with the passing of Premier Zhou Enlai in January 1976, which sparked a spontaneous outpouring of mourning over the beloved leader and indignation against Maoist fanaticism. These sentiments were expressed in the form of classical poems, 1,500 of which were later collected in an anthology. The crackdown on mourner–protesters in Tiananmen Square came to be known as the April Fifth Incident. A month after Mao died on September 9, 1976, Hua Guofeng (b. 1921), Mao's handpicked successor as CCP chairman, ordered the arrest of the Gang of Four. All of them ended up serving life sentences. Jiang Qing committed suicide in 1991, and the others died of illness.

By late 1978, Hua Guofeng had lost power to Deng Xiaoping, whose rule in the following decade ushered in the New Era (*Xin shiqi*). Abandoning the xenophobic insulation of the Cultural Revolution, Deng opened China to the free world and made economic and technological reform his top priority. He launched the "Four Modernizations" (*sige xiandaihua*) of agriculture, industry, national defense, and science and technology. In the cultural sphere, the Third Plenum of the Eleventh Party Congress in December 1978 encouraged writers and intellectuals to "liberate thought." The liberalizing, forward-looking atmosphere made possible a "thaw" in the literary scene.

The first sign of a thaw appeared as early as 1976, when several major journals, such as the *Poetry Journal* and *People's Literature*, were revived. Writers who had been persecuted were "rehabilitated" from 1978 to 1980 and were free to write and publish again; some (such as Ding Ling and Ai Qing) were given prominent positions in the literary establishment. Collectively, these "rehabilitated" writers may be called the "returnees" (*guilaizhe*). Mu Dan's "tree of wisdom" is nourished with "bitter juice" and Niu Han's "half-tree" is mutilated by lightning but still standing.

The return of critical realism is demonstrated by fiction, drama, and reportage, such as Liu Xinwu's (b. 1942) "The Homeroom Teacher" (Banzhuren), Bai Hua's (b. 1930) play *Light of Dawn* (*Shu guang*), Xu Chi's reportage "Goldbach's Conjecture" (Gedebahe caixiang), and Liu Binyan's reportage "Between Human and Monster" (Renyao zhijian).

The burst of creative energy in post-Mao China came not so much from the new establishment as from the underground. On October 11, 1978, Huang Xiang, Li Jiahua, Fang Jiahua, and Mo Jiangang journeyed from Guiyang to Beijing and posted the inaugural issue of *Enlightenment* (*Qimeng*) on a wall in the Xidan district. Huang Xiang also recited his long poem "God of Fire: A Symphonic Poem" (Huoshen jiaoxiangshi) to a large crowd that had gathered spontaneously. The wall soon came to be known as the Democracy Wall (*minzhuqiang*). From late 1978 to spring 1981, many articles and underground journals were posted here, such as "The Fifth Modernization – Democracy and Other Things" (Diwuge xiandaihua – minzhu ji qita) by Wei Jingsheng (b. 1950, under the pen name Jin Sheng); *April Fifth Forum* (*Siwu luntan*), edited by Liu Qing (b. 1946), Yang Jing, Xu Wenli, Zhao Nan, and others; "A Manifesto of Human Rights in China" (Zhongguo renquan xuanyan) by Ren Wanding (b. 1944); and *Fertile Soil* (*Wo tu*) and *Beijing Spring* (*Beijing zhi chun*), edited by Hu Ping (b. 1947) and Wang Juntao (b. 1958). Known as Beijing Spring, this period marked the first demand for democracy in post-Mao China; it came to an end with the arrest of some of the editors and writers.

The one underground journal devoted exclusively to literature is *Today* (*Jintian*). Launched in late December 1978, *Today* brought together a group of writers and artists led by Bei Dao (who initiated the idea) and Mang Ke (who gave the journal its name). The original group comprised Lu Huanxing, Huang Rui (b. 1952), Zhang Pengzhi, Sun Junshi, Tao Jiakai, Ma Desheng (b. 1952), and E Fuming. In the inaugural issue, the editors proclaimed, "History has finally given us a chance, allowing our generation to sing out that which has been buried in our hearts for ten long years." The celebration of the newfound freedom was the perfect prelude to a literary renaissance in which the journal played a seminal role.

One of the works published in *Today* was the novella *Waves* (*Bodong*) by Bei Dao (under the pen name Ai Shan), which depicts "the lost generation" of the Cultural Revolution through the extensive use of stream of consciousness, montage, and interior monologue. Bei Dao's poetry expresses disillusionment with political reality and reaffirms human dignity, as simply stated in these lines from "Ending or Beginning" (Jieju huo kaishi): "I don't want to be a hero. / In an age without heroes, / I just want to be a man." Since 1989, Bei Dao has mostly lived outside mainland China, taking up writer-in-residence and teaching stints at universities in Europe, North America, and Hong Kong. He continues to be prolific in both poetry and prose.

In Mang Ke's poetry, the sun is a "bloody shield" rising in the sky and people are "sunflowers in the sun." An ironic twist to the stock symbolism of Chairman Mao as the red sun, the sunflowers try to break the chains that enslave them to the sun. After composing two long poems in the 1980s, Mang Ke effectively stopped writing poetry. He published the novel *Wild Things* (*Ye shi*) in 1995, which depicts the protagonist's sexual escapades against the bleak background of the Cultural Revolution. He also penned a collection of vignettes of his writer-friends, from Shizhi and Genzi to poets of the younger generation, titled *Look, These Guys!* (*Qiao, zhexie ren!*).

Today folded under political pressure in December 1980, after nine issues. By that time, several poets published therein had won national reputation and their works were appearing in official journals. Aside from Bei Dao and Mang Ke, Gu Cheng (1956–1993) also came from Beijing. "A Generation" (Yidai ren, 1979) was a manifesto of the youth of the Cultural Revolution for the triumph of optimism over tragedy, hope over darkness: "Dark night has given me dark eyes / But I use them to look for light." Dubbed the "Fairytale Poet," Gu Cheng employed the persona of the child and expressed a childlike delight in nature – whether it be a flower, a cricket, or a raindrop. He regarded Hans Christian Andersen (1805–1875) as his "esteemed teacher" and acknowledged the influences of Federico García Lorca (1898–1936) and Walt Whitman.

In "Bulin's File" (Bulin de dang'an) written in 1981 and 1982, the wide-eyed child in Gu Cheng's early work morphed into Bulin – a mischievous boy reminiscent of the Monkey King in *Journey to the West*. The fantastic images presaged a stylistic change as well as an intense interest in poetics, Daoism, and the relation between the unconscious and language. Such interests would lead to a poetry of dreamlike states, stripped of normal syntax and thought processes. In 1988, Gu Cheng and his wife Xie Ye (1958–1993, also a writer) moved to Waiheke, an island off the coast of Auckland, New Zealand, where they lived a secluded but impoverished life. On October 8, 1993, in the middle of a marital crisis, he murdered Xie Ye and committed suicide.

A factory worker, Shu Ting (b. 1952) lived in Xiamen in Fujian Province. Mentored by the senior poet Cai Qijiao (1918–2007), she rendered tributes to lasting love between man and woman – a taboo subject during the Cultural Revolution – that won the hearts of millions. Her comparison of lovers to two trees standing side by side, or to two boats on a stormy sea, emphasizes equality, independence, and mutual respect. Shu Ting was also among the first in the New Era to critique the role of women in a patriarchal society. "Goddess Peak" (Shennü feng) refers to a peak by the Wu Gorge whose shape resembles that of a woman. According to one myth, the peak is the physical embodiment of a goddess who waits in vain for her lover to return. Speaking against female martyrdom idealized in Chinese culture, the poet proclaims, "Instead of being on display on the cliff for a thousand years / I'd rather have a hearty cry on my lover's shoulder for a single night." Shu Ting has written little poetry since the 1990s.

Jiang He is best known for the personal perspective and contemplative tone of his poems that comment on recent history. "An Unfinished Poem" (Meiyou xiewan de shi) memorializes Zhang Zhixin (1930–1975), a CCP member who was executed on April 4, 1975, for speaking out against Mao's cult of personality during the Cultural Revolution. Each of the five sections of the poem presents an interior monologue by Zhang (except for the second section, spoken by Zhang's mother). The opening lines put Zhang in a long line of martyrs who are "nailed to the wall," being pecked at by crows and thrashed by wind and rain. The image evokes a Promethean heroine who suffers unspeakable pain – Zhang's vocal chords were cut to prevent her from protesting before the execution – for her beliefs.

Other poets associated with *Today* included Duo Duo, Yan Li, Tian Xiaoqing (b. 1953), Yang Lian (b. 1955), Wang Xiaoni (b. 1955), and Xu Jingya (b. 1953), to name just a few. Yan Li started writing poetry and painting in the early 1970s. He was a founding member of the Stars Painting Association (Xingxing huahui, 1979), the first underground organization of artists in the New Era. In 1985 Yan Li went to New York to study; two years later he founded the poetry journal *One Line* (*Yi hang*), which lasted until 1992. In 1993 Yan Li returned to China and now lives in Shanghai, where he continues to paint and write.

Duo Duo (a.k.a. Bai Ye, Duoduo) showed a keen awareness of the independence of poetry as art in his early writings. Contrary to the official ideology, he spoke of the interior world of angst and alienation, and defined poetry as "handicraft." The charged language, grotesque and surrealistic imagery, and sardonic tone of his work distinguished him from his contemporaries. A poet's poet, Duo Duo was not recognized nationally until the 1990s and has since become arguably the most influential poet of his generation. After living in Europe for fifteen years, he returned to China in 2004 and is currently a professor at Hainan University.

Yang Lian was introduced to *Today* by Gu Cheng. In the early 1980s, he and Jiang He advocated "modern epics," which incorporated archaeological findings, historical sites, and mythology. Their rewriting of ancient myths (such as Nüwa, Kua Fu, Jing Wei, and Hou Yi) made them leading proponents of the Roots-Searching School (Xungen pai). Yang Lian tried to recover traditional Chinese culture, considering it essential to dynamic interaction with foreign resources. A representative work is "Banpo," a Neolithic village near Xi'an unearthed in the 1950s, which, for the poet, symbolizes the birth of Chinese civilization. Yang has made London his home since 1994. Unlike Jiang He, who stopped writing poetry after he moved to New York in the late 1980s, Yang Lian has been prolific.

In July and August 1980, the first Youth Poetry Gathering (Qingchun shihui) was organized by the *Poetry Journal*. Seventeen rising stars were invited to Beijing to attend a series of writing workshops with senior poets. Aside from several *Today* poets (Shu Ting, Gu Cheng, Wang Xiaoni, and Xu Jingya), Liang Xiaobin (b. 1954) was among the invitees. Liang had gained a national reputation for "China, I've Lost My Key" (Zhongguo, wo de yaoshi diu le). The poem recalls the loss of innocence as a Red Guard (symbolized by an album of childhood photos) and the effort to retrieve the lost self (symbolized by a key).

Scar Literature

Much of the literature at the beginning of the New Era can be broadly categorized as scar literature. Derived from Lu Xinhua's short story "Scar" (Shanghen, 1978), the term refers to works in the late 1970s and early 1980s that portray the psychological "scars" that resulted from the Cultural Revolution. Kong Jiesheng's (b. 1952) "By the River over There" (Zai xiaohe nabian, 1979) depicts a sister and brother who, separated since childhood by their parents' politically motivated divorce, unwittingly commit incest. Zheng Yi's (b. 1947) "Maple" (Feng, 1979) shows a husband and wife who belong to opposing factions of the Red Guard and who end up destroying each other.

Another taboo that writers began to tackle was life in prison or labor camps. These authors usually endured persecution in the Anti-Rightist Campaign and were now "rehabilitated." Cong Weixi (b. 1933), along with Wang Meng, Deng Youmei (b. 1931), and Liu Shaotang (1936–1997), was one of the Four Black Swans in 1957 and went through twenty years of "reeducation" through labor. Zhang Xianliang (b. 1936) was incarcerated several times. Cong and Zhang are generally considered founders of "high wall literature" (*da qiang wenxue*).

Zhang Xianliang's *Half of Man Is Woman* (*Nanren de yiban shi nüren*, 1985) is set in the Cultural Revolution. The protagonist is a political prisoner sentenced to twenty years. While working on a state farm one day, he sees a beautiful woman bathing nude in the river. He meets her again eight years later and they get married. The marriage turns sour as the protagonist suffers from impotence after he finds out that he is cuckolded by the Party secretary. Through the prism of sex, the novel offers an analysis of the physical and mental castration that a totalitarian society inflicts on citizens by politicizing every aspect of life, both public and private. Furthermore, impotence is inseparable from the destruction of language. The meanings of words are turned upside down and intellectuals are forced to keep silent. The intertwining of sex and politics made the book controversial.

Wang Meng published *Bolshevik Salute* (*Buli*) as well as many short stories after he was rehabilitated in 1979. These works are considered modernist for their minimalist plot, the use of stream of consciousness to break down the boundary between space and time, and the emphasis on subjective states of mind.

Reflection went beyond recent history as many came to see the Cultural Revolution as the culmination of a deeply flawed system, rather than a temporary aberration in a generally sound system. As if awaking from a nightmare, people began to ask, "What happened?" "Why did it happen?" and, most importantly, "What was my role in it?" At its most meaningful, "literature of introspection" (*fansi wenxue*) is more than victimology, offering intense soul-searching. A major form it takes is the memoir.

Yang Jiang's *Six Chapters at the Cadre School* (*Ganxiao liu ji*, also translated as *My Life from "Down Under"*) records the two years that she and her husband Qian Zhongshu spent separately at May Seventh Cadre Schools in rural Henan Province from 1970 to 1972. Yang shuns all references to violence and refrains from any emotional display or didactic comment. She simply presents an account of the mundane details of daily life with candor, self-deprecation, and compassion. Echoing Lu Xun's famous verdict that Chinese culture is "cannibalistic," Yang describes the puppy at her cadre school as kinder than humans. The reeducation that millions were forced to go through was in vain after all, as Yang admits: "After undergoing more than ten years of reform, plus two years at the cadre school, not only had I not reached the plateau of progressive thinking that everyone sought, I was nearly as selfish now as I had been in the beginning."

Probably the most influential memoir in post-Mao China, Ba Jin's *Random Thoughts* (*Suixiang lu*) contains one hundred and fifty essays that the veteran author wrote for a column in the *Dagongbao* in Hong Kong from December 1, 1978 to August 20, 1986. They include reminiscences of fellow writers of the May Fourth generation, exposés of systemic problems and psychological malaise in Chinese society, and calls for creative freedom and a free spirit. Ba Jin refuses to portray himself as a hapless victim but confesses his own complicity in the system and swears never to allow himself to be turned into a "beast" again. Before he died, his repeated call for the founding of a Cultural Revolution museum fell on deaf ears.

Memoirs represent the voices of conscience that began to be heard in the New Era. The underlying critical spirit is also found in fiction, drama, poetry, reportage, and film. To name but a few: *In the Files of Society* (*Zai shehui de dang'an li*) by Wang Jing (the pen name of Bu Anli), *Lady Thief* (*Nü zei*) by Li Kewei, *What If I Were Real* (*Jiaru wo shi zhen de*) by Sha Yexin (b. 1939),

Chinese Fairies (Feitian) by Liu Ke, *Bitter Love (Ku lian)* by Bai Hua (b. 1930), "Dissatisfaction" (Buman) by Luo Gengye (b. 1951), "Please Raise a Forest of Hands, Stop!" (Qing juqi senlin yiban de shou, zhizhi) by Xiong Zhaozheng (b. 1952), "General, You Can't Do This" (Jiangjun, bu neng zheyang zuo) by Ye Wenfu (b. 1944), and *Hibiscus Town (Furong zhen)* by Gu Hua (b. 1942).

What If I Were Real (1979) was based on a true story that took place in Shanghai. Passing himself off as the son of a high-ranking Party official, the protagonist uses his new connections to obtain a coveted transfer from the country to the city. The young man is caught. At the trial he declares, "Where I go wrong is that I am not real. If I were real, everything I've done would be legitimate."

After decades of collectivization and class struggle, there was a hunger for humanistic values. *Love Must Not Be Forgotten (Ai, shi buneng wangji de,* 1978) by Zhang Jie (b. 1937) depicts a woman writer who gets out of a loveless marriage and falls in love with an old CCP member, against societal norms. Zhang's insistence on true love as the only moral foundation for marriage made the novel immensely popular. Chen Rong's *People in Middle Age (Ren dao zhongnian)* revolves around an ophthalmologist who has dedicated her life to serving patients at the expense of her family and her own health. Living in harsh conditions, she has little support, much less appreciation or reward.

If the above works sought to restore faith in humanity, others tried to preserve the old China that was fast disappearing after decades of repression and demagoguery. The focus on local cultures with distinct dialects, folklore, customs, and lifestyles gave rise to "fiction of the marketplace" (*shijing xiaoshuo*), also known as "fiction of the native place" (*xiang tu xiaoshuo*), which may be seen as a precursor of roots-searching literature. Representative are Liu Shaotang's *Catkins and Willows (Puliu renjia,* 1980), about Tongzhou in Hebei Province; Lu Wenfu's (b. 1928) *The Gourmand (Meishijia,* 1983), about Suzhou cuisine; Deng Youmei's *Na the Fifth (Nawu,* 1983) and *Snuff Bottle (Yanhu,* 1984), about Manchu bannermen in Beijing in the Republican period; Lin Jinlan's (b. 1921) *Charms of Low Stool Bridge (Aidengqiao fengqing,* collected in 1987), about Wenzhou in Zhejiang Province; and Feng Jicai's (b. 1942) *The Golden Lotus (Sancun jinlian)*, about female footbinding.

Gao Xiaosheng (1928–1999) was labeled a rightist in 1957 for advocating literature as a means of "breaking free of doctrines, intervening in living, and scrutinizing life." Between 1978 and 1980, he published a series of stories about peasants. In "Chen Huansheng Goes to Town" (Chen Huansheng shang cheng, 1980), Chen collapses from a fever and is taken to a hostel in the county secretary's car. When he wakes up and is asked to pay five dollars for the room, his attitude changes from gratitude to resentment. He no longer cares about soiling the bedding with his dirty clothes or damaging the sofa. He derives satisfaction from the thought of bragging to the villagers about his "connection" and the "luxuries" in town. With irony and humor, the author offers insight into "peasant mentality": kind and conservative, simple yet ignorant, hardworking but petty.

In contrast to Gao's realist approach, lyrical treatment of rural life characterizes the work of Wang Zengqi. After decades of silence, Wang published a series of short stories in the early 1980s. "Initiation into a Monk's Life" (Shou jie) is a free-flowing narrative interspersed with vignettes of local landscape and descriptions of folk customs. The storyline could not be simpler: seventeen-year-old Minghai becomes a Buddhist monk. Along the way, we see the burgeoning love between Minghai and the ferryman's daughter. The vivid colloquial language, rooted in traditional oral literature, has an elegant simplicity that parallels the innocent love between the protagonists. Wang's work was inspiring to writers of roots-searching literature in the mid- and late 1980s.

Misty poetry and the Anti-Spiritual Pollution Campaign

On March 30, 1979, Deng Xiaoping announced the "Four Basic Principles" (sige jiben yuanze), or "Four Principles" for short, as the foundation of the Four Modernizations: the socialist path, proletarian dictatorship, leadership of the CCP, and Marxism–Leninism–Maoism. It was not long before he ordered a crackdown on literary works with "bourgeois liberal" tendencies. Bai Hua's Bitter Love was denounced for posing the defiant question, "You love your country, but does your country love you?" It was interpreted as critical of the fatherland and making the insidious distinction between patriotism (love of China) and socialism (love of the CCP). Bai was one of the five writers labeled the "Five Poisonous Weeds" (wuke da ducao). The others were Liu Binyan for "Between Human and Monster," Sha Yexin for What If I Were Real, Wang Jing for In the Files of Society, and Liu Ke for Flying Fairies and Lady Thief.

A nationwide controversy about the new poetry, mostly by younger poets, erupted. It began in August 1980 with Zhang Ming's "The Infuriating Mistiness" (Ling ren qimen de menglong), which criticized the opaqueness of some recent poems. Here and elsewhere, Gu Cheng's "Arcs" (Huxian) and

"The End" (Jieshu), Bei Dao's "The Reply" and "A Bouquet" (Yishu), Shu Ting's "Remembrances" (Wangshi er san) and "Fatherland, ah My Fatherland" (Zuguo a zuguo) were singled out for critique. Collectively known as "misty poetry," these and other works were accused of "bourgeois liberalism," an umbrella term that included such Anglo-European maladies as individualism, nihilism, and skepticism.

Three essays came to the defense of misty poetry: "Face the New Rising" (Zai xin de jueqi mianqian, 1980) by Xie Mian (b. 1932) at Peking University, "A New Aesthetic Principle Is Rising" (Xinde meixue yuanze zai jueqi, 1981) by Sun Shaozhen (b. 1936) at Fujian Normal University, and "A Group of Poets on the Rise" (Jueqi de shiqun, 1983) by the poet Xu Jingya. Collectively known as the Three Rises, these essays affirmed the new poetry's historical significance, iconoclasm, and modernity.

The attack on bourgeois liberalism merged into the Anti-Spiritual Pollution Campaign, which went on from October 1983 to February 1984. The campaign ostensibly took aim at such social problems as crime, corruption, and pornography, but in reality it targeted scholars, journalists, writers, and artists. All the leading misty poets were critiqued. The pop songs of Deng Lijun (Teresa Teng, 1953–1995), the superstar from Taiwan, were banned for being "pornographic." Gao Xingjian's *Bus Stop* (*Chezhan*, 1983) was banned after six performances in Beijing. In the play, people from different backgrounds and age groups wait at a bus stop on a Saturday afternoon. They watch the buses come and go, without being able to get on. After waiting for ten years, they decide to walk away. In both its absurdist plot and minimalist language, *Bus Stop* is reminiscent of *Waiting for Godot* by Samuel Beckett (1906–1989). The sense of wasted time and the reference to "ten years" had obvious political overtones.

In the next few months (having been misdiagnosed as dying from lung cancer), Gao Xingjian journeyed on foot along the Yangzi river, from its source in Qinghai to Shanghai where it flows into the East China Sea. The experience led to the writing of *Primitive Man* (*Yeren*, 1985), probably the first play about ecological awareness in the PRC, as well as the novel *Soul Mountain* (*Ling shan*, 1989).

A similar journey was undertaken by Zheng Yi during the Anti-Spiritual Pollution Campaign. He bicycled five thousand miles through more than twenty counties along the Yellow River. The experience led to the writing of *Remote Village* (*Yuan cun*, 1984) and *Old Well* (*Lao jing*, 1986). *Old Well* unfolds along two intersecting lines: the thwarted love of Sun Wangquan and his effort to dig a well after his father dies trying. Adapted to the silver screen with Zheng Yi's script, *Old Well* was the first contemporary Chinese film to win international recognition. Zhang Yimou (b. 1951), who was the cinematographer and played the lead role, went on to become an internationally renowned director. The film was critiqued by the CCP for exposing the dark side of peasant life.

At the Fourth Writers' Representatives Assembly in December 1984, CCP Chairman Hu Yaobang (1915–1989) called for "creative freedom," thus putting an end to the Anti-Spiritual Pollution Campaign. After four decades of ideological control, the thaw in the New Era developed into a full-blown renaissance, a new Age of Enlightenment. Three types of intellectual and artistic resources made this possible.

First, there was a movement to reinterpret the May Fourth legacy and reassess Chinese culture. The intense, comprehensive reflections that individual scholars, journals, and civil organizations engaged in in the 1980s are known as the Cultural Discussion or Culture Fever (*wenhua re*). The themes addressed ran a wide gamut, from humanism, instrumental rationality, and revived Confucianism, to Western liberalism, civil society, and hermeneutics. The writings of Li Zehou (b. 1930) and Liu Zaifu (b. 1941) had a major effect on aesthetics and literary theory.

Second, reevaluations of modern literature were also under way; works by Chinese writers that had been overlooked were rediscovered. The introduction of scholarship from outside China aided the process. For example, C. T. Hsia's *History of Modern Chinese Fiction* (1961) was translated into Chinese and published in Hong Kong in 1979. A refreshing alternative to the CCP canon, Hsia highlights Shen Congwen, Eileen Chang, and Qian Zhongshu, among others, based on artistic merit and depth of humanistic vision. His book not only helped revive interest in these writers but also stimulated the rewriting of literary history in 1988 and 1989, spearheaded by Chen Sihe (b. 1954) at Fudan University and Wang Xiaoming (b. 1955) at the East China Normal University (Huadong shifan daxue).

The third resource is the extensive translation of world literature hitherto unavailable. These translations presented a broadened vista and had a profound impact on readers and writers alike. One of the first and most comprehensive was the four-volume *Anthology of Modernist Works from Foreign Countries* (*Waiguo xiandai pai zuopin xuan*, 1980–1985). Edited by Yuan Kejia, Dong Hengzhuan, and Zheng Kelu, the anthology contains poetry, fiction, and drama representative of various schools of modernism in Europe, America, Japan, and India. The impact of this and similar anthologies of world literature cannot be overestimated. As in previous eras in China, Taiwan, and Hong Kong, translations played a formative role in the development of Chinese literature.

Roots-searching and the avant-garde

Literature became a new way of reimagining China beyond established modes of thinking. Rejecting the master discourse of the nation and the grand narrative of history, writers turned to the hitherto repressed or marginalized aspects of Chinese culture and history for alternative meanings of Chineseness. Although they shared the critical spirit of May Fourth, they were skeptical of rational modernity and favored the "primitive," the mystical, and the irrational, and were inspired by mythology, ancient philosophy, and ethnic minority cultures. At the same time, they found deep affinities with international modernism, in particular Kafka, Faulkner, and, above all, magical realism as represented by the Argentinian author Jorge Luis Borges (1899–1986) and the Colombian author Gabriel García Márquez (b. 1928).

Experimental literature in the 1980s is often subsumed under the labels of "roots-searching" and "avant-garde" (xianfeng). The division is misleading, however, in that the two "schools" are by no means mutually exclusive and in fact often overlap. Both may be traced to scar, introspection, and marketplace/native place literature in fiction, as well as to misty poetry. The avant-garde also overlaps with neo-realism (xinxieshi zhuyi) and new historicism (xinlishi zhuyi) in fiction, terms coined in the late 1980s.

In December 1984, Shanghai Literature and two Zhejiang organizations cosponsored a conference in Hangzhou, bringing together writers, editors, and literary critics from Beijing, Shanghai, Hunan, and Zhejiang. The theme of the conference was "Literature of the New Era: Retrospect and Prediction" (Xinshiqi wenxue: huigu yu yuce). The essays that came out of the conference formed the core of the aesthetics of roots-searching literature, including Han Shaogong's (b. 1953) "The 'Roots' of Literature" (Wenxue de "gen"), Zheng Wanlong's (b. 1944) "My Roots" (Wo de gen), Li Hangyu's (b. 1957) "Sorting out Our 'Roots'" (Li yi li women de "gen"), Ah Cheng's "Culture Constrains Humankind" (Wenhua zhiyue zhe renlei), and Zheng Yi's "Across the Cultural Fault Zone" (Kuayue wenhua duanliedai).

Roots-searching is expressed, in one way, in the re-creation of regional or ethnic culture, such as in Jia Pingwa's (b. 1958) Shangzhou series, Li Hangyu's Gechuan River series, and Wure'ertu's (b. 1952) Ewenki culture of Inner Mongolia. Han Shaogong's BaBaBa (1985) features Bingzai, a retarded midget who can say just two words, namely "Baba" and "F— Mama," and is the only witness of the decline of the community as a result of superstition and violence. Bingzai seems to personify the collective unconscious of the Chinese: ugly and dim-witted, yet possessing a mysterious power and a strong instinct for survival.

Han's concern with the Chinese psyche was to resurface in 1996 in *Dictionary of Maqiao* (*Maqiao cidian*). Maqiao is a remote village in northern Hunan, where Han spent six years as an "educated youth." Drawing on the local dialect, the entries in the "dictionary" contain customs, legends, anecdotes, idiomatic expressions, and memories categorized by the number of strokes in the character as in a real Chinese dictionary. By representing a linguistic community whose language use differs drastically from that of the outside world, Han deconstructs the modes of thinking and norms of behavior that we take for granted. For example, in Maqiao, to be "scientific" is to be lazy, to be "sweet" is to be gullible or to die young, and to be "cheap" is to live beyond the age of thirty-six. Han implies that behind the proverbial language barrier lie fundamental differences in perception and moral and social values.

Roots-searching literature found a powerful representation in *King of Chess* (*Qi wang*) by Ah Cheng. Published in the July 1984 issue of *Shanghai Literature*, the novella features Wang Yisheng, whose given name means literally "one life" or "one student." An "educated youth" raised by a widowed mother, Wang is only interested in two things in life: having enough to eat and playing chess. In contrast to the other chess players in the story, Wang is not bound by book learning or motivated by the desire for success and fame. Like a Daoist, he does not "discriminate" and learns from "people everywhere," especially the old garbage collector who tells him, "Playing chess nourishes your nature, and your livelihood could damage your nature." By living in the simplest form and "playing Daoist chess," Wang is ready to embark on a spiritual journey.

In the climax of the story, Wang plays against nine finalists in a championship game: "[He] was sitting alone in the room facing us, his hands on his knees, a slender pillar of iron that seemed to hear and see nothing." "Nothing" evokes the Daoist mind of nonbeing and noninterference, the shedding of egotism and forgetting of all worldly concerns. It is at this moment that Wang has completed the self-transformation from a "chess freak" (*qi chi*) at the beginning of the story to a "chess king."

Other important works of roots-searching fiction include *Living Ghosts* (*Huo gui*) by Zhang Yu (b. 1952), *Amusing Tales of Strange Towns* (*Yixiang quwen*) by Zheng Wanlong, *A Chronicle of the Mulberry Grove* (*Sangshuping jishi*) by Zhu

Xiaoping (b. 1952), *Bao Village* (*Xiaobao zhuang*) by Wang Anyi (b. 1954), and *Wheat Straw Stacks* (*Maijie duo*) by Tie Ning (b. 1957).

The discovery or recovery of local history and marginalized cultures is a salient feature of roots-searching literature. Not only does it provide a perspective outside the official ideology and the dominant Han culture, it is also a source of renewal of creativity. Zhang Chengzhi (b. 1948), a Muslim of the Hui minority, depicts life on the Mongolian grassland and in the Muslim communities in the Great Northwest. He depicts these peoples as possessing a natural nobility and enduring beauty even as they live in harsh conditions.

In poetry, Yang Lian's roots-searching work in the early 1980s inspired many writers in Sichuan whose long poems drew on local cultures, such as "Hanging Coffin" (Xuan guan) by Ouyang Jianghe (b. 1955), "The Great Buddha" (Da fo) by the brothers Song Qu (b. 1963) and Song Wei (b. 1964), and "Songkran" (Poshui jie) by Shi Guanghua (b. 1958). Before these, a new kind of "frontier poetry" had come from Zhou Tao (b. 1946), Yang Mu (b. 1944), and Zhang Deyi (b. 1964) in Xinjiang, and from Li Laoxiang (b. 1943) and Lin Ran (b. 1947) in Gansu.

Born in western Hunan, Chang Yao (1936–2000) joined the People's Liberation Army in 1950 and served in the Korean War. In 1957 he was persecuted as a Rightist and sent to Qinghai Province or Koko Nor in Mongolian (both the Chinese and the Mongolian names mean "Blue Lake"), where he stayed for the rest of his life. With clear, hard images and a classic lyric language, his poetry conjures up the expansive spirit and mysterious power of the landscape and the people on the prairie.

Another remote landscape, Tibet appeared as subject matter in visual art as early as 1980 in the paintings of Chen Danqing (b. 1953) and Zhou Chunya (b. 1955). Fiction set in Tibet came from Ma Yuan (b. 1953), Ma Jian (b. 1953), and Zhaxi Dawa (b. 1959). Ma Jian's (b. 1953) "reportage," titled "Show Your Tastebuds or Nothing at All" (Liangchu nide shetai huo kongkongdangdang, 1987), depicts sexual ritual and the sexual exploitation of women in Tantric Buddhism. The work came under attack for its negative portrayal of the culture. Liu Xinwu, chief editor of *People's Literature*, which published the story, was fired; the issue in which the story appeared was recalled.

Tibetan writer Zhaxi Dawa's "Souls Tied to the Knots on a Leather Cord" (Xizai pishengkou shang de hun, 1985) recounts a journey with no clear beginning or ending. After the protagonist fails to reach his destination of Shambhala, the author himself appears to resume the journey with the woman character. In a setting dominated by white (snow) and black (abyss), the destination seems both unattainable and irrelevant. Their destiny is to travel on.

The writing style of these authors also deserves attention. In *The Temptation of Gangdisi*, Ma Yuan addresses the reader directly, while his short story "Fiction" begins this way: "I am a Han person named Ma Yuan. I write fiction." The authorial presence is purposely intrusive rather than invisible; he often interrupts the narrative flow to speak directly to a character or imagined reader. Metafiction (*yuan xiaoshuo*) had a large following in the 1980s and continued into the 1990s, as seen in the writings of Hong Feng (b. 1957), Su Tong (b. 1963), Ge Fei (b. 1964), Sun Ganlu (b. 1959), Ye Zhaoyan (b. 1957), and Bei Cun (b. 1965). Other examples of metafiction include Wang Anyi's *Realism and Fiction* (*Jishi yu xugou*), Pan Jun's *Wind* (*Feng*), Lü Xin's *Caress* (*Fumo*), Liu Ke's (b. 1953) *The Blue Rainy Season* (*Lanse yuji*), Li Dawei's (b. 1963) *Dream Collector* (*Jimeng aihaozhe*), Lin Bai's (b. 1958) *Keeping Watch of Empty Years* (*Shouwang kongxin suiyue*), Wang Xiaobo's (1952–1997) *Temple of Longevity* (*Wanshousi*), Wang Meng's *The Season of Lost Love* (*Shilian de jijie*), and Liu Zhenyun's (b. 1958) *Hometown Flows Everywhere* (*Guxiang xiangchu liuchuan*).

One of the most important avant-garde writers, Can Xue (b. 1953, née Deng Xiaohua), burst onto the scene with "Little House on the Hill" (Shanshang de xiaowu), "Yellow Mud Street" (Huangni jie), and "Old Floating Clouds" (Canglao de fuyun) in 1985. These stories present a haunting world where the surreal and the strange reign supreme. Taking the device of defamiliarization to an extreme, they are full of eerie metamorphoses, grotesque images, and enigmas, all of which are delivered in a matter-of-fact tone. No stability, security, or finality exists in reality, only transmutation, menace, secrecy, and indeterminacy. Paradoxically, Can Xue's world can be simultaneously nightmarish and poetically beautiful. Hailed as the "Chinese Kafka," she has written essays on her favorite authors, including Borges, Calvino, and Kafka.

Mo Yan (which literally means "do not speak") is the pen name of Guan Moye (b. 1956). Born to a peasant family in Gaomi, Shandong Province, Mo Yan became a soldier in the People's Liberation Army. "Red Sorghum" (Honggaoliang, 1986) catapulted him onto the national scene; the story was incorporated, along with four other novellas, into *Red Sorghum: A Family Saga* (*Honggaoliang jiazu*).

Set in northeast Gaomi, where red sorghum grows, the family saga spans the Republican period and the Second Sino-Japanese War. The plot proceeds along two lines: the legendary love story of the narrator's grandparents, and the valiant fighting of the militia led by Grandpa Yu and Father against the Japanese. At the end of the story, during an ambush on a Japanese truck fleet, Grandma is killed, as is most of the militia; Grandpa and Father are the only two left standing in the red sorghum field.

The color red takes on multiple symbolic meanings. It suggests the ancestral spirit of the land, the blood shed in the war, and the primeval life force in the men and women who love and hate, laugh and cry. With an array of evocative scenes, such as the invocation of the wine god, a primitive drumbeat, wild sex in the red sorghum field, and Grandpa Yu pissing into the wine vats (producing the best wine ever), the story celebrates the Dionysian spirit. *Red Sorghum* the film (1987) was directed by Zhang Yimou in his directorial debut and featured Gong Li (b. 1965). It won the Golden Bear Award at the Berlin Film Festival in 1988.

Mo Yan went on to become one of the most prolific writers in contemporary China. If he has created an unforgettable north, then Su Tong (the pen name of Tong Zhonggui), born in Suzhou and raised in Nanjing, is the tireless storyteller of the south. Parallel to the lush, exquisite landscape of the Jiangnan region are tales permeated with a sensual, decadent beauty, depicting lust, treachery, revenge, violence, insanity, and death. *Wives and Concubines* (*Qi qie chengqun*, 1989; film version *Raise the Red Lantern*, 1991) focuses on Cheng Songlian, a nineteen-year-old college student whose father committed suicide after going bankrupt. To support herself, she chooses to become the fourth wife of a rich merchant. In the traditional household she quickly learns that the only way for the wives to empower themselves is to satisfy the master's sexual needs and bear his children. It is not long before the strong-headed Cheng finds herself failing in both. After witnessing at night the adulterous third wife being thrown into the old well, she goes insane. The recurrent images of the well and the wisteria flowers in the rear garden are both symbols of death: the well beckons Cheng to death and the flowers wither on the pergola as her situation goes from bad to worse.

Symbolism is also central to Su Tong's *Rice* (*Mi*, 1995). A rags-to-riches story with a sinister twist, the novel depicts how Five Dragons, an orphan and flood refugee, becomes a rich rice merchant. Rice is a symbol of survival in a world propelled by hunger for food and sex. Five Dragon's idiosyncratic habit of stuffing rice into the vagina of every woman he sleeps with suggests a constant need to fill the void inside. His wealth, his wives, and the prostitutes (from whom he contracts syphilis, which kills him) cannot give him the sense of security and wholeness that rice can. Five Dragons dies on a mountain of rice loaded on a train.

Insanity is equally ubiquitous in the early work of Yu Hua (b. 1958). *One Kind of Reality* (*Xianshi yizhong*, 1988) presents the dismal, myopic world of a rural family that consists of two brothers and their wives and children. The story is a dark, anti-Confucian satire that turns family and patrilineality on its head. "Family" is represented by Grandma, who watches the internecine vendettas that unfold before her eyes and shows little concern for the deaths of her sons and grandsons, preoccupied only with her own death.

Yu Hua went on to write more stories about the Chinese family, although his approach has become more realist than symbolist, more sympathetic than satiric. *To Live* (*Huo zhe*, 1992) depicts the many unpredictable vicissitudes and heart-wrenching tragedies that befall the protagonist. By the end of the story, all of his family and close friends are dead, yet he bears no grudges and harbors no bitterness. According to Yu, the story was inspired by the American folksong "Old Black Joe" by Stephen C. Foster (1826–1864). Indeed, the protagonist's life resembles that of a black slave in the old American south, who has little control over his fate and is resigned to a life of privation. *To Live* won the Grinzane Cavour Award in Italy in 1998.

A native of Beijing, Liu Heng (b. 1954) attracted much attention with *Damned Foodstuff* (*Gou ri de liangshi*) and *Fu Xi, Fu Xi*. The latter story begins with a fifty-something widower, Yang, who exchanges twenty acres of farmland for a young virgin named Judou for the purpose of producing a male offspring. When he becomes impotent, he vents his anger by physically abusing her. Judou carries on an illicit affair with Yang's seventeen-year-old nephew Blue Sky and gives birth to a baby boy, White Sky. White Sky refuses to acknowledge Blue Sky, who commits suicide out of guilt. In Chinese mythology, Fu Xi mates with his sister to create the universe. It is ironic that in *Fu Xi, Fu Xi* the so-called "incest" reveals the oppression of women by patriarchy: Judou is a tool of procreation and White Sky is the agent of karma that punishes the lovers for their transgression. Liu Heng went on to write several well-received scripts, including *Autumn Chrysanthemum Takes It to Court* (*Qiuju da guansi*) and *Pretty Mama* (*Piaoliang mama*). The resulting films both featured Gong Li.

Also born in Beijing, Li Rui (b. 1950) went to Mount Lüliang in Shanxi Province in 1969 as an "educated youth" and lived in a tiny village for five years. *Fertile Earth: Vignettes of Mount Lüliang* (*Houtu – Lüliangshan yinxiang*, 1986) opens with this question and answer: "What is China? China is an overripe autumn." The severity and melancholy traditionally associated with autumn permeates the entire collection. In "Double Burial" (*He fen*, 1986), a student goes to a remote mountain village during the Cultural Revolution and drowns when a dam breaks. Fourteen years later, the villagers, led by the retired branch secretary, find her a husband – a deceased man of compatible age and horoscope – and bury them together. The plot centers on the exhumation of the body and the burial of the husband and wife. The image of the skeleton clutching the Little Red Book drives home the pathos of Mao's betrayal of idealistic youth.

The clash between ideology and humanity underscores Li Rui's *Windless Tree* (*Wufeng zhishu*, 1996) as well. In the end it is humanity that renders ideology powerless and irrelevant. The novel relies on monologue and dialogue, and employs multiple first-person narrators, each telling the story from a unique perspective, even that of a donkey. Like a pointillist painting, the sixty-three chapters present a multiplicity of points of view that adds up to great scope and depth.

Urban literature and the newborn generation

Roots-searching literature is grounded in rural China, but other writers turned to the city. While roots-searching literature is mostly based on the experience of the "educated youth" during the Cultural Revolution, other writers explored the angst of urban youth. Writers of the latter group are not necessarily younger than the roots-searching writers, but the world they depict is vastly different. There is no national allegory or reflection on history; what we find instead is youthful rebellion against authority, accompanied by excitement as well as frustration. Examples are Liu Suola's (b. 1955) "You Have No Choice" (Ni biewu xuanze, 1985), Xu Xing's (b. 1956) "A Variation without Theme" (Wuzhuti bianzou), and Chen Cun's (b. 1954) *Young Men and Young Women, Seven in All* (*Shaonan shaonü, yigong qige*, 1985). Fiction focusing on urban youth would become a popular trend in the 1990s and early 2000s.

Due to its brevity, poetry can be published and circulated underground far more easily than fiction. This was the case during the Cultural Revolution, and it holds true for the New Era. If fiction writers depended mainly on official outlets to publish their works, poets turned to the underground circuit of production and distribution. For this reason, poetry maintained a higher degree of autonomy and freedom. Although there was some overlap between them, there were essentially two poetry scenes in the New Era: the official and the nonofficial (or underground). In the 1980s and 1990s, underground journals mushroomed. With a small press run (a few hundred to several thousand copies), the journals were financed by the poets themselves and circulated privately all over China. They ran the risk of being shut down and confiscated by the authorities since they were not registered.

A new generation of poets arose in the second half of the 1980s. Known as the "third generation" (*disan dai*) or the "newborn generation" (*xinsheng dai*), they both drew on and reacted against the groundbreaking canonical misty poetry. By and large, poets of the newborn generation were younger, college-educated, and widely exposed to translations of world literature. A few were even fluent in a foreign language. The main influences for the misty poets were Russian, French (e.g. Baudelaire), and early modern Chinese, while the newborn generation was familiar with contemporary American poetry, such as Sylvia Plath (1932–1963), Allen Ginsberg (1926–1997), John Ashbery (b. 1927), and Gary Snyder (b. 1930). More importantly, whereas for the misty poets the Cultural Revolution was an indelible part of their formative experience, the newborn generation grew up in a more open and prosperous society in the midst of a cultural renaissance. While misty poetry was their collective rite of passage to poetry, they also felt a sense of belatedness and anxiety of influence.

Two anthologies provided an early look at the newborn generation: *Anthology of New Wave Poetry* (*Xinchao shiji*, 1985), edited by Lao Mu (b. 1963); and *Chinese Modernist Poetry Groups 1986–1988* (*Zhongguo xiandai zhuyi shiqun daguan 1986–1988*), edited by Xu Jingya, Meng Lang (b. 1961), Cao Changqing (b. 1953), and Lü Guipin (b. 1956). Both anthologies give generous space to misty poetry but also feature a dazzling array of up-and-coming poets and poetry groups from all over China.

Consisting largely of self-proclaimed iconoclasts, the newborn generation is far from being a homogeneous group and displays a wide range of styles and aesthetic positions. Nevertheless, we may detect two general tendencies. The first is an explicit revolt against misty poetry in terms of subject matter, perspective, and language. Without the historical pathos and humanist orientation, the newborn generation embraces quotidian, urban experiences, and celebrates carnivalesque, Bohemian lifestyles. Instead of the contemplative voice, the newborn generation adopts a light-hearted tone, sometimes satirical, sometimes self-mocking. Instead of metaphoric, lyrical language, the newborn generation prefers a prosaic, colloquial language that has few embellishments and is even anti-lyrical. Overall, there was a tendency toward desublimation and deconstruction. Even some of the titles are indicative: "The Taxi Always Comes at a Moment of Despair" (Wang Xiaolong), "Heroes Have to Eat Too" (Yu Yu), "Thinking of Someone but Can't Remember Her Name" (Shang Zhongmin), "I Want to Board a Slow Ship to Paris" (Hu Dong), "Thinking of a Czech Movie but Can't Remember Its Title" (Wang Yin),

"A Man at a Government Agency Becomes Degenerate as His Talent Goes Unrecognized" (Zhang Feng).

The other tendency of the newborn generation is toward confessional poetry, poetry expressing nostalgia for nature, and the pursuit of the mystical and the transcendent. The subject matter presented in these poems varies from the intensely personal and psychological to the idyllic, the abstract, and the sublime. The voice is solitary, and the language dense. One development of this tendency is the rise of women's poetry, as represented by Zhai Yongming (b. 1955), Yi Lei (b. 1951), Lu Yimin (b. 1962), Tang Yaping (b. 1964), Zhang Zhen, and Tong Wei (b. 1956). Zhai Yongming's *Woman* (1984), a sequence of twenty poems, is a pioneering piece of feminist poetry. Distinguished from their predecessors, the women of the newborn generation are bolder in their exploration of a woman's emotional and psychological world: repressed desires, sexuality, maternal relationships, and clashes with society. It is darker, too, dealing with loneliness, anger, paranoia, despair, and, above all, death. Sylvia Plath is frequently invoked. Together, the women of the newborn generation created a confessional poetry that had a large following in the 1990s.

Since the 1980s, the writing of classical-style poetry has also made a come-back. Numerous classical poetry societies were formed across China and works of the members appeared in print and on the Internet. Unlike underground poetry, classical poetry societies were officially registered cultural organizations and received subsidies from and were supervised by the state. The interest in classical-style poetry writing seemed to converge with the broader trend to preserve and revive Chinese cultural heritage, such as the Read the Classics Movement (*du jing yundong*).

Literature in Post-June Fourth China

In December 1986, thousands of college students took to the streets in Beijing demanding political reform and protesting rising inflation. In the ensuing Anti-Bourgeois Liberalization Campaign, many newspapers, journals, literary works, and films were subjected to criticism and censorship. Gao Xingjian's *The Other Shore* was banned in 1986; the next year he emigrated to France, where he applied for and received political asylum. Several films – including *One and Eight* (*Yige he bage*, 1983), by Zhang Junzhao; *Yellow Earth* (1984), by Chen Kaige (b. 1952); *The Black Cannon Incident* (*Heipao shijian*, 1985), by Huang Jianxin (b. 1954); and *Hibiscus Town* (1986), by Xie Jin (1923–2008) – were banned. Three leading intellectuals, the astrophysicist Fang Lizhi (b. 1936), the veteran journalist Wang Ruowang (1918–2001), and the writer Liu Binyan, were stripped of their CCP memberships. Liu Zaifu, director of the Institute of Literature, Chinese Academy of Sciences, was accused of "anti-Marxism." Even Party General Secretary Hu Yaobang was forced to step down and was replaced by Zhao Ziyang (1919–2005).

The call for political reform did not stop, however. On January 6, 1989, Fang Lizhi addressed a letter to Deng Xiaoping, asking for the release of political prisoners, including Wei Jingsheng. The letter was followed by a petition signed by thirty-three scholars and writers on February 13. These events were a prelude to the democracy movement in the spring of 1989. The movement started out as a memorial organized by students in honor of Hu Yaobang, who had died of a heart attack on April 15. On April 18, ten thousand students staged a sit-in on Tiananmen Square. On April 21, the night before Hu's funeral, some 100,000 students took part in a march at the square. They came from colleges and universities, and were supported by professors and other intellectuals. Rejecting the Party-controlled student associations on the campuses, they set up their own "self-governing associations," demanding reform within the CCP, democracy, and an end to corruption. From Beijing the movement spread to other cities, such as Shanghai, Xi'an, Changsha, Chengdu, and Urumqi.

On May 13, two days before the state visit of Mikhail Gorbachev (1931–2007), thousands of students occupied Tiananmen Square and hundreds went on a hunger strike. On May 19, Premier Zhao Ziyang paid them a visit; his address began with an apology and ended with an assurance of a dialogue with the government if they would end the strike. On May 30, a statue of the Goddess of Democracy, made by students of the Central Academy of Fine Arts, was erected on the square. On May 20, Deng Xiaoping declared martial law and Yang Shangkun (b. 1907) ordered troops to crack down on the demonstrators. At 10:30 on the night of June 3, armored personnel carriers and armed troops fired indiscriminately and beat with sticks those who sought refuge or tried to flee. By 5:40 a.m. on June 4, Tiananmen Square was "cleared."

In the aftermath of the Tiananmen Massacre (or simply "June Fourth" in China), Zhao Ziyang was released from all posts and placed under house arrest indefinitely. Wang Meng, minister of culture since 1986, resigned. Twenty-one student leaders of the democracy movement were on the most-wanted list; many were caught and imprisoned while a few managed to escape overseas. Poets Zhou Lunyou (b. 1952), Liao Yiwu (b. 1958), Li Yawei (b. 1963), and Jiang Pinchao (b. 1967) were jailed. The *Index of Banned Books and Periodicals* in three volumes was circulated internally, silencing many writers and intellectuals.

Some of them, such as Liu Binyan, Zheng Yi, Liu Zaifu, Su Xiaokang (b. 1949, the main author of the controversial television documentary *The River Elegy* (*Heshang*, also translated as *Deathsong of the River*), 1988), Yan Jiaqi (b. 1942), Bei Dao, Duo Duo, Yang Lian, Gu Cheng, Hu Dong, Song Lin (b. 1958), Hong Ying (b. 1962), and Ha Jin (the pen name of Jin Xuefei, b. 1956) went into exile. Those who stayed, such as Wu Zuguang, Yang Xianyi (b. 1915), and Liu Xiaobo (b. 1955), who was fired from the faculty of the Beijing Normal University, had to find publishing outlets abroad, mainly in Hong Kong and Taiwan.

The incident put an abrupt end to the cultural discussion of the 1980s; the idealism and utopianism that underscored the Age of Enlightenment evaporated. The exile of many intellectuals and writers, as well as the disillusionment of those who remained, led to a mood that was more somber, pessimistic, and cynical. The suicide of the poet Haizi (the pen name of Zha Haisheng, 1964–1989) on March 26, and the death of Luo Yihe (1961–1989) on May 31 in Tiananmen Square as the result of a stroke, were retrospectively seen as omens of the end of an era. The world that Haizi had created in his poetry already seemed so far away:

> Starting tomorrow, be a happy man.
> Feed the horse, chop wood, travel around the world.
> Starting tomorrow, care about food and vegetables.
> I have a house facing the ocean, where spring warms and flowers bloom.

If Haizi's ambitious project of writing the ultimate Great Poem – the Indian name for "epic" – represents the newborn generation in viewing poetry as a form of religious dedication, his suicide is mourned as martyrdom, the ultimate sacrifice a writer could make for art's sake. Haizi's death contributed to a cult of poetry in the 1990s, inspiring a large following in writing about rural beauty.

Faced with domestic demoralization and international condemnation, Deng Xiaoping resigned from his official post, although he remained powerful until his death in 1997. Not only did he handpick Jiang Zemin (b. 1926), mayor of Shanghai since 1985, as general secretary (and later president from 1993 to 2003), but he also named Hu Jintao (b. 1942) as Jiang Zemin's successor. To this date, the Tiananmen Massacre has remained a political taboo. Repeated pleas for "reversal" have fallen on deaf ears, and those who investigate or write about the incident have suffered consequences.

From January 18 to February 21, 1992, Deng Xiaoping visited Wuchang, Shenzhen, Zhuhai, and Shanghai. His speeches during this "southern tour of inspection" called for a faster pace of economic reforms and an opening up to more foreign trade and investment. The Fourteenth Congress later that year declared that the main task of the CCP was to create a "socialist market economy." The policy put China on a path to an economic boom that has not slowed until very recently. Deng's catchphrase "to get rich is glorious" opened a floodgate of entrepreneurship and commercialization. "Look toward money" (*xiang qian kan*) – punning on the homophones "forward" and "money" – became the mantra for the entire population. Many quit writing to "plunge into the ocean" (*xia hai*), to jump on the bandwagon of moneymaking. Some switched from poetry to the more profitable fiction, or from fiction to the even more profitable areas of television, publishing, advertising, and so on.

The market economy that has generated enormous wealth has also created a huge demand for entertainment and diversion. Popular culture – from martial arts sagas, romance, and tabloids to pop music, video games, television, and film – has gradually replaced literature since the 1990s. In the 1980s, popular culture from Taiwan and Hong Kong enjoyed sensational success in China. In addition to pop music, the romance novels of Qiong Yao, Yi Shu, and Cen Kailun; the martial arts sagas of Jin Yong, Gu Long, and Liang Yusheng; and the essays of San Mao, Lin Qingxuan (b. 1953), Bo Yang (the pen name of Guo Yidong, 1920–2008), and Li Ao (b. 1935) were extremely popular.

Since the 1990s, the market for popular literature has greatly expanded to include many niches: historical fiction, martial arts sagas, biography and memoir, crime fiction, detective stories, punk literature, grunge fiction, teen literature, and so on. Jin Yong was voted one of the most influential writers of twentieth-century China and received an honorary doctoral degree from Peking University. Qiong Yao has turned her romances into television series produced on the mainland. A trilogy about the Qing emperors by Eryuehe (the pen name of Ling Jiefang, b. 1946) created a new height in television drama not only in the PRC but overseas as well, as did Yu Qiuyu's (b. 1946) prose about the "cultural journey." Wang Shuo (b. 1958) defined the tenor of the 1990s with his stories filled with wise-cracking youth who couldn't care less about societal convention. Some of the titles indicate the tone: *Please Don't Call Me Human* (*Qianwan bie ba wo dang ren*), *Playing for Thrills* (*Wan de jiushi xintiao*), *I Am Your Papa* (*Wo shi ni baba*), *Ferocious Beasts* (*Dongwu xiongmeng*), *Have Fun then Die* (*Guobayin jiu si*), *I Love You and There's No Deal* (*Aini mei shangliang*). Wang is credited as the creator of "hooligan literature" (*pizi wenxue*), which both reflects and helps define "cool" in the post-New Era. Ten of his stories have been made into films, including *In the Heat of the Sun*

(*Yangguang canlan de rizi*, 1994) based on *Ferocious Beasts*. Even Stephen King (b. 1947), the American writer of horror stories, refers to him as the "most influential cultural icon in China."

Poetry polemics

Although the 1990s witnessed a "craze" over the love poetry of Xi Murong (b. 1943) from Taiwan and the uplifting epigrammic verses of Wang Guozhen (b. 1956), poetry was increasingly marginalized in a more diversified, visually oriented, and commercial culture. The days when poetry was widely read by students, and leading poets were treated like rock stars, were gone. The rising tide of commodification (*shangpin da chao*) since the early 1990s is a double-edge sword, however. If many have stopped writing and "plunged into the ocean," they have also started to use their new fortunes to support poetry in the forms of publications, prizes, and festivals. For example, the poet Wan Xia (b. 1962) became an independent publisher and funded the two-volume *Anthology of Post-Misty Poetry* (*Hou Menglongshi quanji*, 1994), which he coedited with Xiao Xiao. It remains the most comprehensive collection of the newborn generation. In January 2004 the *Coquette* (*Sajiao*) poetry journal was revived almost twenty years after its first issue. Its editor, Mo Mo (b. 1964), also founded the Coquette Academy in Shanghai, providing residencies for visiting poets and space for poetry readings. After a brief hiatus, poetry journals began to flourish again. As we move into the twenty-first century, the old distinction between official and underground poetry, or, more generally, between official and nonofficial literature, has blurred, perhaps even become obsolete. It is still illegal to publish a book without an ISBN or "book number" (*shu hao*) in China, which is allocated to publishing houses by the General Administration of Press and Publication. Taking advantage of loopholes in the regulation, however, publishing houses can sell book numbers to privately run presses, known as the "second channel." Presses in the second channel in turn can sell them to individuals at anywhere between RMB 15,000 and RMB 30,000. The existence of the second channel renders it difficult for the government to contain pirating.

In poetry, there has been a veering away from the ebullient idealism of the 1980s. Ouyang Jianghe coined the term "middle-age writing" (*zhongnian xiezuo*), bidding farewell to the "youthful writing" of the New Era. The dominant mood tends to be either elegiac–introspective or ironic–parodic. Although romanticism and lyricism still have a following, many have turned to narrative poetry, a plainer and more colloquial style, and quotidian experiences as subject matter.

Some poets emphasize the intrinsic value of poetry as an art and as a craft. Zang Di (b. 1964) defines poetry as "a kind of slowness" (*yizhong man*). If the relentless pursuit of speed and efficiency characterizes contemporary culture – from information technology to the mass media and material life – the slowness required in the writing (and reading) of poetry is in itself an act of resistance.

Other poets prefer colloquial language to the more refined "poetic" language. Seeing poetry as coterminous with "life" rather than with "art," they use the vulgar to parody reality and deconstruct convention. Yu Jian denounces poetic language and criticizes overt westernization. The clash between these two aesthetic positions came to a head in 1999 in the Panfeng Debate (*Panfeng lunzhan*). Named after the hotel in Beijing where a poetry conference was convened in April 1999, the heated debate went on for two years between the self-proclaimed "popular poets," who initiated the discussion, and the "intellectuals," who were on the defensive. These two groups' aesthetic differences led to disagreement, but not to constructive dialogue or thoughtful arguments. Problematic binary oppositions such as westernized versus Chinese, elitist versus populist, art versus life, hegemony versus marginality, were used. Full of personal attacks, the debate demonstrated a shockingly high level of intolerance and incivility, as it fed the media's hunger for sensationalism and whetted the public's appetite for scandals.

The Panfeng Debate involved only a dozen or so poets on each side. Many poets were not interested in, and rather turned off by, the war of words. Some of them grouped together and called themselves the "third path" (disantiao daolu). The younger generations have also arrived on the scene, known as the "post-70 generation" (*qishi hou*, those who were born in the 1970s) and the "post-80 generation" (*bashi hou*, those who were born in the 1980s).

Body writing

With precedents traced to the mid-1980s, the use of the irreverent was taken to an extreme by two groups: "Lower body" (*xiabanshen*) and "trash" (*laji*, pronounced as *lese* in Taiwan). The lower-body poets shocked the public with their explicit descriptions of carnal desire and sexual acts in rejection of the "upper body" (such as intellect, emotion, tradition). The lower body also contributed to the trend of "body writing" (*shenti xiezuo*) at the turn of the century. In fiction, body writing is best represented by two Shanghai writers, Wei Hui (b. 1973) and Mian Mian (the pen name of Wang Xin, b. 1970). Wei Hui's *Shanghai Baby* (*Shanghai baobei*, 1999) and Mian Mian's *Candy* (*Tang*, 2000) became best sellers after they were banned for their descriptions of sex and drugs. The women authors also ushered in the market for "beauty writers" (*meinü zuojia*).

It is no accident that Wei Hui and Mian Mian both wrote about Shanghai, the most affluent and cosmopolitan city in China. Deng Xiaoping declared that it was acceptable for a minority of the population to get rich first, and Shanghai has had the lion's share of the wealth. Already in the late 1980s, Chi Li's (b. 1957) *A Life of Cares* (*Fannao rensheng*, 1987) and Fang Fang's (b. 1955) *Landscape* (*Fengjing*, 1987) depicted those in the middle and lower echelons of society as they try to survive in the urban jungle. Their naturalist approach continued in Liu Zhenyun's *Chicken Feathers All over the Ground* (*Yi di jimao*, 1991), in which the taxing minutiae of everyday life are "feather-light," but add up to a considerable stress that drains one of time and energy, killing off any romance or idealism in life. Liu's *Cell Phone* (*Shouji*, 2003) was made into a film by Feng Xiaogang (b. 1958) to wide critical acclaim.

Feminist awareness emerged in the 1980s and has developed into a major trend since the 1990s. Known as "private writing" (*sirenhua* or *gerenhua xiezuo*), the works of Lin Bai (the pen name of Lin Baiwei, b. 1958), Chen Ran (b. 1962), Xu Xiaobin, and Hai Nan are prominent representatives. Lin Bai's *A War of One's Own* (*Yigeren de zhanzheng*, 1994) focuses on female sexual desire and experience, including masturbation, abortion, lesbian relationships, and adultery. Chen Ran's protagonists tend to be female, intellectual, and urban. *A Private Life* (*Siren shenghuo*, 1996) is a self-declared manifesto of feminism, addressing such themes as memory, sexuality, femininity, and madness. Also since the 1990s, overseas women writers, such as Ai Bei (b. 1956), Yan Geling (b. 1957), and Hong Ying, have won recognition for their stories about women's plight and triumph. Hong Ying's award-winning *Daugher of Hunger* (*Ji'e de nüer*, translated as *Daughter of the River*, 1997), in particular, offers a riveting account of a young woman's struggle for self-fulfillment.

The city and sense of place

Economic reform has literally changed the face of China, which has been jokingly referred to as one giant construction site. It is perhaps not surprising that many writers look to the past to re-create the city of their origin. The city of Xi'an in Jia Pingwa's *Abandoned Capital* (*Fei du*, also *Ruined Capital* or *Defunct Capital*) evokes ennui and degeneration. The protagonist Zhuang Zhidie is a successful middle-aged writer who regains his sexual prowess when he has an affair with Tang Waner, a young married woman. After she is abducted by her husband and dies as a result of physical abuse, Zhuang becomes impotent again and loses his will to write. The novel was banned in 1994 for its "pornographic" content, made more titillating by the little blocks taking the place of characters on the page followed by a bracketed explanation – "Here the author has expunged 400 characters" – which is an old device in traditional Chinese erotica.

Qin Opera (*Qin qiang*, 2005) returns to Jia Pingwa's rural hometown and portrays his father's generation. Qin Opera is the name of a local clapper opera, which dates back to the Qin dynasty and is still a favorite pastime among peasants in northern Shaanxi. Told from the perspective of the madman as he roams about the village seeing, hearing, and sensing things unknown to others, the story presents a panorama of village life as it witnesses the rapid decline of traditional culture. Another major author from the Xi'an area who specializes in writing about rural Shaanxi is Chen Zhongshi (b. 1942), whose novel *White Deer Plain (Bailu yuan)* has won many prizes, including the Mao Dun Literary Prize.

Nanjing is the city Ye Zhaoyan, the grandson of Ye Shengtao (1894–1988), returns to again and again. *Nanjing 1937: A Love Story (Yijiusanqi de aiqing,* 1996) presents an unlikely courtship against the backdrop of the Rape of Nanking. The juxtaposition of the national crisis and the protagonist's personal transformation brings both comic moments and tragic consequences. The quixotic quest is as hopeless as the ancient capital on the verge of demise.

Shanghai is the recurrent centerpiece in Wang Anyi's work. *Song of Unending Sorrow (Changhen ge,* 1999) opens with the seventeen-year-old Wang Qiyao winning the third place in the Miss Shanghai Pageant in 1946. She becomes the mistress of Director Li of the GMD regime, who dies in a plane crash – likely an assassination – as the CCP takes over the mainland. In the 1950s, Wang manages to preserve some of her old Shanghai lifestyle, such as playing mahjong by laying a thick blanket on the table to minimize the shuffling sound of the tiles. She gives birth to a child whose father runs away. The last part of the novel takes us to the 1980s, when Wang is fifty-seven years old and has an affair with her daughter's friend. She loses this lover, even after trying to offer him the gold bars that Director Li gave her forty years ago. The gold bars become the cause of her death.

The narrative emphasizes that Wang Qiyao is the "typical *nongtang* girl." She is the personification of *nongtang*, a narrow alley that leads to a residential neighborhood. It is a place that witnesses the historical vicissitudes embodied by the male characters – the glamour and elegance of the Republican period, the repressiveness of Maoist China, and the uncouth materialism of the New Era.

Re-creation of place finds another powerful expression in Alai (b. 1959), a Tibetan who came from Maerkang County in northwestern Sichuan. His first novel, *When the Dust Has Settled* (*Chen'ai luoding*, also *Red Poppies*, 1994), is set in the 1940s in Abei, a Tibetan region traditionally governed by eighteen chieftains. The narrator is the younger son of the chieftain. Significantly, he has no name and is simply referred to as Idiot because of his retardation. He is both an eyewitness to, and a major player in, the rise and fall of his tribe. Like a tapestry, the story is rich and intricately designed, at once a family saga, a mirror of the Tibetan caste system, and a *Bildungsroman*. The protagonist is reminiscent of the Western archetype of the fool or court jester, as well as the Daoist whose apparent stupidity belies great wisdom. (Some Chinese readers compare him to Forrest Gump in the Hollywood movie.) The expression "when the dust has settled," in Chinese as in English, denotes a clearing of vision. What emerges from the "sound and fury" is clarity with regard to human nature and impermanence. Idiot's honest, unflinching look at human desires and foibles, including his own, is what allows him to transcend even death itself. As he says, "Yes, Heaven let me see and let me hear, and placed me in the middle of everything while having me rise above it all. It was for this purpose that Heaven made me look like an idiot."

According to Alai, his favorite writers are Faulkner and Hemingway. One may identify affinities with both in *When the Dust Has Settled*: regional culture from one and terse language from the other. It also reminds us of Shen Congwen in the May Fourth period and the roots-searching writers of the 1980s. In 2000, Alai became the youngest fiction writer to win the Mao Dun Literary Prize. (Wang Anyi also won for *Song of Unending Sorrow*, along with Zhang Ping and Wang Xufeng.)

The voice of the individual

In October 2000, Gao Xingjian won the Nobel Prize in Literature. He had left China in 1987 and had been living in France. His work was published in Taiwan and unavailable on the mainland. *Soul Mountain* (1991) and *One Man's Bible* (*Yigeren de shengjing*, 1995) both recount a journey in search of oneself and the freedom to be oneself and live an ordinary life. *One Man's Bible* adopts a dual narrative perspective, alternating between a "he" during the Cultural Revolution and a "you" in the 1990s. In his Nobel acceptance speech, Gao shared his view on literature: "A writer does not speak as the spokesperson of the people or as the embodiment of righteousness. His voice is inevitably weak, but it is precisely this voice of the individual that is more authentic." The Nobel Prize Committee sums up his *oeuvre* this way: "In the writing of

Gao Xingjian, literature is born anew from the struggle of the individual to survive the history of the masses." The observation is equally applicable to the whole of Chinese literature of the past three decades.

Taiwan

Literature and democratization

The Native Literature Movement in 1977 and 1978 brought to the surface long-standing disenchantment with the GMD regime among intellectuals and writers. Throughout the 1970s, a democracy movement had steadily gained momentum as some of its leaders won local and national elections and articulated their dissent in unofficial periodicals. Under the banner of Dangwai ("Outside the Party"), the movement posed a challenge to the GMD that could no longer be ignored.

In June 1979 *Formosa* (*Meilidao*) was launched in Gaoxiong. The magazine further galvanized the democracy movement; within five months it boasted a circulation of 140,000. On the evening of December 10, it organized a parade in commemoration of international Human Rights Day. A scuffle with the police broke out, which resulted in the arrest and conviction of the major organizers. All were sentenced to imprisonment. Despite the outcome, the Formosa Incident won widespread sympathy among people in Taiwan and abroad. One of the lawyers on the defense team was Chen Shuibian (b. 1950).

Throughout the 1980s the democracy movement spread like wildfire. At a Dangwai meeting on September 28, 1986, the Democratic Progressive Party (DPP or Minjindang) was founded. The first real opposition party in Taiwan's history, the DPP would go on to win the presidential elections in 2000 and 2004, overturning long-standing GMD rule.

Under mounting pressure, President Chiang Ching-kuo lifted martial law on July 15, 1987, followed, in January 1988, by the lifting of restrictions on the mass media and overseas travel. For the first time since 1949, media outlets were open to private ownership and civilians were allowed to visit mainland China. In February 1988, Li Denghui (Lee Teng-hui, b. 1923), who had been vice president under Chiang Ching-kuo since 1984, became president after Chiang passed away.

The democracy movement drew energy from college students as well. On March 16, 1990, nine students from the National Taiwan University organized a demonstration demanding further political reform. Calling itself Wild Lily (*yebaihe*), an indigenous flower also known as Formosan Lily, the movement drew students and faculty from colleges throughout Taiwan, and as many as six thousand protestors occupied the square in front of Chiang Kai-shek Memorial Hall. It was reminiscent of the student-led democracy movement in Tiananmen Square a year earlier, but Wild Lily ended in peace, with President Li agreeing to student demands.

Taiwan underwent rapid economic growth and industrialization in the 1970s and 1980s. GNP per capita rose from under $300 in 1970 to over $1,400 in 1978, to about $3,500 in 1986. The "Taiwan miracle" won the island a seat among the Four Little Dragons of Asia, along with Hong Kong, South Korea, and Singapore. Taiwan came to be known as a major player in the global market for its high-tech and information industries, which drew investments from multinational corporations and were largely staffed by returned Taiwanese engineers. Since late 1980 the Xinzhu Science Park (Xinzhu kexue yuanqu) has developed into the Silicon Valley of Taiwan.

As the island became more urbanized, such social issues as overpopulation, crime, and environmental devastation also came to the fore. As the island became more affluent, a sizable middle class emerged to become avid consumers of modern amenities and luxury goods. As the island became more cosmopolitan and globalized, it was increasingly exposed to and influenced by international currents, from entertainment and consumer culture to social agendas and intellectual discourses. Young people dubbed themselves the "new new humankind" (xin xin renlei) – an advertising jingle from a 1992 Oolong Tea commercial designed by the poet Zeng Shumei (b. 1962) – and the N-generation (N for Net or Internet).

By the early 1980s, the nativist discourse had split into the so-called "Taiwan consciousness" and "Chinese consciousness." These differ in how the relationship between Taiwan and mainland China is viewed – that Taiwan is part of China and should be reunited with it eventually, or that Taiwan has been independent of China since 1895 and should be treated as a nation in its own right. Heated debates took place between the reunification (tong) and the independence (du) camps.

"Taiwan consciousness" gained ascendancy as democratization became increasingly equated with nativization. Although different positions existed on a spectrum running from "green" (independence) to "blue" (reunification), the recognition of Taiwan as a unique historical, political, and cultural entity had irrefutable legitimacy. The triumph of nativist consciousness underscored the transfer of power from the GMD to the DPP in the presidential election, first in 2000 and again in 2004, in which Chen Shuibian won.

Under the DPP, a policy of de-Sinicization (qu Zhongguo hua) was implemented to eradicate all "Chinese" imprints, from street names to landmarks associated with the previous regime. New school curricula emphasized native history and culture, including the teaching of Hoklo. Departments of Taiwanese history and literature were established at universities. Taiwan PEN was founded in 1987 in distinction from the Chinese PEN (originally established in China in 1930 and revived in Taiwan in 1950). Grants and prizes were awarded to Taiwan-focused projects and artworks. One positive outcome is the unearthing of Taiwanese literature from the Japanese colonial period. Translations of many works (from Japanese to Chinese) have become available for the first time; new studies have not only filled the lacunae in literary history but revised the old canon and provided a more comprehensive picture. On the other hand, nativization has strained Taiwan's relationship with China, even as Taiwanese investments on the mainland have grown steadily. China passed the Anti-Secession Law (*Fan fenlie fa*) in March 2005.

Taking advantage of the liberalizing trend of the 1980s, writers breached erstwhile taboos, such as the February 28th Incident and the White Terror. The little theater movement (*xiao juchang yundong*), which emerged in the first half of the 1980s, was motivated by artistic ideals as well as social activism. The seeds of experimental theater were sown in the 1960s and 1970s. Ma Sen's (b. 1932) modernist one-act plays departed from May Fourth realism to explore the existential condition of modern men and women. Zhang Xiaofeng (Chang Hsiao-feng, b. 1941), also a major essayist, rewrote Chinese Classics as allegories of the quest of spiritual belonging. Above all, Yao Yiwei (1922–1997) promoted original scripts, and innovative direction and performances. His play *A Suitcase* (*Yikou xiangzi*, 1977) veered away from realist theater on the one hand and commercial theater on the other. In July 1980, Yao launched the annual Experimental Theater Festival; by October 1985, forty-three plays had been presented on the stage.

In 1976, Gengxin Experimental Theater Group (Gengxin shiyan jutuan) was founded. Renamed Lan Ling Theater Workshop (Lanling ju fang, named after the ancient legendary warrior Lord Lanling) in 1980, it incorporated such theories and practices as those of the New York-based La MaMa Experimental Theatre Club (founded in 1961) and the Poor Theater of Jerzy Grotowski (1933–1999). One of the two new plays performed at the first Experimental Theater Festival, *Lotus Pearl's New Match* (*Hezhu xin pei*), ushered in the little theater movement in Taiwan. An adaptation from Peking Opera by Jin Shijie (b. 1951), the play brings together traditional and modern techniques and stylistics in a satire about greed.

The second generation of the little theater arose in the mid-1980s, as represented by such new troupes as Excellence (You juchang), Rive-Gauche

(Hezuoan jutuan), Surrounding Ruins (Huanxu juchang), and Marginalia Theater (Biji juchang). They took up many social issues, including environmental devastation, nuclear power plants, deforestation, overpriced real estate, and corruption.

Literature found fertile ground in the literary supplements, or *fukan*, to newspapers, which provided not only entertainment but also a public forum for cultural discussions and creative writing. The modern poetry debate and the native literature movement could not have taken place the way they did without this forum. In the mid-1970s, the two leading newspapers, *United Daily* and *China Times*, also began to sponsor literary prizes, which launched the careers of many writers.

Literary prizes proliferated in the 1980s and 1990s, as did all kinds of media outlets, including newspapers, journals, publishing companies, and television and radio stations, in the post-martial law era. The euphoria was short-lived, however. As the number of newspapers and television stations tripled, competition for readers and viewers became brutal. The space for literary supplements was diminished to make room for more entertaining topics (such as travel, leisure, lifestyle, and sports). Against the backdrop of the media boom that began in the early 1990s, literature has steadily declined in print media as well as in the book market. In recent years the circulation of the leading newspapers has dropped significantly, and 2007 has been declared by the publishing industry as the worst year in history, worse even than 2003 when SARS caused a big dip in the market. The notion of the "death of literature" has been bandied about, and poetry, with a few exceptions, is considered "poisonous to the market."

Despite the changing cultural milieu, literature has continued to thrive. Even the most marginalized genre, poetry, has enjoyed a loyal following among the young and has even affected mainstream culture and helped shape the language. The fact that many poets are professional editors and publishers helps keep poetry in the public eye. Although poetry societies in the traditional sense have declined since the 1990s, the rise of the Internet has proven especially beneficial to poetry. The marriage of the oldest form of literature and the newest technology has been a success (see Section IV of this chapter). Above all, since the late 1970s, artistic innovation and individual talents, such as Yang Ze (the pen name of Yang Xianqing, b. 1953), Chen Li (the pen name of Chen Yingwen, b. 1954), Luo Zhicheng (b. 1955), Xiang Yang, Xia Yu (preferred spelling Hsia Yü, the pen name of Huang Qingqi, b. 1956), Jiao Tong (the pen name of Ye Zhenfu, b. 1956), Liu Kexiang (b. 1957), Chen Kehua (b. 1961), Lin Yaode (1962–1996), Hong Hong (the pen name of Yan

Hongya, b. 1964), and Xu Huizhi (b. 1966), have injected much vitality into the poetry scene.

While people welcomed the arrival of fully fledged democracy, one of the negative consequences has been an identity politics based on the division between *benshengren* and *waishengren*. The division has consistently been manipulated by politicians to gain power. In the meantime, there have been epochal changes on the global scene: the collapse of the Soviet Union and the end of the Cold War, peaceful revolutions in Eastern Europe, the reunification of Germany, the forming of the European Union, the rise of China, Islamic fundamentalism and terrorist attacks, and so on. Combined with domestic conditions, these events have stimulated reflections on Taiwan's past, present, and future. International movements and trends – from feminism and environmentalism to new historicism and postmodernism, from the Frankfurt School and deconstruction to queer and postcolonial theories – have provided new paradigms for intellectual discourses and inspired artistic expressions. What all the recent trends and movements have in common is a critique of the grand narrative, be it nationalism, patriarchy, or history as teleological and monolithic, which is necessarily a partial and distorted view that serves the interest of power and suppresses alternative narratives. Literature since the early 1980s has broken free of old paradigms, challenged old narratives, and deconstructed old myths on many fronts. Two broad themes may be identified, namely a concern with historical memory and subjectivity, and a focus on urban life and global experience.

Rediscovery and demystification

Long repressed and distorted under the GMD, Taiwan's history has been rediscovered and reevaluated. Zheng Qingwen's "Three-legged Horse" (Sanjiao ma, 1979) depicts those Taiwanese who worked for the Japanese. Zhong Zhaozheng's *Taiwanese People: A Trilogy* (*Taiwanren sanbuqu*, 1980) and Li Qiao's *Cold Night: A Trilogy* (*Han ye sanbuqu*, 1980) depict the struggles of Taiwanese people under Japanese rule. Based on personal experience, Huan Fu's "Messenger Pigeon" (Xin ge) portrays a Taiwanese conscript fighting for Japan in World War II. Li Minyong's (b. 1947) "Memento" (Yiwu) presents the widow of a Taiwanese soldier. Bai Ling's (the pen name of Zhuang Zuhuang, b. 1951) "On hearing the claim that 'comfort women' were volunteers" (Wen weianfu ziyuan shuo) condemns the exploitation of Taiwanese (and other Asian) women as sex slaves by the Japanese military during the war. Dongfang Bai (the pen name of Lin Wende) published the epic *Waves Sifting Sand* (*Lang tao sha*, 1992), based on the legendary life of Qiu Yaxin (b. 1900), the first female doctor from Taiwan. Finally, Shi Shuqing (b. 1949) re-creates the old hometown in *A Journey through Lugang* (*Xingguo Luojin*, 2003) and *Dust in the Wind* (*Feng qian chen'ai*, 2008), two parts of her *Taiwan Trilogy*.

Shi Mingzheng (1935–1988), the older brother of the political activist Shi Mingde (b. 1941), was imprisoned for five years in the early 1960s. "The Man Who Thirsts for Death" (Ke si zhe) and "The Man Who Drinks Urine" (He niao zhe) are both set in the era of the White Terror. In the latter, Mr. Chen is a GMD snitch responsible for a dozen deaths. Ironically, he lands in prison for spying against the GMD. Each morning he drinks his own urine, claiming that it is a miracle cure for his internal injuries. The closed circuit implicit in the self-abusive act suggests inescapable guilt. In the other story, a mainland émigré is sentenced to seven years in prison for shouting reactionary slogans. After several failures, he resorts to a creative method to end his life:

> He takes off the blue beltless pants that prisoners wear, wraps one pant leg around his neck and ties it to the handle of the iron door, which comes up to the navel of a person of average height. Half squatting and half sitting, with both legs stretched out straight and the buttocks a few inches off the ground, he hangs himself with determination.

This grotesque image bespeaks a horror that is almost exquisite. In 1988, in support of his brother Shi Mingde on a hunger strike in prison, Shi Mingzheng also refused food for four months and died.

Grotesqueness is completely absent in *Moon Seal* (*Yueyin*, 1984) by Guo Songfen (1938–2005). Straddling World War II, the story revolves around young Wenhui and her husband Tiemin, a talented playwright bedridden with tuberculosis. She nurses him back to health. He befriends some young men and women from the mainland through his doctor and spends much time away from home. In a fit of jealousy, Wenhui reports to the police a locked chest of books that Tiemin keeps at home. It turns out that he has been involved in underground communist activities. Along with his doctor and mainland friends, he is executed, leaving her an inconsolable young widow.

Moon Seal offers a microcosmic view of the February 28th Incident and the White Terror. There is no direct reference to political turmoil, which is downplayed as a mere inconvenience in daily life (such as food rationing, the occasional power outage). The contrast between the naive narrator and the harsh reality brings to the fore the confusion and terror that enshrouded postwar Taiwan. Wenhui dreams of a pastoral, married life, while Tiemin dreams of a life of Tolstoyan humanitarianism. Each somewhat misguided, their romanticisms clash and end up destroying them. The image of the "moon seal" refers to Tiemin's birthmarks and derives from a folk myth about the Mother Goddess. The birthmarks suggest that Wenhui is the Mother Goddess, who gives Tiemin life only to take it away. The folk myth also evokes a local tradition in contrast to the strange and beautiful "motherland," to which Tiemin is drawn.

Chen Yingzhen's "Bellwort" (Lingdanghua, 1983), "Mountain Path" (Shan lu, 1983), and *Zhao Nandong* (1987) also deal with the White Terror. In "Mountain Path," Cai Qianhui is dying, but her doctor cannot find the cause; she has simply lost the desire to live. Qianhui came to the Li family thirty years ago, after her "fiancée" Guokun was executed for leftist activities. She toiled selflessly to raise the younger brother, Guomu, who has become a successful certified public accountant. After Qianhui passes away, Guomu comes upon the letter she left behind for Huang Zhenbo. The letter reveals that in the early 1950s, Qianhui was engaged to Huang, Guokun's close friend. Both Huang and Guokun were victims of the White Terror, and it was Cai's elder brother who betrayed them in order to save his own skin. To atone for her brother's sin, Qianhui pretended to be Guokun's fiancée so that she could help his poor family. "I came to your house to suffer," she says to Guomu repeatedly. When she reads in the newspaper about Huang Zhenbo's early release from prison, however, she is pained by the realization that she has raised Guomu to be a "tamed animal" indifferent to politics and accustomed to material comfort. She chooses to end her life of "failure."

The tragedy lies in the irony that despite Qianhui's good intentions and self-sacrifice, she is no less a traitor than her brother. While her betrayal does not result in imprisonment or execution, she has unwittingly been complicit with capitalism, thus betraying the ideals that Guokun died for. "Mountain Path" castigates the corruption of capitalism and laments the death of socialist idealism. A Marxist identifying with the PRC, Chen Yingzhen has marginalized himself and become a controversial figure in Taiwan.

"Political poetry" arose in the early 1980s, as represented by Chen Jianong (the pen name of Chen Fangming), Song Zelai (b. 1952), Li Qin'an (b. 1951), Ku Ling (the pen name of Wang Yuren, b. 1955), and Zhan Che, among others. Liu Kexiang's "Young Revolutionaries" (Geming qingnian) tells the story of three generations of a Taiwanese family from the February 28th Incident to the 1980s. Like his father, the narrator has lost his idealism and social commitment, and is resigned to a conventional life of security and material comfort. The same cycle is being repeated in the next generation: like his father, the narrator wants his son to go abroad when he grows up. In plain language, Liu Kexiang ponders the history of Taiwan with its tragic ambiguity and ironies.

Literary representations of historical trauma culminated in the film *A City of Sadness* (*Beiqing chengshi*, 1989), written by Wu Nianzhen (b. 1952) and Zhu Tianwen (b. 1956), and directed by Hou Hsiao-hsien (b. 1947), a leading representative of the new cinema. Portraying the February 28th Incident through the prism of a family in Taipei, the film won the Golden Lion Award at the Venice Film Festival and put Taiwan on the map of international cinema. As a result, the word *beiqing* ("sadness") entered common parlance as a code word for historical trauma caused by political oppression.

Demystification and deconstruction of the grand narrative characterize the fiction of Huang Fan (the pen name of Huang Xiaozhong, b. 1950) and Zhang Dachun (b. 1957). In Zhang Dachun's "The General's Monument" (Jiangjun bei), General Wu lives in elegant retirement in Taiwan after a glorious career in the Republican period. His bachelor son is a professor of sociology. Estranged from his father, he remains single perhaps as a subconscious way to avenge his mother, who was driven to suicide by his father. History, according to the general, is built on patriotism, heroism, and glory. Behind these lofty words, however, lie dogmatism (nationalism and patriarchy), ruthlessness, pride, and self-interest. The story points to the constructed nature of history, and the smashing of the monument at the end symbolically debunks the grand narrative that the general subscribes to and wants people to believe.

Political allegory is a popular genre in the contemporary period as politicians at the highest level play out soap operas of machination and corruption in public. Examples are Song Zelai's *Taiwan the Wasteland* (*Feixu Taiwan*, 1985); Lin Yaode's *Dragon Time* (*Shijian long*, 1993); Zhang Dachun's *Grand Liar* (*Da shuohuang jia*, 1989), *No One Wrote a Letter to the Colonel* (*Meiren xiexin gei shangxiao*, 1994), and *Liar's Disciples* (*Sahuang de xintu*, 1996); and Huang Fan's *A Bipolar Nation* (*Zaoyu de guojia*) and *College Thugs* (*Daxue zhi zei*, 2003). These works offer scathing critiques of those in power. *A Bipolar Nation* sums up the situation thus: "Do you know what real terror is? You don't? Let me tell you, real terror is – behind power."

Nostalgia and *Juancun* literature

Resumption of contact with mainland China since 1988 has brought to the surface the uprootedness suffered by the post-1945 émigrés and the experiences of their Taiwan-born descendants. Li Yu's (b. 1944) *Tales of Wenzhou Street* (*Wenzhoujie de gushi*, 1992) offers vignettes of mainland émigrés in the 1960s. For émigrés who left families on the mainland in 1949, their journeys home and reunions can be bittersweet, disconcerting, or disappointing. After nearly four decades of separation resulting in vastly different life experiences, one cannot go back to the way things were. Such experiences find expressions in the fiction of Liu Daren (b. 1933) and Li Li (the pen name of Bao Lili, or Lily Hsueh, b. 1948), and in the poems of Luo Fu, Chen Yizhi, Zhang Mo, and others.

This topic also finds its way into experimental theater. Stanley Lai (Lai Shengchuan, b. 1954) founded the Performance Workshop (Biaoyan gongzuo-fang) in 1984. His signature piece, *Secret Love in Peach Blossom Land* (*Anlian Taohuayuan*, 1986), juxtaposes and blends two different plays under rehearsal: a tragedy of separated lovers and a comedy of adultery. Forced to share the same stage, the directors and casts of the two plays divide the stage in half and rehearse at the same time. Over the course of the rehearsals, the two plays coalesce into one as the actors complete each other's lines.

Perhaps no one has written more about the descendants of émigrés than Zhu Tianxin (b. 1958). *I Remember . . .* (*Wo jide . . .*) and *Thinking of My Juancun Brothers* (*Xiang wo juancun de xiongdimen*) depict the bond between Juancun (military village or compound) residents based on their identification with Old China and the effort to preserve it through the dialects, regional cuisines, and homesickness. Zhu seems to be reminding readers of a unique chapter in the history of Taiwan, however politically incorrect it may be. Juancun literature has also been produced by Sun Weimang (b. 1955), Zhang Qijiang (b. 1961), Zhang Dachun, Ai Ya (the pen name of Li Ji, b. 1945), Su Weizhen (b. 1954), and others. In the rapidly changing cityscapes, Juancun has come to represent a fast-disappearing subculture. In 2006, the City of Taipei sponsored the first Juancun Culture Festival.

For many youths who pursue advanced education and careers abroad, the issue of roots is especially complicated. In Zhang Xiguo's (Hsi-kuo Chang, b. 1944) *Wrath of Yesterday* (*Zuori zhi nu*), the protagonist finds herself in the absurd position of being a triple stranger – to China with which she is disillusioned, to the US where she is an immigrant, and to Taiwan from which she has been away for so long. She finally chooses to return to Taiwan. Home is also the theme of Ping Lu's (the pen name by inversion of Lu Ping, b. 1953) "Death in the Cornfield" (*Yumitian zhi si*). The protagonist is a homesick Taiwanese-American who commits suicide in a cornfield because it resembles the sugarcane fields back home.

Nostalgia for rural tranquility and natural beauty finds expression in the prose of Chen Guanxue (b. 1934), Meng Dongli (b. 1937), and Li Yun (the pen name of Li Zhaoxiong). In fiction, an early representative is Xiao Lihong's

(b. 1950) best seller *A Thousand Moons on a Thousand Rivers* (*Qian jiang you shui qian jiang yue*, 1980), which takes place in a coastal town in southern Taiwan in the 1970s. A bittersweet love story, it also celebrates traditional culture as an integral part of everyday life.

Pastoral themes may be seen as part of nature writing, which has been an active part of the green movement since the 1980s. Such writers as Hong Suli (b. 1947), Xin Dai (the pen name of Li Bihui, b. 1949), Lai Chunbiao, Chen Huang (b. 1954), Chen Lie (pen name of Chen Ruilin, b. 1946), Ling Fu (b. 1952), Liu Kexiang, Liao Hongji (b. 1957), and Wu Mingyi (b. 1971) have raised environmental awareness through their prose, fiction, and poetry. Many of them are involved in the study of the natural history of Taiwan and the preservation of the flora, fauna, waters, and wild areas of the island.

The idea of home receives a radically different treatment in the fiction of Li Yongping (b. 1948), who was born and raised in Sarawak, Malaysia. "Rain from the Sun" (Ritou yu) is one of the twelve stories that comprise *Legends of Jiling* (*Jiling chuqiu*, 1986). It recounts the gang-rape of Changsheng, the young wife of the coffin-maker, which takes place during the bodhisattva Guanyin's birthday parade. She hangs herself and her husband goes about "settling the account" with the rapists and their accomplices, including the prostitute Red Spring, who runs a brothel and lets the hoodlums use her bed for the brutal crime. The repeated juxtaposition between Guanyin, the Goddess of Mercy, and Changsheng suggests the sacrilegious nature of the rape, and the color contrast between white (her skin and clothes) and red (Red Spring's red quilt) reinforces the contrast between purity and depravity, good and evil.

For Li Yongping, the notion of a "cultural China" (*wenhua Zhongguo*) is a myth. The only way to counter it, as suggested in *East Sea Blue: A Taipei Fable* (*Haidongqing: Taibei de yize yuyan*, 1992), lies in the written language; that is, in the archaic and arcane words he uses liberally. It is as if the author is trying to conjure up a China through the alchemy of words.

Poetry as alchemy and the postmodern condition

Alchemy is exactly the word Luo Zhicheng uses to define poetry. With fanciful imagery and precise language, Luo conjures up a self-sufficient world of beauty and order that is magical. It is precisely this magic in language and form that characterizes Chen Li's poetry. "War Symphony" (Zhanzheng jiaoxiangqu, 1994) is a powerful antiwar poem that uses both typography and the shapes and sounds of four characters to represent the beginning, middle, and end of war. The poem moves from soldiers marching off in magnificent formation to the breakup of the formation as soldiers are maimed and killed on the battlefield, to the return of formation, this time in row after row of graves. Another of his concrete poems, "A Lesson in Ventriloquy" (Fuyu ke), uses contrasts in typography and sound to create the effect of strangeness and imbalance, which connotes the lopsided relationship between marginalized Taiwan and powerful China.

Arguably the most influential poet in the past two decades is Xia Yu. Refusing commercial channels of publication, she designed her first collection, *Memoranda* (*Beiwanglu*, 1984), in an atypical size and shape, written in her childlike handwriting with cartoonish illustrations. This would set the pattern for all of her books since: *Ventriloquy* (*Fuyushu*, 1990), *Rub•Indescribable* (*Moca•bukemingzhuang*, 1995), *Salsa* (1999), and *Pink Noise* (*Fenhongse zaoyin*, 2007). Xia Yu's approach to love is defiantly unconventional and antiromantic. Her parody of patriarchy is directed at male stereotypes of women and the male-dominated literary tradition.

Since *Memoranda*, experiments with language have become more and more central to Xia Yu's poetry. She created pseudocharacters in "Séance III" (Jianglinghui III), while *Rub•Indescribable* is entirely composed of collages made with cut-up fragments of the poems from *Ventriloquy*. *Pink Noise* contains thirty-three poems on transparencies; each poem is presented in the original English (or French, in one case) in black and in Chinese translation in hot pink. The English poems are collages while the Chinese translations are done by the computer translation software Sherlock, resulting in mistranslations and strange-sounding Chinese that is a nightmare for any teacher of the Chinese language. Through the device of extreme defamiliarization, the line between "original" and "translation," between "host language" and "target language," is blurred, in the process expanding the signifying horizon of Chinese.

Not only are Xia Yu's poems set against an urban background, but the sensibility is clearly urban. Approximately 70 percent of Taiwan's population is concentrated in cities, and greater Taipei (including Keelung) is the most populous area, with more than six and a half million residents. But it was Lin Yaode who, in 1989, announced the arrival of urban literature, which explores the "spell of the city" and "urban spirit."

As early as 1985, Lin Yaode referred to "burgeoning postmodernism," using such concepts as deconstruction, collage, synchronicity, and so on as markers. The same year, Huang Fan's "How to Measure the Width of Underground Sewage" (Ruhe celiang shuigou de kuandu) was considered the first example of postmodern metafiction, characterized by extensive self-references, disjunctive nonlinear time, and direct addresses to the reader. Luo Qing's "A Farewell Poem about Farewell" (Yifeng guanyu juebie de juebieshi, 1985) also experimented with metawriting. The poem uses elements of a famous letter by Lin Juemin (1887–1911), a martyr in the Republican revolution, who wrote a farewell missive to his wife expressing his love for the country and the people. Luo Qing borrows the salutation and signatory of Lin's letter but fills the text with trivial tautologies and self-references. The last stanza asks readers to leave the poem alone, addressing them as historians, archaeologists, literary critics, editors, and "voyeurs."

A student of Zhang Dachun, Luo Zhicheng, and Yang Ze at the National Culture University, Luo Yijun (b. 1967) probes the existential enigma by turning convention on its head and blurring the line between reality and fiction. The blending of sadness and obscenity, lyricism and black humor characterizes his approach to death, the central motif of such stories as "The Man Who Transports a Corpse" (Yun shi ren).

Indigenous literature and ethnic writing

With the rise of nativist consciousness, there has been a movement to fight for the rights of indigenous peoples and to preserve their languages and cultures. The earliest inhabitants on the island of Taiwan go back to Paleolithic times; they are Malayo-Polynesians whose languages belong to the Austronesian family. In 1988, the term "original inhabitants" or *yuanzhumin* was officially adopted to replace the older names with their derogatory connotations. In 1990, indigenous writers Walis Norgan (Wu Junjie, b. 1961), Liglave A-wu (b. 1969), and others founded the journal *Hunter Culture* (*Lieren wenhua zazhi*), which evolved into a research center two years later. In 1993, the boulevard facing the Presidential Palace in Taipei was renamed Ketagalan in honor of the indigenous tribe that used to inhabit north Taiwan. In the same year, Sun Dachuan (b. 1953) founded the *Mountains and Seas: Taiwan Indigenous Voice Bimonthly* (*Shanhai wenhua*). In 1996 the Council of Indigenous Peoples (Yuanzhumin weiyuanhui) was established as the key government agency for handling indigenous affairs. To date, thirteen tribes have been recognized, encompassing a population of approximately 435,000.

A few indigenous authors, such as Kowan Talall (Chen Yingxiong, b. 1941), have been active since the 1960s. But it is in the past two decades that we have witnessed a blossoming. Monaneng (Zeng Shunwang, b. 1956) published the first book of poetry by an indigenous writer, titled *Beautiful Rice Grains* (*Meili de daosui*, 1989). Rimui Aki (Zeng Xiumei), Topas Tamapima (Tian Yage, b. 1960), Adaw Palaf (b. 1949), Syman Rapongan (Shi Nulai, b. 1957), Badai (b. 1962), Dadelavan (Tu Yufeng, b. 1962), and Sakinu (Dai Zhiqiang, b. 1972) have all received wide recognition. In 2003, INK published the *Anthology of*

Taiwan Indigenous Literature in Chinese in seven volumes. Indigenous literature is both celebratory and critical. It critiques systemic discrimination and injustices to which indigenous peoples have been subjected under foreign colonizers and Han Chinese. Poverty, prostitution, unemployment, alcoholism, and deprivation of education have plagued them for generations. On the other hand, it celebrates a bond with nature, close-knit communities, and pride in native languages that are central to indigenous cultures.

Not all literature about indigenous peoples is written by indigenous writers. Wu He (literally "Dancing Crane," the pen name of Chen Guocheng, b. 1951) is a good example. Dancing Crane is the Japanese name for the ancestral home of the Ami tribe in eastern Taiwan. Wu He did extensive field work, in 1997 and 1998, on the Wushe Incident – the bloodiest confrontation between indigenous people and Japanese colonizers – which took place from October to December 1930. His novel *Remains of Life* (*Yu sheng*) uses official records, historical documents, and fragmented memories of the Atayal survivors to shed light on the time before, during, and after the incident. Written as one continuous paragraph, the novel leaves readers breathless as they face unanswered questions and the complexity of history. At the end of the novel, the ancestral soul, personified by the girl who claims to be Atayal Chief Mona Rudao's granddaughter, returns to the tribe, suggesting a glimmer of hope for the people.

It is common to refer to four major ethnic groups in Taiwan: Hoklo, Hakka, Indigenous Peoples, and *Waishengren*. For many writers, pride in one's ethnic identity means writing in one's native tongue. The GMD banned the use of Hoklo in public and made Mandarin the only official language. As early as the 1970s, however, poems were written in Hoklo, and since the 1990s they have been thriving. Best known are the works of Xiang Yang and Lu Hanxiu (the pen name of Wang Zhicheng, b. 1958). Similarly, the Hakka Affairs Commmittee (Kejia shiwu weiyuanhui) of the Executive Yuan was established in 2001, and Hakka-speaking television programming began in 2003. In literature, Du Pan Fangge (b. 1927) was the first writer to publish works in Hakka. Other writers publishing in Hakka include Ye Risong (b. 1936), Zeng Guihai (b. 1946), Li Yufang (b. 1952), Chen Ninggui (b. 1957), Huang Hengqiu (b. 1957), and Zhang Fangci (b. 1964).

Gender and sexuality

In the 1970s, women activists and scholars such as Annette Lu (Lü Xiulian), Bao Jialin, Yang Meihui, and Li Yuanzhen introduced feminism to Taiwan. Since the mid-1980s, various women's organizations have emerged to address such issues as the legalization of abortion, equal pay, property and inheritance rights, the banning of child prostitution, and opposition to beauty pageants. In light of rising feminist consciousness, a new generation of women writers arrived. The term "superwoman" (*nüqiangren*) was coined by the fiction writer Zhu Xiujuan (b. 1936) to refer to well-educated, independent career women. Xiao Sa (the pen name of Xiao Qingyu, b. 1953) is best known for her "problem fiction," which features teenagers faced with problems like premarital sex, pregnancy, and prostitution. Liao Huiying (b. 1948) used "Rapeseed" (Youmacai zi, 1982) to symbolize the fate of women: like rapeseed that takes root wherever it happens to fall, a woman is at the mercy of fate. Su Weizhen's stories of love are typically narrated by a single female entangled in an extramarital relationship. Defiance (the decision to love as she pleases) and a sense of doom (the ephemerality of the affair) pull her in opposite directions, but the latter always wins out, leading to escape, insanity, or death.

Yuan Qiongqiong's (b. 1950) "A Sky of One's Own" (Ziji de tiankong, 1980) depicts the transformation of the protagonist from a traditional wife to an independent woman after her divorce. Conversely, "The Mulberry Sea" (Cangsang) presents a reversal of fortune for the protagonist who has an affair, leaves her husband and children, and ends up poor and bitter. Her encounter with her erstwhile neighbor and best friend reveals that lurking beneath the surface is a tangled web of jealousy and remorse.

Finally, Zhu Tianwen's *Fin de Siècle Splendor* (*Shijimo de huali*, 1990) contains seven stories about different facets of life in Taipei. The title story presents Mia, a twenty-five-year-old fashion model who sees herself going downhill professionally and does not expect her affair with a much older married man to last. She builds a world of the senses around her, filled with scents, colors, and textures. Her effort to dry flowers and herbs is not born from a love of nature or a concern with the environment, but rather is an act of remembrance and preservation of beauty, youth, and love. The irony in building a future with memory points to the splendid decadence suggested in the title of the story.

Shifting the setting from the present-day metropolis to a small coastal town in the past, Li Ang's *The Butcher's Wife* (*Sha fu*, literally "murdering husband," 1983) focuses on the plight of women in a patriarchal society. Li draws a parallel between the butchering of pigs (rendered in gory detail) and sexual abuse. At the end of the story the butcher's wife stabs her husband to death, symbolically reversing the roles of butcher and pig. Through the character of the widow living next door, the novel also shows how women can become accomplices in a patriarchal society, victimizing one another even when they are victims themselves.

Li Ang's work since the 1990s, including *Dark Night* (*Anye*), *The Lost Garden* (*Miyuan*), and *The North Harbor Incense Burner* (*Beigang xianglu renren cha*), explores the relationship between sex and power in contemporary society, and focuses on female sexual desire rather than female victimhood. Sexual politics and body politics have become a dominant theme in literature and scholarly discourse on female subjectivity and female desire. In November 1998, Jiang Wenyu (b. 1961) at the National Taiwan University brought together a group of twelve poets to form the first women's poetry society, named She-Whale (Nüjin shishe). Through writings, readings, and seminars, they advocate "female writing."

Homosexuality has received attention as well. Bai Xianyong's *Crystal Boys* (*Niezi*, 1982; translated into English in 1995) breaches the taboo, centering on a group of young homeless gay men who gather at New Park in Taipei at night for love and money. Rejected by the Confucian society outside the park, they live and die in the dark. *Crystal Boys*, whose original title literally means "sons born of sin," is a pioneering work of queer literature, variously known as "homosexual" (*tongxinglian*), "comrade" (*tongzhi*), or "cool babe" (*kuer*) literature in Chinese. Queer literature has flourished as gay and lesbian movements have gained momentum and recognition since the early 1990s.

Chen Kehua has written many poems about homosexuality. Alternating between lyricism and sarcasm, he can be a romantic bard or a postmodern provocateur. Qiu Miaojin (1969–1995), who committed suicide in Paris, left behind *Alligator Diary* (*Eyu shouji*, 1991) and *Last Letters from Montmartre* (*Mengmate yishu*, 1995). Candid descriptions of the longing, alienation, self-loathing, possessiveness, and despair that accompany her quest for love make a riveting read. Other representative works of queer fiction include *Tomboy's Dance* (*Tongnü zhi wu*, 1991) by Cao Lijuan (b. 1960), *Biographies of Deviant Vampires* (*Yiduan xixiegui liezhuan*, 1995) by Hong Ling (b. 1971), *The Book of Evil Woman* (*Enü shu*, 1995) by Chen Xue, *The World of the Senses* (*Ganguan shijie*) by Ji Dawei (Chi Ta-wei, b. 1972), and *The Two Faces of Oedipus* (*Shuangmian Yidipasi*, 2003) by Lin Junying (b. 1960). The celebration of *jouissance* derived from "deviant" sexuality aligns queer literature with what critics have called neo-sensationalism (*xin ganguan*) or erotic literature (*qingse wenxue*).

Prose writers

The essay has always been a popular genre in Taiwan. Since the 1980s the genre has thrived, its terrain greatly enlarged as authors take on an impressive range of themes and incorporate elements of poetry, fiction, and drama. Among the representative writers of this genre are such senior essayists as Qi Jun, Zhang

Xiuya, Yu Guangzhong, Lin Wenyue (b. 1933), Yang Mu, Zhang Xiaofeng, and Jiang Xun (b. 1947). Essayists of the next generation include Ah Sheng (the pen name of Yang Minsheng, b. 1950), Liao Yuhui (b. 1950), Chen Xinghui (b. 1953), Fang Zi (the pen name of Lin Lizhen, b. 1957), Zheng Baojuan (b. 1957), Cai Shiping (b. 1958), and Jian Zhen (b. 1961). Examples of younger writers are Wu Junyao (b. 1967), Zhong Yiwen (b. 1969), and Yang Jiaxian (b. 1978). Most of this prose writing is occasional in nature and expands on minute details of everyday life: a person remembered, a book read, a place visited, an incident encountered, an experience treasured.

Yang Mu's autobiographical prose is a milestone in the genre. *Mountain Wind and Ocean Rain* (*Shanfeng haiyu*, 1987), *Return to Zero* (*Fangxiang gui ling*, 1991), and *Then I Set Forth* (*Xi wo wang yi*, 1997), which comprise the *Qilai Trilogy* (*Qilai qianshu*, 2003), record the poet's physical, emotional, and spiritual journey, which began in his childhood in postwar Hualian and ended with poetry as a lifelong calling. In dense, lyrical language, Yang Mu presents the dialectical relationship between reality and imagination, between experience in the world and its transformation into art. The poetic quest is equated with the quest for spiritual and intellectual beauty, love, and the divine. This conviction is elaborated in *The Skeptic: Notes on Poetic Discrepancies* (*Yi shen*, 2003).

At the other end of the spectrum is prose that comments on political, social, and cultural issues from an analytical standpoint. Four influential political analysts and cultural critics are Bo Yang, Li Ao, Long Yingtai (Ying-tai Lung, b. 1952), and Yang Zhao (b. 1963). Through their writings over the decades, they have achieved the stature of cultural icons in Taiwan, and some of them in China as well.

"I write, therefore I am"

Contemporary literature in Taiwan has demonstrated great diversity and heterogeneity against totalizing forces. In a cultural milieu in which literature has been marginalized, remarkable bursts of creativity are expressed in a wide spectrum of themes and styles. Whether the goal is the creation of a spiritual homeland, subjectivity, or historical verity, the quest takes myriad routes. In the final analysis, literature is its own subject.

This literary self-reflection underlies *My Kid Sister* (*Wo meimei*, 1993) by Zhang Dachun. The novella is the second book of a *Bildungsroman* trilogy, the other books being the immensely popular *The Weekly Journal of Young Big Head Spring* (*Shaonian Datouchun de shenghuo zhouji*, 1992) and *Wild Kid* (*Ye haizi*, 1996). All three are told by the first-person narrator Big Head Spring. In the first book, he is a middle school student who tells it like it is in a weekly journal submitted to his teacher. In the second, he is a twenty-seven-year-old writer from a dysfunctional family who empathizes with his younger sister. In the last, he is a fourteen-year-old school dropout who runs away from home and joins a gang.

The Weekly Journal of Young Big Head Spring is the funniest, while *My Kid Sister* is the darkest of the trilogy. The father in *My Kid Sister* is emotionally manipulative and abusive; he drives the mother insane and is doing the same to his live-in girlfriend. The mother is disconnected from her children and, eventually, from reality. For the narrator and his sister, love is possessiveness and sex is a "redundant ceremony of the flesh." At the reception for his father's art exhibition, the sister grabs the microphone to introduce her "work" to the audience: she has just got an abortion and has no idea who the father was, and her mother is in a sanatorium.

At a deeper level, *My Kid Sister* is about writing and "the ability to tell stories." At different points the narrator gives four definitions of writing: telling lies, escape, therapy, and self-empowerment. While each definition is valid, collectively they point to the power of literature to resist the void and confront death.

This theme finds a unique angle in Zhu Tianwen's *Notes of a Desolate Man* (*Huangren shouji*, 1994). The first-person narrative features a forty-year-old gay man whose childhood friend and one-time lover is dying of AIDS. He has been living in isolation and fear as he reminisces about his long-term lovers and one-night stands and reflects on his intellectual influences in copious allusions to literature, film, philosophy, music, and pop culture. Knowledge and travel do not dispel the ennui or bring meaning to life, however. The man decides that only through writing will he be able to transcend finitude and the void: "For myself, I must write. When I write, I can ward off forgetting. I write, therefore I am."

Hong Kong

Borrowed place, borrowed time

Known as a global financial center with a vibrant popular culture including a world-renowned film industry, Hong Kong has often been portrayed as a cultural desert where no serious literature and art exist. This is far from the truth. Since the 1950s, original and experimental literature has been part of the culture. Between 1997 and 2008, between one and six new journals appeared each year. Although bookstores must move ever higher in commercial buildings due to exorbitant rents, they remain scattered throughout the city; some hold poetry readings and "cultural salons." Veteran authors – such as fiction writers Liu Yichang and Xi Xi; prose writers Liang Xihua, Ye Hui, Huang Guobin, and Zhong Lingling (b. 1948); and poet Ye Si – have all shown unabated vitality, as younger writers break new ground, such as poets Zhong Guoqiang (b. 1961), Luo Feng (the pen name of Chen Shaohong, b. 1964), Chen Mie (the pen name of Chen Zhide, b. 1969), and Liao Weitang (b. 1975), and fiction writers Huang Biyun (Wong Bik-wan, b. 1961), Xie Xiaohong (b. 1977), Yuan Zhaochang (b. 1978), and Han Lizhu. Writers who move to Hong Kong – such as Shi Shuqing and Dong Qiao (Tung Chiao, the pen name of Dong Cunjue, b. 1942) from Taiwan; Huang Canran, Zheng Danyi (b. 1963), and Meng Lang from the mainland; and Lin Xingqian (b. 1963) from Malaysia – inject new energy into the literary scene.

A bridging between the media and other genres has taken place in recent years. For instance, Ye Si has collaborated with photographers, dancers, and installation artists, creating synergy between poetry and other art forms. Two artists Li Zhihai and Jiang Kangquan published *Great Hijack – Comics of Hong Kong Literature* (*Daqijie – manhua Xianggang wenxue*, 2000), which draws on short stories, poems, and prose by twelve Hong Kong writers: Liu Yichang, Cai Yanpei, Kun Nan, Xi Xi, Ye Si, Wu Xunbin, Dong Qizhang (b. 1967), Yin Jiang (the pen name of Liu Yizheng, b. 1949), Huai Yuan, Luo Guixiang (b. 1963), Huang Biyun, and Han Lizhu. Border-crossing is also a salient feature of *Fleurs des lettres* (*Zihua*), a literary journal launched in 2005 and edited by a group of young writers and artists: Xie Xiaohong, Yuan Zhaochang, Zhang Lijun, Deng Xiaohua, Guo Shiyong, Li Zhihai, Chen Zhihua, Deng Zhengjian, Jiang Kangquan (art director), and Chen Jiayong (art designer). The multigenre and multimedia content of the journal has made it a rare financial success.

The single most significant event in recent decades is the handover of Hong Kong from Britain to China. In September 1982, Prime Minister Margaret Thatcher (b. 1925) paid a visit to Beijing to negotiate the handover. In her discussion with Deng Xiaoping, the request of an extension of Britain's lease of Hong Kong was met with firm rejection. Deng Xiaoping expressed his determination to restore Chinese sovereignty over Hong Kong (including Hong Kong Island, Kowloon, and the New Territories) at the end of the ninety-nine-year lease of the New Territories. At the Fifth Session of the Fifth National People's Congress, the PRC Constitution was amended to include a new clause, which provided the legal basis for the policy of "One Country, Two Systems." The amendment would be instrumental in settling the issue of sovereignty over Hong Kong with Britain, and over Macau with Portugal.

On December 19, 1984, the Sino-British Joint Declaration (*Zhong Ying lianhe shengming*) was signed by the two prime ministers in Beijing; it was ratified on May 27, 1985 and registered at the United Nations on June 12, 1985. In the declaration, the two governments agreed that the handover of Hong Kong would go into effect on July 1, 1997. The PRC also announced its basic policies toward Hong Kong. In accordance with the "One Country, Two Systems" principle agreed on by Britain and China, the socialist system of the PRC would not be practiced in the Hong Kong Special Administrative Region (HKSAR); Hong Kong's capitalist system and its way of life would remain unchanged for fifty years. These policies would be stipulated in the Hong Kong Basic Law. On April 29, 1988, China issued a draft constitution for Hong Kong that would grant considerable autonomy in economic, trade, cultural, and political affairs for fifty years beginning in 1997. Critics of the draft said that it would give China veto power over laws passed by the Hong Kong legislative body. They were also concerned that the draft could effectively outlaw political dissent.

At midnight on July 1, 1997, in a solemn ceremony, China resumed sovereignty, ending 156 years of British colonial rule in Hong Kong. The British delegation was headed by Prince Charles (b. 1948), Prince of Wales, Prime Minister Tony Blair (b. 1953), Secretary of State for Foreign and Commonwealth Affairs Robin Cook (1946–2005), and the last governor of Hong Kong, Chris Patten (b. 1944). The Chinese delegation was headed by President Jiang Zemin, Premier Li Peng, Vice Premier Qian Qichen (b. 1928), and designate chief executive of HKSAR Tung Chee-hwa (Dong Jianhua, b. 1937), who stepped down in March 2005.

From the early 1980s to July 1, 1997, the handover was both eagerly awaited and dreaded by the people of Hong Kong. Eagerly awaited because it would end a century and a half of humiliation at the hands of Western colonialism – the sense of national pride was genuine and profound. Dreaded because of the uncertainty inherent in the transfer of power in light of the fundamental differences in the social, political, and economic systems between mainland China and Hong Kong. Many people in Hong Kong had originally fled the mainland in 1949 and 1950. In subsequent decades, political turmoil on the mainland had sent waves of refugees to Hong Kong. After the handover, people wondered, would Hong Kong's economy be adversely affected? And what restrictions would be imposed on civil rights and democratic processes? The Tiananmen Massacre of June 4, 1989 did nothing to allay such fears. The military crackdown on students and other peaceful demonstrators in Beijing was met with horror in Hong Kong, where over a million protestors took to the street on June 5.

Uncertainty about the future had a significant impact on all aspects of Hong Kong society. Negotiations between China and Britain were rocky and at times rancorous, which at various points led to the devaluation of the Hong Kong dollar, a sharp decline in the value of real estate, and food hoarding by citizens. Anxiety about the handover also opened a floodgate of emigration, mostly to Canada (which had a more open immigration policy) and Britain (which granted citizenship to fifty thousand households from Hong Kong). Those with means left en masse. Although many eventually came back or maintained dual residencies, for a decade and a half a deep-seated sense of crisis permeated the city. Under the shadow of the "'97 final end" (*jiuqi da xian*), people in Hong Kong were living in a "borrowed place" on "borrowed time."

This historical watershed sparked widespread reflections among intellectuals and writers on the identity and subjectivity of Hong Kong. If the question "what does it mean to be a Hongkongnese?" had hardly been in public consciousness, now it came to the fore with a sense of urgency. Projects to preserve and record the history and culture of Hong Kong in words, images, and sounds were launched in an effort to define Hong Kong in its own terms rather than the terms of others, to allow Hong Kong to be heard in its own voice rather than being spoken for. In literature, this desire translated into the compilation of literary histories and archives, the editing of anthologies, and the publication of scholarly studies, oral histories, and memoirs.

In January 1985, *Hong Kong Literature* (*Xianggang wenxue*) was launched. Initially edited by Liu Yichang, and after September 2000 by Tao Ran (the pen name of Tu Naixian, b. 1943), the journal aims to call readers' attention to "serious literature" in Hong Kong, to affirm its place in the global network of Chinese literature, and to set rigorous standards. The journal not only publishes materials of literary history and sponsors literary prizes, but it also provides a venue for Chinese writers around the world. Hong Kong literature has been incorporated into the curricula in the education system. The Hong Kong Arts Development Council was founded in June 1995 to provide public funding for literary festivals, prizes, and publication grants for local writers and artists.

Nostalgia and constructed memory

In the 1980s and 1990s, images of Hong Kong were presented through a wide range of media. *Red Checker Bistro* (*Honggezi jiupu*, 1994), by Xin Qishi (b. 1950), follows its characters through three decades of collective memory, including the Protecting Diaoyutai Movement, the movement to establish Chinese as an official language, the Sino-British Joint Declaration, and the Tiananmen Massacre. Xi Xi's *My City* (*Wo cheng*, 1983) and "A Strange Tale of the Floating City" (*Fucheng zhiyi*, 1986) present different aspects of Hong Kong in a magical realist mode. The novel conveys a hopeful message about the vitality of the city and the possibility of renewal, whereas the short story expresses anxiety and restlessness, with the city neither rising nor falling but floating in midair, as are the people. A mirror in the story that only reflects the back side of objects also suggests a grim view of the future.

The picture becomes much grimmer in the fiction of Huang Biyun. Since the early 1980s, she has created a nightmarish world of pathology and extreme violence that includes nausea, incest, self-mutilation, insanity, sadism, necrophilia, and cannibalism. "Lost City" (*Shi cheng*, 1994) links pathology to Hong Kong's historical condition. Concerned about post-handover Hong Kong, Chen Luyuan (whose given name means "distant road") emigrates with his wife and children to Canada. The loneliness and isolation of living in a foreign land drives the couple to the verge of a nervous breakdown. They return to Hong Kong only to find "my city" no longer recognizable after a mere three years. With Bach's cello music in the background, Chen Luyuan calmly bludgeons his wife and four children to death with an iron club and asks his neighbor to come in for a cup of coffee and call the police.

The association of history with violence and insanity is ubiquitous in Huang Biyun's work. "Moon over the Twin Cities" (*Shuang cheng yue*) resurrects Qiqiao, the protagonist from Eileen Chang's *The Golden Cangue*, only to have her suffer horribly through the subsequent decades on the mainland before she flees to Hong Kong. There, a young man, tormented by the memory of his mother's death, is so attracted to her mad gaze that he mutilates his own body as he masturbates before he hangs himself, all the while videotaping himself.

No Hong Kong writer has shown a deeper affinity for Eileen Chang than Zhong Xiaoyang (b. 1962). Born to a Chinese-Indonesian father and a Chinese mother from Manchuria, Zhong became famous when she won a string of awards in Hong Kong and Taiwan between 1979 and 1981. *A Brief Encounter* (*Tingche zhan jiewen*, 1981) spans the period from the Second Sino-Japanese War (1937–1945) to the 1960s, moving from Manchuria, the protagonist's home, to Hong Kong, where she is reunited with and subsequently loses the man she loves. The vivid description of Manchuria, the elegant language, and the wistful, dreamlike atmosphere make for a heart-wrenching story about the entanglement of love, decay, and death.

With the 1997 handover looming on the horizon, nostalgia played a conspicuous role in popular culture. Li Bihua (or Lilian Lee, pen name of Li Bai, b. 1959) focused on the themes of passion, betrayal, karma, and fate, often by adapting freely from Chinese history and classic tales. Many of her works have been made into films, most notably *Farewell, My Concubine* (*Bawang bieji*, 1993), *Temptation of the Monk* (*You seng*, 1993), *Blue Snake* (*Qing she*, based on the folktale of the White Snake, 1993), and *Rouge* (*Yanzhikou*, 1987).

Rouge, Li Bihua's first novel, opens in 1987 as a beautiful ghost follows a young reporter and begs him to place an ad for her. He realizes that she is the famous courtesan Fleur who fell in love with the playboy Chen Zhenbang in 1934. Faced with family opposition and poverty, the lovers decided to commit double suicide so they could be together in the underworld forever. Fleur comes back to the world of the living to look for her lover. With the reporter's help, she finds him. The truth is that Chen did not die and has been making a living as a stand-in in Cantonese Opera. Old and haggard, he has been carrying the burden of guilt for fifty years. Fleur returns the rouge case that he gave her when they were in love and leaves the world of the living for good.

The novel deals with betrayal in two senses of the word. Fleur is betrayed by Chen, but the deeper betrayal is perpetrated by time itself. Attitudes toward love and the city of Hong Kong have both changed. Just as the love Fleur died for turns out to be illusory, so the old Hong Kong is lost forever. The novel was adapted into an award-winning film, directed by Stanley Kwan (Guan Jinpeng, b. 1957) and featuring Anita Mui (Mei Yanfang, Mui Yim-fong, 1963–2003) and Leslie Cheung (Zhang Guorong, Cheung Kwok-wing, 1956–2003).

The Hong Kong story

Shi Shuqing moved to Hong Kong in 1978 and lived there for sixteen years. Her trilogy about Hong Kong consists of *Her Name Is Butterfly* (*Ta mingjiao Hudie*, 1993), *Hong Kong Orchids All over the Mountain* (*Bian shan Yangzijing*, 1995), and *The Lonely Garden of Clouds* (*Jimo yunyuan*, 1997). The saga centers on Huang Deyun, who was abducted from Guangdong and sold into a brothel in Hong Kong in 1892 at the age of thirteen. She has an affair with Adam Smith, a young British administrator. Their sexual relationship is described with colonial metaphors, comparing her body to a conquered land and a preyed-upon animal. Paradoxically, she is also feared as a vampire and a "yellow-winged butterfly" (a species that according to the author is found only on Hong Kong) that pulls Smith into the "licentious hell." When she becomes pregnant with Smith's child, he abandons her. She gives birth to a son and goes on to become a successful entrepreneur. That Huang Deyun prospers despite her abject beginnings is also the story of Hong Kong.

Allegories of Hong Kong take on more ambiguity in Dong Qizhang's *Collected Maps: Archeology of an Imaginary City* (*Dituji: yige xiangxiang de chengshi de kaoguxue*), which represents history as full of self-revision, self-concealment, and self-subversion. In short, history is no less fictionalized than fiction. "The Prosperity and Decline of Yongsheng Street" (Yongshengjie xingshuai shi, 1995) sums it up well:

> Few people know as little about the place where they grew up as we do. But you can't blame us for that; a colony has no need for memory. As the colony marches toward the end, however, we suddenly realize there is a void in our brains and we become anxious to trace our identity. Then we discover that other than fiction, other than fictionality, there is nothing we can rely on.

Gender and sexuality

Dong Qizhang's "Androgyny" (Anzhuozhenni, 1996) is narrated by a female biologist. The story develops along two parallel lines: a biology report and the life of the biologist. Researching her report, the biologist journeys to a mountain to look for an extinct species of androgynous lizard. The trip also lets her get away from her caring yet controlling husband. On the mountain she meets a reticent gardener (named Man), who finds the lizard for her and rapes her. In the end, she completes the report, finds herself pregnant, and possibly commits suicide by poison.

Subtitled "An Evolutionary History of a Non-existent Species," the story presents the feminist ideal of women's complete independence of men, but true independence remains beyond reach. Both men in the story are associated with male oppression through knowledge and physical force. The story ends on a hopeful note: "If it isn't me, then maybe someday my daughter, or my daughter's daughter, will be able to shake off the shackles."

Homosexuality is another important theme in contemporary Hong Kong literature. It was Hong Kong writers who initiated the ironic use of "comrade" to refer to homosexuals. In "Resurrection or No Resurrection Is a Hurricane" (Fuhuo bu fuhuo shi qixuan, 1994) by Cai Zhifeng, a gay teenager comes from a loving but conservative family. His father is a successful businessman, his mother a devout Christian, and his elder sister engaged to be married. After being rejected by the classmate to whom he expresses love, he has sexual encounters with strangers. In the final scene, he goes to a gay bar and runs into his father.

Whether it is about being a homosexual vis-à-vis mainstream society or about a postcolonial city newly incorporated into China, stories of Hong Kong are often about marginality, about in-betweenness. For writers like Ye Si and Dong Qizhang, it is "a city of memory, a city of fictionality." Travel is a recurrent motif in their work. As travelers situated between cultures and historical moments, both authors are wary of any reductionist, commercially motivated expression of nostalgia, wary as well of any grand narrative of the motherland imposed on Hong Kong. For more than two decades, Hong Kong writers have offered nuanced and self-reflexive perspectives. It is through these perspectives that "Hong Kong consciousness" finds its most powerful articulations.

IV. Recent changes in print culture and the advent of new media
By Michel Hockx

During the last decades of the twentieth century, Chinese writers started to publish their works in new ways, in new places, and through new media. Now, at the beginning of the twenty-first century, Chinese writers have access to unprecedented opportunities to present their works to readers all over the world. This section provides a brief overview of the major changes in literary production following the dismantling of what Perry Link has called "the socialist Chinese literary system." It also provides a brief and preliminary overview of ways in which the rise of digital interactive media is transforming habits of reading and writing.

Changes in the domestic system of publishing

During the 1980s and 1990s, the socialist Chinese literary system, which relied heavily on state subsidies, was gradually replaced by a profit-driven system. The number of state-employed writers was reduced to a minimum, the state-run Xinhua bookstores were overtaken by commercial bookstores, and publishing houses, though still state-owned, became competitive enterprises. Currently, the state invests very little money in the system, but continues to exercise control over the nature and content of publications. Specifically, the state controls the official number of publishing houses and the ISBN numbers allocated to those houses through the General Administration of Press and Publication (GAPP) (xinwen chuban zongshu). Unlike in other countries, publications without ISBN numbers are considered illegal in China. It has, however, become customary for the state-owned publishing houses to take advantage of various legislative loopholes in order to sell off their own ISBN numbers to a wide variety of private publishers, often with their own distribution or sales networks. This activity has further enhanced competition as well as profit-making opportunities. It is widely expected that this so-called "second channel" of publishing will eventually be legalized, with the GAPP itself taking over the selling of ISBN numbers to both state-owned and private businesses in open competition, to bring in extra revenue for the state.

The other major form in which the state exercises control of the publishing industry is, and will likely continue to be, the censorship system. This system involves numerous government and public security offices; the editors of publishing houses also carry out anticipatory cuts and revisions in manuscripts, aiming not at improving literary quality but at diminishing sensitivity. Generally speaking, since the 1980s, the censorship system has become less prescriptive and more prohibitive. Writers and publishers are no longer told what to produce, but are penalized if a publication is retrospectively deemed offensive or illegal. Assessing the risks of publishing sensitive works and weighing these risks against the advantages to be gleaned from media attention have become important skills for producers of literature. Some writers have been catapulted to fame because their books were banned while others have suffered serious personal consequences, including imprisonment. Among books of similar content or nature, some have ended up banned while others became best sellers.

Probably the most popular novelist of the 1980s, Zhang Xianliang managed to stay on the right side of the censors most of the time, despite touching on politically sensitive topics in novels such as *Half of Man Is Woman* (*Nanren de yiban shi nüren*) that deal with life in the labor camps during the 1960s and 1970s and contain some mildly explicit descriptions of sex. His masterpiece, *Getting Used to Dying* (*Xiguan siwang*, 1989), a complicated work featuring a threefold protagonist ("I", "you," and "he") and addressing more incisively the cruelties of "reeducation," was banned within months of publication. The vast majority of Chinese writers who write for the Chinese market today (this includes many writers living outside China) accept the fact that their works are subject to censorship and are willing to make the necessary adjustments. How small those adjustments can sometimes be is best illustrated by the case of Ma Jian's story collection *The Noodle Maker* (*Lamianzhe*), first published abroad in an English translation and later "adapted" for publication in China by changing a date in one of the stories from "June Fourth" to "June Third." Nobel Prize-winner Gao Xingjian, who left China in the late 1980s after several run-ins with the censors, is rare among contemporary mainland Chinese writers in consistently refusing to adjust his work to censorship demands and therefore does not publish in the PRC.

Compared to the socialist system, the current system has generally enhanced the variety and quality of publications as well as created better working conditions for successful writers in most genres. The system whereby writers were paid by the word has been replaced by a system of advances, fees, and royalties, similar to that in Western countries. Moreover, mainland Chinese writers now have ample opportunity to publish their work, either directly or through literary agents, outside the mainland, especially in Taiwan.

Cross-straits publishing and the international publishing rights trade

An important reason why so many successful Chinese writers are better off today than they were under the socialist system is that there is a sizable market for mainland literature, especially fiction, in Taiwan. After the political changes that took place in Taiwan in the late 1980s, the government embargo on mainland literature was lifted. Taiwanese publishers were given the freedom to publish works by mainland writers and began doing so with considerable commercial success, resulting in previously unimaginable fees and royalties for the writers involved. A further attraction for mainland writers to publish in Taiwan is the lack of political censorship. Many works by established mainland authors first appear in Taiwan (sometimes in Hong Kong) in an uncensored version before being adapted for mainland publication. Publishing rights are typically sold to the Taiwanese publisher for the traditional-character edition standard in Taiwan, while a mainland publishing house receives the rights to the adapted simplified-character edition. (The simplified (*jianti*) script introduced by the PRC government from the 1950s onwards is not used in Taiwanese publications. Publications in the traditional (*fanti*) script that come out in Taiwan are considered separate editions for copyright purposes.) The uncensored Taiwanese (or Hong Kong) edition tends to be the one used for translation into foreign languages, a trend which will be discussed further in the following section.

Another more significant aspect of cross-straits publishing is the publishing rights trade. From the late 1980s onwards, direct trade in publishing rights between mainland China and Taiwan has flourished. To the extent that the import of publishing rights into the mainland vastly exceeds its export to Taiwan, this has so far been a one-sided trade. Though much of this trade does not involve literary works, it does include, for instance, the rights to publish popular Taiwan authors such as Qiong Yao, as well as the rights to produce Chinese translations of foreign works. Since China joined the Berne Convention in 1992 and the World Trade Organization in 2001, the Chinese government has had to clamp down on the pirating of copyrighted works, making the rights trade even more important. In addition to Taiwanese publishers, leading Western publishing firms have also flocked to the Chinese market. It is worth noting that such companies are involved not only in the rights trade but also in the direct sale of foreign-language works, since the market for the latter is no longer inhibited by the existence of "internal bookstores" (*neibu shudian*) which used to sell officially sanctioned pirated copies of foreign works to Chinese consumers under the socialist system. Foreign-owned companies are also allowed to be active in the distribution and sales of Chinese books, but not yet in publishing itself, which, as mentioned above, remains the preserve of GAPP-licensed state-owned publishing houses.

The global literary market

For literary writers and their agents, the sale of translation rights can be an important source of income. Fiction from China, especially work considered "exotic," "dissident," or both, is in demand on the global literary market, while there are also niche markets for translations of critically acclaimed "serious" literature. Translation rights are often brokered directly on behalf of Chinese authors by Western agents and in some cases by the translators themselves. Chinese publishers are also getting involved in these transactions, which typically take place at large book fairs all over the world, although, as noted above, they rarely hold the rights to the uncensored editions that the authors would like to see translated. After the translation rights have been purchased and a draft translation has been produced, it is not unusual for the foreign publisher to demand further revisions or rewrites in order to make the work more accessible to its target audience. Good examples are the English translation of Mo Yan's *The Garlic Ballads* (*Tiantang suantai zhi ge*), which has a different ending from the original novel, and the English translation of Zhang Xianliang's *Getting Used to Dying*, in which the threefold narrative perspective was changed to a two-person perspective ("I" and "he") to make the work more accessible for the Western reader. It seems ironic that the latter change was considered necessary, when the same narrative structure in Gao Xingjian's Nobel Prize-winning novel *Soul Mountain* (*Lingshan*) was maintained in translation and duly praised by many Western critics.

Chinese authors whose works are successful in translation will often enter into long-term relationships with foreign publishers or agents, receiving contracts and cash advances for new work. In some cases, especially if the author in question lives abroad, heavily edited translations of his or her manuscripts will appear in foreign languages first before ever making it to the Chinese market, if indeed they make it there at all. There has been some debate, especially in China, about the extent to which the hope of success in translation has had an impact on the writing habits of Chinese authors as well as on the preferences of non-Chinese readers and critics. It is certainly true that in today's global literary market there are many kinds of "Chinese literature," and a given kind that appeals to one community may well find indifferent reception in another. A typical example is the work of Gao Xingjian, which is generally considered disappointing by mainland Chinese readers who have managed to gain access to it, while simultaneously winning the Nobel Prize in 2000 and earning critical acclaim in its translated versions.

The new media

The rapid development of digital interactive media, especially the World Wide Web, has in recent years had a massive impact on the Chinese literary world. Although it is too early to assess if this impact will last, those newly emergent literary practices that have stabilized over the past five years are worth discussing in detail.

Literature written for publication on the World Wide Web is referred to in China as *wangluo wenxue*, a term which is translated as "Web literature," "online literature," and "cyber literature" ("Web literature" will be used below). Most Chinese Web literature is traditional linear writing, rather than hypertext or multimedia writing, and as such is not formally distinct from printed literature. Nevertheless, the label "Web literature" continues to be attached to these writings even if they are later reproduced in print. This has led to the paradoxical situation in which Web literature has become an identifiable category of printed literature. Many bookshops, for instance, reserve shelf space for printed editions of Web literature, as if it were a separate genre of writing. There are also special literary prizes and competitions for Web literature, the only distinguishing feature being that the competing works must have been first published on a website.

Due to the late arrival of the Internet in mainland China, the earliest Chinese-language Web literature was produced outside China. As scholars and critics are starting to write the history of this new "genre" of Chinese literature, there seems to be an emerging consensus that the first works of Chinese Web literature appeared in the online journal *China News Digest–Chinese Magazine* (*Huaxia wenzhai*), established by Chinese students in the United States in 1991. US-based Chinese students also posted their creative writings to the Chinese-language newsgroup *alt.chinese.txt*. In the mid-1990s, the first Chinese-language literary websites were set up in countries outside China and viewed only by small numbers of early Internet users inside China. Those same users, based mainly on university campuses, started to produce their own Web literature on so-called bulletin board systems (BBSs), which allowed for some measure of interaction and discussion among users. From 1997 onwards, the first literary websites began to emerge in the mainland, including the successful Shanghai-based site Under the Banyan Tree (Rongshu xia), which claims to be the largest website for original Chinese-language writing in the world.

Meanwhile, Chinese-language Web literature was also emerging in Taiwan and the first Chinese-language author to gain celebrity status for an online work was the Taiwanese author Cai Zhiheng. Using the pseudonym Pizi Cai ("Ruffian Cai"), he serialized the novel *First Intimate Contact* (*Di yici de qinmi jiechu*) online in 1998, while still a graduate student at National Cheng Kung University. *First Intimate Contact* is a popular romance dealing with the world of online dating and virtual romance. In that same year, the printed version of the novel became a best seller in Taiwan, while the online version became hugely popular among Internet users in mainland China. A year later, a simplified-character edition appeared in print in mainland China. It too became an instant best seller, familiarizing many readers with both Web literature and cyber culture, and paving the way for the Web literature craze that continues to occupy millions of Chinese Internet users on a daily basis.

Discussion forums

In recent years, Web literature production as well as discussion about Web literature has started to coalesce around online interactive discussion forums, known in Chinese as *luntan* and sometimes still referred to by the old term "BBS." Most literary websites host forums devoted to specific genres or themes, and often also include classical-style writing, which is undergoing a remarkable revival online. Most discussion forums operate on the principle that only registered members of the site can upload their works, but that both members and non-members may read the works and comment on them.

Comments on a particular work are automatically appended to the work itself, creating so-called "threads" of discussion in which the author of the original work may also become involved. This aspect of direct interaction between author and reader constitutes the main distinction between Web literature and printed literature in China.

Discussion forums normally appear on-screen as a list of titles and (pen) names of authors, followed by statistics such as the number of "hits" and the number of responses. In most cases, texts that have elicited recent responses are at the top of the list; as long as new responses are added, they will continue to receive attention. Once a text has been pushed off the front page, it tends no longer to be read or discussed, but will continue to be available for a long time. As these works require relatively little server space, some literary discussion forums have online archives containing literally millions of works.

Most discussion forums are overseen by moderators (*banzhu*) who ensure that works are submitted to the appropriate forums and, if necessary, delete inappropriate or unwanted content, including content that might catch the eye of Internet censors. Originally, online forums allowed members to see their contributions on-screen almost instantly, but many moderators now take a more cautious attitude and will screen postings before allowing them to be displayed. Moderators are also responsible for keeping a forum lively and active, for instance by organizing competitions or suggesting specific topics for writing, and by taking an active part in the discussions. Often, moderators are also involved in selecting works for inclusion in special online publications known as "webzines" (*wangkan*). Most literary websites, especially those operated by small groups of like-minded associates, will publish regular webzines to showcase the best writing published on their forums. Such webzines are normally carefully designed and edited, with a layout similar to printed literary magazines, and are devoid of interactive functions; that is, they are meant to be read and not commented on.

Discussion forums have taken the Web literature world by storm in recent years. For many users, the forums are not much more than glorified chat rooms and online meeting places, or simply a place to practice writing as a hobby, but more serious sites try to devote themselves to high-level creation, criticism, and discussion. The Web has also produced new avant-garde groups, especially in the genre of poetry, providing space for shocking anti-establishment writing that cannot easily appear in print. A famous example is the "Poetry Vagabonds" (*Shi jianghu*) website, birthplace of the school of "lower body poetry" (*xiabanshen shige*).

Censorship

Much has been published in recent years about the Chinese state's efforts to establish comprehensive Internet censorship, often called "the Great Firewall of China." As far as Web literature is concerned, the basic principles of state censorship are no different from those applied to printed literature: registration, pre-publication self-censorship, and post-publication screening. As with book publications and ISBN numbers, all Chinese Internet domains must display a registration number provided by the relevant local authority. Members of discussion forums must sign an agreement promising not to post illegal content. Moderators fulfill the same function as publishing house editors in ensuring that no sensitive content is published. The state can check online publications, declare them illegal, shut down the website in question, and prosecute those deemed responsible. Since systematic checking of the content of all Web pages is not humanly possible, the state is believed to rely on automatic filters and keyword detectors to trace possible offensive content. In reality, however, it seems equally impossible for Internet censors to sift through the staggering numbers of Web pages that happen to trigger one of the automatic detection mechanisms. As a result, post-publication censorship is sporadic. Most literary websites prefer to play it safe, making sure that no potentially offensive content makes it past the moderators. In short, control of Web literature relies heavily on self-censorship and is based on the assumption that those responsible for running the websites want to stay out of trouble.

The relationship between Web literature and printed literature

As mentioned above, there are generally no formal differences between Chinese Web literature and printed literature. Although some Web authors (*xieshou*, as opposed to *zuojia* or print authors) insist on being active only online, most of those who find success on the Web sooner or later move into print. Nevertheless, even those who are successful in making the move to print, such as the popular author known as Ann Baby (Anni baobei), who started her career on Under the Banyan Tree, find it difficult to shake off the "Web literature" label. Conversely, publishing companies are happy to invest in literary websites as a means to find new audiences and market their products. For instance, Under the Banyan Tree was for a number of years owned by the German publishing giant Bertelsmann, who used the site to promote its products and also sponsored an annual "Bertelsmann Cup" writing competition for Web authors, with the winners being offered contracts for printed publications.

The possibility of publishing literary works in both printed and electronic format has also been instrumental in changing patterns of censorship. This became clear in the banning of Hu Fayun's *This Is How It Goes@sars.com* (*Ruyan@sars.com*), described as "the hottest novel of 2006," about a middle-aged woman who discovers the Internet and becomes entangled in a love triangle and a web of political intrigue as she tries to expose the truth about the government's handling of the SARS crisis. The novel was first serialized in a small regional journal, whose circulation skyrocketed as a result. In October 2006, it was published as a book and also in electronic format on the popular portal sina.com. Then, in January 2007, the director of GAPP mentioned at a meeting that this novel was among eight works that had been pulled off the shelves and banned. The online version, however, stayed online and continued to attract responses from readers on a daily basis. Hu Fayun himself spoke out against the decision to ban his work, calling the censorship system "childish" and "secretive" and adding that, since trying to ban anything in the age of the Internet was ridiculous, the authorities had to revert to sinister methods that were not backed up with any officially communicated decisions. GAPP never officially acknowledged the ban, and the printed version of the book remained on sale in Internet bookshops. In the fall of 2008, the ban was apparently lifted, as Hu Fayun's book had by then become available in bookstores in Beijing.

Many well-known print culture authors are increasingly establishing their own presence on the Web, whether by participating in "serious" discussion forums, taking part in "Web chats" with their readers, or hosting their own websites or (as is the latest fashion) writing their own weblogs or "blogs" (*boke*). It is safe to say that Web literature and literary websites have become an inseparable part of the contemporary Chinese literary landscape.

Epilogue

Sinophone writings and the Chinese diaspora

JING TSU

The development of modern Chinese literature into a national tradition followed a tumultuous and innovative trajectory. In pursuit of a new relationship with the past and with the world, modern literature reinvented itself at several crucial junctures. Though at times precariously maintained, a unity has often been asserted out of a sense of nostalgia. This map of reading continues to change, however, as new visions of the geopolitical imagination abound in current Sinophone literature. With the potential to reshape the field in important ways, these visions have propelled new literary production in places that are neither monolingual nor nationally Chinese. Without converging on one cultural vision or a single aesthetics, current efforts to create alternative literary histories of the Chinese diaspora are introducing new questions while reinvigorating past debates. These efforts seek to extend the horizon of modern Chinese literature beyond the historical scope of this volume.

Though "Chinese-language literature" (*huawen wenxue*) is not unfamiliar to the Chinese-speaking world, it is only in recent years that scholars have begun to reevaluate its relationships with the different histories of literary production in Chinese communities throughout the world, mainly in Hong Kong, Malaysia, Singapore, Taiwan, Western Europe, and North America. The term "Chinese" encompasses conflicting notions of ethnicity, cultural affiliation, and linguistic center. Chinese, furthermore, is not the only language of the Chinese literary diaspora. If one were to consider this diaspora from within, the complex relation between indigenous and Han scripts in the making of minority literary traditions in the latter half of the twentieth century reveals a carefully planned process of assimilation rather than a history of a shared, natural language. Viewed from without, the diaspora includes the mixing of different host languages and mother tongues that do not always agree on the primacy of the modern Chinese language as the vehicle of literary expression. The increasing bilingualism among Chinese writers further pushes the analytical scope of modern Chinese literature.

Taken together, these issues renew the importance of language, dialects, and national affiliation in contemporary Chinese literary studies. Whether Sinophone literature belongs to, or rather revises the notion of, "national literature" will remain a hotly contested issue for some time. It has already begun to prompt critics to reflect on the practice of national literary studies in general, as transnational writing and mobility pose new challenges to existing disciplinary divides and questions of canonicity.

Certainly "diaspora" has been invoked to mean different things to different communities. Unlike Francophone or Anglophone, Lusophone or Hispanophone, however, the mere designation of "Chinese-speaking," or Sinophone, encompasses a wide range of dialectal variety with differences that can be greater than those between Spanish and French. Currently, dialects and mother tongues are presented as forms of cultural allegiance that are more compelling than national affiliation. In light of the traditional neglect of these dialects in the official representation of modern Chinese writing, the current attempt at revitalization seeks to restore materiality to lost and forgotten voices. The increasingly important role of dialects in contemporary literature and literary debates – Fujianese, Hakka, Teochiu, or Cantonese, for example – helps to reassert nativist ideologies against the predominance of nationalism. By using dialect to challenge the authority of the official language, be it Taiwanese against Mandarin (*putonghua*), or Chinese against Malay, diasporic writers turn the very medium of national language (*guoyu*, *hanyu*) into an instrument of dissent. While some insist on writing in their first language and home dialect, exposure to second or third languages in their host countries offers the additional possibility of playing on the notion of identity through shifting and combined linguistic allegiances.

Amidst the multilingualism that defines the diasporic experience, a given writer's choice to write in Chinese while living outside of China carries a particular significance. In a host environment dominated by a national tongue other than Chinese, writing in Chinese insists on language, rather than physical place, as the marker of one's cultural belonging. Writers choose language as their home and invest it with real and imagined origins of authenticity. One Malaysian-Chinese writer, Li Yongping, recounts his own discovery of the pure Chinese language in the process:

> An education in foreign languages has cultivated in me an ability to judge the capacity of language – what is Chinese, what is English. I cannot bear the kind of Chinese that has been "aggressively Westernized." The manner of trading and doing business with language and culture is desecration of the worst

kind . . . and so I later wrote *Retribution: The Jiling Chronicles*. For eight years, on and off, I painstakingly worked on it so as to build a pure, Chinese literary form. To purify myself through the purification of the Chinese language . . . also to purify the language brought from one's native land: to de-nativize, and to get rid of the impure sediments from one's native home.

Regarded as one of Taiwan's most prominent writers, Li charges modern Chinese with straying from its cultural essence. Responding to the "aggressive Westernization" of Chinese, marked by the intrusion of foreign vocabulary and grammatical forms, he takes on the self-appointed task of purifying the Chinese language. His painstaking efforts are well rewarded in the evident success of his novel, *Retribution*, which is written in a vernacular style reminiscent of northern Chinese dialects but does not itself correspond to the colloquialism of any real locality. Set in the town of Jiling, the story recounts the events unfolding around an incident of rape, which is retold from different perspectives in twelve short stories.

As a diasporic writer, Li's allegiance to an idealized mother tongue is striking. The Mandarin Chinese he himself writes in is a standardized national language and, though originally based on the Beijing dialect, has little to do with the mother tongue. It is significant that a diasporic writer should declare the development of the modern Chinese language to be a corruption. Instead of simply expressing a nostalgia that characterizes the impossible desire of the diaspora, Li's case demonstrates the recognized capital of language, precisely because a given language can be consecrated as an ideal tongue and continually reified as a lost art against any dominant language.

If Li's migratory experience from Southeast Asia to Taiwan prompts him to return to a pure, original language, then Zhang Guixing, his contemporary, reconstitutes that experience as a new hybridity at the margins. Expressing a strong tie to his native Borneo, Zhang makes lavish use of the rich flora and fauna of the tropics to stage a reinvented genealogy and primitive exoticism. In such novels as *My South Seas Sleeping Beauty* (*Wo sinian de changmian zhong de Nanyang gongzhu*), *Elephants* (*Qunxiang*), and *Monkey Cups* (*Houbei*), tropical mythology doubles as a setting for ethnic, colonial, and racial violence between native inhabitants, European and Japanese colonialists, and Chinese settler migrants. Far from purifying language, Zhang creates thickly textured narratives that reflect the mix of racial lineages and languages by making the Sinoscript part of the morphology of life and decay.

Both Li and Zhang try to find, in their own ways, a thread to a displaced past that is founded on a certain vanishing point. For them, as for countless writers throughout the twentieth century and beyond, the power of history to consecrate certain narratives while banishing others to silence has provided an inexhaustible source of inspiration and rebellion. The Malaysian-Chinese woman writer Li Zishu, in a poignant allegory, reimagines "History" as an abject beast that relieves others of past trauma by reliving it for them as its own horrific physical deformities. As though history can only be renarrated with the paradoxical hope of forgetting, the idea of China has undergone similar processes of distortion, reinvention, and translation.

Indeed, representations of China and Chinese writing have been disseminated in many parts of the world not only through Mandarin Chinese but also through English, French, and other languages. Once in the realm of other national tongues, Sinophone literature takes on the additional complexity of bilingualism. Given the current climate of globalizing national literatures by increasing the representation of other languages within one national tradition, the role of diasporic literatures in accommodating these new expansive visions of "-phone" literatures has yet to be sufficiently examined. Whether one writer can be claimed by several literary canons and whether the diasporic frontiers of different nations can happily overlap without controversy over new questions of belonging remains to be seen.

Regardless of future struggles, however, one can hardly avoid acknowledging writers who had already traversed those national bounds without calling themselves diasporic. Chinese students who studied abroad beginning in the late nineteenth century spearheaded efforts to introduce and exchange knowledge about China and the world. They opened up a channel of cosmopolitanism that facilitated the negotiation between foreign ideas and self-representations. The early Republican novel *An Unofficial History of Studying in Japan* (*Liudong waishi*) is one of the first compositions in the genre of displacement, modernization, and early national consciousness. Writers of the May Fourth generation who studied in Europe and America founded Chinese and bilingual journals, signifying a new awareness of audiences and readerships beyond national boundaries. Gu Hongming and Lin Yutang are among the best examples of this sensibility in earlier individual writers.

The genre that has come to be known as the "literature of students abroad" (*liuxuesheng wenxue*) has since remained a consistent nexus for the national and global imaginary. Chinese emigrant women writers of the 1960s, 1970s, and 1980s such as Hualing Nieh, Lihua Yu, and Geling Yan brought the new female voice to overseas writing in English through original compositions and translations. Their experimentations with narrative techniques and themes resonated other similarly driven, consciously reinvented voices in Asian-American women's literature by writers such as Maxine Hong Kingston and Malaysia-born American Anglophone writer Shirley Geok-Lin Lim. The circle of exiles and student immigrants in the earlier phase of overseas Chinese literature in North America, including important figures such as Bei Dao and Bai Xianyong, has expanded to encompass writers in secondary and tertiary diaspora around the world. Formerly UK-based writer Hong Ying, for instance, is part of the post-1980s wave of Sinophone writers dispersed throughout western and northern Europe whose works have been widely translated and read, along with that of France-based writers such as François Cheng, Dai Sijie, and Gao Xingjian. This group enjoys a well-established literary presence not only as writers of fiction and poetry but also as directors and playwrights.

If Chinese diasporic literature can be written in any language, there hardly seems to be a need to identify it as Chinese at all. Taiwan-based Malaysian-Chinese writer and critic Huang Jinshu (Ng Kim Chew), in fact, recently called for the "de-Sinicization" (*qu Zhongguo hua*) and "de-nationalization" (*qu guojihua*) of Chinese-language literature. Yet neither writers nor literary critics can dispense with the historical weight of the common script. It is difficult to imagine a scenario in which distinct tongues would cease to matter and everyone would forego their own identity in favor of a pure community and pure language. At the same time, it is even harder to maintain that standard written Mandarin will remain unchanged throughout the historical, living process of language contact. Perhaps one is always dealing with a fundamental and necessary duplicity at the heart of one's allegiance to one's own language, or, to recall Li Yongping's sentiment, "doing business" with the mother tongue. Such are the difficult questions about origin, nativism, modernism, and authenticity that are raised by the current state of Sinophone literature.

The diverse contexts of diasporic writing, furthermore, highlight the problem of borders and territories in the typography of modern Chinese literature. Where, for example, does the national canon end and the diasporic counter-canon begin? Even if one recognized that such lines are not possible or ultimately fruitful to draw, they remain a central point of contention. Despite the optimism often expressed in putting forward diaspora as an antinational force of globalization, Sinophone literature seems to raise the living specter of a nation behind the diaspora. That national literary tradition suppresses minor, especially nonnative, literary traditions has not lessened the appeal of a post-national identity; the desire for community fuels the continual investment in claims of national literatures and cultures. For diasporic writers writing under the condition of multiple marginalizations, the situation is especially poignant.

The different ways in which literature about China is consumed around the world in translation give important indications of the circuits through which Sinophone literature is propagated and pluralized. Such consideration touches on questions of literary awards, global recognition, and the power of translation to mediate as well as to mask the divergent tastes and discontinuities between reading cultures. How Sinophone literature itself reflects the global phenomenon of mediated cultural consumption provides a meaningful look at the redistribution and new concentrations of capital and power. One might take a cue from the earlier example of Eileen Chang, the most influential mainland Chinese woman writer of the twentieth century, who has attracted a wide following among such contemporary writers as Li Tianbao, Zhu Tianwen, and Su Weizhen. Widely revered and emulated for her penetrating narratives of the Chinese family through the perspective of the female psyche, Chang stood out for her solitary voice and insistent silence on politics. When a friend asked whether she would ever write about the proletariat, she replied that she knew more about the lives of invisible, domestic figures like housekeepers. Her works have established an indomitable style for literary explorations of the self, which have been the focus of a sizable body of studies of her life and works. Reaching fame in the 1940s, she wrote a novella, *Jinsuo ji*, that she herself later translated into English as *The Golden Cangue*. The story follows the female protagonist Qiqiao through the torments of widowhood and mistreatment by her husband's family, until she becomes a figure of torture herself.

The story, widely popular among the Chinese readership, was rewritten three more times in two languages between 1943 and 1967. Chang's attempt to convey her story in two language worlds, however, did not meet with equal success. When *Rouge of the North*, an expanded novel-length version based on the plot of *The Golden Cangue*, was published in 1967, Chang had already serialized it in Chinese as "Embittered Women" (Yuannü) in Hong Kong and Taiwan a year earlier. Although the serialized novel was an immediate success, critics in the Anglophone world gave the English version a lukewarm appraisal. Her story failed to speak to the Anglophone world with the same intimacy as it did to a Chinese readership.

Commercial failure notwithstanding, Chang's attempt at self-translation is significant for other reasons. As someone who always refused to subordinate literature to political imperatives, Chang wished to engage audiences outside the Chinese-speaking world and so extended a gesture toward a new literary space that framed her concerns in a different tongue. Her attempt to cross over into a different linguistic world, often carried out under the pressure of financial hardship, also calls into question whether bilingualism facilitates one's literary appeal or condemns the native language to untranslatability. A counterexample can be found in the English translations of Lao She's two famous novels, *Rickshaw Boy* (*Luotuo Xiangzi*) and *The Yellow Storm* (*Sishi tongtang*). Lao She's translators altered the plot of *Rickshaw Boy* and added chapters to *The Yellow Storm* in order to increase their appeal to American audiences; as a result, literary critics and book clubs greeted the two altered translations with great enthusiasm.

Displacement and exile have generated a desire for a language that can articulate the uniqueness of individual sojourns away from China. Gao Xingjian's *Soul Mountain* epitomizes this search through a narrative of self-conscious wanderings, reconstituting the historical subject "I" through the multiple addresses of "you" and "he" – first- and third-person perspectives that oscillate between the present and historical memory. Gao expressed an interest in the problem of time and historical consciousness already in his early short stories, sharing the widely felt need among writers after the Cultural Revolution to renew their artistry so as to reflect on the catastrophic scale of that event. This preoccupation persisted in the writings of Gao and other authors throughout the rest of the century, finding rich articulation in experiments with modernist aesthetics and the more familiar realist mode, especially during the root-seeking movement of the mid-1980s. Gao propelled the effort by writing a programmatic essay that ignited fervent debates about which new literary modes could provide an artistic inroad to the highly politicized historiography of the twentieth century. By relocating the foundations of cultural myths and political legends in the exotic and primordial regions of the hinterland and countryside, writers like Gao sought to reinvent a space for reexamining the accountability of history, nostalgia, and their own personal memories.

Having begun his literary career in Chinese, Gao's international success as the first Chinese to be awarded the Nobel Prize in Literature in 2000, however, puts him in a unique position. Although well received by readers outside of China, Gao has been less enthusiastically acknowledged in mainland China. The tastes of and standards for international recognition do not always coincide with the desired national image of China, especially since some consider Gao's international fame to be garnered at the expense of portraying China's cultural and political barbarism. Success in languages other than the mother tongue, in this case, becomes politicized in such a way that a writer's loyalty to his cultural and national roots is called into question, further reinforcing the kind of political scrutiny that perhaps compelled writers like Eileen Chang and Gao Xingjian to seek literary expression in a foreign tongue.

The question of whether or not to use one's mother tongue pivots on historically entangled issues of national identity, artistic freedom, the public and private spaces of literature, and an increasing reliance on an international audience. One might consider the success of the contemporary writer Ha Jin in the Anglophone world as a testimony to the politics of native language. Unlike Gao, Ha Jin has built his literary career entirely in English. Having published little prior to his migration to the United States in 1985, Ha Jin has attracted attention with his deceptively simple and linear narrative style that evokes something foreign in its expressiveness. While some observe that his lack of previous experience in writing in Chinese actually freed Ha Jin from having to make the cumbersome transition from a native grammar, others criticize his unacknowledged transference of Chinese language and idioms through direct translation into English. Though he is decidedly an Anglophone Chinese writer, Ha Jin's unusual success with writing about modern China in the English language has attracted much attention from Chinese readers.

A major hurdle to how diasporic literature might revise our understanding of modern Chinese literature is whether writers and critics can agree on the terms of the debate. "Chineseness" (*Zhongguoxing*), "modernism" (*xiandaixing*), and "nativism" have each generated extensive discussion in modern Chinese literary historiography. The role of "native soil" – or "local soil" (*bentu*) – in forging the literary imagination of the diasporic world is also tied to the advent of "native soil fiction" (*xiangtu wenxue*) in defining the national modern Chinese literary canon. Lu Xun, in his introductory essay to an anthology of modern fiction collected as part of the *Compendium of Modern Chinese Literature* (*Zhongguo xin wenxue daxi*, edited by Zhao Jiabi in 1935–1936), first defined the category of native soil fiction by describing writers from other provinces as "residential sojourners" (*qiaoyu*) in the city of Beijing who could only write about a home that was not present. They embodied for the mainstream culture of the national metropolis the lost nativism displayed through their distinctive literary voice as writers from afar.

The diasporic writer, similarly, is the necessary nomadic figure that helps to distinguish the local from the sojourner, the foreigner from the national. Implied in Lu Xun's distinction is a geographical hierarchy that places urban areas, as opposed to provincial areas, at the center of the production of national literature. The term "sojourner," incidentally, is embedded in a historical context of systemic prejudice, as it has been used throughout the twentieth century to describe the Chinese migrant. The migrant's stay abroad was meant to be short-term, as seen in the term "sojourn," which implies not a desire to find belonging in a foreign place but a temporary, even involuntary, exile from home.

This deep ambiguity at the heart of the sentiment of nativism has been generally accepted in critical discourse as a form of nostalgia. The concept of nostalgia, as embodied in a wide range of nativist writings – aboriginal, local, national – has, however, not always been used successfully in addressing the complexity of contemporary diasporic literature. Different versions of nativism continue to compete with each other for a larger share of the global audience. Diaspora, rather than pointing at an unspecified desire that can easily be mapped anywhere onto the idea of China, generates tensions not only between nations but also between dispersed Sinophone communities vying to protect their hard-won capital of distinction.

Though Sinophone literature and the literature of diaspora compel us to reexamine the lines of demarcation drawn between them, it has not been easy either to challenge or to circumvent the attachment to Chinese literature as a national legacy. Neither those in favor of its necessity nor those objecting to its monolithic status have fully addressed its continual currency between different Sinophone and diasporic communities. The increasing mobility of writers adds to the problem of identifying any one place as home, while the traditional model of accepting one center as the locus of hegemony is gradually giving way to an alternative understanding that accounts for the flow of cultural power between multiple centers.

The recurring issue is not the right to disengage, but rather the right to claim one's own writing as the more compelling voice in capturing the nomadic essence of Sinophone writing. Even as some scholars criticize the heuristic assumption behind the ethnicizing marker "Chinese" in Western academic discourse, it nonetheless survives its conceptual contradictions as a necessary specter for comparisons and contestations. In this sense, the dialogue between national and Sinophone literature will continue to prompt new reflections and questions. Whether these different voices can be forged into a new unity or even agree enough to disagree is a question essential to the foundational issue of what constitutes a national, world, or world national literature.

Select Bibliography

Chapter 1: Literature of the early Ming
to mid-Ming (1375–1572)

Barr, Allan H. "The Later Classical Tale." In *The Columbia History of Chinese Literature*, ed. Victor H. Mair. New York: Columbia University Press, 2001, 675–696.

Birch, Cyril, ed. *Anthology of Chinese Literature, Vol. 2: From the 14th Century to the Present Day*. New York: Grove Press, 1972.

Brokaw, Cynthia J., and Kai-wing Chow, eds. *Printing and Book Culture in Late Imperial China*. Berkeley: University of California Press, 2005.

Brook, Timothy. *The Confusions of Pleasure: Commerce and Culture in Ming China*. Berkeley: University of California Press, 1998.

Brook, Timothy, Jérôme Bourgon, and Gregory Blue. "*Lingchi* in the Ming Dynasty." In their *Death by a Thousand Cuts*. Cambridge, MA: Harvard University Press, 2008, 97–121.

Bryant, Daniel. *Great Recreation: Ho Ching-ming (1483–1521) and his World*. Leiden: Brill, 2008.

—. "Poetry of the Fifteenth and Sixteenth Centuries." In *The Columbia History of Chinese Literature*, ed. Victor H. Mair. New York: Columbia University Press, 2001, 399–409.

Buck, Pearl S., trans. *All Men Are Brothers*. 2 vols. New York: John Day, 1933. Repr. New York: Grove, 1957.

Chan, Hok-lam. *Legends of the Building of Old Peking*. Hong Kong and Seattle: The Chinese University of Hong Kong and University of Washington, 2008.

Chan, Wing-tsit. *Instructions for Practical Living and Other Neo-Confucian Writings by Wang Yang-ming*. New York: Columbia University Press, 1963.

Chang, Kang-i Sun. "The Circularity of Literary Knowledge between Ming China and Other Countries in East Asia: The Case of Qu You's *Jiandeng Xinhua*." In *NACS Conference Volume: On Chinese Culture and Globalization*, ed. Lena Rydholm. Stockholm: University of Stockholm Press, forthcoming.

—. "Gender and Canonicity: Ming–Qing Women Poets in the Eyes of the Male Literati." In *Hsiang Lectures on Chinese Poetry, vol. 1*, ed. Grace S. Fong. Centre for East Asian Studies Research, McGill University, 2001, 1–18.

Chang, Kang-i Sun, and Haun Saussy, eds. *Women Writers of Traditional China: An Anthology of Poetry and Criticism*. Stanford: Stanford University Press, 1999.

Chaves, Jonathan, ed. and trans. *The Columbia Book of Later Chinese Poetry*. New York: Columbia University Press, 1986.

Ch'en Hsiao-lan and F. W. Mote. "Yang Shen and Huang O: Husband and Wife as Lovers, Poets, and Historical Figures." In *Excursions in Chinese Culture: Festschrift in Honor of William R. Schultz*, ed. Marie Chan, Chia-lin Pao Tao, and Jing-shen Tao. Hong Kong: The Chinese University Press, 2002, 1–32.

Chia, Lucia. *Printing for Profit: The Commercial Publishers of Jianyang, Fujian (11th–17th Centuries).* Cambridge, MA: Harvard University Asia Center, 2002.

Chow, Kai-wing. *Publishing, Culture, and Power in Early Modern China.* Stanford: Stanford University Press, 2004.

Chu, Hung-lam. "Textual Filiation of Li Shimian's Biography: The Part about the Palace Fire in 1421." *East Asian Library Journal* 13, no. 1 (2008): 66–126.

Dent-Young, John, and Alex Dent-Young, trans. *The Broken Seals: Part One of The Marshes of Moung Liang, A New Translation of the Shuihu Zhuan or Water Margin.* By Shi Nai'an and Lo Guanzhong. Hong Kong: The Chinese University Press, 1994.

—, trans. *The Tiger Killers: Part Two of the Marshes of Mount Liang.* By Shi Nai'an and Lo Guanzhong. Hong Kong: The Chinese University Press, 1997.

—, trans. *The Gathering Company: Part Three of the Marshes of Mount Liang.* By Shi Nai'an and Lo Guanzhong. Hong Kong: The Chinese University Press, 2001.

—, trans. *Iron Ox: Part Four of the Marshes of Mount Liang.* By Shi Nai'an and Lo Guanzhong. Hong Kong: The Chinese University Press, 2002.

Dreyer, Edward. *Early Ming China: A Political History.* Stanford: Stanford University Press, 1981.

Dudbridge, Glen. *The His-yu chi: A Study of Antecedents to the Sixteenth-Century Chinese Novel.* Cambridge: Cambridge University Press, 1970.

Ebrey, Patricia Buckley. *Cambridge Illustrated History of China.* Cambridge: Cambridge University Press, 1996.

Elman, Benjamin. *A Cultural History of Civil Examinations in Late Imperial China.* Berkeley: University of California Press, 2000.

Fei, Faye Chunfang, ed. and trans. *Chinese Theories of Theater and Performance from Confucius to the Present.* Ann Arbor: University of Michigan Press, 2002.

Fong, Grace S. "Poetry of the Ming and Qing Dynasties." In *How to Read Chinese Poetry: A Guided Anthology*, ed. Zong-qi Cai. New York: Columbia University Press, 2008, 354–378.

Ge, Liangyan. *Out of the Margins: The Rise of Chinese Vernacular Fiction.* Honolulu: University of Hawai'i Press, 2001.

Goodrich, L. Carrington, and Chaoying Fang., eds. *Dictionary of Ming Biography, 1368–1644.* 2 vols. New York: Columbia University Press, 1976.

Hanan, Patrick. *The Chinese Short Story: Studies in Dating, Authorship, and Composition.* Cambridge, MA: Harvard University Press, 1973.

—. "The Early Chinese Short Story: A Critical Theory in Outline." *Harvard Journal of Asiatic Studies* 27 (1987): 168–207.

Hansen, Valerie. *The Open Empire: A History of China to 1600.* New York: Norton, 2000.

Harmon, Coy L. "Trimming the Lamp: The Literary Tales of Ch'ü Yu." In *Excursions in Chinese Culture: Festschrift in Honor of William R. Schultz*, ed. Marie Chan, Chia-lin Pao Tao, and Jing-shen Tao. Hong Kong: The Chinese University Press, 2002, 125–148.

Hayden, George A. "A Skeptical Note on the Early History of *Shui-hu chuan.*" *Monumenta Serica* 32 (1976): 374–399.

Hegel, Robert E. *Reading Illustrated Fiction in Late Imperial China.* Stanford: Stanford University Press, 1998.

Hsia, C. T. *The Classic Chinese Novel: A Critical Introduction.* New York: Columbia University Press, 1968.

Hucker, Charles. *A Dictionary of Official Titles in Imperial China.* Stanford: Stanford University Press, 1985.

Idema, Wilt L. *The Dramatic Oeuvre of Chu Yu-Tun.* Leiden: Brill, 1985.

—. "Male Fantasies and Female Realities: Chu Shu-chen and Chang Yu-niang and Their Biographies." In *Chinese Women in the Imperial Past: New Perspectives,* ed. Harriot T. Zurndorfer. Leiden: Brill, 1999, 19–52.

—. "Traditional Dramatic Literature." In *The Columbia History of Chinese Literature,* ed. Victor H. Mair. New York: Columbia University Press, 2001, 785–847.

Idema, Wilt L., and Stephen H. West. *Chinese Theater 1100–1450: A Source Book.* Wiesbaden: Franz Steiner, 1982.

Irwin, Richard G. *The Evolution of a Chinese Novel: Shui-hu chuan.* Cambridge, MA: Harvard University Press, 1953.

—. "Water Margin Revisited." *T'oung Pao* 58 (1960): 393–415.

Johnson, Linda Cooke, ed. *Cities of Jiangnan in Late Imperial China.* Albany, NY: State University of New York Press, 1993.

Kroll, Paul W., trans. "The Golden Phoenix Hairpin." By Qu You. In *Traditional Chinese Stories,* ed. Y. W. Ma and Joseph S. M. Lau. New York: Columbia University Press, 1978, 400–403.

Ku Chieh-kang. "A Study of Literary Persecution during the Ming." Trans. L. Carrington Goodrich. *Harvard Journal of Asiatic Studies* 3 (1938): 254–311.

Li, Peter. "Narrative Patterns in San-kuo and Shui-hu." In *Chinese Narrative: Critical and Theoretical Essays,* ed. Andrew H. Plaks. Princeton: Princeton University Press, 1977, 73–84.

Li, Wai-yee. "Full-length Vernacular Fiction." In *The Columbia History of Chinese Literature,* ed. Victor H. Mair. New York: Columbia University Press, 2001, 620–658.

Liu, Wu-chi, and Irving Yucheng Lo, eds. *Sunflower Splendor: Three Thousand Years of Chinese Poetry.* New York: Anchor Books, 1975.

Lo, Andrew Hing-bun. "*San-kuo chih yen-i* and *Shui-hu chuan* in the Context of Historiography." Ph.D. diss., Princeton University, 1981.

Lowry, Kathryn A. *The Tapestry of Popular Songs in 16th- and 17th-Century China: Reading, Imitation, and Desire.* Leiden and Boston: Brill, 2005.

Lynn, Richard John. "Mongol-Yüan Classical Verse (Shih)." In *The Columbia History of Chinese Literature,* ed. Victor H. Mair. New York: Columbia University Press, 2001, 383–398.

—. "Tradition and the Individual: Ming and Ch'ing Views on Yüan Poetry." *Journal of Oriental Studies* (University of Hong Kong) 15 (1977): 1–19.

Ma, Y. W., and Joseph S. M. Lau, eds. *Traditional Chinese Stories: Themes and Variations.* New York: Columbia University Press, 1978.

Mackerras, Colin, ed. *Chinese Theater: From Its Origins to the Present Day.* Honolulu: University of Hawai'i Press, 1983.

Mair, Victor H., ed. *The Columbia Anthology of Traditional Chinese Literature.* New York: Columbia University, 1994.

—. *The Columbia History of Chinese Literature.* New York: Columbia University Press, 2001.

Mair, Victor H., Nancy S. Steinhardt, and Paul R. Goldin, eds. *Hawai'i Reader in Traditional Chinese Culture.* Honolulu: University of Hawai'i Press, 2005.

Marmé, Michael. "Heaven on Earth: The Rise of Suzhou, 1127–1550." In *Cities of Jiangnan in Late Imperial China*, ed. Linda Cooke Johnson. Albany, NY: State University of New York Press, 1993, 17–45.

Metzger, Thomas A. *Escape from Predicament: Neo-Confucianism and China's Evolving Political Culture.* New York: Columbia University Press, 1977.

Mote, F. W. "The Ch'eng-hua and Hung-chih Reigns, 1465–1505." In *The Cambridge History of China, Vol. 7, pt. 1: The Ming Dynasty, 1368–1644*, ed. Frederick W. Mote and Denis Twitchett. Cambridge: Cambridge University Press, 343–402.

—. *Imperial China: 900–1800.* Cambridge, MA: Harvard University Press, 1999.

—. *The Poet Kao Ch'i.* Princeton: Princeton University Press, 1962.

Murck, Christian F. "Chu Yün-ming and Cultural Commitment in Suchou." Ph.D. diss., Princeton University, 1978.

Naquin, Susan. *Peking: Temples and City Life, 1400–1900.* Berkeley: University of California Press, 2000.

Nienhauser, William H. Jr., ed. and comp. *The Indiana Companion to Traditional Chinese Literature.* 2 vols. Bloomington: Indiana University Press, 1986–1998.

Ong, Chang Woei. *Men of Letters within the Passes: Guanzhong Literati in Chinese History, 907–1911.* Cambridge, MA: Harvard University Asia Center, 2008.

—. "The Principles are Many: Wang Tingxiang and Intellectual Transition in Mid-Ming China." *Harvard Journal of Asiatic Studies* 66, no. 2 (2006): 461–493.

Paludan, Ann. *The Imperial Ming Tombs.* Foreword by L. Carrington Goodrich. New Haven: Yale University Press, 1981.

Plaks, Andrew H. *The Four Masterworks of the Ming Novel.* Princeton: Princeton University Press, 1987.

Rexroth, Kenneth, and Ling Chung, ed. and trans. *Women Poets of China.* New York: New Directions, 1972.

Roberts, Moss, trans. *Three Kingdoms: A Historical Novel.* Attributed to Luo Guanzhong. Berkeley: University of California Press, 1991.

Robinson, David M. "Images of Subject Mongols under the Ming Dynasty." *Late Imperial China* 25, no. 1 (2004): 59–123.

Rolston, David L., ed. *How to Read the Chinese Novel.* Princeton: Princeton University Press, 1990.

—. *Traditional Chinese Fiction and Fiction Commentary: Reading and Writing between the Lines.* Stanford: Stanford University Press, 1997.

Santangelo, Paolo. "Urban Society in Later Imperial Suzhou." Trans. Adam Victor. In *Cities of Jiangnan in Late Imperial China*, ed. Linda Cooke Johnson. Albany, NY: State University of New York Press, 1993, 81–116.

Schlepp, Wayne, trans. "Lament for a Song Girl." By Tang Shi. In *Hawai'i Reader in Traditional Chinese Culture*, ed. Victor H. Mair, Nancy S. Steinhardt, and Paul R. Goldin. Honolulu: University of Hawai'i Press, 2005, 456–457.

—. *San-ch'ü: Its Technique and Imagery*. Madison: University of Wisconsin Press, 1970.

Tan, Tian Yuan. "Qu Writing in Literati Communities: Rediscovering Sanqu Songs and Drama in Sixteenth-Century North China." Ph.D. diss., Harvard University, 2006.

—. "The Wolf of Zhongshan and Ingrates: Problematic Literary Contexts in Sixteenth-Century China." *Asia Major* series 3, 20, pt. 1 (2007): 105–131.

Tong, James W. *Disorder under Heaven: Collective Violence in the Ming Dynasty*. Stanford: Stanford University Press, 1991.

Tsai, Shih-shan Henry. *Perpetual Happiness: The Ming Emperor Yongle*. Seattle: University of Washington Press, 2001.

Tu, Ching-i. "The Chinese Examination Essay." *Monumenta Serica* 31 (1974–1975): 393–406.

Tu Wei-ming. *Neo-Confucian Thought in Action: Wang Yang-ming's Youth (1472–1509)*. Berkeley: University of California Press, 1976.

Waley, Arthur, trans. *Monkey*. London: John Day, 1942. Repr. New York: Grove Press, 1958.

Waltner, Ann. "Writing Her Way out of Trouble: Li Yuying in History and Fiction." In *Writing Women in Late Imperial China*, ed. Ellen Widner and Kang-i Sun Chang. Stanford: Stanford University Press, 1997, 221–241.

West, Stephen H., and Wilt L. Idema, ed. and trans. *The Story of the Western Wing*. By Wang Shifu. Berkeley: University of California Press, 1995.

Wixted, John Timothy. "Poetry of the Fourteenth Century." In *The Columbia History of Chinese Literature*, ed. Victor H. Mair. New York: Columbia University Press, 2001, 390–398.

Wu, Yenna. "Outlaws' Dreams of Power and Position in *Shuihu zhuan*." *Chinese Literature: Essays, Articles, Reviews* 18 (1996): 45–67.

Ye, Yang, trans. *Vignettes from the Late Ming: A Hsiao-P'in Anthology*. With annotations and introduction by Yang Ye. Seattle: University of Washington Press, 1999.

Yoshikawa Kōjirō. *Five Hundred Years of Chinese Poetry, 1150–1650*. Trans. John Timothy Wixted. Princeton: Princeton University Press, 1989.

Yu, Anthony C. "History, Fiction, and Reading Chinese Narrative." *Chinese Literature: Essays, Articles, Reviews* 10 (1988): 1–19.

—, ed. and trans. *The Journey to the West*. 4 vols. Chicago: University of Chicago Press, 1977–1983.

—, ed. and trans. *The Monkey and the Monk: A Revised Abridgment of the Journey to the West*. Chicago and London: University of Chicago Press, 2006.

Yu, Pauline. "Formal Distinctions in Chinese Literary Theory." In *Theories of the Arts in China*, ed. Susan Bush and Christian Murck. Princeton: Princeton University Press, 1983, 27–53.

Chapter 2: The literary culture of the late Ming (1573–1644)

Barr, Allan H. "The Wanli Context of the 'Courtesan's Jewel Box' Story." *Harvard Journal of Asiatic Studies* 57 (1997): 107–141.

Birch, Cyril, trans. *Mistress and Maid.* By Meng Chengshun. New York: Columbia University Press, 2001.

—, trans. *The Peony Pavilion: Mudan ting.* By Tang Xianzu. Bloomington: Indiana University Press, 2002.

—, trans. *Stories from a Ming Collection: Translations of Chinese Short Stories Published in the Seventeenth Century.* Bloomington: Indiana University Press, 1958.

Brokaw, Cynthia J., and Kai-wing Chow, eds. *Printing and Book Culture in Late Imperial China.* Berkeley: University of California Press, 2005.

Carlitz, Katherine. *The Rhetoric of Ch'in p'ing mei.* Bloomington: Indiana University Press, 1986.

Chang, Kang-i Sun. *The Late-Ming Poet Ch'en Tzu-lung: Crises of Love and Loyalism.* New Haven: Yale University Press, 1991.

Chang, Kang-i Sun, and Haun Saussy, eds. *Women Writers of Traditional China: An Anthology of Poetry and Criticism.* Stanford: Stanford University Press, 1999.

Chia, Lucille. "Of Three Mountains Street: The Commercial Publishers of Ming Nanjing." In *Printing and Book Culture in Late Imperial China*, ed. Cynthia J. Brokaw and Kai-wing Chow. Berkeley: University of California Press, 2005, 107–151.

Chou, Chih-p'ing. *Yuan Hong-tao and the Kung-an School.* Cambridge: Cambridge University Press, 1988.

Chow Kai-wing. *Publishing, Culture, and Power in Early Modern China.* Stanford: Stanford University Press, 2004.

Clunas, Craig. *Superfluous Things: Material Culture and Social Status in Early Modern China.* Cambridge: Polity Press, 1991.

Dardess, John W. *Blood and History in China: The Donglin Faction and Its Repression, 1620–1627.* Honolulu: University of Hawai'i Press, 2002.

Guo Qitao. *Ritual Opera and Mercantile Lineage: The Confucian Transformation of Popular Culture in Late Imperial Huizhou.* Stanford: Stanford University Press, 2005.

Hanan, Patrick. *The Chinese Vernacular Story.* Cambridge, MA: Harvard University Press, 1981.

—. "The Making of The Pearl-Sewn Shirt and The Courtesan's Jewel Box." *Harvard Journal of Asiatic Studies* 33 (1973): 124–153.

—. "Sources of the *Chin P'ing Mei*." *Asia Major*, new series 10, no. 2 (1963): 23–67.

—. "The Text of the *Chin P'ing Mei*." *Asia Major*, new series 9, no. 1 (1962): 1–57.

Hegel, Robert. *The Novel in Seventeenth-Century China.* New York: Columbia University Press, 1981.

—. *Reading Illustrated Fiction in Late Imperial China.* Stanford: Stanford University Press, 1998.

Huang, Martin, ed. *Snakes' Legs: Sequels, Continuations, Rewritings, and Chinese Fiction.* Honolulu: University of Hawai'i Press, 2004.

Idema, Wilt L., and Beata Grant. *The Red Brush: Writing Women of Imperial China.* Cambridge, MA: Harvard University Asia Center, 2004.

Kafalas, Philip A. *In Limpid Dream: Nostalgia and Zhang Dai's Reminiscences of the Ming.* Norwalk, CT: Eastbridge, 2007.

Ko, Dorothy. *Teachers of the Inner Chambers: Women and Culture in Seventeenth-Century China.* Stanford: Stanford University Press, 1994.

Li, Wai-yee. *Enchantment and Disenchantment: Love and Illusion in Chinese Literature*. Princeton: Princeton University Press, 1993.

McLaren, Anne E. "Constructing New Reading Publics in Late Ming China." In *Printing and Book Culture in Late Imperial China*, ed. Cynthia J. Brokaw and Kai-wing Chow. Berkeley: University of California Press, 2005, 152–183.

Mote, F. W., and Denis Twitchett, eds. *The Cambridge History of China, Vol. 7, pt. 1: The Ming Dynasty, 1368–1644*. Cambridge: Cambridge University Press, 1988.

Owen, Stephen. "Salvaging Poetry: The 'Poetic' in the Qing." In *Culture and State in Chinese History*, ed. Theodore Huters, R. Bin Wong, and Pauline Yu. Stanford: Stanford University Press, 1997, 105–125.

Plaks, Andrew. *The Four Masterworks of the Ming Novel*. Princeton: Princeton University Press, 1987.

Rolston, David L. *Traditional Chinese Fiction and Fiction Commentary: Reading and Writing between the Lines*. Stanford: Stanford University Press, 1997.

Roy, David Tod, trans. *The Plum in the Golden Vase or, Chin P'ing Mei: Volume One, The Gathering*. Princeton: Princeton University Press, 1997.

—. *The Plum in the Golden Vase or, Chin P'ing Mei: Volume Two, The Rivals*. Princeton: Princeton University Press, 2006.

—. *The Plum in the Golden Vase or, Chin P'ing Mei: Volume Three, The Aphrodisiac*. Princeton: Princeton University Press, 2006.

Shang Wei. "*Jin Ping Mei* and Late Ming Print Culture." In *Writing and Materiality in China: Essays in Honor of Patrick Hanan*, ed. Judith T. Zeitlin, Lydia Liu, and Ellen Widmer. Cambridge, MA: Harvard University Asia Center, 2003, 187–238.

Sieber, Patricia. *Theaters of Desire: Authors, Readers, and the Reproduction of Early Chinese Song-Drama, 1300–2000*. New York: Palgrave Macmillan, 2003.

Tian, Xiaofei. "A Preliminary Comparison of the Two Recensions of 'Jinpingmei.'" *Harvard Journal of Asiatic Studies* 62 (2002): 347–388.

Volpp, Sophie. "The Literary Consumption of Actors in Seventeenth-Century China." In *Writing and Materiality in China: Essays in Honor of Patrick Hanan*, ed. Judith T. Zeitlin, Lydia Liu, and Ellen Widmer. Cambridge, MA: Harvard University Asia Center, 2003, 133–186.

Ward, Julian. *Xu Xiake (1587–1641): The Art of Travel Writing*. London: Routledge, 2000.

West, Stephen H. "A Study in Appropriation: Zang Maoxun's Injustice to Dou E." *Journal of the American Oriental Society* 111 (1991): 283–302.

Widmer, Ellen, and Kang-i Sun Chang, eds. *Writing Women in Late Imperial China*. Stanford: Stanford University Press, 1997.

Wu, Laura Hua. "From Xiaoshuo to Fiction: Hu Yinglin's Genre Study of Xiaoshuo." *Harvard Journal of Asiatic Studies* 55 (1995): 339–371.

Yang, Shuhui, and Yunqin Yang, trans. *Stories Old and New: A Ming Dynasty Collection*. By Feng Menglong. Seattle: University of Washington Press, 2000.

—, trans. *Stories to Caution the World: Ming Dynasty Collection, Volume 2*. By Feng Menglong. Seattle: University of Washington Press, 2005.

Ye, Yang, trans. *Vignettes From the Late Ming: A Hsiao-p'in Anthology*. With annotations and introduction by Yang Ye. Seattle: University of Washington Press, 1999.

Chapter 3: Early Qing to 1723

Barr, Alan. "Disarming Intruders: Alien Women in *Liaozhai zhiyi*." *Harvard Journal of Asiatic Studies* 49, no. 2 (1989): 501–517.

—. "The Early Qing Mystery of the Governor's Stolen Silver." *Harvard Journal of Asiatic Studies* 60, no. 3 (2000): 385–412.

Bryant, Daniel. "Syntax, Sound, and Sentiment in Old Nanking: Wang Shih-chen's (Wang Shizhen) 'Miscellaneous Poems on the Ch'in-huai (Qinhuai).'" *Chinese Literature: Essays, Articles, Reviews* 14 (1992): 25–50.

Chang, Kang-i Sun. "The Idea of the Mask in Wu Wei-yeh (1609–1671)." *Harvard Journal of Asiatic Studies* 48, no. 2 (1988): 289–320.

—. *The Late-Ming Poet Ch'en Tzu-lung: Crises of Love and Loyalism*. New Haven: Yale University Press, 1991.

Chaves, Jonathan. "Moral Action in the Poetry of Wu Chia-chi (Wu Jiaji, 1618–1684)." *Harvard Journal of Asiatic Studies* 46, no. 2 (1986): 387–469.

—. "The Yellow Mountain Poems of Ch'ien Ch'ien-i (Qian Qianyi): Poetry as Yu chi." *Harvard Journal of Asiatic Studies* 48, no. 2 (1988): 465–492.

Epstein, Maram. *Competing Discourses: Orthodoxy, Authenticity, and Engendered Meanings in Late Imperial Chinese Fiction*. Cambridge, MA: Harvard University Asia Center, 2001.

Fong, Grace. "Inscribing Desire: Zhu Yizun's Love Lyrics in *Jingzhiju qinqu*." *Harvard Journal of Asiatic Studies* 54, no. 2 (1994): 437–460.

—. "Writing from Experience: Personal Records of War and Disorder in Jiangnan during the Ming–Qing Transition." In *Military Culture in Imperial China*, ed. Nicola Di Cosmo. Cambridge, MA: Harvard University Press, 2009, 257–277.

Hanan, Patrick. *The Invention of Li Yu*. Cambridge, MA: Harvard University Press, 1988.

Hegel, Robert. *The Novel in Seventeenth-Century China*. New York: Columbia University Press, 1981.

—. *Reading Illustrated Fiction in Late Imperial China*. Stanford: Stanford University Press, 1998.

Huang, Martin. *Desire and Fictional Narrative in Late Imperial China*. Cambridge, MA: Harvard University Asia Center, 2001.

—, ed. *Snakes' Legs: Sequels, Continuations, Rewritings, and Chinese Fiction*. Honolulu: University of Hawai'i Press, 2004.

Idema, Wilt, Wai-yee Li, and Ellen Widmer, eds. *Trauma and Transcendence in Early Qing Literature*. Cambridge, MA: Harvard University Asia Center, 2006.

Kafalis, Philip Alexander. *In Limpid Dream: Nostalgia and Zhang Dai's Reminiscences of the Ming*. Norwalk, CT: Eastbridge, 2007.

Ko, Dorothy. *Teachers of the Inner Chambers: Women and Culture in Seventeenth-Century China*. Stanford: Stanford University Press, 1994.

K'ung Shang-jen (Kong Shangren). *Peach Blossom Fan (Taohua shan)*. Trans. Chen Shih-hsiang and Harold Acton, with the collaboration of Cyril Birch. Berkeley: University of California Press, 1976.

Li, Wai-yee. *Enchantment and Disenchantment: Love and Illusion in Chinese Literature*. Princeton: Princeton University Press, 1993.

—. "Full-length Vernacular Fiction." In *Columbia History of Chinese Literature*, ed. Victor H. Mair. New York: Columbia University Press, 2001, 620–658.

—. "Heroic Transformations: Women and National Trauma in Early Qing Literature." *Harvard Journal of Asiatic Studies* 59, no. 2 (1999): 363–443.

—. "The Representation of History in the Peach Blossom Fan." *Journal of the American Oriental Society* 115, no. 3 (1995): 421–433.

Li Yu. *The Carnal Prayer Mat (Rou putuan)*. Trans. Patrick Hanan. Honolulu: University of Hawai'i Press, 1996.

—. *Silent Operas (Wusheng xi)*. Trans. Patrick Hanan. Hong Kong: Chinese University Press, 1990.

—. *A Tower for the Summer Heat (Shi'er lou)*. Trans. Patrick Hanan. New York: Columbia University Press, 1998.

Lu, Tina. *Persons, Roles, and Minds: Identity in* Peony Pavilion *and* Peach Blossom Fan. Stanford: Stanford University Press, 2001.

Lynn, Richard John. "Orthodoxy and Enlightenment: Wang Shih-chen's Theory of Poetry and Its Antecedents." In *Unfolding of Neo-Confucianism*, ed. William Theodore de Bary and the Conference on Seventeenth-Century Chinese Thought. New York: Columbia University Press, 1975, 217–257.

McCraw, David. *Chinese Lyricists of the Seventeenth Century*. Honolulu: University of Hawai'i Press, 1990.

McMahon, Keith. *Causality and Containment in Seventeenth-Century Fiction*. Leiden: Brill, 1988.

Meyer-Fong, Tobie. *Building Culture in Early Qing Yangzhou*. Stanford: Stanford University Press, 2003.

—. "Packaging the Men of Our Times: Literary Anthologies, Friendship Networks, and Political Accommodation in the Early Qing." *Harvard Journal of Asiatic Studies* 64, no. 1 (2004): 5–56.

Owen, Stephen. *Readings in Chinese Literary Thought*. Cambridge, MA: Council on East Asian Studies, Harvard University, 1992.

—. "Salvaging Poetry: the 'Poetic' in the Qing." In Theodore Huters, R. Bin Wong, and Pauline Yu, eds. *Culture and State in Chinese History*. Stanford: Stanford University Press, 1997, 105–125.

Pastreich, Emmanuel. "The Pleasure Quarters of Nanjing and Edo as Metaphor: The Records of Yu Huai and Narushima Ryūhoku." *Monumenta Nipponica* 55, no. 2 (2000): 199–224.

Peterson, Willard. *Bitter Gourd: Fang I-chih and the Impetus for Intellectual Change*. New Haven: Yale University Press, 1979.

Plaks, Andrew. "After the Fall: *Hsing-shih yin-yuan chuan* (*Xingshi yinyuan zhuan*) and the Seventeenth-Century Chinese Novel." *Harvard Journal of Asiatic Studies* 45, no. 2 (1985): 543–580.

Pu Songling. *Strange Stories from a Chinese Studio (Liaozhai zhiyi)*. Trans. John Minford. London: Penguin Books, 2006.

Rolston, David, ed. *How to Read the Chinese Novel*. Princeton: Princeton University Press, 1990.

—. *Traditional Chinese Fiction and Fiction Commentary: Reading and Writing between the Lines*. Stanford: Stanford University Press, 1997.

Shang Wei and David Wang, eds. *Dynastic Crisis and Cultural Innovation: From the Late Ming to the Late Qing and Beyond*. Cambridge, MA: Harvard University Asia Center, 2005.

Spence, Jonathan. *The Death of Woman Wang*. New York: Viking Press, 1978.

—. *Emperor of China: Self-Portrait of Kang Hsi*. New York: Vintage Books, 1988.

—. *Return to Dragon Mountain: Memories of a Late Ming Man*. New York: Viking, 2007.

Strassberg, Richard. *The World of K'ung Shang-jen: A Man of Letters in Early Qing China*. New York: Columbia University Press, 1983.

Struve, Lynn. "History and the *Peach Blossom Fan*." *Chinese Literature: Essays, Articles, Reviews* 2, no. 1 (1980): 55–72.

—. "Huang Zongxi in Context: A Reappraisal of His Major Writings." *Journal of Asian Studies* 47, no. 3 (1988): 474–502.

—. *The Ming–Qing Conflict, 1619–1683: A Historigraphy and Source Guide*. Ann Arbor: Association for Asian Studies, 1998.

—. *Voices from the Ming–Qing Cataclysm: China in Tiger's Jaw*. New Haven: Yale University Press, 1993.

Tung Yüeh. *The Tower of Myriad Mirrors: A Supplement to Journey to the West*. Trans. Shuen-fu Lin and Larry L. Schulz. 2nd edn. Ann Arbor: Center for Chinese Studies, University of Michigan, 2000.

Volpp, Sophie. "The Literary Circulation of Actors in Seventeenth-Century China." *Journal of Asian Studies* 61, no. 3 (2002): 949–984.

Wakeman, Frederic Jr. *The Great Enterprise: The Manchu Reconstruction of Imperial Order in Seventeenth-Century China*. Berkeley: University of California Press, 1985.

—. "Romantics, Stoics, and Martyrs in Seventeenth-Century China." *Journal of Asian Studies* 43, no. 4 (1984): 631–655.

Wang, John. *Chin Sheng-t'an*. New York: Twayne, 1972.

Widmer, Ellen. "The Epistolary World of Female Talent in Seventeenth-Century China." *Late Imperial China* 10, no. 2 (1989): 1–43.

—. "The Huanduzhai of Hangzhou and Suzhou: A Study in Seventeenth-Century Publishing." *Harvard Journal of Asiatic Studies* 56, no. 1 (1996): 77–122.

—. *Margins of Utopia: Shui-hu hou-chuan and the Literature of Ming Loyalism*. Cambridge, MA: Council on East Asian Studies, Harvard University, 1987.

Widmer, Ellen, and Kang-i Sun Chang, eds. *Writing Women in Late Imperial China*. Stanford: Stanford University Press, 1997.

Wu Pei-yi. *The Confucian's Progress: Autobiographical Writings in Traditional China*. Princeton: Princeton University Press, 1990.

Wu Yenna. *The Chinese Virago: A Literary Theme*. Cambridge, MA: Council on East Asian Studies, Harvard University, 1995.

—. *The Lioness Roars: Shrew Stories from Late Imperial China*. Ithaca: East Asian Program, Cornell University, 1995.

Yim, Lawrence C. H. "Qian Qianyi's Theory of Shishi during the Ming–Qing Transition." *Occasional Papers* (Institute of Chinese Literature and Philosophy, Academia Sinica) 1 (2005): 1–77.

Yu, Pauline. "Canon Formation in Late Imperial China." In *Culture and State in Chinese History*, ed. Theodore Huters, R. Bin Wong, and Pauline Yu. Stanford: Stanford University Press, 1997, 83–104.

Zeitlin, Judith T. *Historian of the Strange: Pu Songling and the Chinese Classical Tale*. Stanford: Stanford University Press, 1993.

—. *The Phantom Heroine: Ghosts and Gender in Seventeenth-Century Chinese Literature.* Honolulu: University of Hawai'i Press, 2007.

—. "Shared Dreams: The Story of the Three Wives' Commentary on the *Peony Pavilion*." *Harvard Journal of Asiatic Studies* 54, no. 1 (1994): 127–179.

Chapter 4: The literati era and its demise (1723–1840)

Brokaw, Cynthia. *Commerce in Culture: The Sibao Book Trade in the Qing and Republican Periods*. Cambridge, MA: Harvard University Asia Center, 2007.

Brokaw, Cynthia, and Kai-wing Chow, eds. *Printing and Book Culture in Late Imperial China*. Berkeley: University of California Press, 2005.

Cao Xueqin. *The Story of the Stone: Volume 1, The Golden Days*. Trans. David Hawkes. Harmondsworth, Middlesex: Penguin Books, 1973.

—. *The Story of the Stone: Volume 2, The Crab-Flower Club*. Trans. David Hawkes. Harmondsworth, Middlesex: Penguin Books, 1977.

—. *The Story of the Stone: Volume 3, The Warning Voice*. Trans. David Hawkes. Harmondsworth, Middlesex: Penguin Books, 1980.

Cao Xueqin and Gao E. *The Story of the Stone: Volume 4, The Debt of Tears*. Trans. John Minford. Harmondsworth, Middlesex: Penguin Books, 1982.

—. *The Story of the Stone: Volume 5, The Dreamer Wakes*. Trans. John Minford. Harmondsworth, Middlesex: Penguin Books, 1986.

Chan, Leo Tak-hung. *The Discourse on Foxes and Ghosts: Ji Yun and Eighteenth-Century Literati Storytelling*. Honolulu: University of Hawai'i Press, 1998.

Chang, Kang-i Sun. "Ming–Qing Women Poets and the Notions of 'Talent' and 'Morality.'" In *Culture and State in Chinese History*, ed. Theodore Huters, R. Bin Wong, and Pauline Yu. Stanford: Stanford University Press, 1997, 236–258.

Chang, Kang-i Sun, and Haun Saussy, eds. *Chinese Women Poets: An Anthology of Poetry and Criticism from Ancient Times to 1911*. Stanford: Stanford University Press, 1999.

Chaves, Jonathan, ed. and trans. *The Columbia Book of Later Chinese Poetry*. New York: Columbia University Press, 1986.

Chow, Kai-wing. "Discourse, Examination, and Local Elite: The Invention of the T'ung-ch'eng School in Ch'ing China." In *Education and Society in Late Imperial China, 1600–1900*, ed. Benjamin Elman and Alexander Woodside. Berkeley: University of California Press, 1994, 183–220.

—. *The Rise of Confucian Ritualism in Late Imperial China: Ethics, Classics, and Lineage Discourse.* Stanford: Stanford University Press, 1994.

Duara, Prasenjit. "Superscribing Symbols: The Myth of Guandi, Chinese God of War." *Journal of Asian Studies* 47, no. 4 (1988): 778–795.

Elman, Benjamin. *Classicism, Politics, and Kinship: The Ch'ang-chou School of New Text Confucianism in Late Imperial China*. Berkeley: University of California Press, 1990.

—. *A Cultural History of Civil Examinations in Late Imperial China*. Berkeley: University of California Press, 2000.

—. *From Philosophy to Philology: Intellectual and Social Aspects of Change in Late Imperial China*. Cambridge, MA: Harvard University Press, 1990.

Fei, Faye Chunfang, ed. and trans. *Chinese Theories of Theater and Performance from Confucius to the Present*. Ann Arbor: University of Michigan Press, 1999.

Fong, Grace S. *Herself an Author: Gender, Agency, and Writing in Late Imperial China*. Honolulu: University of Hawai'i Press, 2008.

Guy, Kent. *The Emperor's Four Treasures: Scholars and the State in the Late Ch'ien-lung Era*. Cambridge, MA: Harvard University Press, 1987.

Hanan, Patrick. *Chinese Fiction of the Nineteenth and Early Twentieth Centuries*. New York: Columbia University Press, 2004.

Hegel, Robert. *Reading Illustrated Fiction in Late Imperial China*. Stanford: Stanford University Press, 1998.

Hsia, C. T. *The Classic Chinese Novel: A Critical Introduction*. New York: Columbia University Press, 1968.

Hua, Wei. "How Dangerous Can the *Peony* Be? Textual Space, *Caizi Mudan ting*, and Naturalizing the Erotic." *Journal of Asian Studies* 65, no. 4 (2006): 741–762.

Huang, Martin. *Literati and Self-Re/Presentation: Autobiographical Sensibility in the Eighteenth-Century Chinese Novel*. Stanford: Stanford University Press, 1995.

—, ed. *Snakes' Legs: Sequels, Continuations, Rewritings, and Chinese Fiction*. Honolulu: University of Hawai'i Press, 2004.

Idema, Wilt, and Beata Grant. *The Red Brush: Writing Women of Imperial China*. Cambridge, MA: Harvard University Asia Center, 2004.

Ko, Dorothy. *Teachers of the Inner Chambers: Women and Culture in Seventeenth-Century China*. Stanford: Stanford University Press, 1994.

Kuhn, Philip. *Origins of the Modern Chinese State*. Stanford: Stanford University Press, 2002.

Li, Wai-yee. *Enchantment and Disenchantment: Love and Illusion in Chinese Literature*. Princeton: Princeton University Press, 1993.

Lin, Shuen-fu. "Chia Pao-yü's First Visit to the Land of Illusion: An Analysis of a Literary Dream in an Interdisciplinary Perspective." *Chinese Literature: Essays, Articles, and Reviews* 14 (1992): 77–106.

Mackerras, Colin P., ed. *Chinese Theater: From Its Origins to the Present Day*. Honolulu: University of Hawai'i Press, 1983.

—. *The Rise of the Peking Opera 1770–1870: Social Aspects of the Theater in Manchu China*. Oxford: Oxford University Press, 1972.

Mair, Victor H., ed. *The Columbia History of Chinese Literature*. New York: Columbia University Press, 2001.

Mann, Susan. *Precious Records: Women in China's Long Eighteenth Century*. Stanford: Stanford University Press, 1997.

Miles, Steven B. *The Sea of Learning: Mobility and Identity in Nineteenth-Century Guangzhou*. Cambridge, MA: Harvard University Asia Center, 2006.

Naquin, Susan, and Evelyn S. Rawski. *Chinese Society in the Eighteenth Century*. New Haven: Yale University Press, 1987.

Owen, Stephen. "Salvaging Poetry: The 'Poetic' in the Qing." In *Culture and State in Chinese History*, ed. Theodore Huters, R. Bin Wong, and Pauline Yu. Stanford: Stanford University Press, 1997, 105–125.

Platt, Stephen R. *Provincial Patriots: The Hunanese and Modern China*. Cambridge, MA: Harvard University Press, 2007.

Roddy, Stephen John. *Literati Identity and Its Fictional Representations in Late Imperial China*. Stanford: Stanford University Press, 1998.

Rolston, David L., ed. *How to Read the Chinese Novel*. Princeton: Princeton University Press, 1990.

—. *Traditional Chinese Fiction and Fiction Commentary: Reading and Writing between the Lines*. Stanford: Stanford University Press, 1997.

Ropp, Paul. *Dissent in Early Modern China: Ju-lin wai-shih and Ch'ing Social Criticism*. Ann Arbor: University of Michigan Press, 1981.

Rowe, William T. *Saving the World: Chen Hongmou and Elite Consciousness in Eighteenth-Century China*. Stanford: Stanford University Press, 2001.

Schmidt, J. D. *Harmony Garden: The Life, Literary Criticism, and Poetry of Yuan Mei (1716–1798)*. New York: RoutledgeCurzon, 2003.

Shang Wei. *Rulin waishi and Cultural Transformation in Late Imperial China*. Cambridge, MA: Harvard University Press, 2003.

Shen Fu. *Six Records of a Floating Life*. Trans. Leonard Pratt and Su-hui Chiang. Harmondsworth, Middlesex: Penguin Books, 1983.

Waley, Arthur. *Yuan Mei: Eighteenth Century Chinese Poet*. London: George Allen & Unwin Ltd, 1956.

Wan, Margaret Baptist. "The Chantefable and the Novel: The Cases of *Lümudan* and *Tianbaotu*." *Harvard Journal of Asiatic Studies* 64, no. 2 (2004): 367–388.

Widmer, Ellen. *The Beauty and the Book: Women and Fiction in Nineteenth-Century China*. Cambridge, MA: Harvard University Asia Center, 2006.

Wu Jingzi. *The Scholars*. Trans. Yang Hsien-yi and Gladys Yang. Beijing: Foreign Language Press, 1957. Repr. New York: Columbia University Press, 1992.

Yee, Angelina C. "Self, Sexuality, and Writing in *Honglou meng*." *Harvard Journal of Asiatic Studies* 55, no. 2 (1995): 373–407.

Yu, Anthony. *Rereading the Stone: Desire and the Making of Fiction in* Dream of the Red Chamber. Princeton: Princeton University Press, 1997.

Yu, Ying-shih. "The Two Worlds of *Hung-lou Meng*." *Renditions* 2 (1974): 5–21.

Zeitlin, Judith T. "Shared Dreams: The Story of the Three Wives' Commentary on *The Peony Pailion*." *Harvard Journal of Asiatic Studies* 54, no. 1 (1994): 127–179.

Chapter 5: Prosimetric and verse narrative

Altenburger, Roland. "Is It Clothes that Make the Man? Cross-dressing, Gender, and Sex in Pre-twentieth-Century Zhu Yingtai Lore." *Asian Folklore Studies* 64 (2005), 165–205.

Bender, Mark. *Plum and Bamboo: China's Suzhou Chantefable Tradition*. Urbana: University of Illinois Press, 2003.

Bender, Mark, and Victor Mair, eds. *The Columbia Reader in Chinese Folk and Popular Literature*. New York, Columbia University Press, forthcoming.

Børdahl, Vibeke, ed. *The Eternal Storyteller. Oral Literature in Modern China*. London: Curzon, 1999.

—. *The Oral Tradition of Yangzhou Storytelling*. London: Curzon, 1996.

Børdahl, Vibeke, and Kathryn Lowe, eds. *Storytelling. In Honor of Kate Stevens. Chinoperl Papers* 27 (2007).

Børdahl, Vibeke, and Jette Ross. *Chinese Storytellers: Life and Art in the Yangzhou Tradition*. Boston: Cheng and Tsui, 2002.

Chen, Li-li. *Master Tung's Western Chamber Romance (Tung Hsi-hsiang chu-kung-tiao), A Chinese Chantefable*. Cambridge: Cambridge University Press, 1976.

Chiang, William W. *We Two Know the Script; We Have Become Good Friends: Linguistic and Social Aspects of the Women's Script Literacy in Southern Hunan, China*. Lanham, MD: University Press of America, 1995.

Ding Yaokang. "Southern Window Dream." Trans. Wilt L. Idema. *Renditions* 69 (2008), 20–33.

Doleželová-Velingerová, M., and J. I. Crump. *Ballad of the Hidden Dragon: Liu Chih-yuan chu-kung-tiao*. Oxford: Clarendon Press, 1971.

Dudbridge, Glen. "The Goddess Huayue Sanniang and the Cantonese Ballad *Chenxiang Taizi*." In his *Books, Tales, and Vernacular Culture: Selected Papers on China*. Leiden: Brill, 2005, 303–320.

Eberhard, Wolfram. *Cantonese Ballads (Munich State Library Collection)*. Taipei: Oriental Cultural Service, 1972.

—. *Taiwanese Ballads: A Catalogue*. Taipei: Oriental Cultural Service, 1972.

Elliott, Mark C., trans. "The 'Eating Crabs' Youth Book." In *Under Confucian Eyes: Writings on Gender in Chinese History*, ed. Susan Mann and Yu-yin Cheng. Stanford: Stanford University Press, 2001, 263–281.

Frankel, Hans H. "The Chinese Ballad 'Southeast Fly the Peacocks.'" *Harvard Journal of Asiatic Studies* 34 (1974): 248–271.

—. "The Formulaic Language of the Chinese Ballad 'Southeast Fly the Peacocks.'" *Lishi yuyan yanjiusuo jikan (Bulletin of the Institute of History and Philology, Academia Sinica)* 39, no. 2 (1969): 219–244.

Grant, Beata. "The Spiritual Saga of Woman Huang: From Pollution to Purification." In *Ritual Opera, Operatic Ritual: "Mulian Rescues His Mother" in Chinese Popular Culture*, ed. David Johnson. Berkeley: Chinese Popular Culture Project, 1989, 224–311.

Idema, Wilt L. "Guanyin's Parrot: A Chinese Animal Tale and Its International Context." In *India, Tibet, China: Genesis and Aspects of Traditional Narrative*, ed. Alfredo Cadonna. Orientalia Venetiana VII. Florence: Leo S. Olschki Editore, 1999, 103–50.

—. *Heroines of Jiangyong: Chinese Narrative Ballads in Women's Script*. Seattle: University of Washington Press, 2009.

—. *Judge Bao and the Rule of Law: Eight Ballad Stories from the Period 1250–1450*. Singapore: World Scientific, 2009.

—. *Meng Jiangnü Brings down the Great Wall: Ten Versions of a Chinese Legend*. With an essay by Haiyan Lee. Seattle: University of Washington Press, 2008.

—. *Personal Salvation and Filial Piety: Two Precious Scroll Narratives of Guanyin and Her Acolytes.* Honolulu: University of Hawai'i Press, 2008.

—. *The White Snake and Her Son: A Translation of* The Precious Scroll of Thunder Peak, *with Related Texts.* Cambridge, MA: Hackett, 2009.

Idema, Wilt L., and Beata Grant. *The Red Brush: Writing Women of Imperial China.* Cambridge, MA: Harvard University Asia Center, 2004.

Johnson, David. "Mu-lien in *Pao-chüan*: The Performance Context and the Religious Meaning of the *Yu-ming pao-ch'uan.*" In *Ritual and Scripture in Chinese Popular Religion: Five Studies,* ed. David Johnson. Berkeley: Chinese Popular Culture Project, 1995, 55–103.

King, Gail Oman, trans. *The Story of Hua Guan Suo.* Tempe: Center for Asian Studies, Arizona State University, 1989.

Leung, K. C. "Chinese Courtship: The *Huajian ji* in English Translation." *Chinoperl Papers* 20–22 (1997–99): 269–288.

Liu, Lydia H. "A Folksong Immortal and Official Popular Culture in Twentieth-Century China." In *Writing and Materiality in China: Essays in Honor of Patrick Hanan,* ed. Judith Zeitlin, Lydia Liu, and Ellen Widmer. Cambridge, MA: Harvard University Asia Center, 2003, 553–609.

McLaren, Anne E. *Chinese Popular Culture and Ming Chantefables.* Leiden: Brill, 1998.

Mair, Victor H. *T'ang Transformation Texts: A Study of the Buddhist Contribution to the Rise of Vernacular Fiction and Drama in China.* Cambridge, MA: Harvard University Press, 1989.

Overmyer, Daniel L. *Precious Volumes: An Introduction to Chinese Sectarian Scriptures from the Sixteenth and Seventeenth Centuries.* Cambridge, MA: Harvard University Asia Center, 1999.

Pian, Rulan Chao. "The Use of Music as a Narrative Device in the Medley Song: The Courtesan's Jewel Box." *Chinoperl Papers* 9 (1979–1980): 9–31.

Pimpaneau, Jacques. *Chanteurs, conteurs, bateleurs.* Paris: Université Paris 7, Centre de publications Asie Orientale, 1977.

Průšek, Jaroslav. "Chui-tzŭ-shu – Folk-Songs from Ho-nan." In his *Chinese History and Literature.* Prague: Academia, 1970, 170–198.

Qiu Jin, "Excerpts of *Stone of the Jingwei Bird.*" In *Writing Women in Modern China: An Anthology of Women's Literature from the Early Twentieth Century,* ed. Amy Dooling and Kristina M. Torgesen. New York: Columbia University Press, 1998, 39–78.

Scott, Mary, trans. "Three *Zidishu* on *Jin Ping Mei,* By Han Xiaochuang." *Renditions* 44 (1995): 33–65.

Shi Yukun and Yu Yue. *The Seven Heroes and Five Gallants.* Trans. Song Shouquan. Beijing: Chinese Literature Press, 1997.

Stent, George Carter. *Entombed Alive and Other Songs, Ballads, Etc. (from the Chinese).* London: William H. Allen, 1878.

—. *The Jade Chaplet in Twenty-four Beads: A Collection of Songs, Ballads, Etc. (from the Chinese).* London: Trübner and Co., 1874.

Stevens, Kate. "The Slopes of Changban: A Beijing Drumsong in the Liu Style." *Chinoperl Papers* 15 (1990): 69–79.

Sung, Marina H. *The Narrative Art of Tsai-sheng-yüan: A Feminist Vision in Traditional Chinese Society.* Taipei: CMT Publications, 1994.

Thoms, Peter Perring. *Chinese Courtship, In Verse*. London: Parbury, Allen and Kingsbury, 1824.

Wan, Margaret Baptist. "The *Chantefable* and the Novel: The Cases of *Lümudan* and *Tianbaotu*." *Harvard Journal of Asiatic Studies* 64, no. 2 (2004): 367–388.

Widmer, Ellen. *The Beauty and the Book: Women and Fiction in Nineteenth-Century China*. Cambridge, MA: Harvard University Asia Center, 2006.

Wimsatt, Genevieve, and Geoffrey Chen, trans. *Meng Chiang Nü (Chinese Drum Song), The Lady of the Long Wall: A Ku Shi or Drum Song from China*. New York: Columbia University Press, 1934.

Chapter 6: Chinese literature from 1841 to 1937

A Selective Guide to Chinese Literature, 1900–1949, Vol. 1: The Novel, ed. Milena Doleželová-Velingerová. Leiden: Brill, 1988.

A Selective Guide to Chinese Literature, 1900–1949, Vol. 2: The Short Story, ed. Zbigniew Slupski. Leiden: Brill, 1988.

A Selective Guide to Chinese Literature, 1900–1949, Vol. 3: The Poem, ed. Lloyd Haft. Leiden: Brill, 1989.

A Selective Guide to Chinese Literature, 1900–1949, Vol. 4: The Drama, ed. Bernd Eberstein. Leiden: Brill, 1990.

Acton, Harold, and Ch'en Shi-hsiang, trans. *Modern Chinese Poetry*. London: Duckworth, 1936.

Anderson, Marston. *The Limits of Realism: Chinese Fiction in the Revolutionary Period*. Berkeley: University of California Press, 1990.

Braester, Yomi. *Witness against History: Literature, Film, and Public Discourse in Twentieth-Century China*. Stanford: Stanford University Press, 2003.

Chang, Hao. *Chinese Intellectuals in Crisis: Search for Order and Meaning (1890–1911)*. Berkeley: University of California Press, 1987.

Chow, Rey. *Woman and Chinese Modernity: The Politics of Reading between West and East*. Minneapolis: University of Minnesota Press, 1990.

Daruvala, Susan. *Zhou Zuoren and an Alternative Chinese Response to Modernity*. Cambridge, MA: Harvard University Asia Center, 2000.

Denton, Kirk, ed. *Modern Chinese Literary Thought: Writings on Literature, 1893–1945*. Stanford: University of Stanford Press, 1996.

Denton, Kirk A., and Michel Hockx, eds. *Literary Societies of Republican China*. Lanham, MD: Lexington Books, 2008.

Dikötter, Frank. *Exotic Commodities: Modern Objects and Everyday Life in China*. New York: Columbia University Press, 2006.

Doleželová-Velingerová, Milena, ed. *The Chinese Novel at the Turn of the Century*. Toronto: University of Toronto Press, 1980.

Doleželová-Velingerová, Milena, and Oldřich Král, eds. *The Appropriation of Cultural Capital: China's May Fourth Project*. Cambridge, MA: Harvard University Asia Center, 2001.

Dooling, Amy D. *Women's Literary Feminism in Twentieth-Century China*. New York: Palgrave Macmillan, 2005.

Dooling, Amy D., and Torgeson, Kristina M., eds. *Writing Women in Modern China: An Anthology of Women's Literature from the Early Twentieth Century*. New York: Columbia University Press, 1998.

Eber, Irene. *Voices from Afar: Modern Chinese Writers on Oppressed Peoples and Their Literature*. Ann Arbor: Center for Chinese Studies, University of Michigan, 1980.

Elman, Benjamin. *On Their Own Terms: Science in China, 1550–1900*. Cambridge, MA: Harvard University Press, 2005.

Galik, Marian, ed. *Interliterary and Intraliterary Aspects of the May Fourth Movement 1919 in China*. Bratislava: Veda, 1990.

Gimpel, Denise. *Lost Voices of Modernity: A Chinese Popular Fiction Magazine in Context*. Honolulu: University of Hawai'i Press, 2001.

Goldman, Merle, ed. *Modern Chinese Literature in the May Fourth Era*. Cambridge, MA: Harvard University Press, 1977.

Gunn, Edward M. *Rewriting Chinese: Style and Innovation in Twentieth-Century Chinese Prose*. Stanford: Stanford University Press, 1991.

Han Bangqing. *The Sing-Song Girls of Shanghai*. Trans. Eileen Chang. Rev. and ed. by Eva Hung. New York: Columbia University Press, 2005.

Hanan, Patrick. *Chinese Fiction of the Nineteenth and Early Twentieth Centuries: Essays*. New York: Columbia University Press, 2004.

Hockx, Michel. *Questions of Style: Literary Societies and Literary Journals in Modern China, 1911–1937*. Leiden: Brill, 2003.

Hsia, C. T. *A History of Modern Chinese Fiction*. New Haven: Yale University Press, 1971.

—. *C. T. Hsia on Chinese Literature*. New York: Columbia University Press, 2004.

Hsia, T. A., *The Gate of Darkness: Studies of the Leftist Literary Movement in China*. Seattle: University of Washington Press, 1968.

Hu, Ying. *Tales of Translation: Composing the New Woman in China, 1898–1918*. Stanford: Stanford University Press, 2000.

Huang, Nicole X. *Women, War, Domesticity: Shanghai Literature and Popular Culture of the 1940s*. Leiden: Brill, 2005.

Huters, Theodore. *Bringing the World Home: Appropriating the West in Late Qing and Early Republican China*. Honolulu: University of Hawai'i Press, 2005.

Karl, Rebecca E., and Peter Zarrow, eds. *Rethinking the 1898 Reform Period: Political and Cultural Change in Late Qing China*. Cambridge, MA: Harvard University Asia Center, 2002.

Keulemans, Paize. "Listening to the Printed Martial Arts Scene: Onomatopoeia and the Qing Dynasty Storyteller's Voice." *Harvard Journal of Asiatic Studies* 67, no. 1 (2007): 51–87.

Kinkley, Jeffery C. *The Odyssey of Shen Congwen*. Stanford: Stanford University Press, 1987.

Kowallis, Jon. *The Subtle Revolution: Poets of the "Old Schools" during Late Qing and Early Republican China*. Berkeley: Center for Chinese Studies, University of California, 2006.

Lackner, Michael, Iwo Amelung, and Joachim Kurtz, eds. *New Terms for New Ideas: Western Knowledge and Lexical Change in Late Imperial China*. Leiden: Brill, 2001.

Larson, Wendy. *Literary Authority and the Modern Chinese Writer: Ambivalence and Autobiography*. Durham, NC: Duke University Press, 1991.

—. *Women and Writing in Modern China*. Stanford: Stanford University Press, 1998.

Lau, Joseph S. M., and Howard Goldblatt, eds. *The Columbia Anthology of Modern Chinese Literature*. New York: Columbia University Press, 1995.

Lau, Joseph S. M., C. T. Hsia, and Leo Ou-fan Lee, eds. *Modern Chinese Stories and Novellas, 1919–1949*. New York: Columbia University Press, 1981.

Laughlin, Charles A. *Chinese Reportage: The Aesthetics of Historical Experience*. Durham, NC: Duke University Press, 2002.

—. *The Literature of Leisure and Chinese Modernity*. Honolulu: University of Hawai'i Press, 2008.

Lee, Haiyan. *Revolution of the Heart: A Genealogy of Love in China, 1900–1950*. Stanford: Stanford University Press, 2006.

Lee, Leo Ou-fan. *The Romantic Generation of Modern Chinese Writers*. Cambridge, MA: Harvard University Press, 1973.

—. *Shanghai Modern: The Flowering of a New Urban Culture in China, 1930–1945*. Cambridge, MA: Harvard University Press, 1999.

—. *Voices from the Iron House: A Study of Lu Xun*. Bloomington: Indiana University Press, 1987.

Link, Perry. *Mandarin Ducks and Butterflies: Popular Fiction in Early Twentieth-Century Chinese Cities*. Berkeley: University of California Press, 1981.

Liu, Lydia He, ed. *Tokens of Exchange: The Problem of Translation in Global Circulations*. Durham, NC: Duke University Press, 1999.

—. *Translingual Practice: Literature, National Culture, and Translated Modernity – China, 1900–1937*. Stanford: Stanford University Press, 1995.

McDougall, Bonnie S. *Fictional Authors, Imaginary Audiences: Modern Chinese Literature in the Twentieth Century*. Hong Kong: The Chinese University Press, 2003.

McDougall, Bonnie S., and Kam Louie. *The Literature of China in the Twentieth Century*. London: Hurst, and New York: Columbia University Press, 1997.

McLaren, Anne E. *Performing Grief: Bridal Laments in Rural China*. Honolulu: University of Hawai'i Press, 2008.

Modern Chinese Literature and Culture Resource Center. http://mclc.osu.edu.

Mostow, Joshua, ed. *The Columbia Companion to Modern East Asian Literature*. New York: Columbia University Press, 2003.

Pollard, David. *The Chinese Essay*. New York: Columbia University Press, 2000.

—, ed. *Translation and Creation: Readings of Western Literature in Early Modern China, 1840–1918*. Philadelphia: J. Benjamins, 1998.

Průšek, Jaroslav. *The Lyrical and the Epic: Studies of Modern Chinese Literature*. Ed. Leo Ou-fan Lee. Bloomington: Indiana University Press, 1981.

Rankin, Mary. *Early Chinese Revolutionaries: Radical Intellectuals in Shanghai and Chekiang, 1902–1911*. Cambridge, MA: Harvard University Press, 1971.

Reed, Christopher A. *Gutenberg in Shanghai: Chinese Print Capitalism, 1876–1937*. Vancouver and Toronto: UBC Press, 2004.

Semanov, V. I. *Lu Hsun and His Predecessors*. Trans. Charles J. Alber. New York: M. E. Sharpe, 1980.

Shih, Shu-mei. *The Lure of the Modern: Writing Modernism in Semi-colonial China*. Los Angeles and Berkeley: University of California Press, 2001.

Starr, Chloë F. *Red-Light Novels of the Late Qing*. Leiden: Brill, 2007.

Tang, Xiaobing. *Chinese Modern: The Heroic and the Quotidian*. Durham, NC: Duke University Press, 2000.

Tsu, Jing. *Failure, Nationalism, and Literature: The Making of Modern Chinese Identity, 1895–1937*. Stanford: Stanford University Press, 2005.

Wang, Ban. *The Sublime Figure of History: Aesthetics and Politics in Twentieth-Century China*. Stanford: Stanford University Press, 1997.

Wang, David Der-wei. *Fin-de-Siècle Splendor: Repressed Modernities of Late Qing Fiction, 1849–1911*. Stanford: Stanford University Press, 1997.

Wang, David Der-wei, and Shang Wei, eds. *Dynastic Crisis and Cultural Innovation: From the Late Ming to the Late Qing and Beyond*. Cambridge, MA: Harvard University Asia Center, 2005.

Wong, Timothy C., trans. *Stories for Saturday: Twentieth-Century Chinese Popular Fiction*. Honolulu: University of Hawai'i Press, 2003.

Wong, Wang-chi. *Politics and Literature in Shanghai: The Chinese League of Left-Wing Writers, 1930–1936*. Manchester: Manchester University Press, 1991.

Wright, David. *Translating Science: The Translation of Western Chemistry into Late Imperial China, 1840–1900*. Leiden: Brill, 2000.

Yeh, Catherine Vance. *Shanghai Love: Courtesans, Intellectuals, and Entertainment Culture, 1850–1911*. Seattle: University of Washington Press, 2006.

Yeh, Michelle, ed. and trans. *Anthology of Modern Chinese Poetry*. 2nd edn. New Haven: Yale University Press, 2003.

—. *Modern Chinese Poetry: Theory and Practice since 1917*. New Haven: Yale University Press, 1991.

Zeitlin, Judith T., Lydia Liu, and Ellen Widmer, eds. *Writing and Materiality in China: Essays in Honor of Patrick Hanan*. Cambridge, MA: Harvard University Asia Center, 2003.

Chapter 7: Chinese literature from 1937 to the present

Ah Lai (Alai). *Red Poppies*. Trans. Howard Goldblatt and Sylvia Li-chun Lin. Boston: Houghton Mifflin, 2002.

Ba Jin. *Cold Nights*. Trans. Nathan Mao and Liu T'sun-yan. Hong Kong: Chinese University of Hong Kong Press, 1978.

—. *Random thoughts*. Trans. Geremie Barmé. Hong Kong: Joint Publishing Company, 1984.

—. *Ward Four: A Novel of Wartime China*. Trans. Haili Kong and Howard Goldblatt. San Francisco: China Books and Periodicals, 1999.

Balcom, John, and Yingtsih Balcom, eds. and trans. *Indigenous Writers of Taiwan: An Anthology of Stories, Essays, and Poems*. New York: Columbia University Press, 2005.

Barnstone, Tony, ed. *Out of the Howling Storm: The New Chinese Poetry*. Middletown, CT: Wesleyan University Press, 1993.

Bei Dao. *Landscape over Zero*. Trans. David Hinton and Yanbing Chen. London: Anvil Press, 1998.

—. *Unlock: Poems*. Trans. Eliot Weinberger and Iona Man-Cheong. London: Anvil Press, 2006.

—. *Waves: Stories*. Trans. Bonnie S. McDougall and Susette Ternent Cooke. New York: New Directions, 1990.

Braester, Yomi. *Witness against History: Literature, Film, and Public Discourse in Twentieth-Century China*. Stanford: Stanford University Press, 2003.

Can Xue. *Old Floating Cloud: Two Novellas*. Trans. Ronald R. Janssen and Jian Zhang. Foreword by Charlotte Innes. Evanston: Northwestern University Press, 1991.

Carver, Ann C., and Sung-sheng Yvonne Chang, eds. *Bamboo Shoots after the Rain: Contemporary Stories by Women Writers of Taiwan*. New York: Feminist Press at the City University of New York, 1990.

Cha, Louis (Jin Yong). *The Book and the Sword: A Martial Arts Novel*. Trans. Graham Earnshaw. Ed. Rachel May and John Minford. New York: Oxford University Press, 2004.

—. *The Deer and the Cauldron: The Adventures of a Chinese Trickster*. Trans. John Minford. Australia: Institute of Advanced Studies, Australia National University, 1994.

Chang, Eileen. *Love in a Fallen City*. Trans. Karen Kingsbury and Eileen Chang. New York: New York Review of Books, 2007.

—. *Lust, Caution*. Trans. and with a foreword by Julia Lovell. Afterword by Ang Lee. With a special essay by James Schamus. New York: Anchor Books, 2007.

—. *The Rice-Sprout Song: A Novel of Modern China*. Berkeley: University of California Press, 1998.

—. *The Rouge of the North*. Berkeley: University of California Press, 1998.

—. *Traces of Love and Other Stories*. Ed. Eva Hung. Hong Kong: The Chinese University of Hong Kong Press, 2000.

—. *Written on Water*. Trans. Andrew F. Jones. Ed. Andrew Jones and Nicole Huang. New York: Columbia University Press, 2005.

Chang Hsi-kuo (Zhang Xiguo). *The City Trilogy*. Trans. John Balcom. New York: Columbia University Press, 2003.

Chang, Kang-i Sun. *Journey through the White Terror: A Daughter's Memoir*. Taipei: National Taiwan University Press, 2006.

—. "What Happened to Lü Heruo (1914–1951) after the February 28th Incident?" In *Taiwan and Its Context*, ed. Ping-hui Liao, Kang-i Sun Chang, and David Der-wei Wang, forthcoming.

Chang, Sung-cheng Yvonne. *Modernism and the Nativist Resistance: Contemporary Fiction from Taiwan*. Durham, NC: Duke University Press, 1993.

Chang Ta-chun (Zhang Dachun). *Wild Kids: Two Novels about Growing Up*. Trans. Michael Berry. New York: Columbia University Press, 2000.

Chen Ruoxi. *The Execution of Mayor Yin and Other Stories from the Great Proletarian Cultural Revolution*. Ed. Howard Goldblatt. Trans. Nancy Ing and Howard Goldblatt. Bloomington: Indiana University Press, 2004.

Chen, Xiaomei, ed. *Reading the Right Text: An Anthology of Contemporary Chinese Drama*. Honolulu: University of Hawai'i Press, 2003.

Ch'en Ying-chen (Chen Yingzhen). *Exiles at Home: Short Stories*. Trans. Lucien Miller. Ann Arbor: Center for Chinese Studies, University of Michigan, 1986.

Cheung, Dominic, ed. and trans. *The Isle Full of Noises: Modern Chinese Poetry from Taiwan*. New York: Columbia University Press, 1987.

Chi, Pang-yuan, and David Der-wei Wang, eds. *The Last of the Whampoa Breed: Stories of Chinese Diaspora*. New York: Columbia University Press, 2003.

Chow, Rey, ed. *Modern Chinese Literary and Cultural Studies in the Age of Theory: Reimagining a Field*. Durham, NC: Duke University Press, 2000.

Chu T'ien-hsin (Zhu Tianxin). *The Old Capital: A Novel of Taipei*. Trans. Howard Goldblatt. New York: Columbia University Press, 2007.

Chu T'ien-wen (Zhu Tianwen). *Notes of a Desolate Man*. Trans. Howard Goldblatt and Sylvia Lizhun Lin. New York: Columbia University Press, 1999.

Dooling, Amy D. *Women's Literary Feminism in Twentieth-Century China*. New York: Palgrave Macmillan, 2005.

Duke, Michael S. *Blooming and Contending: Chinese Literature in the Post-Mao Era*. Bloomington: Indiana University Press, 1985.

—, ed. *Contemporary Chinese Literature: An Anthology of Post-Mao Fiction and Poetry*. Armonk, NY: M. E. Sharpe, 1985.

Duo Duo (Duoduo). *The Boy Who Catches Wasps*. Trans. Gregory B. Lee. Brookline, MA: Zephyr Press, 2002.

—. *Looking Out from Death: From the Cultural Revolution to Tiananmen Square*. Trans. Gregory Lee and John Cayley. London: Bloomsbury, 1989.

Feng Jicai. *The Three-Inch Golden Lotus*. Trans. David Wakefield. Honolulu: University of Hawai'i Press, 1994.

Finkel, Donald, trans. *A Splintered Mirror: Chinese Poetry from the Democracy Movement*. San Francisco: North Point Press, 1991.

Goldblatt, Howard, ed. *Chairman Mao Would Not Be Amused: Fiction from Today's China*. New York: Grove Press, 1995.

Gu Cheng. *Sea of Dreams: Selected Writings of Gu Cheng*. Trans. Joseph R. Allen. New York: New Directions, 2005.

—. *Selected Poems*. Trans. Sean Golden and Chu Chiyu. Hong Kong: Research Centre for Translation, the Chinese University of Hong Kong, 1990.

Gunn, Edward, ed. *Twentieth-Century Chinese Drama: An Anthology*. Bloomington: Indiana University Press, 1983.

—. *Unwelcome Muse: Chinese Literature in Shanghai and Peking, 1937–1945*. New York: Columbia University Press, 1980.

Hockx, Michel, and Julia Strauss. *Culture in the Contemporary PRC*. Cambridge: Cambridge University Press, 2005.

Hsia Yü (Xia Yu). *Fusion Kitsch: Poems from the Chinese of Hsia Yü*. Trans. Steve Bradbury. Brookline, MA: Zephyr Press, 2001.

Hsu, Kai-yu. *Literature of the People's Republic of China*. Bloomington: Indiana University Press, 1980.

—, ed. and trans. *Twentieth-Century Chinese Poetry: An Anthology*. Garden City, NY: Doubleday, 1963.

Huang Chun-ming (Huang Chunming). *The Drowning of an Old Cat and Other Stories*. Trans. Howard Goldblatt. Bloomington: Indiana University Press, 1980.

—. *The Taste of Apples*. Trans. Howard Goldblatt. New York: Columbia University Press, 2001.

Huang Xiang. *A Lifetime Is a Promise to Keep: Poems of Huang Xiang*. Trans. Michelle Yeh. Berkeley: University of California, Institute of East Asian Studies, 2008.

Hughes, Christopher, and Gudrun Wacker, eds. *China and the Internet: Politics and the Digital Leap Forward*. London and New York: RoutledgeCurzon, 2003.

Hung, Eva, ed. *Contemporary Women Writers: Hong Kong and Taiwan*. Hong Kong: Research Centre for Translation, Chinese University of Hong Kong, 1990.

Jia Pingwa. *Turbulence*. Trans. Howard Goldblatt. Baton Rouge: Louisiana State University Press, 1991.

Kong, Shuyu. *Consuming Literature: Best Sellers and the Commercialization of Literary Production in Contemporary China*. Stanford: Stanford University Press, 2004.

Lai Tse-han, Ramon H. Myers, and Wei Wou. *A Tragic Beginning: The Taiwan Uprising of February 28, 1947*. Stanford: Stanford University Press, 1991.

Lao She. *Blades of Grass: The Stories of Lao She*. Trans. William A. Lyell and Sarah Wei-ming Chen. Honolulu: University of Hawai'i Press, 1999.

Lau, Joseph S. M., ed. *Chinese Stories from Taiwan, 1960–1970*. New York: Columbia University Press, 1976.

—, ed. *The Unbroken Chain: An Anthology of Taiwan Fiction since 1926*. Bloomington: Indiana University Press, 1983.

Lau, Joseph S. M., and Howard Goldblatt, eds. *The Columbia Anthology of Modern Chinese Literature*. New York: Columbia University Press, 1996.

Lau, Joseph S. M., C. T. Hsia, and Leo Ou-fan Lee, eds. *Modern Chinese Stories and Novellas, 1919–1949*. New York: Columbia University Press, 1981.

Lee, Gregory. *Dai Wangshu: The Life and Poetry of a Chinese Modernist*. Hong Kong: The Chinese University Press, 1989.

Lee, Leo Ou-fan. *Shanghai Modern: The Flowering of a New Urban Culture in China, 1930–1945*. Cambridge, MA: Harvard University Press, 1999.

Leung Ping-kwan (Liang Bingjun). *Islands and Continents: Short Stories*. Trans. John Minford, with Brian Holton and Agnes Hung-chong Chan. Hong Kong: Hong Kong University Press, 2007.

Li Ang. *The Butcher's Wife and Other Stories*. Ed. and trans. Howard Goldblatt. Boston, MA: Cheng & Tsui Company, 1995.

Li Qiao. *Wintry Night*. Trans. Taotao Liu and John Balcom. New York: Columbia University Press, 2001.

Li Rui. *Silver City*. Trans. Howard Goldblatt. New York: Metropolitan Books, 1997.

Li Yung-p'ing (Li Yongping). *Retribution: The Jiling Chronicles*. Trans. Howard Goldblatt and Sylvia Li-chun Lin. New York: Columbia University Press, 2003.

Liao, Ping-hui, and David Wang, eds. *Taiwan under Japanese Colonial Rule, 1895–1945*. New York: Columbia University Press, 2006.

Lin, Yutang. *Moment in Peking: A Novel of Contemporary Chinese Life*. New York: The John Day Company, 1939.

—. *My Country and My People*. London: W. Heinemann, 1939.

Link, Perry, ed. *Roses and Thorns: The Second Blooming of the Hundred Flowers in Chinese Fiction, 1979–1980*. Berkeley: University of California Press, 1984.

—. *The Uses of Literature: Life in the Socialist Chinese Literary System*. Princeton: Princeton University Press, 2000.

Liu Binyan. *Two Kinds of Truth: Stories and Reportage from China*. Ed. Perry Link. Bloomington: Indiana University Press, 2006.

Liu Jianmei. *Revolution Plus Love*. Honolulu: University of Hawai'i Press, 2003.

Lu, Jie. *China's Literary and Cultural Scenes at the Turn of the 21st Century*. London: Routledge, 2007.

McDougall, Bonnie S., and Kam Louie. *The Literature of China in the Twentieth Century*. London: Hurst, and New York: Columbia University Press, 1997.

Mengin, Françoise, ed. *Cyber China: Reshaping National Identities in the Age of Information*. New York: Palgrave Macmillan, 2004.

Mo Yan. *Big Breasts and Wide Hips*. Trans. Howard Goldblatt. New York: Arcade Publishing, 2004.

—. *Red Sorghum: A Novel of China*. Trans. Howard Goldblatt. New York: Viking, 1993.

Modern Chinese Literature and Culture Resource Center. http://mclc.osu.edu.

Pai, Hsien-yung (Bai Xianyong). *Crystal Boys*. Trans. Howard Goldblatt. San Francisco: Gay Sunshine Press, 1995.

—. *Wandering in the Garden, Waking from a Dream: Tales of Taipei Characters*. Trans. Hsien-yung Pai and Patia Yasin. Ed. George Kao. Bloomington: Indiana University Press, 1982.

Qian Zhongshu. *Fortress Besieged*. Trans. Jeanne Kelly and Nathan K. Mao. Foreword by Jonathan Spence. New York: New Directions, 2004.

—. *Limited Views: Essays on Ideas and Letters*. Trans. Ronald Egan. Cambridge, MA: Harvard University Asia Center, 1998.

Shang Qin. *Feelings above Sea Level: Prose Poems from the Chinese of Shang Qin*. Trans. Steve Bradbury. Brookline, MA: Zephyr Press, 2006.

Shen Congwen. *Imperfect Paradise*. Trans. Jeffrey Kinkley. Honolulu: University of Hawai'i Press, 1995.

Shih Shu-ching (Shi Shuqing). *City of the Queen: A Novel of Colonial Hong Kong*. Trans. Sylvia Li-chun Lin and Howard Goldblatt. New York: Columbia University Press, 2005.

Su Tong. *My Life as Emperor*. Trans. Howard Goldblatt. New York: Hyperion East, 2005.

—. *Rice*. Trans. Howard Goldblatt. New York: W. Morrow and Company, 1995.

Wang Anyi. *Baotown*. Trans. Martha Avery. New York: W. W. Norton, 1989.

—. *Love in a Small Town*. Trans. Eva Hung. Hong Kong: Research Centre for Translation, Chinese University of Hong Kong, 1988.

—. *Love on a Barren Mountain*. Trans. Eva Hung. Hong Kong: Research Centre for Translation, Chinese University of Hong Kong, 1991.

—. *The Song of the Everlasting Sorrow*. Trans. Michael Berry and Susan Chan Egan. New York: Columbia University Press, 2008.

Wang Ban. *Illuminations from the Past: Trauma, Memory, and History in Modern China*. Stanford: Stanford University Press, 2004.

Wang Chen-ho (Wang Zhenhe). *Rose, Rose, I Love You*. Trans. Howard Goldblatt. New York: Columbia University Press, 1998.

Wang, David Der-wei. *The Monster that Is History: History, Violence, and Fictional Writing in Twentieth-Century China*. Berkeley: University of California Press, 2004.

—. *Running Wild: New Chinese Writers*. New York: Columbia University Press, 1994.

Wang, David Der-wei, and Carlos Rojas, eds. *Writing Taiwan: A New Literary History*. Durham, NC and London: Duke University Press, 2007.

Wang, Jing, ed. *China's Avant-Garde Fiction: An Anthology*. Durham, NC: Duke University Press, 1998.

Wang, Lingzhen. *Personal Matters: Women's Autobiographical Practice in Twentieth-Century China*. Stanford: Stanford University Press, 2004.

Wei Hui. *Shanghai Baby*. Trans. Bruce Humes. New York: Pocket Books, 2001.

Xi Xi. *A Girl Like Me, and Other Stories*. Trans. Stephen C. Soong. Hong Kong: Research Centre for Translation, Chinese University of Hong Kong, 1986.

—. *My City: A Hong Kong Story*. Trans. Eva Hung. Illustrations by Xi Xi. Hong Kong: Research Centre for Translation, the Chinese University of Hong Kong, 1993.

Xiao Hong. *Tales of Hulan River*. Trans. Howard Goldblatt. Hong Kong: Joint Publishing, 1988.

Yang Mu. *No Trace of the Gardener: Poems of Yang Mu*. Trans. Lawrence R. Smith and Michelle Yeh. New Haven: Yale University Press, 1998.

Yang Mu, and Lo Ch'ing (Luo Qing). *Forbidden Games and Video Poems: The Poetry of Yang Mu and Lo Ch'ing*. Trans. Joseph R. Allen. Seattle: University of Washington Press, 1993.

Ye Zhaoyan. *Nanking 1937: A Love Story*. Trans. and with an Afterword by Michael Berry. New York: Anchor Books, 2002.

Yeh, Michelle, ed. and trans. *Anthology of Modern Chinese Poetry*. 2nd edn. New Haven: Yale University Press, 2003.

—. *Modern Chinese Poetry: Theory and Practice since 1917*. New Haven: Yale University Press, 1991.

Yeh, Michelle, and N. G. D. Malmqvist, eds. *Frontier Taiwan: An Anthology of Modern Chinese Poetry*. New York: Columbia University Press, 2001.

Yeh, Michelle, N. G. D. Malmqvist, and Xu Huizhi, eds. *Sailing to Formosa: A Poetic Companion to Taiwan*. Seattle: University of Washington Press, 2006.

Yu Hua. *Chronicle of a Blood Merchant*. Trans. Andrew F. Jones. New York: Anchor Books, 2003.

—. *To Live*. Trans. Michael Berry. New York: Anchor Books, 2003.

Zheng Qingwen. *Three-Legged Horse*. Ed. Pang-yuan Chi. New York: Columbia University Press, 1999.

Epilogue: Sinophone writings and the Chinese diaspora

Chang, Eileen. *The Rouge of the North*. Berkeley: University of California Press, 1998.

Chang, Sung-cheng Yvonne. *Modernism and the Nativist Resistance: Contemporary Fiction from Taiwan*. Durham, NC: Duke University Press, 1993.

Chi, Pang-yuan, and David Wang, eds. *Chinese Literature in the Second Half of the Twentieth Century: A Critical Survey*. Bloomington: Indiana University Press, 2000.

Chow, Rey, ed. *Modern Chinese Literary and Cultural Studies in the Age of Theory: Reimagining a Field*. Durham, NC: Duke University Press, 2000.

De Francis, John. *Nationalism and Language Reform in China*. Princeton: Princeton University Press, 1950.

Gao, Xingjian. *Soul Mountain*. Trans. Mabel Lee. New York: HarperCollins Publishers, 2000.

Gunn, Edward M. *Rendering the Regional: Local Language in Contemporary Chinese Media*. Honolulu: University of Hawai'i Press, 2005.

Hassan, Abdullah. *Language Planning in Southeast Asia*. Kuala Lumpur: Dewan Bahasa dan Pustaka, Ministry of Education, 1994.

Li Yung-ping (Li Yongping). *Retribution: The Jiling Chronicles*. Trans. Howard Goldblatt and Sylvia Li-chun Lin. New York: Columbia University Press, 2003.

Liao, Ping-hui, Kang-i Sun Chang, and David Der-wei Wang, eds. *Taiwan and Its Contexts*, forthcoming.

Nieh, Hualing. *Mulberry and Peach*. Trans. Jane Parish Yang and Linda Lappin. New York: Feminist Press, 1998.

Shih, Shumei. *Visuality and Identity: Sinophone Articulations across the Pacific*. Berkeley: University of California Press, 2007.

Tsu, Jing, and David Der-wei Wang, eds. *Globalizing Chinese Literature: Critical Essays*. Brill, forthcoming.

Wang, David Der-wei. *The Monster that Is History: History, Violence, and Fictional Writing in Twentieth-Century China*. Berkeley: University of California Press, 2004.

Wang, David Der-wei, and Carlos Rojas, eds. *Writing Taiwan: A New Literary History*. Durham, NC and London: Duke University Press, 2007.

Wang, Gungwu. *Chinese Overseas: From Earthbound China to the Quest for Autonomy*. Cambridge, MA: Harvard University Press, 2000.

Wang Ning, ed. *China in the Twentieth Century*. Special Issue of *Modern Language Quarterly* 69, no. 1 (2008).

Yin, Xiao-huang. *Chinese American Literature since the 1850s*. Urbana: University of Illinois Press, 2000.

Zhang Er and Chen Dongdong, eds. *Talisman Anthology of Contemporary Chinese Poetry*. Jersey City, NJ: Talisman House Publishers, 2007.

Zhang Guixing. *My South Seas Sleeping Beauty: A Tale of Memory and Longing*. New York: Columbia University Press, 2007.

Glossary

Adou 阿斗
Ah Cheng 阿城 (Zhong Acheng 鍾阿城)
Ah Long 阿壠
Ah Q zhengzhuan 阿Q正傳
Ah Sheng 阿盛
Ah Ying 阿英
Ai Bei 艾蓓
Ai Nanying 艾南英
Ai Qing 艾青
Ai Wu 艾蕪
Ai Ya 愛亞
Aina Jushi 艾納居士
Alai 阿來
Amei 阿美
An Lushan 安祿山
Anbang zhi 安邦志
Anni baobei 安妮寶貝
antou ju 案頭劇
Ba Jin 巴金
bagu wen 八股文
bai 白
Bai Chongxi 白崇禧
Bai Hua 白樺
Bai Juyi 白居易
Bai Lian 白蓮
Bai Ling 白靈 (Zhuang Zuhuang 莊祖煌)
Bai Pu 白樸
Bai Qiu 白萩 (He Jinrong 何錦榮)
Bai Wei 白薇
Bai Xianyong 白先勇 (Hsien-yung Pai; Kenneth Pai)
Bai Yuru 白彧如
Bai Zaimei 白在眉
Bainian yijiao 百年一覺

Baise kongbu 白色恐怖
Baishe zhuan tanci 白蛇傳彈詞
Baitu ji 白兔記
Baixue yiyin 白雪遺音
Baiyangdian 白洋淀
balimen 巴力門 (parliament)
Ban Chao 班超
bangzi xi 梆子戲
Banqiao zaji 板橋雜記
banzhu 班主 or 斑竹
Bao Diao 保釣
Bao Jialin 鮑家麟
Bao Tianxiao 包天笑
Bao Zheng 包拯 (Judge Bao)
Baoen yuan 報恩猿
baogao wenxue 報告文學
Baojian ji 寶劍記
baojuan 寶卷
baqi zidi 八旗子弟
Bashiri huanyou ji 八十日環遊記
Bei Cun 北村
Bei Dao 北島 (Ai Shan 艾珊; Zhao Zhenkai 趙振開)
Beidahuang 北大荒
Beijing zhi chun 北京之春
Beiyou ji 北遊記
benshengren 本省人
bentuxing 本土性
Bi Ruxie 畢汝協
Bi sheng hua 筆生花
Bi Yuan 畢沅
Bian er chai 弁而釵
Bian Gong 邊貢
Bian Sai 卞賽

740

Bian Zhilin 卞之琳
Biancheng 邊城
biao 表
Biaoyan gongzuofang 表演工作坊
Biheguan Zhuren 碧荷館主人
biji 筆記
Bimu yu 比目魚
Bing Xin 冰心
Bingtian shishe 冰天詩社
Bishenghua 筆生花
Bo Yang 柏楊 (Guo Yidong 郭衣洞)
Bo Yun 薄雲
boliang 柏梁
boxue hongci ke 博學鴻詞科
Boyi 伯夷
Cai Qijiao 蔡其矯
Cai Yan 蔡琰
Cai Yuanpei 蔡元培
Cai Zhifeng 蔡志峰
Cai Zhiheng 蔡智恒
caizi shu 才子書
Can Xue 殘雪 (Deng Xiaohua 鄧小華)
Canglang hui 滄浪會
Canglang shihua 滄浪詩話
Cao Cao 曹操
Cao Changqing 曹長青
Cao Chunjiang 曹春江
Cao Hange 曹漢閣
Cao Juren 曹聚仁
Cao Liangwu 曹亮武
Cao Lijuan 曹麗娟
Cao Rong 曹溶
Cao Xinzhi 曹辛之
Cao Xueqin 曹雪芹
Cao Yin 曹寅
Cao Yu 曹禺
Cao Zhenji 曹貞吉
Cao Zhi 曹植
Caotang shiyu 草堂詩餘
Caozhao qiaoya 草詔敲牙
Cen Kailun 岑凱倫
Cen Yifei 岑逸飛
Chang Yao 昌耀
Chang'e 嫦娥
Changbanpo 長阪坡
changben 唱本

Changmen 昌門
Changsheng 長生
Changsheng dian 長生殿
Chaongzhou cipai 常州詞派
Chaozhou gece 潮州歌冊
Chaozhou Liu zhifu quange 潮州柳知府全歌
Che 車
Chen Baichen 陳白塵
Chen Baoyao 陳寶鑰
Chen Boqing 陳伯卿
Chen Canyun 陳殘雲
Chen Chen 陳忱
Chen Cun 陳村
Chen Dakang 陳大康
Chen Danqing 陳丹青
Chen Duansheng 陳端生
Chen Duo 陳鐸
Chen Duxiu 陳獨秀
Chen Fangming 陳芳明 (Chen Jianong 陳嘉農)
Chen Gongyin 陳恭尹
Chen Guanxue 陳冠學
Chen Guoqiu 陳國球 (Leonard Chan)
Chen Hengzhe 陳衡哲
Chen Hongbi 陳鴻壁
Chen Houzhu 陳後主 (Chen Shubao 陳叔寶)
Chen Hu 陳瑚
Chen Huang 陳煌
Chen Jiangfan 陳江帆
Chen Jiayong 陳家永
Chen Jinghan 陳景漢
Chen Jingrong 陳敬容
Chen Jingzong 陳敬宗
Chen Jiru 陳繼儒
Chen Jitong 陳季同
Chen Jiying 陳紀瀅
Chen Kehua 陳克華
Chen Li 陳黎 (Chen Yingwen 陳膺文)
Chen Lian 陳璉
Chen Lie 陳列 (Chen Ruilin 陳瑞麟)
Chen Liulong 陳六龍
Chen Mengjia 陳夢家
Chen Minhua 陳敏華
Chen Ninggui 陳寧貴

Chen Ping 陳平
Chen Qi 陳起
Chen Qiuke 陳秋客
Chen Que 陳確
Chen Ran 陳染
Chen Rong 諶容
Chen Ruixian 陳瑞仙
Chen Ruoxi 陳若曦
Chen San 陳三
Chen Sen 陳森
Chen Shaozhi 陳紹陟
Chen Shi 陳時
Chen Shibin 陳士斌
Chen Shiqi 陳士奇
Chen Shixiang 陳世驤 (Hsi-hsiang Ch'en)
Chen Shou 陳壽
Chen Shoupeng 陳壽彭
Chen Sihe 陳思和
Chen Tong 陳同
Chen Weisong 陳維崧
Chen Wenshu 陳文述
Chen Xinghui 陳幸蕙
Chen Xiumei 陳秀美
Chen Xue 陳雪
Chen Xuzhen 陳序臻
Chen Yingxiong 陳英雄 (Kowan Talall 谷灣‧打鹿勒)
Chen Yingzhen 陳映真 (Chen Ying-chen)
Chen Yinke 陳寅恪
Chen Yizhi 陳義芝
Chen Yuanyuan 陳圓圓
Chen Yujiao 陳與郊
Chen Yuqian 陳遇乾
Chen Zhaolun 陳兆崙
Chen Zhihua 陳志華
Chen Zhilin 陳之遴
Chen Zhongshi 陳忠實
Chen Zilong 陳子龍
Chenbao 晨報
Cheng Fangwu 成仿吾
Cheng Huiying 程蕙英
Cheng Qiong 程瓊
Cheng Weiyuan 程偉元
Cheng Yi 程頤
Cheng Yingshu 成英姝
Chenxiang ting 沉香亭

Chi Li 池莉
Chiang Kai-shek 蔣介石
Chong Ji 崇基
Chong'er 重耳
Chongding xinshang pian 重訂欣賞篇
Chougui 酬鬼
Chu Ge 楚戈 (Chu Ko; Yuan Dexing 袁德星)
Chu Renhuo 褚人獲
chuandan shi 傳單詩
Chuangshiji shishe 創世紀詩社
Chuangzao she 創造社
chuanqi 傳奇
chuanqi xiaoshuo 傳奇小説
Chuci 楚辭
Chunqiu 春秋
Churen 處仁
Chusai 出塞
Chuyun 楚雲
ci 詞
Ci Mulan tifu congjun 雌木蘭替父從軍
Ci pin 詞品
cihua 詞話
cizhang 辭章
Cong Weixi 叢維熙
congshu 叢書
Cui Shu 崔述
Cui'e 翠娥
Cuipingshan 翠屏山
Da Ming hunyi tu 大明混一圖
Da Ming lü 大明律
Da Ming xinglong zhuan 大明興隆傳
Da Tang Qinwang cihua 大唐秦王詞話
Dadelavan 達德拉凡 (Tu Yufeng 塗玉鳳)
Dagongbao 大公報
dagu 大鼓
Dai Houying 戴厚英
Dai Mingshi 戴名世
Dai Tian 戴天
Dai Wangshu 戴望舒
Dai Zhen 戴震
Dai Zhiqiang 戴志強 (Sakinu)
Damuzhi 大拇指
dan 旦
Dan Ying 淡瑩
Dangdai waiguo xiaoshuo 當代外國小説

Dangkou zhi 蕩寇志

danxian 單弦

Daohua 悼花

Daoqing 道情

Datong shu 大同書

Dechao aoqi 得鈔傲妻

demokelaxi 德模克拉西 (democracy)

Deng Hanyi 鄧漢儀

Deng Tuo 鄧拓

Deng Xiaoping 鄧小平

Deng Youmei 鄧友梅

Deng Yuping 鄧禹平

Deng Zhengjian 鄧正健

Di yibai shiyi an 第一百十一案

Di yici de qinmi jiechu 第一次的親密接觸

Dianguan 電冠

Dianshu qitan 電術奇談

diao 調

Diaoyu ji 琱玉集

Dibao 邸報

Ding Jizhi 丁繼之

Ding Ling 丁玲

Ding Shaoguang 丁紹光

Ding Xilin 丁西林

Ding Yamin 丁亞民

Ding Yaokang 丁耀亢

Ding Yi 丁毅

Dingdian 頂點

Dingguo zhi 定國志

Dinü hua 帝女花

Dipingxian 地平綫

Diquan 地泉

Disandai ren 第三代人

Disantiao daolu 第三條道路

Dixing xian 地行仙

Dong Bai 董白

Dong Hengxun 董衡巽

Dong Jianhua 董建華 (Tung Chee-hwa)

Dong Jieyuan 董解元

Dong Qi 董玘

Dong Qiao 董橋 (Tung Chiao; Dong Cunjue 董存爵)

Dong Qichang 董其昌

Dong Qizhang 董啟章

Dong Rong 董榕

Dong Shabei 董沙貝

Dong Yong 董永

Dong Yue (fl. 1480) 董越

Dong Yue (1620–1686) 董說

Dong'er 冬兒

Dongfang Bai 東方白 (Lin Wende 林文德)

Dongguo ji 東郭記

Donglin 東林

Dongling xuedao ren 東嶺學道人

Dongyou ji 東遊記

Dou Tao 竇滔

Doupeng xianhua 豆棚閒話

Du Dengchun 杜登春

Du Fu 杜甫

Du Guoqing 杜國清 (Kuo-ching Tu)

Du Heng 杜衡

Du Hong 杜紅 (Cai Yanpei 蔡炎培)

Du Lisao 讀離騷

Du Mu 杜牧

Du Pan Fangge 杜潘芳格

Du Pengcheng 杜鵬程

Du Shiniang 杜十娘

Du sishu daquan 讀四書大全

Du Yunxie 杜運燮

Duan Caihua 段彩華

Duanhong lingyan ji 斷鴻零雁記

Duanmu Hongliang 端木蕻良

Duo Duo 多多 (Bai Ye 白夜; Li Shizheng 栗世征)

Duo Si 朵思

Duo Yu 朵漁

E Fuming 鄂復明

Eiji Yoshikawa 吉川英治

Er hehua shi 二荷花史

erchen 貳臣

erhuang 二黃

Erke pai'an jingqi 二刻拍案驚奇

Erlang 二郎

Ernü yingxiong zhuan 兒女英雄傳

Ershi yi shi tanci 二十一史彈詞

Ershinian mudu zhi guaixianzhuang 二十年目睹之怪現狀

Ershisi shipin 二十四詩品

Ershisi xiao 二十四孝

Eryuehe 二月河 (Ling Jiefang 凌解放)

Faguo nüyingxiong tanci 法國女英雄彈詞

Fahai 法海

Fan Jingwen 范景文
Fan Junfeng 范俊風
Fan Li 范蠡
Fan Muzhi 范牧之
Fan Zengxiang 樊增祥
Fang Bao 方苞
Fang Chengpei 方成培
Fang Ezhen 方娥真 (Liao Yan 廖湮)
Fang Fang 方方
Fang Han 方含
Fang Jiahua 方家華
Fang La 方臘
Fang Lizhi 方勵之
Fang Qi 方旗
Fang Qing 方卿
Fang Si 方思
Fang Xiaobiao 方孝標
Fang Xiaoru 方孝孺
Fang Xin 方莘
Fang Yizhi 方以智
Fang Zhi 方之
Fang Zi 方梓
Fanhua meng 繁華夢
Fei Ming 廢名 (Feng Wenbing 馮文炳)
Fei Mu 費穆
Feng Fangmin 馮放民
Feng Feng 馮馮
Feng Jicai 馮驥才
Feng Menglong 馮夢龍
Feng Mu 馮牧
Feng qiu huang 鳳求凰
Feng shuang fei 鳳雙飛
Feng Weimin 馮惟敏
Feng Xincheng 封新城
Feng Xuefeng 馮雪峰
Feng Youlan 馮友蘭
Feng Yuanjun 馮沅君
Feng Zhi 馮至
Fenghuang shan 鳳凰山
Fenghuang cheng 鳳凰城
Fenghuo 烽火
Fenglian 鳳蓮
Fengshen yanyi 封神演義
Fengshenbang 封神榜
Fengyu tan 風雨談
Fengyue jingnang 風月錦囊

Fengyue meng 風月夢
Fenshu 焚書
Fenyu cao 焚餘草
Fodongxin 佛動心
Foshuo Yangshi guixiu hongluo
    Huaxian'ge baojuan 佛說楊氏鬼繡紅羅
    化仙哥寶卷
Fu Lei 傅雷
Fu Shan 傅山
Fu Wenzheng 傅文正
fubi 伏筆
fugu 復古
Fugui shenxian 富貴神仙
Furen ji 婦人集
Furong dong 芙蓉洞
Fushe 復社
Fusheng liuji 浮生六記
Fuxing wenyi 復興文藝
Gaiding Yuan xian chuanqi 改定元賢傳奇
Gan Bao 干寶
Gan Huili 甘恢里
Ganmeng shangren 邗蒙上人
Gao Bing 高棅
Gao Changgong 高長恭
gao da quan 高大全
Gao E 高鶚
Gao Lian 高濂
Gao Panlong 高攀龍
Gao Qi 高啟
Gao Xiaosheng 高曉聲
Gao Xingjian 高行健
Gao Xinjiang 高信疆
Gao Yang 高陽
Gao Zhun 高準
Gaomi 高密
Gaosai 高塞
ge 格
Ge dai xiao 歌代嘯
Ge Fei 格非
Ge Nen 葛嫩
Gechuan river 葛川江
Gemalan 葛瑪蘭
Geng Jizhi 耿濟之
Gengyun 耕耘
Gengzi guobian tanci 庚子國變彈詞
Genshi 亙史

gezaice 歌仔冊

gezaixi 歌仔戲

Gezhi huibian 格致彙編

Gong Dingzi 龔鼎孳

Gong Liu 公劉 (Liu Renyong 劉仁勇)

Gong Xianglin 龔翔麟

Gong Zizhen 龔自珍

Gongan pai 公安派

Gongyang xue 公羊學

Gongyang zhuan 公羊傳

Gu Bei 古貝

Gu Cai 顧采

Gu Cangwu 古蒼梧

Gu Cheng 顧城

Gu Chun 顧春 (Gu Taiqing 顧太清)

Gu Ding 古丁

Gu Hua 古華

Gu Jiegang 顧頡剛

Gu Jingfang 顧璟芳

Gu Long 古龍 (Xiong Yaohua 熊耀華)

Gu Qiyuan 顧起元

Gu Sen 顧森

Gu Song yimin 古宋遺民

Gu Xiancheng 顧憲成

Gu Yanwu 顧炎武

Gu Youxiao 顧有孝

Gu Zhenguan 顧貞觀

Gu Zhenli 顧貞立

Gu Zhongyi 顧仲彝

Guan Guan 管管

Guan Jieming 關傑明 (John Kwan Terry)

Guan Jinpeng 關錦鵬 (Stanley Kwan)

Guan Mengnan 關夢南

Guan Nanqian 關南倩 (Nancy Kwan)

Guan Yu 關羽

Guanchang xianxing ji 官場現形記

Guang Song yimin lu 廣宋遺民錄

Guangdong xinyu 廣東新語

Guangling chao 廣陵潮

Guangming bao 光明報

Guazher 掛枝兒

guci 鼓詞

Gufu qu 姑婦曲

Gui Fu 桂馥

Gui Hengkui 桂恆魁

Gui Youguang 歸有光

Gui Zhuang 歸莊

guixiu 閨秀

Gujin mingju 古今命劇

Gujin shishan 古今詩刪

Gujin tan gai 古今談概

Gujin xiaoshuo 古今小說

gundiao 滾調

Guo Jichun 郭季春

Guo Lianghui 郭良蕙

Guo Moruo 郭沫若

Guo Shiying 郭世英

Guo Songfen 郭松棻

Guo Songtao 郭嵩燾

Guo Wenjing 郭文景

Guo Xiaochuan 郭小川 (Guo Enda 郭恩大)

Guo Xun 郭勛

Guo Zhengyu 郭正域

Guohun 國魂

Guose tianxiang 國色天香

Gusheng 觚賸

Gushi gui 古詩歸

Gushi yuan 古詩源

gushu 鼓書

Guwangyan 姑妄言

Guwen yuexuan 古文約選

Guwenci leizuan 古文辭類纂

Guyu 谷雨

Guzhang juechen 鼓掌絕塵

guzici 鼓子詞

Ha Jin 哈金 (Jin Xuefei 金雪飛)

Hai Rui 海瑞

Haiguang wenyi 海光文藝

Haijiao yibian 海角遺編

Haishang qishu 海上奇書

Haishanghua liezhuan 海上花列傳

Haitian Duxiaozi 海天獨嘯子

haiwai huawen wenxue 海外華文文學

Haizi 海子

Han Bangqing 韓邦慶

Han Lizhu 韓麗珠

Han Shaogong 韓少功

Han Shizhong 韓世忠

Han Xiangzi 韓湘子

Han Xiaochuang 韓小窗

Han Yu 韓愈

Handan ji 邯鄲記
Hanke 函可
Hansen qu 寒森曲
Hanye sanbuqu 寒夜三部曲
Hao Ran 浩然
Haoqiu zhuan 好逑傳
Haowangjiao 好望角
he 荷
He Da 何達
He Fan 何凡 (Xia Chengying 夏承楹)
He Furen 何福仁
He Gao 何皋
He Jingming 何景明
He Jingzhi 賀敬之
He Qifang 何其芳
He Qiongrui 何瓊瑞
He xiangu baojuan 何仙姑寶卷
He Yinghe 何映荷
He Zhu 賀鑄
Hedian 何典
Hehuan tu 合歡圖
Helü 鶴侶
Hengren 亨人
Henhai 恨海
Heshen 和紳
Holo 河洛 (Hoklo)
Hong Chengchou 洪承疇
Hong Feng 洪峰
Hong Hong 鴻鴻 (Yan Hongya 閻鴻亞)
Hong Jun 洪鈞
Hong Liangji 洪亮吉
Hong Ling 洪淩
Hong Meng 紅夢
Hong Pian 洪楩
Hong Shen 洪深
Hong Sheng 洪昇
Hong Suli 洪素麗
Hong Xingfu 洪醒夫
Hong Xiuquan 洪秀全
Hong Yanqiu 洪炎秋
Hong Ying 虹影
Hongli ji 紅梨記
Honglou meng 紅樓夢
Honglou meng ying 紅樓夢影
Hou Fangyu 侯方域
Hou qiuxing 後秋興

hou qizi 後七子
Hou Ruhua 侯汝華
Hou Shuihu zhuan 後水滸傳
Hou Xiaoxian 侯孝賢 (Hou Hsiao-hsien)
Hou Yi 后羿
Hou Zhi 侯芝
Houbei 猴杯
Housheng yanju yanjiuhui
　厚生演劇研究會
Hu Dong 胡冬
Hu Fayun 胡發云
Hu Feng 胡風 (Zhang Guangren 張光人)
Hu Guoxian 胡國賢
Hu Juren 胡菊人
Hu Lancheng 胡蘭成
Hu Qixian 胡啓先
Hu Shi 胡適
Hu Tianshi 胡天石
Hu Wenkai 胡文楷
Hu Yinglin 胡應麟
Hu Zheng 胡正
Hua Guan Suo 花關索
Hua Yan 華嚴
Huai Yuan 淮遠
Huailu tang shihua 懷麓堂詩話
Huajian ji 花箋記
Hualidao 華麗島
Huan Fu 桓夫 (Chen Qianwu 陳千武)
Huan Wen 桓溫
Huan Ziye 桓子野
Huang Biyun 黃碧雲 (Wong Bik-wan)
Huang Canran 黃燦然
Huang Chunming 黃春明 (Huang
　Chun-ming)
Huang Daozhou 黃道周
Huang Degong 黃得功
Huang E 黃峨
Huang Fan 黃凡 (Huang Xiaozhong
　黃孝忠)
Huang Guobin 黃國彬 (Kwok-pun Wong)
Huang Hengqiu 黃恆秋
Huang Hesheng 黃荷生
Huang Jingren 黃景仁 (Huang Zhongze
　黃仲則)
Huang Jinshu 黃錦樹 (Ng Kim Chew)
Huang Ke 黃珂

Huang Long 黃龍

Huang Moxi 黃摩西

Huang Ningying 黃寧嬰

Huang Rui 黃銳

Huang Sicheng 黃思騁

Huang Tianfu 黃天福

Huang Tingjian 黃庭堅

Huang Tubi 黃圖珌

Huang Weiliang 黃維樑 (Wong Wai
    Leung)

Huang Xiang 黃翔

Huang Xiangjian 黃向堅

Huang Xieqing 黃燮清

Huang Xiuqiu 黃繡球

Huang Yaomian 黃药眠

Huang Yong 黃用

Huang Yuanjie 黃媛介

Huang Yujin 黃禹金

Huang Yun 黃雲

Huang Zhouxing 黃周星

Huang Zicheng 黃子澄

Huang Zongxi 黃宗羲

Huang Zunxian 黃遵憲

Huang Zuo 黃佐

Huangfu Changhua 皇甫長花

Huangfu Chong 皇甫沖

Huangfu Feilong 皇甫飛龍

Huangfu Lian 皇甫濂

Huangfu Pang 皇甫汸

Huangfu Shaohua 皇甫少華

Huangfu Xiao 皇甫涍

Huangguan 皇冠

Huangjiang Diaosou 荒江釣叟

huangmin hua (Kōminka) 皇民化

Huansha ji 浣紗記

Huanxi yuanjia 歡喜冤家

Huanxu juchang 環墟劇場

Huaqiao ribao 華僑日報

Huaren you 化人遊

Huasheng bao 華聲報

Huaxia wenzhai 華夏文摘

Huayue hen 花月痕

Huayue Sanniang 華岳三娘

Hudie bei 蝴蝶盃

Hui Dong 惠棟

huiguan 會館

Huishang 徽商

Huitou kan jilue 回頭看記略

Huitu lienü zhuan 繪圖列女傳

Hunan shishe 湖南詩社

Huolang dan 貨郎擔

huolang'er 貨郎兒

hutong 胡同

Inoue Enryō 井上円了

ji 記

Ji Bu 季布

Ji Dawei 紀大偉 (Chi Ta-wei)

Ji Gang 紀剛 (Zhao Yueshan 趙岳山)

Ji Hun 羈魂

Ji Xian 紀弦 (Lu Yu 路逾; Luyishi 路易士;
    Louis)

Ji Xingwen 吉星文

Ji Yongren 嵇永仁

Ji Yun 紀昀

Ji, Crazy (Ji Dian) 濟顛

Jia Dao 賈島

Jia Fuxi 賈鳧西 (Jia Yingchong 賈應寵)

Jia Pingwa 賈平凹

Jia xing rizhu 甲行日注

Jia Zhifang 賈植芳

Jia Zhongming 賈仲明

Jian Youwen 簡又文

Jian Zhen 簡媜 (Jian Minzhen 簡敏媜)

Jiandeng xinhua 剪燈新話

Jiandeng yuhua 剪燈餘話

Jiang Bin 江彬

Jiang Chenying 姜宸英

Jiang Chunlin 蔣春霖

Jiang Dehua 姜德華

Jiang Dingyue 蔣定粵

Jiang fei 絳妃

Jiang Gai 姜垓

Jiang Guangci 蔣光慈

Jiang Gui 姜貴

Jiang He 江河 (Yu Youze 于友澤)

Jiang Jingqi 蔣景祈

Jiang Kangquan 江康泉

Jiang Kui 姜夔

Jiang Pinchao 蔣品超

Jiang Qing 江青 (Bai Ping 白蘋)

Jiang Shiquan 蔣士銓

Jiang Ti 江堤

Jiang Wenye 江文也
Jiang Wenyu 江文瑜
Jiang Xun 蔣勳
Jiang Yan 江淹
Jiang Yi 蔣彝
Jiang Yingke 江盈科
Jiang Yun 蔣韻
jiangchang wenxue 講唱文學
Jianghu zaijiu ji 江湖載酒集
Jianghuji 江湖集
Jiangzuo qiaozi 江左樵子
Jiangzuo san dajia shichao 江左三大家詩抄
Jianshazui 尖沙咀 (Tsimshasui)
Jiao Hong 焦竑
Jiao Hong ji 嬌紅記
Jiao Tong 焦桐 (Ye Zhenfu 葉振富)
Jiaoyuan qizi 蕉園七子
Ji'e de nüer 飢餓的女兒
Jie Zhitui 介之推
jietouju 街頭劇
jietoushi 街頭詩
Jigong'an 濟公案
Jigu ge 汲古閣
Jihai zashi 己亥雜詩
Jihusou 畸笏叟
Jili pai 肌理派
Jin Bao 金堡 (Jinshi Dangui 今釋澹歸)
Jin ci yuan 今詞苑
Jin Die 金蝶
Jin He 金和
Jin Lian 錦連
Jin Ping Mei 金瓶梅
Jin Shengtan 金聖嘆
Jin Shijie 金士傑
Jin Yi 金逸
Jin Yong 金庸 (Zha Liangyong 查良鏞; Louis Chia)
Jin Youzi 金幼孜
Jin Zhaoyan 金兆燕
Jin-Cha-Ji shipai 晉察冀詩派
Jinci chuji 今詞初集
Jing Hao 荊浩
Jingbao 京報
jin'ge 錦歌
Jingguang yuan 鏡光緣
Jin'gui jie 金閨傑

Jinghua yuan 鏡花緣
Jingling pai 竟陵派
Jingshi tongyan 警世通言
Jingu qiguan 今古奇觀
Jingwei shi 精衛石
Jingyin shishe 驚隱詩社
jingzhong baoguo 精忠報國
Jingzhong zhuan 精忠傳
Jinmen 金門 (Quemoy)
Jinshang 晉商
Jinsuo ji 金鎖記
jinwen jingxue 今文經學
Jinyu yuan 金魚緣
Jishe 幾社
Jiumei tu 九美圖
jiuqi daxian 九七大限
Jiusong ting 九松亭
Jiuwei gui 九尾龜
Jiuye pai 九葉派
Jiya 祭牙
Juewu 覺悟
Jun Qing 峻青
Juntian yue 均天樂
Kai Yuan 開元 (Shen Qiwu 沈啓無)
kaipian 開篇
Kan Yu 闞玉
Kang Fu 康夫
Kang Hai 康海
Kang Wanmin 康萬民
Kang Youwei 康有為
kaoju 考據
Ke Zhongping 柯仲平
Kejia 客家 (Hakka)
Ketagalan 凱達格蘭
Kong fuzi gu'erci 孔夫子鼓兒詞
Kong Jiesheng 孔捷生
Kong Sanzhuan 孔三傳
Kong Shangren 孔尚任
Kongzi gaizhi kao 孔子改制攷
kouhao shi 口號詩
koutou wenxue 口頭文學
Kowloon 九龍
Ku Ling 苦苓 (Wang Yuren 王裕仁)
Ku Xingcan di 哭星粲弟
kuaibanshu 快板書
Kuaiqu 快曲

kuaishu 快書

Kuaiyuan 獪園

Kuang gushi yuyang sannong
狂鼓史漁陽三弄

Kucheng 哭城

kuer 酷兒

Kun Nan 崑南 (Disiai 狄斯艾; Cen
Kunnan 岑崑南)

kunqu崑曲

Lai Chunbiao 賴春標

Lai He 賴和

Lai Shengchuan 賴聲川 (Stanley Lai)

Lake Luo Bridge 羅湖橋

Lan Liu 藍流

Lan'gao Mingci huixuan 蘭皋明詞匯選

Lanling jufang 蘭陵劇坊

Lanxing shishe 藍星詩社

Lao Can youji 老殘游記

Lao Mu 老木

Lao She 老舍

Lei Haiqing 雷海青

Lei Shuyan 雷抒雁

Lei Zhen 雷震

Leifeng ji 雷鋒記

Leifeng ta 雷峰塔

leishu 類書

Leiyu 雷雨

Li An 李安 (Ang Lee)

Li Ang 李昂 (Shi Shuduan 施淑端)

Li Ao 李敖

Li Bai (701–762) 李白

Li Bai (b. 1959) 李白 (Li Bihua 李碧華;
Lilian Lee)

Li Baichuan 李百川

Li Boyuan 李伯元 (Li Baojia 李寶嘉)

Li Changqi 李昌祺

Li Changxian 李昌憲

Li Dawei 李大衛

Li Dingyi 李定夷

Li Dongyang 李東陽

Li Dou 李斗

Li E 厲鶚

Li Fanying 李範碤

Li Gongpu 李公朴

Li Guangtian 李廣田

Li Guinian李龜年

Li Guiyu 李桂玉

Li Hangyu 李杭育

Li Hanqiu 李涵秋

Li Hanzhang 李含章

Li He 李賀

Li Hongzhan 李鴻章

Li Houzhu 李後主 (Li Yu 李煜)

Li Jiahua 李家華

Li Jiangshu 李江樹

Li Jianwu 李健吾

Li Jiasheng 李家昇

Li Jieren 李劼人

Li Jinfa 李金髮

Li Kaixian 李開先

Li Kewei 李克威

Li Kuang 力匡 (Zheng Jianbo 鄭健伯)

Li Laoxiang 李老鄉

Li Li 李黎 (Bao Lili 鮑利黎; Lily Hsueh)

Li Linfu 李林甫

Li Lüyuan 李綠原

Li Mengyang 李夢陽

Li Minyong 李敏勇

Li Panlong 李攀龍

Li Qin'an 李勤岸

Li Qing 李清

Li Qingzhao 李清照

Li Rui 李銳

Li Ruzhen 李汝珍

Li Sanniang 李三娘

Lisao 離騷

Li Shangyin 李商隱

Li Shimian 李時勉

Li Shimin 李世民

Li Shiniang 李十娘

Li Shoumin 李壽民

Li Shuchang 黎庶昌

Li Shuwei 李束為

Li Su 李素

Li Wen 李雯

Li Xian'e (Huaimin) 李憲墨 (懷民)

Li Xiang 李香 (Li Xiangjun 李香君)

Li Yin 李因

Li Ying 李瑛

Li Yinghao 李英豪

Li Yongping 李永平 (Yung-p'ing Li)

Li Yongzhe 李永喆

Li Yu (ca 1591–ca 1671) 李玉 (Li Xuanyu 李玄玉)

Li Yu (1611–1680) 李漁

Li Yu (b. 1944) 李渝

Li Yuanzhen 李元貞

Li Yufang 利玉芳

Li Yun 栗耘 (Li Zhaoxiong 栗照雄)

Li Yuying 李玉英

Li Yuzhong 李育中

Li Zhaoluo 李兆洛

Li Zhi 李贄 (Li Zhuowu 李卓吾)

Li Zhihai 李智海

Li Zicheng 李自成

Li Zishu 黎紫書

Li Zongheng 李縱橫

Liancheng bi 連城璧

Liang Chenyu 梁辰魚

Liang Desheng 梁德繩

Liang Hongyu 梁紅玉

Liang Peilan 梁佩蘭

Liang Qichao 梁啟超

Liang Qingbiao 梁清標

Liang Shanbo 梁山伯

Liang Shanbo ge 梁山伯歌

Liang Shiqiu 梁實秋

Liang Shuming 梁漱溟

Liang Tianlai gao yuzhuang 梁天來告御狀

Liang Xiaobin 梁小斌

Liang Xiaoyu 梁小玉

Liang Xihua 梁錫華

Liang xumei 兩鬚眉

Liang Yicang 梁亦滄

Liang Yusheng 梁羽生

Liang Zongdai 梁宗岱

Lianxian ban 憐香伴

Lianyan 奩艷

Liao Hongji 廖鴻基

Liao Huiying 廖輝英

Liao Qingxiu 廖清秀

Liao Yan 廖燕

Liao Yiwu 廖亦武

Liao Yuhui 廖玉蕙

Liaozhai liqu 聊齋俚曲

Liaozhai zhiyi 聊齋誌異

Libao 立報

Lidai shilüe guci 歷代史略鼓詞

Liechao shiji 列朝詩集

Lienü zhuan 列女傳

Lieren wenhua zazhi 獵人文化雜誌

Lieshi zhuan 列士傳

Liglave A-wu 利格拉樂 · 阿烏

Lin Bai 林白 (Lin Baiwei 林白薇)

Lin Boqiu 林博秋

Lin Chuanjia 林傳甲

Lin Dai 林玳

Lin Geng 林庚

Lin Haiyin 林海音

Lin Hengtai 林亨泰 (Hengren 亨人)

Lin Hong 林鴻

Lin Huanzhang 林煥彰

Lin Huiyin 林徽因

Lin Jinlan 林斤瀾

Lin Junying 林俊穎

Lin Ling 林泠

Lin Lü 林綠

Lin Mang 林莽

Lin Pu 林蒲

Lin Ran 林染

Lin Renchao 林仁超

Lin Shu 林紓

Lin Wenyue 林文月

Lin Zexu 林則徐

Lin Yaode 林燿德

Lin Yiliang 林以亮 (Song Qi 宋淇; Stephen C. Soong)

Lin Yingqiang 林英強

Lin Yutang 林語堂

Linchuan meng 臨川夢

Linchuan pai 臨川派

Linchuan simeng 臨川四夢

Linchun ge 臨春閣

Ling Fu 凌拂

Ling Mengchu 凌濛初

Ling Shuhua 凌叔華

Ling Xue 凌雪

Lingnan sanjia shixuan 嶺南三家詩選

Lingshan 靈山

Liu Bei 劉備

Liu Binyan 劉賓雁

Liu caizi shu 六才子書

Liu Canyang 柳殘楊 (Gao Jianji 高見幾)

Liu Dakui 劉大櫆

Liu Daren 劉大任

Liu Dongsheng 劉東生

Liu E 劉鶚

Liu Fenglu 劉逢祿

Liu Fu 劉复 (Liu Bannong 劉半農)

Liu gongan 劉公案

Liu Heng 劉恒

Liu Huozi 劉火子

Liu Ji 劉基

Liu Jin 劉瑾

Liu Jingting 柳敬亭

Liu Ke 劉克

Liu Kexiang 劉克襄

Liu Kuibi 劉奎璧

Liu Kun 劉琨

Liu Muxia 柳木下

Liu Na'ou 劉吶鷗

Liu Qing 劉青

Liu Ruoyu 劉若瑀

Liu Rushi 柳如是 (Liu Shi 柳是)

Liu Sanjie 劉三姊

Liu Shahe 流沙河

Liu Shaotang 劉紹棠

Liu Shipei 劉師培

Liu Shu 劉淑

Liu Suola 劉索拉

Liu Tao 劉濤

Liu Tingji 劉廷璣

Liu Tongxun 劉統勳

Liu Wuxiong 劉武雄

Liu Xi 劉錫

Liu Xiang 劉向

Liu Xiang baojuan 劉香寶卷

Liu Xiaobo 劉曉波

Liu Xinwu 劉心武

Liu Xiu zouguo 劉秀走國

Liu Yazi 柳亞子

Liu Yichang 劉以鬯 (Liu Tongyi 劉同繹)

Liu Yizheng 劉以正

Liu Yong 劉墉

Liu Yuqing 劉玉卿

Liu Yuxi 劉禹錫

Liu Zaifu 劉再復

Liu Zeqing 劉澤清

Liu Zhenyun 劉震雲

Liu Zhiyuan zhugongdiao 劉知遠諸宮調

Liu Zongyuan 柳宗元

Liuhua meng 榴花夢

Liushi jia xiaoshuo 六十家小說

Long Yingtai 龍應台 (Ying-tai Lung)

Long Yingzhong 龍瑛宗

Longtu erlu 龍圖耳錄

Longzu 龍族

Loudong 婁東

Lü Bicheng 呂碧城

Lu Dan'an 陸澹安

Lü Di 綠蒂

Lü Dongbin 呂洞賓

Lu Ganzhi 盧幹之

Lu Hanxiu 路寒袖 (Wang Zhicheng 王志誠)

Lü Heruo 呂赫若

Lu Huanxing 陸煥興

Lu Jiachuan 盧嘉川

Lü Jian 呂劍

Lü Kun 呂坤

Lu Li 魯藜

Lu Lin 盧林

Lu Ling 路翎 (Xu Sixing 徐嗣興)

Lü Lun 侶倫

Lü Mengzheng 呂蒙正

Lü mudan 綠牡丹

Lu Qingzi 陸卿子

Lu Shikuan 盧世寬

Lu Shuangqin 魯雙芹

Lu Shusheng 陸樹聲

Lü Tiancheng 呂天成

Lu Wenfu 陸文夫

Lü Xin 呂新

Lu Xinhua 盧新華

Lü Xiong 呂熊

Lü Xiulian 呂秀蓮 (Annette Lu)

Lu Xun 魯迅

Lu Yansheng 魯雁生

Lu Yimin 陸憶敏

Lu Yin (1898–1934) 盧隱

Lu Yin (b. 1935) 盧因

Lu Yingyang 陸應暘

Lu You 陸游

Lü Yuan 綠原

Lu Zhaoling 盧昭靈

Lu Zhiwei 陸志韋

Luanchaigou 亂柴沟
luantan 亂彈
Lüdi 綠地
Lugou Bridge 蘆溝橋
Lulei yuan 露淚緣
Lunyu 論語
Luo Binji 駱賓基
Luo Fu (b. 1928) 洛夫 (the poet, a.k.a. Lo Fu)
Luo Fu 羅孚 (the journalist)
Luo Gengye 駱耕野
Luo Guangbin 羅廣斌
Luo Guanzhong 羅貫中
Luo Guixiang 羅貴祥
Luo Jiyi 羅寄一
Luo Luo 羅洛
Luo Pu 羅普
Luo Qing 羅清
Luo Qing (b. 1948) 羅青 (Lo Ch'ing)
Luo Songchuang 羅松窗
Luo Yihe 駱一禾
Luo Yijun 駱以軍
Luo Zhicheng 羅智成
Luopan 羅盤
Luotuo xiangzi 駱駝祥子
Lüye xianzong 綠野仙蹤
Luyishi 路易士
Lüzhou shishe 绿洲诗社
Ma Desheng 馬德升
Ma Feng 馬烽
Ma Fenghua 馬逢華
Ma Jian 馬建
Ma Jue 馬覺
Ma Ke 馬可
Ma Kelu 馬可鲁
Ma Lang 馬朗 (Ma Boliang 馬博良; Ronald Mar)
Ma Rufei 馬如飛
Ma Sen 馬森
Ma Shiying 馬士英
Ma Shuli 馬叔禮
Ma Shuming 馬書銘
Ma Song 馬松
Ma Xianglan 馬湘蘭
Ma Yu 馬玉
Ma Yuan 馬原

Ma Yueguan 馬曰琯
Ma Yuelu 馬曰璐
Ma Zhiyuan 馬致遠
Ma Zhongxi 馬中錫
Mai Lihao 麥理浩 (Murray McLehose)
Man Han dou 滿漢鬥
Mang Ke 芒克 (Jiang Shiwei 姜世偉)
Manyou suilu 漫游随錄
Manyou yeshi 漫遊野史
Mao Dun 茅盾 (Shen Yanbing 沈雁冰)
Mao Jike 毛際可
Mao Jin 毛晉
Mao Lun 毛綸
Mao Xiang 冒襄
Mao Zonggang 毛宗崗
Mao Zedong 毛澤東
Mei Dingzuo 梅鼎祚
Mei Lanfang 梅蘭芳
Mei Niang 梅娘
Mei Xin 梅新
Mei Yanfang 梅艷芳 (Anita Mui; Mui Yim-Fong)
Meng Chengshun 孟稱舜
Meng Dongli 孟東籬
Meng Haoran 孟浩然
Meng Jiangnü 孟姜女
Meng Jiao 孟郊
Meng Lang 孟浪
Meng Lijun 孟麗君
Meng Qi 孟起
Meng Qi (jinshi 875) 孟啟
Meng Shuqing 孟淑卿
Meng Tian 蒙恬
Mengjiao 夢蛟
Mengying yuan 夢影緣
Mengzhong yuan 夢中緣
Mi Heng 彌衡
Mi, Lady 糜
Mian Mian 棉棉 (Wang Xin 王莘)
Miaoshan, Princess 妙善
Miaozhuang 妙莊
Mideng yinhua 覓燈因話
Min Qiji 閔齊伋
Ming ji 明季
Ming mo 明末
Ming sanshi jia shixuan 明三十家詩選

Ming shi zong 明詩綜
Ming shiji 明史記
Ming wen hai 明文海
Mingfeng ji 鳴鳳記
Mingjiao zhong ren 名教中人
Mingming niao 命命鳥
Mingru xue'an 明儒學案
Minguo ribao 民國日報
Mingyi daifang lu 明夷待訪錄
Mingyuan shigui 名媛詩歸
Mingyuan shiwei 名媛詩緯
minjian wenxue 民間文學
Miu Hong 繆弘
Mo Dan 莫旦
Mo Jiangang 莫建剛
Mo Yan 莫言 (Guan Moye 管謨業)
Moling chun 秣陵春
Monan qu 磨難曲
Monaneng 莫那能 (Zeng Shunwang 曾舜旺)
Mou Dunbai 牟敦白
Mou Zongsan 牟宗三
Moufu sha zi yinyangbao 謀夫殺子陰陽報
moyu 摸魚
Mu Dan 穆旦 (Zha Liangzheng 查良錚)
Mudan ting 牡丹亭
Mulian 目連
Murong Yujun 慕容羽軍
muyuge 木魚歌
muyushu 木魚書
Nahan 吶喊
Naihe tian 奈何天
Nan jiugong pu 南九宮譜
Nan Ling bei Mei 南玲北梅
Nan Song zashi shi 南宋雜事詩
Nan wanghou 男王后
Nanchuang meng 南窗夢
nanci 南詞
Nanci xulu 南詞敘錄
Nangong Bo 南宮搏
Nanke ji 南柯記
Nanren de yiban shi nüren 男人的一半是女人
Nanshan ji 南山集
Nanshe 南社
Nanshe congke 南社叢刻

nanyin 南音
Nanyue 南岳
Nara Singde 納蘭性德
Nei xun 內訓
neibu shudian 內部書店
Ni Bin 倪斌
Ni Huanzhi 倪煥之
Ni Kuang 倪匡 (Ni Yiming 倪亦明)
Ni Yuanlu 倪元璐
Ni Zan 倪瓚
Nianpu xuzuan 年譜續纂
Nie Hualing 聶華苓
Nie Yuanzi 聶元梓
Niehai hua 孽海花
Nigu an 尼姑案
Nishikawa Mitsuru 西川滿
Niu Han 牛漢
Niu Xiu 鈕琇
Nü caizi shu 女才子書
Nü kaike zhuan 女開科傳
Nü zhuangyuan cihuang defeng 女狀元辭凰得鳳
Nüjing shishe 女鯨詩社
Nüsao 女騷
nüshu 女書
Nüwa 女媧
Nüxian waishi 女仙外史
Nüyu hua 女獄花
Ou (surname) 區
Ou Waiou 鷗外鷗 (Li Zongda 李宗大)
Ouluoba 歐儸巴
Ouyang Xiu 歐陽修
Ouyang Yuqian 歐陽予倩
Paian jingqi 拍案驚奇
paiziqu 牌子曲
Pan Chengzhang 潘檉章
Pan Jinlian 潘金蓮
Pan Jun 潘軍
Pan Renmu 潘人木 (Pan Fobin 潘佛彬)
Pan Zhiheng 潘之恆
Panfeng lunzhan 盤峰論戰
Panghuang 彷徨
Pangxie duan'er 螃蟹段兒
paoshu 跑書
Pei Du 裴度
Pei Lihe 裴麗荷

Peiduofei julebu 裴多菲俱樂部

Peng Ge 彭歌

Peng Yan 彭炎

Peng Yaofen 彭耀芬

Pianti wenchao 駢體文鈔

pihuang 皮黃

pin 品

Ping Jintao 平鑫濤

Ping Lu 平路

Ping Shan Leng Yan 平山冷燕

pingdian 評點

pinghua 平話

Pingyao zhuan 平妖傳

Pinhua baojian 品花寶鑑

Pipa ji 琵琶記

Pizi Cai 痞子蔡

Pu Songling 蒲松齡

Puming 普明

putonghua 普通話

Qi Bansun 祁班孫

Qi Biaojia 祁彪佳

Qi Huan 齊桓

Qi Jinggong dai Kongzi wuzhang 齊景公
待孔子五章

Qi Jun 琦君

Qi Lisun 祁理孫

Qian Bingdeng 錢秉鐙

Qian Cai 錢彩

Qian Daxing 錢大昕

Qian Mu 錢穆

Qian Qianyi 錢謙益

qian qizi 前七子

Qian Xiyan 錢希言

Qian Xuantong 錢玄同

Qian Yi 錢宜

Qian Zhongshu 錢鍾書

Qiandao Siming tujing 乾島四明圖經

Qiangtou ji 牆頭記

Qianlong you Jiangnan 乾隆遊江南

Qianzhong lu 千忠戮

Qiao shi 樵史

Qiao tuanyuan 巧團圓

Qiaoying 喬影

qichi 棋癡

Qidengsheng 七等生

Qifeng qiao daoren 七峰樵道人

Qifeng yibian 七峰遺編

Qilu deng 歧路燈

Qimeng 啟蒙

Qin Kuai (Qin Gui) 秦檜

Qin Shouou 秦瘦鷗

Qin Shubao 秦叔寶

Qin Zhaoyang 秦兆陽

Qin Zihao 覃子豪

Qing zhong pu 清忠譜

Qingchun shihui 青春詩會

Qinglian shi zhuren 青蓮室主人

Qingni lianhua ji 青泥蓮花記

Qingpingshan tang huaben 清平山堂話本

Qingshi leilüe 情史類略

Qinhuai 秦淮

Qinhuai zashi shisi shou 秦淮雜詩十四首

Qiong Yao 瓊瑤 (Chen Zhe 陳喆)

Qionghan ci 窮漢詞

Qiren zhang 齊人章

Qitian dasheng 齊天大聖

Qiu Chuji 邱處機

Qiu Dongping 丘東平

Qiu Fengjia 丘逢甲

Qiu Haitang 秋海棠

Qiu Jin 秋瑾

Qiu Jun 丘濬

Qiu Miaojin 邱妙津

Qiu Shuyuan 邱菽園

Qiu Xinru 邱心如

Qiu Yaxin 丘雅信

Qiu Ying 仇英

Qiushui 秋水

Qiuxing 秋興

Qiuye cheng Zhilu xiansheng 秋夜呈芝
麓先生

Qiuying 秋螢

Qixia wuyi 七俠五義

Qiyun shi 栖雲石

Qizi zhi hui 七子之會

qu 曲

Qu Bo 曲波

Qu Dajun 屈大均

Qu Fu 屈復

Qu Juesheng 蘧覺生

Qu Qiubai 瞿秋白

Qu Shisi 瞿式耜

Qu Xiaosong 瞿小松
Qu You 瞿佑
Qu Yuan 屈原
Quan Zuwang 全祖望
Quanti xinlun 全體新論
Quanxiang guben xiyou zhengdao shu 全像古本西遊証道書
Quanzhen 全真
Que Buquan 闕不全
Que Lihou 闕里侯
Queqiao mishi 鵲橋秘誓
Qulü 曲律
Qulun 曲論
Qupin 曲品
quyi 曲藝
Rangdu zhou 禳妒咒
Rao Zongyi 饒宗頤
Ren Tianzhi 任天知
Ren Zhaolin 任兆麟
Renjianshi 人間世
riji 日記
Rizhi lu 日知錄
Rongshu xia 榕樹下
Rou putuan 肉蒲團
Rou Shi 柔石
Ru Zhijuan 茹志鵑
Ruan Dacheng 阮大鋮
Ruan Yuan 阮元
Rukai 魯凱
Rulin waishi 儒林外史
Ruyan@sars.com 如焉@sars.com
Sai Jinhua 賽金花 (Fu Caiyun 傅彩雲)
Saideke 賽德克
Saixia 賽夏
Sakinu 亞榮隆・撒可努
San Mao 三毛 (Chen Maoping 陳懋平)
San Wu youlan zhi 三吳遊覽誌
Sanbao taijian Xiyang ji tongsu yanyi 三寶太監西洋記通俗演義
Sanfu heping Mudan ting Huanhun ji 三婦合評牡丹亭還魂記
Sang Yue 桑悅
sanggu 喪鼓
Sanguo zhi 三國志
Sanguo zhi yanyi 三國志演義
sanqu 散曲

Sanxia wuyi 三俠五義
sanxian 三弦
Sanxiao xinbian 三笑新編
Sanxiao yinyuan 三笑姻緣
Sanyan 三言
Sanzi jing 三字經
Saodang bao 掃蕩報
Sha Yexin 沙葉新
Shafei nüshi de riji 莎菲女士的日記
Shan'ge 山歌
Shancai longnü baojuan 善財龍女寶卷
Shandong kuaishu 山東快書
Shang Jinglan 商景蘭
Shang Qin 商禽 (Luo Ma 羅馬)
Shangshu 尚書
shanglai ti 商籟體
shangpin dachao 商品大潮
Shanhai wenhua 山海文化
Shanhaiguan 山海關
Shanhu shan jinsuo yuanyang ji 珊瑚扇金鎖鴛鴦記
shanshu 善書
Shanyaodan pai 山藥蛋派
Shao Can 邵燦
Shao Jingzhan 邵景詹
Shao Yanxiang 邵燕祥
Shao Zinan 邵子南
Shen Congwen 沈從文
Shen Defu 沈德符
Shen Deqian 沈德潛
Shen Fu 沈復
Shen Guisheng 申貴升
Shen Jiazhe 沈嘉轍
Shen Jing 沈璟
Shen Jiping 沈季平
Shen Junqing 沈君卿
Shen luan jiao 慎鸞交
Shen Nanpin 沈南蘋
Shen Qifeng 沈起鳳
Shen Shanbao 沈善寶
Shen Shixing 申時行
Shen Yixiu 沈宜修
Shen Zhou 沈周
Shen Zizheng 沈自徵
Shenbao 申報
sheng guang hua dian 聲光化電

Sheng Ming zaju 盛明雜劇
Sheng Ming zaju erji 盛明雜劇二集
Shenggen zhoukan 生根周刊
Shengsichang 生死場
Shengyu 聖諭
Shenjiao she 慎交社
Shenlou ji 蜃樓記
shenmo 神魔
Shennüfeng 神女峰
shenti xiezuo 身體寫作
shenyou lengqiao 深幽冷峭
Shenzhou shishe 神州诗社
shi 士 (gentleman)
shi 詩 (poetry)
Shi 蝕
Shi chuangzao 詩創造
Shi diantou 石點頭
Shi duo 詩朵
Shi feng 詩風
Shi gongan 施公案
Shi Guanghua 石光華
Shi Jianghu 詩江湖
Shi Jingtang 石敬瑭
Shi Kangcheng 史康成
Shi Kefa 史可法
Shi lingtu 詩領土
Shi Mingde 施明德
Shi Mingzheng 施明正
Shi Nai'an 施耐庵
Shi Nulai 施努來 (Syman Rapongan)
Shi nüshi 詩女史
Shi Runzhang 施閏章
Shi Shuqing 施叔青 (Shi Shu-ching)
Shi Weiyuan 史惟圓
Shi Yukun 石玉昆
Shi zhanxian 詩戰綫
Shi Zhecun 施蟄存
Shi Zhenyu 石振宇
Shi'er lou 十二樓
Shiba Shirō 柴四郎
Shide tang 世德堂
Shiguan 詩觀
Shiji 史記
shijie 失節
shijing xiaoshuo 市井小説
Shijun dashe 十郡大社

Shikan 詩刊
Shimai 詩脈
Shipai shu 石派書
shiqu 時曲
shishang 士商
Shishi xinbao 時事新報
Shishuo xinyu 世說新語
Shituo ji 石頭記 (Honglou meng 紅樓夢)
shiwen 時文
Shixi jicheng 使西紀程
Shiyu tupu 詩餘圖譜
Shizhii 食指 (Guo Lusheng 郭路生)
Shizi po 十字坡
Shu Ting 舒婷
Shu Xiangcheng 舒巷城 (Wang Shenquan
    王深泉)
Shuahai'er 耍孩兒
Shuangxian ji 雙線記
Shuidong riji 水東日記
Shuihu houzhuan 水滸後傳
Shuihu ji 水滸記
Shuihu zhuan 水滸傳
Shuihui an 水繪庵
Shuihui yuan 水繪園
shuji shi 庶吉士
Shuo Yue quanzhuan 說岳全傳
shuochang wenxue 說唱文學
Shuqi 叔齊
Si chanjuan 四嬋娟
Si Ruixuan 司瑞軒
Si youji 四遊記
Sihang cangku 四行倉庫
Sijiu lu 思舊錄
Sikong Tu 司空圖
Siku quanshu 四庫全書
Sima Ling 司馬翎
Sima Qian 司馬遷
Sima Xiangru 司馬相如
Sima Zhongyuan 司馬中原
Sisheng yuan 四聲猿
Sishi tongtang 四世同堂
Siwen lu 思問錄
Siwu luntan 四五論壇
Song Haiquan 宋海泉
Song Jiang 宋江
Song Lian 宋濂

Song Maocheng 宋懋澄
Song Meidong 宋梅洞
Song Qu 宋渠
Song Wan 宋琬
Song Wei 宋煒
Song Yu 宋玉
Song Zelai 宋澤萊
Song Zhidi 宋之的
Songshi jishi 宋詩紀事
Songyin manlu 淞隱漫錄
Soushen ji 搜神記
Su Guoxun 蘇國勛
Su Hui 蘇蕙
Su Kunsheng 蘇崑生
Su Liuniang 蘇六娘
Su Manshu 蘇曼殊
Su Qing 蘇青 (Feng Yunzhuang 馮允莊)
Su Shaolian 蘇紹連
Su Shi 蘇軾
Su Tong 蘇童 (Tong Zhonggui 童中貴)
Su Weizhen 蘇偉貞
su wenxue 俗文學
Su Xiaoxiao 蘇小小
Su Xuelin 蘇雪林
Suehiro Tetchō 末廣鐵腸
Sui Tang yanyi 隋唐演義
Sui Yangdi 隋煬帝
Sui Yangdi yanshi 隋煬帝艷史
Suishi yiwen 隋史遺文
Suiyuan 隨園
Suiyuan nüdizi shi 隨園女弟子詩
Suiyuan shihua 隨園詩話
Suiyuanle 隨緣樂
Sun Dachuan 孫大川
Sun Deying 孫德英
Sun Dian 孫鈿
Sun Ganlu 孫甘露
Sun Jiarui 孫嘉瑞
Sun Jingwu 孫經武
Sun Junshi 孫俊世
Sun, Lady 孫
Sun Lin 孫臨
Sun Ling 孫陵
Sun Qian 孫謙 (Sun Huaiqian 蘇懷謙)
Sun Quan 孫權
Sun Shaozhen 孫紹振

Sun Weimang 孫瑋芒
Sun Yat-sen 孫逸仙
Sun Yu 孫郁
Sun Zhiyuan 孫志遠
Suye wenxue 素葉文學
Tai Jingnong 臺靜農
Taidong shuju 泰東書局
taige ti 台閣體
Taihe zhengyin pu 太和正音譜
Taiping guangji 太平廣記
Taiping yulan 太平御覽
Taishang gangying pian 太上感應篇
Taishi Zhi shi Qi 太師摯適齊
Taiwan minzhu ge 台灣民主歌
Taiwan ren sanbuqu 臺灣人三部曲
Taixia xinzou 太霞新奏
Taixian man'gao 太仙漫稿
Taiya 泰雅
Taiyang shibao 太陽詩報
Taiyang zongdui 太陽縱隊
Taizhou 泰州
Tan Kai 談愷
Tan Yuanchun 譚元春
Tan Ze 談則
tanci 彈詞
tanci xiaoshuo 彈詞小説
Tang 唐
Tang Bin 湯斌
Tang Junyi 唐君毅
Tang Qi 唐祈
Tang Ren 唐人 (Ruan Lang 阮朗)
Tang Ruxun 唐汝詢
Tang Sai'er 唐賽兒
Tang Shi (1920–2005) 唐湜
Tang Shi (fl. ca.1400) 湯氏
Tang Shunzhi 唐順之
Tang Wenbiao 唐文標
Tang Xian ji 唐仙記
Tang Xianzu 湯顯祖
Tang Yaping 唐亞平
Tang Yin 唐寅
Tang yin 唐音
Tang Ying 唐英
Tang Yongtong 湯用彤
Tangshi biecai 唐詩別裁
Tangshi gui 唐詩歸

Tangshi jie 唐詩解

Tangshi pinhui 唐詩品彙

Tangshi xuan 唐詩選

Tangshi zhengsheng 唐詩正聲

Tanlong lu 談龍錄

Tao Jiakai 陶家楷

Tao Qian 陶潛 (Tao Yuanming 陶淵明)

Tao Ran 陶然

Tao Xiunü 陶秀女

Tao Zhenhuai 陶貞懷

Tao zhi meng 逃之盟

Tao'an mengyi 陶庵夢憶

Taohua shan 桃花扇

Taohua shan kao ju 桃花扇考據

Taoshe 逃社

Taowu cuibian 檮杌萃編

Taowu xianping 檮杌閒評

taozhen 陶真

Tian Han 田漢

Tian Jian 田間

Tian Rucheng 田汝成

Tian Xiaoqing 田曉青

Tian Yage 田雅各 (Topas Tamapima)

Tian Yiheng 田藝衡

Tian Yuchuan 田玉川

Tian Yunshan 田雲山

Tianbao qushi 天寶曲史

Tianbao tu 天豹圖

Tianbao yishi zhugongdiao 天寶遺事諸宮調

Tianhua zang zhuren 天花藏主人

Tianliao nianpu bieji 天寥年譜別集

Tianlu licheng 天路歷程

Tianqi Chongzhen liangchao yishi 天啟崇禎兩朝遺詩

Tiantang suantai zhi ge 天堂蒜薹之歌

Tianyuan zhai 天緣債

Tianyuhua 天雨花

Tie Ning 鐵凝

Tihong ji 題紅記

Tixiao yinyuan 啼笑因緣

tixue guan 提學官

Tongcheng pai 桐城派

Tongjian gangmu 通鑑綱目

Tongmenghui 同盟會

Tongren ji 同人集

Tongsheng she 同聲社

tongsu wenxue 通俗文學

Toubi ji 投筆集

Tu Jingyi 涂靜怡

Tu Long 屠隆

Tu Naixian 涂乃賢

Tu Shen 屠紳

Waiguo lienü zhuan 外國列女傳

waishengren 外省人

wan Ming 晚明

Wan Sitong 萬斯同

Wan Xiliang 萬希良

Wang Aihe 王愛和

Wang Anyi 王安憶

Wang Ao 王鏊

Wang Ayling 王璦玲

Wang Bocheng 王伯成

Wang Chang 王昶

Wang Dao 王道

Wang Daokun 汪道昆

Wang Dongbai 王東白

Wang Duan 汪端

Wang Duanshu 王端淑

Wang Fuzhi 王夫之

Wang Gen 王艮

Wang Guowei 王國維

Wang Guozhen 汪國真

Wang Hongwen 王洪文

Wang Jiaoluan 王嬌鸞

Wang Jiawei 王家衛 (Wong Kar-wai)

Wang Jide 王驥德

Wang Jing 王靖 (Bu Anli 卜安利)

Wang Jingquan 王井泉

Wang Jingwei 汪精衛

Wang Jiusi (Meipi) 王九思 (渼陂)

Wang Juntao 王軍濤

Wang Kaiyun 王闓運

Wang Kemin 王克敏

Wang Lan 王藍

Wang Lanqing 王蘭卿

Wang Lindu 王林渡

Wang Meng 王蒙

Wang Mian 王冕

Wang Miaoru 王妙如

Wang Pan 王磐

Wang Pengyun 王鵬運

Wang Qijiang 汪啟疆

Wang Runhua 王潤華 (Yoon-wah Wong)

Wang Ruowang 王若望

Wang Shaotang 王少堂

Wang Sheng 王昇

Wang Shenzhong 王慎中

Wang Shifu 王實甫

Wang Shilu 王士祿

Wang Shisu 王士驌

Wang Shiwei 王實味

Wang Shizhen (1526–1590) 王世貞

Wang Shizhen (1634–1711) 王士禛

Wang Shuo 王朔

Wang Tao 王韜

Wang Tingxiang 王廷相

Wang Tonggui 王同軌

Wang Tongzhao 王統照

Wang Tuo 王拓

Wang Wan 汪琬

Wang Wei (699 or 701–761) 王維

Wang Wei (1607–1647) 王微

Wang Wenxing 王文興 (Wang Wen-hsing)

Wang Wuxie 王無邪 (Wu Xie 無邪;
   Wucius Wong)

Wang Xianchen 王獻臣

Wang Xiangxu 汪象旭

Wang Xianyang 王憲陽

Wang Xiaobo 王小波

Wang Xiaolong 王小龍

Wang Xiaoming 王曉明

Wang Xiaoni 王小妮

Wang Xiaonong 汪笑儂

Wang Xiuchu 王秀楚

Wang Xufeng 王旭烽

Wang Yangming 王陽明

Wang Yi 王義

Wang Youding 王猷定

Wang Yuesheng 王月生

Wang Yun 王筠

Wang Zaijun 王在軍

Wang Zengqi 汪曾棋

Wang Zhaojun 王昭君

Wang Zhenhe 王楨和 (Wang Chen-ho)

Wang Zhiping 王志平

Wang Zhun 王準

Wang Zuoliang 王佐良

Wang, Fifth Daughter 王五娘

wan'ge 挽歌

wangkan 網刊

wangluo wenxue 網絡文學

Wanguo gongbao 萬國公報

Wanguo gongfa 萬國公法

Wanjuan lou 萬卷樓

Wanli yuan 萬里圓

Wanmin an 萬民安

Wannian qing 萬年青

wei an fu 慰安婦

Wei Changsheng 魏長生

Wei Geng 魏耕

Wei Guan 魏觀

Wei Hai 韋海

Wei Hanying 魏含英

Wei Hui 衛慧

Wei Jingsheng 魏京生 (Jin Sheng 金生)

Wei Liangfu 魏良輔

Wei Wei 魏巍

Wei Xi 魏禧

Wei Yingwu 韋應物

Wei Yuan 魏源

Wei Zhongxian 魏忠賢

Wei Zhuang 韋莊

Wei Zi'an 魏子安

Wen Jianliu 溫健驑

Wen Jie 聞捷

Wen Kang 文康

Wen, Madame 文

Wen Ruian 溫瑞安

Wen Tianxiang 文天祥

Wen Tingyun 溫庭筠

Wen Xiaocun 文曉村

Wen Yiduo 聞一多

Wen Yuren 溫育仁

Wen Zhengming 文徵明

Weng Fanggang 翁方綱

Wenming xiaoshi 文明小史

wenren 文人

wenshe 文社

wentan 文壇

Wenxing 文星

Wenxue gailiang chuyi 文學改良芻議

Wenxue jikan 文學季刊

Wenxue xunkan 文學旬刊

Wenyibao 文藝報

Wenyou tongxun 文友通訊

Wo sinian de changmian zhong de Nanyang gongzhu 我思念的長眠中的南洋公主

Wolong Sheng 臥龍生

Wopao ji 倭袍記

Wotu 沃土

Wu Ang 巫昂

Wu Bing 吳炳

Wu Cheng'en 吳承恩

Wu Erlu 吳爾鹿

Wu Han 吳晗

Wu He 舞鶴 (Chen Guocheng 陳國城)

Wu Hong 巫鴻 (Wu Hung)

Wu Jiaji 吳嘉紀

Wu Jianren 吳趼人

Wu Jinfa 吳錦發

Wu Jingzi 吳敬梓

Wu Junjie 吳俊傑 (Walis Norgan 瓦歷斯·諾幹)

Wu Junyao 吳鈞堯

Wu Kuan 吳寬

Wu Kun 吳琨

Wu Lixian 伍立憲

Wu Mi 吳宓

Wu Mingyi 吳明益

Wu Nianzhen 吳念真

Wu Nichang 舞霓裳

Wu Qiang 吳強

Wu Ren 吳人

Wu Rulun 吳汝綸

Wu Sangui 吳三桂

Wu Sheng 吳晟 (Wu Shengxiong 吳勝雄)

Wu Shuangre 吳雙熱

Wu Song 武松

Wu Weiye 吳偉業

Wu Wenjian 吳文健

Wu Wenxian 伍汶憲

Wu Wushan 吳吳山

Wu Xinghua 吳興華 (Liang Wenxing 梁文星)

Wu Xubin 吳煦斌

Wu Yan 吳炎

Wu Yingji 吳應箕

Wu Yingtao 吳瀛濤

Wu Yuchang 吳毓昌

Wu Yueshi 吳越石

Wu Zao 吳藻

Wu Zetian 武則天

Wu Zhaoqian 吳兆騫

Wu Zhensheng 吳震生

Wu Zhuo 吳焯

Wu Zhuoliu 吳濁流 (Wu Jiantian 吳建田)

Wu Zixu 伍子胥

Wu Zuguang 吳祖光

Wu Zuxiang 吳組緗

wubu liuce 五部六冊

Wuguitang 五桂堂

Wujiang pai 吳江派

Wumingshi 無名氏 (Bu Naifu 卜乃夫)

Wuniang 五娘

Wure'ertu 烏熱爾圖

Wushe shijian 霧社事件

Wusheng laomu 無生老母

Wusheng xi 無聲戲

Wuxia bi 無暇璧

Wuyan lüzu 五言律祖

Wuyue huahui 五月畫會

Wuza zu 五雜組

Wuzhong shizi shichao 吳中十子詩鈔

Xi Chengzheng 席誠正

Xi Murong 席慕蓉

Xi Rong 西戎

Xi Shi 西施

Xi Xi 西西 (Zhang Yan 張彥; Lanzi 藍子)

Xia Guo 夏果

Xia Ji'an 夏濟安 (T. A. Hsia)

Xia Jing 夏菁

Xia Jingqu 夏敬渠

Xia Lun 夏綸

Xia Mianzun 夏丏尊

Xia Yan (1482–1548) 夏言

Xia Yan (1900–1995) 夏衍

Xia Yu 夏宇 (Hsia Yü; Huang Qingqi 黃慶綺)

Xia Yunying 夏雲英

Xia Zengyou 夏曾佑

Xia Zhiqing 夏志清 (C. T. Hsia)

xiabanshen shige 下半身詩歌

Xiachao luntan 夏潮論壇

Xian, Lady 冼

xianci 弦詞

Xiang Hongzuo 項鴻祚

xiang qian kan 向錢看

Xiang Yang 向陽 (Lin Qiyang 林淇瀁)

Xiang Yu 項羽

xiangbao ge 相保歌

Xiangshan baojuan 香山寶卷

xiangtu wenxue 鄉土文學

Xianqing ouji 閒情偶寄

Xianrenzhang 仙人掌

xianzhuang 線裝

Xiao Hong 蕭紅

Xiao hulei 小忽雷

Xiao Jun 蕭軍

Xiao Lihong 蕭麗紅

Xiao Qian 蕭乾

Xiao Sa 蕭颯 (Xiao Qingyu 蕭慶餘)

Xiao San 蕭三

Xiao Tong 蕭統

Xiao Wenhuang 蕭文煌

Xiao Xiangwen 蕭翔文

Xiao Xiao 瀟瀟

Xiao Yin 曉音

Xiaofeng wenyi 曉峰文藝

Xiaolin 笑林

xiaopin 小品

Xiaoqing 小青

xiaoshuo 小說

Xiaoshuo huabao 小說畫報

Xiaoshuo lin 小說林

Xiaoshuo shibao 小說時報

Xiaoshuo shijie 小說世界

Xiaoshuo yuebao 小說月報

xiaoxian 消閒

Xiaozhong yuan 笑中緣

Xiaozi zhuan 孝子傳

Xie An 謝安

Xie Ao 謝翺

Xie Bingying 謝冰瑩

Xie Daoyun 謝道韞

Xie Jin 謝晉

Xie Jinyuan 謝晋元

Xie Liang 謝良

Xie Mian 謝冕

Xie Tiao 謝朓

Xie Xiaohong 謝曉虹

Xie Ye 謝燁

Xie Zhaozhe 謝肇淛

Xie Zhen 謝槙

Xie Zhengguang 謝正光 (Andrew Hsieh)

xieshou 寫手

Xiexin zaju 寫心雜劇

xiguan 戲舘

Xiguan siwang 習慣死亡

Xihu erji 西湖二集

Xihu mengxun 西湖夢尋

Xihu shan 西湖扇

Xihu youlan zhi 西湖遊覽志

Xihu youlan zhiyu 西湖遊覽志餘

Xihu yuan 西湖緣

Xiju chunqiu yuekan 戲劇春秋月刊

Xin Dai 心岱 (Li Bihui 李碧慧)

Xin Di 辛笛

Xin faluo xiansheng tan 新法螺先生譚

xin ganjue pai 新感覺派

Xin jiyuan 新紀元

Xin lieguozhi 新列國志

Xin Qiji 辛棄疾

Xin qingnian 新青年

Xin Qishi 辛其氏

Xin Shitouji 新石頭記

Xin sichao 新思潮

Xin wanbao 新晚報

Xin wenyi 新文藝

Xin xiaoshuo 新小說

Xin yue 新月

Xin Zhongguo weilaiji 新中國未來記

Xinbian dongdiao dashuang hudie 新編東
    調大雙蝴蝶

Xinbian jin hudie zhuan 新編金蝴蝶傳

Xinbian ti Xixiang ji yong shi er yue sai
    Zhu yun fei 新編題西廂記咏十二月賽
    駐雲飛

Xing Fang 邢昉

Xingdao ribao 星島日報

Xingli daquan 性理大全

Xinglin 興林

Xingling pai 性靈派

Xingnan xinwen 興南新聞

Xingshi hengyan 醒世恆言

Xingshi yinyuan zhuan 醒世姻緣傳

Xingxing 星星

Xingzuo 星座

Xinhua yuebao 新華月報

Xinlei shitan 新雷詩壇

Xinshengdai 新生代

xintianyou 信天遊

Xinwen chuban zongshu 新聞出版總署

Xinxi xiantan 昕夕閒談

xinxin renlei 新新人類

Xinya shuyuan 新亞書院

Xinzhongguo weilai ji 新中國未來記

Xiong Foxi 熊佛西

Xiong Hong 夐虹 (Hu Meizi 胡梅子)

Xiong Qingtang 熊慶棠

Xiong Shiyi 熊式一 (S. I. Hsiung)

xipi 西皮

Xiunü baojuan 秀女寶卷

Xiuta yeshi 繡榻野史

Xiuxiang xiyou zhenquan 繡像西遊真詮

Xixiang ji 西廂記

Xixiangji zhugongdiao 西廂記諸宮調

Xiyou bu 西遊補

Xiyou ji 西遊記

xiyuan 戲園

Xiyuan shishe 西園詩社

Xizhou Sheng 西周生

Xu Ben 徐賁

Xu Can 徐燦

Xu Changzuo 徐昌祚

Xu Chi 徐遲

Xu Dishan 許地山

Xu Fuzuo 徐復祚

Xu Guangping 許廣平

Xu Haoyuan 徐浩淵

Xu Hongzu 徐弘祖 (Xu Xiake 徐霞客)

Xu Jiang 徐江

Xu Jin Ping Mei 續金瓶梅

Xu Jing 徐經

Xu Jingya 徐敬亞

Xu Junya 許俊雅 (Hsu Chun-ya)

Xu Kun 許坤

Xu Longshen 許龍深 (Ziqian 子潛)

Xu Nianci 徐念慈 (Donghai Juewo 東海覺我)

Xu Qingshi 許清世 (Xiaoxing 曉星)

Xu Shukui 徐述夔

Xu Su 徐速

Xu Wei 徐渭

Xu Wenli 徐文立

Xu Xi 徐爔

Xu Xian 許仙

Xu Xiaobin 徐小斌

Xu Xiaochang 徐孝常

Xu Xing 徐星

Xu Xu 徐訏

Xu Zhenqing 徐禎卿

Xu Zhenya 徐枕亞

Xu Zhimo 徐志摩

Xu Zhongpei 徐鍾珮

Xu Zhongyan 許宗彥

Xu Ziyun 徐紫雲

xuanjiang 宣講

Xuanshi zhi 宣室志

Xuanzong, Ming (r. 1426–1436) 宣宗

Xuanzong, Tang (r. 712–756) 玄宗

Xue Bogu 薛柏谷

Xue Dan 薛旦

Xue Fucheng 薛福成

Xue Rengui zheng dong 薛仁貴征東

Xue Shaohui 薛紹徽

Xue Susu 薛素素

Xuedeng 學燈

Xueheng 學衡

Xungen pai 尋根派

Xunhuan ribao 循環日報

xunkan 旬刊

xushu 續書

xuwudang xiaoshuo 虛無黨小說

Ya Mo 啞默

Ya Xian 瘂弦 (Wang Qinglin 王慶麟)

yaci 崖詞 (涯詞)

yaji 雅集

Yami, Yamei 雅美

Yan Busun 燕卜蓀 (William Empson)

Yan Dichang 嚴迪昌

Yan Ermei 閻爾梅

Yan Fu 嚴復

Yan Geling 嚴歌苓

Yan Jiagan 嚴家淦

Yan Jidao 晏幾道

Yan Jin 嚴謹

Yan Li 嚴力

Yan Ruoqu 閻若璩

Yan Shang 岩上

Yan Shengsun 嚴繩孫

Yan Xiaodong 燕曉東

Yan Yu 嚴羽

Yan'an zhengfeng 延安整風

Yanagawa Heisuke 井松石根

Yandang shan qiao 雁宕山樵

Yang Chaoguan 楊潮觀

Yang Chichang 楊熾昌 (Shuiyinping 水蔭萍)

Yang Guifei 楊貴妃 (Yang Yuhuan 楊玉環)

Yang Hansheng 陽翰笙

Yang Ji 楊基

Yang Jiang 楊絳 (Yang Jikang 楊季康)

Yang Jiaxian 楊佳嫻

Yang Jiguang 楊際光

Yang Jing 楊靖

Yang Jingxian 楊景賢

Yang Jinshan 楊金山

Yang Kui 楊逵

Yang Li 楊黎

Yang Lian 楊煉

Yang Lianggong 楊亮功

Yang Meihui 楊美惠

Yang Minsheng 楊敏盛

Yang Mo 楊沫

Yang Mu 楊牧 (Ye Shan 葉珊; Ching-hsien Wang 王靖獻)

Yang Naiwu yu Xiaobaicai 楊乃武與小白菜

Yang Pu 楊溥

Yang Qingchu 楊青矗

Yang Ran 楊然

Yang Rong 楊榮

Yang Shangkun 楊尚昆

Yang Shen 楊慎

Yang Shihong 楊士弘

Yang Shiqi 楊士奇

Yang Tinghe 楊廷和

Yang Tinglin 楊廷麟

Yang Wanli 楊萬里

Yang Weizhen 楊維楨

Yang Wencong 楊文聰

Yang Wenguang 楊文廣

Yang Xianyi 楊憲益

Yang Yaoxian 楊瑤仙

Yang Yi 楊儀

Yang Yiping 楊益平

Yang Yiyan 楊益言

Yang Yusheng 楊禹聲 (Chen Wentong 陳文統)

Yang Yushu 楊雨澍

Yang Ze 楊澤 (Yang Xianqing 楊憲卿; Hsien-ching Yang)

Yang Zhao 楊照

Yang Zhouhan 楊周翰

yangbanxi 樣板戲

Yangguang xiaoji 陽光小集

yanglian jin 養廉金

Yangxian 陽羨

Yangyi pian 艷異篇

Yangzhou huafang lu 揚州畫舫錄

Yangzhou meng 揚州夢

Yangzhou qingqu 揚州清曲

Yangzhou shiri ji 揚州十日記

Yanjing wenxue 燕京文學

Yano Ryūkei 矢野龍溪

Yanshan conglu 燕山叢錄

Yanshui sanren 煙水散人

yansipilichun 煙斯披裹純

yanyi 衍譯

Yanyi pian 艷異篇

Yanzi jian 燕子箋

Yao Fulan 姚馥蘭

Yao He 姚合

Yao Jiayi 姚嘉農

Yao Ke 姚克

Yao Nai 姚鼐

Yao Wenyuan 姚文元

Yao Xinnong 姚莘農

Yao Yiwei 姚一葦

Yaxiya de gu'er 亞細亞的孤兒

Ye Gongchao 葉公超

Ye Hui 葉輝 (Ye Dehui 葉德輝)

Ye Lingfeng 葉靈鳳

Ye Risong 葉日松

Ye Rongqing 葉蓉青

Ye Shaojun 葉紹鈞

Ye Shaokui 葉紹楏

Ye Shaoyuan 葉紹袁

Ye Sheng 葉盛

Ye Shitao 葉石濤

Ye Shuting 葉樹亭

Ye Si 也斯 (Ping-kwan Leung 梁秉鈞)

Ye Weilian 葉維廉 (Wai-lim Yip)

Ye Wenfu 葉文福

Ye Xianzu 葉憲祖

Ye Xiaogang 葉小鋼

Ye Xiaoluan 葉小鸞

Ye Xiaowan 葉小紈

Ye Zhaoyan 葉兆言

Ye Zhicheng 葉至誠

Ye Zhou 葉晝

Yecao 野草

Yesou puyan 野叟曝言

Yeya shalong 野鴨沙龍

Yi Da 依達

Yi Lei 伊蕾

Yi Suo 頤瑣

Yigeng 奕賡

Yihang 一行

Yihui 奕繪

Yin Di 隱地

Yin Hao 殷浩

Yin Jiang 飲江

Yin Xueman 尹雪曼

Yin Zhengxiong 銀正雄

Yinfengge zaju 吟風閣雜劇

Yinghuan suoji 瀛寰瑣記

Yingmei'an yiyu 影梅庵憶語

Yingshen qu shi'er shou 迎神曲十二首

Yingying zhuan 鶯鶯傳

Yinling hui 銀鈴會

Yinshi 蟫史

Yinyang pan 陰陽判

Yipeng xue 一捧雪

yishu 譯述

Yiyao zhuan 義妖傳

Yiyuan zhiyan 藝苑卮言

Yizei Liao Tianding 義賊廖添丁

Yizhen 儀貞

yizhong man 一種慢

Yizhong qing 一種情

Yizhong yuan 意中緣

Yongle dadian 永樂大典

Yongxi yuefu 雍熙樂府

Yoshikawa Eiji 吉川英治

You Tong 尤侗

Youlian 友聯

Youmeng ying 幽夢影

Youshi wenyi 幼獅文藝

youxi 遊戲

Youxue ji 有學集

Yu Chanshi cuixiang yimeng 玉禪師翠鄉
一夢

Yu Dafu 郁達夫

Yu Erniang 俞二娘

Yu Guangzhong 余光中 (Kwang-chung Yu)

Yu Hua 余華

Yu Huai 余懷

Yu Jian 于堅

Yu lianhuan 玉連環

Yu Mingchuan 俞銘傳

Yu Pingbo 俞平伯

Yu qingting 玉蜻蜓

Yu Qiuyu 余秋雨

Yu Suqiu 尉素秋

Yu Tiancong 尉天驄

Yu Wanchun 俞萬春

Yu Xiangdou 余象斗

Yu Xiushan 俞秀山

Yu Yingshi 余英時 (Yu Ying-shih)

Yu Yue 俞樾

Yu Zhixin 于植信

Yuan Changying 袁昌英

Yuan Cun 遠村

Yuan gongci 元宮詞

Yuan Hongdao 袁宏道

Yuan Kejia 袁可嘉

Yuan Mei 袁枚

Yuan Qiongqiong 袁瓊瓊 (Zhu Ling 朱陵)

Yuan Shao 袁紹

Yuan Shikai 袁世凱

Yuan Shuipai 袁水拍

yuan xiaoshuo 元小说

Yuan Yuling 袁于令

Yuan Zhaochang 袁兆昌

Yuan Zhen 元稹

Yuan Zhongdao 袁中道

Yuan Zongdao 袁宗道

yuanben 院本

Yuancao 緣草

Yuannü 怨女

Yuanqu xuan 元曲選

Yuanshan tang jupin 遠山堂劇品

Yuanshan tang qupin 遠山堂曲品

yuanyang hudie pai 鴛鴦蝴蝶派

Yuanzai 元宰

yuanzhumin 原住民

Yuchu xinzhi 虞初新志

Yuchuan yuan 玉釧緣

Yue Chong 岳重

Yue Fei 岳飛

Yuefu buti 樂府補題

Yueqiu zhimindi xiaoshuo 月球殖民地小說

Yuewei caotang biji 閱微草堂筆記

Yueyue xiaoshuo 月月小說

yugu 魚鼓

Yugu xinhuang 玉谷新簧

Yuli hun 玉梨魂

Yulong taizi zouguo yinyang baoshan 玉龍
 太子走國陰陽寶扇

Yunduan 蘊端

Yunjian pai 雲間派

Yunmen zhuan 雲門傳

Yushan 寓山 (Qi Biaojia's garden estate)

Yushan 虞山 (Qian Qianyi's Yushan
 School)

Yushi mingyan 喻世明言

Yuwai xiaoshuo ji 域外小說集

Yuyuan Pool 玉淵潭

Yuzhoufeng 宇宙風

Zaisheng yuan 再生緣

Zaizao tian 再造天

zajia 雜家

zaju 雜劇

zan 贊

Zang Di 臧棣

Zang Kejia 臧克家

Zang Maoxun 臧懋循

Zaowu 造物

zawen 雜文

Zazhi yuekan 雜誌月刊

zazu 雜俎

Zeng Guihai 曾貴海

Zeng Guofan 曾國藩

Zeng Jing 曾靜

Zeng Pu 曾樸

Zeng Shumei 曾淑美

Zeng Shunwang 曾舜旺 (Rimui Aki)

Zeng Xinyi 曾心儀

Zeng Zhuo 曾卓

Zengbu Xingyun qu 增補幸雲曲

Zha Shenxing 查慎行 (Zha Silian 查嗣璉)

Zhai Yongming 翟永明

Zhan Bing 詹冰 (Lü Yan 綠炎)

Zhan Che 詹澈

Zhan huakui 占花魁

Zhan Ruoshui 湛若水

Zhanfeng 戰峰

Zhang Ailing 張愛玲 (Eileen Chang)

Zhang Baorui 張寶瑞

Zhang Binglin 章炳麟

Zhang Chao 張潮

Zhang Chengzhi 張承志

Zhang Chunfan 張春帆

Zhang Chunqiao 張春橋

Zhang Cuo 張錯 (Ao Ao 翺翺; Zhang
 Zhen'ao 張振翺; Dominic Cheung)

Zhang Dachun 張大春 (Chang Ta-chun)

Zhang Dafu 張大復

Zhang Dai 張岱

Zhang Daofan 張道藩

Zhang Deyi 章德益

Zhang Ding 張汀

Zhang Dongsun 張東蓀

Zhang Du 張讀

Zhang Fangci 張芳慈

Zhang Fei 張飛

Zhang Guixing 張貴興

Zhang Guorong 張國榮 (Leslie Cheung,
 Cheung Kwok-Wing)

Zhang Heci 張鶴慈

Zhang Heng 張衡

Zhang Henshui 張恨水

Zhang Hongqiao 張紅橋

Zhang Huiyan 張惠言

Zhang Jian 張堅

Zhang Jianzhong 張建中

Zhang Jie 張潔

Zhang Jin 張津

Zhang Jinyan 張縉彥

Zhang Junmai 張君勱

Zhang Kangkang 張抗抗

Zhang Langlang 張郎郎

Zhang Liang 張良

Zhang Lihua 張麗華

Zhang Lijun 張歷君

Zhang Lu 張魯

Zhang Ming 章明

Zhang Mo 張默

Zhang Nanzhuang 張南莊

Zhang Pengzhi 張鵬志

Zhang Pijie 張丕介

Zhang Ping 張平

Zhang Qijiang 張啟疆

Zhang Qijie xiafan Huaiyin ji 張七姐下凡槐蔭記

Zhang Qiyun 張其昀

Zhang Shenqie 張深切

Zhang Shicheng 張士誠

Zhang Shiyan 張士彥

Zhang Shuguang 張曙光

Zhang Tianyi 張天翼

Zhang Wei 張偉

Zhang Wenhuan 張文環

Zhang Wentao 張問陶

Zhang Wenxing 張文興

Zhang Wojun 張我軍

Zhang Xianghua 張香華

Zhang Xianliang 張賢亮

Zhang Xiaofeng 張曉風 (Chang Hsiao-feng)

Zhang Xie zhuangyuan 張協狀元

Zhang Xiguo 張系國 (Hsi-kuo Chang)

Zhang Xinxin 張辛欣

Zhang Xiuya 張秀亞

Zhang Xuecheng 章學誠

Zhang Xueliang 張學良

Zhang Yan (1248–1320?) 張炎

Zhang Yan (1487–?) 張綖

Zhang Yang 張揚

Zhang Yanxun 張彥勳

Zhang Yu (b. 1952) 張宇

Zhang Yu (1333–1385) 張羽

Zhang Yuniang 張玉孃

Zhang Zhidong 張之洞

Zhang Zhixin 張志新

Zhang Zhupo 張竹坡

Zhang Zilan 張滋蘭

zhanghui xiaoshuo 章回小説

Zhangxie zhuangyuan 張協狀元

Zhao Bixian 趙碧仙

Zhao Jiabi 趙家璧

Zhao Lingzhi 趙令畤

Zhao Luorui 趙蘿蕤

Zhao Nan 趙楠

Zhao Ruihong 趙瑞蕻

Zhao Tianyi 趙天儀

Zhao Yi 趙翼

Zhao Yifan 趙一凡

Zhao Yun (mid-17th century) 趙澐

Zhao Yun 趙雲

Zhao Zhixin 趙執信

Zhao Zifan 趙滋藩

Zhao Ziyang 趙紫陽

zhaoying 照映

Zhaxi Dawa 扎西達娃

Zheng Boqi 鄭伯奇

Zheng Chenggong 鄭成功

Zheng Chouyu 鄭愁予 (Wen-tao Cheng 鄭文韜)

Zheng Danruo 鄭澹若

Zheng He 鄭和

Zheng Hui 鄭慧

Zheng Kelu 鄭克魯

Zheng Min 鄭敏

Zheng Qingwen 鄭清文

Zheng Renlai 鄭仁賚

Zheng Xie 鄭燮

Zheng Yi 鄭義

Zheng Zhen 鄭臻 (Zheng Shusen 鄭樹森; William Tay)

Zheng Zhenduo 鄭振鐸

Zheng Zhizhen 鄭之珍

Zhengde you Jiangnan 正德遊江南

zhengzong 正宗

Zhenwen ji 貞文記

Zhenzhu ta 珍珠塔

Zhepai 浙派

Zhexi 浙西

Zhexi liujia ci 浙西六家詞

Zhi 殖

Zhi Gui'er 朱貴兒

zhiguai 志怪

Zhikan ji 芝龕記

Zhinang 智囊

Zhiyanzhai 脂硯齋

Zhizhen 志貞

Zhong Lihe 鍾理和

Zhong Meiyin 鍾梅音

Zhong Wuyan 鍾無艷

Zhong Xiaoyang 鍾曉陽

Zhong Xing 鍾惺

Zhong Yao 鍾繇

Zhong Yiwen 鍾怡雯

Zhong Zhaozheng 鍾肇政

Zhongcheng she 忠誠社

Zhongguo minzhu tongmeng 中國民主
同盟

Zhongjiandai 中間代

zhongnian xiezuo 中年寫作

Zhongshan lang zhuan 中山狼傳

Zhongzi 仲姿

Zhou Enlai 周恩来

Zhou Ji 周濟

Zhou Jing 周京

Zhou Lianggong 周亮工

Zhou Liangpei 周良沛

Zhou Libo 周立波

Zhou Lunyou 周倫佑

Zhou Mengdie 周夢蝶 (Zhou Qishu
周起述)

Zhou Qiong 周瓊

Zhou Shoujuan 周瘦鵑

Zhou Shunchang 周順昌

Zhou Tao 周濤

Zhou Yang 周揚

Zhou Yingfang 周穎芳

Zhou Yu 周瑜

Zhou Zexian 周澤先

Zhou Zhao 周炤

Zhou Zhongling 周忠陵

Zhou Zuoren 周作人

Zhu Chen cun ci 朱陳村詞

Zhu Chusheng 朱楚生

Zhu Da 朱耷

Zhu Di 朱棣

Zhu Guangqian 朱光潛

Zhu Hui 朱卉

Zhu Quan 朱權

Zhu Shenglin 諸聖鄰

Zhu Shi 朱實

Zhu Su 朱橚

Zhu Suxian 朱素仙

Zhu Tianwen 朱天文 (Chu T'ien-wen)

Zhu Tianxin 朱天心 (Chu T'ien-hsin)

Zhu Tingzhen 朱庭珍

Zhu Xi 朱熹

Zhu Xiang 朱湘

Zhu Xiaoping 朱曉平

Zhu Xining 朱西寧

Zhu Xiujuan 朱秀娟

Zhu Xueshu 朱學恕

Zhu Yingtai 祝英台

Zhu Yizun 朱彝尊

Zhu Youdun 朱有燉

Zhu Yuanzhang 朱元璋

Zhu Yun 朱筠

Zhu Yunming 祝允明 (Zhishan 枝山)

Zhu Ziqing 朱自清

Zhu Zumou 朱祖謀

Zhu Zuochao 朱佐朝

Zhuang Cunyu 莊存與

Zhuang Yifu 莊一拂

Zhuangzi 莊子

zhuanzai 傳仔

zhuban ge 竹板歌

Zhuge Liang 諸葛亮

Zhuge Qingyun 諸葛青雲

zhugongdiao 諸宮調

Zhui baiqiu 綴白裘

Zhulin 竹林

Zhuo Renyue 卓人月

Zhuo Wenjun 卓文君

zhuqin 竹琴

Zhuzhi 竹枝

Zi bu yu 子不語

Zichai ji 紫釵記

zidishu 子弟書

Zihua 字花

Ziluolan 紫羅蘭

Zixiao ji 紫簫記

Ziye 子夜

Ziyou jiehun 自由結婚

Ziyu 紫玉

Zizhuan nianpu 自撰年譜

Zong Baihua 宗白華

Zong Chen 宗臣
Zong Pu 宗璞 (Feng Zhongpu 馮鍾樸)
Zong Yuanding 宗元鼎
Zou Difan 鄒荻帆
Zou Diguang 鄒迪光

Zuiyue yuan 醉月緣
Zuo Guangdou 左光斗
Zuo Liangyu 左良玉
Zuo Weiming 左維明
Zuozhuan 左傳

Index

CABRINI COLLEGE

610 KING OF PRUSSIA ROAD

RADNOR, pa 19087-3699